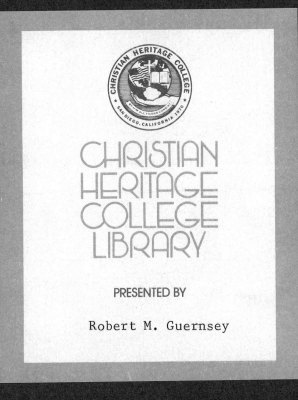

# COMPARATIVE
# POLITICS

# COMPARATIVE POLITICS A READER

EDITED BY *Harry Eckstein* AND *David E. Apter*

**THE FREE PRESS,** *New York*
*Collier-Macmillan Limited, London*

# PREFACE

The task of science is the reasoned interpretation of experience through the discovery of valid generalizations and the application of such generalizations to particular events. Science seeks theoretical and useful knowledge, to which both the unique and the familiar may contribute.

Broadly speaking, students of politics, even political philosophers, have always seen their task as the construction of science in that sense, despite profound differences with respect to the appropriate forms and fashions of the scientific enterprise. Their differences lie in their varied views on what constitutes a reasoned interpretation of events and how to discover the general in the particular. Debates on their differences have certainly not declined in recent times. Witness the bitter sadness of Leo Strauss when, discussing the position of contemporary social science, he charges that the "greatest representative of social science positivism, Max Weber, has postulated the insolubility of all value conflicts, because his soul craved a universe in which failure, that bastard of forceful sinning accompanied by still more forceful faith, instead of felicity and serenity, was to be the mark of human nobility."[1]

Yet elsewhere, Strauss argues for the view that political philosophy is "the attempt to replace opinion about the nature of political things by knowl-edge of the nature of political things," a view of fundamentals that Weber would no doubt share. And surely, "knowledge" of the nature of political things implies knowledge of the empirical world of man and his communities and an understanding of the various political arrangements through which men have, in their various ways and times, sought to live with one another. The acquisition of such knowledge is the end of comparative politics.

Comparative study is, of course, not the only way in which one can acquire political knowledge. However poor it may be in some respects, political science is extremely rich in the ways it has conceived that task. Some in political theory have sought, by reflection and by virtue of their own humanity and perhaps compassion, to consider the various aspects that make up the totality of political life and by their cogitations give it new meaning. This has been one of the tasks of political philosophy. Others have studied the detailed workings of government and its branches, seeking in the relentless gathering of facts some key to the ordering of events and some principles in the events themselves. Still others have sought to compare governments and societies, either in the tradition of the first or in the tradition of the second, in order to reveal, by effective comparison, that which is substantial and real in political life and distinguish the important from the trivial. Their objects of study include those arrangements of man in the state portrayed in history and time, or in a moment in time, and in places both exotic and familiar. The effort of science through comparison is in that sense as old as science itself, for science begins with the effort to order and classify the objects of the universe. That is first a job of comparison, but comparison is not limited to the purely classificatory. It can and must be used as a method for determining useful theories.

Efforts to make comparisons useful for purposes of both classification and theory are to be found today in the work of many political scientists. This Reader is an attempt to illustrate the state of comparison in the political field. Some of the issues, methods, and empirical works with which these aspects of political science are concerned are contained in the present volume. We have sought to use genuinely comparative materials, although by far the larger proportion of the writing in the so-called field of comparative politics is essentially not comparative at all. We have also tried to limit a field that, defined too broadly, excludes almost nothing.

In the field of political science, what seems to fall clearly outside the scope of comparative politics? In the past, the study of comparative politics has been equated with the study of foreign governments, and so it is still, to some extent, today. For certain purposes of comparison, however, indeed for most, American government and politics need also be included in the subject. How, for example, could one analyze the conditions of stable or unstable democracy or the determinants of party structure and behavior or a host of other subjects without referring to American experience? International relations must be included too, for international conditions are certainly one of the elements pressing upon national systems and determining their operation. And since much of the conceptual and theoretical equipment used in comparative politics—not to mention many problems raised in the field—comes from "political philosophy," even that part of political science cannot be readily excluded.

So broad a conception of comparative politics, equating it with political science, makes the former clearly redundant. It deprives the idea of comparative politics of meaning precisely because it makes it all-encompassing. As suggested earlier, one way out of this difficulty is to consider works in comparative politics that, in one way or another, really make comparisons. Essays that deal with a subject or problem by the inspection of a variety of political contexts or that outline methods and analytical frameworks for doing so have been included in the present Reader. Any work dealing with only a single context was automatically ex-

cluded by virtue of that fact—unless the single context was used merely to illustrate a framework for comparative analysis.

Given the present condition of political science, however, this principle of selection entails certain important disadvantages that make it necessary to justify its use. One disadvantage is that a set of readings that includes only multicontextual analyses necessarily leaves untapped many sources of rich and fruitful work—practically the whole vast literature dealing with Western political institutions and processes, accumulated throughout generations of sound, scholarly research, as well as the steadily growing literature on the politics of non-Western societies, much of which makes intelligent use of the concepts and theories of modern social science.

Perhaps more important still, a Reader based on such a principle of selection leaves out much that is relevant to the subjects and problems dealt with in comparative studies. For example, while there is available a certain amount of comparative work dealing with the requisites of effective democracy, much more on this subject can be found in works dealing with particular countries where democracy has worked or failed. Similarly, the comparative literature on the origins of totalitarian dictatorship is rather thin, while some brilliant theorizing on this subject has been done in studies of the rise of Nazism and Soviet Communism. One can, therefore, give no accurate idea of thought in political science on most of the major problems of comparative politics without taking into account much noncomparative work, either work dealing with single contexts only or abstract theory. What is more, if one put such writings together, one could conceivably get more comprehensive and convincing comparative analyses than by considering solely works that are themselves comparative in character, although putting them together would mean, not merely reproducing, but also processing them by the use of comparative method.

For better or worse, however, the object of this Reader is not to give a comprehensive view of the ideas of political scientists on certain topics and problems. Rather, it is to present a broad view of the state of genuinely comparative studies in political science at the present time—to acquaint readers with a particular genre of analysis, some of the procedural problems it involves and most of the substantive uses to which it has been put. The gaps or other shortcomings in the materials presented are due (excepting only some materials we may have overlooked or omitted on other grounds) to nothing but the state of comparative political studies. Comparative politics has long existed in name; but, as the Introduction of the present volume seeks to demonstrate, has only recently been practiced extensively in fact. By reading the text anyone can see for himself how great and important some of these gaps and other shortcomings are. It is only fair to emphasize at the outset, however, that work in comparative politics is at present proceeding at such a pace that some of the gaps may be filled and some of the deficiencies remedied even while the present volume is being processed. By presenting the Reader in the form we have chosen, moreover, we hope to stimulate greater interest on the part of political scientists in extending and improving genuinely comparative political studies. There is plenty of scope for both.

The idea of this volume was conceived while the editors were fellows at the Center for Advanced Study in the Behavioral Sciences, Stanford, California, and some of the initial planning was also done there. One of the editors, Harry Eckstein, wishes to state his gratitude to the Center of International Studies at Princeton, for making available time during which his original contributions to the volume were written.

DAVID E. APTER
HARRY ECKSTEIN

*Berkeley, California*
*Princeton, New Jersey*

*March, 1963*

NOTE

1. Leo Strauss, *What Is Political Philosophy?* (New York: The Free Press of Glencoe, 1959), p. 23.

# Contents

## Constitutions and Constitutional Courts

## Parliamentary vs. Presidential Systems

## Conditions of Stable and Effective Democracy

# Part IV   ELECTORAL SYSTEMS

# Part V   POLITICAL PARTIES

# Part VI   PRESSURE AND INTEREST GROUPS

## Part *VII* TOTALITARIANISM AND AUTOCRACY

## Part *VIII* POLITICAL CHANGE

## *Part IX*   NON-WESTERN GOVERNMENT AND POLITICS

### *Discontinuity and Politics in the Developing Areas*

### *Political Organization*

## *Part X*   COMPARATIVE POLITICS AND POLITICAL THOUGHT:
### Past Influences and Future Development—DAVID E. APTER

## A SELECTIVE INTRODUCTION TO
## THE LITERATURE OF COMPARATIVE POLITICS

I

# I Introduction

# A PERSPECTIVE ON COMPARATIVE POLITICS, PAST AND PRESENT[1]

## Harry Eckstein

The field of comparative politics has a long and honorable past. That its pedigree reaches back as far as Aristotle is not unusual, since just about every discipline can, in one way or another, trace its origin to Aristotle. Comparative politics, however, has a particular right to claim Aristotle as an ancestor because of the primacy that he assigned to politics among the sciences and because the problems he raised and the methods he used are similar to those still current in political studies. From Aristotle stretches an impressive line of other Greats who can be numbered, without too much distortion, among the ancestors of the field: Cicero, Polybius, and Tacitus among the Romans; Machiavelli, among others, in the Renaissance; Montesquieu in the Enlightenment; and an imposing line of sages in the nineteenth century—Tocqueville, Marx, Mill, Bagehot, Mosca, and many more. The general analysis of political systems, the classification of their types, the study of the forms of their development, and the observation of the many varieties of actual political systems are concerns nearly as old as the history of recorded thought. These concerns have at least as time-honored a place in human thought as the concern with political morality.

Yet specialists in comparative politics seem today to be preoccupied, almost paradoxically, with questions we associate not with the maturity but with the infancy of a field of inquiry—questions about the fundamentals, the "first things," that govern the processes and ends of analysis. Such questions are raised only rarely in disciplines that have a highly developed tradition. If we are to understand the present state of comparative politics, we must know what these questions are and why they are being raised at this particular stage in the field's development.

## THE PRESENT STATE OF COMPARATIVE POLITICS

Let us begin with the questions. First of all, a host of procedural—perhaps one should say methodological and epistemological—questions are raised by contemporary students of comparative politics. What, they ask, is the very nature of comparative method: how is it used and what sorts of studies are not comparative? What can be learned by comparisons, assuming that we know how to make them properly? Is the comparative method in the social sciences, for example, really an adequate substitute for experimentation in the natural sciences, as has sometimes been claimed? Can it be used at all in a field like political science—that is, are political systems really comparable—or is each system unique, so that each particular political system is best dealt with by configurative rather than comparative analysis, by constructing a special *Gestalt,* a "profile" as Heckscher has called it? Even if this conclusion is not necessary, does not the comparative method operate usefully only within certain limits: at a relatively low level of theoretical abstraction, where analysis is not very broad in scale but confined, at most, to limited periods in time, certain geographic areas, or similar types of political structure? And what do we mean by concepts like uniqueness, abstraction, similarity? Not only are questions raised about such basic issues, but also about the proper use of specific devices for comparative analysis: for example, the proper uses of ideal and real types, of sampling methods, scaling techniques, and so on.

A second set of questions concerns the use of concepts in the field. These fall primarily into two categories: questions regarding the classification of political systems and questions regarding the elements of such systems.

In political science a bewildering variety of classificatory schemes is available. The most venerable of these schemes is still much in use and was never discarded (only amended, simplified, elaborated) from the time of the Greeks to the nineteenth century. It classifies political systems according to the number of participants in decision-making processes into monarchies, aristocracies, and democracies. Since the middle of the nineteenth century, however, schemes for classifying political systems have multiplied helter-skelter,

3

every man his own taxonomist. Today an almost embarrassing number of such schemes exists, requiring choices we do not really know how to make.

Some writers on politics use schemes consisting of two basic types, not, as in the classic case, of three. Some of these two-term schemes consist of polar types, limiting a continuum along which actual systems may be ranged, while others simply provide two "boxes" into which actual systems are placed. An example of the "box" approach is the classification of systems, now widely used, into Western and non-Western types. The continuum approach is found in a large number of schemes— for example, the division of political systems into constitutional and totalitarian, traditional and modern, or agricultural and industrial types.

Some students of politics choose instead classificatory schemes consisting of three basic terms. Weber, for example, classifies political systems according to the legitimations of authority dominant in them into traditional, rational-legal, and charismatic types. The Marxists classify them, according to the dominant economic class, into feudal, bourgeois, and proletarian systems. Coleman, departing less from the classic typology, characterizes them either as competitive, semicompetitive, or authoritarian. Dahl uses the terms democracy, hierarchy, and bargaining systems. (The last are added, presumably, to accommodate his interest in economic systems in which not "decisions" but, so to speak, mutual "accommodations" are arrived at.) Still another series of writers uses four-term schemes. Apter, for example, labels governments as dictatorial, oligarchical, indirectly representational, and directly representational. Almond once constructed a scheme typifying political systems, obviously on a variety of bases, as Anglo-American, Continental European, totalitarian, and preindustrial.

We can find in the literature schemes even more complicated than these. Edward Shils, for example, has recommended a five-term typology, constructed specifically to deal with the analysis of "new" states: political democracies, tutelary democracies, modernizing oligarchies, totalitarian oligarchies, and traditional oligarchies. Coleman, in another classificatory proposal, has gone Shils one better by dropping one of his categories (totalitarian oligarchy, which, presumably, would not be omitted in the analysis of established as well as new states) and adding two others, "terminal colonial democracy" and "colonial or racial oligarchy." And this is only a partial list, a sample.

We have here a considerable *embarras de richesses*. We can explain why it exists and why it should have come into existence after the middle of the nineteenth century, particularly in very recent times, for this variety of classifications is obviously a reflection of the rapid development of modern social theory and the broadening of the range of materials in the social sciences. The important point, however, is that such a disconcerting wealth of classificatory schemes inevitably raises some fundamental questions: Which scheme is more useful than others for any given purpose and, even more basic, what is the use of any classificatory schemes at all? How ought such schemes properly to be constructed, and how can one distinguish, in principle, a good scheme from a bad one?

The same questions arise in regard to the elements of political systems, taking "elements" to mean the parts into which such systems are divided and out of combinations of which they are, for analytical purposes, constituted. Following early modern usage, we used to think of these elements primarily as three: legislative, executive, and judicial structures and functions; but lately a large variety of alternatives have been proposed and used. Apter, for example, thinks of political systems as consisting primarily of government, political groups, and systems of social stratification. The last he considers the aspect of the social setting most directly and most significantly related to politics. Each of these elements is then further divided and subdivided to arrive at a large series of components of politics, certain of which supposedly "cluster" in typical (frequently found) political systems. Governments, for example, are held to have a certain "format" and to depend for their very existence on five structural requisites: authoritative decision-making, accountability and consent, coercion and punishment, resource determination and allocation, and political recruitment and role assignment. Lasswell presents a breakdown of political systems on the basis of seven functional variables (and explicitly because of his dissatisfaction with the classic separation-of-powers formula): intelligence, recommendation, prescription, invocation, application, appraisal, and termination. (The meanings of these anything but self-explanatory terms are immaterial to the present purpose.) Easton suggests that political systems have essentially two elements—inputs (demands and supports) and outputs (authoritative decisions)—while Almond provides a complicated breakdown of both inputs and outputs into seven so-called functional categories: four for "input" function (political socialization and recruitment, interest articulation, interest aggregation, and political communication) and three for "output" function (rulemaking, rule application, and rule adjudication—the classic formula, but restricted to only one aspect of political systems).

These also are only examples to which a good many others might be added, but they will suffice to illustrate the many different grounds on which a breakdown of political systems might be based— structural categories, functional categories, structural-functional categories, system requisites, elements of formal organization, elements of informal processes. They also show why questions should nowadays be in the air regarding the most basic aspects of such analytical breakdowns: their relative utility, their purpose as such, the "logic"—if there is any—of their construction.

To some extent, the answers to such questions depend on how one answers certain other basic questions that are also very much in the air these days. Is it, for example, more fruitful to treat political systems as autonomous systems or as systems embedded in other aspects of society? If we want to link politics with its larger setting, what aspect of that setting should we stress? Does social stratification really have the explanatory power Apter claims for it, so that we can safely dispense with the examination of other elements of setting? Or are the most significant links to be made with levels of economic development (as Lipset suggests), culture (as Beer implies), or personality (as political psychologists like Lasswell appear to argue)? Even more important for the way we break down and classify our data—and indeed also for our methods —what *is* a political system? What really is our subject matter? Is it "states"—governmental units possessing sovereignty—as the most venerable view in political science has it—or is it any power relationship (Catlin), any influence relationship (Lasswell), any system which allocates social values? And if the last, are we really interested in *any* such allocation or only, as Easton maintains, in *authoritative* allocations? That is to say, does government, in the traditional sense, remain our focus, or do we act upon the recommendations of a whole host of men, from Catlin to March, and examine in the construction of a truly general and comparative political science almost any interpersonal relationship, whether conventionally thought of as political or not?

Once we have dealt with such questions, a host of others, equally basic, remain. For example, what unit of analysis should we use in political studies? Should we use impersonal units, such as "roles" (clusters of expected behavior patterns revolving about a particular function) or "interactions" (acts and the responses they engender)? Or should we use a personal unit—that is, concrete individuals? Or superpersonal units, such as groups, institutions, or organizations (taking these in the specialized senses in which they are used in modern sociology)? What "perspectives" or "orientations" should we use in analyzing these units? Should we still emphasize, as we have traditionally emphasized, the study of formal constitutional structure or apply instead group theory, structural-functional analysis, the decision-making approach, communications theory—to mention only a few of the possible analytical approaches available to us? And what sort of "theories" do we want to construct through these

approaches: empirical "laws," models, causal explanations, functional analyses, equilibrium theories, developmental theories, or still other, as yet unexplored, types of theories?

These questions—about methods, concepts, definition of the field and its elements and boundaries, units of analysis, analytical approaches, and types of theories—will be recognized immediately as the most important metatheoretical and pretheoretical problems arising in any field of inquiry. ("Metatheoretical" refers to theory about theory—methodology, for example. "Pretheoretical" refers to operations that must be performed before the construction of theory proper—that is, before the formulation of testable hypotheses and their testing.) I have listed them here, not because I have any intention of answering them or resolving disputes about them, but solely because they can immediately tell us something important about the present condition of comparative politics.

In most fields of inquiry, such questions, despite their obvious importance, are either not raised at all or are raised only by the way and by men, like the members of the Vienna Circle, who have a special taste for philosophy and fundamentals— and men who are usually more influential outside of their fields than in them. Why then are they raised so much in comparative politics today? After all, students of politics, as I have stated, have had many centuries to reach settled conclusions about them. What is more, preoccupation with such questions, fundamental though they are (indeed just because they are fundamental), probably hinders more than it promotes substantive research. In a way such preoccupation involves a kind of vicarious experience of research. What then can explain the apparent paradox between the venerable age of the field and the infantile questions raised in it?

The answer is both simple and important. Some historians of science tell us that, despite the myth of steady scientific progress that we have inherited from the Enlightenment, the advance of science has not really been steady. Instead, it has been punctuated by revolutionary intervals in which the whole framework of scientific knowledge—all its basic, usually unspoken, assumptions—has come under heated debate: assumptions about the proper purpose of inquiry, about the nature of its subject-matter, about what constitutes satisfactory scientific knowledge. Science always functions within a framework of such preconceptions, but the preconceptions are never opened to examination when a consensus on them exists; men do not argue questions upon which they are agreed. In such cases of consensus one may indeed get the impression of a steady unfolding of a shared perspective upon scientific work. When consensus breaks down, however—when a field is marked by dissent or is in transition from one framework of inquiry to another —the fundamentals always come to the forefront;

the silent major premises cease to be silent. In such periods, if the breakdown of scientific consensus is broad enough, intensive philosophical exploration of a general sort occurs. If the breakdown is restricted to a narrow field, its practitioners will engage in metatheoretical and pretheroretical labors that, to others, may seem exotic and unrewarding, if not irrelevant to actual scientific work.

From this we can infer what is perhaps most basic about comparative politics today: that it is a field acutely in dissent because it is in transition from one style of analysis to another. For just this reason, it is a field in which many different styles of analysis are at present to be found. This being the case, we cannot give any simple account of comparative politics. Instead, to portray the character of the field today we must do three things: provide an historical account of its development, explain how it reached its present state of dissension, and expound the principal discontents and aspirations of its contemporary practitioners.

## THE ORIGINS OF COMPARATIVE POLITICS

Periodization is always hazardous. Nevertheless, we can locate the beginnings of the modern study of comparative politics with fair precision at that point in time when political systems came to be conceived not as natural bodies ("corporations") but as artifacts, created by men and therefore subject to re-creation (reform) by men. In short, its earliest source, leaving the classics aside, is Renaissance political thought, most obviously that of Machiavelli; and it comes to its first full fruition in the Enlightenment, above all in the writings of Montesquieu.

### Machiavelli and the Renaissance

When Burckhardt says that in the Renaissance the state came to be regarded as "a work of art," he does not mean that it was looked upon as something aesthetically pleasing; nor does he mean that political actions were considered to be self-justifying, like artistic creations, rather than subject, like works of morality, to fixed ethical codes; and he certainly does not mean that politics was not regarded as a proper subject for scientific analysis. He means precisely what he says—that the state had come to be regarded as an artifact, something that was made rather than something that simply was; for just that reason, it came to be looked upon in the Renaissance and Enlightenment as a proper subject *in itself* for "reflection and calculation."

We can, of course, reflect on the behavior of natural objects that are only imperfectly subject to human control or not subject to it at all; the natural sciences do almost nothing else. But the more *un-alterably* given we regard phenomena to be (that is, the less susceptible to human engineering), the more likely we are to be intellectually passive in regard to them, to dismiss "scientific" inquiry as futile or as an esoteric taste or to subsume study of the phenomena to the larger contemplation of "being as such"—to metaphysics, ontology, or theology. It is no accident, therefore, that the study of politics through the broad-scale examination of political experience comes to the forefront just when men are beginning to talk about an "art" of governing and of "statecraft." From this standpoint we can also understand why comparative inquiries, conducted to establish generalizations about political behavior and not merely to illustrate them, came first to be carried on when natural law doctrines were on the wane. If one really believes in a natural law that rigidly governs all human relations, then one is likely either to look for it through abstract speculation upon first principles or, even more likely, through very narrow studies of experience, since any limited range of experience—a single government, for example—will then illuminate as much as very broad ranges of experience—and the analysis of very broad ranges of experience is the hallmark of genuinely comparative studies. The point of view most hospitable to such studies is one that sees social life as governed by necessary relations, knowledge of which can be used in controlling, at least to some extent, human affairs.

In the Renaissance this point of view emerged, although art was emphasized far more than nature, and this emphasis is important. If one studies a subject primarily because one believes in the necessity of human engineering in the area it comprehends, inquiry into it is bound to be of a particular kind. Inevitably it will focus upon the discovery of techniques through which such engineering can be effectively carried out: upon *Staatskunst*, not *Staatswissenschaft*. Machiavelli himself is the primary example. What makes a ruler successful? How can power be won, maintained, expanded? What arrangements and practices make a state powerful, stable, free, prosperous? These are the quintessential problems of the political technician, and they are precisely the problems that preoccupied Machiavelli.

Moreover, if one's purpose is to discover directly techniques of statecraft—if, that is, one proceeds from the very beginning with what we now call "policy-oriented" studies—the methods one uses are also likely to be of a certain kind. In all probability they will be "empirical" in the most literal sense of the term; that is, they will involve the examination of experience as if it were a record of trial and error, of a kind of thoughtless experimentation, in which some procedures are revealed to be conducive and others not conducive to certain ends.[2] If anything further is done with such "rules of prudence," it will be to infer generalizations about psychological propensities underlying the rules and to deduce further rules of prudence, not revealed directly by experience, from the psychological propensities. Crude inductions, crude inferences from the inductions, and crude deductions from the inferences will always characterize such direct inquiries into statecraft. Certainly they characterize Machiavelli's. *The Prince* and *Discourses* teem with examples.

Consider only one, by no means the most blatant —the argument against using mercenary soldiers (Chapter XII of *The Prince*). No Prince who relies upon an armed force of mercenaries, says Machiavelli, can ever "stand firm or sure"; such troops are "disunited, ambitious, without discipline, faithless, bold amongst friends, cowardly amongst enemies, they have no fear of God, and keep no faith with men." Why so? Because it is not a man's nature to die for another purely for the sake of a wage; because the more competent a mercenary leader, the more, having no deep bond of loyalty to a Prince, he is likely to aspire to the Prince's place or otherwise to overstep his powers. And what is the evidence for these assertions? The helplessness of the Italian cities before King Charles of France, the oppression of the Carthaginians by their mercenaries, the fickleness of Francesco Sforza toward the Milanese, and the successes, in contradistinction, of Rome, Sparta, and the Swiss. But what about the Venetians and Florentines, who seemed to do well enough with mercenary forces? No matter, for they were "favored by chance": the ambitions of their mercenary captains were diverted elsewhere, and these captains *would* have caused more harm if they had been *more* competent. And so it goes, in nearly every chapter.

## Montesquieu and the Enlightenment

In the Enlightenment, such simple and disingenuous inductions, aiming at the discovery of political rules of prudence, still abound, along with deductive theories of the state influenced by Cartesian philosophy. In some writers of the Enlightenment, however, above all in Montesquieu, we can detect more modern and more sophisticated concerns, if not in method, then certainly in the problems raised and theories proposed. In many ways, *The Spirit of the Laws* is, in fact, a work astonishingly "modern."

To be sure, Montesquieu is interested, like Machiavelli, in using induction primarily for purposes of statecraft. What, after all, is his famous theory of the institutional conditions of freedom if not a rule of prudence based upon very limited and crude induction? But perhaps it would be more accurate to say that Montesquieu was interested not so much in statecraft, as Machiavelli would have understood the term, as in constitutional engineering—not in how rulers should behave but in how governments should be constituted. Unlike Machiavelli, whose argument proceeds from human nature, Mon-

tesquieu thought of right government primarily as a matter of sociology and ecology, of adjusting governmental structure to prevailing conditions. Hence, his interest in some very modern concerns: the relations of political systems to their physical environments, the role in politics of economic factors and of "manners and morals," problems of classifying political systems, and the like.

Any methodical arrangement of *The Spirit of the Laws* immediately gives it a contemporary ring, granted that such an arrangement must be largely imposed by others upon a study for which chaotic is a term of flattery. Take, as an example, the now widely followed scheme by G. Lanson. Montesquieu, according to this scheme, first considers the various types of government: their nature, their structural principles, and the conditions under which they arise and under which they tend to persist or decline (have "viability" or not, as we would say). He goes on to consider the functions of government, including provisions for the safety of the state (civil-military relations), the liberty of the subject, and the raising and expenditure of public monies ("resource allocation," in modern jargon). Then there follow a long series of chapters dealing with those aspects of their "setting" that condition political systems: ecological conditioning factors, such as climate, soil, and population; social institutions, such as the "relations between the sexes"; matters of culture (the "general spirit, the morals and customs of a nation," and religion); and economic conditioning factors (the "interrelation between commerce, morals, poverty, and the types of government"). Finally, there are some very scattered, but suggestive, hints at "developmental theory," at social dynamics no less than social statics.

Anyone *au courant* with modern comparative politics will recognize these topics as a large proportion of its stock in trade. And it is not only the topics that ring familiar, but also the way they are handled. Montesquieu's types of government, for example, are ideal types and quite consciously so in that they are logical structures based upon certain fundamental principles underlying the type, to which actual political systems only more or less correspond. Like modern sociologists, he thought of societies as being interconnected, as patterned structures, as "systems" the parts of which are interdependent in such a way that change in any one part leads to compensating changes in the others or to disintegration of the whole. Therefore, he produced an essentially mechanistic interpretation of social change, in distinction both to the voluntaristic theories prevalent in his time and the eschatological theories of history soon to be propounded. He has been called (by Meinecke, for example) one of the founders of "historicism," but this view is tenable only if we equate historicism with any theory of social change that assigns a role to involuntary social processes or if we use the term to denote any use of the "genetic" approach in social studies and not if we use it to describe grandiose theories of the meaning and goal of history. Montesquieu's modernity lay precisely in the fact that he worked at a nonvoluntaristic theory of social change without going over to the historicist extreme.

Was Montesquieu an aberration, a stranger to his own age? So it is often argued, but surely not correctly, for it is as plausible to regard him as the culmination of past trends of thought as to regard him as the precursor of writers still to come—not to mention other writers of his own time (such as Adam Smith, Hume, and Ferguson). Methodologically, a clear line runs to him from Descartes and through Malebranche. Montesquieu was certainly not the very crude empiricist that Machiavelli was,[3] but understood what it means to assert the existence of "social laws" (as Machiavelli, with his constant harping on chance and fortune, never did). He understood that these laws are to be found by a combination of logic and observation, that proper induction requires the wide-ranging observation of many contexts, and that logic has at least an equal, if not prior, role to play in scientific analysis.

While Montesquieu's method originated in Descartes, his problems, in contrast, were posed largely by Machiavelli and Bodin. His approach to developmental theory may be quite original, but he wrote at a time when social mechanism was very much in the air and sophisticated historiography at least beginning, however little the latter was influenced by the former. His concern with the relations between governments and their settings, especially his concern with physical environment, was anticipated in a large number of "modern" thinkers, including Bodin and Chardin. And his far-ranging empirical work was certainly connected with the very broad outlook of his age: its belief in the uniformity of men beneath their cultural differences and its relative freedom from the nationalistic and provincial biases that predisposed subsequent thinkers to regard political systems as unique and incomparable.

In Montesquieu, then, and in the writings of lesser men of the Enlightenment, we can see emerging a comparative science of politics not so very different from that which present political scientists seem to want: a "science" aiming at the construction of a structural-functional analysis of political systems, a sophisticated typology of such systems, a set of broad generalizations about the links between polity, society, economy, and environment, and a set of mechanistic theories of political dynamics—all in embryo, of course, but, in many cases, in surprisingly sophisticated form. Between the late eighteenth century and the present, however, a number of forces intervened that sidetracked political studies from these paths, so that we can regard the intervening development of comparative political studies as an elaborate veering away from and return to the lines of analysis sketched, however incoherently, by Montesquieu.

## HISTORICISM

Although Montesquieu's ideas had many antecedents, they undoubtedly were aberrations in the sense that very different ideas set the tone in social thought immediately after his time.[4] Not sociological historiography but rampant historicism—universal history, speculations on the first causes and final end of history—became the dominant style of social thought. This style (the style of Bossuet, Vico, and Condorcet rather than of Montesquieu) affected the study of all social phenomena. In the study of political institutions interest now came to be centered primarily upon historical first principles, upon the "cunning of history," upon the construction of audacious developmental theories, unilinear in form, based on single determining principles and more often than not predicting the imminent universality of democracy—theories of change more organic than mechanistic in form. The best examples are obvious and familiar: Condorcet, with his belief in the simultaneous unfolding of reason and democracy; Hegel, with his belief in the unfolding of Reason and Freedom; Comte, with his belief in the unfolding of the scientific spirit (and, in contrast to the prophets of democracy, his prediction of the coming benevolent dictatorship of well-informed bankers); Marx, with his belief in the unfolding of freedom through class conflict.

Although historicism has long since become discredited, the field of comparative politics owes a great deal to this phase in Western social thought. In the first place, many of its concepts are still used and used fruitfully ("class," for example). Many of its problems are still raised, above all, problems about the relations between politics and economic development, politics and education, politics and the "culture" of societies. Historicist theories also directed attention, to some extent at least, to a broad panorama of political experience. Hegel, for example (among many possible examples), was anything but a parochial thinker, his ideas ranging widely, if not very accurately, over China, India, Persia, Judaea, Byzantium, and the Mohammedan world, as well as over ancient and medieval Western history. The historicists were also responsible for much of the subsequent interest in social dynamics—especially in evolutionary theory, which helped, much more than did the less fanciful Montesquieu, to counterbalance the voluntaristic biases of political historians. Most of all, interest in broad-scale theory as such derives, in large part at least, from historicism.

But if the historicists bequeathed to subsequent students of comparative politics much to aim at and much to imitate, they also gave them much to overcome. Their broad-scale theorizing was mainly a matter of abstract and formal speculation upon the broadest conceivable questions; for the canons of accurate observation—for "content," in Hegel's terminology—they had a monumental disregard. Their data, in almost every case, were invoked merely to illustrate, not to test, their theories, so that one searches in vain in their works for a methodologically valid bridge between theory and data. In effect, their work engendered two interests that never really meshed: an interest in the construction of the most ambitious and contentless kinds of theories, on one hand, and an interest in detailed and formless political history, a sort of political ethnography, on the other. They did not, however, engender (if anything, they discouraged) the sort of concerns that every young discipline ought to concentrate upon: the formulation and meticulous empirical testing of "middle-range" hypotheses and the tentative conceptual exploration of a field. The basic charge against the historicists is, consequently, that while they induced an interest in theorizing about wide ranges of data (the essence of any "comparative" study), both their theories and uses of data, and above all the way they related theory and data, ultimately proved sterile. They tried too early to do too much, and so, in the end, contributed very little—except some interesting problems and theoretical approaches, and some very far-ranging misinformation.

Perhaps this explains why the historicists, in the final analysis, had a far greater influence upon politics (through the ideological impact of their theories) than upon political science. Concepts they used continued to be used; questions they raised continued to be raised; but the whole style of the historicists, their basic approach to social analysis, constituted only a swiftly passing phase in the development of social thought—granted the occasional appearance of a throwback to the historicist era. A large number of forces converged in the later nineteenth century to discredit historicism; in the realm of philosophy, the rise of positivism and philosophical pluralism; in politics, the rise of nationalism; in social thought, the impact of cultural relativism; in the general climate of opinion, the reaction against the softer idealisms, the tough-mindedness and perhaps petty-mindedness that followed the great disillusion of 1848. All these conspired against theories inadequately grounded upon observation, blandly optimistic, and assuming a uniformity of development for every society and nation, so that in the end historicism came to be important not so much for the positive influence it exercised as for the reactions to which it led. Certainly this is the case if we confine ourselves to the history of the comparative study of politics.

## REACTIONS AGAINST HISTORICISM

In the study of politics, the reaction against historicism took many different forms, each undoubtedly for good reasons, but each involving also a serious retrogression from the promising lines reached in the eighteenth century. Not Condorcet and his kind only, but Montesquieu and his kind as well, were rejected in the process.

### Abstract Theory

One of the reactions against historicism was emphasis upon purely abstract political analysis, especially criticisms and defenses of democracy on the basis of deductions from metaphysical, ontological, psychological, and legal premises. This reaction has only a remote, though nonetheless significant, bearing on the study of comparative politics. Its relevance is, in gist, that in the post-historicist period, institutional and philosophical political studies, studies with "content" and studies with "form," became more rigidly separated than at any previous time in the history of political thought, a fact with the most momentous significance for the development of comparative political studies. Historicist thought, whatever its shortcomings, had at least one virtue: it joined, however unsatisfactorily, thought and data. The historicists did think about something, not just about thought. Even Hegel, who believed in the autonomy of formal thought from its content, at least undertook to fill the form with concrete matter in order to portray, if not to test, his formal theories. Those who reacted against historicism, however, did not initially attempt to improve upon what had been at best an uneasy marriage of fact and speculation. They resorted instead to outright divorce, so that in the wake of historicism (in the late nineteenth and early twentieth centuries, roughly) political thought tended to become, so to speak, increasingly subjective and the study of political objects increasingly thoughtless.

The contemporary study of politics as a separate field, and of comparative politics as a separate subdivision of the field, begins, unhappily, perhaps disastrously, at this very point in time. That fact tells us a great deal about one of the more remarkable, if not absurd, characteristics of the political science curriculum: the division of the field into the study of political thought and the study of political institutions and behavior. More to the point here, however, is that it tells us a great deal also about the development of comparative political studies in the post-historicist period.

### Formal-Legal Studies

The separation of thought and data is at least partly responsible for a second reaction to historicism that does have a direct bearing upon comparative politics: the increasingly exclusive stress in the study of political actualities on formal political institutions—that is to say, on constitutional and legal structure (then called "public law"). Not all data lend themselves equally well to thoughtless treatment. Those that do so well are unequivocal data, easy to come by and subject to a minimum of interpretation; those that do so best are data that come to us, not in the usual way, inchoate and unordered, but in some already ordered form. And what data in political science present themselves in such a fashion—preprocessed, so to speak? Obviously two sorts: one, political thought itself; the other, formal institutional arrangements, prescribed in documents that are, in fact, mental constructs (and often bad hypotheses), but that can be treated as if they were raw data of political experience, for the political scientist does not invent them, but comes upon them, as he comes upon behavioral data of quite different sorts.

The emphasis in the study of politics upon formal-legal arrangements is thus a natural outgrowth of the positivistic reaction to historicism, simply because primitive positivism, in attempting to restrict the role of thought, naturally leads the analyst to steer clear of the more inchoate data. Primitive, unadulterated positivism insists upon *hard* facts, indubitable and incontrovertible facts, as well as facts that speak for themselves—and what facts of politics are harder, as well as more self-explanatory, than the facts found in formal legal codes? And what other facts are equally conducive to *Wertfreiheit* in analysis, to what purports to be hardheaded, ethically neutral empiricism? Perhaps this argument may seem strange today. Most of the self-labeled positivists in contemporary political science are concerned with precisely the sort of inchoate materials that their predecessors ignored: voting behavior materials, power and influence relations, elite structures, informal political processes, and so on. But this does not controvert the fact that the initial impact of positivism upon the field was to direct attention toward superficial facts, even pseudo-facts; nor does it deny that the positivistic outlook as such creates, even today, a preference for the superficial over the profound.

The emphasis upon formal-legal structure that came to be the dominant empirical style of political studies in the late nineteenth century was not, however, due to the post-historicist dissociation of thought and data alone, although that dissociation alone may sufficiently explain it. One other factor that certainly made for emphasis upon formal-legal structure, especially upon constitutional documents, is simply that the nineteenth century was a great age of constitution-making. In fact, one would be hard-pressed to find "constitutions," in the sense of elaborate formal-legal codes rationally devised to create political organizations and govern political processes, in a previous period.

If we go to earlier periods, we find constitutions in the Burkean and typically British sense of the term (constitutions as historical accretions of institutions and processes that can be stated in, but are not defined by, formal rules); we find one or two prophetic documents, like the *Instrument of Government,* as quaint in their own time as they are common later; and we find charters—bills, and documents called "constitutions"—that are not constitutions in the modern sense at all, but either contractual agreements between princes and subjects (such as municipalities and social groups) or solemn and explicit declarations of historically evolved political relations. This discovery is hardly surprising, for the very idea of a constitution in the modern sense could not have occurred to anyone who regarded the political order as a "natural" thing and is, therefore, properly a product of a time when mechanistic social beliefs, coupled with faith in the powers of human engineering, displaced earlier organicist and historicist ideas. Of course, these beliefs alone were not enough to make political studies focus upon constitutional documents; the documents themselves had to be there to study—as indeed they were, in constantly growing numbers, in the late nineteenth century. But the prevalent mechanistic outlook and faith in social engineering of the period explain at least why constitutional codes were taken so seriously, by politicians and students of politics alike.

Inevitably, these beliefs and interests also left a deep mark on the virgin field of "political science." Indeed, the very fact that political science emerged in this period as a separate, autonomous field of study divorced from philosophy, political economy, and even sociology, may have created a tendency to emphasize the study of formal-legal arrangements, quite apart from any other factors moving the field in this direction. If a study becomes departmentally *sui generis,* it will try also to assume a subject matter and techniques of study that are *sui generis.* And what subject matter can be regarded as purely political? Political behavior, in the larger sense in which we now regard it, is touched upon by the subject matters of all sorts of other disciplines: those of sociology, social and individual psychology, cultural anthropology, and economics. If there is any subject matter at all which political scientists can claim exclusively for their own, a subject matter that does not require acquisition of the analytical tools of sister-fields and that sustains their claim to autonomous existence, it is, of course, formal-legal political structure. Its study, therefore, quite naturally became the focal point of the new discipline of political science in search of a *raison d'être*.

Perhaps we ought to add to this list of factors making for emphasis on formal-legal studies (and it is an emphasis that requires a lot of explaining) still one other: the emphasis in the teaching of politics at this time upon "training"—training for citizenship and for public administration and preliminary training for the law. This emphasis was particularly great in the "new" states of Europe, above all in the newly unified Germany. Sigmund Neumann has pointed out that in the Bismarckian era, the German universities, once the centers of the fight for freedom, were "gradually transformed into guardians of training for leadership in important public offices, the judiciary, the bureaucracy, and the teaching profession." The "value-free" sociology of Weber and others is regarded by Neumann as one illustration of these tendencies; the emphasis on studies in formal public law may be considered another. To what were they due? Neumann attributes them to the regime's authoritarianism and German admiration for the Iron Chancellor's successes; but we can just as plausibly regard them as responses to the new state's need to "socialize" men into new political patterns: to inculcate in them civic loyalty and educate them to play roles in new administrative and legal arrangements. Perhaps this is an even more plausible interpretation than Neumann's, particularly when we take into account the emphatic interest in formal-legal codes in the United States. No authoritarianism, no admiration for successful *Realpolitik*, existed here to dampen the impulse to moral criticism in politics or the drive to uncover the deeper forces determining political actualities.

It is true, of course, that the German universities were extremely influential in America around the turn of the century, but the United States had also in common with Germany a tremendous problem in political "socialization," due in one case to the creation of a new political system and in the other to mass immigration. In both cases, the agencies most readily available for dealing with these functional needs were educational institutions, especially institutions of secondary and higher education. Hence, there was a mushroom growth of civics courses providing indoctrination into citizenship and of courses preparing for participation, in one role or another, in the political structure—above all, courses in public administration, constitutional development, and public law. Courses in political "behavior," as we now use that term, could hardly have performed the same necessary function in either system—might indeed have been dysfunctional in both settings. And it *is* a fact that formal-legal studies were mainly German and American in origin, epitomized in the German case

by the truly gargantuan collection of monographs appearing from 1883 on, the *Handbuch des Oeffentlichen Rechts der Gegenwart* (Handbook of Contemporary Public Law), and in the American case by a study of Woodrow Wilson's, based largely upon the *Handbuch,* which will be discussed presently.[5]

## Configuration Studies

A third reaction against historicism in political studies involved a drift away from comparative studies of all sorts and toward "configurative" analysis—the analysis of particular political systems, treated either explicitly or implicitly as unique entities. Many political studies of the immediate post-historicist period exhibit a considerable narrowing of the analytical attention, a tendency to cover very little ground, and to cover it in great, often indiscriminate detail. This tendency not only restricted attention to one set of political data—formal-legal structure—but also was restricting in a geographic and historical sense. To some extent this narrowing of analysis in time and space may have been the result of the very emphasis on formal-legal structure, for such an emphasis necessarily makes one work within the compass of particular constitutional systems and is, for reasons already mentioned, appropriate only to a limited period in European history. We can see this narrowing influence of the formal-legal approach reflected even in some of the wider-ranging political studies of the post-historicist period, particularly in the large number of compilations of constitutional provisions then published, and taken very seriously. But configuration analysis was also an outcome of some of the factors that produced the emphasis on formal-legal studies itself: the reaction against broad speculative theories of any sort; the influence of nationalism and its roots in the idea of national character, which logically implies that each nation is an analytically unique entity; the emphasis on citizenship training and vocational training in an age of rapidly expanding national bureaucracies.

This is not to say that only narrow political studies, confined to particular nation-states, were produced in this period.[6] There was no dearth of studies ranging over very wide territory indeed, but it is characteristic of these studies that their theoretical import should be almost inversely proportional to the range of material included. Generally speaking, they presented a wide panorama of political materials with a theoretical equipment restricted to little more than Aristotle's classifications of governments and to abstract speculations on abstract questions and with the materials arranged either in terms of the three basic forms of government, in chronological order, or in a combination of chronology and form of government.

An example of this sort of political study—probably the most famous—is Wilhelm Roscher's *Poli-*

*tik,* written intermittently between 1847 and 1892, but chiefly in the last few years of this time span. The revealing subtitle, *Geschichtliche Naturlehre der Monarchie, Aristokratie und Demokratie* (Natural History of Monarchy, Aristocracy and Democracy), of course, gives the whole work away. Its principal theoretical concern is with the proper classification of states, a question Roscher settled by adding a fourth category, Caesarism, to the three classical categories and by distinguishing among plutocratic, proletarian, and middle-class states (still well within the Aristotelian framework). The study is based upon an explicit rejection of the "idealistic" studies of the times—that is, purely abstract treatments like that of Fichte, who, in Roscher's own words, "conceived political science to have only the business of depicting a best state, so that reality appeared to him as real only in so far as it corresponded to the image of this best state." Roscher, on the contrary, sets out to do precisely what the idealists most disdained, namely, to present a *Naturlehre,* a set of "naturalistic descriptions" of the *Notstaaten* so despised by the theorists of the *Idealstaaten.* And this he does very largely, though not exclusively, in the manner of historical narrative within each of the classificatory categories he adopts.

The result is a work displaying, even by Germanic standards, a truly massive learning. Switzerland, Athens, Rome, Gaul—Egypt, Normandy, Sparta, Venice—Spanish America, Tudor England, the Hebrew State—Brahmanism, Buddhism, Jesuitism, Protestantism—Demosthenes, Henry VIII, Hannibal, Napoleon—the book is almost a political encyclopedia. In this it is reminiscent of nothing so much as the more extravagant historicist theories; but the history it presents is history without the "ism," a matter of content with very little form, a pointless display of interminable exactitudes. It is in such works that we see the real impact of the divorce of thought and data on the field of comparative politics, just at the time when its practitioners became conscious of having a separate disciplinary identity.

## TWO SYNTHESES

Political ethnography, purely abstract speculations, formal-legal studies, and configuration studies—these are all different, even antithetical, reactions against historicism. But because they come from a single source, one should not be surprised to see them combined, however uneasily and in however ill-fitting a manner, in the large syntheses of political thought of the period. These "large syntheses" are not necessarily works of great merit. More often than not, in fact, such works are written by secondary figures, by those who ape the styles of the times rather than those who create them; but they do provide a very broad picture of the dominant fashions in analysis. Any number of such studies could be used to exemplify the immediate post-historicist period in comparative politics, but two may suffice here: one, published in 1878 by Theodore D. Woolsey, a former President of Yale, entitled rather grandiosely *Political Science, or the State Theoretically and Practically Considered;* the other, by his later Princeton counterpart, Woodrow Wilson, a work with the even more prolix title, *The State: Elements of Historical and Practical Politics: A Sketch of Institutional History and Administration* (1895).

Both Woolsey's and Wilson's subtitles, like Roscher's, tell us, in the typically ingenuous fashion of the late nineteenth century, the most basic things we need to know about their studies. Each portrays mainly two of the anti-historicist styles we have discussed, though in each may be found examples also of the others.

Woolsey's work, an ambitious and pretentious undertaking indeed, is in effect a combination of purely abstract speculations and purely concrete political ethnography. When Woolsey talks about the state "theoretically considered," he refers primarily to two of the three categories into which German writers on politics had by then come to divide political studies: *Naturrecht* (natural rights—sometimes *Staatsrecht,* public rights) and *Staatslehre* (theory of the state). The first of these, *Naturrecht* (Woolsey calls it the "Doctrine of Rights as the Formulation of a Just State") is, of course, concerned with normative theories of political freedom and obligation. This part of the study bears no relation to anything subsequently said in it, but it is justified in Woolsey's own mind on the ground that no state worthy of the name is unjust, that justice in the state mainly consists of the safeguarding of natural rights, and that, therefore, there is no point in discussing the state without discussing the theory of natural rights—a curious syllogism, to say the least, but one that does encompass in a flimsy way the bifurcation of theory and data that confronted Woolsey.

To this concern with natural rights is added a series of concerns that Woolsey himself identifies as *Staatslehre,* a veritable rag bag of ethical and nonethical questions: "Opinions on the Nature of the State and on Its Origins," "Theories of Sovereignty," "The Proper Ends and Sphere of the State," "The Organization of States" (whether the desire for it is instinctive or habitual, the need for a "constitution," the various departments of government, distinctions between representative and non-representative systems), "Theories of Communism and Socialism," "Limits and Extent of the Punitive Power of the State," and sundry normative questions ("Can the Citizen's or Subject's Connection with the State Terminate?" "What Are the Limits of Loyalty and Obedience?" "What of Conflicts between Law and Conscience?").

All these problems, normative or not, are mainly discussed abstractly in the light of the abstract speculations of other political theorists. Politics "practically considered," on the other hand, turns out to be what the late nineteenth-century Germans understood by *Politik*: the large-scale historical examination of political institutions from earliest to modern times, mainly in terms of the classical categories; the formal examination of the "departments" and "institutions" of central and local government; and, at the very end, a few afterthoughts (one or two quite reminiscent of Montesquieu, whom Woolsey had obviously read but not really understood) on the influences of "Physical Causes on Politics," on "National Character," and on the "Causes of Political Change and Revolutions." In short, the whole book, save only for the very end, is either unmitigatedly abstract or pointlessly concrete, and the quotation cited from it on the relations of the study of rights and the state, which introduces the work, is a good indication of the way Woolsey relates theory to data throughout.

Woodrow Wilson's *The State* is admittedly his minor piece—though anything but a modest one, going on as it does through 1,287 sections, large and small. From our standpoint, however, it is much more worth examining than his more distinguished work, for two reasons: one, that it purports to be a text on politics of unprecedented scope, a summation of the empirical knowledge of the State in his time; the other, that it begins with large claims for comparative politics as the only proper approach to understanding political experience.

But what is "comparative" politics to Wilson? Essentially, it signifies to him, as to Woolsey, a very detailed and far-ranging political ethnography primarily as historical narrative and secondarily through the depiction of contemporary formal-legal structure. About five-sixths of the work is devoted to such bald descriptions. Wilson begins the study with some questions about the probable origins of government—a fact whose significance we shall see later, but this subject, after a cursory consideration of evolutionary and early anthropological theories, soon takes him to the more congenial ground of classical history, where his political ethnography proper begins. The political institutions, first of Greece and Rome, then of "Teutonic Polity" in the Middle Ages, and then of German and French feudalism and monarchy are painstakingly examined; the chapters on them constitute the "institutional history" section of the work. The "practical politics" side of the study involves mainly an indiscriminate detailing of the formal-legal structures of French, German, Swiss, Austro-Hungarian, Swedish-Norwegian, British, and American governments. And all this, counting some historical discussions scattered throughout, takes up nearly a thousand sections.

Not until section 1,121 is any attempt made to draw any "comparative" conclusions. And what are these conclusions? Their modesty is perhaps as remarkable as the ostentatiousness of the data on which they are based. Essentially, Wilson distills from his materials three inferences: political change has taken the form of a very slow process of development from more primitive to more highly developed political organizations; modern political experience confirms the Aristotelian classifications, although modern monarchies, aristocracies, and democracies have some features not found in the ancient world; governments are all pretty much alike—denying the view of those (Wilson claims the great majority) who believe in the uniqueness of political systems—but there are differences between governments, due partly to unique historical backgrounds and partly to "nation-marks," an argument that immediately reinstates the belief in uniqueness, albeit in a milder form. Finally, in a sort of epilogue, Wilson considers some purely abstract questions in primarily an abstract way: sovereignty, the nature of law, the classification of the functions of government, political rights, whether society is greater than government, and so on. That is the total extent of Wilson's *summa*—for a *summa* in a way it is, a summation of all the dominant modes of political thought of his time.

## POLITICAL EVOLUTIONISM

Undoubtedly this is an incomplete account of post-historicist studies in comparative politics. It has dealt only with dominant themes in American and German political studies. As a result, it necessarily is less than just to those writers who were, as some writers always are, out of tune with the dominant trends, who lagged behind the times or marched ahead of them. For example, Bluntschli, in his monumental (and much neglected) *Theory of the State,* begins with an explicit rejection of two "false methods," "abstract ideology" and "mere empiricism," and a special plea for methods of "concrete thinking," and lives up to this position at least to some extent (though Bentley denies it). We can no doubt find other important writers equally at odds with the tenor of the times. This is especially the case in regard to a school of writers who, more than any others, kept comparative politics alive throughout this largely anticomparative period, writers whose works have very wide scope, who combine theory and data almost on the scale of the historicists, and who are alluded to in almost every work on politics of the period, even the narrowest, most abstract, and most formal-legal—the political evolutionists.

Evolutionary studies might of course be considered a particular kind of historicism, and in some forms they do come close to what is nowadays (after Popper) generally meant by that term. Those evolutionary studies which posit some inevitable goal (such as democracy or perfect freedom) for the evolutionary process and a basic evolutionary principle (such as survival of the fittest, economic growth, progressive economic differentiation) as, so to speak, the "spirit" of the process are almost indistinguishable from historicist theories. Most evolutionists rejected, however, the too audacious, often ill-informed, theories of the historicists no less than did the pure philosophers, the formal-legalists, and the political ethnographers, although they rejected them in different ways and for different reasons.

Evolutionary theories about politics involved, in the first place, an empirical reaction against historicism in that the evolutionists paid meticulous attention to data that the historicists had on the whole treated only in the vaguest generalities—particularly primitive, early Western, and non-Western political systems. Evolutionism involved also a theoretical reaction against historicism. Instead of attempting to write universal history, including the future no less than the past, they concentrated upon much more limited problems—particularly the problem of the origin of the modern territorial state. As a general rule, they tried merely to find the processes and laws underlying the development of complex political systems. This is in every sense a more limited concern than that which motivated Condorcet or Hegel. At their best, evolutionary studies combined the respect for data of the ethnographers with the modesty in speculation of contemporary middle-range theorists. Granted that some of the theories the evolutionists produced look very peculiar nowadays—that is less the result of any dubious procedures on their part than of the fact that they proceeded from theoretical presuppositions and asked theoretical questions that have simply gone out of fashion.

### Evolutionary Theories

What sort of theories did the evolutionists produce? Essentially two kinds: theories of sequence—the stages of political development—and theories of the moving forces behind the evolutionary sequences. The most common theory of sequence traced the origin of the modern state to a continuous process of social enlargement and complication beginning with the primordial family. Among many works arguing this point of view probably the most illustrious are Sir Henry Maine's *Ancient Law* (1861) and *Early History of Institutions* (1874), in which political life is depicted as beginning with the patriarchal family and proceeding through two intermediate units, the house and the tribe, before the territorially contiguous form of the state is reached. This argument is based on a meticulous examination of Hebrew, Greek, Roman, and Hindu history.

The principal alternative to this interpretation is one that traces the origin of the state not to the family but rather to the disintegration of primitive social forms—not to the growing size and complexity of social units but to the opposite, the gradual individuation of human beings, their extrication from collectivities in which individuality itself is absorbed into the larger unit. So, for example, Edward Jenks argued, in *A Short History of Politics* and *The State and the Nation,* both published toward the end of the period under consideration (1900 and 1919), that the proper sequence for the emergence of the territorial state is not Maine's, but rather from hunting pack to tribe, from tribe to clan, from clan to family, and from there to nonkinship units, individuals, and the state. In a sense, he reverses Maine's arguments.

As to the moving forces behind these sequences, a much greater variety of theories confronts us. Some evolutionists attributed the rise of the state, particularly the transition from the patriarchal family to the more extended political groups, to religious forces. The usual theory is that of Fraser's *Golden Bough* (for a political scientist's version, see Sir John Seeley's *Introduction to Political Science,* 1896), which traces the evolution of simple patriarchal authority through gerontocrats claiming a special skill in dealing with the world of spirits and through the rule of specialized magicians to that of the priest-king. Fraser's work was based largely on studies of societies with which Maine had not dealt in detail, such as ancient Egypt and primitive societies portrayed in early anthropological studies.

Another group of theorists, especially Oppenheimer in *The State* (1914), find the propelling force leading to the state not in religion but in force, in the building-up of gradually larger units through systematic conquest. Still another theory claims that the state comes into being through the impact of social differentiation on primitive social forms, especially through the appearance of vertical stratification. This view is argued, for example, by W. C. MacLeod in two works, *The Origins of the State* (1924) and *The Origin and History of Politics* (1921), studies in which Darwin, Marx, and early anthropology are all combined in a rather curious mixture.

A fourth theory linked the evolution of political institutions with economic changes, not so much in the style of Marx as in that of Rousseau's *Essay on the Origins of Inequality.* An example is Oppenheimer's *The State,* which, in effect, combines the conquest theory of the state with an economic theory of its origins. Oppenheimer argues that complex forms of government are made necessary by class distinctions based on wealth and that the institution of slavery to build up a labor force is the basic foundation of the state. ("The moment when the first conqueror spared his victim in order to exploit him is of incomparable historical importance. It gave birth to nation and state. . . .") Some writers linked the development of the state with the development of pastoral pursuits as such, others with the accumulation of surplus wealth, still others with the development of the idea of property or population pressures upon resources and resulting wars of conquest or, as we have seen, social differentiation of any sort.

Finally, certain writers produced "diffusion" rather than "convergence" theories of the state. These theories argue, in effect, that the factors leading to the state did not produce it in different places through force of similar circumstances, but that the state came into being only once and in only one place through "natural causes" and then gradually spread, presumably because of its organizational superiority and through a process combining conquest and borrowing, to other societies, like the well-known ripples in the pool. For example, G. E. Smith and W. J. Perry, in *The Origin and History of Politics* (1931), place the origin of the state in Egypt around the year 5000 B.C. Here the state emerged, in their view, through a convergence of religious and economic forces never duplicated elsewhere. From Egypt it spread, by quite another sort of inevitability, to the rest of the world.

### The Legacy of Evolutionism

Developmental theories of this sort have gone out of style in our age of static models, "systemic" theories, and equilibrium analyses; and so they have about them a musty and archaic flavor, an ambience of crumbling volumes in the dark recesses of libraries and of vain debates long since resolved in irreconcilable disagreements. Yet the pursuit of such theories spans a period from mid-nineteenth century to a mere generation ago, a period that overlaps on one end with historicism itself and on the other with the comparative politics of our own time. In fact, the larger syntheses of political evolutionary studies still smell of fresh ink, the best-known perhaps being Book I of MacIver's *The Modern State,* first published in 1926 and reissued last in 1955, and Part II of E. M. Sait's *Political Institutions,* published first in 1938. Sait calls his study *A Preface,* a rather melancholy fact when viewed from the perspective of our time, for it is, in fact, an epilogue and a summing-up. This useful summing-up synthesizes all the divergent tendencies of nearly a century of evolutionary thought about politics, however, as witness the following extract:[7]

The State is composed of three elements: people, government and territory. From the beginning, groups of people are bound together by the cohesive force of kinship and religion. The family is the primordial unit, which expands into sibs (*gentes,* clans) and the tribe.

Among pastoral people, patriarchal discipline prepares the way for tribal government; tribesmen who are accustomed to give unquestioning obedience to their respective family heads naturally accept the authority of the council of elders or patriarchs and of the chieftain who rises out of the council. But the emergence of government—that is, an intensified regulative system—within the kinship group must be associated with economic causes, with the adoption of pastoral pursuits and the accumulation of surplus wealth. Property introduces all sorts of complications. There are disputes within the tribe to be settled; there are raids by avaricious neighbors to be repelled. The situation calls for individual leadership. Some member of the council, more energetic and enterprising than his fellows (and for that reason more wealthy), pushes his way to the front with or without the assistance of religious superstition. He, or some one who later essays the same role, is recognized as chieftain. Since the qualities of leadership are likely to be inherited, the office becomes attached to a particular family and is transmitted like other forms of property. Government exists. But although the pastoralists may confine their wanderings within roughly determined geographical limits, they are still nomads.

The territorial State does not appear until population begins to press upon subsistence. Then one of two courses may be followed: new land may be acquired by migration or the old land put to more productive use. Fertile pasturage, when brought under cultivation, will support a much larger population; and the tribesmen have long been familiar with the possibility of raising grain and vegetables from wild seed. Rather than leave the region to which they have become attached, they supplement the prevailing pastoral economy with the rudiments of agriculture. Gradually the herdsmen become husbandmen. The transition takes place slowly, as, by trial and error or by the imitation of some neighboring agriculturists, the methods of tillage are improved and their potentialities realized. Along with the new system of production come great social changes: above all, the sharpening of class distinctions, the systematic resort to slavery, the emphasis placed upon military life (first for defense, then for conquest), and the establishment of monarchy. With settlement upon the land and the acquisition of fixed abodes, the original kinship tie gives way, naturally but stubbornly, to the new territorial tie . . .

In some such way the State arose.

Because evolutionary political studies have passed out of fashion, their importance is all too easily underrated, but they constituted a tremendously important phase in the development of comparative politics. Above all, they kept comparative study itself alive in a period when it was threatened from every direction. Along with political ethnography they helped to focus attention on political systems other than those of the West just when the academic emphasis on training exerted great pressure toward restricting the political scientist's span of attention. They posed genuine theoretical problems when political scientists were concerned mainly with depicting formal-legal structures. They kept alive a systematic interest in links between political institutions and other aspects of society and kept political science in touch with other social sciences, especially sociology and cultural anthropology, when the newly won departmental autonomy of the field produced attitudes threatening to cut it off from a vast range of relevant data and many useful theories. To be sure, they led in political studies to the consideration of a very limited range of problems, especially concern with the origin of certain widespread political forms and the attempt to discover common sources for similar political institutions in different societies—the chief purpose of E. A. Freeman's celebrated *Comparative Politics*. But that was better at least than no concern at all with problems requiring large-scale comparisons.

## EARLY POLITICAL SOCIOLOGY

Anyone acquainted with political thought in the late nineteenth and early twentieth centuries will realize immediately that some formidable names that might have been mentioned in connection with the state of comparative political studies in this period are still missing from the picture, even after writers like Bluntschli and the evolutionists have been discussed. I refer to a number of men who loom very large in political science (not least in comparative politics) today, but who do not readily fit into any of the categories used here to characterize the political thought of their own time—men like Mosca and Max Weber, Pareto and Michels, the most illustrious of the early modern political sociologists. All constructed large-scale theories of politics, but theories certainly not purely formal in character. With the possible exception of Michels, they all ranged over wide sweeps of data, but not in the pointlessly empirical manner of the political ethnographers. They were more interested in actual power relations than in constitutional documents, more concerned with recurrent actual patterns of authority than with the inherited formal distinctions between types of government.

They did not restrict the subject matter of their studies to the state but branched out into all sorts of other political phenomena, from the government of political parties to that of private groups, and they explored systematically the impact on politics of its setting. In doing these things, they developed novel analytical perspectives for political studies, devised new concepts, proposed empirically relevant hypotheses, and developed unconventional techniques for applying comparative methods. They engaged, in short, in just the sort of conceptual, methodological, and theoretical explorations that would seem to be the major present concerns in comparative politics.

Why then have they been omitted from the story? Simply because only the *creation* of their works belongs to the period we have been discussing. Their impact on the field of comparative politics belongs to a later time, when the concerns of its practitioners had changed in such a manner as to make them more receptive to the sociologists' ideas. But this is not to say that political scientists in general simply ignored the political sociologists. They did read them and they did teach them, but only to some extent, and only in a way: they taught them as if they had been political "philosophers" in the then familiar sense, men concerned primarily with abstract and normative political theory. Without exception, the early political sociologists were represented as "critics of democracy," "irrationalists," latter-day Hobbesians, who attacked the comfortable premises of the defenders of democracy, equality and human reason— in short, as foils to men like Locke, Mill, and T. H. Green. Anyone who becomes familiar with the work of the early political sociologists today will realize that it was a travesty of their intentions, and indeed of what they actually said, thus to represent them, even though some of them—Mosca, for example—certainly invited such treatment by drawing large normative conclusions from their sociological studies. But basically the political sociologists were treated as they were, not because of anything they did themselves, but because the categories with which they dealt seemed naturally to place them, if not outside of political science altogether, then in the area of political theory rather than in the political institutions division of the field. And this is something doubly regrettable, for it means that some of the most promising modern works on comparative political institutions and behavior were long misrepresented in the "political theory" courses, to which they were only indirectly relevant, while they were ignored in the comparative politics courses, on which they had a direct and important bearing.

No wonder that students of comparative politics had to rediscover, and even to relearn, the early political sociologists for purposes of their own work. No wonder either that this rediscovery is something quite recent. In my own undergraduate days Mosca, Michels, and Pareto were still represented mainly as abstract critics of the abstract bases of democratic ideology. I remember, with some horror and some relish, the comment of a venerable teacher (not a "theorist" by any means) on an undergraduate essay about Weber's political sociology: "An interesting analysis of a brilliant but obscure"—yes, obscure—"German thinker."

Today, of course, the names of Weber, Pareto, Mosca, and Michels are among the more luminous in the study of comparative politics. But before they could become this there had to be a reaction against the older conception of comparative politics and the actual lines of analysis pursued in the field. This reaction in fact occurred in the 1920's and '30's.

## "Informal" Politics

One of its first manifestations—not confined to comparative politics, but, in fact, appearing at first mainly in studies of American politics—was a growing interest in political parties and pressure groups. This interest is important because parties and pressure groups are not, strictly speaking, parts of legal-institutional structure and because they link politics to other social phenomena more closely than does the formal-legal framework of a political system. The reasons for the growing interest in "informal" political processes throughout the 1920's and '30's are fairly obvious. Most obvious of all is the fact that parties and pressure groups by this time played a greater role in the politics of most states than they had before. Parties, in the sense we now think of them, developed rather late in the history of representative systems, however much the term itself might have been in use in earlier times. Large-scale, bureaucratized, intensely active pressure groups, especially great economic and other "interest" groups, also belong to a relatively recent period. This fact, however, while important, is not alone enough to explain the increased interest in parties and pressure groups, for the mere fact that something exists and plays an important role in politics does not mean that it will necessarily be studied by political scientists. The analyst's attention must first be prepared by operative preconceptions to seek out the data and to recognize them as significant. What theoretical influences, then, disposed political scientists to look intensively at party and pressure group activities?

One of these influences undoubtedly was political pluralism. By rejecting the idea of sovereignty and by intruding into the Lockean dualism of individuals and the state the concept of groups either mediating between them or coequal with the state, pluralism made all sorts of phenomena appear "political." Under the influence of the monistic theory of the state these phenomena had appeared extraneous to politics. To be sure, the pluralists argued mainly a normative case: that the state was only one social organization among many and that it had no special right to impose obligations upon individuals or their collectivities, that is, no special status above the other associations of society. But this normative position inevitably influenced the way politics was conceived for all theoretical purposes. In breaking down the distinction between the political and the social, the pluralists did not remove the consideration of politics from the study of society, but, quite the contrary, they invested all things social with political significance. Under their influence, one saw politics and government, power and authority, everywhere and in all social collectivities, but first of all, of course, in those collectivities most closely bound up with the state: pressure groups and parties.

There can be little doubt that the pluralistic point of view underlies, consciously or otherwise, the work of such men as Lasswell and Catlin, the undoubted pioneers in enlarging the subject matter of political science from the state to social relations as such. "The writer," says Catlin in the Preface to his *Principles of Politics* (1930), "sees no objection to calling the science of social inter-relations by the good Aristotelian name of Politics." Shortly thereafter, Catlin acknowledges his "profound debt" to Harold Laski, who was, at one time, perhaps the most celebrated of the normative pluralists. Politics he then defines as a particular kind of activity, "not as a thing," specifically as any act of human or social control. A broad definition indeed, but no broader than that with which Lasswell begins his famous *Politics: Who Gets What, When, How* (1936): "The study of politics is the study of influence and the influential," the influential being "those who get the most of what there is to get. . . ."

The growing emphasis on parties and pressure groups can also be attributed to a second major influence on political preconceptions: certain experiences made students of politics more aware than in the past of the great difference between constitutional forms and political reality. In America, the muckrakers had led the way toward the discovery of the "anonymous empire" of lobbyists and influence-wielders, conducting a kind of private government under the public façade of the Constitution and in interplay with formal authorities. This process seemed to the leading "group theorist" of them all, Bentley, to be the total sum and substance of politics.

Perhaps the most crucial experience leading to a disenchantment with constitutional forms was the fate of the Weimar Constitution, that professionally engineered document so widely acclaimed in its time, such a dismal failure in operation, which eventuated in the most extreme of totalitarian regimes. Some political scientists managed to cling to their preconceptions in the face of the Weimar experience (and the equally sorry operation of the French Third Republic) by claiming that it was all the result of faulty constitutional engineering. Many more, however, drifted toward the view that political processes are only imperfectly subject to control by formal rules and mainly the products of social and economic forces, of the interests and attitudes of public and politicians, military officers and public officials, capitalists and trade unionists, and the like. Certainly these experiences helped to make political scientists aware that men like Marx and Pareto, Michels and Mosca, Wallas and Lippman, did not belong merely among the abstract, primarily normative, political theorists, but that they could help one to reach a better understanding of actual political processes than could the constitutional lawyers and writers on formal political structure.

From this growing concern with informal political processes, political competition, semipolitical groups, and actual distributions of power, there naturally followed a growing interest in the links between politics and other aspects of society. From this in turn there followed a growing interest in systematic problem-solving on the middle-range level rather than in the construction of mere morphology. "Political sociology" came by degrees to be reconciled with what had passed for political science. It is clear from the literature of the period that the crisis of democracy in Europe provided the main impetus toward this reconciliation—even more than the widespread influence of Marxism, which certainly had a greater impact on political activists than political scientists in these years.

## THE SYNTHESIS OF DATA

The reaction that took place in the 1920's and '30's against the older conception of comparative politics had also another important manifestation. There appeared in this period a number of studies that attempted to synthesize the findings of configurative studies in large-scale comparative works and, in the course of this synthesis, attempted also to reunite political theory and political data. These syntheses—the most weighty are James Bryce's *Modern Democracies* (1921) and C. J. Friedrich's *Constitutional Government and Democracy* (1937)—are fundamentally different from those of Woolsey, Wilson, and their kind, particularly in two ways. They do not present theory and data simply as cohabitants under a single set of covers but chastely separated. On the contrary, they bring the data directly to bear on the theories, making the resolution of theoretical issues turn at least to some extent upon the evidence of experience rather than exclusively upon the promptings of reflection. And they do not synthesize configurative studies by presenting broad historical narratives in the manner of Wilson (narratives in which each link in the chain still appears as something quite unique in whole or in large part). Rather —and this is especially true of Friedrich—they present data in terms of general functional and structural categories, which, by implication, are elements of all political systems, or of all political systems of a particular sort. Because of this presentation, they are much more obviously "comparative" in nature than Woolsey's and Wilson's syntheses. Perhaps these two tendencies—the reconciliation of theory and data and the use of generalized categories for the analysis of political systems—are still rather primitively developed in the work of Bryce and Friedrich. Perhaps also, the theories are still too much taken from purely abstract political speculations and the generalized categories from the existing corpus of formal-legal studies. This is saying no more than that their work was affected by studies already in the field, as any scientific work must be. There is much that is old-fashioned in both Bryce and Friedrich (and, of course, much more in Bryce than in Friedrich); but there is also much that is original and portentous for the future and much that is derived from the original studies of informal political processes of their own time. Bryce and Friedrich are in effect transitional figures in comparative politics; and just for that reason it is worth looking in some detail at both what is essentially old and what is essentially new in their studies.

## BRYCE'S *MODERN DEMOCRACIES*

Bryce's *Modern Democracies* is in many ways a synthesis in the grand old manner, certainly in scope and to some extent also in content. Much of it consists of old-fashioned configurative studies of a large number of "democratic" countries: ancient Athens, the republics of Latin America, France, Switzerland, Canada, the United States, Australia, and New Zealand. In these configurative studies much space is devoted, in the established manner, to formal-legal structure. But quite apart from the fact that Bryce also gives considerable space to political parties and "the action of public opinion" —subjects not at all discussed by Wilson, whose index of seventeen pages does not even list parties, and discussed only cursorily, in the main abstractly, by Woolsey, who gives them twenty-five pages out of twelve hundred—the whole conception of the work makes it into something unprecedented, in idea, if not in every aspect of the way the idea is carried out.

The configurative studies that Bryce presents are in fact intended only to provide data necessary to achieve a broader analytical purpose. And what is this purpose? Basically, it is to solve a single substantive problem that ties together the whole prolix and often incoherent work, and to solve it by applying a particular procedure that to Bryce is the only proper procedure for comparative analysis. Both of these aspects of his purpose, his problem and his method, furnish evidence of the transitional character of his work.

The basic substantive objective of *Modern Democracies* is to examine the plausibility of the justifications and criticisms of democracy on *empirical* grounds, to see what light actual experience sheds upon the abstract arguments used either for democracy or against it (in his time, chiefly for it). His object, Bryce explains in the Preface, is not to develop "theories" but to state facts and "explain" them. Explaining facts is of course precisely what most of us today understand by developing "theory," but to Bryce theory means something quite different, and significantly different. It denotes what he later refers to as the "systematic" approach: purely speculative thought, unencumbered by data. Such thought, he argues, leads only to "bloodless abstractions," based, more often than not, on supposedly self-evident propositions about man and society, which inevitably give rise to empirically false or dubious conclusions.

The usual procedure in arguments about democracy is, according to Bryce, to establish first certain natural human rights; to argue from these to the logical desirability of democracy (that democracy is "government upright and wise, beneficent and stable"); to posit certain propensities in the nature of man that make it possible to argue that "democratic institutions . . . carry with them, as a sort of gift of Nature, the capacity to use them well"; and then to deduce further a great many not at all self-evident propositions about the desirability of liberty and equality, the educatability of all men, the relations of literacy and political wisdom, the rightness of public opinion, and so on. Bryce himself wants nothing to do with such abstractions, nor with any discussions of schemes of political reform "on general principles." His aim is to subject all such assertions to a single question: are they borne out by political experience and, if not, what propositions fit such experience better? The whole work, then, is intended to be an antidote to abstract theory about questions that the abstract theorists had wrongly pre-empted from the empiricists.

Of course, this very definition of his problem means that the abstract theorists exercised a great influence upon Bryce's study, if only in that his own theoretical problems are derived from them. This fact alone gives the work a curiously old-fashioned tone. Like the abstract political theorists, Bryce is concerned with what is right or wrong with democracy and a host of subsidiary normative problems. (Does power corrupt? Does wealth? Can the arts and sciences flourish under democracy?) Since his data are in most cases not adequate to solve such problems, there is in his work, as in the older syntheses, still a considerable gulf between speculations and data, even though the basic aim is to bring the two together.

Furthermore, just as Bryce's problems are rooted in tradition, so also, in some respects, are his methods of dealing with them. Not only does he present his data in the first instance through a large series of configurative studies, but his whole conception of the relations between facts and theory is primitive and old-fashioned. Nowadays we certainly do not believe that facts speak for themselves, that we need only know them in order to know what follows from them. We believe that facts are dumb and slippery, that they reveal their significance only when we have set all sorts of cunning traps for them—when we have gathered them in various ingenious ways and subjected them to various complicated processing devices: experiments, carefully chosen samples, multivariate analysis, and the like. But Bryce's attitude to facts is essentially that of a methodological innocent, even though, like Machiavelli, he has more than the ordinary amount of shrewd common sense.

Basically, Bryce is the crudest sort of empiricist in that he believes, implicitly at any rate, that facts are really self-explanatory, and in that he decidedly belongs to the past rather than the present. So also he echoes the past, though in a different way, in his basic conception of "comparative method." *Modern Democracies* is indeed represented as a "comparative work"; in fact, its very first chapter, after the introduction, is devoted to an explicit discussion of comparative method, something surprisingly rare in the field. But comparative method to Bryce has only a very special and limited utility; it can yield no direct knowledge of anything he wants to know but only give a more solid grounding to those first principles from which all political positions must be deduced. Comparative method is not really intended by him to be an alternative to the "systematic approach." In the last analysis, he uses comparison only as a way of arriving at basic premises for systematic analysis, a way supposedly superior to the formulation of "self-evident" propositions. While, therefore, the basis of Bryce's arguments is certainly empirical, or meant to be empirical, the arguments themselves, once we leave his country studies behind, sound curiously abstract.

Methodologically speaking, Bryce is in effect both a crude empiricist and a reductionist of the most extreme sort. This combination explains all the essential characteristics of his work: why he is a theorist who uses almost no theoretical equipment and, even more important, why he carries out an explicitly comparative analysis in a basically configurative way. Bryce believes, in effect, that every concrete social pattern is something unique, something ephemeral and nonreplicable, and therefore that it can be adequately represented only by means of configurative analysis. But just because every concrete social pattern is a world unto itself, a precise social science must be based, he argues, upon psychology, upon the constants of human nature that underlie the varieties of social experience.

What then is the comparative method to do? Is it not, upon this view, irrelevant to social science? Not quite; comparative method, to Bryce, does have a role to play in social science, a psychological role: one uses it to discover the fixed characteristics of human nature by examining the differences in actual social phenomena. What we do in comparing is simply that we subtract from actual experience that which is seen not to be "fundamental" to it: anything due to "disturbing influences," such as the influence of race, "external" conditions, historical antecedents, and so on. We are then left, as a residue, with the human constants we need for a precise social science. For the sort of issues Bryce raised, this social science is necessarily deductive once the psychological premises have been established, but for the explanation of concrete social facts it yields a simple *ad hoc* empiricism. To explain any concrete behavior we simply combine the psychological constants with the unique disturbing influences bearing upon the behavior pattern—and there we are.

This sort of procedure is nothing original in Bryce's time—though there is no evidence that he knew anything of Pareto, with whose *Mind and Society* his *Modern Democracies* has much in common, not only in method but, as a consequence perhaps, in manner: particularly in the disorganized presentation of great heaps of information in volume after interminable volume, the whole being sifted here and there for a very few dubious propositions of cosmic import. Psychological reductionism happened to be very much in the air in Bryce's time, not least in political studies. What is important in Bryce's version of it is his insistence on the actual analysis of political systems in order to discover relevant psychological constants, rather than proceeding from common-sense notions about human nature or "self-evident" propositions.

Whatever one may think of reductionism in principle, it is certainly a procedure difficult to carry out in practice. It is no small matter to try to find in the enormous varieties of concrete social life anything constant at all, except variety itself. And so it is not surprising that Bryce is, in the final analysis, not quite true to his method. He actually distills from his configurative materials not only psychological constants but also, with more emphasis and at much greater length, certain broad *ad hoc* generalizations about the essential bases of successful democratic government and the contingent circumstances that help or hinder its existence.

His argument comes down to this: successful democracy, he thinks, requires a legislature rather like the British House of Commons up to the late nineteenth century. It should consist of illustrious men who command great respect and have a high sense of political responsibility, who are not divided into many antagonistic groups and yet not subject to great party discipline either, who are not mere spokesmen for constituents or parties and yet can easily be integrated into majorities for the expeditious discharge of business—a legislature devoid of caucuses, groups, opportunists, and second-rate men. The possibility of the existence of such a legislature depends on the general national character of a people. This character, in turn, Bryce treats not as a simple given fact but as the product of numerous conditioning factors that he never makes explicit but that keep appearing in his analysis: demographic and geographic factors (smallness is absolutely essential: only its great size keeps China from being a successful parliamentary democracy!); the ethnic, religious, and class diversity of a society; occupational structure and economic development (agri-

culture is conducive to democracy, while industry, because it generates occupational diversity and class conflict, and because wealth corrupts, is a threat to democracy); history (especially the gradual development of a desire for democracy and a tradition of self-government); and a mysterious factor he refers to as "racial qualities."

While most of the work thus deals with the "disturbing influences" that condition societies, some of it is devoted, as it must be, to the constants on which these influences work. Bryce's constants resemble those of Michels as much as his method resembles that of Pareto, again without any evidence of acquaintance with Michels' work. What Bryce really discovers is not any psychological constants at all but a sociological principle and certain principles subsidiary to it. This principle is the universal fact of oligarchy in politics. He finds it to be a universal fact because "organization is essential for the accomplishment of any purpose," because the majority of men take little interest in politics and lack sufficient knowledge to play a positive political role, and because the natural capacities of men are unequal. Democracy in its classic form, therefore, is a human impossibility; at most it can mean only the prescription of broad ends and the selection of leaders from among competing elites by the electorate. Bryce thus develops a very early version of Schumpeter's elitist argument in *Capitalism, Socialism and Democracy,* and couples it with some very pessimistic findings about the educatability of men, the usefulness of mass media of communication, and the appetites of men for self-government and authority.

But this is not the place to go fully into Bryce's substantive findings. The important thing is to note the ways in which he presents them and arrives at them. To sum these up: Bryce is, in the first place, still an abstract theorist, but one who insists on the empirical derivation of his first principles. He is also, by conviction, an exponent of configurative analysis, but he insists on using the data of configurative studies for broader theoretical purposes. Finally, he is also something of a middle-range theorist (insofar as he looks for the probable effects of particular conditioning factors like ecology, social structure, and economic structure on particular aspects of political behavior), but he assigns to such middle-range theories a relatively low importance compared with residual first principles and arrives at them through the crudest sort of empiricism. What we should note above all perhaps is that he insists that theories be fully grounded upon data and that data be presented always for theoretical purposes. Politics appears to him an activity embedded in all social relations yet not governed by any single transcendental principle. In these respects, his work represents a long step away from the world of historicism and its aftermath and toward the approach of Montesquieu, who was by Bryce's own admission, along with Tocqueville, the model he sought to emulate.

## FRIEDRICH'S *CONSTITUTIONAL GOVERNMENT AND DEMOCRACY*

In one sense, perhaps, Friedrich's *Constitutional Government and Democracy* is more like the late nineteenth-century syntheses than Bryce's *Modern Democracies*. It is packed with discussions of the abstract political theorists that are in many cases not clearly integrated with the empirical parts of the study. Bryce at least derived from the abstract theorists his analytical problems; in Friedrich, references to the political "theorists" sometimes are little more than displays of erudition, albeit impressive erudition. In many important respects, however, *Constitutional Government and Democracy* takes great strides beyond *Modern Democracies*.

For one thing, there really is no purely configurative analysis in the book. Instead of presenting his empirical materials on a country-by-country basis, Friedrich organizes them in terms of a large number of structural and functional categories, under each of which theoretical speculations and data from a number of political systems (all Western) are given, the data then being sifted for theoretical significance. It is true that information under most of Friedrich's categories is itself presented in a country-by-country fashion, but the intent is clearly to go beyond configurative analysis, the country-by-country approach being used merely as a way of organizing the materials and not as the result of a belief in the uniqueness of each configuration. It should also be noted that many of the categories in terms of which the work is organized refer to formal-legal structure. That may, however, be the result simply of the nature of the materials available to Friedrich rather than of a narrow conception of politics on his part. In any case, the study includes much comparative material on parties, interest groups, and media of political communication; and throughout Friedrich gives considerable attention to the interplay between political forms and social conditions. In *Constitutional Government and Democracy* we thus come upon a full-fledged modern comparative synthesis, although one which still leaves many theoretical strands dangling in empty abstraction and which is still deeply rooted in the formal-legal style of early political science—two facts perhaps inevitable, given the period in which it was written.

Just as the contents of the study and the way they are organized are a mixture of the new and old, so also is the methodology underlying it, although it is a methodology very different from that of Bryce. As we have seen, Bryce's methodology had as its object mainly the establishment of first princi-

ples on empirical grounds. The ultimate purpose of Friedrich's, on the other hand, is to defend crude empiricism in the direct (not the deductive) construction of middle-range theories, although in the course of establishing this position he passes over some of Bryce's methodological ground.

Friedrich is not nearly so optimistic as Bryce about the possibility of scientific precision in political science on any basis. In a methodological appendix that portrays exactly what he does in his substantive chapter (but that is omitted from the later editions of the work, since Friedrich himself no longer holds these views), he rejects the possibility of formulating "laws" about politics and argues that one can at most formulate only "reasonably accurate hypotheses concerning recurrent regularities" in political experience. A reasonably accurate hypothesis about politics seems to him doomed to be always a greatly inaccurate hypothesis. Why so? Because all social phenomena involve the operation of a great many variables, and the greater the number of variables bearing upon a subject, the more inexact generalizations and forecasts about it must be.

The proper method for such a subject matter, among all the methods available to us, is what Mill called the inverse deductive method, and this is simply the method of reductionism: the establishment of psychological constants by reasoning back from cultural variations to invariant underlying conditions. Here we seem to be back with Bryce. But—and this is the rub—to find the constant human nature underlying social experience, argues Friedrich, no complicated procedures are needed; psychology is fully available to common sense, for in talking about human nature, we are only talking about ourselves, and therefore about data available to simple introspection! Friedrich is almost touchingly certain, in fact, that we already know almost everything worth knowing about politics and that any "partially inaccurate" notions we may have about the subject are easily corrected by deeper introspection and a wider inspection of data, for if psychology is the basis of political knowledge, we need "only" look inward to know politics, and if, despite this fact, inaccurate notions about politics become established, the "facts" will soon disabuse us of these notions. In this way, Friedrich, having ruled out scientific precision at the outset, then makes things still easier on political scientists by holding that all "reasonably accurate" hypotheses in political science are immediately accessible to common sense—anybody's common sense, though best of all the common sense of the well-informed political scientist. This "methodology" is nothing more than an argument for ordinary shrewdness, and nothing less than an argument against social "science."

In the substantive chapters of the work Friedrich is faithful to these views. Unlike many social scientists, he knows exactly what he is doing. His actual method in *Constitutional Government and Democracy* (though not in later works) is first to inspect a certain range of behavior (now broad, now narrow) pertaining to one of his subdivisions of constitutional government, then to generalize about it on the basis of common sense (that is, without using any special technical apparatus), and finally to see whether the generalizations so arrived at, when reduced to psychological terms, are congruent with his own common-sense notions about human nature. He collects a set of facts, reflects upon them, and checks the common-sense plausibility of the reflections; this, in his view, is really all that social scientists can do fruitfully.

We get the quintessence of this procedure in the conclusion to his chapter on electoral systems. "Proportional representation," Friedrich says there, "has been found wanting and incompatible with parliamentary government"—as indeed it had to be, for the "natural" effect of P.R. is to splinter political forces and thus prevent the formation of majorities on which stable parliamentarianism depends. The Weimar Republic illustrates the case. But if we look at all the other cases of P.R. that Friedrich cites—Belgium, the Netherlands, Sweden, Norway, Denmark, Ireland—this conclusion seems by no means to follow. What then? Well, "there are special factors to be considered in these several lands." Apparently, P.R. is not incompatible with parliamentary government in constitutional monarchies, or in small countries, or in countries with strong administrative traditions, or in countries where a single emotional issue divides the electorate. And "all this goes to show that the prevalent English and American opinion against proportional representation is practically sound." What we get here is in effect a generalization based on a single case, supported by common sense, and then an almost model exercise in what to methodologists is one of the cardinal sins: "saving the hypothesis" by enlarging it to cover all the cases that seem to falsify it— in this instance, the great majority.

But it is too easy, and quite unjust, to be harsh on Friedrich from a contemporary perspective. Despite the deliberate antiscientism to which Friedrich adhered when he wrote the book, *Constitutional Government and Democracy* deals with a host of middle-range problems that simply cry out for more methodical treatment and includes a large number of theoretical propositions that have furnished issues to comparative politics for a long time now.

The objective that unifies the work is to determine the conditions of success of constitutional government (and, by the way, to develop, through the examination of existing systems, a set of maxims of constitutional prudence). In regard to this basic problem Friedrich chooses an essentially "cultural" solution—that is, the primary significance of what Bentley called "soul-stuff," political ideas and attitudes. Constitutional government and democracy,

he argues, are threatened primarily by "intensity" in politics, especially intense disagreements over fundamental procedures and ultimate political objectives, intensity itself being measured by the extent of political enthusiasm ("consent") and animosity ("restraint") in a society—a finding that, needless to say, he believes to be confirmed both by common-sense psychology and common political experience. This broad hypothesis—which seems commonplace now but was not at all conventional twenty years ago—is the apex of a great many more limited generalizations: for example, that successful constitutional government requires a "balance of social classes" (whatever that might be), that "objective" heterogeneity in a society does not undermine constitutional government so long as there is a minimal unity of political outlook, that the number of parties in a representative system depends upon conditions prevailing in the system prior to the establishment of parliamentary government, that an inflexible constitution is to be preferred over a flexible one in societies that have no firm constitutional tradition but not in societies that have such a tradition—and many more, all based, of course, on artless inferences from very few cases.

At the end, we are left with three sets of theoretical ideas, two substantive and one procedural. First, the study presents what is in effect a set of requisites for successful democracy, many of them truistic, as they must be in view of Friedrich's method, but some not at all obvious. These requisites fall into two categories. One comprises organizational requisites, such as a responsible bureaucracy, an efficient diplomatic service, an effective judiciary with wide powers (including controls upon administration), a legislature organized for fruitful deliberation and not merely accurate representation and unlimited debate, some sort of separation of powers, functional or territorial, a neutral arbiter of constitutional disputes, and broad but rigidly defined executive emergency powers. The other comprises social and cultural characteristics: a viable economy, low intensity in politics, an effective constitutional symbolism, informative media of communication, and a high degree of political integration of economic and other material interests in society. Secondly, Friedrich presents a number of conditions that, while not requisites of effective democracy, do help to create a favorable climate for it: for example, a firmly rooted political tradition (its absence is not fatal, because it can be overcome by proper constitutional devices), judicial review, the plurality systems of elections, and the existence of only two political parties in the system. And third, he provides throughout, chiefly by implication, a number of variables to use in the analysis of the functioning of all political systems, the most important of which are, in his view, political attitudes and constitutional structure, although he also resorts in places to factors such as social structure (note the requirement of a balance of social classes), history and personality (that is, "leadership" as something that is not the product of any social forces).

All in all, then, *Constitutional Government and Democracy* is an early example of the functional approach to political analysis. It is a thoroughly comparative work, partly because a functional conception of a subject is in its very nature more conducive to comparative study than any structural definition. It is a study entirely devoted (leaving aside the generous references to traditional political theory) to the construction of middle-range theory about political institutions and behavior. In other words, its analyses are neither as all-encompassing as those of the historicists nor as narrowly restricted to configurative and formal-legal descriptions as those of the post-historicists. The middle-range theories presented deal mainly with the interplay of formal political processes with political parties and groups, and, in a still larger sense, with cultural, historical, and social forces. These are the "new" elements of the work. On the other hand, *Constitutional Government and Democracy* has no real method (at most, an antimethodical methodology) and uses, geographically speaking, a rather limited range of data.

With Friedrich, however, we are at least to a large extent back in the world of Montesquieu's political sociology. We are not yet very far beyond it or in some respects even abreast of it. But it is no accident that it is Friedrich who really begins to synthesize political science with the political sociologies of Mosca and Pareto, Weber and Michels, to all of whom there are liberal references—though mostly critical references—throughout his study. What is still missing in his work is even that beginning of a systematic and rigorous approach that we can detect in *The Spirit of the Laws*.

## POSTWAR DEVELOPMENTS IN COMPARATIVE POLITICS

By World War II, then, comparative politics was characterized by a reawakened interest in large-scale comparisons, a relatively broad conception of the nature of politics and what is relevant to politics, and a growing emphasis upon solving middle-range theoretical problems concerning the determinants of certain kinds of political behavior and the requisites for certain kinds of political institutions. Comparisons, however, were still made largely without the use of any special technical procedures; speculation and data were only beginning to be deliberately integrated. The subject-matter treated was still predominantly the sovereign state, indeed still mainly the formal aspects of Western nation-states. The concepts used for analysis were largely conventional

rather than technical, no explicit conceptual schemes designed for theorizing were used, and some of the most important aspects of analysis were left implicit. The interwar period was one pre-eminently of *ad hoc* and common-sense theorizing. And this brings us to our own time.

What have been the trends in comparative politics in the postwar period? The most basic have been four. First, the empirical range of the field has been greatly enlarged, primarily through the intensive study of non-Western systems (but also through research into aspects of politics previously little studied). Second, concerted attempts have been made to overcome the lack of rigor and system that characterized the field in the prewar period—to make it more "scientific," if the use of unconventional technical concepts, systematic analytic approaches, and rigorous testing procedures may be called scientific. Third, there has been much greater emphasis upon the political role of social groups (whether explicitly organized for politics or not) and upon social institutions that play a special role in molding political values and cognitions, loyalties and identifications—agencies of political "socialization." Finally, political systems have been analytically dissected and questions raised about them in terms of conceptual schemes largely imported from other social sciences, above all in terms of structural-functional analysis. These trends take us back full-scale at last to the political sociology of Montesquieu, and indeed greatly improve upon it.

I have not listed the trends here in any logical sequence, but neither have I listed them in a merely random way. Granted some unavoidable overlapping, they appear in the order in which emphasis upon them actually developed in the postwar period (save only for the fact that structural-functional analysis has played an important role throughout, but a constantly greater role as the trends unfold), and they appear in this order because each stage in the postwar development of the field helps us to understand why the next was embarked upon.

### The Study of Non-Western Systems

The influences leading to the gradual extension of subject matter to non-Western systems are fairly plain. The most obvious of them is the fact that societies and areas that political scientists interested in current events could once safely ignore became important and obtrusive in the postwar period for a great many reasons: the emergence of many new states in non-Western areas, the impact of the Pacific and North African wars (which certainly made many Westerners intimately acquainted with areas previously regarded as merely exotic), and the fact that only the non-Western areas were uncommitted, or open to a revision of commitment, in the power conflicts of the cold war. There was, consequently, and still is, a considerable demand in the non-academic world for specialized knowledge of these areas, and such a demand for expertise necessarily acts as an impetus toward its acquisition, most of all in a policy-oriented and training-oriented discipline like political science.

Yet it would be much too one-sided to regard the intense postwar interest in the developing areas merely as a response to postwar politics, even conceding that the most obvious academic influence that might have made for this interest, political evolutionism, had played itself out by this time. Why had not this great interest arisen much sooner? Perhaps because financial support for studies of premodern systems was harder to come by in the pre-war period—and such systems are expensive to study—but financial support was scant at the time for almost all projects in the social sciences. Perhaps because international power relations centered heavily upon the European countries; but there was Japan to contend with in the East no less than Germany and Italy in the West, there were riots, demonstrations, and mass arrests in India, there were important upheavals in China and Turkey. There was much to study outside of the West.

Why then did so very few students of comparative politics turn to study other areas? The answer is, at least partly, that their aims and preconceptions as political scientists simply did not direct their attention toward them. Perhaps the most important factor responsible for this was the almost universal emphasis in political science upon the study of democratic institutions, then, and still, to be found mainly in the West. We must remember that even Alfred Cobban's pioneering study *Dictatorship: Its History and Theory,* which now may strike us as very antique, dates only to 1939. And why this emphasis on democracy? The answer was already noted by Bryce: because of an almost universal belief not only in the desirability and possibility but also the inevitability of representative democracy in the development of nations. After all, was not all of Western history itself indicative of this trend? Even the early Soviet Union did not raise any particular problem in this regard, for one could always take its doctrines at face value and persuade oneself to believe that it was itself tending in a democratic direction. So, in their larger-scale political works, political scientists wrote, if not about the modern democracies themselves, then about the Ur-democracies of the ancient world and the historical processes leading from them to the more fully developed democracies of modern times; but it seemed pointless and superfluous to write about contemporary predemocratic, obviously transitional, systems—certainly as long as the end of the transitional process did not seem problematic.

From this standpoint, the interest in non-Western systems in political science is closely bound up with the crisis of democracy in Western Europe, the emergence of Italian and German totalitarianism, and the brutalization of Soviet Communism under Stalin. The declining faith in the inevitability of democracy led not only to a general interest in authoritarian governments, as exemplified by Cobban's own work, but also to two other, and relatively new, interests: in the processes of political change and the forces governing it and in the social forces rather than the legal rules governing politics. All of these interests obviously helped to open the door to the study of nondemocratic, rapidly changing societies lacking highly differentiated political systems and highly articulated formal-legal structures, or possessing them only on the level of colonial authority.

Also as a result of the crisis of democracy, political scientists now undertook a more intensive searching of the early political sociologists in order to gain insights into the cause of the unexpected political experiences of the modern world, and through the works of the political sociologist—certainly through Pareto, Mosca, and Weber—they acquired at least a cursory acquaintance with a wider range of political systems than political scientists had normally possessed.

The great postwar interest in non-Western areas is therefore a reaction to prewar no less than postwar political conditions. At any rate, it is a consequence of certain modes of thought engendered by prewar political experiences. And it may also be regarded as a consequence of a trend more purely internal to the field—namely, the growing interest in middle-range theories as such. The connection here is really quite simple: configurative study is bound, by its very nature, to narrow the empirical scope of studies, and comparative study, for the purpose of formulating, and even more for testing, middle-range theories, is bound to broaden it. This is a truism, but for the present purpose an important one.

## Scientific Rigor

Without slighting the role of external influences, therefore, one might reasonably have expected a broadening of the scope of comparative politics in the postwar period in any event. So also with the postwar interest in scientific method. Already in the 1920's and '30's one can detect a certain unease about the looseness of analysis characteristic of the field. Bryce's chapter on comparative method is about a dubious version of it, but it *is* a chapter on the conditions of rigorous social analysis. Friedrich's epilogue on method is an apologia for his unscientific empiricism, but he does appear impelled to apologize for these aspects of his work. Certainly it is not difficult to see how formulations of middle-range theories about behavior within numerous contexts might lead the analyst, quite without other stimuli, toward increasing rigor of procedure and unconventional concepts and approaches; the moment one begins to question propositions like those which abound in *Constitutional Government and Democracy,* one can hardly avoid such matters, for it is precisely the lack of rigor and unconventionality that gave rise to the propositions.

But the postwar quest for a more rigorously "scientific" comparative politics is also due to certain "external" causes. It is certainly a reflection of the growing postwar cult of "behavioral" science throughout all the social sciences (taking "behavioral science" to denote (1) middle-range theorizing on the basis of (2) explicit theoretical frames of reference with the use of (3) very rigorous, particularly quantitative, procedures for testing the theories). The "behavioral" approach has affected comparative politics primarily through the growing influence upon the field of sociology and cultural anthropology, and this influence in turn may be attributed in large part (though not entirely) to the very fact of increasing interest in non-Western political systems. For one thing, when political scientists turned to the study of non-Western systems, they found other social scientists already occupying the ground, mostly cultural anthropologists but also a growing number of sociologists (or sociologically trained anthropologists); and so they naturally went to school with them and absorbed their techniques and style. For another, the theoretical equipment of political scientists, such as it was, generally failed them when they confronted political systems unlike the highly differentiated, formally organized, predominantly democratic or totalitarian systems of the West. For this reason also they went to school with social scientists who offered more appropriate theoretical tools and learned to use these tools.

## The Emphasis on Setting

Just as the growing interest in non-Western political systems helped to engender a desire for going much farther beyond common-sense propositions and common-sense testing procedures, so also it helped to produce—and much less obliquely—the present emphasis on the social setting of politics and on agencies mediating between the social and the political, such as political groups and agencies of political "socialization." Because political scientists found in such systems much less differentiation between the social and political—that is, few specialized organizations for political decision-making or competition—they simply could not help seeing the extent to which the political is embedded in social relations in such systems, or suspecting that it might be so also in the more highly differentiated political system.

If they were indeed confronted by specialized political institutions and agencies, these, like the whole political system, were generally very much in flux—in process of coming into being or being altered. And when political processes are unsettled—

when patterns of politics are in the making rather than functionally autonomous of the conditions creating them—the nonpolitical is always particularly obtrusive and apparent, as it was to political observers in Europe in the great age of revolutions from 1789 to 1848, and as it was in the era of the rise of totalitarianism. It is worth noting in this connection that the halcyon days of formal-legalism in the study of politics fell precisely in that relatively calm and settled period between the great revolutions and the totalitarian era.

Here again, however, we must add other factors leading in a similar direction. We must remember, for example, that interest in the broader setting of politics, and in its more informal aspects, was already well advanced in the prewar period, above all in studies of American politics. In fact, many of the concepts, methods, and interests now being applied in comparative politics came out of the intensive study of American politics in the interwar and postwar periods—not least because of a gradual awareness on the part of specialists in comparative politics that the study of American politics was far outstripping their own specialty. The great role of the Social Science Research Council's Committee on Political Behavior in stimulating interest in applying comparatively some of the insights and techniques developed in American political studies —not least, its important role in helping to bring into being the SSRC Committee on Comparative Politics, which has done so much to help advance the field in recent years—should certainly be mentioned here.

In a way, also, interest in the setting of politics flowed almost naturally from the desire for scientific rigor in the field. It did so in two ways. First, in so far as the pursuit of rigor led to the more intensive study and emulation of sociology and cultural anthropology, it also led to the introduction into comparative politics of broad frameworks of analysis that, on the whole, regard all social phenomena as interrelated and certainly do not concentrate on any functionally distinctive aspect of society as if it were divorced from all other aspects of it.

Secondly, it is on the whole much easier to develop theories subject to rigorous testing by taking certain social and economic categories and relating them to politics (for example, such easily measurable categories as wealth and economic development, demographic data, occupational distributions —even value-orientation data) than by taking the often unmeasurable "pure" phenomena of politics as such—especially in societies where electoral data, the most easily measurable of all purely political data, are nonexistent, unreliable, or beside the point. As the opponents of rigorous quantitative methods in political science never weary of pointing out, the phenomena of politics, as traditionally conceived, simply do not lend themselves well to rigorous (that is, statistical, logical, mathematical) treatment—but this may (and did) as easily induce political scientists to conceive such phenomena differently as persuade them to give up rigorous methods altogether.

The influence of sociology upon comparative politics can be seen most clearly of all in the postwar emphasis upon a particular constellation of facts in the setting of politics, the facts that Montesquieu referred to as "the general spirit, the morals of a nation" and that have now come to be called "political culture." This term, as presently used, refers in general to politically relevant values (purposive desires), cognitions (conceptions of the nature of reality), and expressive symbols, from language to visual ceremony. It refers in particular to the "internalized" expectations in terms of which the political roles of individuals are defined and through which political institutions (in the sense of regularized behavior patterns) come into being.

The emphasis upon such "cultural" data is clearly a reflection of the influence upon political studies of the presently dominant sociological frame of reference, the action frame of reference, evolved chiefly by Parsons and Shils, upon the basis of Parsons' interpretation of Weber, Durkheim, and Pareto. At any rate, the "political culture" approach has been pioneered in comparative politics chiefly by two writers who freely admit their debt to Parsons and Shils, Gabriel A. Almond (who may rightly claim to have originated the concept in political science) and S. H. Beer. It is mainly through this emphasis on "cultural" data that the study of political "socialization" processes has come to be of great significance in the contemporary field, for if the values, cognitions, and symbols defining men's political conduct are regarded as the primary substratum of their political behavior, then explanations of political behavior must stress *ipso facto* the processes through which values, cognitions, and symbols are learned and "internalized," through which operative social norms regarding politics are implanted, political roles institutionalized and political consensus created, either effectively or ineffectively. This, essentially, is what we mean by political socialization.

At the same time, the concern with political culture helps to explain the emphasis upon the study of political groups, although this emphasis is also a continuation of prewar tendencies and a result of basing middle-range theories about politics upon hard, preferably measurable, facts. The vogue of the group approach to politics reflects the preoccupation with political culture simply in that there are very few societies, even among the most politically centralized, that have homogeneous political cultures, rather than being composed of a variety of political subcultures; certainly there are very few such societies among the emerging or rapidly changing states of the non-Western areas.

# STRUCTURAL-FUNCTIONAL ANALYSIS

Throughout the postwar period, but particularly, as I have pointed out, in very recent years, students of comparative politics have also made increasing use of the perspectives and categories of structural-functional analysis. What precisely does structural-functional analysis denote in this case? The term certainly cannot be left without explication, even when used in discussions of the fields in which it originated, for structural-functional analysis seems to include a very large, perhaps all-comprehending, variety of analytical questions and procedures. One of its principal exponents, M. J. Levy, has even claimed that, as used nowadays by most sociologists, it is merely another term for "talking prose"—that the structural-functional theorists do nothing more than state in a particular language what everybody already states in other languages. That may be so, although it makes one wonder why a structural-functional language should then be used at all; but in the postwar study of comparative politics the term does refer to certain specific, though still somewhat heterogeneous, procedures and problems.

It refers, first, to the very definitions of politics: to what we conceive to be a political system. One can define a political system in two ways: either as a particular set of concrete organizations, such as "governments" or "sovereign states," or as any social structures that perform whatever we conceive to be the function of politics—that is, any social structures that engage in political activities.

The latter may be considered a structural-functional definition, and this kind of definition of the political system has become increasingly common in the field. We tend no longer to think of political systems solely as sovereign states and their formal subdivisions but as any "collective decision-making structure," or as any set of structures for "authoritatively allocating social values," or as structures that perform the function of "maintaining the integration of society," or as structures that perform the functions of "the integration and adaptation of societies by means of the employment, or threat of employment, of more or less physical compulsion"— and in many other ways in similar vein. Some of these structural-functional definitions, like the first two examples cited, simply define a special activity, whatever its effect upon the larger social unit in which it occurs. Others, like the last two examples, define an activity that is presumed to be a requisite of the viability of a larger social unit. The latter definitions are more strictly characteristic of the style of structural-functional analysis than the former, for the problem of the requisites of the viability of social systems, of their stability and efficient operation, is perhaps the most basic substantive concern of those using the structural-functional approach.

Just as we can define a political system in structural-functional terms, so also we can devise analytical breakdowns of political systems—construct schemes of the elements that constitute them—in such terms, and this again in two ways. One way is simply to define the subsidiary activities that go into the larger activity of politics. In effect, this is what Almond does in breaking down political function into four input and three output categories (see p. 4). The other way is to break down the political function into those subactivities, and structures performing the subactivities that are required for the effective performance of the political function, as a viable political system is required for the effective operation of the larger social system. This is what Apter does in breaking down political systems into five "structural requisites" (see p. 4), and this latter procedure also is more strictly characteristic of structural-functional analysis than the former.

The purpose of structural-functional definitions and breakdowns of systems is, of course, to allow one to state and solve certain problems in which structural-functional theorists are particularly interested and that are based upon their preconceptions of the nature of social life. For all intents and purposes, the problems typical of structural-functional analysis can all be subsumed under a single concern: the impact of any social structure or function upon the larger social unit of which it is a part (or, less frequently, upon any other structure or function to which it is related).

Social structures of functions can impinge upon social systems in a variety of ways. The structure or function under consideration may be a "prerequisite" for the larger (or related) pattern, in that it must exist before the larger pattern can exist. It may be a "requisite" for it, in that it is required if the larger pattern is to be maintained. It may be "eufunctional" if it helps the pattern to persist or "dysfunctional" if it helps to undermine it. Its operation may be "manifest" if it is intended and understood by the actors involved or "latent" if its operation is not intended and understood. Questions about such relations between structures or functions and larger social units are obviously not profoundly different from questions often raised in other terms. There is, for example, little difference between saying that something is a requisite or prerequisite for something else and saying that something is a necessary but not sufficient condition for (or cause of) another.

A distinctive preconception of societies does, however, underlie structural-functional analysis that gives to such questions an import, certain overtones, that they do not possess when raised in the language of causality or other theoretical languages. This preconception is that societies are mutually interconnected wholes, every aspect of which impinges upon every other and contributes something to the viability (or lack of viability) of the whole. Societies, upon this view, are equilibrated units which have a tendency toward inertia and which change through the persistent or serious disturbance of any part of their equilibrium. They are "systems" in the technical sense of the term: hence the concern with their functional interrelations.[8]

It is this preconception of the nature of political systems, and of the way they fit into the larger social setting, that has gradually come to the forefront in postwar comparative politics. With it has come an emphatic interest in structural-functional problems, particularly problems regarding the requisites of any viable (stable, effective) political system or of the viability of certain kinds of political systems (for example, representative democracies) and problems regarding the functional consequences upon politics of other social patterns and upon nonpolitical patterns of political structures and activities.

What explains the present vogue in comparative politics of these preconceptions and problems? To some extent, of course, the very fact that social sciences in which structural-functional analysis is widely used have exerted an important influence upon comparative politics in the postwar period. But there are more deep-seated reasons.

Curiously enough, one of these deeper reasons is connected with the rapidly changing character of many contemporary non-Western systems—curiously enough, because structural-functional analysis is often accused of being a purely static approach to social science. It is so represented, however, for two bad reasons: one, the very concept of equilibrium is taken (erroneously) to imply immobility; the other, the major social scientists who have developed structural-functional analysis have in fact emphasized static over dynamic studies—most of them have worked in the anti-Marxist tradition, which assumes integration rather than conflict, and consequently inertia rather than constant motion, as the "normal" state of society. But this fact represents a coincidence rather than a logical relation. Indeed, structural-functional analysis, as depicted here, seems perhaps to lead logically (if it leads logically to anything at all) to theories about the coming into being, transformation, and breakdown of societies rather than to static analyses of fixed social states.

Rather than arguing that structural-functional analysis has a logical affinity to static analysis, one should argue that it is likely to produce a particular approach to social dynamics, different from that produced by theories like Marxism or evolutionary theory—an approach that always sees social change as a transition from one static, equilibrated state to another. Marxist and evolutionary theory are perhaps more *inherently* dynamic than structural-functional analysis in one sense: one cannot imagine, in terms of them, any fixed states, any equilibria other than dynamic equilibria, at all. For the structural-functional analyst, on the other hand, a fixed state is entirely possible and even necessary, although it does not rule out the analysis of changes of state.

At the same time, however, theories like Marxism and evolutionary theory make it difficult, if not impossible, to think of rapid, cataclysmic changes in society; note, for example, the great difficulties created for Marxist theorists by the doctrine of "permanent revolution." Such theories lend themselves chiefly to a conception of orderly, constant flow in social phenomena, one thing leading, never very rapidly or abruptly, to the next, the whole flow being conceived, but only for heuristic purposes, as a series of "stages" through which societies must always pass in their life-histories. Structural-functional analysis, on the other hand, makes it perfectly possible to think in terms of very broad and rapid changes, of one society skipping the stages of growth passed through by another or embarking very rapidly upon a new course of growth, through some large-scale change, however brought about, in one of the functional elements of society. It makes it possible to think of rapid transformations, revolutionary breaks, innovations, and metamorphoses, while other, supposedly more dynamic, approaches make it possible only to think of flows and phases.

Precisely these two characteristics of structural-functional analysis—that it leads to a conception of social change as a process from static states to other static states and offers the possibility of explaining very broad and rapid changes—make it attractive for those concerned with contemporary non-Western political systems. With what kinds of social dynamics do these systems confront us? Certainly not with orderly and constant flow. In such systems one always seems to begin with very static traditional societies, hardly changed in essential respects for centuries—societies exhibiting "fixed states" in any reasonable meaning of the term. And from such beginnings one always seems to proceed to the swiftest and most large-scale changes: from tribalism to the nation-state, from agrarian subsistence economics to modern industrialization, from feudalism to socialism; hurricanes of change strike the societies and swiftly transform them in ways that elsewhere took generations, even centuries.

Perhaps we shall find that this is not really an accurate depiction of what is happening in the "developing" areas. Perhaps the large-scale changes that appear to be occurring in them are merely surface phenomena under which more gradual processes of social flow proceed. But rapid metamorphosis from relatively unchanging states does *seem,*

to naked observation, to be the essence of their contemporary history. For that sort of dynamism a theoretical approach at once static and dynamic is obviously the most appropriate.

Thus, the very study of rapidly changing political and social systems creates a predisposition toward structural-functional analysis, not despite but precisely because of its affinity for static theory. And thus also the present emphasis on social setting and on theoretical rigor in comparative politics has induced an increasing use of structural-functional analysis and directs the analytical attention, more perhaps than any other approach, to the whole web of relationships of which politics is a part: the social phenomena on which politics impinges and those phenomena which impinge upon politics. Structural-functional analysis is the pre-eminent approach to the study of social interconnections. The emphasis on rigor has induced structural-functional analysis because it at least offers the possibility of something more than crude, unsystematic description and induction, without committing the theorist to a premature, perhaps vain, search for social "laws" or for "grand theories" in the historicist manner.

Nor does it commit him to a quest for sufficient "causes" in a realm where multicausality and multivariation operate to such an extent that necessary——or favorable—but insufficient conditions of phenomena are perhaps all we can ever hope to find. Structural-functional analysis, from this standpoint, is the pre-eminent approach to what I have called middle-range theories—theories that go beyond mere description and common-sense generalizations, that are based upon some explicit theoretical frame of reference, that permit some rigor in formulating and testing hypotheses, and that yet do not present ironclad laws or total interpretations of the meaning of social life. Talcott Parsons, whose name is perhaps the most famous of those associated with structural-functional analysis in the contemporary social sciences, defends the approach precisely on this basis:[9]

It may be taken for granted that all scientific theory is concerned with the analysis of elements of uniformity in empirical processes. The essential question is how far the state of theory is developed to the point of permitting deductive transitions from one aspect or state of a system to another, so that it is possible to say that if the facts in A sector are W and X, those in B sector must be Y and Z. In some parts of physics and chemistry it is possible to extend the empirical coverage of such a deductive system quite widely. But in the sciences of action dynamic knowledge of this character is highly fragmentary, though by no means absent.

In this situation there is danger of losing all the advantages of systematic theory. But it is possible to retain some of them and at the same time provide a framework for the orderly growth of dynamic knowledge. It is as such a *second best type of theory* that the structural-functional level of theoretical system-atization is conceived and employed.

In the first place completely raw empiricism is overcome by describing phenomena as parts of or processes within systematically conceived empirical systems. The set of descriptive categories employed is neither *ad hoc* nor sheer common sense but is a carefully and critically worked out system of concepts which are capable of application to all relevant parts or aspects of a concrete system in a coherent way. This makes *comparability* and *transition from one part and /or state of the system to another,* and from system to system, possible. [Italics mine.]

## COMPARATIVE POLITICS TODAY: AN APPRAISAL

Since the postwar tendencies in comparative politics will be illustrated and analyzed in many of the readings that follow, we can conclude this survey without describing and evaluating these tendencies further. And yet, in a sense, we cannot really "conclude" it, for in the contemporary development of the field nothing has really been concluded. It would be nice if we could say at this point of the survey that the study of comparative politics, after its many vagaries and tergiversations, had reached at last a new consensus upon concepts, methods, and analytical approaches capable of yielding a broad and precise science of political institutions. It would be nicer still if we could point to the actual existence of such a science. But there is a great distance still to go before this point is reached, and we are unlikely to reach it without further serious modifications of the field. Given its present state, it is quite inevitable that this survey should end on a note of ambiguity and suspended judgment, primarily for three reasons:

1. The field is today characterized by nothing so much as variety, eclecticism, and disagreement.

2. Disagreement and divergences are particularly great in regard to absolutely basic preconceptions and orientations (in terms of which one *recognizes* "scientifically" valid findings).

3. The tasks contemporary practitioners of comparative politics (especially the more radical ones) have set for themselves are so many and so difficult that they are unlikely to achieve satisfying results without further important changes in their approaches.

### Dissent

It should not be supposed that in describing the four main tendencies in present-day comparative politics—structural-functional analysis, the quest for scientific rigor, concern with non-Western systems, and concern with the broader setting of politics—we have in fact described the whole field

of comparative politics in the postwar period. Not at all; we have only described what is new and progressive in a field that is in fact to a large extent old-fashioned and conservative. It is important to realize that the stages in the development of comparative politics described here did not unfold in an orderly and episodic manner. In the manner of all things historical, these stages overlapped one another, each leaving within the contemporary discipline a certain residue, a particular style of analysis incongruent with other styles in the field.

In the contemporary field of comparative politics, we can in fact find, not two, but three quite distinctive styles; indeed we can sometimes find them in the writings of a single individual. One is the predominantly formal-legal, morphological, essentially descriptive, and configurative style of the immediate post-historicist period. In any of the established texts in the field (Ranney, Hertz and Carter, Cole, Zink, Neumann) that is essentially what will be found. If any approach is today dominant in the field, it is still this one. The second is middle-range theory based upon common-sense concepts and methods—crude empiricism, unguided by any rigorous procedures or explicit analytical frames of reference. That is what one finds in most of the deliberately comparative and problem-solving works of the present day, like Duverger's *Political Parties,* Rossiter's *Constitutional Dictatorship,* or Friedrich and Brzezinski's *Totalitarian Dictatorship and Autocracy.* The third is the broad and self-consciously systematic style distinctive to the postwar period.

### The Concern with Fundamentals

This coexistence in the field of three quite different styles accounts, as pointed out at the beginning, for the present concern in comparative politics with a multitude of pretheoretical and metatheoretical problems. These problems were not raised in earlier times—or not raised with such intensity and by so many people—simply because no one saw anything problematic in them. Political scientists *knew* the proper subject matter of their science: the state. They *knew* what it was most essential to deal with in studying this subject matter: public law. They *knew* how to classify political systems, how to divide them into parts, the nature of the basic units to be used in analysis, and what sort of a finding was a satisfactory and trustworthy finding. Today, precisely because of the variety of approaches in the field, we are not at all sure about these and other basic matters, and so we spend almost as much time and effort in thinking about the field of comparative politics as we spend in the comparative study of politics.

Nowhere are this self-concern and self-criticism more apparent, and nowhere are the depth and intensity of intradisciplinary disagreement more clearly revealed, than in the two general works about the study of comparative politics so far produced in the postwar era, Gunnar Heckscher's *The Study of Comparative Government and Politics* and Roy C. Macridis' *The Study of Comparative Government,* selections from which begin this volume. Macridis and Heckscher—the first speaking for what is essentially "modern" in the field, the second for what is essentially "traditional"— disagree not so much about whether comparative politics is to be a "science," as may appear to be the case in the readings, but—and this is much more serious—about what a political science, properly speaking, ought to be; and that is the deepest and most frustrating disagreement that can arise in any discipline.

Macridis and Heckscher can speak for themselves; there is no need here to reproduce their arguments. In any case, all the essential issues their arguments raise, explicitly or implicitly, are sketched at the beginning of the essay. But it is essential to note one fact about their disagreements: not only do such arguments impede the development of the field by distracting its practitioners from substantive tasks, they also impede the development of the field because, while such issues are unsettled, one cannot even determine when a field has been developed. All science involves building upon tacit assumptions and silent premises; and this means that the moment such assumptions and premises are made explicit by being argued no science can be said to exist. In such cases one can only have methodology and metaphysics, only prolegomena to study, research designs, conceptual proposals, and the like—preliminaries that now in fact afflict comparative politics in tremendous volume. But one cannot have that heaping up of tested theoretical findings ("accumulative research," in the wishful jargon of modern social science) that we generally think of as science.

Would it then be better not to raise questions regarding basic preconceptions? In the final analysis, it is unnecessary to answer this question one way or the other, because we simply have no choice in the matter. Pretheoretical and metatheoretical concerns become significant in fields of inquiry under certain conditions; they arise because it is necessary that they should arise, and once they have arisen, they cannot be wished away. One can operate with agreed preconceptions or one can disagree about preconceptions, but one cannot operate without any preconceptions. Therefore, when preconceptions are being questioned, one can only let the questioning take its course until some general understanding is reached, or, better, one can try, by procedural argument or substantive research, to influence others to accept one's own preferred preconceptions and thus contribute to the outcome of the questioning. In one way or the other—by argument or example—some dominant opinion will sooner or later become established, but in the meantime one can only leave the analysis of the field open-ended—or indulge in prophecy.

## The Need for Simplification

What kind of a comparative politics, then, is likely to emerge out of the present disorder in the field? Whatever the final product—and it might be best to desist from specific forecasts until the contents of the field have been presented in the readings—one thing seems certain. Even if we confine ourselves to the postwar developments in comparative politics, it seems improbable that a coherent discipline could be built upon concerns so various and complicated as are the present concerns of comparative politics. The most obvious need in the field at present is simplification—and simplification on a rather grand scale—for human intelligence and scientific method can scarcely cope with the large numbers of variables, the heaps of concepts, and the mountains of data that seem at present to be required, and indeed to exist, in the field.

Consider what the contemporary practitioner of comparative politics is supposed to know in order to be *au courant* with all the main streams of his field. He is supposed to be at once a political scientist, a logician, and a methodologist. He is supposed to know a good deal of sociological, anthropological, social-psychological, and general systems theory. His knowledge must (ideally) extend not merely to a specific country, nor even a particular region or type of government, but over the whole universe of political phenomena. He must not only know contemporary politics, but be something of a universal historian as well. And there is even a suggestion that his familiarity with political behavior should extend not only to nation-states but to every social relationship in which authority is exercised, or influence wielded, or the allocation of social values carried out. Certainly, the study of public law, in which scholars of the past made rich and busy careers, has become a mere fraction of all the things he is supposed to study. He must also learn all about informal politics, relate politics to its setting (ecological, social, economic), and be able to deal adequately with attitudes and motivations, with culture and socialization processes. These, obviously, are absurd demands to make even of the highest intelligence, the most retentive memory, the busiest industry, the most versatile manipulator of the skills of social science. They are demands that could conceivably be met by a sensible division of labor in the field, but such a division of labor presupposes some agreement on what is being divided, an accord (which we do not possess) on the desirable nature and direction of inquiry. The fact that at present it is very difficult, perhaps impossible, for any specialist in the field to know just how his work fits into any broader picture makes it necessary for everyone to work essentially according to his own lights, in terms of what he conceives to be the ultimate destiny of the field.

Dissent on fundamentals is thus reflected in lack of focus and definition in regard to "circumstantials" in the field, and in a way this is to the good. In the past, comparative politics had clearly defined boundaries only at the cost of too narrow and perhaps too inconsequential a concentration on subject matter, formal-legal structure. Any workable approach to the field, particularly at a time when we are concerned largely with relatively undifferentiated political systems, was bound to depart from such a rigidly constricting focus. But what have we to put into its place? If the answer is that we must deal with everything instead, that nothing can be omitted, then we are lost just as surely—indeed, more surely.

The basic need of the field at present, therefore, is focus and simplification. While we can detect searches for simplified approaches in the contemporary literature about the field, these are so far *only* searches. What is more, the usual tack taken in analytical writings on comparative politics is to throw into proposed schemes everything considered in any sense relevant to political study. Thus, the student of comparative politics today confronts a profoundly serious problem, even a dilemma. He must not focus on formal-legal studies only; we know that from long and disappointing experience. Yet he must not deal with *everything* else—and formal-legal data to boot. He must somehow limit inquiry. Yet the most obvious way to limit political inquiry is to focus on the most obviously political thing there is, as political scientists did in the formative years of their field—namely, formal-legal structure. What, then, are we to concentrate upon? We do not know as yet; that is to say, we are not agreed upon a solution. But the readings which follow may shed light upon the problem, even if they do not manage to solve it.

## NOTES

1. I have called this essay a "perspective" because it is, in a way, a history of comparative politics, without being, in any way, a survey of writings in the field—not even of the most important writings. The object of the essay is to illuminate the present condition of the field by discussing the main phases in its evolution and the forces that have affected it, both in the present and the past. Had it been written as a conventional history, I would have dealt at length with many more writers, especially such great writers as Tocqueville, Herder, Marx, Weber, Ranke, Mill, and Bagehot. I would have dealt more briefly, or not at all, with minor writers whose chief virtue is that they can illustrate, in an exaggerated way, the character of comparative political studies in their periods and not that they have made any important contribution to such studies. I would have taken some care to distinguish national differences in style of analysis in the same periods, rather than speaking of comparative political studies only in over-all terms—and such national differences have always existed and exist today: English writers on comparative politics, for example, were much less affected by what I call here the formal-legal style than others and have been less affected, perhaps for just that reason, by the contemporary reaction against that style. Finally, I would have taken greater pains to show the extent to which the predominant style of any one period is still practiced, with less emphasis, in the periods that follow, although I try to make clear throughout that the development of comparative politics has not proceeded through mutually exclusive phases, but has involved instead a continuous heaping up of strata of analysis, if one may put it that way.

I should perhaps also point out that, since the distinction between comparative politics and other aspects of the study of politics is rather recent in origin, much of this essay is a "perspective" on the whole study of politics, indeed of the social sciences, as well.

I am grateful to the Center of International Studies at Princeton University for making available the time during which the essay was written and to G. A. Almond, S. H. Beer, Hans Daalder, Roy Macridis, Elie Kedourie, and Melvin Richter for criticizing the first draft.

2. I am using the word "empirical" here in its conventional sense, not technically—that is, not with specific reference to the British school of "empirical" psychology and epistemology.

3. I refer to Machiavelli's "method" as viewed from the perspective of social science. I do not refer to the quality of his work as such nor to the aptness of his method when viewed in the light of his avowed aims—which were *not* primarily to produce social science.

4. These ideas set the tone in social science, but certainly did not monopolize it. That Montesquieu's style of thought was not without influence in succeeding generations can be seen most clearly perhaps in Tocqueville's works, although Tocqueville was far from typical of his own period. Large-scale comparative studies flourished also in this period in fields somewhat peripheral to social science: comparative geography, comparative philology, comparative religion, and comparative jurisprudence. A brief treatment of these, with references to more comprehensive works, is given in Fritz Redlich, "Toward Comparative Historiography: Background and Problems," *Kyklos: Internationale Zeitschrift für Sozialwissenschaften,* vol. XI (1958), 362-389. Redlich points out that these fields were influential upon some of the earliest nineteenth-century writings in comparative politics, above all, E. A. Freeman's *Comparative Politics,* New York, 1874.

5. The emphasis on formal-legal studies undoubtedly varied in this period from country to country, depending on special considerations—whether or not, for example, the study of politics is an autonomous branch

of university life, whether there are serious problems of political socialization, whether the country concerned has a written constitution—although in the field as a whole there was a strong trend toward such studies. Perhaps the main exception to the trend can be found in Great Britain. Here there was no written constitution to analyze; here also the common-law tradition, in contrast to the continental Roman law tradition, directed attention to usage and other "informal" aspects of politics. British politics was exceptional, and so also, perhaps necessarily, was British political science. Bagehot's *English Constitution* is certainly not a formal-legal study; nor, in the strict sense of the term, is Dicey's *Law and Opinion*. Yet even British political studies were not totally out of the main stream of development in the field, certainly not so much that we can consider formal-legal political studies in the nineteenth century merely a continuation of a long-standing emphasis upon public law in Roman-law countries. For one thing, theory in Britain in this period reflects the subjectiveness of political thought everywhere, not only in the case of the political "idealists" but even among the utilitarians. Informal political processes were widely neglected—Bagehot, for example, talks about party, but, unlike the monarchy, it is not considered deserving of a special chapter. Lacking a constitutional document, British writers on British government tended to treat actual behavior as if one could read formal-legal rules into it and as if one had "explained" it when

the formal rules it implied had been made explicit. In this connection, it is worth noting that this period is not only the great period of continental constitution-making, but also that of the great codifications of procedure in Britain. Thus, in Britain, there is some tendency toward turning the study of politics into the study of public law, while on the continent the latter practically swallowed the former. British writers did, however, keep alive in this period a broader and more analytical tradition in political study. In this way, they may have contributed to the later revulsion against formal-legal studies.

6. Nor is it to say that narrow, and largely formal-legal studies have nothing to be said for them. Many of them set standards of scholarliness, solidity, and resistance to fads that contemporary practitioners of comparative politics might well emulate. They suffered more from their writers' aims than from a lack of ability.

7. E. M. Sait, *Political Institutions: A Preface,* New York, Appleton, 1938, p. 135.

8. Most contemporary structural-functional theorists treat this as a point of view from which to analyze societies, not, as was once the case, as gospel truth. Anyone interested in the differences between contemporary and the older functionalism should read R. K. Merton, *Social Theory and Social Structure* (1949).

9. Talcott Parsons, *The Social System,* New York, The Free Press of Glencoe, 1951, p. 20.

# II

# II Present Trends in Comparative Politics

## INTRODUCTORY NOTE

We have supplied lengthy introductions to all the sections of readings—except this one. There are two reasons for this exception. One is that practically all the selections reprinted in this Part are themselves in a sense introductory in nature: they provide a kind of preface to the contemporary study of comparative politics. The other is that Part I of this book is meant to be an introduction to Part II, which illustrates and carries forward some of the points made earlier.

In general, the selections reprinted below will give readers some idea of the types of issues that today preoccupy writers in the field of comparative politics, of their principal aims, of the major approaches that they believe will attain these aims, and of the growing empirical scope of their researches.

To supplement these readings, it would be advisable for readers to consult works dealing more generally with the contemporary issues, aims, and approaches of political science. For this purpose we recommend three sets of readings: Heinz Eulau, Samuel J. Eldersveld, and Morris Janowitz, eds., *Political Behavior,* New York: The Free Press of Glencoe, 1956; Roland Young, ed., *Approaches to the Study of Politics,* Evanston, Ill.: Northwestern University Press, 1958; and S. Sidney Ulmer, ed., *Introductory Readings in Political Behavior,* Chicago: Rand McNally & Co., 1961.

# GENERAL METHODOLOGICAL PROBLEMS

## Gunnar Heckscher

A number of the problems discussed, both at the Florence meeting and otherwise, are only superficially—if at all—specific to the study of comparative government. Questions concerning the validity of results, the needs of hypothesising, the establishment of a general theory, etc., obviously relate no more to comparative government than to other aspects of political science. In most cases they are common to all social sciences or even to the whole field of humanistic study. Even when we discuss the applicability, e.g., of Mill's method of differences, this is only superficially a specific problem. Whether or not this method is applicable in the field of comparative government depends almost entirely on the general character of results attained in political science.

It would be tempting simply to leave all these questions aside. They seem to be outside the scope of our subject, and in any case we can hardly expect to solve them at this stage. Unfortunately, such a procedure is impossible in view of the present state of discussion. There is no consensus on these points, but rather general disagreement or even confusion. On the other hand, whatever we try to establish with regard to comparative government has to be based on assumptions of a fairly general character. The methodology of comparison is not a self-contained separate subject, but part of the general method of political science. The fundamental assumptions, therefore, have to be discussed even if the result of the discussions are inconclusive and some of the arguments no more than commonplaces.

For political science as well as for other fields of scholarship and scientific study, the fundamental questions are those concerned with truth and validity. Certain aspects can be disposed of rather quickly. It is against the assumptions of Western civilisation to assert that any science can ever be permitted to deviate for any reason from the quest for truth. This should be self-evident and on the whole is so regarded, but we sometimes forget the

implications. I quote a paper by Professor Beer of Harvard University:

In the United States, for instance, it is not uncommon to speak of the teaching of political science as "education for citizenship." Whether one objects to this or not depends on what it means. But on the face of it, the notion seems to me an abomination. I should prefer the premise—vague as it is—that our task is to try to teach the truth—and that means regardless of its possible consequences on society or the state. Conceivably this premise may conflict with the notion that we are "educating for citizenship." In the bad state, the wise man may be the bad citizen. Or indeed, even in a good state, a wise man may choose not to be, in any real sense, a citizen at all.

As a matter of fact, the talk about "education for citizenship" is probably not as bad as it seems. Those who use it frequently accept the slightly naïve assumption of liberalism that truth will always be triumphant and that the best citizen is he who has acquired the greatest respect for it. But an unsophisticated person may sometimes forget this basic consideration, and where this happens, scientific truth is in danger and scholars may be subjected to witchhunts.

Another point is concerned less with outside influence than with the psychology of scientists themselves. We all hold a great number of theories and assumptions, on which we base our reasoning. These basic assumptions may or may not be generally accepted. In many cases they are *implicit,* although never expressly stated. It is highly desirable that they should be brought to the surface and made *explicit* to the greatest possible extent, since our reasoning may be unintelligible where this is not the case. On the other hand, we are not always conscious of our own assumptions. Particularly where they seem to us (but not necessarily to others) to be self-evident, they may not at all appear on the surface. This is always a danger, but it is particularly dangerous where we move in an international setting or else under circumstances where it can be suspected that basic differences exist among writers on the same or similar subjects. Consequently, a special effort is required to make implicit assumptions and theories explicit if we are to avoid serious misunderstandings and complications.

This brings us to a more fundamental question, that of *criteria of relevance*. It is sometimes argued that our functions are "merely descriptive" and that this should relieve us of a number of considerations which might otherwise be necessary. It is submitted that this is an altogether unrealistic assumption. Photographical description is beyond the realm of possibility, if indeed desirable. It is completely impossible to "merely describe" in the sense of giving "all the facts": facts and data always have to be selected. Consequently, there has to be a basis of selection. What we mean when we say "all the facts" is all the *relevant* facts; it remains to set a standard by which we can decide which facts are relevant or not.

This observation has led some scholars to the conclusion that the selection of data has to be based on a previously established general theory. Undoubtedly, this approach is far from impossible in itself. Provided there is a general theory, and provided it is universally accepted or at least universally regarded as of fundamental interest, it can be used as a criterion of relevance. Some of the theories in the physical sciences, such as the theory of relativity, appear to have been successfully used for such purposes.

We may for the moment leave aside the question whether the circumstances of social sciences in general and of comparative government in particular are such as to warrant the employment of this method even under the most favourable conditions. At any rate, it would be a fatal mistake to regard it as the only possible approach. It is equally reasonable and much more simple to regard the question of relevance in the light of particular problems. These problems may be as limited as we like, and it follows that the standard of relevance need not be absolute. Certain data may be irrelevant in connection with one problem but highly important in the light of another. Let us assume that we are collecting data on the activity of cabinet ministers. If our problem is that of the inner mechanism of a cabinet certain facts are important; if we are concerned with parliamentary leadership we concentrate on others. Certain data may be relevant to both problems, particularly since the two are closely connected; but in a majority of cases our choice of data depends on which of the two problems we are concerned with. And for a third problem the social and educational background of ministers, their moral standards, etc., may be of fundamental importance—which leads us to select a third set of data.

The problem of *validity* is of a more basic and fundamental character. In approaching it social scientists in general and political scientists in particular seem to suffer from a hypnotic preoccupation with the exact natural sciences. Physics, mathema-

tics, chemistry, mechanics, are regarded as preeminently scientific and all other scholars are developing an inferiority complex. Consequently, they yearn for measurable quantities, absolute conclusions on causality, etc.

This seems to be particularly true of those who do not have even a superficial acquaintance with natural science. Closer observation should be encouraging. In the first place natural science is not a monolithic block, and all natural sciences are not equally exact. The standards of biology are indeed very far from those of pure mathematics and mechanics. Secondly, largely as a result of recent development, physics and chemistry also deal to a considerable extent with non-measurable quantities and with approximations. The whole field of nuclear physics is a case in point. And finally, the social sciences are not alone suffering from these limitations. We have to accept the fact that all cultural sciences, including history, law, etc., are rather different from the exact natural sciences in this respect. Some fields, such as the very fashionable one of psychology, offer even less hope of exactitude than do the older humanistic sciences.

Consequently, we have to accept the fact that the social sciences are not "scientific" in exactly the same way and to the same extent as, let us say, physics. In political science, as well as in other cultural sciences, "scientificness" is hardly more than an attitude of mind. This, of course, does not dispense us from considering critically the reliability and especially the validity of our results. We may hope that in some very distant future we shall be able to obtain a reliability and a validity comparable to those of the exact natural sciences. But since the sciences of man deal with realities which are more complicated than those of the former, it is improbable that this desirable result will come in sight within the near future.

Two solutions would then seem to be possible. Either we have to exclude all problems where such an attitude is at present unattainable—which in practice would mean that we shall have to stop working—or else we have to be content with results which are only very approximate in character. The first proposal has never been advanced, and consequently we are left with the latter.

Thus, we have to accept our own limitations. By the same token, however, we must see that we are conscious of them. We may possibly observe general tendencies, but we cannot expect to find "laws of political behaviour." If we promise to do more than we can, we cease to be scientists, but as long as we make it clear to ourselves and to others that our results are imperfect, we may continue to work with a good conscience and make shift with unsatisfactory measures and classifications, hoping that our tools will ultimately improve.

The need for consciousness of our own limitations can hardly be overemphasised. We may, for instance, establish "systems" to illustrate our meaning and to list the components influencing developments (or as many as possible of them). We may hope to prove that these components really are important for the result, but we must not assume that we are able empirically to establish the "weight" or "value" of each of them. We have to accept that our science is "descriptive" instead of regarding this as a term of abuse, while obviously attempting to refine our instruments of description—e.g., by comparative studies. And while our observation will, in a certain sense, always remain superficial, this does not prevent us from attempting as much "depth" as possible in looking for causes as far as possible even beyond those which are immediately apparent.

The attitude just described has much influence on our approach to such things as *predictions*. In a more general way, it even modifies the use of hypothesising.

It might be said that there are sciences of prediction and sciences of explanation; or rather, since science always seeks explanation, that there are certain fields where attempts at explanation may make it possible to predict, and others where this is not the case. This would seem to apply to any statement about the future. The idea that one should distinguish between predictions and forecasts is unintelligible to the present reporter, since general predictions are always made up of specific forecasts and logically lead to other specific forecasts. Any statement about the future, whether of a more detailed or of a more general character, seems to be subject to the same conditions.

Now, the future can be known to us only in so far as the various components influencing events are known to us, not only in the sense that they have all or nearly all been discovered but also, and more particularly, in the sense that we are able to measure them and thus state their relative influence in terms which must not be altogether haphazard, although a certain amount of approximation is permissible. This is what happens in the exact sciences, where deviation from predicted events indicates the presence of an unknown quantity which very frequently is discovered and measured shortly after the deviation has been observed.

In the cultural sciences, this procedure is at present hardly possible. Even where we can find measurements for some of the factors involved, as for instance in the case of public opinion polls, there are always a number of unmeasured and provisionally unmeasurable quantities of real and practically always equal importance. But worse still: even where we deal with "measurable" quantities, they each have measures of their own which can no more be combined than we are able to perform the traditional feat of adding apples to pears. Take the case just mentioned, public opinion polls. We find that the members of one party are in favour of an extension of the suffrage to persons between 18 and 21 and opposed to government control of water resources; while the members of another party are in favour of government control of water resources but opposed to the extension of the suffrage. Does this tell us anything with regard to the possibility of making a deal between the parties to extend both the suffrage and control of water resources? Obviously not. Even if we have figures for the proportion of party members wanting one thing and another, we are unable to measure the intensity of one wish as compared to another; nor can we be certain that the figures mean the same thing in both parties. Consequently, even where we are able to establish the existence of "tendencies" of different types and apparently to find some measure of their strength, we have so far no means of comparing them quantitatively and thus to make sure of what is their strength as components influencing events. Since we invariably deal with conflicting tendencies, this seems to make statements about the future completely unreliable except in the exceedingly rare cases where one tendency is incomparably stronger than the others; and these are precisely the cases where prediction is generally possible to any informed person without the use of scientific methods.

The question of *hypotheses* is an entirely different one. The Evanston report[1] placed great emphasis on hypothesising. It said that comparative government had so far been "insensitive to hypothesising" and insisted that problems should be "stated in such a form as to lead immediately to hypotheses." Undoubtedly, the former may be true to some extent and the latter is not impossible, in so far as the hypotheses refer to and are permitted to remain approximative and related only to tendencies.

Yet even here it is impossible to repress certain doubts. On the one hand, the problem has to be posed before the collection of data begins; on the other hand, hypotheses altogether without basis in facts are apt to be somewhat uninteresting. Consequently, we may pose a problem in the hope that it will lead to fruitful hypotheses, only to find when we have got to the facts that nothing of the sort is practically possible. The problem may be interesting in itself, and it may even be useful to pose it, although at the present stage of knowledge we are not able to make even the most tentative hypotheses with regard to the solution.

Furthermore, on the basis of data collected not only our hypotheses, but even the character of our problem frequently change. There is a continual process of mutual influence between the character of the problem and the collection of the facts. Actually, while a general hypothesis is frequently inherent in the problem, what we can demand is hardly more than that any study of the political process—whether comparative or not—should start from a clearly and explicitly stated problem. One has to agree that this has not always been the case in the past.

So far, we have been dealing more or less with problems common to all cultural sciences. It will be necessary to come back somewhat farther on to the problem of relationship between various fields, and the meaning of the *inter-disciplinary* approach can not be discussed here. It should, however, be mentioned that while co-operation is indeed necessary and exchange of experiences highly useful, there are definite methodological differences between the cultural sciences. It was said by one of the participants who attended both the Evanston and the Florence deliberations that we should "use history, but not as historians do." This applies to all related sciences, including sociology: we should use their results and study their methods but not necessarily copy their jargon.

The place of political science in *relation to other cultural and especially social sciences* is not altogether easy to determine. The unity of science is becoming increasingly evident, and the delimitations are appearing as somewhat futile. Particularly as our work develops the borderline fields grow increasingly important. This, however, does not mean that it is impossible to describe broadly what political science in practice does mean. Indeed, something of this sort is indispensable if we are to attain a coherent and systematic approach to any problems at all.

In a recent paper, Professor S. E. Finer has attempted a general definition of *what is meant by a political predicament*:

If I insist on red curtains but my wife insists on green—a political predicament exists. If I demand free trade, and others protection—a political predicament exists. If Russia wants a disarmed Germany and the Western Powers wish to rearm her—again, a political predicament exists. In all cases, what *I* wish to do is such as automatically to bind *him* to do something he does not want to do: and what *he* wants to do is such as automatically to bind *me* to do something *I* do not wish to do. The characteristic features of the predicament are identical: in the first place the policies pursued are such as by their nature to eliminate the alternatives (and thus involve their champions' compliance with the victorious policy); and in the second place, no unanimity exists as to which policy should be pursued.

(*a*) A political predicament does not arise unless there are two or more actors. Robinson Crusoe was not involved in politics until Man Friday arrived. A neat way, therefore, of solving a political predicament is to make sure it does not exist: i.e. by eliminating everybody else.

(*b*) Nor does a political predicament arise where the policies in question are compatible: for they can be pursued side by side. An untidy but practical way of solving political predicaments is to modify the original, competing policies until they reach this condition.

(*c*) Nor, finally, does the political predicament arise unless there are two or more policies; i.e. unless there is a lack of unanimity. No competition in policy, no

predicament; no predicament, no activity. There is no problem to solve. Sometimes people become bored with this condition. Then they invent predicaments. Such invented predicaments are games and sports, such as cricket, football, boxing matches. They are analogical to politics (as most of our political philosophers, who are usually cricket-mad, do not hesitate to point out).

If we accept these definitions it is obvious that we are concerned not only with forms but with realities, and with *specific* realities. This is true whatever is the object of our study. For instance, the party system in France may be the object not only of political but also of historical and sociological studies. The political scientist is interested in finding out what are the power relations between the parties and within the parties, as well as between parties and other organised and unorganised groups. His primary interest is concerned with the situation as it stands today, but in order to understand this he will frequently have to go back and look for the genesis of the present state of affairs. He will also have to seek a background in contemporary and recent circumstances outside the field of power relations. To the sociologist, on the other hand, power relations are only one of the interesting factors, and hardly the most interesting. To him agreement is frequently of greater interest than conflict, and his question will be concerned, for instance, with the role of party organisation in the social life of communities, status attainable through the individual's influence within the party, etc. The historian, finally, is interested in all these things, but to him the recent situation is no more important than the situation 200 or 300 years ago. The important thing is what changes have taken place, and why; whether these changes are mainly related to the political aspects of the party system or to something else.

On the other hand, it is also sometimes argued that "a political scientist covers the same world in the mind that a statesman covers in action"; this signifies that political science is identical with statecraft. This would seem to be rather ambitious, particularly since in the modern world statecraft is concerned with practically all sides of human life; which political science would fain *not* be.

In attempting to discuss the role of methodology, we may refer to certain general problems mentioned in the introduction. In particular, the problem centres round the general objectives of political science. On the whole, an empirical—or, as it is sometimes called, experimentalist—attitude has found pretty general acceptance. Empiricism, of course, is in itself a methodological principle of the first order, but it is sometimes interpreted so as to dispense with discussion of other methodological problems. Empiricism, then, would be regarded as "a methodology to end all methodologies." But this interpretation is neither necessary nor entirely reasonable. There is also, on the other hand, a very definite hunger for discussion of methodological principles, and notably so in the United States. Probably because of the over-emphasis on pragmatism formerly usual on the Western side of the Atlantic, there is in American political science today a great anxiety to get down to fundamentals —just as the formerly more speculative Europeans are anxious to deal with nothing but solid facts.

While the empirical attitude by no means precludes further study of methods, it is obviously true that methods can be developed and tested only by successful research investigations. But which are the criteria of success? It seems that the results should in the first place be coherent and thus reasonably immune to immanent criticism. Secondly, a successful investigation is one where the results are corrected and developed by further study, but not entirely discarded. Finally, it is sometimes held that the success of the investigation is proved by the fact that predictions contained in it prove to be true. This may be open to some doubt: the results may be purely coincidental, while on the other hand an investigation may be highly useful although a minor flaw prevents it from forming the basis of correct prediction. In any case there is undoubtedly a strong correlation between the empirical approach and the establishment of fruitful hypotheses. In the words of S. V. Kogekar:

An emprical approach to the problems of political science which centre, broadly speaking, round the organization and control of human relations in society, assumes great importance in this task of hypothesising. Not that hypotheses are always and necessarily the product of empirical studies. But such studies may both stimulate our minds in the task of hypothesising and provide a testing ground for the hypotheses arrived at by whatever process.

In any case it would obviously be nonsense to say that no methodology is required, while at the same time maintaining that the correct method is proven by the successful result of investigation where it has been applied. The moment we start to speak of *successful* investigation, we are in need of criteria for success. These criteria can be developed only through methodological discussion, and thus even the extreme empiricist can never avoid consideration of principles in this respect; he can only lose in clarity by making them implicit and not explicit.

What "methodology" is can thus be stated rather simply: to take stock of methods used so far, criticise them on the basis of the results attained in employing them and trying to perfect them further with a view to the future. This is something which we are all doing, consciously or unconsciously. But it is particularly for countries where the study of political science is just beginning that we need to present explicitly our experiences.

On the other hand, we must remain conscious of the limitations of methodological study. Is it supposed to involve a theory or a procedure? Both are probably included, but the inductive approach makes it necessary for us to take special interest in the procedural side. Furthermore, very few methodological rules are universally applicable. On the whole, methodology is usually related to a problem or a group of problems and should be discussed in this context. Methodology in the abstract is hardly very useful, except with regard to a few almost self-evident basic principles; but a study of the methods impressed in a particular investigation or type of investigation can be exceedingly interesting.

As to the basic "universal" principles, it is sometimes maintained that nothing has been done so far. This seems highly surprising. It may be that nothing or almost nothing has been done by political scientists, but in this discipline, as in so many others, it is necessary to draw on the philosophers, who have been anything but unconscious of methodological problems involved in a study of society. We may go back to the "common-sense" philosophers in England in the eighteenth and nineteenth centuries; to a German philosopher like Windelband or a Swede like Hägerström; or we may refer to an economist and sociologist like Max Weber. All these authors will have something of importance to teach us. This does not imply that the last word has been said, and in particular we are in great need of participation by scientists actively engaged in *using* the methods (such as, incidentally, Max Weber). Still there is much to draw on and it would be a serious mistake to assume that we should start from scratch. In fact, more can probably be gained by testing theories already outlined on the basis of results achieved in practical research than by new attempts to develop theories of method *a priori*. The history of social science methodology is a long and interesting one, providing a fertile ground for the growth of new methodological refinements. The problem is not one of inventing ideas but to find out which ideas can be used in practice.

There is undoubtedly in many fields—again particularly in the United States—a desire for the development of a *general theory in political science*. It is hoped by many scholars, as well as probably by laymen, that political science will develop something of direct use for the solution of the problems of our time. To quote Benjamin E. Lippincott in the UNESCO volume on *Contemporary Political Science*:

We have had two world wars and a great depression, yet no political theory has been written by political scientists, indicating, on the evidence of the past, that all these things are possible, indeed were very likely. No political theorist saw, before it was clear to all who had eyes to see, the deadly challenge made by Nazism, and then by Communism, on a global scale; none saw the "cold war," nor Communist aggression by satellite powers. No book in theory has been written in America, the home of modern democracy, to make an advance on John Stuart Mill, whose writtings are still classic ones on the subject; in fact, no one in England or America has produced since his time an analysis of the principles of democratic government equal to his. . . . We may say, in conclusion, that political theory in America will come into its own when political theorists give up their emphasis on the history of political ideas, and on the descriptive approach to political science. It will come into its own when it reaches beyond empiricism, and employs scientific method after the manner of the great physicists. It will begin to perform the task of which it is capable when political theorists take stock of their field, and determine its chief problems. Political theory will become fruitful when its practitioners consult other branches of learning, as well as other fields of political science, for the purpose of testing the operation of its principles.[2]

Political science is also sometimes said to "suffer from indigestion of facts." Karl Loewenstein wants us to continue in the direction of developing what used to be called in Germany *Allgemeine Staatslehre*. The Evanston seminar was apt to regard the development of a general theory alternatively as the main purpose of comparison or even as a necessary basis for establishment of criteria of relevance. And some scholars hope that political science as well as mechanical science is approaching the stage where it can begin to formulate general "laws."

Now, the idea of a "general theory" is by no means unambiguous. It is sometimes understood to mean a theory of "the best system of government." This would imply agreement as to values, since otherwise it is impossible to know what is "best." It would also require a development of political science up to the point where one can make almost infallible predictions as to how given institutions will work in a given environment. Such a development, however, is certainly not yet even in sight. Finally, under the existing circumstances, attempts to create a general theory of this type would lead us almost directly back to the speculative political theory of Rousseau, Montesquieu and Locke and obliterate practically every distinction between political science and politics. It is a very natural desire to find a theory which is able to answer these questions; but we should be very unwise were we to give out any hope of fulfilling such desires.

On the other hand, a general theory is sometimes understood as political philosophy pure and simple. There seem to be certain difficulties in accepting this idea also. At least in so far as comparative government is concerned what we can hope to attain is chiefly what has been called a conceptual framework, giving us the definitions and clarifying the problems with the help of which we should analyse existing political institutions and forces. This is both more and less than a political philosophy. It is less in that it does not attempt an explanation of the real nature of the state or the origins of political relationships; but it is more in that it relates directly to empirical facts and not only to speculation.

A definition given by one of the members of the seminar with regard to a general theory of one particular problem should help to clarify matters. Professor Macpherson, in his paper on political parties, started out as follows:

> By general theory of the party system I mean a statement of the relations, necessary or contingent, between the party system and the purposes of democratic government, and, ultimately, of democratic society. A general theory should be built inductively, but the aim (though not completely attainable) should be to state it deductively, i.e. in principles from which the limits and possibilities of party systems in particular circumstances could be deduced. Are party systems necessary to the purposes of democracy? In what ways are they necessary? What characteristics of form and substance are required in party systems if they are to fulfil those purposes? These are some of the questions that should continually be asked. They have not been asked sufficiently often, or not with sufficient care.

It should be noted that the emphasis here is on deduction, not on induction. In the words of another participant in the seminar, Professor S. E. Finer, we are making an attempt at "describing the political possibilities." Considerable emphasis should be put on the word *describing:* we remain in the humble sphere of description and do not attempt to rise to the more lofty one of speculation. With this limitation, the general theory, and perhaps in particular its component parts, should be highly useful, especially in order to make explicit assumptions or theories which we are always implicitly using.

But it is perhaps important to make one further qualification. Even in the physical sciences the general theory is built up of innumerable problem solutions. It is continually developing, and parts of it are no more than sketchy hypotheses or even question-marks. This seems to be even more true of political science. Unless we know *all* states and *everything* about them, no complete theory will ever be possible. Our general theory will resemble a map where large parts, perhaps the largest, are in white, indicating undiscovered lands and attracting further study. And these further studies will necessitate corrections on the map even of what we regard as comparatively well-known territories, since the borders are long and complicated.

By contrast to those hoping for a complete and infallible theory of politics as an immediate result of our study in comparative government, there are also those who indicate that no general theory should be attempted, let alone permitted to influence our studies. We should not attempt to go by the map, but simply march courageously and practically ahead, noting what we see by the roadside and drawing our own conclusions. But just as the man who starts on a walk without bothering to take a map generally has some sort of an idea in his head as to the character of the territory into which he is going, the political scientist who brags about his lack of interest in general theory frequently has a rather complete theory of his own, although he does not bother to make it explicit. Actually, there are a number of theories of which we are all conscious and which are continually influencing our thought. It should be sufficient to mention three of the most important ones.

The classical, much maligned institutional approach is definitely a theory; and it has been developed in this manner and with a number of variations by authors such as Jellinek, Kelsen and Esmein. Its basic assumptions are that institutions have a (legal) life and importance of their own; that human beings are on the whole alike and will react similarly to the same institutions; but that the number of possible combinations of institutional arrangements is unlimited, thus leading to the great differences between countries and peoples. A variation of this idea is that of an "institutional equilibrium," comparable to the price theory of classical economics and brought forward for the Florence discussions by Professor S. E. Finer.

The pluralistic approach, with the young Harold Laski as its most well-known proponent, is of course even more definitely a general theory. It was formerly regarded as a mere curiosity, but it is becoming more and more widely accepted by political scientists all over the world. This is an important change in the basic assumptions of political science and in particular of comparative government, and it is largely because of this change that some of the earlier characteristics of political science are being criticised today. For pluralism leads us to recognise the fact that what we have to study is not government alone but politics, including a great number of factors formally disregarded. Among those factors are not only the political parties but also more or less organised groups of a seemingly non-political or at least predominantly non-political type—practically on the whole everything which tends to influence public opinion. Quite clearly, the pluralist has to draw much more on economics and sociology than the institutionalist.

Thirdly, there is the power approach: the study of politics as the study of the nature and phenomena of power. This can be combined with either institutionalist or pluralist assumptions. It has so far been important particularly in the United States, but it is spreading all over the world. It deals with all sorts of political situations, including those arising in institutions other than those which we are apt to call political institutions. On the other hand, it has the advantage of providing us with a point of view which is different from those of other social sciences, with the possible exception of political history.

Occasionally, it is argued that the quest for a general theory is opposed to the "problem" approach. On consideration, however, it must be obvious that there is no real conflict between the two, in so far as a theory must always be built up of problem solutions and at the same time points to new problems which have to be solved. Only if a general theory is interpreted so as to mean unfounded statements about generalities does it seem to be opposed to the careful and detailed study of separate problems. On the other hand, of course, problem studies are also possible without reference to a general theory of politics as a whole. It is clearly quite reasonable to attempt an investigation of a practical problem in itself, leaving open its relationships to other questions.

In choosing problems for study, we can never avoid the question of criteria of relevance. Even within the framework of a general theory this may be quite a difficult one since not everything related to the theory is of the same importance. And without a general theory providing the framework of reference, opinions may vary even more as to what is relevant and what is not. There is no difficulty in finding examples of this, and in fact some of the most acrimonious discussions between political scientists have been related exactly to the question of whether certain problems should be regarded as relevant or not. The Evanston report dealt with what it called "narrow-range" and "middle-range" problems: an analysis of the relations between the power of dissolution and ministerial stability in parliamentary systems forming an example of a "narrow-range" problem, whereas the political consequences of rapid industrialisation in underdeveloped areas was cited as an example of "middle-range" problems. "Wide-range" problems, presumably, would be those related to the fundamentals of a general theory of politics. Obviously the choice of problems in all the three ranges is almost unlimited, even with a view to comparative government. Already ten years before the Evanston report Karl Loewenstein presented examples of equal interest:

A genuinely comparative approach should operate freely along trans-national lines. Such problems as political power, leadership (in particular, executive leadership), federalism, civil liberties—whether they have a core of sacrosanctity or are subject to sublimation—are common to every state. Solutions arrived at in one national environment cannot fail to have a bearing on similar situations in one or several other states.

But what should govern our choice of problem?

A specific, "pragmatic" solution is found in what has been called policy-orientation. The problems chosen by political scientists should primarily be the problems confronting statesmen in actual political life. Thus, political science would, so to speak, work to order and present solutions which could be immediately useful to the development of the respective countries and to mankind as a whole.

There are obvious difficulties to this approach. The most obvious one is that those who formulate policies and thus state "policy oriented" problems are unconscious of a great many aspects of political life which tomorrow may prove more important than what politicians are considering today and which require much more prolonged study than time will allow if we are working merely to order. There is at least a chance that some of the problems of tomorrow will be brought up for discussion in time, if political scientists are not too much concerned with the immediate problems of today. On the other hand, a fairly close relation to political life itself has its uses. We should compare ourselves to the economists, who in the recent past have been far more closely involved than political scientists in actual political considerations. The need for immediate "solutions" has sometimes stimulated their work, sometimes proved a hindrance to fundamental research, but more seriously it has sometimes also tempted economists to give some sort of scientific authority to the solutions desired by the holders of political power or, alternatively, by those striving to attain it. Political science would do well to attempt to profit by these experiences in avoiding at least some of the major pitfalls into which economists have been dropping.

One might also consider what could be called "teaching-oriented" problems. The close relationship between teaching and research means not only that teaching has to build on the results provided by research, but also that teaching very frequently puts the spotlight on fundamental problems or on problems not yet sufficiently elucidated by research. This is particularly true in the field of comparative government. Practically no teaching of political science is possible without continual comparison, and thus the teacher is figuratively speaking always working in front of the map. Unknown areas, whether in the literal sense of the word or in the form of problems left aside by the relevant authors, very quickly become apparent in teaching. In fact, it might be argued that teaching provides a better guide than policy orientation for the discovery of problems to be investigated in the field of comparative government. Yet this is certainly not the answer to our question. Teaching may help us to discover the relevant problems, but it does not provide the criteria of relevance. And we are thus left with the highly unsatisfactory conclusion that these criteria are as yet very arbitrary. Perhaps this is what is meant by those who maintain that the study of politics is "an art, not a science."

A final observation might be permitted. It deals with the terms in which we are expressing ourselves. On the whole, political science and politics have the same terminology. There are drawbacks in this apparent simplicity, since the terms of political science frequently suffer from being used as weapons in political discussions. It is tempting to try to develop a separate terminology, sufficiently complicated to deter politicians from using it. This would also demonstrate how "scientific" we are. In the end, it might be developed so as to lead to great precision by avoiding the vagueness of words in common political usage. On the other hand, attempts made so far have frequently proved more ridiculous than precise. And in any case such terminology can be useful only if it is very carefully standardised and maintained over a really long period of time. A varying and changing terminology is more dangerous the more precise it sets out to be.

## NOTES

1. *American Political Review,* Vol. XLVII, No. 3, Sept. 1953.

2. *Contemporary Political Science,* pp. 220 *seq.,* 223.

# A SURVEY OF THE FIELD
# OF COMPARATIVE GOVERNMENT

Roy C. Macridis

## MAJOR CHARACTERISTICS OF THE TRADITIONAL APPROACH

A brief account of the characteristics of the traditional approach and emphasis in the comparative study of government will reveal the source of the current dissatisfaction and will point to the need for reorientation. Comparative study has thus far been comparative in name only. It has been part of what may loosely be called the study of foreign governments, in which the governmental structures and the formal organization of state institutions were treated in a descriptive, historical, or legalistic manner. Primary emphasis has been placed on written documents like constitutions and the legal prescriptions for the allocation of political power. Finally, studies of foreign governments were largely addressed to the Western European democracies or to the political systems of Western Europe, Great Britain, and the Dominions.

It may be worthwhile to discuss briefly each of these characteristics of the traditional approach.

### Essentially Noncomparative

The vast majority of publications in the field of comparative government deal either with one country or with parallel descriptions of the institutions of a number of countries. The majority of texts illustrate this approach. The student is led through the constitutional foundations, the organization of political power, and a description of the ways in which such powers are exercised. In each case "problem areas" are discussed with reference to the country's institutional structure. The right of dissolution is often cited to explain political instability in France, and, conversely, political stability in

England is discussed with reference to the prerogatives of the Crown, with particular emphasis, of course, on the Prime Minister's power of dissolution. The interest of the student is concentrated primarily on an analysis of the structure of the state, the location of sovereignty, the electoral provisions, and the distribution of the electorate into political parties whose ideologies and programs are described. This approach will be found in any standard text and in a number of monographs which aspire to be more comparative in character.[1]

### Essentially Descriptive

It may well be argued that description of the formal political institutions is vital for the understanding of the political process and that as such it leads to comparative study. If so, we hardly ever have any comparison between the particular institutions described. A reading, for instance, of one of the best texts, *Governments of Continental Europe,* edited by James T. Shotwell, will reveal that as we pass from France to Italy, Switzerland, Germany, and U.S.S.R. there is no common thread, no criterion of why these particular countries were selected and no examination of the factors that account for similarities and differences. The same generally applies to Frederic Ogg's and Harold Zink's *Modern Foreign Governments,* and to Fritz M. Marx's *Foreign Governments.* In a somewhat different fashion John Ranney's and Gwendolen Carter's *Major Foreign Powers* has the virtue of addressing itself to only four political systems and of discussing them with reference to some basic problem areas, but again the connecting link and the criterion of selection are missing. Another pioneer book in the field, Daniel Witt's *Comparative Political Institutions,* abandons the country-by-country approach in favor of categories within which comparison is more feasible, but the author is satisfied to include under such categories as "The Citizen and the Government" and "The

Electoral Process" separate descriptions of the institutions of individual countries, and fails to make explicit comparisons.

It should be clearly understood here that these remarks are not meant to reflect on the scholarly quality of the books cited, nor to disparage the descriptive approach. They are meant merely to point out that these books are limited primarily to political morphology or what might also be called political anatomy. They describe various political institutions generally without attempting to compare them; what comparison *is* made is limited exclusively to the identification of differences between types or systems, such as federal versus unitary system or parliamentary versus presidential system or the more elusive differences between democratic and totalitarian systems.

There are two typical approaches in the descriptive study of political institutions. The first is *historical* and the second is *legalistic*. The historical approach centers on the study of the origins and growth of certain institutions. We trace the origins of the British parliamentary system to Magna Carta and study its development through successive historical stages. It is assumed that parallel historical accounts of the evolution of the French parliament or the German representative assemblies will indicate similarities and differences. The approach followed is almost identical with that used by the historian. There is no effort to evolve an analytical scheme within which an antecedent factor is related in terms other than chronological to a particular event or development.[2]

The second most prevalent approach is what we might call the legalistic approach. Here the student is exposed primarily to the study of the "powers" of the various branches of government and their relationships with reference to the existing constitutional and legal prescriptions. This is almost exclusively the study of what can be done or what cannot be done by various governmental agencies with reference to legal and constitutional provisions. Again, this approach, like its historical counterpart with which it often goes hand in hand, describes the political system in a very narrow frame. It does not seek the forces that shape the legal forms, nor does it attempt to establish the causal relationships that account for the variety in constitutional prescriptions from one system to another or from one period to another. A typical illustration of this approach are two recent studies on post-World War II constitutional developments in Western Europe: Arnold Zurcher's *Constitutionalism and Constitutional Trends since World War II,* and Mirkine Guetzevitch's *Les Constitutions Europeènnes*. To a great extent Ivor Jenning's works on the *British Cabinet* and the *British Parliament* rely on the legalistic approach with particular emphasis on the search for precedents that "explain" the powers of various governmental organs.

The combination of the historical and the legalistic approaches is found in the great majority of books published on foreign systems that purport to be comparable. Even though they give us a cameralike picture of the development and relationships of the various political organs in a system, and point to parallel historical development, they do not attempt to devise a general frame of reference in which we can get broad hypotheses about the development and operation of institutions.

### Essentially Parochial

The great number of studies on foreign political systems has been addressed to the examination of Western European institutions. Accessibility of the countries studied, relative ease of overcoming language barriers, and the availability of official documents and other source materials, as well as cultural affinities, account for this fact. France, Great Britain, Germany, Switzerland, and to a lesser extent the Scandinavian countries and the British Dominions have been the countries to which writing and research has been directed and which are being included in the various comparative government courses in the greater number of American universities. Again, however, no systematic effort has been made to identify the similarities and the differences among these countries except in purely descriptive terms. No effort has been made to define in analytical terms the categories that constitute an "area" of study. True, most authors seem to identify these countries in terms of a common historical and cultural background and they often pay lip service to some other common traits, such as their advanced economic systems, particularly institutions, and democracy. What is meant by "advanced" economic systems, however, and, more specifically, what is the relationship between political institutions and the existing economic system? We often find the statement that Germany did not develop a democratic ideology and parliamentary institutions because capitalism developed "late," but no effort is being made to test the validity of such a generalization comparatively—for, after all, capitalism developed "late" in the United States and in some of the British Dominions. Often statements about the existence of a common ideology are made without attempting to define what is "common" and how ideology is related to political institutions.[3]

There is no doubt that references to social and economic configurations, political ideologies, and institutions that can be found in texts should be interrelated into a system that would make comparative analyses of these Western European countries possible. No such effort, however, with the exception of Carl Friedrich's *Constitutional Government and Democracy,* has been made, and even Professor Friedrich is concerned only with the interplay between ideology and institutions. There is no systematic synthesis of the various "characteristics" or "traits" of different political systems. Yet without such a conceptualization no variables can be identified and compared, and as a result no truly comparative analyses of the Western governmental systems have been made by political scientists.

Some notable exceptions, in addition to Professor Friedrich's and Professor Herman Finer's books, are Michel's book on *Political Parties*[4] and the recent comparative analysis of the structure and the organization of political parties and the relationship between structure and ideology by Professor Maurice Duverger.[5] Another good illustration of a more sophisticated study is a current essay on the French political system by François Goguel[6] in which he points out that political, economic, and social instability in France is due to the uneven development of various regions in the country, thus suggesting a relationship between political stability and uniformity of economic development within a country.

Concentration on Western systems cannot be exclusively attributed to some of the considerations suggested above. An even more important factor was the belief at one time shared by many political scientists that democracy was the "normal" and durable form of government and that it was destined to spread throughout the world. In fact, "comparative study" would embrace more political systems only as they developed democratic institutions. James Bryce put this in very succinct terms:

The time seems to have arrived when the actualities of democratic government in its diverse forms, should be investigated, and when the conditions most favorable to its success should receive more attention than students, as distinguished from politicians, have been bestowing upon them.[7]

It was natural that such a point of view should limit comparative study to the democratic systems and that it would call for the study of other systems only for the purpose of identifying democratic institutions and forms. As we shall see, such a preoccupation distorted the analysis and study of non-Western systems by centering upon patterns and institutions that were familiar to the Western observer, such as constitutions and legislatures, but whose relevance to the political process of non-Western countries was only incidental.

## Essentially Static

In general the traditional approach has ignored the dynamic factors that account for growth and change. It has concentrated on what we have called political anatomy. After the evolutionary premises of some of the original works in the nineteenth century were abandoned, students of political institutions apparently lost all interest in the formulation of other theories in the light of which change could be comparatively studied.

The question of sovereignty and its location occupied students of politics for a long time; the study of constitutional structures became a favorite pastime, though no particular effort was made to evaluate the effectiveness of constitutional forms in achieving posited goals or to analyze the conditions underlying the success or failure of constitutionalism. The parallel development of administration was noted, but again its growth was studied with reference to a constitutional setting, as Dicey's work amply illustrates.[8] The growth of political parties was studied, but aside from descriptions of their legal status little consideration was given by political scientists to the radical transformation parties were to bring about in the organization of political power. Henry Maine's and William Lecky's[9] bold hypotheses about the impact on democracy of the development of party government and of the extension of the franchise were abandoned in the light of contrary evidence and were never replaced with new ones. Indeed, Walter Bagehot's[10] analysis of the British Cabinet remained standard until the turn of the century, though the word "party" rarely appears in it, and Dicey's formal statement of the limitations of parliamentary sovereignty were considered for a long time to the most definitive formulation of the problem.[11] The British people, it was pointed out by Dicey, constituting the "political sovereign" body limited the "legal sovereignty" of the parliament and such limitation was institutionalized through the courts. Federalism and its development in the various dominions was also discussed with reference to the legal organization of power and to its relationship with the concept of sovereignty. In all cases the studies made were a dissection of the distribution of powers in terms of their legal setting and left out of the picture altogether the problem of change and the study of those factors —political or other—that account for change.

## Essentially Monographic

The most important studies of foreign systems, aside from basic texts, have taken the form of monographs that have concentrated on the study of the political institutions of one system or on the discussion of a particular institution in one system. Works such as those by John Marriott, Arthur K. Keith, Joseph Barthelemy, James Bryce, Ivor Jennings, Harold Laski, A. V. Dicey, Frank

Goodnow, W. A. Robson, Abbott L. Lowells, Woodrow Wilson,[12] and many others were addressed generally to only one country or to a particular institutional development within one country. The American presidency, the British parliamentary system, the congressional form of government were presented in studies in which the particular institutional forms were placed in the context of the whole tradition and legal system of the country involved. Sometimes such monographs represented great advances over the legalistic approach because they brought into the open nonpolitical factors and institutions or attempted to deal analytically with some of the problems facing the democratic systems. They had a focal point and the description of the institutions was always related to a common theme or was undertaken in the light of a common political problem, such as the relationship between executive and legislature, the growth of administrative law and the institutions of administration, the relationship between national characteristics and political ideology, and the like. The relationships established between political and nonpolitical factors, however, hardly attain a systematic formulation that can be used for comparative study, i.e., for identifying variables and attempting to account for them. Nor is the suggestion ever explicitly made that the particular way in which a problem is studied or certain institutional developments discussed is applicable to parallel phenomena in other countries.

### The Problem Approach in the Traditional Literature

A number of studies dealing with problem areas have employed the traditional approach. Examples are studies of the relationship between democracy and economic planning; of representation and the growth of administrative agencies with new economic and social functions; of the decay of bicameralism; or of the efforts of representative assemblies to reconcile the social and economic conflicts arising in democratic societies between the two world wars.

Such studies have usually been confined to the institutional framework of the country involved. Analyses of policy-orientation have not gone beyond the examination of reforms of the formal institutional structure, as in studies of the reorganization of the House of Lords, the development of functional representative assemblies, the establishment of economic federalism, the delegation of legislative powers to the executive, the association of professional groups in policy-making, the integration rather than separation of policy-making organs, and, finally, measures to combat the growth of antidemocratic parties within democratic systems. The study of such problems has paved the way, however, for the abandonment of the traditional formal categories, for these problems cannot be examined in that restricting frame. They call for the development of a more precise analysis of human behavior and of the relationship between political institutions and social and economic factors. They call for an approach in which politics is conceived as a process that cannot be understood without reference to the contextual factors of a political system.

### The Area Focus

Only recently has the study of foreign systems been cast in a frame that carries more promise for comparative analysis. Partly as the result of the war and the need to acquire better knowledge about certain geographic areas, and partly as the result of the intensive and more systematic study by sociologists and anthropologists of human behavior in various non-Western countries, political scientists have become involved in interdisciplinary studies of "areas." An area is a cluster of countries which, because of certain policy preoccupations, geographic propinquity, or common problems and theoretic interests, can be studied as a unit. The political and economic systems, languages, history, culture, and psychology are jointly explored by representatives of various disciplines in universities and government departments. Area studies have developed rapidly in the United States in the last fifteen years. Every big university now has a number of such programs ranging from Western Europe to the Middle East and Africa.[13]

On its face the so-called area programs provide what many students of comparative government consider to be the best laboratory for comparative analysis. For it has been assumed that an area is a cluster of countries in which there is enough cultural uniformity to make the comparative study of political institutional variables between them possible. Furthermore, it has also been assumed that the interdisciplinary approach provides for a more sophisticated and systematic analysis in which the investigator or group of investigators can gain a "total" picture of the system and subsequently be able to dissect it and compare its component elements.

The interdisciplinary approach has suggested some important organizational concepts on the basis of which data could be gathered, variables identified, and comparative study undertaken. Most important among them have been the concepts of *culture and personality*. The former stresses the particular traits that constitute the configuration of a culture.[14] Culture-traits or culture-patterns can be identified and compared with each other. Yet in most cases comparison here, even among anthropologists, has assumed primarily the character of pointing out differences rather than explaining them. The *personality* concept on the other hand, by pointing out various personality traits or patterns, provides an instrument for the study of motivational aspects and their variations from one culture to another.[15]

It is difficult to assess the contributions of the area approach to the comparative study of politics. Very often, instead of suggesting a systematic analytical frame within which political scientists might attempt intracultural comparisons, the area approach has degenerated into either a descriptive analysis of institutional political structures within the given areas or merely produced monographs in which certain problems were studied with more sophistication with reference to one country. Such books as Robert Scalapino's *Democracy and the Party Movement in Pre-War Japan,* Barrington Moore's *Soviet Politics, the Dilemma of Power,* Alex Inkeles's *Public Opinion in the Soviet Union,* George Blanksten's *Peron's Argentina,* and Merle Fainsod's *How Russia Is Ruled* are the best representative works in area studies, but their excellence lies not so much in their systematic orientation or in the development of analytical concepts for comparison but rather in the sophistication with which the authors relate the political process in the system discussed to the ideological, cultural, and social contextual elements. Institutions are no longer described as if they had a reality which is taken for granted but rather as functioning entities operating within a given context. The descriptive approach gained as a result a richness and flavor which could not be found in the traditional legalistic and historical approach.

But in general, the area approach with its interdisciplinary orientation has failed to provide us with a systematic frame for comparative analysis. For, after all, the very definition of an area is subject to methodological questions with which many of the area specialists never grapple. An area is not a concrete reality as has often been asserted or taken for granted on the basis of considerations of policy or expediency. It is, or rather ought to be, an analytical concept which subsumes certain categories for the compilation of data, provides for certain uniformities which suggest a control situation of the laboratory type within which variables can be studied. Area programs, however, have not attained this level of systematic orientation and as a result their contribution to comparative analysis has been limited. They have enriched our awareness of cultures and institutions in which the political forms vary greatly from the Western forms and they have been suggestive, at least to the political scientist, of the need to broaden his horizon and include in his study of formal institutions many of the informal processes of a system.

## CRITICAL EVALUATION OF THE TRADITIONAL APPROACH

The preceding section presented a general survey of the traditional approach to comparative politics. A brief recapitulation and a critical re-examination are now in order.

### Recapitulation of Major Features of the Traditional Approach

The traditional approach addressed itself primarily to Western political systems.

1. It dealt primarily with a single-culture configuration, i.e., the Western world.

2. Within this culture configuration, comparative study dealt mainly with representative democracies, treating nondemocratic systems until recently as aberrations from the democratic "norms."

3. This prevented the student from dealing systematically not only with nondemocratic Western political systems, but with colonial systems, other "backward" areas, and culturally distinct societies which exhibit superficially the characteristics of the representative process (e.g., India, Japan, etc.).

4. Research was founded on the study of isolated aspects of the governmental process within specific countries; hence it was comparative in name only.

The comparative study of politics was excessively formalistic in its approach to political institutions.

1. It focused analysis on the formal institutions of government, to the detriment of a sophisticated awareness of the informal arrangements of society and of their role in the formation of decisions and the exercise of power.

2. In neglecting such informal arrangements, it proved to be relatively insensitive to the nonpolitical determinants of political behavior and hence to the nonpolitical bases of governmental institutions.

3. Comparison was made in terms of the formal constitutional aspects of Western systems, i.e., parliaments, chief executives, civil services, administrative law, etc., which are not necessarily the most fruitful concepts for a truly comparative study.

The comparative study of politics was preponderantly descriptive rather than problem-solving, or analytic in its method.

1. Except for some studies of proportional representation, emergency legislation, and electoral systems, the field was insensitive to hypotheses and their verification.

2. Even in the purely descriptive approach to political systems it was relatively insensitive to the methods of cultural anthropology, in which descriptions are fruitfully made in terms of general concepts or integrating hypotheses.

3. Thus, description in comparative government

did not readily lend itself to the testing of hypotheses, to the compilation of significant data regarding a single political phenomenon—or class of such phenomenon—in a large number of societies.

4. Description without systematic orientation obstructed the discovery of hypotheses regarding uniformities in political behavior and prevented the formulation, on a comparative basis, of a theory of political dynamics (i.e., change, revolution, conditions of stability, etc.).

A number of factors have accounted for our increasing awareness of the shortcomings of the traditional approach and have led to a reorientation:

1. The prevalent dissatisfaction with the country-by-country approach in teaching and research. The study of foreign governments is not in any sense of the word comparative study. It has been limited, as we have seen, to parallel descriptive accounts of various political institutions and the student is often left to his own devices in noting superficial similarities and differences between political systems.

2. The need to broaden our approach by including in our study non-Western systems and by attempting to relate the contextual elements of any system with the political process.

3. The growing concern with policy-making and policy-orientation. It is probably not untrue to say that research is often related to the broad exigencies of policy making. Its global requirements have suggested the close interrelatedness of a number of factors that were considered to be separate in the past and have shown the fallacy of compartmentalization, i.e., of area studies. Yet the need for reorientation is in a sense the natural outcome of the area study programs developed in this country during the war in many universities. Area specialists were brought together and it was natural that they should be asked to relate their findings. This in itself called for comparison.

4. Finally, comparative analysis is becoming increasingly part and parcel of the growing concern with the scientific approach to politics. Science aspires to the establishment of regular patterns of behavior. Such patterns can be discovered only by studying as many systems as possible in the light of common analytical categories.

Probably with the above factors in mind, Pendleton Herring, in his address to the 1953 meeting of the American Political Science Association, stated:

Careful studies that deal comparatively with the cultures and the ideologies, the historical development and the whole complex of forces that seek final expression politically would lead not only to a better understanding of the countries of the world with which we must deal but should likewise enable us to understand ourselves better....[16]

### Critical Re-examination

Re-examination of the nature and scope of comparative study is a relatively recent development.

In 1944 a committee of the American Political Science Association, reporting in the *American Political Science Review,* pointed out the need for some methodological reorientation and for undertaking substantive studies of a truly comparative nature. The committee observed:

In the voluminous material accumulated by the correspondence and the panel discussion, one fact stands out clearly, i.e., that the branch of political science commonly styled comparative government has emerged from a tedious and stagnating routine and, unless this reporter is badly mistaken, is about to undergo a rejuvenation not hoped for by its most ardent devotees—this much to the surprise of those who at first had referred to comparative government as a discipline in a status of suspended animation, hardly alive under the competitive pressure of the more glamorous "international relations." . . .

Comparative government has ceased to be merely *l'art pour l'art.* It is forced to reorient itself in line with the technological development which is about to weld the world together into a closer union of peoples, if not of states.

Consequently, the majority of the participants in the panel agreed on two basic points: First: comparative government in the narrow sense of descriptive analysis of foreign institutions is an anachronism. As is the case with political science at large, it has to widen its scope to refine and redefine its methods. Second: there is no longer any single technique, neither the orthodox institutional approach nor the strict behaviorist method being sufficient *per se* to gain access to the true *Gestalt* of foreign political civilizations; methods and designs must be blended and kept in elastic touch and mutual penetration. Although some of the elder statesmen raised their warning voice that *qui trop embracé mal étreint,* that a too promiscuous or ambitious application of diversified methods would lead to dilettantism and confusion, the majority seemed agreed that the frontier posts of comparative government must be moved boldly into the precincts of neighboring and collateral disciplines—that, to use an illustration, criminal law is not under the exclusive jurisdiction of the lawyer if it helps to understand the social function of state and government. The prevailing impression among the participants was that comparative government has lost its traditional character of descriptive analysis and is about to assume the character of a "total" science if it is to serve as a conscious instrument of social engineering.[17]

In a recent report[18] also published in the *American Political Science Review* and incorporating the deliberations of a summer seminar on comparative politics held under the auspices of the Social Science Research Council, the participants agreed substantially with the same general criticisms presented in this study. They, too, felt that comparative study had been comparative in name only; that it was addressed primarily to the Western systems and that it lacked systematic orientation. The authors agreed that the "comparative method revolves around the discovery of uniformities, i.e., the analytical formulation of concepts and problems under which real institutional forms can be compared." Noting that "the nineteenth century students of politics indulged primarily in theories and normative speculations," while "today we have many facts but we do not know why we have them and we are unable to decide what to do with them," they pointed out that it was only by suggesting a scheme of inquiry that systematic empirical research and investigation in the field could be undertaken. Their major conclusion on the method of comparative study and by implication their criticisms of the traditional approach may be stated in full:

1. That comparison involves abstraction and that concrete situations or processes can never be compared as such. Every phenomenon is unique; every manifestation is unique; every process, every nation, like every individual, is in a sense unique. To compare them means to select certain types or concepts, and in so doing we have to "distort" the unique and the concrete.

2. That prior to any comparison it is necessary not only to establish categories and concepts but also to determine criteria of relevance of the particular components of a social and political situation to the problem under analysis (i.e., relevance of social stratification to family system, or sunspots to political instability).

3. That it is necessary to establish criteria for the adequate representation of the particular components that enter into a general analysis or the analysis of a problem.

4. That it is necessary in attempting to develop ultimately a theory of politics to formulate hypotheses emerging either from the context of a conceptual scheme or from the formulation of a problem.

5. That the formulation of hypothetical relations and their investigation against empirical data can never lead to proof. A hypothesis or a series of hypothetical relations would be considered proven, i.e., verified, only as long as it withstands falsification.

6. That hypothetical series rather than single hypotheses should be formulated. In each case the connecting link between general hypothetical series and the particular social relations should be provided by the specification of conditions under which any or all the possibilities enumerated in this series are expected to take place.

The formulation of hypothetical series, it should be pointed out, unlike a single hypothesis (which states what consequence will flow from a given antecedent state X), states series of consequences which will flow from state X or several states, X, Y, Z under particular conditions. It is designed to deal with the problem of verification in social sciences, where the absence of experimental situations prevents us from having sufficiently constant situations to determine the role played in them by specified variables. Under such circumstances we can only state hypotheses for varying conditions, i.e., hypothetical series. The specification of such conditions is what gives us a meaningful element of regularity in the absence of experimental situations and allows us to test our hypotheses by finding not only similar but also dissimilar consequences ensuing from given antecedent conditions.

7. That comparative study, even if it falls short of providing a general theory of politics, can pave the way to the gradual and cumulative development of theory by (a) enriching our imaginative ability to formulate hypotheses, in the same sense that any "outsidedness" enhances our ability to understand a social system; (b) providing a means for the testing of hypotheses, and (c) making us aware that something we have taken for granted requires explanation.

8. Finally, that one of the greatest dangers in hypothesizing in connection with comparative study is the projection of possible relationships ad infinitum. This can be avoided by the orderly collection of data prior to hypothesizing. Such collection may in itself lead us to the recognition of irrelevant relations (climate and the electoral system, language and industrial technology, etc.). Such a recognition in itself makes for a more manageable study of data. *Hence the importance attached by the members of the Seminar to the development of some rough classificatory scheme prior to the formulation of hypotheses.*

The members of the seminar generally rejected the arguments made in favor of uniqueness, and argued that comparison between institutions not only can be made, but also may eventually provide— through types of approach to be indicated presently —a general theory of politics as well as a general theory of political change. Before theories can be developed, however, it was suggested that research along the following lines must be undertaken in as orderly a way as possible:

1. Elaboration of a tentative classificatory scheme, however rough;

2. Conceptualization at various levels of abstraction (preferable at the more modest and manageable level of the problem-oriented approach);

3. Hypothesizing, i.e., the formulation of single hypotheses or hypothetical series suggested either by the data ordered under a classificatory scheme or by the formulation of sets of problems; and

4. Finally, the constant testing of hypotheses by empirical data in order to eliminate untenable hypotheses by falsification, making possible the formulation of new and more valid ones.

It is regrettable that none of these approaches has been seriously and methodically used by political scientists. Classification is spotty, and, in most cases, of descriptive, formal character. Conceptualization and hypothesizing have not moved beyond the narrow-gauge problem-approach state—and this with reference to the Western European countries primarily. As for a systematic process for the verification and falsification of hypotheses, it remains practically unknown in our literature.

In calling for a new orientation the authors of this report took particular issue with the descriptive character of the traditional approach and with its lack of systematic orientation. The criticisms of the authors, however, were addressed to the method or rather the lack of method followed by the traditional approach, since it would be unfair to assume that they wanted to abandon description of institutional forms or processes! The authors simply pointed out that description does not mean random description. It does not mean the description of a concrete institutional reality simply because it happens to attract the investigator's attention. In fact there is no such thing as description unless we know what we want to describe. One cannot begin with the observation of facts as we are so often told, unless he has a notion of what a fact is, which in itself implies an abstraction made on the basis of certain criteria which are only too often based upon explicit or implicit theoretical commitments. A man jumps from Brooklyn bridge. It is a fact! And yet this very same fact is looked upon in different ways by the physicist, the policeman, the doctor, the psychiatrist, and the man's wife. It is the way in which we look at the phenomenon that makes it an "observable fact." "What are the facts," writes M. R. Cohen,

is far from being clear and self-evident to the naked or untrained eye. Indeed to find all the relevant facts is the final goal of the carefully elaborated procedure which we call scientific method. But discoveries in science are made only by those who know what to look for, and to do this we must have some preliminary ideas as to the way things are connected. . . .[19]

This applies with particular force not only to comparative analysis but to the very first step on which we build our material for comparisons: namely, description through which we gain an insight into the institutional arrangements of a system and into the working of the system as a whole.

It should be made clear, therefore, at the risk of overstating the obvious that the references here to the inadequacies of the descriptive approach are not meant to underestimate the role and significance of description but rather to indicate the need of conceptual categories in the light of which either political systems as such or specific institutional structures and arrangements are described. The dissatisfaction with the descriptive approach does not stem, in other words, from any dissatisfaction with description, which is, as has been pointed out, basic to the study of politics as well as to any other discipline, but rather from the particular manner in which descriptions of Western and non-Western systems were made on the basis of the traditional approach.

Another criticism was that the traditional approach, in its concern with democratic and representative systems, tended to subordinate empirical investigation of political forms and processes to normative standards. Nondemocratic and nonparliamentary forms were treated as aberrations or deviations from the norm and the resulting confusion between empirical and normative study was extremely damaging to comparative analysis and even to description of non-Western governmental systems. For even when nondemocratic societies were studied, the goal of the investigator was to find elements that approximated the democratic forms. This tended, of course, to obscure the understanding of phenomena such as power configuration, legitimacy, and leadership for the sake of describing formal institutions like constitutions and parliaments which in the non-Western systems were very often mere forms whose descriptive study could not advance our understanding of these societies. To the extent to which the apparently similar constitutions that had evolved in non-Western systems were compared with their Western counterparts, confusion became only confounded since such comparison involved invariably two functionally dissimilar political institutions.

Finally, to the extent to which the traditional approach was policy-oriented it suffered from some basic weaknesses. First, the very formulation of the problem calling for a "policy solution" was not made in a manner that indicated the nature of the comparative study involved. Second, the problem was not systematically studied before recommendations based upon comparative study were made. To quote once more the authors of the SSRC Report:

It was agreed that the formulation of the problem should be as clear and logically coherent as possible. A problem selected should be presented in the following form:

1. The statement and structure of the problem: The problem must be stated precisely; it must be stated in such a form as to lead immediately to hypotheses; it must be analyzed into its component elements; its variables and the relations between them must be spelled out; and all this must be done in operationally meaningful terms.

2. Its relations to a possible general theory of politics: that is, how would the problem fit into a more general theoretical orientation, and what more general questions can illuminate its solution.

3. Demonstration of the manner in which the problem calls for the use of comparative method, and analysis of the level of abstraction which comparison would involve.

4. The enumeration of a recommended research technique for dealing with the problem and justification of the recommendation.

5. The enumeration of possible alternative research techniques.[20]

## SUMMARY

To summarize, the major criticism here of the traditional approach to the study of comparative politics is that it is centered upon the description of the formally established institutions of government; that the expression "comparative government" signifies the study of the legal instrumentalities of government and of political processes conceived as the result of the interaction between the properly constituted organs of government—the electorate, the legislature, the executive, the administration, and the courts; that the traditional approach is in general singularly insensitive to informal factors and processes such as the various interest groups, the wielders of social and economic power and at times even of political power operating outside of the formal governmental institutions, and the more complex contextual forces that can be found in the ideological patterns and the social organization of the system. It lacks a systematic approach. The very word "system" causes a number of people to raise their eyebrows while to others it has connotations of group research that suggest the suppression of the imagination and sensitivity of the observer for the sake of conceptually determined and rigidly adhered to categories. This is far from being the case, however. A systematic approach simply involves the development of categories for the compilation of data and the interrelationship of the data so compiled in the form of theories, i.e., the suggestion of variable relationships. The development of common categories establishes criteria of relevance. Once such categories are suggested, their relevance for the compilation of data through the study of problems in as many political systems as possible should be made. For instance, if it is shown that the composition or recruitment of elites in certain political systems accounts for the degree to which the system is suceptible to change, which in turn may lead us to certain general suppositions about political stability, then a systematic approach would require the examination of the same phenomenon in a number of political systems in the light of the same general categories. While the traditional approach does not claim to be explanatory, a systematic approach claims to be precisely this. For explanation simply means verification of hypothetical propositions. In the field of politics, given the lack of experimentation, it is only the testing of a hypothesis in as many systems as possible that will provide us with a moderate degree of assurance that we have an explanation.

The term "comparative politics" which is favored here in place of "comparative government" is beginning to delineate, therefore, an area of concern and a methodological orientation that differs from the traditional approach. It offers to study the political process and institutions in a truly comparative fashion for the purpose of answering common problems and questions. In so doing it broadens the range of comparison to as many political systems as possible. It abandons the traditional emphasis upon governmental institutions in order to study politics as a social function that involves deliberation and decision-making for the purpose of providing adjustment and reconciliation of the all-prevailing power aspirations. But such a function is neither performed exclusively by the formally constituted governmental agencies nor can it be understood only with reference to the functioning of such governmental agencies. In fact, government is only one of the many factors that enter into the analysis of the political process. In this sense "comparative politics" broadens the range of comparative study by introducing factors that were neglected in the past.

From a methodological point of view "comparative politics" delineates an approach which attempts to identify the characteristics of political systems in terms of generalized categories; it establishes such analytical categories in the light of which identification of political phenomena is made possible for as many systems as possible; it purports above all not only to identify similarities and differences but also to account for them. Explanation, however, requires an exhaustive compilation of data in common categories and the formulation of hypotheses that can be tested. Finally, it aims toward the development of a body of knowledge in the light of which predictions of trends and policy recommendations can be made. In this sense comparative politics becomes a matrix from which theories emerge and at the same time a laboratory for their testing.

## NOTES

1. See for instance some of the best texts: James T. Shotwell (ed.): *Governments of Continental Europe*, New York, The Macmillan Co., 1950; Taylor Cole (ed.): *European Political Systems*, New York, Alfred A. Knopf, Inc., 1953; Gwendolen Carter, John Ranney, and John Hertz: *Major Foreign Powers*, New York, Harcourt, Brace and World, 1952; Frederic Ogg and Harold Zink: *Modern Foreign Governments*, New York, The Macmillan Co., 1953.

2. Some of the best illustrations of this approach are David Thomson: *Democracy in France*, New York, Oxford University Press, 1952; A Soulier: *L'instabilité ministerielle*, Paris, Sirey, 1939; François Goguel: *La Politique des Partis sous la Troisième République*, Paris, Aux Editions du Seuil, 1946.

3. T. D. Weldon: *The Vocabulary of Politics*, London, Pelican, 1953.

4. Herman Finer: *The Theory and Practice of Modern Government*, New York, Henry Holt and Co., 1949; Robert Michels: *Political Parties: A Sociological Study of the Oligarchic Tendencies of Modern Democracies*, New York, Hearst's International Library Co., 1915.

5. Maurice Duverger: *Les Partis Politiques*, Paris, Colin, 1951; and the excellent review articles of Samuel H. Beer: "Les Partis Politiques," *Western Political Quarterly*, 6:512–517 (September, 1953) and Sigmund Neumann: "Toward a Theory of Political Parties," *World Politics*, 6:549–563 (July, 1954).

6. Francois Goguel: "Political Instability in France," *Foreign Affairs*, 33:111–122 (October, 1954).

7. James Bryce: *Modern Democracies*, New York, The Macmillan Co., 1921, Vol. I, p. 4.

8. A. V. Dicey: *The Law of the Constitution*, New York, The Macmillan Co., 1902.

9. Henry Maine: *Popular Government*, London, T. Murray, 1890, and William Lecky: *Democracy and Liberty*, London, Longmans, Green and Co., 1896.

10. Walter Bagehot: *The English Constitution,* London, Oxford University Press, 1936.

11. Dicey, *op. cit.*

12. See John Marriott: *English Political Institutions,* Oxford, The Clarendon Press, 1910, *The Mechanics of the Modern State,* Oxford, The Clarendon Press, 1927, *Second Chambers,* Oxford, The Clarendon Press, 1910; Abbott L. Lowell: *The Government of England,* New York, The Macmillan Co., 1908, *Governments and Parties in Continental Europe,* Boston, Houghton Mifflin and Co., 1897, *Greater European Governments,* Cambridge, Harvard University Press, 1918; Joseph Barthelemy: *Le role du puvoir executif dans les republiques modernes,* Paris, Giard et Briere, 1906, *Le gouvernement de la France,* Paris, Payot, 1925; Woodrow Wilson: *Congressional Government,* Boston, Houghton Mifflin and Co., 1913, *Constitutional Government in the United States,* New York, Columbia University Press, 1913; Arthur B. Keith: *The British Cabinet System* (2nd ed.), London, Stevens and Sons, Ltd., 1952; Frank Goodnow: *Comparative Administrative Law,* New York, G. P. Putnam's Sons, 1893, *Politics and Administration,* New York, The Macmillan Co., 1900; W. A. Robson: *Justice and Administrative Law* (2nd ed.), London, Stevens and Sons, Ltd., 1947; Ivor Jennings: *Cabinet Government,* New York, The Macmillan Co., 1936, *Parliament,* New York, The Macmillan Co., 1940; James Bryce: *Modern Democracies,* New York, The Macmillan Co., 1921.

13. W. C. Bennett: *Area Studies in American Universities,* New York, Social Science Research Council, 1951.

14. Ruth Benedict: *Patterns of Culture,* Boston and New York, Houghton Mifflin and Co., 1934; Melville Herskovits: *Man and His Works,* New York, Alfred A. Knopf, Inc., 1951; Clyde Kluckhohn: *Mirror for Man,* New York, McGraw-Hill Book Company, Inc., 1949.

15. Some of the most illustrative works are: Theodore Adorno and others: *The Authoritarian Personality,* New York, Harper & Brothers, 1950; Gabriel Almond: *The Appeal of Communism,* Princeton, Princeton University Press, 1954; David Levy: *New Fields of Psychiatry,* New York, W. W. Norton & Company, Inc., 1947. See also the excellent review article by Raymond Bauer: "The Psycho-Cultural Approach to Soviet Studies," *World Politics* 7:119–132 (October, 1954).

16. Pendleton Herring: "On the Study of Government," *American Political Science Review,* 47:961 (December, 1953).

17. Karl Loewenstein: "Report on the Research Panel on Comparative Government," *American Political Science Review* 38:540–548 (June, 1944).

18. "Research in Comparative Politics," *American Political Science Review* 47:641–675 (September, 1935), a report prepared jointly by Roy C. Macridis and Richard Cox embodying the deliberations of the Social Science Research Council Interuniversity Research Seminar on Comparative Politics in which the following participated: Samuel H. Beer, Harry Eckstein, George Blanksten, Carl W. Deutch, Richard Cox, Roy C. Macridis, Kenneth Thompson, and Robert E. Ward.

19. Morris R. Cohen: *Reason and Law,* New York, The Free Press, 1950, p. 2.

20. "Research in Comparative Politics," *op. cit.,* pp. 651–652.

# A SUGGESTED RESEARCH STRATEGY IN WESTERN EUROPEAN GOVERNMENT AND POLITICS

## Gabriel A. Almond, Taylor Cole, and Roy C. Macridis

If one compares the literature on American government and politics with that which concerns continental Europe, it is quite evident that the two fields of study in the last decades have proceeded

Reprinted from *The American Political Science Review,* Vol. XLIX, No. 4 (December, 1955), pp. 1042–1049, by permission of the American Political Science Association.

This report was prepared by a subcommittee of the Committee on Research in Comparative Politics of the Social Science Research Council. Gabriel A. Almond acted as reporter.

on somewhat different assumptions as to the scope and methods of political science. This divergence is of relatively recent origin. Before World War I a substantial number of leading American students in this field had their training in European centers of learning, and brought back with them the rich tradition of European historical, philosophical, and legal scholarship.

With noteworthy exceptions the study of continental European political institutions still tends to be dominated by this historical, philosophical, and legal emphasis. The continuity of scholarship in the continental European area has been broken by the two world wars, by totalitarian regimes, by enemy occupation, and by the persistence of internal antagonism and cleavages. With the exception of a few years in the 1920's, the entire era since World War I has been one of catastrophe or the atmosphere of catastrophe in which scientific inquiry and the renewal of the scientific cadres could be carried on only for short periods, under the greatest handicaps, and with inadequate resources.

In the United States, beginning after the First World War and stimulated in some measure by the great European innovators such as Ostrogorski, Bryce, Weber, Pareto, and Michels, the conception of the scope of political science began to undergo a significant change. This development occurred in an experimental and pragmatic way, and with little theoretical explication. As American political scientists discovered that governmental institutions in their actual practice deviated from their formal competences, they supplemented the purely legal approach with an observational or functional one. The problem now was not only what legal powers these agencies had, but what they actually did, how they were related to one another, and what roles they played in the making and execution of public policy. In this respect they were plowing more deeply into ground which had been broken by such English political scientists as Bagehot and Bryce.

Once having departed from the legal framework and method, they began to probe into the non-legal levels and processes of politics, and a substantial literature developed including—in addition to realistic and functional analyses of the presidency, the courts, the Congress, and the bureaucracy—studies of non-legal or semi-legal institutions and processes such as political parties, pressure groups, public opinion, and political behavior.

While this impairment of the unity of the Western European-American tradition of political science is of relatively recent origin and is by no means irremediable, its consequences at the present time are to make comparisons of political institutions and processes as between the European and American areas most difficult. With all its breadth and technical resourcefulness, the branch of political science dealing with American government and politics has been unable to escape a kind of parochialism in which the insights into our own process which can come only from comparison tend to be lost. And with all the refinements of European legal scholarship, the richness of the European historical tradition, and its philosophical and theoretical sophistication, that branch of the political science discipline which deals with continental European government and politics has not been able to escape a certain alienation from reality which always results from too great an emphasis on the formal aspects of institutions and processes.

There has indeed been a continual process of communication between American, British, and continental European scholars, and the contributions of the many European political scientists now teaching in American universities have gone far toward bridging the two fields and combining the merits of both. But a fair appraisal of the state of the two fields cannot escape the conclusion that a great deal more can be done toward reestablishing a common approach and a more effective sharing of methods and insights.

At another level the impulse for this memorandum arises from more urgent and practical considerations. The survival of parliamentary and democratic institutions on the European continent is by no means to be taken for granted. The political communities of the major Western European countries—France, Germany, and Italy—are fragmented into exclusive ideological movements. Large bodies of opinion appear to be alienated from the West, politically apathetic, or actively recruited to communism. The legal-historical-philosophical approach, which characterizes the scholarship dealing with these countries, is not by itself adequate to discover how serious these cleavages and alienations are, for by admission the basic problems of civic loyalty and political cohesion lie in large part outside of the formal governmental framework. Other methods and approaches are necessary if we are to have a proper understanding of the causes of the persistent evils of continental European government and politics—instability, stalemate, and the alienation of large elements of the population from the political community.

What is proposed here is not a sharp innovation, but rather the strengthening of tendencies on both sides of the Atlantic which are already moving in this direction, increasing the resources available for this type of research, concentrating such resources as are, or may become, available more effectively, and facilitating a more effective exchange of insights and skills. Thus both European and American students in this field are already moving into these unknown and partly known areas, and demonstrating the richness and usefulness of this approach. What we suggest here is a broad research strategy which may multiply those efforts and give them more coherence than they now have.

# I. MAJOR TYPES OF RESEARCH NEEDS

In appraising the state of knowledge on the continental European area we may distinguish a number of different types of research needs. First, there are legal institutions and processes, about which literally nothing is known. Second, for the most part our knowledge of formal governmental institutions is primarily historical and legal in character, and there have been relatively few studies of the actual functioning of these institutions. Third, there is the whole field of the non-legal political institutions and processes—parties, pressure groups, public opinion—where research is only in its beginnings. And finally, these areas of ignorance, differences in approach, and unevennesses of development make difficult if not impossible those higher levels of comparative analysis without which genuine understanding is impossible. The comments on these types of research needs which follow are intended to be illustrative rather than exhaustive.

### Areas of Ignorance

While much is known about public administration in the United States, England, and to some extent in France, only the barest legal essentials are known about the contemporary administrative and judicial systems of Germany and Italy. On the European continent, with noteworthy exceptions, the whole field of legislative organization and procedure is a *terra incognita*. At this level of the simple absence of any knowledge whatever, the situation varies sharply from country to country. Most is known about English governmental institutions, but surprisingly enough the state of knowledge in most of the Commonwealth countries is extremely inadequate. In Germany and France we are beginning to get studies of legislative procedure and organization, but in Italy not even the elementary facts of legislative organization are known. Of all the great powers on the continent, Italy presents the most massive gaps in knowledge, due, no doubt, to the 20-year Fascist interruption of research and training.

Thus, a scholar concerned with comparing even on a purely formal basis the organization of governmental powers for the continental European countries would find whole areas in which the basic data are lacking on the legal structure, and where the simple leg-work of drawing such information from working manuals and legal and administrative codes is still to be done.

### The Functional Approach

Once one begins to ask about the actual role and functioning of the executive, the bureaucracy, and the legislature, and their interrelations in the continental European countries, an even more serious research need becomes obvious—the absence of realistic studies of the operations of governmental institutions. This is only in part to be explained by the fact that France, Germany, and Italy are all operating under postwar constitutions, and that the continuity of their scholarship has been interrupted by the events of the last 30 years. The work now being done, with noteworthy exceptions again, is still dominated by the historical and legal-analytical approaches. The task here is not simply that of re-constructing legal structures from codes of one kind or another, but of looking at these constitutions in a different way, of employing observational techniques, and of making case studies of the legislative and administrative processes. While this approach is relatively new in the United States and England, there is nevertheless a rapidly accumulating monographic literature describing the internal organization and functioning of governmental institutions, their interrelations with one another, and the impact of the party system on them. On the European continent the scholars employing such techniques stand out by their uniqueness. Here the research need is one not only of the accumulation of data, but also of the sharing and development of skills.

### Non-legal Institutions and Processes

There are significant phases of the political process in the major countries of Western Europe which have been studied hardly at all by European or American scholars. In the United States studies of public opinion, political communication, pressure groups, and political parties are relatively well advanced both in methodological sophistication and substantive findings. European scholarship has a strong tradition only in the study of parties and electoral sociology, and even here there are serious limitations of resources and of trained personnel. Studies of pressure groups are only in their beginnings, and modern methods of public opinion research have not as yet found widespread acceptance in European university circles.

Thus the scholars who deal with European political systems are seriously handicapped in dealing with the causes of cabinet instability, the fragmentation of the legislature, and the general problem of political *immobilisme*. They lack the scientific tools which would be required to trace the extent of fragmentation of the political community, beyond the legislature and party system into the network of social groupings, and the attitudes of the general population. They tend to stop with the political parties and to extrapolate these tendencies into the political community itself. Some evidence suggests that such speculative conclusions are unsound. To take the French case as an illustration, the percentage of the vote received by the French Communist party has held up since the end of the war, while membership in the party and in the Communist-dominated CGT and the circulation of the Communist press have dropped drastically. This would suggest that a large part of the Communist vote is a negative, or protest vote, and that there is at least the possibility of breaking the hold of the Communist party upon a large part of its following. But our thinking about this problem is seriously hampered by lack of fundamental knowledge of the distribution of political attitudes and the characteristics of political organization in France. We suffer from the same lack of basic information on Italy. And while the problem is of a different kind, our ignorance of political attitudes and political organization in Germany also prevents us from making sound estimates as to future possibilities.

There has thus far been no effective effort to utilize the substantial accumulation of public opinion data on France, Germany, and Italy. With all of its limitations the analysis of this type of material in the United States has demonstrated how useful it can be in suggesting hypotheses as to the structure of public opinion and its ideological characteristics and potentialities. Some of this material has already suggested the special meaning of Communist party affiliation to the French and Italian working class and peasantry. Needless to say, if this whole body of data is analyzed together and compared with American and British patterns, it may yield a substantial number of new insights into the political processes in both the Anglo-American and continental European areas. If these data are analyzed in conjunction with studies of pressure groups and political parties, they may tell us something of the relationship between organized and articulate opinion, and latent feelings and moods in the population. It is from studies of these relationships between the moods and attitudes of groups in the population and the organized expression of group opinion and policy that speculation about the future of politics in these countries may become more informed and reliable, and a sounder appraisal be made of various efforts to effect these developments.

In this field of the newer "research technology" adapted to the study of political attitudes and processes American scholarship has the most to offer, just as it has most to learn from the European tradition of historical scholarship, philosophical depth, and theoretical refinement.

## II. RESEARCH APPROACHES

These types of research needs may be met only by the application of a variety of methods, often used in combination, by a greater concentration of resources than is now available, and by a closer cooperation between European and American scholars. Obviously these needs cannot be met by a single research design. Some of the problems seem to call for fairly large-scale research efforts; others seem to lend themselves more appropriately to the efforts of individual scholars. There may be some value, however, in enumerating the main types of methods which might have their place in a broad program of research intended to fill these needs.

### Historical Studies

What has been said should not by any means be construed as suggesting that historical research has no place in a research program on the Western European area. On the contrary, any research program which failed to place contemporary political developments in continuity with the past would lose one of the most essential dimensions of understanding. It would be hard to find a more important work in the literature of political parties than Ostrogorski's historical-sociological classic *Democracy and the Organization of Political Parties*. Unfortunately, there is nothing comparable to it in the historical dimension for the continental European countries. Certainly the history of European parties and political institutions is one of the most essential areas of research. But here the methodology and tradition are already strong, and the problem is mainly one of resources.

### Institutional Studies

The institutional approach is familiar to students of government and politics both here and abroad. What is suggested is a greater concentration of resources for the making of such studies, and the improvement of standards. The role of a particular institution or class of institutions such as the executive, the legislature, the bureaucracy, the courts, the political parties, and pressure groups, can be understood only if the institution is placed in the context of the total political system of which it is a part. Hence, to understand the role of the political parties in a given country it is not enough to know their history, ideology, and internal organization. It is also essential to see them in their connection with the electoral process, the pressure groups, their constituencies, and their access to the agencies of governmental authority.

For the major countries of the European continent, while what is available is generally of high quality, there is only the beginning of a monographic literature on governmental and political institutions. The student of European government and politics is greatly handicapped by the absence of intensive studies of cabinet systems, bureaucracies, legislatures, executive-legislative relations, patterns of administrative regulation and adjudication, to say nothing of monographic studies of parties and pressure groups. Indeed, the research needs are so great that only an intensified process of scholarly training, and a large increase in the resources available for research, can begin to fill in these glaring gaps in the literature.

### Process Studies of Public Policy Decisions

It has been found in American studies that one of the most effective ways of describing the functions or operational roles of political institutions is through the case study approach. What is meant by a process study of this type is an effort to reconstruct

—through analyzing the documentation and the interviewing of participants—what actually happened in the course of consideration of a legislative enactment, what roles were played by the executive, the bureaucracy, the political parties, pressure groups, the media of communication, and public attitudes and behaviors, in other words, how all of these relevant factors interplayed to produce the particular legislative result. If through time we can accumulate a representative collection of such reconstructions of the political process in a given country, we can begin to develop a set of propositions about the general characteristics of the process, and the particular properties or roles of the institutions and agencies which are involved in it. Certainly our understanding of American politics has been greatly enhanced by such process case studies as those of Schattschneider, Bailey, Latham, Riggs, and Harold Stein. Case studies of this kind may be one of the most useful ways of developing our present knowledge of political institutions and processes on the European continent from its present formal limitations to a more faithful representation of reality.

## Attitude Studies

Students of European politics with noteworthy exceptions have been more reluctant than those concerned with American politics to utilize the methods and findings of public opinion research. Recent studies of elections and of attitudes towards various aspects of public policy in the United States in which such methods have been used have demonstrated convincingly that public opinion research can give us a dimension of the political process which is otherwise unobtainable. Thus the impressive studies of electoral sociology in France leave some of the questions unanswered as to the meaning of the political phenomena which they describe. Survey methods are among the most appropriate devices to gain insight into the condition of the political community. To be sure, the method is expensive. But it does not appear to be cost which stands in the way of the use of this material; there is already available a huge accumulation of public opinion data in England, the Commonwealth countries, Scandinavia, the Low Countries, France, Germany, and Italy which political scientists here and abroad have hardly touched. It would be an unsound procedure to undertake new surveys of political attitudes in these countries until the accumulation of this material is carefully processed and analyzed. The main barriers to its use would appear to be those of skill and tradition. To overcome these barriers two techniques may be useful. First, studies demonstrating the insights and hypotheses which can be derived from these materials may have the effect of encouraging imitation. Secondly, collaborative studies undertaken by European and American

scholars may facilitate the process of training in this particular method of studying political phenomena.

## Community Studies

If studies of political attitudes through the use of public opinion surveys represent an assimilation of social psychological methods and insights into political science, community studies represent an effort to employ social-psychological, anthropological, and sociological methods in combination to enrich our knowledge of the political process. Studies of community political organization and of attitudes are still relatively new in the United States, where the technique and approach developed. Where they have been done in Europe it has been the result of American initiative. What recommends their use, despite the fact that the approach is still largely experimental, is that they make possible "microscopic" investigations of the actual impact of political parties and other types of organizations, and of the meaning of party affiliation and of electoral behavior, at the grass roots level. A community study combines analysis of political institutions at the local level with direct observation of the functioning of the political process and with studies of the distribution of attitudes within different strata of the community. In other words, the scale is sufficiently small to make possible intensive study of the place of politics in the life of the community and of the significant groups which make it up. Obviously, an intensive method of this kind is costly and has to be used selectively. Its use is clearly suggested in problem areas such as Southern Italy, or the "Communist zones" in France and Italy, or in areas in Germany where nationalism or neo-Nazism are strongly entrenched. Studies of such communities will yield the best results if control communities are investigated at the same time, in order to isolate the significant variables.

This brief discussion of research needs in the European area and of the research methods appropriate to meeting them is obviously not a "research project," but rather a statement of a research strategy, and a series of suggestions as to possible tactics or methodological approaches. Some of the approaches suggested are novel and still experimental in the United States, but by and large the approaches proposed are familiar to both European and American scholars specializing in the European area.

Two main lines of action flow from these proposals. First, the above statement of research needs represents the considered views of only a small group of scholars concerned with the field. It will be essential to explore the views of other members of the profession both here and abroad in order to check on the validity of these views and the merits of the proposals. Here, seminars and conferences in which both European and American scholars would participate seem to be indicated. This procedure would have the merit of stimulating research along these lines, as well as enlisting the best minds in the field in a process of self-improvement and development. A second line of action would be the stimulation of research efforts on an individual scale, and of larger-scale comparative research designs where the problems lend themselves to this type of research effort. The Committee on Research in Comparative Politics of the Social Science Research Council hopes that both lines of action may be stimulated by this statement.

# NEW HORIZONS FOR COMPARATIVE POLITICS

Dankwart A. Rustow

The rapid drive of formerly colonial and dependent countries toward independent nationhood has gone hand in hand, over the last decade, with a thorough reorientation in the discipline of comparative politics. In Southeast Asia, on the Indian subcontinent, in the Near East—everywhere, the Western powers have surrendered their former positions of imperial domination. Even in Africa, once the dark continent of colonialism, fully half the population now has emerged to self-government. In all, a score of new nations has joined the roll of sovereign states, and their global importance is attested daily by far-flung programs of economic assistance, by the gradual shift of the cold-war front from Europe to Asia and Africa, and by the recent redistribution of voting power in the United Nations. Little wonder that specialists in comparative government, once snugly secure in their study of the countries of Europe and the Commonwealth, cross the oceans in increasing numbers to study public administration in Egypt, local government in Uganda, economic planning in India, communism in Malaya, or party developments in the Philippines. Not long ago Western man ruled the world: today he studies it.

This sudden shift of interest implies, no doubt, some dangers. The skeptic may warn that the breathless pursuit of the "background of tomorrow's headlines" could induce political scientists to discard the ballast of theoretical notions acquired in their more leisurely and methodical past, or that continued preoccupation with problems of capital formation and of cultural change will tend to turn them into amateur economists and amateur anthropologists. I shall argue in the following, nonetheless, that the current reorientation in comparative politics is a logical stage of growth and development and that it holds out the prospect of genuine theoretical advances.

Some sixty or seventy years ago the systematic study of comparative government began with a historical and analytical examination of the constitutional and legal institutions of the democracies of Western Europe and North America. This narrow focus hid from view a large number of economic, cultural, and historical variables, and thereby permitted the formulation and refinement of a body of closely related theoretical insights. Subsequently, under the influence of men like Bryce, Ostrogorski, Michels, and Lowell, political scientists became alive to the crucial role played by parties and other political groupings in operating the constitutional structure. This shift was accentuated by the study of European dictatorships since the 1920's, which demonstrated, among other things, the totally different practical content that could be given to similar formal institutions. At the same time a closer examination of public opinion and propaganda revealed the importance of social and psychological factors. A widening of empirical horizons thus went hand in hand with a revision and extension of theory. With some significant modifications, the sociologically oriented group theory of politics has been successfully applied to the interaction of such forces as the army, the party, the managerial elite, and the secret police in a totalitarian system.[1] Still, theoretical neatness and precision have been preserved at the price of limited applicability. Embarking upon the investigation of a universe made up of some one

Reprinted from *World Politics*, Vol. IX, No. 4 (July, 1957), pp. 530–549, by permission of the author and publisher.

hundred contemporary political systems, political scientists began by examining first half a dozen, and then as many as fifteen or twenty. By and large, their attention remained centered upon a single major culture—the industrial civilization of modern Europe with its American and East European offshoots.

The new interest in the politics of Asia, of the Near East, and of Africa for the first time suggests the possibility of a global study of comparative politics, based on the entire body of available evidence. To approximate this goal, systematic inquiry must be extended not only to the colonial or newly independent countries but also to the countries of Latin America and to the long-neglected smaller nations of Europe. But surely a science that is resolutely leaping from its accustomed preserve of Britain-France-Germany-and-Russia to such exotic regions as Nigeria, Indonesia, and Afghanistan will be able to reconnoiter Bulgaria, Iceland, and Colombia along the way. Once again the extension of the empirical base must be accompanied by systematic elaboration of the theoretical superstructure. The besetting infirmity of political science has been its preoccupation with current events and with problems of obvious pragmatic relevance. For the first time, perhaps, daily events themselves are providing the needed corrective. Where once they tended to reinforce our parochialism, they now impel us to greater universality. In proportion as the theoretical difficulties can be resolved, comparative politics will become truly world-wide.

## II

No one who has attempted to study political processes in some of the newer locales of political science, or who has tried to distill his findings in the classroom, will lightly shrug off the obstacles ahead. Somewhat schematically, these may be divided into difficulties of data-gathering and difficulties of interpreting the data obtained.

The obvious and urgent need for additional linguistic preparation is perhaps on balance the least formidable among the difficulties of data-gathering—although in the case of languages such as Chinese or Arabic it can be an impressive difficulty indeed. More serious is the fact that many important areas are physically barred to the scholarly investigator. Until the recent relaxation of Soviet policies, travel in Russia and its satellite empire was difficult or impossible; movement in such guerrilla-torn areas as Algeria and Malaya is severely circumscribed; and the Muslim holy cities of Mecca and Medina are generally inaccessible to the unbeliever. While Soviet research can place

reliance on newspapers and other published sources, the scarcity or absence of publications rules out this alternative for many other areas.

The low level of communications within most Asian, African, and Latin American societies hampers research at every turn. Many of the ordinary reference tools for political research are non-existent, inadequate, or unreliable. Census returns are likely to be scanty, full of statistical and arithmetic errors, and outdated; there is a shortage of biographical directories; court decisions may be unpublished or even unrecorded; newspapers lack indices and often substitute editorial opinion for factual report. A widely prevailing notion which equates politics with conspiracy may obscure the investigation of even those political activities that move within the safe bounds of legality. But the difficulty is not so much that a foreign society intentionally withholds information from the investigator. Frequently, the immediate participants in the political process themselves turn out to be quite uninformed about the background factors that provide the setting for their own activity.

The most serious obstacles tend to be psychological. The very presence of the observer in a jungle outpost in Burma, in a Levantine bazaar, or in the highlands of Ethopia is a by-product of modern industrial technology which, spreading from Western Europe, has made the remote parts of the globe geographically accessible and politically interdependent. For most of the peoples exposed to it, the impact of this modern technological civilization has been a painful process, associated with colonial servitude, with the dislocation of time-hallowed habit and custom, and with economic misery no longer accepted as inevitable. Resolutely as he may cling to his chosen role of impartial observer, the student willy-nilly is to some extent an agent and participant in this cultural clash between tradition and modernity. The very notion of scholarly detachment may seem not only novel but patently insincere to his respondents.[2]

Nor does the foreign society meet the student with a single, solid front; hence no dramatic act of penetration will remove the cultural difficulty. Many non-Western societies are fragmented and culturally discontinuous. Even where geographic communication and economic intercourse are highly developed, religious, ethnic, or caste barriers may block intellectual and emotional contact among Turk, Kurd, and Arab, among Hindu, Muslim, and Sikh, among peon, landlord, and merchant, among White, Indian, and Mestizo. The group most readily accessible to the observer—the Westernized intellectuals—may turn out to be the least reliable informants about the remainder of the society. Almost inevitably, the Western education of the upper strata reinforces class divisions by endowing them with a cultural dimension.[3] The

Asian intellectual hence may feel more at home in Oxford, Paris, or New Haven than in the villages or cities of his own country. He may be consumed by a sense of shame at what he considers the "backwardness" of his own society and thus be tempted to adopt elaborate rationalizations whose value as evidence of culture conflict may be great, but whose heuristic utility is likely to be nil.

The difficulties of conceptualization are even more imposing. A political scientist writing a book some twenty years ago on the government and politics of a European country probably was well aware of the political significance of the country's cultural heritage, of its level of economic development, and of its social structure. Yet he generally could condense his treatment of these matters into a single background chapter, at times appropriately entitled "Land and People." Author, reader, and subject matter all were part of the same civilization, and the range of cultural or economic variation within that civilization was not excessive. The author could take it for granted, moreover, that he was dealing with an established political system, embracing a given population, and occupying a given geographic territory. Although he might trace the history of English liberties to Magna Carta, he did not have to start his broader treatment of the British political system with King Alfred, William the Conqueror, or Henry VIII. Finally, whether he was analyzing the role of parties, social classes, and pressure groups in a democracy, or the component structures of a totalitarian system, he was dealing with a set of well-defined and highly articulate organizations.

The contemporary political scientist studying the politics of non-Western countries ventures on an enterprise that, for a variety of reasons, is of vastly greater complexity.

First, he will find it impossible to treat culture either as a fixed datum or as a mere background factor. Again and again he must try to capture in his mind a picture of a highly dynamic and fleeting cultural scene. And although the pace of change in most parts of the world has greatly quickened of late, the quest for an imaginary "fixed point" when traditional culture last appeared in its "pure" form is likely to lead the student on a wild goose chase from Atatürk to the Tanzimat period to Sulaiman the Magnificent and to the Byzantine Empire; or from Gandhi to the 1857 mutiny to Warren Hastings to the Moghuls and back to the Upanishads. A cursory glance at the present-day Asian and African scene, moreover, will convince the observer that culture is not only the setting but also the central theme of politics. In Turkey, in China, in India, in Ghana, or in Saudi Arabia—wherever he turns, he will find that the rate, the extent, and the direction of cultural change are at once the overriding issues and the

prime determinants in the political process. The impact of industrial technology calls into the arena new political forces, such as a trained officer corps, a professional middle class, or an urban proletariat; and in turn political decisions such as the opening of Japan, or secularization of politics and purification of language in Turkey, or the drawing of linguistic state boundaries in India are having profound effects on the content of culture.

Second, the political scientist who ventures beyond the study of the major European powers frequently encounters political systems that lack clear delimitation and are very far from established. In a global context, societies such as China, Japan, or Ethopia which have a historically rooted sense of identity within a set of more or less natural boundaries would seem to be the exception rather than the rule. The unity or division of the Arab countries; the establishment on the Indian sub-continent of one, two, or more independent nations; the adoption in Indonesia and Nigeria of unitary or federal government; separation versus federation in the West Indies and in Central Africa—these have been issues of prime importance influenced by the prevailing political constellation and in turn bound to become determinants of future political patterns. Even the composition of the population in newly independent states has been profoundly affected by such policies as the population exchange between India and Pakistan, or the "Ingathering of the Exiles" in Israel and the corresponding displacement of Arab Palestinians. That the level of economic development also is subject to variation and that it relates to the political process as both cause and effect hardly require special emphasis in this age of international economic assistance.

Third, the student of non-Western politics quite commonly must deal with political issues that are tangled, confused, and but dimly perceived by the protagonists; with political interests that are latent and unorganized; with social and political institutions which, like the state itself, are in a process of gestation. The dairy farmer in Wisconsin and the factory worker in Milwaukee both know that their prosperity and welfare depend largely upon government action. Each belongs to an association that represents his interests both in Madison and in Washington. Politics for them is by and large a rational process and they participate in it with a fair degree of rationality. In voting for political candidates they are likely to judge in terms of the candidates' expressed, organized views. By contrast, no Near Eastern *fellah* and very few Near Eastern townspeople have any political or economic organizations to represent them. Nor is it clear what they expect of their government or what the government would and could do for them. While the peasant is often politically inert, his city cousin is likely to be involved in politics at the first sign of riot or government crisis. In many of the more secluded non-Western countries, it would be a rash over-extension of the term to speak of a "public opinion." Elsewhere, where strategic segments of the population are drawn into the political vortex, their action is likely to be spasmodic, vehement, and self-contradictory.

It has become rather commonplace to assert that the countries which have won their independence in the last decade are "caught between the millstones of two revolutions"[4]—a political revolution for national independence and a socio-economic revolution. This is an undue simplification. In many places there is indeed abundant revolutionary ferment; but no such simple dichotomy can fully account for it. Cultural change, the delimitation of the nation's boundaries and the orientation of its foreign ambitions, centralization versus local autonomy, the quest for a national language, economic development and redistribution, industrialization, patronage and personal power, religion and secularism—all these explosive issues are thrown at once into the cauldron. And the politician's universal compulsion to be all things to all men leaves him to find what foothold he can amid the erratically shifting alignments.

Fourth, the profound differences among non-Western countries and between them and the West pose sharply the question of comparability. Textbooks on European governments have at times been criticized for being little more than collections of country monographs that leave the task of integration and comparison to the baffled reader—and the solid cloth binding. If this is a problem within the traditional Europe-and-Commonwealth orbit, what prospects are there of achieving valid comparisons of the political activities of the auto worker in Detroit, the Bedouin shaykh, and the Calcutta jute mill operator? And where, amid the uncertain boundaries within ex-colonial empires, is the scholar to find the appropriate units of comparison? Are they to be the Fertile Crescent or Syria, Jordan, and Iraq? India and Pakistan or Sind, Bengal, and Madhya Pradesh? Indonesia or Sumatra, Java, and Celebes?

## III

The difficulties are real, yet by no means insuperable. Take first the difficulties of data-gathering and conceptualization. It is well to bear in mind that the discontinuities of cultural context, the lack of communications, and the rapid change of behavior patterns that complicate the task of observation are also among the most crucial substantive features of the political process to be analyzed. A clear grasp and appreciation of the obstacles to data-gathering will therefore go a long way toward solving the problem of conceptualization. As we have already remarked, the interaction of modern Western and traditional cultures, of which the observer's own journey is only a single and belated example, is one of the most pervasive influences on the politics of non-Western countries.

The specialist in non-Western politics, it is true, will at times be perplexed by the many profound differences in the political patterns which he encounters. Even within one and the same world region he discovers pronounced contrasts between, say, the commercial cosmopolitanism of Lebanon and the tribal isolation of Yemen, or between the influence of Buddhism in Burma and Thailand and of Islam in Pakistan and Indonesia. But a broader view reveals that the impact of the West and of modern industrial civilization has resulted in similarities both in the cultural and socio-economic setting and in the political process itself. As a first approximation some of these uniformities and trends may be summarized under the following headings:

### 1. *Economic Development*

The economic problems of what our current jargon terms "underdeveloped countries" have been widely publicized in recent years and hence need not long detain us here. The economies of Asia and Africa, like many of those in Latin America and South and East Europe, are generally characterized by extremely low standards of living and education. Primary production—whether in agriculture or mining—predominates over industry and the service trades. Birth rates are high, communications poor, and rates of capital formation meager.

The Industrial Revolution of Europe and North America was largely a process of non-directed discovery and exploration. The over-all goal of human control over the natural environment was clearly perceived, yet the specific tools of control were fashioned *ad hoc* and *de novo*. In the process of emulative industrialization in Asia and Africa, by contrast, specific goals and techniques are demonstrated with painful vividness by the achievements of the older industrial economies. A dire sense of urgency arises, and the processes of capital formation that were gradual and fortuitous in Europe centuries ago must now be planned, coaxed, and sped along. The major choices seem to be induced saving or foreign assistance—one resulting in a short-run reduction of consumption, the other a threat to national pride. Expectations soar far ahead of performance. The temptation to raise consumption levels at once becomes well-nigh irresistible, and thus endangers the very expansion of the capital base which would ultimately support such raised levels.

## 2. *Cultural Ambivalence*

In the cultural field the impact of the West gives rise to tensions, discontinuities, and amalgams of varying degrees of stability. Because of Western superiority in technology, in economic resources, and in military power, Westernization is not experienced as a self-directed and voluntary process. In colonial areas, it becomes a policy imposed by defeat. In countries defending their independence, it is an imperative of survival. The typical intellectual attitude toward the West thus has been one of ambivalence—of admiration and hate, of eager emulation and indignant rejection.[5]

This ambivalence is epitomized in the peculiar character of non-Western nationalism. National consciousness as a rule has been a direct or indirect product of the Western impact, but it finds its most vigorous expression in the militant struggle for political independence from the West. As Professor Emerson has said, ". . . it is so clearly and strikingly the impact of the West which has brought to fighting consciousness societies which in their own roots derive wholly from non-Western sources."[6] Yet, once victorious in their struggle, nationalist leaders often become a potent force in their societies for continued and intensive Westernization. The Turkish nationalists marched to the War of Independence (1919-1922) to the strains of Mehmed Akif's hymn "To Our Heroic Army," which exhorts the Muslim faithful to rise in arms against the evil designs of "that monster called Civilization which has but one tooth left in its jaw."[7] During the following decades, however, Turkey outdid most other non-Western countries in adopting Western forms of dress, law, alphabet, education, and art. The Jordanian nationalist officers who, late in 1955, engineered the ouster of General John Bagot Glubb as commander of the Arab legion promptly proceeded to replace its Bedouin headgear with a Western-style military cap. In India and Pakistan, English has remained the only *de facto* linguistic link among the political leaders of scores of millions whose native tongues are Hindi, Urdu, Bengali, Gujerati, Tamil, and innumerable others. Ten years after independence, India's government began a concerted drive to unify and translate into the metric and decimal systems a bewildering array of local weights, measures, and coins that had survived with little change under centuries of European rule.

The same ambivalence results in a search for shortcuts to Westernization and hence in a quick acceptance and equally sudden rejection of ephemeral Western ideological currents.[8] The strongest appeal of communism in the ex-colonial and other non-Western countries is precisely that it offers such an apparent shortcut.[9] At the same time, romantic glorification of the distant non-Western past often serves as an effective weapon against the traditionalist influence of the more immediate past and hence as an important device for Westernization.

## 3. *Transformation of the Social Structure*

The pre-Western social structure was generally characterized by a low degree of what Karl Deutsch has called "social mobilization."[10] The strongest feelings of solidarity attached to units, such as the the extended family, the tribe, the village, the caste, the guild, which were much smaller than the modern nation, and often these units were the only seats of effective social power. In some cases, as in precolonial Africa, they were almost fully independent and self-sufficient. Elsewhere—as in China, Japan, and Ottoman Turkey—they were embedded in loosely knit imperial structures. Economic symbiosis among distinct ethnic, religious, or social groups resulted in what has been termed a plural society, or an ethnic division of labor.[11] The acceptance of Western cultural patterns by indigenous elites was likely to accentuate existing cleavages between the ruling class and its subjects, between town and country. Increasingly, however, new channels of mobility opened up as ascription gave way to achievement. With the reception of Western patterns, the smaller units—the tribes, villages, and castes—were enveloped in an emerging larger, national context; at the same time, the Western cultural and military impact put considerable strain on the imperial superstructures—occasionally, as in Mughal India and Ottoman Turkey, leading to their complete disintegration.[12]

## 4. *Disparities Between Constitutional Form and Political Content*

The political similarities among non-Western countries are equally striking.[13] All colonial countries upon gaining independence, and nearly all non-colonial countries, have embraced the outward forms of Western representative institutions. Constitutions are solemnly adopted by national constituent assemblies. Representatives are elected from geographic constituencies. Laws are enacted by parliaments and administered by presidents or prime ministers assisted by their cabinets. Indeed, there is often a boundless trust, unmatched since the days of John Austin, in the omnipotence of legislation. Separation of powers or cabinet responsibility, parliamentary committees, government corporations, independent judiciaries, guarantees of civil rights, federal or unitary administrations—these and other familiar Western themes recur.

But almost as widespread as the tendency to adopt Western representative institutions are the difficulties which non-Western countries confront in operating them. The absence of a strong and established sense of national unity, the prevailing weakness of parties and other voluntary associations, the widespread lack of administrative experience, and the vicissitudes of a turbulent international situation all contribute to these difficulties.

### 5. Insecure Nationalism

For all the militant clamor of nationalist sentiment, nationalism in Asia and Africa is generally weak and inexperienced and rests on a precarious foundation of national unity. In some non-colonial countries such as Iran, Afghanistan, Saudi Arabia, and Ethiopia, the administrative centers never established intimate enough contact with the outlying districts to allow for the attachment of strong loyalties. Elsewhere colonial boundaries were forcibly imposed on a diffuse pattern of traditional organization—joining disparate ethnic elements, as in Nigeria and Libya, or dividing areas such as the Arabic "Fertile Crescent" where a sense of unity was beginning to emerge. In addition, colonialism, by a divide-and-rule policy, often accentuated existing cleavages. Even where colonial empires coincided with geographically well-defined regions, as in India and Indonesia, the removal of foreign rule gave added scope to a variety of divisive tendencies. In plural societies of mixed ethnic settlement such as India and the Near East, the creation of territorially defined national polities led to the wholesale dislocation of minorities, to boundary disputes and irredentism. Local autonomy, far from securing a harmonious balance among the diverse regions, often has posed a threat to national unity and survival—witness the Iranian experience in Azerbaijan and the short-lived Indonesian federal experiment. In the Indian member states and in Ceylon, the desire for a single language in politics, administration, and education has exacerbated feelings among the various linguistic communities.

### 6. Diffuseness of Political Movements

The institutional channels for the expression of political interests and opinions are most imperfectly developed throughout the non-West. In some countries like Iran, Thailand, and many of the Arab states, durable political parties have been totally lacking. Elsewhere, as in India, Burma, Egypt, Turkey, and Ghana, a single party has dominated the scene, the opposition being split, suppressed, or otherwise ineffective. In very few countries has there been that orderly alternation between government and opposition which the traditional Anglo-American theory of representative government presupposes. In the colonial countries, the struggle for independence demanded the concentration of all political forces in a single movement, thus inhibiting any natural differentiation of opinion. Almost everywhere a strong tradition of patrimonial authority on the local or national level has discouraged

free party competition. As a result, many of the existing parties are held together less by a common program or well-defined interests than by the personality of a leader or a common desire for the spoils of office. Other voluntary associations, such as labor unions and business or professional organizations, are non-existent or immature—and hence less than effective in providing political expression for their constituents. The weakness of the party and associational structure has drawn into the political arena a number of extrapolitical organizations. Among these, the army officers and the university students often have the advantage of being among the earnest mediators of Westernizing, modernizing influences and also are among the earliest beneficiaries of social mobility and merit advancement. The armies have the added advantage of expertise in violence in a situation where non-violent processes of decision-making by deliberation and compromise are not customarily employed or are ineffective. Extremist groups such as the Muslim Brethren in Egypt or the Fidaiyan-i-Islam in Iran have combined a traditionalist ideology with highly up-to-date methods of organization and terrorism. And the ubiquitous Communists have done their best to undermine governmental stability in alliance either with extreme nationalists or with bona fide social reformers.

### 7. Administrative Inexperience

The shortage of trained administrative personnel is almost universal—with the partial exception of countries like Japan, China, and Turkey which are the fortunate heirs of ancient indigenous bureaucracies. The situation is immensely aggravated by the enormous expansion of governmental functions, which has perhaps been the single most notable consequence of the impact of modernity on non-Western countries. In bygone days, a sultan or raja might exercise despotic power within his palace and perhaps in his capital. Yet apart from occasional military expeditions, his ability to affect the daily lives of his subjects was severely circumscribed by the inadequacy of transport and by the universal rule of traditional law and custom. Governmental functions consisted largely in the maintenance of a royal court and of a small professional soldiery and in the periodical appointment of governors for the outlying provinces. In the middle of the twentieth century, by contrast, any self-respecting government endeavors to levy taxes on the most diverse economic activities, to provide education and to secure employment, to build up industry and communications, to control domestic prices, to balance foreign payments—in short, to ensure the spiritual and material well-being of millions of subjects. As one ponders this sudden and staggering expansion of the scope of government in non-Western societies, one is inclined to marvel less at the ever-present possibility of inefficiency and corruption than at the skill and dedication which non-Western administrators generally bring to their tasks.

### 8. *Hazards of the International Scene*

The international situation confronting the independent countries of Asia and Africa is too well known to require detailed comment. All of them are left in an international power vacuum. The ex-colonial countries as a rule owe their independence less to their own strength than to the defeat or exhaustion of the colonial powers in two cataclysmic world wars. Similarly, many of the non-colonial countries, such as Iran, Afghanistan, and Thailand, survived precariously amid opposing pressures from rival imperial powers. Nearly all the non-Western states depend on foreign economic and technical assistance to satisfy the urgent aspirations of their newly awakened masses. Most of them since the fall of China find themselves within a radius of 1,000 miles or less from the frontiers of the Soviet bloc, and none of them could expect to resist invasion by itself. But the conclusion and maintenance of effective alliances are made difficult by the same factors that tend to invite aggression in the first place. While quarrels in Palestine, Pushtunistan, Kashmir, and elsewhere pose serious obstacles to regional cooperation, colonial memories cloud relations with the Western powers. Soviet pressure, moreover, presents not only a military but also a political, economic, and psychological threat.

### 9. *Need for Leadership*

The task confronting the leaders of non-Western states today is immense and beyond anything familiar to the West in normal times. They must preside over the founding of new commonwealths, groping for a sense of unity and common purpose in the absence of unitary traditions or established patterns of popular participation. In a period of rapid cultural change, they must (in Professor von Grunebaum's expressive phrase) play "to two galleries at the same time,"[14] legitimizing their actions in the eyes of both the traditionalist and the modernist segments of the population. They must try to satisfy the impatient clamor for economic advancement with the help of administrators lacking in training and experience. They must face the hazards of an ominous international situation over which they have at times little, if any, control.

The most effective form of leadership in such situations appears to be that provided by a small but growing elite dedicated to the service of a wider community and to the task of construction and modernization—an elite that serves its apprenticeship under a traditional order but demonstrates its mastery in building a new one. Such were the Westernized Ottoman officers at the close of the Tanzi-

mat period who formed the Young Turk movement and later provided the key supporters in Atatürk's nationalist transformation. Such were the Japanese military and civilian oligarchy of the Meiji period. And such has been the Indian Congress Party.

At moments of acute crisis the survival of a newly founded political community may depend in addition on the presence of a single charismatic figure—such as Atatürk, Gandhi, Nehru, or Nkrumah. The charismatic leader provides a ready point of attachment for emotional loyalties uprooted by the collapse of tradition; yet by focusing national energies on the constructive tasks ahead, he can transfer these loyalties to the emerging community of the future.[15]

## IV

Systematic empirical investigation will no doubt invalidate or modify many of the generalizations just outlined. Insofar as they have any plausibility, they would seem to justify the hope that the problem of comparison can indeed be resolved. It will be well to remember that comparison presupposes the existence of both differences and similarities—that differences among empirical phenomena are not of themselves an impediment to comparison. Comparability is never a quality inherent in the data; rather, it is bestowed upon them by the observer's mind. As soon as two sets of activities—however remote from one another in time, space, and appearance—can be identified as political, they are, to that extent, comparable.

It would be idle to expect valid comparisons to emerge from a Procrustean treatment that would force Western and non-Western materials alike into the mold of categories, such as the executive, the legislature, the party system, and the rights of citizenship, derived from Western experience alone. Comparison of non-Western countries may take the initial form of a growing and cumulative body of monographs on individual countries and their political problems.[16] Or it may take the form of comparison of a specific institution or problem in several non-Western countries—e.g., studies on the role of the army, of religion, of political leadership, of nationalism, of economic development, or of communism within the political process. Both types of study have important contributions to make, and each to a large extent reinforces the other. For example, the role of military leaders in transforming the Ottoman Empire into a Turkish Republic would have to be analyzed against the background of the social and political structure and the intellectual, religious, and international situation of Turkey since the eighteenth century. But it could be greatly illuminated by systematic comparison with the situation faced by nationalist leaders and other civilian and military reformers in, say, India, Japan, or the Arab countries. There has been a cautious and praiseworthy tendency in the literature on non-Western politics to proceed from the specific to the general. Studies of individual countries thus have generally been followed by comparative studies embracing an entire region.[17] But as the example just given indicates, interregional comparisons, though doubtlessly more difficult to execute, will prove even more rewarding.

Although the non-Western specialist at present, then, will normally center his research interest on a single country or world region, he must not allow himself to become intellectually isolated from other area specialists. Much of the current interest in the politics of non-Western countries stems from a realization that our theorizing in comparative politics has proceeded from too narrow an empirical base.[18] Nothing would be gained by supplementing a parochial study of the politics of continental Europe, of the United States, and of the English-speaking Commonwealth with equally parochial studies of the Near East, of Southeast Asia, or of Tropical Africa.

It would be equally wrong to posit a pervasive dichotomy between Western politics, on the one hand, and non-Western politics, on the other. The contemporary politics of Asia and Africa offers an enormous range of diversity—from the rather closely knit social structure of industrial Japan to the loose tribalism of Afghanistan; from the intense political consciousness of Turkey to the systematic depreciation of human power urges in India; from the monolithic governmental structure of Yemen to the mosaic of Indonesia. Furthermore, many of the more baffling and complex problems of contemporary non-Western politics have their parallels and analogies in the political experience of Europe and America. The impact of Western European industrial technology and military organization had comparable (if far from identical) results in the Russia of Peter the Great and of Lenin, in the Germany of Bismarck, in the Japan of Meiji, in the Turkey of Mahmud II and of Kemal Atatürk, and in the Egypt of Muhammad Ali and Abdul Nasser. The perplexing problem of finding the appropriate unit of political comparison recurs in Southeastern Europe. (Should the entire area, by virtue of its common history of Ottoman-Habsburg and Bolshevik domination, be considered a single unit, or does the rather short-lived separation of Bulgaria, Rumania, Hungary, and Czechoslovakia justify distinct treatment?) The East European successor states to the Ottoman, Habsburg, and Romanov Empires quite generally faced the shortage of administrative talent, the precariousness of nascent nationality in areas of mixed ethnic settlement, the recurrent conflicts between democratic theory and dictatorial practice, and other problems which the ex-colonial successor states are facing in our own day.

The Latin American countries in particular would seem to constitute a perfect connecting link between contemporary Western and non-Western political experience. Their liberation from colonialism preceded that of the Asian and African states by a century and a half. While some of them have developed along very nearly European lines, others appear to offer a modified version of the present non-Western experience. Such features as ethnic and cultural cleavages, major realignments of boundaries, chronic governmental instability, the prominence of personal leadership and of military coups, and the need for economic development—all these are equally characteristic of many Latin as well as many Asian and African countries.[19]

The challenge facing comparative politics is to elaborate a conceptual apparatus in keeping with the vastly extended global scale of its empirical investigations. A systematic re-examination of the Western model would seem to be inevitable. Factors once treated as constants, such as area, population, the level of the economy, and the established existence of a state, are now becoming variables within the over-all political process. Residual categories such as cultural background must be more fully absorbed into the analytical model. Above all, the political scientist is compelled to construct a dynamic rather than a static model of politics—one that will account not only for the interaction of political forces at a given moment, but also for their evolution over longer periods of time.[20] There is every indication that these theoretical revisions, even though prompted primarily by the study of non-Western areas, will be of equal value in the interpretation of many aspects of Western politics.

In this task of rebuilding the political model there is much that political scientists can learn from other social science disciplines. In attuning himself to the particularities of a given foreign culture, the student of non-Western politics will profit from the researches of the comparative linguist, the social anthropologist, and the literary and religious historian. Economists have grappled for some time with the problem of dynamic theory which political science now encounters. The elaboration of sociological theory by Talcott Parsons, Marion Levy, and others provides a large number of concepts that have proved suggestive for political inquiry. There is much room also for interchange with historians, once students of comparative politics resolutely abandon the rather implausible notion—implicit in much of their past work—that man became a political animal around A.D. 1900. Historians, moreover, have long lived with the broader perspectives of interaction among culture, society, economy, and politics which political scientists tend to rediscover in their current endeavors.

There is considerable evidence that this need for interdisciplinary cooperation is well appreciated in the other social sciences. Sociologists and anthropologists, in turning to the study of major non-Western societies, have gathered data and formulated hypotheses that are immediately relevant to an interpretation of non-Western politics.[21] Economists increasingly tend to accord an important place to political factors in their explanation of the process of economic growth.[22] And a group of prominent historians recently concluded their conference with a plea that historians continue "to improve communications with fellow social scientists."[23]

There is equally much that political scientists will be able to learn from one another. The need for cooperation and interchange among the various Western and non-Western area specialists has already been emphasized. Beyond this, it seems likely that the new interest in non-Western politics and the consequent re-examination of traditional concepts and hypotheses may help to bridge the gap that has opened up over the decades between comparative politics and political theory. There probably is no other scholarly discipline in whose academic curriculum "theory" has been so largely equated with "history of doctrine." Even within this context of doctrinal history, the conventional treatment of political theory tends to focus rather narrowly on theories, from Plato to Rousseau and Mill, on such subjects as political obligation, the proper locus of sovereignty, and the respective limits of state powers and of individual rights. Topics such as the rise and fall of political communities, the historical interplay of integrative and disintegrative forces, and the expansion of political functions as a result of intensified social communication are very largely neglected. The seventeenth- and eighteenth-century theory of social contract—which, on the face of it, was an attempt to discover in abstract terms how political communities come into existence—tends to be interpreted as an expository device to explain rights and obligations in existing commonwealths.[24] The Platonic concept of the lawgiver, evolved by Rousseau into a rudimentary theory of how basic institutions are formulated in nascent political systems, appears to have caught the imagination of few historians of political theory.[25] The time-honored theories of comparative politics of Aristotle, Machiavelli, and Montesquieu have been incorporated into the accepted canon. For the nineteenth and twentieth centuries, however, emphasis has been placed largely on the growth of such political-economic ideologies as liberalism, socialism, communism, and fascism—to the neglect of more empirically based theories of men like de Tocqueville, Pareto, Maine, Gierke, and Max Weber. As comparative politics turns with renewed vigor to the elaboration of theoretical concepts, and as political theory becomes less preoccupied with mere exegesis, there is hope for a far more fruitful and organic relationship between research and theory in politics than has generally obtained in the past.

## NOTES

1. See, e.g., Merle Fainsod, *How Russia Is Ruled,* Cambridge, Mass., 1953, and Barrington Moore, *Terror and Progress—USSR,* Cambridge, Mass., 1954.

2. Lucian W. Pye, reporting on his interviews with surrendered guerrilla Communists in Malaya, writes: "The introductory remark that the interview was being conducted in the interest of social science by one attached to an American university, and that it was in no way an intelligence operation, seemed so unlikely and even fantastic to the SEP's [Surrendered Enemy Personnel] that it had to be eliminated for the sake of achieving frankness." *Guerrilla Communism in Malaya,* Princeton, N.J., 1956, p. 123n.

3. See George McT. Kahin, Guy J. Pauker, and Lucian W. Pye, "Comparative Politics of Non-Western Countries," *American Political Science Review,* XLIX (1955), pp. 1022–41.

4. Gamal Abdul Nasser, *Egypt's Liberation: The Philosophy of the Revolution,* Washington, D.C., 1955, p. 41.

5. For a fuller elaboration of the concepts of amalgamation and ambivalence in this context, see Dankwart A. Rustow, *Politics and Westernization in the Near East,* Center of International Studies, Princeton, N.J., 1956, pp. 6 and 10ff.

6. Rupert Emerson, "Paradoxes of Asian Nationalism," *Far Eastern Quarterly,* XIII (1954), p. 133.

7. Cf. Dankwart A. Rustow, "Politics and Islam in Turkey, 1920–1955," in Richard N. Frye, ed., *Islam and the West,* The Hague, 1957, p. 74.

8. For some Near Eastern illustrations, see Rustow, *Politics and Westernization,* pp. 12ff. Similarly, Paul M. A. Linebarger *et al.* describe the Japanese as "always somewhat gullible in seeking the Western fashion in politics and economics" (*Far Eastern Governments and Politics,* New York, 1954, p. 363n.).

9. Cf. Arnold J. Toynbee, *The World and the West,* New York, 1953, p. 15.

10. Karl W. Deutsch, *Nationalism and Social Communication,* New York, 1953.

11. For the former term, see e.g. J. S. Furnivall, *Colonial Policy and Practice,* 2nd ed., New York, 1956, *passim;* for the latter, Carleton S. Coon, *Caravan: The Story of the Middle East,* New York, 1951, p. 27.

12. Meyer Fortes and E. E. Evans-Pritchard observe an analogous effect of colonial rule on the tribal structure of African society. The power of strong chieftains generally was reduced, whereas among the smaller tribes, where no established chieftaincy existed earlier, such positions were fostered. See their *African Political Systems,* London, 1940, pp. 15f.

13. Three members of the Committee on Comparative Politics of the Social Science Research Council have contributed to a penetrating and suggestive dis-

cussion of the Western cultural impact and its political implications which coincides at many points with the above analysis; see Kahin *et al., op. cit.* For a similar position, cf. Gabriel A. Almond, "Comparative Political Systems," *Journal of Politics,* XVIII (1956), pp. 402f.

For particular non-Western regions, see e.g. George Lenczowski, "Political Institutions," in Ruth Nanda Anshen, ed., *Mid-East: World Center,* New York, 1956, pp. 118–72; G. E. von Grunebaum, "Problems of Muslim Nationalism," in Frye, ed., *op. cit.* (note 7); Rupert Emerson, *Representative Government in Southeast Asia,* Cambridge, Mass., 1955; Lennox A. Mills, *The New World of Southeast Asia,* Minneapolis, 1949, pp. 288–342; Philip W. Thayer, ed., *Nationalism and Progress in Free Asia,* Baltimore, 1956, pp. 37–168; and James S. Coleman, "The Problem of Political Integration in Emergent Africa," *Western Political Quarterly,* VIII (1955), pp. 44–57.

14. Von Grunebaum, in Frye, ed., *op. cit.,* p. 26. See also his earlier essays in "Studies in Islamic Cultural History," *American Anthropologist,* Memoir No. 76 (1954), pp. 1–19; and "Islam," *ibid.,* Memoir No. 81 (1955), especially chs. 7, 11, and 12.

15. Kahin *et al., op. cit.,* p. 1025.

16. See, e.g., David E. Apter, *The Gold Coast in Transition,* Princeton, N.J., 1955; Marcel Colombe, *L'Evolution de l'Egypte,* Paris, 1951; Jacob M. Landau, *Parliaments and Parties in Egypt,* Tel Aviv, 1953; J. C. Hurewitz, *The Struggle for Palestine,* New York, 1950; Majid Khadduri, *Independent Iraq,* London, 1951; Stephen Hemsley Longrigg, *Iraq, 1900–1950,* London, 1953; George Lenczowski, *Russia and the West in Iran,* Ithaca, N.Y., 1949; George McTurnan Kahin, *Nationalism and Revolution in Indonesia,* Ithaca, N.Y., 1952; and Robert A. Scalapino, *Democracy and the Party Movement in Prewar Japan,* Berkeley, Calif., 1953.

17. See, e.g., Sydney N. Fisher, ed., *Social Forces in the Middle East,* Ithaca, N.Y., 1955; Alfred Bonné, *State and Economics in the Middle East,* 2nd ed., London, 1955; George Lenczowski, *The Middle East in World Affairs,* 2nd ed., Ithaca, N.Y., 1956; W. Macmahon Ball, *Nationalism and Communism in East Asia,* Melbourne, 1952; Furnivall, *op. cit.;* and the literature cited in note 13.

18. Cf. Roy C. Macridis, *The Study of Comparative Government,* New York, 1955, pp. 9ff.

19. It should be remembered that Latin America includes some areas such as Puerto Rico and the British West Indies which, like much of Asia and Africa, are in the process of transition from colonialism to independence. On Puerto Rico, cf. Henry Wells, "Ideology and Leadership in Puerto Rican Politics," *American Political Science Review,* XLIX (1955), pp. 22–39. For the independent countries of Latin America, see e.g. Asher N. Christensen, ed., *The Evolution of Latin American Government,* New York, 1951; and Miguel Jorrin, *Governments of Latin America,* New York, 1953.

20. Macridis, *op. cit.,* pp. 11ff. Herman Finer, erupting into rhyme in the preface to his most recent work, declares:

> Political science without history has no roots;
> History without political science has no fruits.

(*Governments of Greater European Powers,* New York, 1956, p. ix.) Ernest Barker's essay on *The Development of Public Services in Western Europe, 1660–1930* (London, 1944) and Crane Brinton's *Anatomy of Revolution* (New York, 1938) are outstanding examples of political comparison across the centuries—though both are limited to countries in the West. Such works as Herman Finer's *Theory and Practice of Modern Government* (rev. ed., New York, 1949), Carl J. Friedrich's *Constitutional Government and Democracy* (rev. ed., Boston, 1950), and R. M. MacIver's *Web of Government* (New York, 1947) distinguish themselves from most other general treatments of the subject not only by their systematic (rather than country-by-country) organization, but also by their richer historical and philosophical perspective.

21. See, e.g., Donald E. Webster, *The Turkey of Atatürk,* Philadelphia, 1939; Fortes and Evans-Pritchard, *op. cit.;* Bertram J. O. Schrieke, *Indonesian Sociological Studies,* I, The Hague, 1955; Morroe Berger, *Bureaucracy and Society in Modern Egypt,* Princeton, N.J., 1957.

22. See, e.g., Simon Kuznets, Wilbert E. Moore, and Joseph J. Spengler, eds., *Economic Growth: Brazil, India, Japan,* Durham, N.C., 1955; and Hugh G. J. Aitken, ed., *The State and Economic Growth,* New York, 1959. Both volumes incorporate a series of papers originally prepared for conferences sponsored by the Social Science Research Council's Committee on Economic Growth.

23. Richard D. Challener and Maurice Lee, Jr., "History and the Social Sciences: The Problem of Communications," *American Historical Review,* LXI (1956), p. 337.

24. See, e.g., Bertram Morris, "The Substance of the Social Contract," in Milton R. Konvitz and Arthur E. Murphy, eds., *Essays in Political Theory Presented to George H. Sabine,* Ithaca, N.Y., 1948, pp. 113–29.

25. See Plato, *Nomoi, passim;* and Rousseau, *Contrat Social,* Book ii, ch. 7.

# SOCIAL THEORY AND COMPARATIVE POLITICS

## F. X. Sutton

## 1. INTRODUCTION

In drawing together my ideas for this paper I was surprised to note how many of them could be traced back to Durkheim. One source of the confidence I could muster for a difficult task was the resulting feeling that I did not have to depend on my own strengths. The diffusion of Durkheim's ideas, principally through Radcliffe-Brown and Parsons, had created a kind of flying wedge to propel me through difficulties. The basic point of view in this paper assumes an indissoluble connection between theory and comparative method, and this is, of course, a Durkheimian point of view. As he forcibly put it:

La sociologie comparée n'est pas une branche particulière de la sociologie; c'est la sociologie même, en tant qu'elle cesse d'être purement descriptive et aspire à rendre compte des faits. [Comparative sociology is not a particular branch of sociology; it is sociology itself, in so far as it ceases to be purely descriptive and aspires to account for facts.][1]

In its broadest interpretation this canon of method emphasizes that a proper science deals with the general rather than the unique; a multiplicity of empirical cases must be brought together under the abstract categories of a theory. It does not necessarily imply that we must always be comparative in the "cross-cultural" sense; there are some phenomena presenting enough instances within a given society to permit their scientific study within this restricted locale. But Durkheim's practice was in fact to make "cross-cultural" comparisons, and for a great many social science problems such ranging comparisons are in-

dispensable. The traditional domain of comparative politics has taken in only a limited number of societies, but it has been a study of large-scale social systems and thus logically requires a "cross-cultural" perspective. Much of this paper will consequently deal with "macro-sociology" and the world-wide perspectives that the subject demands.

A brief prospectus may be a helpful addition to the outline I have given above. I assume that general sociological theory has some interest and utility to the political scientist. Its tools are in any case needed for application in later discussion and I supply a brief primer in section 2.1. General theory alone will hardly suffice for the needs of comparative politics and my sections 2.2 and 2.3 offer a more concrete view of the structure and typology of societies. Section 3 attempts to discriminate political systems in the general domain of social systems and charts one approach to comparative politics. The notions of representation, stratification, and integration assume particular importance as the paper proceeds, and my final section 4 offers some suggestions of dynamic analysis in these terms. In many places I maintain a general perspective, but I give special attention to modern industrial societies and their problems of transition from earlier forms.

## 2. SOME GENERAL SOCIOLOGY

### 2.1. The General Analysis of Social Systems

The elaborate complexity of human societies has evoked a variety of responses from scholars. Historians in particular have been mistrustful of generalized approaches to the intricate and delicate interdependences they saw in society and have accordingly put their trust in exhaustive scholarship and intuitive, "humanistic" procedures. Other scholars, with a very different cast of mind, have sought to lift themselves above detail and devise very general theories as guides through complexity. Across a broad spectrum of methodological difference there

The major part of this article appeared with the title "Representation and the Nature of Political Systems," in *Comparative Studies in Society and History,* Vol. II, No. 1 (October, 1959), and is reprinted by permission of the Editorial Committee of that review and the author.

A paper prepared for a conference under the auspices of the Committee on Comparative Politics of the Social Science Research Council, Princeton, N.J., June 2–4, 1955.

seems nevertheless to have been the common assumption that societies display some kind of intelligible coherence. The development of modern sociology has brought a growing explicitness and clarity about this assumption. Conceptions of *social systems* and *societies* now exist in reasonably orthodox forms and provide the base for general bodies of sociological theory. Since I shall view political systems as social systems of a particular kind, it will be useful to recall some fundamentals in the theory of social systems.[2]

The notion of a system implies an orderly patterning in the parts of the system; this is to say that any system, and a social system in particular, has a *structure*. The proper description of structure is thus an essential part of the study of social systems. It provides the setting for and the statement of problems. For if one is to get beyond description into analysis, the orderly patterning of systems must be taken as problematical. The notion of *function* provides the bridge to analysis; it signifies a point of view in which parts and aspects of the system are scrutinized with reference to their significance in the persistence of the system. The acuity and depth of discussion that Professors Parsons, Merton, and Levy have recently addressed to structural-functional analysis have given it a rather difficult and esoteric flavor. I do not think it need or should have this flavor. Like any useful mode of scientific analysis it is "played by ear" all the time, and a working competence in it is certainly not difficult to achieve.[3]

The structural description of social systems requires some specification of elements. A little reflection will show that this specification is not altogether easy and straightforward. It is evident that human action takes place in a physical and biological setting and in a cultural tradition. Any global view of a distinguishable set of action patterns must thus include numerous and heterogeneous elements. (A very able attempt to do this may be found in Chester Barnard's "theory of cooperative systems."[4]) To envisage social systems in such inclusive terms seems necessary, but it threatens to be awkward. If we are to gain a convenient focus of analysis, it is necessary to seek out the more peculiarly "social" in any system of action. This requires a slight step beyond common sense. An attentive person may have noted that I have thus far avoided any talk about social "groups." I have done this deliberately because I am concerned that we recognize a distinction between concrete individuals and their participation in any given social system. The doctrines that "the whole man goes to work in our fair city" or that "militants give the whole of their lives to the Party" are species of dubious sociology. It seems better to seize upon the evident fact that the action of individuals in any social setting responds to *expectations* peculiar to that setting. Hence, the sociologist's preoccupation with *roles* and his use of

them rather than personalities or concrete individuals as structural units in social systems. In this view, any social system, say a parliament, is not just a collection of concrete individuals. It is a system of action built around a set of interlocking roles. The members of a parliament bring their personalities into the chamber, and what they do there will depend in some respects on their personalities. But they will also play the roles expected of them as members, and the coherence of the parliament as a social system (different from others in which the same individuals also play roles) depends on this fact.

Social systems exist in complicated relations to other social systems.[5] A parliament, e.g., contains sub-systems in its committees, party caucuses, etc.; it also has multifarious linkage to other social systems through its members' other roles, its constitutional authority, etc. A structural description of any social system usually must take into account its sub-systems and some other systems as well. Since a role is always a role in a particular system there will be role-structures corresponding to each sub-system and to each overlapping or linked system.

All of this no doubt sounds distressingly complicated but there are compensations; many of the most interesting problems in social analysis arise from the juxtapositions of different roles and systems.

In the terminology I favor, a *society* is a particular kind of social system, viz., one comprehensive and differentiated enough to be self-sufficient (with respect to the diverse functional needs of its members).[6] (Parsons sometimes speaks of "total social systems" to cover the same idea.[7]) In section 2.2 I shall specialize the discussion to societies, but for the present I shall remain on the general level and consider the analysis of any social system.

A general theory of social systems must rest on standard ways of describing social structure and of surveying functional problems. A very useful approach on the structural side is provided by what Parsons now calls "pattern variable" analysis. This approach has, of course, been a part of the working equipment of sociologists since the pioneer work of Maine and Toennies. It derives from the observation that there are recurrent and contrasting patterns which turn up in the norms of social systems. Thus, Toennies saw a contrast between the expected behavior in families and local communities on the one hand and organizations like modern business firms and markets on the other; his famous categories, *Gemeinschaft* and *Gesellschaft,* emerged to become a general tool of analysis for any social system. The discernment of patterns in this fashion has often proceeded very intuitively and unsystematically. Thus Ruth Benedict found patterns of culture among the Zuni, Kwakiutl, Dobuans, Japanese, Thai, and Rumanians; but each society posed new problems, and it was not her interest or talent to forge a standard set of tools for handling any society or social system. Those with a more systematic turn of mind have tried to clarify just what was being patterned, and to discover a standard, exhaustive array of types of patterns. Parsons has worked at this problem over the past two decades. He has, I think, shown conclusively that simple dichotomies such as Maine and Toennies used are not satisfactory; instead of a single dichotomy or variable several must be used. The quest of a definitely exhaustive list has proven to be very difficult, and Parsons' latest work indicates the possible addition of a sixth variable to the five that have been standard in his work for some years. Clarification in this area is certainly one of the most important problems now facing sociological theory, but I am sure that we do not have to await further theoretical advance to make good use of existing tools. The variables Parsons has recently utilized seem to me to have demonstrated their usefulness in many ways. This is not the place for an extended discussion of their nature and I shall confine myself to listing them with brief, illustrative comments. His list is as follows:[8]

1. Affectivity-affectiven neutrality: A distinction exemplified in the obligations to love one's wife but to be "businesslike" with one's secretary.
2. Self-orientation—collectivity orientation: Classically exemplified in the contrast of business firms and governments.
3. Universalism-particularism: The formula that laws should operate "without regard to persons" is a universalistic formula. Kinship behavior, by contrast, tends to be particularistic.
4. Ascription-achievement: This is Linton's well-known distinction. Parsons has interpreted it as resting on emphases on *qualities* or *performances,* and has substituted these terms in recent writings.
5. Specificity-diffuseness: The contrast between the bounded obligations of a contract and the undefined range of obligations between close kinship roles.

In later sections of this paper I shall make considerable use of these variables and I hope to offer some concrete evidence of their interest for the study of comparative politics.[9]

The basic virtue of these pattern variables is that they give a standard means of describing the role-expectations and value-standards in *any* social system. One can by this means identify quickly similarities and differences that are important in comparative analysis, and the technique is applicable from the broadest to the narrowest types of comparison. The same tools can tell us something about the differences between President Eisenhower and Suleiman the Magnificent as well as the differences between President Eisenhower and the spouse of Mrs. Eisenhower.

I might also emphasize that pattern variable analysis is directly applicable to social systems and their inter-relationships. Thus we say, e.g., that a bureaucracy is built on universalistic and achievement norms, or that the contractual relations among business firms are ruled by norms of specificity. The application of these variables at the social system level is again perfectly general; they may be used to discuss international relations, or the place of a clique in a local party organization.

Turning now from structure to function, we find systematic problems of great difficulty. The great generality of the notion of social system makes it evident that generality is necessary in conceiving functional problems.[10] Parsons and Bales seem to have been the hardiest explorers in this tenuous atmosphere. I shall dodge around the formidable difficulties of their systematic treatment and confine myself to a rougher sort of general orientation. The simplest starting point is provided by Bales' array of four functional problems, the "adaptive," the "instrumental," the "expressive," and the "integrative,"[11] which "stated" against a background of preoccupation with small discussion groups. The first relates to the fact that social systems exist in situations to which they must adapt. In a total society, there is evidently the problem of adaptation to the physical environment with all that this implies in terms of "maintenance" activities and technology. The second recognizes the goal orientation of human action and the necessity of contriving action patterns with an appropriate instrumental significance in relation to goals. The third recognizes the fact that the human actors in any social systems have psychological states that require maintenance and symbolic expression. The fourth notes the requirement of internal adjustment and coordination of the system as it meets its other functional problems. Whether or not this scheme represents a tight and exhaustive categorization of functional problems for any social system is, of course, a problem deserving the closest attention, but we cannot stop to wrestle with it here. My hope is that this list gives a sufficient sense of the range of functional problems the sociologist keeps in mind to provide a setting for the special focus of attention to follow.

One of the assumptions of this general approach is that any concrete social system copes with a multiplicity of functional problems. There is no simple correspondence of differentiated social structures to functional problems. If there were, the task of the social scientists would be much simplified, but we must resign ourselves to complexity. In our particular subject of interest here we must not expect that those institutions we call political will have a unique functional significance, or that the "political problem" can be nicely localized in any system. Specialization of social structures about particular functional problems nevertheless does occur in some degree. Those structures we call political seem to have a particularly important link to certain types of integrative problems. I shall not attempt to justify this assertion immediately but I hope that the sense I give to it will become clear as we proceed.

The discussion of integration in the fashion of most interest here requires the conceptual apparatus developed in section 3 of this paper. After we have that apparatus in hand, we can proceed to a more concrete discussion. I venture first, however, to recall the broad classes of questions subsumed under the notion of integration. There are first the problems of integrating individuals into any given social system. This has its "moral" aspects in the problem of individual conformity to the norms and expectations established within the system. It also has its "cathetic" aspects in that individuals react to other individuals by liking or disliking them and some workable arrangement of these cathexes must be at hand in any integrated system. In addition there are problems of meshing and compatibility of the action patterns and sub-systems within the given social system and in its complex relations to other systems.[12]

## 2.2. The Structure of Societies

The study of societies is a more specialized subject than the general study of social systems. While the general theory of social systems has direct applications to the problems of comparative politics and other special fields of social science, we obviously need additional, more specialized approaches. In particular, we need morphologies for the description of societies. In every-day science work we all use structural categories when we talk of kinship systems or bureaucracies or caste systems. These are categories arising in empirical observation of the gross anatomy of societies, and some set of categories of this type seems to me indispensable. I believe it would be very unfortunate, in the field we are here concerned with, if a revulsion against the sterility of formal institutional description should lead to a neglect of careful structural setting of problems. The contemporary social science literature contains many works that seem to me to involve regrettable distortion because the authors did not see their problems in the relevant structural setting.[13] Unfortunately, there is at present no evidence that the requisite categories can be drawn out of the first principles of a general theory. They have a loose kind of relationship to the general functional problems of societies, but the complications of empirical societies have thus far thwarted efforts at systematic derivation of useful categories.[14]

For the broad comparison of societies, there seem to be two general strategies one might follow in structural analysis. On the one hand, one might try to classify sub-structures of particular sorts across the range of all societies. In comparative politics, Weber's famous system of ideal types (of patrimonialism, bureaucracy, etc.) is an outstanding venture. The field of kinship probably offers the best developed model, and illustrates the long and patient development that is necessary in this type of work.[15]

Another possibility is to classify societies and develop analysis within the resulting typology. Since the demise of evolutionary theories, this has been an unpopular procedure, but it has special attractions in the subject of comparative politics. The point of view I take throughout this paper is quite in accord with that expressed by the Report from the 1952 SSRC Seminar on Comparative Politics;[16] this is a field in which the separation of a special set of institutions from their total social context threatens to be very damaging. One is thus led to investigate the possibility of setting comparative problems in a typology of total societies. The scope of the venture is dismaying but there is encouragement to be found in the literature. Durkheim made the discrimination of different "types" of societies one of the rules of sociological method,[17] and Radcliffe-Brown has subscribed to this rule.[18]

I cannot here perform the labors of generations and present a good general typology of societies. I believe it is possible, however, to sketch the basic features of two broad types that are especially important for the study of comparative politics in the present-day world. Social philosophers from Henry Adams to Mr. Oppenheimer have made the sharpness and rapidity of change the crucial feature of the modern world. A proper focus on this massive fact of rapid change seems to require discrimination of types of change. Societies in which modern science and technology have been institutionalized are intrinsically changing societies, but much of the change they induce goes on without alteration of basic social structure. The transition brought on at the beginning of industrialization appears to be a more fundamental type of social change. One is thus led to seek out a specification of the end-points of the transition.[19]

We now talk freely of "modern industrial society" as a type. I believe it is possible to describe this type in some detail without inviting great controversy. The predecessors of modern industrial society on the other hand seem very heterogeneous. In the perspective of modern industrial society, many of them nevertheless show much in common, as Professor Levy has persistently argued.[20] Professor Redfield's "folk society" is doubtless the best-known model for these societies, and its success offers encouragement that useful models are possible. For our purposes I shall sketch out a related type of society based on intensive agriculture that seems to be a reasonable abstraction from the empirical societies that have existed prior to industrialization over much of the world. When juxtaposed against modern industrial societies, it provides a typology akin to Redfield's scheme of "folk" and "urban" societies.

Before plunging into description of these two types of society, I want to restate what I am doing in the hope of clarification. Following Durkheim, I take the view here that comparative politics and other forms of comparative social science need a classification of types of societies. To approach comparison of the French and German political systems with nothing more than a conception of societies in general seems too meager an equipment. One needs a more specialized conception of the type of society that these cases presumably represent, and this type of society will be different from that underlying a comparison between a West African kingdom and an Indian state. The typology I present here is a very crude one, but it will be serviceable in later discussion of political systems. It may also serve to illustrate a sociological perspective on societies and the use of pattern variable analysis.[21]

## 2.3. A Typology of Societies

Two broad types of societies will be distinguished as "intensive agricultural" and "industrial" societies. This grounding of my typology on the "means of production" has great empirical importance, but I do not stress the technological in the actual definitions. I shall stress social structural features without detailed attention to how they may depend on or derive from modes of production.

An "agricultural" society[22] has the following essential characteristics:

1. Predominance of ascriptive, particularistic, diffuse patterns.
2. Stable local groups and limited spatial mobility.
3. Relatively simple and stable "occupational" differentiation.
4. A "deferential" stratification system of diffuse impact.

Some of these brief general characterizations should be immediately comprehensible. Others will require comment and illustration. Ascriptive norms imply stable patterns in the assignment of individuals to roles by birth, sex, age, etc. Continuities of status implies continuity in access to facilities and rewards, and hence strong ties to locality. In the great agricultural societies of the world, stable local communities have been the familiar rule—the demands of agriculture in most places have been such as to require the continuous attention of people who are functionally specialized as cultivators or husbandmen. The villages or scattered local settlements in which these cultivators and their kin groups have lived have been highly particularistic groupings. They have been marked off from outsiders, and matters within the local community have been ruled by norms appropriate to small numbers of people in permanent and intimate association. Urban agglomerations have occurred in all the great agricultural civilizations,

but they have been the homes of a minority of the population; of necessity, the modal pattern has been that of the small, agricultural community.

The role differentiations corresponding to our occupations that occur in these societies may be quite numerous (witness India). By comparison with a modern industrial society they are, however, on a lower level of differentiation. Ascriptive patterns of recruitment also mean that these "occupations" are not subject to the generalizing influences that tend to reduce them to a common character in industrial societies. Instead of having a loose connection to other roles held by an individual, and hence a well-defined character in themselves, the analogues of our occupational roles have disparate qualities and accretions.

In conformity with this relatively weak differentiation of "occupational" roles, class stratification has a diffuse significance and an occupationally concrete character. Land-owners not actively engaged in cultivation but living from rents (in some form) tend to occupy a definite class status that typically has other related occupational features. (Military roles, as in the Western medieval world, are one common example.) The linkage of class status with a limited array of occupational statuses has led people to speak of "estates" or "Staende," whether or not these have means of corporate expression or action.[23]

I have called the typical class stratification system "deferential." By this I mean that class status has a diffuse character and unless expressly excluded is presumed to be a reference point for interaction.[24] The contrasting form of class status I call "egalitarian"; in this sort of system, familiar in our own society, universalistic norms require the avoidance of class as a normal reference point in interaction. Tocqueville and many lesser observers have pointed to the "deferential" character of class stratification in the older structure of the West, and there are ample grounds for thinking that this type of stratification is general to the type.

One might follow Weber and add "traditionalism" to the characterization of this type of society, but I believe that insofar as it is relevant here, this quality is implied by the prevalence of ascription.

As essential sociological features of a *modern industrial society* I suggest the following:

1. Predominance of universalistic, specific, and achievement norms.
2. High degree of social mobility (in a general—not necessarily "vertical"—sense).
3. Well-developed occupational system, insulated from other social structures.
4. "Egalitarian" class system based on generalized patterns of occupational achievement.
5. Prevalence of "associations," i.e., functionally specific, non-ascriptive structures.

I trust that a few comments will serve to illuminate this list and make the necessary explanations of technical terms. The prevalence of universalistic and achievement norms implies a marked restriction of the significance of kinship systems. These norms also act as a kind of solvent to barriers among local, ethnic and other groups. Spatial mobility is facilitated and stimulated by legitimate access to different possible statuses. A highly differentiated occupational system is governed by universalistic and achievement norms. Holding some sort of occupational role becomes a normal expectation for adult men and for those women for whom kinship duties do not take precedence. This is one sense in which the occupational system becomes generalized in the society. There is another sense. Occupational roles have the common features of (1) demanding relatively continuous application, (2) being the principal "instrumental role" activity of the incumbent, (3) money remuneration, which in the typical case is the principal source of income of the jobholder. These common features and the criteria that make any qualified person the potential incumbent of any occupational role serve to produce an effective generalization. Occupations can be and are in fact compared with one another. On the basis of such comparisons individuals choose their jobs and measure their attainments or satisfactions. Sociologists have shown that in several countries of the modern world a scale of prestige rankings of occupation can be elicited with good reliability.[25] These prestige rankings have an intimate connection with the scale provided by the money remuneration of occupations and there are pressures to bring the two scales into close conformity.

The weakness of ascription in modern industrial societies provides scope for the flourishing of a type of social structure scarcely to be found in many societies. These are commonly called "associations" and have as their leading characteristic specificity of purpose and participation. Business firms, governmental agencies, hospitals, universities are "associations" built around occupational participation; the rich array of groupings we call "voluntary associations" (Protestant churches, patriotic organizations, etc.) are another class built primarily on more limited participation of their members. I stress particularly the non-ascriptive and specific character of "associations." New "associations" may be contrived to meet needs as they arise, and individuals may participate in them in the very limited and segmental way made possible by norms of specificity. It is, of course, one of the more remarkable and important features of our own and other modern industrial societies that "associations" are possible.

The importance of occupations and the prevalence of universalistic norms impose limitations on the possible types of class structure in these societies. The prestige ranking of occupations and the associated differences in personal income make for a ranking of kin groups in a class structure. But this class structure lacks sharp discontinuities, and "egalitarian" norms restrict its impact. In the class systems of agricultural societies there are notable discontinuities in values across the various strata: a military aristocrat is expected to be bold, self-assured, and perhaps "cultivated" but not necessarily industrious; the ideal of a peasant cultivator in the same society usually contains contrasting virtues of industry and deferential submissiveness. But in a developed industrial society, the different class statuses tend to be strung out on a chain of common values in conformity with the universalistic expectation that everybody be judged on the same fundamental bases. The occupational sphere carries many strict hierarchical rankings (as in a typical bureaucratic structure); but these are *specific* to the occupational sphere, and universalism forbids their easy extension into "private" lives. The drawing of clear lines of division in the class structure by organizations specifically based on class status is also inhibited by universalistic values. These "egalitarian" class systems thus tend to have an inconspicuous and restrained character that has led some people to argue that countries like the United States have no class system at all.

Weber stressed the prevalence of rationality as a norm for the guidance of social behavior in modern industrial societies. This sort of norm is, I believe, implied by the norms of universalism and achievement. It means a continuous scrutiny of received ways of doing things in terms of their suitability for a similarly scrutinized set of goals. A modern industrial society cannot be a static society; by giving legitimacy to rational criticism from the realm of technology to the intimacies of family life, it is constantly stimulating change and coping with the unforeseen consequences of these changes.

The major societies of the modern world show varying combinations of the patterns represented in the ideal types I have sketched out. Some stand close to the model of industrial society; others are in various transitional states that hopefully may be understood better by conceptions of where they have been and where they may be going.

We are now prepared to turn to a particular feature of social systems and societies that will lead us into the domain of the political.

## 3. REPRESENTATION AND THE NATURE OF POLITICAL SYSTEMS

### 3.1. Representation, Stratification, and Authority

Early in the development of modern sociology, Maine and Weber emphasized that some social systems have a special corporate character. Their notion of a *corporate group* rests on the observation that social systems may possess structures and symbols that permit the whole system to be *represented* over against its individual members and sub-groups, or outside groups and individuals.[26] This feature of social systems has an obvious importance for political science and I shall devote special attention to it.

Obviously, not all social structures are made up of corporate groups. I have at various times argued that all social structures could be viewed as *classifications, reticulations,* or *collectivities*.[27] There are some institutionalized classifications of individuals that carry no direct implications of solidarity or common purposes: sex, age, and education provide familiar examples. Kinship gives a major example of reticulations among roles that cut across solidary groupings. There are, of course, many social structures with definite boundaries and within which the members have a sense of solidarity and of common values and purposes. These are the structures that have been called collectivities.[28]

The lines between these categories tend, of course, to be fluid. One important problem of social integration is found in the tendency of classifications to generate collectivities. We are familiar in the modern world with norms and ideologies directed at controlling these tendencies—e.g., the "Americanization" movement in our society was a movement against emphasis on ethnic status, and I have already noted the universalistic restraints that inhibit organized expressions of class status. In modern industrial societies there are persistent efforts to form representative agencies for social classifications that have some plausible common interests or solidary sentiments; the ease of building "associational" structures is no doubt responsible, and this process is one reason for the peculiarly "dynamic" character of modern industrial societies. Obviously, not all would-be representative agencies make classifications into corporate groups. It may be that all collectivities are corporate groups in the sense indicated above. I am not altogether clear on the point, but it is at least obvious that there are very great differences in the degree to which collectivities have distinct and clear patterns for representation.

The need for some discrimination of *representative* and *autonomous* activities in a collectivity should be evident. In the "foreign relations" of any collectivity it is important that the actions and intentions of the collectivity as such be discriminated from the "private" actions and intentions of its component members. Thus, if business firms are to incur obligations as firms, there must be means of defining just how these are legitimately incurred. Similarly, in a great variety of internal matters it is often essential to know whether or not the shared values and goals of the collectivity are in question or whether matters are the autonomous concern of individuals or sub-systems.[29] An appropriate set of symbols and role differentiations must thus exist to provide regularized channels and contexts of representation. In most societies these symbols and structures have a religious character, for reasons familiar since Durkheim's classic analysis in *The Elementary Forms of the Religious Life*.[30]

The study of corporate groups and representation is a general topic in sociology, underlying such diverse fields as kinship, business organization, and government. I shall take the view here that our special concerns are with a particular kind of representative agency, viz., those arising from the fact that territorial relations have a special character and importance in societies. Claims to spatial locations are obviously fundamental parts of social structure (not only in the familiar legal forms of property but in a much broader sense). These claims must be recognized and maintained by the members of effectively interacting groups. But they are also intrinsically subject to invasion by outsiders who do not share the norms of the resident group. The potential use of force is obviously of especial importance in these matters, and there is a familiar connection between territorial organizations and the control of the use of force. The fact that human beings have physical location means that the diverse social systems in which they participate tend to have an intimate spatial juxtaposition; diverse social systems thus tend to share common location and integrative problems become intimately linked to the facts of territoriality.

The upshot of these remarks is that territorial groupings tend to fall into collectivities and hence require representative agencies. My discussion has been cast in very general terms. Since the suspicion always exists that such discussions are distorted by preoccupation with familiar societies, I think it wise to proceed more empirically at this point with two examples of territorial representation in primitive societies.

EXAMPLE 1. Leach's recent monograph on the Kachins, *Political Systems of Highland Burma*,[31] has given us an admirably analyzed picture of territorial groupings. The Kachins are a patrilineal people living in villages and village clusters. Each village contains members of several patrilineages, but there is one lineage that "owns" the village. Leach calls this the "principal lineage," and in the terminology I am using here it would be the "representative" lineage. Similarly, there is a principal or representative lineage for clusters of villages; one village is considered to be senior to others in the cluster, and its principal lineage becomes the principal lineage for the whole cluster. A male from the principal lineage is in turn a representative figure for the village cluster. The heads of village clusters have a special honorific title, *duwa,* and Leach calls them "thigh-eating chiefs" from their prerogative of receiving a hind thigh from animals sacrificed within the village cluster. Village headmen sometimes claim the title *duwa* but lack other legitimate prerogatives of the thigh-eating chiefs.[32]

The representative or principal lineage "owns" the land of a village or village cluster in a special sense. Rights of usufruct in the land rest with individual households; they "eat it." Chiefly ownership implies little or no economic advantage but rather a bundle of rights:[33] (1) to commit violence on the land, (2) to make offerings to the chief of the sky-spirits, *Madai nat,* (3) to dig ditches around the graves of members of the chiefly lineage, (4) to erect a special kind of house post, (5) to hold a certain kind of communal ceremony called a *manau,* (6) to perform certain annual rituals associated with the earth spirit, *ga nat* or *shadip*.[34]

In the analytical terms I am using here, items (3) and (4) in this list refer to modes of symbolizing a special representative status of the chief. There are normally no "public buildings" in a Kachin village, but the dwelling-place of the headman or chief is differentiated both by its house posts and by containing the setting *(madai-dap)* for the sacrifices to the sky-spirit. Both the chief sky-spirit *(Madai nat )* and the earth-spirits, *ga nat,* rule over matters of general importance to the whole village collectivity. The sky-spirits control wealth and prosperity; the earth-spirits, fertility, both human and agricultural. The chief thus has exclusive right of ritual approach to these spirits. (Ideologically, his right is based on distant affinal kinship to Madai, and his ritual actions preserve prosperity and fertility.) He thus becomes the representative figure for the collectivity's interests vis-à-vis supernatural powers in his capacities (2), (5), and (6). His rights of control over violence in his territory lack an intrinsically communal character, but conform to the universal tendency for these rights to be restricted to territorial representative figures.

A more extended territorial control is vested in certain chiefly lineages. The Kachins have the notion of a "domain" (*mung*) that may contain only a single village cluster, but may be much larger. Where such domains exist, there is a representative lineage. The domain chief (the *mung duwa*) and all subordinate chiefs within the domain are of the same lineage, the subordinate chiefs representing junior branches. (Actually, the Kachins observe ultimogeniture so that the senior lineage is a "youngest son lineage.") The status relations of the chiefly hierarchy are thus grounded in kinship rankings. This is carried further in a system of ranking lineages through their affinal connections (the *mayu-dama* system). Ideally, a chief of any territorial grouping is from a lineage senior to resident lineages with which it has affinal connections.

In general form the characteristics of this society are very familiar. The use of a lineage as a representative agency over a territory is familiar in the monarchies of Western history, in China and throughout the world. Before passing on to another example, I would emphasize the following points:

1. The linkage of representation and high status.
2. The interrelations of representative figures at different levels through ideology, kinship, and stratification.
3. The restriction of collectivity action to the representative figures.

EXAMPLE 2. Because of the peculiarly "acephalous" and "unpolitical" character of their society, I venture to recall a few facts about the Nuer of the Southern Sudan, as described by Evans-Pritchard. The Nuer number some 300,000 and are spread out sparsely in villages over a large region around the upper Nile. They have a common language and culture but are not a collectivity in the sense used here. The largest solidary units are tribes, which are economically self-sufficient and lay exclusive claim on definite territories. Within a tribe there are means for settling disputes and grievances but no such means exist between tribes. Tribes are internally segmented into sections, each with its territory and some degree of solidarity; sub-sections of these primary sections also exist. Villages are grouped into tribal sections; they also tend to fall into districts in accordance with ease of communication and these districts tend to coincide with tertiary tribal sections[35]. At no level in Nuer society is there a figure properly called a chief, i.e., one enjoying representative status and exercising authority and ritual powers accordingly. There is however, a kind of representative status associated with kinship groups. The Nuer have clans segmented at various levels into systems of lineages. Neither clans nor lineages are localized, but members from a given clan or lineage may be found in different tribes, tribal sections, or villages. There is, nevertheless, a special association of kinship groups with territorial groupings. In each tribe there is a clan (usually in numerical minority) that enjoys a special status; its members are aristocrats, *diel,* in that tribe though not in others.[36] Similarly primary tribal sections are associated with maximal lineages and so on down to the village that has a local minimal lineage as its "aristocrats." The "aristocrats" have special prestige in their territorial grouping, some claims to leadership, but no formal authority; they are not the judges of disputes nor the agencies for execution of justice.

The significance of kinship groups as territorially representative groups in this case must apparently be traced to the Nuer needs for conceptualizing social relationships in kinship terms. The relations of tribes and sub-sections are in any case fluid and easily disturbed. Evans-Pritchard emphasizes their relations as ones of hostile *opposition,* occasionally breaking out in feuds and undergoing processes of fission and fusion. These relations are, however, not wholly anarchic; there are restraints on the modes of fighting feuds and wars (e.g., the women and children are not killed or enslaved). A conceptualization of distinctiveness but also of relatedness and overarching unity is provided by the kinship structure through the device of "aristocratic" or representative status for particular clans or lineages.

A close linkage between *representation* and *stratification* stands out in these examples. I shall argue that this is a general characteristic of corporate group structure and a matter of basic importance for political science. Representative contexts and agencies must evoke sentiments related to the common values of a corporate group. They must symbolize these values in a positive fashion. In so far as individuals enter these representative contexts and agencies, they must share in this high positive valuation. In any society, then, representative figures must either be drawn from those possessing a generalized high status in some form, or the roles they fill must have sufficient prestige to assure high status for their incumbents. It also follows that in any society territorially representative institutions must be shaped by the character of the stratification system.

Representation also has intimate links to *authority*. In a highly segmental and traditionalistic society, there is limited need for representative figures to mobilize a total group and commit it to a program of action. Hence, the very weak authority of Kachin chiefs and the practical non-existence of territorial authority figures among the Nuer. But insofar as representation does imply the capacity to commit a group to action or to perform coordinated acts for its general welfare, it implies *authority*. The legitimate bases of this authority are the bases of legitimate representation. Weber's well-known stress on the problem of legitimacy for political systems is a stress that might be applied in any corporate group. As I see the matter, the prominence of legitimacy questions in political systems derives from the delicacy and difficulty of integrating a social system about legitimate representative agencies. All institutionalized structures are "legitimate" in some sense, but representative agencies must have a peculiarly high and difficult kind of legitimacy.

## 3.2. The Nature of Political Systems

The territorial representative agencies I have been discussing would be called political institutions in familiar usages of the term "political." The question immediately arises whether or not they constitute the essential core of political systems. I believe there is good reason to regard them this way. If we accept this point of view, the study of political systems becomes the study in the first instance of representative agencies over territories. The same sort of fuzziness in the boundaries of political systems exists that exists for social systems in general. But on this showing, the study of political systems has a special focus and other features of a total society enter the study only in so far as they bear on the structure and functioning of territorial representative institutions.

I do not believe that this view of the nature of political systems is in any sense radical or original. I would, however, argue that it is a much more convenient and practical definition of the political than some others, in particular than the view that political systems are constituted by all the manifestations of power and authority in a society. The difficulty with this latter view is that any social structure contains patterns of power and authority. A political scientist who took seriously the view that his field is the comprehensive study of power and authority would have to busy himself with families and factories as well as with princes and parliaments. There might for some special purposes be advantages in such catholicity, but for most purposes I believe this would be a confusing and disheartening commission.

Weber's political criterion, viz., exclusive control over the legitimate use of force in a territory, is implied in the view adopted here. In my concluding section I shall discuss why territorially representative institutions become ultimate agencies of social control. I thus conceive that I am not in conflict with Weber's definition, but I see advantages in not putting the control of the use of force in the definitional center. Most of the actual study of political institutions seems to me more directly and intimately connected with their character as representative agencies than with the ultimate sanctions they can exercise.

There is some sociological theory that can be applied directly to the general discussion of the structure of territorially representative agencies (or "political institutions," as I shall now freely call them). For example, the kind of distinction Bagehot made when he talked of the "dignified" and "efficient" parts of the English constitution is observed clearly in many states. In extreme form, the principal symbolic figures may be quite cut off from the effective operation of political authority. Bagehot's queen kept a stubborn grip on affairs, but others, like the Japanese emperors under the Tokugawa Regime, lost it almost completely. The discrimination of functions here rests, of course, on an analytical distinction relevant in any political system. It is that between symbolic representation and executive control. Discriminations of this type have been studied in very general form. Bales has shown that there is a tendency in small discussion groups for two sorts of leaders to appear, the "instrumental leader" and the "integrative leader."

He and Parsons have analyzed the underlying reasons and made instructive applications to the study of kinship.[37] Applications of this sort may prove valuable in comparative politics, but I shall not here attempt to gather together my scattered bits of knowledge that might support this suggestion. I confine myself to the line of analysis begun in 2.2 and 2.3.

### 3.3. Comparative Politics in Different Types of Societies

A general scheme for the study of comparative politics is implied in the conception of political systems as focused about territorial representative agencies. From the preceding discussion it appears that these agencies will reflect the social structures they represent, and the classificatory problems that engaged our attention in section 2 of this paper will be pertinent. Both to illustrate this viewpoint on political institutions and to suggest a division of labor in the study of comparative politics, I shall carry forward the discussion of agricultural and industrial societies begun in 2.3.

It would be very helpful to me at this point if there were a general political science of preindustrial, agricultural societies. Weber's essay on Patrimonialism in *Wirtschaft und Gesellschaft* is an isolated monument reminding us of what is possible, but I scarcely know anything else like it. It seems to me that there ought to be a well-digested body of textbook material that would reach out over the many empirical examples and give us a comparative politics for these societies. But even in Europe the *ancien regime* is left to the piecemeal, nation-by-nation cares of the historian, and I have been told by political scientists that a knowledge of kings, favorites, and tax farmers is no stock in their normal trade. Lacking good professional guidance, I must confine myself to very sketchy treatment.

A unified state in these societies has commonly depended on a representative lineage. The structure of the political system has been basically particularistic in accordance with the character of the underlying society. There have consequently been great problems in maintaining unity over extended areas. Local particularism has meant a kind of federative structure.[38] Most of the members of a local community have not been direct members of the political system in the sense that a modern citizen is. They have entered into the political system through local representative figures who have normally held a diffuse high status. The integration of the state has then depended on the coherence of an aristocratic class and its relations to the royal lineage. The structure of political institutions reflects this general social structure. (Thus, in the Middle Ages in the West, kings were surrounded by aristocratic councils.) Various devices in different states have appeared to counterbalance the claims of local aristocrats to representative statuses. They have usually involved some measure of universalistic recruitment. Some, like the Chinese bureaucracy, were extraordinarily successful over long periods. Others, like the slave households of the Ottomans, have been more desperate measures and correspondingly more susceptible to rapid decay. The executive competence of these "patrimonial governments" looks extremely limited by comparison with modern bureaucratic states. They are often sufficient to the needs of a stable agricultural society but very ill adapted to the efficient direction of social change that is of such central importance in modern bureaucratic governments. They have been hampered in effective operation by fixed particularistic claims, and Weber has shown a universal tendency for a hard-won centralization to crumble into a loose feudalism.

I conceive that a specialized branch of comparative politics might be devoted to these societies and their political systems. Special comparative morphologies are needed to classify the relevant institutions. Many special problems which are of minor or trivial significance in modern industrial societies assume central importance in these pre-industrial societies. One obvious example is the subject I like to call "kingship and kinship." Over the world a great many different arrangements have emerged to assure regular succession to royal status. The fact that kings have siblings and collateral and affinal relatives poses a whole series of integrative problems, and we have considerable understanding of these problems in individual scattered cases. The interest in the incest problem, for example, has led to considerable attention to the famous royal exceptions among the Ptolemies, the Azande, and elsewhere. Royal incest invites comparisons with different devices having similar functional significance. (I think of the Ottoman elimination of problems with their in-laws by slave marriages and problems with siblings by extermination. Other arrangements like those of the Banyankole or the Zulu invite comparative attention.)

In addition to the special apparatus of typology and theory for these societies, one might expect various applications of the general theory of social systems. It is obvious that any general advance in our understanding of ascription and particularism in social systems should throw light on institutions in which these value patterns are prominent.

A general comparative politics for pre-industrial societies would doubtless be of primary interest to pure scholarship, but it might also be a valuable base point for understanding the transitional societies which crowd the contemporary scene.

In the pure type of a modern industrial society we should expect the representative territorial agency to have the following characteristics: (1)

It should be an *association* rather than a lineage or a patrimonial household. (2) In its symbolism and ideology it should reflect the universalistic values of the collectivity it represents. If for no other reason one expects the government to be an association because it must provide rational direction in a continually changing and dynamic society. The universalism in the class structure would probably also require an associational form—there should be no diffusely qualified aristocracy to whom governmental functions might of right be allocated. As in the examples cited above, the symbolism of government must conform to the underlying social structure and its dominant values.

Empirical societies approximate to this model, but with characteristic modifications reflecting their history of transition from agricultural societies. In the Western world the urge toward equality which Tocqueville saw as the dominant passion in the nineteenth century has issued in the universalistic concept of citizenship and the ideology of popular government. The idea of a nation as the underlying collectivity has slowly lost its ambiguities. . . . The stiff autonomy of aristocrats has given way to the assured dependence of salaried officials. Recent history, nevertheless, shows no want of difficulties and instabilities in the structure of representative authority. These difficulties seem to rise in part from the strains of transition and in part from intrinsic problems of industrial societies. I shall devote my final section to a discussion of representative agencies and integrative problems in these societies.

From this general picture, I conclude that there is a legitimate special kind of comparative politics for modern industrial societies. The conclusion is in a sense very trite—no professional student of modern governments need be told that his study has its own special complexities. It may not, however, be trivial to suggest that there are theoretical as well as pragmatic bases for specialization—the earnest student of comparative politics in its familiar Western scope need not then feel that his specialization is merely a practical consequence of limited energy and erudition. Actually, of course, the rapid diffusion of Western-model political institutions has produced many mixed and transitional situations that blur the lines of convenient division. But these should admit of study in precisely the fashion that their labels suggest, viz., as intermediate or mixed forms between generally understood types of societies and political systems.

## 4. SOCIAL INTEGRATION AND POLITICAL INSTITUTIONS

Most of the discussion in this paper might properly be called structural and static. I have emphasized the basic structure of different types of societies and the corresponding structure of political institutions. Before concluding, I should like to give some attention to functional problems and to more dynamic considerations.

The emphasis on representation in this paper points to a special connection between the study of political institutions and problems of social integration. One must assume a diversity of functions for political institutions; governments have many functions (e.g., in economic allocation) that are not directly integrative. But their existence and character is intimately dependent on the general state of social integration, and they in turn serve very important functions in maintaining that integration. In this final section of my paper I shall attempt to make clear how a sociologist looks at the problem of social integration, and how political systems appear in this perspective.

It is empirically obvious that no society is perfectly integrated, and there are good theoretical reasons for believing that none can be. Any social system is built on the conformity of its members to expectations, and this conformity is not automatic. The molding of human raw material in the socialization process achieves much toward making people want to do the things they are expected to do, but the molding is never quite perfect. The diverse functional problems and cultural residues in societies keep their structures from having ideal clarity and consistency. Individuals are thus presented with problems in the duties they must meet and the rewards they may legitimately expect; at a more macroscopic level, there are delicate problems in the balance and intermeshing of solidary groups in the total society. Any society thus has *strains* that are patterned by the question "Qu-est-ce qu'une nation? C'est le souverain et l'aristocratie." Such limitations of the "nation" to its high-status groups seem to represent a natural confusion of collectivities with their representative figures, but the confusion has become progressively less likely. The norms of universalism and the facts of status mobility have fostered the conception of a nation as an undifferentiated mass of citizens. The breakup of local particularism and the decline of ascriptive statuses have produced problems of security for individuals that have given great emotional force to nationalism. Various forms of symbolic participation, through elections and otherwise, have reinforced ideologies of government as representative of all the people.

The form of political institutions as associations built on elective offices and bureaucratic hierarchies is basically compatible with universalistic values. A high seriousness deriving from the force of nationalistic sentiments provides a high status for representative authority without direct dependence on the class status of those who hold governmental offices. The status of persons in government is, of course, integrated more or less closely with status rankings in other social contexts. In no society are legislators and officials drawn indiscriminately from all class strata; the upper strata make disproportionately heavy contributions and this is no mere survival of older patterns.[39] The anarchist (and Marxist) ideal of a government run by genuinely "common" people is incompatible with the extensive authority and technical difficulty of modern governments. A progressive extension of universalistic recruitment has, of course, been characteristic. We find gradual elimination of the disabilities that kept Jews and Social Democrats out of the old German imperial civil service or that kept the French civil service in the hands of the *haute bourgeoisie*.[40] The familiar high status of representative figures is nevertheless maintained, although tempered by an ideology that makes them "servants of the people."

The problems of integration for political systems in modern industrial societies are distinctly different from those I have suggested for agricultural societies. The resistances of local particularism have been removed, and questions of sheer territorial integration are displaced to the international level. In contrast to patrimonial governments, modern bureaucratic governments seem to have lesser problems of organizational basic structure and that evoke *reactions* that again fall into definite patterns. The examination of these strains and reactions is a basic procedure in the study of social integration.[41]

Political institutions become involved in problems of social integration in two important ways: (1) they serve as an agency for the control of individual deviance; (2) they provide a means of control and coordination among the imperfectly integrated groups in the total social system. In both of these matters, political institutions play their role in a general setting where other types of institutions serve similar functions. The magnitude of the integrative problems governments must handle evidently depends on the integration of the underlying social structure, and I shall discuss the control of deviance and over-all coordination with this fact in mind.

*Deviance* from legitimate expectations is a normal potentiality or actuality in any social system. Any functioning social system has some means of dealing with deviance, through a system of social controls for its prevention and through devices for handling actual occurrences of deviance. When deviance occurs, it thus tends to take definite forms and it calls forth definite responses both from the deviating individual and from others.[42]

The social patterning of deviance has led sociologists to talk about "deviant roles" and to serious efforts at categorizing the principal modes of deviance.[43] The criminal, the sick, and the ritually polluted are familiar examples; they have well-defined deviant roles in many or most societies. Since the conception of deviance implies departure from normally approved behavior, deviant roles are in some sense derogated roles. In a well-integrated social system, when an individual deviates, both he and others categorize his behavior as deviant. In some fashion, it is made clear that his behavior is not to be indiscriminately imitated. Normally there is a procedure whereby he is subject to sanctions and then reinstated to his normal role.[44]

A great part of the control of incipient or actual deviance in any society occurs without the use of representative agencies, political or otherwise. The close study of the operation of "private" social controls is only in its infancy, but we are beginning to understand the subtle processes by which individuals are "kept on the rails" in ordinary social life. These studies may seem remote from political science, but they have an important relevance. Strains managed in private contexts might, given other expression, pose problems for the political system. The alternatives sometimes appear in direct and vivid form. In studying modes of control on Communists in our society, I came across numerous instances in which "militants" were subject to serious pressures to view their heated concerns as personal neurosis rather than social iniquity. Whether or not the alternatives appear in this direct form, there is an obvious relief of pressure on political systems if there are other channels for the expression and management of strains.

In addition to "private" agencies, there is in most societies an important control function vested in the political system. The underlying reason is suggested by my remarks above: deviance is an affront to the established norms of a social system and calls for a symbolic demonstration that such actions are improper. The proper agency for this demonstration must be one that can symbolize the common disapproval of the social system. It must thus be a representative agency. In some cases this need not be the ultimate representative agency for all the social systems in intimate juxtaposition. But for certain especially disturbing forms of deviance the ultimate agency must be called into play. Thus the courts and the police system in our society deal with criminals and impose coercive restraints on the more extreme forms of psychotic disorder.

If social systems approached perfect integration, it might be that all behavior would fall clearly into approved and deviant forms, and the problems of political institutions would be correspondingly simple. A simple model of social integration that envisages only conformity and deviance is, however, altogether too simple for the facts of social life. In section 2.1 I made the point that social systems normally contain sub-systems that must somehow be related to one another if the total system is to function with any semblance of coherence and order. A great many of these relationships are established and maintained without the direct involvement of political institutions. Any social system, like a church or university in our society, orients itself constantly to the existence of similar and dissimilar social systems in its society. A local Protestant church, e.g., may declare its solidary affiliation with other churches of the same denomination or with an ecumenical movement. It will also typically declare its solidary loyalty to the nation-state within which it functions. In shaping its organization and practice, it uses various *reference groups*. It may imitate those defined as comparable and similar (like other Protestant churches), and it may deliberately emphasize its distinctiveness or opposition to others (e.g., by avoiding liturgical similarities to Roman Catholicism).[45] While such patterns of intergroup relationship are constantly studied in particular cases and some promising general approaches have appeared,[46] I do not know of any simple and exhaustive scheme for their analysis. Empirical examples like the one just discussed suggest at least four important modes of relationship: solidarity, autonomy, opposition, and relative status ranking. The basis for integration of a total society lies in some combination of these (and perhaps other) modes of relationship.

The view of political institutions advanced in this paper clearly implies their special importance in the total integration of all the tangle of social systems and processes encompassed within a society. As representative agencies over a territory, political institutions serve as a common reference point for all the social systems located in their domain. They thus become the natural focus for the control and adjustment of relations among these sub-systems. Great variations exist in the way these integrative functions are carried out and in the degree of importance they assume in the total integration of the society. In the examples I have earlier cited from primitive societies, representative political agencies served primarily for the symbolic expression of common ties; more typically they have had authority and legitimate command over means of coercion. Even where these powers have been strongly developed, great differences in the mode of over-all integration occur. The totalitarian societies of the modern world represent an extreme effort at achieving integration by denying legitimacy to many types of autonomous subsystems or by eliminating them entirely. In societies of the liberal persuasion, there has been a quite different pattern in which integration has been sought by allowing a responsible autonomy to subsystems and avoiding the strains of close, hierarchical coordination.

Mention of these familiar examples suggests that the political scientist has a special claim to the study of the integration of total societies. I believe this to be the case, at least for those societies in which political institutions play a conspicuous role in over-all integration—as they certainly do in the major societies of the modern world. In this perspective the comparative study of totalitarian and liberal societies is the study of different forms of over-all social integration in modern industrial societies. It is at once a branch of comparative politics and of the general study of societies.

An emphasis on the close connection between political institutions and the general problems of social integration has the unwelcome feature of complicating political science. I suspect, however, that this complication is inescapable, and likely to be rewarding. A great many of the concerns of comparative politics, like the "immobilisme" of the French political system, the shaky repute of parliamentary government in Germany, or the magnitude of the Communist vote in various countries, seem to reflect underlying problems of social integration. On the other side of the matter, good reasons can be adduced for expecting strains arising in the most varied contexts to find expression in the political sphere. It would be desirable if I could offer extended discussion of these propositions, but I shall have to confine myself to a brief exhortation.

Some of the most promising opportunities for the analysis of political systems seem to me to lie in close study of the political consequences of stratification systems. In section 3 I gave some rough outlines of structural interrelations between stratification and political institutions. But much more can be done through a dynamic analysis that traces out the imperfections of stratification systems and their consequences. Tocqueville long ago demonstrated some possibilities. Nowadays, even with lesser talents, we should be able to go much farther. In doing so, we would be following a major strand in the analysis that places political institutions in the general study of social integration, for stratification systems are themselves a principal means of social integration and one comes to understand the consequences of their imperfections against this background.

## NOTES

1. *Les règles de la méthode sociologique* (Paris, 1947), p. 137. [Translation from Emile Durkheim, *The Rules of Sociological Method*, Eighth Edition, translated by Sarah A. Solovay and John H. Mueller and edited by George E. G. Catlin. New York: The Free Press of Glencoe, Inc., 1950, p. 139. Copyright 1938 by the University of Chicago.]

2. Radcliffe-Brown gives Montesquieu and Comte credit for first emphasizing the systematic interconnections in social action. The line of more recent theoretical development that is most familiar to me starts in neo-classical, general equilibrium economics. It was there that Pareto first got the notion of a society as a system. Walras' idea of an economy as an interdependent system provided the framework for Pareto's own work as an economist and the model for his effort (in *The Mind and Society*) to treat total societies as systems. When L. J. Henderson expounded Pareto to a generation at Harvard, he did so with a characteristically stern insistence on the notion of a social system. The recent work of Talcott Parsons grows out of this heritage. His is the system of social theory I grew up on and I shall use it in much of what follows. (*Structure and Function in Primitive Society*, New York: The Free Press, 1952, pp. 4–5.

There now exists a Society for the Advancement of General Systems Theory, organized by L. v. Bertalanffy, Kenneth Boulding, Ralph W. Gerard, and Anatol Rappaport. Boulding's recent emphasis on action at the boundaries of systems converges closely with Parsons' treatment of the economy as a social system in his recent (unpublished) Marshall Lectures.

3. Good general discussion of the method, however, is certainly difficult. I have had a great deal of instruction from the writings alluded to, and I do not mean to disparage the importance of this work.

4. *Functions of the Executive*, Part I.

5. Cf. the discussion by Parsons, Bales, and Shils in *Working Papers in the Theory of Action* (New York: The Free Press, 1953), ch. V, pp. 190–194.

6. An attempt at careful definition may be found in D. F. Aberle *et al.*, "The Functional Prerequisites of a Society," *International Journal of Ethics*, January, 1950. Marion Levy has pursued the question further in his *Structure of Society* (Princeton, N.J., 1952).

7. Talcott Parsons and Edward A. Shils, *Toward a General Theory of Action* (Cambridge, Mass., 1951), p. 196.

8. *Ibid.*, p. 77.

9. One need not, of course, attempt to use precisely this set of variables for all purposes. I do not in fact confine myself to them in this paper, and Professor Levy has used a somewhat different set in his *Structure of Society*. Special problems may call for emphasis on a particular variable (like the representation-autonomy distinction I use later) that does not appear in Parsons' array. If his (or any other array) is truly exhaustive, then all such variables should prove to be "compounds" of the basic variables. This does not mean they should not be used but it will obviously facilitate the advance of knowledge if we can get along with a few basic variables.

10. At one point the author and others thought the full generality of social systems too forbidding and made an effort to treat the special case of a total society. Aberle, *et al.*, *op. cit.*

11. *Interaction Process Analysis*, ch. II, pp. 49 ff. and ch. V.

12. I do not expect that these very general statements will be particularly helpful at this point. My hope is that they may provide an orientation and will become meaningful as detail is supplied later. One of the most useful discussions of this general type that I know is

again that supplied by Chester Barnard in *The Functions of the Executive*, especially Chs. V, XI, XII.

13. The field of national character studies blossoms with examples. I would cite Henry Dicks' studies of Russian refugees and Margaret Mead's study of authority patterns in Russia. For want of explicit recognition that much of the behavior they describe occurs in bureaucracies both of these capable analysts are kept from distinguishing things which reflect the problems of bureaucracies and things traceable to a distinctive Russian character.

14. Talcott Parsons' effort in Chs. II, IV of *The Social System* (New York: The Free Press, 1951) is the most sophisticated one known to me. He in effect breaks off the systematic derivation in Ch. V, and takes a new stance to discuss the structure of actually existing societies.

15. The present state of the subject may be grasped from G. P. Murdock's *Social Structure* (1949) or Radcliffe-Brown's long introduction to *African Systems of Kinship and Marriage* (1950). Systematic work in this field may be dated from Morgan's great study, *Systems of Consanguinity and Affinity* (1870).

16. *American Political Science Review*, v. XLVII, Sept., 1953, pp. 641–675.

17. Durkheim, *op. cit.*, pp. 76–88.

18. It gives me comfort to quote Radcliffe-Brown:
"The immense diversity of forms of human society must first be reduced to order by some sort of classification. By comparing societies one with another we have to discriminate and define different types. Thus the Australian aborigines were divided into some hundreds of separate tribes, each with its own language, organization, customs, and beliefs; but an examination of a sufficient sample shows that beneath the specific diversities there are such general similarities that we can constitute and describe in general terms an Australian type. The type . . . is an abstraction only a little way removed from the concrete reality. When a number of such types have been adequately defined they in turn can be compared with one another and a further step in abstraction can be made. By such a process, obviously requiring the labour of many students over many years, we may reach classifications and abstract concepts more precisely defined and more exactly representing empirical reality than the concepts indicated by such phrases as 'primitive society,' 'feudal society,' 'capitalist society,' that occur so abundantly in contemporary writing." Introduction to *African Political Systems* (1940), pp. xi-xii.

19. Recognizing, of course, that neither end-point need be rigidly static.

20. Much of what follows grows out of discussions in recent years with Marion Levy, John Pelzel, David Landes, David Aberle, and Lloyd Fallers. Most of this group participated in a 1953 SSRC seminar on the comparative analysis of societies.

21. The reader concerned to follow the main flow of the argument may want to skip ahead to section 3.1 and return to the immediately following exposition when it becomes relevant background for 3.3.

22. I shall not preserve the qualifying adjective "intensive," but I mean it to be understood. Hunting and gathering and transhuman pastoral societies are of

course excluded from this type. So also are societies practicing agriculture in casual or auxiliary forms, and probably those practicing a shifting "slash-and-burn" type of cultivation. The boundaries are naturally obscure, but clearly a great many primitive societies are excluded.

23. The nobility in France after the procedures of admission became regularized, and especially after it became hereditary, is an excellent example. Cf. Marc Bloch, *La société féodale,* v. II.

24. This distinction of class systems is discussed more fully in a paper "Achievement Norms and the Motivation of Entrepreneurs," which I presented in a conference at the Center for Entrepreneurial History, Cambridge, Mass., in November, 1954.

25. Alex Inkeles and Peter Rossi have recently shown a close agreement among these scales for the United States, Great Britain, New Zealand, Japan, and Germany. "Cross National Comparisons of Occupational Ratings," *American Journal of Sociology.*

26. I have found Maine's discussion of primogeniture in his *Ancient Law* particularly instructive in the ideas developed in this section. Weber used the notion of a *Verband* extensively in his work. In their translation of the first part of Weber's systematic treatise, *Wirtschaft und Gesellschaft,* Parsons and Henderson have translated *Verband* as "corporate group" (*Theory of Economic and Social Organization,* pp. 145–148).

27. Radcliffe-Brown has used precisely this classification (with different terminology). *Structure and Function in Primitive Societies,* p. 191.

28. Cf. Parsons and Shils, *op. cit.,* pp. 192–195.

29. There are a great many subtleties here of which I cannot hope to give more than a suggestion. Cf. section 4 below.

30. Émile Durkheim, *The Elementary Forms of the Religious Life,* translated by Joseph Ward Swain. New York: The Free Press, 1954.

31. E. R. Leach, *Political Systems of Highland Burma: A Study of Kachin Social Structure.* Cambridge, Mass.: Harvard University Press, 1954.

32. I restrict myself here to *gumsa* organization. There is a different form (*gumlao*).

33. Leach, *op. cit.,* pp. 155–156.

34. Leach omits this last point from his list but from other evidence in his monographs I conclude he did it through oversight.

35. Meyer Fortes and E. E. Evans-Pritchard, *African Political Systems.* London: Oxford University Press, 1940, p. 275.

36. E. E. Evans-Pritchard, *The Nuer: A Description of the Modes of Livelihood and Political Systems of a Nilotic People.* London: Oxford University Press, 1940, pp. 211 ff.

37. Talcott Parsons and Robert F. Bales, in collaboration with James Olds, Morris Zelditch, Jr., and Philip E. Slater, *Family, Socialization and Interaction Process.* New York: The Free Press, 1955.

38. S. F. Nadel's *Black Byzantium* gives a good picture of this kind of structure in a Nigerian kingdom. I have also found instruction in Funck-Brentano's account of French villages before 1789 (*The Old Regime in France,* ch. VIII) and Marion Smith's picture of the integration of Indian villages into wider political structures (*American Anthropologist*). "Federative" is perhaps too loose a term for what I have in mind; where there is a centralized "capital," the solidarity is radial and there is motivated opposition among the points (village communities) at the periphery.

39. Cf. the recent survey of the backgrounds of parliamentary representatives in various European countries (including the Soviet Union) by Mattei Dogan—"L'origine sociale du personnel parliamentaire dans l'Est et l'Ouest de l'Europe," *Transactions of 2nd World Congress of Sociology,* v, II, pp. 175–179 (1954).

40. On this latter, see the paper by Bottomore, pp. 143–153 in the *Transactions* just cited.

41. This is the conceptual scheme underlying studies I have made in the ideology of radical Marxists and American businessmen. The latter study (with Seymour Harris, Carl Kaysen, and James Tobin) contains a general exposition of the scheme and has been published as ch. 15 of Francis X. Sutton. *et al., The American Business Creed.* Cambridge, Mass.: Harvard University Press, 1956.

42. Cf. the excellent example in Raymond Firth's essay on "Authority and Public Opinion in Tikopia," in (ed.) Meyer Fortes, *Social Structure: Studies Presented to A. R. Radcliffe-Brown,* Oxford, 1949. For a related kind of situation in our own society, cf. Margaret Mead, *And Keep Your Powder Dry,* New York, 1942, ch. IX, "The Chip on the Shoulder," pp. 138–157.

43. Cf. Radcliffe-Brown on "Social Sanctions" in the *Encyclopedia of the Social Sciences,* and the essay by John Provinse in (ed.) Fred Eggan, *Social Anthropology of North American Tribes* (Chicago, 1937).

44. Parsons, *The Social Systems,* ch. IX, and Merton's essay, "Social Structure and Anomie," in his *Social Theory and Social Structure* (New York: The Free Press, 1957, rev. ed.)

45. Similar processes, of course, go on among political units. Different states in the United States measure themselves against one another, and the nations of the world maintain delicate patterns of solidarity, opposition, and relative status.

46. Among these I would include (1) the analysis of opposition and balance among corporate groups in the work of Radcliffe-Brown and the British Africanists, and (2) the study of reference groups emerging in the work of Merton, Stouffer, and others.

# A COMPARATIVE METHOD ✓
# FOR THE STUDY OF POLITICS

## David E. Apter

### INTRODUCTION

This essay presents a method which is, at present, inelegant, not parsimonious, and which combines both analytic and descriptive categories. Its purpose is to create a framework for the treatment of governments in diverse social settings in order to make possible some generalization about how the presence, absence, or clustering of certain combinations of variables affect politics.

Implicit in this scheme is a model of politics. Every society has a social stratification system. The dominant motive of social behavior is assumed (whether rightly or wrongly) to be the increased mobility toward the higher ends of the stratification hierarchy. Members of the public join in political groups in order to expand mobility opportunities and, in this respect, make representations to government or to influence or control government in some manner. Government policy must then in part be responsive to the interests of political groups. Depending upon who the group represents, we see that government policy is geared as well to the ultimate alteration of social stratification or aspects thereof. This is, of course, both a traditional and a respectable view of politics. Government is viewed as a maximizer, sending out streams of satisfactions. One is to political group leaders who represent both an information and organizational dynamic. A second is to followers who, depending upon their group composition, represent in some measure the prevailing social stratification system. Assuming that no one is ever truly satisfied with the system of social stratification other than conservatives, we find that the basic motive of politics then is a striving motive to expand mobility opportunities, either for some special group or for large segments of the society.[1]

The scheme laid out here attempts to delineate sets of useful variables in each of three main dimensions—social stratification, political groups, and government—in order to produce manipulative theory out of comparative research. It stems from a tradition associated with Pollock and Maitland, Austin, Maine, and Vinogradoff and the functionalist tradition in modern anthropology and sociology. It is designed to cover societies whether they are industrial or not, tribal, traditional, or technologically advanced.[2] The core of such a scheme is a set of general analytical categories called the "structural requisites" of any government. These represent a minimal set of concerns for any government, whether it be formalized or not. The demands put upon government, initiated in part through parties and originating in mobility strivings, must be met through activities in one or a combination of the structural requisites.

Nor does the format of government have to be democratic. The possible range of representativeness will limit the manner in which actions within each of the structural requisites can be performed. Such structural requisites are more than simply a heuristic device, as we shall hope to indicate.

The problem for which this scheme was undertaken deals with the development of parliamentary government in Africa. Cultural and technological data there range from aspects of the most secular and complex of European governments to tribal life, all within the compass of single societies. Stated generally, we are studying rapidly changing underdeveloped areas in order to indicate some of the general conditions produced by change as reflected in the conditions which are necessary for the development of parliamentary government.[3] The range of events and the materials to be dealt with require treatment in systematic fashion—a treatment that is not methodologically harsh, inappropriate, or stultifying, yet which is sufficient to provide a meaningful focus in comparative work.[4]

We shall in this discussion sketch out very briefly the major components of each of the three dimensions: social stratification, government, and poli-

Reprinted from *The American Journal of Sociology*, Vol. LXIV, No. 3 (November, 1958), pp. 221–237, by permission of The University of Chicago Press. Copyright 1958 by the University of Chicago.

tical groups, with emphasis upon the last. It is a major assumption here that there will eventually result from extensive comparative study typical clusterings of these variables. Departures from typical clusterings should prove challenging and interesting as well, as we attempt to develop theory to explain the phenomena observed.

## UTILITY OF
## SOCIAL STRATIFICATION

Social stratification and government have a close connection. Ultimately, the actions of government affect stratification in some significant manner. Of particular interest are the changes occurring in stratification in hitherto tribal societies under the impact of commercial, colonial, nationalist, and technological forces. Changes in culture include alteration in ideologies, with their expressed valuations on patterns of stratification. Most of all, however, the values and ideas of a changing social system can be expressed in the activities which take place to modify or protect the given pattern of stratification in a particular area.

Stratification is, as well, a useful way of indicating the degree of internal flexibility in a system. Relatively undifferentiated systems tend to be fragile and unable to adapt to changes in the social or political environment with ease. An important query then is similar to the one that Durkheim posed, as follows: In systems in which there is limited division of labor there is little flexibility (a lack of pluralism) or, to put it another way, fragility. Hence the most powerful expression of social solidarity is through an extensive system of repressive law which regards a wide range of socially unsanctioned acts as crimes against basic morality. With an increase in the division of labor there is not only specialization of function but also an increase in local solidary affiliations which become mutually dependent, and a decline in repressive law. These affiliations give rise to defined hierarchies of power and prestige, some based upon ascriptive evaluations and others based upon achievement. These, as well as other factors directly derivative from the pattern of alteration in stratification, set limiting conditions both for the activities of government and for the actions of political parties.[5]

Nor is the utility of stratification limited to societies which are industrializing. Its application is more general, applying as well to "mature" industrial systems, where it retains its intimate association with government and party actions.

Where active modification of the stratification system is going on, members characteristically (1) are status-conscious (i.e., they are aware of their position in the social system vis-à-vis others and, in addition, are aware of the advantages and disadvantages of a given status position which they might occupy); (2) are engaged in role-testing (i.e., they explore the legitimate limits of their roles and experiment to the point where they can expect sanctions of one kind or other to be initiated); and (3) are future-oriented (i.e., they look to changes in their life-chances and attempt to produce conditions leading to secure expectations proximate to what they desire).[6] Where these three conditions prevail, the implications for political development are great.

Three questions about the stratification system need to be answered before it is possible to make meaningful statements about the consequences of changing stratification. The first asks what the system is from the point of view of the members. How are *roles* defined in a given system and how are they ranked in a status hierarchy? Second, what are the institutionalized criteria of stratification? Are they economic, political, religious, generational, educational, etc.? Third, what are the recruitment patterns to the major groups which comprise the system? Are the institutional criteria such that recruitment is relatively open or closed, achievement-based or ascription-based?

For example, common in systems which are undergoing rapid industrialization and commercialization is a decline in power accorded to generational factors and religious factors, although prestige may persist a bit longer. High valuations for both power and prestige result from economic and sometimes political factors. Interesting situations are produced when groups which formerly had economic power and prestige lose the first and seek to maintain the second.

The set of variables to be specified under the dimension of social stratification, once the rank order of status positions has been described [and is shown in the diagram on p. 84].

These categories should, first, indicate what group values and "vested interests" exist in a system. Second, they should illuminate the institutionalized barriers to social mobility, and, third, they should demonstrate the nature of political groupings to the degree such groups reproduce or fail to reproduce the stratification range in their recruitment and membership. Finally, they should provide some guides to the degree of commitment members have to the system, leading to hypotheses about the direction of change. In this usage, change means the degree of alteration in the basic characteristics of the stratification system itself, reflecting alteration in the concrete groupings of the unit under observation.

The ultimate concern here is therefore the relationships between government and social stratification. However, the crucial connecting link is political party, association, or movement, as the case may be. To give equal treatment to each of the three dimensions discussed here is impossible because of lack of space. We shall therefore concentrate the discussion on the *political group* dimension after first specifying its relationship to government as well as to stratification. Before going on to discuss political groups, therefore, we see that a discussion of government is essential.

### 1. *Institutional Criteria of Stratification*

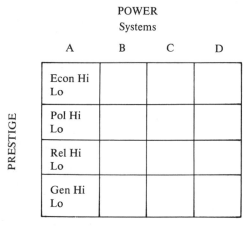

### 2. *Recruitment*

## GOVERNMENT

Very narrow definitions of government exclude a great deal that we intuitively know is relevant to government. Broad definitions tend to have limits which are loose. Legal definitions obscure the relationship between government and the social systems of which they are part.

As used here, "government" refers to a concrete group. It is defined as follows: In a system "government" is the most generalized membership unit possessing (a) defined responsibilites for the maintenance of the system of which it is a part and (b) a practical monopoly of coercive powers.[7] In this usage we can speak of the government of a society, or a church, or a trade union. The same characteristics analytically defined would hold whatever the empirical form the activities of government might take. These general characteristics we can call "structural requisites." In addition, the manner of participation in government of members of a unit can vary. Types of variation we shall call "format." The variation of format will depend upon the degree of representativeness of government. Finally, we are saying that government, although a concrete unit, is distinct from others in the following respect: *it is a concrete structural requisite for any social system.* We are saying, for example, that, while any substructure of a society (or other social system) has relationship to the maintenance of society, government is the most strategic of these. We do not say that, if you set up a government, you automatically create a society. Rather, the minimal requirements for the maintenance of government must be related to society in such a way that both can exist.

The crucial concerns of government are those which threaten the existence of the unit of which it is part. With its practical monopoly of coercive powers, government has an indivisible responsibility for protecting the system. Government handles its responsibilities in terms of certain minimal structures. If any of these structures should fail to operate, government itself must undergo drastic modification, and/or the system itself will undergo drastic modification. Therefore, important threats to the system are, first, threats to the ability of government to work in terms of its structural requisites. Second, they can derive from inadequate performance of government within the structural requisites from the point of view of the system as a whole, i.e., bad policy, inadequate action, etc. We shall discuss these structural requisites very briefly.[8]

### *The Structural Requisites of Government*

Of the broad range of activities which governments undertake, some are "vitally" necessary if the unit is to keep going. Some of the means to insure the performance of such activities are, in a loose way, what we mean by structural requisites. A tentative set of goals can be listed for any government as follows: (1) the structure of authoritative decision-making; (2) the structure of accountability and consent; (3) the structure of coercion and punishment; (4) the structure of resource determination and allocation; and (5) the structure of political recruitment and role assignment.

Decision-making by government involves the posing of alternatives and the selection of one or more for effectuation. Decision-making is presumed to be prompted by demands made outside the government or demands placed upon government by its own plans or the logic of previous actions. Here the important questions are: (a) Who makes the decisions? (b) What is the nature of the issues posed? (c) What is the range of supervision by decision-makers? Significant characteristics to be specified are as follows: the method of arriving at decisions, the scope of those decisions, and the degree of centralization in decision-making (including federal and unitary forms). Decisional legislation can take two forms: *framework legislation,* or broad enabling legislation with scope for initiative and innovation in application left to effectuating agencies, and *supervisory legislation,* involving detailed and continuous scrutiny by decision-makers.[9]

Patterns of accountability and consent involve reference groups for decision-makers significant to the extent that they will make decisions with such groups in mind. Such groups will either modify decisions at the request of government or require formal approval before a final decision is made. In democratic societies there are legally defined and ordered accountability groups (e.g., standing committees of a legislature) and consent groups (e.g., parliaments). In such instances there is symmetry between decision-making and accountability. Where decision-makers can more arbitrarily shift their accountability (e.g., to interest groups or special groups in a party), they have considerable autonomy. "Asymmetry" in such instances can involve a genuine difference between formal and substantive accountability, as in the case of "rubber-stamp" parliaments.[10]

Indeed, where decision-making does not have effective accountability, there is a genuine lack of information on the part of decision-makers, who very often cannot control the consequences of their own decisions or make useful predictions in this regard. Each decision involves an evaluation of consequence. Systems which posit goals of a distant nature and force the pace to their accomplishment normally cannot remain accountable to representatives of the public for very long periods of time. Instead, they would be more likely to be responsible to the technicians and others who are concerned with carrying out the goals. They use specialist information rather than information about public desires.

Where accountability is asymmetrical and shifting (i.e., where decision-makers have considerable autonomy), coercion and punishment are normally extensive. Coercion may take the form of positing new norms, concepts of ideal citizenship (the "New Soviet Man," for example), and social pressures of a variety of kinds. Types of coercion may range from social pressure to the modern arsenal of technological refinements. Both coercion and punishment are consequences too of actions taken without knowledge of consequences. Insofar as the costs of coercion and punishment are financially high and morally corrosive (they break down solidarity except the solidarity of complicity) they reduce the ability of government to devote as much of its resources to modifications in stratification as are perhaps necessary (except by using party, police, or army as patronage).

The general ability of decision-makers to act and the costs of their decisions to the public are determined by the ability of government to define, exploit, and allocate resources. Included here are the important problems of taxation and revenue assessment, which might result in reapportionment of wealth. In the modern social welfare state, and this would include most colonial and recent former colonial states as well, many of the most important ways of modifying social stratification without drastic measures come through welfare measures. Equally, they are a means of keeping the commitment of members to the system itself.

Finally, links between social stratification, party, and government itself are in part determined by the method of recruitment to and the definition of the roles of government. As Duverger has shown very adequately, types of electoral systems, for example, play an important part in determining the pattern of government accountability, the important units of decision-making, and the ability of government to recruit effective participants in government.[11] In some systems elections are the only permissible warrant for making decisions. In others there is co-optation and election. In some systems there are appointments germane to the perpetuation of an oligarchy. In large part the structure of political recruitment and role assignment determine the format of government. Format is extremely important because it is an indication of the formal responsiveness of a regime.

### Format of Government

As we have indicated, we mean by "format" the degree of representativeness of the regime. All regimes can be regarded as oligarchical in some respects, but the important question is whether or not the oligarchy serves the wider purposes of the system or is free to serve its own. However, even totalitarian regimes have some representative feature. Format, then, represents types of systems with respect to their representativeness as follows: (1) dictatorial; (2) oligarchical; (3) indirectly representational; and (4) directly representational. They are important insofar as variations in them involve differences in the performances of structural requisites and indicate degrees of sensitivity to the social stratification system. Depending upon format, as well, political parties have differing roles to play, their potentialities are different, and they have limits put upon their own actions.

It is important to recognize, first, the crucial and strategic role of government in a going social system. Second, the format of government in part determines its actions. Third, that these actions occur within the framework of five structural requisites, failure to perform in any one of which entails the breakdown of government itself. Insofar as government is regarded as a concrete structural requisite of any social system, the social system itself will be altered.

From the point of view of theory the empirical variations in possible actions in each of these structural requisites should be the core of comparative treatment. Ideally, a battery of data would have to be built up based on analysis of widely differing social systems and societies before the theoretical value of many empirical activities could be ascertained. At a minimum, then, these structures should have heuristic value. At a maximum they should produce useful theories.

## POLITICAL GROUPS

Modifications in the stratification system can be brought about by two major groups of entrepreneurs: (a) those who use the factors of production and are primarily *economic* and (b) those whose entrepreneurial activities are essentially devoted to the recruitment of followers who attempt to modify the system either by participation in government or by directing their action against it. These latter will be regarded as *political*. Of groups called "political," those which seek to find positions for their members in government will be regarded as political *associations* if they are composed of intimates and associates (like clubs) and political *parties* if there are regularly prescribed rules for membership and if the members are governed by the rules rather than personal association. If the rules of a political group are vague, not based upon norms for the behavior of intimates, it will be called a *movement*. To be effective, movements require mass membership. They are extraordinarily dependent upon personal leaders. They tend to transform themselves into parties if a stable framework of legitimate government is sufficiently flexible.

Historically, in most Western countries political associations appeared before political parties, but only recently have political movements transformed themselves into parties. Political movements emerge particularly where there are fundamental disequilibria in social stratification and where economic entrepreneurship does not appear as a feasible means of increasing public commitment to that system. In some instances political movements transform themselves into parties if they can capture government and combine economic entrepreneurship with political entrepreneurship through state enterprise. Political movements are normally monopolistic, and opposition groups are despised or their members regarded as traitors.

The actions of political groups depend ultimately upon the social stratification system insofar as there is a search for basic issues and grievances and insofar as recruitment to political groups is deeply affected by social strata. Depending upon who is recruited, considerable limitations are normally imposed upon political parties, upon political associations in particular, and, to a lesser extent, upon political movements. However, political groups have both contingent properties and their own "system" properties. They have certain organizational characteristics which produce changes in their activities and ideologies. Some refer to leadership and to the

abilities of a political group to take advantage of a given situation. Others refer to the specific characteristics of their recruitment and scope. A constant rejuxtaposition of such characteristics provides differences in political group activity. We shall discuss political groups therefore under two general rubrics: the structure of leadership and the structure of membership.

### The Structure of Leadership

Four characteristic types of leadership shall be encompassed here. They are: (1) bureaucratic and durable; (2) personal and fragile; (3) bureaucratic and fragile; and (4) personal and durable.

Normally, bureaucratic and durable parties, such as the Social Democratic party of Germany or the Conservative and Labour parties in England, require a stable and highly participant structure of government with a format of indirect democracy. The leadership in such a party may itself be oligarchical but only within the larger compass of a democratic state. Hence the oligarchical aspect of bureaucratic and durable parties tends to reinforce the democratic system by using its machinery to bring about a correspondence between public demands and government decisions. Democracy within a party does not necessarily lead to effective democracy in government.

Bureaucratic and durable parties have stable oligarchical (and usually middle-aged) leaders. The supporters are normally middle class and are "majoritarian" in their outlook, requiring mass membership less than a stable mass support. Such parties have a large corps of functional experts whose position in the party may involve a full-time appointment and is based upon "expertise" (functionally specific roles). There is, at the very top, a leadership composed of a few persons whose roles are widely varied and who can play, simultaneously, public spokesman, symbol of ideas, parliamentary leader or prime minister, and chief "organizer" of talent. Such leaders are characteristically "political entrepreneurs."[12]

Bureaucratic and durable parties require a stable governmental format, and they help to produce one. They draw their following from widely differing groups in the social stratification system, but they are substantially different from political movements, which also draw their support from widely differing groups in the social stratification system, insofar as they are not temporary amalgams of unhomogeneous elements. Such political parties are normally progressive or conservative and gain their flexibility by appealing to voters within the generally middle-class ranges of the social stratification system. These parties are possible, however, only where the stratification system is relatively wide in range and open in mobility. Bureaucratic and durable parties which do not find such a social stratification system are normally impossible to organize unless they transform the political format of government into a single party state, in which case the party oligarchy becomes the government oligarchy. The case of Turkey has, until recent years, been very instructive here.

The complete obverse of bureaucratic and durable political party leadership is that which is personal and fragile. Normally, in such patterns of leadership, a single figure exercises an extremely powerful moral and legitimizing influence. Members partake of his grace and are a chosen people or the carriers of a special mission. In its extreme form this is the type of leadership that Weber called "charismatic." In its more usual form it involves a highly personal type of control over followers which should not be confused with charisma[13] but which is dependent upon offices and rewards to be supplied by the leader for his followers and, most of all, upon the access to high positions in the social stratification system which the party makes possible.

Personal and fragile parties need crises in order to maintain their followings. Very often they require a revolutionary ideology, although in practice they may not be at all opposed to the social stratification system, but are merely interested in opening avenues for party members to the high power and prestige roles. This is certainly the case for Fascist parties, which characteristically have a "revolutionary" ideology before they assume office—hence recruiting the most mobility-conscious of those in the population whose index of commitment to the stratification system is high but whose opportunities for advancement within it are low—and a conservative ideology as soon as they achieve control of the government. And, because they are fragile, they must produce a state bureaucracy in the absence of a party bureaucracy (i.e., the leader may have followers who perform bureaucratic tasks), but the essence of bureaucracy is that it has regularized and institutionalized roles which cannot be arbitrarily dealt with. Personal and fragile political parties show a constant change in officers. The government, then, serves to produce the bureaucracy which is under the control of the party leader. Such a combination can work quite well until the problem of leader succession arises—a problem which few personal and fragile parties have been able to solve satisfactorily.[14]

This problem is adequately solved by personal and durable leaders. These are, characteristically, leadership roles in which the leader is not important as an individual but in which his position is intensely symbolic and mystical. Divine kingship is the classic example of such a position in government; others are provided by certain monarchical parties where a king or a pretender is in fact the party leader or figurehead in whose name a party leader operates. Personal and fragile parties must, over time, change into either bureaucratic and durable parties or personal and durable parties. An example of a partially unsuccessful attempt to make the transformation was demonstrated in the U.S.S.R. after the death of Lenin. Under Lenin's auspices it appeared as if the party would move more directly toward a bureaucratic and durable leadership. Under Stalin such a process became a menace to his own leadership autonomy, and, through purges and other means, such bureaucratization of the party was halted—though there was a great increase in government bureaucracy, as was discussed above—and, indeed, personal control constantly increased. It is particularly difficult for personal and fragile parties to maintain that type of leadership in systems of indirect representation (i.e., in democratic systems of government) and especially difficult where a single-member constituency parliamentary government is in operation. It is extremely useful to observe personal and fragile parties, which develop out of nationalist movements, in underdeveloped territories where colonial oligarchical governments have been displaced by European parliamentary forms of indirect representative government.

It is very difficult for personal and durable parties to operate for long periods in governments with indirect representation without changing the format of government to at least a nominal oligarchical format, as in Portugal. Equally, personal and durable parties can be transformed into bureaucratic and durable parties by a conflict between a monarchical system and leaders of personal and durable parties. This expresses itself simultaneously in a widening of recruitment to the political party and in demands for more representative government. It helps to explain the phenomenon of Tory radicalism in nineteenth-century England and the expansion of constitutional monarchy.

Personal and fragile political parties usually develop out of political movements catering to wide segments of the social stratification system. Personal and durable political parties usually develop out of select political associations having a narrow recruiting base in the social stratification system. Personal and durable parties are often associated with religious legitimacy, in which the role of the leader has personal characteristics of a sacral nature, while the occupant of the role may change.[15] In personal and fragile parties, it is the person occupying the leadership position who carries with him these characteristics; hence the difficulty of succession.

Bureaucratic and fragile parties are particularly significant where the stratification system is widely disjointed or membership is not on the basis of a movement but upon familiar linkages of social groups normally in contact with one another, such as with political associations based upon members of certain clubs, universities, occupational groups, and religious groups. Normally, they are held together by their overlapping membership in significant reference groups rather than by individual leaders, and they show a marked tendency to fission and reamalgamation with simply a reallocation of defined roles between members. Middle-class nationalist parties in colonial territories show that these propensities and parties break up and re-form with the same old faces and with only the party name being changed. Parliamentary party associations in nineteenth-century England showed some of these characteristics until they sought a more durable base among wider segments of the population dispersed throughout a social stratification system in which middle ranges were increasing. The same has been true in British colonial territories. A mass following helps produce a more stable bureaucracy in party leadership.

Very often, as a symptom as well as a cause of declining membership, a bureaucratic and durable party will transform itself into a bureaucratic and fragile party. This is particularly the case where substantial changes going on in the stratification system are not manifested in changes in the content of decisions in government, if such a party is in government, or if the government does not hold itself accountable to the party. If the index of commitment to the stratification system declines, then fission and fractionalization occurs in the bureaucratic and durable party, changing into a bureaucratic and fragile one. Normally, this is accompanied by growth of personal and fragile parties, especially those having a revolutionary ideology.

The type of party leadership, then, depends a great deal upon what is going on in the region of social stratification (i.e., its sources of recruitment) and its means and manner of representing those groups in relation to government. Personal and fragile parties have an affinity for oligarchical or dictatorial forms of government. Bureaucratic and durable parties have affinities for indirect representation systems of government. If the stratification system is such that the top positions are relatively narrow and closed, yet achievement criteria prevail with widely developed groups in the population having obtained such achievements, a personal and fragile movement is possible. This would promise, in itself, to become a social stratification system, since by virtue of membership it accords both power and prestige. Such situations are normally revolutionary, and, when the movement succeeds and takes over the government, it directs its effort to drastic economic and social reform. If it is to be successful, such reforms must accord a significant number of followers the fruits of revolution at the expense of former high-ranking status-holders. Most bloody revolutions are of this character. On the other hand, if the movement becomes a party and the index of commitment to the system is high enough, it may be possible to satisfy enough of the followers by giving them political appointments without changing the social stratification system. Both instances

are normally found in association with some form of state socialism. In the first instance, the new stratification system comes into being by the party capturing the government, changing its format if necessary, and substantially altering property relations via massive nationalization. In the second instance, property relations are not basically altered, but positions are created in conjunction with the already existing high status positions to be found. The first instance is characteristic of the Communist pattern and the second of the Fascist pattern.

Bureaucratic and durable parties normally are pushed along the same lines by the same impulses in the social stratification system. However, if they are working within the framework of parliamentary government, progressive reform rather than revolutionary change is characteristic. Much then depends upon how the structures of government are operated. Government may use its power of taxation and revenue allocation to minimize conflict in the social stratification sphere; indeed, it may do so drastically. But if the social stratification system is such that important groups in the poulation are highly resistant to such reform (such as in the case of modern France), it is quite possible that government will not be able to carry out its functions. Such impotence will provide opportunities for a drastic change in the society itself.

Personal and fragile parties and movements thrive when changes in social stratification produce uncertainty in social and economic life and in their most extreme case establish a system of legitimacy at variance with that of government. They can produce chaos by making it impossible for the government to carry out any or all of the structural requisites of government. If bureaucratic and durable parties are to be able to cope with such conditions in the social stratification system (which may be produced by depression, or plague, or a host of circumstances), they require a format of government in which the structure of accountability and consent and the structure of authoritative decision-making reflect both the needs and the demands of the population. Normally, a bureaucratic and durable party has a better awareness of incipient discontent in the members of the society and can reflect that awareness within the decision-making apparatus of a representative system of government. Totalitarian or oligarchical governments reach their maximum efficiency just after there has been a dramatic system change and the leaders are in close identification with the public, and, increasingly, they grow remote from the needs and the requirements of the public. Hence they grow increasingly restrictive, and, normally, decision-making is in terms of a postponed goal which has a sentimental and historical attachment to the issues which gave rise to the movement or party in the first place, while they seek to demonstrate their achievements in the future rather than the present.

If these totalitarian or oligarchical governments can accord sufficient satisfactions throughout a changing social stratification system to keep the public reasonably happy, it is possible for them to make their governmental format more representative, increase the accountability of the government, and change the party into a more bureaucratic and durable type. Some observers see signs of this process occurring in the social stratification system in the U.S.S.R. In some underdeveloped territories where a personal and fragile political movement has been transformed into a party operating a parliamentary government, either there must be enough commitment to the social stratification system for governmental activities to be not the exclusive concerns of members of society or the government system must be made oligarchic or dictatorial.[16] When economic entrepreneurship is possible as a major means of reform, this is normally the case. Otherwise the political entrepreneurs transform themselves into economic entrepreneurs through the mechanism of state enterprise.

The impulses thus deriving from types of political group leadership strongly affect the way in which both government format and social stratification will be manifested in society. The activities of government and the social stratification system give rise to types of political group leadership. Such leadership reflects ideological positions which range in their degree of commitment to the social stratification system. The range itself, as a reflection of political group identification with the stratification system, can be specified as follows: *revolutionary* (i.e., a complete system change) and *progressiste* (i.e., extensive alteration in social stratification in any of the categories which describe it, such as changes from achievement rather than ascriptive eligibility to status, or extending or narrowing the range of participation). A *conservative* ideology involves maintenance of substantially the same structure of social stratification with only minor changes. A *revivalist* ideology seeks to restore an already altered social stratification system. Political ideas can serve under more than one of these categories. For example, Communist political ideas are conservative in the contemporary U.S.S.R., according to this usage of ideology, but are revolutionary in the French Cameroons. Political groups of various types can subscribe to various of these ideological positions and can change over time. The National Socialist party of Germany, for example, showed elements of revivalism in its mythology, "revolutionaryism" before the SA purge, and conservatism for most of its governmental tenure. The Reassemblement Démocratique Africaine in French West Africa shows considerable Marxist influence yet remains *progressiste* in its ideology, and has a pragmatic approach aimed at gauging public demands for changes in the social stratification system without allowing

Communist dogma to direct party programs and actions.

Types of leadership can strongly affect the type of ideological position taken, particularly in the case of personal and fragile political groups which (1) feed on crises of increasing intensification, (2) make manifest latent disaffiliation of the public from the system of social stratification, and (3) if they push the government to decisions which contradict their position, or make active the structure of coercion and punishment are forced to an increasingly revolutionary position. This is particularly true where they seek by means of strikes or paramilitary operations to make the structure of coercion and punishment inoperative, hence making government inoperative. Such political groups would require a revolutionary ideology both to justify their position with their following and to seek to create a new kind of society. In underdeveloped areas nationalist movements are normally not of this type. They seek to throw out oligarchical colonial regimes, making them representative, and, by the use of electoral machinery, to take control and then seek reform. Thus they are mostly *progressiste,* although the actual slogans and ideas may sound revolutionary. An excellent example of this is the case of Ghana, where the Convention People's party is today in control of an independent country within a British-type parliamentary system of government, pushing toward moderate reform in the social stratification system. However, if under such circumstances the personal leadership of the party should fail, and the party, becoming more bureaucratic, show signs of fragility, it is possible that the government bureaucracy and the apparatus of the state power can be transformed into the personal weapon of the party leader, and the format of government can change to dictatorship or oligarchy, carrying a revolutionary ideology. The social stratification system would be altered or constrained as the case might be.

However, the range of possibilities open to political leaders is not only dependent upon the social stratification system and the format of government. Much depends on the characteristics of political group membership.

A diagram of leadership and ideological characteristics can be made as [shown on p. 90].

### The Structure of Membership

Variations in leadership patterns and ideology reflect the type of membership which obtains in a political group, whether a movement, a party, or an association. The first basic distinction is whether or not the political group is an *elite* or a *mass* organization. Normally, elite political groups are composed of narrow segments of the social stratification system or of people who have by some means "removed" themselves from it, as in the case of the bourgeois origins of many Communist party members. Where they seek a mass following, they form a party within a movement. An elite political group may or may not have strict rules of membership. Communist or Fascist parties normally do so; so may some nationalist parties which have their roots in situations where they were originally proscribed by governments and therefore show earmarks of operating illegally. Some elite parties openly do not want mass followings, for example, a political party in Uganda which identified itself as a party of "leaders" (i.e., the best people). Such an elite is a "weightier party" type of organization which seeks to influence others by the distinction of the membership.

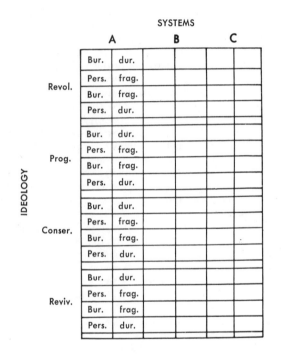

Many of the characteristics of party leadership will also depend upon whether the organization, elite or mass as the case might be, is *urban* or *rural* dominant, *territorial* or *supraterritorial* in those it seeks to affiliate, and *ethnic* or *regional* in its scope.

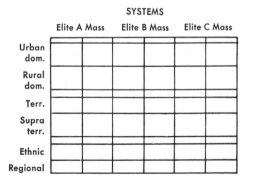

Ethnic and/or regional groups, particularly if they are rural-dominant, mass political movements or political parties, tend to push for local autonomy within a given territory and demand a federal system of government if they support a system of indirect representation and if the ethnic group is smaller than the government of the entire country. They may vary in their ideology, but, if the rural population is poor and disgruntled, and the leadership is urban-dominant, they normally push toward a *progressiste* system of reformism. If the leadership is personal and fragile, and especially if the membership is predominantly rural, this may quickly take the form of a revivalist ideology.

Urban-dominant elite parties, normally territorial in scope, may, depending upon how they recruit from the social stratification system, produce a bureaucratic and fragile leadership, as in the classic case of small, middle-class political parties which show fission and fusion and a conservative or *progressiste* ideology. If they recruit from a disinherited and disenfranchised group in the social stratification system, and if they are barred by an oligarchical government from effective participation, they are likely to produce a personal and fragile leadership moving toward a revolutionary ideology; while an equivalent group which is rural-dominant and ethnic-dominant is normally personal and durable in its leadership and revivalist in its ideology. This is particularly the case in some tribal societies existing in the context of a colonial oligarchical regime, such as the Bataka party in Uganda, and, among right-wing monarchical rural parties in some European countries having indirect representation, for example, in prewar France and Weimar Germany.

Occasionally, a situation exists in which an elite party forms an elect within a political movement, with a personal and durable leadership, an elite membership urban-dominant and supraterritorial in its scope. Communist parties show some of these characteristics, the binding force being a revolutionary ideology reinforced by government actions which use against them the structures of decision-making, coercion and punishment, and sometimes revenue assessment and allocation. Their relative strength depends in large part upon the index of commitment to stratification. If it is high, Communist parties are relatively powerless, and, if it is low, they can be relatively powerful. Insofar as systems of government having indirect representation with bureaucratic and durable parties are normally most capable of determining what the index of commitment is, they are usually the most effective in resisting party activities. The least effective are oligarchical or totalitarian systems, unless they are constantly transforming the social stratification system.[17]

There are special problems when dealing with political parties which are themselves elites, such as a Communist party which bases its ultimate strength upon a number of factors which might be crucial for the Communist party, but for no other party which would normally abide by the more general rules of the game. Hence tactics and strategy for a Communist party, and often a Fascist party, in a parliamentary setting has dangers to that setting which do not normally obtain. However, elite parties which are revolutionary in their ideology require a mass following, that is, people who may belong to a movement but are not, strictly speaking, allowed into the party itself. Now a characteristic of a movement is that, while it may have a well-defined goal, the goal must be ideologically diffuse. It cannot be narrowly programmatic, since movements usually recruit from a wide range of groups having relatively different positions in the social stratification system. The only exception is where a system has a dominant single class, like a working class, more or less permanently disbarred from high positions, as in classic Marxian doctrine. In practice this has been not very rare. Even in Asia movements have been rural in recruitment and urban in leadership with propensities for splitting apart with an increase in programing and scheduling political targets.

Communist parties, particularly in Europe, have the special problem of defining goals more narrowly for their members than for their followers, that is, for those in the movement which support the party. This increases the need for secrecy among party members and builds characteristics of control and discipline into the party which complement other reasons for control and discipline, such as subversion or capturing control of voluntary associations.

In addition, movements, as we have said, are normally "mass type." In classic Leninist doctrine, Communist party membership must remain small and fulfil vanguard functions. Party discipline does not extend to the movement. Hence there must be a considerable degree of symbolic representation of both persons and issues and a high degree of personalization of leadership, which is done less for the sake of party members than for the followers of the movement. A Communist party, therefore, becomes an elect inside a movement with a double standard of behavior, one for members of the party acting as party members and another for members of the party working to rally the movement. Indeed, this situation prevailed in the U.S.S.R. to a large extent. Stalin's crime was to personalize himself to party members as well as to followers of the movement —hence the special sense of outrage in decrying the cult of personality.

Movements are characteristic of certain types of nationalist political groups. In underdeveloped areas they encompass members having regional and ethnic affiliations as well. In Nigeria this has produced political parties which range in their ideology from (1) conservative (the Northern People's party), (2) *progressiste* but dominated by a bureaucratic and durable chiefs' and middle-class leadership (Action Group), and (3) *progressiste* with a more radical program and a clearly urban leadership (the National Council of Nigeria and the Cameroons).

There can be considerable confusion between the broadly based, mass political party, such as those in this country, and a movement. Normally, mass political parties do not require much participation by members except at election time. A movement, on the other hand, tends to be aroused by an issue or series of issues which challenge the status quo in some fundamental manner; while mass parties in substance require the maintenance of the system as it stands. Hence mass parties do not challenge the legitimacy of government, although they might question its activities, that is, they will seek to manipulate and change the content of decisions but not the structure of decision-making. Movements, furthermore, require periodic manifestations of the loyalty of followers in a variety of activities and institutions (protest, strikes, petitions, special organizations like special schools, etc.). They surround their leaders with a mystique. They need considerable solidarity, which mass political parties do not. Their leadership is ordinarily personal and fragile or personal and durable.

Movements are characteristic of those societies in which commitment to the social stratification is low, and they normally change into parties of a mass type, or disintegrate. When an elect exists inside the movement, it tends to become dangerous, because it is difficult to control except by dramatic changes in the social stratification system which are normally brought about by the elect capturing the government and promulgating drastic reconstruction in society or by becoming extraterritorial in scope. Egypt under President Nasser is a case in point; here the extraterritorial basis of the movement is along ethnic lines (pan-Arabism), internal reform is extremely difficult, and the symbolic mystique of the leader personal and fragile. Leadership could become personal and durable, as is true of some other Arab groups, by increasing the religious nature of its leadership, and a pseudo-papal Islamic religious role could be made out of the leadership position.

These additional aspects of political group structure, then, set limiting conditions upon the development of leadership and ideology in political groups. Each of the possible combinations produce different possible consequences and, taken together with the other elements of this comparative scheme, should (a) increase the ability of a research worker to make predictions about the outcome of a given state of affairs in politics and (b) generate theories on the basis of comparative treatment.

It should be possible to outline major consequences of structural relations between types of party organizations and types of government format, for example, modified by the performances of each, the seriousness of which can be measured in the degree to which they support or hinder government in carrying out its structural requisites—in turn, crucial for the maintenance of a given system. For example, when there are bureaucratic and fragile parties participating in a system of government which is indirectly representative (of the parliamentary type), party tendencies to fission produce multiple parliamentary party situations. Multiple parliamentary party situations emphasize differences between parties. Emphasis on differences produces (1) coalitions for government-forming purposes and (2) appeals to voters at the two opposite ends of the political spectrum (i.e., appeals to extremes). Appeals to extremes are modified by immediate coalition prospects and by electoral support, plus potential support of uncommitted voters to an opposition coalition. This is in large part determined by the degree of commitment which exists in the social stratification system.

Bureaucratic and durable parties tend to form middle-spectrum coalitions when there is a multiple-party system in parliament. Where there is a two-party system in parliament, the programs of the government party and the opposition party tend constantly to identity up to the point where marginal voters cease to prefer one party or the other.

Personal and durable parties tend toward a high degree of "traditionalistic" authoritarianism in which tendencies toward fission within the party are regarded as tantamount to treason. In a parliamentary setting they normally form a solid bloc and rarely have wide support, except in theocratic types of societies, and they prefer oligarchical government to indirect representative government.

Personal and fragile parties are dependent upon their degree of deviation from the social stratification system as it stands and cannot long endure under conditions of parliamentary government. They therefore seek to undermine it or else to transform themselves into bureaucratic and durable parties with the same leadership maintained intact. This has been particularly true of political parties which have developed out of a special "struggle," whether in Europe, where the struggle was against a given form of oligarchy with changes sought in both the system of stratification and the format of government, or in underdeveloped areas attacking colonialism and, as a result, achieving self-government. Ghana, Indonesia, and Malaya are all interesting countries to compare in this latter regard.

combinations of these variables in action. If comparative analysis is to be effective, some such treatment is essential. The essence of this approach involves an examination of sample issues which are thrown up for government to deal with, particularly those which imply threats to the structural requisites of any government. Any research done in these terms would therefore, first of all, require a delimitation of core issues which, related to social stratification, on the one hand, and manifested in political group activity, on the other, specify how differing governments, in differing formats, deal with them. The structural requisites of any government then give a guide to the limits of variation to which governments may be subject without being destroyed, and their actual operations in terms of these structures gives a guide to how well they are able to perform.

The possible empirical combinations of these variables are very great. Only a few possible combinations have been discussed. In this respect, as we have indicated, the scheme is very inelegant. It does not have precision. Much of it would be difficult, though hopefully not impossible, to operationalize for fine treatment. A wide variety of research techniques would be appropriate to its use. Refinements in comparative criteria would be essential.

Most of all, a careful comparison of differing societies and their governments can indicate some of the conditions necessary for the working of democracy, an especially acute question in those parts of the world where democratic institutions are new, their social bases weak, and governments are in the position of seeking social change while remaining able to control it. Oligarchical governments and totalitarianism are common, and we know some of the pressures which produce them. Can some of these same pressures be utilized for the working of modern democratic governments as well? In this respect we know far less about the potentialities of democracy than oligarchy. It is through the comparative analysis of democracies under widely differing conditions and through time that we can learn something about their potentialities and ultimate compatability with drastic social change. Equally, a study of some of the newer governments round the world should help to produce a genuine theory of democratic government—a theory having practical as well as ethical implications for our times.

## CONCLUSION

The foregoing represents a "prolegomene" to a comparative method. It seeks to produce theories by developing a scheme in which by comparative treatment of many instances, it is possible to see

## NOTES

1. The model can be stated as follows:

Time 1: $[ss] \rightarrow [pf + pl] \rightarrow [govt] \rightarrow (sr + format)$
$\quad\quad\quad 1 \quad\quad\quad 2 \quad\quad\quad\quad\quad 3$

$$[pf + pl] \rightarrow [ss] \text{ Time 2}$$
$$\quad 4 \quad\quad\quad\quad 5$$

$ss$ = social stratification system
$pf$ = party following (composition)
$pl$ = party leadership
$govt$ = government in terms of:
(a) $sr$ = structural requisites
(b) format = type determined by degree of representativeness

2. Vinogradoff has argued that "we must begin by ascertaining whether certain fundamental ideas recurring in various combinations may be traced as elements of the institution. If such elements exist, the work of each one ought to be analyzed as far as possible by itself before the ways in which it combines with other materials can be studied. The materials for such an analysis may be drawn from a broad and comprehensive collection of ethnological data, because it is only in this manner that we can make sure that nothing essential has escaped our observation" (Paul Vinogradoff, *Outline of Historical Jurisprudence* [New York: Oxford University Press, 1920], I, 93 and 167).

3. This methodological scheme represents work done by the author in conjunction with his colleagues on the West African Comparative Analysis Project. The members of this project are James S. Coleman (University of California at Los Angeles), Gray Cowan (Columbia University), Robert A. Lystad (Tulane University). The work of this group has been made possible through a grant from the Carnegie Corporation, to which gratitude is hereby expressed.

4. More specifically, the concern here is to produce a system of comparative analysis which is integrated with real research. We are not concerned with the basic properties of system qua system. We are concerned here with the treatment of empirical systems in general through the comparative observation of empirical systems in particular. In other words, we are concerned with characteristics which mediate between the most highly general (any system) and the most specific (system $x$), so that we can discuss regularities and irregularities in the variables of systems $x_{1, 2, 3, \ldots} n$.

There are, of course, special difficulties involved in doing comparative work at the gross data level. Analytical categories in use are hard to operationalize for purposes of rigorous manipulation. Scaling techniques seem the most favorable for much of the data-gathering. Another difficulty is that the higher the degree of control over the variables, i.e., the more selectivity employed, and the more precise the operations performed upon them, the lower is the degree of control over the parameters. Testing by other means is difficult because (1) a small data unit may simply affirm general system properties, (2) a small data unit may not exhibit equivalent variables, and (3) criteria of validation are difficult to specify.

5. See Émile Durkheim, *The Division of Labor* (New York: Free Press, 1947), *passim;* and Reinhard Bendix, "Social Stratification and Political Power," *APSR,* Vol. XLVI (June, 1952).

6. Parsons notes: "It has come to be rather widely recognized in the sociological field that social stratification is a generalized aspect of the structure of all social systems, and that the system of stratification is intimately linked to the level and type of integration of the system as a system" (Talcott Parsons, "A Revised Analytical Approach to the Theory of Social Stratification," in Reinhold Bendix and Seymour Lipset [eds.], *Reader in Social Stratification* [New York: Free Press, 1957]). See also S. F. Nadel, *The Theory of Social Structure* (New York: Free Press, 1957), chap. iv.

7. This definition is by no means unusual. A similar one has most recently been put forward by Bertrand de Jouvenel (*Sovereignty* [Chicago: University of Chicago Press, 1957], p. 20).

8. Applications and discussion of the structural requisites of government are given much fuller treatment in another paper, "Government and Economic Growth," in *Economic Development and Cultural Change,* January, 1959.

9. We do not have space for a genuine discussion of this structural requisite. It is strategic from a research point of view as well. If a content analysis is done, for example, on sample legislation in a given area and work can be done on the initiation and direction of bills (or other forms of decisions like orders or commands, etc.), then considerable information about the responsiveness of government can be elicited, along with patterns of leadership and autonomy in government. For a useful discussion of decision-making see R. C. Snyder, H. W. Bruck, and B. Sapin, *Decision-making as an Approach to the Study of International Politics* ("Foreign Policy Analysis Project," Series No. 3 [Princeton, N.J., 1954]).

10. It is held here that even dictators are accountable in some measure to groups in the system. They will normally "spread" that accountability in such fashion that no crucial accountability group can challenge authority. Indeed, many of the crises of dictatorial regimes arise because it is difficult to keep the distribution of accountability such that it does not limit the autonomy of the dictator. The ultimate accountability group in democratic systems is the total responsible and adult membership of the system, i.e., where there is universal suffrage. This represents a residual accountability. Interesting combinations occur where the two extremes merge, i.e., where effective dictatorship occurs with maximum support as expressed in universal suffrage or some equivalent. Popular radical dictatorships are of this nature.

11. For a general discussion of the relationship between party, government, and stratification see M. Duverger, *Political Parties* (London: Methuen & Co., 1954), *passim.* A detailed, if at times unorthodox, discussion of the consequences of differing electoral systems applicable to systems of indirect representation can be found in J. F. S. Ross, *Elections and Electors* (London: Eyre & Spottiswoode, 1955).

12. For a discussion of functionality and bureaucracy see D. E. Apter and R. Lystad, "Bureaucracy, Party and Constitutional Democracy," in G. Carter and W. O. Brown (eds.), *Transition in Africa: Studies in Political Adaptation* (Boston: Boston University Press, 1958).

13. The term "charismatic" has become ill used. Charisma is a most unusual phenomenon and does simply refer to personal magnetism on the part of a leader. Properly speaking, charisma involves special qualities of grace and legitimization which are deeply spiritual and profound (see Max Weber, *The Theory of Social and Economic Organization,* trans., Alexander Morell Henderson and Talcott Parsons [Edinburgh: William Hodge & Co., 1947]).

14. The Spanish example is instructive here, since Generalissimo Franco has apparently chosen to restore the monarchy (i.e., personal and durable leadership) to succeed himself.

15. An excellent example of this in the United States is afforded by the Mormons.

16. When personal and fragile leaders working within a parliamentary system need to change the format of government in order to preserve their leadership, the modern pattern of Populist or radical totalitarianism (which in modern times begins with Napoleon) produces leaders who prefer totalitarianism to oligarchy on the grounds that the former is more "democratic" or at least more compatible with fervent ideals. An oligarchy tends to create a specially privileged group in the social stratification system, while with radical dictatorships oligarchies can be removed. Indeed, this is implicit in the communism of both Leninists and Titoists, and only when it is discovered that a new oligarchy can emerge not based on actual ownership of property is there awareness of how "mischievous" is the doctrine. A good, yet pathetic, example of this "awareness" is to be found in Milovan Djilas, *The New Class* (New York: Frederick A. Praeger, 1957). See also Ernst Cassirer, *The Myth of the State* (New Haven, Conn.: Yale University Press, 1946).

17. They may do this by dramatic economic change (difficult without weakening the entire system), purges, changes in role occupants but not roles, etc.

III

# III Constitutional and Representative Government

# Introduction

## CONSTITUTIONAL ENGINEERING AND THE PROBLEM OF VIABLE REPRESENTATIVE GOVERNMENT

Harry Eckstein

I

Among the many subjects dealt with in comparative politics, pride of place must go, if only for reasons of past emphasis, to the study of representative, constitutional governments. "Representative government" here means government in which leaders are recruited through open and regular competitive processes, "constitutional government," that the scope and procedures of decision-making are defined by formal-legal rules— rules that serve at once as sources of and limitations upon official power. Anyone not too fastidious about terminology may call such governments "democracies" if he wishes.

A generation or so ago, a reader in comparative politics would have been devoted almost exclusively to this subject. Moreover, the selections would have displayed considerable confidence in the viability of representative institutions, in some cases indeed a belief in the inevitability of successful representative government once a nation has reached a certain decent level of "civilization." At the very least, successful cases of representative government, like those of Britain and the United States, would have been considered entirely "normal" (that is, not particularly in need of explanation). Unsuccessful cases, like those of Italy and Germany, would have been treated as the results of aberrations of one sort or another: the dislocations of war, the psychological effect of a supposedly vindictive peace, inflation, depression, and so forth.

Partly because of this comfortable belief in the normality of viable representative and constitutional government, partly for other reasons, the analyses of political scientists would have dealt primarily with issues raised by formal rules and institutions: whether representative governments should use majority electoral systems, proportional representation, or some particular version of one or the other; whether parliamentary government is superior to presidential government, or vice versa; whether the executive should have the power to dissolve the legislature, and, if so, on what terms; whether formal provision should be made for executive emergency powers, and how these provisions should be defined; what formal procedures should be used to exact accountability of bureaucrats; on what terms legislative power should be delegated; whether legislative chambers should be rectangular or semicircular, speakers neutral or partisan, constitutions easily amendable or not; and so on through a host of similar issues.

This emphasis on the formal structures of representative government reflected the belief that, even under very troublesome circumstances, representative government could survive and effectively perform its tasks if only it were rightly constructed —if only executive powers were wisely defined, executive-legislative relations correctly ordered, or electoral systems arranged so as to assure what Bagehot considered the *sine qua non* of parliamentary government, steady and reliable majorities.

Why, for example, did the Nazis come to power in Germany? In the first place, because of the great depression of the early thirties, the great inflation of the early twenties, and the Treaty of Versailles—historic accidents rather than forces emanating from the very character of German society. But, worse than this, the Germans used some very ill-advised formal institutions and procedures. They used proportional representation to elect their members of parliament; they made their Chancellor responsible to both the Reichstag and

the President; and they did not sufficiently circumscribe executive emergency powers or the executive's power of dissolution. And, apart from all
that, Nazism itself would only be a passing aberration in the history of a highly civilized and progressive nation, an adjustment to temporary crisis,
and an attempt to modify an impossible institutional
structure.

In short, it was widely assumed, not much more
than a generation ago, that viable representative
government was nothing less than a corollary of
civilized life; that, apart from the inherent processes of history, it depended—if it depended on
anything—only on the proper arrangement of its
formal parts and reasonable good luck in economic
life and international affairs; and that good structure would serve even in the absence of good luck.
This assumption, to be sure, was not implied in
all works in comparative politics, but it was far
more common to hold such views than contradictory positions, even in the wake of the collapse
of the German Weimar Republic and despite the
growing influence of the political sociologists.

Today, representative government still occupies
the center of the stage (though the stage is much
more crowded) in comparative politics. The whole
approach to the subject, however, has undergone
a marked change. What seemed axiomatic about
representative institutions a generation or so ago
now seems profoundly problematic, or even obviously false.

No one can really believe any longer in the
inevitability of effective and stable democracy without being blind to the most palpable facts of the
political world. Totalitarianism seems entirely able
to entrench itself successfully, and indeed to do
so by means once considered the best safeguards
of popular democracy, like universal education,
mass communications, and a high level of industrial
production. Nontotalitarian autocracies are still
common, and in the developing areas, with very
few exceptions, representative and constitutional
government exists only in the most minimal sense,
if that. Many countries in these areas seem indeed
to have rejected the classic forms of representative government as inappropriate to their social
structures or political purposes.

At the same time, it is more difficult now to
have faith in the viability of representative institutions where they already exist in highly developed form, indeed even where there is a good deal
of commitment to them. The collapse of Italian
democracy in the early twenties and of German
democracy in the early thirties, the *immobilisme*
of the French Third and Fourth Republics and
the dissolution of the latter in violence, the question marks still hanging over the ultimate fate of
de Gaulle's Republic and of Bonn—all these, and
other instances, shed doubt on the ability of representative institutions to function well, or indeed

survive, at least in certain contexts. We have every
reason today to wonder just what conditions are required if representative government is to be viable,
simply because so many nonviable representative
systems have existed even in countries possessing
a rather advanced level of "civilization" (if by
this one means such things as industrialization, urbanization, mass education and communications,
specialization, the prevalence of rationalistic activity and universalistic patterns, and the relatively
small significance of primary group relations and
greater significance of secondary organizations).

A good deal has happened also to shake our
faith in the power of well-conceived formal constitutional structure to bring effectively functioning
government into being. For one thing, political
scientists now know a great deal more than in
the past about the social and economic bases of
political activity, about social forces that exert
their weight through any formal structure. Political
scientists also now know much more than in the
past about the significance of informal political
processes—that is to say, the tendency of actual
political practices to diverge from those prescribed
in formal-legal documents, openly or covertly, as
a result of a society's political habits, or the needs
of its more powerful interests, or the exigencies of
administration and policy-making in the age of
positive government and cold war. These alone are
enough to make one wonder about the effects formally prescribed procedural rules can have on the
operation of representative governments, and further reasons for doubt are furnished by the many
apparently well-conceived constitutions that failed
utterly to survive or really to guide political behavior.

The constitution of the German Weimar Republic, for example, which was carefully engineered
by extremely well-informed and thoughtful people,
was proclaimed in its day as the most perfect of
democratic constitutions. Yet it culminated within
a decade and a half in rampant totalitarianism and
worked very badly while in existence. The constitution of the Fourth Republic made a number of
innovations designed to avert the worst faults of
the Third—for example, requiring governments to
resign only if defeated by an absolute majority of
the members of the National Assembly (not just a
majority of those voting) in order to avoid excessive ministerial instability. Yet governments under
the Fourth Republic were even more short-lived
on the average than governments under the Third,
not least because they tended to resign even when
not constitutionally required to do so. And why?
Because of French political traditions, which an
obscure clause in a little-read document could
hardly hope to change, because of one of the most
basic exigencies of government—the fact that it
made little sense for a cabinet to linger in office
without being able to make policy—and because

the effectiveness of French cabinets was undermined not so much by negative votes in the Assembly as by dissensions among ministers themselves, representing as they did a great many political parties with a great variety of political outlooks and supporters.

One could multiply such cases at great length from the history of recent "constitutional engineering" and indeed find even worse examples. Some of the most striking are provided by postwar Italy, where some constitutional provisions (like those on regionalization) have been blatantly ignored, others (like the provisions on the constitutional court) implemented late and half-heartedly, to the detriment of the prestige and power of the institution, and still others (like many sections in the constitution's grandiose bill of rights) treated as mere pious generality, unrealizable in practice.

We do not want to paint too black a picture. On the face of it, there is about as much to be said on one side of these issues as the other. Although we can no longer believe that representative government is inevitable in history and entirely appropriate to the human condition in all but rude societies, we have as little reason to believe that viable representative government is impossible. It exists in Britain, Scandinavia, the United States, and the older Commonwealth countries, it may be coming into existence in present-day Germany, and it may yet come into existence in France. At the same time, not all tinkering with formal structure has been in vain; for example, the present salutary state of the German party system surely owes something to the provisions of the Bonn Basic Law relating to political parties, and much has been claimed (with some reason) for the efficacy of Article 67 of the Basic Law, the article requiring a "constructive" vote of confidence if an incumbent government is to be forced to resign.

Rather than rejecting old beliefs, we want only to subject them to inquiry. What precisely are the conditions that make viable representative government possible? Are they common or uncommon, likely to be found only in special cases or in the ordinary case? What contribution can formal constitutions make to the viability of representative governments, and how has this problem been regarded, by politicians and political scientists? Can the over-all arrangement of government make a difference—that is to say, do presidential governments, for example, have any inherent advantages over parliamentary governments, or the latter over the former? Can constitutional structure, even if not itself capable of producing viable representative government, be so related to social conditions that it can push a system significantly in the direction of viability?

These are the most significant questions in the study of constitutional and representative government today, and they are explicit or implicit in most of the selections that follow. The questions are not finally answered in these selections, simply because political scientists are still busily engaged in formulating and testing their hypotheses. But the readings should at least help to clarify and to focus the problems, as well as suggesting possible solutions and ways of putting such solutions to the test; and they will certainly indicate how much work and reflection are now required before we can again speak on these issues with the assurance of our forebears.

## II

The first three selections in this section (from J. S. Mill's *Representative Government,* Bryce's *Modern Democracies,* and H. J. Laski's *A Grammar of Politics*) represent the chief pre-modern classics on representative government, those written before the appearance of two works that are still, for all their shortcomings, the best general modern treatments of the subject, Friedrich's *Constitutional Government and Democracy* (discussed at length in Part I of this Reader) and Herman Finer's *Theory and Practice of Modern Government* (dealt with more briefly in the concluding essay). These selections are included mainly to convey some of the flavor of the works from which they are taken, not because they represent accurately and unequivocally the older attitudes toward representative government or even the attitudes of their authors. Mill, Bryce, and Laski were far too wise to accept the old beliefs about representative government whole hog and too sophisticated to have easily classifiable views of their own. Nevertheless, one can detect in their work more than mere echoes of these old beliefs, in what they argued for, and, at times, in what they sought to refute.

Take the very beginning of Mill's *Representative Government:*

By some minds government is conceived as strictly a practical art, giving rise to no questions but those of means and an end. Forms of government are assimilated to any other expedients for the attainment of human objects. They are regarded as wholly an affair of invention and contrivance. Being made by man, it is assumed that man has the choice either to make them or not, and how or on what pattern they shall be made. Government, according to this conception, is a problem, to be worked like any other question of business. The first step is to define the purposes which governments are required to promote. The next, is to inquire what form of government is best fitted to fulfil those purposes. Having satisfied ourselves on these two points, and ascertained the form of government which combines the greatest amount of good with the least of evil, what further remains is to obtain the concurrence of our countrymen, or those for whom the institutions are intended, in the opinion which we have privately arrived at. To find the best form of government; to persuade others that it is the best; and having done so, to stir them up to insist on having it, is the order of ideas in the minds of those who adopt this view of political philosophy. They look upon a constitution in the same light (difference of scale being allowed for) as they would upon a steam plough, or a threshing machine.

Mill thought this view to be absurd if accepted without qualification; in that he is very much with the moderns. But he considered equally absurd the contrary view: that governments should be regarded "as a sort of spontaneous product," that they cannot be constructed by premeditated design, but "just grow" from the nature and life of a people, "a product of their habits, instincts, and unconscious wants and desires, scarcely at all of their deliberate purposes." In his opening paragraphs, Mill thus squarely straddles one of the basic issues raised here: whether and to what extent it is possible to create effective representative government by "invention and contrivance." Despite this noncommittal beginning, however, the whole tenor of his work is in favor of constitutional engineering, and he displays throughout much greater faith in representative institutions than even optimists would allow themselves today.

Take first his views on the likelihood of effective representative government. Provided only that the character of a people is in some fundamental way appropriate to it, viable representative government can be, in Mill's view, effectively constructed anywhere. As to the kind of people required for it, his demands are very modest. He seems to think, in fact, that the necessary human traits are likely to exist in all but the rudest, the most primitive, peoples, those who "have still to learn the first lessons of civilization." Representative government, he thinks, requires a people that at least is not deeply opposed to it, a people not highly apathetic toward politics, not completely submissive to authority, and yet not completely unruly and anarchic. These, obviously, are not very stringent requirements, and Mill seems to think that they are more likely to be satisfied than not among peoples some way beyond the state of savagery.

Mill also has considerable faith in the power of human contrivance in affairs of government. The chapter of his essay reproduced here, dealing with the proper functions of representative bodies, shows this confidence. Only the purest of democrats could take it as an attack on representative institutions. It is really an analysis of the functions best assigned to a legislature if its work and that of the whole government is to be done well. Its maxims, although obviously derived from British experience, are meant to inform the contrivers of representative governments everywhere. This optimism about the possibility of constructing governments so as

to assure their effectiveness emerges also, even more clearly perhaps, from other parts of the work.

Take as an example his views on electoral systems. Mill thinks, his general optimism notwithstanding, that in civilized societies, representative government does face two important dangers: political ignorance, especially among the lawmakers, and the possibility that particular "sinister interests" might dominate the government. But he also argues that both these evils can be averted by a single structural device, a kind of cure-all for the various ills of representative systems: the adoption of Hare's system of proportional representation. This electoral system was designed to mirror the various shades of opinion and interests in the society better than the still existing British system of constituency representation. Mill believed that it would not only do that, preventing the dominance of special interests in government, but that it would somehow improve the quality of a nation's legislators into the bargain.

Many further examples of Mill's faith in structural and procedural contrivance can be found throughout the rest of his work: in the chapters on modes of voting, the duration of parliaments, the role and composition of second chambers, the recruitment and structure of the executive and judiciary, the role of local government, and the conditions under which federal government is preferable to unitary government.

As we have stated, Mill was too wise ever to be simple. While his essay is at bottom a eulogy of the representative system, his faith in representative institutions does not go unqualified. He is aware of the need for some sort of popular agreement on such institutions, though, interestingly enough, he does not speak of a need for consensus on their desirability, as would modern political scientists, but rather of the absence of consensus on their undesirability—and there *is* a difference. For all his faith in democracy, he is at least slightly aware of its dangers when it is too pure; in the chapter here reproduced, for example, he insists on strong executive leadership and considerable executive autonomy, owing to the inherent limitations on government by a representative assembly. But if we subtract some of these intelligent complexities from his work, it may serve well enough as a sample of early attitudes toward representative government, particularly those of lesser men.

Mill's essay was first published in 1861. Bryce's *Modern Democracies,* which was analyzed at length in Part I of this book, and Laski's *A Grammar of Politics* both saw the light of day more than half a century later. Both should be regarded essentially as works of transition. There are new themes in them, but these themes become much more clamorous later and are often drowned out in their works by concerns and arguments about representative government of the traditional sort.

Bryce's work, for example, is certainly a defense of democracy against other forms of government, but his optimism in regard to democratic systems is tempered by important doubts—about the power of wealth and its corrupting effects, for example; about the tendency of democratic politicians to "play for votes" rather than making intelligent and necessary decisions; about the overbearing power of party organizations; and, most striking of all, about the inevitability of oligarchy in democracies, the rule of the few in the guise of the many. Yet there is scarcely a hint in Bryce's work of the problems besetting democratic government that would most concern political scientists today. He mentions ministerial instability, but does not speak of *immobilisme* and paralysis of the decision-making processes. Nor does he seem much worried about the ability of democracy to survive in the face of extremist attacks upon it, to hold fast popular allegiances once these allegiances are gained, and to realize the principal aspirations of a society.

Similarly, Bryce displays a considerable awareness of the impact on a political system of "objective" conditioning factors. (Note his discussion of the impingement of large-scale immigration and capitalist development on American politics, and the contrasts he makes between the politics of predominantly agricultural and largely industrial societies, especially his association of stability with an occupational structure predominantly based on land.) Yet he maintains also a considerable, if somewhat diluted, faith in constitutional engineering. Institutions, to be sure, can only "moderate or mitigate" the propensities inherent in human nature and social conditions, "but that which they can do is sufficient to make it worth the while of those who frame constitutions or lead reforming movements to study the institutions which have in one country or another given good results."

Laski, being a neo-Marxist, is much more aware than either Mill or Bryce of the social and economic foundations of political systems and behavior. "It is not likely," he points out in the selection reproduced below, "that the difficulties of the modern State are such as to be at all seriously remediable by reforms of electoral machinery"—or, presumably, other structural and procedural contrivances. "Mainly, those difficulties are moral in character. We shall meet them rather by the elevation of the popular standard of intelligence, and the reform of the economic system. . . ."

The same selection, however, also makes clear how very seriously he takes the particular arrangements of electoral systems, as well as a great many other matters of formal structure, even relatively minor ones. One should note in this connection his arguments in favor of the sanctification of formal rules in written constitutions themselves; his belief that Mussolini's rise to power was in some way aided by the brevity and vagueness of the Piedmont Statute, the only constitutional underpinning of the pre-fascist Italian representative system; and his elaborate arguments about the proper definition of amending procedures and the relative merits of federal and unitary systems.

Zurcher, in his introduction to the collaborative work, *Constitutions and Constitutional Trends Since World War II* (selections from which are reprinted in this part of our reader), overstates the degree of disillusion with constitutional engineering in the interwar period. Certainly he overstates his case for the early interwar years, the decade following 1918, which produced, after all, that most painstakingly contrived and fatally unfortunate of constitutions, the Weimar Constitution. (In this connection, note Loewenstein's remarks on constitution-making after the first World War, in the essay reprinted below.) By the late thirties, however, the disillusion with constitutional contrivance as well as with optimistic views of the viability of representative government was certainly well advanced.

This disillusion comes out even in the chapter from Friedrich's *Constitutional Government and Democracy* that follows the selections from the "classics" in the readings. The chapter is, of course, a defense of the value and political significance of written constitutions. Such constitutions are, Friedrich argues, real and autonomous political "forces"; but it is clear that Friedrich has in mind throughout another point of view, which he represents, curiously enough, by a quotation from Rousseau. This is the view that there is, or at any rate may be, a considerable difference between the ostensible (formal) and real constitutions of a country. The ostensible constitution is an artifact, something deliberately and consciously contrived. The real constitution, however, is not "graven on tablets of marble or brass, but on the hearts of the citizens"; in other words, it is a matter, in Mill's language, of actual habits, instincts, and unconscious wants, of "national feelings and character," the political reflexes of a people, as it were. Clearly this view must have been very much in the air for Friedrich to make it the touchstone of his analysis. And that analysis itself concedes more to it than might at first sight appear. Constitutions, argues Friedrich, may become autonomous political forces (that is, determinants of the characteristics and performance of political systems), but only if they reflect the real forces of opinion in a society. The real constitution gives force to the formal constitution, and having done so, the formal constitution may itself mold and shape political life, in ways transcending the habits and opinions that originally give it force.

We may take this argument as sufficiently representative of the views of most political scientists of the thirties. They no longer held the views that seem implicit in Mill; but they were, on the average, no more pessimistic about representative government or constitutional contrivances than Bryce or Laski. The situation today is very different.

Let us consider first attitudes toward constitution-making. In the essay mentioned above, Zurcher argues that a great disenchantment with nineteenth-century attitudes toward constitution-making is characteristic of the present day. He himself considers the social bases of politics infinitely more important and singles out for particular emphasis the existence or absence in a society of political consensus—agreement on the basic ends and means of politics. He is aware, of course, of the great energies expended in the postwar world on the contrivance of constitutions, not only in the new states but also in the reconstructed democracies of Western Europe: Germany, Italy, and France. (Between 1945 and 1950 alone some fifty nations acquired new constitutions, a number unparalleled in history.) He is also aware of the fact that these new constitutions tend to be far more ambitious—longer, more detailed, more rationally thought out—than were earlier constitutions and that many of them attempt to constitutionalize (that is, make subject to formal-legal and, hopefully, sacroscanct rules) matters once left everywhere to ordinary political processes. But he does not consider all this very significant. Rather he thinks of modern constitution-making as involving a good deal of mere ritual, a process by which new states, or states being reconstituted, acquire one of the recognized trappings of a modern political order.

In taking this view, Zurcher (and Loewenstein) may be attributing to the world of politics a mood much more prevalent in the world of political science (and by no means universal there). Undoubtedly, constitutions may be mere trappings for those autocratic states—mainly, but not only, Communist—that have acquired them in the postwar period. Undoubtedly also, the expectations that other nations rest in their new constitutions differ from those prevalent in earlier periods. No longer are written constitutions treated as tickets to Utopia, but this is not to say that they are not taken seriously. They may be, indeed are, taken seriously in different ways and for different reasons. In the new nations, they serve as a kind of surrogate tradition where no national political traditions could yet exist. They attempt to prescribe in formal-legal rules what in older nations might be matters of political instinct; hence, they are written at great length and in minute detail, as in the gargantuan Indian constitution.

In the older nations, the principal purpose of constitutions in the postwar period, as both Friedrich and Loewenstein point out, has been to prevent such evils of the past as ministerial instability, decisional paralysis, and the seemingly legitimate destruction of constitutional government by anticonstitutional conspirators. The new constitutions attempt to eliminate past evils by a better mechanical ordering of the political process, more elaborate and better safeguarded bills of rights, and the creation of judicial or quasi-judicial guardians of these rights and processes. To prevent catastrophe and to provide a basis for nationhood may be purposes less sublime than to achieve utopia, but they are serious and important purposes all the same. The vital fact is that postwar constitution-makers have all attributed at least the ability to prevent the worst to constitutional contrivances.

Even in this modest regard, however, the mood among most political scientists is certainly more pessimistic than among the politicians who made the postwar constitutions. As Loewenstein's essay shows, the old question of the formal versus the real constitution (he calls it the "nominal" versus the "living" constitution)—the "ontological" question of the relations between constitutional forms and social forces—is still central to the concerns of political scientists. Nowadays, however, much more is attributed to the social forces than in the past. We simply know too much now about the ways in which constitutional contrivances can be vitiated. They may be modified by usage, coming to embody more and more the very political habits they are supposed to shape. They may simply be ignored in practice— as the power of the executive to dissolve parliament atrophied from disuse in the Third Republic. Behavior may simply not fully conform to them. We also know a good deal now about the obscure and complicated forces that govern the distribution of power and the competition for offices and policy in any society; about the role and influence of informal political processes, like those of pressure groups; and about the importance of "political culture," the ingrained political values, beliefs, and symbols of a society, whether homogeneous or heterogeneous in character. It is certainly a mark of the times that in the readings on conditions of stable and effective democracy that conclude this part, constitutional structure should scarcely be mentioned. That would have been inconceivable a hundred, or fifty, or even thirty years ago.

That there is scarcely more optimism about the likelihood of viable representative government is also shown by these readings. Indeed, the prevalent pessimism about the survival value and decisional effectiveness of representative institutions emerges even from the tenor of the postwar constitutions. As we have pointed out, the overriding purpose of those who framed the constitutions of the newly reconstructed democracies was to protect them against possible disaster. Such a purpose obviously assumes the likelihood of disaster, and those who seek to achieve it must be many worlds removed from men who considered representative government natural to the condition of all but primitive societies. The theme that effective and stable democracy is somehow related to social development persists (note, above all, the essay by Lipset below), but conceptions of the requisites of effective democracy have become much more stringent and complicated. Not only that; the suspicion has grown in the process that these requisites are extremely difficult to satisfy—that, far from being normal, viable democracy may be the exception rather than the rule, even in very advanced societies. This is by no means established, but the possibility must certainly be entertained. At any rate it is very probable in view of recent political history and the fate of older theories of political science, that the roots of viable democracy lie very deep in the social order; and it is practically certain that they lie deeper than in constitutional contrivance. In what they lie, and how much "nominal" constitutions can affect actual political processes, remains to be established.

## III

We have restricted the selections reprinted in this part to those which raise the two fundamental problems of constitutional engineering and the requisites of stable representative government or consider very closely related issues (the role of constitutional courts and the relative merits of presidential and parliamentary systems). This restriction does not mean, of course, that representative government raises no other problems. Those we have singled out are certainly the most fundamental, but others are worth mentioning. For example, there are the problems of adapting institutions of representative government to the development of the social service (or welfare) state, not the least of which is the constant growth of the size and power of bureaucracy. A great many questions concern particular structural aspects of representative government: legislative procedure, the relations between the executive and the legislative branches, types of local government structure and relations between local and central government, the judiciary, the amending procedure, and so on. And many questions arise about the politics of representative systems: electoral processes, parties, and pressure groups.

The last three subjects are dealt with in other sections of the reader. The others we have omitted for a number of reasons. One is space: the subject of representative government is enormous and must here be restricted somehow, and we consider it more desirable to give some vital aspects of it a thorough airing than to allude superficially to all. Another is that the particular problems raised by bureaucracy and special aspects of constitutional structure have been little written about in a truly comparative manner; most studies of them are restricted to particular national contexts. A third is that the few more comprehensive and synthetic treatments of these subjects are quite readily available in other forms and can therefore be treated as readings supplementary to the present selections. We might briefly mention some works that ought to be used by readers who want to range wider than the selections here permit.

The best treatments of representative institutions in general are still C. J. Friedrich, *Constitutional Government and Democracy* and Herman Finer, *The Theory and Practice of Modern Government*, both originally published in the thirties and revised many times since. No one can consider himself fully informed on representative institutions without having read these works, and practically all particular institutional problems of representative government are dealt with in them. For a more recent treatment, H. J. Spiro, *Government by Constitution* (1960) may be recommended, but this book, precisely because it is more recent, focuses less upon institutions, especially formal ones, than the earlier syntheses.

On the whole, excellent treatments of the construction and contents of postwar constitutions can be found in Arnold Zurcher, *Constitutions and Constitutional Trends since World War II,* from which two essays are reprinted here. The other essays included in the volume should certainly be read, as should the references to the subject in Karl Loewenstein, *Political Reconstruction* (1946). Readers may want to supplement these general and comparative studies with works treating constitution-making in particular countries. For France, Gordon Wright, *The Reshaping of French Democracy* (1948), is by far the best work in English on the origins of the Fourth Republic, but a larger number of adequate studies are available on the shaping of the Fifth Republic, including Nicholas A. Wahl, *The Fifth Republic* (1959), Roy C. Macridis and Bernard E. Brown, *The de Gaulle Republic: Quest for Unity* (1960), and S. Hoffmann, "The French Constitution of 1958," *American Political Science Review,* June, 1959. For Germany, a comprehensive treatment is available in John F. Golay, *The Founding of the Federal Republic of Germany* (1958). This can be supplemented with C. J. Friedrich, "Rebuilding the German Constitution," *American Political Science Review,* June–August, 1949, and E. H. Litchfield (ed.), *Governing Post-War Germany* (1953). On constitution-making in Italy, almost nothing is available in English, except the references to the subject in Muriel Grindrod, *The Rebuilding of Italy* (1955).

Anyone who wishes to supplement the readings we have selected on conditions of stable and effective democracy should, above all, read fully the works from which these selections have been taken, adding to them one or two earlier thought-provoking studies, especially Erich Fromm, *Escape from Freedom* (1941), and H. D. Lasswell, *World Politics and Personal Insecurity* (1935). Studies of particular representative systems should of course be read to supplement these more general treatments, but bibliographies about such systems can be found in the standard texts on comparative politics (for example, Beer and Ulam, *Patterns of Government;* Taylor Cole, *European Political Systems;* Robert A. Neumann, *European and Comparative Government;* R. T. Shotwell, *Governments of Continental Europe;* Almond and Coleman, *The Politics of the Developing Areas*) and would take up far too much space here.

The same thing applies to studies of the workings of particular institutional arrangements. Only very few genuinely comparative works are available on these: for example, on federalism: K. C. Wheare, *Federal Government* (1946); on modern execu-

tives and bureaucracies: Jean Meynaud, "The Executive in the Modern State," *The International Social Science Bulletin,* Vol. X, No. 2 (1958), W. J. Siffin (ed.), *Toward the Comparative Study of Public Administration* (1957), and numerous articles in *The Administrative Science Quarterly;* and on executive emergency powers: Clinton Rossiter, *Constitutional Dictatorship: Crisis Government in the Modern Democracies* (1948). Such subjects as the role and definition of the power of dissolution, executive-legislative relations in general, and parliamentary procedure can still by and large be studied only in works dealing with particular governments.

*Classic Studies*

# OF THE PROPER FUNCTIONS
# OF REPRESENTATIVE BODIES

## John Stuart Mill

In treating of representative government, it is above all necessary to keep in view the distinction between its idea or essence, and the particular forms in which the idea has been clothed by accidental historical developments, or by the notions current at some particular period.

The meaning of representative government is, that the whole people, or some numerous portion of them, exercise through deputies periodically elected by themselves the ultimate controlling power, which, in every constitution, must reside somewhere. This ultimate power they must possess in all its completeness. They must be masters, whenever they please, of all the operations of government. There is no need that the constitutional law should itself give them this mastery. It does not in the British Constitution. But what it does give practically amounts to this. The power of final control

Reprinted from John Stuart Mill, *"On Liberty"* and *"Considerations on Representative Government,"* edited by R. B. MacCallum (Oxford: Basil Blackwell, 1948), pp. 161–174.

is as essentially single, in a mixed and balanced government, as in a pure monarchy or democracy. This is the portion of truth in the opinion of the ancients, revived by great authorities in our own time, that a balanced constitution is impossible. There is almost always a balance, but the scales never hang exactly even. Which of them preponderates is not always apparent on the face of the political institutions. In the British Constitution, each of the three co-ordinate members of the sovereignty is invested with power which, if fully exercised, would enable it to stop all the machinery of government. Nominally, therefore, each is invested with equal power of thwarting and obstructing the others: and if, by exerting that power, any of the three could hope to better its position, the ordinary course of human affairs forbids us to doubt that the power would be exercised. There can be no question that the full powers of each would be employed defensively if it found itself assailed by one or both of the others. What then prevents the same powers from being exerted aggressively? The unwritten maxims of the Constitution—in other words, the positive political morality of the country: and this positive political morality is what we must look to, if we would know in whom the really supreme power in the Constitution resides.

By constitutional law, the Crown can refuse its assent to any Act of Parliament, and can appoint to office and maintain in it any Minister, in opposition to the remonstrances of Parliament. But the constitutional morality of the country nullifies these powers, preventing them from being ever used; and, by requiring that the head of the Administration should always be virtually appointed by the House of Commons, makes that body the real sovereign of the State. These unwritten rules, which limit the use of lawful powers, are, however, only effectual, and maintain themselves in existence, on condition of harmonising with the actual distribution of real political strength. There is in every constitution a strongest power—one which would gain the victory if the compromises by which the Constitution habitually works were suspended and there came a trial of strength. Constitutional maxims are adhered to, and are practically operative, so long as they give the predominance in the Constitution to that one of the powers which has the preponderance of active power out of doors. This, in England, is the popular power. If, therefore, the legal provisions of the British Constitution, together with the unwritten maxims by which the conduct of the different political authorities is in fact regulated, did not give to the popular element in the Constitution that substantial supremacy over every department of the government which corresponds to its real power in the country, the Constitution would not possess the stability which characterises it; either the laws or the unwritten maxims would soon have to be changed. The British government is thus a representative government in the correct sense of the term: and the powers which it leaves in hands not directly accountable to the people can only be considered as precautions which the ruling power is willing should be taken against its own errors. Such precautions have existed in all well-constructed democracies. The Athenian Constitution had many such provisions; and so has that of the United States.

But while it is essential to representative government that the practical supremacy in the state should reside in the representatives of the people, it is an open question what actual functions, what precise part in the machinery of government, shall be directly and personally discharged by the representative body. Great varieties in this respect are compatible with the essence of representative government, provided the functions are such as secure to the representative body the control of everything in the last resort.

There is a radical distinction between controlling the business of government and actually doing it.

The same person or body may be able to control everything, but cannot possibly do everything; and in many cases its control over everything will be more perfect the less it personally attempts to do. The commander of an army could not direct its movements effectually if he himself fought in the ranks, or led an assault. It is the same with bodies of men. Some things cannot be done except by bodies; other things cannot be well done by them. It is one question, therefore, what a popular assembly should control, another what it should itself do. It should, as we have already seen, control all the operations of government. But in order to determine through what channel this general control may most expediently be exercised, and what portion of the business of government the representative assembly should hold in its own hands, it is necessary to consider what kinds of business a numerous body is competent to perform properly. That alone which it can do well it ought to take personally upon itself. With regard to the rest, its proper province is not to do it, but to take means for having it well done by others.

For example, the duty which is considered as belonging more peculiarly than any other to an assembly representative of the people, is that of voting the taxes. Nevertheless, in no country does the representative body undertake, by itself or its delegated officers, to prepare the estimates. Though the supplies can only be voted by the House of Commons, and though the sanction of the House is also required for the appropriation of the revenues to the different items of the public expenditure, it is the maxim and the uniform practice of the Constitution that money can be granted only on the proposition of the Crown. It has, no doubt, been felt, that moderation as to the amount, and care and judgment in the detail of its application, can only be expected when the executive government, through whose hands it is to pass, is made responsible for the plans and calculations on which the disbursements are grounded. Parliament, accordingly, is not expected, nor even permitted, to originate directly either taxation or expenditure. All it is asked for is its consent, and the sole power it possesses is that of refusal.

The principles which are involved and recognised in this constitutional doctrine, if followed as far as they will go, are a guide to the limitation and definition of the general functions of representative assemblies. In the first place, it is admitted in all countries in which the representative system is practically understood, that numerous representative bodies ought not to administer. The maxim is grounded not only on the most essential principles of good government, but on those of the successful conduct of business of any description. No body of men, unless organised and under command, is fit for action, in the proper sense. Even a select board, composed of few members, and these specially conversant with the business to be done, is always an inferior instrument to some one individual who could be found among them, and would be improved in character if that one person were made the chief, and all the others reduced to subordinates. What can be done better by a body than by any individual is deliberation. When it is necessary or important to secure hearing and consideration to many conflicting opinions, a deliberative body is indispensable. Those bodies, therefore, are frequently useful, even for administrative business, but in general only as advisers; such business being, as a rule, better conducted under the responsibility of one. Even a joint-stock company has always in practice, if not in theory, a managing director; its good or bad management depends essentially on some one person's qualifications, and the remaining directors, when of any use, are so by their suggestions to him, or by the power they possess of watching him, and restraining or removing him in case of misconduct. That they are ostensibly equal sharers with him in the management is no advantage, but a considerable set-off against any good which they are capable of doing: it weakens greatly the sense in his own mind, and in those of other people, of that individual responsibility in which he should stand forth personally and undividedly.

But a popular assembly is still less fitted to administer, or to dictate in detail to those who have the charge of administration. Even when honestly meant, the interference is almost always injurious. Every branch of public administration is a skilled business, which has its own peculiar principles and traditional rules, many of them not even known, in any effectual way, except to those who have at some time had a hand in carrying on the business, and none of them likely to be duly appreciated by persons not practically acquainted with the department. I do not mean that the transaction of public business has esoteric mysteries, only to be understood by the initiated. Its principles are all intelligible to any person of good sense, who has in his mind a true picture of the circumstances and conditions to be dealt with: but to have this he must know those circumstances and conditions; and the knowledge does not come by intuition. There are many rules of the greatest importance in every branch of public business (as there are in every private occupation), of which a person fresh to the subject neither knows the reason or even suspects the existence, because they are intended to meet dangers or provide against inconveniences which never entered into his thoughts. I have known public men, ministers, of more than ordinary natural capacity, who on their first introduction to a department of business new to them, have excited the mirth of their inferiors by the air with which they announced as a truth hitherto set at nought, and brought to light by themselves, something which was probably the first thought of everybody who

ever looked at the subject, given up as soon as he had got on to a second. It is true that a great statesman is he who knows when to depart from traditions, as well as when to adhere to them. But it is a great mistake to suppose that he will do this better for being ignorant of the traditions. No one who does not thoroughly know the modes of action which common experience has sanctioned is capable of judging of the circumstances which require a departure from those ordinary modes of action. The interests dependent on the acts done by a public department, the consequences liable to follow from any particular mode of conducting it, require for weighing and estimating them a kind of knowledge, and of specially exercised judgment, almost as rarely found in those not bred to it, as the capacity to reform the law in those who have not professionally studied it. All these difficulties are sure to be ignored by a representative assembly which attempts to decide on special acts of administration. At its best, it is inexperience sitting in judgment on experience, ignorance on knowledge: ignorance which, never suspecting the existence of what it does not know, is equally careless and supercilious, making light of, if not resenting, all pretensions to have a judgment better worth attending to than its own. Thus it is when no interested motives intervene: but when they do, the result is jobbery more unblushing and audacious than the worst corruption which can well take place in a public office under a government of publicity. It is not necessary that the interested bias should extend to the majority of the assembly. In any particular case it is often enough that it affects two or three of their number. Those two or three will have a greater interest in misleading the body than any other of its members are likely to have in putting it right. The bulk of the assembly may keep their hands clean, but they cannot keep their minds vigilant or their judgments discerning in matters which they know nothing about; and an indolent majority, like an indolent individual, belongs to the person who takes most pains with it. The bad measures or bad appointments of a minister may be checked by Parliament; and the interest of ministers in defending, and of rival partisans in attacking, secures a tolerably equal discussion: but *quis custodiet custodes?* who shall check the Parliament? A minister, a head of an office, feels himself under some responsibility. An assembly in such cases feels under no responsibility at all: for when did any member of Parliament lose his seat for the vote he gave on any detail of administration? To a minister, or the head of an office, it is of more importance what will be thought of his proceedings some time hence than what is thought of them at the instant: but an assembly, if the cry of the moment goes with it, however hastily raised or artificially stirred up, thinks itself and is thought by everybody to be completely exculpated however disastrous may be the consequences. Besides, an assembly never personally experiences the inconveniences of its bad measures until they have reached the dimensions of national evils. Ministers and administrators see them approaching, and have to bear all the annoyance and trouble of attempting to ward them off.

The proper duty of a representative assembly in regard to matters of administration is not to decide them by its own vote, but to take care that the persons who have to decide them shall be the proper persons. Even this they cannot advantageously do by nominating the individuals. There is no act which more imperatively requires to be performed under a strong sense of individual responsibility than the nomination to employments. The experience of every person conversant with public affairs bears out the assertion, that there is scarcely any act respecting which the conscience of an average man is less sensitive; scarcely any case in which less consideration is paid to qualifications, partly because men do not know, and partly because they do not care for, the difference in qualifications between one person and another. When a minister makes what is meant to be an honest appointment, that is when he does not actually job it for his personal connections or his party, an ignorant person might suppose that he would try to give it to the person best qualified. No such thing. An ordinary minister thinks himself a miracle of virtue if he gives it to a person of merit, or who has a claim on the public on any account, though the claim or the merit may be of the most opposite description to that required. *Il fallait un calculateur, ce fut un danseur qui l'obtint* is hardly more of a caricature than in the days of Figaro; and the minister doubtless thinks himself not only blameless but meritorious if the man dances well. Besides, the qualifications which fit special individuals for special duties can only be recognised by those who know the individuals, or who make it their business to examine and judge of persons from what they have done, or from the evidence of those who are in a position to judge. When these conscientious obligations are so little regarded by great public officers who can be made responsible for their appointments, how must it be with assemblies who cannot? Even now, the worst appointments are those which are made for the sake of gaining support or disarming opposition in the representative body: what might we expect if they were made by the body itself? Numerous bodies never regard special qualifications at all. Unless a man is fit for the gallows, he is thought to be about as fit as other people for almost anything for which he can offer himself as a candidate. When appointments made by a public body are not decided, as they almost always are, by party connection or private jobbing, a man is appointed either because he has a reputation, often quite undeserved, for *general* ability, or frequently for no better reason than that he is personally popular.

It has never been thought desirable that Parliament should itself nominate even the members of a Cabinet. It is enough that it virtually decides who shall be prime minister, or who shall be the two or three individuals from whom the prime minister shall be chosen. In doing this it merely recognises the fact that a certain person is the candidate of the party whose general policy commands its support. In reality, the only thing which Parliament decides is, which of two, or at most three, parties or bodies of men, shall furnish the executive government: the opinion of the party itself decides which of its members is fittest to be placed at the head. According to the existing practice of the British Constitution, these things seem to be on as good a footing as they can be. Parliament does not nominate any minister, but the Crown appoints the head of the administration in conformity to the general wishes and inclinations manifested by Parliament, and the other ministers on the recommendation of the chief; while every minister has the undivided moral responsibility of appointing fit persons to the other offices of administration which are not permanent. In a republic, some other arrangement would be necessary: but the nearer it approached in practice to that which has long existed in England, the more likely it would be to work well. Either, as in the American republic, the head of the Executive must be elected by some agency entirely independent of the representative body; or the body must content itself with naming the prime minister, and making him responsible for the choice of his associates and subordinates. To all these considerations, at least theoretically, I fully anticipate a general assent: though, practically, the tendency is strong in representative bodies to interfere more and more in the details of administration, by virtue of the general law, that whoever has the strongest power is more and more tempted to make an excessive use of it; and this is one of the practical dangers to which the futurity of representative governments will be exposed.

But it is equally true, though only of late and slowly beginning to be acknowledged, that a numerous assembly is as little fitted for the direct business of legislation as for that of administration. There is hardly any kind of intellectual work which so much needs to be done, not only by experienced and exercised minds, but by minds trained to the task through long and laborious study, as the business of making laws. This is a sufficient reason, were there no other, why they can never be well made but by a committee of very few persons. A reason no less conclusive is, that every provision of a law requires to be framed with the most accurate and long-sighted perception of its effect on all the other provisions; and the law when made should be capable of fitting into a consistent whole with the previous existing laws. It is impossible that these conditions should be in any degree fulfilled when laws are voted clause by clause in a miscellaneous assembly. The incongruity of such a mode of legislating would strike all minds, were it not that our laws are already, as to form and construction, such a chaos, that the confusion and contradiction seem incapable of being made greater by any addition to the mass. Yet even now, the utter unfitness of our legislative machinery for its purpose is making itself practically felt every year more and more. The mere time necessarily occupied in getting through Bills renders Parliament more and more incapable of passing any, except on detached and narrow points. If a Bill is prepared which even attempts to deal with the whole of any subject (and it is impossible to legislate properly on any part without having the whole present to the mind), it hangs over from session to session through sheer impossibility of finding time to dispose of it. It matters not though the Bill may have been deliberately drawn up by the authority deemed best qualified, with all appliances and means to boot; or by a select commission, chosen for their conversancy with the subject, and having employed years in considering and disgesting the particular measure; it cannot be passed, because the House of Commons will not forgo the precious privilege of tinkering with it with their clumsy hands. The custom has of late been to some extent introduced, when the principle of a Bill has been affirmed on the second reading, of referring it for consideration in detail to a Select Committee: but it has not been found that this practice causes much less time to be lost afterwards in carrying it through the Committee of the whole House: the opinions or private crotchets which have been overruled by knowledge, always insist on giving themselves a second chance before the tribunal of ignorance. Indeed, the practice itself has been adopted principally by the House of Lords, the members of which are less busy and fond of meddling, and less jealous of the importance of their individual voices, than those of the elective House. And when a Bill of many clauses does succeed in getting itself discussed in detail, what can depict the state in which it comes out of Committee! Clauses omitted, which are essential to the working of the rest; incongruous ones inserted to conciliate some private interest, or some crotchety member who threatens to delay the Bill; articles foisted in on the motion of some sciolist with a mere smattering of the subject, leading to consequences which the member who introduced or those who supported the Bill did not at the moment foresee, and which need an amending Act in the next session to correct their mischiefs. It is one of the evils of the present mode of managing these things, that the explaining and defending of a Bill, and of its various provisions, is scarcely ever performed by the person from whose mind they emanated, who probably has not a seat in the House. Their defence rests upon some minister or member of Parliament who did not frame them, who is dependent on cramming for all his arguments but those which are perfectly obvious, who does not know the full strength of his case, nor the best reasons by which to support it, and is wholly incapable of meeting unforeseen objections. This evil, as far as Government bills are concerned, admits of remedy, and has been remedied in some representative constitutions, by allowing the Government to be represented in either House by persons in its confidence, having a right to speak, though not to vote.

If that, as yet considerable, majority of the House of Commons who never desire to move an amendment or make a speech would no longer leave the whole regulation of business to those who do; if they would bethink themselves that better qualifications for legislation exist, and may be found if sought for, than a fluent tongue and the faculty of getting elected by a constituency; it would soon be recognised that, in legislation as well as administration, the only task to which a representative assembly can possibly be competent is not that of doing the work, but of causing it to be done; of determining to whom or to what sort of people it shall be confided, and giving or withholding the national sanction to it when performed. Any government fit for a high state of civilization would have as one of its fundamental elements a small body, not exceeding in number the members of a Cabinet, who should act as a Commission of legislation, having for its appointed office to make the laws. If the laws of this country were, as surely they will soon be, revised and put into a connected form, the Commission of Codification by which this is effected should remain as a permanent institution, to watch over the work, protect it from deterioration, and make further improvements as often as required. No one would wish that this body should of itself have any power of *enacting* laws: the Commission would only embody the element of intelligence in their construction; Parliament would represent that of will. No measure would become a law until expressly sanctioned by Parliament: and Parliament, or either House, would have the power not only of rejecting but of sending back a Bill to the Commission for reconsideration or improvement. Either House might also exercise its initiative, by referring any subject to the Commission, with directions to prepare a law. The Commission, of course, would have no power of refusing its instrumentality to any legislation which the country desired. Instructions, concurred in by both Houses, to draw up a Bill which should effect a particular purpose, would be imperative on the Commissioners, unless they preferred to resign their office. Once framed, however, Parliament should have no power to alter the measure, but solely to pass or reject it; or, if partially disapproved of, remit it to the Commission for reconsideration. The Commissioners should be appointed by the Crown, but should hold their offices for a time certain, say five years, unless removed on an address from the two Houses of Parliament, grounded either on personal misconduct (as in the case of judges), or on refusal to draw up a Bill in obedience to the demands of Parliament. At the expiration of the five years a member should cease to hold office unless reappointed, in order to provide a convenient mode of getting rid of those who had not been found equal to their duties, and of infusing new and younger blood into the body.

The necessity of some provision corresponding to this was felt even in the Athenian Democracy, where, in the time of its most complete ascendancy, the popular Ecclesia could pass Psephisms (mostly decrees on single matters of policy), but laws, so called, could only be made or altered by a different and less numerous body, renewed annually, called the Nomothetæ, whose duty it also was to revise the whole of the laws, and keep them consistent with one another. In the English Constitution there is great difficulty in introducing any arrangement which is new both in form and in substance, but comparatively little repugnance is felt to the attainment of new purposes by an adaptation of existing forms and traditions. It appears to me that the means might be devised of enriching the Constitution with this great improvement through the machinery of the House of Lords. A Commission for preparing Bills would in itself be no more an innovation on the Constitution than the Board for the administration of the Poor Laws, or the Inclosure Commission. If, in consideration of the great importance and dignity of the trust, it were made a rule that every person appointed a member of the Legislative Commission, unless removed from office on an address from Parliament, should be a Peer for life, it is probable that the same good sense and taste which leave the judicial functions of the Peerage practically to the exclusive care of the law lords, would leave the business of legislation, except on questions involving political principles and interests, to the professional legislators; that Bills originating in the Upper House would always be drawn up by them; that the Government would devolve on them the framing of all its Bills; and that private members of the House of Commons would gradually find it convenient, and likely to facilitate the passing of their measures through the two Houses, if instead of bringing in a Bill and submitting it directly to the House, they obtained leave to introduce it and have it referred to the Legislative Commission. For it would, of course, be open to the House to refer for the consideration of that body not a subject merely, but any specific proposal, or a Draft of a Bill *in extenso,* when any member thought himself capable of preparing one such as ought to pass; and the House would doubtless refer every such draft to the Commission, if only as materials, and for the benefit of the suggestions it might contain; as they would, in like manner, refer every amendment or objection which might be proposed in writing by any member of the House after a measure had left the Commissioner's hands. The alteration of Bills by a Committee of the whole House would cease, not by formal abolition, but by desuetude; the right not being abandoned, but laid up in the same armoury with the royal veto, the right of withholding the supplies, and other ancient instruments of political warfare, which no one desires to see used, but no one likes to part with, lest they should at any time be found to be still needed in an extraordinary emergency. By such arrangements as these, legislation would assume its proper place as a work of skilled labour and special study and experience; while the most important liberty of the nation, that of being governed only by laws assented to by its elected representatives, would be fully preserved, and made more valuable by being detached from the serious, but by no means unavoidable, drawbacks which now accompany it in the form of ignorant and ill-considered legislation.

Instead of the function of governing, for which it is radically unfit, the proper office of a representative assembly is to watch and control the government: to throw the light of publicity on its acts: to compel a full exposition and justification of all of them which any one considers questionable; to censure them if found condemnable, and, if the men who compose the government abuse their trust, or fulfil it in a manner which conflicts with the deliberate sense of the nation, to expel them from office, and either expressly or virtually appoint their successors. This is surely ample power, and security enough for the liberty of the nation. In addition to this, the Parliament has an office, not inferior even to this in importance; to be at once the nation's Committee of Grievances, and its Congress of Opinions; an arena in which not only the general opinion of the nation, but that of every section of it, and as far as possible of every eminent individual whom it contains, can produce itself in full light and challenge discussion; where every person in the country may count upon finding somebody who speaks his mind, as well or better than he could speak it himself—not to friends and partisans exclusively, but in the face of opponents, to be tested by adverse controversy; where those whose opinion is overruled, feel satisfied that it is heard, and set aside not by a mere act of will, but for what are thought superior reasons, and commend themselves as such to the representatives of the majority of the nation; where every party or opinion in the country can muster its strength, and be cured of any illusion concerning the number or power of its adherents; where the opinion which prevails in the nation makes itself manifest as prevailing, and marshals its hosts in the presence of the government, which is thus enabled and compelled to give way to it on the mere manifestation, without the actual employment, of its strength; where statesmen can assure themselves, far more certainly than by any other signs, what elements of opinion and power are growing, and what declining, and are enabled to shape their measures with some regard not solely to present exigencies, but to tendencies in progress. Representative assemblies are often taunted by their enemies with being places of mere talk and *bavardage*. There has seldom been more misplaced derision. I know not how a representative assembly can more usefully employ itself than in talk, when the subject of talk is the great public interests of the country, and every sentence of it represents the opinion either of some important body of persons in the nation, or of an individual in whom some such body have reposed their confidence. A place where every interest and shade of opinion in the country can have its cause even passionately pleaded, in the face of the government and of all other interests and opinions, can compel them to listen, and either comply, or state clearly why they do not, is in itself, if it answered no other purpose, one of the most important political institutions that can exist anywhere, and one of the foremost benefits of free government. Such "talking" would never be looked upon with disparagement if it were not allowed to stop "doing"; which it never would, if assemblies knew and acknowledged that talking and discussion are their proper business, while *doing,* as the result of discussion, is the task not of a miscellaneous body, but of individuals specially trained to it; that the fit office of an assembly is to see that those individuals are honestly and intelligently chosen, and to interfere no further with them, except by unlimited latitude of suggestion and criticism, and by applying or withholding the final seal of national assent. It is for want of this judicious reserve that popular assemblies attempt to do what they cannot do well—to govern and legislate—and provide no machinery but their own for much of it, when of course every hour spent in talk is an hour withdrawn from actual business. But the very fact which most unfits such bodies for a Council of Legislation

qualifies them the more for their other office—namely, that they are not a selection of the greatest political minds in the country, from whose opinions little could with certainty be inferred concerning those of the nation, but are, when properly constituted, a fair sample of every grade of intellect among the people which is at all entitled to a voice in public affairs. Their part is to indicate wants, to be an organ for popular demands, and a place of adverse discussion for all opinions relating to public matters, both great and small, and, along with this, to check by criticism, and eventually by withdrawing their support, those high public officers who really conduct the public business, or who appoint those by whom it is conducted. Nothing but the restriction of the function of representative bodies within these rational limits will enable the benefits of popular control to be enjoyed in conjunction with the no less important requisites (growing ever more important as human affairs increase in scale and in complex) of skilled legislation and administration. There are no means of combining these benefits except by separating the functions which guarantee the one from those which essentially require the other; by disjoining the office of control and criticism from the actual conduct of affairs, and devolving the former on the representatives of the Many, while securing for the latter, under strict responsibility to the nation, the acquired knowledge and practised intelligence of a specially trained and experienced Few.

The preceding discussion of the functions which ought to devolve on the sovereign representative assembly of the nation would require to be followed by an inquiry into those properly vested in the minor representative bodies, which ought to exist for purposes that regard only localities. And such an inquiry forms an essential part of the present treatise; but many reasons require its postponement, until we have considered the most proper composition of the great representative body, destined to control as sovereign the enactment of laws and the administration of the general affairs of the nation.

# MODERN DEMOCRACIES

James Bryce

## COMPARISON OF THE SIX DEMOCRATIC GOVERNMENTS EXAMINED

The examination contained in Part II [of *Modern Democracies*] of the institutions which Democracy has given itself in different countries and of the phenomena which their working in each has shown needs to be completed by a comparison of those phenomena, for the rule of the people, taking in each different forms, has shown resemblances as well as diversities, both in the spirit which the institutions evoked and in the tangible results that have followed. No democratic government is typical; each has its merits, each its faults; and a judgment on democratic institutions in general can be formed only by observing which faults are most frequent, and how far each of these is specially characteristic of Democratic government, or rather belongs to Human Nature as displayed in politics. This chapter [Chapter 67 of *Modern Democracies*] is meant to present the comparison in three ways:

First by noting the salient features of popular government in each of the six countries examined, and what each has contributed to political science in the way of example or warning.

Next by showing in which of those countries and to what extent in each the faults commonly charged on democratic government exist.

Thirdly by noting the presence in each country of what may be called the mental and moral coefficients, viz. those qualities in a people that help democracy to work its institutions in the right way, so as to obtain in the largest measure the benefits which governments have been established to secure.

I begin with a brief statement of the features most characteristic of each country.

### I. Summary View of Salient Features

In France administration is highly centralized, much business which is in English-speaking coun-

tries left to local authorities being managed by officials who are appointed by and take their orders from the central government, so local self-government, narrowly circumscribed in its functions, and exciting little interest, does comparatively little for the political education of the people. France, having so far as methods of administration go, preserved the inheritance of the old monarchy, is the least democratic of democracies, for State authority is strong against the individual citizen. Yet although Government is strong, Ministries are unstable, because dependent on majorities in the legislature which fluctuate under the influence, sometimes of party passion, sometimes of personal intrigues. The legislature, or rather its directly elected branch, the Chamber of Deputies, is master of the political situation, and its individual members control individual Ministers, obtaining from them as the price of their support favours for their respective constituencies, and by means of these favours holding their own seats. In matters of moment the Second Chamber, largely composed of able and experienced men with a longer tenure of their seats, exerts a useful guidance or restraint, and the high average quality of the Civil Service makes administration efficient.

Behind both deputies and Ministers stand the great financiers, powerful through their wealth and the influence it enables them to exert upon the newspapers. Their influence, though sometimes steadying, can also be baneful, for it may induce the sacrifice of national interests to private interests, and it has sometimes enveloped public men in a mist of suspicions. The sky is seldom free from signs of storm, for fifty years of republican government have not assuaged the bitterness which divides the various parties, yet the faults of politics which sometimes seem to be a game played in the legislature by a comparatively small class, have not seriously affected the strength and progress of the nation.[1] Foreigners have judged France too much by its politics and its politicians, underrating its spirit and vitality and stability.

The emergence of strong organizations advocating communistic doctrines, and accentuating antagonism between classes, are phenomena now visible all over the world, and the revolutionary movements thence arising would be more threatening under a less popular constitution. French democracy, with difficulties to face greater than any that have tested the other countries we have surveyed, has nevertheless brought the nation safely through a time of unprecedented perils.

Switzerland presents a striking contrast. Nowhere is administration so decentralized, for functions and powers are parcelled out not only between the Federal and the Cantonal Governments, but also between the Cantons and the Communes. The people are called upon to take a more direct and constant part in public work than any other State requires from its citizens, being accustomed to review by their votings the measures passed by their legislatures; and the citizens can, by the Initiative, put forward, without consulting those bodies, legislative proposals which popular voting adopts or rejects. The practice of local self-government has trained the people to fulfill these functions efficiently, keeping their attention fixed upon those who represent them in their assemblies or are entrusted with official business. Party spirit is comparatively free from virulence; elections have aroused little passion; the same member is returned time after time to the legislatures; the same members are retained for many years in the Administrative Councils. The less agreeable side of what may be called "small scale politics" appears in the petty intrigues which affect elections to minor posts in some Communes and Cantons. Though the absence of corruption, both in the Federal and in Cantonal Governments, and the high standard maintained in public life for many years, are partly due to the absence of those temptations which men of great wealth can apply to politicians, much must also be ascribed to the vigilance of public opinion in small communities. In no democracy has the power of money counted for so little, in none has political life had so few prizes to offer. But after all, the most interesting lesson it teaches is how traditions and institutions, taken together, may develop in the average man, to an extent never reached before, the qualities which make a good citizen—shrewdness, moderation, common sense and a sense of duty to the community. It is because this has come to pass in Switzerland that democracy is there more truly democratic than in any other country.

As France shows at its maximum the power of the legislature,[2] and Switzerland the power of the body of citizens voting directly, so the United States is the best example of the strength which party organizations can attain and the control they can wield. Legal authority, divided between the Federal Government and the Governments of the several States, is in both divided also between the elected Executive and the two elected houses of the legislature, the frequently recurring differences between which complicate both administration and legislation. Such co-operation as is needed to make the machinery work is created by the party organizations, which nominate for election both the representatives and (in the several States) the higher officials in each State as well as its Executive head; and as persons elected in the same area at the same time usually belong to the same party, both officials and representatives are expected to carry out its policy. The work which the organizations have to discharge has called into being a large class of professional politicians who live off the offices which they are able to secure for themselves and the various gains which fall to those who can exert private influence. Next to the power of Party, the most salient features of the United States system are the wide application of popular election to the choice of officials, including judges, and the recent introduction in many States of direct popular legislation in the form of Initiative and Referendum, as also of direct popular action on administration in the provisions for the Recall of executive and judicial officials by popular vote. Thus the inordinate number of elections throws on the voter more work than he can properly discharge.

Two of the faults charged on government in the United States are due to exceptional causes. That the Money Power has attained such huge proportions as to assail the virtue of officials and demoralize some State legislatures, must be largely ascribed to the prodigious fortunes which the swift development of a new country's resources created, the possessors of which found it worth while to buy favors from politicians who had them to sell. Similarly, the worst scandals of municipal misgovernment appeared where a sudden influx of old-world immigrants flooded cities that were already growing fast, phenomena unforeseen by those who granted universal suffrage to ignorant crowds who had no interest in honest and economical administration. These supervenient factors have told heavily against the working of democratic institutions. As against the evils they have caused must be set two points in which the institutions of the country have won the praise of foreign observers. One is the action of the Federal Courts in so interpreting and prudently developing the Constitution as to enable it to work well under new conditions that have imposed a heavy strain upon it. Another is the practice of local self-government which, diffusing an amount of political knowledge and creating a sense of civic responsibility, is surpassed only in Switzerland. It has helped to develop that public spirit which has from time to time, and notably in recent years, carried through movements of sweeping reform by which the political atmosphere has been purified.

Canada, Australia, and New Zealand have in common the English frame of parliamentary government, but their economic and social conditions are sufficiently dissimilar to have imprinted a different character on its working in each country.

In Canada two-thirds of the population live by work on the land, and nearly all the farmers own the soil they till. This has given stability to political parties and to the government as a whole. Ministries last on an average ten times as long as does a Ministry in France or in Australia. The legislatures, especially in the Provinces, have not fully maintained the best traditions received from England, for both they and some members of the administrations they install in power have been suspected of abusing their position. Responsibility is, however, pretty well secured by the power of questioning and dismissing Ministers, justice is honestly administered, order is effectively maintained over a vast and thinly peopled Western territory, and the difficulties which the presence of two races speaking different languages presents have been surmounted.

In Australia, where nearly half the population is gathered into a few great cities, the wage-earning class has been fully organized and obtained a political power which in other countries it is still only seeking. The rich, among whom there are no millionaires, take little part, at least openly, in politics. Frequent and hard-fought strikes have roused class antagonisms. The Labour Party created in the legislatures caucuses which, working along with the Trade Councils outside, obtained complete control of the Federal Parliament, and at one time or another of each of the State Parliaments; and their action has shown how the essence of parliamentary government may be destroyed with an apparent respect for its forms. Bold experiments in extending State action to industrial undertakings and in fixing wages by State authority have been tried by Labour Ministries and by others which depended on Labour support, but, except during strikes, law and order as well as a creditable standard of administrative efficiency and judicial purity have been maintained.

New Zealand has an agricultural landowning population larger in proportion to the whole than in Australia, but smaller than in Canada. The urban hand-workers, though they have never obtained a majority in Parliament, have been strong enough to secure legislation which in some points anticipated that of Australia in extending State functions, fixing wages, and taking over branches of business or industrial production. Parties, less organized than in Australia, have been less strictly disciplined. As the dominance of the parliamentary caucus has been Australia's most distinctive contribution to the art of politics, so has State Socialism been the contribution of New Zealand. Ministries have been stable, and public business not ill managed, though with scant regard to economy and a tendency to purchase parliamentary support by improvident grants to local purposes. Apart from this form of jobbery, government has been honest, and except among the wage-earners who show their discontent by frequent strikes, a spirit of general good-will bears witness to the country's prosperity.

In these three British Self-governing Dominions members of the legislatures receive salaries, but no class of professional politicians has arisen except in so far as the officials of Trade or Labour Unions, occupying themselves with politics as well as with purely industrial matters, can be so described.

## II. Defects Observable in the Six Governments

a. INSTABILITY OF THE EXECUTIVE GOVERNMENT OWING TO FREQUENT CHANGES. This, most conspicuous in France, has been conspicuous in Australia also, both in the Commonwealth and the State Governments. In the United States it is prevented by the constitutional arrangements which install an administration for a fixed period. It is not seen in Canada and New Zealand, and least of all in Switzerland.

b. FAILURE OF THE EXECUTIVE TO MAINTAIN LAW AND ORDER. In America this is evident in some only of the States, where lynching and other disorders have been tolerated. Against none of the other democracies is it chargeable. Strike riots have been frequent in Australia, France, and New Zealand, to a less extent in Canada; and though such breaches of the law occur in all countries, they are doubtless more frequent and more serious where the fear of losing votes by offending strikers deters an Executive from action.

c. ADMINISTRATIVE EXTRAVAGANCE. Economy, once expected to be among the strong points of democracy, has proved to be its weakest. Financial waste is worst in the United States National Government, owing to the desire to win votes by grants from the public treasury to localities, but the same evil is rampant in Canada and New Zealand, and to a less extent in France and Australia.

d. WANT OF HONESTY IN ADMINISTRATORS, LEGISLATORS, AND VOTERS. Though no democracy has sunk so low as either the ancient republics or many autocracies, such as those of Russia, Turkey, and China, the atmosphere has not been altogether wholesome in France, in Canada, and in many of the American States. In the United States Federal Government the tone is now satisfactory. Bribery occurs sporadically in the United States and Canada, but to a less extent than it did in England before that country had been democratized. Australia, New Zealand, and Switzerland have a good record.

e. FAULTY ADMINISTRATION OF JUSTICE. In many of the American States where the Judicial Bench is filled by popular election, the Judges are far from competent; and in a few they are suspected of corruption. Everywhere the administration of criminal justice is so defective that a very high authority has called it "a disgrace to American civilization."[3] In France the inferior judges are not altogether trusted. In the other four countries the character of the Bench stands high.

*f*. THE SPIRIT AND POWER OF PARTY. Party spirit is no stronger in these democracies than it has often been under other governments, and it everywhere rises and falls according to the circumstances of the time. Party organization is a comparatively new phenomenon, first developed in the United States, where a strong and skilfully constructed system grew up between 1826 and 1860. It has rendered some services, but far greater disservices, in the land of its birth, and has been more or less imitated in Australia, New Zealand, Canada, and Great Britain, in all of which it is possibly the source of more evil than good. In France it counts for little, and in Switzerland for less.

*g*. PROFESSIONALISM IN POLITICS. The growth of a class which makes its living out of politics, due partly to the number of persons needed to work a party organization and partly to the existence of legislative and administrative posts sought as a livelihood and obtainable by party patronage, tends to pervert and even debase politics by making it a business occupation, in which the motive of civic duty is superseded by the desire of private gain. The class, large in the United States, exists in the other democracies, again excepting Switzerland, but is nowhere numerous, though it may increase with that raising of legislative salaries, recently effected in France and Australia, and now demanded in Britain, which makes a seat in the legislature more desired.

*h*. THE POWER OF WEALTH. Democracy was expected to extinguish this ancient evil, for every citizen is interested in preventing men from using money to secure gains for themselves at the expense of the community. It has, however, proved as noxious in republics as it was in the days when the favorites of kings could be bribed, though the methods now in use are less direct. Of the six countries, the United States has been that in which money has been most generally powerful during the last sixty years, France that in which it is probably most powerful now, while Canada comes next, Australia, New Zealand, and Switzerland being practically exempt, though of course a party or a group of men with ample funds for elections and able to run newspapers in its interest enjoys everywhere an advantage.

### III. Presence or Absence of Favouring Conditions

We have so far been considering the results which democratic institutions, differing more or less in their features, have produced in six countries. These results have, however, been due not merely to the greater or less excellence either of the institutions or of the external conditions of the countries described, but also to the intellectual capacity and public spirit of the peoples that work them. Let some paragraphs be therefore given to this branch of the comparison.

*a*. The intelligence of the Average man, and the sense of civic duty which leads him to try to understand and vote honestly upon the questions submitted at elections, are most largely developed in Switzerland, next in the United States, in Canada, and in New Zealand, with Australia perhaps a little behind. In France it is certainly not intelligence that is deficient, but a feeling among the peasantry and *petite bourgeoisie* that every citizen ought to make his opinion felt and his voice heard. As nothing approaching an absolute quantitative test can be applied to determine the volume of the health-giving ozone of public spirit in the atmosphere, one can do no more than conjecture whether it is increasing. In all the countries, France included, it seemed to me to be growing, though slowly, while improvement is perhaps most evident in the United States, where a reforming spirit is abroad.

*b*. The extent to which the best-educated class, including many besides those who would be called the intellectual *élite* of the nation, exert themselves in public affairs, is to be measured not merely by their taking a hand in legislative or administrative work, but also by the contributions they make to thought on public questions and by their influence in the formation of national opinion.

Here the results of observation are disappointing. The extension of the functions of government and the increasing magnitude and complexity of the subjects falling within those functions have not elicited a corresponding will to serve the community on the part of those best fitted to serve it. In some countries one is told of a decline: but this may be because the want is more felt, not because the supply has fallen off: there is not less water, but more thirst. It is in France that public life seems to draw out most brilliance of talent, in Switzerland the most of sober wisdom. In none of the other countries does the traveller feel that the class to which wealth or knowledge or capacity gives social influence is doing its full duty to the State. Administrative work attracts a fair number of competent men, but neither the legislatures nor more than a few of the Ministers seem equal to their tasks. The causes of this, already explained in the accounts given of each country, are much the same everywhere, but have in some been increased by the disposition to require from candidates a pledge to speak and vote with the majority of their party, whatever their individual opinion, a pledge which men of spirit refuse to give. It was thought, fifty years ago, that the extension of the suffrage and the growth of the sentiment of equality, coupled with the diffusion of education and the cheapening of elections, would draw new streams of talent, energy, and unselfish patriotism into the service of the State. But this has nowhere happened. Though the number of those who, belonging to classes formerly excluded, have now entered the legislatures, has increased, and though legislation is everywhere directed far more than formerly towards ameliorating the conditions of health and labour, there is no more talent, no more wisdom, no more of the disinterested zeal which subordinates all other interests to the common good. The more educated class, to whatever political party they belong, are in many countries heard to complain that public life is being vulgarized, that the laws which determine national prosperity are being misunderstood or ignored because abstract theories and vague sentimentalities fill the public mind, and that social classes are being alienated from one another for want of mutual understanding and the sense of a common interest. If and so far as there is any truth in these complaints, is not a principal cause to be found in the failure of the most educated and most thoughtful to take the part that belongs to them in public life?

*c)* The existence of a sentiment of national unity and of an intelligently active public opinion. These two things go together, for if the former be weak, if the clashing of sectional interests and tenets diverts each section from its loyalty to the common good, sympathy is chilled and reciprocal comprehension lessened. I have dwelt in a previous chapter (Chapter XV [of *Modern Democracies*]) on the advantages of government by Public Opinion as compared with the mechanical though indispensable methods of government by voting, and have sought to show that the value of Public Opinion depends on the extent to which it is created by that small number of thinking men who possess knowledge and the gift of initiative, and on the extent to which the larger body, who have no initiative but a shrewd judgment,[4] co-operate in diffusing sound and temperate views through the community, influencing that still larger mass who, deficient both in knowledge and in active interest, follow the lead given to them. Taking the rule of Opinion in this sense, it is most fully developed in Switzerland and the United States, rather less so in Canada and New Zealand. In France, great as is the devotion to national glory and the Sacred Soil, the assimilative and unifying influence of opinion is weakened by the sharp divisions on religious questions, as it is in Australia by a like division upon Labour and class issues, a source of acerbity which has begun to appear also in such countries as Belgium, Holland, and Italy. The diffusion from one country into another of new types of economic doctrine and new schemes for the regeneration of society preached by enthusiastic missionaries has increased those forces that disunite nations, as in the sixteenth century there were Protestants who renounced their loyalty to a Roman Catholic king, and Roman Catholics prepared to revolt against a Protestant. Such phenomena may be transient, but for the present they disintegrate national opinion and subject democracy to an unexpected strain.

Neither the presence nor the absence of the three conditions just enumerated can be ascribed to democratic institutions, for much depends on the racial qualities and the history of each people, but their presence or absence is nevertheless a credit or discredit to those institutions, because it indicates how far they tend to accompany and strengthen democracy, enabling the machinery to play freely and smoothly without shocks and jars. It is a sign that something is wrong with a government if it fails to attract to its service enough of such talent as the country possesses; it is an evidence of its excellence if the will of the people is amply and clearly brought to bear on the governing authorities through the means by which opinion expresses itself in the intervals between the moments when it is delivered at the polls.

The examination and comparison made above have shown that however marked the differences are between one modern democracy and another, all have some defects in common. Wherever rich men abound the power of money is formidable in elections and in the press, and corruption more or less present. I will not say that wherever there is money there will be corruption, but true it is that Poverty and Purity go together. The two best-administered democracies in the modern world have been the two poorest, the Orange Free State before 1899 and the Swiss Confederation. In every country but Switzerland financial administration is wasteful, and that form of political jobbery which consists in angling for political support by grants of money to constituencies is conspicuously rife. So, too, the rise of a class of professional politicians must be expected if large salaries are paid to representatives. Such a class grows in proportion to the work party organizations have to do, and patronage is misused for party purposes wherever lucrative posts or so-called honours are at the disposal of a party Executive. These phenomena are all natural, the inevitable result of tendencies sure to operate where circumstances invite their action; and only two, the habit of buying support by grants to localities and by bills intended to capture votes from some section of the voters, are directly due to the system of party government by the votes of the masses. The existence of a class who make their living by politics, though ascribed to democratic government, is no worse than was the bestowal of places and pensions on Court favorites, or on the relatives or friends of Ministers, in monarchies or oligarchies. Unscrupulous selfishness will have its way under one system as well as another.

These observations may be summed up by saying that the chief faults observable in the democracies described are the following:

(1) The power of money to pervert administration or legislation.

(2) The tendency to make politics a gainful profession.

(3) Extravagance in administration.

(4) The abuse of the doctrine of Equality and failure to appreciate the value of administrative skill.

(5) The undue power of party organizations.

(6) The tendency of legislators and political officials to play for votes in the passing of laws and in tolerating breaches of order.

Of these faults, the first three have been observed in all governments, and the first not worse under Universal suffrage than it is to-day, though the forms of all three are now different and their consequences more serious; for the number of useless or undeserving persons who lived off the public revenue under the English oligarchy of the eighteenth century was smaller in proportion to the population than that of persons of the same type who live off it in the United States to-day, and the waste of public money in favours bestowed on constituencies and individuals under that English oligarchy or under the Prussian oligarchy down to 1914 was less in proportion to the total revenue than it is now in France or the United States or Canada. As the third fault is in Switzerland not visible, and the second only in a slight degree, these are plainly inseparable from democratic institutions. The evils attributable to the fourth, fifth, and sixth sources may be more definitely connected with popular government. The new democracies in particular suffer from an insufficient appreciation of the need in modern States of legislative and administrative knowledge and skill, an error particularly unlucky in nations which have been piling upon the State new functions for the discharge of which knowledge and skill are required. The years of rapid constitutional development in Australia and New Zealand coincided with the spread of new ideas in populations less well equipped for constructive work than were the older nations, and class antagonisms sprang up before a thoughtful and enlightened public opinion, able to profit by the lessons of experience, had time to establish itself as a ruling force. These things, however, may come: the defects of new countries are less disheartening than the declensions of old countries.

Democracy has opened a few new channels in which the familiar propensities to evil can flow, but it has stopped some of the old channels, and has not increased the volume of the stream. No institutions can do more than moderate or mitigate these propensities, but that which they can do is sufficient to make it worth the while of those who frame constitutions or lead reforming movements to study the institutions which have in one country or another given good results.

Two dangers threaten all these six countries, and indeed all modern democracies. One is the tendency to allow self-interest to grasp the machinery of government and turn that machinery to its ignoble ends. The other is the irresponsible power wielded by those who supply the people with the materials they need for judging men and measures. That dissemination by the printed word of untruths and fallacies and incitements to violence which we have learnt to call Propaganda has become a more potent influence among the masses in large countries than the demagogue ever was in the small peoples of former days. To combat these dangers more insight and sympathy, as well as more energy and patriotism, are needed than the so-called upper and educated classes have hitherto displayed.

## DEMOCRACY COMPARED WITH OTHER FORMS OF GOVERNMENT[5]

As everything in human affairs is relative, so also the merit of any set of institutions can be tested and judged only by comparison with other sets created for similar purposes. All institutions being imperfect, the practical question is which of those that are directed to like ends show the fewest imperfections and best secure the general aim of every political system—the welfare of the nation which lives under it. That form of government is to be preferred which gives the better tendencies of human nature the fullest scope and the most constant stimulus, permitting to the worse tendencies the fewest opportunities for mischief.

Accordingly, to judge democracy aright it must be compared with the two other forms of government to which it was in the ancient world and is still the alternative, Monarchy and Oligarchy. By Monarchy I understand the Thing, not the Name, *i.e.* not any State the head of which is called King or Emperor, but one in which the personal will of the monarch is a constantly effective, and in the last resort predominant, factor in government. Thus, while such a monarchy as that of Norway is really a Crowned Republic, and indeed a democratic republic, monarchy was in Russia before 1917, and in Turkey before 1905, and to a less degree in Germany and the Austro-Hungarian Monarchy till 1918, an appreciable force in the conduct of affairs.

The merits claimed for Monarchy as compared with Democracy are the following:

It is more stable, better able to pursue, especially in foreign relations, a continuous and consistent policy.

It gives a more efficient domestic administration because it has a free hand in the selection of skilled officials and can enforce a stricter responsibility.

It enables all the services of the State to be well fitted into one another and made to work concurrently and harmoniously together, because the monarch is the single directing head whom all obey.

It makes for justice between social classes, because the monarch, being himself raised above all his subjects, is impartial, and probably sympathetic with the masses of the people whose attachment he desires to secure.

Of these claims, the first is not supported by history so far as foreign relations are concerned, for monarchies have been as variable as democracies, and on the whole more disposed to war and aggression.

Some weight may, however, be allowed to the claims made under the second and third heads, whenever the sovereign happens to be an exceptionally capable and industrious man, or has that gift for selecting first-rate administrators which sovereigns occasionally possess, as did Henry IV, Louis XIV, and Napoleon in France, Frederick II in Prussia, Peter the Great and Catherine II in Russia. The seventeenth and eighteenth centuries saw many reforms in European countries which no force less than that of a strong monarchy could have carried through.

There have been a few kings whose action justified the fourth claim, but modern monarchs in general have chiefly relied on and favoured the aristocracy who formed their Courts, and have allowed the nobles to deal hardly with the humbler classes.

History, however, if it credits some kings with conspicuous services to progress, tells us that since the end of the fifteenth century, when the principle of hereditary succession had become well settled, the number of capable sovereigns who honestly laboured for the good of their subjects has been extremely small. Spain, for instance, during three centuries from the abdication of Charles V, had no reason to thank any of her kings, nor had Hungary, or Poland, or Naples. A ruler with the gifts of Augustus or Hadrian and the virtues of Trajan or Marcus Aurelius can be a godsend to a nation; and if there were any practicable way for finding such a ruler, he and public opinion working together might produce an excellent government. But how rarely do such monarchs appear! If a sovereign turns out to be dissolute or heedless or weak, power goes naturally to his ministers or his favourites, who become a secret and virtually irresponsible oligarchy. In most modern countries, moreover, the disposition to obedience and sense of personal loyalty which used to support a hereditary ruler who could win any sort of popularity, have waxed feeble, nor would it be easy to revive them. The fatal objection to autocracy is that it leaves the fortunes of a State to chance; and when one considers the conditions under which autocrats grow up, chance is likely to set on the throne a weakling or a fool rather than a hero or a sage.

Oligarchies deserve, both because they suffer less from the hereditary principle, and for another reason that will presently appear, more consideration than monarchies. There have been various types. The feudal magnates of mediaeval European countries ruled partly by armed force, partly by the respect felt for birth, partly because their tenant vassals had a like interest in keeping the peasants in subjection. In the virtually independent Italian and German cities of those ages the ruling few were sometimes, as in Bern and Venice, nobles drawing wealth from landed estates or from commerce, sometimes the heads of trading guilds which formed a strong civic organization.[6] The conditions of those days are not likely to return in this age or the next, so that in order to compare modern oligarchies with modern democracies it is better to take such cases as the British and French aristocracies of the eighteenth century, or the nobility and bureaucracy of Prussia since Frederick the Great, the last king whose rule was personal in that country, or the groups of men who governed France under Louis Napoleon, and Russia since the Tsar Nicholas I, and Austria since Joseph II. In these countries real power rested with a small number of civil and military officials, the sovereign being practically in their hands. To such cases there may be added in our own time countries like Chile and Brazil, both republics but hardly democracies, for the real substance of power is in few hands. The difference between these last countries and the monarchical oligarchies[7] of Prussia, Austria, and Russia is that in the latter not only did the personal authority of the sovereign occasionally count for something, but that to the power of the civil officials and of the leading soldiers there was added the influence of the strongest men in the fields of commerce and industry, great bankers, heads of railroad and steamship companies and manufacturing undertakings, for the power of wealth, considerable even in the days when Edward III borrowed money from the Peruzzi in Florence and Charles V borrowed it from the Fuggers of Augsburg, is now greater than ever.[8] Any oligarchy of the future will apparently have to be either a mixture of plutocracy and bureaucracy, or else composed of the leaders of labour or trade organizations; and the wider the extention of State functions, *e.g.* under a Communistic system, the greater will the power of the ruling few be likely to prove in practice. Being of all forms of government that best entitled to be called Natural, for it springs out of the natural inequality of human beings, it takes the particular form which the economic and social conditions of a community prescribe, military, commercial, or industrial, as the case may be; and however often it may be crushed, its roots remain in the soil and may sprout afresh.

Oligarchy has undeniable merits. It has often proved a very stable government, able to pursue a consistent policy and hold a persistent course in foreign affairs, paying little regard to moral principles. Rome could never have conquered the world without a Senate to direct her policy abroad. She escaped the inconstancies which belong to the rule of monarchs, one of whom may reverse the action of his predecessor, and of assemblies which are at one time passionate and aggressive, at another depressed by misfortune or undecided when promptitude is essential. Rome, and Venice in her best days, was prudent as well as tenacious. The two great errors of the English oligarchy, its high-handed action towards the North American colonies in and after 1775 and its failure to pass Roman Catholic Emancipation concurrently with the Parliamentary Union of Ireland with Great Britain in 1800 were not its faults so much as those of King George III, to whom it weakly yielded.

Domestic government has been often efficient under an oligarchy, because the value of knowledge and skill was understood better than has yet been the case in democracies. Unsympathetic to the masses as it has usually been, it has sometimes seen the need for keeping them contented by caring for their material well-being. The Prussian oligarchy, following no doubt in the footsteps of Frederick the Great, settled a tangled land question in the days of Stein, put through many beneficial measures and built up a singularly capable civil service along with a wonderful military machine. Even the government of Louis Napoleon, whose blunders in foreign policy were as much his own as those of his advisers, for he had unluckily taken international relations for his province, did much for the economic progress of France, and left the peasantry contented.

These and other minor merits which oligarchies may claim have, however, been outweighed by their faults.

Class rule is essentially selfish and arrogant, perhaps even insolent, and the smaller the class is, so much the more arrogant. It judges questions from the point of view of its own interest, and seldom does more for the classes beneath it than it feels to be demanded by its own safety. Legislation is stained by this class colour, and administration is likely to suffer from the personal influence which members of the dominant group exert on behalf of their friends.

Oligarchies are apt to be divided into factions by the rivalries and jealousies of the leading families. Where these do not lead to violence, as they often did in ruder ages, they take the form of intrigues which weaken and distract the State, retarding legislation, perverting administration, sacrificing public to private interests.

The pervasive spirit of selfishness and absence of a sense of responsibility to the general opinion of the nation, as well as the secrecy with which business is conducted, gives opportunities for pecuniary corruption. England under Walpole suffered from this cause, so did France under Louis Napoleon, so did Austria, so, and to a greater extent, did Spain also and the Italian Principalities, not to speak of Russia and China, where venal bureaucracies worked the ruin of both countries, creating habits which it may

take generations to cure, and destroying the respect of the nation for the sovereigns who tolerated it. England, in the years between 1770 and 1820, is almost the only case of a country in which this weed was quickly eradicated without a revolutionary change.

Lastly, where a people advancing in knowledge and prosperity finds itself ruled, even if efficiently ruled, by a class—and the example of Prussia shows that it may sometimes be so ruled—it is sure to grow restive, and troubles must be expected like those which England, and still more Scotland and Ireland, witnessed during the half century before the Reform Act of 1832. That these troubles did not culminate in civil war, was due to the traditions and good sense of the Whig section of the aristocracy which espoused the popular cause. When aristocracies are seriously divided the end of their dominion is near. It was a scion of one of the oldest patrician families of Rome who destroyed the rule of the Optimates, though for this a civil war all over the Roman world was needed. A people in which the springs of ancient reverence have run dry will trust no class with virtually irresponsible power.

There are points in which a democratic Government suffers by comparison with an oligarchic, for the latter is more likely to recognize the importance of skill in administration and of economy in the management of finance, since it is not tempted to spend money in satisfying the importunities of localities or of sections of the population. It draws as much ability as democracy into the service of the State, for although the upward path is not so open, more trouble is usually taken to discover and employ conspicuous talent; and it is less disposed to legislate in a recklessly vote-catching spirit. The executive vigor with which it is credited is, however, qualified by the fear of provoking resistance or disaffection by the use of force, just as in a democracy the Executive begins to shake and quiver when votes are in question. The selfishness of those old days, when Venice kept her Slav subjects ignorant lest they should be restless, and when the English landowners enclosed commons with little regard for the interests of the humbler commoners, began in later years to be corrected—as in Prussia—by the need felt for keeping the masses in good humour. In the matter of purity, there is, if we look at concrete cases, not much to choose. The German Governments maintained a higher standard of honour among their ministers than some of the Canadian Provinces have done, and among their judges than some of the American States have done. The fear of social censure proceeding from the members of a highly placed profession may be as powerful a deterrent in an oligarchy as is the fear of public displeasure in a democracy.

Crediting Oligarchy with all these merits, it nevertheless remains true that few who have lived under a democracy would exchange its rule for that of an oligarchy; few students of history would honour the memory of a great oligarch like Bismarck as they honour the memory of men like Cavour or Cobden or Abraham Lincoln. Individual liberty has a better chance—even if not a complete security—with the People than with a class. There is less room for the insolence of power. The sense of civic duty and the sense of human as well as civic sympathy are more likely to flourish. Government is more just and humane, not because it is wiser, for wisdom does not increase with numbers, but because the aim and purpose of popular government is the common good of all. An enlightened monarch, or even a generous and prudently observant aristocracy, may from time to time honestly strive to help and raise the masses, but wherever power rests with a man or a class, a scornful selfishness sooner or later creeps back and depraves the conduct of affairs. So long as democracy holds fast to the principle that it exists for the whole people and makes its officials truly responsible to the whole people it will deserve to prevail.

So far I have spoken of the Rule of the Few as being the rule of a Class. There is, however, another sense in which the Few may rule and do rule, which needs to be considered, for it is of wide import.

## OLIGARCHIES WITHIN DEMOCRACIES[9]

No one can have had some years' experience of the conduct of affairs in a legislature or an administration without observing how extremely small is the number of persons by whom the world is governed. Oxenstierna's famous dictum, *Quantula regitur mundus sapientia,* finds its exemplification every day, but it is a criticism not of the flocks who follow but of the shepherds who lead. In all assemblies and groups and organized bodies of men, from a nation down to the committee of a club, direction and decisions rest in the hands of a small percentage, less and less in proportion to the larger and larger size of the body, till in a great population it becomes an infinitesimally small proportion of the whole number. This is and always has been true of all forms of government, though in different degrees. The fact is most obvious in an autocracy. The nominal autocrat, except in so far as the fear of assassination or rebellion obliges him to regard popular feeling, can be a real autocrat, exercising direct personal government, only in two cases, viz. in a small community which he can, like the Sicilian tyrant Agathocles or Chaka the Zulu king, rule directly, or in a wider area when he is, like Julius Caesar or Napoleon, a superman in intellect and energy. In all other cases his personal will plays a small part, and the vast bulk of the business is done by his

Ministers, so that the important part of his function lies in selecting those who are to govern in his name, and trying, if he be capable of the duty, to see that both they and their personal *entourage* continue to deserve his confidence. In a Court like that of Louis XV the powers of the State were, subject to such directions as that voluptuary might occasionally give, divided between three or four high officials and the king's private favourites, with the reigning mistress or her favourites. The Ministers were themselves influenced by their secretaries and favourites, but the total number of persons who guided the destinies of France, exercising, say, nineteen-twentieths of the power over national as distinguished from local affairs, may have been less than twenty. Every Monarchy becomes in practice an Oligarchy.

British India furnishes an excellent example of an enlightened, hard-working, disinterested, very small official class ruling a vast country. Taking together the Central Government and the Governments of the Provinces, the traveller who has good opportunities for observation comes to the conclusion that the "persons who count"—that is, those from whom all the important decisions on policy proceed—do not exceed thirty or forty, including those private secretaries who may sometimes be quite as potent factors as their better-known chiefs. Within the large oligarchy of some hundreds of the higher British officials, this inner oligarchy rules, each member of it having an actual power which is often less or greater than that legally assigned to his office, his personal intelligence and industry making the difference. To take an example on a much smaller scale, that of a country which a democracy left to be governed practically by one man, though subject to the check imposed on him by the necessity of defending his acts in Parliament, and—when the matter was exceptionally important—of persuading his Cabinet colleagues that those acts were defensible, it may be said that the persons who aided and advised the Chief Secretary, and in that way bore a part in ruling Ireland, were, on an average, less than a dozen, viz., three or four of the most experienced officials, two or three of the popular leaders, and a very few private friends on whose advice the Chief Secretary set value,[10] the power of each, *i.e.* the share of each man in the decisions taken, being proportioned to the value which the Minister set upon that man's opinion.[11] In Germany and in Austria the determination of great issues, even the tremendous issues of war and peace which arose in July 1914, lay with seven or eight persons. In large democratic countries like England and France, and above all in the United States, the number of persons who count, swelled as it is by journalists and by the leaders of various organizations that can influence votes, is very much larger in proportion to the population, but that proportion is still infinitesimally small.

Conceive of Political Power as a Force supplied to a machine from a number of dynamos, some with a stronger, some with a weaker, current, and try to estimate the amount of that Force which proceeds from each dynamo. The force which comes from each dynamo that represents an individual man is capable of a rough evaluation, while that force which represented the mass of public opinion is not so evaluable, because it varies with the importance of the issue, which sometimes excites public opinion and sometimes fails to interest it. Whoever tries, in the case of any given decision on a political question, to estimate the amount of the force proceeding from the dynamos which represent the wills of individual men will be surprised to find how high a proportion that amount bears on the average to the whole volume, because in many cases public opinion, though recognized as the supreme arbiter, is faint or uncertain, so that in those cases decision falls to the few, and a decision little noted at the time may affect the course of the events that follow. This is plain enough in the case of the German decision of 1914. It is less evident in a democracy, for there public opinion is more active and outspoken, and when it speaks with a clear voice, omnipotent. But such cases are exceptional. Moreover, even in democracies opinion itself is in the last analysis made by a comparatively small percentage of the nation, the party chiefs being specially powerful among these. Public opinion is in ordinary times deferential to those who hold the reins of government, leaving to them all but the most important decisions.

The members of a representative legislature in a Parliamentary country are presumably men of exceptional ability, each being a sort of leader to his own constituents: yet within every legislature power is concentrated in a few, including the six or seven strongest men among the Ministers, five or six prominent leaders of the various Opposition groups and about ten per cent of the rest, the others practically following the lead given to them, and not merely voting but also mostly thinking and feeling with their party. In the United States House of Representatives business was for many years directed by a very few persons. After the Speaker ceased to be a dictator, it passed to a small Committee, the exigencies of business as well as the interest of the dominant party prescribing this. The selection of the persons to be nominated by the two great parties as candidates for the Presidency of the United States at their national Convention falls in practice into the hands of a small group of politicians, so the nation may be shut up to choose between two men whom few citizens would have selected, the attempt made to ascertain the popular will by the plan of "Presidential Primaries" having virtually failed. In a large popular Assembly, like that of a Greek republic, with hundreds of thousands listening to the speeches of orators, there was no party control, and every citizen voted as he pleased, but the contagion of numbers was powerful, and the dominant feeling swept men off their feet. No ruling assembly ever contained so many men who had intelligence to guide their wills coupled with freedom to express their wills by a vote, as did that of Athens, but that will was the will rather of the crowd than each man's own, and was in the last resort due to the persuasive force of the few strenuous spirits who impressed their views upon the mass. Even where the absolute equality of every voter was most complete, power inevitably drifted to the strong.

What has been said of governments and assemblies is equally true of non-legal organizations. The two great parties in the United States, counting their members by millions, have long been ruled by small cliques: and in every huge city the Organization has its Great General Staff or Ring of half a dozen wire-pullers, usually with a Boss as chief. The much less important party organizations in England are directed by two or three members of the Government and of the Opposition, with a few office-bearers of Conservative and Liberal Associations. But the most striking illustration of the law that the larger the body the fewer those who rule it is furnished by the great Labour Unions that now exist in all industrial countries. The power which the members of the Unions entrust to their delegates to Trade Congresses and the docility with which in some countries they follow whatever lead is given them by a strong will, can, as an able writer who has given special study to the subject remarks, be in those countries paralleled only by the religious veneration given to saints.[12] Ferdinand Lassalle in Germany, Enrico Ferri in Italy, received a loyalty and adulation which hung upon every word. Millions of votes are controlled by perhaps a dozen leaders who have won confidence. This surrender of power by the Many to the Few is admitted by the leaders themselves, who, recognizing its abandonment of the principle of Equality, justify it by the needs of the case. A militant organization is an army which can conquer only as an army conquers, by Unity of Command. It may be said that after victory equality will return. Yes; but so will indifference. A party is most interested and excited when it is militant, and though the leaders may not be of the same type after the battle has been won, they will be still few and powerful.

We are thus driven to ask: Is a true Democracy possible? Has it ever existed?

If one finds everywhere the same phenomena they are evidently due to the same ubiquitous causes, causes that may be summed up as follows:

(1) Organization is essential for the accomplishment of any purpose, and organization means that each must have his special function and duty, and that all who discharge their several functions must be so guided as to work together, and that this co-

operation must be expressed in and secured by the direction of some few commanders whose function it is to overlook the whole field of action and issue their orders to the several sets of officers. To attempt to govern a country by the votes of masses left without control would be like attempting to manage a railroad by the votes of uninformed shareholders, or to lay the course of a sailing ship by the votes of the passengers. In a large country especially, the great and increasing complexity of government makes division, subordination, co-ordination, and the concentration of directing power more essential to efficiency than ever before.

2.) The majority of citizens generally trouble themselves so little about public affairs that they willingly leave all but the most important to be dealt with by a few.[13] The several kinds of interest which the average man feels in the various branches or sides of his individual life come in something like the following order:

First, the occupation by which he makes his living, which, whether he likes it or not, is a prime necessity.

Secondly, his domestic concerns, his family and relatives and friends.

Thirdly, but now only in some countries, his religious beliefs or observances.

Fourthly, his amusements and personal tastes, be they for sensual or for intellectual enjoyments.

Fifthly, his civic duty to the community.

The order of these five interests of course varies in different citizens: some men put the fourth above the second, some so neglect the first as to be a burden to others. But the one common feature is the low place which belongs to the fifth, which for more than half the citizens in certain countries scarcely exists at all. For nearly all—and this will obviously be most true where women possess the suffrage, because domestic cares necessarily come first in the mind and time of most of them—the fifth fills a very small place in the average citizen's thoughts and is allowed to claim a correspondingly small fraction of his time.

3.) Even those citizens who do take some interest in the welfare of their community are prevented, some by indolence, some by a sense of their want of knowledge, from studying political questions. Those who think, those who quickly turn thought into action, inevitably guide the rest. The "common will" to which Rousseau attributes rule, must have begun as the will of two or three, and spread outwards from them.[14]

4.) Inequality of Natural Capacity. Comparatively few men have the talent or possess the knowledge needed for thinking steadily on political questions; and of those so qualified, many are heedless or lazy, and leave politics alone, because they care so much more for other things that they confine themselves to delivering their vote at elections. Thus leadership naturally passes to the men of energy and boldness,

especially if they possess also the power of persuasive speech. They become the Ruling Few. This sort of oligarchy is the natural and inevitable form of government. In a curious little collection of songs written to be sung by citizens during the First French Revolution there is a sort of hymn to Equality which begins, "O sweet and holy Equality, *enfant chéri de la Nature.*" But however sweet the child, Nature is not its parent. Monarchy was natural in some states of society: oligarchy in others, but the direct rule of all citizens equally and alike never has existed or can exist. The propensity to obey is at least as strong as the sense of independence, and much more generally diffused.[15]

As these things are of course familiar to any one who has either read a little history or seen a little of practical politics in any assembly down to a parish meeting, how then did the apostles of democracy come to talk as they did? Where is the Will of the People?[16] What becomes of the rule of the people by the people?

These enthusiasts were not the mere victims of illusions, but as they lived in times of revolt against the misgovernment of monarchies and oligarchies, governments of the Few who selfishly pursued their own class interests, they leapt to the conclusion that the one thing needful for good government was to place it in the hands of the Many, and that the Many, *i.e.* the whole mass of the citizens, would take the same interest in using it for the good of all as the oligarchs had taken in using it for their own class. They saw the people roused as they had not been roused since the religious conflicts of the sixteenth century, to take an eager interest in public affairs, and assumed that this interest would continue when the excitement had died down; and being themselves ardent politicians, they attributed to the mass a zeal like that which they felt themselves. The lapse of years has given us a fuller knowledge. It is time to face the facts and be done with fantasies. As Bishop Butler long ago observed: Things are what they are, and not some other things, and they assuredly are not what we like to believe them to be. The proportion of citizens who take a lively and constant interest in politics is so small, and likely to remain so small, that the direction of affairs inevitably passes to a few. The framers of institutions must recognize this fact, and see that their institutions correspond with the facts.

In one thing, however, the sanguine enthusiasts of whom I have spoken were entirely right. They saw that the chief fault of the bad governments they sought to overthrow lay in their being conducted for the benefit of a class. The aim and spirit were selfish: a government could be made to serve the people only by giving the people the right to prescribe the aims it should pursue. This was done by the overthrow of the oligarchs: and this is one great service democracy has rendered and is still trying, with more or less success, to render. It will have to go on trying, for Nature is always tending to throw Power into the hands of the Few, and the Few always tend by a like natural process to solidify into a Class, as the vapors rising from the earth gather into clouds. Fortunately the Class also, by a like process, is always tending to dissolve. The old Oligarchies of the Sword lasted longest, because in rude feudal times they had seized and anchored themselves to the land. The more recent Oligarchies of the Purse are less stable, because new men are always pressing in, and movable paper wealth may soon pass away from the descendants of those who acquired it. The Oligarchy of Intellect is still more fluid: talent easily enters it, and talent is not transmissible like the shares in a railroad. Philosophers who disliked the oligarchies of rank and feared the plutocracies that succeeded them have dreamed of an aristocracy of Intellect as the best kind of government, but though they knew that a State needs uprightness and public spirit as well as intellect in its rulers, they never succeeded in showing how the possessors of these qualities are to be found and chosen, and they forgot that to both sets of qualities there must be added another which only experience tests, that is, Strength, the power to move and control the minds and wills of men. "The Kingdom of Heaven is taken by violence, and the violent take it by force."

Thus Free Government cannot but be, and has in reality always been, an Oligarchy within a Democracy. But it is Oligarchy not in the historical sense of the Rule of a Class, but rather in the original sense of the word, the rule of Few instead of Many individuals, to wit, those few whom neither birth nor wealth nor race distinguishes from the rest, but only Nature in having given to them qualities or opportunities she has denied to others.

What, then, becomes of Democracy? What remains to the Many? Three rights and functions; and they are the vital strength of free government. Though the people cannot choose and guide the Means administration employs, they can prescribe the Ends: and so although government may not be By the People, it may be For the People. The people declare the End of government to be the welfare of the whole community and not of any specially favoured section. They commit the Means for attaining that end to the citizens whom they select for the purpose. They watch those selected citizens to make sure that they do not misuse the authority entrusted to them. Popular powers, however, though they determine the character and scope of government, are in practice more frequently Negative or Deterrent than Positive. The people can more readily reject a course proposed to them than themselves suggest a better course. They can say, "We dislike this: we will not have it" on many an occasion when they cannot say what else they wish to have, *i.e.* in what form such general benefits as they desire ought to be given.

Of these three functions the most important and most difficult is that of choosing leaders, for though it seems simple to say that government must pursue the common good, the power to discern and decide in any given case what is that good, and what Means best conduce thereto, needs a wisdom and an unselfishness possessed by few. Since the people can seldom do this for themselves, their leaders must do it for them, and be held responsible for the consequences. A nation is tested and judged by the quality of those it chooses and supports as its leaders; and by their capacity it stands or falls.

To realize how much power does rest and must by a law of nature always rest with the few who guide the fortunes of any community, be it great or small, is to indicate the supreme importance of the choice which a free nation is called to make. The larger the nation the more difficult the choice, because opportunities for personal knowledge are slighter. And the choice is also more momentous, because the greater the body and the more numerous the various sections it contains, the more essential is it that strong leaders should be trusted with the powers needed to hold it together.

## NOTES

1. I speak of France as it was in 1914, for the time that has passed since the Great War ended has been too short to judge what effect it has had upon politics.

2. In Britain also the legislature, or, rather, the House of Commons, is legally supreme, but in practice it is much controlled by the Cabinet, who can dissolve it, and can appeal to the party organizations over the country to require members to render steady support. Though, as Bagehot observed, a committee of Parliament, they are a Ruling Committee.

3. President Taft speaking at Chicago in 1909, quoted in Mr. Moorfield Storey's book, *The Reform of Legal Procedure.*

A full and careful examination of this subject may be found in the work of Mr. Raymond B. Fosdick, *American Police Systems,* published in November, 1920. He remarks with truth that the inefficiency of the police in the United States as compared with Europe is largely due to the immense mass of foreign-born population; but this fact does not excuse the faults of criminal procedure.

4. As to this distinction see Pericles as reported by Thucydides in Book II, chap. 40.

5. Chapter 74 of *Modern Democracies.*

6. It is greatly to be wished that we should possess in English a history or histories of mediaeval city oligarchies based on a comparison of the civic institutions of Italy and those of Germany, not without references to those of France, Spain, and England in which there was less independence because royal power was more effective. Separate studies on a considerable scale of the history of such cities as Bern and Geneva, Siena and

Genoa, Lübeck, Hamburg, Ghent, and Augsburg are also wanting in our language, though they might be made both instructive and interesting. Such books exist for Venice and Florence.

7. German writers used to speak of Prussia as a Constitutional Monarchy—so Dr. Hasbach throughout his book, *Moderne Demokratie*—but in actual working it was, down till 1918, more oligarchic than monarchical; and only a superman could have made it a real monarchy.

8. This element was least powerful in Russia because it contained fewer men of great wealth, and in particular very few who combined wealth with such intellectual capacity as distinguished the German plutocrats.

9. Chapter 75 of *Modern Democracies.*

10. Parliament governed Ireland in the sense that its wishes, or what were conjectured as likely to be its wishes, could not be defied, and that where legislation was needed, its consent to that legislation must be obtained, but the majority that gave general support to the Cabinet was usually so disposed to vote as the Cabinet wished that an extremely wide field was left open for the volition of the Irish Government and this volition was the work of the responsible Minister and the handful whom he thought it worth while to consult.

11. The less the Chief Secretary happens to know of Ireland before he is sent there, the smaller will usually be the number of those whom he consults and the greater their influence on decisions.

The view stated in the text is based on the experience I acquired when, many years ago, responsible for the government of Ireland.

12. The views stated in the text which I had reached by other paths are confirmed by an able writer who has given special study to the subject, R. Michels, in his book entitled *Political Parties*, pp. 68-74. I may add that his description of the Socialist parties in Germany is well worth reading. He remarks that the Socialist leaders come mostly (as did Marx) from the bourgeoise, and are often idealists, led by their convictions, not by ambition—though of course they, like all leaders, come to love power—and maintaining an intellectual standard equal to that of German politicians generally. Some have been very striking figures.

13. As to the small minorities by which important questions are decided at votings on Socialist or Labour affairs, see Michels, pp. 55-58, *op. cit.*

14. Rousseau wrote in the *Contrat Social*: "A prendre le terme dans la rigueur de l'acception il n'a jamais existé de véritable démocratie, et il n'en existera jamais. Il est contre l'ordre naturel que le grand nombre gouverne et que le petit soit gouverné."

15. Proudhon observed: "L'espèce humaine veut être gouvernée, elle le sera. J'ai honte de mon espèce." Quoted by Michels, p. 421.

16. The phrase "Will of the People" seems to involve two fallacies, or rather perhaps two implications which induce fallacies, and they spring from the habit of conceiving of the People as One. The first is that the Will of the Majority is apt to be thought of as if it were the Will of All. The second is that as it comes from many it is thought of as issuing alike and equally from many, whereas in fact it originates in few and is accepted by many.

# POLITICAL INSTITUTIONS

## Harold Laski

### I

The modern State, for practical purposes, consists of a relatively small number of persons who issue and execute orders which affect a larger number in whom they are themselves included; and it is of the essence of its character that, within its allotted territory, all citizens are legally bound by those orders.

What are the forms through which they should move to their appointed end? Since the time of Aristotle, it has been generally agreed that political

Reprinted from Harold Laski, *A Grammar of Politics,* 4th ed. (London: George Allen & Unwin Ltd., 1938), pp. 295–318, by permission of the publisher.

power is divisible into three broad categories. There is, first, the legislative power. It enacts the general rules of the society. It lays down the principles by which the members of the society must set their course. There is, secondly, the executive power. It seeks to apply those rules to particular situations; where, for instance, an Old Age Pension Law has been enacted, it pays out the specified sum to those entitled to receive it. There is, thirdly, the judicial power. This determines the manner in which the work of the executive has been fulfilled. It sees to it that the exercise of executive authority conforms to the general rules laid down by the legislature; it may, as in *Ex parte O'Brien*,[1] declare that the particular order issued is, in fact, *ultra vires*. It settles also the relationship between private citizens, on the one hand, and between citizens and the government upon the other, where these give rise to problems which do not admit of solution by agreement.

It may be admitted at the outset that these categories are of art and not of nature. It is perfectly possible to conceive of all these functions being performed by a single body, or even in the name of a single person; and in the modern democratic state the distinction between them cannot, in fact, be consistently maintained. Legislatures often perform executive acts, as when the Senate of the United States confirms the nominations of the President. They perform judicial duties also; the House of Lords is a Court to pass upon impeachments authorised by the House of Commons. Executive bodies, especially in recent times, perform acts it is difficult to distinguish from legislation, on the one hand, and judicial functions on the other; of which the provisional order system in England, and the power of the Ministry of Health in *Arlidge* v. *Local Government Board*[2] are sufficient examples. The judiciary, moreover, is constantly acting as an executive. The English judges issue rules under the Judicature Acts. They act also as a legislature when they give expression to that part of the law not formally enacted by statute;[3] and it is a striking fact that the responsibility of the French State has been largely created by the jurisprudence of the *Conseil d'Etat*.[4] There exist, moreover, in every State powers like that of declaring war and making treaties, of recognising governments already *de facto* as *de jure,* of the veto of legislation by an executive authority, which is no easy matter to classify with any precision. Little, indeed, is gained by the formal attempt—the effort, for instance, to make the judicial power merely a species of executive authority—to distinguish between the different types of function here outlined. For rules formulated to govern particular cases become, if they work satisfactorily, general rules; and general rules, in their turn, are made obsolete by the manner, or the result, of their application.

It may yet be fairly argued that, in every State, some distinction between the three powers is essential to the maintenance of freedom. Since the work of Locke and Montesquieu, we have come generally to admit the truth of Madison's remark that "the accumulation of all powers . . . in the same hands . . . may justly be pronounced the very definition of tyranny."[5] Nor is the reason for this insistence far to seek. Power that is not in some fashion divided is bound to be absolute; and power being, by its very nature, dangerous to those who exercise it, it needs to be limited before it can be exercised with safety. This was put concisely by Montesquieu in some famous sentences:

When the legislative and executive powers are united in the same persons or body, there can be no liberty, because apprehensions may arise lest the same monarch or senate should enact tyrannical laws, to enforce them in a tyrannical manner. . . . Were the power of judg-

ing joined with the legislature, the life and liberty of the subject would be exposed to arbitrary control, for the judge would then be the legislator. Were it joined to the executive power, the judge might behave with all the violence of an oppressor.[6]

It is not, I think, possible so to define the area of each of these three authorities that each remains independent and supreme in its allotted territory. The separation of powers does not mean the equal balance of powers. If it is, broadly speaking, the business of the executive to carry out those principles of general policy enacted by the legislature, it must retain the confidence of the latter body; and such confidence implies the power to compel subordination of the executive to its will. The legislature, that is to say, can directly secure, as a matter of right, that the substance of executive acts is suffused with what it deems to be its purposes. So, too, though more indirectly, with the judiciary. The legislature ought not to dictate to any judiciary the nature of the results it should attain in a particular case; but it is entitled, within the limits hereafter discussed, to provide by statute against the recurrence of a decision of which it is in disagreement with the principles. So, also, when a particular decision, as in the *Free Church of Scotland* case,[7] is likely to result in injustice, a legislative compromise is not an unfair solution of the problems raised. In general, therefore, the powers both of executive and judiciary find their limits in the declared will of the legislative organ.

The case is different in the relationship of executive and judiciary. It is the business of the judge to be the taskmaster of the executive. He has to see that its interpretation of its powers is never so elastic that it either arrogates novelty to itself or bears unequally upon the body of citizens. To such ends as these, it follows that every executive act should be open to scrutiny in the courts; and the decision of the judiciary should always be binding upon the executive unless the legislature otherwise resolves. There should never be the power in an executive body which enables it to escape the scrutiny of men less tempted than itself to identify will with authority. What Professor Dicey has called the rule of law is, with all its implications, fundamental. It means that the State must be put on an equality with all other bodies, that it must answer for its acts; it means, also, that no mysterious prerogative should intervene to prevent the attainment of justice. The power of the judiciary over the executive is, therefore, if contingent, nevertheless essential. The one limitation of substance is that the courts cannot act *propriis motibus*. There must be complaint before decision, and the complaint must come from the citizen body. But when the complaint is proved, the executive should have no authority to transcend the judicial will. Remedy, if remedy be required, is the business of the legislature.

This separation of functions need not imply,

though it has been taken to imply, a complete separation of personnel. Montesquieu's mistaken view of the relation between executive and legislature in England, consecrated as it was by Blackstone, led to the theory that no bridges ought to be built between the organs which represent these various powers. But, as Duguit has pointed out,[8] the execution of any order involves the assistance of all ultimate authorities in the State; and the attempt, as in the American Constitution, rigidly to separate the three powers, has only meant the building of an extra-constitutional relationship between them. The use of the patronage, on the one hand, and the peculiar structure of parties, on the other, has affected by means open to serious question a conjunction between executive and legislature which needs, in any case, to be made. Much the best method of obtaining it is to make the executive, as in England and France, a committee of the legislature. Thereby a variety of ends are served. The executive can only stay in office so long as it retains the confidence of the legislature. A flexibility in its policy is thus assured which prevents that deadlock in action which occurs whenever the American President is at odds with Congress, and that even when his own party is in power. The presence of the executive in the legislature enables it to explain its policy in the one way that ensures adequate attention and organised criticism. It is not attention and criticism in a vacuum. It is attention from, and criticism by, those who are eager to replace the executives if it proves unconvincing. It thus makes for responsibility. It prevents a legislature which has no direct interest in administration from drifting into capricious statutes. It arrests that executive degeneration which is bound to set in when the policy of a ministry is not its own. It secures an essential co-ordination between bodies whose creative interplay is the condition of effective government.

Nor is that all. The executive as a committee of the legislature has an opportunity to drive a stream of tendency through affairs. That is an urgent task. The modern legislature is, of necessity, too large to be left to direct itself; either it loses its centre of equipoise in a mass of statutes unrelated to the posture of affairs, or it gives rise to an interest as against the executive which sets one striving against the other in an effort to win credit from the electorate. The value of an executive which forces the legislature either to accept or to reject its measures is that the latter's efforts are then canalised into something like an organised policy. The play of ideas is not prohibited, but it is limited to the measures upon which men are prepared to risk their political existence. The executive is not made to administer measures it believes mistaken; the policy adopted is one for which it is prepared to make itself responsible. Or, alternatively, a different executive comes into view.

This relationship, moreover, presents a simple means whereby persons fitted to be members of an executive may make known their ability. Certainly whatever may have been the defects of the House of Commons, what has been called its selective function has been amazingly well done. It has proved character as well as talent. It has measured the hinterland between oratorical quality and administrative insight with much shrewdness. I know of no alternative method that in any degree approaches it. Certainly the choice of men for high executive office, as during the war, on the ground of great business capacity, or position in the trade union world, was, generally, a sorry failure. The average American President represents, at the best, a leap in the dark; his average cabinet rarely represents anything at all. But the average member of an English cabinet has been tried and tested over a long period in the public view. He has the "feel" of his task long before he comes to that task. He has spent his earlier career in contact with the operations he is now to direct. To give the executive, by this means, the initiative in law-making, and to build its life upon the successful use of that initiative in the legislature, is an elementary induction from historic experience.

Nothing in this implies the mastery of the legislature by the executive. Under the system, indeed, there have developed experiences so different as those of Great Britain and France. What, rather, is involved is the co-ordination of knowledge, so that each aspect of the governmental adventure is used to enrich the other. The position of the judiciary is different. Its whole purpose is impartiality. It is deliberately set aside from the normal process of conflict out of which law emerges. For its object is, above all, to protect the body of citizens from executive encroachment. To make it in any sense subordinate to the executive is to make impossible the performance of the most urgent function within its province. That is why most political systems have set themselves to protect the independence of judges. The federal judiciary in America, the bench in England, can only be removed by a special and difficult procedure; and it is noteworthy that in the American States, where election of judges usually prevails, a much less high standard of competence prevails. It is, I think, clear that the proper performance of the judicial function implies, first of all, that no judge shall be removed except for physical reasons or for corruption. The executive may dislike his pronouncements. His decisions may be unpopular with the people. Unless he is in a position to know that no penalty follows from doing the right as he sees the right, he is bound to be the creature of the passing phases of public opinion. It implies, secondly, the rule of law. That rule may be enforced through special tribunals, where technical problems, as in the fixation of gas-rates in America, are in issue; but there must be no organ of the executive exempt from judicial inspection.

And, clearly, where the executive itself exercises quasi-judicial functions the judiciary should have such power of scrutiny as will enable it to see that the rules adopted by the executive are such as are likely to result in justice. Executive discretion is an impossible rule unless it is conceived in terms of judicial standards.

I do not think, as has sometimes been suggested, that judicial independence of the executive is attacked in the prerogative of pardon which inheres in the executive.[9] There are three clear reasons for its existence in practically its present form. In the first place, judicial errors do occur. They are, possibly, infrequent, but cases like the Beck case make it imperative that, where they are detected, there should be immediate means of remedy. There is, secondly, the possibility of a wrong assessment of penalty. Judges notoriously vary in the severity of punishment inflicted; it is necessary to have the means of balancing justice by mercy in the necessary cases. There is, thirdly, the fact that cases occur in which the penalty inflicted ought not to be operative for reasons made evident only after it has been assessed. The power to review in cases like these is obviously essential. It may be admitted that, under the first head, judicial pardon would not raise immense difficulties. But judicial action under the second and third would undoubtedly lead to public criticism, and that, in its turn, would bring the judiciary into an atmosphere peculiarly unfavourable to its functioning. When the power is, on the other hand, given to the executive, public criticism has its definite place. The *locale* of the power to pardon (or to mitigate) is simply a matter of convenience of which the utility hardly needs discussion.

The method of appointing judges raises questions which I shall discuss in detail later. Here I would urge only that either popular election, as in America, or legislative election as in Switzerland is neither of them adequate. Appointment by the executive has, on the whole, produced the best results. But it is, I think, urgent to prevent judicial office being made the reward for political services. To that end it is a matter of elementary wisdom to ordain that no member of a legislature, or of the political executive, should be eligible for judicial office. The English tradition, for instance, of giving the law officers of the Crown the refusal of such judicial vacancies as occur is a serious error. The qualities which make a man fit for the judicial function are not necessarily those which make a man a successful attorney-general; and it brings to the bench men accustomed to consider problems from the special angle of executive need, instead of men accustomed to the jealous scrutiny of the effort to satisfy that need. It follows, also, that such a fusion of executive and judiciary as is represented by the office of Lord Chancellor is similarly mistaken. The more complete the separation of the judiciary from politics the better for its quality and independence.

The reverse logically follows. A man who serves in a judicial capacity ought not to be eligible for political office. To make it possible, for instance, for a judge of the Supreme Court of the United States to look forward to the Presidency is inevitably to introduce elements into his decisions of a peculiarly undesirable kind.

I have assumed, in this discussion, that while the judiciary may control the acts of the executive, it ought not to control legislative acts. This raises certain complex considerations which need some further analysis. It is obvious that there are two cases in which the work of a legislature is inevitably subject to the scrutiny of the courts. (1) Where the Constitution is written and the powers of the legislature are defined by it, the authority of the legislature is confined to what the courts hold to be within the competence of its powers. (2) In any federal State, even when the central legislature is left unhampered by such restrictions as those represented by the Fourteenth Amendment to the American Constitution, the question of the area of competence of the different elements of the Federation is also a judicial matter.

Outside of Great Britain, it has been usual in most States to define with some exactitude the powers of a legislative assembly and, as in the United States, to attach to the definition of those powers a system of limitations embodied in a Bill of Rights. We have had experience of a written constitution in England under the Commonwealth; but no attempt has been made since that time to differentiate between constitutional and ordinary legislation. As a result, Parliament can, as a matter of strict law, abolish the Habeas Corpus Act as easily as it changes the laws relating to the liquor traffic. What prevents such an attempt is the tradition which gives to statutes like Habeas Corpus a majesty of a peculiarly impressive kind. Certainly the absence of this differentiation makes for a flexibility that has enormous advantages in a period of great social change. It means that new ideas can make their way without being compelled to pass through the complicated sieve devised to protect ideas deemed fundamental by an earlier period. If England wishes to abolish child labour, that change can be directly affected; but the will of the American Congress is thwarted by the Supreme Court. The English system clearly prevents the judiciary from deciding upon the desirability of legislation the principles of which were unknown, naturally enough, to the generation by which the Constitution was made. And it is obvious that the more the courts can be saved from passing upon such desirability, the more likely they are to retain the respect of citizens.

For it must not be forgotten that much legislation held unconstitutional by the Supreme Court is, in fact, so held not upon principles of strict theory, but upon a view of what is reasonable. The substance of reasonableness does not dwell in the clouds, but is built almost entirely upon the habits and contacts of those estimating it. A few men may be detached enough to project themselves beyond the special circle of their limited experience; most, certainly, will be content to be imprisoned therein without any sense of that captivity. Mr. Justice Braxfield had never a shadow of doubt that the Scottish radicals were criminal, not because of overt acts logically construable as crime, but because men in his own environment did not hold those opinions. Mr. Justice Grantham tried election petitions in the simple belief that a decision in favour of the Tory candidate fulfilled the requirements of justice.[10] The remarks of American judges in the political trials of the last ten years have been more frequently like those of counsel determined to secure a conviction than of men anxious to arrive at an impartial verdict on the facts.[11] To entrust the judge with the power to override the will of the legislature is broadly to make him the decisive factor in the State.

In that sense, a written constitution in which the legislature is so vigorously controlled seems to me a great mistake. For the constitution will always reflect the spirit of the time at which it was made. The judge will, on the average, be better acquainted with that spirit, more bound to the ideas it reflects, than he will be with a later and more novel, ideology. His views on the advisibility, say, of economic legislation are no more likely to be right than those of the legislature, and there seems, therefore, no common sense in allowing his views to prevail.

But, equally, there seems no good reason why a legislature should be able to enforce its will on subjects of great magnitude without control of some kind. There are notions so fundamental that it is necessary in every State to give them special protection. Freedom of speech ought not to be interfered with as easily as the licensing laws. *Ex post facto* laws and bills of attainder are, I think without exception, vicious both in principle and result. Acts of indemnity ought not to be available by the simple process of majority rule. Martial law ought not, as in the Punjab rising of 1919, to be antedated in order to include cases in which, under normal circumstances, it might be difficult to secure a prosecution.[12] Legislation which aims at the disfranchisement of a special class or creed is an outrage upon the whole thesis of citizenship. Powers such as these ought never to be within the compass of a legislature except under severe restrictions as to their exercise.

So also, I would urge, in matters like the period in which a legislature is to retain power, it ought not to be able to prolong its own existence. It ought not to be able to pass financial measures which provide the executive with funds for more than a year at a time. It ought not to be able to ally itself to a particular Church. It ought not, in a word, to be able to alter the basic framework of the State except under special conditions, direct access to which is rendered difficult.

This implies, I think, a written constitution. Ideas so fundamental as these cannot be left to the hazards of a chance majority in the legislature. The action of the Supreme Court in cases concerned with freedom of speech has shown that judicial review is not an adequate safeguard; and the ambit covered by the Defence of the Realm Act shows that a powerful executive may so sweep a legislature off its feet, that fundamental liberties may become the creatures of executive discretion. We need to avoid the unlimited authority of Parliament, on the one hand, and the unique inaccessibility of the American Constitution to amendment on the other. A written constitution which may be amended by a two-thirds majority of the legislature supplies an adequate *via media*. It secures the electorate against the danger that its liberties may be invaded. It prevents the judiciary from exercising more than a limited control over the political sphere. It leaves room for the making of such necessary changes as have a convinced public opinion on their side. It may be added that an age which, like our own, has seen the classic safeguards of representative government thwarted on every side, needs to reinforce its conviction of their urgency. It ought not, for instance, to be possible for a revolution like that of Mussolini to express itself through constitutional forms. Liberty is, in any case, a sufficiently fragile thing for it to be wise to make its suppression less easy than it has become in recent times. Men who are determined to enforce change of this kind by violence will, doubtless, resort to it if no other means lies open. But it is, it may be urged, better that their effort should be plainly revolutionary than that they should be able to pervert the Constitution to their purposes. Atheism, after all, should not be preached from the pulpit of a cathedral.

The situation in a federal State is somewhat different. There not only are the earlier problems in issue, but also those special problems which relate to a somewhat more rigorous distribution of competence than is the case in a unitary State. I do not, indeed, believe that the problems are qualitatively different; it is as urgent for Manchester to control its special needs as it is for Alberta or Tennessee. But the range of competence in a federal State is likely to be wider than elsewhere, and special provision needs to be made for it. Here, I think, the lesson of experience is tolerably clear. A written constitution is the only method by which the effective control of the powers allotted to the constituent parts of a federation can be guaranteed to them; and the judicial review of the exercise of those powers is the most certain way of securing the maintenance of a reasonable equilibrium. Certainly the Supreme Court of the United States has been remarkably successful in holding the balance even between centrifugal and centripetal tendencies; and decisions like *McCray* v. *United States*,[13] on the one hand, and *Noble State Bank* v. *Haskell*,[14] on the other, show how much elasticity has been provided for in the system.

But it is also obvious that no original distribution of powers will ever be adequate over any long period. While it is possibly too broad a generalization to urge, with Professor Dicey, that federalism is always a stage on the road to unity, it is certainly true that the interests of a developing nation-State need the continual readjustment of the powers allotted. This, it is clear, has been the experience of the United States. Very notably, the control of labour legislation by the States was much more suited to a pre-industrial epoch than to one, like the present, in which uniform manufacturing conditions are implied by large-scale industry. The same is true of matters like company-law, like bills and notes, and, in a very different sphere, like the rules for admission to such professions as the law and medicine. The uniformity obtainable by negotiation between the different States is too arduous a matter for any subject of urgency. The attempt to secure it by indirect means, the use, to take the example of child labour, of powers like the Commerce clause, is mistaken because it perverts the instrumentalities provided by the Constitution to illegitimate uses. What, once more, emerges as essential is that amendment should be reasonably accessible without being too easy of access.

The American method of amendment is, it should be said at once, far too difficult to be satisfactory. It is built upon the supposition that the areas represented by State-lines are still genuine entities for the purpose of creative administration. That may have been true in 1787; it is no longer true to-day. And to maintain the States as the effective power in the amending process is, accordingly, to deprive the central authority of the instrumental needs to fulfill its ends. Nor is the Canadian technique of federal disallowance of provincial acts much more satisfactory. It raises, in the first place, the very difficult problem of the grounds of disallowance, which are, in each case, problems in policy uniquely susceptible to partisan interpretation, and, secondly, it is a merely negative power, where what is required is a method of positive reorganisation.[15] The Australian system, which provides for the elicitation of public opinion by a referendum,[16] suffers from the fact that it is referring to an undiscriminating and uninformed mass a problem which, from its very nature, requires treatment by expert inquiry. The way out, as I think, lies in allowing the central authority to make the adjustment it requires on three conditions. It must secure a two-thirds majority of the legislature for its proposal; it must be able to pass it by that majority in two successive sessions of the legislature; and, in the event of the legislatures of two-thirds of the constituent States presenting a formal protest against the change, it must be able a third time to secure the assent of a two-thirds vote of the Central Legislature. The advantages of such a method of amendment are clear. It makes the burden of change lie within the control of the body charged with the national interest. It makes the period of change slow enough to prevent any hasty or ill-conceived proposal finding its way immediately to the statute-book, and by providing the constituent States with a means of protest, to which consequences are attached, it offers them the assurance that their insistence will be duly weighed. The method, it will be noted, does not at any point impair the power of judicial review; it would still be competent for the courts to hold either federal or State legislation *ultra vires*. But a court decision would no longer be able, as it is able in the United States, to hinder the passage of statutes which have behind them the considered opinion of the central legislature.

I said above that the problem of the distribution of powers in a federal State is only quantitatively different from that in a unitary State. In most countries, local government powers lie completely within the control of the central legislature. Outside of Germany, practically every local authority in a unitary State has merely specified powers; and it can only secure an increment of authority by persuading the central legislature to pass a special act conferring the power desired. This is, as a system, unduly distrustful of local experiment. It prevents the local body from exercising initiative in regions where new ideas are not only valuable in themselves, but add both to the responsibility and to the attractiveness of local politics. If the borough of Fulham desires to run a municipal laundry, I see no reason why parliamentary permission should have to be invoked; if Boston wishes to purchase its tram-lines, it should not need to wait upon the will of the Massachusetts legislature. In any distribution of powers in a unitary State, therefore, we seem to need two categories of authority: we need (*a*) areas to which, at a given standard, the local body must devote its attention; (*b*) areas the control of which is definitely reserved to the central legislature. In the second, indeed, the control may well be, on occasion, merely the control of inspection, the actual administration, as in education in England, being left to local bodies. But in the residuary area, the larger the volume of initiative left to the local body, the more fruitful is its performance likely to be. The central legislature may still be left to amend the technique of distribution between the central executive and the local bodies. But it ought not, I urge, to be able easily to amend that technique. The majority required for the change proposed ought always to be larger than in the case of ordinary legislation. For in every State, the more opportunity is given for the needs of the community to be satisfied rather at the base than at the apex of the social pyramid, the fuller and richer will be the life of that community. Normally and broadly, central control will be more efficient; but, normally and broadly also, such control will never arouse the degree of interest in the process of law-making that local initiative can secure.

A word here is advisable upon the distribution of powers in the aspect of devolution. It is increasingly assumed in political discussion that we have need, not only of central and local bodies, but also of intermediate bodies which will assume control over areas intermediate between, say, Great Britain, on the one hand, and Liverpool on the other. The case of Great Britain may be taken by way of illustration. Parliament, it is said, is overwhelmed by the pressure of its work because it is continually compelled to deal with questions too narrow to be worthy of its scrutiny. Just as, apart from local government, the United States has forty-nine legislatures to cope with its problems, Australia seven, and Canada eight, so should Great Britain have at least four, in order that the Imperial legislature may be free to devote its time to major issues only. The same would apply to France in terms of one or other of the many regional schemes proliferated there in recent years. The Belgian problem, also, could thereby be solved, since Flemings and Walloons would then become autonomous in local concerns.

It may be admitted that the element of nationalism makes the Belgian problem quite distinct from that of the normal unitary State not keenly divided by bitter feeling between its component parts. But devolution in the latter case has nothing of its *a priori* simplicity when it is analysed in detail. The analogy with a federal State is an unjustified one. America, Australia and Canada are all rather continents than countries; Germany presents quite special problems of origin and composition; Switzerland is too small a theatre of events to present comparable issues. And, in any case, the pressure on the normal federal legislature is not less than that upon Parliament; what it gains in the limited area to be discussed it loses in intensity within its allotted field. The pressure is, in fact, the natural result of the transformation of a negative State into a positive State. Anyone, moreover, who studies the list of subjects it is proposed to devolve upon local legislatures will be struck by their comparative unimportance.[17] Education, prisons and public health apart, the majority of them do not occupy a twentieth part of parliamentary time; and of the latter, housing and national health insurance raise financial questions of a magnitude that no local legislature could solve without central control (and therefore parliamentary review) of its decisions. Such a division of powers, further, would involve at every point a judicial review of legislation made by the subordinate legislatures, and thereby multiply largely the business of the courts.[18] There will, further, be an immense increase in the size of the civil service, since for the functions now centrally performed, at least a triplicate staff will be necessary. And this is to omit minor questions like the multiplication of elections in which, outside of Parliament, the stimulation of local interest has become so difficult. Certainly that interest is not increased by giving it new issues of mainly a technical kind to disentangle.

It is, I think, a clear general truth in politics that to secure an adequate legislature two things are necessary. There must, first, be the power in the legislature to solve important questions, and, secondly, consideration must be attached to the position of a private member. Both those conditions are satisfied by the Parliament of the modern State; neither, I think, can be satisfied in the local legislatures suggested. For where, as I have argued, vital questions like education and housing are involved, finance is bound to transfer effective control back to the central legislature; and popular interest in licensing and ecclesiastical measures is not likely to invest the average member with the prestige which comes from the power to handle great questions. The mere multiplication of territorial centres of authority has no contribution to offer to the type of problem we are now seeking to solve. There are, of course, genuine territorial questions; and the problem of area apart, the twofold division into central and local seems fully adequate to their needs. Where other issues arise, it will, I think, be found that the considerations involved are different. We need the central resolution of general principle, as now. But the application of general principle is a matter, not of territorial, but of functional devolution. Our future lies in discovering how to relate genuine industrial units to a central legislature in the same way that we relate territorial units. The distribution of power between those units and the legislature does not raise issues seriously different from those discussed earlier in this chapter. But it is better to postpone discussion of this relationship until we have sought to build our industrial institutions.

II

The legislature of a State is chosen by the citizen-body. How is the choice to be made? What are to be the relations between the persons chosen and the electorate which chooses them? I argued earlier in this book that the modern democratic State has no alternative to universal adult suffrage. It lies, as a State, at the disposal of each of its members to enable him to realise the best in himself; and he is entitled, as a matter of logic, to the vote that he may thereby express what his experience seems to warrant him expressing in the push of affairs. I do not argue that universal suffrage has any practical merits which render it inherently superior to other systems. But, theory apart, no tests of exclusion seem available which assist the State to the furtherance of its end. Property as a basis for the franchise merely limits the interests of the State to those of the owners of property. No technique is known whereby an educational qualification can be made synonymous with political fitness. Exclusion on the ground that a man has been in receipt of public relief is merely to stigmatise economic misfortune as a crime. Exclusion on the ground of conviction by the courts is intelligible if it is confined to a small range of offenses. But, even here, a time-limit ought to operate; for obviously we do not want to exclude men like Jean Valjean from exercising their full part in civic life. Lunacy and mental defect are, of course, different matters. In those cases exclusion is built on the simple ground that attainment of a best self is, in any sense implicit with social meaning, impossible.

But an electorate must be organised to choose. A whole adult population cannot from some vast list select those whom it prefers. It is clear that a local relationship of some kind must develop between the member of the legislature and his constituents. What ought that relationship to be? Broadly, we have a choice between two systems. We may either have equal electoral districts, each returning a single member; or we may have some larger, equal unit area, each returning a number of members upon the basis of proportional representation.

What must be realised at the outset is that the member of a legislature will only be returned as a member of some party or group. The life of the democratic State is built upon the party-system, and it is important at the outset to discuss the part played by party in the arrangement of affairs. Briefly, that part may be best described by saying that parties arrange the issues upon which people are to vote. It is obvious that in the confused welter of the modern State there must be some selection of problems as more urgent than others. It is necessary to select them as urgent and to present solutions of them which may be acceptable to the citizen-body. It is that task of selection the party undertakes. It acts, in Mr. Lowell's phrase, as the broker of ideas. From the mass of opinions, sentiments, beliefs, by which the electorate moves, it chooses out those it judges most likely to meet with general acceptance. It organises persons to advocate its own view of their meaning. It states that view as the issue upon which the voter has to make up his mind. Its power enables it to put forward for election candidates who are willing to identify themselves with its view. Since its opponents will do the same, the electorate, thereby, is enabled to vote as a mass, and decision that would otherwise be chaotic assumes some coherency and direction.

Much time has been spent in the effort to explain the origin of parties. To some they are born of the natural contrast between those who cling to the old and those who embrace the new. To others, they arise from the pugnacious instinct of men. It is, however, clear that no single explanation suffices. There is a conflict of wills in society, and that conflict is decided by the decision of the intermediate mass which is not firmly convinced of the truth of any general cause. To attract its support it is necessary to advertise one's view. Parties are the natural method of effecting that end. Their form is largely dependent upon the conditions of any given time. They may group themselves about religious issues, as in sixteenth-century France; they may group themselves about economic issues, as in the England of our own day. Naturally, they arouse the pugnacious instinct; naturally, also, there will be a tendency for the radical solution to attract the young. What, at least, is certain, is that without parties there would be no means available to us of enlisting the popular decision in such a way as to secure solutions capable of being interpreted as politically satisfactory.

To say, of course, that parties are natural is not to say that they are perfect. They suffer from all the evils of group separatism which I discussed in an earlier chapter. They distort the issues that they create. They produce divisions in the electorate which very superficially represent the way in which opinion is in fact distributed. They secure, at best, an incomplete and compromising loyalty. They falsify the perspective of the issues they create. They build about persons allegiance which should go to the ideas. They build upon the unconscious and they force the judgment of men into the service of their prejudices. Yet, when the last criticism of party has been made, the services they render to a democratic State are inestimable. They prevent popular vagaries from driving their way to the statute-book. They are the most solid obstacle we have against the danger of Cæsarism. Above all, they enable the electorate to choose between alternatives which, even though at best are artificial dichotomy, are the only satisfactory method of obtaining a government. For, on practically every issue in the modern State, the serried millions of voters cannot do more than accept or reject the solutions offered. The stage is too vast to permit of the nice shades of quantitative distinction impressing themselves upon the public mind. It has rarely the leisure, and seldom the information, to do more than indicate the general tendency of its will. It is in the process of law-making that the subtler adjustments must be effected.

If this is true, it follows that a political system is the more satisfactory, the more it is able to express itself through the antithesis of two great parties. Each may contain a certain variety of opinion. Both may fail to attract in their ranks much more than that active minority which is willing to devote itself to political affairs. But the superiority of a two-party system over a multiplicity of groups is above all in this, that it is the only method by which the people can at the electoral period directly choose its government. It enables that government to drive its policy to the statute-book. It makes known and intelligible the results of its failure. It brings an alternative government into immediate being. The group-system always means that no government can be formed until after the people has chosen the legislative assembly. It means that the executive will represent, not a general body of opinion, but a patchwork of doctrines which compromise their integrity for the sake of power. It means, also, short-lived administrations, since reshuffling of the groups to overthrow the government is the most interesting exercise in which the legislature can indulge. Short-lived administrations always mean that no coherent policy can be realised. While the group system probably reflects more accurately the way in which the popular mind is actually divided, it is fatal to government as a practical art. For the essential need in administration is the absence of uncertainty. An executive must be able to plan its way continuously to an ordered scheme of policy. That involves a majority, because it involves strong government. A legislature, otherwise, is so much the master of the executive that the latter is unable to attempt great measures, and the time which should be spent upon them is devoted to manœuvring for positions which are lost almost as soon as they are occupied.

So stated, any electoral system ought to satisfy four general considerations. It ought to enable the legislative assembly to embody the opinions of the majority and the minority on the great issues of public interest. It need not, indeed, if it is to be effective, it cannot, embody the total drift of opinion with any effort after mathematical precision. It must allow all groups of men to make themselves heard; but it is compelled to confine popular selection to predominant groups in order to make the business of government coherent and continuous. The areas, secondly, which return members to the legislature, must be small enough to enable the candidates to be known in a genuine way, and, after election, to be closely related to their constituents so that a personal relation develops between them. There must, thirdly, be a means between elections, of checking the result of a general election by revealing the drift of opinion among the voters: this, it may be added, is admirably secured in England and America by the method of bye-elections. This system, fourthly, must be so organised that the voters are as directly related as possible to the government in power. They must be able to feel that it is their choice and that it is as a government that it will come before them for scrutiny when the term of legislative office expires.[19]

On these grounds we reject the system of proportional representation by which it is sought to obviate the defects caused by the majority-principle. I cannot deal here in detail with the arguments by which it is defended; here it must be sufficient to point out the general grounds of rejection. These are, it may be noted, mainly practical in character. We should be compelled to substitute great multiple member constituencies for the present areas. Thereby, we should intensify the complexity of choice, and increase the power of the professional organiser in politics. We should destroy any prospect of personal relations between the member and his constituents; he would become simply an item in a list, voted for almost entirely on party-grounds. We should get weak government, without that body of support which enables it to operate a great programme. We should multiply the number of vagaries which from time to time, like the supporters of the Tichborne claimant and Mr. Bottomley, obscure the clash of real issues. We should be unable to have bye-elections as a test of changes in opinion; and we should encourage all dissidents within a party to seek that independent structure which, ultimately, means the group-system. Thereby we should transfer the place where governments are made from the country as a whole, to the obscurer recesses of the legislative assembly. Not least, we should diminish the responsibility of the private member by increasing his sense that, whatever his personal effort, the party organisers who maintained the list of candidates would be able to ensure his return. Every such complication of electoral machinery is, I believe, bound to result in a decline of civic interest in the political process.

What compensation does the proportional system offer in mitigation of these defects? It will, it is alleged, result in a better representation of national opinion than is now the case. But, in fact, there are few shades of national opinion which do not already find their expression in a legislative assembly; and, at best, the variety is obtained at a sacrifice that is very dubious. It is said, further, that the system makes opportunities for independent persons that are now largely absent. I do not think there is any substance in this view. For, in the large constituency the system involves, what is important is no longer the individual candidate, but the total impression produced by the list to which he belongs. In that aspect, the more independent a candidate the less chance the list will have of conveying a solid impression to the electorate; and the tendency of the party organiser will be to choose as candidates men who can be trusted not to disturb the regular routine. Nor, I would urge, is there any foundation for the view that in the single-member constituency, the minority is unrepresented, while, in the proportional system, this danger is adequately met. "The horizon of a minority," as Dr. Finer well remarks, "is not limited by the boundaries of a constituency." Government is not carried on by presenting to a legislative assembly alternatives which must be fully accepted or rejected. The process of give-and-take which takes place there enables every minority that is organised to give expression to its views, to exercise its "pull" on the total pressure of which a given measure is the result. Political decisions are not made by an arithmetical process of counting votes. More urgent is the weighing of influences that takes place in the law-making process. And minority-views may find adequate institutions therein for the expression of their opinions and desires.

A word should be said upon one aspect of the system to which too little attention is given. In a single-member constituency, it is argued, I may find no candidate I desire to support. But that may equally happen in a multiple-member area, and whereas in the single-member constituency I can give the full weight of my vote to the party I desire to see in power, in the multiple-member area I can give only a fraction of that weight, and the lower preferences I express have no proportionate relation at all to the positive desire I may feel. Something is to be said for the alternative vote in the single-member constituency, where three parties, clearly destined to permanence, exist. But, even there, there is no real relation between the preferences expressed; and the system may result in the choice of the *pis aller* rather than of the man about whom a genuine intensity of opinion has clustered. It involves the danger that the larger the number of candidates who run on special issues, unrelated to the main streams of electoral tendency, the greater the likelihood first that the composition of the legislative assembly will, if they are elected, be atomic, and if they are defeated, that they merely defeat the effort of their supporters to relate themselves to the government of the day.

One final remark in this regard may be made. It is not likely that the difficulties of the modern State are such as to be at all seriously remediable by reforms of electoral machinery. Mainly, those difficulties are moral in character. We shall meet them rather by the elevation of the popular standard of intelligence, and the reform of the economic system, than by making men choose in proportion to the neatly-graded volume of opinion. Proportional representation, where it has been tried, has not noticeably improved the standards of public life. In Belgium it has tended to eliminate independence. In Switzerland, it has so multiplied the tiny groups, that no coherent opinion has been able to emerge. That always implies weak government, and weak government ultimately means irresponsible government. Minorities can always be sure of reasonable representation in the State so long as they are able to make their views articulate and organised to give them driving power. And, in general, the two-party system produces a conflict sufficiently acute to make both of them anxious for ideas likely to attract popular support. The permeation of parties, rather than the creation of groups, is, therefore, the path along which ideas should normally move. There may, of course, come a time when it is evident that assimilation is impossible and that the only way to realisation is through the making of an independent appeal to the voters. That happened, for example, with the Labour Party in England in the years from 1906. But the test of the adequacy of the Labour Party will lie, as it lies with all rebels, in its ability to create a new two-party equilibrium.

## NOTES

1. [See source.]
2. (1916) A.C. 120.
3. Cf. J. Holmes in *Jensen* v. *Southern Pacific,* 244 U.S. 205.
4. Cf. Duguit, *Les transformations du Droit Public,* chap. vii, and my *Foundations of Sovereignty,* chap. iii.
5. *Federalist,* No. 46 (ed. Ford), p. 319.
6. *Ésprit des Lois,* Bk. xi, chap. vi.
7. See the separate report by Orr.
8. *La Séparation des Pouvoirs,* p. 1.
9. Duguit, *Séparation des Pouvoirs,* p. 99.
10. *Hansard,* 4th series, vol. 160. p. 370; 5th series, vol. 22. p. 366.
11. Cf. the citations in Chaffee, *Freedom of Speech, passim.*
12. In the cases of Kitchloo and Satya Pal, cf. the evidence in *O'Dwyer* v. *Nair,* May 1924.
13. 195 U.S. 27.
14. 219 U.S. 104.
15. Keith, *Responsible Government in the Dominions,* 725-49.
16. Moore, *The Commonwealth of Australia,* 597-606.
17. *Conference on Devolution* (Cmd. 692), 1920, Appendix III, pp. 16-17. See Henderson and Laski in *Economica,* March 1925; and Chiao, *Devolution in Great Britain* (1922).
18. Even if the Murray MacDonald scheme (*ibid,* p. 13) of reference to the judicial committee is adopted; and he does not prevent recourse to the courts of law by private persons.
19. See all this excellently put in Dr. H. Finer's pamphlet, *The Case against Proportional Representation* (Fabian Society, 1924).

# Constitutions and Constitutional Courts

# THE CONSTITUTION AS A POLITICAL FORCE

Carl J. Friedrich

## INTRODUCTION

According to Rousseau, the most important of all laws "which is not graven on tablets of marble or brass, but on the hearts of the citizens" is embodied in what he calls "the real constitution." It "takes on every day new powers, when other laws decay or die out, restores or takes their place, keeps a whole people in the ways in which it was meant to go, and insensibly replaces authority by the force of habit." In this curious passage, reminiscent of Burke and other traditionalists, the great Swiss revolutionary is, according to his own words, "speaking of morality, of custom, above all of public opinion; a power unknown to political thinkers, on which none the less success in everything else depends." Since the days of Rousseau, political scientists have, however, been much occupied with this important power, although not infrequently neglecting its relation to custom and to the constitution. On the other hand, Professor Holcombe stressed the connection when he said: "The fundamentals of state government are predetermined outside of the conventions by public opinion. . . . In so far as this is true, and written constitutional charters set forth the accepted moral standards, customs and public opinion, they themselves constitute a political force of great influence. In a sense this is obvious; for were it not so, there would be little sense in making constitutional charters."

## BILLS OF RIGHTS

The political force of the Constitution is particularly apparent in connection with whatever re-

Reprinted from Carl J. Friedrich, *Constitutional Government and Democracy* (Boston: Ginn and Company, 1950, rev. ed.), pp. 154–159, by permission of the publisher.

straints a bill of rights imposes upon government action. Clearly, such bills of rights differ materially from institutional safeguards such as a separation of powers. If the President is given power to veto a bill passed by Congress, he is thereby enabled to restrain the action of Congress. This type of restraint, entrusted to a living human being, will be attended to by that trustee. It is a procedural restraint. But if it is provided that no person shall be deprived of his property without due process of law, that restraint depends directly upon the political force which the Constitution itself possesses. It is a substantive restraint. These substantive restraints embody a people's ways of life.

The way of life thus safeguarded by the restraints of the Bill of Rights constitutes a specific pattern of freedoms. As everyone knows, the American pattern is sketched in the Constitution. A few comparative comments may be in order. The freedom that seems to be most crucial, although it was not so when it first emerged, is what is commonly referred to as *habeas corpus*—the freedom to one's own corporeal liberty. Very elaborate rules are prescribed in the United States for the conditions under which a man can be seized by the authorities. The American people have enjoyed this freedom for so long without any material interference that they are inclined to think very little of it. People living under the totalitarian regimes feel the loss of this particular freedom more bitterly than the loss of any other.

The second freedom, that of bearing arms, is related to the first, but is not so widely recognized for two reasons. In the first place, people do not ordinarily make a practice of attacking their fellowmen, and in the second place, the greatly increased superiority on the part of organized force, whether it be that of the United States Government or of gangsters, prevents the successful use of arms by an individual. The right to bear arms has its value, though, for instance, in strikes, for it gives organized labor a measure of protection against the abuse of military force by their opponents, self-appointed vigilantes, and the like. The third freedom we may mention is the right to worship as one chooses. This particular liberty was of great importance at the time of the English Revolution and later in the early days of American development; it declined in significance along with the decline in the interest of the people in religion as such, but has recently been assuming renewed significance, as it has been more broadly interpreted to cover conviction.

The fourth freedom, the one most frequently highlighted when people talk about civil liberties, is the freedom of speech, generalized as the freedom of expression. This freedom is, of course, vital in its most obvious manifestations to the operation of a free society and is fundamentally related to the pattern of democracy. It is essential to keep in mind the fact that a menace to this freedom may arise from group pressure just as easily as it may from the government, especially in time of crisis. The development of radio broadcasting has also raised serious issues concerning freedom of speech through the use of radio; the charge of monopoly control is frequently heard and great difficulties have been encountered in apportioning time for presenting both sides of controversial matters. Academic freedom, the freedom of the teacher to say what he wishes, is another facet of the freedom of expression. Closely related to the freedom of speech is (fifth) the freedom of the press. This liberty no longer necessarily means the freedom to use the press to expound any particular view. Today the freedom of the press often means the protection of large business concerns in their use of the printed word for the purpose of making money, regardless of the moral, social, or other effects of that printed word, and regardless of who writes those printed words. The anxious question has been raised: "Is not the freedom of the press becoming an instrument for preventing views from being expressed, instead of making it possible for views to be expressed?" The sixth freedom, that of assembly, the right to hold peaceful meetings, is nowadays often broadened to include the freedom of association, though the latter is not expressly guaranteed in the American Constitution. Like the other freedoms of expression, freedom of assembly cannot be exercised unless protection of peaceful group meetings against interference on the part of hostile groups of citizens is undertaken by the government (see next section). These freedoms can be taken together as primarily concerned with a citizen's right to political self-expression—effective participation in political life, and hence constitutive of democracy itself.

A seventh freedom has in recent decades been much discussed, a new freedom which is not included in the Bill of Rights of the American Constitution. This is the freedom to work, which is essential to the free citizen. It is impossible for a responsible person to maintain his self-respect and therefore to develop sanely, soundly, and completely, without the opportunity of putting his hands to something that is definitely worth while in terms of appreciation by the community, expressed in pay. This is one of the most important freedoms at the present time, and needs to receive a good deal of serious consideration if constitutional government is to continue. Totalitarian dictatorship, both in Russia and Germany, has perverted this emerging freedom to mean that every man is part of the system, working for the state. The much-advertised abolition of unemployment is actually the re-introduction of serfdom. Such serfdom may be preferred by people, if they are too long deprived of employment and the opportunity to participate usefully in communal life. For this, like all the freedoms, has a social as well as an individual value. All the rights, so-called, express points of significant mutual service between the individual and the community.

## SUCH RIGHTS NOT NATURAL BUT POLITICAL

It is customary to look upon the bill of rights in any constitution as the instrumentality through which the arbitrary expansion of government is limited, and a sphere of "natural" rights of each individual is thus safeguarded against political interference. The idea that such basic rights are natural has a long history. It produces the impression that certain rights, like private property, or freedom of assembly, have an existence and meaning quite apart from any government. Yet, in fact, all of them presuppose a government. It would therefore be more appropriate to call these rights social, or political. Although they are not necessarily limited to citizens, they require a government for their enforcement. They are rooted in deep conviction. Bills of rights express the dominant ideas concerning the relations between the individual citizen and the government. Take, as an example, the right of free peaceable assembly. The struggle against the authoritarian governments of the eighteenth century created the impression that interference with the free exercise of this right proceeded necessarily from the government. Closer scrutiny reveals that this impression is not tenable in the light of historical experience. If the community happens to be rent asunder by profound conflicts touching its customs and ways of life, such as are engendered by religious and social dissensions, serious handicaps to freedom of assembly (and freedom of speech) arise from the interference of opposing groups with each other. Communists and Fascists, in this country and abroad, have repeatedly sought to break up the meetings of their opponents. Throughout American history, self-appointed guardians of the public weal have undertaken to interfere with assemblies, no matter how peaceful, of dissident minorities. At all such occasions, the presence of large numbers of police demonstrates very strikingly the need for governmental protection of these supposedly "natural" rights. A further striking proof is the British *Public Order Act* of 1936. It was the purpose of this act "to prohibit the wearing of uniforms and the maintenance by private persons of associations of military or similar character, and to make further provision for the preservation of public order on the occasion of public processions and meetings in public places." It was the view of chiefs of police that the wearing of political uniforms was the source of special provocation. Section 2 of the Act prohibited organizations from training and equipping men for the purpose of enabling them to usurp the functions of the police or of the armed forces. Other sections gave the police power to control processions, dealt with the use of abusive or insulting language or behavior, and the interrupting of meetings. Although the Act was hotly debated in Parliament, it was the general opinion back of this Act that all were willing to recognize the need for protection of their liberties against anti-democratic influences, and thus to protect the democratic system itself. All were agreed that the *government* must proceed to check action calculated to destroy existing liberties.

## CONFLICTS OF PRINCIPLE

If bills of rights express the ideas dominant in the community regarding the desirable relations between the government and individual citizens, such bills of rights must necessarily undergo considerable alterations when these dominant ideas change. For as new interests arise in the community they will clamor for recognition as soon as they become sufficiently weighty to arouse a sizable group of people to rally to their support. The resulting need for adjustment creates sharp tensions. The threat of revolution arises and calls for compromise. And since compromises are well-nigh impossible between mutually conflicting fundamental positions, such compromises often assume a very peculiar form. Two mutually exclusive, conflicting clauses or formulas may be inserted into the constitutional charter, each expressing the outlook of one group. The American Federal Constitution contained very few if any such clauses until the enactment of Amendment XVIII. The courts could settle the conflicts with older rights that arose out of the enforcement of this amendment by maintaining the ancient principle that the later rule of law supersedes the earlier. There are, however, indications that Amendment XVIII was carried by an electorate which was only dimly aware of the implications of

its principle and their effect upon the older rights, and that the movement for the repeal of this amendment gained momentum as these implications were becoming apparent. But what would be the attitude of a court or other official when the original constitutional charter embodied such compromises in the form of contradictory clauses? The German constitution of 1919 was drafted and enacted by what later became known as the Weimar Coalition, a conjunction of Liberals, Catholics, and Socialists. These parties had been united in their opposition to the monarchical government of pre-war Germany. But had they enough in common to draw up a constitutional bill of rights? Even a casual inspection of the second part of the Constitution of the German Republic would incline one to reply with an emphatic: No. These "Rights and Duties of Germans" contained liberal, Catholic, and socialist principles in a motley assortment. Such questions as church and state, the schools, and economic life reveal the indecision of the makers. Private property rights are declared to be inviolable, except where laws provide otherwise—which means that private property rights are not inviolable. The church was excluded from control of the schools, but a majority of the parents were given decisive influence—which meant that at least the Catholic Church would nevertheless control the schools wherever it predominated, and so forth. Nor is the German constitution singular in this respect. Many of the postwar European constitutions contain a mixture of liberal and socialist principles. It was the comparative unanimity of the American Constitutional Fathers in matters of general principle, all of them being more or less liberal in their outlook, which gave the American Constitution its great inner coherence. This coherence has unquestionably contributed to the permanence of the American Constitution. The one point on which there was fundamental cleavage was the Federal issue. The question fought out in the Civil War was: "Are the states sovereign and hence free to secede or not?" Today we are confronted by a growing conflict over private property.

## PREAMBLES

Preambles of constitutional charters are of considerable weight as an indication of the public opinion to which a particular constitution owes its force. The well-known American preamble is characteristic: "We, the people of the United States, in order to form a more perfect union, establish justice, insure domestic tranquillity, provide for the common defense, promote the general welfare, and secure the blessings of liberty to ourselves and our posterity, do ordain and establish this Constitution for the United States of America." It may be contrasted with the German Republican preamble: "The German people united in all its tribes and inspired by the determination to renew and strengthen their Reich in liberty and justice, to preserve peace at home and abroad, and to further social progress has given itself the following constitution." It will be seen that the stress laid upon peace and social progress is indicative of a more recent outlook and one which would doubtless express itself forcefully in the preamble of any American Constitution written today. It is, therefore, often maintained that the *real* Constitution of the American people is no longer fully expressed in the written document. On the other hand, the preamble of the constitution of the Soviet Union sets forth ideas which are as yet quite generally rejected in the United States. Significantly, the former constitutional laws of France had no preamble. Being adopted by people quite convinced that their work would not last, the constitution embodied no substantive principles and no bill of rights. In the twentieth century, however, a school of writers, ably led by M. Duguit, maintained that the *Principes de Droit de l'Homme,* general principles of the rights of man, as framed in 1789, formed an integral part of the constitution of the Third Republic. Insofar as these principles are liberal rather than socialist, M. Duguit's argument sought to secure a constitutional sanction for the interests of those who were opposed to a socialist order of government. Such a sanction would have been unnecessary, if opposition to socialism were part of the *real* constitution of France.

## PARTIES AND PUBLIC OPINION

The first change in insight concerning the power of public opinion since the time of Rousseau turned upon the discovery of the political party. More recently the role of interest groups has been added. The division of the people into more or less lasting groups which carry on the process of creating a public opinion has been found to be an essential feature of popular government. Rousseau obviously assumed popular opinion to be one and indivisible, but we incline to view it as divided. And yet, Rousseau remains in the right as far as the constitution is concerned. There must be some binding elements of unity in outlook on the "rules of the game." If people should be fundamentally at odds, it would be difficult for a constitution to exist. It was superficial, yet characteristic of much nineteenth-century political thought, to assume that constitutional government could be long maintained without regard to this sentiment. However, Burke, Bagehot, and Balfour inclined to make the opposite error of speaking too generally and vaguely about "agreement on fundamentals" as an essential condition for constitutional government. There can be much disagreement on fundamentals, as even a casual glance at English, American, and Swiss history shows. Indeed, the only agreement which is essential is the agreement on the elements of constitutionalism.

Lowell, Lippmann, and other writers on public opinion have been concerned mainly with tracing the psychological and other aspects of divisions in opinion. Lippmann finally came to the conclusion that the "public" is a phantom. This view is owing to an overemphasis upon consciously expressed opinion. Burke, de Maistre, and other writers reflecting upon the reaction to the fundamental challenge of the French Revolution were more concerned with the processes by which a certain measure of common agreement is reached and maintained. Thus even wholly irrational factors of tradition found a place in their view. Marx and the Marxists, who expound the economic interpretation of history and of political institutions, have been preoccupied with the forces which prevent any common agreement. Seeing the community basically divided into classes, they had no use for constitutionalism. Indeed, if parties are formed which embody such class divisions and hence are opposed to each other all along the line, civil war is imminent. Harold Laski, in his pessimistic analysis of *Parliamentary Government in England* (1938), insisted that traditional constitutional principles would break down under such conditions. Ivor Jennings, however, has argued, in *Cabinet Government* (1936), that the Labour and Conservative parties do not embody such diametrically opposed class interests, and on the whole, the development to date seems to support his contention.

## TWO BASIC CLEAVAGES: CULTURAL AND ECONOMIC DIVISIONS

The two most formidable cleavages which divide modern nations are the cultural and the social or economic groupings. People are willing to go to war and to die for a national culture or for the working class. If we accept this willingness to die as the final test of effective allegiance, any citizenship which is divided by such loyalties would seem to be distinctly heterogeneous. The relative size of these heterodox groups is of great importance. The significance of heterogeneity would be small if the ratio were nine to one; it would be very great, if it were one to one. Countries like old Austria or former Czechoslovakia and Poland, which include large numbers of people who are sentimentally attached to other national cultures than that of the majority, or who even strive for complete independence, would seem to be so constituted that constitutional popular government can at best maintain no more than a very precarious existence. However, as the case of Switzerland shows, such heterogeneity can be resolved in a higher unity: the real attachment to the basic principles of constitutional democracy can overcome national cultural divisions, as it has overcome religious and other cleavages in the past. The case is different when the disagreement turns upon the basic institutions of constitutional democracy itself. Countries that have a large organized Communist or Fascist party are equally or perhaps even less likely to maintain such a system of government. Consequently an effective constituent power is non-existent. The constitution is not real enough to become a political force.

## AUTOCRATIC IMPOSITION OF UNITY

The making of culturally united nations has been a long and arduous process wherever it has been accomplished, as in England, France, Holland, Denmark, Sweden, and Norway. In these countries, unification was accomplished before the rise of the international labor movement brought to light a new element of dissention and disunity. In them, the leaders of the labor movement were imbued with a sense of national loyalty even after they had begun to admit a higher allegiance to the international labor community. In Italy and Germany, where national unity came after the rise of the international labor community had already commenced to take hold of their working class, the conflict remained unresolved. The intensification of nationalist emotionalism during and after the war led to a violent reaction against all popular constitutional government. Fascism here, National Socialism there, proceeded to attack ruthlessly the flourishing internationalist labor movement. They resuscitated the methods which were in vogue under the autocratic monarchies of England and France. Such methods, to be sure, started those countries on the road toward their unitary national culture. Once united, the British and French nations in two bloody revolutions asserted their right to rule themselves. There was good reason for placing Mussolini and Hitler in parallel to Cromwell and Napoleon from this viewpoint. All these men reasserted the national unity in an autocratic fashion after a period of confusion attendant upon a revolutionary upheaval. Is it likely that Germany, like France after the collapse of Napoleonic imperialism, will purge itself and evolve a popular constitutional government within the national frame? Doubts may be entertained on account of the persistence of the international class conflict. Furthermore, economic and technological factors point toward an international, rather than a national order. The vigorous participation of Germany and Italy in European unification is highly significant in this connection.

## CULTURAL DISUNITY OVERCOME: SWITZERLAND

Those who object that such a multinational constitutional system is inconceivable, should examine the case of Switzerland. Here popular constitutional government has achieved great stability, though it rests upon three very distinct national cultural groups. To aggravate the difficulty, each of these constituent elements of the Swiss people belongs to one of the most vigorous national cultures on the Continent; French, German, and Italian are the three official languages of the little mountain republic. Nor are the Swiss linked by a common religion. But these three distinct cultural groups are united by a long tradition of common political customs which through centuries separated them from the surrounding monarchical governments. The partly democratic, partly aristocratic member states, today called cantons, were uniformly republican and very proud of it. Protected to some extent by natural geographic conditions, and long surrounded by the halo of their startling victories over much more powerful princes, the Swiss Confederation profited by peace and afforded an asylum to victims of the religious persecutions. Though each of its cultural groups stuck with tenacity to its own language, customs, and habits, none went far in attempting to proselytize the others. The leading French Swiss canton, Geneva, was kept away from France politically by its stern protestantism, and neither Germany nor Italy possessed a united national government to which their Swiss brethren could have rallied on the basis of common national sentiment. Thus a tradition of common political destiny welded the culturally divided cantons into a united whole. Thus, in important respects, the sentiment of nationality in Switzerland resembles that in the United States and in Canada. The racial and cultural elements which play the decisive role in England and France are supplanted by a kind of secular religion: the free political traditions common to different and distinct racial and cultural groups. The shared experience of fighting for these traditions, both spiritually and materially, builds up a common store of memories which finds poetic expression in symbolic paintings and in holidays which emphasize the distinctive contributions.

Switzerland most strikingly illustrates the weight of a common tradition rising from a joint past as the procreator of that *real* constitution which transforms a written charter into a political power of lasting importance. Burke has well stated the need for real unity in favor of a common government as a necessary prerequisite. In his *Appeal from the New to the Old Whigs* he said:

The power of acting by a majority . . . must be

grounded on two assumptions: first, that of an incorporation produced by unanimity; and secondly, an unanimous agreement that the act of a mere majority . . . shall pass with them and with others as the act of the whole.

Now this unanimity at the start of an association or a group (what Burke calls an incorporation) must, in the case of so extensive and complex a group as that which constitutes the citizenship of a modern country, be built upon a fairly long period of living together or upon an overwhelming sense of the need for association, such as existed at the start of the American Federal union.

## CONTRAST BETWEEN GERMANY AND GREAT BRITAIN

It was not pusillanimity, as the radicals charged, when Friedrich Ebert sought to retain the monarchy in 1919, but a sound sense of the fragile foundation of German political tradition. Germany having been united under one government for less than fifty years, the time was not ripe for overthrowing it without jeopardizing the underlying sentiment of unanimity and cohesion. That sense for the need of continuity found expression in the curious phrase of the preamble ". . . to renew and strengthen *their* Reich . . . ," as well as in a lengthy debate over the retention of the word *Reich* itself. There is a great contrast between the use of the word *Reich* in this preamble and the meaning given to it in the preamble of the imperial constitution of 1871. There it was said that

> His Majesty the King of Prussia, . . . His Majesty the King of Bavaria, His Majesty . . . and so forth (enumerating all the ruling German princes and the governments of the free cities of Hamburg, Bremen, and Lübeck) . . . do conclude an everlasting union for the protection of the federal territory and of the rights valid therein, as well as for the furtherance of the welfare of the German people. This union shall bear the name of the German Reich and shall have the German constitution.

In this preamble, then, the term *Reich* is nothing but the name for the union of monarchs ruling in Germany, who even insisted that the emperor be merely German Emperor and not Emperor of Germany. Those members of the republican constitutional convention were doubtless right who maintained that the term *Reich* referred to the monarchical past. But when they contended that the term *Reich* should be eliminated in favor of the term German Republic, Friedrich Naumann and others urged that the word *Reich* was a symbol of German national unity, that it embodied much more than the Bismarckian preamble allowed one

to infer, and should be retained. *Reich* was therefore rendered as commonwealth. "Commonwealth" suggests the analogy to Cromwell's time, and just as Cromwell misused the word "Commonwealth," so the Nazis abused the word *Reich*. For commonwealth, even more than *Reich,* suggests the idea of effective participation by all. It was a stroke of genius when Lord Balfour, in search for a symbolic formula around which sentiments of underlying traditional unanimity could rally within the British Empire, hit upon the expression "British Commonwealth of Nations." For in the days of Cromwell, too, several nations had been united under a common weal.

## SYMBOLS AND STEREOTYPES

The traditionalism of the British in matters of politics has always manifested itself in a strong sense of the importance of symbols. Customs, such as surround the conduct of judicial business, have a definite symbolic value. They greatly aid in strengthening the sense of community; practically all modern nations have peculiar holidays of their own, none more so than the Americans. These patriotic occasions, while often irritating to the more sophisticated (note such deprecatory expressions as "Fourth-of-July oratory"), symbolize the national unity transcending all groups. The ritual of the flag, so consistently observed in the United States, is an everyday illustration of how the symbols of communal unity are instinctively hallowed in a democracy. In recent years, the problem of symbols has received more general attention from political scientists than it used to. Professor Hayes's searching inquiries into the nature of nationalism focused attention upon the important role which flags, national anthems, and the like play in rallying mass sentiment. Walter Lippmann showed that the actions of the mass-man are largely determined by certain fixed notions which Lippmann called stereotypes. These stereotypes elicit more or less predictable responses, and it is obvious that distinct appeals to the senses can be produced by certain combinations of colors, shapes, or sounds. All this is by no means new; for unless shrewd practical men had been aware of these effects, such symbols would not have been created. But what is new is a clear recognition of the bearing these psychological factors have upon the political manipulation of men. It is, however, quite easy to exaggerate the manipulative side. Thurman Arnold, in his *Symbols of Government* (1935) and his *Folklore of Capitalism* (1937) advanced the extreme proposition that most scientific word usages constitute folkloristic ceremonials. In thus making light of all the analytic elements contained in modern economics, jurisprudence, and political science, he finds himself without any coherent analytic terminology. As a result, both his books end on a note of plaintive preaching. Harold Lasswell, in his *Politics: Who Gets What, When, How* (1936) stated a similar view, which he later elaborated in his *Power and Society* (1950). The charge has been made against such opinions that they represent a new Machiavellianism. Maybe they do. But the more important question seems to be: Are these analyses accurate, are they realistic, as they certainly pride themselves on being? For if they are, no highfalutin name-calling will dispose of them. Unfortunately, the answer to such questions leads beyond arguable evidence; certainly their underlying assumptions are different from those of the present study. They are, we believe, also different from those underlying the Western constitutionalist tradition. For their metaphysics is deterministic; it is the metaphysics underlying Freud and the psychoanalytic approach. The human being is seen as motivated largely by drives beyond his control. Charles Merriam called these aspects the "credenda" and the "miranda" of power. There is certainly a great deal of make-believe in social intercouse, and especially in politics. The "constitution" tends to become a symbol, and its provisions become so many symbols in turn. It is this symbolic function of *words* which makes the constitution a political *force*. It is no longer possible for us to look upon traditions and customs as God-given or natural, as was done by Burke and many of his contemporaries and predecessors. We know that even the most hoary tradition has been created by men, that all such traditions can be manipulated, in short, that propaganda permeates our existence on every side.

It is readily apparent how this "disenchantment" of ideas and sentiments through exposure to the glaring searchlight of modern psychology, how this "debunking" of ideals once held to be sacrosanct as "natural rights," shatters the foundations of the unanimity which has been held to be an essential prerequisite of a constitutional order. If all ideas and ideals are merely shrewdly designed veils hiding special interests in their sparring for position, where is that underlying unanimity to come from which can give a constitution lasting force? Are modern communities bound to dissolve into a free-for-all in which the most ruthless will eventually win out by imposing their will, trampling popular constitutional government underfoot? Or are there traditions and customs which, though admittedly created by men, yet do represent habitual preferences and patterns of behavior in certain communities? These questions are more easily raised than answered at this stage of our inquiry.

In the meantime, it may be worth while to cite one of Burke's most telling arguments in favor of English traditionalism. In his *Reflections on the Revolution in France,* he argues as follows:

. . . from Magna Charta to the declaration of rights, it has been the uniform policy of our constitution to claim and assert our liberties, as an *entailed inheritance* derived to us from our forefathers, and to be transmitted to our posterity; as an estate especially belonging to the people of this kingdom, without any reference whatever to any other more general or prior right. By this means our constitution preserves an unity in so great a diversity of its parts. We have an inheritable crown; an inheritable peerage; and a house of commons and a people inheriting privileges, franchises, and liberties, from a long line of ancestors.

This view was expressed by a man who was by no means unaware of the power of propaganda. For in the same essay he speaks of the matter at length, particularly when discussing the alliance which in his opinion commercial wealth and the masses in France had concluded for the overthrow of the landed aristocracy.

Writers, especially when they act in a body, and with one direction, have great influence on the public mind; the alliance therefore of these writers with the monied interest (their connection with Turgot and almost all the peoples of finance), had no small effect in removing the popular odium and envy which attended that species of wealth. These writers, like the propagators of all novelties, pretended to a great zeal for the poor, and the lower orders, whilst in their satires they rendered hateful, by every exaggeration, the faults of courts, of nobility, and of priesthood. They became a sort of demogogues. They served as a link to unite, in favor of one object, obnoxious wealth to restless and desperate poverty.

There is clear realization here of willful influence upon public opinion, the clothing of interests by effective stereotypes.

## CONCLUSION

The Constitution, then, which *is* the process by which governmental action is effectively restrained, *functions* also as the most effective symbol of the unifying forces operative in a community. Our insight into social motivation owing to modern research enables us to distinguish fairly well between the system of institutional safeguards, patterned in many different ways but always designed to prevent the concentration of power, and the congeries of symbols expressive of communal traditions and general agreements. Through recognizing this, we should avoid the cynicism which springs from a naïve rational search for close correspondence between such symbols and the things they refer to. It is equally important to recognize the need for continual change. An appreciation of the symbolic value of the "constitution" need not obscure the dynamic, changing nature of the traditions and agreements which it symbolizes. That is the meaning behind Lincoln's famous remark that:

> Any people anywhere being inclined and having the power, have the right to rise up and shake off the existing government, and form a new one that suits them better. This is a most valuable, a most sacred right. . . . More than this, a majority of any portion of such people may revolutionize, putting down a minority . . . It is a quality of revolutions not to go by old ideas or old laws. . . .

# THE POLITICAL THEORY OF THE NEW DEMOCRATIC CONSTITUTIONS

## Carl J. Friedrich

Any attempt to assess the political theory of the new constitutions is confronted with the problem whether to treat the constitutional documents as prima-facie evidence or to search for underlying trends that these documents may or may not express. When Charles A. Beard threw out his challenge concerning "the economic interpretation" of the American Constitution—a challenge which in later years he sought to soften considerably—he implied, if he did not state explicitly, that the words the constitution-makers at Philadelphia used were modeled upon their economic interests and the views which stemmed from them. In an interesting detailed application of this general thought, Walton Hamilton and Douglass Adair in their *The Power to Govern* argued that the word "commerce" must be interpreted in accordance with what "commerce" meant to the fathers: that a broad, mercantilist notion was what the constitution-makers "intended" to have understood in the commerce clause. An examination of the political thought of the new constitutions in such exacting and refined terms would be a Herculean task, little short of an intellectual and social history of Continental Europe during the last two generations. All that is being attempted here is to indicate the broad framework of general ideas on politics into which these constitutions are set.[1]

The very phrase "political theory" is intended to provide a limiting concept. The new constitutions deal with a great many matters, not strictly "political" in the sense in which that term has come to be specialized for purposes of modern political science. Everything today is "political," of course. But "political" in the stricter sense is confined to the organizational pattern of government, the control relationships, if you please, its functioning processes, and the like. In this sense, the new constitutions represent restorations, rather than revolutions, although they are stases or overturns in the Aristotelian sense. And, yet, closer inspection reveals a revolutionary change of unintended proportions, which I am proposing to designate by the term "negative revolutions."[2]

The revolutions of 1640 and 1789 were carried forward with a positive enthusiasm for freedom. The drama and the failure of both revolutions were dominated by this fact; both revolutions provided the stage for long-drawn-out struggles to write a constitution. Each produced a crop of such constitutions, and eventually a dictator emerged to carry on by force and authority what could not be arranged by co-operation. But the lesson of the struggle for constitutional freedom was not lost; the idea of the rights of man was not dead. In the United States, a group of small, seemingly inconsequential, colonies got together and merged the ideas of both revolutions, forged them into a lasting charter: the Constitution of the United States. In England and in France the same impulse produced constitutional systems in the course of the next generation, and these systems remained.

The same cannot be said for the revolution of 1917. In impulse and in effect it was anticonstitutional. The dictatorship of the proletariat was, in the revolutionary vision, not linked to a constitutional democracy but to a direct democracy of

Reprinted from Arnold J. Zurcher (ed.): *Constitutions and Constitutional Trends since World War II* (New York: New York University Press, 2nd edition, revised 1955), pp. 13–35, by permission of Carl J. Friedrich.

the Rousseauistic model; yet no corresponding realistic appreciation of the limits, as far as size and spirit are concerned, characterized the vision. Both the revolutionaries themselves and the Fascist reaction they brought on stressed total authority and accepted coercion and violence thinly disguised by alleged necessities and dangers.

But now a strange turn has occurred. Out of the battle of revolutionaries, counterrevolutionaries, reactionaries, and innocent bystanders, a third force has emerged. And this third force is spreading. It is recapturing the impetus of the revolutions of 1640 and 1789. In France, in Italy, even in Germany, constitutions have been written by men who are certainly far from the "mad inspiration of history" which Trotsky called a revolution. These constitutions are not the result of any positive enthusiasm for the wonderful future; they flow rather from the negative distaste for a dismal past. What these odd revolutionists are saying primarily is: "No." They do not want Fascism and dictatorship. They do not want Communism and dictatorship. They do not want liberalism and the anarchy of the "free market" and its enterprises growing into gigantic monopolies. What, then, *do* they want? The answer seems to be: "We want peace. We want a chance to live and *if* possible to live well. We want something better than either free enterprise or the planning economy. We insist that there must be an order beyond Communism and Fascism, and we want to try to work it out." That is why I propose to call these revolutions "negative."

France affirms the rights of man of 1789, Italy affirms the rights and duties of Mazzini's good citizen, Germany affirms the dignity of man and abolishes the death sentence and compulsory military service [since restored]. Are these not positive beliefs? Certainly they once were. In 1789, the Declaration of the Rights of man was expected, however, to usher in the millennium. Did the makers of the French Constitution of 1946, reaffirming these rights, share such expectations? Hardly. They only knew that such a program would be less bad than what they rejected: the weakness and confusion of the Third Republic, the glum serfdom of the Vichy dictatorship, the terror of the Communist comrades. Similar observations apply to the other two democratic constitutions. When read with the cynicism of the twenties, or the ideological spectacles of Marxist orthodoxy, these constitutions have, in fact, a hollow ring. There does not pulse in them that passion, based upon the weird mixture of romanticism and scientism, which animated constitution-makers from 1789 to Weimar.

Are the negative revolutions a species of restoration? Do they seek to rebuild what was once there? Admittedly, neither Charles II nor Louis XVIII ever restored the past either; they just tried. But their policies and programs did express the exhaustion of a generation that was tired of enthusiasm, tired of ideas, tired of change. It might seem as if the same exhaustion were sweeping Europe today. Yet, there is a sign that this analogy does not hold, and this sign provides a possible key to the situation. Genuine enthusiasm is felt in many quarters of Europe for the possibility of effective unification. Underlying the strictly practical and pragmatic grounds there exists an undercurrent: a vivid sense of cultural unity and community. It found striking expression in the French Assembly debate that settled Germany's admission to the European Union. This sense of unity, this idea of European culture, unlike the shadowy and somewhat disturbing concept of world culture (behind which lurks the Soviet Russian slogan of world revolution), corresponds to vividly felt realities in spite of the bitter conflicts, and to some extent even because of them.

When T. S. Eliot, during World War II, appealed to the Germans, pleading with those among them who would yet acknowledge the common culture of Europe, he said: "The dominant force in creating a common culture between peoples each of whom has its distinct culture, is religion . . . I am simply stating a fact." This fact has found striking expression in the new constitutions through the stress laid upon the dignity of man. The way in which this broad concept is interpreted is decisively related to the unity of Europe and distinguishes present European trends from both the Soviet Union and the United States. For this dignity of man is interpreted in all European constitutions to mean freedom of expression *and* socialization or, perhaps more broadly, social responsibilities. The first sets off Europe from the Soviet Union, the second from the United States. Maybe it will prove unrealizable. But when taken together with the common recognition of European unity, and the willingness to surrender national sovereignty to such higher unity, it may yet revolutionize Europe and the world.

The political theory of the new constitutions that are democratic[3] in the traditional Western sense (the "people's democracies" are here excluded, because their constitutions are façades to a much greater extent than constitutions necessarily are) revolves, then, around four major focal points which distinguish them from their predecessors: (1) reaffirmation of human rights; *but* (2) efforts to restrict these rights in such a way as to make them unavailable to the enemies of constitutional democracy; (3) stress upon social goals and their implementation through socialization; *but* (4) efforts to circumscribe these goals and their implementation in such a way as to prevent the re-emergence of totalitarian methods and dictatorship. With reference to all four aspects, a comparison reveals that, generally speaking, they are most explicit in the German Basic Law, and least so in the French Constitution of 1946, the Italian Constitution occupying a middle ground. This fact is in keeping with the relative depth of the totalitarian impact, comparatively, in the three countries, as well as with the time sequence of the three constitutions: 1946, 1947, 1948. This sequence deserves attention, because it suggests that we are here face to face with an emergent trend still in the process of crystallization.

At this point the question may well be asked: What right have we to consider the French, the Italian, and the German Constitutions together? Is not the political theory of a constitution bound to be affected by preceding political experience? So put, a certain divergence is explainable: the more intense the experience with Fascism, the more poignant is the political theory of the new constitution. This reflection reinforces the point made earlier about the time sequence. Furthermore, Fascism represents a pattern of ideological reaction to Communism, and we face in any case the related problem of Communist danger. In this respect, France and Italy are today more vulnerable than Germany, considering the breadth of electoral support in these countries for Communism (approximately 30 per cent as against 8 per cent in Germany); but Germany is confronted with the impact of Communist control in the Soviet-occupied zone and the threat of a war in which the country would forthwith be overrun by victorious Soviet armies. These armies would no doubt establish "people's democracies" in their wake.

Another common ground of these three constitutions is the Rousseauistic tradition regarding democracy that the three countries share to a large degree. What I mean by this tradition is not necessarily something to be found in Rousseau himself, but something associated with his work and thought since the French Revolution: radical majoritarianism. It is the view that the majority, as such, provides an implicit and indubitable "legitimacy" in the determination of public policy and general laws. Reinforced by Jacobinism in France, by Mazzini in Italy, and by Kant and the Kantians in Germany, this view inclines to reify the concept of the general will in terms of actual votes taken in elections, referenda, and the like. That is to say, with a general skepticism about the capacity of man to free himself of such prejudice-creating frameworks as his class and economic interest goes the conviction that the general decisions in the body politic result from an act of will, rather than rational deliberation. Also involved is a tendency to disregard (a) the degree of reversibility of decisions, and (b) natural limits to any decision, resulting from the inherent conditions with which the decision is concerned.[4] But politically decisive is the disregard for the minority, including the individual. There is little understanding in this tradition of the delicate balance between the majority's and minority's "rights" in a free society and the persistent difficulties inherent in any scheme which sets out to achieve this balance in such a way that neither of two undesirable results arises: (a) that the minority is tyrannized over by the majority, (b) that the majority is prevented from acting by the recalcitrant minority. Much of the best thought of constitutional theorizing in English-speaking countries has, as everyone knows, gone into the exploration of these issues; Harrington and Locke, the *Federalist* and John Stuart Mill, and a host of others have tried to resolve the numerous problems posited by what I once called "one majority against another: *populus semper virens.*" This problem is, of course, at the heart of constitutional liberty, as Kant well knew and made explicit in spelling out the implications of Rousseau's concept of the general will.[5] But Continental European democrats, in the tradition of the Jacobins, have tended to neglect these problems, with the result that constitutionalism has been a weak ingredient in their democratic ideology.

It is not possible to consider constitutional provisions in detail, let alone the debates in terms of which their meaning becomes clear. It must suffice to indicate some broad lines of analysis to be implemented by the other essays that follow. Relatively small is the influence of British and American constitutional experience upon these new constitutions, in spite of the manifest "success" of these models in mastering the political tasks with which men, working with and through them, have had to deal. Vague excuses, such as "America is different" and "Britain's parliamentary system is inimitable," served to insulate native thought habits from undue disturbance by these Anglo-American traditions. In Germany, this propensity to stick to local habits was, of course, reinforced by the brutal fact of occupation, which made it unattractive for a politician seeking popular approval to appear to copy the occupants' ideas on democracy in detail; it was bad enough to have to "democratize" under instructions. For the Social Democrats, the unscrupulous propaganda of the Communist party exploiting this weakness was a prime factor in making them move with the greatest circumspection in all matters of this kind. Whatever the reasons, the influence of British and American constitutional thought was certainly quite limited.

There is, however, one important feature of American constitutionalism that has taken hold of Continental European theorists to an unprecedented extent, and that is the idea of making the courts, or at least a judicial body, the guardian of the constitution, rather than the legislative and/or executive authorities. Here again, the French provisions are less pronounced than the German and Italian ones. Austria has had a limited constitutional judiciary under its constitution of 1929, now revived.[6] It has always been recognized in the United States that the existence of a federal system greatly contributes to the need for, and the vitality of, a judicial guardianship over the constitution. The absence of such a federal system in France, its emasculated form in Italy with its regions, and its presence in both Austria and Germany undoubtedly explain to some extent the difference, in stress and emphasis, upon judicial review. The French organized merely a "constitutional committee" consisting of the president, who presides; the presiding officers of the two houses of the legislature; and ten members of the houses—seven from the lower, three from the upper—who are chosen annually by proportional representation. It is obvious that such a body, modeled upon a proposal once advanced by Sieyès, is still very close to the legislature (as are similar ones in a number of the German states). Actually, by the end of 1949, it had met only once. By contrast, the Italian Constitution, definitely implemented by a constitutional law, set up a constitutional court (Arts. 134-137) consisting of lawyers (jurists) who serve for twelve years and are nominated one third by the president, one third by parliament, and one third by the judiciary. They may not be parliamentarians. The German Basic Law likewise provides for a constitutional court (Arts. 92-84).

The German Basic Law shoulders the constitutional court with the task of determining who has abused various basic rights "in order to attack the free, democratic basic order" and provides for the court's pronouncing the extent to which any such attackers have forfeited these basic rights. While the intention of this provision (Art. 18) is laudable, insofar as it seeks to prevent to some extent the re-emergence of Fascist-Communist attempts to twist constitutional freedoms into anti-constitutional tools, the article is a dangerous weapon. In the light of experience in older constitutional democracies, it is certainly well that this weapon be placed in judicial, rather than executive, hands. The Constitutional Court is at present (1962) considered the most widely approved institution of the Federal Republic.

This recognition of judicial protection for constitutional charters is of fundamental significance for the political theory of the new constitutions: not only does it relate clearly to the broader and deeper appreciation of the importance of civil rights, but it also clearly signalizes a recognition of the constitution as a fundamental law in a manner not customary in Continental Europe before. It represents a departure from the older, radically majoritarian, position noted earlier in this paper.

Returning now to the general issue of the re-affirmation of human rights, this trend in European constitutional thought is marked, specifically, by a tendency to put such rights into more forthright language than has been customary since the French Revolution. The reason is apparent enough: Fascist and Communist perversion of general paper declarations has shown how useless such declaratory rights can be. There are, of course, still such quali-

fying phrases as suggest interpretation of these constitutional rights by legislation (e.g., Italian, Arts. 14, 21, freedom of the press: "contrary to good custom," etc.; German, Arts. 2, 4, 8, 10). The rather numerous references to such laws in the German case would be more objectionable if the Basic Law did not also provide (Art. 19) that "in no case may a basic right be altered in its essential core (*Wesensgehalt*)."[7] The "constitutions" of the *Länder* in the Soviet zone of Germany, by contrast, contain high-sounding lists of such rights, but their interpretation is left to a committee of the Communist-dominated parliament. While it would be futile to assume that, under Russian bayonets, judicial safeguards would be any better, the complete concentration of power in the hands of a majority party, so called, reveals the central issue of these rights: How can they be enforced?

Both the Italian and the Western German constitutions conceive of these rights as not limited to the individual but as social and economic in their ramifications. In fact, the Italian Constitution, like the discarded French draft, elaborates these social and economic aspects into a broad pattern; the German Basic Law is briefer, but the fundamental outlook is the same. Thus the state appears as the collective assisting in the realization of all these rights, rather than as the antagonist of the individual's self-expression. Education and family life (Italian, Arts. 29-34; German, Arts. 6-7) and the care of the indigent and the under-privileged are thus seen as social rights, while the right to work—and to social security (Italian, Arts. 35-38; German, Art. 12) when unable to work—take their place alongside the right to organize and to conduct strikes (Italian, Arts. 39-40); they are followed, rather than preceded, by the right of private initiative and of property. But these former individual or natural rights are now carefully circumscribed by such expressions as that they must not be contrary to social utility or do damage to security, freedom, or human dignity (Italian, Arts. 41-42; German, Arts. 14-15). These matters deserve the greatest attention; it is easy to laugh off such broadly sketched social philosophy as in no sense a guarantee of individual rights. Those individual rights, the freedoms of expression, and of personal security and privacy, also find their place in these constitutions and at times are carried to much greater length than in older constitutions (e.g., contrast the German Basic Law guarantee, Arts. 3-4, that no one may be compelled to serve militarily against his conscience, with Italian, Art. 52). But there is a definite effort made in these constitutions, as had been done earlier in the Weimar Constitution and in the Austrian Constitution of 1929, to anchor the human rights of the "welfare state" in the constitution. In conclusion, it might be noted that parties are recognized as instrumentalities of democracy and that these parties themselves need to be democratic (Italian, Art. 49; German, Art. 21).

The need for preventing the enemies of the constitutional order from utilizing such broadly conceived rights for the purpose of destroying the constitution itself is more marked in the German than in the Italian Constitution. In the latter, it is merely proclaimed that all citizens have a duty to be faithful to the Republic and to observe the constitution and the laws. The German Basic Law, on the other hand, proposes, as already noted, to put the enemies of the constitution beyond its protective frame. It goes so far as to attempt to provide (Art. 143) a criminal sanction against attacks on the constitution, written apparently with direct reference to Hitler's seizure of power "from within." Similar provisions are found in the several *Land* constitutions.

Socialization and planning are given constitutional sanction in all three constitutions, and there can be no doubt that the political theory of these constitutions encompasses these modern approaches. While rather controversial, they constitute, according to prevailing opinions, extensions rather than perversions of constitutionalism. This is not the place to elaborate such an idea,[8] but there can be no doubt that the makers of these constitutions entertained the hope that such a solution could be found. Thus, Article 25 of the French Constitution provides for an economic council which, apart from advisory legislative duties, "must be consulted in the adoption of a national economic plan for full employment and the rational utilization of resources." Likewise, the Italian Constitution envisages such an economic council (Art. 99). The German Basic Law, in its long list of legislative competencies of the *Bund* (Arts. 74-75), includes socialization and planning among these federal activities. Before the Basic Law came into being, a socialization law, representing a compromise between Christian and Social Democrats, had already been formulated and passed by the legislature of *Land* North-Rhine-Westphalia (in September 1948) but was suspended by the British in order not to anticipate federal legislation in this field; a similar situation prevails in Western Berlin. Likewise, Hesse passed a Shop Council Law, involving the principle of workers' participation in management, similarly suspended by the Americans. This law, too, represented a Christian and Socialist compromise. Finally, the Bizonal Economic Council prepared a "deconcentration law," which is being brought forward under the Basic Law's enabling clause in this field. All these activities, no less than the socialization measures in France and Italy, show that these constitutional provisions represent a broad sweep of political thought, as do efforts to develop national planning, like the Monnet Plan. They have been greatly strengthened by the pressure for implementing the Marshall Plan. But political theory is no longer unaware of the totalitarian potentialities

of a socialized and planned economy. It would be very misleading, however, to pretend that these constitutions or their makers had as yet made any very striking contribution to the solution of the problems of the rival claims of freedom and authority under such conditions. A slogan, the "social-market economy," has become very important in connection with the German Basic Law, giving it a decidedly "liberal" twist.

The slogan of a "social-market economy" (*soziale Marktwirtschaft*) has certainly become the target of numerous angry attacks by German Social Democrats. In these "broadsides" the underlying conflict between the two major elements supporting European democratic constitutionalism is finding vigorous expression. It is important to bear in mind that all three constitutions (as well as the German *Land* constitutions) are the result of compromises between these Christian and Social Democrats, united primarily by their common hostility toward the totalitarianism of right and left (with some significant differences of emphasis in this respect also). But beyond this common adversary, the approaches of the Christians and the Socialists are rather divergent. It is not only that the Christians assign a maximal role to religion in the ordering of social relations—from which an emphasis on education and the like stems—whereas the Socialists, while no longer doctrinaire atheists, prefer to leave religion a private matter and build the constitution upon a civic spirit; but, in keeping with this theoretically significant divergence in their general outlook, the Christians tend to minimize the role of the state in social betterment, while the Socialists consider it decisive. Such compromise legislation as the socialization law, passed in September 1948 in North-Rhine-Westphalia (but suspended by the British occupation authorities), was very difficult to achieve because of this radical divergence in viewpoint; a mixture of the two outlooks is reflected in the law's essential provisions. It is, in this connection, worth while to note the difference in terminology: Continental Europeans often speak of socialization as different from nationalization, in the sense that the latter involves the "state" as owner and manager, whereas the former does not necessarily do so.

This basic divergence in attitude toward the degree of creative potentiality of state action is reflected, in turn, in the two parties' different attitude toward federalism. The Christian Democrats favor whatever degree of regional and local autonomy can be secured under prevailing conditions. Communal autonomy in France, regional autonomy of the provinces in Italy, and states' rights federalism in Germany are merely three cognate expressions of the same underlying partiality for "grass-roots democracy," as Americans like to call it. There are, of course, considerable differences of opinion within the Christian Democratic movements, but the general trend cannot be doubted. The Socialist Democrats, on the other hand, even if not outright centralists, incline toward the solving of social problems by means of state action in all fields. Yet their ideology contains a distinct paradox in this general outlook, for, while favoring the state, they do not favor "bureaucracy"; they are forever insisting that the civil service must be "democratized" and thus brought within the general framework of their "civic responsibility" pattern of political theorizing.

But whether the Christian Democrats and the Socialists work together in a coalition, as in France, Italy, and a number of German states, or whether they confront each other as government and opposition, as in the Federal German Republic and other German states, it is in any case clear that the continuing process of molding constitutional developments is largely the result of their recurrent compromises. For a constitution consists not merely of the compromise arrived at, when its formal provisions were drafted, but of the ever-changing interpretation of these provisions made by those in power as the political situation unfolds. Perhaps these compromises would not be possible if there were not increasing pressure from the partisans of totalitarian solutions inside and outside these countries; no one knows. The essential fact remains that the divergent theorizing of the Christian and Socialist Democrats coalesces into a compromise practice under these constitutions, and that in the course of this development there is unfolding a "common ground" of constitutional democratic theory which is more moderate than the viewpoints of either of the theoretical contestants.

To round out the analysis, one might mention some governmental institutions that represent, at least negatively, a taking of stock of European constitutional thought and an attempt to transcend the challenge of totalitarianism. For one, the establishment of a Council of the Judiciary in both France and Italy, to weaken the bureaucratic hold of the justice ministry upon courts, is noteworthy. French desire to emulate the British Commonwealth policy found expression in the rather ineffective French Union, through which effective participation in government of all those living under French law is eventually going to be brought about. Italy has also made an attempt, albeit a feeble one, to get away from over-centralization by the recognition and organization of regions with a measure of autonomy; while Germany, partly under Allied pressure but also responding to ancient traditions, has re-established a thoroughgoing federalism which, freed from the Prussian incubus, may prove a workable scheme and more truly federal than the Weimar Republic or even the *Kaiserreich*. Germany's Basic Law has also made an interesting attempt to avoid the instability of governments resting upon coalitions in a parliament by making votes of lack of confidence

depend upon the opposition uniting in putting forward a new chancellor, and giving the chancellor the right to dissolve. But this provision (Art. 67) may lead to a dangerous stalemate, since another article provides that a majority consists of the majority of all members of parliament (Art. 121), which suggests that obstructionist minorities, even though they cannot agree on a chancellor, may thwart all legislation by staying away.[9] The difficulty is enhanced by the weakness of emergency powers under the Basic Law. This is a countertrend in Germany; in France and Italy the emergency powers have been strengthened, and these provisions have already proved their value. Up to the end of 1950 this problem was not serious, because behind any such powers of the German Government there stood the authority of the occupying powers, who, under the Occupation Statute, had reserved to themselves the right to resurrect their "full authority," not only in the interest of their own security and obligations, but also "to preserve democratic government in Germany" (Occupation Statute, Art. 3). But once Occupation Statute was abrogated, without any radical amendment in the Basic Law to correct this weakness, a very serious situation developed. The abuse of Article 48 of the Weimar Constitution by the antidemocratic elements around Hindenberg in 1932–1933 has obscured the fact that, as had been intended, this article served the constitutional system when it was under very serious attack in 1923. Both the Communist rebellion in Saxony that year and the so-called beer-hall *Putsch* could probably not have been handled successfully by a government that had had at its disposal only the powers which the Basic Law provides in the case of an emergency. Nor could the *Länder* be expected to step into the breach; their constitutions also contain rather inadequate emergency-power provisions. This is notably true of the two largest states, Bavaria and North Rhine–Westphalia.[10] The resulting lacuna is soon to be filled by a new law that has been extensively discussed.

Perhaps the most startling novel aspect of these constitutions is their abandonment of the idea of national sovereignty as a central presupposition of their political theory. Here, again, the constitutional provisions are increasingly radical, as we compare the French, the Italian, and the German documents. The French Constitution states that "on condition of reciprocal terms, France shall accept the limitations of sovereignty necessary to the organization and defense of peace" (preamble). The Italian Constitution, in Article 11, provides that Italy "consents, on conditions of parity with other states, to limitations of sovereignty necessary to an order for ensuring peace and justice among the nations; it promotes and favors international organizations directed toward that end." The Basic Law's Article 24 elaborates this thought by the following:

1. The Federation may, by legislation, transfer sovereign powers to international institutions.

2. For the maintenance of peace, the Federation may join a system of mutual collective security; in doing so it will consent to those limitations of its sovereign powers which will bring about and secure a peaceful and lasting order in Europe and among the nations of the world.

3. For the settlement of disputes between nations, the Federation will accede to conventions concerning a general, comprehensive obligatory system of international arbitration.

It will be noted that paragraph (2) specifically makes reference to *Europe* as an area to which the national sovereignty might yield its various rights. While this provision does not preclude participation in the looser kind of league that the United Nations constitutes, it unquestionably is intended to be a more inclusive commitment.[11] This tendency was reasserted by a resolution in the Bonn Parliament, passed in July, 1950, instructing its delegation to the Consultative Assembly of the Council of Europe to "work for the establishment of a government and parliament of Europe" and authorizing it "to transfer to such government and parliament all such authority as other European governments and parliaments were prepared to transfer to it." The resolution passed 362 to 40. The French Parliament, likewise, has gone on record in supporting its government in its efforts to establish a government of Europe, and the foreign-policy debates of the French Council and Assembly are full of references to this idea, as are the resolutions of political-party congresses. The M.R.P.F. adopted a radical plank supporting a government and parliament for Europe.

All these innovations point toward what seems to be a central development of political thought in Continental Europe; namely, the establishment of a federal government for Europe as a whole supported by a European "nation." This European sentiment has grown very rapidly, in spite of many setbacks, especially since the establishment of the Common Market of the Community of the Six— France, Italy, Germany, and the three Benelux countries. It is the positive projection of the negative revolutions that occurred in France, Italy, and Germany. By the end of 1950, this novel constituent power had become very active. Transitional institutional forms had been set up in the form of the Council of Europe, consisting of Ministers and a Consultative Assembly, with headquarters at Strasbourg. At the same time, the Schuman Plan, so called, had led to the draft of an international "government" of the coal and steel industries of France, the Benelux, Italy, and Germany (Federal Republic). Plans were afoot for the establishment of a European army and for a "government" of agriculture. These developments represent what is called the "functional" approach

as contrasted with the "federal" approach of the Council of Europe and the more far-reaching plans to convert the latter into a government of Europe. The issue of functionalism versus federalism has been hotly debated and is not settled, by any means. What concerns the student of political thought is the radical turning away from nationalism involved in all these developments and the substitution of a regional internationalism. This regional internationalism could, and in quite a few minds does, involve a new "nationalism" on a broader plane. As it is customary to speak of Chinese or Indian "nationalism," meaning thereby the sentiment of allegiance and political support for the broad cultural entities of China and India, so European culture is very much the focal point of attention of the European movement. Perhaps one should speak of "culturism" rather than nationalism. On the other hand, the peoples of Europe are being referred to, from time to time, as a "nation" already, and a number of the characteristic elements of nationalism are present in much of the thinking and arguing over the "Pan-Europe" of the future. But this Europe-in-the-making must, in view of the diversity of its "national" subcultures, try to organize itself federally. This means that constitutionalism has suddenly acquired new life and significance, for a federal state cannot be organized, except on a constitutional basis. Its characteristic division of powers (or competencies) along regional lines, *i.e.*, between the federal authorities and the local constituent units (states, *Länder*, cantons, etc.), presupposes a written document. This document must be protected by adequate sanctions and calls for continuous interpretation by some kind of judicial body.[12] Such a federal union will not come into existence without a vigorous constituent power, sufficient to overcome local vested interests, sentiments, and ideology. Within the Consultative Assembly at Strasbourg, in the meeting in August, 1950, all this was proposed, but the demand for the election of a constituent assembly was thwarted by opposition in the Council of Ministers, especially opposition by Britain. Britain, which is governed under an ancient and deep-rooted constitution, has not experienced the rise of such a constituent will to create a new constitutional order as is found on the Continent. Her constitutional tradition is "organic," in the sense that the *grown*, as contrasted with the *made*, constitution appears to her people the sound and natural process. No federating of discordant elements under outside pressure was involved in the process either—the union with Scotland having been brought about by quasi-dynastic methods. This view is sensible, if there is adequate *time* for such growth. For actually "growth" is a slow accumulation of rules and institutions over a long period of time. But there are situations when a new organization has to be created *at one time*. This sort of event is characteristically involved in the founding of federal states as they emerge from a preceding congeries of independent units. The Europeans who insist upon the federal, as against the functional, approach are convinced that such a time has arrived for them. They have come to this view mainly for three reasons: first, the need for achieving some measure of military security in the face of the Soviet Union, without so much dependence upon the United States as is at present required; second, the need for much larger market areas unimpeded by tariffs, foreign exchanges, and the like; and, third, the desire to eliminate the destructive intra-European warfare (and, at present, reconstruction to overcome its effects). In other words, European union has a military, an economic, and a broad political objective in view. To each of these major objectives there corresponds a series of activities, roughly N.A.T.O., O.E.E.C., and the Council of Europe. But behind these immediate objectives, and giving them meaning and significance, is the sense of European culture as a precious heritage to be preserved, a vital challenge to be met.

A great deal of theorizing is going on in Europe at the present time concerning these developments. This theorizing is essentially constitutional in nature. It has significantly intensified the grasp of the inherent meaning of constitutionalism as a system of effective regularized restraints upon a legally organized government. Past Fascist experience, as well as the specter of Soviet dictatorship, have combined to focus attention upon a number of interrelated propositions: that the German problem cannot be solved without a united Europe within which Germany may develop economically and otherwise; that the Communist problem cannot be solved without a united Europe, one that will have a large and prosperous economy; that the Fascist problem cannot be solved without a united Europe in which the appeal of emotional mass nationalism will be attenuated by supranational allegiance. This supranational allegiance found expression in the adoption of a charter of basic rights at Strasbourg in August, 1950. The charter represents the thought of the three constitutions we have already studied. It is not novel, any more than they are. Ancient truth, *das alte Wahre* in Goethe's sense, has been embodied in this document. And yet there is something profoundly significant, from the standpoint of political thought, in this common action. *Si duo faciunt idem, non est idem.* It is fulfillment of the universalism of the English and French revolutions. Both are here being transcended; their specifically local and national orientations have been left behind, and a more truly human embodiment has been given to these ideas. For if all Europeans are now equal before the law, it means that they all acknowledge themselves to be equal to each other. National conceits and pretensions are being laid aside, or at any rate recede into the background.

Before concluding this general sketch of the political theory of the new European constitutions of a Western democratic type, it seems important to note one rather striking divergence from the American, if not from the British, climate of opinion. Nowhere on the Continent is there to be found any genuine "belief in the common man," as that belief is taken for granted in the United States. In fact, the very term is nonexistent and hence untranslatable. This extraordinary personification of American democratic traditions is, throughout Continental Europe, confused with the mass man. Attacks upon the mass man, such as Ortega y Gasset's, have achieved very wide currency among Europeans of presumably democratic convictions. Not only Europe's deep attachment to culture, but the Marxist insistence upon the class-conscious elite (in the socialist sector), and the corresponding elite notions in the catholic tradition, have combined to prevent the rise of any such confidence in the common man's ability to deal with common concerns of the community as is generally accepted in America, even by people with sophisticated ideas about the workings of democracy. Somehow, this shortcoming in European democratic thought seems related to the exaggeration of the majority's views on one side and to the role of the state on the other. In both cases, we must recognize in European democratic theory a stronger emphasis upon the collective aspects of society and government and a corresponding weakness, when it comes to the individual. Characteristically, European parliaments make quite inadequate provisions for the contact between the citizen and his representative. European party leaders tend to become rather authoritarian, as soon as they have achieved a measure of status and authority. The resulting reaction of the people at large is one of indifference, cynicism, and even antidemocratic (though not necessarily protototalitarian) sentiments. Whether a belief in the common man could be generated to remedy these defects seems doubtful. As the gentleman was the embodiment of England's ideal of man in an aristocratic age, so the common man seems America's personal "mirror of man." Some of the more thoughtful European theorists appreciate the weakness resulting from the absence of such a personal projection of democratic ideals, especially in the face of an aggressive totalitarian challenge. But is that enough?

In sum, the negative revolutions that have occurred in Western Europe as a result of the victory of British and American arms over Fascism are animated by a spirit of reconstruction. The political theory associated with these revolutions and with the resulting constitutions is one of moderation and compromise. It seeks to transcend the totalitarian challenge, not by a blind appeal to the past, but by a patient effort to recapture the essentials of human freedom and dignity. The political thought of the negative revolutions is motivated by the social and economic ills of an aging industrial society, rent by violent revolutionary claims for radical improvement. Yet, on the whole, it is still true that Continental Europeans stress abstract principles, rather than specific procedures and concrete solutions. Quite a few years ago, John Stuart Mill wrote:

The common-places of politics, in France, are large and sweeping practical maxims, from which as ultimate premises men reason downwards to particular applications, and this they call being logical and consistent. For instance, they are perpetually arguing that such and such a measure ought to be adopted, because it is the consequence of the principle on which the form of government is founded; of the principle of legitimacy or the principle of the sovereignty of the people.[13]

It is a curious but undeniable fact that these observations still hold true to a remarkable degree, not only of France, but of Italy and Germany as well. If Mill thought that "it would be often a much stronger recommendation of some practical arrangement, that it does not follow from what is called the general principle of the government, than that it does," I believe that this thought is as "weird" and "incomprehensible" to Europeans today as it was nearly a hundred years ago. From which it follows that the political *theory* of these constitutions is probably a good deal more important than an Englishman or American is likely to assume. This reflection may serve as a humble excuse for seeking to elucidate the theorizing of those who have developed these new constitutions: rejecting the totalitarian dictatorship, they are groping for workable principles of social order with genuine theoretical concern.

## NOTES

1. The constitutions to be considered here include the French Constitution of 1946, the Italian Constitution of 1947, and the German Basic Law of 1949—with occasional references to the German *Land* constitutions of 1946 to the present; attention is also given to the emergent Constitution of Europe. Regarding leading commentaries for the French Constitution, mention might be made of Maurice Duverger, *Manuel de droit constitutionnel et de science politique* (5th ed.; Paris, 1948), Julien LaFerriere, *Manuel de droit constitutionnel* (2d ed.; Paris, 1947), Georges Burdeau, *Manuel de droit public—les libertés publiques, les droits sociaux* (Paris, 1948), Marcel Prélot, *Précis de droit constitutionnel* (Paris, 1948); for Italy, Oreste Raneletti, *Istituzioni di diritto pubblico* (13th ed.; Naples, 1948), P. B. di Ruffia, *Diritto costituzionale (lo stato democratico moderno)* (Vol. I; Milan, 1949); on the Italian Con-

stitutional Assembly, V. E. Orlando's *La costituzione della repubblica italiana*, which gives textual extracts and an interesting introduction by the editor, is valuable; the Italian text is contained in the volume published by the general secretariat of the Chamber of Deputies in 1949, entitled *L'assemblea costituente,* which also contains other legislation in summary; for Germany, no good commentaries have yet made their appearance. Three divergent American accounts may be mentioned, however: A. Brecht, "The New German Constitution," *Social Research,* XVI (December 1949), 425–73; Hans Simons, "The Bonn Constitution and Its Government," *Proceedings* of the Twenty-sixth Institute of the Norman Wait Harris Memorial Foundation, pp. 204–14; and Carl J. Friedrich, "Rebuilding the German Constitution," *American Political Science Review,* XLIII (1949), 461–82 and 704–20. The text of the important constitutional documents is contained in *Germany Under Occupation, Illustrative Materials and Documents,* eds. Pollock, Meisel, and Bretton (Ann Arbor, 1949). See also, for a general discussion of the constitutions within the longer perspective of constitutional development, Carl J. Friedrich, *Constitutional Government and Democracy* (Boston, 1950), and the literature cited there at length for the constitution of the Fifth French Republic cf. May article in *Harvard Law Review, LXXII,* 801 ff. (1959).

2. See for this the author's "The Negative Revolutions and the Union of Europe," in *Perspectives on a Troubled Decade,* eds. Bryson, Finkelstein, and McIver (New York, 1950), pp. 329 ff.

3. Throughout this chapter the word "democratic" is used in the prevailing Western sense, which was adumbrated by the American Government through its occupation authorities in an effort to differentiate itself clearly from the Soviet position, on July 9, 1946. It stressed, *inter alia,* (1) frequent popular elections in which "not less than 2" parties effectively compete, these parties to be "voluntary associations," (2) guarantee of basic rights, (3) "rule of law"; see for this Carl J. Friedrich and others, *American Experiences in Military Government in World War II* (New York, 1948), App. C. Consideration is focused upon the constitutions of France, Italy, and Germany, the latter term referring to Germany under Western occupation whose constitution (Basic Law) claims to represent all Germany, from a democratic standpoint, just as the republic that has been erected in the Soviet zone claims to do from a Communist ("people's democracy") standpoint. It might have been well to include also the constitutions of the several German states *(Länder);* there are twelve of them, and all but three have constitutions that resemble the Basic Law sufficiently to reinforce the analysis given here.

Austria was permitted to reactivate the constitution of 1929, to annul at the same time all laws made after March 5, 1933, and especially the Fascist Constitution of 1934—an inadequately noted and belated recognition that Fascism came to Austria at the same time it came to Germany, though in attenuated form. The constitutional situation in Austria deserves and requires separate analysis.

4. For a more detailed discussion of these problems, see my *The New Image of the Common Man* (Boston, 1942; new ed., 1950), chap. iv; for a contrary view, see Edwin Mims, Jr., *The Majority of the People* (Toronto, 1941), and Willmore Kendall, "The Majority Principle

and the Scientific Elite," *The Southern Review,* IV, No. 3 (1939). Neither author deals with (a) above.

5. See for this my *Inevitable Peace* (Cambridge, 1948), as well as Professor Lewis W. Beck's Introduction to his selections of Kant.

6. See Ludwig Adamovich, *Grundriss des oesterrischischen Verfassungsrechts* (4th ed.; Vienna, 1947), esp. pp. 303 ff., where the narrow limits of judicial review in Austria are indicated.

7. We are concentrating in this discussion upon the Italian and German provisions, because the French relegated the statement of basic rights to the preamble. However, the earlier French draft that was rejected by the voters on May 5, 1946, *did* contain such a bill of rights, which to a considerable extent fits into the analysis above (not, however, into the anti-Communist part of it). Cf. Georges Burdeau, *Manuel de droit public.* The authoritative *Précis de droit constitutionnel* by Marcel Prélot, a member of the constitutional committee, entirely discards the preamble and speaks of the rights having been "eliminated," and in the author's view rightly so.

8. *Constitutional Government and Democracy,* chap. xxiii.

9. These provisions are given especial attention by Brecht, *op. cit.* Actually, similar provisions have worked reasonably well in Baden–Württemberg; they have now also been incorporated into the new constitution of North–Rhine–Westphalia. See, for an interesting comparative analysis, Friedrich Glum, *Das parlamentarische Regierungssystem in Deutschland, Grossbritannien und Frankreich* (Munich, 1950), esp. chap. xiii. Dr. Glum takes a critical view of this new system, which he believes will end by leading to minority cabinets that will have to yield to a determined anticonstitutional opposition (cf. pp. 333 ff.).

10. Art. 60 in the latter constitution only provides for the special case in which the *Landtag* (legislature) is prevented from sitting. The Bavarian provisions resemble those of the Basic Law.

11. Whether membership in the United Nations entails an infringement of national sovereignty has been a subject of dispute. The Charter explicitly states that the member states are "sovereign"—as did the United States Articles of Confederation (in Art. II). On the other hand, member states can be committed to actions involving war without their consent, except for those states that exercise a veto power in the Security Council. Yet what this commitment actually amounts to, the Korean crisis has revealed. It seems fair to conclude that, at present, the United Nations Charter leaves member states sovereign; moves to alter this situation have so far not succeeded.

12. See the theory of federalism given in my *Constitutional Government and Democracy,* previously cited, chap. xi.

13. John Stuart Mill, *Logic* (1st ed.; London, 1843), II, 618.

# REFLECTIONS ON THE VALUE OF CONSTITUTIONS IN OUR REVOLUTIONARY AGE

Karl Loewenstein

## THE ONTOLOGICAL APPROACH

The epidemic of constitution-making in the wake of World War II has no parallel in history. Since 1945 some fifty-odd nations have equipped themselves with new constitutions.[1] In some countries the new constitution symbolizes statehood and independence attained. In others, a previously serviceable document did not survive the authoritarian hurricane and had to be completely recast in the light of past experience. In others again, the changes in the location of political power caused by revolution required a redefinition of the political organization.

Reprinted from Arnold J. Zurcher (ed.), *Constitutions and Constitutional Trends since World War II* (New York: New York University Press, 1951), pp. 191–224, by permission of Karl Loewenstein.

In practically all cases the procedure of constitution-making followed the classical democratic pattern: by elections, everywhere pretending to be free and unconstrained, the people, exercising the *pouvoir constituant,* called into being constituent assemblies or constitutional conventions which, in turn, drafted and adopted the instrument of government. Popular ratification occurred (*France* and some of the *Länder* in *Western Germany*) but was not the rule. In a few instances only the customary procedure was deviated from by injecting into it appointed, instead of popularly elected, constituent bodies. Outwardly at least the entire process seems to reflect the triumph of the ideology of democratic legality.

Though it is historically permissible to distinguish "families" of constitutions which, as a rule, embody similar or identical "patterns of government,"[2] practically all new constitutions are surprisingly alike in structure in that they operate uniformly with the traditional tripartite division of functions into legislative, executive-administrative, and judicial organs of the state. Almost without exception they have a comprehensive and ambitious bill of rights which, in addition to the classical libertarian freedoms from state interference, professes the ideal of social justice to a degree amounting almost to standardization.

Does the seeming universality of the process indicate that at long last, after the dark night of lawless despotism, the bright young day of democratic constitutionalism is dawning? Does the phenomenon of constitutionalism mean that all nations alike attach a paramount importance to a formalized constitutional order, or do they merely follow the laws of diffusion and imitation? And, further, are the constitutions "real" and "living" in the sense that the competitive struggle for political power is actually conducted within the frame offered by the constitution, or is the latter manipulated by the ruling class or classes without permitting the sharing of political power by all sociopolitical forces of the community?

Such questions are rarely asked, since the interpretation and application of a constitution is usually monopolized by relatively small groups of technicians—politicians, lawyers, judges, civil servants—to whom, in a society managed by plural power groups, the constitution serves as the instrument for the attainment and preservation of special interests. "Constitutionalysis" and "constitutionology," to speak with Thomas Reed Powell, overshadow what may be called the ontology of constitutions, that is, the investigation of what a written constitution really means within a specific national environment; in particular, how real it is for the common people, who after all are everywhere, in this alleged age of the common man, the addressees of political power.

The following discussion is a pioneering—and, therefore, most tentative—attempt to implement the customary legalistic and functional analysis by an approach that focuses primarily on the congruity, or lack of it, between political reality and ideological intent of the constitution, or on the distinction between the nominal validity and the actual value of a constitution. The question is: Are the constitutions suitable to satisfy, and do they satisfy, the needs and the aspirations of the people living under them? The volume of new constitutions is an invitation for such a comparative investigation.[3]

## THE "CLIMATE" OF
## CONSTITUTION-MAKING

Constitutions, as the rationally conceived and formalized rules for the exercise and, thereby, for the restraining control of political power, are a relatively recent experience of the *homo politicus.* As long as power was based on the traditional forces of irrational state mysticism—the divinely ordained authority of the legitimate hereditary dynasties and the classes affiliated with them—there was no need for the formalization of the *"lois fondamentales du royaume"* (France), to observe which the traditional power holder was believed to be divinely obligated. The idea of a written constitution was the result of a long-drawn revolutionary struggle for the secularization of political power (Lecky). It was primarily an English discovery[4] in the Puritan revolution when the lower gentry and the middle classes forced on Stuart absolutism their share in political power. For Cromwell, religiously conscious of the inherent moral limitations of political power, the answer was a self-limiting "Instrument of Government" (1653) rather than a "constitution." For the British a written constitution was no necessity, because power shifted to the new social classes pragmatically and without recourse to natural law. But subsequently the increasing ascendancy of natural law gravitated the eighteenth century toward a written constitution as the moral basis of a well-ordered society. The goal was reached, rather for practical than theoretical reasons, first in the American colonies, thereafter in the European key state of France. Here Rousseau's general will provided the moral and the metaphysical incentives, mobilized by the social contract and translated into practice by Sieyès' *pouvoir constituant,* both as "subversive" of the existing order as Marxism proved a century later. The constitution was considered the solemn manifestation of the social contract and the functional implementation of the imaginary oath that the general will had taken for its self-realization.

But it is by no means accidental that the climate for the birth of the written constitution was the eighteenth century, fascinated not only by what were believed to be the imperatives of natural law but also by the application of the laws of nature to social dynamics. The science of mechanics was transferred to the science of government. The well-balanced constitution, with its liberty-guaranteeing checks and balances, was intended to establish, by functionally separated powers, the ideal equilibrium of the social forces.[5] In the environment of the Enlightenment the constitution was primarily a moral necessity and a functional achievement only subsidiarily. The constitution itself and the process of constitution-making were surrounded by a sort of collective magic, which belies the rational logicism accompanying it. In their naïve optimism the political theorists and the politicians themselves believed that all that was needed for a well-ordered society was a well-ordered constitution. Well-ordered meant well-equilibrized. Unaware of the demonism of political power, the written constitution would automatically offer the solutions of all social ills and guarantee the happiness of the people living under it. Being a "good" constitution and operated by "good" people it would be self-executing by harmonious cooperation in the interests of the whole society. The first result was the preposterously unworkable French Constitution of 1791, preceded by the greatest seminar in political theory the world has ever known.[6]

The French Revolution did not hesitate to disown the naïve trust of its initiators in human nature and to prove, by streams of blood, that functional utility cannot be neglected with impunity, lest political power might become uncontrolled and destroy political liberty. In the search for the magic formula for taming political power while preserving the freedom of the general will, the constitutional laboratory of the Revolution provided the world with all possible "forms of government," that is, the functional co-ordination of powers: constitutionally limited monarchy; parliamentary government and its perversion of assembly government (gouvernement conventionnel); the intricate checks and balances of the Directory pattern; and, last but not least, the legalized authoritarianism of the First Consul. But in the process, not surprising with so rational a people as the French, the pristine spell of the sacrosanctity of the constitution as the manifestation of the social contract was definitely lost, never to be recaptured again. The Americans are the only nation which for socioeconomic reasons, irreproducible elsewhere, has retained the original spirit of the constitution as "basic" and irrefragable.

## CONSTITUTIONS IN THE NINETEENTH CENTURY

During the nineteenth century most states "constitutionalized" themselves, following certain prominent patterns such as the United States Constitution in Latin America, the French Charte Constitutionnelle (1814) for the semiauthoritarian technique of monarchical legitimism, and the Belgian Charte (1831) for the parliamentary constitutional monarchy.[7] But the transcendental value with which the process had been imbued in the eighteenth century was no longer attached either to the creation or the operation of the constitution. What happened was that the industrial and commercial bourgeoisie asserted itself as the ruling class and that, wherever it took—or was grudgingly granted—its share in political power, the constitution merely legalized the shift that had occurred before. In spite of the constitutional semantics, popular sovereignty was nominal only, using the representative ideology for what was at best an oligarchy of wealth, actually, however, the political monopoly of the propertied classes. The competition for power was conducted at first between the bourgeoisie and the royal pre-

rogative, which was successfully whittled away; subsequently, after the victory of the propertied oligarchy, between the latter and the lower middle classes and labor. Its political core was the suffrage rather than the constitution itself. That the constitutions, on the whole, succeeded in rationalizing the power conflict by subjecting it to the regulatory procedures of positive law was due to the fact that they were applied to a relatively self-contained and homogeneous society, not yet exposed to the challenges of social forces basically opposed to the existing distribution of political power. Constitutions function well so long as the competition for power is confined to different groups of the same social class; but they are strained to the limit, and often break, when their rules become insufficient to accommodate the power ambitions of a class excluded by its very rules. The considerable esteem in which the nineteenth century held the constitutions as a method for the peaceful compromise of political dynamics was responsible also for their improved functional utility, devoid of any emotional or transcendental implications. Compared with, for example, the functional matter-of-factness of the Bismarckian Constitution of 1871, the American Constitution reads like a dissertation on political philosophy.

## CONSTITUTIONS AFTER WORLD WAR I

The magic spell of the constitution was briefly and deceptively recaptured after World War I. The conceptual heritage of the French Revolution—popular sovereignty—gained emotional strength in some of the older states, which were offered an opportunity for wiping the slate clean of the residues of the monarchical tradition. To the host of new states emerging from the ruins of the Czarist, Austro-Hungarian, and Ottoman empires, the constitutions became the symbols of nationhood and independence, in line with Wilson's political ethics of national self-determination, internationally applied. Democratic parliamentarism (France and Britain) had won the war; monarchical authoritarianism had lost. Constitutional democracy was like an incantation invoked everywhere, regardless of how little the professionals and the masses were socially, morally, and politically prepared for it. Constitutions were inspired and carried by the bourgeoisie, which subconsciously expected to tame labor by tying it down to constitutionalism. Labor went along because it hoped to gain power by constitutional majorities. A refreshing wind blew over the world, which once again, for a fleeting moment, believed that democratic fundamentalism would be as permanent as it was deemed absolute. The constitutions of this period, no longer confined to functional mechanics, are boldly constructive,[8] filled with the spirit of experimentation and socially conscious in their bills of rights. The Mexican Constitution (1917) in this hemisphere and the Weimar Constitution (1919) are outstanding illustrations. Simultaneously, the new constitutions were functionally perfected, leaving nothing to chance, trying to bridle all potential power elements by legal arrangement. It was, in short, the maximum effort to "constitutionalize" political power.

The Indian summer of constitutional democracy lasted less than a decade. Almost without exception the new constitutions became the victims of the revolt of the masses. The practice of violence, which, in the meantime, had been raised to the rank of a potent political theory, triumphed over the *juste milieu* of bourgeois rationalism. By and large, the constitutions were anachronistic at the time they were written. The error of the *bourgeoisie* consisted in the assumption that labor and the dispossessed lower classes could be paid off with promises or, at the most, token installments of economic security, and that the dominant position which the ruling capitalistic *bourgeoisie* had obtained in its struggle with landed wealth would be permanent.

The aftermath of the brief interlude of constitutional universalism was the dislodgment of constitutional democracy and, with it, of the constitution it had fashioned. Dictatorship spread like wildfire over Europe, sparing only those nations where ingrained tradition of political compromise resisted mass emotionalism, and also over Latin America with similarly shallow constitutional habits. Fascism did not require formalization of political power, which, however sweepingly formulated, would have been a limitation on its exercise. Where authoritarianism resorted to the device of a constitution, as in Poland (1935), it served merely as a frame to make the existing configuration of power "legally" unchallengeable.

## CONSTITUTIONS AFTER WORLD WAR II

The expectation that the nations liberated from Nazi-Fascist despotism would return to their constitutions with jubilation did not materialize. Return they did. What else could they do? But it was a far cry from the democratic *élan* the preceding generation had exhibited. In some marginal states (the Benelux countries and Norway) the existing constitutions, which had been virtually preserved through governments in exile, were put into application without requiring any changes; here the monarchical continuity proved useful.[9] But in the Continental key states of France, Germany, and Italy, the pre-Fascist instruments having been weighed and found wanting, new ones were created. The business of constitution-making was attended to dutifully and without enthusiasm. Very few people in Western Europe

will admit that their constitutions partake of the quality of the "higher law," except in the purely formal sense that they establish certain regulatory norms for the conduct of the governmental business. For the tired, neurotic, cynical, disenchanted society of the West, divided against itself, the importance of the written constitution has visibly faded. And in the people's democracies of the East where the powers that be played up to the limit the symbolism of the new order, who would dare to pretend that they embody what democracy prides itself on, the identity of the governors and the governed?

The reasons for the evanescence of the emotional attachment to a constitution lie deeper than the mere mental fatigue of nations after occupation and war. True, the people relish that no longer, in the small hours of the night, will the bell ring for the uncertain fate arbitrariness may have in store for them. But this generation has seen too much of the viscera of the political process and the demonism of power to put much store by the protection of paper documents. War and postwar inflation have brought about a revolutionary change in social stratification. The bottom has fallen out from under the economic stability of the propertied middle classes, major proportions of which are precariously close to outright proletarianization. There are few antidotes to economic materialism, and what purports to be the "philosophy" of the period—pessimism disguised as existentialism—is not among them. This generation has become alienated from its governments, realizing that political power is the monopoly of party oligarchies, vested-interest cliques, and pressure groups. After the emotionalization by the dictators, the mass mind has not yet found a new center of moral gravity. Liberty the constitutions could and did promise, but not bread and the modicum of economic security the little man yearns for. To him it is the plain and unadorned truth that the political decisions which are vital for the well-being of all no longer occur within the frame of the constitution. The social forces move—and battle—extraconstitutionally, because the constitutions did not even attempt the required solutions.[10] Constitutions are considered stale compromises and extemporizations of the accidental party configuration. It is not difficult to realize that for the cynic, the disillusioned, and the desperate among the laboring and salaried masses the blandishments of Communist collectivism, which they are told have reversed the class situation in their favor, cannot fail to be attractive.

But even the constitutional lawyer whose vision is not blinded by his profession will find little moral comfort in the study of the new constitutions. He realizes with suspicion that those of the Soviet orbit are technically too simple, functionally too straightforward, to allow for a fair adjustment of the power conflict. On the other hand, the Western constitutions, appraised as a group, are stationary and strangely retrospective, overly legalistic and complex, and yet timid and evasive. Both the French Constitution of 1946 and the Bonn Constitution in many respects are merely responsories to 1875 and 1919, respectively, trying to find foolproof answers to past mistakes. In general, these remedial efforts are understandable and commendable. Illustrations are the prohibition of delegated legislation in France (Art. 13), and the "neutralization" of presidential powers by election through a constitutional convention instead of through the people in Western Germany (Art. 54). By the same token, the attempts at rationalizing parliamentary dynamics (vote of nonconfidence and dissolution) and similar efforts to obtain a stable government are useful. Contrariwise, the constitutions reflect diffidence in the people themselves, with the hardly unintended result of playing the actual exercise of political power into the hands of the party oligarchies. Compared with France and Western Germany, Italy's Constitution is much more optimistic and self-confident. With the elimination of the monarchy, Italian parliamentarism could start from scratch without the inhibitions of adverse past experience.

## THE SO-CALLED "FORM OF GOVERNMENT"[11]

The term "form of government" usually describes the functional arrangement—co-ordination or subordination—of the various organs in the process of determining the will of the state. Here the postwar constitutions did not add anything new to the traditional repertory. None turned to the monarchical solution: in Italy and Bulgaria monarchy was voted out of existence formally by plebiscite; in other Balkan states it was dismissed informally; and India (1949) not only severed the Commonwealth link with the British Crown (though not with Great Britain) but also made short shrift of indigenous residues of monarchical feudalism. All constitutions, those behind the Iron Curtain no less than the others, profess the democratic fundamentals; all adhere, with varying accents, to the functional division of powers (though not to their separation). Outwardly they are very similar, and if one would strike off the U.S.S.R. Constitution (1936), chapters I and X, it would be next to impossible to realize that this is the model of a new social order.

The separation-of-powers pattern of government found no favor outside the sphere of influence of the United States, such as in Latin America where, however, more recently a tendency toward approximation to parliamentarism is discernible, or China (1947) and Southern Korea (1948), serving here a protective coloration for unmitigated authoritarian government. The generally favored pattern is parliamentary government in the sense that the govern-ment requires the continuous support of a majority party or a coalition of parties (France, Italy, India, Israel, and others). An interesting variation was produced in Western Germany for which the name "demo-authoritarian" may seem appropriate; the Federal Chancellor can be removed from office by vote of confidence only if the absolute majority of all members of the *Bundestag* simultaneously have elected a successor (Art. 67). This implies that the Chancellor is virtually irremovable during the four-year term of the parliament except when the government coalition breaks and a substantial part of it combines with the opposition. Similar efforts to stabilize the government were undertaken in some of the Western German *Länder,* and the same device, though in a most hypothetical manner, figures also in the constitution of Eastern Germany (*Deutsche Demokratische Republik*) (Arts. 95, 2). The cabinet system, under which the Prime Minister, by virtue of strict party discipline and the threat of dissolution, is in undisputed exercise of political power between elections, is so much predicated on the interplay of two parties that none of the new constitutions could effectively institutionalize it.

The real surprise, however, is the revival, in the Soviet orbit, of the historically discredited and half-forgotten pattern of assembly government, which not only prevails in the U.S.S.R. itself but also in practically all[12] satellite states including Eastern Germany (German Democratic Republic and *Länder*). Why the Soviets abandoned their previous (1918, 1923) undisguised rule of the new proletarian agencies in favor of the more orthodox assembly government cannot be discussed here. But the archdemocratic pattern of the omnipotence of the popularly elected assembly, free from any checks and balances and, therefore, also from conformance with the separation of functions, lent itself perfectly to the rule of the single party, confirming the historical experience that assembly government is the convenient façade behind which the dictatorship of a person, group, party, or ruling clique can be disguised. Since the rule of the assembly is nominal only—it meets rarely and at great intervals—the Presidium, its permanent steering committee, is a logical innovation.[13] At least in Eastern Germany, where the pretense of the multiple-party state is maintained, assembly government is implemented by the "block technique,"[14] the prearranged (by persuasion, pressure, and other means) unanimity of the parliamentary parties and cabinets. The ingenious device serves for the "voluntary" elimination of the opposition and presents to those who wish to believe it the picture of a monolithic democracy. In the Eastern German Republic the technique is even institutionalized in the constitution (Art. 92): Any party with forty deputies *must* be represented in the government according to its strength in the lower house (*Volkskammer*). Suppression of the opposition certainly is nothing new; but to make a coalition government mandatory in the constitution is evidently the limit of "constitutional" democracy.

## THE "LIVING" CONSTITUTION: SHADOW AND SUBSTANCE

For an ontological evaluation of constitutions it is essential to recognize that the reality of a specific functional arrangement of powers depends to a large measure on the sociopolitical environment to which the pattern is applied. From its own experience the politically advanced Western world is apt to draw the conclusion that, once a constitutional order has been formally accepted by a nation, it is not only valid in the sense of being legal but also real in the sense of being fully activated and effective. If this is the case, a constitution is *normative*. To use a homely simile: The constitution is a suit made to measure and is actually worn. It is, however, an assumption that requires verification in every single case.

There are other cases where a constitution, though legally valid, is actually not lived up to. Its reality and activation are imperfect. This should not be confused with the universally recognized situation that the constitution as written differs from the constitution as applied. Constitutions change, not only by formal constitutional amendments, but even more so, imperceptibly, by constitutional usages. What is aimed at here is the factual state of affairs that a constitution, though legally valid, has no integrated reality. The American Constitution is the law of the land in all the United States, but the Fourteenth Amendment is not fully activated in, for example, Mississippi and Alabama. To continue the simile: It is a ready-made suit which is not worn; it hangs in the closet. In this case the constitution is merely *nominal*.

Finally, there are cases in which the constitution is fully applied and activated, but it is merely the formalization of the existing location and exercise of political power. The mobility of power dynamics, to adjust which is the essential purpose of any constitution, is "frozen" in the interest of the actual power holder. The suit is no suit at all but a fancy dress or a mere cloak. In this case the constitution is nothing but *"semantic."*

The normative constitution prevails in the West where it serves as the procedural frame for the compromise of the power contest. Of the new constitutions, in addition to those of France, Germany, and Italy, those of Israel, India, and Ceylon come under this category, the first because it is manipulated by an intellectually Westernized people, the latter two because of the education the political élite had received in contacts with the British. Burma (constitution of 1947) can hardly be counted here,

her experience with self-government being too scanty.

The nominal constitution, on the other hand, is merely a declaration of constitutional intent, a blueprint expected to become a reality in the future. Its habitat is in nations where Western constitutionalism is implanted into a colonial and/or agrarian-fuedal social structure. Literacy, of course, is indispensable for the reality of a constitution. But even where literacy is extensive it may seem that the rationality of Western constitutionalism is alien, at least for the time being, to the Asiatic or African mind. This situation prevails definitely in states accustomed to authoritarianism like China (Chiang Kai-shek's constitution of 1947), Southern Korea (1948) and Siam, and possibly also in the Philippines and most of the Arab states. But it is also not uncommon in Latin America where, however, Brazil, Argentina, Chile, Colombia, Uruguay, and Cuba must explicitly be exempted and ranked with Western normativism. The borderline may often be fluid. In the Latin American *ambiente,* constitutions are frequently abolished and rewritten, or suspended by the state of siege, according to shifts of the power cliques temporarily in control of the army.[15] The existence or nonexistence of a constitution does, as a rule, not much affect the life of the business community or the common people.

The case of Japan (constitution of 1946) defies classification. Even the older (1889) constitution was not normative in the sense that it served as the frame for the orderly adjustment of the power conflict. In spite of its Westernized "neutrality," it was wholly subservient to the ruling groups of industrial and agrarian feudalism and the army. The new constitution is S.C.A.P. inspired, S.C.A.P. dictated, and S.C.A.P. enforced, the democratically elected Diet operating as a mixed chorus. In the political vacuum of foreign occupation, under a foreign general as pseudo-Mikado and with party dynamics strictly controlled by him, there can hardly be a reality of the constitution even for a nation so adaptable as the Japanese.

Finally, where the written constitution is advisedly used for "legalizing," stabilizing, and perpetuating an existing configuration of power, it cannot serve as the procedural frame for the competitive power elements. This is probably the generic characteristic of all or most authoritarian constitutions, with the instruments of the years VIII and X in France or the constitution of Napoleon III (1852) as historical and the Pilsudski Constitution of 1935 as more recent examples. The existence of the written constitution is merely the face-saving gesture demanded by the present-time universal belief in democratic legitimacy. If no constitution existed at all, the prevailing power monopoly of a person, group, class, or party would not be changed to a substantial degree. At the most, such constitutions regulate the assignment of high-level jurisdictions as the formal basis for the orderly conduct of the governmental business no state can do without. In the narrow sense of the term these instruments are positivist in that they "freeze" the existing power situation. Actually their purpose is semantic camouflage.

Under this category come most of the Soviet satellite constitutions,[16] but equally so those of other states of quasi-feudal structure (Egypt, Iran, Iraq). In underdeveloped countries the distinction between the semantic and the nominal constitution cannot always be applied with satisfactory precision.

## COMPARATIVE OBSERVATIONS ON THE FUNCTIONAL STRUCTURE

### 1. The Legislative-Executive Relations

The legislative-executive relationship—whether in co-ordination or in subordination—is the essence of the "form of government." The solutions attempted reveal the differences between the normativism of the West and the semanticism of the East. In the fully developed "people's democracy," exemplified by Hungary (1949), the problem offers no difficulty. In the place of co-ordination and co-operation there exists, by a curious inversion characteristic of assembly government, a strictly hierarchical system of subordination. The parliament, allegedly "the highest state organ" (Art. 10), is completely dominated by its presidium (called "Presidential Council of the People's Democracy," Arts. 20 and 21), which, in turn, completely controls the Council of Ministers, spoken of as the "highest organ of state administration" (Art. 22) and controlling the local councils hierarchically. All levels are of course linked together by the Communist party (or, in other satellites, the National Front) concerning which the document is semantically silent. No simpler, less complex, and more direct technique for the exercise of political power ever has been put on paper.

In the Western climate, on the other hand, the executive-legislative relationship continues to remain the core of constitutional engineering. There is no longer the eighteenth-century illusion that government and parliament could be harmoniously equilibrized or mutually balanced. The alternatives are either a strong government superior to the parliament, at the expense of responsiveness to public opinion, or a government continually dependent on the whims of the parliamentary parties. The controlling viewpoint is the avoidance of cabinet crises occasioned by the lack of stability of the party coalition supporting the government.

The framers of the new constitutions were visibly impressed by the one hundred-odd cabinets that had occurred under the Third Republic in France within sixty-five years and the twenty-odd under Weimar within fourteen years. A sizable number thereof, being accidental and without deeper political implications, could have been avoided by rationalized parliamentary procedures. Consequently, technical efforts are now made to limit them by the injection of cooling-off periods between the motion for, and the vote of, nonconfidence, or the requirement of a minimum of signatures for the former (Italy, Art. 94) and of absolute majorities for the latter (France, Art. 45; Germany, Bonn, Arts. 67, 68). But the danger of recurrent cabinet crises seems somewhat overemphasized. The record will disclose that many, if not the majority, of the cabinet changes were occasioned by justified demands of the opposition for a change in legislative policies to which the new government conformed. This, after all, is the inherent function of parliamentary government. The exceptional situation under Weimar, to the effect that heterogeneous and basically antidemocratic opposition parties combine "unconstructively" for the overthrow of the government without being able or willing to form an alternative government, may not easily present itself elsewhere. Moreover, breaks in governmental continuity are often mitigated by the "replastering" technique in constituting the new cabinets. Outside France the record of governmental stability since 1945 leaves little to be desired, perhaps with the exception of Belgium while laboring under the singular pressure of the *question constitutionnelle* (the struggle for the removal of Leopold III). Moreover, it may seem doubtful whether cabinet crises are actually the congenital vice of parliamentarism, or whether it is the inability of any "pattern of government" to reconcile political opposites refusing to agree on the socioeconomic fundamentals of the common existence. The common people, with their unstunted sense of realities, are much more aware of this basic dilemma than the politicians and party manipulators themselves.

At any rate, the search for the magic formula to establish a crisis-proof system continues, but the circle remains as unsquared as before. Where the distrust of the strong executive is nationally ingrained as in France, the recourse to unmitigated parliamentarism seems the lesser evil. The French rely largely on the skill of their parliamentarians. Where, as in Germany, the strong executive is an article of national faith, the legislature—and with it the democratic fundamentals—have to foot the bill. The Germans try to ward off spontaneous eruptions of the power conflict by making the Chancellor quasi-irremovable during the four-year term of the *Bundestag* and strengthening his hands, with the *dolus eventualis* of authoritarian government, by the ominous "legislative emergency powers" (Art. 81), under which even if defeated he can operate without parliamentary support for at least six months. The historically less inhibited Italians trust the natural balance of the political forces and the fear of Communism holding together the artificial majority of the Christian Democrats. Evidently parliamentary crises are the price to pay for multiple parties, which Continental politics seemingly cannot be disabused of.

## 2. Dissolution

In the authentic form of parliamentary government,[17] dissolution is the democratic fulcrum of the entire process of adjusting power conflicts by making the electorate the ultimate policy-determining factor. Compared with the period after 1919 dissolution takes a serious beating in the new constitutions even though the French have at long last cautiously revived it (Arts. 51, 52). The curbs to which it is subjected in France and Bonn, Germany, come under the same heading of the search for the crisis-proof constitution. Only in Italy (Art. 88) does the institution preserve its genuine plebiscitary function. Five years of experience in France have demonstrated that the party oligarchies, shifting power among themselves, are as afraid of the people as before, meaning the Communists to the left and the de Gaullists to the right. In Germany, likewise, where dissolution has been resorted to frequently under the empire and Weimar, it seems destined to wither on the vine. Moreover, as F. A. Hermens has emphasized,[18] dissolution loses much of its plebiscitary effect if conducted under proportional representation, which tends to stabilize the existing party pattern. Dissolution, of course, is incompatible with assembly government except in the remote contingency of self-dissolution (Hungary, Arts. 18, 1).[19]

## 3. Position of the President

Within the same context of legislative-executive relations the position of the President has been noticeably weakened in comparison with 1919 and after. Because of its greater democratic prestige, popular election is no longer favored except where, as in Latin America, the American pattern is followed. The President is generally confined to state integrating and ceremonial functions. He retains, however, the designation of the Prime Minister (France, Italy, Israel, India); in Western Germany this function has shifted to the *Bundestag* by election (Art. 63) and in Eastern Germany the strongest party automatically is charged to name the executive-designate (Art. 92). The discretionary powers of the President in dissolution are completely eliminated in France (Arts. 51, 52) and severely restricted by the mechanization of the entire procedure in Western Germany (Arts. 58, 63, 4). Assembly government as a rule dispenses with the office altogether, its functions being performed by the Presidium; for reasons of expediency, however, the office is retained without an actual share in power, in the U.S.S.R., Eastern Germany, Poland, Czechoslovakia, and Yugoslavia.

## 4. Second Chambers

Except in federal states the unicameral organization is now generally preferred. The final emasculation of the British House of Lords by the Labour government is paralleled by the powerless Council of the Republic in France and reflected, to some extent, in the position of the Federal Council (*Bundesrat*) under Bonn, which, while strengthening the position of the territorial subdivisions in matters affecting them, is confined to a suspensive veto in federal affairs and without influence on federal political dynamics. Italy has seen fit to restate full-fledged bicameralism with political equality of the Chamber and the Senate, the latter based on a spurious effort to achieve a different composition by "Regions" and, at least in theory, capable of overthrowing the government.

If an "upper" house were to serve as the brake on, or balance of, accidental party fluctuations within the lower house, it would require a different composition, based on corporate units, specific social strata, more mature age groups, or meritorious individual personalities. But this traditional function of the second chamber has become largely obsolete; an exception is the strictly consultative Senate in Bavaria (constitution of 1946, Arts. 34 ff.). While, thus, the decay of the second-chamber technique is a universal phenomenon, it may seem regrettable that corporativism, whose natural location would be the second chamber, though discredited by totalitarian abuse, has not been given the chance of a democratic trial; the Economic Council in France is weaker than other applications (in Czechoslovakia and Weimar Germany) after 1919. The professional stratification of socioeconomic life in organized power groups is one of the undeniable realities of countries professing a free economy; the powerful combines of labor, cooperatives, management, agriculture, civil servants, professional and other interest groups, deprived of legitimate participation in the formation of public policies, are forced to operate either through political parties or to exert power outside the constitution itself. On this score the postwar constitutions have not been able to face realities.

Under assembly government in nonfederal states the second chamber is at variance with the political doctrine and has been discarded everywhere.

## 5. Federalism

Federalism is on the decline, and this in spite of various institutionalizations in the West and the East. Experience in the oldest and best integrated federal states, the United States and Switzerland, demonstrates that, whatever strength of tradition and emotional values of political theory federalism is still imbued with, the economic imperatives of the technological state require unified if not uniform economic policies throughout the entire territory and do not brook that kind of economic fragmentation which goes with effective member-state sovereignties.[20] To point it up sententiously: A state with a federal income tax is no longer a genuinely federal state. On the other hand, the realization is equally general that, even in relatively small areas, decentralization enhances administrative efficiency. Federalism as an organizational device cannot be divorced from the general political philosophy of the age. Federalism is a product of liberal thinking. It applied the (relative) freedom of the individual to the (relative) freedom of organization of territorial entities. It thrives as long as a free economy thrives. Speaking again sententiously: Economic planning is the DDT of federalism. Constitutions, therefore, that take their federal premises too seriously can hardly escape becoming anachronistic.

However, federalism is essential and indispensable where strong tendencies of multinational or tribal diversity prevail. The Indian Constitution, trying to organize and govern a multinational subcontinent, could not operate without evolving a sort of superfederalism, being applied, in terms of the First Schedule to Article 1, to at least three different categories of states and territorial subdivisions with different legal status in regard to their relations to the Union. This kind of "quantitative" federalism obviously is imperative for the growing together of literally hundreds of socially widely divergent separate communities. Federalism in India, and also in Burma, likewise a "Union," seems a method of social integration rather than of perpetuated diversification.

Of the Iron Curtain constitutions, only that of Yugoslavia follows the Soviet federal pattern. But if the inclusive evidence permits an evaluation, the emphasis, as in the U.S.S.R., is on cultural autonomy rather than political self-government. How far the new collectivist way of life, emanating from planning, has succeeded in overcoming the age-old nationalism of the Croats, Montenegrins, and Macedonians, and their resentment of Serb ascendancy, remains to be seen. Whatever may be the degree of effectiveness of cultural autonomy, the social-planning mechanism extends uniformly to all subdivisions. With the older type of federalism in the West it has evidently nothing in common but the name. Federalism of the five *Länder* in Eastern Germany is wholly semantic, as can be easily seen from the unitarian constitution of the German Democratic Republic.

Nor is federalism in Western Germany any longer the genuine article, belying the endless labor of the military governments and the Germans in fashioning it. On the surface the constitution of Bonn is less unitarian than Weimar. But the facts of economic interdependence of the area militate against genuine federalism, except in certain cultural matters. Actually the elaborate and ambitious *Land* constitutions of the Western zones mean little for the people. The decisive socioeconomic issues, such as economic policies, social security, codetermination, and tax distribution, devolve on the federal government in Bonn. In Italy the new "Regions"[21] remain to date a dead letter (except, to a limited extent, in Sicily, Sardinia, and Alto Adige), and this for the same reasons as elsewhere; namely, that local autonomy cannot but be subservient to nation-wide economic and social policies. Federalism in Latin America (Argentina, Brazil, Venezuela, Mexico) finally never amounted to much in practice because of the constitutionally legalized and frequently used practice of federal intervention.

## 6. Suffrage, Electoral System, and Political Parties

Democratic equality for the formation of the will of the state is no longer problematic. Universal suffrage with, in some instances, a considerably lowered voting age is the general standard. All censitory vestiges have disappeared. But it is indicative of the existing cleavage between constitutional nominalism and political reality that, while proportional representation is universally favored, the operative technique of this (and any) electoral system, the political party, is almost universally ignored. Political parties are mentioned, it is true, in the Bonn (Art. 21) and the Italian (Art. 49) Constitutions as recognized instruments for the formation of the political will of the people. But the fact is carefully ignored that proportional representation, more than any other electoral system, puts the actual exercise of political power into the hands of the party oligarchies and their bureaucracies, which are entirely beyond popular control. The ubiquitous result is the political vacuum in which the party-manipulated parliaments everywhere operate. The general lack of prestige of the political congeries called political parties cannot fail to be reflected in the waning respect the people have for the parliaments themselves.

It is readily admitted that the integration of the political party into the mechanism of the frame of government—recognition of the party within the bill of rights as a phenomenon of the individual right of political association is, of course, merely declaratory—is one of the most difficult aspects of constitutional renovation. The issue may, for the time being, be inaccessible to legal formulas. But it is equally obvious that silence of all constitutions on the emergence of new elites—in the West the party bosses and their bureaucracies, the parliamentary oligarchies, and, in the East, the powerful layer of the officials of the state party and the managerial technicians of the state-owned industries —is a much more potent reality than the ubiquitously proclaimed "sovereignty of the people" France, Art. 3, 1; Italy, Art. 1, 2; Germany, Bonn, Art. 20, 2). Sovereignty actually is located in the political parties.[22] The statement (Germany, Bonn, Art. 38, 1) that the individual deputies in parliament represent the entire nation is a piece of undiluted semantics.

The situation is aggravated by the visibly declining emphasis on participation of the people in the political process. It is confined to elections of the parliament at regular intervals or in the (rare) case of dissolution. Initiative and referendum—the latter only in connection with the amending process (France, Art. 90; Italy, Art. 138)—are conspicuous by their absence in Western Europe, let alone elsewhere, probably because of the inconclusive result of direct democracy in the constitutions after 1919. Monopolization of political power by the party oligarchies makes the new constitutions less democratic than their predecessors.

In the monopolization of the popular will by the single or state party, the people's democracies are more honest, and probably can afford to be. The constitution is not a blueprint to be activated in the future, but it closely reflects, and is synchronized with, the actual power configuration reached in the particular country. The paramount function of the single party is admitted and exalted. No longer an abstraction, it is a stark reality, incorporated in the frame of government proper. In the Soviet Constitution of 1936 the Communist party as "the vanguard of the toilers" is an official state organ (Arts. 126, 141). Since in the earlier elaborations of the Soviet system the transition to the single-party state was not completed, the Communist party (or its equivalent) could not yet be given the privileged position. But in the Hungarian Constitution (1949) the "People's Democracy bases itself on the organization of the class conscious workers" and "the leading force in [such] political and social activities is the working class" (Art. 56, 2). Of the thirty-six times the "workers," "working class," or "class conscious workers" are mentioned in this document, not a few refer to the workers as activators of political power rather than as its addressees. And the constitution of the German Democratic Republic could openly assign (Art. 92) the position of the Minister-President to the strongest party because the power apparatus could by now be trusted to identify this as the Socialist Unity party.

## 7. Constitutional Amendment

In this revolutionary age constitutions, however carefully projected into the future, cannot aspire to make permanent their political solutions. In this

they differ from the optimism of the eighteenth century; the Directory Constitution of 1795 was practically unamendable. Consequently, the process of constitutional amendment everywhere is kept sensibly elastic, neither too rigid to invite, with changing conditions, revolutionary rupture, nor too flexible to allow basic modifications without the consent of qualified majorities. However, the amending procedure is rationalized in the sense that it can no longer be "by-passed." In France the Constitutional Committee (Arts. 91 ff.) determines whether a law passed by the National Assembly requires a revision of the constitution; this is a sort of substitute for judicial review of the constitutionality of statutes. In Western Germany the amendment requires the effective change of the text of the constitution (Art. 79, 2). All the more surprising is the increasing illusion that certain fundamentals can be made "unamendable" (republican form of government, Italy, Art. 139; France, Art. 95; federal structure and basic rights, Germany, Bonn, Art. 79, 3). The Indian provision (Sec. 305), to the effect that certain minorities (Muslims, Scheduled Castes, etc.) shall not be deprived of their seats in the federal and state legislatures for a period of ten years, is one of functional utility rather than of governmental philosophy.

## 8. Judicial Power and the Judicialization of Political Power

Western constitutionalism believes traditionally in the clear-cut separation of the judicial function from the other two branches of government and, correspondingly, in the independence of the judiciary secured by tenure. The Soviet approach deliberately discards the separation of powers in whatever form and under whatever disguise. Assembly government, therefore, does not countenance any *capitis diminutio* either by an independent judiciary or by judicial review of legislation. In spite of some face-saving semantics the judicial function is strictly subordinated to the legislative by election and recall through the parliament, for example in the German Democratic Republic (Arts. 130, 131) or Hungary (Art. 39).

In the West serious efforts were undertaken to protect appointment and promotion of the judiciary from extraneous influence or political pressure. Neutralization of the patronage by the political parties is sought in France through the Supreme Council of the Magistrature (Arts. 83 ff.), and in Italy by the creation of the magistrature as an autonomous organization, charged with the exclusive responsibility for the composition and supervision of the judiciary (Arts. 104 ff.). Western Germany has gone furthest in setting up the judicial branch as co-equal with the other two. While the technical arrangements may seem impeccable, they do not go into the core of the problem. In Germany the judges are public officials and, therefore, not independent of the state. De-Nazification has not succeeded in breaking their class consciousness. Basically the independence of the judiciary resolves itself into the sociological dilemma of a judicial caste, a situation with which the American public in its own environment is thoroughly familiar.

Judicial review of the constitutionality of laws that previously had been recognized only for federal-state relations is now viewed with more favor. In Italy (Art. 134) and Germany, Bonn (Art. 93), it is assigned to a special Constitutional Court. It is generally implied in the judicial function in Japan (Art. 76, 3, 8), while in France it is attenuated to the determination, by the Constitutional Committee acting only on a joint request by the President and the Council of the Republic, whether a law passed by the National Assembly would actually require a constitutional amendment (Arts. 91 ff.). Unavoidable differences of opinion in the interpretation of the new constitutions may well call for an objective judicial decision; but it may seem doubtful whether the institution will integrate itself into political life as the unique regulatory force it is in the United States.

But perhaps more important may become what may be called the judicialization of political power; namely, the efforts to tame the power conflict by subjecting political dynamics to judicial decisions. In Italy (Arts. 134 ff.) and Germany, Bonn (Art. 93), the constitutional tribunal is charged with deciding "conflicts of jurisdiction between the powers of the state" or, in the German version, "disputes concerning rights and duties of the supreme federal organs." Insofar as such conflicts are determinable by positive constitutional norms—the rare exception —judicialization may lead to beneficial results. If, however, jurisdictional attributions of the constitution are being used by the various state organs—for example, by the President against the government or by the government against the parliament—in the competition for political power, the belief that power aspirations can be "decontaminated" by legal formulas may seem to overtax the function of the judiciary. Seemingly the poor showing of the German Supreme Court in an analogous power conflict between the Prussian and the Reich Governments in 1932 was no deterrent. In older and wiser countries the courts exercise self-restraint by refusing to pass on "political questions" or *actes de gouvernement,* which the Germans call *"justizlose Hohheitsakte."*[23] The basic issues of the power process are not justiciable. Reliance on normative legality may impede rather than promote the need for political compromise.

## 9. The Function of the Bill of Rights

Particularly pertinent for the inquiry into the ontological meaning of the constitutions are the principles contained in the bill of rights. In the earlier development of written constitutions the libertarian and equalitarian postulates of the bills of rights were as important as the functional arrangements of the frame of government. The French Declaration of 1789 has assumed the quality of a superconstitutional validity and reality even if the constitution, as, for example, that of 1875, did not contain a restatement or failed to refer to it *expressis verbis.* The (second) constitution of 1946, therefore, could confine itself to a global incorporation by confirming it in the preamble, with some additional socioeconomic rights which the revolutionary fathers could not foresee. But during the nineteenth century, when liberalism was taken for granted, the accent shifted definitely to the functional organization, which, if properly arranged, could be expected to accommodate any socioeconomic system the majority desired to establish by constitutional means. That the Bismarckian Constitution of 1871 failed to register a bill of rights was not due to the authoritarian neglect of the framer but rather to the belief generally adhered to in the period that a constitution should confine itself to functional arrangements and that the main virtue of the declaration of rights consisted in symbolizing the state under the rule of law.

The constitutions after World War I, in whose elaboration the Socialist parties shared for the first time, appear more alerted toward the need of implementnig the classic catalogue of libertarian and equalitarian freedoms from the state by a new socioeconomic pattern of economic security and social justice. But again the concept prevails that, beyond certain programmatic aspirations, the decision should be left to the social and political forces contending for power within the framework of the constitution itself. The sociopolitical content of the bills of rights became more important but still not important enough actually to determine and control the functional arrangements in the form of government.

Nothing is more indicative of the parting of the roads between West and East after World War II than the changed position of the bill of rights. In most of the "people's democracies" the relationship between the functional and the ideological parts of the constitution is reversed. What is variously called socioeconomic structure or organization[24] is not only separated from the classical libertarian rights and freedoms—whose actuality under the police state is obviously nominal—but is moved forward into the body of the functional provisions and, thus, considered as binding as the latter. Nationalization of natural resources, state ownership of the means of production, economic planning, the foreign-trade monopoly of the state, and the restrictions on private ownership and property that go with them are no longer programmatic aspirations; they are now part and parcel of the structure of government necessitating a new type of administrative organization. The functional organization is conditioned on the socioeconomic pattern.

In the West the program of the bills of rights has not materially advanced beyond what was reached after World War I. The bills are still large-scale and pretentious catechisms of socioeconomic, cultural, and educational postulates, nowhere raised to the rank of subjective rights the individual can enforce against the state or, what amounts to the same, implying duties of the state to carry out and implement the program by positive legislation. Moreover, without corresponding judicial protection even most of the libertarian freedoms are of paper value only. On the other hand, Bonn, Germany, is more advanced in converting the basic rights into positive rules of law immediately binding legislation, administration, and adjudication (Art. 1, 3) and opening, by way of a general clause, access to the courts for redress against any violation of the constitutionally guaranteed private sphere by governmental or administrative action (Art. 19, 4).

What may seem more important is the twilight zone in which the political philosophy moves. The bills of rights are as articulate and comprehensive as they are evasive on the decisive social issues of labor-management relations and the property complex as the key to the alternatives of private capitalism or socialization, *laissez faire* or planning. These temporizations are due, of course, to the structure of the party coalition, which was primarily responsible for them (in the three key states dominated by the Christian Democrats). That the elusiveness of the socioeconomic program deprives the most vital parts of the constitution of attraction for the masses can be easily realized by a comparison with Great Britain, where the unformalized character of the basic order permitted the general election of 1945 to become the plebiscite inauguarating a social revolution of the first magnitude.

# ON THE CRAFTSMANSHIP
# OF CONSTITUTIONS

The sociological implications of the craftsmanship in writing a constitution—the drafting skill and the "style"[25]—are still unexplored. The symbolic value of the American Constitution, no less than its functional utility, derives to a considerable degree from the unusually felicitous combination of form and content. Craftsmanship is conditioned, besides national traditions, on the sociological and professional composition of the constituent assembly; the intellectual climate of the period; and foreign influences or even foreign intervention

(as in the cases of the recent Japanese and German constitutions). A nation starting its constitutional life from scratch is probably less inhibited than a people whose new constitution is merely another link in the traditional chain of the national manifestations of the political will, as in Germany or in France. The indifferent craftsmanship of the French Constitution of 1875, merely a bundle of unrelated organic laws, reflects the *"attente monarchique."* Instruments drafted by an individual leader for his own use are, as a rule, consistent and responsive to the actual power configuration, as evidenced by Napoleon's Constitution of the year VIII or Bismarck's Constitution of 1871.[26] The craftsmanship of constitutions emanating from party coalitions is bound to reflect the compromises of conflicting aspirations. It is also fairly obvious that the more a constitution aims at ultimately "neutralizing" and regularizing the power process by injecting into it checks and balances, the more complex it must become, and complexity taxes drafting skill. Since the Iron Curtain instruments merely confirm the existing power situation, they can afford to be simple, straightforward, and direct and can dispense with the complex strategy of distributing functions among various state organs to avoid abuse of power by any one of them. Regarding their stylistic craftsmanship a considered judgment is possible only for one who can read the originals; in translation they all sound alike and are alike drab. The French Constitution of 1946, owing to its being grafted on a previous instrument, does not live up to the national reputation, while both the constitution of Italy and the (draft) constitution of Israel are distinguished by clarity and logical arrangement.

A related problem is that of elaborateness and length. The ideal constitution will contain *only* the essentials of the national political order— organs, functions, jurisdictional delineation—but, at the same time, *all* the essentials. If a constitution wishes to be crisis proof—that is, in practice, to avoid deadlocks between the constituted organs —it can leave nothing to chance and must spell out all contingencies. In trying to be "gapless" it approximates the substance of a code that is necessarily more lengthy and complex. Other constitutions, setting greater store by the wisdom and moderation of their manipulators to compromise the power conflict, need be less specific. Once again the semantic constitutions of the East have the advantage of brevity and conciseness in the functional arrangements because they are not likely to be exposed to the strain of competitive political forces.

On the whole, the recent vintage of constitutions is more verbose and articulate than the previous families of constitutions. But here the national "style" tradition comes into focus. Anglo-Saxon legal training and habits of statutory formulation, which try to cover all foreseeable eventualities, are responsible for the length and the minutiae of the Indian Constitution whose 315 articles and 8 schedules fill a book, with the Burmese Constitution of 234 articles running a close second. Much of this is, of course, due to the conditions of a multinational federalism and religious differences. In the West the Bavarian Constitution of 1946 holds the record in the number of words without claiming the palm of craftsmanship.

There is no evidence that any of the new constitutions will attain either the symbolic value or the rank of a piece of classic literature that distinguishes the American Constitution. They are instruments written by lawyers for lawyers. Excessive legalism in craftsmanship necessarily minimizes the appeal to, and the emotional attachment of, the people. This, in turn, cannot fail to reflect adversely on the potential integration of the new constitutions in the minds of the people as the addressees of political power.

## THE PEOPLE AND THE CONSTITUTION

At this point the crucial question may be raised: What do constitutions, in our time, mean to the people? Are they "living" in the sense that they are essential for the life not of the professionals manipulating them but of the common people? Or, somewhat more emotionally pointed up: Is the constitution instrumental for the pursuit of happiness of the people? There is no parallel to the phenomenon of the American Constitution as a living reality for the American people, which, beyond its well-advertised quality as a social myth, is essential because it served, and still serves, for the peaceful (and at times even playful) adjustment of the power conflict. It is, of course, a patriotic distortion to attribute the absence of the class struggle in this country to the constitution; rather, the reverse is true. The continued congruity between constitutional form and socioeconomic substance can be preserved because there is no social class to which the functional organization of the constitution denies its share in political power. With the exception of the War between the States no major social conflict has challenged it. The New Deal was accommodated within the constitutional frame with relative ease.

The new constitutions will find it difficult to integrate themselves in the minds of the people. They mean next to nothing, or very little, to the little man ground between the nether and the upper millstones. To be sure, most people value the return of legal security and administration conducted without galling arbitrariness. But the constitutions are indifferent toward the realities of the life of the people, incapable of satisfying the minimum of social justice and economic security that the common people believe themselves entitled to, the pretentious bills of rights to the contrary notwithstanding. The vital issues are no longer decided by constitutional processes but by the pressure groups operating outside and often in opposition to them. The constitution cannot, and does not, bridge the gap between poverty and wealth. Everywhere, with the possible exception of Britain and the marginal monarchies of Western and Northern Europe, the people distrust their governments, their officials, their parties and parliaments, and their constitutions. What is true for the sophisticated West may even be truer for the East wherever the education of the masses for the Communist eschatology is still incomplete. If the constitution means little for the citizen in Bordeaux or Frankfurt, how much can it mean for the illiterate coolie in Shanghai? The moral crisis of this age cannot fail to vitiate the moral value of a constitution that fails to provide tangible remedies for tangible grievances.

The actual value of a constitutional order can be tested only in the wear and tear of the political process. Predictions, therefore, are mere speculations. Since the constitutions in the Soviet orbit are formalizations of the specific power entrenchment of single-party control and not destined to serve for free power competition, they will not last a day longer than Communist coercion will last. This may be long, and longer than the people living thereunder would desire. How the new constitutions in the West will stand up under the strain of a serious economic or political crisis remains to be seen. In spite of hectic efforts to make them crisis- and shockproof, the inherent defects of the representative parliamentary system have not been exorcised. Authoritarianism remains the skeleton in the closet, except in a political environment with the traditional wisdom of the parliamentary elite trained to govern and, perhaps, the stabilizing influence of respected monarchies.

But obviously the causes for the ambivalence of Western constitutionalism lie deeper than in the inadequacy of functional arrangements. We have not yet begun to investigate the ontological causality between the form of government a constitution endorses and the socioeconomic structure of the society to which it is applied. The inquiry is hampered by still existing residues of the naïve optimism of the eighteenth century that a functionally well-constructed constitution can adjust peacefully any power conflict. That much can be learned from the crude materialism of the Soviet-orbit constitutions; viz., that a definitely chosen socioeconomic pattern requires a commensurate institutionalization of the power situation. The Communists realized that not every constitution can accommodate any form of society, and that a specific society requires a specific constitutional order. The concept that the constitution, confined to the jurisdictional determination of authority, can be "neutral" and "objective" toward the power process is as much a by-product of liberal relativism as is the concept that the written constitution itself is a child of liberal rationalism. In the light of our—admittedly limited—historical experience, it seems likely that an inner congruity exists between constitutional form and societal substance.

To state the thesis in more concrete terms: Athenian direct democracy was predicated on the nontechnological economy of a small and socially homogeneous community based on slavery. The absolute monarchy of the prerevolutionary period corresponded to the social stratification of landed wealth and the hereditary privilege of an aristocratic society. Parliamentary democracy, or rather oligarchy, was suitable for the dominance of the middle-class *bourgeoisie*, rooted politically and economically in *laissez faire*. Liberal constitutionalism could afford to raise the rule of law to the dignity of an absolute value. When finally the laboring masses, unwilling to abide by the rules of liberal capitalism, claimed their share of economic and political power, this form of government was bound to become inadequate. The transformation of capitalism into all-out socialism by planning and nationalization of the natural resources, the means of production and trade, required the authoritarian form of government for the new ruling class. It is most unlikely that this will be more than a transitional stage in the never-ending political experimentation of mankind. On his appointed day the new Montesquieu will arise.

## NOTES

1. The following enumeration is incomplete: *Germany:* two federal constitutions (1949), one each for the Western (*Deutsche Bundesrepublik*) and the Eastern part (*Deutsche Demokratische Republik*); each of the four *Länder* in the United States zone (1945–1946); three in the French zone (in addition to the Saar); five in the Soviet zone (1946–1947); two in the British zone (North-Rhine-Westphalia and Schleswig-Holstein (1950); those in Lower Saxony and Hamburg are in the process of completion. Berlin adopted two constitutions (1946 and 1948). *France:* two constitutions (1946); the first, of April 27, 1946, was rejected by referendum. Other new constitutions in Western Europe are: *Italy* (1947); *Iceland* (1944). In Eastern Europe new constitutions were adopted by the Soviet satellite states of *Yugoslavia* (1946); *Albania* (1946), which was reportedly supplanted by a new constitution in 1950; *Bulgaria* (1947); *Czechoslovakia* (1948); *Ru-*

*mania* (1948); *Hungary* (1949); *Poland* confined itself to an adaptation of the older constitution of 1920. Latin America has had nine new constitutions since 1945: *Bolivia* (1945); *Brazil* (1946); *Ecuador* (1946); *El Salvador* (1945); *Guatemala* (1945); *Haiti* (1946); *Nicaragua* (1948); *Panama* (1946); *Venezuela* (1947). Among the new constitutions in Asia are: *China* (1946); *Japan* (1946); *Siam* (Thailand) (1949); *Korea* (1948); whether Northern Korea had a constitution is not known. Others, in the British sphere of influence, are *India* (1949); *Ceylon* (1946); *Burma* (1948). In Pakistan and Indonesia, constitutions are under preparation. *Israel,* after a draft constitution (1948), operates on the basis of an *interim* or "little" constitution (1949). *Transjordan* adopted a constitution in 1946.

Reliable texts are not easily obtainable except in the case of Western Europe and Latin America; a good collection of the latter is edited by Russell H. Fitzgibbon, *The Constitutions of Latin America* (Chicago, 1948). For the Arab world, see Helen Miller Davis, *Constitutions, Electoral Laws, and Treaties of the States in the Near and Middle East* (Durham, N.C., 1947). The ambitious undertaking by Amos J. Peaslee, *Constitutions of Nations* (Concord, N.H., 1950), to assemble in three volumes the constitutions of all states seems, at least to the author of this section, a complete and unmitigated failure. Translations are often far from accurate even if obtained from American embassies abroad. The factual data (in some cases even concerning the very date of the constitution) are shot through with crude errors; the introductions of the editor are often without understanding. Much of the tabulatory material is worthless. The bibliographies are neither up to date nor properly selective. Misspellings abound. It is regrettable that the author's efforts have resulted in so amateurish a compilation.

2. See Karl Loewenstein, *Political Reconstruction* (New York, 1946), pp. 317 ff.

3. No student desirous of divesting himself from the stereotypes of constitutional legalism will ignore the work of Max Weber and Guglielmo Ferrero's trilogy: *Bonaparte in Italy* (London, 1939); *The Reconstruction of Europe* (New York, 1941); *The Principles of Power* (New York, 1943). Relevant materials may be found in: John A. Hawgood, *Modern Constitutions since 1787* (New York, 1939); Karl Loewenstein, "The Balance between Legislative and Executive Power," *Chicago Law Review,* V (1938), 566 ff.; Georges Burdeau, *Traité des sciences politiques* (3 vols.; Paris, 1949, 1950) (Vol. III contains the general theory of constitutions); Maurice Duverger, *Manuel de droit constitutionnel et de la science politique* (Paris, 1948); Dietrich Schindler, *Verfassungsrecht und soziale Struktur* (Zurich, 1932); J. Allen Smith, *The Growth and Decadence of Constitutional Government* (New York, 1930); Samuel L. Sharp, *New Constitutions in the Soviet Sphere* (Washington, D.C., 1950).

4. See, for example, Egon Zweig, *Die Lehre vom pouvoir constituant* (Tübingen, 1909); Walther Rothschild, *Der Gedanke der geschriebenen Verfassung in England* (Tübingen and Leipzig, 1903); Richard Schmidt, *Die Vorgeschichte der geschriebenen Verfassung* (Leipzig, 1916).

5. See, for example, *The Federalist,* No. 51, and the interesting observations by Hans J. Morgenthau, *Politics among Nations* (New York, 1949), pp. 125 ff. See

also, on the problem of political equilibrium, Carl Schmitt, *Verfassungslehre* (Munich and Leipzig, 1928), pp. 183 f.

6. See Robert Redslob, *Die Staatstheorien der französischen Nationalversammlung von 1789* (Leipzig, 1912); Karl Loewenstein, *Volk und Parlament nach der Staatsauffassung der französischen Nationalversammlung von 1789* (Munich, 1922).

7. See John A. Hawgood, *Modern Constitutions since 1787* (New York, 1939), pp. 93 ff., 131 ff., who calls the two patterns the "condescended" and the "negotiated" state, respectively.

8. See Arnold J. Zurcher, *The Experiment with Democracy in Central Europe* (New York, 1933).

9. See Karl Loewenstein, *Political Reconstruction* (New York, 1946), pp. 138 ff., 168 ff.

10. A striking illustration is the issue of industrial codetermination in Western Germany, to all intents and purposes the most significant development in management-labor relations in postwar Europe. The Bonn Constitution was prudently silent on it; the federal parliament unable to solve it. When the pressure of the labor unions in coal and steel forced the issue, the *Bundestag* had to yield. The constitutional machinery was used merely for ex post facto ratification.

11. For a detailed discussion of the postwar patterns of government, see Karl Loewenstein, "The Presidency Outside the United States," *The Journal of Politics,* XI (1949), 447 ff.

12. Albania, Bulgaria, Hungary, Yugoslavia, Rumania. Poland and Czechoslovakia are exceptions, the former having re-established, with some streamlining, the constitution of 1920 (Constitutional Act of February 19, 1947); the latter rewrote the constitution of 1920 in 1948.

13. See, for example, Hungary (Arts. 19–22), where it is called "Presidential Council." It does not exist, however, in the German Democratic Republic and is seemingly less well endowed with power in Czechoslovakia and Poland.

14. The leading discussion is Alfons Steiniger, *Das Blocksystem* (Berlin, 1949).

15. Venezuela's Constitution of 1947 (now suspended) is the twenty-second in one hundred and thirty-six years.

16. Samuel L. Sharp, in "Communist Regimes in Eastern Europe," *Foreign Policy Reports,* XXVI, No. 16 (January 1, 1951), 183, states that, "in accordance with Stalinist doctrine, constitutions merely register situations of fact already achieved." This explains convincingly that the still existing differences of the constitutions in the Soviet-controlled area, between themselves as well as with the Soviet prototype, are due to the gradualism of evolution toward the Soviet pattern. Hungary, as the latest formulation (1949), is closest and without Westernized pretenses of objectivity. It may be added that the comparative affinity of the Eastern German constitutions (which Sharp does not discuss) to the Western system is occasioned by the desire not to antagonize the Western Germans directly. Therefore, the multiple-party system is nominally preserved.

17. Robert Redslob's *Die parlamentarische Regierung* (Tübingen, 1918) (French edition, *Le Régime parlementaire* [Paris, 1924]), most influential after 1919, is now almost forgotten.

18. Ferdinand A. Hermens, *Mehrheitswahlrecht oder Verhältniswahlrecht?* (Munich, 1949); *Europe between Democracy and Anarchy* (Notre Dame, 1951). See also Maurice Duverger, *L'Influence des systèmes électoraux sur la vie politique* (Paris, 1950).

19. See also the equally unlikely case of dissolution in Art. 95, 6, of the Eastern German Constitution.

20. The case of Switzerland is particularly illustrative. The partial revision of the constitution in 1947 (Arts. 31 ff.) practically not only modified the policy of economic *laissez faire* but subjected the entire economic life of the Swiss confederation to federal control.

21. See Pietro Virga, *La regione* (Milan, 1949).

22. Constitutional theory, on the other hand, has become widely aware of the changed situation. See, for example, Pascal Arrighi, *Le Statut des partis* (Paris, 1948); Pedro J. Frias, *El ordenamiento legal de los partidos politicos* (Buenos Aires, 1944); Wilhelm Grewe, *Zum Begriff der politischen Partei,* Festgabe für Erich Kaufmann (Sutttgart, 1950), pp. 65 ff.

23. See, for example, Werner Weber, *Weimarer Verfassung und Bonner Grundgesetz* (Göttingen, 1949).

24. Hungary (social structure, Arts. 4–9); Rumania (social and economic structure, Arts. 5–15); Yugoslavia (socioeconomic organization, Arts. 14–20); Bulgaria (public economic organization, Arts. 6–14). In the German Democratic Republic the break with the tradition is less visible because the economic order (Arts. 19–29) is placed together with other categories of rights under a common heading, "Substance and Limits of Sovereignty."

25. See Heinrich Triepel, *Vom Stil des Rechts* (Heidelberg, 1947). The issue is of practical importance, for example, in dealing with the positive validity of preambles, which are a common feature of most recent constitutions.

26. Unique in the history of constitution-making is the poetic vision incorporated by Gabriele d'Annunzio in his constitution for Fiume, *"La reggenza italiana del Carnero";* see *Il Popolo d'Italia,* September 1, 1920.

# THREE CONSTITUTIONAL COURTS: A COMPARISON

Taylor Cole

Two years ago, when an astute critic made a half-century appraisal of comparative politics in the United States, he reminded us that the American Political Science Association was founded in 1903 as an outgrowth of moves to establish a National Conference on Comparative Legislation.[1] During the more than half-century that followed, the writings in comparative government and politics have reflected the influences which have made themselves felt in the discipline as a whole. The attention given by Charles E. Merriam after World War I to "informal government," "underlying processes and relations," and "social bases of political cohesion" is fully appreciated now by those who are projecting comparative studies of political socialization.[2] In the 1930s, Carl J. Friedrich's writings pointed up the need for more adequate conceptualization when combined with appropriate appreciation of empirical research.[3] Mention should also be made of the earlier works of Herman Finer.[4] In their respective ways, albeit in varying degrees, all of these writers recognized the need for an increased emphasis upon the informal and extra-legal factors affecting the political process, and for more concern with generalization and theory.

Prior to World War II, there had been a growing belief in some quarters that much of the work in comparative government was a mere parochial accumulation of facts about Western institutions.[5] The needs experienced during the War called for far more systematic classification and interpretation of existing data, as well as for the use of new sources of information. Developments of the postwar period—the cold war, the anti-colonial movements, and the growth of nationalism in various parts of the globe—helped place a premium on policy-oriented research.

In this setting, and cognizant of the efforts in the social science disciplines to seek for a greater comparability of research findings, the Committee on Comparative Politics of the Social Science Research Council was established in 1954. On the basis of some common orientation and with a bias for functional analysis, this committee has encouraged a large number of studies focused on political groups in Western and non-Western countries.[6] These efforts are necessarily experimental. They have provoked some questions as to whether the interest group approach will lead to better understanding of political institutions and behaviors than would other approaches.[7] Notwithstanding, this "pioneering" represents one of the most promising and provocative group research efforts in comparative politics today.

Work in comparative administration has also developed rapidly since World War II under the auspices of governments, universities, and professional societies. Moreover, serious attempts are being made to move beyond the "action research" which has held the center of the stage in the past.[8] New American journals have appeared, such as the *American Journal of Comparative Law,* and *Comparative Studies in Society and History.* Both foreign and domestic institutes and centers are directing greater attention to research in comparative politics. This is also true of the international associations, including the International Political Science Association. *The Study of Comparative Government and Politics,* edited by Gunnar Heckscher,[9] and *Interest Groups on Four Continents,* edited by Henry W. Ehrmann,[10] embody some of the reflections of foreign and American political scientists on the scope, methodology, objectives, and trends in comparative politics.

As Charles S. Hyneman recently reminded us in his *The Study of Politics,*[11] there are many paths for the laborer to follow in this vineyard. Each of us will doubtless be guided in that direction to which his interest, training, and experience point.

This evening, we have set for ourselves a modest assignment in an area which has received too little

Reprinted from *The American Political Science Review,* Vol. LIII, No. 4 (December, 1959), pp. 963–984, by permission of The American Political Science Association.

Presidential address delivered at the annual meeting of the American Political Science Association, Washington, D.C., September 3, 1959.

attention and which is deserving of more study in the future. That will be to examine, comparatively, the Constitutional Courts of three Western European countries—those of West Germany, Italy, and Austria. We shall discuss the reasons for their creation, some of their most significant decisions, and the general position which they occupy in their own political systems.

# I

Constitutional Courts have been established in the three countries in accordance with the provisions of their respective Constitutions, as implemented by the necessary legislation. These Constitutions are the Austrian one of 1920 (as amended in 1925 and 1929) which was reinstituted during the uncertain postwar period in 1945, the Italian Constitution of 1948, and the West German Basic Law of 1949. Though the Austrian Constitution presents a special case, all three may be classed as of post-World War II vintage. The Constitutions of West Germany and Italy were the product of negative revolutions, reflecting a deep distaste for the "dismal past." As characterized by our Chairman of this evening,

> The political theory of the new Constitutions which are democratic in the traditional Western sense . . . revolves . . . around four major focal points which distinguish them from their predecessors: (1) reaffirmation of human rights, *but* (2) efforts to restrict these rights in such a way as to make them unavailable to the enemies of constitutional democracy, (3) stress upon social goals and their implementation through socialization, *but* (4) efforts to circumscribe the goals and their implementation in such a way as to prevent the reëmergence of totalitarian methods and dictatorship.[12]

To achieve these goals, the specially provided Constitutional Courts were to play an important part.

In seeking the explanations for the adoption of these special Courts, we are reminded that judicial review in continental Europe, as in the United States, had its roots in the higher law background and conceptions of ancient and medieval times. The precedents for special courts to protect the fundamentality of the Constitution can be traced at least as far back as the 18th century, when written constitutions came into being,[13] with the proposals of Abbé Siéyès in the 1790s for the creation of a constitutional jury. The work of a succession of distinguished advocates of judicial review, who refused to accept some of the implications and influences stemming from the French Revolution, followed at later periods.

That this heritage and this special advocacy were alone inadequate to account for the later creation of Constitutional Courts is evident from a glance at the history of Western Europe. It was not until postmortems on World War I that the Austrian Constitutional Court came into being. And there were particular considerations after World War II which gave an impetus to the establishment of special courts in West Germany and Italy.

The most obvious influence was that of national precedent. In the case of West Germany, there were precedents which could be traced from the constitutional proposals of the National Assembly of 1848 down to the history of the National Supreme Court (*Reichsgericht*), and of the High Court (*Staatsgerichtshof*) of the Weimar period. The High Court had jurisdiction over the settlement of disputes between states (*Länder*) and between states and the *Reich,* as well as over impeachment cases. The Supreme Court passed upon the compatibility of state laws with federal laws, and it reviewed the constitutional validity not only of state, but also in several instances of federal legislation. But there were various limitations which operated to restrict the scope and effectiveness of the activities of these Courts. In Austria, traces of the Austrian Constitutional Court can be found in constitutional developments of the period between 1848–1851, and especially in the establishment in 1867 of the Court of the Empire (*Reichsgericht*). As time went on, this Court exercised jurisdiction over the claims of the provinces (*Länder*) against the Empire and *vice versa;* it dealt with conflicts of competence between judicial and administrative authorities at both the provincial and national level, and with complaints of citizens over the violation of constitutionally guaranteed political rights after other remedies had been exhausted. As for Italy, though there were certain pre-1922 procedures and institutions which pointed toward judicial review, these were of limited significance. The first noteworthy Italian precedent was provided by the Sicilian High Court, created by the Regional Statute of May 15, 1946.

Foreign example can also be stressed. Certain of the practices and procedures in Switzerland, particularly the use of the constitutional complaint, were given serious attention during the drafting of the Bonn Basic Law. The exercise of judicial review by the United States Supreme Court has received continued attention in European countries. As one Italian professor has observed, the "impact of *Marbury* vs. *Madison* was felt in Italy almost a century and a half after the decision."[14] To these considerations may be added indirect pressures which were brought to bear by the occupying powers after 1945, especially by the United States in Germany. However, evidence that direct Allied pressure was responsible for the final action taken is lacking in all three instances.[15]

But it was definitely the reaction to excesses of

the Fascist and Nazi regimes which was the most important factor in the decisions finally taken in Austria to restore her Constitution of 1920, as amended in 1925 and 1929, with its provision for a Constitutional Court; and in Italy and Germany, to establish new Courts. There was remarkable unanimity among most of the democratic parties in all three countries to grant the power of judicial review to some type of court. This same reaction helps explain the incorporation of elaborate bills of rights, to protect the individual, and of federalistic arrangements which, while borrowing from the past, were directed against the centralization of the Fascist period. Judicial review, in some hands, was widely accepted as necessary to safeguard these guaranteed liberties and arrangements. Disagreements existed over the type of court, its organization and composition, and over the method of selecting the judges. The answers were provided by the special Constitutional Courts. In short, external influences and pressures combined with domestic concerns to explain the final decisions which were taken.

The most controversial of these decisions, as evidenced in the debates in the Constituent Assembly in Austria in 1919–20, and in the German Parliamentary Council and the Italian Constituent Assembly between 1946–49, turned on the manner of selecting the judges. These discussions were concerned with the degree of independence to be accorded the Court from the political departments, especially from the parliament. In all three instances, compromises were effected, which provided for a method of selection differing from that used in choosing the judges of the highest regular court and which allowed for some participation by both houses of parliament in the selection process. Today, in Germany the 20 judges of the two Senates, or "twin courts," are selected by parliament, one-half of them by the *Bundestag* and one-half by the *Bundesrat;* six of them are chosen from the judiciary for life and the remainder for 8-year terms. In Italy, one-third of the 15 judges are chosen by the magistracy of the three highest Courts (Cassation, Council of State, and Accounts), one-third by the two houses of parliament sitting together, and one-third by the President—all eventually to hold office for 12-year terms. In Austria, the President, the Vice President, and 6 of the additional 12 judges, as well as 3 substitutes, are appointed by the President from nominees of the Federal Government; the remaining 6 judges, and 3 substitutes, are appointed in part on the recommendation of the lower house, the National Council, and in part on the recommendation of the upper house, the Federal Council. Unlike a majority of the German justices and all of the Italian justices, these are appointed for life. No instances of the use of the removal power over members by the Courts[16] during the post-World War

II period have been recorded, though there have been resignations. In the three countries, provisions are made for the appointment to the Courts of practicing judges and high administrative officials, as well as professors of law. Indeed, the substantial percentage of professors on all of the Courts[17] reflects the long-established practice in continental European countries to look toward the universities in making high judicial appointments.

Partisan considerations have played their part in the selections, though it has not always been possible to document the extent to which such factors have been controlling. The many early criticisms of the German procedure of selection have been based in part on the charge that political affiliation was more important than professional attainment, but it should be noted that all of the German judges except two have been elected unanimously, and re-election has been customary. The operation of *Proporz,* that is, the proportional allocation of administrative and other posts on the basis of the strength of the two major coalition parties, was discussed in 1957, in connection with the appointment of a new president of the Austrian Constitutional Court.[18] Italy had the greatest difficulties in securing the enabling legislation necessary to implement the constitutional provisions regarding the Court[19] and in selecting the judges after the implementing legislation had been finally passed in 1953. The requirement that 5 of the judges must be selected by a three-fifths majority of the two houses of parliament, where approximately 40 per cent of the seats were held by the left-wing parties which demanded representation, presented particular difficulties and provided the background for much of the maneuvering which occurred.[20]

But, withal, there has been only limited criticism of the judges after their selection; on the contrary, there has been general commendation, though the anonymity attached to the method of making decisions and the absence of dissenting opinions may offer protection from public criticism of the partisan and incompetent judge. In short, the judges have become "judicialized" rather than "politicalized" with the passage of time.

The jurisdiction of the West German Constitutional Court is the most extensive and that of the Italian Court the most limited of the three Courts. With variations as to scope and application, the Courts in all three countries have the power to review the constitutionality of federal and state, or provincial and regional, legislation.[21] They pass upon disputes involving "conflicts of competence" between the central governments and the states, provinces, or regions, as well as between these latter political units. They also can decide jurisdictional disputes between "organs" of government at the national level in West Germany and Italy, and between the courts, or courts and administrative authorities, in Austria. They can try impeachments or accusations against certain officials at the national level in West Germany and Italy, or against federal and provincial officials in Austria. Both the Austrian and West German Courts have some jurisdiction in cases involving disputed elections and international law. In addition, each Court possesses some special competences which are unique to it. For example, the West German Court may pass upon the constitutionality of political parties and the forfeiture of basic rights. Advisory opinions were authorized by legislation in Germany until the repeal of the empowering provisions in 1956.

But a mere mention of the competences of the Courts will tell little, without a recognition that their functioning depends heavily upon the nature of the social structures within which they operate. These societies have been referred to as fragmented ones in which there is sharp competition between political cultures. The extent of political involvement by the citizen and the development of institutional pluralism vary in the three countries; the degree of consensus, on procedural if not substantive matters, is lower in all instances than that to be found, for example, in Britain.[22] The legal backgrounds of the three countries, with their differing ingredients of Roman and Germanic law, affect the position of the judges. And there are many other considerations which have a bearing on the role of the Courts. The federalism of West Germany and Austria, and the "attenuated federalism" of Italy, merit particular attention. The nature of the party system (with the trend toward the two-party system in West Germany, government by party cartel "with built-in opposition" in Austria,[23] and shifting coalitions based upon a mass party in the center in Italy) affects the legislative product of the parliaments which is subject to review by the Courts. We must of necessity leave these matters with only passing mention, though with a full appreciation of their significance in appraising the work of the Constitutional Courts.

## II

In examining the work of the Courts, some attention may be directed to selected decisions dealing with (1) equality before the law, (2) federalism, (3) delegation of legislative powers, and (4) legislation and public service relationships dating from the Fascist and National Socialist periods.

The Constitutions of each of the three countries contain an almost identical guarantee that "all persons shall be equal before the law."[24] In addition, they include certain other clauses which are to make more specific the general guarantees. The differences among these reflect the varied historical circumstances under which these constitutional provisions had their origins.

The significance of the equality-before-the-law guarantees must be viewed in the light of the accessibility of the Courts in question. West Germany, to speak generally, provides a more liberal access to the Court than either Austria or Italy. For the individual, two avenues are open to the German Court, the most widely used being the constitutional complaint.[25] Under this arrangement, any person can question before the Court a law, an act having the force of law, or an administrative decision and order, which violates his constitutional guarantees, including equal protection before the law. He likewise may, during proceedings in regular courts, secure the judicial review of legislation, which allegedly infringes his rights, though the courts themselves must determine whether the access to the Constitutional Court is justified. While the Austrian system also provides two somewhat comparable modes of access, they are more narrowly construed than in Germany. In Italy, the access to the Constitutional Court is still more limited, as there is only the one procedure of judicial review. The institution of constitutional complaint, as it exists in Germany and, in a modified form in Austria,[26] is unknown in Italy.

The West German Court, in the cases before it, has applied the general principle that equal protection prohibits differential treatment of that which is essentially equal but "it does not prevent that which is essentially unequal from being treated by the legislature differentially in proportion to its inequality."[27] There must be a reasonableness of classification in all instances, even outside the range of the specific prohibition of discrimination on the grounds of sex, race, descent, language, place of birth, or religious belief. At the same time, the Court—applying the guarantee of equal rights to men and women—has recognized permissible distinctions involving the biological and functional differences of the sexes. Thus, on May 10, 1957[28] the Court rejected two constitutional complaints by male plaintiffs who alleged that the provisions of the Criminal Code under which they had been committed violated Article 3 of the Basic Law, in that these provisions provided no punishment for women convicted of comparable offenses. In a highly publicized decision announced on July 29, 1959,[29] the Court held that certain provisions of the Civil Code[30] violated Article 3, Sections 2 and 3 (as well as Article 6) of the Basic Law in that they denied the equal status of man and wife with regard to their children. Several housewives had brought constitutional complaints before the Court alleging that these statutory provisions accorded to the father the right of legal representation and certain other rights with respect to the child, and thereby discriminated against the mother. The Court found no biological or functional differences between man and wife which justified the statutory differentiations.[31]

This was the first major instance involving family relations where the Court had based its decision specifically upon the provisions of the Basic Law concerning equality of the sexes. The Austrian Court had in the previous year held the provisions of Section 26, paragraph 3, of the Income Tax Law of 1953, providing for joint taxation of man and wife, to violate Article 7 of the Constitution in differentiating between the sexes for tax purposes.[32] This case, and others involving the granting of concessions and the treatment of public employees, illustrate the extension of the applicability of the equality before the law provisions to new aspects of social relationships.

Aside from the fact that access of the individual to the Courts is limited in Italy, there are other considerations which explain why the Italian Court seems to have accepted the most restrictive view on equal protection. In review cases, it allows the widest discretion to a legislative finding of facts. Said the Court in a decision in 1957: "the evaluation of the relevance of the diversity of situations in which the individuals subject to the legal regulations find themselves cannot but be reserved to the discretion of the legislature, as long as the limits specified in the first paragraph of Article 3 are observed";[33] however, the "principle of equality is violated when the legislators subject to an indiscriminate discipline situations which they consider themselves and declare to be different."[34]

It has been particularly in cases involving equality before the law that the West German Federal Constitutional Court has given some evidence of its recognition of a higher law above the positive law, that is, of a superior and unwritten constitutional law. Though there were earlier statements by the Court to which natural law adherents might point, the Court perhaps gave its clearest expression of the acceptance of a "hierarchy of norms within the Basic Law" and of certain natural law "guidelines" in a decision of December 18, 1953,[35] involving the equality of the rights of men and women. There the Court did acknowledge the possibility in "extreme cases" of conflicts between the positive law of the Basic Law and of the higher law.[36] The Court was here reflecting something of the natural law revival in post-World War II Germany, which had resulted in part from a reaction against the earlier positivist justifications for the Nazi regime. Since 1953, it appears that the Court has been deliberately more careful in its references. It has tended more to stress the "basic principles" of the Constitution as expressed in the specific provisions of the Basic Law, and it is being cautious in providing continuing opportunity to reopen the debates on "unconstitutional constitutional norms."[37]

Of the three Courts, the Italian Court has been the most careful to confine its reasoning narrowly to the provisions of the Constitution and to avoid overt reference to value judgments based on natural law in its decisions. Certainly, the Italian Court has insisted that its jurisdiction is limited to examination of the compatibility of laws and of acts having the force of law with the Constitution, and that it is not competent to pass upon the constitutionality of constitutional norms. The position of the Austrian Court appears to be different from the other two: it has not rejected completely the review of constitutional norms, as has the Italian Court, nor has it claimed the right to subject constitutional provisions to review in the light of higher or natural law precepts. In its much discussed decision on provincial citizenship on December 12, 1952,[38] the Court recognized that it could not review the substance of constitutional provisions in the light of higher or supra-positive ideas "since, in general, any standard for such an examination is missing."[39] It has, however, insisted upon its power to decide whether a proposed amendment involves a "total revision of the Constitution" and hence is subject to a popular referendum.[40] In this instance, the Court must go beyond the formal requirements of enactment to a consideration of those basic constitutional principles whose alteration would involve "total revision."[41] Thus, in all three countries, the quest of the judges for foundations on which to base some of their decisions regarding individual rights and, specifically, the application of the equality before the law provisions of the Constitutions, continues.

The restraints which are imposed by a federalistic system and by federalistic arrangements upon the exercise of arbitrary power at the center were recognized by many of the framers of the Bonn Basic Law and the Italian Constitution. They also helped influence the sequence of events in Austria in 1919–20 and, again, during 1945–46. Since only four of the regions in Italy have as yet been created, the relationships in that state can be called only pseudo-federalistic. Nevertheless, the regions which have been established are guaranteed a significant degree of autonomy which can be altered only by constitutional amendment.

It is easy to overstress the centralizing trends in West Germany, unless there is adequate appreciation of the functioning of the *Bundesrat* and of the Federal Constitutional Court. Two of the most significant decisions of the Federal Constitutional Court, in particular, have evidenced its efforts to draw the lines between the competences of the Federal and the state governments. In the highly controversial Concordat case, decided on March 26, 1957,[42] while the Court recognized that the Concordat of 1933 was still a binding treaty, it did sustain the school legislation of Lower Saxony as falling under its reserved powers.

Several events in the spring and early summer

of 1958 provided the setting for the much publicized atomic rearmament referenda cases involving the states of Hamburg, Bremen, and Hesse and decided on July 30, 1958.[43] In the play of party politics, the Social Democratic Party had sought and failed to secure the passage by the *Bundestag* of an act to provide for a national referendum on atomic rearmament. It resorted to other tactics to secure what it termed "consultative plebiscites." The states of Hamburg and Bremen, both with legislative bodies containing Social Democratic majorities, passed legislation for holding referenda at the state level. At the request of the Federal Minister of Interior, the Federal Constitutional Court issued on May 27, 1958, restraining orders to prevent the implementation of state laws pending a final decision by the Court as to their constitutionality. The Court, in following certain selected arguments of the Federal government in its joint decision, found the acts of Hamburg and Bremen to be unconstitutional. They represented attempts to provide for the participation of the citizens "in an area within the exclusive jurisdiction of the Federal Government." In addition, "instructions" through referenda from the people of the state to "representatives" were violative of the Basic Law. The Court, in its brief decision, was particularly parsimonious in its discussion of Article 28 of the Basic Law, which recognizes the right of the states to deal with their own constitutional organization as long as they meet "republican, democratic, and social rule of law" requirements. But, recognizing the restricted grounds on which it based its decisions, the Court did give evidence that it would impose limits on the efforts of the states to explore at the behest of a political party uncharted jurisdictional areas under the federal system. These, and other recent decisions,[44] indicate some of the efforts of the Federal Constitutional Court to draw the lines between the competences of the federal and state governments.

The Constitutional Court in Austria has been faced with equally complex problems. After World War II, this Court has taken again as a basis for some of its decisions the theory of freezing of the distribution of competences (*Versteinerungstheorie*) at a given time in the constitutional development during the First Republic. The date chosen was that of the effectiveness of the first constitutional amendment on October 1, 1925.[45] Nevertheless, certain general trends in the decisions of the Court may be noted. During the first years after 1946, the Court's decisions were seemingly directed toward the protection of the modest sphere of reserved powers of the provinces.[46] However, in later years, the Court has more frequently decided in favor of the Federation. Thus, by a decision in 1951, the Constitutional Court upheld the second Nationalization Law of March 26, 1947, which recognized the power of the Federation to nationalize electricity and power plants.[47] Again

in 1952, the Court sustained the law of 1949 providing for the equalization of economic burdens as falling within federal jurisdiction.[48] In a suit brought in 1953, while several provisions of the law establishing the Federal Chamber of Commerce were invalidated, the essential contentions of the plaintiff government of Vienna were rejected.[49] In 1954, the Court recognized that the control of radio fell entirely within the jurisdiction of the Federation;[50] in 1956, the first Nationalization Law of 1946 was sustained.[51] These decisions must, of course, be compared with those which have favored the provinces.[52] But they must also be read in the light of the realities of the coalition government and of the changing international status of Austria, which have served to encourage federal legislation tending to narrow progressively the area of provincial autonomy.

Though the constitutional provisions have been only partially implemented, regionalism in Italy has provided more than its share of legal controversy. Indeed, more than half of the 381 cases "disposed of" by the Italian Constitutional Court prior to March 31, 1957 involved disputes between the central government and the regions.[53] The most controversial questions have involved the relations between the Sicilian High Court, which was created in accordance with Articles 24–30 of the Special Statute for Sicily on May 15, 1946, and was authorized to pass upon the constitutionality of laws enacted by the Sicilian legislature and the compatibility of national laws with the Regional Statute.[54] After the Italian Constitutional Court began to function in 1956, the problem of the relationship of the two Courts arose. In a decision of February 27, 1957[55] the Constitutional Court refused to recognize the possibility of a coexisting and competing jurisdiction with the High Court, at least over subjects within the competence of the Constitutional Court. But there are still unsettled questions involving the relationships between the two, as recent decisions of the Constitutional Court bear witness.[56] Indeed, the Italian Constitutional Court has evidenced a cautious approach in its efforts to demarcate the autonomous sphere of the sensitive regions.[57]

Thus, the West German Court is looked upon more as a protector of the reserved powers of the states than is the Austrian Court. The decisions of the Federal Constitutional Court appear to be of the greater significance in the total political picture, but its competences are broader. Its decisions have commanded more attention, but it is the newer creation. There has been less concern generated by the decisions of the Austrian Court, possibly because there is little evidence that its decisions have threatened major parts of the legislative program of the coalition government. The jurisdictional controversies between the central government and the regions in Italy, while occupying much of the Court's attention, necessarily have limited application.

The concern over the dangers of unlimited delegation of legislative powers was reflected in the attempts of the Constitution makers to place constitutional restraints upon such delegation, as, for example, in Article 80 of the Basic Law in West Germany. This Article, empowering legislative bodies to authorize the Federal Government, a minister, or a state government to issue decrees implementing legislation, requires that the "content, purpose, and scope" of the statutory basis be specific. In 1956,[58] and again in 1958,[59] the Court has found provisions of legislation to be lacking in clarity as to "content, purpose, and scope" insofar as they authorized certain implementing decrees. But, said the Court in 1958, in a case involving designated paragraphs of the Price Law of 1948,[60] it is not necessary that "content, purpose, and scope" be expressly stated in the statutory basis; it suffices if they can be deduced from the whole statute, its styling, its meaning in context, its history. "This can be done in the present case."

In Italy, Article 76 of the Constitution provides that "the exercise of the legislative function cannot be delegated to the Government unless directive principles and criteria have been determined and only for a limited time and for definite purposes." There the Court has recognized that the determination of cases involving the unconstitutional delegation of legislative powers is one of its most important tasks.[61] The Court has invalidated, as being in effect "unconfined and vagrant," a law which left to the administrative authorities the determination of contributions (and of the persons required to contribute) to the tourist offices.[62] While it did not do so, the Court might well have borrowed from the language used by Justice Cardozo in 1935 in dissenting in the *Panama Refining Co.* and in concurring in the *Schechter* cases.[63]

The complicated history of restraints on legislative delegation, and of the legality of "law-amending ordinances" in Austria, defies brief summarization. But, according to numerous decisions of the Court, Article 18 of the Constitution permits the legislature to authorize the issuance only of implementing and not of "law-amending" ordinances; in order to justify the implementation, the statutory basis must prescribe the essential limits within which the intended regulations will be confined and the purposes toward which they will be directed.[64] The Court has not hesitated to strike down statutory provisions which have violated these requirements. In short, in differing ways but with rather similar results, the Constitutional Courts of the three countries have been concerned with the application of constitutional provisions designed to prevent the legislature from leaving ill-defined and broad discretion in the hands of the administrator.

The Courts have been called upon to pass on the constitutionality of post-World War II legislation which dealt with public officials and military personnel in service during the Nazi regime in Germany, and of legislation enacted during the Fascist and Nazi regimes in Italy and Austria and affecting the private rights of individuals.

In West Germany, Article 131 of the Bonn Basic Law provides that the legal relationship of persons, including refugees and expellees, who were in the public service on May 8, 1945 and had been excluded from the public service on other than civil service or salary grounds, and who had not received positions comparable to their previous posts, was to be regulated by law. Such a law was passed on May 11, 1951. The Court rejected on December 17, 1953,[65] constitutional complaints of certain public officials who alleged that various constitutional rights had been violated by the law. The Court pointed out that, while under international law the state had retained its identity after 1945, the public service relationship had fundamentally changed during the Nazi regime. Consequently, the legislature could, in the exercise of its discretion, determine the status of the plaintiffs without allowing them any grounds for constitutional complaint against the law based upon their previous public service relationships. Similarly, the Court held that the *Wehrmacht* ceased to exist with the unconditional surrender of German military forces in 1945, and rejected the constitutional complaints entered by various officers, officials, and members of the former *Wehrmacht* directed against the Law of May 11, 1951.[66] In particular, the Court in a constitutional complaint of a former official of the *Gestapo*, took the opportunity to answer various criticisms of its previous "131" decisions and presented a lengthy and devastating analysis of the nature of the public service relationship during the Third Reich.[67] The tenor of the Court decisions, in passing upon the rights of officialdom of a previous totalitarian regime, has been consistent with its application of Article 21 of the Basic Law, under which the Nazi-oriented Socialist Reich Party was dissolved and its assets confiscated in 1952,[68] and the successor case, decided in 1956,[69] in which the Communist Party of West Germany was subjected to the same penalties.

In Italy, a large percentage of the "civil liberties cases" have involved the constitutionality of legislation which was enacted during the Fascist period (including the Criminal Code, the Code of Criminal Procedure, and the Police Law of 1931). Indeed, roughly one-third of the first forty decisions of the Court involved the constitutionality of criminal laws and regulations, most of them of Fascist vintage.[70] To take a few examples: in 1956, Article 157 of the Police Law of 1931 providing for repatriation to the community of origin by administrative decree was held to be incompatible with the Articles of the Constitution guaranteeing the inviolability of personal liberty and freedom of travel;[71] in 1957, a section of the Police Law of 1931 requiring notification in case of religious ceremonies outside of churches, irrespective of the place where held, was considered inconsistent with the Constitution;[72] in the following year, the Court invalidated the provisions of a Law of 1942, which left to administrative officials the discretion to authorize the opening of private schools.[73] "Such a system," preserved "even after the collapse of the regime which established it," said the Court, "is incompatible with the meaning which the Republican Constitution attributes to the freedom of the school."

Under the provisional Constitution of Austria of 1945, two constitutional transitional laws were passed, the one to nullify constitutional provisions of the period after 1933, and the other, to deal with the period after 1938.[74] The latter of these transitional laws provided that "all laws and ordinances . . . passed after March 13, 1938 which are incompatible with the existence of a free and independent Austria or with the principles of true democracy, or which contradict the legal conceptions of the Austrian people or reflect typical National-Socialist ideas, are abrogated." This provision which, at least after 1953, the Court has held to be applicable without any governmental ordinance designating the laws or ordinances to be abrogated, has provided the basis for several decisions of the Austrian Court.[75]

There is no need to mention the several illustrations which might be cited. Suffice it to say that in Austria, as in Italy, the Court has been continuously concerned with an examination of legislation, or legal norms, dating from the previous regimes and has invalidated many of them which have been violative of the Constitution. In so acting, the Courts in these two countries have perhaps offered some instigation to parliaments which have been slow to revise legislation still bearing some of the Fascist and National-Socialist substance as well as imprint.

If we have dwelt at some length on certain selected decisions of these Courts, it has been to indicate the ways in which the Constitutions are being interpreted by the judges of the Constitutional Courts. They have clearly pointed out some of the effective constitutional limits beyond which the legislator and the administrator cannot go in their actions affecting individual rights.

## III

Any conclusion regarding the role of the Constitutional Courts must be highly tentative and subject to much more critical examination. The record of the West German Constitutional Court has occasioned more comment than that of either Italy or Austria, possibly because of the breadth of its jurisdiction, its daring during the formative years, and the controversial character of some of its decisions.

In the relation of the Constitutional Courts to other governmental organs at the national level, there have been crisis periods in each of the countries. The German crisis occurred during 1952-53, when the consideration of the European Defense Community Treaties eventuated in what one critic called a "period of judicial frustration."[76] However, despite the critical position taken at that time in certain official quarters, the Adenauer Government has looked with increasing sympathy upon the Court in recent years. The *Bundesrat* has furnished more friendly support for the Court than has the governmental coalition in the *Bundestag*. The Social Democratic Party, as the opposition party, and the governments of certain of the states, as the weaker elements in the federal system, have viewed the Court as the protector of the rights of minorities. Although there have been various proposals coming from several circles for the reform of the Court, such minor changes in composition, organization, and jurisdiction as were made by legislation in 1956 and 1959, have emanated from the Court itself.

The crises in the brief history of the Italian Court were those which took place during the long period of delay after 1948, before implementing legislation could be enacted, and after 1953, before the judges were finally appointed. The assortment of internal and external problems faced by the Court, culminating in the final resignation of its first President, De Nicola, in 1957, were brought sharply to public and parliamentary attention. However, the reticence of the Court to go behind a legislative finding of facts in Italy and the limited exercise of the power to invalidate statutes enacted since 1948 have kept parliamentary criticism at a minimum.

In Italy, dissatisfied groups and organizations have on occasion attacked decisions of the Court. For example, the Communists have objected to certain ones respecting land reform legislation; the Church, to others involving the application of constitutional provisions regarding freedom of worship. Some opposition to the Court has also come from the lower bureaucracy. But the really violent opposition has emanated from the regions, especially from Sicily. These reactions, when coupled with the lethargy of the Italian populace toward the Constitution, have combined to create a negative image of the Court which is gradually being erased.

In Austria, neither of the major political parties nor any important pressure groups have made the Constitutional Court a target for continuing criticism. There have been past occasions, as in 1956-57, when partisan differences almost involved the Court, but these were exceptional instances. The relationship between the Constitutional Court and the other highest courts has provoked some controversy,[77] and there has been continuing academic discussion of the right of access to and the jurisdiction of the Court. Those who favor an expansion of its jurisdiction sometimes look toward West Germany; those who favor a more restricted status, may point toward Italy. But the recent constitutional law and legislation of 1958 dealing with the Court have resulted in only slight changes in its jurisdiction and organization. In Austria, as in West Germany and Italy, there has been general acceptance of the Court, though without either generous enthusiasm or violent criticism.

There have been problems of implementation of decisions. Some have been considered in West Germany, in connection with the atomic rearmament referenda cases, and others with decisions requiring parliamentary action.[78] The failures on the part of the parliament and the bureaucracy in Italy, to accept his strictures as to implementation, help explain De Nicola's threatened resignation in 1956 as President of the Court. But the record does not show any situation comparable to the effective nullification of a Court's decision, as occurred in the United States during President Jackson's administration following the Cherokee Indian cases.[79] There have been more warnings to the Federal Constitutional Court of Germany to exercise "intellectual humility," and "self restraint" in not pushing its jurisdictional bounds beyond the limits of the feasible and the practicable, than there have been in Italy and Austria, where the more limited jurisdiction of the Courts and the greater hesitancy to question legislative enactments have been evidenced. Its record indicates that the West German Court is seeking to follow this advice, and is sensitive to the charges of "judicial legislation," but it apparently has been unable to extricate itself from involvement with what the United States Supreme Court would call political questions.

The Constitutional Courts in Europe are in part the products of reaction against a gloomy past, as previously mentioned. Some of their activities have been devoted to a liquidation of this heritage and to a prevention of its repetition. But, today, the Courts are increasingly faced with the new issues which have developed during the post-World War II period. These new issues, as well as the old ones, have continued to involve the application of the pertinent constitutional provisions regarding equality before the law, federalism, and the delegation of legislative powers.

The idea that courts, or some judicial body, should serve as the final guardian of the constitution had its roots and origins in Europe. It has seen its widest acceptance and expansion in the United States. In turn, American application and judicial experience have helped undergird the European precedents and theoretical support for the formation of special judicial bodies to guarantee the fundamentality of their constitutions.

Today, there are those who believe that the significance of judicial review in the United States is diminishing and that our Supreme Court can no longer serve as an effective protector of individual liberties and minority rights against legislative majorities and executive discretion. Is it possible, asked one thoughtful observer, that we may borrow in the future from the experience of these European Constitutional Courts rather than contribute to it—that there will be another period in the "give-and-take between the new and the old worlds?"[80]

However, it is still too early in their history to speculate about the future of these Constitutional Courts. During the past decade, they have not faced that type of crisis which economic adversity, the messianic leader, or foreign military experiment might provide. Until such a time there will be uncertainty as to the degree to which constitutional democracy today reflects an active faith, and the extent to which it is the formal expression resulting from Allied political pressure, a prosperous economy, and anti-totalitarian resentment.[81] Only then will we know how deeply rooted are the constitutions for which these Courts serve today as interpreters and guarantors.

## NOTES

1. Sigmund Neumann, "Comparative Politics: A Half-Century Appraisal," *Journal of Politics,* Vol. 19, pp. 369–90 (1957).

2. Note particularly his *Making of Citizens* (Chicago, 1931), with the subtitle, "A Comparative Study of Methods of Civic Training," in which Merriam sought to summarize and provide a central interpretation for eight country studies in a series on civic training.

3. See the introductory chapter of his *Constitutional Government and Politics* (Boston, 1937), subsequently published in revisions under the title of *Constitutional Government and Democracy.*

4. Esp., *Theory and Practice of Modern Government* (2 vols., London, 1932).

5. *E.g.,* Roy C. Macridis, *The Study of Comparative Government* (New York, 1955).

6. Over 100 articles, and formal and informal papers, have resulted from the work of the Committee. For an explanation of its evolving rationale, see Gabriel A. Almond, "A Comparative Study of Interest Groups and the Political Process," *The American Political Science Review,* Vol. 52, pp. 270–82 (1958), and Lucian W. Pye, "Political Modernization and Research on the Political Socialization Process" (mimeo, July, 1959). The major collective and interpretive effort of this Committee to date is the forthcoming volume, *The Politics of the Underdeveloped Areas,* which deals with the characteristics and classification of the political

systems and the process of political development in the new countries of Africa, South America, South Asia, and the Middle East, by Gabriel A. Almond, James S. Coleman, Lucian W. Pye, George O. Blanksten, Dankwart A. Rustow, and Myron Wiener.

7. Joseph LaPalombara, "The Utility and Limitations of Interest Group Theory in Non-American Field Situations, *Journal of Politics,* p. 6.

8. Note the current program of the American Society for Public Administration. On the literature, see, for example, Robert V. Presthus, "Behavior and Bureaucracy in Many Cultures," *Public Administration Review,* Vol. 19, pp. 25–35 (1959).

9. (London, 1957).

10. (Pittsburgh, 1958).

11. (Urbana, 1959).

12. C. J. Friedrich, "The Political Theory of the New Democratic Constitutions," *Review of Politics,* Vol. 12, pp. 217–18 (1950).

13. David Deener, "Judicial Review in Modern Constitutional Systems," *The American Political Science Review,* Vol. 46, pp. 1079–83 (1952).

14. Giuseppino Treves, "Judicial Review of Legislation in Italy," *Journal of Public Law,* Vol. 7, p. 345 (1958).

15. Even in Germany, there is considerable evidence for the view expressed by Rudolf Katz, Vice President of the Federal Constitutional Court, that there was no necessary causal relationship between the original Allied demands and the final German action. See comments and literature cited in the author's "The West German Federal Constitutional Court: An Evaluation after Six Years," *Journal of Politics,* Vol. 20, pp. 283–84 (1958), and "The *Bundesverfassungsgericht,* 1956–1958: An American Appraisal," *Jahrbuch des Öffentlichen Rechts,* Vol. 8, pp. 29–47 (1959).

16. In West Germany, by the Federal President upon the request and with the consent of the Court; in Italy and Austria, by the Courts acting directly.

17. Of the present 20 justices on the German Federal Constitutional Court, seven are professors (who retain their professional status on a part-time basis); and of the 15 justices in Italy at the end of 1958, some 10 held the title of professor. The President and Vice President, as well as other members of the Austrian Constitutional Court today, are professors in Vienna and other universities. The Constitutional Council of the Fifth French Republic (which can hardly be designated as a "constitutional court") contains no professor of law for special reasons. See Stanley H. Hoffmann, "The French Constitution of 1958: I. The Final Text and Its Prospects," [The American Political Science Review], Vol. 53, p. 341, n. 37 (1959).

18. See *Berichte und Informationen,* Dec. 6, 1957, and *Die Wochen-Presse,* Dec. 29, 1956 and Jan. 19, 1957; also Herbert P. Secher, "Coalition Government: The Case of the Second Austrian Republic," *The American Political Science Review,* Vol. 52, p. 799 (1958).

19. One of the several reasons for this delay was the hesitancy of parliament to set up a body which would restrict parliament's powers. See John Clarke Adams and Paolo Barile, "The Italian Constitutional Court in Its First Two Years of Activity," *Buffalo Law Review,* Vol. 7, pp. 250–265 (1957–58). This difficulty has reminded these two authors of the legendary story of Bertoldo, who was sentenced to be hanged and then was entrusted with the responsibility of finding an appropriate tree. In Bertoldo's case there were explainable delays.

20. Note the account in David G. Farrelly, "The Italian Constitutional Court," *Italian Quarterly,* Vol. 1, pp. 53–56 (1957).

21. All three differentiate between "incidental" proceedings, arising out of a pending trial, and "principal" proceedings, *i.e.,* those instituted by a governmental organ.

22. Note the provocative comparisons in Herbert J. Spiro, *Government by Constitution* (New York, 1959), ch. 22.

23. An expression used by Otto Kirchheimer, "The Waning of Opposition in Parliamentary Regimes," *Social Research,* Vol. 24, pp. 127–56 (1957); *cf.* Charles A. Gulick, "Austria's Socialists in the Trend toward a Two-Party System: An Interpretation of Postwar Elections," *Western Political Quarterly,* Vol. 11, pp. 539–62 (1958).

24. West Germany: Art. 3; Austria: Art. 7; Italy: Art. 3. In the following discussion, I am heavily indebted to Mr. W. R. Dallmayr for his assistance.

25. Though a number of nuisance and facetious complaints are submitted, the Court in West Germany has based an increasing percentage of its important decisions on selections from the 4,800 complaints which had been made prior to December, 1958. An illustration of the facetious complaint was one which contended that the refusal of police to extend the time during which "bars" might be kept open violated the constitutionally guaranteed right of freedom of assembly.

26. Against individual decrees and acts of the administration, but not against laws, ordinances, or court rulings.

27. 1 *Entscheidungen des Bundesverfassungsgerichts* (hereafter cited as *B.V.G.E.*) 52; *cf.* Gerhard Leibholz, *Die Gleichheit vor dem Gezetz* (2nd ed., Berlin and Munich, 1959), pp. 1–12.

28. 6 *B.V.G.E.* 389.

29. 1 *BvR* 205/58.

30. Secs. 1628 and 1629, paragraph 1. These provisions had not been altered by the Equal Protection Law of June 18, 1957. See J. Leyser, " 'Equality of the Spouses' under the New German Law," *American Journal of Comparative Law,* Vol. 7, pp. 276–87 (1958).

31. We cannot avoid quoting from an editorial in an American newspaper which commented on this decision: "Thus from Karlsruhe comes the news that father no longer has the last word. It is triumph for the species. Of course, at this point, the German wife has only acquired a sort of deadlock. There is no last word. Give her time, however, and we may be sure that she not only will have deprived mere man of the last word but will, as has her American counterpart, have appropriated it, herself." *Durham Sun,* July 5, 1959, p. 3.

32. Decision of March 29, 1958; G 1, 2, 3, 5, 29, 30/58. The Federal Constitutional Court in West Germany had in 1957 invalidated somewhat comparable provisions of the Income Tax Law of 1951, but, while expressing some doubts as to the compatibility of these statutory provisions with Art. 3 of the Basic Law, the West German Court had based its decision on the grounds of violation of Art. 6, paragraph 1, of the Basic Law. 6 *B.V.G.E.* 55.

33. *Raccolta Ufficiale delle Sentenze e Ordinanze della Corte Constituzionale* (hereafter cited as *R.U.*), No. 3, Vol. 2, 1957, p. 21, at 27.

34. *R.U.*, No. 53, Vol. 6, p. 68 (1958); also cited in Treves, "Judicial Review of Legislation in Italy," *loc. cit.*, p. 351.

35. 3 *B.V.G.E.* 225.

36. Such words and phrases as "supra-positive basic norms," "natural justice," "fundamental postulates of justice," "norms of objective ethics," etc., have been used in cases. *Cf.* Heinrich Rommen, "Natural Law in Decisions of the Federal Supreme Court and of the Constitutional Courts in Germany," *Natural Law Forum*, Vol. 4, pp. 1–25 (1959); Gottfried Dietze, "Unconstitutional Constitutional Norms? Constitutional Development in Postwar Germany," *Virginia Law Review*, Vol. 42, pp. 1–22 (1956).

37. *Cf.* the author's "The West German Federal Constitutional Court: An Evaluation after Six Years," *loc. cit.*, pp. 300–304, and the literature there cited.

38. *Sammlung der Erkenntnisse und wichtigsten Beschluesse des VGH* (hereafter cited as *Slg.*), No. 2455.

39. For pertinent comments by the three Presidents of the Court during the period since 1946, note Ludwig Adamovich, "Probleme der Verfassungsgerichtsbarkeit," *Juristische Blätter*, Vol. 72, p. 73 (1950), and "Die Verfassungsmässige Funktion des Richters," *Osterreichische Juristenzeitung*, Vol. 9, p. 410 (1954); Gustav Zigeuner, "Zehn Jahre Verfassungsgerichtshof in der Zweiten Republik," *Juristische Blätter*, Vol. 78, pp. 631–32 (1956); and the somewhat more natural-law oriented position of the present President, Walter Antoniolli, "Gleichheit vor dem Gesetz," *ibid.*, Vol. 78, pp. 611 ff. (1956).

40. See Constitution, Arts. 44 and 140.

41. At this point, as Professor Felix Ermacora has said, "the Constitutional Court is . . . the guardian of the Constitution and also the guarantor of the implementation of the requirements of direct democracy." "Die Bedeutung der Überprüfung von Bundesverfassungsgesetzen durch den Österreichischen Verfassungsgerichtshof," *Juristische Blätter*, Vol. 75, p. 539 (1953).

42. 6 *B.V.G.E.* 309.

43. 2 *BvF* 3/58 and 2 *BvF* 6/58. See also 2 *BvG* 1/58 of July 30, 1958.

44. Note the decision of June 16, 1959, in which the Court held a Federal Law concerning the Payment of Compensation Claims of 1956 to be incompatible with Article 120 of the Basic Law in that it required the states to bear expenditures which represented obligations of the Federal Government (2 *BvF* 5/56); and the decision of July 14, 1959, in which the Court held that the 1957 Federal Law for the Establishment of a Foundation called "Prussian Cultural Property" and the Transfer of Assets of the former *Land* Prussia was not in violation of Article 135 of the Basic Law. 2 *BvF* 1/58.

45. *Slg.*, Nos. 2217 (1951), 2319 (1952), 2546 (1953), and 2721 (1954).

46. Note *Slg.*, No. 2087 (1951), where the Court criticized the Federation for using the powers granted in Art. 12, Sec. 1 (under which the *Bund* lays down the "basic principles" and the province retains the power of execution) in such a way as to infringe upon the competences of the province by providing detailed regulation of the subject matter in question. For earlier post-war cases, see Paul L. Baeck, "Postwar Judicial Review of Legislative Acts: Austria," *Tulane Law Review*, Vol. 26, pp. 76–77 (1951–52).

47. *Slg.*, No. 2092 (1951).

48. *Slg.*, No. 2264 (1952). See the criticisms of this decision in Hans Spanner, "Die Prüfung von Gezetzen und Verordnungen durch den Verfassungsgerichtshof in der Zeit von 1950–1952," *Österreichische Zeitschrift für Öffentliches Recht*, Vol. 6, pp. 181–82 (1954).

49. *Slg.*, No. 2500 (1953). See also H. P. Secher, "Representative Democracy or Chamber State" (mimeographed paper delivered at the 1959 Annual Meeting of the Midwest Conference of Political Scientists), pp. 9–10.

50. *Slg.*, No. 2721 (1954).

51. *Slg.*, No. 3118 (1956).

52. For references to certain of these cases, including ones involving hunting, real estate transactions, area planning, etc., see Felix Ermacora, "Die Entwicklung des Österreichischen Verfassungsrechts seit dem Jahre 1951," *Jahrbuch des Öffentlichen Rechts*, Vol. 6, p. 339 (1957), and *Der Verfassungsgerichtshof* (Vienna, 1957), pp. 145–46. Note, particularly, a decision of June 28, 1958 (G 32/58) in which the Court declared unconstitutional a federal law of 1957 levying import duties on certain products.

53. Adams and Barile, *loc. cit.*, p. 258.

54. The Sicilian Statute was converted by the Constituent Assembly, under pressure of time, into a Constitutional Law of Feb. 26, 1948, No. 2.

55. *R.U.*, No. 38, Vol. 2, p. 375.

56. *E.g.*, a decision of January 24, 1958. *R.U.*, No. 7, Vol. 5, p. 61 (1958).

57. Note the discussion by P. Biscaretti di Ruffia, "The First Two Years of Functioning of the Italian Constitutional Court," *Il Politico*, Vol. 23, pp. 477 ff. (1958).

58. 5 *B.V.G.E.* 71.

59. 7 *B.V.G.E.* 282.

60. 8 *B.V.G.E.* 274.

61. Note the comments of President Azzariti at the beginning of the second year of activity of the Court, in *R.U.*, Vol. 3, pp. 13–14 (1957). The Italian Court has held that both the law of delegation and the authorized act are subject to its review. *R.U.*, No. 3, Vol. 2, p. 21 (1957). *Cf.* Giovanni Cassandra, "The Constitutional Court of Italy," *American Journal of Comparative Law*, Vol. 8, pp. 4–5, n. 8 (1959); Gaetano Sciascia, "Die Rechtsprechung des Verfassungsgerichtshofs der Italienischen Republik," *Jahrbuch des Öffentlichen Rechts*, Vol. 6, pp. 7–9 (1957).

62. *R.U.*, No. 47, Vol. 2, p. 507 (1957).

63. 293 U.S. 388 (1935) and 295 U.S. 495 (1935); Adams and Barile, *loc. cit.*, p. 259.

64. *E.g.*, *Slg.*, Nos. 2109 (1951), 2276 (1952), 2462 (1953), and 2664 (1954).

65. 3 *B.V.G.E.* 58.

66. 3 *B.V.G.E.* 288.

67. 6 *B.V.G.E.* 132.

68. 2 *B.V.G.E.* 1.

69. 5 *B.V.G.E.* 85.

70. Since the Constitution was silent on this point, there was doubt as to whether the Court has the power to pass upon the constitutionality of "anterior legislation," but the Court in its first decision laid all questions at rest as to its jurisdiction. *R.U.*, No. 1, Vol. 1, p. 25 (1956). See David G. Farrelly and Stanley H. Chan, "Italy's Constitutional Court: Procedural Aspects," *American Journal of Comparative Law*, Vol. 6, p. 326 (1957).

72. *R.U.,* No. 45, Vol. 2, p. 491 (1957); *cf. R.U.,* Nos. 13 and 14, Vol. 5, pp. 101–107 (1958).

73. *R.U.,* No. 36, Vol. 5, p. 231 (1958).

74. *StGBl.,* Nos. 4 and 6.

75. For example, in 1953, in the decision which declared governmental proclamation unnecessary, the Court abrogated a National Socialist Law of November 5, 1935 on Exchanges, Vocational Guidance, and Procurement of Apprentices, which had been extended to Austria after the Nazi *Anschluss,* as reflecting "typical National Socialist ideas" and as "being incompatible with . . . true democracy." *Slg.,* No. 2620 (1953). The plaintiff had, moreover, been deprived of certain rights guaranteed under Article 12 of the Basic Law of 1867 and under Article 83, paragraph 2, of the Constitution.

71. *R.U.,* No. 2, Vol. 1, p. 41 (1956).

76. Karl Löewenstein, "The Bonn Constitution and the European Defence Community Treaties, A Study in Judicial Frustration," *Yale Law Journal,* Vol. 64, pp. 805–39 (1955).

77. See *Juristische Blätter,* Vol. 79, pp. 263–65, and 287–89 (1957).

78. 8 *B.V.G.E.* 1, of June 11, 1958.

79. *Cherokee Nation v. Georgia,* 5 Peters 1 (1831), and *Worcester v. Georgia,* 6 Peters 515 (1832).

80. Gottfried Dietze, "America and Europe—Decline and Emergence of Judicial Review," *Virginia Law Review,* Vol. 44, p. 1272 (1958).

81. *Cf.* Leonard Krieger, *The German Idea of Freedom* (Boston, 1957), p. 468.

# *Parliamentary vs. Presidential Systems*

# ANALYSIS OF POLITICAL SYSTEMS

Douglas V. Verney

## PARLIAMENTARY GOVERNMENT

Parliamentarism is the most widely adopted system of government, and it seems appropriate to refer to British parliamentary experience in particular because it is the British system which has provided an example for a great many other countries. Nowadays when it is fashionable to speak of political systems and theories as "not for export" it is worth bearing in mind the success with which a system adopted piecemeal to suit British constitutional developments has proved feasible in different situations abroad. This is not to imply that the British parliamentary system should be taken as the model and that others are, as it were, deviations from the norm, although generations of Englishmen have been tempted to make this assumption. Mr. Churchill remarked, when plans for a new House of Commons were being discussed, that it should be oblong in shape like the old.

Reprinted from Douglas V. Verney, *Analysis of Political Systems* (London: Routledge and Kegan Paul Ltd., 1959; New York: The Free Press of Glencoe, 1959) pp. 17–56, by permission of the publishers.

Logic, which has created in so many countries semi-circular assemblies with buildings that give to every member, not only a seat to sit in, but often a desk to write at, with a lid to bang, has proved fatal to Parliamentary Government as we know it here in its home and in the land of its birth (393 *H.C. Debates* 5s., cols. 403–4.)

Yet of the eleven west European countries which are members of the Inter-Parliamentary Union only one, The Netherlands, has an oblong chamber like the British; and in all the chambers, the Netherlands included, Members of Parliament have their own seats. These arrangements do not appear to have been "fatal" to parliamentary government.

Indeed an examination of parliamentarism in various countries indicates that there are two main types of parliamentary procedure, the British and the Continental. In British parliamentary procedure, as adopted in the Commonwealth and Ireland, legislation is initiated in the full Assembly and not in committees. Private members speak only from their places, not from a tribune. Continental procedure is sometimes called "French" but seems to have parallel origins in Sweden and Norway. Moreover according to Hawgood in practice "it was

Belgium, and not Britain, France, Sweden or Norway, that became the pattern and prototype for constitutional monarchies everywhere during the century following 1831" (*Modern Constitutions since 1787*, pp. 145–6)—the year in which the Belgian Constitution came into force.

This analysis of parliamentarism is concerned less with distinguishing the various forms of parliamentarism than with establishing the highest common factors in different parliamentary systems. It is not therefore necessary to account for all the political institutions existing in parliamentary countries, still less to describe devices such as federalism which are common to all three types of government, presidential and conventional as well as parliamentary. It may surprise those who have tended to regard British government as the model as well as the Mother of Parliaments to know that the United Kingdom could abolish the Monarchy, adopt a single code of constitutional laws on the pattern of the French or American Constitutions, transform the House of Lords into a Senate (or even do away with it), introduce a multi-party system based on proportional representation, institute a number of parliamentary committees to deal with specific topics such as finance and foreign affairs, and still possess a parliamentary system.

There would seem to be a number of basic principles applicable to both of the chief varieties of parliamentary government. These can be analysed and later used for purposes of comparison with presidential and convention government.

## 1. The Assembly Becomes a Parliament

Where parliamentary government has evolved rather than been the product of revolution there have often been three phases, though the transition from one to the other has not always been perceptible at the time. First there has been government by a Monarch who has been responsible for the whole political system. Then there has arisen an Assembly of members who have challenged the hegemony of the King. Finally the Assembly has taken over responsibility for government, acting as a Parliament, the Monarch being deprived of most of his traditional powers.

This has certainly been the pattern in Britain. As late as the seventeenth century King James I could still preach the doctrine of the Divine Right of Kings. Addressing the Houses of Parliament in 1609 he said, "For Kings are not only God's Lieutenants upon earth, and sit upon God's throne, but even by God Himself they are called Gods." In France the Charter of 1814, framed on the restoration of the French Monarchy during Napoleon's exile to Elba, assumed the divine right of the Bourbons to the throne. During this first phase, if such it may be called, the "Government" consisted of Secretaries who helped the King in his administration. If there

was a "Parliament" it was partly because a high court of justice was necessary and partly because the Monarch wanted a sounding-board of public opinion and needed support, especially of a financial nature, for his foreign policies. Between 1302 and 1614 the French States-General met as a whole in less than forty-two years. Even in England the Houses of Parliament met in only 198 of the years between 1295 and 1614—though whereas the English Parliament was about to assert its real authority by the end of the period the States-General was to meet for the last time until 1789. The foundations of the English Parliament's strength were maintained and strengthened in the Tudor period and it required considerable finesse on the part of the Monarch to manage the two Houses. But there was as yet no question of challenging the supreme position of the Monarch as Executive. "To act without the King, to coerce his action, prescribe his policy, and hold his ministers accountable before Parliament, does not enter any man's mind." (D. L. Keir, *The Constitutional History of Modern Britain,* 3rd ed., p. 151.)

However, by establishing their power over the purse, Assemblies were ultimately able to claim their own area of jurisdiction. Henceforth the Monarch's role was increasingly that of an Executive dependent ultimately on the goodwill of the Legislature. Constitutional development entered a second phase in which the term "legislative power" was given to Assemblies to distinguish them from the "executive power" of the King. The English Civil War and the 1688 Revolution did not establish parliamentarism in England but made explicit this division of executive and legislative power between the King and the two Houses. No doubt, as we can now see, the ultimate supremacy of the Houses of Parliament could never be challenged again, but John Locke was quite right to say, as he did in his *Second Treatise of Civil Government,* that both authorities could in a sense claim to be supreme. During the eighteenth century division of responsibility became generally acknowledged and thanks to the writings of Montesquieu and Blackstone this device of government became widely celebrated as the "separation of powers." Whereas on the Continent of Europe despotic governments were the rule there was in Britain a division of power between the King and the Houses of Parliament which Englishmen considered to be the "guardian of their liberties and a bulwark against tyranny."

A similar trend is discernible in Scandinavia early in the nineteenth century. Sweden passed from the first to the second phase with the introduction of a new Constitution in 1809. Gustavian absolutism gave way to the rule of the Bernadottes under a system where "the King alone shall govern the realm" (Article 4) but where at the same time the Riksdag was made *solely* responsible for taxation (Article 57).

But even as the theory of the separation of

powers was coming into vogue the transition to the third and present phase was under way in Britain. In the eighteenth century the King was already losing his executive power to Ministers who came to regard the Assembly, not the Monarch, as the sovereign to whom they were really responsible. Ministers were increasingly chosen from among members of the Assembly and resigned when the Assembly withdrew its confidence from them. The change was slow and it was not until the reign of Queen Victoria that parliamentary government as we know it today was fully established. As late as 1867 Bagehot could still feel it necessary to deny that the executive and legislative powers were separated in Britain, and to argue that in the British political system there was a "fusion of powers." By this time parliamentary government was already formalized in the Belgian Constitution. In Sweden, where the separation of powers had only recently been established, the introduction of parliamentarism had to wait until the formation of Liberal Governments in the first two decades of the twentieth century.

In parliamentary monarchies such as Britain, Belgium and Sweden, the Monarch has ceased in practice (though not in form) to exercise even the executive power. Government has passed to "his" Ministers who are responsible to the Legislature. Parliamentary government implies a certain fusion of the executive and legislative functions, the body which has been merely an Assembly of representatives being transformed into a Parliament.

In short, the first phase ended in Britain about the time of the death of Elizabeth I, the last of the Tudors. The following century (1603–1714), known as the Stuart period, saw the rise of Parliament and the recognition of its distinct sphere of influence and power. But the gradual transition to the third and present phase of parliamentary government, which began with the appointment of Walpole as First Minister in 1721, was not completed until the reign of Victoria (1837–1901) since when parliamentary government has been in operation.

It is somewhat confusing, however, to find the term "Parliament" commonly used to describe the Assembly throughout all three phases. Clearly the English Parliament of the sixteenth century was a very different body from the British Parliament of today. For the sake of clarity, the term "Assembly" or "Houses of Parliament" is used in this study to describe the British Parliament as it was before the introduction of parliamentary government, that is to say before the Government came to consist of members of Parliament responsible to that body rather than to the Monarch.

Equally confusing is the use of the term "Parliament" at the present time in two different senses. The statement "Parliament is supreme" refers to Parliament as a whole, members of the Government included, and is correct usage. On the other hand the phrase "The Government is responsible to

Parliament" presumably means that the Government is dependent upon the support of *other* members of the Legislature, the Government excluded. In the one instance "Parliament" is used broadly, to include both members of the Government and "private members" as they are often called in Britain, and in the other it connotes these private members only. Unfortunately there is no generic term to describe the private members, either in Britain or abroad. (The term "private member"—and still less "back-bencher"—hardly does justice to the eminent office of Her Majesty's Leader of the Opposition, or even to his colleagues on the Opposition Front Bench.) This fact alone demonstrates the fusion of powers which has taken place, and for all practical purposes the Assembly as such has ceased to exist. Indeed, it is arguable that to insist upon the drawing of a distinction is to encourage a misunderstanding of the nature of parliamentary government, which has so successfully obliterated it.

It is true that for the most part the use of the term "Parliament" at one time to include the Government and at others to exclude it seems to cause little difficulty, provided some knowledge of the parliamentary system is assumed. In a comparative study of political systems, however, such ambiguity presents certain problems if like is to be compared with like. It therefore becomes necessary to insist on a more precise usage. "Parliament" will at all times signify a body which includes the Government. When it is necessary to refer to the Legislature excluding members of the Government the term "Assembly" will be used.

According to Montesquieu's classical exposition there were not two powers but three, the third being the judicial. However, the independence of the judiciary in the sense of non-interference by the Government is now well-established and is a characteristic of all three theories of government. In over half the countries of the world judicial independence is thought to mean the right of judges, as guardians of the constitution, to overrule the legislative and or executive branches. This legacy of the theory of the separation of powers is frequently found in parliamentary systems.

Not all parliamentary systems are monarchical, and in those countries which are republics another personage, usually called the President, takes the place of the constitutional monarch as Head of State. A noteworthy feature of several republics is that at one time they too were monarchies, but during revolutions the monarchy was swept away. The process of constitutional development was often crowded into a very short period, some republics passing straight from a state of monarchical despotism to a form of parliamentarism.

In fifty-three days the representative assembly of France had been transformed from a medieval gathering of the King's principal subjects, grouped into three distinct classes, into a modern parliament composed of the

Deputies of the people. (Lidderdale, D. W. S., *The Parliament of France*, pp. 6–7.)

In such circumstances it is hardly surprising that the process of transformation was not as smooth as in Britain or Scandinavia.

The first characteristic of parliamentarism may now be summarized. It is a political system where the Executive, once separate, has been challenged by the Assembly which is then transformed into a Parliament comprising both Government and Assembly.

## 2. The Executive Is Divided into Two Parts

One important consequence of the transformation of the Assembly into a Parliament is that the Executive is now split in two, a Prime Minister or Chancellor becoming head of the Government and the Monarch or President acting as Head of State. Usually the Monarch occupies his throne by hereditary title (though elected monarchies, e.g. in Malaya, are not unknown), while a President is elected by Parliament. It does not follow that the Head of State fills a purely formal or decorative office. Constitutional monarchs still have important prerogatives and even if those which they do not (or dare not) use are left out of consideration there remains a considerable field in which their powers are politically significant.

In principle there should be no objection to, and perhaps much to be said for, a clear statement of the respective functions of Head of State and Government. But the British view appears to be that the relationship of the two parts of the Executive is better left to the operation of flexible convention than written into the law of the Constitution. In several European monarchies there has been a similar transfer of power from Monarch to Ministry, but without a re-statement of their respective functions. Thus Article 4 of the Swedish Constitution still reads: "The King alone shall govern the realm." Part of Article 30 of the Norwegian Constitution reads:

Everyone who holds a seat in the Council is in duty bound to express fearlessly his opinions, to which the King is bound to listen. But it remains with the King to take a resolution according to his own judgement.

The Governments of these countries are thus shielded by the Constitution when they claim freedom of action on the part of the Crown whose powers they wield.

Where the Head of State is a President there is less reticence about making the duties of the divided Executive explicit, presumably because the President is elected by Parliament. In constitutional monarchies experience has shown that if the Monarch does not have his duties constitutionally defined and protected greater flexibility is possible. (In other words, the King can be deprived of more and more of his prerogative powers.) There is an important exception to this rule in Japan. Fear that the Emperor might not accept the role of a constitutional Monarch has led to the explicit withdrawal of all governmental functions from him in the new constitution. Executive power is vested expressly in the Cabinet. In parliamentary republics there is a fairly general apprehension lest the President engross the powers which pertain to the Government. The Constitution of the French Fourth Republic accordingly stated what powers the President of the Republic (Articles 29–44) and the President of the Council of Ministers (45–54) might wield.

On the other hand Presidents are sometimes allowed a greater authority than Monarchs because their status is achieved, not ascribed as a result of inherited title. The French President, for example, had a temporary veto over legislation which Monarchs might possess in theory but certainly do not exercise in practice. But where, as in the Fifth Republic and in Finland, the President has special rights comparable with or superior to those of the Ministry, the system ceases at this point to be truly parliamentary.

It is a characteristic of hereditary monarchies that the King cannot be held personally responsible and so his Ministers must bear responsibility for him. No such inhibition seems to affect republics, where the President is elected. Consequently when the President oversteps his position he is subject to impeachment, for high treason in France, for unconstitutional activity in the Federal German Republic, and for both in Italy.

The second characteristic of parliamentarism may now be summarized. The Executive is divided into a Head of State and a Government whose relationship with the Head of State may or may not be precisely formulated.

## 3. The Head of State
### Appoints the Head of Government

The value of a divided Executive in constitutional monarchies is fairly obvious. For one thing, the proper business of State can be carried on by a Government responsible to the Legislature while the mystique of Monarchy is preserved. There seems no apparent reason, at first glance, for dividing it in Republics. Admittedly it is useful to have someone above the day-to-day political warfare to receive ambassadors and to decorate ceremonial occasions, but this hardly seems to justify the expense of such an office. After all, the President of the United States, who as head of the American government bears the greatest responsibilities of any statesman in the world, manages to combine with his high and lonely eminence the even higher office of Head of State.

However, it is in the very nature of the parliamentary system that there shall be two distinct offices, and that the head of the Government shall be appointed by the Head of State. Were the electorate itself to perform this task, directly or through a special College of electors as in the United States or Finland, the system would become, in this respect at least, presidential in character. For Parliament to elect the head of the Government would be to adopt the procedure which is characteristic of the convention system. The different methods of selecting the head of the Government distinguish as clearly as anything else the three theories of governmental organization.

Nor is the duty of apointing the head of the Government a mere formality. It is true that the Head of State is bound by the results of parliamentary elections and must appoint the head of the party which is clearly the victor. But this is the situation only where one party or stable coalition has obtained an absolute majority of seats, which is called appropriately in Scandinavia "Majority-parliamentarism." But in many parliamentary systems, especially multi-party systems, no party has an absolute majority and "minority-parliamentarism" prevails. In selecting the Prime Minister who can best obtain a working majority the Head of State may have to use his personal discretion. The last occasion on which such a situation arose in Britain was in 1931, and the role of the Monarch during this crisis is still disputed. Even where there is majority-parliamentarism problems may occur. The Prime Minister may resign for personal reasons, as Sir Anthony Eden did in 1957, without leaving an obvious successor, and then the Monarch has to make a very important personal decision. The Conservative Party was criticised on this occasion for not appointing a leader before this situation arose, and no doubt the Queen's selection would have been merely a formality had this been done. But it is quite possible that on some future occasion, for example when a party is divided about a new leader, the Head of State may once again be compelled to use his or her discretion. It may be desirable that where the Head of State is a Monarch the selection of the head of the Government shall be a formality but this can by no means be guaranteed in a parliamentary system.

Some parliamentary republics, notably Western Germany and the French Fourth Republic, have escaped from this dilemma by the introduction of an element of convention theory whereby selection of a Prime Minister has three stages. The President nominates a candidate, the Assembly shows its approval by electing him (in Germany) or by giving him a vote of confidence (in France) and then the President appoints him as Prime Minister.

Parliamentarism, therefore, implies some balance of power even though the separation of institutions still characteristic of presidential government has given way to fusion. Unlike convention government it is not government by Assembly, nor is it the absorption of the Executive by the Assembly. It is the creation of a completely new institution in the political system, a Parliament, in which the Assembly and the Government are somehow miraculously blended. The duty of the Head of State to appoint the head of the Government—the third characteristic of parliamentarism—is as necessary to preserve that balance as the popular election of both President and Assembly is to preserving the balance in presidential systems.

### 4. The Head of the Government Appoints the Ministry

An interesting feature of parliamentarism is the distinction made between the Prime Minister and other Ministers. The former is appointed by the Head of State; the latter are nominated by the Prime Minister after his appointment. Usually the selection of various Ministers allows a certain amount of personal choice to a head of Government, which cannot usually be said of the appointment of a Prime Minister by the Head of State. Ministers are formally appointed by the Head of State, who may often no doubt exert an informal influence upon appointments—but so may the state on party alignments and factions in the Assembly. It remains a cardinal principle that the Prime Minister alone is responsible for the composition of the Ministry. Where, as in Australia, Ministers are sometimes elected by their party this is a departure from the parliamentary principle in the direction of convention government.

### 5. The Ministry (or Government) Is a Collective Body

The transfer from the monarchical Executive to a Council of Ministers has meant that a single person has been replaced by a collective body. Whereas under anciens régimes it was the King's pleasure (le Roi le veult), under parliamentarism the Prime Minister is merely first among equals (primus inter pares), though no doubt some Prime Ministers are more forceful than others. Criticism of an American study of the office of Prime Minister (by Byrum Carter) has been directed against its assumption that the Prime Minister's role can be discussed separately from that of the Ministry as a whole. In the United States, of course, the President is sole Executive, but it is a hallmark of the parliamentary system that the Government shall be collective.

### 6. Ministers Are Usually Members of Parliament

Members of the Government have a double role to play in the parliamentary system. They are not only Ministers but are at the same time members of Parliament, elected (unless they are members of the British House of Lords) like the members of the Assembly and equally dependent upon the goodwill of their constituents. The problem of distinguishing between Parliament and Assembly is most acute when this role is analysed. In Britain there is no law that Ministers must be members of one of the Houses of Parliament (though it is required that at least three members of the Cabinet must be drawn from the House of Lords) but there is a convention that they are in fact always members of one or other. Thus when Mr. Bevin became Minister of Labour in 1940 a seat was found for him in the House of Commons. When Sir Percy Mills joined Mr. Macmillan's Government in 1957 he was made a peer. The Constitution of the French Fourth Republic specifically stated that Ministers are collectively and individually responsible to the National Assembly and there is an implication that they should be members of that body.

Since, according to the usage adopted in this chapter, Parliament comprises both Government and Assembly, a member of the Government is *ipso facto* a member of Parliament, but by definition he cannot be a member of the Assembly. In fully parliamentary countries such as the United Kingdom where Ministers are members of Parliament it is difficult to make the distinction between Government, Parliament and Assembly clear. Indeed the attempt to make one seems artificial.

However, not all parliamentary countries have accepted the necessity for Ministers to be members of one of the Houses of Parliament. In Sweden up to a third of the Ministry of fifteen members have on occasion in recent years not been Members of Parliament. In the Netherlands, Norway and Luxembourg, Ministers are actually forbidden to be Members of Parliament after their appointment. Here there is a relic of the old doctrine of the separation of powers when Ministers were responsible to the Monarch. (Traces of the doctrine may be found elsewhere, for example, in the traditional French rule that Ministers may not be members of parliamentary committees.)

Generally speaking, nevertheless, it is usual for most if not all Ministers to be Members of Parliament. Where they are not, the system may still be said to be of the parliamentary type if they can take part in parliamentary debates and are truly responsible to the Assembly for the conduct of the Executive. In Norway, Sweden, the Netherlands and Luxembourg, all parliamentary monarchies, these conditions are fulfilled. In the French Fifth Republic, where the Government is not responsible to Parliament for the conduct of the President, they are not.

## 7. The Government Is Politically Responsible to the Assembly

In parliamentary systems the Government is responsible to the Assembly which may, if it thinks that the Government is acting unwisely or unconstitutionally, refuse to give it support. By a formal vote of censure or by simply not assenting to an important Government proposal the Assembly can force the Government to resign and cause the Head of State to appoint a new Government.

In the *anciens régimes* of Europe Ministers were responsible not to the Assembly but to the King, as in Nepal today. They were truly Ministers of the Crown. The question "To whom is the Monarch responsible?" was not one which a constitutional lawyer or a political scientist would care to answer, though a moral philosopher would probably say that he was governed by the moral law or the spirit of the constitution. There was no institution charged with the enforcement of his responsibility and no definition of what constituted responsible and irresponsible action. Legally as "God's Lieutenant," though not morally, the King could do no wrong. Hobbes went so far as to assert in the mid-seventeenth century that there should be no limits to the Sovereign's power and that in practice an absolute sovereign power was better than the alternative— anarchy. To this day Monarchs as a rule cannot be held constitutionally responsible for their actions.

An escape from this dilemma was first provided by the introduction of a rule that Ministers could be held responsible by the Assembly for the advice which they rendered. Thus although Article 30 of the Norwegian Constitution stressed the right of the King to act according to his own judgement, Article 5 stated: "The King's person shall be sacred; he cannot be blamed or accused. The responsibility shall rest upon his Council." During the period of what may be termed "limited monarchy" or the "separation of powers" before parliamentarism was established the Assembly was supposed to hold Ministers responsible by this device.

In comparison with the present-day procedure of an adverse vote the method adopted was complicated and not altogether successful. Ministers were required to countersign all documents issued by the King-in-Council before they became law. A committee of the Assembly examined these documents and held the countersigning Minister responsible for their contents. In certain countries, such as Sweden, a distinction was drawn between advice which was unwise and proposals which were unconstitutional. Where the committee of the Assembly decided that due regard had not been paid to the welfare of the State it could advise the Assembly to request the Monarch to dismiss the offending Minister. But no action could be taken to ensure that this request was acceded to. Where Ministers were deemed to have acted unconstitutionally they could be impeached before a special court. Neither means of checking the Government proved effective in Sweden in the nineteenth century and today these provisions of the Constitution are a dead letter. Yet some Swedish authorities have been reluctant to accept the notion that day-to-day political pressure in the Assembly has replaced them, partly, no doubt, because Sweden has only recently (1917) emerged from a century of limited monarchy. It is particularly difficult for constitutional lawyers to recognize conventions which run counter to the letter of the Constitution.

Countersignature still has its uses in republics as a last resort to prevent the Head of State from acting unconstitutionally. A President elected by the Assembly is more likely in a time of crisis to claim to represent the real public interest. Unless he can obtain a countersignature for his actions he leaves himself open to criticism and can, if necessary, be impeached. Although a dead letter in the constitutions of parliamentary monarchies, the requirement of a countersignature has been written into several recent constitutions in parliamentary republics.

## 8. The Head of Government May Advise the Head of State to Dissolve Parliament

In the pre-parliamentary monarchies of Europe the Monarch could, if dissatisfied with his Assembly, dissolve one or more Houses in the hope of securing a more amenable selection of representatives after a new election. Today, when the Executive is divided, it is still the Head of State who dissolves Parliament, but he does so on the request, and only on the request, of the head of Government. In Denmark the Constitution actually states that either the King or the Prime Minister may dissolve Parliament. But where the Head of State acts independently, as President Macmahon did in France in 1877, parliamentarism is not being practised.

For parliamentary dissolution is very different from the earlier form of dissolution. In the old days a challenge by the Assembly to the Executive did not lead to a change of Executive but to a change (or attempted change) of the Assembly. Nowadays a defeat of the Government by the Assembly causes the Prime Minister either to resign or to request a dissolution. But the dissolution is not of the Assembly but of Parliament, that is to say of the Government as well—although the Government (in Britain at least) stays in power until the new Parliament assembles. The conflict between the two parts of Parliament is left to the electorate to resolve.

The power of the Government to request a dissolution is a distinctive characteristic of parliamentarism. Some British writers consider that the threat of dissolution is essential in order that the Ministry may secure the loyal support of its party, but other parliamentary systems survive without Whips who whisper hints of dissolution to recalcitrant back-benchers.

Nevertheless, dissolution must remain the ultimate sanction. Commenting on the failure of the Chilean experiment with parliamentary government in the period 1891-1925 Professor Karl Loewenstein has observed:

However, genuine parliamentarism could not evolve because the President lacked the power to appeal to the people through dissolution of the chamber, and dissolution is the pivot around which genuine parliamentarism revolves. (*Journal of Politics*, 1949, p. 455.)

Certain states generally regarded as parliamentary severely restrict the right of the Executive to dissolve the Assembly. In Norway the *Storting* dissolves itself, the Head of State being allowed to dissolve only special sessions, but this is a departure from parliamentarism inspired by the convention theory of the French Revolution. In France, where the right of the Government of the Fourth Republic to request a dissolution of Parliament was restricted by the Constitution, the political system also exhibited certain convention characteristics.

## 9. Parliament as a Whole is Supreme Over Its Constituent Parts, Government and Assembly, Neither of Which May Dominate the Other

The notion of the supremacy of Parliament as a whole over its parts is a distinctive characteristic of parliamentary systems. This may seem a glimpse of the obvious to those accustomed to parliamentary government, but it is in fact an important principle, all too often forgotten, that neither of the constituent elements of Parliament may completely dominate the other. The Government depends upon the support of the Assembly if it is to continue in office, but the Assembly is not supreme because the Government can, if it chooses, dissolve Parliament and appeal to the electorate at the polls. Many parliamentary systems have failed because one or other of them has claimed supremacy, and Parliament as a whole has not been supreme over both Government and Assembly.

In practice the nature of parliamentary supremacy varies from country to country. In the United Kingdom and Scandinavia the emphasis is on the Government's role in Parliament and in Britain the system is actually called "Cabinet Government." In others, notably the French Third and Fourth Republics, the dominant role in Parliament was played by the Assembly. Generally speaking, where there is majority-parliamentarism the Government has a sense of security, subject only to the sudden onset of a crisis. No Government has been defeated on a motion of confidence in the House of Commons for about thirty years, though it took merely a drop in his customarily large majority to cause Mr. Chamberlain to resign as Prime Minister in 1940. Governments lacking the support of an absolute majority of members are in a much more exposed position, and in France for example, changes of Government following loss of confidence by the Chamber of Deputies or National Assembly were fairly frequent.

Many countries appear in practice to depart from the parliamentary ideal of a balance between the Government and the Assembly. On the one hand there are states like France where the capacity of the Assembly to change Governments at will has been an indication not, as is sometimes thought, of an interesting variation of the parliamentary principle, but of a departure from it in the direction of Assembly government. On the other there are countries like the United Kingdom where the increasing tendency for the Government to dominate parliamentary business may be a departure from the parliamentary principle in the opposite direction. The United Kingdom is by no means alone. It has been said of the Danish political system for example:

> "Private members" bills have little chance of passage —which means that virtually all legislation is sponsored by the government (that is the ministry), and the constitution provides that all laws must be considered by the ministry. Under the parliamentary system, *of course,* the ministry has in reality an absolute veto on legislation. (B. A. Arneson, *The Democratic Monarchies of Scandinavia*, p. 90. My italics.)

It would be more in keeping with parliamentarism as it is defined in this study to deny the right of either Government or Assembly such absolute authority. Parliamentarism implies co-operation between the executive and legislative branches, neither dominating the other and both recognizing the supremacy of the larger institution, Parliament as a whole.

The notion of parliamentary supremacy described in this section is not to be confused with the legal notion of parliamentary sovereignty. Whereas the former explains the relation of Parliament to its component parts, the latter is concerned with its external relations. All Parliaments are supreme over the Governments and Assemblies which compose them. But not all are sovereign, that is to say legally unrestricted in their powers. In Britain Parliament is sovereign in the sense that the Queen-in-Parliament is not limited legally by the Constitution. In other parliamentary states, however, the power of Parliament and the Head of State is limited by the terms of written constitutions. It need hardly be emphasized therefore that parliamentary sovereignty, which plays so large

a part in British politics, is by no means a characteristic of parliamentary systems generally.

And of course parliamentary supremacy or sovereignty is strictly a governmental notion affecting relations between the branches of government. It is compatible with the belief that in a very real sense it is the electorate which is ultimately supreme: hence the notion of popular sovereignty, taken for granted in the United States and assumed in the United Kingdom by those who believe that government should act in accordance with a mandate from the people.

## 10. *The Government as a Whole Is Only Indirectly Responsible to the Electorate*

A parliamentary Government, though directly responsible to the Assembly, is only indirectly responsible to the electorate. The Government as a whole is not directly elected by the voters but is appointed indirectly from amongst the representatives whom they elect to the Assembly. The earlier direct relationship of Monarch and people whereby persons could petition their Sovereign disappeared as parliamentarism was introduced. Today the route to the Government lies through elected representatives though in Britain, for example, one may still formally petition the Monarch. It is true that members of the Government, like other members of Parliament, must (unless they are peers) stand before their constituents for election. However, they do so not as members of the Government but as candidates for the Assembly in the ordinary way. The responsibility for transforming them, once elected, into Ministers rests with the Prime Minister alone (and of course with the Monarch in the case of the Prime Minister).

As late as the nineteenth century in Britain it was thought to be bad form for a member of the Government, including the Prime Minister, to appeal to the electorate in general as well as to his constituents during an election. Not until after the second Reform Bill of 1867 was there a departure from this tradition. Today elections are fought on a national basis, Government and Opposition appealing as national parties to a national electorate. There has also grown up an important channel of direct communication between Ministries and the public, and even Prime Ministers have their public relations advisers. Nevertheless, this growth in direct communication has not been accompanied by a feeling of direct responsibility to the electorate. A Prime Minister returning from an important international conference does not usually address the public either by Press or television until he has first reported to Parliament.

It may still be argued that in reality, if not in constitutional theory, there is an exception to this principle of indirect responsibility, at least in two-party states. Are not, it may be asked, the people at election time presented in fact with two alternative Governments for one of which they vote? In a broad sense this is no doubt true, but there is a world of difference between, say, the election of the American President by the American people and the appointment of a British Government. The individual British voter, unlike his American counterpart, elects only a member of the Assembly. He may even, if he is a Liberal, Independent or Communist, vote for a particular candidate or party with full knowledge that he cannot have anything to do with the formation of a Government, at least in the immediate future. Should the voter elect a Labour Member of Parliament and then discover that the Labour Party is to form the new Government, his responsibility is indirect, as is that of all Labour voters. The people have not directly elected a Government: what they have done is to elect a party whose leader is called upon by the Monarch to form a Government of *his* own choosing.

This point is not always well taken. In a recent book, *The British Political System,* a French writer, André Mathiot, describes the British Cabinet under the heading "A Government Chosen by the People." He rightly points to the plebiscitary element in British elections as a result of the two-party system. It is true that "The electorate actually votes for members of Parliament, but they are really choosing the government by deciding which party is to have a majority in the House of Commons." But Mathiot slurs over the fact that *members* of the Government are selected neither by the people nor by the victorious party. It is a misleading oversimplification to state that "the Prime Minister and the Cabinet are appointed by the Queen but really chosen by the people." Ministers are in fact chosen by the Prime Minister, and as for the premiership itself this has been transferred on many occasions without any consultation of the people. There were no general elections preceding the appointments of Lloyd George in 1916, Stanley Baldwin in 1923, Winston Churchill in 1940 or Harold Macmillan in 1957.

Where there is a multi-party system in which no party has a majority the relation of Government and voters is much more indirect. Of course nobody knows which parties will increase their representation, but even if this can be guessed the nature of the coalition Government may be unknown. The task of forming a Government falls to party leaders and the Head of State after the results are announced, and is hardly the direct result of the election. In such circumstances the electors clearly are responsible directly only for candidates and parties, the Government being the responsibility of those leaders who are successful in the election.

## 11. Parliament Is the Focus of Power in the Political System

The fusion of the executive and legislative powers in Parliament is responsible for the overriding ascendancy of Parliament in the political order. It is the stage on which the drama of politics is played out; it is the forum of the nation's ideas; and it is the school where future political leaders are trained. For parliamentarism to succeed, the Government must not fret at the constant challenge which the Assembly offers to its programme, nor wince at the criticism made of its administration. The Assembly in turn must resist the temptation to usurp the functions of Government. Here is a delicate balance of powers which check each other without the benefit of separate institutions.

Above all, politicians, party militants and voters have to accept the parliamentary spirit of give and take. They must be loyal to Parliament as well as to their party, not doubting the good faith of those with whom they disagree. Where this confidence is lacking or is betrayed, parliamentarism falls into disrepute and the system may become unworkable. The weakness of parliamentarism in France has been due in large measure to the unwillingness of large numbers of Frenchmen to give their Parliament this trust and loyalty. Many party militants on the Right have wanted to abolish Parliament and replace it with a separated Executive and Assembly as in presidential theory. Many on the Left would have preferred to see power transferred to the Assembly as in the brief days of the Convention and the Commune. In all parties, within and without the National Assembly, there were those who could not be true parliamentarians because they doubted the suitability of parliamentary government for France. In such circumstances parliamentarism cannot flourish. It must be, if it is to succeed, the focal point of the nation's political interest, the centre of the political system.

In conclusion it may be helpful to summarize the definitions of some of the main terms used in this chapter. The *political system* is the generic term for all those institutions which contribute to the formation and execution of policy within and without *government,* which according to the traditional classification comprises the executive, legislative and judicial powers. The *Executive* in parliamentary theory comprises both the *Head of State,* whether Monarch or President, and the *Government* proper consisting of the Prime Minister and other Ministers. The *Government* is that part of the Executive which comprises the Ministry. It does not, therefore, include the Head of State. The Assembly is the body of representatives who act as watchdogs over the Government and as partners in legislation. All Government bills must be passed by the Assembly before becoming law. Taxes cannot be raised or money spent without its authority. *Parliament* is not to be confused with the British Houses of Parliament. It connotes an institution which comprises both the Government and Assembly. The former is usually composed of persons who are individually elected as members of Parliament. The latter also consists of elected representatives (or, in Britain, peers), but they are not officeholders. It excludes the Head of State. (Where reference is made to both Head of State and Parliament another term, for example *Queen-in-Parliament* in the United Kingdom and *Stats-makterna* in Sweden, is adopted.)

There is an important difference between *parliamentary supremacy,* the superiority of the Government and Assembly acting together as Parliament over either of these bodies individually, and *parliamentary sovereignty,* the power of the Government and Assembly as Parliament to act without any legal restraint upon their authority. Since nowadays Parliaments are dependent upon the support of the electorate a distinction must of course be made between *legal sovereignty* which may lie with Parliament as it does in the United Kingdom, and *popular* sovereignty, whereby at election time the electorate shows itself to be ultimately supreme.

Where an Assembly enjoys both executive and legislative power there is *Assembly supremacy* and government is carried on by a committee or committees. This may be called the *convention* system.

In diagrammatic terms the system is as follows:

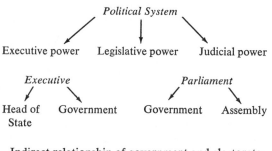

Indirect relationship of government and electorate:

## PRESIDENTIAL GOVERNMENT

Presidential government is often associated with the theory of the separation of powers which was popular in the eighteenth century when the Amer-

ican Constitution was framed. Two writers in particular drew attention to this notion. John Locke, writing at the end of the seventeenth century, suggested that the long conflict between the British Monarch and the Houses of Parliament would best be resolved by the separation of the King as Executive from the two Houses as Legislature, each body having its own sphere. In the mid-eighteenth century a French observer of the British political scene, Montesquieu, pronounced himself in favour of the British system of government as one which embodied, in contrast to the despotism of the Bourbons, the separation of the executive, legislative and judicial powers. Historically the theory as expounded by Locke and more especially Montesquieu is important for an understanding of the climate of opinion in which the American Constitution was framed.

However, it is one thing to study this celebrated theory for historical purposes but quite another to trace its contemporary significance for an understanding of presidential government. It was, after all, based on the assumption that a Monarch would act as Executive and an Assembly as Legislature. The theory was considered to be an improvement on the absolute monarchies of the Continent, which it undoubtedly was, and was praised with them in mind. There was as yet no experience of parliamentarism. Today such constitutional monarchies as still survive are based on the parliamentary principle.

Another offspring and successor of the theory is presidential government, but the substitution of an elected President for a hereditary Monarch has, as we have seen, created a system hardly comparable with pre-parliamentary limited monarchies. If presidential government is regarded simply as a direct form of expression of the eighteenth century doctrine of the separation of powers then (as indeed many people have thought) the Americans may, by adopting their rigid Constitution, have artificially prevented their political system from developing into parliamentarism. But if, as it is argued here, the system is a successor to that doctrine then it is not like limited monarchy, the precursor of parliamentary government, but one of its two offsprings, the other being parliamentarism.

Indeed the use of the term "separation of powers" to describe the presidential system is something of a misnomer, as is its counterpart the "fusion of powers" of parliamentarism. In theory it is possible to conceive of complete separation of the executive, legislative and judicial functions, but there is no evidence of its practical feasibility. If government is to be carried on the powers must be co-ordinated and must overlap. Thus in the United States the President (the Executive) wields legislative power when he signs or vetoes bills sent to him by Congress. Congress (the legislative branch) shares in the Executive's authority when it ratifies treaties and confirms appointments. The Supreme Court (the Judiciary) may use its power to interpret the Constitution so as to encroach on both the executive and legislative spheres. In parliamentary theory, despite the fusion of powers implied by parliamentary supremacy, an important distinction is drawn between the three branches, and textbooks on constitutional law begin with an account of the separation of powers. It is still considered everywhere to be one of the bulwarks against tyranny and dictatorship—except perhaps in the Vatican. (Article I of the Fundamental Law of the City of the Vatican states: "The Sovereign Pontiff, sovereign of the City of the Vatican, has full legislative, executive and judicial powers.") If the powers are not really separated in presidential systems, neither are they altogether fused in parliamentary states.

Where presidential and parliamentary governments *do* differ is over the separation not of powers but of institutions and persons. In the parliamentary system there is a single institution called Parliament which combines two other institutions and their personnel—the Government and the Assembly. It may, as in the United Kingdom, combine part of the Judiciary as well (the House of Lords being the highest court of appeal) and thus Parliament may seem to wield executive, legislative and judicial power. There is no such combination of functions in presidential systems, the Executive being quite separate from the Assembly as an institution. Moreover the personnel of the two institutions, and of the Judiciary, are different.

The term "separation of powers" is therefore an inadequate and misleading description of the theory underlying presidential government. It is inadequate because as stated by Montesquieu and Blackstone it applied to a monarchical Executive which has since been generally replaced by parliamentarism, and because it does not explain the theory of presidential government. It is misleading because the powers are separated in both presidential and parliamentary theory. These are distinguished partly by the degree of separation of powers but more particularly by the separation of institutions and persons which is so marked a characteristic of presidential but not parliamentary theory.

In parliamentary government, where the legislative and executive powers have to a marked degree been fused, it is sometimes difficult to draw a distinction between the Government and the Assembly which together form Parliament. In presidential government, on the other hand, a clear distinction *is* drawn between these two branches of the political system. The President is the Executive, being both Head of State and head of Government, and is quite separate from the Assembly. Indeed the use of the terms "Government" and "Ministry" employed in parliamentarism to distinguish the repository of real political power from the Head of State is inappropriate in the

presidential context. Americans tend to use the expression "Administration" to describe the President and his aides. The term "Parliament" is never used because in presidential systems there is no place for an institution which combines the executive and legislative powers.

The term *presidential* has been chosen because in this system the offices of head of Government and Head of State are combined in a President. The term is as expressive as *parliamentary* was to describe the system where the Government and Assembly are fused in a Parliament.

It seemed appropriate to begin an analysis of parliamentary government by reference to British political institutions. It is equally valuable to study presidentialism by first examining the American political system. The United States was the first important country to break with the European monarchical tradition and to shake off colonial rule. The break occurred in the eighteenth century when Britain was still a limited monarchy and the theory of the separation of powers was in vogue. The American Constitution bears witness to these influences and to the colonial government of Governor and Legislature, an elected President replacing the King or Governor as the Executive power. A number of countries—all twenty American republics, Liberia, the Philippines, South Korea and South Vietnam—have followed the example of the United States, though rarely with comparable success. The American political system is therefore the model and prototype of presidential government. Yet the United States, like the United Kingdom, could abolish or transform many of its institutions and remain based on the same theory of government. For example, the framers of the 1787 Constitution could have proposed an elective Monarch instead of a President, a House of Lords rather than a Senate, and a unitary political system instead of a federal union of states without destroying the presidential principle—though the name "presidential" would hardly be suitable for a system where the Executive was an elective Monarch. Presidential, like parliamentary, theory has certain basic characteristics irrespective of any particular political system.

The nature of presidential theory can best be understood by re-stating the eleven propositions of Chapter II [of *Analysis of Political Systems,* pp. 176-184 of this book] as they apply to presidential government.

## 1. The Assembly Remains an Assembly Only

Parliamentary theory implies that the second phase of constitutional development, in which the Assembly and Judiciary claim their own areas of jurisdiction alongside the Executive, shall give way to a third in which Assembly and Government are fused in a Parliament. Presidential theory on the other hand requires the Assembly to remain separate as in the second phase. The American Revolution led to a transfer from colonial rule to the second stage of separate jurisdiction, and there have been some observers who have thought that the rigid Constitution has prevented the "natural" development of the American political system towards parliamentarism. This is not so. By abolishing the Monarchy and substituting a President for the King and his Government, the Americans showed themselves to be truly revolutionary in outlook. The presidential system as established in the U.S.A. made parliamentarism both unnecessary and impracticable in that country. The Assembly (Congress in the United States) remains an Assembly.

## 2. The Executive Is Not Divided But Is a President Elected by the People for a Definite Term at the Time of Assembly Elections

The retention of a separate Executive in the United States was made feasible because the Executive remained undivided. It was not, of course, the same institution as the pre-parliamentary monarchical Executive. Such a Monarch governed by virtue of an ancient tradition into which he was born, and with all the strength and potential weaknesses that this implied. The presidential Executive is elected by the people. In an era when Governments have had to rely not on some mystique but on popular support the Americans have found a solution which has enabled their separate single Executive to withstand criticism. The suggestions that the United States should adopt parliamentarism have proved abortive largely because it cannot be said of the Presidency, as it could of hereditary Monarchy, that the institution lacked democratic roots.

An undivided Executive obviously requires no delineation of the respective functions of Head of State and the Government. The powers of the Executive are defined vis-à-vis the Assembly and the Judiciary and each checks the others to ensure that the balance of power is not unduly disturbed. Yet this has not prevented a change in their status and role. In the United States as late as 1884 Woodrow Wilson (then a professor of political science, not President of the United States) could regard the Senate and House of Representatives as the pivot of the system and could call his book on American politics *Congressional Government*. Today, as the title of this chapter ["Presidential Government"] indicates, the influence of the President has appreciably extended. In other presidential systems the President usually wields very considerable powers. If there is any trend it is away from parliamentarism, not towards it.

The President is elected for a definite term of office. This prevents the Assembly from forcing his resignation (except by impeachment for a serious misdemeanour) and at the same time requires the President to stand for re-election if he wishes to continue in office. It seems desirable that the chief Executive's tenure should be limited to a certain number of terms. For a long time there was a convention in the United States that no President should run for a third term.

When the question of a possible third term for President Coolidge arose, the Senate passed a resolution declaring that any departure from the two-term tradition "would be unwise, unpatriotic, and fraught with peril to our free institutions." (Swarthout, J. M., and Bartley, E. R., *Principles and Problems of American Government*, 2nd. ed., p. 381.)

President Roosevelt swept the convention aside in 1940—but some of his most loyal friends refused to support his candidacy. After his re-election for the fourth time in 1944 there was a movement to make it unconstitutional to run more than twice. An amendment to the Constitution to this effect was passed by Congress in 1947 and adopted by the necessary three-quarters of the States by 1951.

Equally important for the proper operation of the presidential system is the election of the President at the time of the Assembly elections. This associates the two branches of government, encourages party unity and clarifies the issues. Admittedly in the United States simultaneous elections do not prevent the return of a Republican President and a Democratic Congress, but the tensions would be even greater if the President was elected for a seven-year term as in France. General de Gaulle was elected as President in 1958 about the time of the Assembly elections, but the opportunity to make this coincidence permanent was not seized. However, since the de Gaulle Constitution allows for dissolution of Parliament as well as the resignation of the Government (but not the President) serious difficulty may be avoided.

## 3. The Head of the Government Is Head of State

Whereas in pre-parliamentary Monarchies the Head of State was also the head of the Government, in the presidential system it is the head of the Government who becomes at the same time Head of State. This is an important distinction because it draws attention to the limited pomp and circumstance surrounding the presidential office. The President is of little consequence until he is elected as political head by the electorate and he ceases to have any powers once his term of office has expired. The ceremonial aspect of his position is but a reflection of his political prestige.

Presidential theory, if it is to be successfully applied, demands a certain sophistication of the electorate. In parliamentary states, as Sir Winston Churchill once noted, war victories are celebrated by a cheer for the Head of State; defeats by a change of Government. In presidential systems a voter who may oppose the President as head of the Government has nevertheless to be loyal to the President as Head of State.

In the appointment of a political Executive it is a characteristic of parliamentary systems that the head of Government shall be appointed by the Head of State. The absence of any distinction between the two offices in presidential systems makes such an appointment unnecessary. Nor is the Executive elected by the Assembly since this would be contrary to the doctrine of the separation of powers. It is the mark of presidential government that both Executive and Assembly should be selected by the electorate.

### 4. The President Appoints Heads of Departments Who Are His Subordinates

In parliamentarism the Prime Minister appoints his colleagues who together with him form the Government. In presidential systems the President appoints Secretaries (sometimes called Ministers) who are heads of his Executive Departments. Formally, owing to the rule whereby appointments are subject to the confirmation of the Assembly or one of its organs (in the United States the Senate, in the Philippines the commission on appointments) his choice may be restricted to persons of whom that body approves. In practice the President has a very wide choice. Whereas in parliamentary systems Ministers are usually selected from those who have served a political apprenticeship in the Assembly, it is by no means customary in presidential systems for heads of Departments (or for that matter the President himself) to have had experience in the legislative branch of government.

### 5. The President Is Sole Executive

In contrast to parliamentary government, which is collective, the Prime Minister being first among equals, presidential government tends to be individual. Admittedly the term "Cabinet" is used in the United States to describe the meetings of the President with his Secretaries, but it is not a Cabinet or Ministry in the parliamentary sense. There is a famous story of Abraham Lincoln meeting with his Cabinet. He put a proposal to them and then took a vote in which he alone supported his suggestion. He then remarked: "Noes 7, Ayes 1. The Ayes

have it." In this respect the "loneliest office in the world" bears some resemblance to pre-parliamentary Monarchies where the King alone wielded executive power. President Truman made the point even more succinctly as President by placing a notice on his desk: *The buck stops here.* Such being the nature of the presidential Executive it would seem inappropriate to use the term "Cabinet" at all.

Most of the business consists of reporting on departmental problems; there is little discussion of general policy. Several cabinet members stay on after the meetings to discuss privately with the President matters that they feared to bring up in the meeting because of possible opposition or leaks to the press. (Burns, J. M. and Peltason, J. W., *Government by the People,* 3rd. ed. 1957, pp. 433-4.)

"Cabinet" is one of the few parliamentary terms to be adopted out of context by Americans.

Mexico and the Philippines, like the United States, give the President sole executive power, but most of the American republics require a counter-signature from a Minister before Presidential orders become valid legally. In three countries (Bolivia, Costa Rica and El Salvador), Ministers are made jointly responsible for the actions of the Executive. However, the motive in each case seems to be to provide a check on the President, not to introduce the notion of collective responsibility.

The great exception to the rule is provided by Uruguay, which in other respects conforms to presidential theory. Executive power is vested here in the hands of a National Council of Government consisting of nine persons elected by the people for four years. The presidency of the Council is by yearly rotation from among those members who were elected from the majority party. The National Council is not itself a Ministry. Nine Ministers of State are appointed by the Council to be heads of Departments.

### 6. Members of the Assembly Are Not Eligible for Office in the Administration and Vice-Versa

Instead of the parliamentary convention or law whereby the same persons may be part of both the executive and legislative branches of government, it is customary in presidential states for the personnel to be separate. Neither the President nor his aides may sit in the U.S. Congress. Few of the other American republics have copied the complete separation practised in the United States. While Ministers may not be members of the Assembly (except in Cuba and Peru) they are usually entitled to attend and take part in debates. This appears to accord with the practice of some pre-parliamentary Monarchies where, despite a strict rule that the Monarch should not attend debates, Ministers were often allowed to be present whether members or not. In a few countries (Costa Rica, Bolivia, El Salvador and Panama) Ministers give up their seats to alternates (*suplente*) for the period they hold office.

### 7. The Executive
### Is Responsible to the Constitution

The President is not, like parliamentary Governments, responsible to the Assembly. Instead he is, like pre-parliamentary Monarchs, responsible to the Constitution. But whereas in the *anciens régimes* this was but a vague notion, in presidential systems it is usually laid down with some precision in a constitutional document. Acts of the President may, as in the United States, be declared unconstitutional by the Supreme Court, though as Chief Justice Marshall discovered when attempting to protect the rights of the Cherokee Indians, it is one thing to hand down a decision and another to enforce it. However, should a President persist in acting unconstitutionally the Assembly can take action itself and impeach him or his aides. (The term "civil officer" is used to describe them in the United States.)

Impeachment in pre-parliamentary Monarchies was confined to Ministers who were held responsible for the King's actions through an elaborate system of counter-signature. The Monarch himself could only be dealt with by drastic action for which there was no constitutional procedure. He could be forced to abdicate without any right of self-defence, as happened to James II of England, Gustav IV of Sweden, Kaiser Wilhelm II of Germany, and Napoleon I, Charles X, Louis Philippe and Napoleon III of France. If he appeared to stand in the way of important political and social changes he might even be executed like Charles I of England or Louis XVI of France. In presidential systems, however, both Ministers and Presidents may be impeached. Where, as in Honduras and Paraguay, there is no provision for impeachment the system is not, in this important respect, presidential. In several South American Constitutions there are provisions which compel the President to dismiss his Ministers through political pressure as well as after impeachment. Thus in Peru ministers must resign after a vote of no-confidence.

It is usually the Assembly which holds the President ultimately responsible to the Constitution by the impeachment process. This does not imply that he is responsible to that body in the parliamentary sense of depending on its confidence in any political capacity. Impeachment enforces *juridical* compliance with the (constitutional) letter of the law and is quite different from the exercise of political control over the President's ordinary conduct of his office. Political responsibility implies a day-to-day relationship between Government and Assembly; impeachment is the grave and ultimate penalty (only one American President, Andrew Johnson was impeached, unsuccessfully) necessary where ordinarily the Executive and Assembly are not mutually dependent.

The President may not be dependent on the Assembly for his political survival but he is very dependent on its goodwill for the furtherance of his policies. The Budget, foreign programmes, senior appointments all require its acquiescence. If there is no agreement the Assembly may decide to take no action. It cannot however replace the President.

### 8. The President Cannot Dissolve
### or Coerce the Assembly

The Assembly, as we have just seen, cannot dismiss the President. Likewise the President may not dissolve the Assembly. Neither, therefore, is in a position to coerce the other, and it is not surprising that this system is, par excellence, one of checks and balances. In countless ways almost incomprehensible to those accustomed to parliamentarism the presidential system exhibits this mutual independence of the executive and legislative branches of government. In the United States, President Eisenhower declined for some time to take issue in 1954 with Senator McCarthy on the grounds that a Senator's conduct was primarily the responsibility of the U.S. Senate, not the Executive. In 1957, after the suicide of the Canadian Ambassador to Egypt, the President was unable to assure the Canadian people that congressional committees would in future exercise more discretion since he was not responsible for the behaviour of the Senate. Conversely, the Senate, whose Southern members had blocked civil rights legislation for over half a century, did nothing in 1948 when President Truman abolished racial segregation in the armed forces—even in the South. For as President Mr. Truman was Commander-in-Chief and could act without reference to Congress.

The position of a President is very different from that of a pre-parliamentary Monarch who could dissolve his Assembly if he felt that this was desirable. A President may call a special session of the Assembly if he fails to obtain his demands at the ordinary session and he may, if the Houses disagree, adjourn their meetings (though no American President has attempted the latter). But he may not appeal to the electorate to think again about its choice of a legislative branch of government by dissolving the Assembly. Where the President does have the constitutional authority of dissolution, as in Haiti and Paraguay, the system does not conform to the presidential pattern.

## 9. The Assembly Is Ultimately Supreme Over the Other Branches of Government and There Is No Fusion of the Executive and Legislative Branches as in a Parliament

It was remarked of parliamentary systems that neither the Government nor the Assembly is supreme because both are subordinate parts of the parliamentary institution. In presidential systems such fusion of the executive and legislative powers is replaced by separation, each having its own sphere. As we have just observed, constitutionally the Executive cannot interfere in the proceedings of the Assembly, still less dissolve it, and the Assembly for its part cannot invade the province of the Executive.

In practice the relation of the two, at least in the United States, is much more subtle than the theory of the separation of powers and checks and balances would indicate. The President is head of the Government and leader of his party. He controls an immense amount of patronage. He is responsible for the preparation of major legislation (even if technically it is introduced by members of the Assembly) and for securing its successful passage through the Assembly. Certainly Franklin D. Roosevelt effectively dominated the United States Congress in the famous "Hundred Days" of 1933. Conversely, to say that Congress cannot invade the province of the Executive does not mean that it cannot obstruct his policies, or, if it so choose, refuse the appropriations which are usually necessary for their implementation. If the United States Congress refused to grant the President the funds he required he would have to go without. In practice a compromise is nearly always reached, and the President is left to mind his own Executive business. In certain Latin American countries the President can automatically decree the budget if the Legislature fails to vote it. There is also a provision to this effect in the constitution of the French Fifth Republic.

Since there is no Parliament there can be no parliamentary supremacy. Where, then, does supreme power lie in the event of a serious controversy? It has been demonstrated that the Assembly cannot force the resignation of the President any more than he can dissolve the Assembly. Moreover, both branches of government may find that their actions are declared unconstitutional by yet a third power, the Judiciary. In a sense the Constitution is supreme. The short answer is that it is intended in presidential government that the different branches shall check and balance one another and that none shall predominate.

Yet in a very real sense it is the Assembly which is ultimately supreme. The President may have considerable authority allocated to him in the Constitution but he may be powerless unless the Assembly grants him the necessary appropriations. If he acts unconstitutionally the Assembly may impeach him. In the event of a serious conflict even the Judiciary must bow to the will of the Assembly because this body has the right to amend the Constitution. The American Constitution is not, as is sometimes asserted, simply "what the judges say it is."

It may be suggested that the position does not appear to be altogether different from that in parliamentary states where ultimately the legislature may amend the Constitution. This is not so. In parliamentary states the Constitution has to be amended by both Government and Assembly acting as Parliament, whereas in presidential systems the Assembly may amend the constitution without regard to the President. For example, the American Congress has limited the presidential tenure of office to two terms.

It is true that this authority of the Assembly is sometimes qualified. In the United States three-quarters of the State legislatures or conventions must ratify amendments to the constitution. In states which possess unitary constitutions it is often thought desirable that amendments shall be passed only if there is a two-thirds majority in favour or if, following a general election, a new Assembly gives further approval. The "sovereign people" themselves are thus consulted. But in each instance it is an Assembly, not the Executive or Judiciary, which has the power to change the constitution: it is the legislative branch which is supreme.

## 10. The Executive Is Directly Responsible to the Electorate

Governments in parliamentary countries are appointed by the Head of State; they are not elected. By contrast the presidential Executive is dependent on a popular vote and the President alone (and Vice-President if there is one), of all the persons in the political system, is elected by the whole body of electors. Whereas the pre-parliamentary Monarchies could not in the end withstand the pressure of the people's representatives upon their control of government a President can say to members of the Assembly: "You represent your constituency: I represent the whole people." There is no reply to this argument, and it is perhaps not surprising that in many South American countries and in France at various times the President has been able to go one step further and to assert that he *alone* represented the people.

Admittedly in form the President of the United States is still indirectly elected by an Electoral College, but so long as there are two main parties and one candidate who obtains at least fifty per cent of the vote in the College the result is a foregone conclusion after the national elections. The growth of political parties and the realities of political life have in practice placed the nomination of candidates for the Presidency in the hands of the parties, and elections in those of the electorate. If one of the various proposals to abolish the College were adopted, it might alter the balance of power among the States but it would make no difference to the fundamentally direct relationship of President and people. In other presidential countries, without exception, election is direct.

It is a distinctive feature of the system that the President should owe his position not, as in parliamentary government, to appointment, nor, as in convention theory, to selection by the Assembly, but to the electorate at election time. Between elections the President speaks to the voters directly, not indirectly through an Assembly. He cannot, except on special occasions, deliver a speech to the Assembly and unlike Prime Ministers in parliamentary states he may not use it as a forum. Hence in the United States there has grown up the fireside chat, the television appearance, and above all the weekly press conference where the President is the host.

The electorate in presidential countries therefore bears a double burden. The voters elect representatives from their own districts to the Assembly, but instead of leaving the selection of the Government to the Assembly and Head of State they also elect a President as Executive. In their wisdom they may prefer a President who belongs to a party which has only minority status in the Assembly. They will, nevertheless, at least in the United States, expect the two branches of government to reach a workable compromise.

## 11. There Is No Focus of Power in the Political System

The political activities of parliamentary systems have their focal point in Parliament. Heads of State, Governments, elected representatives, political parties, interest groups and electorates all acknowledge its supremacy.

It is tempting to assume that there must be a similar focal point in presidential systems. This is not so. Instead of concentration there is division; instead of unity, fragmentation. In the design of Washington, D.C., the President's home, the White House, is at the opposite end of Pennsylvania Ave. to the capitol where Congress meets. Geographical dispersion symbolizes their political separation.

Nor is it accurate to say that the difference is simply one of degree of fusion: that instead of one focus there are several. It would hardly be less apposite to say that the difference between a political system in which there is only one political party and others in which there are two or more lies simply in the number of parties. In both

instances there is a difference in kind more fundamental than the obvious one of degree.

In parliamentary systems, for example, there cannot for long be profound differences of opinion between Government and Assembly. Where a division appears it is in the nature of parliamentarism either for the Government to resign or for an election to take place. The differences must be resolved in order that mutual confidence between Government and Assembly, essential to the operation of the system, be restored. Differences are confined to political parties, which exist to express the various opinions in the matter.

In presidential systems there are also differences between parties and where there is federalism there may be important differences between regions as well. But in addition there is a gulf between the President and the Assembly (to say nothing of possible differences between members of his Administration, bound together by no ties of collective responsibility). Moreover, these differences, especially those between the President and Assembly, are part of the system, friction and discord being an indication not of imminent chaos but of its proper operation. In the late spring of every year the *New York Times* remarks on the unwillingness of Congress to enact the President's programme and tries to forecast the probability of his most important measures passing into law. Later in the summer as Congress recesses it lists those which have been successful. In 1957 they amounted to barely half of President Eisenhower's 155 bills.

Parliamentarians often find it incredible that the Executive in a presidential system should at times have so little control over legislation. "What is the use," they ask, "of a Government which does not govern?" But of course in a presidential system there is no Government. There is no recognized centre of the political system on which people and politicians focus their interests and aspirations. Unlike parliamentarism, which ensures the co-ordination of the various branches of the political system, the presidential system assumes that the executive and legislative branches shall be constantly checking and balancing each others' activities. It may therefore prevent action from being taken unless there is wide agreement and considerable pressure (hence the role of pressure groups in the United States).

Those who admire efficient government may be inclined towards the Cabinet government form of parliamentarism. Those who prefer more limited government may turn towards presidentialism. It should not be assumed, however, that the presidential form, because it is divided, is necessarily one of weak government. Admittedly, where presidential leadership is lacking the system may even appear to be on the verge of breaking down. But where there is a vigorous Executive he may in fact dominate the Assembly, as several American Presidents (notably Franklin D. Roosevelt) have succeeded in doing.

Miraculously, in the United States this domination has never gone too far. In much of Central and South America, where there is the form of presidential government but not the substance, the presidential system has been distorted by dictatorship.

It is difficult to explain the failure of presidential government in so many parts of South America and it is perilous to confine such explanation to purely political factors. Historically and culturally South and Central America are utterly different from the United States. However, there are a number of particular political features of these countries' systems which deserve note, not least of which is the multi-party system which characterises several of them. Where a President is elected by what is in effect a minority vote instead of by the clear majority customary in the United States he lacks that sense of being the people's representative which is so marked a feature of the American presidency. At the very least it adds a complicating factor to the relations of President, Assembly and people, and in all probability contributes to political instability.

Where there is a multi-party system there is the temptation to add to the President's status and independence by giving him a longer term of office than the Assembly. Not surprisingly the French Fifth Republic's constitution gives the President a term of seven years compared to the Assembly's four. Such a long term, while of small moment in a parliamentary system, may make a President in a non-parliamentary system a powerful figure.

Finally it may be observed that few countries have been able to enjoy the clear distinction between President and Assembly so characteristic of the United States. There has been an attempt to introduce something of the "responsibility" common to parliamentary systems. Thus there is a separate "Government" in the new French constitution, and this "Government" (but not the President) is responsible to the Assembly and may be dismissed by it. Yet the history of the Weimar Republic, to say nothing of Latin America, has shown that in practice (as if to confirm political theory) the President (i.e. the real Government) may be unaffected by such a procedure and it then becomes an ineffective weapon in the hands of the Assembly. If he *is* affected, then the system becomes parliamentary and the attempt to create a separate Executive has failed.

For there should be either a separation as in the United States and *no* focus of the political system; or a fusion with Parliament as the focus.

# THE ENGLISH CONSTITUTION: THE CABINET

Walter Bagehot

The efficient secret of the English Constitution may be described as the close union, the nearly complete fusion, of the executive and legislative powers. No doubt by the traditional theory, as it exists in all the books, the goodness of our constitution consists in the entire separation of the legislative and executive authorities, but in truth its merit consists in their singular approximation. The connecting link is *the cabinet*. By that new word we mean a committee of the legislative body selected to be the executive body. The legislature has many committees, but this is the greatest. It chooses for this, its main committee, the men in whom it has most confidence. It does not, it is true, choose them directly; but it is nearly omnipotent in choosing them indirectly. A century ago the Crown had a real choice of ministers, though it had no longer a choice in policy. During the long reign of Sir R. Walpole he was obliged not only to manage parliament, but to manage the palace. He was obliged to take care that some court intrigue did not expel him from his place. The nation then selected the English policy, but the Crown chose the English ministers. They were

Reprinted from Walter Bagehot, *The English Constitution,* Oxford University Press; first published in 1867.

not only in name, as now, but in fact, the Queen's servants. Remnants, important remnants, of this great prerogative still remain. The discriminating favour of William IV made Lord Melbourne head of the Whig party when he was only one of several rivals. At the death of Lord Palmerston it is very likely that the Queen may have the opportunity of freely choosing between two, if not three statesmen. But, as a rule, the nominal prime minister is chosen by the legislature, and the real prime minister for most purposes—the leader of the House of Commons—almost without exception is so. There is nearly always some one man plainly selected by the voice of the predominant party in the predominant house of the legislature to head that party, and consequently to rule the nation. We have in England an elective first magistrate as truly as the Americans have an elective first magistrate. The Queen is only at the head of the dignified part of the constitution. The prime minister is at the head of the efficient part. The Crown is, according to the saying, the "fountain of honour"; but the Treasury is the spring of business. Nevertheless our first magistrate differs from the American. He is not elected directly by the people; he is elected by the representatives of the people. He is an example of "double election." The legislature chosen, in name, to make laws, in fact finds its principal business in making and in keeping an executive.

The leading minister so selected has to choose his associates, but he only chooses among a charmed circle. The position of most men in parliament forbids their being invited to the cabinet; the position of a few men ensures their being invited. Between the compulsory list whom he must take, and the impossible list whom he cannot take, a prime minister's independent choice in the formation of a cabinet is not very large; it extends rather to the division of the cabinet offices than to the choice of cabinet ministers. Parliament and the nation have pretty well settled who shall have the first places; but they have not discriminated with the same accuracy which man shall have which place. The highest patronage of a prime minister is, of course, a considerable power, though it is exercised under close and imperative restrictions—though it is far less than it seems to be when stated in theory, or looked at from a distance.

The cabinet, in a word, is a board of control chosen by the legislature, out of persons whom it trusts and knows, to rule the nation. The particular mode in which the English ministers are selected; the fiction that they are, in any political sense, the Queen's servants; the rule which limits the choice of the cabinet to the members of the legislature are accidents unessential to its definition—historical incidents separable from its nature. Its characteristic is that it should be chosen by the legislature out of persons agreeable to and trusted by the legislature. Naturally these are principally its own members—but they need not be exclusively so. A cabinet which included persons not members of the legislative assembly might still perform all useful duties. Indeed the Peers, who constitute a large element in modern cabinets, are members, nowadays, only of a subordinate assembly. The House of Lords still exercises several useful functions; but the ruling influence—the deciding faculty—has passed to what, using the language of old times, we still call the lower house—to an assembly which, though inferior as a dignified institution, is superior as an efficient institution. A principal advantage of the House of Lords in the present age indeed consists in its thus acting as a *reservoir* of cabinet ministers. Unless the composition of the House of Commons were improved, or unless the rules requiring cabinet ministers to be members of the legislature were relaxed, it would undoubtedly be difficult to find, without the Lords, a sufficient supply of chief ministers. But the detail of the composition of a cabinet, and the precise method of its choice, are not to the purpose now. The first and cardinal consideration is the definition of a cabinet. We must not bewilder ourselves with the inseparable accidents until we know the necessary essence. A cabinet is a combining committee—a *hyphen* which joins, a *buckle* which fastens, the legislative part of the state to the executive part of the state. In its origin it belongs to the one, in its functions it belongs to the other.

The most curious point about the cabinet is that so very little is known about it. The meetings are not only secret in theory, but secret in reality. By the present practice, no official minute in all ordinary cases is kept of them. Even a private note is discouraged and disliked. The House of Commons, even in its most inquisitive and turbulent moments, would scarcely permit a note of a cabinet meeting to be read. No minister who respected the fundamental usages of political practice would attempt to read such a note. The committee which unites the law-making power to the law-executing power—which, by virtue of that combination, is, while it lasts and holds together, the most powerful body in the state—is a committee wholly secret. No description of it, at once graphic and authentic, has ever been given. It is said to be sometimes like a rather disorderly board of directors, where many speak and few listen—though no one knows.[1]

But a cabinet, though it is a committee of the legislative assembly, is a committee with a power which no assembly would—unless for historical accidents, and after happy experience—have been persuaded to entrust to any committee. It is a committee which can dissolve the assembly which appointed it; it is a committee with a suspensive veto—a committee with a power of appeal. Though appointed by one parliament, it can appeal if it chooses to the next. Theoretically, indeed, the power to dissolve parliament is entrusted to the sovereign only; and there are vestiges of doubt whether in *all* cases a sovereign is bound to dissolve parliament when the cabinet asks him to do so. But neglecting such small and dubious exceptions, the cabinet which was chosen by one House of Commons has an appeal to the next House of Commons. The chief committee of the legislature has the power of dissolving the predominant part of that legislature—that which at a crisis is the supreme legislature. The English system, therefore, is not an absorption of the executive power by the legislative power; it is a fusion of the two. Either the cabinet legislates and acts, or else it can dissolve. It is a creature, but it has the power of destroying its creators. It is an executive which can annihilate the legislature, as well as an executive which is the nominee of the legislature. It *was* made, but it *can* unmake; it was derivative in its origin, but it is destructive in its action.

This fusion of the legislative and executive functions may, to those who have not much considered it, seem but a dry and small matter to be the latent essence and effectual secret of the English Constitution; but we can only judge of its real importance by looking at a few of its principal effects, and contrasting it very shortly with its great competitor, which seems likely, unless care be taken, to outstrip it in the progress of the world. That competitor is the Presidential system. The characteristic of it is that the President is elected from the people by one process, and the House of Representatives by another. The independence of the legislative and executive powers is the specific quality of the Presidential Government, just as their fusion and combination is the precise principle of Cabinet Government.

(First,) compare the two in quiet times. The essence of a civilized age is, that administration requires the continued aid of legislation. One principal and necessary kind of legislation is *taxation*. The expense of civilized government is continually varying. It must vary if the government does its duty. The miscellaneous estimates of the English Government contain an inevitable medley of changing items. Education, prison discipline, art, science, civil contingencies of a hundred kinds, require more money one year and less another. The expense of defence—the naval and military estimates —vary still more as the danger of attack seems more or less imminent, as the means of retarding such danger become more or less costly. If the persons who have to do the work are not the same as those who have to make the laws, there will be a controversy between the two sets of persons. The tax-imposers are sure to quarrel with the tax-requirers. The executive is crippled by not getting the laws it needs, and the legislature is spoiled by having to act without responsibility: the executive becomes unfit for its name since it cannot execute

what it decides on; the legislature is demoralized by liberty, by taking decisions of which others (and not itself) will suffer the effects.

In America so much has this difficulty been felt that a semi-connexion has grown up between the legislature and the executive. When the Secretary of the Treasury of the Federal Government wants a tax he consults upon it with the Chairman of the Financial Committee of Congress. He cannot go down to Congress himself and propose what he wants; he can only write a letter and send it. But he tries to get a chairman of the Finance Committee who likes his tax;—through that chairman he tries to persuade the committee to recommend such tax; by that committee he tries to induce the house to adopt that tax. But such a chain of communications is liable to continual interruptions; it may suffice for a single tax on a fortunate occasion, but will scarcely pass a complicated budget —we do not say in a war or a rebellion—we are now comparing the cabinet system and the presidential system in quiet times—but in times of financial difficulty. Two clever men never exactly agreed about a budget. We have by present practice an Indian Chancellor of the Exchequer talking English finance at Calcutta, and an English one talking Indian finance in England. But the figures are never the same, and the views of policy are rarely the same. One most angry controversy has amused the world, and probably others scarcely less interesting are hidden in the copious stores of our Anglo-Indian correspondence.

But relations something like these must subsist between the head of a finance committee in the legislature, and a finance minister in the executive.[2] They are sure to quarrel, and the result is sure to satisfy neither. And when the taxes do not yield as they were expected to yield, who is responsible? Very likely the secretary of the treasury could not persuade the chairman—very likely the chairman could not persuade his committee—very likely the committee could not persuade the assembly. Whom, then, can you punish—whom can you abolish— when your taxes run short? There is nobody save the legislature, a vast miscellaneous body difficult to punish, and the very persons to inflict the punishment.

Nor is the financial part of administration the only one which requires in a civilized age the constant support and accompaniment of facilitating legislation. All administration does so. In England, on a vital occasion, the cabinet can compel legislation by the threat of resignation, and the threat of dissolution; but neither of these can be used in a presidential state. There the legislature cannot be dissolved by the executive government; and it does not heed a resignation, for it has not to find the successor. Accordingly, when a difference of opinion arises, the legislature is forced to fight the executive, and the executive is forced to fight the legislative; and so very likely they contend to the conclusion of their respective terms.[3] There is, indeed, one condition of things in which this description, though still approximately true, is, nevertheless, not exactly true; and that is, when there is nothing to fight about. Before the rebellion in America, owing to the vast distance of other states, and the favourable economical condition of the country, there were very few considerable objects of contention; but if that government had been tried by the English legislation of the last thirty years, the discordant action of the two powers, whose constant co-operation is essential to the best government, would have shown itself much more distinctly.

Nor is this the worst. Cabinet government educates the nation; the presidential does not educate it, and may corrupt it. It has been said that England invented the phrase, "Her Majesty's Opposition"; that it was the first government which made a criticism of administration as much a part of the polity as administration itself. This critical opposition is the consequence of cabinet government. The great scene of debate, the great engine of popular instruction and political controversy, is the legislative assembly. A speech there by an eminent statesman, a party movement by a great political combination, are the best means yet known for arousing, enlivening, and teaching a people. The cabinet system ensures such debates, for it makes them the means by which statesmen advertise themselves for future and confirm themselves in present governments. It brings forward men eager to speak, and gives them occasions to speak. The deciding catastrophes of cabinet governments are critical divisions preceded by fine discussions. Everything which is worth saying, everything which ought to be said, most certainly *will* be said. Conscientious men think they ought to persuade others; selfish men think they would like to obtrude themselves. The nation is forced to hear two sides—all the sides, perhaps, of that which most concerns it. And it likes to hear—it is eager to know. Human nature despises long arguments which come to nothing—heavy speeches which precede no motion—abstract disquisitions which leave visible things where they were. But all men heed great results, and a change of government is a great result. It has a hundred ramifications; it runs through society; it gives hope to many, and it takes away hope from many. It is one of those marked events which, by its magnitude and its melodrama, impress men even too much. And debates which have this catastrophe at the end of them—or may so have it—are sure to be listened to, and sure to sink deep into the national mind.

Travellers even in the Northern States of America, the greatest and best of presidential countries, have noticed that the nation was "not specially addicted to politics"; that they have not a public opinion finished and chastened as that of the Eng-

lish has been finished and chastened. A great many hasty writers have charged this defect on the "Yankee race," on the Anglo-American character; but English people, if they had no motive to attend to politics, certainly would not attend to politics. At present there is *business* in their attention. They assist at the determining crisis; they assist or help it. Whether the government will go out or remain is determined by the debate, and by the division in parliament. And the opinion out of doors, the secret pervading disposition of society, has a great influence on that division. The nation feels that its judgement is important, and it strives to judge. It succeeds in deciding because the debates and the discussions give it the facts and the arguments. But under a presidential government a nation has, except at the electing moment, no influence; it has not the ballot-box before it; its virtue is gone, and it must wait till its instant of despotism again returns. It is not incited to form an opinion like a nation under a cabinet government; nor is it instructed like such a nation. They are doubtless debates in the legislature, but they are prologues without a play. There is nothing of a catastrophe about them; you cannot turn out the government. The prize of power is not in the gift of the legislature, and no one cares for the legislature. The executive, the great centre of power and place, sticks irremovable; you cannot change it in any event. The teaching apparatus which has educated our public mind, which prepares our resolutions, which shapes our opinions, does not exist. No presidential country needs to form daily, delicate opinions, or is helped in forming them.

It might be thought that the discussions in the press would supply the deficiencies in the constitution; that by a reading people especially, the conduct of their government would be as carefully watched, that their opinions about it would be as consistent, as accurate, as well considered, under a presidential as under a cabinet polity. But the same difficulty oppresses the press which oppresses the legislature. It can *do nothing*. It cannot change the administration; the executive was elected for such and such years, and for such and such years it must last. People wonder that so literary a people as the Americans—a people who read more than any people who ever lived, who read so many newspapers—should have such bad newspapers. The papers are not so good as the English, because they have not the same motive to be good as the English papers. At a political "crisis," as we say— that is, when the fate of an administration is unfixed, when it depends on a few votes, yet unsettled, upon a wavering and veering opinion—effective articles in great journals become of essential moment. *The Times* has made many ministries. When, as of late, there has been a long continuance of divided parliaments, of governments which were without "brute voting power," and which depended on intellectual strength, the support of the most influential organ of English opinion has been of critical moment. If a Washington newspaper could have turned out Mr. Lincoln, there would have been good writing and fine argument in the Washington newspapers. But the Washington newspapers can no more remove a president during his term of place than *The Times* can remove a lord mayor during his year of office. Nobody cares for a debate in Congress which "comes to nothing," and no one reads long articles which have no influence on events. The Americans glance at the heads of news, and through the paper. They do not enter upon a discussion. They do not *think* of entering upon a discussion which would be useless.

After saying that the division of the legislature and the executive in presidential governments weakens the legislative power, it may seem a contradiction to say that it also weakens the executive power. But it is not a contradiction. The division weakens the whole aggregate force of government—the entire imperial power; and therefore it weakens both its halves. The executive is weakened in a very plain way. In England a strong cabinet can obtain the concurrence of the legislature in all acts which facilitate its administration; it is itself, so to say, the legislature. But a president may be hampered by the parliament, and is likely to be hampered. The natural tendency of the members of every legislature is to make themselves conspicuous. They wish to gratify an ambition laudable or blameable; they wish to promote the measures they think best for the public welfare; they wish to make their *will* felt in great affairs. All these mixed motives urge them to oppose the executive. They are embodying the purposes of others if they aid; they are advancing their own opinions if they defeat; they are first if they vanquish; they are auxiliaries if they support. The weakness of the American executive used to be the great theme of all critics before the Confederate rebellion. Congress and committees of Congress of course impeded the executive when there was no coercive public sentiment to check and rule them.

But the presidential system not only gives the executive power an antagonist in the legislative power, and so makes it weaker; it also enfeebles it by impairing its intrinsic quality. A cabinet is elected by a legislature; and when that legislature is composed of fit persons, that mode of electing the executive is the very best. It is a case of secondary election, under the only conditions in which secondary election is preferable to primary. Generally speaking, in an electioneering country (I mean in a country full of political life, and used to the manipulation of popular institutions), the election of candidates to elect candidates is a farce. The Electoral College of America is so. It was intended that the deputies when assembled should exercise a real discretion, and by independent choice select the president. But the primary electors take too much interest. They only elect a deputy to vote for Mr. Lincoln or Mr. Breckenridge, and the deputy only takes a ticket, and drops that ticket in an urn. He never chooses or thinks of choosing. He is but a messenger—a transmitter: the real decision is in those who chose him—who chose him because they knew what he would do.

It is true that the British House of Commons is subject to the same influences. Members are mostly, perhaps, elected because they will vote for a particular ministry, rather than for purely legislative reasons. But—and here is the capital distinction—the functions of the House of Commons are important and *continuous*. It does not, like the Electoral College in the United States, separate when it has elected its ruler; it watches, legislates, seats and unseats ministries, from day to day. Accordingly it is a *real* electoral body. The parliament of 1857, which, more than any other parliament of late years, was a parliament elected to support a particular premier—which was chosen, as Americans might say, upon the "Palmerson ticket"—before it had been in existence two years, dethroned Lord Palmerston. Though selected in the interest of a particular ministry, it in fact destroyed that ministry.

A *good* parliament, too, is a capital choosing body. If it is fit to make laws for a country, its majority ought to represent the general average intelligence of that country; its various members ought to represent the various special interests, special opinions, special prejudices, to be found in that community. There ought to be an advocate for every particular sect, and a vast neutral body of no sect—homogeneous and judicial, like the nation itself. Such a body, when possible, is the best selector of executives that can be imagined. It is full of political activity; it is close to political life; it feels the responsibility of affairs which are brought as it were to its threshold; it has as much intelligence as the society in question chances to contain. It is, what Washington and Hamilton strove to create, an electoral college of the picked men of the nation.

The best mode of appreciating its advantages is to look at the alternative. The competing constituency is the nation itself, and this is, according to theory and experience, in all but the rarest cases, a bad constituency. Mr. Lincoln, at his second election, being elected when all the Federal states had set their united hearts on one single object, was voluntarily re-elected by an actually choosing nation. He embodied the object in which every one was absorbed. But this is almost the only presidential election of which so much can be said. In almost all cases the President is chosen by a machinery of caucuses and combinations too complicated to be perfectly known, and too familiar to require description. He is not the choice of the nation, he is the choice of the wire-pullers. A very large constituency in quiet times is the necessary, almost the legitimate, subject of electioneering management: a man cannot know that he does not throw his vote away except he votes as part of some great organization; and if he votes as a part, he abdicates his electoral function in favour of the managers of that association. The nation, even if it chose for itself, would, in some degree, be an unskilled body; but when it does not choose for itself, but only as latent agitators wish, it is like a large, lazy man, with a small, vicious mind,—it moves slowly and heavily, but it moves at the bidding of a bad intention; it "means *little,* but it means that little *ill.*"

And, as the nation is less able to choose than a parliament, so it has worse people to choose out of. The American legislators of the last century have been much blamed for not permitting the ministers of the President to be members of the Assembly; but, with reference to the specific end which they had in view, they saw clearly and decided wisely. They wished to keep "the legislative branch absolutely distinct from the executive branch"; they believed such a separation to be essential to a good constitution; they believed such a separation to exist in the English, which the wisest of them thought the best constitution. And, to the effectual maintenance of such a separation, the exclusion of the President's ministers from the legislature is essential. If they are not excluded they become the executive, they eclipse the President himself. A legislative chamber is greedy and covetous; it acquires as much, it concedes as little as possible. The passions of its members are its rulers; the law-making faculty, the most comprehensive of the imperial faculties, is its instrument; it will *take* the administration if it can take it. Tried by their own aims, the founders of the United States were wise in excluding the ministers from Congress.

But though this exclusion is essential to the presidential system of government, it is not for that reason a small evil. It causes the degradation of public life. Unless a member of the legislature be sure of something more than speech, unless he is incited by the hope of action, and chastened by the chance of responsibility, a first-rate man will not care to take the place, and will not do much if he does take it. To belong to a debating society adhering to an executive (and this is no inapt description of a congress under a presidential constitution) is not an object to stir a noble ambition, and is a position to encourage idleness. The members of a parliament excluded from office can never be comparable, much less equal, to those of a parliament not excluded from office. The presidential government, by its nature, divides political life into two halves, an executive half and a legislative half; and, by so dividing it, makes neither half worth a man's having—worth his making it a continuous career—worthy to absorb, as cabinet gov-

ernment absorbs, his whole soul. The statesmen from whom a nation chooses under a presidential system are much inferior to those from whom it chooses under a cabinet system, while the selecting apparatus is also far less discerning.

All these differences are more important at critical periods, because government itself is more important. A formed public opinion, a respectable, able, and disciplined legislature, a well-chosen executive, a parliament and an administration not thwarting each other, but co-operating with each other, are of greater consequence when great affairs are in progress than when small affairs are in progress—when there is much to do than when there is little to do. But in addition to this, a parliamentary or cabinet constitution possesses an additional and special advantage in very dangerous times. It has what we may call a reserve of power fit for and needed by extreme exigencies.

The principle of popular government is that the supreme power, the determining efficacy in matters political, resides in the people—not necessarily or commonly in the whole people, in the numerical majority, but in a *chosen* people, a picked and selected people. It is so in England; it is so in all free countries. Under a cabinet constitution at a sudden emergency this people can choose a ruler for the occasion. It is quite possible and even likely that he would not be ruler *before* the occasion. The great qualities, the imperious will, the rapid energy, the eager nature fit for a great crisis are not required—are impediments—in common times. A Lord Liverpool is better in everyday politics than a Chatham—a Louis Philippe far better than a Napoleon. By the structure of the world we often want, at the sudden occurrence of a grave tempest, to change the helmsman—to replace the pilot of the calm by the pilot of the storm. In England we have had so few catastrophes since our constitution attained maturity, that we hardly appreciate this latent excellence. We have not needed a Cavour to rule a revolution—a representative man above all men fit for a great occasion, and by a natural, legal mode brought in to rule. But even in England, at what was the nearest to a great sudden crisis which we have had of late years—at the Crimean difficulty—we used this inherent power. We abolished the Aberdeen cabinet, the ablest we have had, perhaps, since the Reform Act—a cabinet not only adapted, but eminently adapted, for every sort of difficulty save the one it had to meet—which abounded in pacific discretion, and was wanting only in the "demonic element"; we chose a statesman who had the sort of merit then wanted, who, when he feels the steady power of England behind him, will advance without reluctance, and will strike without restraint. As was said at the time, "We turned out the Quaker, and put in the pugilist."

But under a presidential government you can do nothing of the kind. The American government calls itself a government of the supreme people; but at a quick crisis, the time when a sovereign power is most needed, you cannot *find* the supreme people. You have got a Congress elected for one fixed period, going out perhaps by fixed instalments, which cannot be accelerated or retarded—you have a President chosen for a fixed period, and immovable during that period; all the arrangements are for *stated* times. There is no *elastic* element, everything is rigid, specified, dated. Come what may, you can quicken nothing and can retard nothing. You have bespoken your government in advance, and whether it suits you or not, whether it works well or works ill, whether it is what you want or not, by law you must keep it. In a country of complex foreign relations it would mostly happen that the first and most critical year of every war would be managed by a peace premier, and the first and most critical years of peace by a war premier. In each case the period of transition would be irrevocably governed by a man selected not for what he was to introduce, but what he was to change—for the policy he was to abandon, not for the policy he was to administer.

The whole history of the American civil war—a history which has thrown an intense light on the working of a presidential government at the time when government is most important—is but a vast continuous commentary on these reflections. It would, indeed, be absurd to press against presidential government *as such* the singular defect by which Vice-President Johnson has become President —by which a man elected to a sinecure is fixed in what is for the moment the most important administrative part in the political world. This defect, though most characteristic of the expectations[4] of the framers of the constitution and of its working, is but an accident of this particular case of presidential government, and no necessary ingredient in that government itself. But the first election of Mr. Lincoln is liable to no such objection. It was a characteristic instance of the natural working of such a government upon a great occasion. And what was that working? It may be summed up—it was government by an *unknown quantity*. Hardly any one in America had any living idea what Mr. Lincoln was like, or any definite notion what he would do. The leading statesmen under the system of cabinet government are not only household words, but household *ideas*. A conception, not, perhaps, in all respects a true but a most vivid conception, what Mr. Gladstone is like, or what Lord Palmerston is like, runs through society. We have simply no notion what it would be to be left with the visible sovereignty in the hands of an unknown man. The notion of employing a man of unknown smallness at a crisis of unknown greatness is to our minds simply ludicrous. Mr. Lincoln, it is true, happened to be a man, if not of eminent ability, yet of eminent justness. There was an inner depth of Puritan nature which came out under suffering, and was very attractive. But success in a lottery is no argument for lotteries. What were the chances against a person of Lincoln's antecedents, elected as he was, proving to be what he was?

Such an incident is, however, natural to a presidential government. The President is elected by processes which forbid the election of known men, except at peculiar conjunctures, and in moments when public opinion is excited and despotic; and consequently, if a crisis comes upon us soon after he is elected, inevitably we have government by an unknown quantity—the superintendence of that crisis by what our great satirist would have called "Statesman X." Even in quiet times, government by a president is, for the various reasons which have been stated, inferior to government by a cabinet; but the difficulty of quiet times is nothing as compared with the difficulty of unquiet times. The comparative deficiencies of the regular, common operation of a presidential government are far less than the comparative deficiencies in time of sudden trouble—the want of elasticity, the impossibility of a dictatorship, the total absence of a *revolutionary reserve*.

## NOTES

1. It is *said* that at the end of the cabinet which agreed to propose a fixed duty on corn, Lord Melbourne put his back to the door, and said, "Now is it to lower the price of corn, or isn't it? It is not much matter which we say, but mind, we must all say *the same*." This is the most graphic story of a cabinet I ever heard, but I cannot vouch for its truth. Lord Melbourne's is a character about which men make stories.
2. It is worth observing that even during the short existence of the Confederate Government these evils distinctly showed themselves. Almost the last incident at the Richmond Congress was an angry financial correspondence with Jefferson Davis.
3. I leave this passage to stand as it was written, just after the assassination of Mr. Lincoln, and when every one said Mr. Johnson would be very hostile to the South.
4. The framers of the constitution expected that the *vice*-president would be elected by the Electoral College as the second wisest man in the country. The vice-presidentship being a sinecure, a second-rate man agreeable to the wire-pullers is always smuggled in. The chance of succession to the presidentship is too distant to be thought of.

# Conditions of Stable and Effective Democracy

## POLITICAL MAN

### Seymour Martin Lipset

### ECONOMIC DEVELOPMENT AND DEMOCRACY

**D**emocracy in a complex society may be defined as a political system which supplies regular constitutional opportunities for changing the governing officials, and a social mechanism which permits the largest possible part of the population to influence major decisions by choosing among contenders for political office.

This definition, abstracted largely from the work of Joseph Schumpeter and Max Weber,[1] implies a number of specific conditions: (1) a "political formula" or body of beliefs specifying which institutions—political parties, a free press, and so forth—are legitimate (accepted as proper by all); (2) one set of political leaders in office, and (3) one or more sets of recognized leaders attempting to gain office.

The need for these conditions is clear. *First,* if a political system is not characterized by a value system allowing the peaceful "play" of power, democracy becomes chaotic. This has been the problem faced by many Latin-American states. *Second,* if the outcome of the political game is not the periodic awarding of effective authority to one group, unstable and irresponsible government rather than democracy will result. This state of affairs existed in pre-Fascist Italy, and through much, though not all, of the history of the Third and Fourth French Republics, which were characterized by weak coalition governments, often formed among parties having major interest and value conflicts with each other. *Third,* if the conditions for per-

petuating an effective opposition do not exist, the authority of the officials in power will steadily increase, and popular influence on policy will be at a minimum. This is the situation in all one-party states, and by general agreement, at least in the West, these are dictatorships.

This chapter will consider two characteristics of a society which bear heavily on the problem of stable democracy: economic development and legitimacy, or the degree to which institutions are valued for themselves and considered right and proper. Since most countries which lack an enduring tradition of political democracy lie in the underdeveloped sections of the world, Weber may have been right when he suggested that modern democracy in its clearest form can occur only under capitalist industrialization.[2] However, an extremely high correlation between such things as income, education, and religion, on the one hand, and democracy, on the other, in any given society should not be anticipated even on theoretical grounds because, to the extent that the political subsystem of the society operates autonomously, a political form may persist under conditions normally adverse to the *emergence* of that form. Or a political form may develop because of a syndrome of unique historical factors even though the society's major characteristics favor another form. Germany is an example of a nation where growing industrialization, urbanization, wealth, and education favored the establishment of a democratic system, but in which a series of adverse historical events prevented democracy from securing legitimacy and thus weakened its ability to withstand crisis.

Key historical events may account for *either* the persistence *or* the failure of democracy in any particular society by starting a process which increases (or decreases) the likelihood that at the next critical point in the country's history democracy will win out again. Once established, a democratic political system "gathers momentum" and creates social supports (institutions) to ensure its continued existence.[3] Thus a "premature" democracy which survives will do so by (among other things) facilitating the growth of other conditions conducive to democracy, such as universal literacy, or autonomous private organizations.[4] In this chapter I am primarily concerned with the social conditions like education, which serve to *support* democratic political systems, and I will not deal in detail with the internal mechanisms like the specific rules of the political game which serve to *maintain* them.[5]

A comparative study of complex social systems must necessarily deal rather summarily with the particular historical features of any one society.[6] However, the deviation of a given nation from a particular aspect of democracy is not too important, as long as the definitions used cover the great majority of nations which are considered democratic or undemocratic. The precise dividing line between "more democratic" and "less democratic" is also not basic, since presumably democracy is not a unitary quality of a social system, but a complex of characteristics which may be ranked in many different ways. For this reason I have divided the countries under consideration into general categories, rather than attempting to rank them from highest to lowest, although even here such countries as Mexico pose problems.

Efforts to classify all countries raised a number of problems. To reduce some of the complications introduced by the sharp variations in political practices in different parts of the earth I have concentrated on differences among countries within the same political culture areas. The two best areas for such internal comparison are Latin America, and Europe and the English-speaking countries. More limited comparisons can also be made among the Asian states and among the Arab countries.

The main criteria used to define European democracies are the uninterrupted continuation of political democracy since World War I *and* the absence over the past twenty-five years of a major political movement opposed to the democratic "rules of the game."[7] The somewhat less stringent criterion for Latin America is whether a given country has had a history of more or less free elections for most of the post-World War I period.[8] Where in Europe we look for stable democracies, in South America we look for countries which have not had fairly constant dictatorial rule (see Table 1).

## ECONOMIC DEVELOPMENT IN EUROPE AND THE AMERICAS

Perhaps the most common generalization linking political systems to other aspects of society has been that democracy is related to the state of economic development. The more well-to-do a nation, the greater the chances that it will sustain democracy. From Aristotle down to the present, men have argued that only in a wealthy society in which relatively few citizens lived at the level of real poverty could there be a situation in which the mass of the population intelligently participate in politics and develop the self-restraint necessary to avoid

**TABLE 1—Classification of European, English-speaking, and Latin-American Nations by Degree of Stable Democracy**

| EUROPEAN AND ENGLISH-SPEAKING NATIONS | | LATIN-AMERICAN NATIONS | |
|---|---|---|---|
| Stable Democracies | Unstable Democracies and Dictatorships | Democracies and Unstable Dictatorships | Stable Dictatorships |
| Australia | Albania | Argentina | Bolivia |
| Belgium | Austria | Brazil | Cuba |
| Canada | Bulgaria | Chile | Dominican Republic |
| Denmark | Czechoslovakia | Colombia | Ecuador |
| Ireland | Finland | Costa Rica | El Salvador |
| Luxembourg | France | Mexico | Guatemala |
| Netherlands | Germany | Uruguay | Haiti |
| New Zealand | Greece | | Honduras |
| Norway | Hungary | | Nicaragua |
| Sweden | Iceland | | Panama |
| Switzerland | Italy | | Paraguay |
| United Kingdom | Poland | | Peru |
| United States | Portugal | | Venezuela |
| | Rumania | | |
| | Spain | | |
| | U.S.S.R. | | |
| | Yugoslavia | | |

succumbing to the appeals of irresponsible demagogues. A society divided between a large impoverished mass and a small favored elite results either in oligarchy (dictatorial rule of the small upper stratum) or in tyranny (popular-based dictatorship). To give these two political forms modern labels, tyranny's face today is communism or Peronism; while oligarchy appears in the traditionalist dictatorships found in parts of Latin America, Thailand, Spain, or Portugal.

To test this hypothesis concretely, I have used various indices of economic development—wealth, industrialization, urbanization, and education—and computed averages (means) for the countries which have been classified as more or less democratic in the Anglo-Saxon world and Europe, and in Latin America.

In each case, the average wealth, degree of industrialization and urbanization, and level of education is much higher for the more democratic countries, as the data in Table 2 indicate. If I had combined Latin America and Europe in one table, the differences would have been even greater.[9]

The main indices of *wealth* used are per capita

**TABLE 2—A Comparison of European, English-speaking, and Latin-American Countries, Divided into Two Groups, "More Democratic" and "Less Democratic," by Indices of Wealth, Industrialization, Education, and Urbanization**[a]

A. Indices of Wealth

| | Per Capita Income [b] | Thousands of Persons Per Doctor [c] | Persons Per Motor Vehicle [d] |
|---|---|---|---|
| European and English-speaking stable democracies | U.S.$ 695 | 0.86 | 17 |
| European and English-speaking unstable democracies and dictatorships | 308 | 1.4 | 143 |
| Latin-American democracies and unstable dictatorships | 171 | 2.1 | 99 |
| Latin-American stable dictatorships | 119 | 4.4 | 274 |
| *Ranges* | | | |
| European stable democracies | 420–1,453 | 0.7–1.2 | 3–62 |
| European dictatorships | 128–482 | 0.6–4 | 10–538 |
| Latin-American democracies | 112–346 | 0.8–3.3 | 31–174 |
| Latin-American stable dictatorships | 40–331 | 1.0–10.8 | 38–428 |

| | Telephones Per 1,000 Persons [e] | Radios Per 1,000 Persons [f] | Newspaper Copies Per 1,000 Persons [g] |
|---|---|---|---|
| European and English-speaking stable democracies | 205 | 350 | 341 |
| European and English-speaking unstable democracies and dictatorships | 58 | 160 | 167 |
| Latin-American democracies and unstable dictatorships | 25 | 85 | 102 |
| Latin-American stable dictatorships | 10 | 43 | 43 |
| *Ranges* | | | |
| European stable democracies | 43–400 | 160–995 | 242–570 |
| European dictatorships | 7–196 | 42–307 | 46–390 |
| Latin-American democracies | 12–58 | 38–148 | 51–233 |
| Latin-American stable dictatorships | 1–24 | 4–154 | 4–111 |

B. Indices of Industrialization

| | Percentage of Males in Agriculture [h] | Per Capita Energy Consumed [i] |
|---|---|---|
| European stable democracies | 21 | 3.6 |
| European dictatorships | 41 | 1.4 |
| Latin-American democracies | 52 | 0.6 |
| Latin-American stable dictatorships | 67 | 0.25 |
| *Ranges* | | |
| European stable democracies | 6–46 | 1.4–7.8 |
| European dictatorships | 16–60 | 0.27–3.2 |
| Latin-American democracies | 30–63 | 0.30–0.9 |
| Latin-American stable dictatorships | 46–87 | 0.02–1.27 |

income, number of persons per motor vehicle and thousands of persons per physician, and the number of radios, telephones, and newspapers per thousand persons. The differences are striking on every score (see Table 2). In the more democratic European countries, there are 17 persons per motor vehicle compared to 143 for the less democratic. In the less dictatorial Latin-American countries there are 99 persons per motor vehicle versus 274 for the more dictatorial.[10] Income differences for the groups are also sharp, dropping from an average per capita income of $695 for the more democratic countries of Europe to $308 for the less democratic; the corresponding difference for Latin America is from $171 to $119. The ranges are equally consistent, with the lowest per capita income in each group falling in the "less democratic" category, and the highest in the "more democratic."

*Industrialization,* to which indices of wealth are of course clearly related, is measured by the percentage of employed males in agriculture and the per capita commercially produced "energy" being used in the country (measured in terms of tons of coal per person per year). Both of these show equally consistent results. The average percentage of employed males working in agriculture and related occupations was 21 in the "more democratic" European countries and 41 in the "less democratic";

## TABLE 2—A Comparison of European, English-speaking, and Latin-American Countries (Cont'd.)

### C.  Indices of Education

|  | Percentage Literate [j] | Primary Education Enrollment Per 1,000 Persons [k] | Post-Primary Enrollment Per 1,000 Persons [k] | Higher Education Enrollment Per 1,000 Persons [l] |
|---|---|---|---|---|
| European stable democracies | 96 | 134 | 44 | 4.2 |
| European dictatorships | 85 | 121 | 22 | 3.5 |
| Latin-American democracies | 74 | 101 | 13 | 2.0 |
| Latin-American dictatorships | 46 | 72 | 8 | 1.3 |
| *Ranges* | | | | |
| European stable democracies | 95–100 | 96–179 | 19–83 | 1.7–17.83 |
| European dictatorships | 55–98 | 61–165 | 8–37 | 1.6–6.1 |
| Latin-American democracies | 48–87 | 75–137 | 7–27 | 0.7–4.6 |
| Latin-American dictatorships | 11–76 | 11–149 | 3–24 | 0.2–3.1 |

### D.  Indices of Urbanization

|  | Per Cent in Cities over 20,000 [m] | Per Cent in Cities over 100,000 [m] | Per Cent in Metropolitan Areas [m] |
|---|---|---|---|
| European stable democracies | 43 | 28 | 38 |
| European dictatorships | 24 | 16 | 23 |
| Latin-American democracies | 28 | 22 | 26 |
| Latin-American stable dictatorships | 17 | 12 | 15 |
| *Ranges* | | | |
| European stable democracies | 28–54 | 17–51 | 22–56 |
| European dictatorships | 12–44 | 6–33 | 7–49 |
| Latin-American democracies | 11–48 | 13–37 | 17–44 |
| Latin-American stable dictatorships | 5–36 | 4–22 | 7–26 |

a. A large part of this table has been compiled from data furnished by International Urban Research, University of California, Berkeley, California. Not all the countries in each category were used for each calculation, as uniform data were not available for them all. For instance, the data available on Albania and East Germany are very sparse. The U.S.S.R. was left out because a large part of it is in Asia.

b. United Nations, Statistical Office, *National and Per Capita Income in Seventy Countries,* 1949, Statistical Papers, Series E, No. 1, New York, 1950, pp. 14-16.

c. United Nations, *A Preliminary Report on the World Social Situation, 1952,* Table 11, pp. 46-48.

d. United Nations, *Statistical Yearbook, 1956,* Table 139, pp. 333-38.

e. *Ibid.,* Table 149, p. 387.

f. *Ibid.,* Table 189, p. 641. The population bases for these figures are for different years than those reporting the numbers of telephones and radios, but for purposes of group comparisons, the differences are not important.

g. United Nations, *A Preliminary Report . . . , op. cit.,* Appendix B, pp. 86-89.

h. United Nations, *Demographic Yearbook, 1956,* Table 12, pp. 350-70.

i. United Nations, *Statistical Yearbook, 1956, op. cit.,* Table 127, pp. 308-10. Figures refer to commercially produced energy, in equivalent numbers of metric tons of coal.

j. United Nations, *A Preliminary Report . . . , op. cit.,* Appendix A, pp. 79-86. A number of countries are listed as more than 95 per cent literate.

k. United Nations, *A Preliminary Report . . . , op. cit.,* pp. 86-100. Figures refer to persons enrolled at the earlier year of the primary range, per 1,000 total population, for years ranging from 1946 to 1950. The first primary year varies from five to eight in various countries. The less developed countries have more persons in that age range per 1,000 population than the more developed countries, but this biases the figures presented in the direction of increasing the percentage of the total population in school for the less developed countries, although fewer of the children in that age group attend school. The bias from this source thus reinforces the positive relationship between education and democracy.

l. UNESCO. *World Survey of Education,* Paris, 1955. Figures are the enrollment in higher education per 1,000 population. The years to which the figures apply vary between 1949 and 1952, and the definition of higher education varies for different countries.

m. Obtained from International Urban Research, University of California, Berkeley, California.

52 in the "less dictatorial" Latin-American countries and 67 in the "more dictatorial." The differences in per capita energy employed are equally large.

The degree of *urbanization* is also related to the existence of democracy.[11] Three different indices of urbanization are available from data compiled by International Urban Research (Berkeley, California): the percentage of the population in communities of 20,000 and over, the percentage in communities of 100,000 and over, and the percentage residing in standard metropolitan areas. On all three of these indices the more democratic countries score higher than the less democratic for both of the areas under investigation.

Many people have suggested that the higher the *education* level of a nation's population, the better the chances for democracy, and the comparative data available support this proposition. The "more democratic" countries of Europe are almost entirely literate: the lowest has a rate of 96 per cent; while the "less democratic" nations have an average rate of 85 per cent. In Latin America the difference is between an average rate of 74 per cent for the "less dictatorial" countries and 46 per cent for the "more dictatorial."[12] The educational enrollment per thousand total population at three different levels—primary, post-primary, and higher educational—is equally consistently related to the degree of democracy. The tremendous disparity is shown by the extreme cases of Haiti and the United States. Haiti has fewer children (11 per thousand) attending school in the primary grades than the United States has attending colleges (almost 18 per thousand).

The relationship between education and democracy is worth more extensive treatment since an entire philosophy of government has seen increased education as the basic requirement of democracy.[13] As James Bryce wrote, with special reference to South America, "education, if it does not make men good citizens, makes it at least easier for them to become so."[14] Education presumably broadens man's outlook, enables him to understand the need for norms of tolerance, restrains him from adhering to extremist doctrines, and increases his capacity to make rational electoral choices.

The evidence on the contribution of education to democracy is even more direct and strong on the level of individual behavior *within* countries than it is in cross-national correlations. Data gathered by public opinion research agencies which have questioned people in different countries about their beliefs on tolerance for the opposition, their attitudes toward ethnic or racial minorities, and their feelings for multi-party as against one-party systems have shown that the most important single factor differentiating those giving democratic responses from the others has been education. The higher one's education, the more likely one is to believe in democratic values and support democratic prac-

tices.[15] All the relevant studies indicate that education is more significant than either income or occupation.

These findings should lead us to anticipate a far higher correlation between national levels of education and political practice than we in fact find. Germany and France have been among the best educated nations of Europe, but this by itself did not stabilize their democracies.[16] It may be, however, that their educational level has served to inhibit other antidemocratic forces.

If we cannot say that a "high" level of education is a *sufficient* condition for democracy, the available evidence suggests that it comes close to being a *necessary* one. In Latin America, where widespread illiteracy still exists, only one of all the nations in which more than half the population is illiterate—Brazil—can be included in the "more democratic" group.

Lebanon, the one member of the Arab League which has maintained democratic institutions since World War II, is also by far the best educated (over 80 per cent literacy). East of the Arab world, only two states, the Philippines and Japan, have since 1945 maintained democratic regimes without the presence of large antidemocratic parties. And these two countries, although lower than most European states in per capita income, are among the world's leaders in educational attainment. The Philippines actually rank second to the United States in the proportion of people attending high schools and universities, and Japan has a higher educational level than any European nation.[17]

Although the evidence has been presented separately, all the various aspects of economic development—industrialization, urbanization, wealth, and education—are so closely interrelated as to form one major factor which has the political correlate of democracy.[18] A recent study of the Middle East further substantiates this. In 1951–52, a survey of Turkey, Lebanon, Egypt, Syria, Jordan, and Iran, conducted by Daniel Lerner and the Bureau of Applied Social Research, found a close connection between urbanization, literacy, voting rates, media consumption and production, and education.[19] Simple and multiple correlations between the four basic variables were computed for all countries for which United Nations statistics were available (in this case 54) with the following results:[20]

| Dependent Variable | Multiple Correlation Coefficient |
|---|---|
| Urbanization | 0.61 |
| Literacy | 0.91 |
| Media Participation | 0.84 |
| Political Participation | 0.82 |

In the Middle East, Turkey and Lebanon score higher on most of these indices than do the other four countries analyzed, and Daniel Lerner, in reporting on the study, points out that the "great post-war events in Egypt, Syria, Jordan and Iran have been the violent struggles for the control of power—struggles notably absent in Turkey and Lebanon [until very recently] where the control of power has been decided by elections."[21]

Lerner further points out the effect of disproportionate development, in one area or another, for over-all stability, and the need for co-ordinated changes in all of these variables. Comparing urbanization and literacy in Egypt and Turkey, he concludes that although Egypt is far more urbanized than Turkey, it is not really "modernized," and does not even have an adequate base for modernization, because literacy has not kept pace. In Turkey, all of the several indices of modernization have kept pace with each other, with rising voting participation (36 per cent in 1950), balanced by rising literacy, urbanization, etc. In Egypt, the cities are full of "homeless illiterates," who provide a ready audience for political mobilization in support of extremist ideologies. On Lerner's scale, Egypt should be twice as literate as Turkey, since it is twice as urbanized. The fact that it is only half as literate explains, for Lerner, the "imbalances" which "tend to become circular and to accelerate social disorganization," political as well as economic.[22]

Lerner introduces one important theoretical addition—the suggestion that these key variables in the modernization process may be viewed as historical phases, with democracy part of later developments, the "crowning institution of the participant society" (one of his terms for a modern industrial society). His view on the relations between these variables, seen as stages, is worth quoting at some length:

The secular evolution of a participant society appears to involve a regular sequence of three phases. Urbanization comes first, for cities alone have developed the complex of skills and resources which characterize the modern industrial economy. Within this urban matrix develop both of the attributes which distinguish the next two phases—literacy and media growth. There is a close reciprocal relationship between these, for the literate develop the media which in turn spread literacy. But, literacy performs the key function in the second phase. The capacity to read, at first acquired by relatively few people, equips them to perform the varied tasks required in the modernizing society. Not until the third phase, when the elaborate technology of industrial development is fairly well advanced, does a society begin to produce newspapers, radio networks, and motion pictures on a massive scale. This, in turn, accelerates the spread of literacy. Out of this interaction develop those institutions of participation (e.g., voting) which we find in all advanced modern societies.[23]

Learner's thesis, that these elements of modernization are functionally interdependent, is by no means established by his data. But the material presented in this chapter offers an opportunity for research along these lines. Deviant cases, such as Egypt, where "lagging" literacy is associated with serious strains and potential upheaval, may also be found in Europe and Latin America, and their analysis— a task not attempted here—will further clarify the basic dynamics of modernization and the problem of social stability in the midst of institutional change.

## Economic Development and the Class Struggle

Economic development, producing increased income, greater economic security, and widespread higher education, largely determines the form of the "class struggle," by permitting those in the lower strata to develop longer time perspectives and more complex and gradualist views of politics. A belief in secular reformist gradualism can be the ideology of only a relatively well-to-do lower class. Striking evidence for this thesis may be found in the relationship between the patterns of working-class political action in different countries and the national income, a correlation that is almost startling in view of the many other cultural, historical, and juridical factors which affect the political life of nations.

In the two wealthiest countries, the United States and Canada, not only are communist parties almost nonexistent but socialist parties have never been able to establish themselves as major forces. Among the eight next wealthiest countries—New Zealand, Switzerland, Sweden, United Kingdom, Denmark, Australia, Norway, Belgium, Luxembourg and Netherlands—all of whom had a per capita income of over $500 a year in 1949 (the last year for which standardized United Nations statistics exist), moderate socialism predominates as the form of leftist politics. In none of these countries did the Communists secure more than 7 per cent of the vote, and the actual Communist party average among them has been about 4 per cent. In the eight European countries which were below the $500 per capita income mark in 1949—France, Iceland, Czechoslovakia, Finland, West Germany, Hungary, Italy, and Austria—and which have had at least one postwar democratic election in which both communist and noncommunist parties could compete, the Communist party has had more than 16 per cent of the vote in six, and an over-all average of more than 20 per cent in the eight countries as a group. The two low-income countries in which the Communists are weak—Germany and Austria —have both had direct experience with Soviet occupation.[24]

Leftist extremism has also dominated working-class politics in two other European nations which belong to the under $500 per capita income group —Spain and Greece. In Spain before Franco, anarchism and left socialism were much stronger than moderate socialism; while in Greece, whose per capita income in 1949 was only $128, the Communists have always been much stronger than the socialists, and fellow-traveling parties have secured a large vote in recent years.[25]

The inverse relationship between national economic development as reflected by per capita income and the strength of Communists and other extremist groups among Western nations is seemingly stronger than the correlations between other national variables like ethnic or religious factors.[26] Two of the poorer nations with large Communist movements—Iceland and Finland—are Scandinavian and Lutheran. Among the Catholic nations of Europe, all the poor ones except Austria have large Communist or anarchist movements. The two wealthiest Catholic democracies—Belgium and Luxembourg—have few Communists. Though the French and Italian cantons of Switzerland are strongly affected by the cultural life of France and Italy, there are almost no Communists among the workers in these cantons, living in the wealthiest country in Europe.

The relation between low per capita wealth and the precipitation of sufficient discontent to provide the social basis for political extremism is supported by a recent comparative polling survey of the attitudes of citizens of nine countries. Among these countries, feelings of personal security correlated with per capita income (0.45) and with per capita food supply (0.55). If satisfaction with one's country, as measured by responses to the question, "Which country in the world gives you the best chance of living the kind of life you would like to live?" is used as an index of the amount of discontent in a nation, then the relationship with economic wealth is even higher. The study reports a rank order correlation of 0.74 between per capita income and the degree of satisfaction with one's own country.[27]

This does not mean that economic hardship or poverty *per se* is the main cause of radicalism. There is much evidence to sustain the argument that stable poverty in a situation in which individuals are not exposed to the possibilities of change breeds, if anything, conservatism.[28] Individuals whose experience limits their significant communications and interaction to others on the same level as themselves will, other conditions being equal, be more conservative than people who may be better off but who have been exposed to the possibilities of securing a better way of life.[29] The dynamic in the situation would seem to be exposure to the possibility of a better way of life rather than poverty as such. As Karl Marx put it in a perceptive passage: "A house may be large or small; as long as

the surrounding houses are equally small it satisfies all social demands for a dwelling. But if a palace arises beside the little house, the little house shrinks into a hut."[30]

With the growth of modern means of communication and transportation both within and among countries, it seems increasingly likely that the groups in the population that are poverty-stricken but are isolated from knowledge of better ways of life or unaware of the possibilities for improvement in their condition are becoming rarer and rarer, particularly in the urban areas of the Western world. One may expect to find such stable poverty only in tradition-dominated societies.

Since position in a stratification system is always relative and gratification or deprivation is experienced in terms of being better or worse off than other people, it is not surprising that the lower classes in all countries, regardless of the wealth of the country, show various signs of resentment against the existing distribution of rewards by supporting political parties and other organizations which advocate some form of redistribution.[31] The fact that the form which these political parties take in poorer countries is more extremist and radical than it is in wealthier ones is probably more related to the greater degree of inequality in such countries than to the fact that their poor are actually poorer in absolute terms. A comparative study of wealth distribution by the United Nations "suggest[s] that the richest fraction of the population (the richest 10th, 5th, etc.) generally receive[s] a greater proportion of the total income in the less developed than in the more developed countries."[32] The gap between the income of professional and semiprofessional personnel on the one hand and ordinary workers on the other is much wider in the poorer than in the wealthier countries. Among manual workers,

there seems to be a greater wage discrepancy between skilled and unskilled workers in the less developed countries. In contrast the leveling process, in several of the developed countries at least, has been facilitated by the over-all increase of national income . . . not so much by reduction of the income of the relatively rich as by the faster growth of the incomes of the relatively poor.[33]

The distribution of consumption goods also tends to become more equitable as the size of national income increases. The wealthier a country, the larger the proportion of its population which owns automobiles, telephones, bathtubs, refrigerating equipment, and so forth. Where there is a dearth of goods, the sharing of such goods must inevitably be less equitable than in a country in which there is relative abundance. For example, the number of people who can afford automobiles, washing machines, decent housing, telephones, good clothes,

or have their children complete high school or go
to college still represents only a small minority
of the population in many European countries.
The great national wealth of the United States or
Canada, or even to a lesser extent the Australasian
Dominions or Sweden, means that there is relatively little difference between the standards of
living of adjacent social classes, and that even classes
which are far apart in the social structure will
enjoy more nearly similar consumption patterns
than will comparable classes in Southern Europe.
To a Southern European, and to an even greater
extent to the inhabitant of one of the "underdeveloped" countries, social stratification is characterized by a much greater distinction in ways of life,
with little overlap in the goods the various strata
own or can afford to purchase. It may be suggested, therefore, that the wealthier a country, the
less is status inferiority experienced as a major
source of deprivation.

Increased wealth and education also serve democracy by increasing the lower classes' exposure
to cross-pressures which reduce their commitment
to given ideologies and make them less receptive
to extremist ones. The operation of this process
will be discussed in more detail in the next chapter,
but it means involving those strata in an integrated
national culture as distinct from an isolated lower-
class one.

Marx believed that the proletariat was a revolutionary force because it had nothing to lose but its
chains and could win the whole world. But Tocqueville, analyzing the reasons why the lower strata
in America supported the system, paraphrased and
transposed Marx before Marx ever made his analysis by pointing out that "only those who have
nothing to lose ever revolt."[34]

Increased wealth also affects the political role
of the middle class by changing the shape of the
stratification structure from an elongated pyramid,
with a large lower-class base, to a diamond
with a growing middle class. A large middle class
tempers conflict by rewarding moderate and democratic parties and penalizing extremist groups.

The political values and style of the upper class,
too, are related to national income. The poorer a
country and the lower the absolute standard of
living of the lower classes, the greater the pressure
on the upper strata to treat the lower as vulgar,
innately inferior, a lower caste beyond the pale of
human society. The sharp difference in the style
of living between those at the top and those at the
bottom makes this psychologically necessary. Consequently, the upper strata in such a situation tend
to regard political rights for the lower strata, particularly the right to share power, as essentially
absurd and immoral. The upper strata not only resist democracy themselves; their often arrogant po-

litical behavior serves to intensify extremist reactions
on the part of the lower classes.

The general income level of a nation also affects
its receptivity to democratic norms. If there is
enough wealth in the country so that it does not
make too much difference whether some redistribution takes place, it is easier to accept the idea that
it does not matter greatly which side is in power.
But if loss of office means serious losses for major
power groups, they will seek to retain or secure
office by any means available. A certain amount of
national wealth is likewise necessary to ensure a
competent civil service. The poorer the country,
the greater the emphasis on nepotism—support of
kin and friends. And this in turn reduces the opportunity to develop the efficient bureaucracy which
a modern democratic state requires.[35]

Intermediary organizations which act as sources
of countervailing power seem to be similarly associated with national wealth. Tocqueville and other
exponents of what has come to be known as the
theory of the "mass society"[36] have argued that
a country without a multitude of organizations
relatively independent of the central state power
has a high dictatorial as well as revolutionary
potential. Such organizations serve a number of
functions: they inhibit the state or any single source
of private power from dominating all political resources; they are a source of new opinions; they
can be the means of communicating ideas, particularly opposition ideas, to a large section of the
citizenry; they train men in political skills and
so help to increase the level of interest and participation in politics. Although there are no reliable
data on the relationship between national patterns
of voluntary organization and national political
systems, evidence from studies of individual behavior demonstrates that, regardless of other factors,
men who belong to associations are more likely
than others to give the democratic answer to questions concerning tolerance and party systems, to
vote, or to participate actively in politics. Since
the more well-to-do and better educated a man is,
the more likely he is to belong to voluntary organizations, the propensity to form such groups
seems to be a function of level of income and
opportunities for leisure within given nations.[37]

## The Politics of Rapid
## Economic Development

The association between economic development
and democracy has led many Western statesmen
and political commentators to conclude that the
basic political problem of our day is produced by
the pressure for rapid industrialization. If only
the underdeveloped nations can be successfully
started on the road to high productivity, the as-

sumption runs, we can defeat the major threat to newly established democracies, their domestic Communists. In a curious way, this view marks the victory of economic determinism or vulgar Marxism within democratic political thought. Unfortunately for this theory, political extremism based on the lower classes, communism in particular, is not to be found only in low-income countries but also in newly industrializing nations. This correlation is not, of course, a recent phenomenon. In 1884, Engels noted that explicitly socialist labor movements had developed in Europe during periods of rapid industrial growth, and that these movements declined sharply during later periods of slower change.

The pattern of leftist politics in northern Europe in the first half of the twentieth century in countries whose socialist and trade-union movements are now relatively moderate and conservative illustrates this point. Wherever industrialization occurred *rapidly*, introducing sharp *discontinuities* between the pre-industrial and industrial situation, more rather than less extremist working-class movements emerged. In Scandinavia, for example, the variations among the socialist movements of Denmark, Sweden, and Norway can be accounted for in large measure by the different timing and pace of industrialization, as the economist Walter Galenson has pointed out.[38] The Danish Social Democratic movement and trade-unions have always been in the reformist, moderate, and relatively non-Marxist wing of the international labor movement. In Denmark, industrialization developed as a slow and gradual process. The rate of urban growth was also moderate, which had a good effect on urban working-class housing conditions. The slow growth of industry meant that a large proportion of Danish workers all during the period of industrialization were men who had been employed in industry for a long time, and, consequently, newcomers who had been pulled up from rural areas and who might have supplied the basis for extremist factions were always in a minority. The left-wing groups which gained some support in Denmark were based on the rapidly expanding industries.

In Sweden, on the other hand, manufacturing industry grew very rapidly from 1900 to 1914. This caused a sudden growth in the number of unskilled workers, largely recruited from rural areas, and the expansion of industrial rather than craft unions. Paralleling these developments in industry, a left-wing movement arose within the trade-unions and the Social Democratic party which opposed the moderate policies that both had developed before the great industrial expansion. A strong anarcho-syndicalist movement also emerged in this period. Here again, these aggressive left-wing movements were based on the rapidly expanding industries.[39]

Norway, the last of the three Scandinavian countries to industrialize, had an even more rapid rate of growth. As a result of the emergence of hydroelectric power, the growth of an electrochemical industry, and the need for continued construction, Norway's industrial workers doubled between 1905 and 1920. And as in Sweden, this increase in the labor force meant that the traditional moderate craft-union movement was swamped by unskilled and semiskilled workers, most of whom were young migrants from rural areas. A left wing emerged within the Federation of Labor and the Labor party, capturing control of both in the latter stages of World War I. It should be noted that Norway was the only Western European country which was still in its phase of rapid industrialization when the Comintern was founded, and its Labor party was the only one which went over almost intact to the Communists.

In Germany before World War I, a revolutionary Marxist left wing, in large measure derived from workers in the rapidly growing industries, retained considerable support within the Social Democratic party, while the more moderate sections of the party were based on the more stable established industries.[40]

The most significant illustration of the relationship between rapid industrialization and working-class extremism is the Russian Revolution. In Czarist Russia, the industrial population jumped from 16 million in 1897 to 26 million in 1913.[41] Trotsky in his *History of the Russian Revolution* has shown how an increase in the strike rate and in union militancy paralleled the growth of industry. It is probably not coincidental that two nations in Europe in which the revolutionary left gained control of the dominant section of the labor movement before 1920—Russia and Norway—were also countries in which the processes of rapid capital accumulation and basic industrialization were still going on.[42]

The revolutionary socialist movements which arise in response to strains created by rapid industrialization decline, as Engels put it, wherever "the transition to large-scale industry is more or less completed . . . [and] the conditions in which the proletariat is placed become stable."[43] Such countries are, of course, precisely the industrialized nations where Marxism and revolutionary socialism exist today only as sectarian dogmas. In those nations of Europe where industrialization never occurred, or where it failed to build an economy of efficient large-scale industry with a high level of productivity and a constant increase in mass-consumption patterns, the conditions for the creation or perpetuation of extremist labor politics also exist.

A different type of extremism, based on the small entrepreneurial classes (both urban and rural), has emerged in the less developed and often culturally backward sectors of more industrialized societies. The social base of classic fascism seems to arise from the ever present vulnerability of part of the middle class, particularly small businessmen and farm owners, to large-scale capitalism and a powerful labor movement. Chapter V [of *Political Man*] analyzes this reaction in detail as it is manifest in a number of countries.

It is obvious that the conditions related to stable democracy discussed here are most rapidly found in the countries of northwest Europe and their English-speaking offspring in America and Australasia; and it has been suggested, by Weber among others, that a historically unique concatenation of elements produced both democracy and capitalism in this area. Capitalist economic development, the basic argument runs, had its greatest opportunity in a Protestant society and created the burgher class whose existence was both a catalyst and a necessary condition for democracy. Protestantism's emphasis on individual responsibility furthered the emergence of democratic values in these countries and resulted in an alignment between the burghers and the throne which preserved the monarchy and extended the acceptance of democracy among the conservative strata. Men may question whether any aspect of this interrelated cluster of economic development, Protestantism, monarchy, gradual political change, legitimacy, and democracy is primary, but the fact remains that the cluster does hang together.[44]

. . . Examination of some of the requisites of democracy which are derived from specifically historical elements, particularly those which relate to the needs of a democratic political system for legitimacy and for mechanisms which reduce the intensity of political conflict, . . . although related to economic development, are distinct from it since they are elements within the political system, and not attributes of the total society.

## Methodological Appendix

The approach in this chapter is implicitly different from some other studies which have attempted to handle social phenomena on a total societal level, and it may be useful to make explicit some of the methodological postulates underlying this presentation.

Complex characteristics of a social system, such as democracy, the degree of bureaucratization, the type of stratification system, have usually been handled by either a reductionist or an "ideal-type" approach. The former dismisses the possibility of considering these characteristics as system-attributes as such, and maintains that the qualities of individual actions are the sum and substance of sociological categories. For this school of thought, the extent of democratic attitudes, or of bureaucratic behavior, or the numbers and types of prestige or power rankings, constitute the essence of the meaning of the attributes of democracy, bureaucracy, or class.

The "ideal-type" approach starts from a similar assumption, but reaches an opposite conclusion. The similar assumption is that societies are a complex order of phenomena, exhibiting such a degree of internal contradiction that generalizations about them as a whole must necessarily constitute a constructed representation of selected elements, stemming from the particular concerns and perspectives of the scientist. The opposite conclusion is that abstractions of the order of "democracy" or "bureaucracy" have no necessary connection with states or qualities of complex social systems which actually exist, but comprise collections of attributes which are logically interrelated but characteristic in their entirety of no existing society.[45] An example is Weber's concept of "bureaucracy," comprising a set of offices which are not "owned" by the officeholder, continuously maintained files of records, functionally specified duties, etc.; so is the common definition of democracy in political science, which postulates individual political decisions based on rational knowledge of one's own ends and of the factual political situation.

Criticism of such categories or ideal-types solely on the basis that they do not correspond to reality is irrelevant, because they are not intended to describe reality, but to provide a basis for comparing different aspects of reality with the consistently logical case. Often this approach is quite fruitful, and there is no intention here of substituting another in its place, but merely of presenting another possible way of conceptualizing complex characteristics of social systems, stemming from the multivariate analysis pioneered by Paul Lazarsfeld and his colleagues on a quite different level of analysis.[46]

The point at which this approach differs is on the issue of whether generalized theoretical categories can be considered to have a valid relationship to characteristics of total social systems. The implication of the statistical data presented in this chapter on democracy, and the relations between democracy, economic development, and political legitimacy, is that there are aspects of total social systems which exist, can be stated in theoretical terms, can be compared with similar aspects of other systems, and, at the same time, are derivable from empirical data which can be checked (or questioned) by other researchers. This does not mean that situations contradicting the general relationship may not exist, or that at lower levels of social organization quite different characteristics may not be evident. For example, a country like the United States may be characterized as "democratic" on the national level, even though most secondary organizations within the country may not be democratic. On another level, a church may be characterized as an "unbureaucratic" organization compared to a corporation, even though important segments of the church organization may be as bureaucratized as the most bureaucratic parts of the corporation. On yet another level, it may be quite legitimate, for purposes of psychological evaluation of the total personality, to consider a certain individual "schizophrenic," even though under certain conditions he may not act schizophrenically. The point is that when comparisons are being made on a certain level of generalization, referring to the functioning of a total system (whether on a personality, group, organization, or society level), generalizations applicable to a total society have the same kind and degree of validity that those applicable to other systems have, and are subject to the same empirical tests. The lack of systematic and comparative study of several societies has obscured this point.

This approach also stresses the view that complex characteristics of a total system have multi-variate causation and consequences, in so far as the characteristic has some degree of autonomy within the system. Bureaucracy and urbanization, as well as democracy, have many causes and consequences, in this sense.[47]

From this point of view, it would be difficult to identify any *one* factor crucially associated with, or "causing," any complex social characteristic. Rather, all such characteristics (and this is a methodological assumption to guide research, and not a substantive point) are considered to have multi-variate causation, and consequences. The point may be clarified by a diagram of some of the possible connections between democracy, the initial conditions associated with its emergence, and the consequences of an existent democratic system.

The appearance of a factor on both sides of "democracy" implies that it is both an initial condition of democracy, and that democracy, once established, sustains that characteristic of the society —an open class system, for example. On the other hand, some of the initial consequences of democracy, such as bureaucracy, may have the effect of *undermining* democracy, as the reversing arrows

indicate. Appearance of a factor to the right of democracy does not mean that democracy "causes" its appearance, but merely that democracy is an initial condition which favors its development. Similarly, the hypothesis that bureaucracy is one of the consequences of democracy does not imply that democracy is the sole cause, but rather that a democratic system has the effect of encouraging the development of a certain type of bureaucracy under other conditions which have to be stated if bureaucracy is the focus of the research problem. This diagram is not intended as a complete model of the general social conditions associated with the emergence of democracy, but as a way of clarifying the methodological point concerning the multi-variate character of relationships in a total social system.

Thus, in a multi-variate system, the focus may be upon any element, and its conditions and consequences may be stated without the implication that we have arrived at a complete theory of the necessary and sufficient conditions of its emergence. This chapter does not attempt a *new* theory of democracy, but only the formalizing and empirical testing of certain sets of relationships implied by traditional theories of democracy.

## SOCIAL CONFLICT, LEGITIMACY, AND DEMOCRACY

### Legitimacy and Effectiveness

The stability of any given democracy depends not only on economic development but also upon the effectiveness and the legitimacy of its political system. Effectiveness means actual performance, the extent to which the system satisfies the basic functions of government as most of the population and such powerful groups within it as big business or the armed forces see them. Legitimacy involves the capacity of the system to engender and maintain the belief that existing political institutions are the most appropriate ones for the society. The extent to which contemporary democratic political systems are legitimate depends in large measure upon the ways in which the key issues which have historically divided the society have been resolved. While effectiveness is primarily instrumental, legitimacy is evaluative. Groups regard a political system as legitimate or illegitimate according to

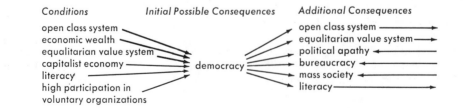

Conditions    Initial Possible Consequences    Additional Consequences

open class system
economic wealth
equalitarian value system
capitalist economy                democracy
literacy
high participation in
voluntary organizations

open class system
equalitarian value system
political apathy
bureaucracy
mass society
literacy

the way in which its values fit with theirs. Important segments of the German Army, civil service, and aristocratic classes rejected the Weimar Republic, not because it was ineffective, but because its symbolism and basic values negated their own. Legitimacy, in and of itself, may be associated with many forms of political organization, including oppressive ones. Feudal societies, before the advent of industrialism, undoubtedly enjoyed the basic loyalty of most of their members. Crises of legitimacy are primarily a recent historical phenomenon, following the rise of sharp cleavages among groups which are able, because of mass communication, to organize around different values than those previously considered to be the only acceptable ones.

A crisis of legitimacy is a crisis of change. Therefore, its roots must be sought in the character of change in modern society. Crises of legitimacy occur during a transition to a new social structure, if (1) the *status* of major conservative institutions is threatened during the period of structural change; (2) all the major groups in the society do not have access to the political system in the transitional period, or at least as soon as they develop political demands. After a new social structure is established, if the new system is unable to sustain the expectations of major groups ·(on the grounds of "effectiveness") for a long enough period to develop legitimacy upon the new basis, a new crisis may develop.

Tocqueville gives a graphic description of the first general type of loss of legitimacy, referring mainly to countries which moved from aristocratic monarchies to democratic republics: ". . . epochs sometimes occur in the life of a nation when the old customs of a people are changed, public morality is destroyed, religious belief shaken, and the spell of tradition broken . . ." The citizens then have "neither the instinctive patriotism of a monarchy nor the reflecting patriotism of a republic; . . . they have stopped between the two in the midst of confusion and distress."[48]

If, however, the status of major conservative groups and symbols is not threatened during this transitional period, even though they lose most of their power, democracy seems to be much more secure. And thus we have the absurd fact that ten out of the twelve stable European and English-speaking democracies are monarchies.[49] Great Britain, Sweden, Norway, Denmark, the Netherlands, Belgium, Luxembourg, Australia, Canada, and New Zealand are kingdoms, or dominions of a monarch, while the only republics which meet the conditions of stable democratic procedures are the United States and Switzerland, plus Uruguay in Latin America.

The preservation of the monarchy has apparently retained for these nations the loyalty of the aristocratic, traditionalist, and clerical sectors of the population which resented increased democratization and equalitarianism. And by accepting the lower strata and not resisting to the point where revolution might be necessary, the conservative orders won or retained the loyalty of the new "citizens." In countries where monarchy was overthrown by revolution, and orderly succession was broken, forces aligned with the throne have sometimes continued to refuse legitimacy to republican successors down to the fifth generation or more.

The one constitutional monarchy which became a fascist dictatorship, Italy, was, like the French Republic, considered illegitimate by major groups in the society. The House of Savoy alienated the Catholics by destroying the temporal power of the Popes, and was also not a legitimate successor in the old Kingdom of the Two Sicilies. Catholics were, in fact, forbidden by the church to participate in Italian politics until almost World War I, and the church finally rescinded its position only because of its fear of the Socialists. French Catholics took a similar attitude to the Third Republic during the same period. Both the Italian and French democracies have had to operate for much of their histories without loyal support from important groups in their societies, on both the left and the right. Thus one main source of legitimacy lies in the continuity of important traditional integrative institutions during a transitional period in which new institutions are emerging.

The second general type of loss of legitimacy is related to the ways in which different societies handle the "entry into politics" crisis—the decision as to when new social groups shall obtain access to the political process. In the nineteenth century these new groups were primarily industrial workers; in the twentieth, colonial elites and peasant peoples. Whenever new groups become politically active (e.g., when the workers first seek access to economic and political power through economic organization and the suffrage, when the *bourgeoisie* demand access to and participation in government, when colonial elites insist on control over their own system), easy access to the *legitimate* political institutions tends to win the loyalty of the new groups to the system, and they in turn can permit the old dominating strata to maintain their own status. In nations like Germany where access was denied for prolonged periods, first to the *bourgeoisie* and later to the workers, and where force was used to restrict access, the lower strata were alienated from the system and adopted extremist ideologies which, in turn, kept the more established groups from accepting the workers' political movement as a legitimate alternative.

Political systems which deny new strata access to power except by revolution also inhibit the growth of legitimacy by introducing millennial hopes into the political arena. Groups which have to push their way into the body politic by force are apt to overexaggerate the possibilities which political participation affords. Consequently, democratic regimes born under such stress not only face the difficulty of being regarded as illegitimate by groups loyal to the *ancien régime* but may also be rejected by those whose millennial hopes are not fulfilled by the change. France, where right-wing clericals have viewed the Republic as illegitimate and sections of the lower strata have found their expectations far from satisfied, is an example. And today many of the newly independent nations of Asia and Africa face the thorny problem of winning the loyalties of the masses to democratic states which can do little to meet the utopian objectives set by nationalist movements during the period of colonialism and the transitional struggle to independence.

In general, even when the political system is reasonably effective, if at any time the status of major conservative groups is threatened, or if access to politics is denied to emerging groups at crucial periods, the system's legitimacy will remain in question. On the other hand, a breakdown of effectiveness, repeatedly or for a long period, will endanger even a legitimate system's stability.

A major test of legitimacy is the extent to which given nations have developed a common "secular political culture," mainly national rituals and holidays.[50] The United States has developed a common homogeneous culture in the veneration accorded the Founding Fathers, Abraham Lincoln, Theodore Roosevelt, and their principles. These common elements, to which all American politicians appeal, are not present in all democratic societies. In some European countries, the left and the right have a different set of symbols and different historical heroes. France offers the clearest example of such a nation. Here battles involving the use of different symbols which started in 1789 are, as Herbert Luethy points out, "still in progress, and the issue is still open; every one of these dates [of major political controversy] still divides left and right, clerical and anti-clerical, progressive and reactionary, in all their historically determined constellations."[51]

Knowledge concerning the relative degree of legitimacy of a nation's political institutions is of key importance in any attempt to analyze the stability of these institutions when faced with a crisis of effectiveness. The relationship between different degrees of legitimacy and effectiveness in specific political systems may be presented in the form of a four-fold table, with examples of countries characterized by the various possible combinations:

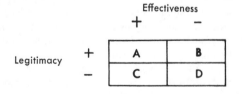

Societies which fall in box A, which are, that is,

high on the scales of both legitimacy and effectiveness, have stable political systems, like the United States, Sweden, and Britain.[52] Ineffective and illegitimate regimes, which fall in box D, are by definition unstable and break down, unless they are dictatorships maintaining themselves by force, like the governments of Hungary and eastern Germany today.

The political experiences of different countries in the early 1930s illustrate the effect of other combinations. In the late 1920s, neither the German nor the Austrian republic was held legitimate by large and powerful segments of its population. Nevertheless, both remained reasonably effective.[53] In terms of the table, they fell in box C. When the effectiveness of various governments broke down in the 1930s, those societies which were high on the scale of legitimacy remained democratic, while such countries as Germany, Austria, and Spain lost their freedom, and France narrowly escaped a similar fate. Or to put the changes in terms of the table, countries which shifted from A to B remained democratic, while those which shifted from C to D broke down. The military defeat of 1940 underlined French democracy's low position on the scale of legitimacy. It was the sole defeated democracy which furnished large-scale support for a Quisling regime.[54]

Situations like these demonstrate the usefulness of this type of analysis. From a short-range point of view, a highly effective but illegitimate system, such as a well-governed colony, is more unstable than regimes which are relatively low in effectiveness and high in legitimacy. The social stability of a nation like Thailand, despite its periodic *coups d'état,* stands out in sharp contrast to the situation in neighboring former colonial nations. On the other hand, prolonged effectiveness over a number of generations may give legitimacy to a political system. In the modern world, such effectiveness means primarily constant economic development. Those nations which have adapted most successfully to the requirements of an industrial system have the fewest internal political strains, and have either preserved their traditional legitimacy or developed strong new symbols.

The social and economic structure which Latin America inherited from the Iberian peninsula prevented it from following the lead of the former English colonies, and its republics never developed the symbols and aura of legitimacy. In large measure, the survival of the new political democracies of Asia and Africa will depend on their ability to meet the needs of their populations over a prolonged period, which will probably mean their ability to cope with industrialization.

### Legitimacy and Conflict

Inherent in all democratic systems is the constant threat that the group conflicts which are democracy's lifeblood may solidify to the point where they threaten to disintegrate the society. Hence conditions which serve to moderate the intensity of partisan battle are among the key requisites of democratic government.

Since the existence of a moderate state of conflict is in fact another way of defining a legitimate democracy, it is not surprising that the principal factors determining such an optimum state are closely related to those which produce legitimacy viewed in terms of continuities of symbols and statuses. The character and content of the major cleavages affecting the political stability of a society are largely determined by historical factors which have affected the way in which major issues dividing society have been solved or left unresolved over time.

In modern times, three major issues have emerged in Western nations: first, the place of the church and/or various religions within the nation; second, the admission of the lower strata, particularly the workers, to full political and economic "citizenship" through universal suffrage and the right to bargain collectively; and third, the continuing struggle over the distribution of the national income.

The significant question here is: Were these issues dealt with one by one, with each more or less solved before the next arose; or did the problems accumulate, so that traditional sources of cleavage mixed with newer ones? Resolving tensions one at a time contributes to a stable political system; carrying over issues from one historical period to another makes for a political atmosphere characterized by bitterness and frustration rather than tolerance and compromise. Men and parties come to differ with each other, not simply on ways of settling current problems, but on fundamental and opposed outlooks. This means that they see the political victory of their opponents as a major moral threat, and the whole system, as a result, lacks effective value-integration.

The place of the church in society was fought through and solved in most of the Protestant nations in the eighteenth and nineteenth centuries. In some, the United States, for example, the church was disestablished and accepted the fact. In others, like Britain, Scandinavia, and Switzerland, religion is still state-supported, but the state churches, like constitutional monarchs, have ceased to be major sources of controversy. It remains for the Catholic countries of Europe to provide us with examples of situations in which the historical controversy between clerical and anticlerical forces has continued to divide men politically down to the present day. In such countries as France, Italy, Spain, and Austria, being Catholic has meant being allied with rightist or conservative groups in politics, while being anticlerical, or a member of a minority religion, has most often meant alliance with the left. In a number of these countries, newer issues have been superimposed on the religious question. For conservative Catholics the fight against socialism has been not simply an economic struggle, or a controversy over social institutions, but a deep-rooted conflict between God and Satan.[55] For many secular intellectuals in contemporary Italy, opposition to the church legitimizes alliance with the Communists. And as long as religious ties reinforce secular political alignments, the chances for compromise and democratic give-and-take are weak.

The "citizenship" issue has also been resolved in various ways. The United States and Britain gave the workers suffrage in the nineteenth century. In countries like Sweden, which resisted until the first part of the twentieth century, the struggle for citizenship became combined with socialism as a *political* movement, thereby producing a revolutionary socialism. Or, to put it in other terms, where the workers were denied both economic and political rights, their struggle for redistribution of income and status was superimposed on a revolutionary ideology. Where the economic and status struggle developed outside of this context, the ideology with which it was linked tended to be that of gradualist reform. The Workers in Prussia, for example, were denied free and equal suffrage until the revolution of 1918, and thereby clung to revolutionary Marxism. In southern Germany, where full citizenship rights were granted in the late nineteenth century, reformist, democratic, and nonrevolutionary socialism was dominant. However, the national Social Democratic party continued to embrace revolutionary dogmas. These served to give ultra-leftists a voice in party leadership, enabled the Communists to win strength after the military defeat, and, perhaps even more important historically, frightened large sections of the German middle class who feared that a socialist victory would end all their privileges and status.

In France, the workers won the suffrage but were refused basic economic rights until after World War II. Large numbers of French employers refused to recognize French trade-unions and sought to weaken or destroy them after every union victory. The instability of the French unions, and their constant need to preserve militancy in order to survive, made the workers susceptible to the appeals of extremist political groups. Communist domination of the French labor movement can in large part be traced to the tactics of the French business classes.

These examples do not explain why different countries varied in the way they handled basic national cleavages. They should suffice, however, to illustrate the way in which the conditions for stable democratic government are related to the bases of diversity. Where a number of historic cleavages intermix and create the basis for ideological politics, democracy will be unstable and weak, for by definition such politics does not include the concept of tolerance.

Parties with such total ideologies attempt to create what the German-American political scientist Sigmund Neumann has called an "integrated" environment, in which the lives of the members are encased within ideologically linked activities. These actions are based on the party's assumption that it is important to isolate its followers from the "falsehoods" expressed by nonbelievers. Neumann has suggested the need for a basic analytic distinction between parties of representation, which strengthen democracy, and parties of integration, which weaken it.[56] The former are typified by most parties in the English-speaking democracies and Scandinavia, plus most centrist and conservative parties other than religious ones. These parties view their function as primarily one of securing votes around election time. The parties of integration, on the other hand, are concerned with making the world conform to their basic philosophy. They do not see themselves as contestants in a give-and-take game of pressure politics, but as partisans in a mighty struggle between divine or historic truth on one side and fundamental error on the other. Given this conception of the world, it becomes necessary to prevent their followers from being exposed to the cross-pressures flowing from contact with outsiders which will reduce their faith.

The two major nontotalitarian groups which have followed such procedures have been the Catholics and the Socialists. In much of Europe before 1939 the Catholics and Socialists attempted to increase intra-religious or intra-class communications by creating a network of social and economic organizations within which their followers could live their entire lives. Austria offers perhaps the best example of a situation in which two groups, the Social Catholics and the Social Democrats, dividing over all three historic issues and carrying on most of their social activities in party or church-linked organizations, managed to split the country into two hostile camps.[57] Totalitarian organizations, fascist and Communist alike, expand the integrationist character of political life to the furthest limit possible by defining the world completely in terms of struggle.

Efforts, even by democratic parties, to isolate their social base from cross-pressures clearly undermine stable democracy, which requires shifts from one election to another and the resolving of issues between parties over long periods of time. Isolation may intensify loyalty to a party or church, but it will also prevent the party from reaching new groups. The Austrian situation illustrates the way in which the electoral process is frustrated when most of the electorate is confined within parties of integration. The necessary rules of democratic politics assume that conversion both ways, into and out of a party, is possible and proper, and parties which hope to gain a majority by democratic methods must ultimately give up their integrationist emphasis. As the working class has gained

complete citizenship in the political and economic spheres in different countries, the socialist parties of Europe have dropped their integrationist emphasis. The only nontotalitarian parties which now maintain such policies are religious parties like the Catholic parties or the Calvinist Anti-Revolutionary party of Holland. Clearly the Catholic and Dutch Calvinist churches are not "democratic" in the sphere of religion. They insist there is but one truth, as the Communists and fascists do in politics. Catholics may accept the assumptions of political democracy, but never those of religious tolerance. And where the political conflict between religion and irreligion is viewed as salient by Catholics or other believers in one true church, then a real dilemma exists for the democratic process. Many political issues which might easily be compromised are reinforced by the religious issue and cannot be settled.

Wherever the social structure operates so as to isolate *naturally* individuals or groups with the same political outlook from contact with those who hold different views, the isolated individuals or groups tend to back political extremists. It has been repeatedly noted, for example, that workers in so-called "isolated" industries—miners, sailors, fishermen, lumbermen, sheepshearers, and longshoremen—who live in communities predominately inhabited by others in the same occupation usually give overwhelming support to the more left-wing platforms.[58] Such districts tend to vote Communist or socialist by large majorities, sometimes to the point of having what is essentially a "one-party" system. The political intolerance of farm-based groups in times of crisis may be another illustration of this same pattern, since farmers, like workers in isolated industries, have a more homogeneous political environment than do those employed in most urban occupations.[59]

These conclusions are confirmed by studies of individual voting behavior which indicate that individuals under cross-pressures—those who belong to groups predisposing them in different directions, or who have friends supporting different parties, or who are regularly exposed to the propaganda of different groups—are less likely to be strongly committed politically.[60]

Multiple and politically inconsistent affiliations, loyalties, and stimuli reduce the emotion and aggressiveness involved in political choice. For example, in contemporary Germany, a working-class Catholic, pulled in two directions, will most probably vote Christian-Democratic, but is much more tolerant of the Social Democrats than the average middle-class Catholic.[61] Where a man belongs to a variety of groups that all predispose him toward the same political choice, he is in the situation of the isolated worker and is much less likely to be tolerant of other opinions.

The available evidence suggests that the chances for stable democracy are enhanced to the extent that groups and individuals have a number of cross-cutting, politically relevant affiliations. To the degree that a significant proportion of the population is pulled among conflicting forces, its members have an interest in reducing the intensity of political conflict.[62] As Robert Dahl and Talcott Parsons have pointed out, such groups and individuals also have an interest in protecting the rights of political minorities.[63]

A stable democracy requires relatively moderate tension among its contending political forces. And political moderation is facilitated by the system's capacity to resolve key dividing issues before new ones arise. If the issues of religion, citizenship, and "collective bargaining" are allowed to accumulate, they reinforce each other, and the more reinforced and correlated the sources of cleavage, the less likelihood for political tolerance. Similarly, the greater the isolation from heterogeneous political stimuli, the more the background factors "pile up" in one direction, the greater the chances that the group or individual will have an extremist perspective. These two relationships, one on the level of partisan issues, the other on the level of party support, are joined by the fact that parties reflecting accumulated unresolved issues will further seek to isolate their followers from conflicting stimuli. The best conditions for political cosmopolitanism are again those of economic development—the growth of urbanization, education, communications media, and increased wealth. Most of the obviously isolated occupations—mining, lumbering, agriculture—are precisely those whose relative share of the labor force declines sharply with industrialization.[64]

Thus the factors involved in modernization or economic development are linked to those which establish legitimacy and tolerance. But it should always be remembered that correlations are only statements about relative degrees of congruence, and that another condition for political action is that the correlation never be so clear-cut that men feel they cannot change the direction of affairs by their actions. And this lack of high correlation also means that for analytic purposes the variables should be kept distinct even if they intercorrelate. For example, the analysis of cleavage presented here suggests specific ways in which different electoral and constitutional arrangements may affect the chances for democracy. These are discussed in the following section.

### Systems of Government

If crosscutting bases of cleavage make a more vital democracy, it follows that, all other factors being constant, two-party systems are better than multi-party systems, that the election of officials on a territorial basis is preferable to proportional representation, and federalism is superior to a unitary state. Of course there have been and are stable democracies with multi-party systems, proportional representation, and a unitary state. In fact, I would argue that such variations in systems of government are much less important than those derived from the basic differences in social structure discussed in the previous sections. Nevertheless, they may contribute to over-all stability or instability.

The argument for the two-party system rests on the assumption that in a complex society parties must necessarily be broad coalitions which do not serve the interests of one major group, and that they must not be parties of integration but must seek to win support among groups which are preponderantly allied to the opposition party. The British Conservative or American Republican parties, for instance, must not basically antagonize the manual workers, since a large part of their votes must come from them. The Democratic and Labor parties are faced with a similar problem vis-à-vis the middle classes. Parties which are never oriented toward gaining a majority seek to win the greatest possible electoral support from a limited base—a "workers" party will accentuate working-class interests, and a party appealing primarily to small businessmen will do the same for its group. For these splinter parties, elections, instead of being occasions for seeking the broadest possible base of support by convincing divergent groups of their common interests, become events in which they stress the cleavages separating their supporters from other segments of the society.

The proposition that proportional representation weakens rather than strengthens democracy rests on an analysis of the differences between multi-party and majority party situations. If it is true, as suggested above, that the existence of many parties accentuates differences and reduces consensus, then any electoral system which increases the chance for more rather than fewer parties serves democracy badly.

Besides, as the German sociologist Georg Simmel has pointed out, the system of electing members of parliament to represent territorial constituencies rather than groups (as proportional representation encourages), forces the various groups to secure their ends within an electoral framework that involves concern with many interests and the need for compromise.[65]

Federalism increases the opportunity for multiple sources of cleavage by adding regional interests and values to the others which crosscut the social structure. A major exception to this generalization occurs when federalism divides a country across the lines of basic cleavage, e.g., between different ethnic, religious, or linguistic areas, as it does in India and Canada. Democracy needs cleavage within linguistic or religious groups, not between them. But where such divisions do not exist, federalism seems to serve democracy well. Besides creating a further source of crosscutting cleavage, it provides the various functions which Tocqueville noted it shared with strong voluntary associations—resistance to centralization of power, the training of new political leaders, and a means of giving the out party a stake in the system as a whole, since both national parties usually continue to control some units of the system.

I might emphasize again that I do not consider these aspects of the political structure essential for democratic systems. If the underlying social conditions facilitate democracy, as they seem to in, say, Sweden, then the combination of many parties, proportional representation, and a unitary state does not seriously weaken it. At most it permits irresponsible minorities to gain a foothold in parliament. On the other hand, in countries like Weimar Germany and France, where a low level of effectiveness and legitimacy weakens the foundations of democracy, constitutional factors encouraging the growth of many parties further reduce the chances that the system will survive.

### Contemporary Challenges: Communism and Nationalism

The characteristic pattern of stable Western democracies in the mid-twentieth century is that they are in a "post-politics" phase—that is, there is relatively little difference between the democratic left and right, the socialists are moderates, and the conservatives accept the welfare state. In large measure this situation reflects the fact that in these countries the workers have won their fight for full citizenship.

Representatives of the lower strata are now part of the governing groups, members of the club. The basic political issue of the industrial revolution, the incorporation of the workers into the legitimate body politic, has been settled.[66] The key domestic issue today is collective bargaining over differences in the division of the total product within the framework of a Keynesian welfare state, and such issues do not require or precipitate extremism on either side. However, even though the working class of the Western democracies is incorporated into the society, it still possesses authoritarian predispositions which, under certain conditions, appear in support of extremist political and religious movements.

In most of Latin and Eastern Europe, the struggle for working-class integration into the body politic was not settled before the Communists appeared on the scene, and this fact drastically changed the political game. Communists could not be absorbed in the system in the way that the socialists have been. Communist workers, their parties and trade-

unions, cannot possibly be accorded the right of access to actual political power by a democratic society. The Communists' self-image, and more particularly their ties to the Soviet Union, lead them to accept the self-fulfilling prophecy that they cannot secure their ends by democratic means. This belief prevents them from being allowed access, which in turn reinforces the Communist workers' sense of alienation from the government. The more conservative strata in turn are strengthened in their belief that giving increased rights to the workers or their representatives threatens all that is good in life. Thus the presence of Communists precludes an easy prediction that economic development will stabilize democracy in these European countries.

In the newly independent nations of Asia and Negro Africa the situation is somewhat different. In Europe the workers were faced with the problem of winning citizenship from the dominant aristocratic and business strata. In Asia and Africa the long-term presence of colonial rulers has identified conservative ideology and the more well-to-do classes with subservience to colonialism, while leftist ideologies, usually of a Marxist variety, have been identified with nationalism. The trade-unions and workers' parties of Asia and Africa have been a legitimate part of the political process from the beginning of the democratic system. Conceivably such a situation could mean a stable democracy, except for the fact that these political rights predate the development of a stable economy with a large middle class and an industrial society.

The whole system is standing on its head. The left wing in the stable European democracies grew gradually during a fight for more democracy and gave expression to the discontents created by the early stages of industrialization, while the right retained the support of traditionalist elements in the society, until eventually the system came into an easy balance with modifications on both sides. In Asia the left wing is now in power during a period of population explosion and early industrialization, and will have to accept responsibility for all the consequent miseries. And, as in the poorer areas of Europe, the Communists, who capitalize on all these discontents in a completely irresponsible fashion, are currently a major party—the second largest in most Asian states.

Given the existence of poverty-stricken masses, low levels of education, an elongated-pyramid class structure, and the "premature" triumph of the democratic left, the prognosis for political democracy in Asia and Africa is bleak. The nations with the best prospects—Israel, Japan, Lebanon, the Philippines, and Turkey—tend to resemble Europe in one or more major factors: high educational level (all except Turkey), a substantial and growing middle class, the retention of political legitimacy by conservative groups. The others are committed more deeply to a certain tempo of economic development and to national independence, under whatever political form, than they are to the pattern of party politics and free elections which exemplify our model of democracy. It seems likely that in countries which avoid Communist or military dictatorship, political developments will follow the pattern developing in countries such as Ghana, Guinea, Tunisia, or Mexico, with an educated minority using a mass movement and leftist slogans to exercise effective control, and holding elections as a gesture toward ultimate democratic objectives and as a means of estimating public opinion rather than as effective instruments for a legitimate turnover in office.[67] With the pressure for rapid industrialization and the immediate solution of chronic problems of poverty and famine, it is unlikely that many of the new governments of Asia and Africa will be able to support an open party system representing basically different class positions and values.[68]

Latin America, economically underdeveloped like Asia, is politically more nearly like Europe in the early nineteenth century. Most Latin-American countries became independent states before the rise of industrialism and Marxist ideologies and so contain strongholds of traditional conservatism. The countryside is often apolitical or traditional, and the leftist movements secure support primarily from the industrial proletariat. Latin-American Communists, for example, have chosen the European Marxist path of organizing urban workers, rather than the "Yenan way" of Mao, seeking a peasant base.[69] If Latin America is allowed to develop on its own and is able to increase its productivity, there is a good chance that many Latin-American countries will follow in the European direction. Recent developments, including the overthrow of a number of dictatorships, reflect the effects of a growing middle class and increased wealth and education. There is, however, the great danger that these countries may yet follow in the French and Italian direction rather than that of northern Europe, that the Communists will seize the leadership of the workers, and that the middle class will be alienated from democracy. Once a politically active middle class is in existence, the key distinction between "left" and "right" political tendencies no longer suffice as a means of differentiation between supporters and opponents of democracy. As Chapter V [of *Political Man*] shows, the further distinction between left, right, and center, each with a characteristic ideology and social base, and each with a democratic and an extremist tendency, clarifies the problem of "authoritarianism," and its relationship to the stage of economic development.

## NOTES

1. Joseph Schumpeter, *Capitalism, Socialism and Democracy* (New York: Harper & Bros., 1947), pp. 232–302, esp. 269; Max Weber, *Essays in Sociology* (New York: Oxford University Press, 1946), p. 226; see also the brilliant discussion of the meaning of democracy by John Plamenatz in his chapter in Richard McKeon, ed., *Democracy in a World of Tensions* (Chicago: University of Chicago Press, 1951), pp. 302–327.

2. See Max Weber, "Zur Lage der bürgerlichen Demokratie in Russland," *Archiv für Sozialwissenschaft und Sozialpolitik,* 22 (1906), pp. 346 ff.

3. See S. M. Lipset, "A Sociologist Looks at History," *Pacific Sociological Review,* 1 (1958), pp. 13–17.

4. Walter Galenson points out that democracy may also endanger economic development by allowing public pressure for consumption to divert resources from investment. The resultant conflict between the intense commitment to industrialization and the popular demand for immediate social services in turn undermines the democratic state. Thus, even if democracy is achieved by an underdeveloped nation, it is under constant pressure from the inherent conflicts in the developmental process. See Walter Galenson, ed., *Labor and Economic Development* (New York: John Wiley & Sons, 1959), pp. 16 ff.

5. See Morris Janowitz and Dwaine Marvick, *Competitive Pressure and Democratic Consent,* Michigan Governmental Studies, No. 32 (Ann Arbor: University of Michigan Press, 1956); and Robert A. Dahl, *A Preface to Democratic Theory* (Chicago: University of Chicago Press, 1956), esp. Chap. 4, pp. 90–123, for recent systematic efforts to specify some of the internal mechanisms of democracy. See David Easton, "An Approach to the Analysis of Political Systems," *World Politics,* 9 (1957), pp. 383–400, for discussion of problems of internal analysis of political systems.

6. No detailed examination of the political history of individual countries will be undertaken, since the relative degree or social content of democracy in different countries is not the real problem of this chapter.

7. The latter requirement means that no totalitarian movement, either fascist or communist received 20 per cent of the vote during this time. Actually all the European nations falling on the democratic side of the continuum had totalitarian movements which secured less than 7 per cent of the vote.

8. The historian Arthur P. Whitaker has summarized the judgments of experts on Latin America to be that "the countries which have approximated most closely to the democratic ideal have been . . . Argentina, Brazil, Chile, Colombia, Costa Rica, and Uruguay." See "The Pathology of Democracy in Latin America: A Historian's Point of View," *American Political Science Review,* 44 (1950), pp. 101–18. To this group I have added Mexico. Mexico has allowed freedom of the press, of assembly, and of organization to opposition parties, although there is good evidence that it does not allow them the opportunity to win elections since ballots are counted by the incumbents. The existence

of opposition groups, contested elections, and adjustments among the various factions of the governing *Partido Revolucionario Institucional* does introduce a considerable element of popular influence in the system.

The interesting effort of Russell Fitzgibbon to secure a "statistical evaluation of Latin American democracy" based on the opinion of various experts is not useful for the purposes of this paper. The judges were not only asked to rank countries as democratic on the basis of purely political criteria, but also considered the "standard of living" and "educational level." These latter factors may be conditions for democracy, but they are not an aspect of democracy as such. See Russell H. Fitzgibbon, "A Statistical Evaluation of Latin American Democracy," *Western Political Quarterly,* 9 (1956), pp. 607–19.

9. Lyle W. Shannon has correlated indices of economic development with whether a country is self-governing or not, and his conclusions are substantially the same. Since Shannon does not give details on the countries categorized as self-governing and nonself-governing, there is no direct measure of the relation between "democratic" and "self-governing" countries. All the countries examined in this chapter, however, were chosen on the assumption that a characterization as "democratic" is meaningless for a nonself-governing country, and therefore, presumably, all of them, whether democratic or dictatorial, would fall within Shannon's "self-governing" category. Shannon shows that underdevelopment is related to lack of self-government; my data indicate that once self-government is attained, development is still related to the character of the political system. See the book edited by Shannon, *Underdeveloped Areas* (New York: Harper & Bros., 1957), and also his article, "Is Level of Development Related to Capacity for Self-Government?" *American Journal of Economics and Sociology,* 17 (1958), pp. 367–82. In the latter paper Shannon constructs a composite index of development, using some of the same indices, such as inhabitants per physician, and derived from the same United Nations sources, as appear in the tables to follow. Shannon's work did not come to my attention until after this chapter was first prepared, so that the two analyses can be considered as separate tests of comparable hypotheses.

10. It must be remembered that these figures are means, compiled from census figures for the various countries. The data vary widely in accuracy, and there is no way of measuring the validity of compound calculated figures such as those presented here. The consistent direction of all these differences, and their large magnitude, is the main indication of validity.

11. Urbanization has often been linked to democracy by political theorists. Harold J. Laski asserted that "organized democracy is the product of urban life," and that it was natural therefore that it should have "made its first effective appearance" in the Greek city states, limited as was their definition of "citizen." See his article "Democracy" in the *Encyclopedia of the Social Sciences* (New York: Macmillan, 1937), Vol. V, pp. 76–85. Max Weber held that the city, as a certain type of political community, is a peculiarly Western phenomenon, and traced the emergence of the notion of "citizenship" from social developments closely related to urbanization. For a partial statement of his point of view, see the chapter on "Citizenship" in *General Economic History* (New York: The Free Press of Glencoe, 1950), pp. 315–38.

12. The pattern indicated by a comparison of the averages for each group of countries is sustained by the ranges (the high and low extremes) for each index. Most of the ranges overlap; that is, some countries which are in the "less democratic" category are higher on any given index than some which are "more democratic." It is noteworthy that in both Europe and Latin America, the nations which are lowest on any of the indices presented in the table are also in the "less democratic" category. Conversely, almost all countries which rank at the top of any of the indices are in the "more democratic" class.

13. See John Dewey, *Democracy and Education* (New York: Macmillan, 1916).

14. James Bryce, *South America: Observations and Impressions* (New York: Macmillan, 1912), p. 546. Bryce considered several classes of conditions in South America which affected the chances for democracy, some of which are substantially the same as those presented here. The physical conditions of a country determined the ease of communications between areas, and thus the ease of formation of a "common public opinion." By "racial" conditions Bryce really meant whether there was ethnic homogeneity or not, with the existence of different ethnic or language groups preventing that "homogeneity and solidarity of the community which are almost indispensable conditions to the success of democratic government." Economic and social conditions included economic development, widespread political participation, and literacy. Bryce also detailed the specific historical factors which, over and above these "general" factors, operated in each South American country. See James Bryce, *op. cit.,* pp. 527–33 and 580 ff. See also Karl Mannheim, *Freedom, Power and Democratic Planning* (New York: Oxford University Press, 1950).

15. See C. H. Smith, "Liberalism and Level of Information," *Journal of Educational Psychology,* 39 (1948), pp. 65–82; Martin A. Trow, *Right Wing Radicalism and Political Intolerance* (Ph.D. thesis, Department of Sociology, Columbia University, 1957), p. 17; Samuel A. Stouffer, *Communism, Conformity, and Civil Liberties* (New York: Doubleday & Co., Inc., 1955); Kotaro Kido and Masataka Suyi, "A Report of Research on Social Stratification and Mobility in Tokyo" (III), *Japanese Sociological Review,* 4 (1954), pp. 74–100. This point is also discussed in Chap. IV.

16. Dewey has suggested that the character of the educational system will influence its effect on democracy, and this may shed some light on the sources of instability in Germany. The purpose of German education, according to Dewey, writing in 1916, was one of "disciplinary training rather than of personal development." The main aim was to produce "absorption of the aims and meaning of existing institutions," and "thoroughgoing subordination" to them. This point raises issues which cannot be entered into here, but indicates the complex character of the relationship between democracy and closely related factors, such as education. See John Dewey, *op. cit.,* pp. 108–10.

17. Ceylon, which shares the distinction with the Philippines and Japan of being the only democratic countries in South and Far East Asia in which the Communists are unimportant electorally, also shares

with them the distinction of being the only countries in this area in which a *majority* of the population is literate. It should be noted, however, that Ceylon does have a fairly large Trotskyist party, now the official opposition, and while its educational level is high for Asia, it is much lower than either Japan or the Philippines.

18. This statement is a "statistical" statement, which necessarily means that there will be many exceptions to the correlation. Thus we know that poorer people are more likely to vote for the Democratic or Labor parties in the U.S. and England. The fact that a large minority of the lower strata vote for the more conservative party in these countries does not challenge the proposition that stratification position is a main determinant of party choice.

19. The study is reported in Daniel Lerner's *The Passing of Traditional Society* (New York: The Free Press of Glencoe, 1958). These correlations are derived from census data; the main sections of the survey dealt with reactions to and opinions about the mass media, with inferences as to the personality types appropriate to modern and to traditional society.

20. *Ibid.,* p. 63. The index of political participation was the per cent voting in the last five elections. These results cannot be considered as independent verification of the relationships presented in this paper, since the data and variables are basically the same (as they are also in the work by Lyle Shannon, *op. cit.*), but the identical results using three entirely different methods, the phi coefficient, multiple correlations, and means and ranges, show decisively that the relationships cannot be attributed to artifacts of the computations. It should also be noted that the three analyses were made without knowledge of each other.

21. *Ibid.,* pp. 84–85.

22. *Ibid.,* pp. 87–89. Other theories of underdeveloped areas have also stressed the circular character of the forces sustaining a given level of economic and social development, and in a sense this paper may be regarded as an effort to extend the analysis of the complex of institutions constituting a "modernized" society to the political sphere. Leo Schnore's monograph, *Economic Development and Urbanization: An Ecological Approach,* relates technological, demographic, and organizational (including literacy and per capita income) variables as an interdependent complex. Harvey Leibenstein's recent volume, *Economic Backwardness and Economic Growth* (New York: John Wiley & Sons, 1957), views "underdevelopment" within the framework of a "quasi-equilibrium" economic theory as a complex of associated and mutually supportive aspects of a society, and includes cultural and political characteristics—illiteracy, the lack of a middle class, a crude communications system—as part of the complex. (See pp. 39–41.)

23. Lerner, *op. cit.,* p. 60. Lerner also focuses upon certain personality requirements of a "modern" society which may also be related to the personality requirements of democracy. According to him, the physical and social mobility of modern society requires a mobile personality, capable of adaption to rapid change. Development of a "mobile sensibility so adaptive to change that rearrangement of the self-system is its distinctive mode" has been the work of the twentieth century. Its main feature is *empathy,* denoting the "general capacity to see oneself in the other

fellow's situation, whether favorably or unfavorably." (See pp. 49 ff.)

Whether this psychological characteristic results in a predisposition toward democracy (implying a willingness to accept the viewpoint of others) or is rather associated with the antidemocratic tendencies of a "mass society" type of personality (implying the lack of any solid personal values rooted in rewarding participation) is an open question. Possibly empathy (a more or less "cosmopolitan" outlook) is a general personality characteristic of modern societies, with other special conditions determining whether or not it has the social consequence of tolerance and democratic attitudes, or rootlessness and anomie.

24. It should be noted that before 1933–34, Germany had one of the largest Communist parties in Europe; while the Socialist party of Austria was the most left-wing and Marxist European party in the Socialist International.

25. Greece, economically the poorest political democracy in Europe, "is now the only country in Europe where there is no socialist party. The Socialist party (ELD), established in 1945 by individuals who collaborated with the Communists during the Occupation, dissolved itself in August 1953, a victim of its fickle and pro-Communist policy. The whole field was then surrendered to the Communists with the justification that conditions were not mature enough for the development of a socialist movement!" Manolis Korakas, "Grecian Apathy," *Socialist Commentary,* May 1957, p. 21; in the elections of May 11, 1958, the "Communist directed" Union of the Democratic Left won 78 out of 300 parliamentary seats and is now the second largest party in the country. See New York *Times,* May 16, 1958, p. 3, col. 4.

26. The relationship expressed above can be presented in another way. The seven European countries in which Communist or fellow-traveling parties have secured large votes in free elections had an average per capita income in 1949 of $330. The ten European countries in which the Communists have been a failure electorally had an average per capita income of $585.

27. William Buchanan and Hadley Cantril, *How Nations See Each Other* (Urbana: University of Illinois Press, 1953), p. 35.

28. See Emile Durkheim, *Suicide: A Study in Sociology* (New York: The Free Press of Glencoe, 1951), pp. 253–54; see also Daniel Bell, "The Theory of Mass Society," *Commentary,* 22 (1956), p. 80.

29. There is also a considerable body of evidence which indicates that those occupations which are economically vulnerable and those workers who have experienced unemployment are prone to be more leftist in their outlook. See Chap. VII [of *Political Man*], pp. 231–37.

30. Karl Marx, "Wage-Labor and Capital," in *Selected Works, Vol. I* (New York: International Publishers, 1933), pp. 268–69. "Social tensions are an expression of unfulfilled expectations," Daniel Bell, *op. cit.,* p. 80.

31. A summary of the findings of election studies in many countries shows that, with few exceptions, there is a strong relationship between lower social position and support of "leftist" politics. There are, of course, many other characteristics which are also related to left voting, some of which are found among

relatively well paid but socially isolated groups. Among the population as a whole, men are much more likely to vote for the left than women, while members of minority religious and ethnic groups also display a leftist tendency.

32. *United Nations Preliminary Report on the World Social Situation* (New York: 1952), pp. 132–33. Gunnar Myrdal, the Swedish economist, has recently pointed out: "It is, indeed, a regular occurrence endowed almost with the dignity of an economic law that the poorer the country, the greater the difference between poor and rich." *An International Economy* (New York: Harper & Bros., 1956), p. 133.

33. *United Nations Preliminary Report . . . , ibid.* (See also Table 2.) A recently completed comparison of income distribution in the United States and a number of western European countries concludes that "there has not been any great difference" in patterns of income distribution among these countries. These findings of Robert Solow appear to contradict those reported above from the U.N. Statistics Office, although the latter are dealing primarily with differences between industrialized and underdeveloped nations. In any case, it should be noted that Solow agrees that the relative position of the lower strata in a poor as compared with a wealthy country is quite different. As he states, "in comparing Europe and America, one may ask whether it makes sense to talk about relative income inequality independently of the absolute level of income. An income four times another income has different content according as the lower income means malnutrition on the one hand or provides some surplus on the other." Robert M. Solow, *A Survey of Income Inequality since the War* (Stanford: Center for Advanced Study in the Behavioral Sciences, 1958, mimeographed), pp. 41–44, 78.

34. Alexis de Tocqueville, *Democracy in America*, Vol. I (New York: Alfred A. Knopf, Vintage ed., 1945), p. 258.

35. For a discussion of this problem in a new state, see David Apter, *The Gold Coast in Transition* (Princeton: Princeton University Press, 1955), esp. Chaps. 9 and 13. Apter shows the importance of efficient bureaucracy, and the acceptance of bureaucratic values and behavior patterns for the existence of a democratic political order.

36. See Emil Lederer, *The State of the Masses* (New York: Norton, 1940); Hannah Arendt, *Origins of Totalitarianism* (New York: Harcourt, Brace & World, 1951); Max Horkheimer, *Eclipse of Reason* (New York: Oxford University Press, 1947); Karl Mannheim, *Man and Society in an Age of Reconstruction* (New York: Harcourt, Brace & World, 1940); Philip Selznick, *The Organizational Weapon* (New York: McGraw-Hill Book Co., 1952); José Ortega y Gasset, *The Revolt of the Masses* (New York: Norton, 1932); William Kornhauser, *The Politics of Mass Society* (New York: The Free Press of Glencoe, 1959).

37. See Edward Banfield, *The Moral Basis of a Backward Society* (New York: The Free Press of Glencoe, 1958), for an excellent description of the way in which abysmal poverty serves to reduce community organization in southern Italy. The data which do exist from polling surveys conducted in the United States, Germany, France, Great Britain, and Sweden show that somewhere between 40 and 50 per cent of the adults in these countries belong to voluntary associations, without lower rates of membership for the less stable democracies, France and Germany, than among the more stable ones, the United States, Great Britain, and Sweden. These results seemingly challenge the general proposition, although no definite conclusion can be made, since most of the studies employed noncomparable categories. This point bears further research in many countries. For the data on these countries see the following studies.

For France, see Arnold Rose, *Theory and Method in the Social Sciences* (Minneapolis: University of Minnesota Press, 1954), p. 74 and O. R. Gallagher, "Voluntary Associations in France," *Social Forces,* 36 (1957), pp. 154–56; for Germany see Erich Reigrotski, *Soziale Verflechtungen in der Bundesrepublik* (Tübingen: J. D. B. Mohr, 1956), p. 164; for the U.S. see Charles R. Wright and Herbert H. Hyman, "Voluntary Association Memberships of American Adults: Evidence from National Sample Surveys," *American Sociological Review,* 23 (1958), p. 287, J. C. Scott, Jr., "Membership and Participation in Voluntary Associations," *American Sociological Review,* 22 (1957), pp. 315–26 and Herbert Maccoby, "The Differential Political Activity of Participants in a Voluntary Association," *American Sociological Review,* 23 (1958), pp. 524–33; for Great Britain see "Mass Observation," *Puzzled People* (London: Victor Gollanz, 1947), p. 119 and Thomas Bottomore, "Social Stratification in Voluntary Organizations," in David Glass, ed., *Social Mobility in Britain* (New York: The Free Press of Glencoe, 1954), p. 354; for Sweden see Gunnar Heckscher, "Pluralist Democracy: The Swedish Experience," *Social Research,* 15 (1948), pp. 417–61.

38. See Walter Galenson, *The Danish System of Labor Relations* (Cambridge: Harvard University Press, 1952); see also Galenson, "Scandinavia," in Galenson, ed., *Comparative Labor Movements* (Englewood Cliffs, N.J.: Prentice-Hall, 1952), esp. pp. 105–20.

39. See Rudolf Heberle, *Zur Geschichte der Arbeiterbewegung in Schweden*, Vol. 39 of *Probleme der Weltwirtschaft* (Jena: Gustav Fischer, 1925).

40. See Ossip Flechtheim, *Die KPD in der Weimarer Republik* (Offenbach am Main: Bollwerk-Verlag Karl Drott, 1948), pp. 213–14; see also Rose Laub Coser, *An Analysis of the Early German Socialist Movement* (unpublished M.A. thesis, Department of Sociology, Columbia University, 1951).

41. Colin Clark, *The Conditions of Economic Progress* (London: Macmillan, 1951), p. 421.

42. The Communists also controlled the Greek trade-unions and Socialist Labor party. The Greek case while fitting this pattern is not completely comparable since no real pre-Communist labor movement existed and a pro-Bolshevik movement arose from a combination of the discontents of workers in the war-created new industry and the enthusiasm occasioned by the Russian Revolution.

43. Friedrich Engels, "Letter to Karl Kautsky," Nov. 8, 1884, in Karl Marx and Friedrich Engels, *Correspondence 1846–1895* (New York: International Publishers, 1946), p. 422; see also Val R. Lorwin, "Working-class Politics and Economic Development in Western Europe," *American Historical Review,* 63 (1958), pp. 338–51; for an excellent discussion of the effects of rapid industrialization on politics, see also Reinhold Niebuhr, *The Irony of American History*

(New York: Charles Scribner's Sons, 1952), pp. 112–18.

44. In introducing historical events as part of the analysis of factors *external* to the political system, which are part of the causal nexus in which democracy is involved, I am following in good sociological and even functionalist tradition. As Radcliffe-Brown has well put it: ". . . one 'explanation' of a social system will be its history, where we know it—the detailed account of how it came to be what it is and where it is. Another 'explanation' of the same system is obtained by showing . . . that it is a special exemplification of laws of social psychology or social functioning. The two kinds of explanation do not conflict but supplement one another." A. R. Radcliffe-Brown, "On the Concept of Function in Social Science," *American Anthropologist,* New Series, 37 (1935), p. 401; see also Max Weber, *The Methodology of the Social Sciences* (New York: The Free Press of Glencoe, 1949), pp. 164–88, for a detailed discussion of the role of historical analysis in sociological research.

45. Max Weber's essay on "'Objectivity' in Social Science and Social Policy," in his *Methodology of the Social Sciences, op. cit.,* pp. 72–93.

46. The methodological presuppositions of this approach on the level of the multi-variate correlations and interactions of individual behavior with various social characteristics have been presented in Paul F. Lazarsfeld, "Interpretation of Statistical Relations as a Research Operation," in P. F. Lazarsfeld and M. Rosenberg, eds., *The Language of Social Research* (New York: The Free Press of Glencoe, 1955) pp. 115–25; and in H. Hyman, *Survey Design and Analysis* (New York: The Free Press of Glencoe, 1955), Chaps. 6 and 7. See also the methodological appendixes to Lipset, *et al., Union Democracy* (New York: The Free Press of Glencoe, 1956), pp. 419–32; and to Chap. XII of *Political Man.*

47. This approach differs from Weber's attempt to trace the origins of modern capitalism. Weber sought to establish that *one* antecedent factor, a certain religious ethic, was crucially significant in the syndrome of economic, political, and cultural conditions leading up to the development of Western capitalism. Our concern is not to establish the causal necessity of any one factor, but rather the syndrome of conditions which most frequently distinguish nations which may be empirically categorized as "more democratic" or "less democratic," without implying any absolute qualities to the definition.

48. Alexis de Tocqueville, *Democracy in America,* Vol. I (New York: Alfred A. Knopf, Vintage ed., 1945), pp. 251–52.

49. Walter Lippman in referring to the seemingly greater capacity of the constitutional monarchies than the republics of Europe to "preserve order with freedom" suggests that this may be because "in a republic the governing power, being wholly secularized, loses much of its prestige; it is stripped, if one prefers, of all the illusions of intrinsic majesty." See his *The Public Philosophy* (New York: Mentor Books, 1956), p. 50.

50. See Gabriel Almond, "Comparative Political Systems," *Journal of Politics,* 18 (1956), pp. 391–409.

51. Herbert Luethy, *The State of France* (London: Secker and Warburg, 1955), p. 29.

52. The race problem in the American South does constitute one basic challenge to the legitimacy of the system, and at one time did cause a breakdown of the national order. This conflict has reduced the commitment of many white southerners to the democratic game down to the present. Great Britain had a comparable problem as long as Catholic Ireland remained part of the United Kingdom. Effective government could not satisfy Ireland. Political practices by both sides in Northern Ireland, Ulster, also illustrate the problem of a regime which is not legitimate to a major segment of its population.

53. For an excellent analysis of the permanent crisis of the Austrian republic which flowed from the fact that it was viewed as an illegitimate regime by the Catholics and conservatives, see Charles Gulick, *Austria from Hapsburg to Hitler* (Berkeley: University of California Press, 1948).

54. The French legitimacy problem is well described by Katherine Munro. "The Right wing parties never quite forgot the possibility of a counter revolution while the Left wing parties revived the Revolution militant in their Marxism or Communism; each side suspected the other of using the Republic to achieve its own ends and of being legal only so far as it suited it. This suspicion threatened time and time again to make the Republic unworkable, since it led to obstruction in both the political and the economic sphere, and difficulties of government in turn undermined confidence in the regime and its rulers." Quoted in Charles Micaud, "French Political Parties: Ideological Myths and Social Realities," in Sigmund Neumann, ed., *Modern Political Parties* (Chicago: University of Chicago Press, 1956), p. 108.

55. The linkage between democratic instability and Catholicism may also be accounted for by elements inherent in Catholicism as a religious system. Democracy requires a universalistic political belief system in the sense that it accepts various different ideologies as legitimate. And it might be assumed that religious value systems which are more universalistic, in the sense of placing less stress on being the only true church, will be more compatible with democracy than those which assume that they are the only truth. The latter belief, which is held much more strongly by the Catholic than by most other Christian churches, makes it difficult for the religious value system to help legitimate a political system which requires as part of its basic value system the belief that "good" is served best through conflict among opposing beliefs.

Kingsley Davis has argued that a Catholic state church tends to be irreconcilable with democracy since "Catholicism attempts to control so many aspects of life, to encourage so much fixity of status and submission to authority, and to remain so independent of secular authority that it invariably clashes with the liberalism, individualism, freedom, mobility and sovereignty of the democratic nation." See "Political Ambivalence in Latin America," *Journal of Legal and Political Sociology,* 1 (1943), reprinted in A. N. Christensen, *The Evolution of Latin American Government* (New York: Henry Holt, 1951), p. 240.

56. See Sigmund Neumann, *Die Deutschen Parteien: Wesen und Wandel nach dem Kriege* (Berlin: Junker und Dünnhaupt Verlag, 1932) for exposition of the distinction between parties of integration and parties of representation. Neumann has further distinguished between parties of "democratic integration" (the Cath-

olic and Social Democratic parties) and those of "total integration" (fascist and Communist parties) in his more recent chapter, "Toward a Comparative Study of Political Parties," in the volume which he edited: *Modern Political Parties, op. cit.,* pp. 403–5.

57. See Charles Gulick, *op. cit.*

58. See Chap. VII of *Political Man,* pp. 233–35, 249.

59. This tendency obviously varies with relation to urban communities, type of rural stratification, and so forth. For a discussion of the role of vocational homogeneity and political communication among farmers, see S. M. Lipset, *Agrarian Socialism* (Berkeley: University of California Press, 1950), Chap. 10, "Social Structure and Political Activity." For evidence on the undemocratic propensities of rural populations see Samuel A. Stouffer, *op. cit.,* pp. 138–39. National Public Opinion Institute of Japan, Report No. 26, *A Survey Concerning the Protection of Civil Liberties* (Tokyo, 1951) reports that the farmers were the occupational group by far the least concerned with civil liberties. Carl Friedrich, in accounting for the strength of nationalism and Nazism among German farmers, suggests similar factors to the ones discussed here; that "the rural population is more homogeneous, that it contains a smaller number of outsiders and foreigners, that it has much less contact with foreign countries and peoples, and finally that its mobility is much more limited." Carl J. Friedrich, "The Agricultural Basis of Emotional Nationalism," *Public Opinion Quarterly,* 1 (1937), pp. 50–51.

60. Perhaps the first general statement of the consequences of "cross-pressures" on individual and group behavior may be found in a work written over fifty years ago by Georg Simmel, *Conflict and the Web of Group Affiliations* (New York: The Free Press of Glencoe, 1956), pp. 126–95. It is an interesting example of discontinuity in social research that the concept of cross-pressures was used by Simmel, but had to be independently rediscovered in voting research. For a detailed application of the effect of multiple-group affiliations on the political process in general, see David Truman, *The Governmental Process* (New York: Alfred A. Knopf, 1951).

61. See Juan Linz, *The Social Bases of German Politics* (unpublished Ph.D. thesis, Department of Sociology, Columbia University, 1958).

62. See Bernard Berelson, Paul F. Lazarsfeld, and William McPhee, *Voting* (Chicago: University of Chicago Press, 1954), for an exposition of the usefulness of cross-pressure as an explanatory concept. Also, see Chap. VI [of *Political Man*] for an attempt to specify the consequences of different group memberships for voting behavior, and a review of the literature.

63. As Dahl puts it, "If most individuals in the society identify with more than one group, then there is some positive probability that any majority contains individuals who identify for certain purposes with the threatened minority. Members of the threatened minority who strongly prefer their alternative will make their feelings known to those members of the tentative majority who also, at some psychological level, identify with the minority. Some of these sympathizers will shift their support away from the majority alternative and the majority will crumble." See Robert A. Dahl, *A Preface to Democratic Theory* (Chicago: University of Chicago Press, 1956), pp. 104–5. Parsons suggests that "pushing the implications of political difference too far activates the solidarities between adherents of the two parties which exist on other, nonpolitical bases so that members of the political majority come to defend those who share other of their interests who differ from them politically." See Parsons' essay "Voting and the Equilibrium of the American Political System," in E. Burdick and A. Brodbeck, eds., *American Voting Behavior* (New York: The Free Press of Glencoe, 1959), p. 93. A recent discussion of this problem in a Norwegian context points up "the integrative functions of cross-cutting conflict . . . [when] the conflict lines between the voter groups cut across the divisions between readers of newspapers of different political tendencies and this places a considerable proportion of the electorate in a situation of cross-pressure . . . In the Norwegian situation there is an interesting two way process of mutual restraints: on the one hand a majority of the Socialist voters are regularly exposed to newspaper messages from the opposition parties, on the other hand the non-Socialist papers, just because they in so many cases dominate their community and address themselves to a variety of politically heterogeneous groups, are found to exercise a great deal of restraint in the expression of conflicting opinions." Stein Rokkan and Per Torsvik, "The Voter, the Reader and the Party Press" (Mimeographed, Oslo: 1959).

64. Colin Clark, *The Conditions of Economic Progress* (New York: Macmillan, 1940).

65. Georg Simmel, *op. cit.,* pp. 191–94. Talcott Parsons has recently made a similar point that one of the mechanisms for preventing a "progressively deepening rift in the electorate" is the "involvement of voting with the ramified solidarity structure of the society in such a way, that, though there is a correlation, there is no *exact* correspondence between political polarization and other bases of differentiation." Talcott Parsons, *op. cit.,* pp. 92–93.

66. T. H. Marshall has analyzed the gradual process of incorporation of the working class into the body politic in the nineteenth century, and has seen that process as the achievement of a "basic human equality, associated with full community membership, which is not inconsistent with a superstructure of economic inequality." See his brief but brilliant book *Citizenship and Social Class* (London: Cambridge University Press, 1950), p. 77. Even though universal citizenship opens the way for the challenging of remaining social inequalities, it also provides a basis for believing that the process of social change toward equality will remain within the boundaries of allowable conflict in a democratic system.

67. See David Apter, *The Gold Coast in Transition* (Princeton: Princeton University Press, 1955), for a discussion of the evolving political patterns of Ghana. For an interesting brief analysis of the Mexican "one-party" system see L. V. Padgett, "Mexico's One-Party System, a Re-evaluation," *American Political Science Review,* 51 (1957), pp. 995–1008.

68. As this chapter was being edited for publication, political crises in several poor and illiterate countries occurred, which underline again the instability of democratic government in underdeveloped areas. The government of Pakistan was overthrown peacefully on October 7, 1958, and the new self-appointed president announced that "Western-type democracy cannot function here under present conditions. We have only 16 per cent literacy. In America you have 98 per cent."

(Associated Press release, October 9, 1958.) The new government proceeded to abolish parliament and all political parties. Similar crises have occurred, almost simultaneously, in Tunisia, Ghana, and even in Burma, since World War II considered one of the more stable governments in Southeast Asia, under Premier U Nu. Guinea has begun political life as a one-party state.

It is possible that the open emergence of military semi-dictatorships without much of a democratic "front" may reflect the weakening of democratic symbols in these areas under the impact of Soviet ideology, which equates "democracy" with rapid, efficient accomplishment of the "will of the people" by an educated elite, not with particular political forms and methods.

69. Robert J. Alexander, *Communism in Latin America* (New Brunswick: Rutgers University Press, 1957).


# THE POLITICS OF MASS SOCIETY

## William Kornhauser

### TWO VIEWS OF MASS SOCIETY

The theory of mass society has two major intellectual sources, one in the nineteenth century reaction to the revolutionary changes in European ·(especially French) society, and the other in the twentieth-century reaction to the rise of totalitarianism, especially in Russia and Germany. The first and major source may be termed the *aristocratic* criticism of mass society; the second, the *democratic* criticism of mass society. The first centers in the intellectual defense of elite values against the rise of mass participation. The second centers in the intellectual defense of democratic values against the rise of elites bent on total domination. The defensive posture of the aristocrats has been adopted by democrats who, having won the nineteenth-century war of ideas and institutions with the former, now seek to preserve their values against the totalitarian challenge.

Not all intellectual rejections of revolutionary change have been based on the idea of mass society. Criticisms of nineteenth century trends that may properly be termed theories of mass society found the decisive social process to be *the loss of exclusiveness of elites and the rise of mass participation in cultural and political life*. Burckhardt[1] and Gustave Le Bon[2] were among the leading aristocratic critics of mass tendencies in the nineteenth century; Ortega y Gasset[3] and Karl Mannheim,[4] in his discussions of elites, are twentieth century representatives of this approach.[5]

Similarly, not all democratic criticisms of totalitarianism are based on a theory of mass society. Those which may properly be termed theories of mass society find the decisive social process to be *the loss of insulation of non-elites and the rise of elites bent on total mobilization of a population.* Emil Lederer[6] and Hannah Arendt[7] are leading representatives of this conception of the nature of mass society.[8]

Paradoxical as it may appear to be, these democratic critics have come to rely heavily on the intellectual weapons employed by aristocratic thinkers against the rising flood of democratic ideologists during the nineteenth century. The central idea taken over by these democratic theorists from their aristocratic critics is that *the preservation of critical values (especially freedom) requires the social insulation of those segments of society that embody them.* Aristocratic and democratic critics of mass society agree on this, even as they disagree on the content of the values to be preserved—especially the nature of freedom—and, correspondingly, on the segments of society that embody them.

The aristocratic notion of freedom emphasizes the conditions that permit men to act as they *ought* to act, that is, in accordance with standards of right conduct. Mannheim has noted that this idea of freedom is counterposed to an egalitarian conception: "Men, . . . [the aristocratic theorists] claimed are essentially *unequal,* unequal in their gifts and abilities, and unequal to the very core of their beings."[9] Standards of right conduct are most highly developed in the upper reaches of society, and therefore the "true bearers," the "true subjects" of liberty are the "organic communities" of aristocratic elites. "The 'liberty' of the different estates under feudalism which meant their 'privileges,' and the distinctly qualitative and non-egalitarian flavour

Reprinted from William Kornhauser, *The Politics of Mass Society* (New York: The Free Press of Glencoe, 1959), pp. 21–38, 74–101, 194–211.

which was contained in the medieval concept, is here revived once more."[10] The traditional order based on moral law insulates aristocratic elites and thereby perserves liberty.

The democratic notion of freedom, on the other hand, implies the minimizing of social control (including that of the traditional order), that is, the removal of as many external constraints on the individual as is consistent with the freedom of his fellows. Freedom so conceived is dependent on *equality of rights.* This value is embodied in the whole community. Therefore, it is the independent group life of the non-elite which functions to preserve liberty, as independent groups insulate people from domination by elites.

In sum, these two versions of the mass society differ in their conception of freedom and the social foundations of freedom. One sees mass society as a set of conditions under which elites are exposed to mass pressures. The other conceives of mass society as a set of conditions under which non-elites are exposed to elite pressures. Nevertheless, they share a common image of mass society as the *naked society,* where the direct exposure of social units to outside forces makes freedom precarious. We shall attempt to formulate a general theory of mass society that incorporates elements from both the aristocratic and democratic criticism.

But to reach this goal, it is necessary to explicate partial and polemical versions of the theory. Therefore, we consider first the major argument of the aristocratic criticism of mass society, and then we analyze the democratic criticism of mass society. First a word about the bases for distinguishing these two views.

Our interest is in analyzing the theoretical basis of each approach, rather than in examining the value orientation typically associated with each of them. The two approaches have been distinguished according to whether the condition of elites or the condition of non-elites is identified as the basic criterion of "mass society." This means that any theory that locates the decisive feature of mass society in the exposure of accessible elites to mass intervention is classified as "aristocratic," while any theory that locates the essential feature of mass society in the exposure of atomized non-elites to elite domination is classified as "democratic." The choice of the terms "aristocratic" and "democratic" to describe these two theories should not obscure the fact that the classification is based on an *analytical* rather than a value distinction. However, there is an affinity between each of these theoretical positions and each value orientation. Most writers on mass society whose *theories* have focused on the loss of insulation of elites have also advocated aristocratic *values,* while most of those whose theories have focused on the loss of insulation of non-elites have also advocated democratic values. Nevertheless, there are some exceptions, for some writers hold values of the one type and expound theories of the other. When this occurs, the contributions are classified according to the theoretical, not the value, position of the writer. This explains why Mannheim, for example, is cited as a representative of the "aristocratic" approach; though committed to the preservation of democratic *values,* his *theory* of mass society tends to stress the way in which mass participation undermines elite functions.[11]

There is a second point, relating to the theoretical nature of the classification (rather than its value relevance), that should be borne in mind. Our interest is in the logic of each argument, rather than in the work of particular theorists. A separate series of logically connected propositions about the nature of mass society is related to the major premise of each approach. A particular theorist may well incorporate aspects of both arguments in his writings, without thereby providing a clear outline of either argument or a general and systematic statement of the theory of mass society. It may sometimes happen, therefore, that the same writer is at one time cited in support of a proposition embodied in the aristocratic approach, and at another time cited in support of a proposition embodied in the democratic approach. This will occasion no confusion if it is recalled that *ideas, not men, are the objects of classification.* On the whole, it is true that those who adopt the major premise of one school tend to ignore the social processes central to the major premise of the other school. Yet there are some exceptions, particularly De Tocqueville, who analyzed not only the need for insulation of elites, but also the role played by multiple autonomous groups in the insulation of non-elites.

What follows is not an historical reconstruction of ideas on mass society, but a logical reconstruction of two major intellectual traditions that are intermingled in the literature on mass society. *Our integrated statement of mass-society theory is based on elements drawn from both traditions. At the same time, it accepts the democratic concern with the identification of conditions favorable to the preservation of democratic values.*

### The Loss of Authority in Mass Society

During the nineteenth century, aristocratic critics of bourgeois society spun a rhetoric of pessimism concerning the value-standards men live by in an age of increasing materialism and equalitarianism. Le Bon crystallized this theme in sociological terms when he depicted the times as an "era of crowds," and spoke bitingly of crowds as vehicles in the downfall of civilization: "the populace is sovereign, and the tide of barbarism mounts."[12] Ortega popularized this thesis as the "revolt of the masses," a situation which leads to the "sovereignty of the unqualified."[13] Such present-day critics as T. S. Eliot[14] use the term "mass society" in this pejorative sense to designate the alleged destructiveness of popular pressures on traditional values and elites.

Aristocratic theorists believe that liberty and equality are incompatible: "The spread of democratic equal rights facilitates, as Nietzsche prophesied, the equal violation of rights."[15] The paradigmatic experiences underlying this imagery were the French Revolution and the 1848 revolutions against the ancient regimes. The heart of the imagery itself is the *equalitarian society,* without excellence, distinction, style, meaning. Such a (mass) society is viewed as lacking the moral basis for resisting Caesarism, for preventing political tyranny as well as cultural decay.

Thus De Tocqueville has written:

I believe that it is easier to establish an absolute and despotic government among a people in which the conditions of society are equal than among any other; and I think that if such a government were once established among such a people, it not only would oppress men, but would eventually strip each of them of several of the highest qualities of humanity.[16]

Thus Burckhardt has written:

So long as the masses can bring pressure on their leaders, one value after another must be sacrificed: position, property, religion, distinguished tradition, higher learning.[17]

Thus Mannheim has written:

The open character of democratic mass society, together with its growth in size and the tendency towards general public participation, not only produces far too many elites but also deprives these elites of the exclusiveness which they need [to perform their functions]. . . . The lack of leadership in late liberal mass society can . . . be . . . diagnosed as the result of the change for the worse in selecting the elite. We must recognize further that it is this general lack of direction in modern mass society that gives the opportunity to groups with dictatorial ambitions.[18]

Thus Lippmann has written:

Where mass opinion dominates the government, there is a morbid derangement of the true functions of power. The derangement brings about the enfeeblement, verging on paralysis, of the capacity to govern.[19]

The conception of mass society contained in such writings as these includes three major terms: (a) growing equalitarianism (loss of traditional authority); (b) widespread readiness to support anti-aristocratic forms of rule (quest for popular authority); (c) rule by the masses (domination by pseudo-authority). In this universe of discourse, "mass society" is the opposite of aristocratic order. Mass society is the condition under which rule by the masses—either directly or through the popularly supported demagogue—displaces aristocratic rule. This condition is equality of voice in the determination of social policy. Therefore, mass society is the equalitarian society, in which the masses seek to raise up leaders in their own image. As a result, it produces rule by the incompetent.

However, the incompetence of the many is not what distinguishes mass society, according to the aristocratic criticism. Mass society is new, whereas there always has been widespread ignorance in society.[20] Mannheim observes in this connection that the student of such changes as the loss of distinctive art styles, the increasing intellectual indecisiveness, or the decline of leadership, "if he is not used to noticing the social mechanisms at work behind the immediate concrete events is inclined to believe . . . that human beings are today less talented and less creative and have less initiative than in earlier periods."[21] What has changed is the structural relationship between the many and the few. In the mass society, there is a marked increase in opportunities for the many to intervene in areas previously reserved to the few. These opportunities invite the determination of social policies and cultural standards by large numbers who are not competent to make such decisions.

Mass society from this standpoint is the society in which there is a *loss of exclusiveness of elites*:[22] it is a social structure possessing high access to governing groups. High access to elites results from such procedures as direct popular elections and the shared expectation that public opinion is sovereign. When elites are easily accessible, the masses pressure them to conform to the transitory general will: "the voice of the masses [is] preponderant."[23] Therefore, loss of authority on the part of institutional elites results from widespread opportunities to participate in the formation of major social policies.

A system in which there is high access to elites generates popular pressures on the elites that prevent them from performing their creative and value-sustaining functions. People are not expected to have particular qualifications to make different kinds of decisions. Public opinion, viewed as the transitory general will, is regarded as the *immediate* as well as ultimate arbiter of all matters of policy and taste. Therefore, *anyone* is qualified; anyone may feel justified in judging or trying to influence any decision. As a result, the aristocratic critics claim, it is not simply that a large number of individuals is unqualified, but rather, it is the very *system* that is unqualified. For the system makes no provision for separating the qualified from the unqualified, and therefore excellence (whether in governing, in art, or in any other sphere) can neither be discovered, developed, nor protected.[24] It is a situation in which elites cannot be creative nor can they deeply influence society. But only elites can perform these functions: "Civilizations as yet have only been created and directed by a small intellectual aristocracy, never by crowds. Crowds are only powerful for destruction."[25]

Insofar as popular participation cannot be controlled, it destroys liberty as well as authority. Equalitarianism is judged to be incompatible with individual liberty, for "liberty is preserved not by mass-will nor by counting noses but by tiny, heroic natural-aristocracies and by the majesty—beyond mob majorities—of moral law."[26]

But is it the mere quantitative fact of widespread participation in the setting of social policy which destroys elite functions and thereby liberty? Aristocratic critics would not deny that if people intervened only at certain points in the decision-making process, and in a manner regulated and controlled according to set rules, then elites would be protected from undue interference and could fulfill their critical functions. They assume, however, that popular participation will not be of this kind. Thus Le Bon[27] uses such terms as suggestible, unconscious, impulsive, capricious, and the like, to characterize popular participation where elites are accessible. And Ortega[28] speaks of the indocility of the masses in a similar vein. These aristocratic critics are arguing that when people intervene in decision-making processes in an excitable and intractable manner, liberty is threatened.

We must ask the aristocratic critics how *equality* of opportunity to participate leads to *unrestrained* intervention, as in political strikes. We may agree that high access to elites is a permissive condition for recurrent mass behavior of this sort. But it is not a sufficient condition, since *non-elites may be restrained on their side, by means of their own groups and values*. That is, those members of society who identify themselves with the central values of a constitutional order are not likely to exploit opportunities to subvert elites. On the other hand, people who are *alienated* from society may express their resentment by using the most accessible instruments of action to impose their will. In short, the source of mass behavior cannot be located *only* in the structure of elites. It also must be found in the structure of non-elites, in a set of conditions close to the personal environment of the people who engage in mass behavior. Open elites can provide the "pull" for unrestrained participation in the vital centers of society, but not the "push." Since the democratic criticism specifies a set of conditions under which people will be propelled into mass actions, the aristocratic view of mass society may be strengthened by taking these additional conditions into account.[29]

## The Loss of Community in Mass Society

From the democratic viewpoint, the threat posed by mass society is less how elites may be protected from the masses and more how non-elites may be shielded from domination by elites. This difference is part of the larger difference dividing the two approaches: concern with opportunities for and functions of the few, on the one hand, versus concern with widespread opportunities for large numbers of people to participate in the collective life, on the other hand. The aristocratic position judges the formulation of broad social policy to be the responsibility and capability of the few, whereas the democratic position implies that potentially all members of society share in this responsibility.

Aristocratic critics attribute loss of liberty to the rise of popular participation in areas previously limited to the specially qualified: mass society is a condition under which there is too much control by the many over the few. Democratic critics, in their turn, attribute loss of liberty to the rise of mass manipulation and mobilization in areas previously left to the privacy of the individual and the group: mass society is a condition under which there is too much control by the few over the many. In short, one conception views mass society as unlimited democracy ("hyperdemocracy" in Ortega's terms), the other as unlimited tyranny.

Now, of course, these two states could be intimately related. In fact, one student of the problem has stated the belief that "a whole literature on mass behavior and mass psychology [has] demonstrated and popularized the wisdom, so familiar to the ancients, of the affinity between democracy and dictatorship, between mob rule and tyranny."[30] It is the thesis of this study that such an affinity is caught by the concept of mass society; but the fact remains that unlimited democracy is not unlimited tyranny, even though it may become so. Therefore, it remains to be clarified how a theory of mass society may specify this relationship.

Another difference between the two approaches to mass society concerns the consequences of equalitarianism. The democratic criticism does not find equality of condition inherently inimical to liberty, nor does it look only to elites for the defense of liberty. From this point of view, the chief characteristic of the mass is not brutality and backwardness, as the aristocratic criticism implies, but isolation and amorphous social relations. Furthermore, *mass behavior may characterize people in high status positions as well as those from lower classes;* "highly cultured people were particularly attracted to mass movements [in post-war Europe]."[31]

What concerns the democratic critics is the possible emergence of another elite modeled after those thrown up by the Nazi and Bolshevik revolutions, with the consequent destruction of political democracy. The core of this imagery is the *atomized society*. Mass society is a situation in which an aggregate of individuals are related to one another only by way of their relation to a common authority, especially the state. That is, individuals are not directly related to one another in a variety of independent groups. A population in this condition is not insulated in any way from the ruling group, nor yet from elements within itself. For insulation requires a multiplicity of independent and often conflicting forms of association, each of which is strong enough to ward off threats to the autonomy of the individual. But it is precisely the weakness or absence of such social groups, *rather than their equality,* which distinguishes the mass society, according to these theorists. In their absence, people lack the resources to restrain their own behavior as well as that of others. Social atomization engenders strong feelings of alienation and anxiety, and therefore the disposition to engage in extreme behavior to escape from these tensions. In a mass society there is a heightened readiness to form hyper-attachments to symbols and leaders. "Such loyalty can be expected only from the completely isolated human being who, without any other social ties . . . derives his sense of having a place in the world only from his belonging to a movement."[32] Total loyalty, in turn, is the psychological basis for total domination, i.e., totalitarianism.

There are three major terms implied in the democratic criticism of mass society: (a) growing atomization (loss of community); (b) widespread readiness to embrace new ideologies (quest for community); (c) totalitarianism (total domination by pseudo-community). In this universe of discourse, mass society is a condition in which elite domination replaces democratic rule. Mass society is objectively the *atomized* society, and subjectively the *alienated* population. Therefore, mass society is a system in which there is *high availability of a population for mobilization by elites.*

People become available for mobilization by elites when they lack or lose an independent group life. The term *masses* applies "only where we deal with people who . . . cannot be integrated into any organization based on common interest, into political parties or municipal governments or professional organizations or trade unions."[33] The lack of autonomous relations generates widespread social alienation. Alienation heightens responsiveness to the appeal of mass movements because they provide occasions for expressing resentment against what is, as well as promises of a totally different world. In short, *people who are atomized readily become mobilized.* Since totalitarianism is a state of total mobilization, mass society is highly vulnerable to totalitarian movements and regimes.

We must ask the democratic critics at this point whether mass society is totalitarian, or only may become so. Democratic critics tend to construe totalitarianism as mass society, because elite domination based on a mobilized population is the central meaning of their conception of totalitarianism. However, they also tend to designate societies that are vulnerable to totalitarianism as mass society. For example, both Weimar Germany and Nazi Ger-

many have been called mass societies. This obscures the problem of developmental patterns, since factors which encourage totalitarian movements in political democracies are not necessarily the same as those which *sustain* totalitarian regimes once they are in power. It is necessary, therefore, to distinguish between a mass society and a totalitarian society.

We must next inquire whether an available population constitutes by itself a condition sufficient to result in numerous mass movements, as the democratic theorists imply. There are at least three reasons why high access to elites must also be present. In the first place, it is apparent that in order for available masses to become mobilized at all, agents of mobilization—for example, Communist spokesmen and organizations—must have opportunities to contact and appeal to large numbers of people. This requires readily accessible channels of communication. Moreover, if the paths to power were not open, there would be little incentive to mobilize and incite masses. In this sense, an accessible elite can serve as a magnet, both to would-be totalitarian leaders and to discontented masses. People in the mass (i.e., an undifferentiated and amorphous collectivity) are highly susceptible to total mobilization; but unless there is access to the means of communication and power, counter-elites (such as Communist leaders) will not be able to seize the opportunity provided by the mass for the conquest of total power.

Secondly, the success of totalitarian movements is contingent upon the vulnerability of existing elites. An accessible elite should not be equated with a vulnerable elite, for the strength or weakness of elites depends upon a host of factors other than their degree of accessibility. Nevertheless, an accessible elite is more vulnerable than one which is not accessible, other things being equal. When access is low, elites are relatively immune to popular pressures, so that mass movements peter out without overturning elites or infiltrating elite positions. Accessible elites more easily succumb to the attacks of totalitarian movements.

There is yet a third reason for suggesting that an available population does not automatically call forth elite domination. Totalitarian regimes are installed by new elites who have successfully mobilized an available population. But if this were in fact the sole condition required for the seizure of total power by new elites, how is it that the old elites, favored by this very same condition (i.e., an atomized population available for mobilization), have not themselves absorbed total power? Evidently *elites may be restrained on their side by means of their own relations and values.* Old elites generally lack the will and capacity to mobilize a large population. The one major exception is when the very existence of the social order is believed to be threatened, as in war or revolution. That is, mobilized movements led by representatives of existing institutions tend to be military ventures against external or internal enemies. Such mass movements may be developed in response to the mobilization of forces by another nation or by a revolutionary group, or in response to the expectation of such an enemy mobilization. It is under these conditions that a mass society may move toward totalitarianism under the direction of institutional rather than anti-institutional leadership. The model of the "garrison state"[34] is precisely such a state of mobilization by established elites in the name of national security.

The "garrison state" undoubtedly is a possible course along which mass society can move. But there are a number of factors which militate against mobilization of large numbers by existing elites (except under conditions of total war). In the first place, these elites are part of a going concern, and this alone makes for an essentially mundane orientation. Activism entails a readiness to reject routine modes of activity, and therefore tends to be eschewed by groups whose very power is bound to established routines. It usually requires a new elite devoid of the restraints incident upon institutional participation to mobilize widespread activism. As a form of charismatic leadership, the totalitarian elite is "outside the realm of everyday routine" and is "foreign to all rules."[35]

Another reason why existing elites infrequently set in motion a large population is the presence of leadership rivalries. These conflicts between leaders operate as checks on the power of each, including any attempts to expand power by mobilizing masses.

In addition, existing elites may be restrained by their value commitments. They ordinarily have a strong stake in preserving the social order, for their own positions are legitimated by established values. Those who are successful are often more amenable to abiding by the rules of the game. Further, the achievement of high position may reflect or induce a heightened sense of responsibility for and awareness of institutional values.

Thus it is that popular mobilization generally is the work of counter-elites, since they are not inhibited by commitments to the social order, nor by constraints resulting from participation in a balance of power.[36] These counter-elites are pushed towards making allies among the masses, since this is the only way to gain total power in mass society. Finally, established elites in a mass society not only lack the capacity to mobilize a large population; they also are ill-equipped to protect their organizations from penetration by counter-elites bent on destroying an existing order.

We may therefore conclude that high vulnerability to the *development* of totalitarianism presupposes accessible elites as well as available non-elites. A rising totalitarian movement finds its prey not only in an exposed mass but also in an exposed elite. The penetration of an existing elite by a successful totalitarian movement (as the Nazis pene-

trated the Weimar government) is *prima facie* evidence of its accessibility. On the other hand, the maintenance of a population in a state of mobilization by a given (totalitarian) elite requires low access to elites; otherwise the ruling group would not be able to maintain its power.

Thus, the concept of mass society, in order to be useful for a theory of the transformation of democratic into totalitarian society, *necessarily* presupposes accessible elites. *The democratic criticism of mass society requires for its completion the notion of accessible elites provided by aristocratic critics.* It now may be shown that the negative consequences of accessible elites envisioned by aristocratic critics are greatly increased when non-elites are available by virtue of the loss of community.

Aristocratic theorists assume that whenever people are given the opportunity to participate in the shaping of social policies, they will do so in a destructive manner. But the opportunity for widespread participation in society does not automatically call forth mass action unrestrained by social relations and cultural norms. Not all members of a society, but only *people in the mass* are disposed to seize the opportunity provided by accessible elites to impress mass standards on all spheres of society, and to do so in an unrestrained manner. This is true for two reasons. First, when large numbers of people are interrelated only as members of a mass, they are more likely to pressure elites to provide satisfactions previously supplied by a plurality of more proximate groups. Second, they are likely to do so in a direct and unmediated way, because there is a paucity of intervening groups to channelize and filter popular participation in the larger society. As a result, mass participation tends to be irrational and unrestrained, since there are few points at which it may be checked by personal experience and the experience of others. Where people are not securely related to a plurality of independent groups, they are available for all kinds of adventures and "activist modes of intervention" in the larger society. It is one thing for a population to participate at specified times and in institutional ways for defined interests—for example, through trade associations and trade unions, or in elections. It is quite another to create *ad hoc* methods of direct pressure on critical centers of society, such as the "invasion" of a state legislature, street political gangs, etc.[37] It is the latter form of collective activity that the aristocratic theorists fear, but they err in assuming that equal access to elites is sufficient to produce it: widespread availability attendant upon social atomization also must exist.

Thus, each conception of mass society requires the other for its completion. Together they provide the basis for a general theory of mass society.

# STRUCTURE OF MASS SOCIETY

We can conceive of all but the simplest societies as comprising three levels of social relations. The (first) level consists of highly personal or primary relations, notably the family. The (third) level contains relations inclusive of the whole population, notably the state. The (second) level comprises all intermediate relations, notably the local community, voluntary association, and occupational group. These intermediate relations function as links between the individual and his primary relations, on the one hand, and the state and other national relations, on the other hand. It must be emphasized that voluntary associations are not the only kind of intermediate relation; all organized relations that mediate between the family and the nation, such as local government and the local press, are classified as intermediate structures in the present study. Voluntary associations are used as the main empirical indicators of intermediate structures in this study because the best data are available for this kind of intermediate relation.

The logic of our model dictates that the structure of mass society must be of such a nature as to support a high rate of mass behavior by fulfilling the two requirements for mass behavior, namely, accessible elites and available non-elites. Such a structure may be shown to be one in which intermediate relations of community, occupation, and association are more or less inoperative, and therefore one in which the individual and primary group are directly related to the state and to nation-wide organizations. The members of mass society, then, are interconnected only by virtue of their common ties to national centers of communication and organization. It is in this sense that we speak of mass society as the *atomized* society.

Mass society lacks intermediate relations, but it is not to be conceived merely as the absence of social relations. The central feature of primary groups in mass society is not so much their internal weakness as it is their external *isolation* from the larger society. The isolation of primary groups means that by themselves they cannot provide the basis for participation in the larger society. Again, mass society is not to be thought of as lacking relations inclusive of the whole population. On the contrary, modern mass society possesses a highly *politicalized* organization, as "everything that people know or feel Society will not undertake is simply heaped on to the . . . State."[38] This results in the centralization of the social structure, especially a centralized state. The centralization of communication and decision-making means that to the extent people do participate in the larger society, they must do so through the state, and other inclusive (nation-wide) structures.[39]

We shall elaborate this model of the structure of mass society by examining it on each of its three levels: (1) the weakness of intermediate relations, (2) the isolation of primary relations, and (3) the centralization of national relations.

## Weakness of Intermediate Relations

Weak intermediate relations leave elites and non-elites directly exposed to one another, and thereby invite widespread mass behavior; for in the absence of intermediate relations, participation in the larger society must be direct rather than filtered through intervening relationships.

The lack of strong independent groups undermines multiple proximate concerns, and thereby increases mass availability. Consider a man's relation to his work. While there often are important sources of intrinsic satisfaction derivable from the work itself, nevertheless the gratification derived from a sense of fellowship and control over the conditions of work are at least as important for firm occupational attachments. It is precisely these latter sources of interest and participation in work that require independent groups for their realization. Informal work groups supply some basis for fellowship and control at work, but with the growth in scale and complexity of the factory, office, and work institutions generally, they are insufficient. Therefore, all kinds of formal work associations, such as trade unions and professional associations, are needed.[40] To the extent that they fail to develop, or, at the other extreme, themselves grow so far out of the reach of their members as to no longer be capable of providing the individual with a sense of participation and control, people are less likely to find the whole sphere of work an interesting and rewarding experience. Consequently, people may cease to care about their work, though of course they continue to work, despite their alienation from their jobs.

Similar factors shape a man's relation to his community. Unless a variety of forms of association are open to him, the individual is not likely to take an active interest in civic affairs—particularly in the metropolis, where the size of the population and the specialization of activities place a premium on voluntary associations as bases of political participation. Or, in the absence of associations such as the P.T.A. to provide channels of communication and influence between parents and school, the individual is less likely to develop or sustain interest and participation in the education of his children. Examples may be easily multiplied, but these are sufficient to suggest why independent groups are indispensable bases for the maintenance of meaningful proximate concerns.

The lack of a structure of independent groups also removes the basis for self-protection on the part of elites, because it permits direct modes of intervention to replace mediated participation in elites. In the first place, intermediate groups, even though they are independent of top elites, operate to protect these elites from arbitrary and excessive pressures by themselves being responsive to the needs and demands of people. They carry a large share of the burden of seeking to fulfill the interests of people who would otherwise have to rely exclusively on national agencies to minister to their needs. Secondly, the leaders of intermediate groups, irrespective of their particular aims (so long as these aims are not contrary to the integrity of the community), help to shore up the larger system of authority with which their own authority is inextricably bound. Third, intermediate groups help to protect elites by functioning as channels through which popular participation in the larger society (especially in the national elites) may be directed and restrained. In the absence of intermediate groups to act as representatives and guides for popular participation, people must act *directly* in the critical centers of society, and therefore in a manner unrestrained by the values and interests of a variety of social groups.

These reasons why the weakness of intermediate groups characterize mass society are at the same time reasons why the strength of such groups characterizes the pluralist society. A strong intermediate structure consists of stable and independent groups which represent diverse and frequently conflicting interests. The opposition among such groups restrains one another's power, thereby limiting the aggregate intervention in elites; that is, a system of social checks and balances among a plurality of diverse groups operates to protect elites as well as non-elites in ways we have indicated. Furthermore, the separation of the various spheres of society— for example, separation of religion and politics— means that access to elites in one sphere does not directly affect elites in other spheres. The various authorities are more or less autonomous in their own spheres, in that they are not directly determined in their membership or policy by authorities in other spheres. These same factors protect non-elites from elites, since independent groups guard their members from one another, and since overlapping memberships among groups, *each of which concerns only limited aspects of its members' lives*, restrains each group from seeking total domination over its membership.

The state in pluralist society also plays a vital role in support of individual freedom, for it is above all the state which has the capacity to safeguard the individual against domination by particular groups. Durkheim saw more profoundly than most that it is the *combination* of the state and what he called "secondary groups" that engenders individual liberty, rather than one or the other social structure alone. We shall quote him at length because he brings out with great clarity the special competence of each type of social structure for the advancement of individual freedom:

[The individual] must not be curbed and monopolised by the secondary groups, and these groups must not be able to get a mastery over their members and mould them at will. There must therefore exist above these local, domestic—in a word, secondary—authorities, some over-all authority which makes the law for them all: it must remind each of them that it is but a part and not the whole and that it should not keep for itself what rightly belongs to the whole. The only means of averting this collective particularism and all it involves for the individual, is to have a special agency with the duty of representing the overall collectivity, its rights and its interests, vis-à-vis these individual collectivities. . . . It is solely because, in holding its constituent societies in check, it [the state] prevents them from exerting the repressive influences over the individual that they would otherwise exert. So there is nothing inherently tyrannical about State intervention in the different fields of collective life; on the contrary, it has the object and the effect of alleviating tyrannies that do exist. It will be argued, might not the State in turn become despotic? Undoubtedly, provided there was nothing to counter that trend. In that case, as the sole existing collective force, it produces the effects that any collective force not neutralized by any counter-force of the same kind would have on individuals. The State itself then becomes a leveller and repressive. And its repressiveness becomes even harder to endure than that of small groups, because it is more artificial. The State, in our large-scale societies, is so removed from individual interests that it cannot take into account the special or local and other conditions in which they exist. Therefore when it does attempt to regulate them, it succeeds only at the cost of doing violence to them and distorting them. It is, too, not sufficiently in touch with individuals in the mass to be able to mould them inwardly, so that they readily accept its pressure on them. The individual eludes the State to some extent—the State can only be effective in the context of a large-scale society—and individual diversity may not come to light. Hence, all kinds of resistance and distressing conflicts arise. The small groups do not have this drawback. They are close enough to the things that provide their *raison d'être* to be able to adapt their actions exactly and they surround the individuals closely enough to shape them in their own image. The inference to be drawn from this comment, however, is simply that *if that collective force, the State, is to be the liberator of the individual, it has itself need of some counterbalance; it must be restrained by other collective forces, that is, by . . . secondary groups . . . it is out of this conflict of social forces that individual liberties are born.*[41]

It has been said that medieval society was in fact essentially pluralist.[42] But of course medieval society did not permit democratic control. The confusion here resides in the notion of pluralism: shall it be conceived as referring merely to a multiplicity of associations, or in addition, to a multiplicity of *affiliations?* Where individuals belong to several groups, no one group is *inclusive* of its members' lives. Associations have members with a variety of social characteristics (e.g., class and ethnic identities) and group memberships (e.g., trade unions may possess members who go to various churches, or even belong to church-affiliated trade union associations such as ACTU). Warner found that in Newburyport, Massachusetts, one-third of the 357 associations that were studied had members from three out of the six classes he identified, another third had members from four classes, and one-sixth from five or six classes. Almost two-thirds of the 12,876 members of associations belonged to associations in which four or more of the six classes were represented. Over three-fourths belonged to associations in which three or more of the ten ethnic groups were represented. Over one-half belonged to associations in which two or more of the four religious faiths were represented.[43] Such extensive *cross-cutting solidarities* favor a high level of freedom and consensus: these solidarities help prevent one line of social cleavage from becoming dominant, and they constrain associations to respect the various affiliations of their members lest they alienate them. Socially heterogeneous religious organizations are also important pluralistic agencies; they may be contrasted with situations in which religious and class lines tend to closely correspond, as in France where anti-clericalism is largely a working-class phenomenon. Political parties which draw their support from all major social segments constitute still another kind of cross-cutting solidarity. In this respect, the highly heterogeneous and decentralized American parties may be contrasted with the highly centralized, class-based Socialist parties and religious-based Catholic parties characteristic of European multiparty systems.

Our conception of pluralism includes that of multiple affiliations, which means that medieval society was not pluralist in our use of the term. So long as no association claims or receives hegemony over many aspects of its members' lives, its power over the individual will be limited. This is a vital point, because the authority of a private group can be as oppressive as that of the state.

A plurality of groups that are both independent and non-inclusive not only protects elites and non-elites from one another but does so in a manner that permits liberal democratic control. Liberal democratic control requires that people have *access* to elites, and that they exercise *restraint* in their participation. Independent groups help to maintain access to top-level decision-making by bringing organized pressure to bear on elites to remain responsive to outside influence. Each group has interests of its own in gaining access to elites, and has organized power not available to separate individuals for the implementation of these interests. These interests require not only that elites pay attention to the demands of the group, but also that other groups do not become so strong as to be able to shut off this group's access to the elite. Since independent groups seek to maintain their position by checking one another's power as well as the power

of higher-level elites, the interaction of these groups helps to sustain access to decision-making processes in the larger society.

A plurality of independent groups also helps to regulate popular participation by integrating people into a wide range of proximate concerns. Where people possess multiple interests and commitments, attachments to remote objects, such as loyalty to the nation-state, are mediated by proximate relations.[44] Therefore, people in pluralist society engage in relatively little *direct* participation in national decisions, not because elites prevent them from doing so, but because they can influence decisions more effectively through their own groups. Furthermore, people tend to be *selective* in their participation, limiting their direct involvement in the larger society to matters that appear to them of particular concern in light of their values and interests. Since pluralist society engenders a variety of values and interests, self-selective involvement in national politics tends to limit the number of people who are vitally concerned with any given issue.

The intermediate structure of pluralist society helps to maintain access to elites by virtue of its *independence* from elites. The intermediate structure of totalitarian society, on the other hand, helps to prevent access to the elite by virtue of its *domination* by the elite. By means of intermediate groups instituted and controlled from above, the totalitarian regime is able to keep the population in a state of mobilization. Such organizations as Soviet trade unions have the primary function of activating and channelizing the energies of workers in directions determined by the regime. If there were no controlled intermediate organizations in all spheres of society, people would be free to regroup along lines independent of the regime. That is why it is of the utmost importance to totalitarian regimes to keep the population active in these controlled groups. Totalitarian regimes search out all independent forms of organizations in order to transform them or destroy them. In certain other societies, the natural decline of independent forms of association prepares the way for the rise of totalitarian movements.

The intermediate structure of communal society helps to maintain traditional authority and community in that its constituent groups are independent of the highest elites, while at the same time exercising *inclusive* control over their members— who are not free to leave the group or to join another group.[45] This kind of intermediate structure is exemplified in the corporations of the Middle Ages.

In the Middle Ages men thought and acted corporately. The status of every man was fixed by his place in some community—manor, borough, guild, learned University; or convent. The villein and the monk scarcely existed in the eye of the law except through the lord of the manor and the Abbot of the monastery. . . . The unit of medieval society was neither the nation nor the individual but something between the two—the corporation.[46]

The corporation protected the individual from outside coercion—for example, from undue interference by the king; but at the same time, the individual had little control over his corporate group, for he had neither status nor rights apart from the group. "As a human being, or as an English subject, no man had 'rights' either to employment or to the vote, or indeed to anything very much beyond a little Christian charity."[47]

The intermediate structure corresponding to each of our four types of society has been analyzed along two dimensions: (a) the strength of intermediate social organizations, especially their capacity to operate as autonomous centers of power; and (b) the inclusiveness of intermediate organizations, that is, the extent to which they encompass all aspects of their members' lives. The results of our analysis may be summarized in Table 1.

## TABLE 1

|  | INTERMEDIATE GROUPS ARE: | |
|  | Strong | Weak |
| Inclusive | Communal society | Totalitarian society |
| INTERMEDIATE GROUPS ARE: | | |
| Non-Inclusive | Pluralist society | Mass society |

France provides a good illustration of a society in which intermediate relations are weak and non-inclusive. A closer look at this aspect of French life may help to clarify our conception of mass structure.

French society tends to be highly organized on the national level, in the form of a highly centralized state bureaucracy, and on the family level. There is a relative paucity of intermediate structures to link these two levels of life. Since voluntary associations are major forms of intermediation in the democratic society, the weakness of this social form in France, compared with England or the United States, is one important indication of the atomization of that society.

France has a long history of hostility toward voluntary associations:

French tradition has not been favourable to the growth of associations. . . . It is only within the last thirty years that the bonds of a restraining vigilance have been finally relaxed. . . . It seems clear enough that what associations, whether religious or secular, were able to exist, were the offspring of a privilege tardily given and illiberally exercised.[48]

Freedom of association was not granted full legal recognition until 1901; but even since that time, a marked retardation in voluntary organiza-

tion has persisted in France. Arnold Rose reports, on the basis of interviews with a number of French leaders,

. . . the almost uniform impression that what social influence associations [those actively directed toward an outside purpose] there are in France are largely "paper" organizations and that even if they claim a large membership they do not involve the members' interests and emotions very deeply. . . . The general impression is that associations play but a small role, both in the functioning of the community or nation and in the lives of the average citizens.[49]

Another recent study of French society also observed "the relative scarcity of voluntary organizations in France as compared with the massive American proliferation of channels whereby individuals engage themselves in public enterprise."

The absence of active civic participation is evident in all social classes in France. There are very few "clubs" of the sort developed by the upper social groups in Britain. Among the middle class there are few parallels of Rotary, Kiwanis, and Lions . . . [or of] the Parent-Teachers' Association, the League of Women Voters, and the Association of University Women. . . . Among the working class only the labour union has made any headway, but even it hardly touches the French worker in his daily life—offering him neither educational opportunities, recreational facilities, consumers' cooperatives, nor social diversions.[50]

Voluntary groups generally tend to be shut out from participation in the performance of vital social functions in France, with the consequence that they are incapable of helping to adapt people to changing social circumstances. This appears to be true for associations nominally oriented toward change as well as for associations with conservative ideologies; French trade unions and working-class parties, for example, frequently resist change just as strenuously as do agricultural organizations and business associations. A study of associations in two French communities arrives at the conclusion that French associations are less capable of mediating social change than are their American counterparts: "The association in the United States may be a mechanism for integrating or mediating change, but in the French community, associations appear to be oriented toward the prevention of change."[51]

Harold Laski believed that the "division of French parties into a plethora of groups owes its origin less to any inherent naturalness or to a proved benefit in the performance of party-functions than to the possibility that such division affords for the erection of a system of loyalties external to that of the state."[52] Yet, even political parties do not absorb the attention of very many Frenchmen. When asked, "Do you think it would make much difference whether one party or another were in power?" thirty-nine per cent of a national sample answered negatively and an additional 12% had no opinion. In answer to the question, "Do questions concerning politics interest you?" only 10% indicated a great interest, 39% expressed little interest, and 51% said they had no interest at all.[53] These data suggest that French political parties are not by themselves very effective links between a large portion of the population and the national society.

Local government in France also does not function as an independent intermediate structure, since it operates more as a part of the national bureaucracy than as an expression of the autonomy of the local community. The key agent of local government, the Prefect, is appointed by the Minister of the Interior and exercises the national government's powers in a local area (department). Since these powers are great, including as they do extensive executive and financial control, local self-government is small. Local government is a mechanism of national authority, and not a basis for local participation and control. Therefore, it does not serve to involve the individual in the public realm, nor does it serve to protect the individual against control by the state.

To an inconceivable degree Empire and Republic have completed the work of the monarchy and extinguished all trace of autonomy and independence in communes and departments. The first and most important answer to the question of who rules France must be that it is ruled by ninety agents [Prefects] of the Ministry of the Interior.[54]

The local community and parish in France may provide certain satisfactions for the individual. The cafe and public parks are bases of participation in the local community.[55] But institutions of this type, no matter how much they may enrich communal life, are nevertheless not capable of linking either the individual or the community to the larger society. Furthermore, increasing geographic mobility is weakening these informal social relations. As for the parish, a recent inquiry notes that "the larger part of even rural France consists of 'parishes indifferent to Christian traditions'" and concludes that "the church does not have much hold over a majority of the French today."[56] The apparent ineffectiveness of local government, community, and parish as bases of participation in the larger society creates a social vacuum in French life. This may be a reason why a study of a French community, after reporting that associations are "generally not very important" and "cut into the lives of their members very little," nevertheless concludes that "without the associations, [people] would live in almost complete isolation."[57]

We may conclude from this brief analysis of French group life that independent social forms are more or less inoperative as sources of mediation between elites and non-elites. As a result, large numbers of people are available for mass appeals, as evidence in the success of communism, Gaullism, and Poujadism in recent years. Since World War II no other Western democracy has witnessed such widespread mass attacks on the constitutional order. More than one hundred years ago, De Tocqueville also argued that French political upheavals were related to the lack of independent group life; and over fifty years ago Durkheim stated his belief that France suffered from the paucity of what he called "secondary groups" intermediate between state and individual:

Our political malaise thus has the same origin as the social malaise we are suffering from. It too is due to the lack of secondary organs intercalated between the State and the rest of the society. We have already seen that these organs seem necessary to prevent the State from tyrannizing over individuals; it is now plain that they are equally essential to prevent individuals from absorbing the State. They liberate the two confronted forces, whilst linking them at the same time. We can see how serious this lack of internal organization is, which we have noted so often: this is because it involves in fact something of a profound loosening and an enervation, so to speak, of our whole social and political structure. The social forms that used to serve as a framework for individuals and a skeleton for the society, either no longer exist or are in course of being effaced, and no new forms are taking their place. So that nothing remains but the fluid mass of individuals. For the State itself has been reabsorbed by them. Only the administrative machine has kept its stability and goes on operating with the same automatic regularity.[58]

Germany appears to be similar to France and different from England and the United States in respect to the development of multiple independent groups that participate in the direction of public affairs. In a recent study of West German society, the author described the crucial differences between Germany, on the one side, and England and the United States, on the other, as follows:

In Germany, there is a sharp break between the public and the private spheres. Political and social responsibility is an attribute of office, whether in the parliaments, the ministries, the churches, the trade-unions, or the interest-groups. What is more, within these various political structures a strong hierarchical spirit dominates, so that political responsibility and communication tend to be confined to the very heights of these institutions. In England and the United States, on the other hand, there is a gradation from public to private. Private association for public purposes is not confined to political parties and interest-groups, but includes a variety of general and special public-interest groups concerned with policy issues of all kinds at all levels of the governmental process. Power and communication are more or less decentralized within these organizations. . . . The shortcomings of democratic society in Germany result from absence of such institutional pluralism.[59]

France and Germany suffer from the failure to have developed and sustained an intermediate structure of independent groups. The centralization of national organization is one major consequence. Conversely, whenever there is expropriation of major social functions by large organizations, smaller groups lose their reasons for existence (except perhaps as administrative agencies). This loss of function, in turn, undermines the meaning smaller groups possess for their participants. No group can lose its character-defining functions and remain a source of meaning and belonging. An organization whose performance falls far short of its avowed purposes loses meaning: the subjective response of the individual is tied to the objective role of the group. Thus, the role of local organization becomes attenuated as decision-making and communication shift toward a national center, with the consequence that rank and file members find little basis for participation in it. Similarly, the role of a job in the fashioning of a product becomes attenuated as that job becomes increasingly subdivided and removed from the worker's control, with the consequence that the individual finds little basis for a sense of workmanship and status in it.[60] In like manner, as the role of the local community in leisure activities progressively gives way to the national media of entertainment, the individual finds less to interest him in his community.[61] In sum, the attenuation of association, occupation, and community characterizes the intermediate structure of mass society.

## Isolation of Personal Relations

Personal as well as intermediate relations become increasingly peripheral to the central operations of the mass society. This is shown by the change in social position of the family from an extended kinship system to an *isolated* conjugal unit following upon the loss of many social functions. The family gives up its educational role to a public school system, its mutual aid role to a social security system, and so on. The loss of functions sharply limits the public meaning of the family, though not necessarily its private meaning, and diminishes its capacity for relating the individual to the larger society. Kinship units may be too narrow in scope and too far removed from the public realm to be able to provide an effective basis for developing interest and participation in it.

With this argument in mind, many students of mass society imply that mass society lacks family ties as well as intermediate social relations. This view is open to serious question. In the first place, since the family by itself is inherently incapable of linking the individual to large-scale society, it is theoretically unnecessary to assume that such relations are absent in order to have a mass society. In other words, it is entirely possible to have a society in which there are family ties but which is still a mass society due to the lack of intermediate relations. Furthermore, since the individual who is *totally* isolated (that is, without even family ties)

for long periods is not likely to possess that minimum of personal organization required by collective activity, the loss of all family life leads to personal deviance—in the extreme case, mental disorders and suicides—rather than to mass behavior. But it is mass behavior which marks the mass society.

Data showing that extreme personal deviance and extreme political behavior do not vary together lend support to this view, for they indicate that different social conditions may give rise to each. Thus, if the proportion of the electorate which supports the Communist party may be taken as an indicator of the extent of extremist political behavior in a society, and if the proportion of the population recorded as suicides, manslayers, and alcoholics may be used as indicators of the extent of personal deviance in a society, then it may be shown that countries characterized by relatively strong Communist movements are not generally characterized by relatively high rates of personal deviance; and, conversely, countries with relatively small Communist electorates do not tend to have relatively low rates of personal deviance. More precisely, if Australia, Canada, Denmark, Finland, France, Italy, Norway, Sweden, Switzerland, United Kingdom, and United States are ranked by size of the Communist vote in the first election after 1949, and if they are ranked by proportion of suicides in 1949, *the rank order correlation between suicide rate and Communist vote is —.26.* If the same countries are ranked according to rate of homicides rather than suicides, *the rank order correlation between proportion of manslayers and of Communist voters is —.08.* If these countries are ranked by proportion of alcoholics and of Communist voters, the correlation is —.38.[62] We may conclude that there is *no evidence here for a positive relation between conditions that favor mass deviance and those that favor personal deviance.* If anything, there may be a slight negative relation, since all three coefficients are negative.

The same conclusion is reached when we compare changes in the suicide rate with changes in the Communist vote *within each country.* Comparing the direction of change in the per cent Communist vote with the direction of change in the crude suicide rate for each pair of election years in twelve European countries between 1921 and 1954,[63] we find that they change in *opposite* directions in 36 out of the 60 comparisons, or 60% of the time. In only two out of the twelve countries do the two measures change in the same direction (increase or decrease together) in a majority of cases. The following observations on the social conditions underlying support of communism in Sweden are consistent with these data.

The kind of social isolation which is associated with Communist voting behavior is ordinarily not caused by individual maladjustment. *Those who vote Communist usually seem to have satisfactory primary group relations in the home, factory, and community.* Furthermore, the suicide rate in Sweden is not positively correlated with the Communist vote. Suicides are least frequent in the "reddest" country.[64]

Thus, there are good theoretical and empirical reasons (although the data are far from conclusive) for not assuming that the loss of family life is a necessary condition underlying mass tendencies. Rather, we contend that it is the *isolation* of the family and other primary groups which marks the mass society.

Since social isolation, as the term will be used herein, refers to the lack of social relations to the larger society, individuals may be isolated even though they possess family ties—so long as the family groups in turn are not linked to the larger society in any firm way. For isolated families (or other kinds of primary associations, such as friendship groups) cannot by themselves provide the basis for understanding or managing the impersonal environment with which the individual also must grapple. Therefore, whereas the isolation of a small group does not entail the isolation of its members from one another, the individual member of such a group may nevertheless be isolated from the common life of the "great society." A central proposition of this study states that meaningful and effective participation in the larger society requires a structure of groups intermediate between the family and the nation; and the weakness of such a structure creates a vulnerability to mass movements. Participation in small but isolated groups such as the family is no substitute for participation in intermediate groups and may even be favorable to participation in mass movements, since the individual is more likely to engage in new ventures when he receives support from his close associates, and because the member of even a small group is a more accessible target for mass agitation than is a completely unattached person. In other words; the totally isolated individual (that is, the person without *any* social ties) will be unable to maintain his personal organization sufficiently to engage in cooperative ventures of any kind, whereas the individual who has personal ties but no broader ties in the society is more likely to be available for mass movements.

## Centralization of National Relations

The organizing principle of large-scale mass society centers on the national level. This is indicated by the proliferation of governmental functions in previously autonomous spheres of activity, by the growth of national organizations, and by the concomitant shift in power from local to national centers. Structures on the national level develop in response to the size and complexity of society; they expropriate functions formerly reserved to intermediate groups and the family.

Modern mass society is characterized by the great degree to which this transference has taken place, so that the state and national organization assume the central role in the direction of all kinds of collective activity. Mass society finds a major basis of integration in large-scale organization. Therefore, we would be misconstruing mass society if we were to describe it as a state of social disorganization.

National organization that is centralized at the expense of smaller forms of association helps to create amorphous masses. People are more easily manipulated and mobilized when they become directly and exclusively dependent on the national organization for the satisfaction of interests otherwise also met in proximate relations. When the national organization is atomized, its members find it increasingly difficult to orient themselves to the larger society. They cannot understand the workings of the over-all system, in part because "there are far few positions from which the major structural connections between different activities can be perceived, and fewer men can reach these vantage points."[65] Furthermore, increasing distance between centers of decision and daily life make it more difficult for people to grasp the meaning of issues at stake. Faced with the impersonality and incomprehensibility of national relations, and at the same time lacking an independent group life, the individual may withdraw from participation in the larger society. Or he may act in spite of the lack of group relations. Certain spheres of mass society are based on such unmediated participation of large numbers of individuals.

Large-scale communication is based on mass participation when it is divorced from intermediate relations, and prevails over other modes that are anchored in such relations. Agencies of large-scale communication are not necessarily mass media, however. They become so when they lose their ties to local and personal forms of communication. Mere growth in size of these agencies makes mass relations more probable (but certainly not inevitable), as it encourages national centralization and discourages local relations of those who manage the media.[66] Thus, the genuine community newspaper forms a link in the local chain of gossip and discussion, as its staff members participate in face-to-face relations with their readers. By contrast, the mass media lack such intermediate associations; as a result, instead of sharing a community of value and interest with their audience, they substitute organizational and market relations on a national level.

In general, formal organizations are to be identified as mass organizations, not by their size, but when they lack intermediate units which have some autonomy from the central leadership. In the absence of a structure of smaller groups, formal organizations themselves become remote from their members. That is, they get beyond the reach of their members, and as a result cannot deeply influence them nor command their allegiance in the face of competition for member loyalties. Consequently, members of excessively bureaucratized organizations may become mobilized by totalitarian elites. This is illustrated by the Nazi success in capturing many youth groups in Germany during the 1920's.

Prior to World War I, Germany witnessed a great upsurge of youth movements, filled with young men and women who were alienated from existing religion, politics, business, education, art, literature, and family life. The youth movements themselves were "at bottom random, 'goalless,' but persistent attempts to replace the crumbled value system . . . with another which would in some way focus the longing for a sacred experience."[67] But the prewar youth movement sank into routine in the early 1920's. Esoteric and intimate aspects of the movement became commonplace. The initially spontaneous charismatic leadership grew matter-of-fact and even traditional. The tendency toward tutelage by adults created centralized and routinized office staffs for many youth organizations. The whole movement became bureaucratized. Hitler, Goebbels, and Rosenberg seized the opportunity to exploit the widespread yearning for action on the part of both leaders and members of the youth movements. By 1923, the Nazis proclaimed the establishment of the Greater German Youth Movement to capture these restive youths. Funds were appropriated for an intensive propaganda campaign. By the end of 1924, Nazi youth groups were shooting up throughout Upper Saxony. After Hitler announced the creation of the Hitler Youth as a party auxiliary at the 1926 party convention, the organization spread rapidly.[68]

Members or clients of an organization who are alienated from the leadership are favorite targets for mass movements. Communist successes among unemployed trade unionists in England during the depression have been related to the lack of close ties between the central Trade Union Congress and the local Trade Councils. In the absence of effective communication and organic bonds, the national leadership was insufficiently responsive to the distress of its members, with the result that the local organizations "were left without either lead or help from the centre and were thus easily led to back the Communists."[69] Communist (and Nazi) penetration of the unemployed ranks in Germany likewise was facilitated by poor relations between trade union leadership and the ranks, in this instance in part because union functions were being absorbed by the state. German trade union connections with the workers were "unquestionably weakened by the increased activity of the state in the regulation of wages and conditions of unemployment." The vast array of economic functions

administered by the state induced workers to believe they no longer needed unions.[70] At the same time rank and file members were becoming less and less committed to their unions, the leadership of both the trade unions and the Social Democratic party was becoming more and more entrenched and entwined in the government apparatus.[71] As a result, there developed "an increasing gap between what the average worker hoped and expected, and what was being said and done by the reformist, government-affiliated bureaucracy of the SPD and the unions."[72] Membership in the socialist unions declined, and, especially as unemployment rose, both the Communists and the Nazis won increasing working-class support.

When, on the other hand, unions have developed strong locals, clubs, and the like, which perform important economic and social functions for their members, these members possess multiple relations to the organization, and to the larger social order —commitments they are not likely to endanger by supporting extremist movements. A study of the International Typographical Union shows how independent subgroup formation not only ties printers to the union, but also how it facilitates democratic processes within it.[73] The I.T.U. is perhaps the most democratic union in America. Its distinguishing feature is a permanent two-party system, which guarantees an ever-present source of criticism of and alternative leadership to the incumbent administration. The two parties are not the only independent groups within the union to relate the rank and file and leadership, however. In addition, and supportive of the party-system as well as the union, there are strong and relatively autonomous locals, large enough to protect their members from undue outside coercion, and small enough to provide an interpersonal basis for participation in the union's affairs. Furthermore, the printers possess a flourishing "occupational community," organized around a plurality of independent benevolent organizations, newspapers, athletic teams, lodges, social clubs, and informal relations. Although these subgroups are not part of the union, nor explicitly political in any way, they serve to increase political participation in the union (for example, by increasing contact of non-political printers with those who already are active in union politics), to train new union leaders (especially as a result of filling their own leadership needs for club officials), and to give their members a greater stake in maintaining the social order of the occupation, including the union and its party system. In short, through parties, locals, clubs, and friendships, as well as a result of other factors (such as the insulation of the printing occupation from other manual trades), printers develop multiple ties to their work, their union, and the larger social order of which they are a part.

Nisbet argues that unless all kinds of large-scale organizations are rooted in partially autonomous subgroups, they intensify rather than counteract the process of atomization:

> The labor union, the legal or medical association, or the church will become as centralized and as remote as the national State itself unless these great organizations are rooted in the smaller relationships which give meaning to the ends of the large associations. . . . Only thus will the large formal associations remain important agencies of order and freedom in democracy.[74]

Large-scale organizations that fail to develop or sustain independent subgroups tend to be characterized by low levels of membership participation. Because they are not close enough to their members to allow for effective participation, mass organizations engender widespread apathy. Furthermore, the lack of a pluralist structure within organizations, like its absence in the larger society, not only discourages membership participation. It also discourages the formation of an informed membership, the development of new leadership, and the spread of responsibility and authority, so that the wide gap between the top and the bottom of mass organizations tends to be bridged by manipulation.[75]

At the same time that mass relations permit extensive manipulation of people by elites, they also encourage manipulation of elites by non-elites. Elites are more directly influenced by non-elites in the absence of intermediate groups because they are less insulated. Elites lose their insulation since demands and impulses of large numbers of people that formerly were sublimated and fulfilled by intermediate groups now are focused directly on the national level. Higher elites absorb functions formerly reserved to intermediate elites and therefore no longer can depend on these groups to siphon off popular pressures and to regulate participation. Furthermore, popular participation in the higher elites is all the stronger and less restrained for being in part a substitute for diversified participation in intermediate groups—especially in times of crisis.

In conclusion, the growth of centralized organizations at the expense of intermediate groups constrains both elites and non-elites in efforts to directly manipulate the other. Media of communication that command the attention of millions of people simultaneously are major instruments of this manipulation by those who command them, but also by the audience upon which their success or failure directly is dependent. Centralized decision-making also may cut two ways: if the populace can make its voice felt more easily when it can influence directly one master decision, rather than having to influence many smaller decisions to achieve the same result, then by the same token elites also may grasp one major lever of power more readily than many smaller ones. Centralization of decision-making functions does not preclude direct intervention either by the mass or the elite,

although it certainly does prevent people from expressing and implementing *individual* views on public matters. When centralized national relations are combined with weak intermediate relations and isolated family relations, elites are unprotected from mass pressures and masses are unprotected from elite pressures. The structure of mass society thus provides extensive opportunity for mass movements. The character of that structure may now be summarized.

Social groups larger than the family and smaller than the state operate to link elites and non-elites, so that the nature of these groups shapes the political relation. Where intermediate groups do not exist or do not perform important social functions, elites and non-elites are directly dependent on one another: there is non-mediated access to elites and direct manipulation of non-elites. This kind of social arrangement leaves society vulnerable to anti-democratic movements based on mass support. Centralized national groups do not mitigate mass availability; neither do isolated primary groups. For the one relationship is too remote and the other is too weak to provide the individual with firm bases of attachment to society. This is the situation of mass society.

Where many social groups are operative, the question is whether they are autonomous, that is, free from domination by other groups, and of limited scope, that is, influential with respect to only limited aspects of their members' lives. Where groups are influential with respect to the whole of their members' lives (for example, where "the status of every man was fixed by his place in some community—manor, borough, guild, learned University or convent"[76]), the political structure tends to be authoritarian but not totalitarian, since each community is to some degree independent and therefore capable of limiting the power of a central elite. This is the situation of more complex communal societies, such as medieval society with its corporations that protected the individual from undue external interference, for example, by the monarchy, but that did not give him much leeway with respect to the corporate authority itself.

Where, on the other hand, social groups are not only inclusive of their members' lives but also are themselves controlled by a central elite, then the political structure tends to be totalitarian. For in this case the individual is available to the central elite through his intermediate affiliations, which are instituted by the elite precisely for this purpose. Thus, whereas the medieval guild could help prevent the state from easy manipulation of its members by virtue of the guild's independence of the king, the state-dominated trade union is an instrument of the political elite for the mobilization of workers (as in the Soviet Union today). Where the trade union is not only independent of the state, but in addition the worker is not under the domination of his union except with reference to limited areas of life, then it supports a liberal democratic rule. The trade union must fulfill important social functions, however, for otherwise it becomes merely another organization without the ability to define and protect its members' position in the larger society. Intermediate groups whose functions have been absorbed by national structures mark the mass society. A wide variety of independent, limited-function organizations permits democratic control but also insulates both elite and non-elite from undue interference in the life of the other. This is the situation of pluralist society.

Social arrangements may encourage tendencies that transform the political system. This is especially true of the mechanisms of mass society, for they permit an abundance of mass movements. A major objective of this study is to identify the social origins and social bases of mass movements. On the basis of our model of mass society, we expect to find that mass movements are facilitated by the atomization of social relations, since unattached people are disposed to engage in mass action.

McCarthy had no political organization, but his following constituted an incipient mass movement which had considerable working-class support. A Gallup poll taken in March, 1954, found 45% of manual workers expressing a favorable opinion of McCarthy. The neo-Fascists in Italy obtain about one-third of their support from the working class (urban and rural). It is more difficult to estimate the proportion of Nazi votes which are attributable to workers in Hitler's successful bid for power, but the composition of the party in 1933 was well over one-third urban and rural workers.[78] The same is true for the Italian Fascist party in 1921.[79]

Fascist movements, then, are not adequately conceived as middle-class phenomena, nor are Communist movements to be understood merely as working-class phenomena. In the latter case, in addition to the figures just given, we may recall that middle-class intellectuals have played a decisive role in Communist movements, everywhere providing leadership for nascent Communist parties. In the former case not only do Fascist movements rely on working-class support for a significant portion of their following; but in at least one in-

## MARGINAL MIDDLE CLASSES

Any political enterprise which aspires to power on the basis of popular support will have to command the allegiance of sizable numbers of people from both the middle and working classes, because the size of these classes makes it a necessity. This is true even when a political group depends for primary support upon only one class.

As Table 2 shows, the Republican party receives disproportionate support from the middle class; but at the same time, a large minority of its votes is cast by workers (note the large increase in the proportion of the Republican vote coming from workers in that party's victory in 1952). By the same token, the Democratic party requires large numbers of middle-class votes to turn its working-class majority into a national majority. In England, too, the Conservative party depends on workers for a large share of its votes. The Labor party commands proportionately many fewer middle-class votes, but that is one of its major electoral problems.

Political mass movements are no exceptions to this rule. The French Communists receive thirty per cent of their electoral support from middle-class voters, according to a survey taken in 1952. The Italian Communist-Nenni Socialist coalition also depends on middle-class voters for about one-third of its electoral base. Although no figures are available on the composition of the Communist voters in the United States, one study[77] reports that the party's membership is over one-half middle-class (including students; if students are excluded, the proportion is a bit under one-half).

TABLE 2—**Class Composition of Electorate of Parties in Several Countries**

| Party | PER CENT OF PARTY ELECTORATE WHO ARE | |
|---|---|---|
| | Middle Class | Working Class |
| United States (1952) | | |
| Republican | 63 | 37 |
| Democratic | 41 | 59 |
| United States (1948) | | |
| Republican | 76 | 24 |
| Democratic | 40 | 60 |
| Great Britain (1951) | | |
| Conservative | 51 | 49 |
| Labor | 14 | 86 |
| Germany (1955) | | |
| Christian Democratic | 60 | 40 |
| Social Democratic | 28 | 72 |
| France (1952) | | |
| Gaullist | 68 | 32 |
| MRP (Catholic) | 74 | 26 |
| Socialist | 52 | 48 |
| Communist | 30 | 70 |
| Italy (1953) | | |
| Fascist | 66 | 34 |
| Christian Democratic | 70 | 30 |
| Social Democratic | 69 | 31 |
| Communist, Left Socialist | 37 | 63 |

SOURCES: Data recomputed from University of Michigan Survey Research Center surveys of 1948 and 1952 (U.S.); John Bonham, *The Middle Class Vote* (London: Faber and Faber, 1954), p. 168; Morris Janowitz, "Social Stratification and Mobility in West Germany," *American Journal of Sociology*, LXIV (1958), 22; Philip Williams, *Politics in Post-War France* (London: Longmans, Green, 1954), p. 446; and *Italian Political Party Preferences*, a report prepared for the Center for International Studies of M.I.T. (unpublished MS, 1953). The distinction between working class and middle class in this table is essentially one between manual and nonmanual occupations.

stance (the Peronist), a Fascist-like movement had a predominantly working-class base; and in another instance (Italian fascism) the original cadres (led by Mussolini) came out of the socialist movement.

These observations suggest that what from the standpoint of class analysis is the "deviant" portion of a totalitarian party's social base (e.g., the working class vote for a Fascist party) is from the standpoint of mass analysis an expression of its basic character. The fact remains, however, that even though there is a "totalitarian appeal" common to both movements, fascism has a greater affinity for the middle classes and communism for the working classes. We shall not attempt to analyze this class differential here (it has been described in numerous studies), nor more broadly how dispositions to engage in mass movements get channelized along the lines of one extreme or the other. What we are after is the identification of kinds of people who support mass movements of whatever kind. Therefore, in this section on the middle classes, support for Fascist and proto-Fascist movements will be used as the main indicator of mass susceptibility; and in the following section on the working classes, support for Communist movements will be used in a similar fashion.

We wish to show that there are marked similarities between the condition of middle-class people who support mass (especially Fascist) movements and the condition of working-class people who support mass (especially Communist) movements. The similarity of condition is one of mass availability resulting from lack of social integration. Thus, it is the more marginal sections of the middle classes which manifest the greater susceptibility to mass movements; specifically, poorly-established business rather than well-established business, and small business rather than big business.

## Marginal Big Business

Since big business in highly developed capitalist systems tends to possess a network of organizations for the defense of its interests, as well as a high involvement in voluntary associations of all kinds, its willingness to risk the destruction of an existing democratic order should, in the ordinary course of events, be relatively low. For its multiple stakes in that order require, among other things, that big business protect its position by maintaining continuous access to policy-making institutions, and this access would be jeopardized by support of extremist movements unless they gave strong promise of success.

The attitudes of capitalist groups toward the policy of their nations are predominantly adaptive rather than causative, today more than ever. Also, they hinge to an astonishing degree on short-run considerations equally remote from any deeply laid plans and from any definite "objective" class interests.[80]

This argument, of course, is diametrically opposed to the Marxist theory of fascism, which claims to find in the most highly organized business groups the main impetus and base for fascism. The fact that the most highly developed capitalist societies have experienced the smallest Fascist movements and the strongest commitments to democratic values on the part of the business community, and that it has been in the less industrial countries (e.g., Italy) and in countries in which the state assumed a major responsibility for industrial development (e.g., Germany) that Fascist movements have been strong and have commanded at least some important business support, sharply contradicts the Marxist theory. Furthermore, within countries that went Fascist, it was the less established business groups that backed Fascist movements earlier and with greater vigor.

National Socialism received little big business support in its initial period, but picked up considerable aid from this source during its rapid growth following the depression. Prior to the depression, when the movement was small and weak, what little support was forthcoming from big business centered in the local South German producers. Nationwide industrial leaders were not much interested in sponsoring the Nazis until after 1928.[81] "The German economy did not raise up Hitler. . . . To be sure, he did approach big capital—though as a blackmailer, not as a lackey. But in that springtime of self-confidence [prior to the depression], there was nothing to be had from capital by blackmail."[82] This matter of the timing of big business support for the Nazis is an important one, for it is one thing to latch on to an already successful totalitarian party for opportunistic reasons, and quite another ardently to cast one's lot with a young and struggling movement of highly uncertain outcome. If nazism were indeed to be understood as the "last stand of capitalism," big business would not have withheld its support until the Nazis achieved more power than the conservatives. In Germany, and elsewhere when Fascist parties have triumphed, big business does not so much *create* these totalitarian movements as it attempts to use them once they are ascendant. In general, "the evidence . . . will not support those who attribute to German industrialists (. . . with noteworthy exceptions) a dynamic role in the advent of National Socialism."[83]

If big business for the most part did not rally early to Hitler, neither did it support the Republic.[84] By 1930, however, faced with great pressures on their economic position and confronted with a powerful Nazi movement, portions of big business did give considerable financial backing to Hitler. What is of specific note for the present analysis is the apparent fact that this support did not emanate from big business as a whole, but from its newer sections. "It would appear that the old industrial families of the Ruhr feared

Hitler's budding totalitarianism much more strongly than did the directors of the anonymous companies who live on big salaries, instead of on individual profits."[85]

Thus, although before 1930 apparently no central organ of industry made financial contributions to the Nazis,[86] and at no time *before* the Nazi victory does it seem that German industry as a whole or as an organized group supported nazism, those large contributions which were forthcoming by 1930, and which played a crucial role in the following years, came particularly from leaders of heavy industry, especially steel.[87] This was the sector of German business which developed late and failed to achieve an autonomous position in the economic order. Heavy industry was more strongly affected by the authoritarianism of the Prussian monarchy than the rest of the middle classes,

. . . because its period of rapid expansion coincided with the consolidation of the Bismarck Reich and was made possible in considerable part by the protectionist and armament policies of that regime. . . . On the condition that it accept a subordinate role in this authoritarian bureaucratic regime, heavy industry was given the advantages of a large, protected internal market, the prospect of social acceptance by the aristocracy and court, and gratification of national pride through the rapid rise to power of the second Reich."[88]

This orientation encouraged militant resistance to unionization and active support of extreme national groups such as the Pan-German League prior to the war, and opposition to the Weimar Republic after the war. When the depression hit, several of the big industrial concerns that faced the greatest economic difficulties began to pour large sums of money into the Nazi organization.[89] While some were looking for a "savior," most were more calculating in their support of nazism. The latter, according to a leading Conservative who himself at first cooperated with Hitler, believed that nazism was a patron of order and security that would help restore profits.

The restoration of "order," the disciplining of the workers, the ending of politically fixed wages and profit-destroying social services, the abolition of the workers' freedom of association, and the replacing of the continual alteration of short-lived parliamentary governments by a stable political system that permits long-range calculation—all these things tempt leaders of industry and finance and of society to shut their eyes to the fundamental difference between the true motives with which the dynamic dictatorships are set up and the motives which lead the conservative elements to support them.[90]

Even among those large industrialists who supported the Nazis, there were many who did not fully close their eyes, and who were fearful lest they be totally absorbed by the Nazi movement. In consequence, part of their objective in support-ing Hitler was to restrain him, particularly on economic matters.[91] The better part of the big industrial concerns, "while welcoming Hitler as an ally against labor, would have preferred him being used as a mere tool in the hands of a cabinet controlled by industry and the Junkers."[92] Some cautious industrialists, to be on the safe side, continued their membership in other political parties while quietly acquiring membership in the Nazi party.[93] In general, it would appear that big businessmen were more opportunistic toward nazism than the other classes were, since they had the greater stake in preserving the existing economic order; at the same time, newer sections of big business, having less at stake than the old industrial families, rallied to Hitler's side once his ascendancy became apparent.

An old and rooted upper class, with established traditions, tends to strike an attitude of *noblesse oblige* toward the disinherited, and to seek accommodation via amalgamation rather than subversion of the system. The new rich, on the other hand, when faced with great pressures on their position in the existing order, more often will support extremist movements. In the United States, the little support which Huey Long received from the wealthy came from "mavericks of one sort or another who 'did not belong' because of their ancestry, the sources of their money, or their accent."[94] McCarthy also was supported by newly wealthy individuals (e.g., Texas oil millionaires) during a period of prolonged prosperity. At such times, all social barriers to the power and prestige of new fortunes are felt to be great shackles imposed by the old upper class. In general, new wealth is more liable to make common cause with the disaffected of all classes, since it is rootless.[95]

### Marginal Small Business

Big business as a whole occupies a central position in industrial democracies, and therefore except for its more marginal elements has not been especially attracted to mass movements. Small business, on the other hand, increasingly is marginal in modern society and as a result has been more susceptible to mass movements. Small business is less and less assimilated into a world of rationalized enterprise, but it also cannot find security in a declining world of individual enterprise. Squeezed between the pressures of big business and big labor, the class interests of small business are inherently ambiguous, finding allies neither in the classes above nor in the classes below. The central difficulty facing small business is the relative absence of realistic possibilities for improving its long-run economic position in a world increasingly dominated by large-scale organization. Big business finds bureaucratic organization congruent with its interests; and industrial workers have ready recourse to trade-union organization as a counter to big business organization. Even white-collar employees increasingly have the possibility of using collective means to protect their interests, as their conditions of work become rationalized (for example, as office workers are massed together in large numbers, and as their work is standardized, more of them join unions). But the small businessman faces much greater difficulty in rationalizing his enterprise or his relations with other small businessmen. He is truly the marginal man in the industrialized society, and therefore he is readily available for nihilistic mass movements.

There is widespread agreement among students of anti-democratic movements that small businessmen contributed substantial support to the Fascists in Italy, the Nazis in Germany, the Poujadists in France, and the McCarthyists in America. Considering first the Italian Fascists, it has been established that three-fourths of the provincial party secretaries came from the lesser bourgeoisie.[96] But the lower-middle class did not respond uniformly to the appeals of fascism. The *urban* sections figured more prominently in the leadership and active cadres of the Fascist movement. Furthermore, it was the more marginal and unintegrated members of the urban lower-middle class who provided the bulk of active members. These were people who remained outside of the established middle-class organizations, and therefore were "ready to rush in any direction."[97]

In post-war Italy, artisans in business for themselves have given less support to the democratic parties than have other middle-class groups (see Table 3).

Small businessmen also contributed much more than their share to Hitler's mass base. These self-employed members of the lower-middle class felt themselves squeezed between the industrial workers and industrialists, "whose unions, cartels, and parties took the center of the stage."[98] The Nazis responded directly to the small businessman's resentments by attacking those features of industrialism that were most threatening to small business. Following their accession to power, however, the Nazis terminated their support of small busi-ness, since they had no interest in deliberately limiting the opportunities for industrial growth and large-scale distribution.[99]

Another section of the middle class that disproportionately supported the Nazis consisted of the lower white-collar employees. This is evidenced by the growth of anti-democratic and pro-Nazi organizations of white-collar people, and the concomitant decline in white-collar organizations that favored democracy.[100] White-collar support for Hitler cannot be accounted for in the same terms as small business support, since white-collar employees are not marginal to large-scale enterprise. Rather, it would appear to be based on resentment against a system which failed to fulfill its promises of status and security within rationalized organization. In other words, white-collar people appear to have reacted more to the *crisis* of industrial capitalism than to the *order* of industrial capitalism, whereas small businessmen reacted against the order itself.[101] Thus, white-collar people have not generally responded to mass appeals except during the depression (and then in only a few countries), whereas small businessmen have on certain occasions responded to mass appeals even during periods of relative prosperity. Poujadism and McCarthyism are two recent examples of this.

Poujade fashioned a large if amorphous movement out of the resentment of small businessmen against the representatives of modernization, especially big business, big labor, and big government. Yet salaried employees not only rejected the movement; they have constituted a favorite target for Poujade, who complained bitterly against their social security, family allocations, and other economic gains.[102] Poujadism in its initial and primary face is the revolt of merchants and artisans residing in small towns and rural areas, lacking organizations of their own to protect their interests, and taking a dim view of all political parties. The first adherents and local directors by and large were small merchants or artisans, who, in the words of one of the earliest militants of the movement, "were tired, discouraged, without hope, without anything . . . who worked harder and longer than

## TABLE 3—Preference for Anti-Democratic Parties by Type of Middle-Class Occupation, Italy, 1953

| PER CENT WHO PREFER | AMONG THOSE WHO ARE | | | |
|---|---|---|---|---|
| | Free Artisans | White Collar | Employers | Professionals or Executives |
| Anti-democratic parties | 52 | 36 | 24 | 16 |
| Fascists | 14 | 11 | 11 | — |
| Monarchists | 14 | 18 | 7 | 8 |
| Nenni Socialists | 15 | 2 | 6 | 8 |
| Communists | 9 | 5 | — | — |
| Democratic parties | 48 | 64 | 76 | 84 |
| Total | 100% | 100% | 100% | 100% |

SOURCE: Data recomputed from *Italian Political Party Preferences,* a report prepared for the Center for International Studies of M.I.T. (unpublished MS, 1953), p. 12.

before the war and than their parents did but who lost ground rather than advanced."[103] Thus, out of the 52 Poujadists elected in 1956, 26 are merchants and the other 26 are either artisans or heads of small or medium enterprises, plus a school director and two students.[104]

The Poujadists have been strongest in those areas which have benefited least by the modernization of French economic life. Poujadists gained their major electoral success in the economically stagnant south and west of France, and have had very little appeal in those regions where industrialization has developed furthest. Within departments, Poujadists generally have succeeded better in the rural cantons than in the urban and industrial ones. Poujadism is rooted in marginal areas and supported by marginal members of the middle classes; for it has flourished in those areas by-passed in the rationalization of French society and among those people who have been most frustrated by this process. Poujade succeeded above all in mobilizing unorganized sections of the rural middle classes in the backward Center and Midi. The marginality characteristic of Poujade's adherents is linked to the mass behavior of the movement: its reliance on direct action (exemplified in the physical resistance to tax collections), anti-parliamentarism, and early collaboration with the Communists (a collaboration apparently so thorough that when Poujade broke with the Communists he complained "they went so far as to tell me what I must say"); in some areas the Communists supplied the leadership of the Poujadist movement, and even many of the voters.[105]

In prosperous post-war America, there is some evidence to indicate that it also has been the small businessman rather than the white-collar employee who voices support for McCarthyism, another mass movement with certain anti-democratic overtones. A study of the social base of McCarthy in Bennington, Vermont, in 1954 (the height of McCarthy's popularity) reports that less than 30% of salaried employees approved of McCarthy, as compared with over 50% of the small businessmen.[106] What is of special note is the finding that the small businessmen were much more favorable to McCarthy than white-collar people of *similar education*. This is to say that the difference is

truly one of occupation and not merely an artifact of the lower educational level of small businessmen.

Table 4 shows that education does make an important difference in level of support for McCarthy, especially as between those who have been to college and those who have not. Among both small businessmen and white-collar employees, support for McCarthy decreases as education increases. But the differences between these two occupational groups remain, even on the college level. A clue to the source of these differences between small businessmen and salaried workers of similar education is provided by an analysis of their attitudes toward the growth of large-scale organization. The Bennington study shows that small businessmen are more likely than are people in other occupations to believe that *both* big companies and labor unions have too much power. Among those with less than four years of high school, 41% of the small businessmen but only 25% of the salaried employees and 29% of the manual workers believe that both big business and labor have too much power. It is among the small businessmen who hold such beliefs that McCarthy receives overwhelming approval: almost 3 out of 4 in this subgroup were McCarthy supporters. "Here is evidence that a generalized fear of the dominant currents and institutions of modern society was an important source of McCarthy's mass appeal, not *only* among small businessmen, but perhaps especially among a group like small businessmen whose economic and status security is continually threatened by those currents and institutions."[107]

In sum, small businessmen have provided strong support for fascism, nazism, Poujadism, and McCarthyism. However, it does not follow that these movements themselves may be understood simply as expressions of small business. Mass movements, especially Fascist movements, acquire much wider support than that supplied by one occupational grouping alone. This may be shown by a consideration of the role of the farmer in the rise of mass movements.

### Marginal Farmers

Differences between large farmers and small farmers parallel in part those which have been observed to obtain between big businessmen and small businessmen. Small farmers tend to back both communism and fascism to a greater extent than do large farmers. In both France and Italy, the poorer the farmer the higher the support for the Communist party; and small farmers in Italy support the neo-Fascists twice as frequently as do the large farmers.[108] In Germany, a major source of support for National Socialism was the small, independent family farmer rather than the large landowner. An ecological study of voting in Schleswig-Holstein, the only election district in which the Nazis obtained a majority of the valid votes

**TABLE 4—Support for McCarthy by Occupation and Education**

| LESS THAN HIGH SCHOOL GRADUATES | | HIGH SCHOOL GRADUATES | | SOME COLLEGE OR MORE | |
|---|---|---|---|---|---|
| Small Business | White Collar | Small Business | White Collar | Small Business | White Collar |
| 65% | 38% | 58% | 36% | 32% | 22% |
| N (52) | (53) | (38) | (78) | (44) | (124) |

SOURCE: Martin Trow, "Small Businessmen, Political Tolerance, and Support for McCarthy," *American Journal of Sociology*, LXIV (1958), 274.

cast in the July, 1932, election, found a positive correlation between the proportion of people employed on small farms and the percentage of votes received by the Nazis in 1932. At the same time, large landowners were found to be less inclined to vote Nazi and more to vote Conservative.[109] Studies of other regions in Germany reveal similar patterns of Nazi strength among small rather than large farmers.[110]

It is not only the worse economic position of small farmers, compared with large farmers, which creates their greater affinity for mass movements. It is also their *group isolation* and the *alienation* from society which this isolation breeds. Where farmers lose their ties to the larger social order, they are more available for extremist movements. Thus, a factor which favored the success of Hitler among the small farmers was the relative paucity of social relations between people living on small farms *and* the larger society (farmers were likely to have multiple ties *within* a farming area). Where intermediate relations existed, nazism was less successful. In Bavaria, for example, farmers organized by the Catholics (as well as workers organized by the Socialists) were relatively immune to the appeals of nazism.[111]

In critical situations, smaller and poorer farmers often back the political extremes rather than the democratic parties, in part because they lack established organizations and leaders to summon their loyalties. Table 5 shows that while one-half of

**TABLE 5—Membership in Farm Organizations by Economic Level of Farmers, United States, 1943**

| | | PER CENT BELONGING TO | | | |
|---|---|---|---|---|---|
| Economic Level | Farm Bureau | Grange | Farmers Union | Other | None |
| High | 30 | 5 | 6 | 16 | 50 |
| Medium | 18 | 4 | 1 | 8 | 71 |
| Low | 6 | 2 | 1 | 4 | 87 |
| Total | 18 | 3 | 2 | 9 | 71 |

SOURCE: Hadley Cantril (ed.), *Public Opinion 1935-1946* (Princeton, N.J.: Princeton University Press, 1951), p. 5.

the wealthy farmers in the United States belong to one or more agricultural organizations, only about one-eighth of the poor farmers have any such affiliation. Even the populist Farmer's Union has, if anything, a higher proportion of wealthy members than do the more conservative Bureau and Grange. In farmer-run organizations in other countries, the wealthier producers also are more active than the poorer farmers. In France, for example, the confederation of farmers has been faced with loss of membership among small holders and tenants.[112] Peasants who have turned to the Communists in France lack their own leaders, since leadership in agricultural organizations has fallen to the more prosperous farmers.[113] In the villages

of Russia in 1917, an inferior political consciousness born of non-participation in the larger society permitted the peasants to be swayed one way and the other, depending on the intensity and persistence of pressure applied by the various competing movements. "Apparently often there was a herd and it did stampede."[114]

Extremism among farmers is associated with their isolation ". . . from the larger body politic. . . . They do not command the established means of communications."[115] The loss of contact with centers of power and communication accompanying the rise of the city has bred agrarian antagonism to symbols of urban pre-eminence and it has encouraged glorification of the rural past. The first readily has been transformed into anti-Semitism; and the latter easily is perverted into ethnocentric, extremist politics (much as religious revivalism first began in rural areas in part as a reaction against urbane religion). Thus the Nazi glorification of rural living and the *volk,* as well as Nazi hostility toward the Jews and finance capitalism, was highly congenial to German peasants. Furthermore, "the rural population constitutes the compact mass which stands behind the uncompromising emotional nationalism. That is perhaps the most important reason why movements like National Socialism and fascism are first of all supported by the peasants."[116] Anti-Semitism and anti-urbanism were also manifested by rural movements in North America, including the Populist party and the Social Credit party.

Poorer farmers have been especially receptive to xenophobic appeals because they have not been very successful in forging new ties to replace those relations which were eroded by urbanization. Wealthier farmers, on the other hand, have been more fully integrated into urban society. Comparison of twentieth century with nineteenth century America reveals this change. In the nineteenth century nearly all farmers were inevitably isolated; but with the widespread diffusion in the last fifty years of the automobile, radio, telephone, mail order purchasing, and the like, the well-to-do farmers have become able to participate in the same cultural milieu as their urban counterparts. But if the rapid development of communication and transportation has pulled the wealthier farmer into the mainstream of society, it has left much less of a mark on the poorer farmer. "With these changes there has developed in the American countryside a disparity in living standards and outlook between the most affluent and the least privileged that almost matches anything the city has to show."[117] Therefore, the poorer and more isolated farmers, like their counterparts in business, are especially vulnerable to the appeal of the demagogue. Huey Long, Talmadge, and Bilbo, for example, gained their main following from among small farmers rather than large farmers in the South.[118]

In conclusion, the middle classes are not uniformly vulnerable to the appeal of mass movements. The *old* middle classes, both urban and rural, are more vulnerable than the *new* middle classes; and the *lower* middle classes are more vulnerable than the *upper* middle classes. Mass theory helps to account for these differences by adding to the economic factor of poorer market opportunities for the small entrepreneur and peasant, the social factor of their loss of social ties and status in the larger society. As the situation of the small entrepreneur continues to deteriorate in the face of the growing rationalization of the economic order, we may expect new mass movements to gain adherents from the old middle classes, and especially their lower sections.

## NOTES

1. Jacob Burckhardt, *Force and Freedom* (New York: Meridian Books, 1955).

2. Gustave Le Bon, *The Crowd* (London: Ernest Bonn Ltd., 1947).

3. José Ortega y Gasset, *The Revolt of the Masses* (New York: W. W. Norton, 1940).

4. Karl Mannheim, *Man and Society in an Age of Reconstruction* (London: Kegan Paul, 1940), pp. 79–96.

5. Catholic critics of nineteenth century society, like Bonald and De Maistre, share certain views with aristocratic critics. So do such aesthetic critics as Arnold. In the most general sense, all anti-bourgeois intellectuals of the nineteenth century shared certain ideas which were congenial to a theory of mass society. For a brief review of conservative ideas since the French Revolution, see Peter Viereck, *Conservatism from John Adams to Churchill* (Princeton, N.J.: D. Van Nostrand, 1956).

6. Emil Lederer, *State of the Masses* (New York: W. W. Norton, 1940).

7. Hannah Arendt, *The Origins of Totalitarianism* (New York: Harcourt, Brace and World, 1951).

8. Hannah Arendt, "Authority in the Twentieth Century," *Review of Politics,* XVIII (1956), 403–417, closely follows the aristocratic criticism of mass society.

9. Karl Mannheim, *Essays on Sociology and Social Psychology* (New York: Oxford University Press, 1953), p. 106.

10. *Ibid.,* p. 107.

11. Critics of the theory of mass society generally fail to differentiate between the aristocratic and democratic versions of that theory. A recent example is Daniel Bell's "The Theory of Mass Society, A Critique," *Commentary, xxxii* (July, 1956), 75–83.

12. Le Bon, *op. cit.,* pp. 14, 207.

13. Ortega y Gasset, *op. cit.,* p. 25

14. T. S. Eliot, *Notes towards the Definition of Culture* (London: Faber and Faber, 1948).

15. Peter Viereck, "The Revolt against the Elite," in *The New American Right,* ed. Daniel Bell (New York: Criterion Books, 1955), p. 96.

16. Alexis de Tocqueville, *Democracy in America* (New York: Knopf, 1945), vol. II, p. 322.

17. Quoted by Viereck, *Conservatism from John Adams to Churchill, op. cit.,* p. 159.

18. Mannheim, *Man and Society . . ., op. cit.,* pp. 86–87.

19. Walter Lippmann, *The Public Philosophy* (New York: Mentor Books, 1956), p. 19.

20. Thus, Ortega remarks that mass society is "entirely new in the history of our modern civilization." *Op. cit.,* p. 21.

21. Mannheim, *Man and Society . . ., op. cit.,* p. 87.

22. The term "elite" as used in this study refers to a relatively small circle of people who claim and are charged with the responsibility for framing and sustaining fundamental values and policies in their area of competence.

23. Le Bon, *op. cit.,* p. 15. Ortega also speaks of "the predominance . . . of the mass," *op. cit.,* p. 16.

24. Cf. Philip Selznick, *The Organizational Weapon* (New York: McGraw-Hill, 1952), p. 278, and Mannheim, *Man and Society . . ., op. cit.,* pp. 82 ff.

25. Le Bon, *op. cit.,* p. 18.

26. Viereck, "The Revolt against the Elite," *op. cit.,* p. 104.

27. Le Bon, *op. cit.*

28. Ortega y Gasset, *op. cit.*

29. Several aristocratic thinkers also have been concerned with this problem and have influenced the formulations of later democratic theorists. But it has remained for the latter to provide a basic understanding of sources of mass behavior in the transformation of community. Thus, a present-day conservative thinker has written: "I think that one of the principal errors of conservatively-inclined men has been their neglect of the need for true community." Russell Kirk, *Prospects for Conservatives* (Chicago: Gateway Books, 1956), p. 129.

30. Arendt, *Origins of Totalitarianism, op. cit.,* pp. 309–310.

31. *Ibid.,* p. 310.

32. *Ibid.,* pp. 316–317.

33. *Ibid.,* p. 305.

34. Harold D. Lasswell, "The Garrison State," *American Journal of Sociology,* XLVI (1941), 455–468.

35. Max Weber, *The Theory of Social and Economic Organization* (New York: Oxford University Press, 1947), p. 361.

36. A recent review of the literature on community conflict in the United States notes that "both community organizations and community leaders are faced with constraints when a dispute arises; the formation of a combat group to carry on the controversy and the emergence of a previous unknown as the combat leader are in part results of the *immobility of responsible organizations and leaders.* Both the new leader and the new organization are freed from some of the usual shackles of community norms and internal cross-pressures which make pre-existing organizations and leaders tend to soften the dispute." James S. Coleman, *Community Conflict* (New York: The Free Press of Glencoe, 1957), p. 13.

37. Selznick, *op. cit.,* p. 294.

38. Burckhardt, *op. cit.,* p. 203.

39. Centralization, it must be emphasized, does not necessarily mean authoritarianism. Thus, Lasswell and Kaplan, in *Power and Society* (New Haven: Yale University Press, 1950), pp. 224–225, 235, distinguish between "centralization" and "concentration" of power, and include the latter but exclude the former on a list of seven definitive characteristics of despotic as against democratic rule.

40. Durkheim judged occupational groups to be the basic kind of intermediate organization in modern society. *Professional Ethics and Civic Morals* (New York: The Free Press of Glencoe, 1958), pp. 1–41, 96–97.

41. Durkheim, *op. cit.,* pp. 62–63; italics added.

42. See, for example, Clark Kerr, "Industrial Relations and the Liberal Pluralist," in *Proceedings of the Seventh Annual Meeting of the Industrial Relations Research Association,* ed. L. Reed Tripp (Madison, Wis.: Industrial Relations Research Association, 1955), p. 4.

43. W. Lloyd Warner and P. Lunt, *The Social Life of a Modern Community* (New Haven: Yale University Press, 1941), pp. 341, 346, 349.

44. See Morton Grodzins, *The Loyal and the Unloyal* (Chicago: University of Chicago Press, 1956), pp. 29–30, for a discussion of the combination of direct and indirect ties to the nation-state in pluralist society: "National loyalty has a variety of roots. It springs from direct involvement in the nation's grandeur, from direct response to the symbols of the nation. It is an indirect product of satisfactory private life, loyalties to voluntary groups being transmitted to, and culminating in, national loyalty."

45. Simmel has remarked that the "peculiar character of group formation in the Middle Ages" lies in the fact that "affiliation with a group absorbed the whole man." *Conflict and the Web of Group Affiliation* (New York: The Free Press of Glencoe, 1955), pp. 148–149.

46. G. M. Trevelyan, *History of England:* Vol. I, *From the Earliest Times to the Reformation* (New York: Doubleday, 1953), p. 239.

47. *Idem.*

48. Harold J. Laski, *Authority in the Modern State* (New Haven: Yale University Press, 1919), p. 321.

49. Arnold J. Rose, *Theory and Method in the Social Sciences* (Minnesota: University of Minneapolis Press, 1954), p. 77.

50. Daniel Lerner, "The 'Hard-Headed' Frenchman," *Encounter,* VIII (March, 1957), p. 29.

51. Orvell R. Gallagher, "Voluntary Associations in France," *Social Forces,* XXXVI (1957), p. 159.

52. Laski, *op. cit.,* p. 322.

53. Rose, *op. cit.,* pp. 111–113.

54. Herbert Luethy, *France against Herself* (New York: Meridian, 1957), p. 20.

55. See Rose (*op. cit.,* pp. 105–6, 110, 112). Cf. Mannheim's statement: "France, too, has the smaller cities and the provinces as counter-forces to protect it against the mechanisms of mass society" (*Man and Society . . . , op. cit.,* p. 88); and Luethy's statement: "The empty and impoverished life of most French villages and provincial towns, whose monuments bear witness to a former vitality, is the result of [the centralization of French society]" (*loc. cit.*).

56. Rose, *op. cit.,* pp. 106–107.

57. Charles Bettleheim and S. Frère, *Une Ville Française Moyenne: Auxerre en 1950,* p. 282 (cited in *ibid.,* p. 75).

58. Durkheim, *op. cit.,* p. 106.

59. Gabriel A. Almond, "The Politics of German Business" in *West German Leadership and Foreign Policy,* ed. Hans Spier and W. Phillips Davison (Evanston, Ill.: Row, Peterson, 1957), pp. 238–239.

60. Of the voluminous literature on the alienation of labor, the writings of Karl Marx are especially noteworthy. *Capital* (New York: Random House), pp. 395–400, 708–709. See also Erich Fromm, *The Sane Society* (New York: Holt, Rinehart, Winston, 1955), pp. 125–131, 177–184, and Hannah Arendt, *The Human Condition* (Chicago: University of Chicago Press, 1958), pp. 248–257.

61. On the alienation of leisure, see Fromm, *op. cit.,* pp. 131–37, and Riesman, *et al., The Lonely Crowd* (New York: Doubleday, 1953, abridged edition).

62. Statistics on suicide, homicide, and alcoholism are from Fromm (*op. cit.,* pp. 8–9). Canada and the United Kingdom are not included in the correlation of alcoholics and Communist vote, because data on number of alcoholics were not given.

63. Suicide data are from World Health Organization, *Epidemiological and Vital Statistics Report,* IX, no. 4 (1956), pp. 250–253.

64. W. Phillips Davison, "A Review of Sven Rydenfell's *Communism in Sweden,"* *Public Opinion Quarterly,* XVIII (1954–55), p. 378; italics added.

65. Mannheim, *Man and Society . . . , op. cit.,* p. 59.

66. The change in the *Manchester Guardian,* a leading English newspaper, has been considered in this light (Taylor, 1957, p. 12). "The *Manchester Guardian . . .* has ceased to represent Manchester except in name . . . it is now a national paper pure and simple. . . . The London office provides most of the paper. . . . Now the editor plays little part in local politics."

67. Howard Becker, *German Youth: Bond or Free?* (New York: Oxford University Press, 1946), p. 51.

68. *Ibid.,* pp. 145–146.

69. G. D. H. Cole, *A History of the Labour Party from 1914* (London: Routledge and Kegan Paul, 1948), p. 148.

70. Franz Neumann, *European Trade-Unionism and Politics* (New York: League for Industrial Democracy, 1936), pp. 31–32.

71. Carl E. Schorske, *German Social Democracy, 1905–17: The Development of the Great Schism* (Cambridge, Mass.: Harvard University Press, 1955), pp. 127–128.

72. Otto Kircheimer, "West German Trade-Unions: Their Domestic and Foreign Policies," in Spier and Davison, *op. cit.,* p. 138.

73. S. M. Lipset, M. Trow, and J. Coleman, *Union Democracy* (New York: The Free Press of Glencoe, 1956).

74. Robert A. Nisbet, *The Quest for Community* (New York: Oxford University Press, 1953), p. 277.

75. Cf. Selznick, *op. cit.,* p. 290.

76. Trevelyan, *op. cit.,* p. 239.

77. Gabriel A. Almond, *The Appeals of Communism* (Princeton: Princeton University Press, 1954), p. 189.

78. Hans H. Gerth, "The Nazi Party: Its Leadership and Composition," in *Reader in Bureaucracy,* ed.

Robert K. Merton *et al.* (New York: The Free Press of Glencoe, 1952), p. 106.

79. Herman Finer, *Mussolini's Italy* (London: Victor Gollancz Ltd., 1935), p. 143.

80. Schumpeter adds that "at this point Marxism degenerates into the formulation of popular superstitions." *Capitalism, Socialism, and Democracy* (New York: Harper and Bros., 1947), p. 55.

81. George W. F. Hallgarten, "Adolf Hitler and German Heavy Industry, 1931–1933," *Journal of Economic History,* XII (1952), 225.

82. Konrad Heiden, *Der Fuehrer, Hitler's Rise to Power* (Boston: Houghton Mifflin, 1944), .p. 264.

83. Gabriel A. Almond, "The Politics of German Business," *op. cit.,* p. 198.

84. Alan Bullock, *Hitler, A Study in Tyranny* (London: Odhams Press, 1952), p. 57.

85. Hallgarten, *op. cit.,* p. 243.

86. Edward Peterson, *Hjalmar Schacht: For and Against Hitler; A Politico-Economic Study of Germany, 1923–1949* (Boston: Christopher Publishing House, 1954), pp. 112–117.

87. F. Thyssen, *I Paid Hitler* (New York: Farrar and Rinehart, 1941), p. 102. Thyssen (in 1932) made the largest financial contribution to the Nazis.

88. Almond, "The Politics of German Business," *op. cit.,* pp. 195–156.

89. Hallgarten, *op. cit.,* p. 245.

90. Hermann Rauschning, *The Revolution of Nihilism* (New York: Alliance Book Corp., 1939), pp. 105–106.

91. Louis P. Lochner, *Tycoon and Tyrant: German Industry from Hitler to Adenauer* (Chicago: Henry Regnery, 1954), p. 20.

92. Hallgarten, *op. cit.,* p. 245.

93. Lochner, *op. cit.,* pp. 22–23. Among the Reichstag members in 1928 connected with I. G. Farben, one sat with the DNVP, one with the DDP, and one with the Center Party. I. G. Farben contributed to all these parties, and later to the Nazis. Richard Lewinson, *Das Geld in der Politik* (Berlin: Fischer Verlag, 1930), pp. 84–85.

94. V. O. Key, *Southern Politics* (New York: Knopf, 1949), p. 163.

95. S. M. Lipset, "The Sources of the 'Radical Right,'" in *The New American Right,* ed. Daniel Bell (New York: Criterion Books, 1955), p. 195.

96. Harold D. Lasswell, *The Analysis of Political Behavior* (London: Kegan Paul, 1947), p. 161.

97. A. Rossi, *The Rise of Italian Fascism, 1918–1922* (London: Methuen, 1938), pp. 340–342.

98. Harold D. Lasswell, "The Psychology of Hitlerism," *Political Quarterly,* IV (1933), p. 374.

99. Arthur Schweitzer, "The Nazification of the Lower Middle Class and Peasants," in *The Third Reich,* ed. Maurice Baumont *et al.* (New York: Praeger, 1955), pp. 580–582.

100. Peter Gay, *The Dilemma of Democratic Socialism* (New York: Columbia University Press, 1952), pp. 209–211. Cf. Franz Neumann, *European Trade Unionism and Politics* (New York: League for Industrial Democracy, 1936), p. 20.

101. Martin Trow, "Small Businessmen, Political Tolerance, and Support for McCarthy," *American Journal of Sociology,* LXIV (1958), pp. 278–279.

102. Stanley Hoffman, *Le Mouvement Poujade* (Paris: Librairie Armand Colin, 1956), p. 28.

103. Quoted by Hoffmann, *ibid.,* p. 36

104. *Ibid.,* p. 190.

105. *Ibid.,* pp. 38–40.

106. Trow, *op. cit.,* p. 278.

107. *Ibid.,* p. 277.

108. J. Stoetzel, "Voting Behavior in France," *British Journal of Sociology,* VI (1955) 18; *Italian Party Preferences,* a report prepared for the Center for International studies of M.I.T. (unpublished MS, 1953), p. 12.

109. Rudolf Heberle, *Social Movements* (New York: Appleton-Century-Crofts, 1951), pp. 228–30.

110. Charles P. Loomis and A. Beagle, "The Spread of German Nazism in Rural Areas," *American Sociological Review,* XI (1946), pp. 724–34.

111. *Ibid.*

112. G. Wright, "Agrarian Syndicalism in Postwar France," *American Political Science Review,* XLVII (1953), pp. 402–416.

113. Henry Ehrmann, "The French Peasant and Communism," *American Political Science Review,* IV (1952), p. 41.

114. Oliver H. Radkey, *The Election to the Russian Constituent Assembly of 1917* (Cambridge: Harvard University Press, 1950), pp. 70–71.

115. Sigmund Neumann, *Permanent Revolution* (New York: Harper and Bros., 1942), pp. 98–100.

116. Carl J. Friedrick, "The Agricultural Basis of Emotional Nationalism," *Public Opinion Quarterly,* VI (1937), pp. 50–61.

117. Richard Hofstadter, *The Age of Reform* (New York: Knopf, 1955), p. 128.

118. See Rudolf Heberle and A. Bertrand, "Factors Motivating Voting Behavior in a One-Party State," *Social Forces,* XXVII (1949); and Key, *op. cit.*

IV

# IV  *Electoral Systems*

# Introduction

# THE IMPACT OF ELECTORAL SYSTEMS ON REPRESENTATIVE GOVERNMENT

Harry Eckstein

I

In the preceding section, we raised two problems: under what conditions in general can representative governments be stable and effective and what in particular can formal-legal rules (constitutional structure) contribute to the viability of such governments? In this part we can pursue the latter question still further and in greater particulars, for electoral systems are the parts of constitutional structure most frequently singled out by political scientists as crucial to the workings of representative institutions. A few political scientists believe that practically the whole fate of representative government depends on electoral arrangements; almost all believe that such arrangements have some sort of important effect on the way representative governments work.

It is not difficult to see why this should be the case. Social scientists, like other scientists, are always in search of simple, economical theories—theories that can explain a great deal with very little. The hypothesis that the fate of representative governments turns mainly on their electoral arrangements certainly fills that bill, whether one believes, with Mill, that proportional representation is a kind of cure-all for democracy, or, with Hermens, that it is its fatal poison. Moreover, it is difficult to think of anything more fundamental to representative government than the electoral process. It scarcely matters whether the particulars of electoral systems are actually specified in written constitutions (as used to be the case almost invariably) or whether they were left to ordinary legislative enactments under only the broadest and vaguest constitutional guidance (as tends to be the case in the postwar constitutions). Clearly, no other aspect of representative government can be considered more truly "fundamental" to it, more truly

"constitutional," if by that term we mean political arrangements that should not be matters of constant pragmatic adjustment to contingent circumstances nor left to the whims and interests of passing majorities. After all, we have defined representative government as government in which open and regular competition for offices occurs, and it is through the electoral system that such competition is conducted and by it that its basic outcome is decided. In that sense, electoral arrangements are certainly basic to the whole of representative government; and from thinking something basic to thinking it a determinant is a small, perhaps irresistible, step.

In fact, many postwar constitutions leave the particulars of electoral arrangements to ordinary law for just that reason, not because their framers considered such arrangements to be mere "circumstantials" in the representative system. By not prescribing constitutionally such particulars, it is possible to carry on a certain amount of experimentation with electoral procedure, to discard what proves to be pernicious in practice and to strengthen what turns out beneficial. This has, in fact, been done in most of the reconstructed European democracies, all of which have had numerous electoral laws since their reconstruction. One may question the wisdom of this state of affairs. Constant experimentation with the fundamentals of governmental structure, even for unselfish purposes (and some of the recent tinkering with election laws in Europe has not been unselfish), is certainly not calculated to embed a constitution in the "effective stereotypes" of society, to help it acquire that aura of sanctity, of autonomy from human will, that turns nominal into "living" constitutions (see p. 101). Yet, if electoral systems have crucial effects upon the whole efficacy of representative government, there may also be something to be said for making them readily accessible to control in light of experience.

At any rate, electoral processes are something that

can be controlled, more readily by far than levels of economic development, degrees of political consensus, the associational structure of society, or authority relations in nongovernmental structures. That fact alone may recommend theories about their crucial significance to political scientists. Few people like to feel themselves subject to implacable forces. And in the case of electoral systems, there is little difficulty in seeing connections between the alleged cause and its supposed consequences. Successful representative government, especially in parliamentary systems, obviously requires clear party majorities or persistent, working coalitions. Clear party majorities obviously emerge only rarely from very fragmented party systems, and working coalitions are also more likely where there exist a few large parties rather than many small ones, and where men of different political persuasions hold their opinions moderately enough to work effectively with one another. The party system (especially the number and size of parties) and the political climate obviously decide in some basic way the stability and decisional effectiveness of representative governments, and both can be related easily to the operation of electoral systems. By deciding who gets to be represented, such systems affect the life chances of political organizations engaged in the competition for office and thus, presumably, help determine the number of parties in the arena. For the same reason they may also be presumed to have certain consequences upon the character of party organizations and party appeals and through the latter upon the whole atmosphere of political competition.

All this explains the modern vogue of theories relating electoral systems to the larger problems of representative government. Such theories have in fact been popular for well over a century, certainly since Mill wrote his celebrated *Considerations on Representative Government* (1861). Yet that very fact should give one pause. After a hundred years, the problem of the impact of electoral processes on other institutions is still a problem, still a subject for practical trial and error. No single theory on the subject has yet been successfully tested, and a very great many have been proposed. That in itself proves nothing, but it makes one wonder. Can it be that so obviously basic a matter as electoral procedure may nevertheless be causally negligible in regard to the operation of representative systems? In what ways, and how profoundly, do different electoral systems in fact affect representative government? What do they affect? Are they always important, never, or only under particular conditions?

These are the principal questions that the present section is meant to provoke in readers' minds. Their relevance to the larger issues of the preceding section—the requisites of viable representative government and the significance of constitutional structure—should be obvious.

## II

For purposes of discussion, we can begin by distinguishing between two sorts of electoral systems: proportional representation (PR) and the plurality system. The latter is also sometimes called, not quite so accurately, the "single-member constituency" system, or the majority system, or, more aptly but awkwardly, the "first-past-the-post" system. In the typical plurality system, the country is divided, as in Britain and the United States, into a number of constituencies electing a single representative, the candidate receiving the most votes being elected. Under proportional representation, an effort is made, by one means or another, to apportion parliamentary seats to parties in proportion to the number of their supporters in the electorate. Ideally in such a system the whole nation would be treated as a single constituency and parliamentary seats allotted in strict proportion to national electoral support, but it is in fact more common for very large electoral districts to be used and to restrict the operation of PR to these, rather than to conduct it entirely without constituencies.

An unusually "pure" system of PR was used in the Weimar Republic, and this may serve as an example of PR in actual operation. Under the Weimar system, Germany was divided into thirty-odd electoral constituencies. In each of these areas, one seat was awarded to every party for every 60,000 votes it received. Unused remainders from the basic local constituencies (note that if a party received three seats locally for 230,000 votes, it "wasted" 50,000 of these votes) were transferred to a smaller number of electoral districts, where again each party received one seat for every 60,000 votes—provided only that it had satisfied certain not very exigent qualifications on the local level. And remainders from the district pools were totaled at the national level, one seat again being given for every 60,000 votes, again with very slight qualifications.

Under this system it was possible for some votes to go unrepresented, but only very few. The Weimar system thus came very close to the ideal of PR, the faithful representation of all shades of opinion. This quintessentially democratic ideal certainly does not provide the main animus behind the plurality system. The idea of the single-member constituency originated rather in predemocratic days, when legislators were supposed to represent corporate bodies as such rather than numerical agglomerations of individuals—when representation was to be of localities, universities, economic corporations, and the like, rather than of individual persons. It was this idea of representation which justified for so long the existence of rotten boroughs in England, constituencies consisting of virtually defunct communities, with which certain aristocrats could do pretty much as they pleased. Democratization in Britain involved the reform of the more conspicuous anomalies of the old system of representation, but never made inroads on the very idea of constituency representation. From Britain the plurality system was exported to many other countries, including a great many that had no similar feudal heritage.

This division of electoral systems into two varieties, however, will serve only for purposes of very broad discussion. The world of actual electoral systems is far more complicated. It consists of a great many variations on both basic systems, as well as mixtures of the two and some procedures that are virtually unclassifiable under one heading or the other.

Systems of proportional representation, for example, differ from one another in nearly every way conceivable. They differ in size of electoral districts, some, as in Weimar Germany, being very large, others, as in the Fourth Republic, little larger than constituencies used in some plurality systems. They differ also in regard to the way people vote. In some cases, one can vote only for a list of candidates, not for individuals, those heading the lists normally receiving the seats allotted to a party; in others, voters may express their preference among candidates on a single list; in still others they may cross-vote, that is, split their votes among candidates on different lists. And systems of proportional representation differ, in still more complicated ways, in the ways seats are allocated among parties. The Weimar method is generally called the "quota" system and is by far the simplest. Under it, of course, the size of parliament changes from election to election depending on the number of voters. There are also methods for allocating fixed numbers of parliamentary seats, the so-called "highest average" and "highest remainder" systems, which we need not dwell upon for the present.

Plurality systems are on the whole less variable than PR systems, but they do involve important variations. It is perfectly possible, for example, to use multimember rather than single-member constituencies (the American states are multimember constituencies for purposes of elections to the Senate). It is also possible to use a two-ballot rather than a one-ballot system. Most of the elections under the French Third Republic were in fact conducted by the two-ballot, or run-off, method; if no candidate in a constituency received a majority of votes in the original election, a second balloting took place in that constituency a week later, and in the run-off election a mere plurality of votes was needed for election.

Nor do the variations with which electoral systems confront us stop there (even if we ignore those non-European nations and territories that divide their electorate into racial or tribal sections and use almost unfathomable arithmetic devices for calculating the outcome of elections). Germany, today, for example, uses an electoral system that appears to be half PR and half plurality, but that works as if it were nearly all PR in some respects (the actual allocation of seats) and plurality in others (the way campaigns are conducted). Some PR countries award special bonuses of seats to particularly successful parties. Some require a fairly successful showing of a party before it can use its votes to receive seats under PR at all. New methods of voting, counting votes, and allocating seats are constantly being devised. It is the easiest thing in the world to get inextricably tangled among the complexities of electoral systems. For just that reason, however, it is wise to begin reflecting on the effects of such systems by keeping in mind only the basic distinction between plurality elections and proportional representation.

## III

For a defense and justification of PR, the arguments presented by John Stuart Mill in his *Considerations on Representative Government* have scarcely ever been bettered. The particular version of PR that Mill defended was first sketched by Thomas Hare in his *Treatise on the Election of Representatives* (1859) and has been known since as the "Hare system." It is a complicated system, to put it mildly, but it has essentially three aspects:

1. Voters indicate their order of preference among as many candidates as they wish (at any rate a sizable number) on a national or other large geographic basis.

2. A quota of votes required for election is established by dividing the number of voters by the number of parliamentary seats.

3. Seats are awarded to candidates who achieve the quota by counting, to begin with, only first choices, then second choices, then third, and so on, until a full complement of legislators is elected.

(For the actual details, readers may be referred, as they are referred by Mill, to Mr. Hare's treatise —and to the selection from F. A. Hermens' *Democracy or Anarchy* included here.)

Mill defended PR, in the first place, on the simple ground of democratic values, at any rate as he conceived them. PR would lessen the possibility of a tyrannous majority by assuring minorities of some sort of representation. It would help to make parliament into something like a faithful image of the nation, rather than distorting representation in favor of the majority by forcing minorities to waste their votes on the constituency level. Furthermore, in addition to assuring the representation of minorities, PR would make certain that the majorities of parliament really reflect the majorities in the country; it would assure *true* majority government. Mill's much quoted argument on this subject may be worth quoting once again:

There is not equal suffrage where every single individual does not count for as much as any other single individual in the community. But it is not only a minority who suffer. Democracy, thus constituted, does not even attain its ostensible object, that of giving the powers of government in all cases to the numerical majority. It does something very different: it gives them to a majority of the majority; who may be, and often are, but a minority of the whole. All principles are most effectually tested by extreme cases. Suppose then, that, in a country governed by equal and universal suffrage, there is a contested election in every constituency, and every election is carried by a small majority. The Parliament thus brought together represents little more than a bare majority of the people. This Parliament proceeds to legislate, and adopts important measures by a bare majority of itself. What guarantee is there that these measures accord with the wishes of a majority of the people? Nearly half the electors, having been outvoted at the hustings, have had no influence at all in the decision; and the whole of these may be, a majority of them probably are, hostile to the measures, having voted against those by whom they have been carried. Of the remaining electors, nearly half have chosen representatives who, by supposition, have voted against the measures. It is possible, therefore, and not at all improbable, that the opinion which has prevailed was agreeable only to a minority of the nation, though a majority of that portion of it whom the institutions of the country have erected into a ruling class. If democracy means the certain ascendancy of the majority, there are no means of insuring that but by allowing every individual figure to tell equally in the summing up. Any minority left out, either purposely or by the play of the machinery, gives the power not to the majority, but to a minority in some other part of the scale.

This potential power of a minority is illustrated most clearly, of course, where parties have won great parliamentary majorities without even a slight majority in the country, an occurrence familiar enough in plurality systems.

It is important to add that, for Mill, the case for PR did not rest solely on democratic values. In his view, PR also "attains incidentally several other ends of scarcely inferior importance": it makes government not only more representative, but more effective. (Nowhere than in this argument does the old belief that what promotes numerical democracy also promotes good government emerge more strikingly.) For various reasons (readers should consult Chapter VII of Mill's essay) Mill felt that PR would strengthen the ties between constituents and their representatives, improve the intellectual qualities of representatives, and, by strengthening and making more constructive the opposition in parliament, still further improve its legislative product.

Therefore, Mill recommends PR on grounds both of democracy and good government, and thereby poses the two essential problems of the "grand debate" in political science about electoral systems. Does PR or the plurality system better satisfy the ideals of democratic representation? Does one system or the other better promote efficient government, government that is stable and decisionally effective?

Understandably enough, few have questioned the superiority of PR as a system of democratic representation. The constituency system, after all, did originate in predemocratic days, and, for all subsequent adjustments, has never been entirely democratized. The minority in a constituency does wind up with nothing to show for its vote; great distortions of popular opinion do occur on the parliamentary level; some sizable social groups can scarcely hope for any sort of representation. It is true that some systems of PR do not, in fact, mirror public opinion very closely in the legislature, but none distort it quite so much as plurality elections. On the other hand, a very strong attack has been made in recent years on the notion that PR promotes effective as well as representative democracy. Some political scientists indeed consider it the source of all the essential ills of democracy and thus confront us with a poignant dilemma: in making democracy more representative, we also lessen its chances of effective functioning, and indeed of survival.

F. A. Hermens, whose main (by no means only) attack on PR is reprinted in this volume, is the principal exponent of this point of view—although certainly not the first. Even in Mill's day some views like those of Hermens were in the air, for Mill addresses himself to them. Arguments against PR nearly as strong as those of Hermens can be found in Herman Finer's famous Fabian pamphlet of 1924, *The Case against Proportional Representation;* and similar views can be found in Laski's *A Grammar of Politics* and Friedrich's *Constitutional Government and Democracy.* But nowhere is the logical case against PR, and the empirical corroboration of the logical case, made to seem more overwhelming than in Hermens' work. The details of that case can be left to the selection we reprint, but the gist of the argument and its main basis ought to be summarized here to indicate its force and extensiveness.

Hermens argues that the probable results of proportional representation are the "pluralistic stagnation" of representative government, through pluralistic stagnation a general malfunctioning of democracy and disaffection from it, and through these the probable collapse of democratic institutions. By pluralistic stagnation, he means mainly (though not only) the incapacitation of democracy's decision-making processes, which occurs as a result of a number of consequences flowing from PR. The first and most important is the splintering of political parties into large numbers of small organizations. Such splintering takes place chiefly because nothing under PR seems to compel any large-scale cooperation between groups with different political views. All societies, even the most consensual, consist of a great many segments having different political interest and opinions. In plurality systems, however, these segments (so the argument goes) become aggregated in a small number, perhaps only two, organizations of electoral competition, since no group can reasonably hope to win any representation without mobilizing large numbers of supporters in some constituencies—that is to say, without affiliating itself to an organization that integrates several shades of interest and opinion. This situation obviously does not exist under PR, and it is the less likely to exist the more an actual PR system corresponds to the pure type. Moreover, PR radicalizes as well as splinters political forces—makes them more dogmatic, more "ideological," more incapable of compromise, and thus impedes integration on the parliamentary no less than the electoral level.

In plurality systems the basic point of electoral competition seems to be to win over undecided voters in order to augment a party's committed supporters and thus give the party a majority or plurality of all voters. Since undecided voters are, presumably, more moderate than committed voters, party programs and party styles are pulled in a moderate direction and the whole of political life is made thereby less intense and hyperprincipled— and more consensual, for parties compete for the support of the same small group of people. The undecided, curiously enough, decide the whole tone of the system. Clearly (or so it seems) the logic of PR is the reverse. Nor is there anything under PR to keep parties from becoming mere organs of the special interests in society, rather than brokers of a variety of interests. The over-all result is a parliament split into a larger number of groupings, more concerned with the pursuit of vested interests than with their integration and less capable of the pragmatic compromise needed to form stable coalitions and reach positive decisions. And the result is either great ministerial instability and decisional inefficiency, or blatant parliamentary *Kuhhandel*— shameless "cattle-dealing" among the spokesmen of particular interests—or the dishonest compromise of dogmatically professed principles, whenever coalitions are formed and decisions actually made. In either case, democracy is the loser.

Nor does Hermens stop there. He launches a frontal attack also on Mill's argument that PR improves the quality of legislators, adducing numerous reasons for holding that it has precisely the opposite effect. And he even attacks the idea that PR is preferable to the plurality system on grounds of democracy, by arguing that it vitiates democratic relations on the intraparty level—though that part of his case is less plausible than the others, in view of what was known even when Hermens wrote about the chances of intraparty democracy under any electoral system.

The temptation is strong, in the light of such arguments, to grant Mill half of his case and his opponents half of theirs: to admit that PR is more faithfully representative of opinions and the plu-

rality system more conducive to good government, and to draw from this whatever conclusions follow for a workable theory of democratic government. But it is far from certain that this is the right tack to take. There are reasons for thinking that one should not grant either party even half its case, but argue instead that the issue is far more complicated than they make it out to be or that electoral systems have little, if anything, to do with the character and performance of representative systems, compared with the deeper, more intractable factors discussed in the preceding section. For all their belief in the efficacy of electoral contrivances, Lakeman and Lambert, in the selection reprinted, provide plenty of ammunition for either of these positions.

Do PR systems really fragment and dogmatize party conflict? and plurality systems really integrate and moderate it? If we look mainly at Great Britain and Weimar Germany, the theory holds well enough. But the moment one looks further, it comes to seem much more uncertain. Readers will recall from the Introduction to Part I to what extent Friedrich had to modify his theories about PR when he looked at practically all the countries but Germany that used PR in his day (see p. 22). The present day furnishes equally striking exceptions to the supposed rule. Italy today uses PR, but there has occurred in Italy neither any fragmentation nor any radicalization of party life. If anything, the opposite has occurred: the Christian Democrats are a very large multi-interest party very much in the American and British style; the coalition of Communists and fellow-traveling socialists furnishes a sort of opposition bloc; and among the more extreme socialists, as well as on the right, dogma and intensity seem to be waning rather than increasing. Although the present German electoral system works very much like pure PR in operation, there has taken place in postwar Germany a constant trend toward the polarization of politics in two great electoral blocs and dogmatic ideology has almost totally disappeared. Such unexpected cases can also be found among plurality systems. Most elections under the French Third Republic, for example, were conducted under the plurality procedure, yet party competition was highly fragmented and radical, while parliament displayed every symptom of pluralistic stagnation. Then, too, there is the unfortunate case of pre-Civil War Spain, where the introduction of the English system of elections led to anything but an English type of political competition.

One could multiply such cases, on both sides of the issue, at considerable length (the Lakeman and Lambert selection may be used to augment those mentioned), but the cases cited above will suffice at least to cast some doubts on easy generalizations about the consequences of electoral systems. At the very least, they indicate a need for considering alternative positions. If the more popular hypotheses about electoral systems cannot really hold when tested by sufficiently broad comparisons, one of four other positions must be the right one.

One is the position that electoral systems do affect the workings of representative government in important ways, but that hypotheses about them must be much more complicated than those we have discussed. After all, as we have seen, even electoral systems in the same basic category, PR or plurality, differ from one another in important ways; and it may be that even slight variations on a basic system make that system have effects greatly different from its effects in a pure form.

Take the Third Republic as an obvious example. To be sure, the great majority of its elections were conducted under the plurality system. But the version of the plurality system used in the Third Republic did not correspond exactly to the British; instead, it required for election an absolute majority on the first ballot and made provisions for *ballotage* (run-off elections) if no candidate obtained such a majority. This version of the plurality system, it might be argued, tends to have effects similar to PR, or at any rate different from purer forms of plurality election. For example, the run-off system may not compel electoral collaboration among groups that are somewhat but not very like-minded in the first election, since the whole system minimizes the winning chances of their more serious opponents before the run-off. It may also lead to purely temporary alliances among formally independent groups for purposes of the run-off elections, based on the local performance of the various parties in the first election, and thus prevent the more permanent, national electoral alliances among political groups that characterize a two-party system. It may thus have no lasting integrative effects on party structure. This tendency, it has in fact been argued, is what really developed in the Third Republic. Many figures could be cited to show that, under the pure plurality conditions prevailing in French run-off elections, a pronounced tendency toward the integration of parties occurred. (Most constituency seats were decided either by an absolute majority on first ballot or in two-cornered or three-cornered contests, much in the British manner, on the second.) Electoral alliances, however, differed from constituency to constituency and rarely survived from one election to the next.

Such a case might also be made about the past and present German electoral systems. It is true that the electoral processes of the Bonn Federal Republic work practically like the pure PR of Weimar from the standpoint of allocating seats among the qualifying parties. But it is also true that under the dual system elections are conducted as if they were practically pure plurality elections: half the parliamentary seats are given to individuals who win single-member constituency elections, so that elections tend to revolve around persons rather than party lists, nearly as much as in countries using a straight plurality procedure. Furthermore, no German splinter-group at all can today hope to be represented at the federal level, for it now takes a certain minimum performance (three single-member seats or 5 per cent of the total votes in the Federal Republic) to qualify for the benefits of PR.

These changes, it might be argued, make all the difference, not just some slight difference, to the party system and the manner of party competition, and through these to the functioning of the whole government. Simple generalizations about plurality and proportional systems of election from this point of view are bound to be inadequate, but one can still maintain that electoral systems matter a great deal to the workings of democracy and defend constitutional engineering via such systems, by taking into account the particular nuances as well as the general characteristics of electoral procedures—or rather by focusing entirely on the nuances.

That is one alternative to broad generalizations about PR and plurality elections. A second is to argue that the particular environments in which electoral systems are used, more than the procedural variations they embody, decide their consequences —or that both do so. It may well be that every electoral system has certain political effects inherent in it, certain "logical" consequences; and it may be that these are fully discoverable by logical reflection. It may also be the case, however, that the inherent tendencies of electoral processes can manifest themselves only under certain particular environmental conditions—only, in effect, if nothing in a society prevents them from being the primary influences on other aspects of government. Even the most ardent electoral-systems theorists will grant that the performance of governments is affected by all sorts of other forces, and from this it is a short step to granting that these other forces might not merely reduce the significance of electoral systems in certain cases but sometimes even nullify or reverse their "logical" tendencies.

To take a simple instance: suppose that plurality elections really do normally have a moderating effect on politics by concentrating party efforts on undecided voters; but now suppose the undecided voters are not moderates, that they are extremists, undecided between the extremism of the left and of the right? What then? Obviously then the effect of plurality elections will be, if anything, just the reverse. And this supposition is not far-fetched: the latent extremist who has not yet settled on an object for his extremism is not perhaps as uncommon as one might think.

Of course, this is only a hypothetical example. Just what the conditions are that may nullify or reverse the logical tendencies of electoral systems we do not as yet know. But one thing seems certain. Whatever the logical effects of electoral systems might be, they cannot manifest themselves in actuality unless politicians adjust their actions to these systems. Politicians, however, are unlikely to do so unless their primary object is to attain office within a given governmental system or unless the adjustments they must make to a system do not themselves lessen their chances of election or require actions running counter to deep and unadjustable beliefs. A really dogmatic politician is unlikely to give up his dogmas merely for the sake of electoral advantage; what use is electoral victory to him if in achieving it he frustrates his dogmatic purposes? An opportunistic politician representing dogmatic constituents will think twice, just because he is an opportunist interested in election, before he compromises his constituents' ideals. And politicians who are more interested in public attention than a seat, or more intent upon undermining a government than playing a role in it, or more concerned with representing particular interests than the complex business of "aggregating" interests, are not unknown. In other words, electoral systems can manifest their inherent tendencies only if politics and politicians are predominantly of a certain kind; certain conditions may give them great causal significance, others prevent them from having it—granted that, to make this argument strict, one should be a good deal more specific about these conditions than we have been here.

Both these alternative positions to simple generalizations about PR and plurality systems—that their effects depend upon other conditions and upon the particular arrangements more than the general character of an electoral process—give rise, however, to a common problem. If one once begins to qualify general hypotheses with all sorts of particular conditions, where does one stop? How stop short of giving up general hypotheses altogether? One might then be forced to argue, for example, that political party life under the Weimar Republic was fragmented and radicalized, not because of PR, but because of the particular version of PR used under the particular conditions prevailing in Weimar Germany. Similarly, one might argue that it is not the system of plurality elections that gives Britain two moderate political parties, but the particular plurality system used in Britain under the particular conditions prevailing in Britain. How, then, does one know that it was indeed PR in Weimar Germany and plurality elections in Britain that had the consequences attributed to them and not something else about these societies, quite independent of their electoral systems? And how does one discover what particular nuances of the electoral procedures, or what particular aspects of social and political life, among all those that might be emphasized, are really worth emphasizing? How

does one test theories about such matters, if not by comparisons?

Once one starts in that direction, the end would seem to be the one Mackenzie, in the lecture reprinted here, arrives at: to give up comparatively tested generalizations almost altogether and to present instead descriptive surveys of particular electoral processes, interpreted in offhand ways according to the particular inspiration of the interpreter. That is the third alternative position one can take on the analysis of electoral systems. Mackenzie sees some point in it, but it is difficult to see just what Mackenzie sees in it—what findings useful to political science (not cultivated conversation and BBC talks) might emerge. Rather than settle for that position, it might be better to explore a fourth: that electoral systems do not in fact have important consequences for other aspects of the political process but only express, whatever their character may be, the deeper determinants of the politics of a society.

## IV

Needless to say, political science has not yet settled these issues; otherwise, there would be little point in raising them here. But readers who want to explore them further should consult certain materials supplementary to those appearing below, for there is certainly more to be said about them than we have said.

Unfortunately, a very important monograph, perhaps the best on the subject, by Maurice Duverger and others on the broad effects of electoral systems, has not been translated from the French; Duverger's ideas, however, can be found in his book, *Political Parties: Their Organization and Activity in the Modern State* (1954), and in a long article, "The Influence of the Electoral System on Political Life," published in *The International Social Science Bulletin* (Summer, 1951). A basic general treatment of electoral systems is given in W. J. M. Mackenzie, *Free Elections* (1958), and the works by Hermens and Lakeman and Lambert, from which excerpts appear below, should, of course, be read in full, as should a later work by Hermens, *Europe between Democracy and Anarchy* (1951).

These general treatments might well be augmented by studies of the electoral systems of particular countries. The list of these is very large, and references can be found easily in the bibliographies of the standard comparative politics texts, but a few of the better ones in English dealing with Western European systems might be mentioned: for Britain, D. E. Butler, *The Electoral System in Britain, 1918–1951* (1953), and the Nuffield General Election Studies, the most recent of which is

Butler and Rose, *The British General Election of 1959* (1960); for France, Peter Campbell, *French Electoral Systems and Elections* (1958); for Germany, James K. Pollock, editor, *German Democracy at Work* (1955), and Uwe Kitzinger, *German*

*Electoral Politics* (1960). Very useful also, especially for making large-scale comparisons, are the short descriptions of elections and electoral systems throughout the world issued periodically by the Institute of Electoral Research, London.

# THE DYNAMICS
# OF PROPORTIONAL REPRESENTATION

## F. A. Hermens

When analyzing what we may call the dynamics of P.R. we shall, for the time being, omit any reference to the various systems of P.R., such as, for example, the Hare system and the list system. The number of P.R. systems that have been invented so far exceeds three hundred, and many more might still be presented to us. Medieval schoolmen might well have concluded that if there are so many different varieties of a doctrine which claims to be the absolute truth, something must be wrong with the premises from which it is claimed that all of these different conclusions have been drawn. Monsieur Georges Lachapelle, the veteran leader of the P.R. forces in France, seems to provide ammunition for such arguments when in his defense of P.R. he frankly states: "There do not exist different ways of ensuring absolute electoral justice; only one way can exist."[1] It is not necessary for us to enter at this juncture into a consideration as to whether this be true or not. Let it suffice to say that all systems of P.R. are bound to have one feature in common: A certain number of candidates are to be elected from one constituency,[2] and prominent supporters of P.R. will usually admit that this number should not be less than five. Candidates are then to be elected in proportion to the number of votes cast for them. Nothing else but these two conditions which represent truisms are underlying the following analysis of the principal results of P.R. They, therefore, apply to all different brands of P.R.

Reprinted from F. A. Hermens, *Democracy or Anarchy?* (Notre Dame, Ind.: The Review of Politics, University of Notre Dame, 1938), pp. 15–74, by permission of the author.

## P.R. AND THE SPLITTING-UP OF PARTIES

The clearest proof of the assertion that electoral systems are a dynamic rather than a neutral factor lies in the fact that the majority system promotes a concentration of parties, and that P.R. facilitates —and thereby creates—a multiplication of parties. Under the majority system, the number of candidates who have a chance to win is restricted. All political groups are aware of the fact that there is only one way of making sure of success, and that is to have an absolute majority over all other parties. Only a party which can hope to achieve this can risk fighting the electoral battle alone. The others realize that if they fight under their own banner exclusively they risk turning over the coveted seats to their opponents. Hence voters with somewhat similar views will be ready to combine in support of the same candidate. The best chance of success is enjoyed when there is warrant for the expectation that more than fifty per cent of the votes will be cast for their man. And since those on the other side of the fence will also aim at having more than fifty per cent the result will be a tendency for the voters to concentrate on two great parties. To be sure, this tendency is at first confined to the individual constituencies only. But if and insofar as the situation is similar in other constituencies, a two-party system will develop, and the political line-up will be as simple as democratic institutions permit.

The result will be somewhat different if in the various constituencies a different set of parties fight for a majority. Under such conditions the majority

THE DYNAMICS OF PROPORTIONAL REPRESENTATION

system will not create a system of two parties. It will rather engender a tendency to set up two great political blocs, which may operate in much the same fashion as two major parties. Wherever one party has little hope to carry a constituency itself, it will be inclined to support the candidate of a party with similar views, if only for the purpose of defeating the candidate of some other party to which it is definitely opposed. Reciprocity may be expected, and often such electoral coalitions are concluded for the entire country. The rank and file of the voters—whose unfailing political instinct clearly and rightly regards parties as means to an end rather than as ends in themselves—consider such arrangements so natural that they will often spontaneously form coalitions in the elections even without the guidance of their political leaders. Such mutual support means that the parties concerned are no longer independent of one another. Their parliamentary strength is based upon a common electorate, and this will tend to enforce a common policy. It implies that such parties will suppress as far as possible the points upon which they differ and emphasize the points they have in common. Ultimately, out of an electoral alliance there may develop a fusion, and the system of two blocs may become a system of two parties.

So much for the majority system. If elections are fought under a P.R. system, it is no longer necessary to have a majority of the votes cast in order to record a victory. The percentage of votes actually required to secure a seat varies with the brand of P.R. employed. Complete "proportionality" would be attained only if the whole area covered by the elections formed one big constituency. In this case the percentage of votes required would be determined by the number of seats that were available. If, for example, in the United States the four hundred and thirty-five members of the House of Representatives were to be elected in one huge constituency, the fraction required would be one four hundred and thirty-fifths, or about one-fifth of one per cent.[3] But the friends of P.R. have always been afraid of carrying proportionality to this extreme and have therefore divided the country into a number of smaller constituencies. Such constituencies return a smaller number of members; hence the percentage required in order to gain a seat is greater. In order to have a practical basis of comparison, let us on this occasion consider the electoral system which was in force in the German Reich from 1920 until 1933.[4] A total of 60,000 votes was required in a normal constituency (*Wahlkreis*), of which constituencies there were thirty-five. With the exception of East Prussia each of these constituencies was combined with one or two others into a district constituency (*Wahlkreisverband*). If more than 30,000 votes had been polled for a given party in a constituency, and if the remainder of the district constituency provided enough votes to insure a total of 60,000 that party was entitled to a seat. Small parties concentrated their efforts on winning these first 30,000 votes, experience demonstrating that this could often be done with only three per cent of the votes cast. This may be taken as fairly representative of the situation created by the P.R. system. On the other hand, we may safely assume that if a party tried to capture a seat under the majority system it would have to poll at least twenty-five per cent of the votes.[5] Hence if we disregard the many qualitative elements which a quantitative comparison cannot take into account, we may say that it is eight times as easy to succeed with a new party under P.R. as it is under a majority system. It need not be emphasized that this difference is of material importance. After every election the battlefield is strewn with the remains of defeated candidates and unsuccessful parties. With P.R. many more will be successful, and soon the political map of the country may be radically changed.

It is obvious that the implications of this fact are greater than the supporters of P.R. assume. In their view P.R. will only achieve the "just representation" of those groups which have been organized under a majority system but failed to obtain as many seats as would correspond to the number of votes received.[6] Actually, however, the new conditions created by P.R. will produce entirely new groups, the emergence of which was quite unforeseen when the new electoral system was adopted—groups of which nobody ever dreamed and for which most supporters of P.R. would have been far from demanding "electoral justice." Any group can win which has the required number of followers, full though it be of faddists and cranks. In Germany things went so far that the midwives could threaten the Minister of the Interior that they would set up a party of their own unless their demands were met. It is true that even under P.R. most of these parties will fail. But some will succeed. It matters little that at the first attempt the measure of success has been small; the voters have been convinced that the new party is a practical proposition and that the votes cast for it are no longer "thrown away." Thus the few members of parliamentary bodies who have been elected will act, as it was termed in Belgium, as a "center of infection," and the new party is bound to grow until it reaches the limit set for it by the appetites of rival parties likewise desirous of gaining seats under the easy conditions provided by P.R. From our point of view it is interesting to note that the change is not confined to the composition of parliaments; it deeply affects the political complexion of the country as a whole. Many, perhaps most, of those who vote for a new party are persons who would not have thought of doing so a few years before. They were then quite satisfied to pursue their political activities within the framework of those major parties which the majority system had created. But given the chance at reorientation afforded them by P.R., they now consider it natural that there be a party to represent every shade of political opinion. This means that political differences are not only more clearly expressed, but multiplied and intensified. The new parties will evolve a central and local leadership which thinks exclusively in the narrow terms of the new group and its interests. After they have been molded by the new situation in which they find themselves, they will try to mold their followers in the same way. For this purpose they will develop a party literature and a party press. Those actively interested in politics will receive their political education from this source. Those who fail to read the press will be exposed to the propaganda of the new concepts in political meetings or in discussions with their neighbors on the street or in the workshop. As a result, a new political tradition will have been formed and the "will of the people" made quite different from what it was under the majority system. Is it not clear that P.R. is not at all what its friends claim it to be, a map which faithfully reproduces on a minor scale the territorial divisions of the country? Rather, it is a device which divides the nation against itself.

## RADICALIZATION OF PARTIES

There is another point to be considered. The parties created by P.R. differ in their very nature from those that have been molded by the majority system, the most powerful agency of moderation yet devised. This system forces every party desiring a seat to capture a majority. The major hurdle which the rules of this game require contestants to take is not the getting of votes from the bulk of the old party members. Most of them will vote for the party in any event. It is necessary only to keep their enthusiasm alive and make them missionaries for the party, impressing others with their overwhelming numbers and winning converts by their active endeavors. The real obstacle which all the party efforts are exerted to overcome is the doubtful allegiance of the undecided voters, who may vote for this party or that as their notions or their convictions dictate. It is the candidate who can win them into his flock who stands the best chance of winning the race. But these people are not easy to win over. Disraeli spoke of them as "conscientious men" and "deeply meditative individuals," distinguished not only by their "pensive turn of mind," but by "a charitable vein that seems to pervade their being."[7] They often wait until the last minute before they make up their minds, and they never tell before the election how they intend to vote. Every party manager hates them, but democracy needs them badly. Because they belong to no party organization they are free to enforce their will upon all parties. More than any other body of voters they judge a party not according to the beauty of its written programs but on the basis of its concrete achievements in the past or the hope it holds out for concrete achievements in the future. If they are disappointed with the party for which they voted in the last election, or if they have decided that it is time for the opposition to have its turn, they shift their votes from one party to the other without any sentiment in the matter. We call them the marginal voters. They govern political life in the same way that marginal utility, according to some economists, governs the price of commodities.

The existence of an influential group like this means the death knell of radicalism. It makes it possible for democracy to live. An example will serve to make this clear. Suppose there should be a constituency in which ten per cent of the voters belong to the extreme Right and the same number to the extreme Left, thirty per cent each to the moderate Right and the moderate Left, and the remaining twenty per cent form the marginal vote. What happens under such conditions is most clearly evidenced in those instances where (as was the case in Republican France) there are two ballots. If no candidate has obtained an absolute majority on the first ballot, run-off elections are held and the candidate with the greatest number of votes is proclaimed elected. Under such circumstances each party puts up its own candidates for the first ballot, with no risk involved, and the division of votes occurs as above. For the run-off elections, however, the picture will have to be simplified. If the members of the party of the extreme Right continue to vote for their own candidate, they run the risk that the followers of the extreme Left may be more practical and vote for the candidate of the moderate Left, thus more or less assuring his victory. Hence both parties of the extremes will probably withdraw their candidates, and a straight fight ensues between the moderate Right and the moderate Left. The issue is decided by the marginal voters of the center, who once more demonstrate their strong tendency to eliminate the more radical of the two candidates.

So it is that the extremist parties have to bear the cost of the bargain. They are far away from the marginal voter and his sympathies. Even if we modify the illustration given above so that the extremists of the Right have thirty per cent of the voters and the moderate Rightists only ten per cent the former are not likely to succeed. The moderate Rightists might vote for their candidate to the last man, but the marginal voters would be likely to be scared into the support of the candidate of the moderate Left, who would then be elected. Radicals[8] all over the world are aware of this and complain bitterly of the injustice[9] of the majority system. As they express it, they are not allowed to vote *for* a candidate, but must vote *against* somebody else in order to prevent the most undesirable man from being elected. A witty Frenchman neatly put it as follows: "De la modération, sapristi, si l'on veut vraiment la révolution"—"Moderation, mind you, if you really want revolution."

Advocates of P.R. of whose democratic convictions there can be no doubt have frequently joined the extremists in complaining of these results of the majority system. In their view the effect of the majority system has merely been to drive the Radicals underground; it would have been better, they argue, if they had been allowed to come out into the open and discuss their grievances, as a P.R. system would permit. These people overlook the fact that the blow dealt to Radicals by the majority system is so severe that the evil is cured once and for all. The first ones to change their attitude are, for reasons mentioned above, the bulk of the party members. They might have continued to support a radical party if it had been a practical proposition; but since it is not they are angry with their leaders who have enticed them into throwing their votes away and are ready to support a more moderate party. This gives them at least the satisfaction of having been on the winning side. Actual or potential political leaders may be more reluctant to change sides. As a rule, however, their ambitions will not be satisfied with service in the ranks of the Radicals if this service brings no recognition and no results. Sometime or other many of them will join the ranks of more moderate parties, which then, of course, will be strong enough to assimilate them. Republican France, in particular, was full of illustrations of this truth. It is well known that such men as Gambetta, Clemenceau and Millerand started out as leaders of the radical Left, but came to power only after they had discarded the radical ways of their political youth. If radical leaders are unwilling to make this change, they will be generals without an army. Like Charles Maurras and the brilliant band of intellectuals whom he gathered around himself in the "Action Française," they will be a nuisance rather than a danger for the democratic statesmen of their country.

This change from radicalism to moderation may at first be based on purely tactical reasons, convictions remaining radical even if words and actions are no longer so. But this is not likely to continue for any length of time. It does not contribute to a man's success to be without faith in the rightness of what he does. And, as William James has pointed out, convictions tend to follow actions. Moreover, in a democracy one is continually called upon to explain and defend what one does. It is necessary to find as good reasons for one's actions as possible, and since one must repeat these reasons again and

again he is likely in the long run to become convinced himself. When we consider the well-known statesmen mentioned above we find no reason whatsoever to doubt that they sincerely believed what they did was right. In the case of more than one we know how bitter was the inner struggle that led to the change of view. But the reasons given for the decision are so convincing to the outsider as to leave no doubt that those who set them forth were themselves thoroughly convinced.

In the practical working out of problems in government, the outcome of events seems to justify the course of moderation. On the one hand, the members of the extreme Left have to travel the same road as their counterparts on the extreme Right, which means that radical groups can no longer mutually provoke one another. Such moderation tends to oil the machinery of democracy. Parties with moderate views will readily cooperate in order to form a government; friction between them will be comparatively slight; and the work of government will go on in a satisfactory manner. The voters will not fail to take notice, and so, in spite of the war of words which is inseparable from the workings of democratic government, there will be agreement on basic matters. To be sure, there will still remain a handful of unconvinced Radicals, and they will manifest their dissatisfaction from election to election by running candidates of their own. But the vote of the people will defeat them as often as they try their luck; they will lose their prestige and in time may be considered nothing short of a public nuisance. It is not probable that such groups will resort to revolutionary means to gain their ends. They are unlikely to be strong enough to do so. If they do, the government will have the full moral support of the country if it employs all the weapons of state in battle against them, and their inevitable defeat will be hailed as a victory for democracy.

It has often been asserted that if democratic government is to be workable there must be a basic homogeneity of views and interests among the people concerned. In this connection, the famous remarks of Lord Balfour in his preface to Walter Bagehot's *English Constitution* are frequently quoted:

Our alternating Cabinets, though belonging to different Parties, have never differed about the foundations of society. And it is evident that our whole political machinery pre-supposes a people so fundamentally at one that they can safely afford to bicker; and so sure of their own moderation that they are not dangerously disturbed by the never-ending din of political conflict. May it always be so.[10]

From the above analysis we are inclined to assume that it will indeed "always be so" if and when in a country like England the majority system is retained. For in this case the integrating effects of the electoral system will give battle to whatever dis-integrating forces there are in the country and it seems that in this fight the distribution of forces is such that democracy is bound to come off vic-toriously. In other words, the majority system of voting, instead of presupposing basic hemogeneity in a country, will tend to create it. This is a rather far-reaching conclusion, supported ·by arguments which the author purposes to go into more fully on another occasion. Suffice it here to say that condi-tions are basically different as soon as a P.R. sys-tem is adopted. Members of a radical party may be a comparatively small minority, but they will be able to pick up a seat here and there, and if the electoral law permits them to utilize their surpluses all over the country their parliamentary groups will easily number one or two dozen members in a short time. Under normal conditions they may not, in spite of P.R., be able to achieve more than that. Nevertheless, the help given them by the possession of these few seats is of inestimable value. The can-didates of the party remain on the official ballots; elections give them a chance to advertise themselves under favorable conditions; their force must be taken into account in every constituency, hence their opponents must attack them everywhere, and these attacks often do them more good than harm by giving them publicity. Finally, let it be stated that the privileges enjoyed by members of parlia-ment are invaluable. Their salaries provide a living for their professional agitators; a certain percentage may be levied upon them to pay the major part of the party expenses; and last but not least, the privi-lege of immunity given to members of parliament-ary bodies in most democratic countries is used to the limit as a cover for their defamation of their opponents, an essential part of radical propaganda. Thus, if P.R. gives to these radical groups, under normal conditions, only a comparatively small num-ber of seats, it at least contributes greatly toward keeping them alive; whereas under the majority system they sustain failure after failure, with the result that they tend to disappear completely from the political scene.

It must be further noted that P.R. creates for these groups a heaven on earth when economic conditions grow bad. Then comes their great chance —to profit from the protest vote which such con-ditions invariably create. The experience of every great country demonstrates that with an economic crisis comes a landslide. People blame everything—unemployment, high taxes, low profits in business, and so on and so forth—on the government, until millions of voters are induced to change their poli-tical allegiance. The majority system gives them little choice. There is only the one great and comparatively moderate democratic opposition—whether a single party or a bloc of parties—and this big basin is the normal reservoir for the waters of discontent. The voters know all too well that if they vote for one of the more radical small parties, the temper of which may more adequately express their angry mood, their votes are thrown away. There will be a three-cornered fight and the old government which they dislike so much will have a good chance to be returned to power with a mere plurality of the votes cast. Hence most voters will support the moderate opposition, which will be swept into power, take up its work with renewed vigor, and lead the country out of the depression. The desired result will have been accomplished by democratic methods.

Under P.R., however, the extremist parties do have a chance to get the protest vote, and they exploit it to the utmost, blaming existing difficulties not only on one of the democratic parties but on the "democratic system" as a whole. The more incensed the voters are by reason of the distressed condition of the country and the apparent failure of the government to do anything about it, the more they will be inclined to fall into the well-placed nets of the extremists. These are in an excel-lent position. It is part and parcel of their policy never to compromise themselves by taking active part in a democratic government or voting for un-popular measures. In the United States they might well hold forth like this: "To be sure, the Republi-cans have led the country into this depression. But the Democrats won't do anything about it. Have you forgotten the many mistakes—nay, crimes—which they have been guilty of during their periods in power? We of the xxx have never been tainted with the corruption of democratic politics. We never will be, for when we come into power we will make an end of all the democratic mecha-nism which creates corruption; we will drive the Jews and the foreigners out, and establish a truly American government for Americans." Is it any wonder that such arguments are effective?

Again, such extremists are bound to have most excellent allies in those whom they declare to be their greatest foes, the extremists on the other side of the fence. In Europe after the War, for example, corresponding to the extremism of the Fascist groups at the Right was the extremism of the Com-munists at the Left. Such groups always declare that they hate each other to the death. So they do. But this does not prevent them from giving each other all possible help. So the Fascists are able to win great popularity by playing up the Red scare. Many peaceful citizens who ordinarily take no inter-est in politics rally enthusiastically to the banners of a party which claims that it alone can terminate the Communist menace to house and home. To prove the imminence of the Communist danger the Fascists will point to the Communists in parliament and to the hundreds of thousands of voters who sent them there—not mentioning that most of these voters had nothing in mind other than to lodge a protest against economic misery. The Communists, in their turn, will play the same game. "Look what the insolent Fascists are doing. They combine all the forces of reaction in order to enslave the workingman and drag him along the way that leads to exploitation and to war." Many Leftists, workers in particular, will be frightened by these dire warnings and vote for the Communists. And it will not be long before a substantial portion of the electorate is rallying behind one or the other of these extremist groups in order to defend themselves against a danger which they themselves are creating.

The crisis comes when each of the two radical groups gains a numerical strength in parliament which approaches one-half of the available seats. In this case the remaining democratic parties can form a majority only if they all support the government. This seems quite the natural thing to do. So, in September 1930, when in Germany the National Socialists and Communists between them had 184 seats out of the possible 577 the Socialist leader and Prussian Premier, Otto Braun, called for a "Koalition aller Vernünftigen," a "coalition of all reasonable men." He overlooked the fact that no matter how necessary this coalition might be, it would sap all the vigor and force from democracy, for it meant the end of the democratic opposition. A democracy needs such an opposition as much as it needs a government.[11] The opposition is the only effective instrument whereby the electorate can check up on the government and see to it that the will of the people is obeyed. But suppose that a democratic opposition does not exist. What then can the people do but vote for its non-democratic substitute? The result is that the rules of the game are falsified: the democrats have a monopoly of responsibility, and their opponents a monopoly of opposition and irresponsibility. Further, the burden of responsibility is more difficult to carry than it ever was before. On the one hand, the depression has created problems which it would be difficult for any government to solve; on the other hand, this type of government is more seriously hampered by internal strife than any other. It consists of a number of democratic parties which claim to be widely different from one another and would normally be facing one another as government and opposition. Cooperation will be most reluctantly given, since views will differ on every question that may arise; hence there will always be delayed action, precisely what ought not to happen in a period of crisis. The extremists are swift to denounce such coalition as immoral. The democratic parties, they say, used to be willing to fight for their convictions, but they are so no longer; they stand together now, despite their recent animosity, solely in order to get all the spoils without having to risk a fight for them. And sometimes the additional charge will be made that these democratic parties are all so corrupt that an effective opposition led by any of them

would compromise them all, hence they prefer to cooperate and hush everything up.

The average democratic voter, human as he is, naturally ends by getting so disgusted with his old democratic parties that he turns his back on them and swells the forces of the extremists.[12] He does not realize that after a time his protest becomes *too* effective. The two extremist groups may, at the next election, gain an absolute majority of seats, as they did in Germany twice in 1932. The trouble with this majority is that between its two constituent parts cooperation for securing positive legislation is impossible; they are only waiting for the moment when they can cut each other's throats. Thus no government can be formed; the mechanism of democracy has been broken by people whose whole desire and intent in the main was to develop democracy. Inevitably, however, a dictatorship of some description is bound to follow: whichever one of the minority groups, which have temporarily combined to beat the democratic parties, is swift enough and unscrupulously brutal enough to demolish its momentary collaborators first will as quickly as possible impose the will of its minority on the entire people and wipe out all opposition, even to the abolition of any expression, even unofficial, of dissenting opinion. Thus, much of the support for P.R. —the opportunity for every shade of opinion to be expressed—will be shown to be as false as the claim that P.R. brings added vitality to democracy. The dictatorship will, of course, lose no time in abolishing all elections, and a considerable number of citizens will think it the right thing to do under the circumstances since universal suffrage had proved itself to be destructive anyway. And so P.R. will have achieved what Charles Maurras, the famous "Master" of the "Action Française," called "the abdication of the (democratic) sovereign." Maurras and his followers thought of this as something it would be difficult to bring about, since it seemed to imply recognition on the part of the voters that they were incapable of governing themselves. But under P.R. this may be accomplished with ease. The voters are led by a roundabout path to the point where they sign their own political death warrant. Those who went with the extremists merely meant to make as efficient a use of their rights as possible, but it is in precisely this way that the sovereign people secure their own abdication.[13]

Therefore, is it too much to say that P.R. is *the* Trojan Horse of democracy?

But apart from consideration of the people's motives, this is, in the case described above, the outstanding fact: Democracy has not been defeated by an assault from without; it has been *voted* out of existence. The democrats have been beaten at their own game. If they are fair, can they protest against the result? Whoever does not admit that the rules were falsified will indeed have to concede that he has witnessed a *"reductio ad absurdum"* of democracy. There is now no moral force in those who still believe in democracy and, even after such elections have occurred, would like to fight for it. They have no positive alternative for dictatorship; the only thing they can demand is a dictatorship of another sort. To most of them this will seem futile, and so they will submit to the encroachments of the totalitarian group which has seized the reins of power. They may even believe that they are good democrats when they submit, inasmuch as the people apparently wanted the dictatorship. The situation is different for those who realize that the reason the people did not vote for a strong democratic government was only that the electoral system gave them no chance to do so. *Their* faith in democracy will remain unshaken, and it will be their part to give it back to those who through the perversion of an excellent institution were led to throw it away. But they will be opposed at every step by the supporters of P.R., who will not fail to state over and over again that the countries in which democracy broke down were not ripe for the system. Unconsciously and with the best of intentions, they are the best allies that Fascist propaganda can find.

## THE CHANGE IN PARTY STRUCTURE

The destruction of democracy will be further facilitated by the fact that P.R. radically changes the character of the remaining democratic groups. First, it will tend to make them adopt a rigid creed, a "world outlook," which will make it difficult for them to discharge their functions. For the reasons mentioned above, the majority system leaves little room for rigid programs.[14] In the first place, the marginal voter prefers issues to programs which he feels instinctively do not correspond to reality. In the second place, parties under a majority system will as a rule be so large—or form part of such large combinations—that the responsibility of running the government is always within close range, and responsibility kills doctrinal rigidity as a spring frost nips the blossoms in the bud. As mentioned above, facts are not concerned with following the textbook outline of a rational program, and whoever is concerned with facts will soon throw all the elements of a rational program overboard. The result will be that all parties will look pretty much alike, resembling, as the famous comparison puts it, "empty bottles with different labels." Let us hasten to add, however, that this fact, far from destroying their value, is what makes parties really serviceable. The absence of doctrinal rigidity in organizations which comprise only a part of the nation means that no artificial barriers are erected between the different elements in the population. Furthermore, parties which are more or less alike can comparatively easily perform their function of

gathering a majority of the people for the purpose of providing a majority for a government. This indeed is the *"raison d'être"* of political parties and, little as the writers devoted to pure theory have understood it, the need for such instruments has caused parties to grow, just as in organic life the function creates the organ. Combined with this task of being instruments of government is the other purpose of parties, namely, to provide a mechanism for the selection of leadership. A democracy needs an "elite" of policy-setting personalities as does any other form of government. This it secures by the method of perennial competition. Whoever desires to try out his gifts for political leadership may do it within a political party of his own choice. If he is the right man, he will succeed and may soon rise to the top in the hierarchy of leadership; if he fails, he will have only himself to blame. Competition is the essence of this selection. If it were to cease,[15] cooptation and favoritism would supplement the existing leadership, and it would soon degenerate. Hence political parties are a vital necessity even if they only bring about a selection of leadership, and if therefore their fight is only a struggle of the "ins" against the "outs." After all, if the "ins" are worn out, it is all to the good that there is some mechanism which can be used to drive them out of office and give a new team a chance to prove its value.

To the adherents of P.R. parties are an abuse if they merely serve the purpose of getting certain persons elected and fail to be dignified by a "program." Over and over again we are told that it is regrettable that the majority system tends to make of an election a duel between persons, or, as it is sometimes put, a "gladiators' fight." From Victor Considérant on, almost every advocate of the new electoral system who has been aware of its implications has decried the way in which the majority system forces parties to throw their programs overboard.[16] They have followed their great predecessor in suggesting P.R. as the remedy for this evil. There can be no complaint that in this regard P.R. fails to live up to the expectations of its friends. It makes the various parties independent of the marginal voter in the center, who has so little appreciation of programs,[17] and makes it possible to limit its appeal to those voters who appreciate programs. Naturally, this possibility becomes a necessity, since every shade of political tendency now has a chance to form an organization of its own, and parties can maintain their hold on the greatest possible number of voters only if they satisfy the desire on the part of the "characteristic" members of their parties for a "clear program." These "characteristic" members are the local and provincial leaders, whose zeal for party purity has been commented upon in an earlier part of this discussion. Under the conditions produced by P.R. they come into their own and become in the highest degree influential.

A further point for consideration is the fact that under P.R. political parties have a remoter prospect of having to assume the responsibility of government. They may, like the antiparliamentarian parties, refrain for the most part from assuming responsibility as long as democratic institutions stand; or they may be unable to assume the responsibility of office except as they act in coalition with other parties. In the former case, there is of course no extreme to which the party may not go in developing and cherishing its own "world outlook." And since this "world outlook" is never confronted with the stubborn facts of real experience, it can go on indefinitely, unfolding a life of its own imagining. In the second case, the responsibility which a party assumes is only partial, and partial responsibility is no responsibility at all. If the government fails to act in accord with the creed of a given party which is a member of the coalition, the members of that party can always "pass the buck." When they encounter protest or adverse criticism they point to the fact that they are only one of several elements in the combine and insist that it is the fault of the others if things are not as they should be. And naturally, the other partners in the coalition do the same. Thus several different "world outlooks" find it possible to survive an experience in the business of government which would have been fatal to any one of them engaging in it alone.

Once such unnatural creeds have been allowed to take root, there is no end to the process of their ramification and development. Since these different creeds are mutually exclusive, the party leaders take great care that they exert an exclusive influence over their members. Other parties are looked upon as a different political sect, and contact with them means contamination, a menace to the spiritual well-being of the faithful. Party members, therefore, must keep their social intercourse confined within the limits of the party. In order that this requirement may be fulfilled the party undertakes to regiment its members socially by setting up a number of subsidiary organizations. This social organization lays hold on the members at an early stage. The little Socialist boy, for example, must go to a "red" kindergarten, where he cannot be subjected to bourgeois influence. When he grows up and plays soccer, a game which all European boys love, he must join the Socialist team. There is manifestly an enormous difference between workers' sports and bourgeois' sports, and any party member who fails to understand this simple fact is badly in need of political education. When the boy grows up and founds a family he must avoid a church ceremony, for the class-conscious worker is a freethinker. When he and his wife do their shopping, it must be done in a Workers' Cooperative, for this is the only way to avoid contact with the capitalistic profit system. And when a member of the family dies, it is up to the Association for Cremation, to which practically all party members worthy of the name have contributed for years, to take care of his remains. Thus the party watches over its members from the cradle to the crematorium.

Social autarchy in this extreme form has been confined thus far to Socialist and Communist groups. But conditions have been similar in other parties; sports and cooperatives have, in most P.R. countries, been organized along party lines to a considerable extent. Silly as such lines of cleavage are, both those who draw them and those who are expected to heed them take them very seriously indeed. It does not take long for all sense of humor to disappear from countries whose political life has been disorganized by P.R.; political differences are considered too serious a matter to be permitted "undignified" treatment. So the last barrier which common sense could erect to hold back the flood of political dogma is removed, and the field is free for the party prophet. This important functionary goes about his work in a very thorough manner. Somehow the stand of the party must be related to philosophical assumptions. This relation is carefully traced—if necessary, invented. After some time a beautiful mixture of metaphysics and politics is produced and held up for the admiration of the party members. Of course, after one party has availed itself of such a trump card the others cannot allow themselves to be outdone. Even a party so obviously based on economic interests as was the "Economic Party of the German Middle Classes" will have its theoretical defense in terms of ultimate values. A diligent philosopher will set himself to work and presently emerge with a *"Weltanschauung"* which the party proclaims as the true reason for its existence. After such a *Weltanschauung* has been created, the party members must, of course, be indoctrinated with it. To this end there will be instituted training courses for local and provincial leaders, for the youth, and for the women's group. Those who graduate from these courses will then go out into the country as duly qualified missionaries of the new creed, and it will not be long before each party has injected its world outlook into all members who are in any way actively interested in politics. The result is obvious: artificial lines are drawn, and national unity is destroyed. Under a majority system no such development could possibly take place; but once P.R. has prepared the way for division it will easily proceed, gathering strength as it grows by reason of the conditions which it creates.

## P.R. AND INTEREST GROUPS

### Interest Groups in General

P.R. involves another set of consequences which simultaneously create a new type of party and alter the structure of the old democratic parties. We refer to the grouping of political parties according to economic interests. Such parties rarely develop under a majority system. As a rule, the members of a particular interest group do not form a majority in any given constituency; and even where they do, many of them would prefer voting for a political party rather than for a new organization confined to the "representation" of their economic interests. Interest parties, therefore, under a majority system, have no reasonable prospect of success though efforts in this direction have been repeatedly made over a long period of years. But this does not mean that economic interests are not "represented." On the contrary, all interest groups submit their demands to the candidates put up by the various parties in the field, who will be ready to comply with them if they can. But they will be able to do so only if such action on their part does not result in alienating other groups from them. Consequently, candidates for office are forced to consider the claims of these special interests in relation to the well-being of the community as a whole. They can pledge themselves to the fulfillment of the demands of any given group only if and when they can convince rival groups that they will not be unduly harmed by the course they contemplate. This process of education has excellent results in all directions. The candidate, confronted with the conflicting demands of various groups, has to acquaint himself with the economic situation of every group; he has to keep his eye on the whole of the nation rather than upon its separate parts. And the same applies to the interest groups themselves. Each has to take into account the fact that since it is only one of several groups which have diverse interests its own demands can be fulfilled only on terms acceptable to the others. Thus the interest groups as well as the candidates are compelled by the nature of the electoral system to consider the community as a whole, not merely their own narrow economic concerns.

Introduce P.R. and the picture is changed. No longer is there need to appeal for a majority; any interest group with a minimum number of members is privileged to set up a party of its own. At first only a fraction of those constituting this group may choose to vote for the new party; but the first success will bring others in its train, and soon the new party may be solidly established. Let this be accomplished by one element, and others will be bound to follow suit, fearful lest a disproportionate political influence be exercised by the group that has seen fit to organize. One need not dwell at length upon the logical consequences of this fact. The members sent to parliament by these new parties will be pledged to the consideration of one interest only—that of the group to which they appealed for support. They have been asked to vote on the basis of their own interests exclusively.[18]

Nobody has told them that there are other groups in the community for which it is the duty of parliament to legislate wisely and well. Inevitably they will become even more disposed than before to think in terms of their own demands. They will become in every respect more self-conscious. They will discover that they suffer from wrongs which have previously gone unnoticed; and their party, which profits by capitalizing upon such complaints, will impress upon them that their grievances are altogether just and demand redress. Once more P.R. will have shown its power to produce untoward conditions such as never existed before.

Many observers of political life in countries where P.R. has been adopted have found nothing so depressing as this interpenetration of politics and economic interests. Big national issues tend to disappear from the scene, to be replaced by items of controversy brought forward by people whose interests are solely economic. An element of insincerity necessarily enters in. After all, the great issues of foreign and domestic politics do exist, and they must be dealt with in one way or another. But those who have been sent to parliament as members of the new parties have been brought up in ignorance of these vital questions. The voters who sent them there are united only by their economic interests, and matters not affecting their material well-being in a definite and direct way are carefully excluded from the platform, for fear that any stand taken may alienate members of the party whose influence they cannot afford to lose. When the successful candidates of such groups come to parliament, non-economic questions such as marriage and divorce, the relation between church and state, a proposed treaty of friendship or alliance with a foreign country, come up for discussion and vote. But on these matters they have received no popular mandate. Whatever decision they make will, in contravention to the principles of democracy, be made by themselves alone.[19] It is only natural that they subordinate such matters to the economic interests of their group. What they do is to let it be known that they are ready for a bargain on this sort of basis: You of the political parties agree to vote for measures designed to promote our economic interests, and we in turn will vote on non-economic questions in whatever way you desire. When such bargains become common, political life has reached a low level indeed, and the voters will not in the long run be content. The time will come when they turn in utter disgust against these *"Interessenhaufen"* (agglomerations of people with particular interests), and join the extremist parties, which are based on a political principle, namely, a violent negation of the existing democratic institutions. Such parties have at least the merit of being concerned with what they conceive as the general good. For this reason many a sincere idealist will support them as a preferable alternative.

## The Deterioration of the Political Elite

Of no less importance is this consideration, that the appearance of interest parties means deterioration in the political leadership in the country. Supporters of P.R. are inclined to overlook the importance of good political personnel; in their view, only the program matters in politics, and some have gone so far as to recommend that the voter cast his ballot only for a program, leaving it to the party to appoint and recall the deputies. In practice, of course, much depends upon the quality of the "political class" to which the government of a country is entrusted. Their capable management can enable the country to weather a storm in which a poorly piloted ship of state might take serious harm; their weakness may allow it to drift into dangerous waters and expose it to peril even when the sea is comparatively calm.

As a matter of experience, the types of candidates that "make the grade" are altogether different under the two electoral systems. The majority system awards the prize of success to the man who can appeal to the majority of the voters in his constituency. As a rule, those candidates are favored who are not too narrowly identified with any particular economic interest, else the party might lose the support of important elements in the electorate. The candidate with the best prospects is one who enjoys an all-round popularity. If he has earned the people's confidence through his success as a lawyer, a physician, a college professor, or a high school teacher, such experience will be to his advantage, for the practice of those professions involves varied contacts and makes for resourcefulness in dealing with both problems and people. This holds true insofar as the knowledge of history is concerned, and law, and the social sciences. Further, the college or university graduate is more likely than other candidates to enjoy the advantage of an acquaintance with foreign languages. This is of little importance in a vast country like the United States with one prevailing tongue, but it means much in the smaller European countries where one cannot travel many hours on a fast train without crossing a border. There, no one who does not speak the current languages can be regarded as competent to represent his country in negotiations with the representatives of foreign powers, or before an international conference. Moreover, the social and economic problems of our times exhibit remarkable similarities in different countries. One who has a knowledge of several foreign languages will be able to study the experience of other countries before he endorses a new piece of legislation in his own, and thus in some cases be able to save his fellow citizens from engaging in a costly experiment of doubtful value. Likewise he will be in a position to recommend, on the basis of this broader acquaintance, measures which it would not occur to his fellow legislators to propose.

It must be admitted, however, that only a small percentage of college graduates have marked ability along political lines. The majority of them are more or less indifferent to politics. And it is further to be emphasized that democracy has a real place for the self-made man, of whatever rank, who has had no chance to get long years of schooling at the expense of his parents. The majority system takes care of him as well as of his better educated brothers. No college graduate is going to be given a seat solely because he has a college degree; nor will anyone be excluded because he is not a college graduate. Everything depends upon the voter's opinion as to the fitness of the candidate; and it is the testimony of experience that the voter ordinarily decides in favor of a rather fortunate blend of the various elements. College graduates will succeed—great numbers of them. But workingmen and merchants and farmers will always be among those who enter parliament, the place they occupy in national life depending upon their personal ability.

Now the interest groups which succeed on account of P.R. have a different mode of selection. A candidate need not be the kind of man who appeals to a majority of the citizens; he need only be acceptable to those who defend a particular interest. Professional men—lawyers, physicians, teachers, and their sort—find themselves as a rule excluded from politics. The members of interest parties are a radical set; according to them everything in politics is determined by one's position in life, and if a physician were elected by a group of house owners he might easily betray the interests of those who voted for him. There is a chance for him in the new party only if he is a house owner himself, and if his voters can be convinced that he will think first and foremost as a house owner. For, say the voters, if he is primarily a physician, let him join with the other physicians and found a party of physicians, who will then get their just percentage of parliamentary seats just as the house owners do. And the supporters of P.R. will give their approval. The result to which such reasoning leads in obvious: To be "of the profession"—any profession—comes to be a *privilegium odiosum,* and the country is deprived of some of the choicest of its leadership material.

A further unfortunate consequence of the system is that interest groups fail to select the highest type of candidate from among their members. The workers, the farmers, and the house owners who place high on the lists of their respective parties are not of the same type as the workers, the farmers, and the house owners who are elected under the majority system. Before P.R. was adopted the members of all professions joined existing political parties. They were put up as candidates if they seemed politically promising—in other words, if they were thought to have the qualities which mark the politician as well as the statesman. Candidates of the interest parties formed under P.R. are, however, selected for their ability to serve particular economic interests. They must be well acquainted with their party's demands and energetic in pressing for their fulfillment. The result of applying this criterion is, at best, the selection of a number of specialists who are well acquainted with their own chosen field but who suffer from the general defect of specialists, namely, a curious inability to see anything other than the subject on which they have elected to concentrate. This defect is intensified by the fact that the interest parties naturally tend to favor those who have been active in the various organizations formed for the defense of their interests, particularly the paid secretaries of such organizations. To be sure, these secretaries are more thoroughly acquainted with the demands of their organizations than the independent members. They have made tours of the country, have done their share of lobbying, and generally "know their stuff." But they are bureaucrats rather than politicians. Their work is administrative work of a routine character. In this routine they are master performers; but let them be confronted by an extraordinary task and they do not know what to do. Lacking the resourcefulness which the able politician has, they cannot be expected to be experts in the forming of policies or the planning of maneuvers.

## The Influence of Interest Groups upon the Surviving Democratic Parties

The influence exerted by interest groups upon politics is not confined to the immediate effect of their numerical importance in parliaments. In time, all other parties will be contaminated by the spirit which animates them. First, the deterioration of the élite will become a general phenomenon. Other parties can compete with the interest groups only if they can point to representatives of interest groups on their own lists. They will then say, "Farmer, you don't have to vote for the Farmers' Party in order to be properly 'represented' in parliament. Look at our list. Right at the top you will find Mr. Brown, who is a farmer, every inch of him. If you vote for him, your vote will help to elect one of your own number." Such arguments do get results. The consequence is, that whatever political parties remain, eventually hand over most of their seats to members of different interest groups. It must be borne in mind, however, that they are not free to select the candidates they deem best fitted for office. To be sure of success, they have to secure the endorsement of the economic organizations backing the various groups. These organizations will not be slow to sense their new power and, though in theory non-political, they will try to force the men of their choice on all the parties for which any substantial number of their members can be expected to vote. The men whom these organizations recommend are, of course, organization men. They may have comparatively little sympathy with the party on which they are thrust, and after election they will not forget that "their" party was only a minor factor in returning them to parliament. And even if they are well disposed toward the party, they cannot, for the reasons mentioned above, serve it as well as did the old-time politician. Indeed, it is even doubtful whether they are good material, from the point of view of the organization. It has happened that such organizations have forced political parties to take men of whom they themselves were tired, thinking that the best way to get rid of them was to send them into parliament and let the taxpayers take care of their remuneration. It is hardly necessary to emphasize what it means for the political élite of a country if most of its members are selected in this manner. We can readily understand why Max Weber, after he had seen this tendency at work during the first P.R. elections in Germany, predicted that soon the Reichstag would be "a parliament of idiots, incapable of forming in any way the basis for the selection of political leaders."[20]

The result of this forcing of representatives of economic interests upon political parties is that the parties lose their unity of action. The members of one interest group will try to drag the party in one direction, the members of another in a different direction. Before a party can do anything, it will have to take stock of all its component groups. To be sure, this is something that every big political party has to do, since interests and views are bound to vary increasingly as the party grows in size. But the difference is this. Under a majority system every single member of the parliamentary group of a given party had to decide in favor of the party and pledge himself, in effect, to put party interests first, before he could be elected. If after his election he should emphasize one interest to the exclusion of others, he would endanger his reelection. Under P.R., however, the deputy is more indebted to the members of his economic group and to their organization than he is to his party. In case of conflict, he will put his economic group first, and his party second. Thus a party exhibits no longer the old degree of unity. It is like a holding company, composed of a number of loosely grouped corporations, each of which has very definite interests of its own. Whenever the holding company tries to enforce its will upon a reluctant member corporation, the owners of the major portion of the shares will go their own way and break with the group to which they belong. It is something like this that happens to parties which have been forced to make concessions to interest groups. They can no longer act in a normal way. It requires long drawn-out negotiations to win the consent of its different contingents to proposals that are made, and the result may be that in certain controversial matters the party is unable to take any action at all.

## THE HARE SYSTEM AND
## THE LIST SYSTEM OF P.R.

The preceding pages have, when the influence of interest groups on the structure of the remaining parties was discussed, already touched upon problems which may be somewhat different under the two major modern types of P.R., namely, the Hare system and the list system. For this reason let us now briefly discuss the differences between the two systems.

Under the Hare system the voter casts his ballot for individual candidates. He gives his first choice to the man whom he likes best, his second choice to the candidate whom he likes second best, and so on. To be elected a candidate is supposed to obtain a certain number of votes, the "quota," which may be a number fixed by the law or may differ according to the number of votes cast and the number of candidates to be elected. If a candidate obtains first preference votes in excess of the quota, the surplus is attributed to another candidate to whom his supporters gave their second preferences. If, by following through with this process,[21] not enough candidates have obtained their quota yet, the weakest candidates are eliminated, and their votes are transferred to the stronger ones, until ultimately the successful candidates have been determined.

So far as the list system is concerned there are two rather important variations: the "rigid list" and the "free list." In the first case the competing lists are drawn up by party committees, who arrange the candidates in a certain order. After the counting is over, it is first determined how many seats each party obtains; when this has been done, those candidates are declared elected who are at the top of the list. If, for example, a party obtained five seats, the first five candidates on the party list would be elected. This is different in cases in which a "free list" is used. The voter is then given the opportunity to express individual preferences for one or more candidates; sometimes he is allowed to give his preferences to candidates of more than one party list. The electoral law determines how much weight is to be given to these preferences. It might be provided, for example, that after the number of seats to be attributed to a given party list has been determined, those candidates are elected who have obtained the highest number of personal preferences, irrespective of the places given them on the list of their party.

If we try to compare these two systems of P.R.

it is necessary to establish a proper basis of comparison. In England and in the United States the supporters of P.R. usually advocate the Hare system, and call it the "best system of P.R." and the list system "an inferior system." In this form the two adjectives "best" and "inferior" are subjective value-judgments, without scientific meaning. The only standard with the help of which we can decide about the claim for perfection made on behalf of the two systems is in relation to the logical premises of P.R. The question must be asked: Representation of what and in proportion to what? There is no doubt that the objects for which "representation" is sought are, as mentioned above, parties or "opinions" or something similarly impersonal, and proportionality simply means that these bodies of "opinion" share the seats in an elective body in proportion to the votes cast for them. The person of the "representative" is, in this process, fully subordinated to that more objective entity.[22] Whoever glances through the literature written in defense of P.R. will not fail to realize how strongly the majority system is attacked for the very reason that it emphasizes the "subjective" element of persons rather than the "objective" element of parties. The Hare system, however, if it operates as intended, focuses the attention of the voter on persons rather than on parties. For this reason it is an illogical form of P.R., whereas the list system, which makes elections primarily an option among parties, is its most logical form.

It might be said that rigid adherence to logic is not a political requirement, and that matters should be considered from a more practical point of view. Even if we do so, the Hare system of P.R., when compared with the list system, does not fare as well as its supporters assume. If we take the consequences of P.R. mentioned in the foregoing pages (multiplication of parties, encouragement of radical parties and promotion of interest groups), the Hare system, considered in itself, is worse than the list system because it increases the three disintegrating effects of P.R. mentioned. If we consider the multiplication of parties first,[23] it is obvious that under a list system the foundation of a new party remains a risk; the risk is much smaller than under the majority system, but it remains a risk. If the quota be 60,000 then the members of a new party which obtains fewer than 60,000 will still end up by having "thrown their votes away." For the promoters of new parties this is a serious handicap, which they are often not able to overcome. The Hare system removes this source of trouble. It operates like a re-insurance arrangement. If it is not certain whether the members of a new party will be numerous enough to obtain a quota, they can be instructed to give one of their minor preference votes to the candidate of a party who is sure of election. This will induce many voters to support a new party who would not have done so under the list system of P.R. Needless to say, among these new parties will be radical parties and interest groups.[24]

The supporters of the Hare system of P.R. will, however, point to the practical experience in the countries in which elections were held under the system which they advocate; in these countries the disintegrating effects of P.R. have indeed, as we shall see later, not been as intense as in countries where the list system was applied. The reason for this, however, is not the Hare system in itself. As mentioned above any system of P.R. is more or less "proportional," and therefore, more or less destructive, according to whether the constituencies formed are larger or smaller. If, for instance, only three candidates are to be elected from one constituency any party which polls more than 50% of the total will be sure to obtain two of the three seats. Such arrangements, of course, operate to the disadvantage of small parties and to the advantage of larger ones. Needless to say, the supporters of P.R. ought to oppose such results as abridgments of the proportionality which they desire; they ought to demand the election of members of legislative bodies over the whole country at large—which Thomas Hare[25] indeed did.

On the other hand, the discouragement of the multiplication of parties which small constituencies bring about is nothing peculiar to the Hare system. On the contrary the list system, since it offers no chances of effecting a re-insurance between small and larger parties, would obtain the same end even more efficiently.

There is some reason, however, why the supporters of the Hare system of P.R. are nowadays in favor of small constituencies, no matter how much the proportionality of the result suffers thereby. Suppose all the 435 members of the United States House of Representatives were elected by the Hare system, the whole country forming one huge constituency. It is fair to assume that in this case there would be at least 5000 candidates in the field. When faced with such a number the average voter would be helpless. A certain percentage of the voters—much higher than under the majority system—would cast invalid ballots. Others might wish to vote for a few candidates about whom they had a fairly clear idea, and they might be able to go through the ordeal of finding their names out of 5000 printed on the ballot. But none of these candidates might be certain of election; and some might obtain more than their quota on the first count, with the result that additional votes cast for them would no longer be counted for them. To whom shall the voters then give further preferences? In all probability they will, by that time, have become bewildered. They may cease to mark any more preferences, and then their votes will not count, as the ballot becomes "exhausted." Or they may do what voters have done so often when the Hare

system was applied in municipal elections in the United States, namely, resort to "alphabetical" voting. After having given their first preference or preferences to the candidate or candidates for whom someone may have instructed them to vote, they will just mark the name of the candidate who is closest on the ballot to those for whom they voted first. Naturally, the result is that through the complications of the system of voting the voter has been deprived of a chance to make his will prevail.

Let it be added that the total of "invalid and exhausted" ballots, even in comparatively small constituencies (as in New York, for example) has reached twenty per cent. In a nationwide constituency a much higher percentage of those who go to the polls would see themselves deprived of the opportunity of making their influence felt in an election. And, of course, when this happens we cannot say—as the proponents of P.R. have so often said—that if some voters fail to understand the technical aspects of the Hare system of P.R.[26] this matters as little as when people who cross a bridge do not understand the engineering aspects of its structure. In this case as in so many others we must be on our guard against improper analogies. The proper analogy to choose is this: Suppose there is a new, intricately constructed bridge, greatly liked by the engineers because of its novel technical features. However, up to twenty per cent of the cars driving across it are involved in fatal accidents. It is proven that good drivers manage to cross the bridge safely enough, but the police would probably not be impressed by this observation. They would decide that we must take human nature as it is, and that as long as twenty per cent of those who have to use the bridge lose their lives we have to condemn the new bridge and make the engineers revert to the old type of structure, which experience has proven to be reasonably safe.[27]

Then there comes the problem of counting the votes. Counting takes long enough in some American city elections already. In such cases remedy might be found in the future by the use of voting machines. But the voting machine which will take care of thousands of candidates does not exist, and it can probably never be constructed. Hence, the delay in the count would, if the Hare system were applied nationally, be endless, and it is doubtful whether the voters of any country would like to go through such an experience a second time, if they had once been exposed to it.

In addition, there is the element of chance. It is rather technical, and we shall trace only the barest outline of the problem here. More detailed treatises written by the proponents of the Hare system of P.R. emphasize the great need of using a sufficiently reduced quota;[28] it may be due to failure to comply with this necessity which produces results such as the following:

In Christchurch, New Zealand, the ballots were counted over three hundred times, and in the end they could not determine who the last two successful candidates to be elected should be, so the ballots were put in a hat and the returning officer backed up to the hat like this (indicating), put his hand into the hat, and pulled out a name. That man was elected. He then repeated the performance and pulled out another name, and that was the final selection.[29]

Let us assume that such things will not happen if the proper quota is applied. However, even then there will be difficulties. In the first place it is customary that when the surplus votes of a candidate who has more than his quota are transferred, those ballots are counted for their subsequent preferences which have not been counted before. This means that it is a matter of chance whether the ballots of such voters will be counted for one candidate or the other. Theoretically this could be avoided by recounting all the ballots; practically, this would be so complicated that it is not done. Second, it usually happens that not enough candidates obtain their quota even on the final count. In this case the remaining seats are filled by the candidates with the highest vote. The implication is that a political group whose candidates obtain just enough votes to be elected will obtain more seats than a group whose candidates poll a higher vote than necessary.

This goes to show again that the list system is much more germane to the spirit of P.R. than the Hare system. Under the list system, the voter can cast his vote for one of the lists without the slightest difficulty. Such lists may be presented in comparatively small regional constituencies, because the surplus votes obtained by any party can easily be transferred to a National List. The combination of regional and national lists can then, in a way as easy as it is practical, ensure a hundred per cent proportionality between votes cast for a party and seats attributed to it. The counting is so easy that for the whole country the result may be known during the election night. It goes without saying that voting machines can easily be used.

To summarize briefly: If we examine the claim that the Hare system is "the best system of P.R." we find that the Hare system is contrary to the spirit of P.R., and that in practice it can be made workable only by interfering strongly with the desired proportionality between the number of votes cast for a certain party and the number of seats attributed to it. Also, when faced with the claim (which is never supported by any detailed evidence) that whatever defects the list system of P.R. had in Europe would not have occurred under the Hare system, one is reminded of what Sir Austen Chamberlain had to say when faced with a similar question: "If one system of proportional representation fails, it is not the fault of the principle, it is merely that its exponents hit upon the wrong method. We

are told to try another, and if that fails the supporters of this system are not disconcerted; they are hardly surprised, and they will produce you another."[30]

To avoid any possible objection we shall, however, in the following paragraphs, try to specify in every case what differences might be said to exist between the practical effects of the Hare system and the list system of P.R.

# DESTRUCTION OF THE DEMOCRATIC CHARACTER OF PARTIES BY THE LIST SYSTEM OF P.R.

It is easy to realize to what extent P.R. must interfere with the democratic character of political parties, in particular if a system of rigid lists is used.[31] Under a majority system a party has to be democratic, for the most important unit of its organization is close to the voters and can be effectively controlled by them. The electoral battle is fought independently in every individual single-member constituency,[32] and the final success is the sum of the successes achieved in the individual constituencies. A party administration based on small and independent constituencies cannot but be democratic. It is so small that the members of the committee which directs the affairs of the constituency will be personally known to many of the voters. If the voters want a certain change in politics, they know to whom they can address their demands. Moreover, when the party committee is reelected it will be comparatively easy for the voter to reach the place where the election is held, to register his vote (unless a primary is held which enables him to cast his vote in his local community). It can be assumed that a committee whose members are in such close contact with a great many electors know the voters' wishes and are willing to comply with them. If this is not the case, the voters have an easy way of rectifying matters. They may stay at home, may vote for the candidate of another party, or may put a candidate of their own into the field. In the first two cases the result of a comparatively small defection of party voters may give the seat to the opposing party. The party committee will do its utmost to prevent this, and so will endeavor to keep in line with the party members. When the dissident voters put a candidate of their own into the field, the situation is more serious. If the candidate is successful we may safely assume that the party will welcome him back into the fold, and that the old local leadership will be turned out and replaced by a new one which is in harmony with the victorious candidate. As has been remarked, the party authorities will be inclined to deal gently with a dissident candidate who has put up a good fight, even though he has failed to be elected. As Ramsay MacDonald put it, "If there is a Liberal Independent or a Conservative Independent who kicks the machine over and tells the party managers and whips to mind their own business and fights, and fights well and is defeated, what happens to him? The doors are opened to him and fattened calves killed in his honor."[33]

One further result of this situation will be a close relationship between the deputy and the voter. The comparatively small size of the constituency enables the candidate to know every part of it. In elections for the United States House of Representatives, for instance, it often happens that a candidate will pay a visit to every town in his constituency no matter how small it may be and plead his cause before the voters there. Thus every voter who has an interest in politics can catch a glimpse of the candidate, at least. Many will have the opportunity to ask him questions at the meeting, and perhaps, if they so desire, talk with him at leisure after the meeting is over. It follows that the members of the party are keenly interested in the fate of the candidate. Much of what they do during the campaign will be inspired by personal loyalty to him. They will be ready to acclaim his every success, and they will do their best to destroy the effect of any failure in the electoral campaign. When the man is elected, the party members will regard the victory as a material reward for their efforts. They will be filled with pride, and the torchlight or bandwagon parade in which they may give expression to their feelings will be an additional triumph for the candidate. The new deputy will try to keep in contact with his constituents by periodic visits to the more important towns of his district. He may not go so far as did a certain French deputy, who as a candidate told the voters that if they ever came to Paris and had no other place in which to leave their umbrella he would take care of it for them in his hotel room. But he will not neglect them, or hold himself aloof. He knows too well that within a few years he will come up for re-election and will need the renewed support of the electorate.[34]

A similarly democratic relationship will prevail between the deputies and the leaders of the party. In a parliamentary system of government the national leader of the party is as a rule elected by the members of the party group in parliament. He must therefore be a man in whose superior ability the deputies voluntarily put their trust. They elect him on the assumption that he is better able than anyone else to lead them in their fight. Such a leader will normally be able to rely on the support of the deputies and need not resort to the expedient of securing pressure from without. This statement, to be sure, does require qualification. In modern democracy there exists a direct relationship between the national party leader and the masses of the

voters. The deputies can never elect anyone to the leader's place who has no appeal for the electorate. This means that if, and as long as, the national leader of the party is sure of the masses, he may be able to enforce his will upon any individual deputy or group of deputies. This is necessary because otherwise the party would not have the degree of unity which it needs for the successful support of the government. However, the ultimate arbiter between the individual member and his national leader is always the voters in the constituency. If they think that "their" member is unfairly treated by the leadership of the party, they let it be known that they are on his side. The deputy is aware of the fact that in such a case he can rely not only upon the registered members of his own party but also on a fair proportion of other voters, including members of other political parties which have no candidate in this particular constituency. Hence the position of the deputy is relatively strong. The party leader, aware of this fact, will always be willing to use persuasion rather than force upon the members of his parliamentary group. It is well known that this happens even in a country where the independence of the individual member is comparatively small, as in England. Whenever Mr. Baldwin, for example, whose national popularity has in certain periods been overwhelming, was planning an important step, he first carefully sounded out the mood of Parliament. Before he brought the abdication issue to a head, he made sure that the great majority of the members of his party were with him. Moreover, the ultimate result of the Hoare-Laval plan demonstrated that when a revolt of a group of deputies of his own party was supported by public opinion it was the Prime Minister who had to give in, not the revolting members of the party.[35] The relationship between individual deputies and the national leader under a majority system strongly tends, we conclude, to be truly democratic.

Under the list system of proportional representation, however, the party organization can be democratic neither in its local nor in its central branches. The small single-member constituency disappears, and in spite of all efforts to combine P.R. with single-member constituencies it is now admitted that reasonable proportionality requires constituencies with at least five members. As a result the local units of the party organization will be five times as large as before. This means that the committee formed for this constituency can no longer rest upon as popular a basis as the old single-member constituency. A comparatively small percentage of the voters will be personally acquainted with the members of this committee; hence it can easily happen that the provincial leadership of the party loses that direct contact with the voters which is so important. Furthermore, the voter cannot make his wishes felt as effectively as under the majority system. If he stays at home or votes for another party, his defection will involve a comparatively small loss for the party, probably not enough to bring defeat. There remains, of course, the third means of expressing dissatisfaction. The dissenting voters have it in their power to set up a party of their own. But this is so expensive a course of action that a small group of independent voters will seldom record its protest in such a fashion. All of which means that the local organization of the party is no longer as democratic as it was before.

A similar change occurs in the relationship between the individual candidate and the voters. It is practically impossible for a candidate to make speeches in every important town and village of the constituency, and the voters can no longer know him personally. Moreover, if the list system is applied, the voters have no chance to vote for an individual candidate. They must vote for the list as a whole, although they might prefer to elect only certain ones among the candidates and reject the others. The system of rigid lists does not admit of discrimination. The voters must either cast their votes for the entire list as it stands, or they must vote for some other list which has the same defect. They feel—and justly—that their power is considerably curtailed. Too, they cannot consider any particular candidate as "their" candidate as people do in a single-member constituency. In the same way the successful candidate cannot consider any particular group of voters as "his" voters. Since all who cast their ballots for him have voted for his successful running mates likewise, the new deputy will be unable to concentrate his efforts upon a comparatively small area which he regards as his own peculiar responsibility. He will have to travel around the whole constituency, feeling really at home nowhere. The impossibility of maintaining a satisfactory contact with the voters on whom he relies breeds indifference on his part. In time the voters will resent his lack of attentiveness and transfer this resentment to the democratic institution which made such neglect possible. In this case as in others they will not realize that it is a perversion of the principle of democracy that has stirred them to revolt rather than its real substance.

The democratic character of all parties will be destroyed at the top as well as at the bottom of their organization. The individual deputy is no longer independent; he lacks the support of his constituents.[36] The selection of candidates depends upon provincial committees, and the national leader of the party may, by various devices, gain control of them. This is merely a matter of efficient organization, a problem of business management rather than statesmanship, and one of the most satisfactory solutions is by way of financial domination of the party's newspapers. In such a case the national party leader becomes a kind of dictator. The individual members have to obey his command because if they refuse he will have power to destroy their political career by inducing the provincial committee to refuse the deputy a place on the party list at the coming election. It is small comfort for the rebellious deputy that he has the right to set up a rival organization of his own, for he knows that this would require more time and money than are his to command. The national party leader can bring dozens of parliamentary careers to an end by a mere stroke of the pen.[37] We have mentioned above how different the situation would be under a majority system. By way of demonstrating from actual experience we may profitably consider an incident in the recent history of the United States. During the Supreme Court fight dozens of senators belonging to the Democratic party refused to follow the advice of their national leader. Now, this national leader had a stronger popular appeal than any of his predecessors had enjoyed. According to all indications the party committees in the various states were with him as well as the electorate. Under a list system of P.R. there is no doubt that the situation would have been simple. The President would have asked the Democratic committees in their respective areas to wire their senators that if they did not comply with the wishes of the Administration their names would not be placed on the party's lists again. Naturally, many senators would have preferred to obey rather than commit political suicide. But the United States has a majority system, which means that the recalcitrant senators could not be deprived of their seats except by the waging of a difficult war against each of them in his home constituency. There the revolters had many friends who would have liked them to go along with the President but who would at the same time refuse to desert them just because they declined to support the Court reorganization bill. Furthermore, the attempt to replace the incumbent senators by other candidates was considered an interference with the independence of the voters, and some of them seem to have voted to send the same senators back to Congress just to make it clear that they did not propose to have the national headquarters act as director of their local affairs. Then too, many Republican voters would have supported the Democratic senators who were in conflict with their own party, even if such support entailed their registering as Democrats in the primaries. Thus the attempted "purge" failed; none of the opposed senators was defeated in the primaries, and only one Representative succumbed, whose case was not typical since much of the opposition to him followed from the fact that he was regarded as a Tammany man.

How will the Hare system of P.R. affect the democratic character of political parties? Much depends upon the size of the constituencies adopted. If constituencies were as large as Thomas Hare wanted them to be the effects of the Hare system would not differ much from those of the list system. As Walter Bagehot put it:

. . . The only way to obtain (i.e., an effective use of the votes cast for a certain candidate) is to organize. A man who wanted to compose part of a Liberal constituency (i.e., secure the election of a particular Liberal candidate) must not himself hunt for 1,000 other Liberals (Bagehot assumes that 1,000 is the quota); if he did, after writing 10,000 letters, he would probably find that he was making part of a constituency of 100, all of whose votes would be thrown away, the constituency (i.e., the number of voters) being too small to be reckoned. Such a Liberal must write to the great Registration Association in Parliament Street; he must communicate with its able managers, and they would soon use his vote for him. They would say: . . . Here is our list. If you do not want to throw your vote away, you must be guided by us: here are three very satisfactory gentlemen (and one is an Honourable): you may vote for either of these, and we will write your name down; but if you go voting wildly, you'll be thrown out altogether.

And Bagehot continues:

The evident result of this organization would be the return of party men only. The member-makers would look, not for independence, but for subservience—and they could hardly be blamed for so doing. . . . Upon this (in theory) voluntary plan, you would get together a set of members bound hard and fast with party bands and fetters, infinitely tighter than any members now.[38]

With this prediction we are bound to agree as much as with the following one:

As in the case of a dissenting congregation, one great minister sometimes rules it, while ninety-nine ministers in the hundred are ruled by it, so here one noted man would rule his electors, but the electors would rule all the others.[39]

This last sentence reads as if it had been written to characterize the control which Adolf Hitler was able to exercise over the National Socialist party! It goes without saying that under such a set-up there would be but little chance for the independent candidate. As Walter Bagehot again puts it: "And there would be no appeal for a common-minded man. He is no more likely to make a constituency for himself (i.e., to obtain a quota) than a mole is likely to make a planet."[40] To a surprising extent this prediction has been borne out in New York City, where so far the Hare system of P.R. has been applied in constituencies numbering more voters than any other constituency that ever used the Hare plan. We also observe what reflection leads us to expect, namely, that the votes cast for independent candidates will be largely wasted and that this fact may give a majority of the seats to a closely-knit and well disciplined group, such as Tammany Hall, even when it is supported by only a minority of the voters.

Will conditions differ greatly from this picture if the Hare system is applied in comparatively small constituencies? In detail everything will depend upon just how large the constituency is. It will be somewhat easier for the individual candidate to make himself known to the voters. On the other hand, the smaller the number of candidates to be elected, the larger the percentage of the votes which a candidate needs in order to be successful. Some of the effects of the majority system will then be approximated, although there will remain this one important difference that an independent candidate will not have to encounter the objection that votes for him will be thrown away. As mentioned before, he can effect a re-insurance arrangement; his supporters may be invited to give their first preference to him and their minor preferences to candidates who are more likely to be elected. The existence of such a chance should be expected to assist independent candidates and small parties in the same way as does the institution of the second ballot, as it was used in the France of the Third Republic, or the so-called "preferential ballot," which has often been advocated as a substitute for a "second ballot." Needless to say, to the extent that this is so, the splitting up of parties will be favored.

## LOSS OF VITALITY
## AS A RESULT OF P.R.

P.R. not only deprives parties of their democratic character, it also destroys their vitality. The majority system provides automatically for the survival of the fittest. Every candidate must, first of all, fight in his own constituency against all challengers, and only a man with a goodly amount of fighting quality in his makeup can hope to win. Others are eliminated at the outset. Once having entered the race, a candidate has to push through to the end in a way that calls for vigor and vitality, both physical and mental. These qualities are no less helpful after the race has been won, for the legislator has an exacting, exhausting task which requires a strong body as well as a resourceful mind. And in the event that democracy is subjected to attack, these qualities become invaluable. Only those who are real fighters will be able to campaign in its defense. Under a majority system which has seen to it that only men with fighting blood in their veins and stamina in their bodies have been admitted to parliament, the anti-democratic agitators have no easy task on their hands. And what holds true for the average deputy holds true also for the national party leaders. They must usually have become deputies first and then entered into competition with other deputies for leadership in the party. As a rule they will get to the top of the party pyramid only if they are stronger than their rivals. So we may safely assume that, insofar as the possession of fighting qualities is concerned, the national leaders will, under a majority system, be distinctly above the average level of the deputies in parliament, who in turn exemplify the survival of the fittest.

But what shall be said of the rigid list system of P.R.? Just this, that it destroys vitality once and for all. Only a limited number of candidates have a chance to win in the election. If they are placed at the top of the list of their party they need not fight at all. As long as their party continues to win at least a few seats they will be elected. After their nomination they may, if they so desire, take a train to a pleasure resort and return when the election is over. The situation is less agreeable for those who occupy doubtful places on the party list and who may or may not be elected. Even their success, however, practically never depends upon their personal efforts. If they take a vigorous part in the campaign and increase the vote of their party, the benefit may go to others and not to themselves at all. Under such circumstances many people will seek a nomination which it would never occur to them to desire if they had to meet the test of a battle in a single-member constituency. In addition, those in control of a party will soon form a kind of reinsurance company and reappoint one another from election to election to the highest places on the party lists. All of which is to say that under such a system the possession of fighting qualities has nothing to do with a man's getting into parliament nor with his keeping his seat after it has been won.

And the evil goes farther. Men who do have in them the stuff of which fighters are made will fail to develop their capacity. In this case, as in biological development, the function develops the organ; conversely, if the function ceases, the organ will atrophy. As a result a rather strange phenomenon will be observed. In the first parliaments elected under proportional representation the party leadership will count many members who have been elected first under the majority system, and have been able to pass the tests which this system imposes upon a candidate. They have been good fighters. But after a few years of P.R. they lose their vigor. There is no need for it in the process by which they are maintained in their positions of leadership. Then later when they are called upon to withstand the kind of assault which the anti-parliamentarian groups deliver upon the democratic parties, they are helpless—bewildered that such a thing could come to pass in a country which they believed themselves to be able to control so easily. And it may happen that when the hour of decision comes they will meekly prefer to submit rather than to fight, even though their chances to win are better than good.

The foregoing has in the main been written with regard to the list system, and once more the question is to be answered as to what degree the results differ under the Hare system. Owing to the great similarity existing in this respect among all systems of P.R., a certain amount of repetition is inevitable. Nevertheless, most of the creative results peculiar to the struggle for election under the majority system are lost under the Hare system as well as under any other system of P.R. The available seats are in theory at least divided among the competing parties according to their approximate strength. Hence, there is no longer a struggle for victory and defeat. Inevitably campaigns diminish in vigor when it is no longer possible to elect or to defeat one of the large parties or party combinations which under the majority system fight for a majority in the country as a whole. The fact that it is no longer possible to elect or defeat individual candidates is also responsible for a slackening of interest. The results of elections in single-member districts are well known. One personality is confronted with another, which makes the contest so much more lively than the set-up under P.R. The best example is offered when under the majority system the opposing candidates appear on the same platform: The voters will flock to their debates in large numbers, and when they make a decision between them, they will feel that they really exercised the sovereign power in a democracy. At the same time, such debates may dramatize the issues of the day before a nationwide audience, as the famous Lincoln-Douglas debates did, or more recently, the debates between Senator Taft and Senator Bulkley before the 1938 elections. Such features any system of P.R. destroys without providing for a substitute.[41]

Will the Hare system of P.R. interfere with the vitality of democratic parties? Needless to say, if the Hare system is applied in large constituencies, the necessity of rigid party control of the voters will weaken vitality as much as it weakens the democratic character of political parties. In small constituencies matters will again be different. Yet, it will hardly be denied that there cannot be such a fight for the survival of the fittest as occurs under the majority system. Therefore, the quality of the members of parliamentary bodies is bound to decline. And, of course, the one type of fight which is peculiar to the Hare system will not be generally regarded as welcome. We refer to the fact that every candidate of a party has to rival with the candidates of his own party as well as with others. His fate depends upon the votes cast for him personally, upon first preference votes in particular, since without a sufficient number of these he will soon be out of the running. Such rivalry does not make for good feeling. It is true enough that whatever resentment there is will as a rule be suppressed. Every candidate will try not to antagonize other candidates of his own party because he hopes to obtain the minor preferences of the supporters of that candidate. These votes become available if the latter is eliminated, or if he has so many votes that those which are in excess of the quota will be counted for the candidate to whom minor preferences have been given. However, if such conflicts are suppressed, it does not mean that they do not exist!

## LACK OF CHANCES
## FOR YOUNG PEOPLE

The list system of P.R., by eliminating the need for a type, will at the same time impose a serious handicap upon ambitious young men. The young are natural fighters, and under a majority system their ability along this line is appreciated as a party asset. All the leaders realize that aggressive young candidates will be ready to undertake a contest for their party even in a constituency where the chances of success are not great. In such a case the unexpected not infrequently happens, and the youthful candidate carries off a seat, thus contributing to a rejuvenation of the leadership of the party. Whoever has watched a young candidate putting up his fight in a single-member constituency will not be surprised at the victory won under such difficult circumstances. The young candidate has an appeal because of his very freshness and enthusiasm, and may quickly become popular with voters old and young, who feel that at last something new is being offered to them. He will be acclaimed by other young folk who will make his cause their own.

On the other hand, any system of P.R. narrows the basis from which a selection for leadership is made. Under P.R. only a limited number of seats change hands from election to election, and real fighting is restricted to them. Only a few incumbent deputies are in danger of defeat and have to give of their best in order to be re-elected; only a few newcomers have a chance to win their first success. The majority system, however, frequently produces a large turn-over of seats; it creates thereby lively struggles over large sections of the country, and gives many a newcomer a chance. In addition, there will, under a majority system, always be many candidates who will fight for a seat in a constituency even if they know the task to be hopeless. Their campaign gives them a chance to distinguish themselves and if they make the best of difficult conditions, they know that their party may give them a better chance the next time. This provides for the continuous insertion of new blood into party leadership, for which there is no parallel under any system of P.R. Under a majority system it will indeed happen that many young people previously indifferent to politics flock to the headquarters of the candidate and offer their services. Some of them may do their work in a rather amateurish way, but others will make a success of it, and all are likely to discover in themselves abilities which they and others have failed to observe in the past. Moreover, they will add industry to their ability, holding meetings in behalf of their candidates wherever they can and losing no chance to talk against the candidates of other parties at meetings called by their opponents. This means that the members of the local party organization will come to realize that these young workers do their job much more effectively than the old committeemen. The older people grow more willing to accord the young a place of larger influence; and if the young candidate is elected, he may be allowed to reorganize the committee—which means the replacement of seasoned party workers by younger ones all along the line.

If, moreover, under the majority system a party resists too long the infusion of new blood, the young voters can easily stage a revolt. It will cost them no great amount to put a candidate of their own into the field, and if their man is elected a rejuvenation of the party will have been brought about automatically. If he loses, the cause may have been well served nevertheless, provided there has been a defection of voters sufficient to stir up the older people in command of the party, who are well aware that the loss of comparatively few votes may swing the seat over to the enemy. If this happens the election will have repercussions all over the country. The veteran leaders will everywhere be reminded that if they continue to offer the people unsatisfactory candidates—who in many cases have bought their way into the party—they will provoke active dissension on the part of the young members of their party. The national headquarters will then press upon all local committees the need for more acceptable candidates—which, as a rule, means younger ones—and the process of rejuvenation will follow in the natural course of events. Older men, realizing that they are not equal to the strain which an electoral campaign imposes upon all who actively participate, will resign of their own free will and yield their places to younger and sturdier spirits.

Under a list system of P.R. this mechanism of rejuvenation is destroyed. Old men are no longer inclined to retire voluntarily. Since it requires no effort to stick to their place on the list, they do so just as long as they can, the voters meanwhile waiting for them to create a vacancy by dying. The chances of young candidates are correspondingly less, for they cannot by sheer ability and enterprise win a new seat for their party. All they can do is to demand a place on the party list, which is practically equivalent to asking the party leaders for a gift. They can point to no merit which would justify their claim, for they have had no chance to exhibit their qualities of leadership. As for the party leaders, granted they are willing in some cases to nominate younger men as candidates, they simply do not know whom to select. The majority system makes it possible to open the doors of opportunity to a number of aspirants and then select those who have proved their worth. But P.R. does not. Only a few can be nominated, and the system of rigid lists is such that they cannot achieve a success which could be attributed beyond any doubt to their personal efforts. If young candidates are appointed, it must be done by the method of cooptation, which is characteristic of autocratic rather than democratic governments. In order to make this cooptation less arbitrary, party leaders as a rule protect themselves by choosing the professional secretaries of youth organizations, who are all too often highly unsuitable. The kind of work in which they have distinguished themselves is bureaucratic; and a young bureaucrat is no better than an old one. Moreover, such people are known to be of the sort who make a profession of being young, claiming to speak as interpreters of youth when they themselves have reached the forties. It would be much better to have young candidates elected who without any declaiming about the rights of youth go into their constituencies, show what they can do in the field of practical politics, and get themselves nominated and elected on their demonstrated merits. But this is, of course, impossible under the list system of P.R.

For all these reasons there is bound to be a wide gap between the old political parties and the young people of the country. The old democratic parties are in the hands of the older men, and the young know that it is almost impossible for them to gain any influence. If they continue to stand by these old-line parties they will do so rather out of a sense of duty than in a spirit of enthusiastic devotion, and so be unlikely to induce other young people to support the democratic party to which they belong. On the other hand, the antidemocratic parties are full of members of the younger generation. The radical negation of the existing political institutions and the wholesale condemnation of all the abuses connected with them cannot but appeal to the reforming, crusading spirit of youth. Then too these radical parties furnish abundant opportunity for the young. Most of them have been founded by young people, and most of their leaders are young; hence a young man need fear no belittling criticism if he aspires to a place of leadership. The general situation in the country is such that the difference between democratic and non-democratic parties coincides with the difference in age. The young—leaders and voters—associate themselves with the anti-democratic groups, while the older ones stick to democracy. There arises then in the popular mind the idea that democratic institutions represent the outworn ideal of a generation which is about to pass from the scene. Needless to remark, this does not add to their prestige.

Will the Hare system of P.R. give young people a better chance than the list system? If the Hare system were applied in large constituencies, the party leaders would undoubtedly decide as much about the candidates to be elected as they do under a system of "rigid lists." If small constituencies are used, young candidates whom their party leaders do not favor would once more have to obtain a rather large percentage of the total vote in order to be elected. Therefore, so far as the different systems of P.R. are concerned, it would seem that young people would have the best chance under a "free list." The party committee could not avoid placing one or more young party members on the list, and their friends could assure their success by giving them their personal preferences. Yet, there is a great difference between the young candidate who is elected under the majority system and the one who is elected under P.R., no matter whether the Hare system or a "free list" is used. It is the difference between the man who is chosen by an entire constituency because he is deemed best to do the job, and the one who comes to parliament as just another representative of a group interest. This latter situation agrees badly with the innate idealism of youth.

## P.R. AND POLITICAL STAGNATION

It is one of the advantages of the majority system that political conditions are kept in a constant state of flux. A small change in the distribution of voters may create a considerable change in the distribution of seats, and consequently in the composition of parliament. Parties may come into power which before the election seemed to have little chance or none. At the same time there will be a change in political personnel, and this will occur irrespective of whether there is a material change in the distribution of seats among the different parties. If a party holds two hundred seats before the election and the same number afterwards, it is probable that among this number there may be many who were not in the old parliament, whereas a corresponding number of old deputies will have been defeated. Both sorts of change—in the political strength of the various parties and in the political personnel—are welcomed by the body of voters. In fact, the voter is often heard to express himself very emphatically on this point in the days before the election. If he is a German, he says, "Das muss anders werden." If he is a Frenchman, he echoes, "Il faut que ça change." More recently, in certain localities in the United States, success has been achieved under the slogan: "It's time for a change!" In fact, whenever a considerable change occurs, the voter is pleased. He has gotten what he wanted, and it strengthens his conviction that in a democracy he is the real master of his country's destinies.

Under any system of P.R. there comes to be, instead of political change, political stagnation. (The supporters of P.R. call it stability, but the meaning is the same.) Whenever a change occurs in the distribution of votes, there follows a corresponding change in the distribution of seats. The latter change will be slight, however, and therefore, under normal conditions, the new parliament will be much the same as the old one. As a Belgian Senator put it after the country had begun to witness the results of P.R.: "We are governed by His Majesty the Status Quo" and as another Belgian observer remarked, "it (P.R.) engenders sleeping sickness."[42] Stability as regards the relative strength of the various parties will be matched by stability in the political personnel. Members of the old parliament will be found in the new one as well. This, however, is not likely to please the voter, who will consider that such a small change has hardly been worth the trouble of an election. Under these contions he falls easy prey to the anti-democratic agitators who din it into his ears that no matter what he does in the elections he continues to be governed by the same old democratic oligarchy.

It goes without saying that so far as political stagnation is concerned, no difference can be claimed to exist between the Hare system and the list system of P.R.

## GOVERNMENT UNDER THE CONDITIONS CREATED BY P.R.

Let us now consider in some detail the consequences of P.R. as concerns the formation of a government. The first result is that majorities are cut down; at a later stage they are destroyed. The cutting down of majorities is inevitable. The majority system ordinarily gives the majority party more seats than would correspond to the number of votes cast for it, and this gain is immediately destroyed by P.R. As a result majorities will often be so small that the smooth working of the machinery of government becomes impossible. Every member is expected to be present to vote with his party; the margin of safety which so greatly facilitates the work of the majority no longer exists. One single vote may tip the scales. Thus the health bulletin—or the honeymoon—of one member may become political news of first-rate importance, and a general uneasiness prevails, everyone realizing that a trifling accident may mean the frustration of long and arduous effort. Moreover, those more or less unimportant revolts which are wont to occur now and then when certain party members object to a decision can no longer be regarded with tolerance by the government. The crack of the party

whip resounds louder than before in the halls of parliament—not without its effect on the mood of the members, who miss their good old safety valve, the privilege of an occasional dissent.

Government efficiency is of course much more affected when P.R. destroys the majority which existed before its adoption—which, as we shall see, is what it nearly always does. In all cases in which under a majority system a two-party alignment would have continued to exist, the machinery of government will work in a much less democratic, much less efficient manner than before. First and foremost, a parliamentary oligarchy will replace the plebiscitary democracy which was previously in command. Under a two-party system the people vote directly upon the government of the country. Their vote implies that the leader of the party which secures a majority is to form the government. The leader of the new cabinet is thereby given a prestige which no other member of the party enjoys; he has been designated for his position by the people themselves. The new premier, therefore, can select the prominent members of his party. There are, it is true, certain outstanding individuals whom he cannot well ignore; but even in regard to them he has a considerable freedom of choice as to the type of office he confers upon them. To all minor offices he will be perfectly free to appoint the people whom he personally prefers—though he will, of course, be inclined to favor persons sufficiently capable to make a success of their work and so contribute to the success of the cabinet as a whole. It is reasonable to expect, under such conditions, that the cabinet will be as homogeneous a group as human limitations permit.

A further point worthy of mention is this. When the voters elect[43] the prime minister of the country they at the same time make a direct decision upon the issues involved in the electoral campaign. The leaders of both parties are called upon to declare their stand, before the elections, on the most important problems confronting the nation. The vote therefore has to do not only with persons but with policies. Often it will happen that an election is called for the one purpose of seeking a popular verdict on a certain question, in which case it is a direct plebiscite. After such an election the government has a mandate to pursue the policy which has been approved by the voters. This should eliminate all doubt as to what course the cabinet is to steer and thus facilitate its work.

When P.R. destroys the two-party system it takes out of the hands of the electorate decisions affecting both measures and men. Since no party has obtained a majority, the government will have to be formed by arranging a coalition of several parties. In this connection it must be borne in mind that the parties under P.R. differ from their predecessors of majority system days. There has been no need for electoral alliances; each party has been able to declare in the campaign that it is independent of all others. Thus the successful candidates of the various parties have been elected only by the votes of those belonging to their own party, and the electorate has not determined that a certain group of parties should cooperate in taking over the government of the country. This means that after the elections are over the parties in parliament are free to form a government in whatever way they see fit, a state of affairs which reminds one of what Rousseau said about the English people of his time: "The English people think they are free, but they sadly deceive themselves. They are free only when they elect the members of parliament. As soon as they are elected the people are slaves,—they are nothing."[44]

At the same time the voters have not been able to register a decision upon the major problems confronting the country. The numerous parties will present them with numerous issues. Most of them will manage to dodge concrete issues altogether, confining themselves to the exposition of an abstract and nebulous "world outlook." After the elections are over each party will claim that its "program" expresses the will of the people, when as a matter of fact the will of the people has not been expressed at all. The voters have spoken with so many voices that one drowns out the other. The deference of the party to the people is only theoretical; in reality the members of parliament, once elected, do as they please.

The multiplicity of parties makes it inevitably difficult to form a government. Sometimes this proves an impossible task; in other cases long negotiations are required before success is achieved, and the authority of the government is correspondingly weakened. Before the new government can take office there is an interim of doubtful constitutionality. These interim governments are like the former "lame duck" presidents in the United States. It may happen that during the time they are in office a question arises which can be satisfactorily settled only by immediate action. When this is not forthcoming the country suffers loss of some sort, perhaps even permanent harm. Furthermore, the negotiations leading to the formation of a government coalition are sure to be attended by many untoward incidents, the effect of which is to dim the prestige of the government. When negotiations begin, the claims of the different parties seem to be mutually exclusive. If a reconciliation is to be made, some of the demands that have been made must be dropped. But which ones? The party that makes a demand and then backs down is made to appear insincere, and the government which it supports seems to be similarly lacking in principle. Like difficulties will arise over the distribution of cabinet posts among the partners in the coalition. Each party will try to get as many portfolios as it can wrest from the unwilling hands of the others, and this scramble may go on for weeks. This process

is, naturally, as painful to the political leaders as it is to the political observer, and there are bound to be permanent scars left by the wounds of battle.

All of these difficulties persist even after a cabinet has been formed. Its members do not form an organic unit, and anything resembling real team work is impossible. The cabinet members, considering themselves delegates of their respective parties, think in terms of their party rather than of the coalition. As a matter of fact, they have to put forth considerable effort to convince the members of their party that their participation in the coalition does not mean that they have renounced their party's creed. In theory these cabinet members should be the strongest individuals in their respective parties and should lead them in unanimous support of the government. In actual fact, parties will often refuse to have their strongest men placed in cabinet posts. They prefer to have this responsibility put upon some inconspicuous member of their parliamentary group whose action they can disavow at pleasure. They may go so far as to delegate to the cabinet men who do not belong to that group, who perhaps are not even registered members of the party. This, of course, makes it still easier for the party leaders to free themselves from responsibility for the actions of the cabinet. But even if the real leaders of the party become members of the cabinet, they will not be able to commit their party to the support of the ministry; for there develops in every party a curious tendency to replace their leading cabinet members by others. These latter may be persons of mediocre political quality, whose only merit, in the eyes of the members of the party, consists in the fact that they have had no share in the coalition or its compromises. Nevertheless they will consider themselves called upon to play the part of supervisor—be a sort of watchdog—over the cabinet members of their party and be ready to criticize them before the councils of the party whenever they deem it necessary.

In such a cabinet the prime minister is no longer a leader; he is no more than a *primus inter pares*. He has little influence in the selection of cabinet ministers, and it may even happen that a party will place a man in a cabinet post with the express intention of using him as a check upon the prime minister and prevent his exercising any real authority. When such conditions prevail it is impossible for a prime minister to fuse the members of his cabinet into an organic whole. As soon as he tries to assert himself in any way that implies genuine leadership, he meets with a negative response and soon learns that he must abandon any attempt of this kind. Let public opinion and the press urge him as they will to be a real leader and enforce his will upon a recalcitrant party; he knows from experience that this cannot be done, since there is no positive power behind his personal will, and he knows too that no general will go into battle unless he has a fighting force with which to meet the onslaughts of the enemy.

Under such conditions as have been described, the various parties involved naturally do not give wholehearted support to the cabinet. Many measures may be enacted by the coalition government which the party actively dislikes, and tolerates only because it sees no way to sidetrack them. Moreover, if the ministry is a success, the credit may go to only one of the parties in the coalition—probably the one which the prime minister represents—although the others have contributed largely to that success. Thus for some of the parties that have entered into the coalition the success of the cabinet means only that the popularity of their competitors is enhanced at their expense.

It is obvious that if all the parties concerned are resolved to maintain their identity while participating in the government, the latter's unity of action is destroyed. The cabinet works in much the same way as an international conference. The different ministers are comparable to the representatives of sovereign states. As such they will insist upon their rights and often refuse to yield an inch. In such case delayed action is the result; and delayed action is sometimes as bad as no action at all. A workable compromise[45]—which, of course, is in the essence of democracy—cannot be arrived at. The respective parties have developed their attitudes before the voters without any regard to later agreements with other parties; as mentioned above, P.R. is regularly advocated exactly because it makes such action possible. Parties elected on such a basis do not want to make concessions, and if after long wrangling something is accomplished which is given the name of a compromise, it will more often than not either be unworkable, or fail to provide real action at all—being what Carl Schmitt[46] calls a "dilatorisches Formelkompromiss," which in reality consists in leaving matters just as they are. Considering the difficulties involved in the process of arriving at an agreement, coalition governments often refrain from attacking vital questions at all. They simply let matters drift, waiting for a *deus ex machina* to come out and end the controversy. There are cases, however, in which such waiting cannot be prolonged for more than a few weeks— as, for an outstanding example, in the matter of the ever-recurring problem of the budget. The old budget law expires on a fixed date. Afterwards, there may be no legal basis for the continuation of most government activities; yet the government of the country cannot be suspended. So, if provision for it cannot be made in the manner prescribed by the Constitution the government may think that the situation empowers and even obliges it to provide for the necessary measures by decree. Public opinion may support this view, but nothing can ward off the evil result. The authority of the fundamental law of the land is undermined. The Constitution required the budget law to be passed by Parliament, and if the government provides for a budget by decree the Constitution has apparently been flouted. The anti-parliamentarian parties will not fail to play up the fact that the democrats have not been able to run the government under the rules which they themselves set up, and many voters will let themselves be convinced that the decree laws have been unconstitutional. If such a government takes measures against illegal activities on the part of anti-democratic groups, these will come back with the unanswerable charge that the government itself has broken the law and can hardly require anything any more in the name of justice and right.

## P.R. AND THE RIGHT OF PARLIAMENTARY DISSOLUTION

In this connection it must be added that P.R. destroys the usefulness of one of the most important weapons with which any government can defend itself against recalcitrant parties, namely, the right to dissolve parliament. The exercise of this right is entirely democratic, for it means that when there comes to be a difference of views between the government and parliament the case is submitted to the people for their decision, which is final. At the same time, the right of dissolution is an essential counterpart of the right of parliament to overthrow a government. If parliament has the right to throw a government out of power, it follows that the government should have the right to bring the legal existence of this parliament to an end. Otherwise the members of parliament would be irresponsible as long as their term in office lasted and could with impunity cause a government to be overthrown. The overthrow of a government is so momentous an act that it should certainly not be left to an irresponsible group of deputies.

Under a majority system the weapon of dissolution is a keen-edged instrument. If parliament is dissolved, a small change in the distribution of votes may, as mentioned before, cause a landslide. This may work in favor of the opposition, but then again it may not. At any rate, those of the opposition know that they run a very serious risk. They will realize that any election requires money and strenuous physical efforts. Very often the treasury of the party has not yet recovered from the deficit incurred during the last election. Moreover, the individual members of the parliamentary opposition will realize that, over and above the hazard of a party defeat, there is a personal risk for every one of them. Their party cannot assure them of re-election even in the event of a party victory. Consequently every single deputy will think a long time before he casts a vote which might lead to an overthrow of the government, and the party leaders find it not so easy to induce their followers to do so. They must be able to show that such a course is not dangerous or that a vote of this kind is an absolute necessity. At the same time the party leaders themselves may have personal reasons for caution. Every one of them has to fight for re-election, and experience has demonstrated that the voters have little respect even for the leaders who have served them longest, and may not hesitate to give preference to a new candidate. Hence the party leaders will think twice before they vote against the government. The same applies to the members of the party or the group of parties which support the government. In general, it is expected that the opposition will vote according to the old slogan. "The duty of the opposition is to oppose," and the government will have to rely upon the members of its own majority. But the unpopularity which sometimes follows from the continuous support of the government may bear heavily on the members of the majority, who are inclined on occasion to give themselves a holiday from party regularity and vote against their own government. Now an occasional lapse of this kind may not meet with strong objection provided the issue is not too important. But in all essential matters the government will insist on having the support of its followers. If too many of them refuse, the cabinet will be forced to dissolve parliament. Fearing such action, the members of the government party will be inclined to go along with their official leaders as long as circumstances permit. It is not even necessary for these leaders to preface every important vote with the announcement that if they are not upheld they will dissolve parliament. The members of that body know that the big stick of dissolution is always ready for use, and they tend to avoid trouble by acting with discretion.

The first result of P.R. in this connection is that under normal conditions there is no fear of a landslide. If the opposition, or certain elements of the government party, antagonize the cabinet to the extent of causing a dissolution of parliament, the risk they run is comparatively small. At the worst they will lose a certain number of seats; the relative strength of the various parties will remain about as before. Furthermore, the party leaders need have no fear for their own fate. Their names will again appear at the head of the party lists, and they will be safely re-elected. The danger is greater, of course, for the members of their parliamentary group who are not so high on the list. It is quite likely that some of them will not be re-elected, and they know it; but, for the reasons mentioned above, they will feel obliged to comply with the wishes of their party leaders at whatever cost to themselves. Well they know that if they do otherwise they will lose their place on the party list and before long disappear from the political scene. Thus, under the conditions created by P.R., the weapon of dissolution will remain in the government arsenal, but its edge will be blunted. It may be used, to be sure, for in the face of multiplying difficulties the government will have to use any available method or means whereby to strengthen its position, even temporarily. But when the voters observe that after every dissolution the same evil conditions prevail, they will come to the conclusion that it is sheer folly to start up the expensive machinery of new elections when the prospect of a decent return is so small.

## NOTES

1. G. Lachapelle, *Les Régimes électoraux* (Paris, 1934), p. 167.
2. H. Finer, *The Case against Proportional Representation,* Fabian Tract No. 211 (London, 1935), p. 6.
3. In practice the percentage might be still lower on account of the votes lost by parties which are too small to obtain this percentage.
4. In theory it has continued to exist, with comparatively unimportant alterations, throughout Hitler's dictatorship.
5. This, of course, is possible only if more than three candidates of almost equal strength are in the race. In a straight fight more than half of the votes are required.
6. As a matter of fact, most advocates of P.R. are either members of such groups or sympathizers.
7. *Coningsby,* Bk. 5, chap. 4.
8. It is necessary to make some remarks here concerning the term "Radical." "Radicalism" can be defined in two ways: first, as to the ends sought and second as to the means employed to gain those ends. In the first sense, a Radical is somebody who wants to go to the "roots" of existing institutions and to replace existing things by something altogether new. In the second sense, a "Radical" is somebody who uses—or is willing to use, if he is allowed to do so—violent means in order to attain his ends, whereas in comparison with him everybody is a moderate who resorts to peaceful means only no matter how "radical" his ultimate ends may be. Throughout this book, the term "radical" is as a rule used in the second sense of the word. For example, the German Socialists are not called "Radicals" although they advocated radical changes in the social structure, because they confined themselves strictly to the employment of democratic means in the advocacy of their ends. This distinguished them from the German Communists, who employed every means at their disposal, illegal as well as legal, to further their aims. In the same way, the English Conservatives are "moderate" because they adhere to democratic processes, whereas Sir Oswald Mosley's Fascists are clearly "Radicals" (or "Extremists") because in order to gain power they would be quite willing to employ the same undemocratic means employed by the followers of Mussolini and Hitler, if only the police and the courts would allow them to do so. In a few instances, however, the terms "Radical" and

"Moderate" will be used in a merely comparative sense. A group may be called more "moderate" than another because it is closer to a "middle of the road" policy than another.

9. Needless to say, it is a complete misunderstanding of the rules of the game of democratic government if the members of radical groups call this result "unjust." Majority rule is democratic on account of the process required to obtain a majority, and not merely on account of the fact that a majority is a majority, or a plurality a plurality. To put it more concretely: Government by majority is government by persuasion. Whoever is able to obtain a majority of the votes has made the most successful effort of persuasion; he has been able to win the largest number of people of different creeds, of different social groups and of different attitudes on the question of the day, together. The "moderates" are successful because they are prepared to play this game—because they are willing to see the other fellow's point of view and to build a political house in which they can all live peacefully together. Nobody prevents the "Radicals" from trying their hand at the same game. They have complete liberty to go out and to try to convince as many fellow citizens of their views as anybody else. But if they fail to do so, it is because they did not measure up to the standards which democracy must set and maintain in their own interests. As will be shown below, we should risk the utter destruction of democracy if we would dispense the "Radicals" from the need of recruiting in some electoral district the majority of the voters before they can enter parliamentary bodies.

10. W. Bagehot, *The English Constitution,* "The World's Classics," p. xxiv.

11. As a matter of fact, the distinctive feature of democracy when compared with an autocratic form of government is that it permits the existence of a legal opposition.

12. It will be noticed that this feeling indicates the existence of a second type of protest vote. Protest is directed not only against economic conditions, but also, and to an increasing extent, against the inefficiency of the democratic "system," which is the result of P.R.

13. Will supporters of P.R. be able to point to any instance in which elections creating such a heterogeneous majority of irreconcilable groups have occurred under the majority system?

14. As Ramsay MacDonald put it: "It (the majority system) discourages sectionalism and tends to destroy dogmatic and academic differences in parties which have no value in actual life." (*Socialism and Government,* London, 1909, p. 138.)

15. The fact that it does cease in anti-parliamentarian parties as soon as they have won a victory and secured a political monopoly is the major reason for the assumption that modern dictatorships will no more solve the problem of succession than their predecessors have. Cf. F. A. Hermens, "Parlamentarismus oder was sonst," *Hochland,* March, 1932.

16. Considérant complains bitterly that in an election under the majority system parties do not openly display their banners. He continues: "There is, therefore, in all parties an evident tendency to complement each other, at any rate in words and promises, and to borrow for themselves mutually what all of them lack as a result of their exclusive character." Considérant regrets that situation because it blurs the dividing lines between parties; he adds that if one wants to have a clear expression of all different "opinions," the necessity of making concessions which characterizes the majority system must be abolished. Instead, the voters must possess the liberty to organize as they please. This can easily be done, for: "Generally speaking, change the conditions in which people find themselves with regard to each other, and you will change the character of the relations between them." We do not subscribe to this latter statement when expressed in such general terms, but adherents of P.R. who deny the dynamics of its consequences might well take into account what Considérant had to say on this matter.

17. John Stuart Mill, to whom, after Considérant, we owe what there is in the way of theoretical defense of P.R., does not fail to notice this. He takes the marginal electors energetically to task and calls them "the most timid, the most narrowminded and prejudiced" of all voters. (*Considerations on Representative Government,* London, 1861, pp. 136–7.)

On the other hand, Ramsay MacDonald once again formulates the issue clearly when he says: "Proportional Representation seeks to fix in our system of government those evils which attend times of political transition and instability, to emphasize the irreconcilable dogmatic differences which the élite consider to be precious, and to prevent the intermingling of opinion on the margin of parties and sections of parties which is essential to ordered and organic social progress. Unfortunate will be the country which, having started on better ways, is either driven into these bad ones or in mistake adopts them of its own free will." (*Op. cit.,* p. 165.

18. Therefore, it is not correct to say that P.R. would have the advantage of mitigating the evils of pressure groups by "bringing them into the open." As A. V. Dicey put it: "Sixty-seven anti-vaccinators who might accidentally obtain seats in the House of Commons, e.g., as Conservatives or Liberals, would, be it noted, constitute a very different body from sixty-seven members sent to the House of Commons to represent the cause of anti-vaccination. The difference is this: In the first case each anti-vaccinator would often perceive that there were matters of more pressing importance than anti-vaccination; but the sixty-seven men elected under a system of proportional representation to obtain the total repeal of the vaccination laws would, one may almost say must, make that repeal the one dominant object of their parliamentary action." (*Introduction to the Study of the Law of the Constitution,* London, 1920, p. lxxii.)

See also F. A. Hermens, "Democracy and Proportional Representation," *Public Policy Pamphlet No. 31,* University of Chicago Press, September 1940, pp. 13–15.

19. As Ramsay MacDonald expressed it: "Under this system of anarchistic, individual and able-man representation (the Hare system of P.R.) you get a man elected in a huge constituency on one point, and he comes there and, except on that point, does not represent his constituency at all. . . . It is a most absurd idea of representation." (G. Horwill, *Proportional Representation, Its Dangers and Its Defects,* London, 1925, p. 123.)

20. The passage in question deserves to be quoted in full in the original language: "Bei den nächsten Wahlen wird eintreten, was bei diesen sich erst im

Keim zeigte: die Berufsverbände (Hausbesitzer, Diplominhaber, Festbesoldete, Bünde aller Art) werden die Parteien zwingen, lediglich zum Zwecke des Stimmenfanges deren (der Berufsverbände) besoldete Sekretäre an die Spitze der Liste zu stellen. Das Parlament wird so eine Körperschaft werden, innerhalb derer solche Persönlichkeiten, denen die nationale Politik 'Hekuba' ist, die vielmehr, der Sache nach, unter einem imperativen Mandat von ökonomischen Interessenten handeln, den Ton angeben: ein Banausenparlament, unfähig in irgendeinem Sinne eine Auslesestätte politischer Führer darzustellen." (*Berliner Börsenzeitung,* February 25, 1919. Reprinted in *Gesammelte Schriften zur Politik,* Duncker and Humblot, München, 1921, p. 391.)

21. For details see C. G. Hoag and G. H. Hallett, Jr., *Proportional Representation* (New York, 1926), pp. 77 ff.

22. For some advocates of P.R. the person of the candidate is so immaterial that in their opinion the only object of elections should be to determine the number of places to be given to each party. After that, the party could fill the seats with whatever persons it chooses, with the understanding that such deputies would be subject to recall by the party. (Cf. H. Kelsen, *Das Problem des Parlamentarismus,* Vienna and Leipzig, year of publication not indicated, pp. 16-19.)

23. So far as the multiplication of parties under the Hare system is concerned, it is good to remember that Thomas Hare himself not only predicted it, but obviously saw in it a distinct advantage. For example, he says: "Many more candidates will be everywhere put in nomination," and in later pages he is even more explicit: "minorities . . . (will, under the single-transferable vote) far exceed the entire number of any minorities now existing, by the operation of numberless affinities and compulsions, which, in a state of liberation, *will dissolve the present majorities.*" (Italics mine) (See T. Hare, *The Election of Representatives, Parliamentary and Municipal,* 4th ed (London, 1873), pp. xv and 26-7.)

24. Supporters of the Hare system claim that under it the splitting up of parties would be limited, because voters who disagree with the wishes of the party leaders could, instead of founding a party of their own, support a member of their old party as a candidate who shares their views. If this should happen it would, however, have effects in no way different from a splitting up of parties. Parties are units of action, and their ultimate purpose is to develop a coherent policy and to find a majority for it. A party whose unity is destroyed by the election of candidates of different views who have nothing in common but a party label is not able to fulfill its functions.

It is interesting to note that the leading French (and Italian!) advocates of P.R. used to demand P.R. for the purpose of creating strong party organizations, which at the time of the introduction of P.R. did not exist in their countries. It is evident that under these conditions only the list system of P.R. could qualify for recommendation; the Hare system might have made existing matters worse. Therefore, the leading French supporters of P.R. were almost unanimous in demanding the list system, and this has been done after as well as before the breakdown of the German Republic. (See G. Lachapelle, *Les Régimes électoraux, op. cit.,* pp. 170-1; *Elections législatives,* 26 *avril et* 3 *mai* 1936, pp. xiv-

xvi, Paris, 1936.) In addition to the argument that existing party organizations need strengthening, Lachapelle quite rightly demands the list system for reasons of consistency, because it is the only method which can ensure full proportionality.

25. According to Hare, the entire United Kingdom, including Ireland, was to form one constituency so far as the computation of the quota is concerned. The voter "will have a schedule before him, containing the names not only of the candidates for his own particular constituency, but of the candidates for all the other constituencies of the kingdom." (*Op. cit.,* p. 125.) In a later passage he says that the voter would be given "a freedom of choice, not only of the two or three (candidates who offer themselves under the majority system) but probably of two or three thousand candidates." (P. 140.) However, hundreds of "constituencies" would nevertheless be formed in the country, and the intention obviously is to have the voter concentrate on those candidates who offer themselves expressly for the constituencies to which the voter belongs.

There are other features in Hare's proposal, which do not lend themselves easily to summarization; the reader is referred to Hare's book for all details that might interest him.

26. Walter Bagehot makes the following statement about Mr. Hare's "scheme": "No common person readily apprehends all the details in which, with loving care, he has embodied it. He was so anxious to prove what could be done, that he has confused most people as to what it is. I have heard a man say, 'He never could remember it two days running.'" (*op. cit.,* p. 132.)

27. Proponents of P.R. might say that under the majority system even more than twenty per cent of the votes are "wasted." That objection would, however, imply a begging of the question. It can be made only upon the basis of the claim that "The object of a representative body is to represent." For us, elections do not have the ultimate purpose of "representation"; instead, they constitute a process of integration, an essential feature of which consists in the making of a decision directly by the voters. As long as that is the case no vote is wasted because it belongs to the minority; there simply have not been enough votes cast for its candidates to make it a majority. On the other hand, all votes have been wasted if the elections have failed to create a legislative body which possesses a majority able and willing to cooperate for the common good. Such a result, for which the two elections to the German Reichstag held in 1932 constitute the best example, will be generally regarded as the *reductio ad absurdum* of the process of voting, and will pave the way for dictatorship, which means that all free voting will come to an end.

28. See, for example, Hoag and Hallett, *op. cit.,* pp. 378 ff.

29. J. R. MacNichol in: "Special Committee on Elections and Franchise Acts, Minutes of Proceedings and Evidence," Session 1936, House of Commons (Ottawa, 1936), p. 81. Such developments have never occurred in the use of P.R. for local elections in the United States. They are not entirely unknown, however, where P.R. is applied for elections in private bodies. As a gentleman who occupies a position of trust in his profession wrote me: "In a Union election I tallied . . . we followed the Hare system faithfully and found several cases where it was left to those who

counted the ballots to decide whether one candidate was elected rather than another."

30. Horwill, *op. cit.,* p. 126. Sir Austen then asks the question: "If that does not succeed, do you think you have come to the end of the story?" He answers it by discussing a pamphlet of a proponent of P.R., at the end of which its author deals with the results of the Hare system of P.R. in Tasmania and concludes: "There are said to be over three hundred methods of proportional representation already devised. The problem is to find one which will preserve the good results that Tasmania has already experienced, and reduce to a negligible quantity the dangerous effects which the recent election has brought into startling prominence." (*Ibid.,* pp. 127-8.) Sir Austen uses rather strong language when he continues after this quotation by saying: "Are we to go on trying all these three hundred nostrums which the quack doctors offer us?" (*Ibid.,* p. 128.)

31. The reason why so much attention is given to the rigid list system of P.R. is that this system was used in pre-Nazi Germany. Of all the dictatorships which have become possible on account of thé weakening of democratic institutions brought about by P.R., that of Hitler has been most disturbing for the political life of the world.

32. We are not unaware that in some instances the majority system has been combined with the list system, several candidates being elected in a relatively large constituency. Such cases are, however, exceptional.

33. Horwill, *op. cit.,* p. 122.

34. The beneficial character of these close relations between the electors and the elected has been well expressed by Sir Austen Chamberlain in these words: "I sat for more than twenty-one years for a single constituency which in that time grew from an electorate of 10,000 to an electorate of 25,000 or 27,000. There is nothing that I value more, and there is nothing that I regretted so much by my severance of that connection in order to accept the candidature in another constituency, which had special personal ties for me, than that long personal connection between the Member and his constituents. I knew them and they knew me, and it was a good thing and a strength to both of us that it was so." (Horwill, *op. cit.,* p. 128.)

35. Mr. Neville Chamberlain, it is true, for a long time treated both Parliament and the cabinet in a rather autocratic manner. However, in the end the House of Commons did manage to force his resignation, and ever since Mr. Churchill became Prime Minister, Parliament has been treated with the utmost consideration. On the general subject of the relation between the English government and the members of the House of Commons, see W. I. Jennings, *Parliament* (New York, 1940), pp. 119 ff., 152 ff., 224 ff.

36. It may be charged that elections in small constituencies make the deputy the slave of local interests. The proper answer has been given by Abbé Lemire, who said during the French P.R. debate of 1909: "Election in single-member districts means dependence of the deputy in little matters, but his independence and pride in large ones." (Quoted from Jean Mistler, "Rapport fait au nom de la Commission du Suffrage Universel," Chambre des Députés, N. 6326, Quinzième, Législature, Session de 1936, p. 28.)

37. This makes it easy for anti-parliamentarian parties to adjust themselves to the conditions of democracy. Their principles demand that their central leaders be in absolute command over the party, the deputies included. Under a single-member constituency this would not be possible, since every deputy would have to win a constituency for himself, and in this constituency he would be a factor with which the party would have to reckon.

38. Bagehot, *op. cit.,* pp. 135-6.

39. *Ibid.,* p. 138.

40. *Ibid.,* p. 139.

41. The remarks on this subject are so short that they should be supplemented by what has been written previously on the subject, in particular by C. Mierendorff, "Die Gründe gegen die Verhältniswahl und das bestehende Listenverfahren," in: J. Schauff, *Neues Wahlrecht* (Berlin, 1929), pp. 22-6.

42. J. Barthélemy, *L'Organisation du Suffrage et l'Expérience Belge* (Paris, 1912), p. 655.

43. So far as the details are concerned, matters are different in different countries. In the United States the President is at the present time directly elected by the people, although, as we shall later see, this would soon be different under P.R. In countries with the parliamentary system of government the Prime Minister is not formally elected by the people, but as a rule appointed by the head of the State. If there is a two-party system, or a system of two blocs, and if the victorious party or bloc has a recognized leader, then the head of the State will not fail to appoint him as Prime Minister, which means that ultimately the designation is made by the people.

44. *Contrat Social,* Chapter XV. This statement of Rousseau no longer holds true of the English Parliament. The improved means of communication and especially the press and the radio make it possible now for the English voters to check the political activities of their deputy throughout his term in Parliament. The deputies try to act in conformity with the wishes of their electorates, in so far as that is possible. For some details see Jennings, *op. cit.,* pp. 28 ff.

45. For the different types of compromise see C. Schmitt, *Verfassung und Verfassungsrecht* (Munich, 1928), pp. 31-6.

46. *Ibid.,* p. 32.

> *"Government is a trust, and the officers of the government*
> *are trustees; and both the trust and the trustees*
> *are created for the benefit of the people."*
> —HENRY CLAY, speech at Ashland, Kentucky, 1829.

# VOTING IN DEMOCRACIES

## Enid Lakeman and James D. Lambert

### SOME POLITICAL ASPECTS OF P.R.

Proportional methods of election are, it is generally agreed, better adapted than is majority method to producing an "image of the feelings of the nation," the first of our aims which an electoral system should fulfil. But their adoption is often opposed on grounds other than the technical objections discussed in the previous chapter. Proportional systems, it is asserted, increase unduly the number of parties securing representation, thus preventing any one party from obtaining a working majority; therefore, government has to be based on a coalition or on a single party which depends for its majority on the support of allies. This results in greater likelihood of unstable government.

In the first place, however, opponents of proportional representation exaggerate its tendency to facilitate an increase in the number of parties, and ignore the fact that a multiplicity of parties may arise from many causes and often exists under majority systems. It would be more correct to say, not that proportional representation creates parties, but that when those parties have been called into being by other causes it secures their reflection in Parliament. In Tasmania,[1] the voters find their needs met by only two parties and Independents, and half a century of P.R. has not changed this position. On the other hand, the French voters tend, for a variety of reasons, to divide among many parties, and the use of a majority system has never checked this tendency.

Table 1 shows the number of parties represented in the Lower House in various European countries just before the outbreak of the 1914-18 war. It is evident from Table 1 that the number of parties

in a country has little relation to its voting system, and in particular that the salient examples of the multiplication of parties cannot have arisen from proportional representation. All the countries in [Table 1] which were then using majority systems later adopted proportional representation. Their experience under the new system is discussed in the next section (pp. 284-303). In no case was the change followed by any marked increase in the number of parties, and in some instances there was a decrease. The indications are, therefore, that proportional representation does not encourage the formation of parties but only reflects in the Parliament whatever tendencies towards fusion or division may exist in the country at the time of the election.

While that general conclusion follows from experience of all proportional systems in actual use, it should be pointed out that in this respect the single transferable vote is likely to differ materially from party list systems. Where votes have to be cast for a party list, any dissident element within a party can seek representation only by submitting a separate list. This forces the voter into a choice between the one group and the other; moreover, it entails the creation of some sort of organization, which may tend to make the splinter group a permanent party, remaining after the occasion of the split has disappeared. If, however, the voter has a free choice among different candidates of the same

### TABLE 1*

| First-Past-the-Post | Second Ballot | | Proportional Systems | |
|---|---|---|---|---|
| Denmark 4 | Germany | 21 | Finland | 6 |
| | France | 12 | Belgium | 4 |
| | Italy | 10 | Sweden | 3 |
| | Netherlands | 10 | | |
| | Switzerland | 5 | | |
| | Norway | 3 | | |

* All figures are from official returns, Braunias' *Das Parlamentarische Wahlrecht* or contemporary newspapers.

Reprinted from Enid Lakeman and James D. Lambert, *Voting in Democracies* (London: Faber & Faber Ltd., 1955), pp. 149–199, by permission of the publishers.

party, and especially if he can, in addition, indicate his agreement with certain of the candidates in other parties, the dissident group will probably be able to secure its due representation without constituting itself a separate party. Those conditions are fulfilled most completely under the single transferable vote.

Moreover, if a split does occur, the single transferable vote enables it to be more easily healed when the circumstances producing it have changed. This is illustrated by an incident in the history of the Irish Labour Party. In 1944, the National Labour Party split off from the Labour Party owing to a dispute over alleged Communist influence in Irish branches of British trade unions. This split, however, had no serious effect on the Labour movement's electoral fortunes, as it would have had under other voting systems, for supporters of the one section were free to give their later preferences to candidates of the other, and a sufficient number did so to enable the two together to secure nearly their proportional share of the seats.[2] Thus, the bitterness that would have arisen if the two parties had spoiled one another's chances was avoided, all Labour voters were encouraged to remember that their two parties still had much in common, and they were re-united before the election of 1951.

It is often objected that if three (or more) parties obtain representation, the third party may, by holding the balance of power, be able to exact from one of the larger parties concessions in return for its own support. In other words, a certain amount of minority legislation might be possible through party bargaining. But the fear of this is exaggerated, for both partners in any such bargain will be aware that it may lose them many votes at the next general election, and possibly at a by-election. Any attempt by a smaller party to abuse its balancing position, or acquiescence in this by a larger party, will be dangerous to the party itself.

But even if the danger associated with a balancing party in Parliament is real, it is less serious than the risk of control by a very small group of voters. The Parliamentary party has to vote openly, and can be called to account at the next election; the electors vote by secret ballot and are accountable to nobody. A balancing party in the House of Commons representing probably two or three million voters may decide this or that action of the government; a few thousand voters, by changing sides, may decide which government takes office.

It is indeed this very power of the "floating voter" which supporters of the two-party system give as a reason for thinking two parties sufficient. Each of those parties, they say, in its anxiety to win over people not firmly attached to either of them, adopts policies that will appeal to those people, so that "simple majority voting produces a certain moderation in the government."[3] But the result may not be

moderation; one or both parties may be wooing extreme groups and the government may therefore find itself committed to extreme policies certainly not desired by the bulk of the voters. The "floating voters" may be thoughtful people of moderate views, or thoughtless people easily swayed by trivialities, or organised pressure groups offering their votes to whichever party will pledge its support to their particular interests.

Moreover, the influence of the minority, whether moderate or extreme, must, under a majority system, be very uncertain. In a constituency where the result is expected to be close, a tiny pressure group can exercise influence out of all proportion to its importance; where there exists a large permanent majority for one party, the legitimate claims of a far larger body of voters can be ignored with impunity. Under a proportional system, on the contrary, the influence of such a group cannot be either much greater or much less than its size warrants.

Proportional representation may indeed lead such a group to seek and obtain representation as a separate party, but to deny it the right to do so is to deny it any remedy if the major parties ignore its claims. Opinions of minorities expressed merely at the polls can never be the equivalent to that represented in the House of Commons. As John Stuart Mill said,[4] "in the absence of its natural defenders, the interest of the excluded is always in danger of being overlooked; and, when looked at, is seen with different eyes from those of the persons whom it directly concerns." A similar opinion was expressed by John Morley[5]—"the best guarantee of justice in public dealings is the participation in their own government of the people most likely to suffer from injustice."

A further danger of the two-party system is rule by a minority; rule, that is to say, by a minority of the nation which happens to have a majority in the government party. In nineteenth-century Britain that danger was not so great as it is to-day. The parties were then comparatively loose associations, on the one hand of people generally disposed to experiment and improve, and on the other hand of people preferring the existing order and averse to change. An M.P. was committed to an attitude rather than to a programme. Nowadays, however, to vote for a party is to commit oneself to a series of proposals which a candidate is expected to support completely. Some of those proposals may have been accepted by only a small majority of the party, and may be unacceptable to all or most of its opponents—that is to say, in total, to a majority of the voters—but if that party becomes the government those proposals will nevertheless be put into effect along with the rest of its programme. The country may thus be involved against its will in a course of action from which there is no retreat.[6]

The risk of such minority legislation is reduced

if there are more than two parties. The programmes of those parties are sure to overlap to a greater or less extent, giving the voters the possibility of choice between different combinations of the same policies, and this effect will be increased if the voters can be given, within each party, a choice between candidates of different shades of opinion. Moreover, if there are three or more parties, it becomes much less likely that any one of them will have such a Parliamentary majority as will enable it to act, regardless of criticism from outside or even from within its own ranks.

It is true that the absence of an assured Parliamentary majority for the whole of one party's programme would involve some departure from established British practice. It would be necessary for the largest party to accept the fact that, while it was entitled to the leadership of the House and could expect to achieve much of what it desired, it might on occasion have to give way and consent to practise some form of cooperation with members of other parties. It is also true that politicians have not shown much readiness to accept such a change. There are frequent complaints that both the major parties show more inclination to make party capital out of the problems of the day than to cooperate in solving them. Only rarely is the nation's course of action in any matter agreed upon by both; much more often it is safe to assume that anything proposed by the Government will be resisted by the Opposition, and safer still to assume that, if the matter comes to a division, every member will go into the lobby with his own party and against the other. The parties are often made to appear more sharply divided and more completely opposed to one another than in reality they are. The belief that the two-party system is the only practicable method of governing will, it is hoped, be shown to be erroneous in our later examination of electoral experience in other countries.

## STABLE AND EFFECTIVE GOVERNMENT

The wish to limit the number of parties to two is connected with the belief that government can be carried on effectively only by a single party. One party, it is said, must have unhampered power for the time being to carry out its programme; if the electors are dissatisfied with its conduct of affairs, their remedy is to replace it with another party at the next general election. An opposition party is held to be necessary for this purpose and also to supply criticism of the government. The desirability of such criticism is acknowledged by advocates of "strong" one-party government; for example, Professor Hermens admits that a government majority can be too large and suggests electoral devices to

"secure for the opposition a number of seats large enough to make it possible for it to oppose the majority vigorously in Parliament."[7]

It is assumed, firstly, that the functions of government and opposition are separate, to be carried out by two different bodies of people, and, secondly, that a sufficient guarantee against the danger that a government will ignore criticism is provided by the prospect that the "swing of the pendulum" will bring the critics into power. The parliamentary minority is regarded as the potential government but, for the time being, is excluded from the responsibilities of administration. The system has "the incurable weakness that it tends to make the 'out' party always a destructive party."[8]

However, in some advanced democracies generally regarded as particularly well-governed—notably in Switzerland and in Scandinavia—the conditions so widely regarded in Britain as essential are seldom or never fulfilled. There is no one party with power to carry out its whole programme, no other party whose function is to oppose the government now and replace it in the future. Government is usually carried on either by two or more parties in coalition or by one party that must obtain some support from outside its own ranks for the passage of any given measure. That support does not necessarily always come from the same quarter; a critic of the government on one issue may be a supporter of it on another. Moreover, a government defeated on a particular question, not a vote of confidence, does not necessarily feel called upon to resign; it continues to govern but, on that question, submits to the majority will of Parliament.

In those countries, a general election is usually followed, not by the formation of a completely new government, but by a modification of the old one —a larger share of ministerial posts for one party, a smaller for another; the replacement of one minister by another. This introduces an element of stability which is lacking in countries depending on the "swing of the pendulum"—there is much greater continuity in policy. A measure that has required the assent of several parties, backed by a genuine majority of the voters, is unlikely to be reversed. On the other hand, modifications found desirable in the light of experience may be accepted more readily when the parties are accustomed to the idea of compromise.

In Britain, the introduction of a proportional system would tend to promote a spirit of compromise by removing an incentive for an opposition party to seize upon any opportunity to overthrow the government. Under a majority system, such a party may gamble on the knowledge that quite a small movement of public opinion may give it many more seats; there is a strong temptation to force an election. But under a proportional system no large change in the composition of Parliament can take place without a comparable change in the country. There is no object in forcing an election if no considerable change is likely. The parties therefore have to adapt themselves to the existing situation. Though to some extent they must do this under any form of proportional representation, they will cooperate more easily if the form used is one that puts less emphasis on the divisions between parties and more on what they hold in common. The single transferable vote meets these requirements most fully, because it allows the voter to support candidates acceptable to him, whether they all belong to one party or not.

Coalitions are not here advocated for their own sake. Single-party government, provided it represents the country's wishes, has decided advantages and it may well result from proportional representation. But even if it does not, a coalition backed by a majority of the voters is preferable to a single-party government supported only by a minority. Under the single transferable vote, moreover, coalition is free from the most serious objections raised against it in Britain, for no election pacts would be involved in the constituencies; any number of candidates can seek the support of the electors without "splitting the vote," and parties can therefore cooperate on one question without sacrificing their right to differ on others.

Stability and continuity require, of course, a sense of balance and toleration on the part of both the nation and its representatives. To deny that such an ability exists amongst the British electorate and parties would be absurd. Government without an assured Parliamentary majority is no new thing in British politics. It existed, and worked well, during three periods—from 1846 to 1852, from 1886 to 1892, and from 1910 to 1915. In all three periods the minority government was able to survive for a longer period than the average, and to carry difficult and controversial measures. In 1924 and 1929 it was attempted more half-heartedly, and without success. Coalition governments also have proved successful, though it has needed times of crisis to call them into being. In normal times single-party government, with a real or fictitious majority, is considered the only choice. But if a more democratic and a more mature conception of government can be approached through the agency of a fairer and more scientific voting system, it is surely preferable to a two-party system which, as Sir Winston Churchill said,[9] places us "in the strange position that although four-fifths of each of the great parties agree about four-fifths of the things that ought to be done at home and abroad, and although if the worst happened we should all sink or swim together, we seem to be getting ever more bitterly divided as partisans."

## EXPERIENCE UNDER PROPORTIONAL REPRESENTATION: LIST SYSTEMS

Some indication of the relative merits of majority and proportional voting systems can be found in the experience of certain countries under both methods. Ever since the latter part of the last century, there has been a strong tendency for the countries of Continental Europe to discard a majority system in favour of a porportional one. With a single exception, these proportional systems have all been based on the party list, while on the contrary every English-speaking country that has adopted proportional representation has chosen the single transferable vote form.[10] Experience under list systems will be dealt with here, leaving the next chapter for a discussion of the system with which English-speaking readers are more closely concerned. Some countries have later modified the system of proportional representation originally adopted, or have extended its application to organs of their national or local government not at first affected. In only a few instances has a proportional system been abandoned once it has been adopted.

The following pages deal briefly with the history of electoral changes and their effects in European countries where democratic government still exists. It has not been thought necessary to include those countries now behind the Iron Curtain whose electoral experiments have been quite overshadowed by other factors in their turbulent history. The mechanics of the voting systems used have been explained elsewhere; in these chapters the emphasis is on the motives that inspired a change in electoral methods and on the influence this change itself exerted on administration and on party structure.

Two major criticisms of proportional representation have been discussed (p. 281): that it results (a) in an excessive multiplication of parties and consequently (b) in a lack of effective government. The facts show the fear of these consequences to be exaggerated, while on the other hand there is evidence that in many cases proportional representation has produced political harmony. This is especially true of countries with a more mature experience in self-government, where there has grown up a truer understanding of democracy and an increased sentiment of national unity.

### Scandinavia

By 1921, the Scandinavian countries had each adopted some system of proportional representation for the election of all or many of their national and local political assemblies. These systems differed one from another. It is noteworthy that none of them has been discarded, even for a brief period. In some cases, experience revealed defects in the system as first adopted, but this led to improvements which, far from altering the basic principle of proportionality, strengthened its application.

DENMARK. The first national elections embodying the principle of proportional representation took place in Denmark in 1856. The particular method employed was a form of the single transferable vote devised by the Danish statesman, Carl Andrae.[11] Its application, however, was limited to the election of 55 out of the 80 members of the single-chamber Rigsraad. In 1866, under a later constitution which established a second chamber (abolished again in 1953), the system was restricted to the indirect election of the Landsting or Upper House, by electoral colleges which after 1915 were themselves chosen by a party list form of proportional representation. Andrae's system, like Hare's, was later improved by the adoption of the smaller (Droop) quota[12] and the utilization of unsuccessful candidates' votes as well as of surpluses. However, its full effects in producing free and equitable representation could not be seen in elections where the voters were confined to small electoral colleges composed of disciplined party representatives.

Until 1915, the Lower House (Folketing)[13] was elected by the British system. During the preceding years, political power had been shared chiefly by the Conservatives and Liberals, but two parties of the Left (Radicals and Social Democrats) were developing in strength because of an extension of the franchise. In the earlier years of the present century, neither of the two older parties could obtain a working majority, despite the operation of the majority system. In order to achieve some political stability, the practice grew up of concluding pacts between the parties. It was seldom that all four contested one seat. Conservatives and Liberals on the one hand, and Radicals and Social Democrats on the other, usually preferred to come to an understanding. There was therefore in practice a tendency towards an uneasy party dualism, with the Liberals threatening to absorb the Conservatives and the Radicals and Social Democrats becoming an opportunist fusion. These artificial alliances of parties naturally opposed to one another were an increasingly unsatisfactory factor in the life of the nation.

In an attempt to eliminate unrest caused by these alliances, and give fairer representation to the Left, an element of proportional representation was superimposed on the single-member majority elections by a law of 1915, which operated in the general election of 1918. Following public protests against the inadequacy of this reform, the whole system was put on a proportional basis in 1920, and later modifications have increased the accuracy with which the parties' votes are reflected in the House.[14] Within the party list system, the order of election of individual candidates is determined by a form of transferable vote, but the voter is limited to the expression of his *first* preference, transfers being carried out according to the order of the candidates' names on the ballot paper. This method is very similar to the Belgian.[15] but tends to give a more local character to the representation, because, in each district within the constituency, the candidate nominated by residents of that district appears on the ballot paper as the first of his party's list.

Under proportional representation in Denmark, there has been some tendency for the number of parties to increase. The four chief parties, however, have continued to dominate the Folketing as under the majority system, with two to four minor ones (including the Communists) securing only an ineffective share.[16] Table 2 shows the party representation from the last majority election onwards.

It will be seen that none of the four chief parties has been able to secure a clear majority in any one election. Therefore, administrations have been based on a coalition, or on government by a single party, dependent for its majority in any division on support from some part of the "Opposition," although it should be realized that in Denmark the term "Opposition" has no such connotation as it has in Britain. Table 3 shows that the life of these governments has been relatively long.

The reasons for the stable and satisfactory nature of such administrations are common to all the Scandinavian countries and are dealt with in succeeding pages.

NORWAY. The Norwegian Parliament (Storting)[17] is elected for four years and consists of 50 members from the towns and 150 from the country districts.[18] These are now chosen by a proportional system in 11 urban and 18 rural constituencies returning from 3 to 7 members each. Before 1921, they were elected by the second ballot in single-member constituencies. Representation was shared among three parties (Conservative, Liberal and Socialist), the first two of which contained divisions which did not always collaborate and on two occasions split off to form separate parties. There existed the practice of political alliances usually associated with the second ballot. The Conservatives and Liberals generally combined against the Socialists, thus placing the Left under a permanent electoral disadvantage. The introduction of a proportional system was designed to remedy this.

Under the new system, the number of parties contesting elections increased from five in 1921 to nine in 1933, and in 1949 was six. Not all, however, were successful in winning seats, and the effective parliamentary strength remained concen-

## TABLE 2—Elections to the Folketing, 1913-53*

| | Conservative | Liberal | Radical | Social Democrat | Communist | Others | Number of Parties |
|---|---|---|---|---|---|---|---|
| 1913 | 7 | 44 | 31 | 32 | — | — | 4 |
| 1918 | 22 | 46 | 31 | 39 | — | 2 | 5 |
| April, 1920 | 28 | 49 | 17 | 42 | — | 4 | 5 |
| July, 1920 | 26 | 52 | 16 | 42 | — | 4 | 5 |
| Sept., 1920 | 27 | 52 | 18 | 48 | — | 4 | 6 |
| 1924 | 28 | 45 | 20 | 55 | — | 1 | 4 |
| 1926 | 30 | 47 | 16 | 53 | — | 3 | 5 |
| 1929 | 24 | 44 | 16 | 61 | — | 4 | 5 |
| 1932 | 27 | 39 | 14 | 62 | 2 | 5 | 6 |
| 1935 | 26 | 29 | 14 | 68 | 2 | 10 | 7 |
| 1939 | 26 | 30 | 13 | 64 | 3 | 10 | 9 |
| 1943 | 31 | 28 | 13 | 66 | — | 11 | 8 |
| 1945 | 26 | 38 | 11 | 48 | 18 | 7 | 7 |
| 1947 | 17 | 49 | 10 | 57 | 9 | 6 | 6 |
| 1950 | 27 | 32 | 12 | 59 | 7 | 12 | 6 |
| 1953 | 26 | 33 | 13 | 61 | 7 | 9 | 6 |

* In this and similar tables, 'others' may include several parties and Independents; Independents are not counted as a party. It should be noted that a party continuing under the same name may change its nature radically in the course of years. The table omits a mainly uncontested election in 1915. The elections of July and September 1920 were occasioned by the incorporation of Schleswig into Denmark.

trated in the hands of Conservatives, Agrarians, Liberals, and Socialists. The Socialists' progress received a setback in 1923, when, after the repudiation of Moscow by the moderate element, the left wing broke away to form the Communist party. This had some success, especially in 1945, but by 1949 its support had fallen again below the level necessary to secure a seat even in a seven-member constituency. In the 'thirties, the Socialists, while not attaining an absolute majority in the Storting, won sufficient seats to enable them to form a minority government, which, by a modification of the more extreme points in its programme, was able to command the required majority. Table 4 shows the changes in party strengths in the Storting between 1915 and 1952.

In the first years following the introduction of proportional representation there was an alternation of minority or coalition administrations, whose nucleus was usually the Liberals and against which the Socialists formed the Opposition. In 1933, however, the Socialists emerged as the most powerful single element, strong enough to form a minority government. And since 1945 they have governed alone, with a clear majority.

SWEDEN. Sweden formerly used the British system, except for Stockholm which formed one constituency returning 22 members by the block vote.

## TABLE 3—Danish Administrations, 1913-52

| Type | Duration |
|---|---|
| Radical Liberal with Social Democrat support | June, 1913–March, 1920 |
| Non-party | March–April, 1920 |
| | April–May, 1920 |
| Moderate Liberal | May, 1920–October, 1922 |
| | October, 1922–April, 1924 |
| Social Democrat | April, 1924–December, 1926 |
| Moderate Liberal | December, 1926–April, 1929 |
| Social Democrat and Radical Liberal | April, 1929–November, 1935 |
| | November, 1935–April, 1940 |
| During the occupation, coalitions of all the major parties and Independents. No Danish Government between August 1943 and the liberation | April–July, 1940 |
| | July, 1940–May, 1942 |
| | May–November, 1942 |
| | November, 1942–August, 1943 |
| | May–November, 1945 |
| Moderate Liberal | November, 1945–November, 1947 |
| Social Democrat | November, 1947–October, 1950 |
| Moderate Liberal and Conservative | October, 1950– |

### TABLE 4—Elections to the Storting, 1915-52

| | Conservative | Agrarian | Liberal* | Socialist | Communist | Others | Number of Parties |
|---|---|---|---|---|---|---|---|
| 1915 | 21 | — | 78 | 24 | — | — | 3 |
| 1918 | 50 | 3 | 54 | 18 | — | 1 | 4 |
| 1921 | 57 | 17 | 39 | 29 | — | 8 | 5 |
| 1924 | 54 | 22 | 36 | 24 | 6 | 8 | 6 |
| 1927 | 31 | 26 | 31 | 59 | 3 | — | 5 |
| 1930 | 44 | 25 | 34 | 47 | — | — | 4 |
| 1933 | 31 | 24 | 25 | 69 | — | 2 | 6 |
| 1936 | 36 | 18 | 23 | 70 | — | 3 | 6 |
| 1945 | 25 | 10 | 20 | 76 | 11 | 8 | 6 |
| 1949 | 23 | 12 | 21 | 85 | — | 8 | 5 |

* Braunias (*Das Parlamentarische Wahlrecht*, p. 394) lists separately from the Liberals a small Radical group appearing in 1918 with three members and decreasing to one in 1930.

Representation was seriously distorted, especially under the block vote,[19] and agitation for a change began as early as 1867, at the time of the first introduction of proportional representation into Denmark. Along with this movement went a demand for the reform of the franchise, which rested on property qualifications. A law passed in 1907 established manhood suffrage and proportional representation under the system described in Appendix vi [of *Voting in Democracies*]. It was applied first to the election by local Councils of representatives in the Upper House, and in the following year to the election of the Stockholm Town Council and all the provincial Councils; the first general election to the Lower House of Parliament under this system was in 1911.

Before 1911, Sweden had three parties—Conservative, Liberal and Social Democrat. This pat-

### TABLE 5—Norwegian Administrations, 1913-52

| Type | Duration |
|---|---|
| Liberal | Jan., 1913–June, 1920 |
| Conservative | June, 1920–June, 1921 |
| Liberal | June, 1921–Mar., 1923 |
| Conservative–Independent Liberal | Mar., 1923–May, 1923 |
| Conservative–Independent Liberal | May, 1923–July, 1924 |
| Liberal | July, 1924–Feb., 1926 |
| Conservative–Independent Liberal | Feb., 1926–Jan., 1928 |
| Labour | Jan., 1928–Feb., 1928 |
| Liberal | Feb., 1928–May, 1931 |
| Agrarian | May, 1931–Mar., 1932 |
| Agrarian | Mar., 1932–Mar., 1933 |
| Liberal | Mar., 1933–Mar., 1935 |
| Labour | Mar., 1935–June, 1945 |
| Labour–Conservative–Liberal | June, 1945–Nov., 1945 |
| Labour | Nov., 1945–Nov., 1951 |
| Labour | Nov., 1951– |

tern has persisted without major change. Only one large new party has grown up, the Agrarian Party, which split off from the Conservatives. Though remaining in sympathy with them it has lately turned more towards social reform. The Liberals split on the prohibition question into two groups (elections of 1924, 1928 and 1932) which later re-united to form what is now known as the People's Party. The Communists have had some success but are now declining; a Swedish Nazi Party never succeeded in winning a seat.

Table 6 shows the party strengths from 1911 to 1952. The variations from one election to the next are larger than in most countries using proportional systems, but small compared with those in British elections.

During the 1920's, administrations were usually based on one party, which had no clear majority but relied for support on allied groups within the Chamber. In the early 'thirties, the Social Democrats secured an ascendancy which has endured until the present day, and in 1940 they won a clear majority of the seats. When lacking a clear majority, they either have followed the same plan of relying on Parliamentary support from other parties or have formed a coalition with the Agrarians. It will be seen from Table 7 that these administrations have varied in duration from three months to over six years and have tended to become more and more long-lived. In the last eighteen years there have been only four governments, and each of these has contained some of the same elements as its predecessor; there has thus been continuity of policy.

FINLAND. Finland first adopted a proportional system in 1906, while she was still a Grand Duchy within the Russian Empire, exercising home rule through a Diet consisting of four Houses (Nobility, Clergy, Burghers, Peasantry). Following a *coup d'état* in 1899, the country remained for some time in a turbulent state, and it became increasingly

### TABLE 6—Elections to the Swedish Lower House, 1911-52

|  |  | Conservative | Agrarian | Liberal | Independent People's | Social Democrat | Communist | Others | Number of Parties |
|---|---|---|---|---|---|---|---|---|---|
|  | 1911 | 65 | — | 101 | — | 64 | — | — | 3 |
| Spring, | 1914* | 86 | — | 71 | — | 73 | — | — | 3 |
| Autumn, | 1914* | 86 | — | 57 | — | 87 | — | — | 3 |
|  | 1917 | 59 | 12 | 62 | — | 86 | — | 11 | 5 |
|  | 1920 | 70 | 30 | 48 | — | 75 | — | 7 | 5 |
|  | 1921 | 62 | 21 | 41 | — | 93 | 7 | 6 | 6 |
|  | 1924 | 65 | 23 | 5 | 28 | 104 | 5 | — | 6 |
|  | 1928 | 73 | 27 | 4 | 28 | 90 | 8 | — | 6 |
|  | 1932 | 58 | 36 | 4 | 20 | 104 | 2 | 6 | 7 |
|  | 1936 | 44 | 36 | 27 | — | 112 | 5 | 6 | 6 |
|  | 1940 | 42 | 28 | 23 | — | 134 | 3 | — | 5 |
|  | 1944 | 39 | 35 | 26 | — | 115 | 15 | — | 5 |
|  | 1948 | 23 | 30 | 57 | — | 112 | 8 | — | 5 |
|  | 1952 | 30 | 27 | 59 | — | 109 | 5 | — | 5 |

* The second election in 1914 was due to a constitutional crisis precipitated by a speech by the King.

clear that a radical reconstruction was necessary to place Finnish democracy on a firm foundation. To this end, the constitution of 1906 was drawn up, which is remarkable for the original and democratic nature of its provisions. These included the introduction of universal suffrage at the age of 24, and the establishment of a single-chamber legislature.

The electoral system, which was devised at the same time, was essential to the success, and indeed to the acceptance, of this constitution. As a contemporary Finnish pamphlet[20] points out, the four estates of the realm (i.e. the Nobility, Clergy, Burghers, and Peasantry) would certainly not have surrendered their respective powers and privileges to a single-chamber assembly, if they had not been assured that each of them would receive a fair deal, and that there would exist no possibility of the assembly's being dominated by an extremist minority. An important factor behind their acceptance

### TABLE 7—Swedish Administrations, 1917-52

| Type | Duration |
|---|---|
| Liberal–Social Democrat | Oct., 1917–March, 1920 |
| Social Democrat | March, 1920–Oct., 1920 |
| "Administrative" | Oct., 1920–Feb., 1921 |
| "Administrative" | Feb., 1921–Oct., 1921 |
| Social Democrat | Oct., 1921–April, 1923 |
| Conservative | April, 1923–Oct., 1924 |
| Social Democrat | Oct., 1924–June, 1926 |
| Liberal | June, 1926–Oct., 1928 |
| Conservative | Oct., 1928–June, 1930 |
| Liberal | June, 1930–Sept., 1932 |
| Social Democrat | Sept., 1932–June, 1936 |
| Agrarian | June, 1936–Sept., 1936 |
| Social Democrat–Agrarian | Sept., 1936–Dec., 1939 |
| National Coalition | Dec., 1939–July, 1945 |
| Social Democrat | July, 1945–Oct., 1951 |
| Social Democrat–Agrarian | Oct., 1951– |

lay in the check placed on the power of the assembly by a standing provision that certain important Bills could not become law until after the next general election. This provision was similar in intention to the power of delay possessed by the British House of Lords, but was made more effective because Finland's electoral system allows the voter a greater opportunity to express any conclusions that he may have formed during the period of delay. In Britain, delay until after a general election cannot be relied upon to reveal the electors' will regarding the measure in question, because a vote can express only general approval of a whole political programme. The Finnish electoral system, on the other hand, does make possible an expression of public opinion regarding particular items in such a programme, for (besides giving each party its proportional share of the seats) it permits the voter, within each party, a large degree of choice among different candidates, who may hold various views on the delayed measure.[21]

The new constitution was accepted unanimously by three of the four Houses, and by a majority of 100 to 8 in the House of Nobility. Its initial success has been maintained in such a degree that no substantial changes have been thought necessary. Moreover, under it there has existed that strong government which alone could have maintained the independence of Finland in the face of grave and repeated threats. This strength certainly does not rest on a large Parliamentary majority for one party, for such a thing has never existed since Finland attained independence in 1917. It is not associated either with stability in the sense that the government continues unchanged for long periods; on the contrary, Finland has a new Prime Minister on an average about every eighteen months. The government's strength springs rather from a broad popular consent. Cabinets are usually coalitions of three or four parties, and their complexion has changed gradually with developments in public opinion, preserving continuity and avoiding abrupt reversals of policy.[22] J. Hampden Jackson,[23] writing on the situation of Finland after the Second World War, said that it called for "a patience, a degree of tact, a mixture of solidarity and subtlety on the part of the Finns which would be an unparalleled test of a democratic character." He went on to show that this test had been well met: "It is no accident," he observes, "that Finland is the only surviving democracy in the Russian sphere of influence." Such a survival has been largely due to strongly developed democratic qualities, with a machinery of government that has permitted the effective expression of such qualities.

SCANDINAVIAN EXPERIENCE. In most of these countries there has been a tendency for the number of parties to increase after the adoption of P.R., but in all of them Parliamentary representation has been shared predominantly by four major parties. One or other of these has usually been in a position, if not to form a majority government by itself, at least to provide the nucleus of a stable administration in collaboration with a second party with a programme not too dissimilar from its own. The Scandinavian peoples are often credited with a stronger grasp of democratic principles, and greater ability to translate them into political action than have many countries, not excluding Great Britain. Their success in solving the problems of minority government, when this has been necessary, may be attributed to this natural or acquired capacity. But a considerable contribution has also undoubtedly been made by the political machinery they have adopted; both their electoral systems and the great use made of Parliamentary committees have helped to render cooperation between parties and the spirit of compromise acceptable and normal. Whereas in Great Britain recent attempts (in 1923 and 1929) to carry on the government of the country without a single-party majority were short-lived and disappointing and ended in bitterness and recriminations, minority governments in Scandinavia have functioned successfully and for long periods. As a French observer says of Sweden,[24] the nation is remarkably united on essentials. The processes of compromise in committee lead to virtually unanimous reports and hence to Bills backed by all parties; unanimous votes in the Parliament itself are not unusual. Few countries in the world can point to such general stability of government or to what may be even more important, such continuity of government policy in both home and external affairs.

## Switzerland

In examining the electoral experience of Switzerland, it is necessary to remember the political and racial structure of the country. Switzerland is a federation of cantons which can broadly be divided as regards race into German, French, and Italian, the people of German stock far outnumbering the rest. Within certain cantons themselves there are racial and religious minorities, and conflict has often in the past been serious. Although Switzerland is today a well-integrated federation, the Swiss still thinks first and foremost in terms of his canton, and the cantons retain, and jealously guard, a considerable degree of autonomy. The Swiss system of government is indeed based on a still smaller unit, the commune, where an active democracy expresses itself through meetings of all the adult males.[25] Swiss parties were for long organized on a cantonal basis, and became national bodies only in the later years of the last century. Cantonal elections therefore have more significance than the local elections of most other countries.

Discussion on the suitability of electoral systems began in Switzerland during the first half of the nineteenth century. A system for the election of a Constituent Assembly for Geneva was suggested by Victor Considérant in 1842 and elaborated by him in 1846. This influenced the *Association Réformiste,* founded in 1865, which was partly responsible for the first step taken to revise the Swiss electoral laws. The demand for this revision arose out of the bitterness of political divisions exacerbated by a majority system of election in circumstances where racial and religious differences themselves put a strain upon national unity. In 1847, the predominantly Roman Catholic cantons attempted to secede from the Federation, but their revolt was suppressed by the superior strength of the Protestants in the Sonderbund war. At later dates, several elections gave rise to disturbances involving loss of life.

One such incident occurred in the canton of Ticino in 1889.[26] The election of that year gave the Conservatives 77 seats for 12,783 votes, while the Liberals, with almost as many votes (12,166), got only 35 seats. The resulting dissensions were ended by the intervention of the Federal Council, which recommended a proportional system. This was used first for the election of a constituent assembly, and was incorporated into the cantonal constitution in 1891, for the election of the Cantonal Council, constituent assemblies and Municipal Councils. The law was approved by referendum the following year and has remained in force ever since.[27] The object of pacifying the canton was attained, and the success of proportional representation in Ticino encouraged its adoption for other Swiss elections.

In the canton of Geneva, the Protestants and Catholics were nearly equal in numbers but the operation of the block vote resulted in domination of the council by the former. This led to great friction, particularly where legislation connected with religious matters was concerned. In 1892, Geneva followed the example of Ticino by introducing a proportional system. The effect was to reduce considerably the disturbances caused by unfair representation. The influence of the two systems can be seen in the cantonal elections of November 1892 compared with the elections for the National Council in the same canton the following October. While the cantonal elections passed off calmly and were followed by no disturbances, in the Federal elections (still under a majority system) political antagonism gave rise to rioting.

Such were the diametrically opposite influences of the majority and the proportional systems in a country where racial and religious differences were potential threats to national unity and local harmony. As will be seen later, this situation was approximately repeated in the case of Belgium.

The use of proportional representation gradually extended, so that by 1909 it was in force for some or all local elections in ten more cantons. The cantons' experience in turn influenced public opinion with regard to Federal elections, an effect that is clearly seen in three successive initiatives. Advocates of proportional representation for the election of the National Council[28] first secured a popular vote on the subject in 1900, when the change was rejected by a three-to-two majority of the citizens voting and by 11½ cantons to 10½. Ten years later, the number voting for the change had increased by half, the number of opponents remaining nearly stationary and constituting only a bare majority, and 12 cantons voted in favour to 10 against. By 1918, the supporters of proportional representation had increased by a further 25 per cent while its opponents had fallen by nearly one-half; the proposition was carried by 299,550 votes to 149,035 and 19½ cantons to 2½, and became law in time for the election of 1919. The system then introduced[29] has remained in force ever since, without important change.

Under the majority system before 1919, the Radical Party controlled the Council most of the time. For example, the first Council elected under the new Constitution of 1848 consisted of over a hundred Radicals (who, broadly speaking, were

Protestants) compared with some eight Conservatives (Catholics), although the latter represented about half the population. In some cantons the Radicals invariably secured all the seats, with a bare majority of the votes cast. Towards the end of the last century, the Radicals, under the impact of newer political doctrines, began to lose their cohesion, despite the operation of the electoral law. Their apprehension of the threat to their dominance was shown by their opposition to the efforts made in 1900 and 1910 to introduce an element of proportionality into Federal elections. Despite the continuance of majority voting, however, the Radicals began to lose ground to the Catholics and to newer parties; by 1917, the Social Democrats had secured 19 seats in a Council of 182. Thus, the majority system did not prevent the rise of new parties. Had the system continued, it is probable that the Social Democrats in their turn would have dominated the Council and the Radicals would have become the victims of unfair representation, just as the British Liberals did.

The effect of the change in the voting system in 1919 was to reduce Radical representation sharply from 102 seats to 58 (31 per cent of the seats for 29 per cent of the votes), near which level it has remained ever since. Part of the seats lost by the Radicals went to the new Peasant Party, which already existed in embryo as a section of the Radical Party, and nearly all the rest to the Social Democrats, who more than doubled their representation. A number of splinter parties did present candidates, but they never won more than a very few seats and most of them disappeared again very quickly.

The proportional system has not in the least caused or favoured . . . a multiplication of little parties. On the contrary, if there is any conclusion to be drawn from the four proportional elections so far held, it is that there is a tendency for the voters to concentrate in the great historic parties.[30]

Table 8 shows the development of the Swiss political parties under a proportional system since 1917.

**TABLE 8—Elections to the National Council, 1917-52**

|      | Radicals | Conservative | Social Democrat | Liberal Democrat | Peasants | Communists | Others | Number of Parties |
|------|----------|--------------|-----------------|------------------|----------|------------|--------|-------------------|
| 1917 | 102      | 42           | 19              | 12               | —        | —          | 7      | 6                 |
| 1919 | 58       | 41           | 41              | 9                | 31       | —          | 9      | 9                 |
| 1922 | 58       | 44           | 43              | 10               | 35       | 2          | 6      | 8                 |
| 1925 | 59       | 42           | 49              | 7                | 31       | 3          | 7      | 9                 |
| 1928 | 58       | 46           | 50              | 6                | 31       | 2          | 5      | 9                 |
| 1931 | 52       | 44           | 49              | 6                | 30       | 3          | 3      | 8                 |
| 1935 | 48       | 42           | 50              | 6                | 21       | 2          | 18     | 10                |
| 1939 | 50       | 43           | 45              | 7                | 22       | —          | 10     | 8                 |
| 1943 | 47       | 43           | 54              | 8                | 22       | —          | 20     | 8                 |
| 1947 | 52       | 44           | 48              | 7                | 21       | 7          | 15     | 9                 |
| 1951 | 51       | 48           | 49              | 5                | 23       | 5          | 15     | 8                 |

In considering the effects of the voting system in Switzerland, other characteristics of that country's political structure must be borne in mind. The Swiss citizen shares in his own government much more directly than most. He is expected to take part in a large number of elections and local assemblies, and (together with a specified minimum number of his fellows) may challenge Federal or cantonal legislation or even initiate legislation: the law in question is confirmed or vetoed by a popular referendum. The Federal Council is not, like the British Cabinet, a body of Ministers chosen by the leader of the largest party; it is elected by the Federal Parliament and is chosen so as to include representatives of all the main parties and of the different types of cantons. That is to say, the proportional principle is extended beyond the election of the Parliament to the formation of its Executive. It has also become a tradition that the maximum legal duration of the Federal Council of four years shall not be terminated prematurely, even if any of its proposals are rejected either by the Parliament or by the country on referendum.

Switzerland has long been of interest to constitution-makers, and in many parts of the world today a federal form of government is being considered. In Africa it seems probable that several large areas, on the verge of attaining self-government and containing differing races, cultures and languages, will find federation suited to their problems. The experience of Switzerland with regard to electoral methods in a multi-racial population would seem to be apposite.

### Belgium

The political experience of Belgium under both a majority and a proportional system of election has, in one respect at least, been similar to that of Switzerland. The disputes of the two racial sections of the population (Flemings and Walloons), which menaced the unity of the nation during the last century, have been to a large extent resolved by the substitution of a proportional for a majority system.

The majority system, employed until 1899,[31] resulted in Flanders returning Catholics and Wallonia, except for certain rural areas, returning Liberals or, between 1894 and 1899, chiefly Socialists.[32] Within each region there were minorities which, deprived of any hope of representation in national, or even in local, politics, formed enclaves of discontent.

In the national legislature,[33] until 1894, two solid blocks each represented exclusively the majority in its respective half of the country. They differed irreconcilably on the question of whether Belgium should be a secular State, and on problems created by the privileged position that French (the language of Wallonia) held, to the detriment of most Flemings, in administration, law and education. Both Catholics and Liberals tended to concentrate upon,

and magnify, these issues at the expense of broader and more constructive policies, which would have been beneficial to the nation as a whole,[34] for they allowed little room for non-sectarian opinion within their ranks. Such a state of affairs was, it should be remembered, found in local as well as in national politics.

But the introduction in 1899 of a proportional system for Parliamentary elections[35] enabled the votes of Belgian minorities to become effective, and the representatives of the three main parties, Catholics, Liberals and Socialists, instead of being concentrated within one or other racial area, to be distributed more evenly over the country.[36] Thus, there were returned to the national legislature members whose sectarian views were qualified by other considerations which exercised a moderating influence; when some Catholics represented industrial cities and some Liberals rural areas, it became easier for them to find some measure of common ground than when their representation was confined respectively to opposite types of constituency. Furthermore, within the constituencies proportional representation contributed to making all parties less insistent on sectarian policies and encouraged them to assume the character of national movements, for no party could any longer be assured, as it was under the former system, that an appeal to the majority alone would secure all the seats. The general effect on the nation as a whole was to integrate the different racial and social elements.

The experience of Belgium under proportional representation contradicts the repeated assertion that this system promotes such a large number of parties that any effective government is rendered virtually impossible. The system from the outset assisted the revival of the Liberal Party, which previously appeared to be in process of being eliminated.[37] The only new party to gain representation before 1914 was a minor and short-lived one, the Dansistes. In later years, three additional parties did return members, but the majority of seats was shared by the three older parties, though the incidence of their representation varied. Of the new groups, the Communists alone still retain (1953) any representation. Since 1945 the number of parties in the Chamber has remained stable at four. The table of the various parties in the Belgian Lower House since 1898 (Table 9) shows that the number of parties winning seats since the introduction of proportional representation has not been excessive.

In Belgium, administrations have been more numerous under proportional representation than they were before 1899, but the duration of administrations, or the existence of a government able to ride roughshod over the rights of minorities, is not the sole criterion of good government. In Belgium, the effects of more frequent changes of government have caused less disturbance to the national welfare than the long periods of uninterrupted and arbitrary rule by purely Catholic or purely Liberal administrations.

Belgian governments (which have been largely coalitions since 1900) by no means present the chaotic picture which some critics paint. They have had the merit of giving the nation, in many ways so composite, a far more representative government than previously, and one which, as any examination of the reforms introduced will show, has been far from ineffective in its legislative achievements. There have, admittedly, been times of serious party deadlock. Because these have been resolved either by royal intervention or by government decree, the proportional system has been indicted.[38] But if such a crisis does arise, in which the people's elected representatives are unable to agree on the right course and a more or less arbitrary decision has to be taken, it is surely better that this should be done by the Crown on behalf of the whole nation, or by a government that has come to power with the backing of a majority of the voters, and has had to listen to all points of view, rather than by a party that holds fortuitous power through an unrepresentative electoral system.

Table 10 shows the changes in administration since 1918. A large proportion of these were, as will be seen, merely minor reshuffles in the composition of the cabinet, and not the complete substitution of one government for another. In other instances, they resulted from a general election, held at the legal four-yearly interval.[39] In many of these changes, the basic composition of the government was preserved (even after an appeal to the country). In this respect, continuity, which undoubtedly has

many advantages, has been ensured to a greater degree than in many countries using a majority system.

The advantages that proportional representation can bring to a country are demonstrated in Belgium. The system has succeeded in softening many racial antipathies which hindered the growth of true national unity, and which a majority system was making more acute.

### The Netherlands

The Netherlands first adopted a proportional system in 1917 for elections to the Second Chamber of the States-General[40] and to the various provincial assemblies and local communal councils. Before that year, the Second Chamber was elected by the second ballot in single-member constituencies. For local elections, multi-member constituencies were used. From the granting of the constitution of 1848 this system encouraged a provincial and sectarian conception of politics and prevented the emergence of effective national parties. It cannot be claimed that the change to a proportional system has eradicated these weaknesses from Dutch politics, but it has certainly not accentuated (much less introduced) them. Moreover, it has eliminated one vice of the majority system, namely, that of promoting within the constituencies alliances based rather on the pursuit of immediate electoral advantage than on any real community of principle between the parties, and of distorting the representation of such alliances.

In the years immediately following 1848, three

**TABLE  9—Elections to the Chamber of Representatives, 1898-1952**

|        | Catholic | Liberal | Socialist | Communist | Flemish Nationalist | Rexist | Others |
|--------|----------|---------|-----------|-----------|---------------------|--------|--------|
| 1898   | 112      | 13      | 27        | —         | —                   | —      | —      |
| 1900   | 86       | 34      | 31        | —         | —                   | —      | 1      |
| 1902   | 96       | 34      | 34        | —         | —                   | —      | 2      |
| 1904   | 93       | 42      | 29        | —         | —                   | —      | 2      |
| 1906   | 89       | 46      | 30        | —         | —                   | —      | 1      |
| 1908   | 87       | 43      | 35        | —         | —                   | —      | 1      |
| 1910   | 86       | 44      | 35        | —         | —                   | —      | 1      |
| 1912   | 101      | 44      | 39        | —         | —                   | —      | 2      |
| 1914   | 99       | 45      | 40        | —         | —                   | —      | 2      |
| 1919*  | 75       | 33      | 69        | —         | 7                   | —      | 2      |
| 1921   | 83       | 31      | 68        | —         | 3                   | —      | 1      |
| 1925   | 78       | 23      | 78        | 2         | 6                   | —      | —      |
| 1929   | 76       | 28      | 70        | 1         | 11                  | —      | —      |
| 1932   | 79       | 24      | 73        | 3         | 8                   | —      | —      |
| 1936   | 63       | 23      | 70        | 9         | 16                  | 21     | —      |
| 1939   | 73       | 33      | 64        | 9         | 17                  | 4      | 2      |
| 1946   | 92       | 17      | 69        | 23        | —                   | —      | 1      |
| 1949†  | 105      | 29      | 66        | 12        | —                   | —      | —      |
| 1950‡  | 108      | 20      | 77        | 7         | —                   | —      | —      |

* Adult male suffrage and votes for about 8,000 women (e.g., certain war widows). Remainders were utilized on a Provincial scale.

† Women were enfranchised on the same terms as men, and the number of seats in the Chamber was raised to 212.

‡ Election occasioned by the dispute over King Leopold.

principal movements competed for the support of a limited electorate: the Liberals, the Calvinists and the Catholics; to these were added a few Conservatives who represented the more aristocratic element.[41] The problem of whether the Netherlands should be a secular State or not (on this, Liberals were opposed to the two denominational movements) and, in addition, a doctrinal issue between the Calvinists and the Catholics, became the preoccupations on which the Dutch parties were to concentrate, often to the exclusion of more important questions. Under the majority system then in force, there was inaccurate representation of the opinions of the electorate, and also weak government. The Liberals could sometimes muster an absolute majority in the Second Chamber; when they failed to command this, the alternative was an ineffective and uneasy coalition of the two con-

fessional groups, supported by the Conservatives.

The religious question which divided the parties was complicated in the later decades of the century by the political demands of the unenfranchised working classes whose interests[42] none of the traditional groups represented. Under the impact of these demands, the existing parties began to lose their cohesion and to break up into various factions. As early as 1878, the impossibility of constituting a party administration led to the formation of a non-party ministry.

The new constitution of 1887 extended the franchise and increased the number of members in the Chamber, but left the method of election untouched. The religious problem, chiefly in the guise of denominational versus secular education, and the demand for a still wider franchise, remained two of the chief party issues. To safeguard denominational

### TABLE 10—Belgian Administrations, 1918-52

| | | |
|---|---|---|
| Delacroix | Nov., 1918–Dec., 1919 | Catholic-Liberal-Socialist |
| *Delacroix | Dec., 1919–Nov., 1920 | Catholic-Liberal-Socialist |
| Carton de Wiart | Nov., 1920–Dec., 1921 | Catholic-Liberal-Socialist-Non Party |
| *Theunis | Dec., 1921–May, 1925 | Catholic-Liberal-Non Party |
| (reconstructed† March, 1924) | | |
| *Vande Vyvere | May–June, 1925 | Catholic-Liberal-Socialist |
| Poullet | June, 1925–May, 1926 | Catholic-Liberal-Socialist |
| Jaspar | May, 1926–Oct., 1929 | Catholic-Liberal-Socialist |
| (reconstructed Jan., 1927., Nov., 1927, and in 1928) | | The Socialists left the Administration in Nov., 1927 |
| Jaspar | Oct., 1929–June, 1931 | Catholic-Liberal-Non Party |
| (reconstructed May, 1931) | | |
| Renkin | June, 1931–Oct., 1932 | Catholic-Liberal |
| (reconstructed May, 1932) | | |
| de Broqueville | Oct., 1932–March, 1935 | Catholic-Liberal-Non Party |
| (reconstructed Dec., 1932, Jan., 1934) | | |
| Van Zeeland | March, 1935–June, 1936 | Catholic-Liberal-Socialist |
| *Van Zeeland | June, 1936–Nov., 1937 | Catholic-Liberal-Socialist |
| Janson | Nov., 1937–May, 1938 | Catholic-Liberal-Socialist |
| Spaak | May, 1938–Jan., 1939 | Catholic-Liberal-Socialist |
| Spaak | Jan.–Feb., 1939 | Catholic-Liberal-Socialist |
| *Pierlot | Feb., 1939–Sept., 1944 | Catholic-Liberal-Socialist-Non Party |
| (returned after the General Election of April 1939; reconstructed Sept. 1939 and continued in office in London during the occupation) | | |
| Pierlot | Sept., 1944–Feb., 1945 | All party, including Communists, who resigned in Nov., 1944 |
| ‡Van Acker | Feb., 1945–Jan., 1946 | All party, but the Catholics§ resigned in July, 1945 |
| *Spaak | March, 1946 | Socialists and Technicians |
| ‡Van Acker | March–July, 1946 | Liberal-Socialist-Communist |
| Huysmans | Aug., 1946–March, 1947 | Liberal-Socialist-Communist |
| Spaak | March, 1947—Aug., 1949 | Catholic-Socialist |
| (resigned in Nov., 1948, but resumed office in that same month) | | |
| *Eyskens | Aug., 1949–June, 1950 | Catholic-Socialist |
| *Duvieusart | June–Aug., 1950 | Catholic |
| Pholien | Aug., 1950–Jan., 1952 | Catholic |
| Van Houtte | Jan., 1952– | Catholic |

* Following a General Election.
† Only the major reconstructions are noted.
‡ Van Acker resigned in January 1946 and following the General Election of February 1946 there was a period of political crisis dur-

ing which several party leaders attempted to form administrations. M. Spaak succeeded in forming one for a few days.
§ Towards the end of 1945, the Catholic Party was renamed the Christian Social Party (*Parti Social Chrétien*).

schools, an alliance was forged between the Anti-Revolutionaries (Calvinists) and the Catholics. But the former group, by democratizing its platform, antagonized its right wing, which formed a new party, the Christian Historicals. In 1896, a further electoral law doubled the electorate, which, however, still remained restricted in comparison with that of other democracies. During the following years, the number of parties increased further by the disintegration of the Liberals and the rise of the Socialists and (far less marked) of the Communists. The insistence of the parties on a sectarian approach to religious, franchise or economic issues again necessitated a resort to an extra-parliamentary and non-party ministry. In a further revision of the constitution in 1917, manhood suffrage at the age of 25[43] was conceded by the parties of the Right in return for equal treatment for religious endowed schools, and proportional representation was introduced.

The majority system employed until 1917 had failed to restrict the number of parties. The introduction of proportional representation at first somewhat accentuated the tendency of Dutch political groups to break up into splinter parties, for there was a continued emphasis by Dutch politicians on doctrinal issues and on academic differences of opinion on social and economic problems. However, for the most part, representation in the legislature continued to be monopolized by the half-dozen existing parties. After 1945, the number of small parties that had succeeded in securing one or two representatives diminished considerably. As has been observed elsewhere, when a group ceases to have an adequate *raison d'être* it is not perpetuated by the proportional system. Thus, in 1918, in the first proportional election, eight small groups obtained representation, but by 1952 the number had dropped to two.[44]

Dutch cabinets since 1918 have all been coalitions. Their lives have on the whole been long, though there have been fairly numerous cabinet

reconstructions. In some cases, the formation of an administration has been unduly delayed because of the tendency of groups to haggle over their share of portfolios. Between 1918 and 1940, these coalitions were usually composed of the three denominational parties, which were cemented chiefly by an opposition to the anticlericalism of the Liberal and Labour groups. The first coalition cabinet formed under the proportional system lasted, with some reconstruction, from 1918 to 1925 (surviving a general election); during this time it was twice defeated, but its resignation was refused by the Chamber.[45] Later coalition cabinets had more difficulty in maintaining stability, and, as a solution, there was an increasing tendency to entrust the government to a body of "experts," drawn from as many parties as possible. This practice has been followed since 1945, when the growing urgency of economic problems has shown more clearly than ever the futility of making academic questions a basis for government. Table 11 shows the development of the Dutch parties between 1913 and 1952, and Table 12 shows the Dutch administrations between 1918 and 1952.

Whilst proportional representation may not have eliminated from Dutch political life a certain traditional insistence on sectarian issues, it has certainly allayed any bitterness that might have been felt under a majority system by parties deprived of fair representation or made the victims of opportunist electoral pacts. Moreover, though from time to time it has been possible to form an administration only after hard bargaining, an administration once constituted has usually of late had a long and useful life, because it has been the outcome of a genuine attempt to find common ground. Such a practice, despite its disadvantages, is preferable to the precarious existence of a hastily created stop-gap administration. Finally, proportional representation has made its contribution to the introduction into Dutch political life of a more cooperative spirit. Thus, for example, the Social

### TABLE 11—Elections to the Second Chamber, 1913-52

|  | Catholics | Anti-Rev. | Christ. Hist. | Liberals* | Lib. Dem. | Social Dem.† | Comm. | Others | No. of Parties |
|---|---|---|---|---|---|---|---|---|---|
| 1913 | 24 | 11 | 9 | 32 | 7 | 15 | 2 | 2 | 10 |
| 1918 | 30 | 13 | 7 | 10 | 5 | 22 | 2 | 12 | 15 |
| 1922 | 32 | 16 | 11 | 10 | 5 | 20 | 2 | 3 | 10 |
| 1925 | 30 | 13 | 11 | 9 | 7 | 24 | 1 | 1 | 11 |
| 1929 | 30 | 12 | 11 | 8 | 7 | 24 | 2 | 2 | 12 |
| 1933 | 28 | 14 | 10 | 7 | 6 | 22 | 4 | 9 | 14 |
| 1937 | 31 | 17 | 8 | 4 | 6 | 23 | 3 | 8 | 10 |
| 1946 | 32 | 13 | 8 | 6 | — | 29 | 10 | 2 | 7 |
| 1948 | 32 | 13 | 9 | 8 | — | 27 | 8 | 3 | 8 |
| 1952 | 30 | 12 | 9 | 9 | — | 30 | 6 | 4 | 8 |

* This party included two groups in 1913 and 1918. In 1946, the bulk of the Liberals formed the present People's Party for Freedom and Democracy, while a left-wing section combined with the Social Democrats to form the Labour Party.

† Labour Party—see preceding note.

Democrats, while disagreeing with the more conservative confessional groups on some points, have found enough common ground with them to participate in the government. In post-war years, therefore, the Netherlands has presented the picture of a nation facing, with an increasing degree of unity, the many difficulties created by years of war.

## Israel

Proportional representation elections took place during the Palestine Mandate, and the same system has been continued in the new State of Israel. It is a rigid party list system in which the whole country is treated as one constituency.

This gives the maximum encouragement to small parties, which in any case are likely to be numerous in a new country with a large immigrant population drawn from widely differing lands. Nevertheless, the bulk of the votes have been concentrated on only a few parties (five in 1944, four in 1949, three in 1951) and extreme groups have had very little success.[46] The municipal elections of 1950 (under the same form of proportional representation) showed even more markedly a tendency for the voters to ignore splinter groups.

The provisional government of Ben Gurion was confirmed in power by the 1949 election and again in 1951, his party (Mapai or Labour) being consistently much the largest. It has never had a clear majority, and has governed with the help of one or more of the other moderate parties.

There is some dissatisfaction with the impersonal nature of the voting system, though it seems that most Israelis regard the party as by far the most important consideration in an election. There can, however, be no reasonable complaint about the strength or stability of the resulting government. Considering the difficulties with which it has had to cope (particularly the economic ones associated with the policy of unlimited immigration which no Israeli government could at present reverse), it can only be regarded as very successful.

In all the foregoing countries, proportional representation is associated with stable and generally satisfactory government; its alleged evil effects in this respect are completely absent. We now come to four countries—Germany, Italy, Greece, and France—which are likely to be cited as instances of a contrary character.

## Germany

Representative institutions had existed in Germany for nearly fifty years before 1918, and a party system had been built up, but the real power resided elsewhere. Bismarck bequeathed as his political legacy a nation untrained in self-government, which remained accustomed to having its affairs directed by outstanding statesmen and a strong executive despite the fact that it possessed the semblance of representative institutions. The electorate and their representatives were not allowed the experience of self-government needed to train them in political wisdom.

Excluded from any true responsibility, the parties tended to become, not so much national movements, but pressure groups for the rival regional, sectional and confessional elements which were rooted in German history and character. Any union between them was based upon a bargaining (*Kuhhandel*) which sought to attain limited and selfish objectives.

The electoral system of the country abetted this emphasis on narrow sectarian issues. The Reichstag was chosen from single-member constituencies

**TABLE 12—Dutch Administrations, 1918-52**

| | | |
|---|---|---|
| Ruys de Beerenbrouck | Sept., 1918–Sept., 1922 | Catholic, Anti-Rev. |
| Ruys de Beerenbrouck | Sept., 1922–Aug., 1925 | Catholic, Anti-Rev. |
| Colijn | Aug., 1925–Mar., 1926 | Catholic, Anti-Rev. |
| de Geer | Mar., 1926–Aug., 1929 | Extra-Parliamentary, under a Christ. Hist. |
| Ruys de Beerenbrouck | Aug., 1929–May, 1933 | Catholic, Anti-Rev. |
| Colijn | May, 1933–May, 1935 | "National," composed of Cons. groups |
| Colijn | July, 1935–May, 1937 | "National," composed of Cons. groups |
| Colijn | July, 1937–July, 1939 | "National," composed of Cons. groups |
| Colijn | July, 1939–Aug., 1939 | "National," composed of Cons. groups |
| de Geer | Aug., 1939–Sept., 1940 | Catholic, Anti-Rev., Labour, Non-party |
| Gerbrandy | Sept., 1940–June, 1945 | National |
| | (reconstructed several times whilst in exile in London) | |
| Schermerhorn | June, 1945–June, 1946 | National |
| Beel | June, 1946–July, 1948 | Catholic, Labour |
| Drees | July, 1948–Jan., 1951* | Labour, Catholic, Christ. Hist., Liberal |
| Drees | March, 1951–June, 1952 | Labour, Catholic, Christ. Hist., Liberal |
| Drees | Sept., 1952– | Labour, Catholic, Christ. Hist., Liberal |

* Dr. Drees resigned, and a crisis lasting some fifty days ensued before he again took office.

by the second ballot.[47] This gave opportunity for discreditable electoral bargaining, and often increased the disproportion between the votes cast and the seats won. For example, in 1907, the Social Democrats secured 28.9 per cent of the votes cast and were leading in 73 constituencies, or 18.4 per cent of the whole—that is to say, under the first-past-the-post system they would have had 18.4 per cent of the seats. But combinations of other parties against them on the second ballot reduced this already too low proportion of seats by nearly half, to 10.8 per cent.[48]

The same pattern of party politics reappeared after 1918 under the proportional system adopted by the Weimar Republic, and it must be emphasized that this was the old pattern, not a new one called into being by proportional representation.[49] Although the particular form of proportional representation adopted offered the maximum encouragement to small groups,[50] the number of parties in the Reichstag under that system never exceeded the number in 1912, even if we subtract from the latter the purely local parties that disappeared automatically with the provinces Germany lost in 1918.[51] As early as 1896 the Reichstag was "subdivided to an astonishing degree,"[52] containing 15 parties, no one of them with as much as one-quarter of the seats, and by 1912 the number of parties had risen to 21. Those parties were no more co-operative before 1918 than afterwards, and according to Lowell[53] "the worst feature of the existing (1896) condition of politics is the constant diminution of the moderate elements."

This situation, however, was more dangerous under the Republic than it had been before. The Imperial regime did give Germany a certain unity. The numerous groups pursuing opportunist policies for their own benefit might be ineffectual and often irresponsible, but they were allowed merely the shadow of power; its substance resided in a strong monarchy and efficient executive. With the disappearance of the Kaiser, these politically ill-educated parties were called upon to provide a government. Moreover, they were handicapped by the association of the Republic with defeat, they were faced with acute economic difficulties, and the Weimar regime (unlike that of the Empire) was constantly threatened by the campaign of certain elements whose avowed intention was to destroy it.

Between 1919 and 1932, no coalition of the Right or of the Left could achieve a majority. In such circumstances the Centre held the balance of power. But, owing to the differing and narrow aims (principally economic and social) of its component parts, this Centre group could never formulate a continuous policy nor one that would permit it to ally itself for long with the Right or with the Left. Some homogeneity was, however, introduced by a common religious attitude, and provided a stability which prevented its members from drifting to the Right or to the Left in sufficient numbers to enable either of those groups to form a stable administration. Thus, under Weimar, the Centre was the maker and breaker of cabinets. It was represented in 17 out of the 20 Administrations of the regime, and its erratic policy largely contributed to their downfall.

A further cause of the instability of the Republic's governments was the clash between centralism and federalism. The life of the national government depended not only upon a stable coalition within the Reichstag, but also on the character of the seventeen local assemblies of the Länder (the largest of which represented about 63 per cent of the German population). Party politics within the Länder tended to take on an independent local pattern, which resulted in numerous and sharp disagreements between them and the Reich Government, and often placed the central authority in jeopardy.[54]

Such were some of the broad factors that led to instability, to the failure of the attempt at democratic government, and consequently to dictatorship. To attribute this dictatorship to the operation of the electoral system is an over-simplification of the facts.[55] The Weimar system proved incapable of solving Germany's numerous difficulties for other reasons, and by 1932 the Reichstag elections showed that a majority of the electorate (that is, Communist and National Socialist voters taken together) desired its overthrow. Those electors, disillusioned by the experiment in democracy, were prepared to turn to any element which seemed to offer economic salvation and national rehabilitation. It is alleged that proportional representation led to the triumph of the Nazi Party by enabling it to win seats while it still represented only a small minority of the electors, but winning of a few seats in its first three elections was not a major factor. By 1930, the German elector was in a mood to follow any party showing ruthless determination to give Germany "a place in the sun," whether or not that party already had some members in the Reichstag. Once public opinion had turned to the Nazis, an election under a majority system would have resulted in a landslide in their favor.[56] Under proportional representation, the party never won a majority in the Reichstag in a free election.

The impression that splinter parties were created by proportional representation is fairly widespread within Germany itself, and the system has been opposed also on the ground of its impersonality (there was no provision for choice between candidates within the list). Hence, when the country made a fresh start after 1945, the electoral system of the Weimar Republic was changed. Local elections were held while Germany was still being administered by the Occupying Powers. In the

**TABLE 13—Seats Won by German Parties under (1) the Second Ballot (1912); (2) Party List P.R. (1919-33); and (3) the Mixed System (1949)**

| | 1912 | 1919 | 1920 | May, 1924 | Dec., 1924 | 1928 | 1930 | July, 1932 | Nov., 1932 | Mar., 1933 | | Aug., 1949 |
|---|---|---|---|---|---|---|---|---|---|---|---|---|
| Social Democrats | 110 | 163 | 102 | 100 | 131 | 153 | 143 | 133 | 121 | 120 | Social Democrats | 131 |
| Centre | 91 | 91* | 64 | 65 | 69 | 61 | 68 | 75 | 70 | 74 | Centre | 10 |
| National Liberals | 45 | — | — | — | — | — | — | — | — | — | | |
| Conservatives | 43 | — | — | — | — | — | 4 | — | — | — | | |
| Prog. People's Party | 42 | 19 | 65 | 45 | 51 | 45 | 30 | — | — | — | Free Democrats | 52 |
| Poles | 18 | — | — | — | — | — | — | — | — | — | | |
| Reich Party | 14 | — | — | — | — | — | — | — | — | — | German Right | 5 |
| Guelphs | 5 | — | — | — | — | — | — | — | — | — | | |
| Reform Party | 3 | — | — | — | — | — | — | — | — | — | Reconstruction | 12 |
| Farmer's Union | 3 | — | — | — | — | — | — | — | — | — | | |
| Christian Social Party | 3 | — | — | — | — | — | 14 | 3 | 5 | 4 | Christian Democrats | 139 |
| Alsace-Lorrainers | 3 | — | — | — | — | — | — | — | — | — | | |
| Alsace-Lorrainers Centre Party | 3 | — | — | — | — | — | — | — | — | — | | |
| Economic Union | 2 | — | — | * | * | 23 | 23 | 2 | 1 | — | | |
| German Social Party | 2 | — | — | — | — | — | — | — | — | — | | |
| German Peasants' League | 2 | 4 | 4 | 10* | 17* | 8 | 6 | 2 | 3 | 2 | Bavarian Party | 17 |
| Bavarian Peasants' League | 2 | — | } | — | — | — | — | — | — | — | S. Schleswig Party | 1 |
| Independent Lorrainers | 1 | — | — | — | — | — | — | — | — | — | | |
| Danes | 1 | — | — | — | — | — | — | — | — | — | | |
| Alsatians | 1 | — | — | — | — | — | — | — | — | — | | |
| German Nationalists | — | 44 | 71 | 95 | 103 | 73 | 41 | 40 | 54 | 52 | | |
| Bavarian People's Party | — | —* | 21 | 16 | 19 | 17 | 19 | 22 | 20 | 18 | | |
| German Hanoverians | — | 1 | 5 | 5 | 4 | 4 | 3 | — | 1 | — | | |
| German Democrats | — | 75 | 39 | 28 | 32 | 25 | — | 4 | 2 | 5 | German Party | 17 |
| Independent Socialists | — | 22 | 84 | — | — | — | — | — | — | — | | |
| Communists | — | — | 4 | 62 | 45 | 54 | 77 | 89 | 100 | 81 | Communists | 15 |
| National Socialists | — | — | — | 32 | 14 | 12 | 107 | 230 | 196 | 288 | Freedom Party | 2 |
| Land League | — | — | — | 10 | 8 | 3 | 21 | — | — | — | | |
| Saxon Peasants | — | — | — | — | — | 2 | — | — | — | — | | |
| Christian National Peasants | — | — | — | — | — | 9 | 14 | — | — | — | | |
| State Party | — | — | — | — | — | — | — | 7 | 11 | 2 | | |
| Others | 2 | 2 | — | 4 | — | 2 | 6 | — | — | 1 | Independents | 3 |
| **Total seats** | 397 | 421 | 459 | 472 | 493 | 491 | 577 | 607 | 584 | 647 | | 404 |
| **Parties represented** | 21 | 10 | 10 | 12 | 12 | 15 | 15 | 11 | 12 | 11 | | 11 |

* Parties in alliance.

The 1912 and 1949 figures are taken from official returns, the 1932 and 1933 figures from *Europa*, and the rest from Braunias' *Das Parlamentarische Wahlrecht*, I, 88.

American and French Zones, these elections were under the old Weimar system, but in the British Zone a compromise between this and the first-past-the-post system was adopted, under the impression that a large element of personal choice would thereby be introduced.[57] This mixed system, with minor modifications, is now used for all elections in Western Germany. It is less accurately proportional than the old one, but has avoided any serious distortion of the voters' wishes; in the 1949 election of the Bundestag there was only a slight over-representation of the two largest parties.[58]

The tendency to many parties remains. Thirteen parties, besides Independents, contested the 1949 election and eleven of them got some representation. On the other hand, most of those parties won very few seats and there are signs of a concentration of votes upon a few major parties, a process that had already begun under the Weimar Republic.[59] The only Government so far has been a coalition of Christian Democrats and Free-Democrats headed by Dr. Adenauer (Christian Democrat). It has at least shown itself capable under strong leadership of carrying through successfully a drastic currency reform, and pursuing consistently its policy of cooperation with the Western Powers. The stability of the Adenauer administration confirms the opinion, therefore, that the failure of the Weimar governments was due to causes other than the electoral system.

## Italy

For nearly all the time from her creation as an independent state to 1919, Italy elected her Chamber of Deputies by the second ballot in single-member constituencies. An exception was the period from 1882 to 1891, when the constituencies each elected two to four members by the block vote or five members by the limited vote (four votes for each elector). In 1919, the country adopted party list proportional representation, and, as in the case of Germany, it has been alleged that this contributed to the later rise of a dictatorship. The roots of Fascism, however, existed already, and were nourished by the political circumstances in Italy under the older electoral systems.

Following the establishment of the kingdom of Italy, the parties of the Right enjoyed a period of some fourteen years as the government until 1876. In the last years of the century, power passed to the Left, to a group of politicians possessing little homogeneity or capacity for effective rule and disinterested service. This situation persisted up to the first World War. Thus, true Parliamentary government had never become an integral part of the national life; it even acquired discredit in the eyes of the electorate. Parties were to a great extent mere personal factions, and a conservative estimate of their number in 1913 was ten. Italy was ruled

by "coalition Governments with weak and inconsistent programmes propped by the bought support of groups."[60] The political experience of Italy (like that of Germany) under majority systems of election before 1919 demonstrated that these methods do not necessarily divide Parliamentary representation into two homogeneous bodies of opinion, and certainly do not do so within a country that is still politically immature. In Italy, these majority systems resulted in a tendency to elect a Deputy for his local influence rather than for his political opinions, and the elected Deputy, having no fixed political allegiance, bartered his vote with the administration.

It was in these political circumstances that proportional representation was introduced in 1919. Elections under it were held in 1919 and 1921. There was no substantial increase in the number of parties on the introduction of proportional representation. There was a distinct tendency for the parties to become, instead of personal factions, real political groups with national programmes; far from preventing the emergence of stable groups, the new system promoted them.[61]

The Socialists, who had been gradually gaining in strength, won about one-third of the seats in the new Chamber in 1919, and formed the most effective opposition to the dominant Liberal group; close behind them came a new group, with clerical and peasant associations, the Popular Party. The Catholics for the first time took part in the election as a party. These new elements were not disposed to acquiesce in the manipulations practised by the older political leaders, but, partly owing to their political immaturity, they proved unequal to the task of finding a satisfactory solution to the country's problems. The Socialists refused to collaborate in government, and promoted (with the use of force) industrial unrest which the government did little to check. This, with other factors, inspired the rise of nationalist groups which in their turn resorted to violence.[62] In the 1921 election, these elements, which included Mussolini's Fascists, secured 45 seats, won from the Socialists largely as a reaction from the latter's unconstitutional methods. The formulation of a party programme promising Italy far-reaching reforms was enough in the existing circumstances to set Fascism on the road to success.

The rise of Fascism was assisted by the ineffective policies and dissensions amongst other groups. By 1922, Mussolini was able to form a cabinet, based on a coalition of four parties. He introduced a new electoral law under which the country was divided into fifteen constituencies, and each party submitted national lists of candidates. The party with the largest poll was entitled to two-thirds of the seats (356), while the remaining seats were divided proportionally among the other parties. As it turned out, the "premium" for the largest party was not needed to secure a Fascist victory; they polled not short of two-thirds of the votes, and the end of the first experiment in Italian democracy was at hand.

With the restoration of Parliamentary government in Italy after 1945, a proportional system was again adopted, for the election first of a Constituent Assembly and later of the two Chambers that were created.[63] Of the 556 seats in the Constituent Assembly, 426 were shared among the three largest parties (Christian Democrat, Socialist and Communist), and those parties, with the addition of two Republicans and one Liberal, formed the Government under Signor de Gasperi (Christian Democrat) as Prime Minister. This government led a precarious existence in the face of economic difficulties, but de Gasperi remained in power until his resignation as a result of the election in 1953.

Ten parties obtained some representation in the Chamber. Thus, following this second introduction of proportional representation, there has again been no increase in the number of parties represented. A fear that the system would breed splinter parties (the usual bogey of opponents of proportional representation) has proved unjustified; on the contrary, there has actually been in the Italian Parliament a consolidation, tending to produce only three main parties. This effect might have been more marked if the new system introduced had been the single transferable vote.

It would have also removed one ground for the demands arising a little later for a departure from proportional representation. One motive for changing the electoral law was the desire that all non-Communist parties should be able to pool their strength; under the single transferable vote they could have done this to any extent that the voters wished. The new law, passed in 1953 in the teeth of most bitter opposition, not only provided for *apparentement* but awarded two-thirds of the total seats to any party or alliance polling, over the whole country, more than half the votes. In the event, this weakened the Government coalition, for public resentment against the electoral law contributed to a fall in the government poll to 0.2 per cent below the required half.

## Greece

Greece has never had settled political conditions at any time since her first constitution was granted in 1843. Geographical factors militate against the unification of the country and impede the growth of great national parties such as we know in Britain. There have been four new or revised constitutions ·(1863, 1911, 1926, and 1935), the last of which was suspended under the Metaxas dictatorship and restored in 1944. The Crown has fre-

quently been the subject of dispute, and Greece was a republic from 1924 to 1935. The electoral system has been changed many times, but no form of proportional representation was used until 1926; before that date, majority systems were in force, election being generally by the block vote in large constituencies.

Table 14 records the changes of administration between 1919 and the beginning of the Metaxas dictatorship in 1936. It will be seen from the table

### TABLE 14

| Year | Election | Prime Minister (or Dictator) |
|---|---|---|
| 1919 | | Gounaris |
| 1920 | Majority | Gounaris |
| 1921 | | Gounaris |
| 1922 | | Protopapadakis* |
| 1923 | Majority | Venizelos |
| 1924 | | Papanastasiou |
| | | Sophoulis |
| | | Michalakopoulos |
| 1925 | | Pangalos* |
| 1926 | | Kondylis* |
| | Proportional | Zaimis |
| 1927 | | Zaimis |
| 1928 | Majority | Venizelos |
| 1929 | | Venizelos |
| 1930 | | Venizelos |
| 1931 | | Venizelos |
| 1932 | | Papanastasiou |
| | Proportional | Venizelos |
| 1933 | Majority | Tsaldaris |
| 1934 | | Tsaldaris |
| 1935 | Majority | Tsaldaris |
| | | Demertzis* |
| 1936 | Proportional | Demertzis |
| | | Metaxas* |

* Assumed power as the result of a *coup d'état*. Metaxas became Prime-Minister constitutionally on the death of Demertzis, but made himself dictator and dissolved Parliament four months later.

that the instability of Greek governments certainly cannot be attributed to proportional representation. Changes in administration, brought about either by constitutional or by unconstitutional action, have been frequent under the majority system.[64] When a government with great strength in Parliament has emerged from an election under a majority system, it has not always been to the advantage of the country; the 1920 election was followed by a disastrous war, which was denounced by the Opposition as well as by Greece's allies and therefore might have been averted if the Opposition had had its just representation of about half the seats. On the other hand, the absence of a Parliamentary majority for any one party has not always meant weak government; the coalition government following the 1926 election instituted reforms which probably no one party could have carried through alone.[65]

The great need of Greece is for the development of a much greater capacity for co-operation among her politicians. Proportional representation, by preventing a large Parliamentary majority for one party, did force upon the parties some attempt at co-operation. That attempt would have had a better chance of success if the particular system chosen had been one less dependent on the division of candidates into party lists. With the single transferable vote, some of those parties that appeared as separate entities might have found sufficient expression as wings of one larger party, and the voters could have given expression to the elements of agreement that exist between one party and another.

### France

Contrary to a widespread belief, France has never at any time elected her Parliament by any proportional system except in 1945 and 1946. Confusion on this point arises partly from the repeated use of the second ballot, which many erroneously imagine to be a method of obtaining proportional results,[66] and partly from a system introduced in 1919, by which some of the seats were filled by a proportional method.

Under the Third Republic there was controversy over the merits of single- or multi-member constituencies as such, apart from the voting system applied within them. The single-member constituency (scrutin d'arrondissement) is claimed by its supporters to give the elector a greater hold on his representative, establishing a more intimate relationship between the Parliament and the electorate. This is held to provide a bulwark against any possible coup d'état, a danger to which the country was particularly exposed in the years immediately following the creation of the Third Republic. Moreover, in the Chamber itself, deputies tended to unite into small groups, a factor that militated against rule by large blocs or the exploiting of such blocs by an individual. Thus, the fear of Royalism in 1875, and of Boulangism in 1889, inspired the reintroduction of single-member constituencies. On the other hand, the single-member system is alleged to be more corrupt than a system of multi-member constituencies (scrutin de liste), inducing in deputies a parish-pump mentality and undue sensitiveness to pressure from local interests, and also tending to produce instability of government. Supporters of the large constituency hold that it leads a deputy to take a wider view of his responsibilities, and produces combinations of groups with broader interests, stimulates the formulation of national policies and gives the elected body a more national character.

Throughout most of its existence, the French Republic has used one or other of two systems, each with minor variations: (a) single-member constituencies with the second ballot;[67](b) a majority system in multi-member constituencies (usually coinciding with Departments), with or without a second ballot. The electoral law alternated between one system and the other no less than eight times from 1831 to 1919, the former system predominating.

During the early years of this century, the Socialists in particular, and the smaller groups of the Right and Centre, began to agitate for proportional representation. Jean Jaurès characterized the majority systems as "une acte de défiance envers le suffrage universal," and the success of a proportional system in neighbouring Belgium stimulated the movement for its introduction into France. As in many other countries, the post-war atmosphere of 1919 was favourable to a change. However, the advocates of proportional representation, in their readiness to compromise with the advocates of a majority system, made concessions that quite destroyed the proportional character of the system.[68] The most important of these was the provision that if, in any one constituency, any one party or alliance of parties secured an absolute majority of the votes, that party or alliance took all the seats in the constituency, whether any other party had secured a quota or not. This alone would suffice to make a proportional result very unlikely, but in addition the law gave scope for party manœuvres, especially for the combination of party lists in such a way as to make sure that one such combined list would poll at least 51 per cent of the votes. In 1919, the parties of the Right were the most successful in forming such combinations, while in 1924 it was the parties of the Left which profited; hence the "swing of the pendulum" between those two elections was greatly exaggerated.

This system was abandoned after the 1924 election, and France reverted to the second ballot in single-member constituencies, which continued to be used up to the war. In October 1945, a real proportional system was applied to the election of the first Constituent Assembly. This was a pure party list system, with no panachage or preferential voting; seats were allotted according to the d'Hondt rule.[69] The system was applied without substantial alteration to the election of the second Constituent Assembly in June 1946, and of the National Assembly (formerly the Chamber of Deputies) in the following November. It was criticized in various quarters for several reasons. The impersonality of the voting was widely disliked, and some concession to this dislike was made in the third election, voters being allowed to express a preference for a particular candidate within the party list. In practice, however, this was quite valueless, for such a preference became effective only if expressed by more than half of the voters supporting that party.[70]

Very few voters did express a preference. The Socialists wished also to introduce *panachage,* but this was opposed by the Communists and the *Mouvement Républican Populaire* (M.R.P., or Christian Socialists), who saw in it a danger of their "fringe" voters being seduced, and it was never adopted. A different objection came from the smaller parties, in particular the Radicals, who wanted the unused votes in each constituency to be utilized on a national scale. The d'Hondt rule does slightly favour the larger parties,[71] and it was also true that in a number of constituencies the Radicals fell a little short of the quota, which caused them to win fewer than their proportional share of seats. In the election of June 1946, the average numbers of votes needed to obtain one seat were as follows:

| | |
|---|---|
| Communists | 36,000 |
| M.R.P. | 35,000 |
| Socialists | 36,000 |
| Parties of the Right | 41,000 |
| Radicals | 59,000 |

The differences in these figures are much smaller than those commonly found under majority systems, but the handicap happened to operate against the very party (the Radicals) that, under the second ballot, had been over-represented owing to the concentration of its strength in certain districts where it was sure of a majority.[72] The Radicals, therefore, failing to secure national utilization of remainders, pressed for a return to the second ballot.

A further objection was that the new system did not permit two parties to combine forces against a third, as they used to do on the second ballot. As the time approached for the election of the second National Assembly in 1951, the moderate parties who formed the government became more and more anxious that they should be able to combine against their opponents, and, moreover, that those opponents' representation should be reduced as far as possible. There was fear of, on the one hand, the Communists, and, on the other, General de Gaulle's *Rassemblement du Peuple Français* (R.P.F.), which had taken shape as a party since the previous election. A prolonged dispute followed, which from the first was unlikely to end in any reasonable solution because each party seemed mainly concerned with devising an electoral system that would give it as many seats as possible and its opponents as few as possible. After several abortive attempts, there was finally adopted, just in time to permit elections in June 1951, an electoral law bearing a strong resemblance to that of 1919. Parties presenting separate lists of candidates were allowed to declare that they wished the votes cast for those lists to be pooled (in any one constituency) for purposes of calculating the allotment of seats. In

addition to this, the method of voting over the greater part of the country was changed. In the Seine and Seine-et-Oise (where there are some districts with strong Communist majorities), proportional representation was retained, but with the method of the largest remainder,[73] which favours small parties rather than large ones. In the rest of Metropolitan France (where the Government parties were almost everywhere in a majority), if no one party or alliance of parties obtained a clear majority of the votes, the seats were to be divided proportionally (but using the d'Hondt rule, which favours the largest parties[74]), but if any one party or alliance did get a clear majority, however small, it would take all the seats in that constituency.

This system certainly served its purpose in giving the parties then forming the government an advantage over their Communist and Gaullist opponents.

The advantage of the government parties would have been still greater if they had made fuller use of the provisions for *apparentement.* As it was, with alliances in 83 out of the 95 constituencies to which this system applied,[75] they gained an absolute majority, and therefore swept the board, in 41 constituencies, each returning from two to ten members. Even where an absolute majority was not obtained, and the seats were shared on a proportional basis, the result was sometimes unfair because a party forming part of an alliance could win more seats than a party obtaining more votes but outside the alliance.[76] That might be justified if the parties forming the alliance had a real unity, but this was not necessarily the case; their combinations depended rather on considerations of electoral tactics, and varied from one constituency to another. The general effect of the system was that the two largest parties (amounting to nearly half the electorate) were deprived of all representation in 35 constituencies, covering approximately one-third of the country. This, however, did not enable the other parties to carry on government with any more success than before. No cabinet that could survive a vote in the Assembly was formed until eight weeks after the election of June 1951, and five Prime Ministers held office between that election and the end of 1953.

The period during which France used proportional representation was too short to afford reliable evidence as to the effects of that system on the political life of the country. There was, however, no increase in the already existing tendency to splinter parties and to unstable governments; indeed the number of parties represented in the Assembly was lower than before. The existence of numerous parties and the instability of administrations cannot be put down to proportional representation, for they have been common features in French politics for many generations. Under the Third Republic, that is to say for over twenty years during which she used two types of a majority system, France had more than 90 cabinets, compared with 20 in Great Britain. Long before 1939, the broad divisions of the Right, Centre, and Left were split into numerous sections, and acted merely as loosely allied and opportunist cartels.

The causes of this multiplicity of parties and instability of governments are too various and fundamental to be cured by a change in the electoral system alone.[77] Unlike Great Britain, France has no long tradition of parties organized on a national scale with strong central and local executives. Political organizations in the constituencies still often owe but a loose allegiance to the national party. Deputies, while nominally returned with a party label, have been, and to a large extent still are, more susceptible to public opinion within their constituencies than responsive to the policy of their party chiefs. Moreover, though elections might be fought by candidates under the aegis of the various parties, it has always been the case that parliamentary groups representing shades of opinion within the national parties were formed in the Chamber after the elections. Candidates who climbed on the band-wagon of a party in an election did not consider themselves necessarily pledged to support that party if they were successful.

This inevitably affected the stability of administrations. They were composed of representatives (not always the leaders) of various groups, and sometimes were headed by politicians less influential in one way or another than many of their colleagues. Such administrations were liable to disintegrate rapidly because of the independence of individual deputies, the criticism of other groups, and the friction within their own ranks.

Moreover, for Parliamentary reasons the power of the Chamber was great enough to exert a disruptive influence upon the executive. The parliamentary groups formed the Committees of the Chamber, and it was these Committees (cabinets in miniature) that were largely responsible for the fate of legislation, government or private, in the House. The order of business in the Chamber was divided, not by the government, but by the leaders of the groups; deputies had wide powers through interpellations to raise questions of policy, and they had great latitude in promoting or impeding legislation.

Another important fact to be considered is that the defeat of a French Government is not normally followed by a dissolution. A group or combination of deputies can, therefore, bring about the fall of a government without involving themselves in the expense of a new election or the risk of losing their seats. It is true that, under the Constitution of the Third Republic, a limited power of dissolution was possessed by the Administration. The President of the Republic could dissolve the Chamber on the advice of his Ministers and with the consent of the Senate. This right, however, was exercised but once, in 1877, in circumstances that created a prejudice

against dissolutions.[78] Under the Fourth Republic, the Council of Ministers can dissolve the Assembly when defeated on a motion of confidence or of censure, but only if two cabinets have been thus defeated within a period of eighteen months (excluding the first eighteen months of the Assembly's life).

## Experience under Party List Systems

In considering the several countries using the list system, it has been seen that proportional representation does not lead to an inordinate multiplicity of parties or to unstable government. In no country previously free from them have these disadvantages developed through changing to a proportional system. Countries that have used proportional representations continuously over long periods include the most stable democracies of Europe—Switzerland, the Scandinavian countries and Finland (also Czechoslovakia during her independence). In those countries, the system did indeed encourage the rise of one or two additional parties, but these represented emerging sections of public opinion. They took their place in the Parliamentary sphere, and often as elements of the administration, to the general advantage of the nation.

In certain other countries, such as Italy and France, it has been shown that the introduction of proportional representation was not responsible for the large number of parties and political instability; these conditions had already existed under the discarded majority system. As a corollary to a denial that proportional representation leads to numerous parties and unstable governments, it is clear that a majority system fails to prevent them either; it does not always crystallize public opinion within a few national parties, one of which is sufficiently powerful to support for any length of time a strong administration. This is amply illustrated by an examination of the political history of France and Holland in particular.

Proportional representation has removed from the political life of certain nations disadvantages which a majority system was imposing, to the detriment of their well-being. In Switzerland and Belgium especially, it has been shown that the suppression of minority representation was creating serious internal dissension; those countries are certainly more united as a consequence of having adopted proportional systems.

Two of the most successful democracies (Switzerland and Finland) have gone further than others in modifying the party list system so as to give the voter, rather than the party, power to elect the individual he wishes to act as his representative. This is an advantage, for a body elected under a proportional system of voting (whether the party list or the more elastic single transferable vote) may call for a degree of toleration between groups which may not be demanded by a majority system. The more the voters are allowed to show that there are gradations of opinion within each party, and that people in one party have affinities with people in others, the less sharp and bitter are likely to be the divisions within the nation, and the better are the prospects for cooperation of its component elements, for the give and take which is required if no one party is in a position to dictate. Moreover, the greater the degree of choice among candidates of any one party, the less need there is to form a new party for the promotion of a particular point of view.

The single transferable vote gives more freedom to the voter to choose his representative than is possible under any list system. The next chapter [of *Voting in Democracies*[79]] is devoted to an examination of experience in countries using this method.

# NOTES

1. See Lakeman and Lambert, *Voting in Democracies*, p. 208.

2. See Lakeman and Lambert, *op. cit.*, Appendix ii, p. 224.

3. Prof. W. A. Robson, *International Social Science Bulletin*, Summer 1951, pp. 362-3.

4. *Representative Government* (Everyman Edition), p. 209.

5. *On Compromise* (Macmillan, 1886), p. 326.

6. Cf. Wertheimer, *Portrait of the Labour Party*, p. 207.

7. *Europe between Democracy and Anarchy*, p. 96. Professor Hermens does not, however, suggest any criterion of what is "large enough"; he only refuses to accept the proposition that the opposition should be as large in proportion as the number of its supporters among the electorate.

8. Alistair Cooke in his *Letter from America*, B.B.C. Home Service, 3 November 1950.

9. B.B.C. Home Service, 3 May 1952.

10. In the countries of Continental Europe, political parties were given legal recognition long before the adoption of proportional representation, and parties are often required to register as such in order to obtain the right to nominate candidates. In the United Kingdom, on the contrary, parties, as such, have no official existence in electoral law, none of the official machinery of nomination or election depends on them, and a candidate's party is never mentioned on the official documents required for those purposes.

11. A year after Andrae's system was introduced, Thomas Hare in England independently put forward very similar proposals. These are described in Appendix iii, p. 245 [of *Voting in Democracies*]. The successful working of Andrae's system, and its similarity to Hare's proposals, are discussed in a report from the Secretary of the British Legation in Copenhagen, 1 July 1863.

12. See Lakeman and Lambert, *op. cit.*, pp. 105 and 129.

13. The Folketing consists of 150 members, elected for a period of four years.

14. See Lakeman and Lambert, *op. cit.*, Appendix vi, p. 281.

15. *Ibid.*, p. 92.

16. The Communist representation rose to 18 in 1945 and has since declined to 7. The Justice Party (Georgeist) has lately increased rapidly in strength and in 1950 equalled the Radicals.

17. The Storting elects 38 of its members to form a separate House, the Lagting, the remainder constituting the Odelsting. Legislation must be considered by each House separately; the Lagting can only approve or reject it. If there is disagreement between the Houses, a two-thirds majority at a joint sitting is required for a decision.

18. This division (which favoured the country districts) was abolished in 1952.

19. In 1887, the Liberals had a majority of 20 in the Riksdag, but the following year this was reduced to a minority of 2, because one of the Stockholm members was found to be 13s. od. in arrear on his taxes for 1881-2. This invalidated his election and all the 6,700 ballot papers on which votes were cast for him; a recount then resulted in the defeat of all the 22 Liberal members for Stockholm and the election of 22 Conservatives. (See R. Dickinson, *Summary of the Constitution and Procedure of Foreign Parliaments*, 2nd edition, 1890, p. 151.)

20. *The Finnish Reform Bill of 1906* (Helsinki, 1906).

21. For details of the system, see Lakeman and Lambert, *op. cit.*, Appendix vii, p. 282.

22. See the *Finland Year Book*, 1947, p. 68.

23. *International Affairs*, October 1948, p. 506. For further discussion of recent Finnish history, see this article and the P.R. Society pamphlets No. 95 (p. 24) and No. 96 (p. 22).

24. Marc Ullmann, *Le Monde*, 6-7 June 1954.

25. In some of the smaller cantons (Appenzell, Glarus, Unterwalden), the legislative power of the canton is exercised directly by all male adult citizens meeting in a public assembly called the Landesgemeinde.

26. For the full story, see *La Démocratie Tessinoise et la Représentation Proportionnelle* by Professor J. J. Galland, Grenoble, 1909.

27. Its application was extended in 1892, 1895 and 1898 to the election of the Executive Council, jurors and Communal Councils. In 1904, however, the Liberal majority on the Executive Council secured a change in its method of election to the limited vote. This system was less favourable to the minority, and gave the Liberals four seats out of five instead of three out of five.

28. The Federal Parliament consists of the Council of States, whose members are elected by the cantons, and the National Council, which is the most important body and is elected directly by the male citizens. Each canton has one National Council member per 24,000 of its population. The executive body, the Federal Council, is elected by the Federal Parliament for a period of four years.

29. See Lakeman and Lambert, *op. cit.*, p. 95.

30. *Statistik der Nationalratswahlen*, 1919-28, p. 31.

31. Election was by the second ballot, in constituencies most of which returned from 2 to 4 members each; there were 9 single-member constituencies, and

one (Brussels) returning 18 members. The restricted electorate was increased tenfold by the law of 1894. This law also introduced the plural vote for certain family, property and educational qualifications; this was abolished in 1919.

32. See Lakeman and Lambert, *op. cit.,* p. 63.

33. The Belgian legislature is composed of two Chambers: the Senate, one half of which is elected directly, the rest being elected indirectly or co-opted; and the Chamber of Representatives (the more important), which now numbers 212 Deputies and is elected for four years by universal adult suffrage.

34. Differences between the Catholics and Socialists centred at first on social, industrial, and franchise problems. The rise of a Catholic left wing forced the more traditional Catholic elements to compromise. Nevertheless, strong feeling over religious and racial differences persisted for some years.

35. As in Switzerland, a trial had been made of proportional representation in municipal elections; it had proved successful in improving civic spirit and administration.

36. The extension of the suffrage also contributed to this effect.

37. There is, however, a tendency to draw too sweeping conclusions from too few elections. The graph given by Maurice Duverger (*L'Influence des Systèmes Electoraux sur la Vie Politique,* p. 58) shows a sharp fall in Liberal representation from 1890 to 1898, but does not show that 1890 was a peak year which had been preceded by several other wide fluctuations in the number of Liberal Members.

38. Hermens, *Democracy or Anarchy?,* pp. 306-7.

39. Up to 1914, elections were biennial, covering half the country on each occasion.

40. The national legislature, the States-General, comprises two Chambers. The first is chosen by Colleges of the Provincial States; the second (and more important) is directly elected for four years by universal adult suffrage.

41. These groups could hardly be called parties in the modern sense of the word until later in the century. In 1878 the Anti-Revolutionary Party (Calvinist) was formed; in 1884, the Liberal Union; in 1889, the Social-Democratic League, and in 1896, the Catholic Party.

42. Lakeman and Lambert, *op. cit.,* p. 55.

43. The franchise was extended to women in 1922, and the voting age was lowered to 23 in 1945. Voting is compulsory.

44. The particular form of proportional representation chosen was one offering great encouragement to very small parties. Although voting takes place in eighteen districts, the lists of candidates nominated in those districts can, and usually do, declare themselves to be part of a national party list, and seats are then allocated on the basis of their national total. The law has undergone minor modifications to the disadvantage of the small parties (see Braunias, *Das Parlamentarische Wahlrecht,* Vol. ii, p. 251).

45. It dissolved finally over the religious issue of diplomatic relations with the Vatican.

46. See Lakeman and Lambert, *op. cit.,* Appendix ii, p. 240.

47. If no one candidate had a clear majority on the first ballot, the second ballot took place between the two leading candidates only.

48. J. H. Humphreys, *Proportional Representation,* p. 291.

49. Hermens and others who contend that proportional representation causes a multiplication of parties support this contention by quoting German statistics beginning in 1919. This is misleading if no figures for earlier years are given for comparison.

50. Any party polling 60,000 votes over the entire country obtained one seat.

51. By the time Hitler seized power "there was a general tendency for a concentration of parties and the possibility of only four or even three parties emerging was great." Erich Roll, *Spotlight on Germany* (Faber & Faber, 1933), p. 249.

52. A. L. Lowell, *Governments and Parties in Continental Europe,* Voi. ii, p. 42.

53. *Ibid.,* p. 43.

54. In theory the law of the Reich was supreme, but the lack of adequate police and other machinery often made its enforcement impossible.

55. Under almost exactly the same system, operating over the same period between the wars, Czechoslovakia was the most stable and successful democracy in Eastern Europe.

56. Goering's evidence in his trial for war crimes was that under the British system the Nazis would have won every seat in the 1933 election.

57. See Lakeman and Lambert, *op. cit.,* p. 96.

58. *Ibid.,* Appendix ii p. 243.

59. See Erich Roll, *Spotlight on Germany* (Faber & Faber, 1933), p. 249.

60. Bolton King and Thomas Okey, *Italy To-day* (Nisbet, 1901), p. 20.

61. See the majority and minority reports of the Italian Parliamentary Committee on the electoral law, 1923.

62. Too many Italians, unfortunately, had yet to learn the lesson that "in a self-governing people, all parties are responsible for the maintenance of government; . . . a party that refuses all share of responsibility for the maintenance of government may render a great disservice to the country. For Parliamentary government implies government as well as loyalty to Parliament. Parliamentary parties who refuse to assist in permitting the wishes of the majority to have effect, are in revolt against Parliamentary government itself; in the resulting chaos Parliamentary government may disappear." See John H. Humphreys, *Representation,* August 1923, p. 19.

63. In the Senate, 236 members were elected; 107 others sat of right as ex-Premiers, ex-Presidents of the Chamber, or ex-Deputies who had spent more than five years in prison under Fascism.

64. See for example Braunias, *Das Parlamentarische Wahlrecht,* Vol. i, p. 194.

65. See A. W. Gomme, *Greece* (O.U.P., 1945), p. 68, and S. Forster, *A Short History of Modern Greece* (Methuen, 2nd ed., 1946), p. 164.

66. See for example Hermens, *Democracy or Anarchy?,* p. 143.

67. There has been no restriction on the number of candidates in the second ballot, and as a rule the leader in this second ballot has been declared elected even if lacking a clear majority. The 1831 law, however, provided that in the latter circumstances a third ballot should be held between the two leading candidates only.

68. See *Elections Législatives du 16 novembre 1919,* by Georges Lachapelle, pp. 9 ff.

69. See Lakeman and Lambert, *op. cit.,* p. 87.

70. An effective choice between candidates was introduced in local elections.

71. See Lakeman and Lambert, *op. cit.*, p. 89.

72. Compare *ibid.*, p. 26.

73. *Ibid.*, p. 86.

74. *Ibid.*, p. 89.

75. The R.P.F. (Gaullists) formed alliances in twelve constituencies, the Communists in none. In five constituencies, government parties figured in two rival alliances. See Peter Campbell, *Revue Française de Science Politique*, October-December 1951, p. 498.

76. For example, in the Marne the M.R.P. secured 36,509 votes out of a "coalition" total of 75,595 and received two seats, whereas the Communists and R.P.F. each polled about 10,000 votes more but obtained only one seat apiece.

77. See Dorothy M. Pickles, *The French Political Scene* (Nelson, 1938), pp. 39 ff.

78. This dissolution appeared to the public as a move to override their elected representatives and seize power for President MacMahon and the Monarchists.

79. Lakeman and Lambert, *op. cit.*, Chapter X.

> ... *a deliberate attempt to transpose into political science the technique of the "working model," that is, fundamentally, to restore to favour, in a new guise, the methodical use of hypothesis in science.*
> MAURICE DUVERGER, Political Parties, *p. xiv.*

# MODELS, THEORIES, AND THE THEORY OF POLITICAL PARTIES

## Colin Leys

## 1. INTRODUCTION

The doctrine that party systems are wholly or largely determined by electoral systems seems now to be as widely rejected as once it was widely accepted; yet few textbooks banish its central postulates wholly from their pages. From this prevalent fence-sitting we can draw an important methodological moral, and from the elements of this particular doctrine we can construct a revised theory which, though modest in scope, is tenable, and which it may be possible to extend.

Professor Duverger's formulation of the doctrine in question is the most recent systematic exposition of it, and for convenience I shall refer to it as the *"Duverger doctrine,"* although its pedigree is ancient, as democratic theory goes.[1] At its simplest, the doctrine states that the simple-majority single-ballot system of voting, in single-member constituencies, "favours" two-party systems while proportional systems of representation favour multipartism. Duverger developed a strong form of the doctrine:

Of all the hypotheses that have been defined in this book (*Political Parties*) this approaches most nearly perhaps to a true sociological law. An almost complete correlation is observable between the simple-majority single-ballot system and the two-party system: dualist countries use the simple-majority vote and simple-majority vote countries are dualist.

"The exceptions," he added, "are very rare and can generally be explained as the result of special conditions."[2]

The commonest criticism of the doctrine consists in pointing out that instances of this "law" are in fact as rare as the exceptions, and in arguing that so many "special conditions" need to be invoked to explain the exceptions that nothing remains of the generality (and so the explanatory force) of the "law."[3] This ground of criticism we may call *the adequacy of the theory to the facts to be explained*, with the general diagnosis that the inadequacy is due to reliance on too few factors to explain a multifactorial phenomenon. But although this is virtually a universal form of criticism of the Duverger doctrine, it is not the only one possible.

Two others may be mentioned here. One of them is as rare as the one discussed above is common; this is to argue that the theory is really neither adequate nor inadequate but inherently unusable, on grounds of *logic,* that it is self-contradictory (leads to mutually incompatible conclusions), or leads to conclusions which are incompatible with those to which it is supposed to lead.[4] This ground of criticism we may call the *logic of the model* (using the word "model" in a sense which is explained more fully below), and although few writers seem to have appreciated it, it is really a weakness of this kind which vitiates the Duverger doctrine in its familiar form.

One of the aims of this article will be to analyse the *logical* deficiency of the Duverger doctrine. But it is interesting to ask, first of all, why so little attention has been paid to it (since it is sufficiently obvious), and why the main trend of criticism has borne on the issue of whether or not the doctrine takes into account enough of the significant factors: particularly in view of the fact that most exponents of the Duverger doctrine have themselves been foremost in acknowledging the part played by other factors, have hedged the doctrine around with qualifications, so that they sometimes seem to be claiming no more for the influence of the electoral system than their critics are in any case prepared to allow it.[5] The reason is, I think, that neither exponents nor critics have clearly distinguished the precise nature of the facts to be explained, or had a clear enough picture of the necessary ingredients, so to speak, of *any* theory which might serve to explain them; in particular, they have not distinguished between a *theory* of the behaviour of some set of phenomena, and the logical *model* of which a theory is an interpretation, and which gives it its explanatory force. A logically sound model is no guarantee of a good theory; but a model which is logically defective cannot furnish a theory at all, or at least not the theory we need. I will, I think, help to clarify the general problem involved in constructing an adequate theory of party systems, as well as the defects of the Duverger doctrine, if these distinctions are first examined a little more closely: this is the object of section 2, and an analysis of the Duverger doctrine follows in section 3.

There remains, however, a third ground on which a theory may be criticized, and which it is relevant to mention here. This is *the realism of its assumptions*.[6] It is highly significant that the *psychological postulates* involved in the Duverger doctrine do not seem ever to have been challenged. Indeed, it seems to be largely the appeal of these assumptions which is responsible for the fact that the Duverger doctrine, in spite of repeated convictions for failing to explain the facts, has not (yet at least) been altogether dislodged from the textbooks: firmly expelled through the exit marked "empirically inadequate," it repeatedly sneaks back through the side entrance marked "psychologically plausible." Such resilience is not to be despised. The problem is to try to make use of it: to formulate the Duverger doctrine afresh, to arrive at least at a logically consistent and apposite model. Such logical improvement of the model will not necessarily improve the empirical adequacy of the theory—though it may. This, at any rate, is the task of section 4.

## 2. MODELS AND THEORIES

"Model analysis" in the sense required here is the analysis of the relations between phenomena of the real world by means of formally constructed analogues, which are logical calculi. Formally defined "opposite numbers" of the real-world phenomena under investigation serve as the *variables* of a model:[7] the *model* consists of these variables and statements of the properties which they are assumed to have; such statements together define the logical relations between the variables and constitute the *assumptions* of the model: and the conclusions which we can deduce from them about the variables constitute the model's *behaviour*. Substituting for the model's variables the real-world phenomena to which they are intended to correspond, and interpreting the logical relations between the variables as causal relations between the phenomena of the real world, we have a *theory* of how these phenomena are determined; a good theory if the world behaves as it leads us to expect, and a bad one if not. The value of the model is that it shows what we need to assume in order to make the model's variables behave like the phenomena of the real world—and what we can ignore. A long run of successful prediction with the theory increases our confidence in the relevance of the model; but if our predictions are wrong, then either factors are at work in the real world, determining the behaviour of the phenomena under investigation, of which the theory takes no account (the model contains too few variables or the wrong ones); or factors which have been correctly isolated as the dominant ones operate in some different ways from that which the theory supposes (the model contains the right variables but makes wrong assumptions). Of course other reasons—such as simplicity, consistency with other branches of theory, etc.—may make us value a theory, in spite of predictive shortcomings;[8] but for the purpose of prediction too wide a divergence between the behaviour of the model and that of the real world ultimately renders it a bad one, due for overhaul or replacement.

This account may be illustrated with an example.[9] Malthus believed that living-standards were falling because population was growing faster than food production. He built a model as follows. Population, as a variable in his model, had only two characteristics: (*a*) it needed a fixed minimum of food per head to support life, and (*b*) unchecked, it reproduced faster than the rate at which it would merely replace itself. Food production, as a variable, had only one characteristic: (*c*) it was expanding, at the fastest, by a fixed amount every twenty-five years. Thus "population, when unchecked, increases in a geometrical ratio. Subsistence increases only in an arithmetical ratio"; so that, in this model, there is *necessarily* always less food per head at any given time than at any given previous time—a logical conclusion drawn from assumptions (*b*) and (*c*). Moreover, with the help of assumption (*a*) we can deduce a further conclusion, namely that this process will stop only when the output of food per head is barely enough to keep people alive, and when any further increase in population is limited by starvation to the rate of expansion of food production.

The theory of increasing misery which was founded on this model has, fortunately, so far proved wrong, at least in Britain. The reason is partly that the model did not include all the relevant variables; for instance, the rate of expansion of oversea sources of food supplies, which could be exchanged for manufactures. The model also contained unrealistic assumptions: emigration could reduce the rate of growth of mouths to feed, even if the birth-rate were as high as Malthus assumed, and birth control could reduce the birth-rate; while revolutionary changes in technique were to raise agricultural productivity beyond Malthus's expectations. Any theory, and particularly any very long-run theory of this kind, is subject to falsification in this sort of way; the theorist has to make the best judgment he can of what assumptions are reasonable or sound, and will justify them, as Malthus did, as being either "obvious" or truistic, or the most cautious and conservative (or the most generous, as the case may be) that anyone could reasonably make: and it is plainly in the selection of variables and assumptions about them that the skill of a theorist consists. Of this process, however, there is unhappily nothing general to be said.

What may be said concerns only the treatment of the variables and the assumptions of a model, once they have been selected, and the relationship of a model to a theory; it is necessary to make two observations here under this heading. The first is that the assumptions of the model—the statements which together define the characteristics of the variables and the relations which obtain between them—must be completely specific, altogether precise: "The model is abstract and complete; it is an 'algebra' or 'logic.' . . . There is no place in the model for, and no function to be served by, vagueness, maybe's, or approximations. The air pressure is zero, not 'small,' for a vacuum: the demand curve for the product of a competitive producer is horizontal (has a slope of zero), not 'almost horizontal.' "[10] The reason for this is sufficiently obvious; we cannot deduce conclusions from premises of that kind, and so no model which we might try to build with such material can furnish a theory with definite predictions which the facts may then be seen definitely

to confirm or invalidate. On the other hand, the question whether the facts do or do not confirm a prediction *will* often be a matter of judgment (e.g., a decision as to which test of statistical significance is appropriate); approximations of fact may be held to support (or invalidate) a theory, but there must be no approximations in the model, or there is nothing for the facts to approximate (or to fail to approximate) to. Secondly, it is essential to provide reasonably precise and unambiguous rules for identifying the real world phenomena to which the variables of the model are intended to correspond. These are what are often called "operational definitions." Without them, of course, there is no means of checking the theory which the model is supposed to provide; it becomes metaphysical, and lies open to the abuse of varying the operational definitions so as to exclude evidence which tends to invalidate the theory, and admit evidence which appears to confirm it.

## 3. THE DUVERGER DOCTRINE

Duverger postulates (*a*) a "natural dualism" of parties, and (*b*) a tendency to the proliferation of parties (through splits in old parties and the formation of new ones). The first of these is explicit (*Political Parties*, pp. 215-16). The second is implicit, an acknowledged actual phenomenon of all the countries which Duverger studies. The electoral system, according to Duverger, determines which of these forces shall dominate. Although he speaks of the problem as one of finding factors which "thwart" the natural tendency (*a*) to dualism, he does not provide any reason for holding that, for example, PR "thwarts" such a tendency; on the contrary, he tries to show how majoritarian systems "thwart" the tendency (*b*) to greater fragmentation, or the continuation of an established multipartism. In fact, his exposition conforms in its details to the scheme of earlier ones, and his assumption (*a*) is superfluous.

His model is set up as follows. It is assumed (*c*) that third ("i.e. the weakest") parties are always "under-represented" ("i.e. its percentage of seats [is] inferior to its percentage of the poll") and it is also assumed (*d*) that supporters of third parties transfer their *votes* to one of the two leading parties. For a system of PR, however, assumptions (*c*) and (*d*) are dropped.

Now it is obvious that assumption (*d*) is too strong. It simply cancels assumption (*b*); in fact it assumes the very thing that has to be explained. What is needed is an assumption from which the behaviour described in (*d*)—the transference of their supporters' votes away from third parties—may be derived as a conclusion; and for Duverger, as for other exponents of the doctrine, this is the assumption ($d'$) that under the simple-majority vote system, in single-member constituencies, voters realize that a vote for a third candidate is wasted (and may be assumed to act rationally in accordance with this realization). To all protagonists of the doctrine known to me (and, apparently, to many of its critics) the assumption of ($d'$) has seemed to fill the gap satisfactorily and create a working model of the kind required.

But, psychologically plausible though it may be, a brief consideration shows that it does nothing of the sort. So far from constituting the requisite dynamic element in the model, it totally immobilizes it, for it states, in effect, that supporters of parties which are third (or weaker) in their constituencies abandon them in favour of one or other of the two which are in first and second place, *no matter which two these are* (since the transfer of their votes is dictated solely by the consideration that they would be wasted on parties other than those in first or second place); and from this it follows that, other things being equal, all those parties will be established permanently in the field which are initially in first or second place in any constituency. If, to begin with, there are five parties represented in the legislature, *at least* five will always survive, since five come *first* in at least on constituency each: not to mention those which may also come second in one or more constituencies, although winning none.

The trouble is, in other words, that a vote for a party which is third or worse in terms of representation in the legislature is *not* wasted in those constituencies in which it holds first or second place: and the theory suggested by the model is not a theory of bipartism at all, but a theory of the *status quo;* a theory of *immobilisme,* perhaps, but one which states strictly nothing about the absolute number of parties in any political system.

At various points in his exposition Duverger, unlike some other exponents of the doctrine, shows an awareness of this fundamental difficulty; but because he draws no clear distinction between his model, his theory, and the evidence, the trouble is never isolated and cured, but leads to ambiguities and qualifications within the model, and variations and obscurities in its interpretation and application to the facts as theory. The "true effect" of the simple-majority system, we are told, for instance, "is limited to local bipartism"; this is undeniable on the assumptions which have been made, as we have seen. But instead of finding this conclusion inconsistent with the claim that this electoral system produces national bipartism, Duverger declares that none the less

the increased centralisation of organisation within the parties and the consequent tendency to see political problems from the wider, national standpoint tend of themselves to project on to the entire country the localised two-party system brought about by the ballot procedure.[11]

But of this evidently crucial assumption, vague as it is, no further explanation is offered. At other times Duverger speaks as if his "psychological factor" (assumption ($d'$), called by Duverger the "polarization effect") operates against parties which are third or weaker in terms of the total number of votes in the country at large; but as we have seen, this is too strong if it is simply assumed, and such behaviour cannot be deduced as the logical consequence of a rational response to the single-member constituency system.

The secondary weaknesses of Duverger's exposition of the doctrine, which flow more or less directly from this logical deficiency in the model, may be partially summarized as follows:

1. The logically necessary character of the model, and so the specific character of the predictions of the theory, are abandoned; the Friedman rule against "maybe's and approximations" is broken. For example we are told that "on the whole" PR only "maintains *almost* intact the structure of parties at the time of its appearance" (my italics), although we learn also that it has a "deep-seated tendency which always triumphs over the barriers set up against it" to produce a few more.

2. There are variations in the operational definitions of the variables; some facts are treated rather high-handedly. Britain, for example, is said to have a two-party system not on a "restricted and fragmentary view" but on examination of the "general tendencies of the system"; that is, if before the First World War the Irish Nationalists, and now the Liberals, are regarded as outside the general tendency. Elsewhere, however, the Liberals are included in the reckoning; what is meant is evidently that we have a two-party system in the sense that third parties are always either coming or going. But this depends, of course, on our accepting some theory which says that they they must always be doing this, and it must be said at least that it took more than the electoral system to get rid of the Irish. Here the definition of a "two-party" system varies. Similar variations sometimes occur with respect to "multipartism"; in one case a growth in the *size* of certain small parties is described as "having much the same effect" as a growth in their number, in another a fourth party with only one seat is ignored with the words "in practice therefore three parties alone were represented." Sometimes such variations matter, sometimes they may be less cases of varying defiintions than of legitimately varying interpretations of the facts: the point is that a logically sound model would in most cases render them unnecessary.

3. The "explaining" of "exceptions" is inconsistent; the consequences of the logical weakness of the

model are here direct. Canada and pre-1920 Denmark are said not to be real exceptions because they have displayed bipartism at the constituency level, which is the system's "true effect." Why, then, does not Britain have multipartism in parliament and bipartism only locally?[12] Duverger cannot legitimately appeal to other factors to account for this difference, for then it is a fair question whether factors strong enough to explain this (e.g. national sentiment) will not explain bipartism without any help from the electoral system. This comes out clearly in Duverger's appeal to the key evidence, the contrast between the elimination of the Liberal Party in Britain and elsewhere, and its survival in Belgium after introduction of PR. Since the doctrine provides no reason why the electoral system should have led Liberals to transfer their votes to other parties in Britain, this evidence is neither consistent nor inconsistent with it.

4. Assumption (c)—that third and weaker parties are always under-represented—is superfluous. In spite of some criticism[13] this assumption remains in general highly realistic; the trouble is that no connexion is established by Duverger which would enable it to contribute to the desired behaviour of the model. It is a matter of indifference to a Liberal voter, for example, that the Liberals receive x per cent fewer seats than their percentage of votes in the country at large, if the electoral system will make him desert them only when they are not in first or second place in his constituency. None the less, this assumption can be made relevant to a reformulated version of the doctrine, by an adaptation which will by now probably seem obvious to the reader.

## 4. TOWARDS A NEW THEORY OF THE INFLUENCE OF ELECTORAL SYSTEMS ON PARTY SYSTEMS

We may assume, with Duverger (*Political Parties*, p. 220), that the elements of 'full' democracy— free and fair elections, wide franchise, etc.—are present.

Let $p$ be the number of parties, defined as parties legally registered, or running one or more candidates at any election, or whatever other criterion may be appropriate for defining the notion of "parties in the field." We are interested only in their number, and disregard size, colour, etc. Let $o$ be the number of "bodies of political opinion," defined as groupings of public opinion which give rise to the formation of political parties in the sense already given.

We assume (we may label this assumption (B), to correspond with Duverger's assumption (b)) that there is a tendency for $o$ to increase as a lagged

function of *the number of parties receiving electoral support at elections,* so that for any number $p_1$ which receive support at any election $e_1$ there will be a larger number $p_2$, corresponding to a proliferation of bodies of opinion, at the next election $e_2$. This assumption may be justified as corresponding to experience or to a human tendency to political disagreement; in relying on the support given to parties at elections we may justify it on the grounds that people will be discouraged from further differentiation (the formation of more parties) if some of those already formed can raise no electoral support at all, and we may take such devices as the forfeiture of deposits as working definitions of "lack of support" in this sense. So long as we assume that $o_2$ is greater than the number of parties $p_1$ which received electoral support, it does not matter whether we assume the tendency to proliferate to be violent or relatively weak; a weak assumption would be $p_2 = p_1 + 1$, and a stronger one, which we illustrate in Figure 1, would be $p_2 = 2p_1$. The FO curve (representing the formation of bodies of opinion) is a lagged function of the V curve (representing the parties which receive electoral support).

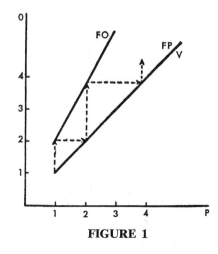

**FIGURE 1**

These assumptions are illustrated in Figure 1. If there is initially only one party, it receives electoral support at the first election to be considered; so that a further body of opinion is formed (raising the total to two), and, to give effect to it, a second party. The formation of the latter is indicated by the FP curve of party formation which, on our present assumptions, coincides with the V curve. At the second election, however (since the coincidence of the V and FP curves means that all parties which are formed get electoral support), both parties are supported by the voters, after which there is a further subdivision of opinion; $o$ (and therefore $p$) increases to 4 for the next election; and so on.

## Case I. "Pure" Simple-Majority or "Dictator" Case

We now introduce a system of elections, and confine ourselves at first to a case in which the only elections held in a country are periodic elections of one man to a single office by a simple majority of all the votes cast throughout the country; and we make the polarization assumption $(D)$ (corresponding to Duverger's assumption $(d')$) that to avoid wasting votes, supporters of "third" party candidates desert them in favour of one or other of those which came first or second in the previous poll. This is to be justified as a legitimate assumption that people respond rationally to the system. If you oppose the party in power (i.e. whose candidate won last time) you lose nothing by supporting the candidate of the party which came second at the last election. People will therefore vote freely for the latter party and the $V$ curve, which shows the parties which receive support, as distinct from those which are formed, remains at 45 degrees up to two parties, and thus far continues to coincide with the $FP$ curve. Beyond that point, however, voting behaviour departs from the behaviour of the political activists whose formation of new parties marks the process of proliferation of bodies of opinion: the $V$ curve becomes inelastic as the "wasted vote" consideration leads electors to withhold support from fresh parties even though they may be sympathetic towards them (Figure 2).

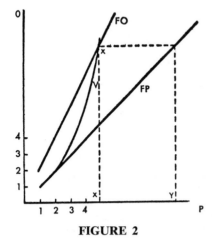

**FIGURE 2**

It will be seen that, so far, we are supposing that the features of the system which makes voters withhold support from fresh parties do not also influence the potential formers of such parties, and deter them from trying. Some unrealism on the part of political "extremists" seems to be a fact of political life, and one which ambivalent behaviour by the electors themselves may foster; for instance,

voters in Britain readily support Liberal candidates at by-elections but desert them at general elections, and Professor Rustow has observed how in Denmark, where a party which is not already represented in the legislature must get 10,000 signatures to a petition to be allowed to enter the campaign, "repeatedly nascent parties have gathered the requisite number of signatures without receiving anywhere near that number of votes in the subsequent election."[14] A more important question is, however, whether continued experience of this polarization by the electors must not be assumed to "feed back" into the conclaves of the political extremists in the course of time, and so attenuate the tendency to proliferation (reduce the slope of the $FO$ curve). After all, assumption $(D)$ is more plausible if we assume that electors have some experience of actually wasting votes, as well as *a priori* grounds for thinking that votes may be wasted, and we should surely therefore be ready to suppose that political activists may profit from experience too.

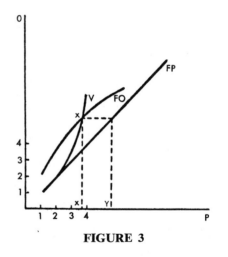

**FIGURE 3**

This may be represented (Figure 3) as a shift in the position of the $FO$ curve with the accumulation of experience; we may call it the "consensus effect," as the tendency to form independent groups and ideologies is diminished because it is seen to be electorally unprofitable. (On similar grounds we might also assume a long-run shift in the right-hand end of the $V$ curve, towards greater inelasticity.)

The equilibrium of the system at $x$ is determined by the intersection of the $FO$ and $V$ curves; for any smaller number of parties receiving votes new bodies of opinion will be formed, entailing the formation of new parties, some of which will be supported electorally, and so on, while for any larger number of parties a number will fail to get electoral support, and with the $FO$ curve lying below the $V$ curve there will be a tendency not to form but to disband parties. At the equilibrium point $x$, of course, there will on the present assumptions be more parties in existence ($Y$) than the voters will support ($X$); this would only cease to be true if the tendency to proliferate were entirely eliminated at a number of parties no greater than the number beyond which the $V$ curve becomes inelastic. The distance $XY$ thus measures one kind of "frustration" incidental to this system; that is, the difference between the number of parties people would in one sense "like" to have, and the number which the system makes it seem "safe" to vote for. The consensus effect naturally reduces $XY$.

Only if we assume that experience ultimately reduces the $FO$ curve to the horizontal will the equilibrium number of parties be *two* in this model. The actual number will depend on the positions we assume for the $FO$ and $V$ curves in the long run, but this particular assumption seems too strong, and we may therefore say that "at least three" parties may be expected to exist under any plausible assumptions for a model of this kind. At the same time, unless there is a tie, only *one* party is *represented*. Case I has therefore no relevance to the phenomenon of bi-partism, in any sense of the concept.

### Case II. "Pure" PR, or "Liechtenstein" Case

We may now consider a system under which a whole country is treated as one multimember constituency for the election of some number of representatives, such as the Diet of Liechtenstein's fifteen members. Should we assume any polarization? It is not obvious that we should not. If there is polarization when there is only one seat to be filled (as in the "dictator" case) does the phenomenon wholly disappear when there are two seats, three, and so on? When the number of seats is small the "quota" of votes needed to elect a candidate to one of them will be relatively large and the activists of very small political groups may well face a possibility that votes for their candidates may be "wasted." The potential relevance of this consideration to systems of PR in which there are only three or four seats per constituency is obvious; for although most writers seem to assume that the polarization assumption has no place in the analysis of any PR system, a weakened polarization assumption may be highly plausible.[15] We may, however, assume that there is a definite number of seats—or that as the ratio of seats to votes increases, there is a definite critical range of its value—above which the polarization factor may be assumed to be negligible. In this case the $V$ curve and the $FP$ curve (representing the parties formed for any given number of bodies of opinion, a curve of 45 degrees) coincide. The electoral system is then neutral, and there is on assumption ($B$) (see page 307 above) no equilibrium, opinions and parties proliferating continuously without check. To get an equilibrium

we may assume *either* a downward shift in the $FO$ curve (experience teaching that further proliferation of parties is futile because so many more already exist than can possibly win any seats) *or* a polarization effect, which shifts the $V$ curve upwards (similar experience having similar effects on the electorate). It is probably plausible to assume that both influences operate to some extent, and that as in Case I, any polarization by the electorate will reinforce the tendency of the $FO$ curve to shift downwards. As an illustration Figure 4 assumes that polarization begins after $p$ becomes equal to $s$, the number of seats to be filled.

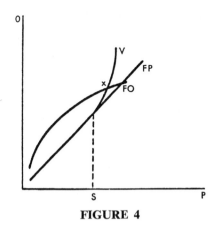

**FIGURE 4**

However we assume that an equilibrium is reached, it will plainly be, on the present assumptions, one of markedly greater multipartism than Case I,[16] whereas this will not necessarily be true of a model in which the number of seats to be filled is relatively small. In reality, of course, most PR systems are not "pure" in the sense of Case II, but divide countries into many constituencies, sometimes with quite small numbers of seats per constituency.[17]

The sort of assumptions suggested above for establishing an equilibrium for the "pure" PR model provoke an interesting incidental line of thought. They were suggested on the same grounds which support the "polarization" assumption itself —that is, as being plausible as the rational response of voters and political activists to *obvious* features of their political situation (in this case the *obvious* futility of forming or voting for new parties beyond a certain point). But what if the electoral system is full of uncertainties? Suppose the consequences of forming or voting for new parties are *not* obvious? If, for instance, a system of "pure" PR were adopted abruptly, with a large number of seats, the first reaction might be one of energetic proliferation, based on the rational calculation that virtually any group may hope to gain enough voters to win at at least one seat. After one or two elections, however, $p$ becomes very large, although still not as large as the number of seats to be filled, which we may take, for the sake of example, to be 100. Long before there are 100 parties (but not until there actually are many), a fresh consideration may be assumed to come into play; from the point of view of parliamentary advantage (e.g. seats in coalition cabinets), it becomes clear that there is much to be gained from fusion with similar groups, and there will be a sharp contraction in their numbers.

In other words, while the number of parties is very small, there is at first no evident limit to the desirability of forming new ones; for low values of $p$ the FO curve, as shown in Figure 5, is indefinitely high. But the higher the number of parties grows, the stronger is the incentive to reduce it; the righthand end of the FO curve is therefore very low. An actual contraction to a small number of parties, however, renews the attractions of schism; and accordingly an oscillation (which, it is plausible to assume, will diminish rather than increase in vio-

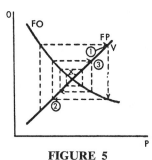

**FIGURE 5**

lence)' will occur around an equilibrium determined by the slope of FO, which will be the equilibrium number of parties, finally reached after a number of elections. This process is represented in Figure 5; the initial multiplication of parties to point 1 is followed by a contraction to point 2, a fresh growth to point 3, and so on till $x$ is reached, a final balance having been established, by experience of the system, between schism and consensus.[18]

In the same way the introduction of devices such as minimum vote quotas, aimed at excluding very small groups from representation, could obviously produce uncertainties of a related kind, operating both directly on small-group activists, and indirectly on them through direct effects on voters; for such devices are intended to ensure that votes cast for very small parties will be wasted, and, knowing this, voters may well polarize voluntarily in favour of larger groups.[19] This kind of uncertainty would produce instability through the process illustrated in Figure 6; that is, the FO curve is shifted, by the introduction of a quota device, from $FO_1$ to $FO_2$, thus reducing the equilibrium number of parties from $x_1$ to $x_2$. But if experience of the actual operation of this device shows that it does not penalize small parties as severely as was feared, the FO curve will shift upwards again, for instance to $FO_3$.

Each introduction of uncertainty may therefore produce two such shifts, one an insurance against the worst, the second an adjustment to experience. Experience may of course prove even worse than expectations, so that a *further* downward shift in the FO curve might occur, or again, experience may

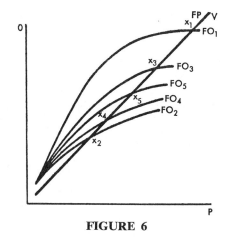

**FIGURE 6**

confirm fears exactly, and no further movement in the FO curve will take place. Figure 6, however, illustrates the introduction of a second quota device after experience of the first has led to a fairly strong reaction ($FO_3$) against the initial downwards "insurance" shift of the FO curve to $FO_2$, and the repetition of this process in response to the second quota. The experience of Holland after the introduction of PR in 1917 (see Duverger's diagram in *Political Parties*, p. 254) suggests the possibility of an explanation of this kind.

### Case III. Simple-Majority Voting in a Number of Single-Member Constituencies: The "British" Case

What changes are required for this case in the assumptions of Case I? If the polarization assumption ($D$) is left unaltered it simply stabilizes the *status quo* in all constituencies. There will be at least three parties in the field in each constituency but they may be different in different areas. The model will exhibit no tendency to bipartism; as we saw, this is the difficulty of Duverger's account.

We assume instead ($E$) that polarization occurs in favour *not* of the two parties which are in the lead locally, but *in favour of the two parties which have the largest number of seats in Parliament, regardless of their local strength*. I think this assumption can be seen to be fully as plausible as assumption ($D$), which it contradicts. The rational response to the system which is assumed here is that in which a vote is felt to be wasted, even if it helps to elect the candidate for whom it is cast in any particular constituency, if it does not contribute towards the parliamentary strength of a party which is "obviously" within reach of gaining an absolute majority of parliamentary representation. On this assumption polarization may occur against the candidate of a party which is, locally speaking, established in first or second place, and throughout the system this process will continue until the two parties which are entrenched behind the polarization effect are the same in all constituencies.

It may be thought at first that assumption $(E)$ commits the same fallacy as that of assumption $(d)$ of the Duverger doctrine (see page 307 above), of simply assuming what has to be explained. But it is at this point that assumption $(c)$ of the Duverger doctrine, which plays no useful role in the traditional account, comes into service. For this assumption $((C)$ in the present model), that all parties after the one which comes first in the total poll get fewer seats than votes, is only appropriate to simple-majority systems (or PR systems which are so "impure" as to be only slight modifications of the simple-majority principle): and in effect it states that the smaller any party's share of the total poll, the greater the disproportion between its share of the poll and its share of the seats. Thus, it is the peculiar feature of such systems that the chances of any "third" party gaining an absolute majority of seats are severely reduced, and its remoteness from power is made dramatically *obvious,* by its exaggeratedly small share of seats. Assumption $(E)$ may therefore be regarded as a rational response to a situation which is peculiarly apt to arise under the simple-majority system in a country divided into single-member districts; and it corresponds, moreover, to what we know of electoral psychology, in that voters in Britain and the U.S.A. do conceptualize the local struggle in terms of the national party scene.

An important distinction must be drawn at this point between bodies of opinion which are *inherently* local in character—e.g., nationalist or agrarian movements—and those which are not. It is obvious that the former type will largely be immune both to under-representation and to the motivations implicit in assumption $(E)$. Their supporters will *ex hypothesi* not attach first importance to voting for the candidate of a party which is within reach of an absolute majority, for the impossibility of such a party's gaining one is generally obvious from the census returns. Not only will they not polarize against it, at least to the same extent; but it will also be less likely to be under-represented since, again by hypothesis, its supporters will not be dissipated over the country at large. Of course most parties, however broadly national in appeal, enjoy for various reasons pockets of strength in certain geographical areas, offset by weaknesses in others, and such empirical relations between votes and seats as the "cube law" in Britain express the in-

fluence of such variations in the distribution of support between the major parties in any country. But such parties will not be immune from under-representation and polarization on the assumptions of the present model.

The equilibrium number of parties in the field in Case III will, therefore, be the same as in Case I, *plus* the number of inherently local parties (i.e. "at least three" plus the latter number).[20] The number *represented* in the legislature, on the other hand, *must in the long run be no more than two, plus the number of inherently local parties,* since only two will be entrenched behind the polarization mechanism in all constituencies other than those where inherently local parties come first or second. We have, therefore, to this extent a definite two-party model (in the sense of a two-party monopoly of representation).

### Case IV. A System of Several (or Many) Multi-Member Constituencies

This case must be considered for the sake of completeness; the complications which it introduces into the model used in Case II may be left to be analyzed by the reader. It corresponds to most PR systems in common use.

## 5. CONCLUSION

Several claims may, I think, be made for the model developed above. It appears to be logically consistent, and its behaviour is, unlike the conclusions to be derived from the traditional formulations of the Duverger doctrine, the sort of behaviour we need for a theory of bipartism. At the same time, it makes clear what it will *not* explain: it suggests, for example, nothing about the alternation of parties in office, nor about the nature of the parties in a two-party system, although it suggests some possible lines of analysis whereby, by the use of extra assumptions, further conclusions of this sort might be drawn. In particular, it draws certain important distinctions which are essential if a theory of parties is to be specific and verifiable: between parties having a majority of representation and parties having merely some representation: between the latter and parties "in the field" or in existence: between parties which are formed and those which receive electoral support. And in general it draws crucial distinctions between types of electoral system which in the past seem all too often to have been lumped ambiguously together. Moreover the "instability" phenomenon derived in Case II seems to be not only worth exploring further as a promising theory of Dutch political development, but also to be of general interest as involving a concept—uncertainty—which is of very wide significance in politics. Lastly, the model relies on the concept of the "obviousness" of the important facts of the political environment, and in particular of the broad features of the parliamentary party scene, not on a sophisticated psychological calculation by the ordinary voter.

But do such "internal" improvements of the model furnish a valid theory? It is, I think, obvious that the model does not furnish a general theory of party systems; but it may possibly furnish a valid theory of bipartism. The formation of new parties obviously may be caused by many different factors which are all subsumed under assumption (*B*) of our model, so that many other variables and assumptions will be necessary to a general theory of party systems. To explain bipartism, however, a much simpler model may be sufficient.

To test this possibility a fresh examination of evidence is necessary, which is beyond the scope of this article. It will be less in the nature of a review of evidence already collected than of a search for the fresh sorts of evidence which are called for by the greater refinement of the model. This is illustrated by the fact that some evidence previously felt by Duverger and others to be recalcitrant "exceptions" to the doctrine now seems *prima facie* to offer some support for it. Thus *federal* systems of government are plainly hybrids for any model which makes the state of the parties in the legislature a crucial variable; which legislature? The former national multipartism of Canada, for instance, may possibly be accounted for in terms of a number of "inherently local" parties, the agrarian-reform CCF and Social Credit parties; but we might also assume a *conflict of polarization* for, for example, Saskatchewan electors (Liberals and Conservatives dominating the national parliament, but CCF and Liberals the provincial parliament), and explain the long continuance of CCF representation at Ottawa along the following line.

During the years of overwhelming Liberal dominance at Ottawa the attention of Saskatchewan voters may be thought of as mainly directed towards the provincial scene, where the leading position of CCF and the Liberals led to polarization against the Conservatives, an influence which "spilled over" and offset the opposite polarization tendency emanating from Ottawa in national elections in Saskatchewan constituencies. After the limited Diefenbaker victory in 1957, however, the national parliamentary situation was transformed; a change of national government was a reality, and a large Tory majority a real possibility. In the 1958 election the national parliamentary scene in fact became virtually the only issue of the campaign— to give or not to give such a majority to Mr. Diefenbaker; and so for the first time the "overspill" of provincial polarization and the national representation of the CCF was decimated.[21]

## NOTES

1. See M. Duverger, "The Influence of the Electoral System on Political Life," *International Social Science Bulletin* (Summer, 1951), pp. 314–52; the well-known account by E. E. Schattschneider, in *Party Government* (New York, 1942), pp. 65-84; and (in a speculative form) H. J. Laski, *A Grammar of Politics* (London, 1925), pp. 315-18. The doctrine is of course implicit in Mill's *Representative Government* (Everyman edition, pp. 258-63).

2. M. Duverger, *Political Parties* (London, 1954), p. 217.

3. A forceful summary of this criticism is made by Peter Campbell in *French Electoral Systems and Elections 1789–1957* (London, 1958), pp. 30-32, and his conclusion will serve as typical of many: ". . . a country's party system is determined far more by its political institutions and traditions in general and by the social factors affecting its politics than by the electoral system. . . . The accurate reflection of the electorate's divisions is a matter of machinery: the nature and number of the parties depend on forces stronger, slower, and less mutable than the electoral system" (*Ibid.*, pp. 32 and 45).

4. Donald V. Smiley uses an argument of this kind in "The Two-Party System and One-Party Dominance," *The Canadian Journal of Economics and Political Science,* vol. xxiv, No. 3 (Aug., 1958), at pp. 316-17: e.g., "The traditional explanation [i.e., the Duverger doctrine] . . . has been used to account for the persistence of the two-party system, but it could have been used equally logically to explain the existence of other kinds of party patterns. If in Canada or the United States . . . political life had been dominated by several sectionally based parties, orthodox political scientists would no doubt argue that the electoral system of single-member districts lay at the base of this phenomenon" (p. 317).

5. Compare the following judgments: "The electoral system works in the direction of bipartism: it does not necessarily and absolutely lead to it in spite of all obstacles. The basic tendency combines with many others which attenuate it, check it, or arrest it" (Duverger, *Political Parties,* p. 228). "It can of course be conceded that the normal workings of the method of single-member districts do impose very considerable handicaps on a minor party outside its area of strength and that in a nation such as Great Britain where sectional influences are weak it is thus difficult for such parties to exist" (Smiley, loc. cit., p. 317).

6. It has been effectively argued by Professor Milton Friedman that the only proper test of the value of a theory is the success of its predictions, so that a theory may be none the worse for resting on "unrealistic" assumptions if it continues to furnish valid predictions. (See his *Essays in Positive Economics* [Chicago, 1953], pp. 16-23.) On the other hand a theory which predicts wrongly may as well be doing so for this reason as any other.

7. I.e., both parameters and dependent variables.

8. I.e., this account deliberately stresses the constructive relationship between model-building and the-

orizing. Yet models are useful largely because they introduce a drastic measure of simplification into our thinking, and it is often true that the simpler they are made, the clearer the conclusions they yield. As the real world is complex, this clarity may usually be increased only at the expense of realism; yet clarity may often be the more important objective. "If there is any justification for the investigation of . . . oversimplified models . . . it is that, *because* of [their] unreality, [they] may bring into prominence certain relations or ideas which will still play their part in more realistic representations" (I. M. D. Little, "Classical Growth," *Oxford Economic Papers* (n.s.), vol. ix, No. 2 (June, 1957), p. 154).

9. I owe this to Mr. P. P. Streeten of Balliol College.

10. Friedman, *op. cit.*, pp. 24-25.

11. Duverger, *Political Parties*, p. 223.

12. This is essentially the objection raised by Smiley, quoted above, p. 128, n. 3.

13. Smiley, *op. cit.*, pp. 316-17, provides figures showing how in Canada the CCF and the Progressives have in the past been over-represented, while the Conservatives have been under-represented, although winning the second largest number of seats and votes. The significance for such observations for assumption (c) is further discussed below.

14. In S. Neumann (ed.), *Modern Political Parties* (Chicago, 1956), p. 178 n.

15. See below, Case IV.

16. The experience of Israel, under a system which treats the whole country as one multi-member constituency, is apparently consistent with the behaviour of this model; see E. Lakeman and J. D. Lambert, *Voting in Democracies* (London, 1955), pp. 181-2 and 240.

17. Duverger notes that few countries have "full" PR (*Political Parties,* p. 253) but by "full" PR he means PR unqualified by anti-splinter devices, such as minimum quotas, etc., and not "pure" PR in our sense of a system which treats the whole country as one constituency; see Case IV below.

18. Since the lag in the relation between the $V$ and $FO$ curves has been assumed to be the time which elapses between elections, it might be more realistic to represent the $FO$ curve in this case as initially like that in Figure 1—i.e. rising steeply to the right, representing continuous party proliferation through more than one election in the first years of the working of the new system; and only shifting to the position shown in Figure 5 when the number of parties has grown very large. More realistically speaking, the type of uncertainty assumptions used in Figure 5 probably belong in a model of *permanent* party instability, with no fixed equilibrium; i.e. in which the $FO$ curve intersects the $V$ curve with a slope of 45 degrees.

19. This would be represented by an upward shift of the $V$ curve.

20. Of course the parties in "third" place may differ from one constituency to another so that unless we introduce further assumptions we cannot conclude that the absolute number in the field in Case III will be limited to the same number as in Case I.

21. A similar analysis of the United States party scene would also take into account the electoral psychological consequences of voting for a President, which might be held responsible for imposing on a situation fully as "hybrid" as Canada's a superficial bipartimorphism beneath which multiparty situations akin to Canada's have often been detected.

# THE EXPORT OF ELECTORAL SYSTEMS

## W. J. M. Mackenzie

### THE SITUATION

This lecture,[1] I am afraid, is concerned primarily with some rather dry questions about the tactics of research in politics, and I hope therefore that you will excuse me if I begin by indicating, in a more personal way, the situation which may give these some present interest. Through the kindness of various sponsors I was able

Reprinted from *Political Studies,* Vol. V, No. 3 (1957), pp. 240–257, by permission of the author and the Clarendon Press, Oxford.

last summer to pay a brief visit to East and Central Africa. There are seven British territories there;[2] in all of these, and in the Sudan too, discussion about the development of elections lies close to the centre of politics. Indeed, there exists already a surprisingly large number of separate electoral systems, because of the introduction of separate electorates for separate communities. I can reckon at least fifteen of them, and this takes no account of the ingenuity of District Commissioners in devising new systems to fit local circumstances, as they are urged to do under the policy of "democratizing" tribal institutions. These homemade electoral systems vary a good deal, and include some useful devices which are not in the textbooks.[3]

This outbreak of a sort of epidemic of electoral systems is at first a little startling to a politics don, more startling than the related outbreaks of Speakers and maces, Permanent Secretaries and Cabinet Secretariats, Federations and County Councils. It has been the fashion in political research, in countries where democracy is well established, to deflate the nineteenth-century notion that in a free election the voter decides rationally between persons and policies:[4] and much excellent work has been done to analyse Western elections on the basis of such concepts as voting habits, the party image, the association of political attitudes with types of personality, the relation of such attitudes to more general economic and social factors. We have begun to see Western elections in terms of what Bagehot used to call "a *cake* of custom":[5] and in doing so we have learnt much, consciously or unconsciously, from the writings of social anthropologists about the life of isolated pre-literate societies. We no longer underrate the political wisdom of non-Western peoples, and in consequence we have become increasingly sceptical about the possibility that one can in any real sense make constitutions for them; yet it is in this period that the construction of constitutions has become an industry on a grand scale. There has been much talk of the expansion of Communism, but there are few Marxist constitutions outside the U.S.S.R. and China: whereas the fashion for government based on free elections has run round the world. Earlier attempts to establish Western constitutions in the Middle East and in Latin America have at least partially failed: yet to these old experiments has been added a series of new ventures in Africa, in the West Indies, the Pacific, South-East Asia, and the countries of the old Indian Empire. There have been such inconceivably gigantic operations as the introduction of universal suffrage in India:[6] at the other extreme is the spontaneous imitation of Western democracy by small groups of people like the 2,000 people of the south coast of Manus Island, where "wait-council" time is so warmly described in Miss Margaret Mead's recent book, *New Lives for Old.*

An ingenious person might construe this as the march of a new type of imperialism, a device for captivation. On the contrary, the "imperialists," British, French, Dutch, Belgian, Australian, to a slightly less extent American, are no longer Wilsonian: they insist nowadays that it is absurd to suppose that Western institutions can possibly be made to work in oriental or African countries without long apprenticeship. We have not imposed Western institutions; they have been demanded, one might say extorted, from us, and we are thus committed against our will to an extraordinary adventure. We share the commitment because we furnished the

model and will be involved in the consequences of success or failure. But now the experiment is launched we are not invited to participate, indeed we have neither the wisdom nor the power to do so. Nevertheless, there is a challenge to gain at least an intellectual grasp of the situation: it is after all an article of faith within the cycle of beliefs to which free elections belong that it is good for a rational being to give an account of himself. If from academic observation comes knowledge useful to countries where the transition has scarcely begun, so much the better: but so far as practical justification is needed it must lie primarily in the fact that independent observation and analysis is in itself a part of free government as we understand it.

## THE POSSIBILITY OF RESEARCH

But if political researchers are to enter this field their first problem is that of Buridan's ass, where to begin. There is a great deal of material, and it is not inaccessible to research. Electoral studies in general have this advantage over other branches of our subject, that their base is relatively secure. There is a limited range of theory about the proper character of choice by large electorates, and a limited range of devices from which to choose a prescription suited to a defined set of normative premisses and of economic and social factors. The range of permutations is inexhaustible, but the materials, the pieces in the building set, are easier to grasp and to define than material about party organization, about the interplay of pressure groups and personal cliques, or about the highest levels of executive government. Indeed, there is a certain element of ritual about elections: the doing of certain familiar things in a familiar order is part of the magic by which they command allegiance. Psephology and liturgiology are akin.[7]

This is therefore a relatively "tidy" subject: it also offers special advantages as a point of entry to the study of politics anywhere. In any country where elections are taken seriously they constitute a sort of bottleneck in the political process, a narrow strait or channel in which political life is for a short period concentrated under the eye of the observer. Orators, party bosses, chiefs, villagers, market women, civil servants, priests, newspapermen, all kinds of sections and pressure groups, in so far as they think about politics at all, think for a short time about one kind of politics only, electoral politics. This jostling multitude of political interests would be unmanageable, but that the formal structure of an election imposes external order on them; a student who sets out shrewdly the main influences that bear on an election thereby gives quite an orderly conspectus of the country's politics.

It should be emphasized that he gives a conspectus, not an analysis, and that an electoral survey raises far more questions than it answers: but at least it is as good a way as any in which to start unravelling the skein.[8]

There are also other advantages. Many of the countries now introducing elections are small and relatively self-contained: the limits of literacy and of other channels of mass communication are such that it is not impossible for a single observer to judge what is reaching the voter from sources at the centre of politics; and both politicians and administrators have felt so much pride and enthusiasm in making new things that they have welcomed friendly observers and have accepted any comment that is not patronizing. There are difficulties of language, and there are difficulties in the extreme intricacy of the local situations on which the new pattern of elections is imposed. But if these difficulties are to be accepted as final, the whole idea of the comparative study of governments separate in time or sphere must be dismissed as a delusion. Complex as are the affairs of the Gold Coast or Nyasaland, they are not—they cannot be—more complex than those of the U.S.A. or Russia, of Georgian England or France of the revolution, subjects which we attempt to teach to second- and third-year students.

## TECHNIQUES

Assuming then that there is something here which is at least worth attempting, how should it be done? —in terms of method, I mean, not in terms of financial resources and men available. (This separation between methods and men is an abstraction, and is apt to do harm in discussions about the next steps in social research, but I hope that it can be excused for the moment.)

To begin with, I should like to make a working distinction between techniques and tactics, a distinction which is intended to evade certain problems, not to resolve them. Discussion about the methodology of the social sciences is apt to become a disguised sort of ethics and metaphysics, and I am anxious not to become involved in this.

It seems to me that the range of techniques available is wide, the choice of tactics limited. Techniques I should classify arbitrarily as arts techniques, science techniques, and techniques of access.

The unity of arts techniques is perhaps mainly an historical one, in that they are those which most of us in this University learn first, remnants of a rather old tradition in education: the capacity to use our own language with awareness of its limits and its ambiguities; to use two or three other languages more crudely, and to grasp in general the sort of problems which arise in translation from one language to another: to handle printed or written sources in a comprehensive and orderly way: to assess the value of these and other scraps of evidence about doubtful matters: above all, to present conclusions in such a way that the reader trusts the author's judgement but is not bound by it.

To my mind, the scientific techniques have a similar unity of tradition, and seek a similar objectivity by a different route, that which combines measurement and mathematics. Probably we have now passed the time when extreme views were held one way or the other about the place of measurement in the social sciences. The problems of obtaining data worth using are now quite generally understood, and so are the limits of mathematical analysis in extracting truth from crude and inaccurate figures. Perhaps the greatest values of big experiments in social measurement (at least in the field of politics) has been not to make discoveries but to elucidate problems about standards of proof and about the status of our conclusions. Even a general notion of what is meant by "operational definition" is a useful razor in cutting away rambling generalities: and there are many incidental ways in which a correct use of questionnaires and samples can help to buttress an argument. But full-scale experiments have generally proved too slow, cumbersome, and expensive for the ordinary man. In this country, it seems to me, the skill chiefly required is that of extemporizing utility variants of elaborate schemes worked out in America, so as to get cheaply and quickly just what is wanted and no more, a business which needs judgement and administrative skill as well as competence in statistics.

My third heading, techniques of access, is, I am afraid, a piece of jargon coined merely to emphasize the importance of common sense and good manners in political research. We all know people otherwise highly qualified whom we should not care to turn loose as observers of a hotly contested election. One of Oxford's most conspicuous contributions to political studies in this country has been to establish that academic observers can be politically neutral and personally charming, and in so doing Oxford has perhaps created in the minds of British politicians a presumption very useful to the rest of us, that people from the Universities are quite trustworthy, sometimes interesting, never in the way. Obviously such success is in part due to the social tradition of this University, and it may seem inappropriate to refer to that "easy consciousness of effortless superiority" as a technique. But it is something that can be learnt, by apprenticeship if not otherwise, and it is a necessary tool of the trade.

Doubtless the ideal research worker has all these techniques at his command: doubtless no one starts at all without some limited capacity in each branch. But being armed, how then to join battle?

## TACTICS

### 1. Electoral Law

May I put on one side first the approach through electoral law? Every electoral system needs a code or textbook of electoral law and practice, something comparable to the massive volumes of Schofield on Parliamentary Elections and Schofield on Local Government Elections. Elections cannot work smoothly and effectively unless there is something in the nature of a prayer book or book of drill, to establish certainty about complex procedure involving a great many people. It is an extremely difficult piece of scholarship to prepare such a textbook satisfactorily: but it is not part of its purpose to add to existing knowledge about open questions. Electoral law is not lawyers' law; it throws up few issues of importance to jurisprudence, and it is of political interest only when we come to look at the relation between form and content, between electoral law and political practice, a matter which perhaps goes beyond the sphere of law as a discipline.

If research on electoral systems has a general purpose it is to elicit new and interesting points about this relationship; an electoral system has a precise formal structure, it is set within a complex and moving political situation. How does one affect the other? How are changes in parts of one related to changes in parts of the other? Our conclusions are not likely to be very interesting or very practical unless we can achieve some analysis of this sort. It is beautiful, even comforting, to regard a political situation simply as an interacting whole, something that is "aye growing" while men "are sleeping."[9] But, as Mill pointed out, this is an unrealistic sort of "political fatalism":[10] in politics as in other branches of knowledge one must fragment in order to gain a point of leverage for action or explanation.

Are there perhaps in theory two methods of approaching this task, methods which are in practice always combined, even by those who think they have separated them? Each separately, I should maintain, is arid; the art of tactics lies in combination.

### 2. Hypothetics"[11]

One method, of course, is that of conceptual framework, hypothesis, and verification; the other is that of history, or (as it is more usually called in this context) "case-study." The former requires that there should be a central system of interrelated propositions about the nature of man in society, from these are to be deduced more limited hypotheses about the behavior of men in particular situations, these hypotheses are to be confirmed or refuted by carefully designed observations. If they are confirmed, the structure of the science is thus enlarged, and strengthened: if they are not confirmed, or are confirmed subject to certain reservations, there must follow a process of checking fundamental theory so as to increase its refinement and exactness. It is to this procedure, we are told, that natural science owes its power: this is what is needed to make the study of politics "a genuine scientific discipline."[12] I quote from a recent conference report in the *American Political Science Review:* the same sort of theme was made familiar, in a less dogmatic way, by the work of Graham Wallas and the Webbs fifty years ago. Indeed, it is no more than the latest version of the old attempt to "introduce the experimental method of reasoning into moral subjects."[13] In its present form its main tactical maxims are that before we start research we should settle carefully the object of each piece of research, by reference to an existing framework of interlocking definitions; that we should handle one question at a time, or at the most a small range of questions, using something analogous to the old method of concomitant variations: and that we should prove each step in the chain properly, according to some defined standard of proof, before we put our weight on it and take a step forward.

I cannot help feeling that this is too weak a hook with which to catch Leviathan. There is not "world enough and time": political problems are too big for us and move too fast for such a method, taken alone, to be of much value. It may be that there has been some misunderstanding of the methods of the natural sciences; what is described seems to be a method of proof or criticism and of exposition, rather than a tactic of discovery. But my own judgement is affected mainly by the analogy of the rather archaic science or discipline in which I was brought up, that of classical philology. Whatever its logical status, the study of language is certainly the most highly developed and the most rigorous of the social sciences; the analogy between politics and language is (I know) vulnerable at some points, but it is at least as persuasive as those between politics and physics or between politics and biology.[14]

There are then three points which this analogy suggests to my mind. The first is that the construction of an effective grammar for a single language is not dependent on the existence of a comprehensive theory of linguistics. To know the grammar of one language may help one to grasp that of a cognate language, may perhaps hamper one in grasping a language radically different: knowledge of several grammars encourages a search for generalization at a higher level, and perhaps this may in time require further thought about how each grammar is organized. But a grammar is valid and useful for its own language without such generalization and revision. One can hope (on this analogy) to frame and to use a reasonably exact grammar of British, or American, or Russian politics without waiting for some new sort of "Grammar of Politics" in general.[15] Secondly, making and learning grammars is a subordinate part of the business, at least for most scholars. The primary task is to understand and to translate. It is indeed possible to set out in terms of general rules, hypotheses, and verifications the business of translating a hard passage or of reconstructing and translating a fragmentary papyrus or inscription. But one is not here working from a specific experiment to a general rule, but from the rule to the meaning of this specific and unique passage; and it is most unusual to set out the structure of proof explicitly—our internal computing machine works much too fast for that, so fast that for the most part we feel we have gone straight to the meaning, and we begin to worry consciously only when we come to the business of translation.[16] Explicit appeal to deduction and verification is used as a last resort if we are stuck and need some mechanical aid in checking over what the meaning may be: or if we are involved in controversy and must defend ourselves. For the most part we proceed, as Housman said in one of his Prefaces, "by the capricious and arbitrary method of putting forward first one foot and then, with strange inconsistency, the other."[17] My third point is that it is extremely rare in dealing with an established literary language to attempt to amend the grammar itself by a process of hypothesis and verification. This is outside my experience, but it is doubtless a different matter if one seeks to elucidate for the first time the grammar of an unwritten language or to follow changes in the grammar of spoken English. I appreciate that some theory of general linguistics may be of value here to emancipate the searcher from the bonds of familiar grammars and to set him going on the most promising line of work. But general linguistics will not help him much unless he also has direct acquaintance with several languages of different types; and even here the object of the research is not primarily to find general laws but to grasp and explain, to make intelligible the particular case.

This is as far as this analogy carries me. As the present Professor of Poetry said in his inaugural lecture,

Man is an analogy-drawing animal; that is his great good fortune. His danger is of treating analogies as identities, of saying, for instance, "Poetry should be as much like music as possible." I suspect that the people who are most likely to say this are the tone-deaf. The more one loves another art, the less likely it is that one will wish to trespass upon its domain.[18]

I am therefore anxious not to go farther, in particular not to suggest that I think the ideas of theoretical discipline and of rigorous proof have no place in political studies. What troubles me about the analogy drawn from natural science is the conclusion deduced from it, that scholarship is idle, in language or in politics, except when it is proving new rules; and I think the assumption is a bad guide to the tactics of research in politics. For the sake of an analogy, which is no more than an analogy, it involves the researcher in grave practical difficulties. One of these is that things move very fast in contemporary politics: not faster than the human mind, but too fast for the step-by-step process of hypothesis and consolidation. Another difficulty is that we are too rich in hypotheses: hypotheses not about external verities, but about extremely interesting and pressing questions of action. To take merely the export of electoral systems, there is a bubbling fountain of hypotheses to be found in an American article on Western institutions in non-Western societies published in 1955:[19] as many more can be derived from the work of Professor Duverger and other French scholars[20] and from the handbook on electoral problems compiled by a German group as a basis for electoral reform in Germany.[21] There are enough hypotheses in circulation already to found a new science or translate all the odes of Pindar; unfortunately the only ones which can be proved fairly easily tend (as Professor Evans-Pritchard has it) "to become mere tautologies and platitudes on the level of common sense deduction."[22] Rigorous proof or disproof of serious hypotheses, even quite small ones, can generally be obtained only with great expense and after considerable delay. There are some famous examples of such thoroughness, but, as I said earlier, they have perhaps been successful primarily as research into methods of research, establishing new standards and devices of proof and elucidating the difficulties of applying them. This is valuable work; but need we all do nothing else?

### 3. Case-Studies

I should prefer to call the extreme into which one reacts the method of case-studies rather than the method of history; there is some risk of confusion, but "case-studies" is the fashionable phrase and at least it sets aside some of the problems which trouble introspective historians.[23] In particular I would like to emphasize at the outset that the tactics of description may—indeed must—use all techniques that come to hand, whether called "humane" or "scientific." It would be absurd, for instance, to think of describing a large election without using electoral statistics.

As it is understood by simple souls, the case-study method is to establish the facts and let them speak for themselves; put the reader in the position of informed spectator and let him use the material as he pleases. He may wish to judge or generalize;

he may merely learn by experience the feeling of a variety of situations.

It need hardly be said that this too, like the notion of an experimental method, is merely a limiting abstraction, not a practical way of proceeding. It is a commonplace that any narrative of events is in some respects both deductive and selective. A narrative is deductive in that the evidence for it is used on the basis of general experience outside the immediate field of study: it is selective in that much of the evidence is not available, and also because some choice has to be made among the evidence which might be used. Case-studies of contemporary events are usually selective in both these ways. Some important evidence is missing: sometimes one knows that it is missing, sometimes one does not know, sometimes one is left in a sort of limbo of discretion, possessing evidence, but unable to argue from it lest its source be betrayed. Other evidence must be neglected because it is too voluminous to be manageable.

Such problems are extremely hard to deal with satisfactorily, yet a case-study is pointless if what it says is determined by chance. The author, in so far as he is skilled, knows how to control his material in accordance with certain criteria of relevance. These criteria may be extremely complex; so complex that he could never explain them fully, not even if the narrative were held up indefinitely during the explanation. To understand what is being said the reader must either share the author's criteria of relevance or learn them by practice as he reads. In this sense the case-study is a means by which the student can grasp in a concrete way the judgement of a more experienced person about what is most important and interesting in a particular situation. Like good history a good case-study is comprehensive: but it is also orderly, and it is sharply, even ruthlessly, selective; and it does not waste time on explanations of its procedure.

It must be ordered also in another way, or in two closely related ways, which are more straightforward and more directly relevant to electoral studies. First, every narrative needs platforms or pausing places, where the narrator halts for a little to sketch the background of the story; however lightly this is done, the account must have form, and its form commits the writer to certain implicit generalizations about what is relevant. Secondly, a narrative must move through time, and if it relates, as electoral studies must relate, to events taking place within a set form of procedure, it falls almost as a matter of course into certain chapters, and these divisions turn up in much the same way in studies made independently. There have been differences in style and personality between the four Nuffield College studies of British general elections, but each has included chapters on the candidates, the campaign, the main organs of mass communication, and the results, and they have all dealt also with the issues of the election as defined by its immediate antecedents, with electoral machinery, and with party organization. In addition, they have usually included a number of case-studies of separate constituencies, each study following the same sort of pattern as the main study but on a smaller scale. The four books rarely use the form of hypothesis and verification, and yet clearly they have reached some sort of generalization about the things that are important in British elections. This generalization could notionally (I suppose) be broken down into a set of separate propositions; many of these propositions, taken separately, would be hard to prove, taken together they give a convincing account of what happens, and this account is the expression of a coherent view set out in an orderly way. The authors believe, and their readers agree, that certain things are relevant to the narrative of a British election, and that other things are not relevant. It is usually relevant, for instance, to discuss the age and education of the candidates, but not their weights or their waist-measurements or the colour of their wives' eyes. It may well be relevant to discuss the weather: it is not deemed relevant to discuss the progress of First Division football clubs, or the state of the London theatre, or the current fashion in women's dress. These may seem outrageous examples, but such matters have sometimes been relevant to politics in the past, and they may turn up again. A future author may feel bound to bring new factors into the narrative, so that it takes a new shape. If a man can do this and convince his readers that he is talking sense, he is not only amusing them, he is also in some way establishing new knowledge, a new but acceptable variant of an existing canon of relevance.

The situation to be described varies a little from one British election to another: it varies still more between a British election and a French election, between an election in Europe and an election in Africa. The author of an electoral survey must contrive to look at each afresh, lest he miss what is most important in it; nevertheless, he proceeds from experience of what has been found relevant elsewhere, and he contributes to and modifies this common stock. We assume when we launch ourselves on a field of study, like the study of elections, that it has some order and some unity: in so far as these exist, they will emerge if shrewd observers experienced in elections expound to intelligent readers what they find, because certain themes will repeat themselves with variations more or less insistent. As Miss Margaret Mead says: "Our capacity to see, to recognize, to isolate significant variables, is a function of which other people, how many other cultural groups, we have seen and studied, for how long and with what conceptual and practical tools."[24]

To talk in this way is to describe one of the

main currents in British political research since the war. It is a form of tactics which we know very well: and we perhaps begin to see its limits. If elections do in fact repeat themselves so that the same pattern serves for several studies without much variation, we begin to say, as the social anthropologists might, that the latest study "lacks theoretical interest"; a case-study may be wholly admirable as a record, and yet fail to break new ground, because there is not in this area new ground to break. One might say that studies of that particular sort of election, like Greek tragedy as described by Aristotle, stop changing when they have found their true nature;[25] and there is then room for generalization, which can be made safely and even rigorously without recourse to a step-by-step process of hypothesis and verification. A recent example of this sort of scholarship is Professor Schapera's excellent book *The Government and Politics of Tribal Societies*:[26] he has the advantage of better field material than has generally been available to political scientists, but at least one can say that this is the sort of thing that political scientists did from the time of Aristotle to the time of Bryce, and still do when they can find courage and material. This, after all, is what the Rector of Exeter has done in his book on *Government by Committee*.[27]

Of course such generalizations are more limited and less stable than those of natural science. They rest firmly enough on the opinion of experienced observers, confirmed by that of their readers, and they can be buttressed by examples which are at least rhetorically convincing. On the other hand, there are no crucial instances on which a chain of reasoning can be based, there is no means of estimating the probabilities involved, there is no clear line between what changes and what is permanent. The research worker in politics is more liable than any other to be caught by events which change the emphasis of institutions, and make nonsense of his conclusions before he has published them, or very shortly afterwards. As in ancient medicine, "opportunity is fleeting, experience treacherous, judgement difficult": and it seems natural to continue the quotation from Hippocrates, translating more freely. "The trouble is that the research worker has to cope with the patient, the bystanders and external circumstances, as well as with his own deficiencies."[28]

## SUMMARY

May I now summarize what I have said so far —and I know, or at least suspect, how many issues it has set aside? I think that for British scholars the best tactics in approaching the problem of electoral systems in non-Western countries is to begin from the method of electoral surveys, which in general we understand pretty well. I do not think that this is an evasion of the challenge to face problems and reach general conclusions, because, given a reasonably wide spread of field work, conclusions emerge from this method more swiftly than from the step-by-step method of hypothesis and verification, and do not lack standing as contributions to knowledge. And I do not think that it evades the requirements of rigorous scholarship: or that it excludes the use of techniques of measurement.

But I recommend these tactics only subject to certain reserves. Repetition of surveys contributes to political science as distinct from historical research only so long as new points of interest continue to emerge. As surveys enter the phase of diminishing returns, the time is ripe for someone to try his hand at generalization, and for others to widen the area of research. The "experimental method" may then be of great value to establish particular points, and also to test methods and set standards of proof. Peculiarity of local circumstances will suggest special problems for investigation: and there will be crises which deserve study simply for the record. In the end, if elections become established outside the West, they will take a settled place within a working system of politics, and it may be wise then to turn from study of the short, critical period of elections, to that of the more normal flow of political life, a more difficult task comparable to that which political scientists face in this country and in the U.S.A.

In effect this concludes my argument, but it is hard to avoid reference to what is perhaps really a false question. This kind of research seems necessary because it is of some general importance to the world to see how this experiment goes. Will research help the experiment to succeed? And behind that question is another—will it help us to assess whether the experiment is succeeding or failing?

## PRACTICAL RECOMMENDATIONS

As regards the first question, I cannot put the matter more succinctly than in the words of Professor Evans-Pritchard: "Social anthropology," he says, and this applies to the electoral studies, "may occasionally resolve problems of administration. It makes for a sympathetic understanding of other peoples. It also provides valuable material for the historian of the future."[29] This is a minimum claim; so much is certain, one might perhaps go a little further. Politics, as we understand it in developed societies, is always to some extent concerned with formal institutions, man-made and by law established. "In studying political organization," wrote the late Professor Radcliffe-Brown, "we have to deal with the maintenance or establishment of social order, within a territorial framework, by the organized use of coercive authority through the use, or the possibility of use, of physical force."[30] This will serve for political science as well as for social anthropology: but one must add that in the analysis of Western societies we are forced to add another level of discussion. As emerges from the volume on African political systems from which I have quoted, and also from Professor Schapera's book, in tribal societies change in institutions is not itself institutionalized. In the West, on the other hand, political institutions are conspicuously institutions for changing other institutions, including political institutions. The export of elections is part of a larger movement for the export of this notion of explicit man-made forms of government. We are accustomed, as I have said, to look rather cynically at our own claim to reason, and to regard changes in electoral systems in the West as reflecting a balance of forces rather than an effort at improvement. The objection generally made by political scientists to the introduction of a single transferable vote in Britain is not that it is impracticable or unjust, but that it is politically naïve to imagine that a great party would ever be prepared to sponsor it. But in spite of this ingrained cynicism, or positivism, we know that constitution-making goes on all the time, in large affairs and small ones, and we never dream of suggesting that it is unreasonable to talk about the success or failure of changes in the organization of government departments, or of the nationalized industries, or of a political party machine. There may be some things which we think it unreasonable to discuss because we believe that they cannot be affected by the sort of reorganization contemplated: but even to say this is to make a practical contribution to a discussion about organization.

I do not think, therefore, that we can, like our colleagues in social anthropology, evade responsibility for recommendation and assessment, particularly in a matter of this sort, in which the special interest of the problem is that it is an attempt to construct new institutions on a grand scale. But what we can do in this sense is narrowly limited, by the nature of things as well as by lack of resources. Experience about the export of elections cannot be gathered and presented systematically in time to help much in this present phase, which is perhaps the decisive phase for the future of Western forms of government in non-Western societies. We can offer perhaps to the countries concerned some indication of what are in our experience reasonable and attainable standards in electoral practice,[31] some competent comment on matters of tactics and party organization, perhaps some sense that because of its growing unity the world has a considerable interest in what may seem small

matters, even to the local people, such as the franchise in British Guiana, or Mauritius, or Fiji.

In the process we will perhaps learn as much about our own political practice as about that of others. It is, for instance, obvious in non-Western countries that many of the issues of politics turn on relations between traditional authorities and a new middle-class who are educated in the Western style and fill roles in an economy of the Western type. In each separate instance the numbers of men and women involved are quite small, and it is possible to see with some clarity how tradition, economic change, and forms of educaton react upon one another and upon the structure of politics. There is a similar interaction in Britain, imperfectly studied because it is very complex and changes slowly: men accustomed to observe such changes elsewhere will be better qualified to record it here. Our study of our own politics has already gained much through the opportunity to see ourselves in another guise—"mutato nomine de te Fabula narratur"—in the politics of the Nuer and the Manus, the Zulu and the Makah Indians; it will gain more if we can grasp more clearly the relation between change of institutions and change of circumstances.

## SUCCESS OR FAILURE

There is finally the question of success or failure. It has been said that nothing imported would survive British withdrawal from Africa except the game of football: I should hazard a guess that elections would also survive, in some form. But what sort of elections? Certainly not the sort which we are seeking to export. An institution newly introduced must change unless it rests on some general public understanding of how it worked in its original place, and of how it is supposed to work now. Such understanding is of necessity dim: even formal teaching is very inadequate as a means of conveying how institutions work and is at best an adjunct to apprenticeship. The institution complete, or moderately complete, can only be taught by participation; people must move with it, as they did to the Dominions of settlement.

Professor Oakeshott's analogy of cookery books and cooking[32] and Professor Polanyi's analogy of connoisseurship[33] are in point. It is certain that, even though they continue to be based on free elections, politics in the Gold Coast or the Federation of Rhodesia and Nyasaland or Malaya or British Guiana will never in practice greatly resemble politics of Britain. These are different places and different people, and formal identity of electoral systems will do little to make them more alike.

I have forebodings, therefore, that in the future we shall hear much about how Western elections have failed in Indonesia, or failed in the Southern Sudan, or failed in British Guiana—and so on: and one is tempted to answer in advance that this sort of statement is nonsensical, because there can be neither success nor failure in this sort of venture. The only thing that can be predicted with certainty about the export of elections is that an electoral system will not work in the same way in its new settings as in its old.

Indeed this is a general point. It is possible to measure success or failure in constitution-making by comparison with an original model. It may be true that the Presidency of the United States is modelled on the monarchy of George III, that of France on the monarchy of Queen Victoria: but it is mere nonsense to use that sort of comparison for purposes of judgment, the crudest confusion between origin and function. Is it, however, possible to seek greater generality by comparing function with function?

The trouble here is that we are not at the moment very certain of the function of elections in our own society. We have on the whole ceased to think that their function is to ensure government by the people, in any sense intelligible to Rousseau or Jefferson or John Stuart Mill: yet we continue to believe most heartily in their necessity; and this Western loyalty to elections has been strengthened by events of the last generation and of the last year. Free elections—elections in which the voters believe that they have a real though limited choice in some matter of importance to the state and to themselves—perhaps offer two advantages of a very general kind: they offer a means of continuity in succession not available to personal or party governments, and they commit the people to a sense of responsibility for their own betterment more effectively than any form of public exhortation yet devised by Ministries of Propaganda or of Information. To say this is not to offer a theory of the function of elections in Western societies, but to indicate that there is no adequate theory. Nevertheless, it seems clear enough that they are essential to us as props of the sentiment of legitimacy and the sentiment of participation: and that these sentiments break easily and are hard to repair. There is perhaps here a measure which can be at least crudely applied: elections once exported may work in odd ways, but they may be said to succeed—in India, for instance, or in Africa or in South-East Asia—if the offer of choice to the elector continues to play a vital part in the continuity of the state. In all these countries the situation demands absolutely that government should be given a new basis. Traditional government may be able to survive in a few of the larger territories, such as Morocco, Siam, Ethiopia, and Saudi Arabia, but it generally operates in units too small to be viable. The only obvious alternatives to it are army rule or party rule. These may solve at least temporarily the prob-

lem of order, but they have never yet solved the problem of popular participation or the problem of peaceful succession without civil war, and recent examples tell against them. At least for the present, there is a general sentiment that there is no answer available except the adoption of a régime based on free elections: and it is in this driving sense of necessity that there lies the greatest hope of success.

## ARTICLES, ETC., RELATIVE TO LOCAL ELECTIONS IN TANGANYIKA

Hans Cory: *The Indigenous Political System of the Sukuma and Proposals for Political Reform, East African Institute of Social Research,* 1954.

B. J. Dudbridge and J. E. S. Griffiths: "The Development of Local Government in Sukumaland," *Journal of African Administration,* vol. iii (1951), p. 141.

J. V. Shaw: "The Development of African Local Government in Sukumaland," *ibid.,* vol. vi (1954), p. 171.

J. Gus Liebenow, Jr.: "Responses to Planned Political Change in a Tanganyika Tribal Group" (the Wasukuma), *American Political Science Review,* vol. 1 (1956), p. 442.

J. Gus Liebenow, Jr.: "Local Government Reform in Tanganyika," *Journal of African Administration,* vol. viii (1956), p. 132.

C. H. Winnington Ingram: "Reforming Local Government in a Tanganyika District" (North Mara), *ibid.,* vol. ii (1950), p. 10.

L. E. Kingdon: "African Rural Councils in the Rungwe District," *ibid.,* vol. iii (1951), p. 186.

C. I. Meek: "A Practical Experience in Local Government" (the Waarusha), *ibid.,* vol. ii (1950), p. 21.

P. H. Johnston: "Chagga Constitutional Development," *Journal of African Administration,* vol. v (1953), p. 134.

K. G. Mather: a forthcoming article in the *Journal of African Administration* on a new method of electing a District Council for Rungwe District.

I. H. Morton: "An Inter-Racial Local Council in Tanganyika" (Newala District), *ibid.,* vol. viii (1956), p. 26.

F. A. Montague and F. Page-Jones: "Some Difficulties in the Democratization of Native Authorities in Tanganyika," *ibid.,* vol. iii (1951), p. 21.

## NOTES

1. The Sidney Ball Lecture, delivered by Professor Mackenzie in the University of Oxford, 21 Feb. 1957.
2. Uganda, Kenya, Tanganyika, Zanzibar, Nyasa-

land, the two Rhodesias. I exclude Somaliland, which has problems of rather a different kind.

3. As an example, a brief bibliography, for Tanganyika alone, is noted at the end of this paper.

4. For a clear and moderate statement and summary see D. E. Butler, *The British General Election of 1951* (1952), p. 3.

5. *Physics and Politics*, Longmans ed. of 1915, vol. viii, p. 18.

6. See the Report of the Chief Election Commissioner, Mr. Sukumar Sen (Manager of Publications, Delhi, 1955).

7. A political form is effective for large numbers of people only if it is δέσμιος φρενῶν, like the song of the Erinyes: elections have form and order, but one of the difficulties of establishing them in new settings is that they do not at once appeal to the Primary and Secondary Imagination, as Auden expounds them in his lecture on *Making, Knowing and Judging* (1956, pp. 27 ff.). It is very hard to regard them as sacred or as beautiful, except in terms of some specific myth of national history such as exists in Britain, France, and the U.S.A.

8. This resembles, but does not venture so far as, the method used by Professor Clyde Mitchell in *The Kalela Dance* (Rhodes-Livingstone Papers, no. 27, 1956): "By working outwards from a specific social situation in the Copperbelt the whole social fabric of the Territory is taken in" (p. 1).

9. John Stuart Mill, *Representative Government* (1861 ed.), p. 4.

10. Ibid., p. 3.

11. Not in Samuel Butler's sense: *Erewhon,* chap. xxi.

12. Harry Eckstein, reporting a conference on "Political Theory and the Study of Politics," *American Political Science Review,* vol. 1 (June 1956), p. 476.

13. Hume, *A Treatise of Human Nature.* Graham Wallas (*Men and Ideas* (1940), p. 22) quotes an exact equivalent from an unpublished work of Bentham.

14. It was used also by Professor Evans-Pritchard in his Marett Lecture, to illustrate a rather different point (*Man,* no. 198, Sept. 1950). It is characteristic of the present phase of opinion that in a recent article on methodology, which casts its net very wide indeed, nothing is said about the study of language; or about research and practice in medicine, both very old political analogies (Jean M. Driscoll and Charles S. Hyneman, "Methodology for Political Scientists: Perspectives for Study," *American Political Science Review,* vol. xlix (1955), p. 192).

15. Laski's *Grammar,* whether to be approved or disapproved, was certainly not framed by the rules of "hypothetics."

16. This problem of how to communicate a "meaning" in another language is one of the "aesthetic" problems of political science referred to by W. Harrison in his article on "Understanding Politics," *Occidente,* vol. ii (1955), p. 259.

17. Preface to edition of Juvenal; reprint of 1931, p. xv.

18. W. H. Auden, *Making, Knowing and Judging,* p. 24.

19. Kahin, Pauker, and Pye, "Comparative Politics of Non-Western Countries," *American Political Science Review,* vol. xlix (1955), p. 1022.

20. M. Duverger, *Political Parties,* published in French in 1951, in English translation, 1954; and (ed.) M. Duverger, *L'Influence des systèmes électoraux sur la vie politique* (1950).

21. *Grundlagen eines deutschen Wahlrechts; Bericht der vom Bundesminister der Innern eingesetzen Wahlrechtscommission* (Bonn, 1955).

22. *Social Anthropology* (1951), p. 57. The books of Professor Apter on the Gold Coast and of Dr. Fallers on Busoga perhaps illustrate this point. I cannot help feeling that their conceptual framework actually impedes them in sharing their great knowledge and acute sense of politics with the reader [David E. Apter, *The Gold Coast in Transition* (Princeton, 1955), and L. A. Fallers, *Bantu Bureaucracy* (1956)].

23. I am inclined to think Professor Evans-Pritchard also evades this, in his comparison between history and social anthropology (*Man,* no. 198, Sept., 1950) (for instance, the problems of historical "explanation," of the historian as poet and myth-maker, of the continuous revision—"all history is contemporary history").

24. She continues: "Deciding what one ought to do next is tied tightly to what one has done before—in the social sciences, long experience is the analogue of the rigorous formulations essential in the natural sciences," *New Lives for Old,* p. 14.

25. Aristotle, *Poetics,* 1449.

26. 1956.

27. K. C. Wheare, *Government by Committee* (1955).

28. Hippocrates, *Aphorisms,* I. i. The first part is the translation of W. H. S. Jones in the Loeb edition, vol. iii, p. 99.

29. Op. cit., p. 123.

30. *African Political Systems,* ed. Fortes and Evans-Pritchard (1940), p. xiv.

31. "Therefore to say that headmen have regular sources of income on the side is rather like saying 'water is wet.' It would be utterly incorrect to call public tribal life corrupt. The only question that matters is whether the procedure remains within traditional limits" (Hans Cory, *Sukuma Political System,* p. 59). Most Western electoral systems are in some respects "wet."

32. Inaugural lecture, *Political Education,* now reprinted in *Philosophy, Politics and Society,* ed. Laslett (1956); see my comment on this point in "Political Theory and Political Education," *Universities Quarterly,* vol. ix, no. 4 (1955), p. 351.

33. Essay on "Skills and Connoisseurship" (Methodological Congress, Turin, 1952). See also Professor W. H. Morris-Jones's recent inaugural lecture, *Taste and Principle in Political Theory* (1957).

V

# V · *Political Parties*

# INTRODUCTION

## David E. Apter

Although a growing literature has been devoted to their examination, political parties remain a perplexing feature of the study of comparative politics for several reasons. In the first instance, no matter how central we regard political parties, it is generally understood that they are more or less spontaneous growths whose rise and fall is dependent in large measure upon the nature of the political system. The American constitution does not mention political parties, nor do most others. Indeed, not so long ago, the term "party" meant "faction," and in our own society faction was regarded as harmful to the body politic. Madison considers this question most carefully in his most famous essay, Number X of the *Federalist Papers*. Reading it, one is led to the conclusion that the system of checks and balances is not only a product of the fear of tyranny but of the consequences of faction as well.

## I

One common view of parties regards them simply as vehicles for conflicts among politicians. In this sense individuals who support parties merely support their favorite politicians. The Jeffersonian and Hamiltonian views of the nature of government were occasions for conflict between the two men, and parties resulting from their conflict were occupied with an interpretation of the nature of the Constitution and its application. This is a particularly American view, for in America personality counts for much in party politics. American political parties are not centers of passion. Today they are part-time organizations, kept alive 'between special elections by minor ones, state and local, by patronage, and by some spoils. Although the occupation of party politicians is not regarded as particularly permanent, honorable, or prestigious, we accord high regard to politicians of excellent character who do exceptional things at crucial times in history.

Despite many ambiguities in the way we regard party politics, we see politicians more than parties; the latter appear to be epiphenomena in the system of representative government rather than fundamental aspects of it. Parties do not appear to stand for anything very meaningful. Perhaps their most outstanding characteristic is their very lack of ideology. On the other hand, we recognize that political parties offer political choices. They provide a peaceful selection of alternative governments. They offer differences in views and policy priorities. Through parties, issues can be identified and preferences indicated by the electorate.

These ambiguous attitudes toward parties disguise the fact that there is a widespread belief that the most significant characteristic of democracy is the multiparty system. Even when parties look alike, and the electoral process seems a bit like a carnival, we nonetheless believe that there is tougher metal in the back room and that the total process is more significant than the sum of its parts.

In the case of foreign countries, however, we often believe that party rather than personality is important. The classic case is Great Britain. If the American system can be regarded as a special case limited to the peculiarities of our large and dispersed society, it is the British that we regard almost with a sense of relief for an illustration of party government. If we turn to history to explain this important achievement, we find the answers disappointing. Party politics is not a very old and recognized institution in England. It developed in the last half of the nineteenth century partly as a response to political insobriety on the part of politicians, ineffectiveness within parliamentary institutions, such obsolete practices as the rotten borough system, and, of course, the extension of the franchise. Indeed, early British party history is not too different from the American experience. It is above all factional and personalistic. British party development is studded with great names—Walpole and Fox, Peel and Canning, Disraeli and Gladstone. Like Jefferson and Hamilton in our case, these great figures were cause for faction; but how did faction become transformed into that complex of institutions we regard as the party system in England? Why did the English system evolve so differently from our own?

There is no simple answer to these questions. British factions were originally organized around political clubs. The two most famous British political clubs, the Carlton and the Reform, originated during the period of agitation for expansion of the franchise. Their object was the control of parliamentary organization. "Loyalty to a party meant loyalty to a club. Membership of the club thus became both a token of adherence in the party and to the outside world a badge of allegiance."[1]

Few could regard the eighteenth- and early nineteenth-century political environment in Britain as very prepossessing. British practice was clearly no more honorable than the American. Corruption, the buying and selling of political office, and rampant patronage were the by-products of party politics. Nor did the parties have consistent political ideologies. If the Whigs were interested in electoral reform, the Tories were interested in social reform —and were not entirely averse even to some electoral reforms. Nevertheless, there emerge from them both very different patterns of party politics. Disciplined parties, effective parliamentary organization, a high standard of ethics, all these now characterize the British political party system in spite of occasional lapses from political virtue and internal cohesion.

It could not, of course, be expected that the British and American party systems should show signs of major similarity. If nothing else, the vast differences in constitutional machinery would cause them to vary. Nor do British parties easily compare with those of France and Germany. In France the parties endured even when the constitution did not. In Germany parties originally operated in a political climate where they were merely tolerated and contributed little but talk to the process of government. Parliamentary institutions were restricted. Certainly this was so under Bismarck.

These comments are designed to show that there is something special about political parties. They are peculiarly linked into that combination of social life and history, political instruments and leadership, which make them extremely difficult to compare in any effective manner. It is therefore not surprising that few successful efforts at comparison between political parties have been made. The study of parties is rather confined to a description of characteristics obtaining in each particular party, its relations to government, its recruitment and leadership, its objectives and programs, and its electoral performance. Analysis of political parties has been primarily concerned with improving representative government. Hence, there is a large literature on electoral methods, on the virtues of proportional representation, on the single or multimember constituency, and on the resulting political effects as registered in the parliamentary party composition of legislatures. What is lacking is a theory of political parties.

So far we have concerned ourselves with those parties that contribute to representative government. There are others, less benign, that have as their object the overturning of the state. Instead of functioning within the limits of the constitutional rules of the state, this form of party regards the state as an expression of the party. Not limited to representing views, the militant party is aimed at directing the public. Instead of supporting electoral competition, the party seeks to bring it to an end.

From the standpoint of representative government, such parties are inevitably extremist. The fascist concept of party government in that sense is similar to the communist in organization. Totalitarian parties have become recurrent phenomena of modern times. Moreover, because totalitarian parties also exist in democratic societies, along with democratic parties, they present special threats to them, anxious as they are to transform democracy into something else. The comparative study of political parties thus includes the role and function of totalitarian parties.[2]

If it is difficult to find a general theory of political parties, at least a clear distinction can be made between those which are totalitarian and those which are democratic. Even here, however, we run into certain logical difficulties. In Western practice, a political party is a function of the larger system in which it operates; that is, it is a servant of the constitutional framework. Totalitarian parties are different; and to understand their role, it is necessary to examine totalitarian societies and governments. In other words, the totalitarian party is coterminous with the state itself.

Can any theory of party politics encompass two such diverse notions of party under the same rubric? Neumann suggests that it cannot, and perhaps he is right. The Communist view of the role of political parties contains one answer to this question. It states a proposition about the functioning of political parties that is both general and consistent, namely, that parties represent class interests. Parties are instruments of the class war; whether proletarian or bourgeois, their function remains the same. Having such a convenient theory, which bypasses the representative and parliamentary significance of Western party government, Communist theoreticians have little more to say about political parties. Essentially they assign a class interest to each party and consider the class interest in relation to the state. Indeed, if one accepts their view of the rise of the proletariat as a change from bourgeois to proletarian dictatorship, parties no longer need to exist once their class basis disappears.[3]

A fresh concern with political parties has arisen with respect to the new nations. If a concern with totalitarianism and totalitarian parties was of major significance during the interwar period, the role of political parties in the new states is now achieving new prominence. The role of the political parties in the new states lies athwart the democratic and totalitarian views of party indicated above. Naturally, our first concern, expressed in efforts to ascertain the position of political parties within the political system, is whether they appear more similar to the democratic or to the totalitarian pattern of political parties. We are troubled about the erosion of democracy in some of the new states, and we recognize that political parties are highly significant instrumentalities in both democratic and totalitarian politics.

A second concern is with political parties as shapers of new communities. Are they effective in strengthening conciliar control over the executive, the representation of interests, provision of electoral choice, and other factors central to the habitual functioning of democracy? One easy answer is that certain of the new states, such as Guinea or Ghana, appear to be moving in a totalitarian direction because they are increasingly one-party states. The political party assumes a role not dissimilar to that of a Communist party in a Soviet bloc nation. Whether or not the easy answer is the correct one remains more obscure.

Defenders of these new nations are quick to point out that democracy and multiparty systems are not equivalents—that democracy is quite independent of any particular pattern of parties. For example, they argue that factionalism within the party can provide some of the same functions that several parties perform in recognized democratic societies. The question is whether political democracy and multiparty systems are more or less coterminous. Indeed, many of the new nations regard the presence of more than one party as a threat to unity. The terms of their argument are not entirely different from the objections to faction raised by Madison.[4]

These then are some of the important questions the new nations pose: Is more than one party essential to the workings of democratic government? Can representative institutions operate without several competitive parties? Are there in new nations political clubs, voluntary associations, and the like that, operating within a single party framework, perform some of the same or equivalent functions as political parties in Western countries?

Our selection of articles is designed to point out some of the differences between political parties and to consider their complexities. Perhaps the best introduction to their study is the stimulating overview provided by the selection from Neumann, who considers the status of current thinking about political parties in terms of the three areas mentioned above —namely, the democratic society, the totalitarian society, and the new nations.

## II

We have pointed out that the concern over political parties is central to any comparative political analysis. Yet comparison is difficult in the absence of a general theory. One way out of this impasse is to point out a possible direction in which a theory might be sought. There have been several attempts to do this, the most notable recent effort being Duverger's. As he points out in the preface to his book, *Political Parties,*

It is at the present time impossible to give a valid description of the comparative functioning of political parties; yet it is essential to do so. We find ourselves in a vicious circle: a general theory of parties will eventually be constructed only upon the preliminary work of many profound studies; but these studies cannot be truly profound so long as there exists no general theory of parties. For Nature answers only when questioned and we do not yet know what questions this subject demands.[5]

We have already considered three significantly different views of political parties. In democratic traditions they are brokers between the public and the government; or, as J. P. Dean and Edward Suchman put it, "Political parties were formed to implement the objectives of interest groups, and gradually they became an essential political institution."[6] In the more totalitarian tradition parties represent the exclusive interest of a particular group or class. In the new nations the position of parties tends to waver between these two poles.

In the democratic tradition political parties assume a constitutional framework of government and operate within its rules. In the totalitarian tradition parties change the rules to serve their own purposes, and the state is thus subordinated to the party. In the new nations the legitimacy of the state and the effective discipline of the party often vary independently of one another, thus causing political parties to have special responsibilities for the establishment of a constitutional framework.

Implicit in all these concepts of party are three relationships. First there is the relationship of the party to the state, for one indication of the difference between democratic and totalitarian systems is precisely in the nature of that relationship. Does the party make the rules or live within them? Second is the relationship between the party and the community. Is the party a broker or an organizational weapon? Third is the relationship among parties. Are they monopolistic or pluralistic?

Where the parties are brokers, authority resides in the people and elections are the means of certifying their right to represeent them. Where the parties are organizational weapons, authority resides in the objectives that the party puts forward in the name of the people. Until these objectives are achieved,

## TABLE 1—Party Relationships and Characteristics

| Social Units | Democratic Parties | Totalitarian Parties |
|---|---|---|
| Party | *Pluralistic:* competitive with other parties | *Monopolistic:* seeks to eliminate other parties |
| Community | *Representative:* seeks to incorporate divergent views in order to win widest following | *Directive:* seeks to amalgamate grievance to overthrow existing order, or if in power, to bend the community towards goals laid down by the party |
| Government | *Constitutional:* party action is limited by constitution, convention and electoral rules | *Extraconstitutional:* accepts legal order only insofar as it is forced to. When in control the party bends the government and constitution to its own ends. Party makes the state subservient to itself. |

the party must press the public rather than respond to it. In the first case, it is the representative framework and the constitution that govern the behavior of the parties. In the second it is the party program that defines the policy.

Parties that are pluralistic must compete with one another for public favor, thereby strengthening both the electoral and representative mechanisms. Where they are monopolistic, electoral and representative institutions are transformed into manifestations of solidarity. We can sum up these relationships in Table 1.

This simple paradigm leads only to further explorations in the comparison of political parties. Depending upon how political parties tend to fall with respect to the paradigm, their roles will vary in the community and so, therefore, will their functions. For example, one would expect that a party that makes its own rules of action in the state, determines its ends and directs the community accordingly, and exercises monopolistic practices would require a totalitarian machinery of government in order to play its proper role. Moreover, its functions would be largely devoted to (1) inducing solidarity through education, propaganda, the manipulation of symbols, and the like, and (2) directing all other features of organized life through pervasive control over them.

In sharp contrast, in those systems where the party is governed by convention and constitution, reflects group ends, and is pluralistic, one finds a very different set of functions for it. These are (1) control over the executive, (2) representation of interests, and (3) recruitment to office. Moreover, the state within which such a system functions must make provision for electoral machinery and legislative lawmaking.

The research questions centering around the totalitarian mode relate to problems of political resistance to the regime and the forms that opposition might take within the political system. In the second instance, research questions reflect the need to improve the functional efficiency of the political system.

Take, for example, the first function, parliamentary control. Political parties in a democracy are examined in terms of that function, particularly with regard to limitations on arbitrary power and, as well, the ability of parties to express the public will. Control over the executive ultimately means control by the public through its elected officials. It will readily be seen that the efficiency of representation, electoral techniques, and party-constituency relations all assume central importance in the analysis of the party politics of democracy.

We could indicate similar concerns growing out of the other two functions. First, it should be seen that in addition to the paradigm of party relationships shown in Table 1 we can specify a second (Table 2) with respect to function.

## TABLE 2—Paradigm of Party Functions

| Democratic System | Totalitarian System |
|---|---|
| 1. Control over the executive | 1. Inducing solidarity |
| 2. Representation of interests | 2. Direction |
| 3. Recruitment to office | |

These two paradigms taken together lead us to a set of core concerns in the politics of political parties. While not themselves specifying a general theory, they form a possible device for denoting important problems in the study of party politics according to Duverger's suggestions. In a democratic system, for example, control over the executive can be examined in the relation of party to government, including parliamentary party organization and tactics. It can be studied as well with respect to party-community relations—that is, how effectively public demands are transmitted to the executive and formed into policy. Finally, with respect to interparty relationships and control over the executive, we can ascertain differences in party ideology and policy and the degree to which each prevails in the conflict between parties.

In the case of our second function—representation of interests—we can readily see that in a democratic polity the way in which the party operates at the party-state level—the ways and means it has to integrate interests, compromise, and maximize policy effectiveness—becomes a central concern. At the level of party-community those interests must fit the widest possible political spectrum in order to gain widespread support and voting strength for the party. This function illuminates the interest we have in specific techniques of manipulation and information that political parties use both to persuade the public to vote for them and to gain knowledge of public wants. Finally, on the interparty level, the pluralistic quality of democratic parties means that they do not challenge one another's legitimate right to exist but, rather, contend for the support of various interests.

The third function is, of course, obvious. On the party-state level it is the job of the political party to win an electoral majority and to place as many as possible of its incumbents in office. On the party-community level, the party must diversify its recruitment to appeal to all sections and significant groups in the population and find suitable candidates for public office. Finally, at the interparty level, recruitment to office involves the internal mechanisms and functions of the party itself. The ways and means of recruitment and selection make up a mysterious process, and to be initiated into the process involves probing some of the most delicate workings of party machinery and leadership.

Hence, in examining our three functions in terms of the three party relationships with other social units, we find a broad basis for comparing the meaning and form of political party systems in democracies. We could do the same for totalitarian systems. We might ask how solidarity is induced at the party-state, party-community, and party-party levels (although in the last instance this would no doubt need to be rephrased as party-faction). Similarly, one is concerned not only with coercion and party propaganda but also with recruitment, since in totalitarian societies party recruitment is a key means for rewarding friends and punishing enemies.

These remarks are designed not to provide a theory but to clarify the various materials covered by the study of political parties. By denoting their possible functions within a given society, it becomes possible to compare those between societies, thus giving political parties a comparative focus. The best effort at genuine comparison remains Duverger's *Political Parties*. He is aware of earlier theories of parties, both of the liberal and totalitarian persuasions, including such analysts as Ostrogorski, Weber, Michels, Pareto, Lenin, and Mosca. Moreover, in tracing the operations of political parties, he includes a discussion of electoral mechanisms,

such as single- versus multiple-member constituency systems as well as plurality, list, and proportional voting—matters discussed separately in this volume. Duverger also compares the nature of totalitarian and democratic parties most effectively.

There are, of course, many noncomparative studies of political parties in single countries. Perhaps the best of these is R. T. McKenzie's *British Political Parties*.[7] This is a detailed historical study of British political parties. It should be read in conjunction with studies on voting and elections in England, perhaps the best of which are the works of David Butler and others on general elections.

Two volumes, one dealing with political parties and elections (covering both the Western and Eastern party systems), and the other with West Africa are particularly worthy of mention. These are S. Neumann, *Modern Political Parties*,[8] and Mackenzie and Robinson, *Five Elections in Africa*.[9] Forthcoming on Africa is a comparative study of political parties in Africa edited by Coleman and Rosberg and note should be made of the recent book by G. Carter, *Single Party Systems in Africa*. No similar work exists for comparative political parties in Asia or the Middle East, although there are many exhaustive studies of particular countries.

We conclude our introduction with special mention of two rather interesting theories of democracy in which political parties play central roles. The first, only indirectly concerned with parties, is announced in Robert Dahl's book, *A Preface to Democratic Theory*.[10] More centrally concerned with political parties, about whose behavior he develops a large list of *a priori* propositions, is Anthony Downs' *An Economic Theory of Democracy*. According to Downs, who is concerned with parties in the context of a general theory of democracy, political parties play a central and crucial role according to an explicit set of rules. The political system of democracy is embodied in these rules. Democracy is itself a system of choices. Voters are the political equivalents of consumers in economic life, and the electoral system is to politics what the market-and-price system is to a free economy. Parties are like firms, their products being decisions and benefits, packaged to appeal to the largest number of voters. Like the theory of perfect competition in economics, the entire model is based upon man's rationality. It is an ingenious theory, and it is an alternative to more sociological theories of party.

Party and faction, party and freedom, party and power, party and change, party and unity, all these are fit subjects of study and of major concern to political scientists. With luck and hard thinking, a more general theory of parties may come forward to serve us in our studies. As these selections will show, much of the spadework has been done.

## NOTES

1. See Norman Gash, *Politics in the Age of Peel* (London: Longmans Green, 1953), pp. 398–399.

2. One of the most valuable of such studies, not well known in this country, is by T. Ferle, *Le Communisme en France* (Paris: Documentation Catholique, 1937), a detailed examination of the structure and organization of the French Communist Party before the war.

3. See Lenin's Appendix II, "Lenin on the Critique of the Gotha Program" in C. P. Dutt (ed.), edition of Marx's *Critique of the Gotha Programme* (Moscow: Cooperative Publishing Society of Foreign Workers in the U.S.S.R., 1937).

4. See, for example, Adande, "In the Phase of National Construction the Fusion of Parties Becomes a Categorical Imperative." Congress of Cultural Freedom, Ibadan Papers, 1959.

5. See M. Duverger, *Political Parties, Their Organization and Activity in the Modern State,* North translation (London: Methuen, 1954), p. xiii.

6. See Berelson, Lazarsfeld, and McPhee, *Voting, a Study of Opinion Formation is a Presidential Campaign* (Chicago: University of Chicago Press, 1954), p. 153.

7. See R. T. McKenzie, *British Political Parties* (London: Heinemann, 1955).

8. See S. Neumann, ed., *Modern Political Parties* (Chicago: University of Chicago Press, 1955).

9. See Mackenzie and Robinson, *Five Elections in Africa* (London: Oxford University Press, 1958).

10. See R. A. Dahl, *A Preface to Democratic Theory* (Chicago: University of Chicago Press, 1956).

# PARTY PERSPECTIVES:
# A SURVEY OF WRITINGS

## Neil A. McDonald

Political parties are regarded in various ways by those who have studied and written about them. In some instances the writers deal directly with the question of the general nature of a party, but in most instances the writer's notion of the general nature of party must be inferred. Thus a combination of definitions, approaches to specific problems, notions about origin, purposes, activities and consequences, and the special interests of particular students all must be used to shed light on what students of parties have thought about party per se.

In order to secure the maximum benefit from an examination of the ways party has been regarded it is necessary to set forth the various approaches in as systematic a fashion as possible. To systematize, however, means to adopt a scheme of organization, and since there is no well-defined and standardized scheme for this field it may be helpful to indicate briefly the basic approach used in this chapter.

The level of generality required to organize the approaches to parties is suggested here by the phrase "social formation." Since party writings either care-

From *The Study of Political Parties,* by Neil A. McDonald. © Copyright 1955 by Random House, Inc. Reprinted by permission.

fully and deliberately, or inadvertently without serious thought, classify parties in a number of ways, it seems advisable to examine these actual ways. For the most part then the categories are drawn from party literature itself and do not represent a superimposed scheme, except in so far as the concept "social formation" is introduced to relate obviously similar but not identical phenomena.

At the outset, then, party is regarded as a category of an intermediate type of social phenomenon called social formation. Social formations may be distinguished and grouped or classified in terms of origin, basic structural characteristics, characteristic function and functioning, objects of concern, and legal status. This latter category is an imposed one and although it is of a different order than the others it seems advisable to disengage it for separate treatment in the interest of clarity. Actually structure, function, and objects may be affected or determined by legal action. Differences in one or all or any combination of these aspects may distinguish a particular type of social formation.

The phrase "party system" is not generally used interchangeably with political party. This creates a presumption that party system denotes a different kind of social formation than political party. Thus it is of importance to take separate note of the way party system has been regarded by some writers.

Just as party theory must deal with the question of what distinguishes a party or party system from other social formations, it must also deal with the various kinds of parties and party systems that are recognizable and meaningful. For example, within the category of political party there are parties with individual membership and those with group members, there are doctrinaire and nondoctrinaire parties, and so on. Likewise there are single-party systems and multiparty party systems.

How is party distinguished and classified as a social formation and how are parties and party systems distinguished, one from another? Party must be part of a more general whole and it must be related in a parallel fashion to other clusters of human behavior. Parties must be regarded as parts of the natural order and not as freaks. Otherwise inquiry would be pointless, except perhaps to produce museum pieces.

## PARTY AS SOCIAL FORMATION

### Origin

There are essentially two general ways in which any social formation can originate. Thus it is possible to characterize any formation in terms of the nature of its origin and development. Stated in simple terms, terms familiar to classic and traditional political speculation, social formations can be regarded as being either natural or artificial. To regard a social formation as natural is to regard it as emerging and taking on identity and special function in a kind of unplanned and automatic fashion. The natural theory of origin even suggests that the social formation is something of a by-product turned out rather unintentionally over a long period of time in the pursuit of other goals. The origin of the family is often regarded as being natural in the sense that it is a kind of an automatically produced by-product of the impulse to perpetuate the species.

An artificially originated social formation is, by way of contrast with the natural kind, one which is deliberately and calculatedly created by man. Business corporations, partnerships, armies, or government bureaus are deliberately created for specified purposes. In terms of essential form and character rather than in terms of origin and development, the natural-artificial difference is substantially the same as the difference between *Gemeinschaft* and *Gesellschaft* as developed by Tönnies and between communal and associational formations as developed by American sociologists. This difference will be more fully developed subsequently.

There seems to be very little explicit writing on the nature of party origin in the terms suggested here, but most writings nevertheless tend to reveal a point of view. Ostrogorski, for example, viewed parties as being ideally formations that could be made and unmade at will. The tendency to discuss party activity in military language also indicates indirectly a conception of a deliberately created entity. Other writers take a more naturalistic approach. The very titles of books often indicate the approach. For example Henry Jones Ford's classic work is entitled *The Rise and Growth of American Politics* and W. E. Binkley's party history is entitled *American Political Parties, Their Natural History*.

One further example perhaps will suffice to make the distinction clear. A. N. Holcombe in his *The More Perfect Union* indicates his preference for the naturalistic theory of origin, at least as applied to American parties. His chapter on party origins is entitled "The Unplanned Institution of Organized Partisanship." What this indicates about his approach is pretty well confirmed by the following more general application.

A political study of American Constitution leads inevitably to a fresh view of Lowell's hypothesis that "men, like animals, may attain a self consistent and harmonious system of conducting their affairs by a process of striving for immediate intentional objects, if the conditions happen to be such to lead to a system of that kind; and this although the actors themselves do not contemplate it, or even if the result is quite contrary to their preconceived ideas." . . . Americans above all other men have a right to believe that the history of the world should be regarded as the realization of a hidden plan of nature to bring about the more perfect union of the nation as the only state in which all the capacities implanted by her in mankind can be fully developed.[1]

Any firm conclusions about the most generally valid theory of party origins can perhaps best be left until other aspects of parties are examined. It can be noted at once, however, that contemplation of American and British parties seems to give much more support to the naturalistic approach, that is, to the dominance of naturalistic elements in party origin and development.

### Structural Characteristics

What kind of thing is it that is distinguished when a person carefully uses group and association to emphasize a difference between two social formations? One answer is that it is a complex of distinctive traits. For present purposes, however, it will be helpful to stress that it is a structural trait with emphasis upon what in biology would be the morphological sense of structure. Structure is used here very much in the sense of form but the scheme adopted conceives of unique form consisting of structural, functional, object, and legal traits. When writers refer to a party as being a group they generally mean to emphasize more than a structural trait if structural is narrowly and rigidly conceived. What is emphasized here in distinguishing group, association, organization, institution, and system as essentially structural distinctions is that all form qualities that are not predominantly functional in nature, or which do not emphasize the objects with reference to which the social formation functions, are regarded as structural. Thus rather than being too sharply defined, it has some qualities of being a residual category.

Structurally, then, it is possible to view party as a group. It is also possible to conceive of group as denoting what is essentially a group-like structural quality which might exist in varying degrees in any social formation. In this sense to say of party that it is a group might be interpreted to mean that structurally the group-like properties are dominant. Despite the fact that there is a strong tendency to classify party as one of the structural types examined here, it is possible to regard party as a structural complex which combines the structural qualities associated with each group, association, organization, institution, and system. In the end it should be realized that analysis requires that distinctions be made tentatively and for useful purposes and that there is nothing eternal in any scheme. Its sole justification is to advance understanding. The tendency to use group, association, and like terms to characterize party must, however, be dealt with because they are so widely and yet differently used, and because each when used suggests the structural character of a party model which inevitably becomes important in directing research and reform programs.

It should be noted that most, if not all, of these terms for designating basic form have both a general common-sense usage and a more technical usage which has been developed and refined by students of the field. In the discussion of how each form is thought to characterize political parties it will be necessary to take account of this distinction and reconcile the differences as fully as seems possible.

PARTY AS GROUP. The term group has two main usages. One is common sense and nontechnical. Under it group is used to denote small social formations in which the interaction pattern is characterized by the intimacy and intensity of the relations. In accordance with this type of usage a few bridge-playing neighbors meeting in a home would be easily and readily called a group. Nevertheless to refer to all of the people of a city or of a nation as a group would not readily suggest itself and would require explanation. More technical usage often finds group used to refer to any social unit or aggregate, regardless of structure, size, complexity, or sharpness of qualities of distinctiveness and hence to be used in about the same fashion as social formation is used here. But even when group is used to indicate great generality its restricted meaning often seems implicitly to emphasize the qualities of a so-

cial formation generally associated with what are called primary groups. And it is precisely this tendency to vest the term group itself with a specialized meaning that requires the substitution of social formation for group.

It is obvious that a political party is not in itself a primary group. It may be viewed as being composed of primary groups as basic units, but this would neither explain nor characterize the nature of the tie that binds the various groups into a more comprehensive social formation. Does the party resemble a group in the nature of the effect that the group as an entity has on its members, participants, or adherents?        ,

In its study of the 1952 presidential election, the Survey Research Center of the University of Michigan sought, among other things, to ascertain the role of party identification in shaping electoral choice. Party influence was examined along with that of candidates and issues. To distinguish between the three motivational factors, as they were called, required the formation of an hypothesis about the nature of the party as an influencer. The report on the study considers party identification as a kind of *group* identification, but it exercises care in defining group as "any aggregation of individuals who share a sense of common characteristics or common goals."[2] The report stresses that a group may be anything from small face-to-face contacts to a more diffuse and impersonal relationship in which there is little or no ritual of membership. The way the group notion of party is used in the study is clearly set forth as follows:

The sense of personal attachment which the individual feels toward the group of his choice is referred to in this chapter as identification and, with respect to parties as groups, as party identification. Strong identification is equated with high significance of the group as an influential standard.[3]

Although the authors in this study define group in the broadest possible terms, their hypothesis about the nature of the party identification is strongly suggestive of the type of identification that is thought to be especially significant with reference to small units of more intimate human relations. Some uncertainty is revealed in the fact that in another place the major political parties are referred to as "sprawling, loosely knit organizations, relatively quiet during the off election years. . . ."[4]

PARTY AS ASSOCIATION. Party is often regarded as an association. The term association, like the term group, has its general common-sense use as well as its more precise and technical meaning. Occasionally it is used interchangeably with group. More commonly it indicates important differences. Two of the many approaches to the distinctive nature of an association seem especially worth examining in relation to political party. The first has already been suggested in the discussion of the origin of parties. The distinction made by the German Tönnies between *Gemeinschaft* and *Gesellschaft* has been developed by American sociologists into a distinction between community and association. Although Maurice Duverger, writing in French, is the only party student who uses the term community to refer to party, nevertheless the distinction between community and association is necessary to understand one approach to association distinctiveness, and in a broader sense to understand party. As contrasted with community, association is regarded as artificial, secular, contractual, mechanical and ideational.

Robin Williams develops the differences under four headings upon which the following discussion is based.[5] The association emphasizes formal, legal, and administrative controls as opposed to a minimum of specialized controls, and greater reliance on accepted values and goals which is characteristic of community or natural formations. Moreover, the association tends to be more instrumental in pursuit of goals outside of itself, whereas in the communal type the greater emphasis is on the relation and the formation itself. A third distinction, as developed by Williams, emphasizes the role of respect, affection, loyalty and similar emotions in communal relations.

> . . . associational relations typically imply a separateness of interacting persons, whereas in communal relations it is presupposed that the participants are linked together by many common activities and values. . . . The prototype is the narrowly contractual relation of buyer and seller in an open market exchange transaction, in which everything is wholly irrelevant to the transaction except considerations of price, quantity, and quality of the goods being exchanged.[6]

Williams notes that it is the indefiniteness of the common activity and ends in communal organization that lends great importance to symbolism in them. By way of contrast the emphasis in the associational type is on objective rights and overt performance and in the communal type stress is on meaning, intent, motive, and feeling.

The final distinction is that the association is built upon relations conceived as being emotionally neutral and feelings of the participants are regarded as being formally irrelevant.

There has been relatively little specific discussion of whether a party is best regarded as a community (natural type of formation) or as an association (artificial). Most of the discussions of party which emphasize the need for party responsibility implicitly suggest a party model of the associational type, but there is a tendency to move back and forth between the terms association and organization. The more general implications of this approach will be noted in discussing organization as a type of social formation.

A second discussion of association that needs to be noted is that developed by David Truman. Truman comes to a consideration of the nature of association by way of a study of interest groups. Individuals in groups, he maintains, strive for equilibrium or stable expectations, but when an individual functions in more than one group, as all individuals do, the demands that one group relation makes may upset the equilibrium of the other group. Functioning in more than one group creates what Truman calls tangent relations between the groups. When tangent relations lead to the formation of another social unit mainly to restore or maintain the equilibrium of each group the resulting creation or created entity is a special type called association.

> An associaton is said to emerge when a considerable number of people have established tangent relations of the same sort and when they interact with one another regularly on that basis. It is a group of a continuing pattern of interactions, that functions as a "bridge" between persons in two or more institutionalized groups or subdivisions thereof.[7]

Truman's notion of the nature of association is not incompatible with that previously developed. It is, in fact, complementary to it. It might be expected that after his careful development of association Truman would, when he came to discuss political parties, classify parties as associations or at least discuss parties in terms of his associational analysis. This, however, is not the case. In his chapter on political parties he apparently does not consider parties either as interest groups or as associations. To his great credit he refuses to oversimplify in order to achieve conceptual neatness. At the same time he seems too readily to attribute an unnecessary degree of formlessness to parties, or at least to do so without sufficient examination. He leans especially heavily upon the notion of party developed by Pendleton Herring which emphasizes the element of personal relations in national parties without fully recognizing that Herring, writing a decade earlier, was anxious to moderate the tendency to view parties as formalistic devices. Truman's thoughts about the nature of parties are well summed up by him as follows:

> The meanings to be attached to the term "political party" are thus extremely varied. The activities implied by the designation depend upon the time and place, the level of government, and the section of the country involved. Viewed from the national level the so-called party-system gives an impression of disorganization, if not of unrelieved chaos. Such an impression is not strictly accurate, but it is apparent that the national party at any given time is fluid and unstable, consisting more of temporary personal alliances than of continuing institutionalized relationships. It follows that the relations between political parties and other political interest groups will be similarly protean. The appropriateness of the political party as a means of group access to government proper will depend, therefore, not only on the claimant groups involved but also upon the

characteristics of the party at the particular time, place, and level of government under discussion. Generalization in the area is hazardous.[8]

It seems quite clear that both technical and common-sense usage distinguish between group and association. It is equally clear that both are relevant to a consideration of the characteristic structure of party as a social formation. And finally it is clear that thus far most of the notions about the basic structural category to which party belongs must be ascertained indirectly.

PARTY AS ORGANIZATION. Party is often referred to as an organization. The phrase party organization is used in such a manner as to suggest that organization is a general phenomenon of which party is a special kind. But both in explicit discussions of party and in casual remarks there is also the practice of referring to "the organization" as if party were the broader term and organization a specialized aspect of it. Clearly there is confusion here.

Social organization is used by some to be equivalent to social phenomena in which only pattern is indicated and social organization is contrasted only with social disorganization. By others it is used in about the same general sense as social formation is used here.

It is tempting to say that the use of some form of the term organization to denote a particular social formation, or to single out certain qualities of a social formation, is simply a way of distinguishing formality in the pattern of relationships. But the referents of formality are no longer self-evident, if they ever were. Nevertheless, to stress organization and formal relationship suggests explicitness in relations, effectiveness, hierarchy, high probability that expectations will be fulfilled, the notion of office as the basic unit in opposition to the more personal role, and sharper lines separating those who belong and those who are on the outside.

The extent to which some of the above qualities are suggested where organization is discussed is indicated by the discussion of organizational systems in action in a recent report on an intensive inquiry into organization behavior and international politics.[9]

Thus, to regard party as an organization is to stress such qualities of structure and process as formality, definition, explicitness, efficiency, determinateness of authority, and like qualities.

E. E. Schattschneider in his perceptive and important book, *Party Government,* uses organization extensively and the implicit party model which he seems to use bears out the above contention that to regard party as an organization is to emphasize certain qualities of structure and process. "A political party is first of all an organized attempt to get power."[10] He goes on to define power as control of the government and to point out that the aim to get control of government is what distinguishes a party

from a pressure group. "Only when an *organization* is in control of the government or is able to create and maintain a widespread expectation that it will take over the government soon does it become a major party or real party."[11] He further says: "Since control of the government is one of the most important things imaginable, it follows that a *real* party is one of the most significant *organizations* in society."[12]

To regard political parties as determinant organizations with reasonably defined boundaries, which are potentially capable, as formations, of taking over the government much as a contractor would take over a construction task, is a rather natural way to consider such a social formation. M. Ostrogorski in his great pioneer work, *Democracy and the Organization of Political Parties,* regards parties ideally as bodies deliberately organized to mobilize and express mass opinion in connection with public questions, and he finds weakness in the strong tendency of any temporary organization to try to become permanent and to create an interest and an opinion of its own. It is the organizational qualities of political parties that Ostrogorski regretfully finds dominant. For Schattschneider, parties in the United States are regretfully inadequate as organizations. Roberto Michels, who dramatized the hierarchical aspect of any organization by referring to it as the manifestation of the "iron law of oligarchy," finds that it is the organizational aspect of political parties that makes a democratic party well-nigh impossible. Schattschneider seems to concede this but finds escape in the democracy that is possible between the parties.[13]

As was indicated previously there is a strong tendency to regard parties rather indiscriminately as associations and organizations but in so doing to stress the common elements that have been suggested.

PARTY AS INSTITUTION. Even a casual examination of party literature and studies will turn up many references to parties as institutions. Like other terms we have noted, institution as a term seems at first to refer to different things depending upon who uses it. What qualities seem to be emphasized when a social formation is called an institution? When we speak of a social formation as having become institutionalized, what do we mean has happened to the formation of which we say this, and how is it to be distinguished from one which has not been institutionalized?

As used in general conversation, institution refers to a wide variety of phenomena, from some local character to a mental hospital, and to the state itself. What seems common to these common-sense references is that they all imply uniqueness and permanence or stability that is not dependent on physical nature or structure. The more explicit considerations of institutions are not especially antagonistic to the more casual usage.

R. M. MacIver develops distinctions between custom and association on the one hand and institution on the other. An institution implies a more definite recognition of a regularity than does custom. For example, he would regard a marriage feast as an institution and courtship as a custom.

Institutions have external insignia, marks of public recognition, which customs as such do not require. Again a custom is always a social mode of conduct, whereas an institution is often only a social condition of conduct. Thus no one would call property a custom though it is certainly an institution.[14]

He distinguishes institutions from associations by noting that we belong to associations but not to institutions.

If we are considering something as an organized group, it is an association; if as a mode or a means of service, it is an institution.[15]

Associations have their characteristic institutions; the church, for example, as an association has its institution of communion and so on. We think of the institution as

. . . the system of controls which extends beyond personal relations, which is the bond between the past and the present and between the present and the future, which links men not to their families and their neighbors but to their ancestors and their gods, and which ramifies into the greater organizations of the political and economic life.[16]

David Truman says that when group patterns are characterized by a high degree of stability, uniformity, formality, and generality they are usually called institutions, and a group that has these qualities is thought of as an institutionalized group.[17] In Parsons' and Shil's general theory formulation, institution is used in contrast with culture to emphasize particular actors in particular institutions.

Situations are grouped, according to regularities of action in them, into *institutions;* an institution is thus a concept which states that many separate situations have features in common, in terms of principles of abstraction or order, and in which, in the same terms, actors exhibit the same or closely similar actions. These similar actions are said to be *institutionalized* if the actors expect them to occur and there are cultural sanctions opposing non-conformity with expectations. In the formal description of institutions the position of the actor is described by saying that he occupies a *status*. When he acts in his status he is said to be acting out a *role*. Thus institutions are in another sense systems of roles. Institutions, or systems of roles, are grouped into larger systems called social systems.[18]

What these definitions seem to have in common is their emphasis upon institution as stressing the regularity of action pattern, its nonpersonal aspect, and the expectations that it creates. To regard party as an institution would be in some measure to single out for stress something that might be called the party way of doing things, something that might be designated by the phrase "party politicking" in order to distinguish it from other types of "politicking."

Despite the many casual references to parties as institutions it is surprising that there is very little in the way of explicit discussion of the significance of the institution concept as applied to parties as social formations.

Those who have adopted the notion of party government, indicating party government as a distinctive variety of government, have generally tended to regard the party as ideally an organization rather than an institution. Thus instead of the *party way* of running a government, suggesting a mode of government with its party institution aspect, it suggests a more or less formal organization as taking over and operating government. Likewise those who emphasize the role of adjustment and compromise as being either the essence of government or of democratic government suggest but do not develop the role of the party as *a way of governing,* but in general they tend to fuse all "politicking" and "party politicking" in such a manner that no regard is had for the distinctive nature of the party phenomenon.

Attention has previously been called to the chapter title "The Unplanned Institution of Organized Partisanship" under which Professor Holcombe discusses the rise of parties in the United States. Earlier it was the term "unplanned" that was singled out. Now we return to the chapter title as an instance of parties being regarded as institutions, that is, as institutions of partisanship.

Holcombe is generally clear and explicit in what he means by the unplanned nature of parties and by organized partisanship. He assumes the meaning of institution, however, and the fact that he moves back and forth in discussing the parties and the party system indicates that he did not carefully work out distinctions. Nevertheless he did choose institution and not association, for example, as he might have done. And there is indirect evidence of a certain considerateness in this selection. In the chapter, Holcombe regards parties as a kind of a *process* involving the coordination of factional interests, the presentation of a leading personality element, and the sublimation and merging of interests. The stress upon the interplay of these elements suggests what might well be regarded as an institutional approach. This is emphasized by the recurring suggestion that party character is determined by the conditions which make for durability in the factions' relations in a party. In general there is greater emphasis on party as a durable patterned way of doing things than upon it as a more static physical entity. The unarticulated emphasis is institutional rather than associational or organizational.

PARTY AS SYSTEM. The concept system as applied to party creates some difficulty and danger of confusion. Any single party may be regarded as a system the same as it may be regarded as an association or organization. In this case parties would be regarded as system-type social formations. This is not a common usage. In referring, however, to a complex unit of related individual parties, or in characterizing the relation of a party to a government, for example, it is common to speak of a party system, or the party system. The general usage of system supports the latter use, whereas the more technical and specific usage supports its use for both. It is common to distinguish a bank from the banking system, to cite only one example. Any party may be regarded internally as being a system or a type of social system. Parties in the United States, considered in terms of the external relations of each to other parties, to the government, and to the society at large, may also be regarded as a system. It seems advisable to reserve most of the system discussion until party systems as types of social formation are considered. That a single party has system-like qualities may be simply indicated here by quoting the following from a recent thorough consideration of the nature of social action.

The most general and fundamental property of a system is the interdependence of parts or variables. Interdependence consists in the existence of determinate relations among the parts or variables as contrasted with randomness of variability. In other words, interdependence is *order* in the relationship among the components which enter into a system. This order must have a tendency to self-maintenance or a stable equilibrium. It may be an ordered process of change—a process following a determinate pattern rather than random variability relative to the starting point. This is called a moving equilibrium and is well exemplified by growth. Furthermore, equilibrium, even when stable, by no means implies that process is not going on; process is continual even in stable systems, the stabilities residing in the inner relations involved in the process. A particularly important feature of all systems is the inherent limitation on the compatibility of certain parts or events within the same system. This is indeed simply another way of saying that the relations within the system are determinate and that not just anything can happen.[19]

Those who write on parties use system to denote party system, a complex of parties, rather than consider a party as a system. Samuel Lubell is an exception in this matter. He is challenged by the fact that the political parties in the United States seem always about to fly to pieces yet they do not do so. Contemplation of this fact leads him to regard parties as systems.

The dynamics of conflict which hold a political coalition together are indeed akin to those of the sun. Astronomers tell us that the sun is a seething mass of broken atoms, in violent movement and constantly threatening to whirl off into space, but held together by gravitational pull. The American political party is also a powerful magnet, which draws together, in constantly colliding coalition, a bewildering variety of conflicting elements. That these elements can continue in alliance seems to defy every law of logic. But, like the sun, this apparently unstable mass has its own gravitational equilibrium.

In their ceaseless friction, the different elements give both positive and negative charges of political electricity. They both repel and attract one another. The common binding attraction is the desire of each element to win dominance in the party. When any one element becomes disaffected the power of antagonistic elements is automatically enhanced—so is their attachment to the party. Precisely because the party elements are so hostile to one another, the bolt of one helps to unify the others.[20]

To speak of a particular social formation as being a group, an association, an organization, an institution, or a system is to say that it predominantly exhibits those qualities of structure and process generally associated with each of the five types enumerated. In the foregoing an effort has been made to specify the dominant qualities that are generally specified by each name, and to indicate an example or two of its implicit or explicit use in discussing parties. When some more specific and distinguishing meaning is given to each term, it appears that no one of them fully characterizes the party phenomenon in all of its variety and complexity; that parties as they are known even casually have some characteristics from each of the five kinds of formation; and that if certain general meanings are attributed to some of the five what they denote becomes so broad as to serve little purpose in naming distinguishable phenomena.

It seems quite clear that structure process alone is not sufficient to exhaust the characteristic qualities of party as a social formation, at least not until other qualities that distinguish one category of social formation from another have been examined as they have been applied to parties.

## PARTY AS PERFORMER OF FUNCTIONS

Any social formation may be distinguished by the distinctiveness of the functions it performs, or by a combination of its distinctive functions and the distinctiveness of the method or mode by which it performs them. Presumably, in some degree at least, structure may remain constant but function and mode of functioning may vary and distinguish a social formation, and vice versa. The interplay here must be and is recognized, but analysis demands some duplication and simplification.

In approaching this aspect of party and of any social formation, two independent but related aspects must be recognized and dealt with. A party functions by entering into the behavior pattern of individuals. It apparently does this by a psychological process in which the individual perceives the party or forms a mental image of it or its symbols and is impelled to react favorably or unfavorably or to see things in a different light because of his perception of the party. Thus party may be viewed as performing functions in direct relation to individual behavior patterns.

In the second place party may be viewed as one social formation which, as a unit, entity, or formation performs functions in relation to other social formations. One social formation may be a part of a more inclusive formation or may perform functions with relation to parallel and related but no more inclusive formations. Likewise the whole formation under study may be regarded as performing functions with reference to less inclusive formations and individuals. Generally, this latter aspect was emphasized in considering structure and process above. Here the main concern will be with the functions and mode of functioning which are widely attributed to parties as they operate in a wider universe of individuals or social formations.

## Party Function and Individual Behavior

It is increasingly clear that a social formation may be mainly the calculatedly merged efforts of diverse individuals, and that the specific object of the merged relationship is so completely dominant in the minds of the individuals involved that there is no consciousness of the pattern of merger of *efforts* as creating an independent entity or formation. In this case the formation need only be considered in relation to its objective. It is equally clear that consciousness of the merger pattern as forming a distinctive entity may shape behavior somewhat distinctively from a specific objective of the merged or cooperative effort. Some students of party have dealt with this aspect of the party phenomenon and their efforts deserve attention in trying to get at the nature of party.

A. N. Holcombe seems to have had this aspect of party function in mind when he discussed the role of sublimation in party-building. According to Holcombe, three main techniques are used in party-building. They are: (1) to coordinate diverse and antagonistic interests; (2) to exploit a popular leader; and (3) to sublimate the private interests by finding principles that merge them with a general interest. He finds examples of this sublimating process in the American System of Clay, in Washington's identification of public interest with the more perfect union, and in Jefferson's identification of liberty and union.

Washington's and Jefferson's successful sublimation of their specific political program by means of devotion to such transcendent interests perhaps goes further than other parts of their general political strategy to explain the glorious success of their efforts to rally the scattered opposition and form them into effective administration parties.[21]

That this sublimation of which Holcombe speaks comes to be symbolized and perpetuated in party seems clear, and this development is implied but not quite explicitly stated by Holcombe. In commenting on the rise of the Republican party Holcombe points out that the ability of the new party to sublimate the issues springing from the slavery question was one of its greatest sources of strength. There can be little doubt but what a great deal of the additional power of anyone who spoke in the name of the Republican party in the years that followed the Civil War came from this sublimation or myth quality with which the Republican party was infused.

The nature and function of the psychological aspect of party is noted by Lord Macaulay, and endorsed by Henry Jones Ford.

A typical result is that curious accumulation of traditions and tenets which give to party communion almost the sanctions of religious faith. On this point, with great sagacity, Macaulay has said: "Every political sect has its esoteric and its exoteric school, its abstract doctrines for the initiated, its visible symbols, its imposing forms, its mythological fables for the vulgar. It assists the devotion of those who are unable to raise themselves to the contemplation of pure truth by all the devices of superstition. It has its altars and its deified heroes, its relics and its pilgrimages, its canonized martyrs and confessors, and its legendary miracles."[22]

The psychological approach to the study of politics had its earliest explicit statement by Graham Wallas. Wallas wrote in something of a spirit of revolt against the excessive preoccupation with the legalistic and formalistic approach in politics. This led him to discuss both the state and the party in terms of the kinds of psychological responses they evoke. He suggests that when men are grouped together under common political names the names or the grouping per se may acquire emotional associations in addition to the intellectually analyzable meaning. An association becomes an entity and emotions, affections, and interests may be directed toward the entity and with different results than those which might be expected solely on the basis of deliberate observation and analysis of the facts.[23]

Wallas takes note of the great number of voters and the inability of the human psyche to deal with more than a few of its fellow men and the separate objects of political thought and feelings and concludes that

. . . something is required simpler and more permanent, something which can be loved and trusted, and which can be recognized at successive elections as being the same thing as was loved and trusted before, and a party is such a thing.[24]

In explaining why it is hard, virtually impossible, for a person to be elected to public office except under the party label, he observes of voters and candidates:

The party prepossessions and party expectations of its constituents alone make it possible for them to think and deal with them. When he speaks there is between him and his audience the party mask, larger and less mobile than his own face, like the mask which enabled actors to be seen and heard in the vast open air theatres of Greece.[25]

Later he speaks of party as an entity, "with an existence in the memory and emotions of the electorate, independent of their own opinion and actions."[26]

Despite the suggestiveness of Wallas's observations concerning the psychological nature of party, both theoretical and empirical exploration of this aspect of party have lagged behind in the study of parties.

When a person approaches a decision and there is a high probability that he will act in a certain determinate way even when the calculated reasons for his so acting seem obscure, he is said to be predisposed to act in a certain way. This emphasizes a situation in which he might act in the unexpected fashion and overcome the predisposition, but unless there are extra strong countervailing reasons his action will accord with the predisposition. There is considerable evidence to indicate that attachment to a party predisposes the individual to act in a certain way on some political questions.

One of the most explicit developments of the predisposition in connection with party is that advanced in connection with the panel survey that was conducted during the 1940 election under the general direction of Paul Lazarsfeld.[27] Basically this is a study of how voters make up their minds in a campaign. To a large degree, then, it is a study of the nature of the campaign effect on decision-making in the election. The campaign is found to have three effects: activation, reinforcement, and conversion. It is noted that in a presidential election most persons know how they are going to vote even before the nominating conventions have chosen candidates and platforms. Thus the campaign builds upon the predisposition and makes a vote out of a tendency. But beyond this the initial party preference or predisposition also does much to determine the kind of campaign effort the voter comes into contact with.

The political predisposition and group allegiances set the goal; all that is read and heard becomes helpful and effective in so far as it guides the voter toward his already "chosen destination."[28]

The study observes that in 1940 there was a great deal more Republican campaign material available than there was Democratic, yet this was offset by party preference and predisposition, and this evened up the reinforcement effect of the campaign.

But, of course, actual exposure does not parallel availability. Availability plus predisposition determine exposure—and predisposition leads people to select communications which are congenial, which support their previous position. More Democrats than Republicans listened to Roosevelt and more Republicans than Democrats listened to Willkie. The universe of campaign communications—political speeches, newspaper stories, newscasts, editorials, columns, magazine articles—was open to virtually everyone. But exposure was consistently partisan, and such partisan exposure resulted in reinforcement.[29]

The very fact that conversions as a result of the campaign were relatively few and never certain is further testimony to the existence and strength of the predisposition that arises from party preference.

The point that has been emphasized in this discussion of the psychological function of social formations suggests that the political party or a political party has a certain amount of capacity to influence behavior almost regardless of what is actually done in the name of party by its authorized spokesmen. *Being* as well as *acting* is important. This aspect may be viewed as a blind following of a name or symbol, but it may also be viewed as an organizing and systematizing force in the minds of persons to whom the party consideration is important and enters into their consideration and decision-making. In any event there can be little doubt that some social formations cast a psychological spell and that this is a highly relevant aspect of party formations.

An indication that a social formation is widely perceived as having a kind of an independent existence in people's minds is a widespread practice of personifying or reifying the party; that is to say, speaking of it as a readily indentifiable person or thing. The tendency to speak of parties as if they lived and breathed, or as if they could be readily drawn or photographed, indicates the great importance that must be attached to the psychological function of parties.

### Party Function in Society

In the final analysis any social formation functions in the bigger world of which it is a part by influencing or modifying individual behavior. Thus the psychological impact of a social formation is part of its total impact, or, to put it another way, its total impact is ultimately psychological in nature. But patterns of individual behavior can be emphasized at one time and patterns of interaction with emphasis on the interaction pattern as a unit may be stressed separately from the pattern of the *individual*. This is essentially the transition we now make in turning from the way social formations function in the mind of the individual to a consideration of how they function *among* other social formations.

In approaching the question of what function party-type social formations perform in a society it is necessary to develop further the separateness and the relatedness of parties on the one hand and party systems on the other. The reason for this is that most writing and analysis tend unconsciously to merge the two and to move back and forth between them, presumably assuming that a party system is merely a sum of the parties in the undefined system.

It was indicated earlier that one party could be regarded as a system type of formation but that system is generally applied when discussing the functions, not the structure, of the parties in a society. A few typical and meaningful uses of the system concept should make its nature and distinctiveness clear and permit us then to pass on to consider the social functions performed by parties and party systems.

Merriam and Gosnell's textbook is entitled the *American Party System*. Despite the fact that the authors make no sharp distinction between parties and party system, the insight which impelled them to emphasize system in their title arose from a correct sense of the need for such a concept. In the following they seem on the verge of more explicit recognition.

> The party system may be regarded as an institution, supplementary to the government, aiding the electorate in the selection of official personnel and in the determination of public policy, and in the larger task of operating or criticizing the government. In this sense the party may be regarded as a part of the government itself, an extension of officialism, shading out from very definite responsibility for official acts to the less definite responsibility for shaping and guiding the course of public opinion.[30]

Later on the system concept is still further suggested.

> The parties move in and out among these social and governmental groups and mechanisms in what may seem a mysterious way. Bi-partisan and non-partisan arrangements and agreements at times erase party lines or blur them almost beyond recognition. Through it all, however, the party habit, the party attitude, party institution persists, rendering a service to the political community.[31]

R. M. MacIver is not explicit concerning the system concept and parties but he recognizes the relevance of the system idea. He observes that throughout history there have been political groups which have rallied to the support of principles and leaders

> . . . but these groups did not establish any continuous organizations and therefore can hardly be called parties in our sense. *There was no party system.*[32]

An even clearer recognition is to be found in the following passage:

> The party system originated in the opposing fronts of two parties, but while this type prevailed for cen-

turies in England it has been superseded or greatly modified, except in the United States of America and a few other countries, by a more elaborate diversification.[33]

As notions about party functions are examined, note will be made of instances in which the systems approach as opposed to the specific party approach seems to be significant in terms of clarifying the nature of party.

Party literature reveals that parties or party systems are variously regarded, in a functional sense, as a connection, manager-operator, mediator-broker, nominator, and organizer. In most writing, it is needless to say, it is a matter of party being regarded as predominantly, not wholly, one or the other of these function performers.

PARTY AS CONNECTOR. Edmund Burke's famous definition of a political party emphasizes party as a group bound together by common and shared principles. This definition has obscured Burke's stress on the importance of party as connection. There is the implication in Burke that the connection which is party can lead to shared views and it presupposes that the connection *could* exist prior to the sharing of views. This notion of party functioning primarily as connection was also stressed by Henry Jones Ford over a century after Burke wrote.

> . . . party action being a social product is an organic connection with all the processes of thought and feelings which pertain to human nature, and is subject to the play of their influence.[34]

Ford's most explicit statement of the connection aspect of party is:

> Party organization acts as a connective tissue, enfolding the separate organs of government, and tending to establish a unity of control which shall adapt the government to the uses of popular sovereignty.[35]

PARTY AS MANAGER-OPERATOR. Social formations may function primarily as managers or operators of the more comprehensive social entity of which they are a part. Under this view the party is seen as operating or managing some enterprise, usually government. This seems to be essentially the view taken in a report by the Committee on Political Parties of the American Political Science Association. This report operated on the assumption that something needed to be done to improve parties in the United States. In general it reflected a notion that parties should be devices which could take over and manage the government for a period of time.

> An effective party system requires, first, that the parties are able to bring forth programs to which they commit themselves and, second, that the parties possess sufficient internal cohesion to carry out these programs.[36]

and also that

Parties have the right and the duty to announce the terms to govern participation in the common enterprise. The emphasis in all consideration of party discipline must be on positive measures to create a strong and general agreement on policy. A basis for party cohesion in Congress will be established as soon as the parties interest themselves sufficiently in their Congressional candidates to set up strong and effective campaign organizations in the constituencies.[37]

In still another place the report rejects the notion of parties as "mere brokers" and says that they must function as agencies. A very substantial part of the party literature which stresses the need for increased party leadership and party responsibility seems to view parties as functioning properly and characteristically when they act as managers or operators of the government.

PARTY AS BROKER-MEDIATOR. It may be noted above that the Committee explicitly rejected the broker notion of political parties. Under the broker approach the typical party leader is a person engaged primarily in mediating, adjusting, and pulling divergent views into sufficient harmony for action. The notion of parties as brokers was first and most explicitly set forth by A. Lawrence Lowell.[38] Lowell regards the role of broker in the business world as a form of division of labor. In the political world people are absorbed in their own affairs and have little time to attend to affairs of state. Yet they must be brought together on some middle ground.

. . . it requires a species of brokerage, and one of the functions of politicians is that of brokers. Perhaps it is their most universal function in a democracy, because, in the caustic language of Sir Henry Maine, the mincing of political power into small morsels naturally makes the wire puller a leader.[39]

"If politicians are largely brokers," Lowell goes on to say, "party is the chief instrument with which they work."[40] The politician functions as a party man and in so doing he focuses and frames issues for the popular verdict.

Pendleton Herring advances similar but more developed views in his very provocative and important work on parties, *The Politics of Democracy.* Herring is sharply critical of the overformalistic view of politics in general and of parties in particular.

The task of leadership is to bring the diversity of our society into a working harmony. Our system of political parties is designed to implement this purpose. Through such organizations the politician can contribute to the process of adjustment.[41]

Lowell had talked about brokering and compromise as a kind of a second best, below the level of real statesmanship, yet regrettably necessary in a less than perfect world. Herring's mediating and compromising role grows out of a more positive conception of the role of compromise and media-

tion. The dignity of the individual depends upon his not being unduly imposed upon. The most important thing, under this view, is to preserve the democratic way of arriving at joint decisions. Maintaining the democratic *way* requires the maintenance of the democratic *system.* This sometimes requires forward movement and at other times conserving action. For Herring the party system's proper mode of functioning grows out of this analysis.

Our party system tries to reconcile conservative elements with the forces making for change. Such reconciliation is achieved not by debate alone. Common loyalty to an organization is no small factor in bringing men of contrary interests together. This straddle presumably can stretch only so far; but before the breaking point is reached, concessions are often made out of loyalty to the organization which both sides value. Our present system does not mean the negation of policies because the parties seem so similar in viewpoint. There is ample room for positive programs, but our parties are not the channels best suited for their initiation. The real springs for policy occur without reference to the formal organization of parties and the legal framework of government.[42]

PARTY AS ORGANIZER. Closely related to the mediator-broker mode of functioning is that of organizer. As symbol or myth the party functions as a kind of automatic organizer of opinion. Similarly party workers and officials perform organizing work among the electorate and officials. The organizer type of function casts the party in a more positive and active role. Rather than being mediated or brokered, opinions and interests are positively fashioned or shaped into a policy. R. M. MacIver emphasizes this role in the following way:

Public opinion is too variant and discursive to be effective unless it is organized. It must be canalized on a broad line of some major division of opinion. Party focuses the issues, sharpens the differences between the contending sides, eliminates confusing cross currents of opinion. Each party formulates its platform, grooms and selects its candidates, enables the public to make its choice between sufficiently distinct alternatives.[43]

V. O. Key in his extremely valuable work on the political situation in the South is impressed with the difference in the organizing function.[44] He notes the tendency in the North and in general, to belittle the organizing function performed by parties, but he concludes that in this respect their performance is heroic beside "a pulverized factionalism."[45] He distinguishes between factions that form and reform and which come to have no permanence or continuity in the mind of the voter. Being continuously confronted with new faces and choices leaves the voter in a kind of a state of nature.

A. N. Holcombe conceives of parties functioning mainly as organizers and concludes that they perform that function quite well in the electorate but inadequately in mobilizing and organizing support behind officials so they can put into operation a coherent scheme of public policy.[46]

PARTY AS NOMINATOR. The role of parties as nominators may be of a somewhat different order than the others that have been discussed, but note needs to be taken of the fact that many students of party find in the nominating function the most unique and exclusive function performed by parties. It is regarded as their dominant mode of functioning and all else either follows or is of subordinate importance. All students of parties would agree that the nominating function is important and unique. E. E. Schattschneider sets out the importance of the nominating way of life.

The nominating process is obviously one of the points at which parties can be studied most advantageously for no other reason than that the nomination is one of the most innately characteristic pieces of business transacted by the party. A party must make nominations if it is to be regarded as a party at all. By observing the party processes at this point one may hope to discover the locus of power within the party, for he who has the power to make the nomination owns the party. If the simplicity of the English process results from a centralization of authority in English parties, it is easy to imagine that the great elaboration of formal and public nominating procedures in the United States is a mark of the decentralization of American parties.[47]

Nominating can be regarded as a kind of professional *initiative-taking* in connection with the filling of public offices. The initiative-taking function is nowhere provided for in the Constitution or in law and parties, it may be argued, have made it their characteristic or most distinctive function in the political system. Most constitutions rest heavily upon a probability theory, the probability that someone will contest for and accept each of the various public offices. Party makes an effort to reduce randomness of choice and to guard against the failure of the voluntary method of filling public offices.

PARTY AS ORGANIZATIONAL WEAPON. Consideration of the nature of the Communist party may have contributed an important notion about a function common to all political parties. At least the notion should not be rejected out of hand when generally applied. Philip Selznick conceptualizes the Communist party as an "organizational weapon." This he conceives as a model, defined as follows:

We shall speak of organizations and organizational practices as weapons when they are used by a power seeking elite in a manner unrestrained by the constitutional order of the arena within which the contest takes place.[48]

In developing the notion of the organizational weapon Selznick stresses two things: its aims are general and unlimited, and it tends to transform a voluntary association into a managerial structure, and to make members into agents. A party which is an organizational weapon he calls a combat party.

Selznick is specific and explicit in restricting the notion of the organizational weapon to those formations which operate outside *and against the established order.* He is anxious to show that there is a fundamental difference between the Communist party, for example, and the Democratic and Republican party. This restrictiveness seems unnecessarily to limit the usefulness of the model which he rather carefully constructs. The *general purpose* nature of some aspects of political parties is striking. Party leaders are often thought of as a group of persons who can get a variety of governmental jobs done. Most of the problems of organizational weapons that he discusses, such as winning allegiance to the entity in general as distinct from winning allegiance for rigidly specific goals, are shared by most social formations in some degree.

In trying to construct a helpful model for increasing the understanding of bolshevik parties, Selznick is highly suggestive concerning all political parties. This seems to warrant our considering the possibility that any party may function as an organizational weapon.

## OBJECTS OF PARTY OPERATIONS

In the foregoing discussion of party function in the social and political system the emphasis is upon function as a type of process. Thus for a party to function as a broker is to say that it functions by the brokering process. Party function may also be stated in terms which emphasize more the objects or specific type of phenomenon upon which they operate or with reference to which they function.

The question of whether parties function most characteristically with reference to the electorate or officialdom is explained in greater detail in Chapters Four and Five [of *The Study of Political Parties*] and can be passed over here with simply a notation that the difference in the emphasis suggested may make a difference in forming an image of the party model. This will, in turn, influence research efforts and reform suggestions.

There is also an important difference in emphasis between those who regard parties as operating predominantly on opinions and opinion clusters or upon interests and interest groups. Some, of course, take the position that opinions derive from interest and that hence there is no difference. Still, even if opinions are regarded as being purely derivative from interest or attachment, the two represent different stages of development in time and it would be possible to argue that parties are properly more operative in coaxing opinions out of interests or in shaping opinions to affect interest or interests. In any event the reality of the difference indicated may be illustrated by the party writings of R. M. Mac-Iver and C. A. Beard. MacIver discusses parties under the heading "organization of opinion" and refers to them as the major political vehicle of opinion. He argues that modern democratic government represents a development toward government by opinion, through representation of opinion, and away from government by interest and representation of interests. He clarifies the difference by referring to the Middle Ages. In the Middle Ages,

> The many for whom the one stood did not constitute an opinion-group, did not have a political platform. The representative stood for a total area, a total community. The cardinals represented the undivided Church, the Electoral Princes represented the people as a whole. Then in England there appeared the representatives of "estates." The representatives became the delegates of constituencies, but again the constituencies were conceived of as wholes, were represented as wholes. The one stood for the collectivity, for the corporate part of a corporate entity. If the one stands for the whole in this sense, he cannot represent opinion. The only policy he can logically stand for is presumptive interest of the whole he represents.[49]

MacIver argues that the party, as an agency for representing opinion, has recently developed out of the class as an agency that represented interest. He notes the continuation of a strong similarity in democracies between party and classes, with the interest base of party which it implies, but he insists that the party even then is not "the sheer class struggle."[50] He notes that some men choose party aside from class affiliation and interest attachment and he comes to characterize the party system as the democratic translation of the class struggle.

Generally speaking and taken as a whole the works of Charles A. Beard develop the notion that economic interests are the most important single factor in causing and hence explaining politics. It would therefore be expected that he would see parties mainly in terms of interests and would regard opinion as derivative in nature, merely the gloss of sound and fury which had to be penetrated in order to get at reality.

This is substantially the case. In one of his later works[51] he finds faults with a pat definition of parties because it left out of party composition "varieties of interests." It also ignored the "role of fate in national history."

Beard is generally inclined to talk about sentiment, propensities and economic interests finding expression in "disputes, parties and factions."

Parties he regards as mainly agencies of interest but also capable of drawing interests together in such a way as to become a motor or an independent force. Beard is never clear about where the rationality implicit in the concept opinion comes from, except as he makes some vague references to leadership.

## PARTY AS LEGAL CREATURE

In general all social formations can be divided into those which are legal creatures, that is, created by legal action, and those which are the result of voluntary or private association. Examples of the first type would be purely governmental agencies such as a legislature or a bureau. Reasonably clear-cut examples of the pure private type would be the evening bridge club, the country club, and the family. In between these two extremes are four commonly recognized intermediate situations. First there is the governmentally created or chartered corporation. Certain corporate legal character was early given to public utilities or natural monopolies, then to formations with charitable purposes, and then to economic associations to limit liability. In each of these instances an associational unit had conferred upon it by an act of sovereign certain specified legal duties and rights. In the second place law recognized certain social formations as conspiracies and made all *members* liable for illegal plotting, even though a member or co-conspirator might not join in all acts. In the third place the law has imposed specific regulations upon most otherwise private social formations, or voluntary associations, as they are called in law. A business may have to take out certain licenses, for example. Finally there are political parties which in the United States started out as purely private associations, having no corporate or entity recognition in law, and have come to be what might be called quasi-legal formations.

The course of the development of the legal form and quality of parties in the United States began with the recognition that the person who, in a variety of types of political contests, could claim with little or no challenge that he spoke or contested in the name of one or the other of recognized named parties had a significant edge over persons with no party label. Once party label gave *additional* support, the means of getting the party label and the nature of the party label became matters of great interest. This interest led to four steps which in less than a hundred years converted parties from private social formations to quasi-public agencies. In the first step, under the guise of controlling the names on the official ballot ushered in by adoption of the Australian secret and official ballot, state laws made persons who acted in the name of parties conform to standards of conduct similar to those imposed on public officials. Hiring a contender to withdraw from a contest became bribery, for example. In a second and related step the states passed laws regulating the management of internal party affairs in the name of democratizing them. Thus the direct primary method of choosing candidates was generally required of a party which wanted its candidate and his party label on the official ballot. In some places, chiefly in the South, the direct primary party elections were run by parties but regulated by law, whereas in most northern states the state government took over the actual conduct of the party elections.

In these two steps in the development of legal character there was no particular explicit development of party theory. The standard way in which the law singled out the formations and even the particular parties it wanted to regulate was to define a legal party as one which at the preceding election polled for its leading candidate 10 per cent, more or less depending on the state, of the total votes cast. In most states this was quite adequate to extend the control scheme that followed to only the Republican and Democratic parties. The implicit test of whether a party had legal character under these developments was really whether its label gave a substantial edge to its candidates. In most instances the states permitted unsuccessful parties to retain most of their private character and form.

Two more recent stages mark the emergence of the present legal character of parties in the United States and have tended to increase their legal character. One line of development saw the United States Supreme Court hold that for the Democratic party in the South to exclude Negroes from participation in its internal affairs was the equivalent of the State excluding Negroes from the vote contrary to the Fifteenth Amendment to the Constitution. For this purpose at least, and even in the absence of specific statutes conferring power on the Democratic party, party action on internal party affairs is regarded as the same as state action. Southern states attempted to circumvent this ruling by repealing most of their election laws. By this method they sought to divest parties of their official character but were rebuffed.

In the case of which the almost inherent legal nature of an effective party was set forth the Court said:

We think this statutory system for the selection of party nominees for inclusion on the general election ballot makes the party which is required to follow these legislative directions an agency of the state in so far as it determines the participants in a primary election. The party takes its character as a state agency from the duties imposed upon it by state statutes; the duties do not become matters of private law because they are performed by a political party. . . . When primaries become a part of the machinery for choosing officials, state and national, as they have here, the same tests to determine the character of discrimination or abridgement should be applied to the primary as are applied to the general election. If the state requires a certain electoral procedure, prescribes a general election ballot made up of party nominees so chosen and limits the choice of the electorate in general elections for state offices, practically speaking, to those whose names appear on such a ballot, it endorses, adopts and enforces the discrimination against Negroes, practiced by a party entrusted by Texas law with the determination of the qualifications of participants in the primary. This is

state action within the meaning of the Fifteenth Amendment.[52]

The foregoing opinion seemed possibly to leave open some way in which white leaders in the South could still divest the Democratic party of official status. South Carolina tried to repeal all laws which dealt with party nominations in particular and parties in general. This effort at circumvention was rebuffed by lower federal courts and review was denied by the Supreme Court. In the course of his court of appeals opinion Circuit Judge Parker said in part:

The fundamental error in the defendant's position consists in the premise that a political party is a mere private aggregation of individuals, like a country club, and that the primary is a mere piece of party machinery. The party may, indeed, have been a mere private aggregation of individuals in the early days of the Republic, but with the passage of the years, political parties have become in effect state institutions, governmental agencies through which sovereign power is exercised by the people. Party primaries are of more recent growth. Originating in the closing years of the last century as a means of making parties more responsible to the popular will in the nomination of candidates for office, they had been adopted by 1917 in all except four of the states of the union as a vital and integral part of the state election machinery.[53]

The basis of Judge Parker's opinion seems to be in part that the state laws give effect to what is done in a primary election, and that this either gives the character of official action to the party primaries, or that the question of official character is irrelevant in that any effective exclusion from voting is somewhat like a conspiracy to turn state agencies to constitutionally forbidden purposes. There is the further suggestion in the opinion that the action is unconstitutional because party officials are state officers *de facto* if not *de jure* and are thus bound by the Constitution. South Carolina made still another attempt but was rebuffed again, this time by the Federal District Court.[54]

The Supreme Court finally upheld the lower courts by holding that even an association which made a preprimary selection of candidates that was, in fact, effective in excluding Negroes was unconstitutional. This decision, however, split the Court and it is not clear whether the preprimary-designating association is a party acting illegally, a type of illegal conspiracy, or whether its acts are illegal because many of its members are public officials which infuses its action with official and hence forbidden quality. The decision drew a dissent from Mr. Justice Minton.

In his dissent Mr. Justice Minton argues for a return to a simpler and more formalistic approach. Without disturbing the accepted rationale concerning the quasi-official nature of political parties in the South in matters of racial exclusion, he developed what might be called a pressure-group theory of the Jaybird Association, the name of the pre-primary nominating association. He finds that its action is private action and thus beyond the reach of the constitutional and federal law. Commenting upon the success of this association in excluding Negroes, Mr. Justice Minton goes on to say:

This seems to differ very little from situations common in many other places far north of the Mason-Dixon line, such as areas where a candidate must obtain the approval of a religious group. In other localities candidates are carefully selected by both parties to give the proper weight to Jew, Protestant and Catholic and certain posts are considered the sole possession of certain ethnic groups.[55]

The final stage of legal investiture has come with efforts to distinguish the Communist party and to impose special disabilities upon it as a social formation. To regulate the Communist party, since it assumes the character of a party, and not to regulate other parties takes some legal defining. This has progressed in three stages. In the Sedition Act of 1940, advocating or conspiring to advocate the necessity or desirability of violent overthrow of the government is made unlawful. The Act is applied and its constitutionality upheld in convicting eleven leaders of the Communist party, but party membership was not illegal per se, nor prima-facie evidence of a conspiracy. In 1950 the Internal Security Act defined a category of Communist front organizations and of Communist action organizations and put special restrictions on them. Communist action organizations were defined by describing the Communist party. Foreign control, illegal objectives, and conspiratorial methods were made the touchstone of distinction. In 1954 the Communist party was named and the law attempted to withdraw any legal privileges it might have and to make intentional membership or affiliation a crime. Following the 1950 act the illegal quality seems to be imparted by foreign control, illegal objectives, unlimited objectives and conspiratorial and clandestine methods. As a corollary it would seem safe to conclude that a party to be legal must be under native control, confine itself to legal and thereby limited objectives, and use open and above board methods.

The steady increase in giving legal form and quality to parties and party processes in the United States has led one commentator to observe with great validity:

American parties have ceased to be voluntary associations like the trade union or the good government club or the churches. They have lost the right freely to determine how candidates shall be nominated, leaders chosen, and platforms framed, and even who shall belong to the party. The state legislatures have regulated their structure and function in great detail.[56]

# KINDS OF POLITICAL PARTIES

In the foregoing discussion an effort was made to ascertain the possible components of party distinctiveness. Thus the approach was in the nature of setting forth a variety of ways in which party could be and has been distinguished from all other social formations and phenomena that are not of the party type. That this attempt was based very heavily upon the American literature which in turn is based upon contemplation of American parties there can be no doubt. It can only suggest additional approaches for the study of all parties.

Just as there are different kinds of social formations of which party is one, there are different kinds of parties within the party class or category. Moreover, it needs to be recognized that there is a difference between kinds of parties and kinds of party systems.

Political parties may be classified in many different ways. For present purposes a useful two-way classification can be made between parties sorted out according to the substantive character of the basic organizing nucleus, and according to the form of basic organizational unit. Under the general heading of substantive organizing nucleus, a distinction may be made between those which are essentially doctrinal and those which are essentially nondoctrinal. This distinction is admittedly a matter of degree and emphasis. But it is none the less important and useful.

## Doctrine-Based Parties

A party based on doctrine is characterized by the fact that its leaders and its basis of appeal function largely in the realm of principles and moral argumentation. Socialist parties which are not based upon trade union membership, as is the socialist party in England, may be regarded as a type of doctrinal party. This is true whether the basis for the socialism is mainly a theory of the inevitable nature of things, or whether it is a matter of moral principles to guide consciously wrought change. Generally speaking so-called capitalistic parties are not as doctrinaire in their approach as are the socialist parties. Nevertheless capitalism provides the basis for a doctrinal party since it involves expounding and defending a political principle. Conservative and liberal parties, if the terms are not just proper names, also suggest the existence of doctrine, since arguments about the principles of social development which are involved are matters of doctrine. A party which conceives of its task as being to moderate change and which rests its notion of its task upon a general view of the way things happen or should happen is a doctrinal party. Likewise a party which is essentially revolutionary rather than liberal or gradual, and which bases its revolutionary advocacy upon a theory of the nature of revolution in the scheme of things is a doctrinal party. Thus the Communist parties in most, if not all, countries are regarded as a doctrinal party both on the score of the substantive program it advocates and the methods which it adheres to as a matter of principle.

Whiggery was a doctrinal element in parties in the United States and England, and probably at one time the doctrine dominated. Party-based doctrines may embody notions of the whole social order on one hand or confine themselves to notions of government more narrowly conceived. Party doctrine may be derivative of religious doctrine. There is some evidence to suggest that doctrinal parties tend increasingly to de-emphasize the doctrinal element as they share or monopolize political authority, and that any party whose leaders and representatives are in the habit of dominating the government loses most of its ideological content. Thus the doctrines of both the Labor and Conservative parties in England seemed to have been greatly modified, if not shoved aside, in recent years.[57]

This suggestion that doctrine may be a variable in party bases suggests that doctrine may derive from and vary with party function, rather than that party derives from and varies with doctrine. This would lead to distinguishing parties, one from the other, in functional terms. But if doctrine often seems to have strong functional elements in it, what about nondoctrinal and nonfunctional bases?

## Nondoctrinal Parties

Parties whose appeal and organizing basis rests upon a shared interest or identity constitute the bulk of party bases which may be regarded as essentially nondoctrinal in nature. The most common actual nondoctrinal bases for parties are socioeconomic classes, charismatic leadership, church, trade union, shared nationality, coalition or alliance, and public office or spoils as it is sometimes called. Every party has its nondoctrinal base or elements, and the existence of these two elements in every party suggests that within any party there might be something in the way of a tension between these two elements. This actually tends to be the case. It was noted earlier that a difference between the socialist parties in England and France was to be found in the correspondingly great role played by the trade unions in England and by doctrine in France. Yet within the British Labor party there has always been something of a split between the doctrinal emphasis and the sort of bread-and-butter emphasis that is characteristic of the British trade union movement in general.

Marriages of convenience between competing groups usually involve a de-emphasis on doctrine and give rise to a party or party alliance based upon a shared desire to govern. One nondoctrinal party

basis of great practical importance is derived from the possession of official political authority. A party whose leaders control the government or who share the power either as coalition or as loyal opposition has an important additional basis consisting of governmental control itself. Again this suggests the function. Region or section may furnish a party basis, and the regional or sectional homogeneity may be an important aspect of either a doctrinal or nondoctrinal element in a party.

In the view taken here the Catholic-based parties which are to be found in Germany and Italy today would be classed as nondoctrinal parties. The Church furnishes a kind of a basic organizing device but in most social and political issues there is apparently no substantial attempt to view a particular position as necessary for Church doctrine. In the United States, in the sense used here, both of the major parties would be regarded as essentially nondoctrinal. They might well be regarded as complexes of all of the nondoctrinal bases which have been discussed here.

In discussing the bases for parties it seems advisable to distinguish between the starting of a party and its perpetuation. Most any one of the organizing bases which have been enumerated might well serve to get a party started, but as it is perpetuated as a party it tends more and more to reach out and combine the various bases, both doctrinal and nondoctrinal. But more on this later.

## Organizational Bases

Nothing is more striking when one becomes conscious of it than the great differences that exist between political parties. Preoccupation with leftness and rightness, with middle class and proletariat, has all but obscured the differences in party structure. This fact has recently been called forcefully to our attention by Maurice Duverger.[58] If Ostrogorski, Michels, and Weber may be taken as earlier examples, it seems to take continental scholars to keep this aspect of party study alive.

Duverger discusses and distinguishes parties in terms of what he calls direct and indirect structure, and in terms of whether the basic organizational unit is a caucus, a branch, a cell, or a militia-type unit.

Parties with direct structure are those whose members or affiliates are related directly—that is, a party which has individuals as members. Indirect parties are those which are built upon other social formations as their basic component units. The individual comes to his party membership or affiliation by virtue of his membership in a nonparty agency. Trade-union affiliation with the British Labor Party is an example.

Parties made up of loose caucuses loosely tied together into a larger formation constitute one characteristic kind of party and represent an organizational stage in the development of most parties. They tend to confine themselves to the narrowly political and informally to co-opt members. Duverger notes that this type of party is admirably suited to middle-class politics as it minimizes collective action. Parties in the United States are of this type.

The party whose main organizational unit is the branch is characteristic of democratic socialist parties. The branch is more formal and an agency of more general purpose than the caucus. It is apt to run counter to the traditional lines on which a society is based and this accentuates the organizational aspects. In all countries there has been a trend toward organizational definition and professionalization, the degree of which may serve to differentiate parties.

The cell-based party has been developed by adherents to communist doctrine. The main difference between a cell and a branch or caucus is that the cell is organized around the job or profession and is very small and conspiratorial in its mode of operation. It is well suited for revolutionary purposes and not suited for winning electoral contests.

The militia-based type of party has qualities suggested by the name. Members are an elite, they wear distinctive insignia, a uniform or a colored shirt, and they drill and march. The militia-type unit finds its main use in practicing a kind of a quasi-legitimate violence in pursuit of its members' or leaders' purposes. The existence of a militia-type party is based upon the notion that it is possible to distinguish between quasi-legitimate violence and, on one hand, legal coercion and on the other hand naked or raw violence.

Generally speaking Duverger tends to equate the caucus- and branch-based type of party with democracy and the cell- and militia-based type with totalitarian and revolutionary political systems. This emphasis is confirmed when he discusses the different modes by which these basic units are articulated into a whole party. Here he finds that the more close the articulation the more totalitarian and the looser the articulation the more democratic parties are. As has been indicated, the cell and militia type lend themselves better to tight articulation into a greater organization.

## KINDS OF PARTY SYSTEMS

The term system is generally used to refer to a party complex composed of all parties that are closely related one to the other or to a common entity, such as a given state. It may also be used to refer to a single party to emphasize party in all of its regularized and patterned relations. System tends to be used to designate social formations characterized by a high degree of regularity and com-

plexity and a low degree of formality in the interaction pattern. Because of the way national boundaries sharply cut off most party relations, a party system is usually a national or state party system. It is, for example, common to speak of the party system of the United States. It would be meaningful to speak of the Communist party system as one which does, and purports to, transcend national boundaries. But in this respect the Communist party system is almost in a class by itself. It may be that an international party system is gradually developing around the activities of the United Nations. This would be an expected development as the United Nations became more effective. As it is, each national state has its own party system and it is possible to classify and compare countries by the types of party systems they possess. The most obvious distinction rests upon the number of parties in each country. In addition to a number-based classification, party systems can also be classified into totalitarian and nontotalitarian, constitutional and unconstitutional, democratic and nondemocratic and so on. Moreover, they can be classified as class based or ideologically based.

Again Maurice Duverger, since he has written recently and thoughtfully, furnishes the main points around which to develop a discussion of the kinds of party systems. He states his conviction that the two-party division of the kind characteristic of the United States is based upon a natural division. Since the natural tendency is toward only two parties in a system some other forces must intervene to produce and sustain multiparty party systems and one-party party systems. In England the nineteenth-century two-party system broke up temporarily with the advent of the Labor Party, but the two-party pattern has effectively reasserted itself. Contrary to the British experience, in other countries, Belgium, Australia and Canada, for example, the rise of a socialist party seems to have imposed a multiparty party system.

Multiparty party systems, according to Duverger's analysis, arise either from splits or overlappings in a natural two-way division. A split may come within either bourgeois or socialist parties and may be encouraged by the electoral system. Splitting creates a centrist position which is highly unstable because the center position represents a tentative and compromised position only for any one person. That is, it is a synthetic position.

Overlapping comes about as a result of a noncoinciding dualism in a society. For example, if a society is divided into two classes and two sections, but classes and sections do not coincide, there is a strong tendency for four parties to rise.

Duverger distinguishes two kinds of multiparty party systems. One he refers to as the 1900 type. It came into existence because the existing parties would not accommodate the emerging views of the socialists. Thus there was no alternative political choice for an increasingly popular point of view. The other type he calls Australian. Under this type the agrarian interests find a congenial party home in neither the socialist-labor nor in the bourgeois-type party. Thus the agrarians create their own party. The lack of homogeneity of interest within the agrarians' ranks makes the formation of a party difficult and thus this type of what Duverger calls "multi-partism" is not very common. Agrarian interests in the other parties are always a cause of cleavages.

One-party party systems are not necessarily totalitarian. The one party may provide an arena in which ordered conflict can take place, and it may be limited in its aspirations. There are different kinds of one-party party systems. Some arise in the form of a governing elite. The party name may be merely a name for the praetorian guard of a dictator. In other cases it may be more fully developed in terms of doctrine and tradition. Overwhelmingly strong emphasis may be placed upon either social or national unity and lead to the notion that only one party can be tolerated in the interests of achieving the goal. Emphasis upon national unity suggests a fascist-type party system whereas emphasis upon social unity indicates a communist system. In a similar way a party may be regarded as the bearer of an ideology or it may be regarded as the vanguard of a class. Duverger distinguishes between a one-party party system which tries to stabilize the regime of which it is a part, and another which tries to keep it stirred up. He observes that although the Fascist and Nazi parties came into power with a revolutionary movement they soon became dedicated to the prevention of change. The Communists, however, are forever shaking up the regime with purges or other actions of a comparable nature.

Although Duverger's discussion of party systems is only tentative and exploratory in nature, it is important for being one of the very few recognitions of the systems concept as applied to parties. A political party considered by itself is such a dependent formation that it often seems highly unrealistic to study it in more or less of isolation. There is a growing tendency to recognize this and to study a party in the context of an electoral system. What is here called the systems approach goes one step further and views as a fruitful object of study the social formation which is a complex of parties with different names and its relation to the government and even the society in which they are found. It will not be known how derivative and how much of an independent political force party systems are until they are studied as systems.

## CONCLUSION

Under the approach taken in this chapter there is a presumption that a distinctive party phenomenon exists. Positing its existence and distinctiveness, however, is only the beginning of knowledge and understanding of the phenomenon. The distinctive qualities, in terms of origin, structure, function, object, and legal status remain to be established, clarified, and delineated. There are many ways to add to understanding. One of these is to bring into some kind of systematic arrangement the various ways the party phenomenon has been regarded by some of the more important students of party. For purposes of presenting this an organizational scheme has been used which derives largely from the various party studies themselves. For purposes of logical completeness categories occasionally are added which represent no well-known point of view.

At the outset, party is regarded as a kind or class of social formation. It may be thought of as a major type of formation or as a subdivision of a major type such as group or association. The phrase "social formation" is used because it is more general and less vested with specific attributes than most terms that might otherwise be used. As a kind of social formation party may be regarded in a variety of ways. The principal ways are grouped and examined under the headings of origin, form, function, object, and legal status. The examination of these theoretical approaches did not reveal any consensus but it did produce a kind of an inventory of approaches or elements which are useful for further theorizing in the form of both hypothesis and model-building.

A party is a kind of social formation but there are different kinds of political parties. For purposes of examining some of the literature on this point a division is made into the kinds or classes of political parties that are posited, and the kinds of party systems. Party system is regarded as the more inclusive category, and thus parties can be classified within a system or between and in relation to various systems. Parties are classified as being essentially or predominantly based upon doctrinal or nondoctrinal considerations. Then they are further classified in terms of the form of the basic organizational components. The standard way of classifying party systems into one-, two-, and multiparty party systems is noted and some differences in each are brought out.

However a political party or a party system is regarded, it represents a cleavage within the society and the political system in which it exists and functions. Where there is only one party it represents a cleavage between those who are regarded as being within the party and all others. Where two or more parties exist side by side there is a cleavage between parties, and between those who adhere to some party and to no party. It is possible to shed light on particular parties and the party phenomenon in general by ascertaining the distinctive qualities of the persons who bear a steady and particular relation to a particular party. The methods by which such information can be gathered and the results of some inquiries are set forth in Chapter Three [of *The Study of Political Parties*].

## NOTES

1. Reprinted by permission of the publishers from A. N. Holcombe: *The More Perfect Union*, Cambridge, Harvard University Press, 1950, p. 428, by The President and Fellows of Harvard College.

2. Angus Campbell, Gerald Gurin, and Warren Miller: *The Voter Decides*, Evanston, Ill., Row, Peterson and Company, 1954, p. 88.

3. *Ibid.*, pp. 88-89.

4. *Ibid.*, p. 88.

5. Robin Williams: *American Society*, New York, Alfred A. Knopf, Inc., 1951, pp. 450-455.

6. *Ibid.*, pp. 451-452.

7. David Truman: *The Governmental Process*, New York, Alfred A. Knopf, Inc., 1951, p. 40.

8. *Ibid.*, p. 282.

9. Richard C. Snyder, H. W. Bruck, and Burton Sapin: *Decision-Making: An Approach to the Study of International Politics*, Princeton, Princeton University Press, 1954.

10. E. E. Schattschneider: *Party Government*, New York, Holt, Rinehart & Winston, Inc., 1942, p. 35.

11. *Ibid.*, p. 36. (Italics added.)

12. *Ibid.*, p. 37. (Italics added.)

13. M. Ostrogorski: *Democracy and the Organization of Political Parties*, New York, The Macmillan Company, 1902; Schattschneider, *op. cit.*; Robert Michels: *Political Parties*, New York, The Free Press, 1949.

14. Robert M. MacIver: *Society: A Textbook of Sociology*, New York, The Macmillan Company, 1927, p. 15.

15. *Ibid.*, p. 16.

16. *Ibid.*, p. 15.

17. Truman, *op. cit.*, p. 26.

18. Reprinted by permission of the publishers from Talcott Parsons and Edward A. Shils (eds.): *Toward a General Theory of Action*, Cambridge, Harvard University Press, 1952, p. 40. Copyright 1952 by The President and Fellows of Harvard College.

19. *Ibid.*, p. 107.

20. Samuel Lubell: *The Future of American Politics*, New York, Harper & Brothers, 1952, pp. 202-203.

21. Holcombe, *op. cit.*, p. 93.

22. Henry James Ford: *The Rise and Growth of American Politics*, New York, The Macmillan Company, 1898, p. 129.

23. Graham Wallas: *Human Nature and Politics*, Boston, Houghton Mifflin Co., 1909, p. 98.

24. *Ibid.*, p. 83.

25. *Ibid.*, p. 91.

26. *Ibid.*

27. Paul Lazarsfeld, Bernard Berelson, and Hazel Gaudet: *The People's Choice* (2nd ed.) New York, Columbia University Press, 1948.

28. *Ibid.*, p. 83.

29. *Ibid.*, p. 89.

30. Charles E. Merriam and Harold Gosnell: *The American Party System* (4th ed.), New York, The Macmillan Company, 1949, pp. 464-465.

31. *Ibid.*, pp. 480-481.

32. Robert M. MacIver: *The Web of Government*, New York, The Macmillan Company, 1947, p. 209. (Italics added.)

33. *Ibid.*, p. 214.

34. Ford, *op. cit.*, pp. 128-129.

35. *Ibid.*, p. 215.

36. American Political Science Association, Committee on Political Parties: *Toward a More Responsible Two Party System*, New York, Holt, Rinehart & Winston, 1950, p. 1.

37. *Ibid.*, p. 2.

38. Specifically in *Public Opinion and Popular Government*, New York, Longmans, Green and Company, 1913.

39. *Ibid.*, pp. 61-62.

40. *Ibid.*, p. 64.

41. E. Pendleton Herring: *The Politics of Democracy*, New York, W. W. Norton & Co., 1940, p. 64.

42. *Ibid.*, p. 105.

43. MacIver, *The Web of Government*, *op. cit.*, p. 213.

44. V. O. Key: *Southern Politics*, New York, Alfred A. Knopf, Inc., 1949.

45. *Ibid.*, p. 303.

46. Holcombe, *op. cit.*, p. 100.

47. Schattschneider, *op. cit.*, p. 100.

48. Philip Selznick: *The Organizational Weapon*, New York, McGraw-Hill Book Company, 1952, p. 2.

49. MacIver, *The Web of Government*, *op. cit.*, p. 210.

50. *Ibid.*

51. Charles A. Beard: *The Republic*, New York, Viking Press, 1943.

52. 321 U.S. 649 (1944).

53. Quoted from *Rice* v. *Elmore*, 165 F. 2nd 387 (1947) in Emerson and Haber (eds.): *Political and Civil Rights in the United States*, Buffalo, N.Y., Dennis & Co., 1952, p. 300.

54. *Brown* v. *Raskin* 78 F. Supp. 933 (1948).

55. *Terry* v. *Adams* 345 U.S. 461 (1953).

56. Howard Penniman: *Sait's American Parties and Elections* (4th ed.), New York, Appleton-Century-Crofts, 1948, p. 190.

57. A very recent example of this contention is William Carleton: "The Triumph of the Moderates," *Harper's Magazine*, April, 1955, pp. 31-37.

58. Maurice Duverger: *Political Parties*, London and New York, Methuen and Co., Ltd., 1954.

# TOWARD A COMPARATIVE STUDY
# OF POLITICAL PARTIES

## Sigmund Neumann

## I. A PRELIMINARY DEFINITION

A definition of "party'" might as well begin with its simple word derivation. To become a "party" to something always means identification with one group and differentiation from another. Every party in its very essence signifies *partnership* in a particular organization and *separation* from others by a specific program.

Such an initial description, to be sure, indicates that the very definition of party presupposes a democratic climate and hence makes it a misnomer in every dictatorship. A one-party system (*le parti unique*) is a contradiction in itself. Only the coexistence of at least one other competitive group makes a political party real. Still the fact remains that the term has been widely used by modern autocrats, and for a very obvious reason: to keep the semblance of a "peoples' rule" in their post-democratic dictatorships. But it is also true that even the totalitarian party depends upon a functioning opposition. If one does not exist, it must still be assumed by the dictators, since under monolithic rule the dictatorial parties must constantly justify their existence in view of the ever present threat of a counterrevolution, hidden or imaginary though its organization may be. The opposition party is the *raison d'être* of the dictatorial movement and its all-pervasive controls through institutions, propaganda, and terror.

Thus parties must prevail under the total structure, too. Yet here again, as in all other strata of the political pyramid, divergent political systems are hidden behind the same nomenclature. Just as "leaders" and "lieutenants" carry different meanings in democracies and dictatorships, so do "parties" also.

Reprinted from *Modern Political Parties,* by Sigmund Neumann, by permission of The University of Chicago Press. Copyright 1956 by The University of Chicago. All rights reserved. Copyright under the International Copyright Union, 1956.

Between the two extremes of "democracy" and "dictatorship" there are wide variations. The British, American, French, Indian, and Scandinavian democratic structures differ as greatly among themselves as do the totalitarian regimes of the Soviet Union, Fascist Italy, Nazi Germany, and Peronist Argentina. In short, the peculiar character of each party system must be defined in terms of the political order of which it is an integral part, if not its kingpin.

What is common to all parties, beyond partnership in a particular organization and separation from others, is their *participation* in the decision-making process, or at least the attempt at and a chance for such a mobilization for action. This ever present readiness alone makes them political in a genuine sense, for only in their fight for control and in their conscious influence on political forces, do parties gain meaning and importance. It is therefore not accidental that the beginning of modern political parties is closely tied up with the rise of a parliament. When political representation broadens and a national forum of discussion develops, providing a constant opportunity for political participation —wherever those conditions are fulfilled, political parties arise. This happened in England in the revolutionary seventeenth century; in France on the eve of the great Revolution of 1789; in Germany around 1848. Even where contingent influences may create political groups of an awakened intelligentsia, as in nineteenth-century tsarist Russia, they assume political dimensions only where some degree of participation is made possible.

While the hour of birth for the political party in every nation can well be defined by such a simple derivation from its original meaning, the same is true of the critical period of a party system. By its very definition, "party" connotes not only the co-existence of different competing entities, with their characteristic partnership, separation, and participation, but also a fourth feature, most significant and yet often forgotten—the essential inclusion of every separate group as *a part in a whole*. Only where the specific interests of parties are imbedded in a common whole does the political struggle not lead to disintegration of the entire group. Only when essentials uniting the political adversaries are constantly reaffirmed can differences be balanced. Just as children are ready to accept the rules of the gang only as long as they are willing to continue their group life, so can sacrifices be asked from each political opponent as long as the preservation of the community seems worth while. A common field of activity, a basic homogeneity, a common language, are presuppositions for a functioning party system. Such a common basis alone makes compromise, sacrifice, and even defeat bearable. Wherever this body politic becomes questionable, the crisis of parties seems the necessary result. The viability of a party system becomes a test for the stability of a social and political order. The strength of the Anglo-American party system is founded largely upon a basic national unity which makes the differentiations of political groups "differences in degree but not in kind."

This interdependence of the fate of political parties with the fate of the national whole is the very result of their "political" character; for political they are not only because of their claim to political power but even more so on account of their fulfilment of their political function of integration.

To summarize: we may define "political party" generally as *the articulate organization of society's active political agents, those who are concerned with the control of governmental power and who compete for popular support with another group or groups holding divergent views.* As such, it is *the great intermediary which links social forces and ideologies to official governmental institutions and relates them to political action within the larger political community.*

A party's concrete character can be spelled out only in time and space. What "this buckle" (to paraphrase Bagehot's description of the British cabinet) actually links up depends on a nation's specific constitution (i.e., the system of its correlated institutions) and its peculiar parallelogram of social forces. It is only in such a substantial situation that the functions, structure, and strategy of parties can be fully revealed.

## II. FUNCTIONS OF POLITICAL PARTIES: DEMOCRATIC AND DICTATORIAL

It has often been stated that the primary task of political parties is to organize the chaotic public will. "They bring order out of the chaos of a multitude of voters" (Lord Bryce). They are brokers of ideas, constantly clarifying, systematizing, and expounding the party's doctrine. They are representatives of social interest groups, bridging the dis-

tance between the individual and the great community. They maximize the voter's education in the competitive scheme of at least a two-party system and sharpen his free choice. The coexistence of a competitor, therefore, is paramount to an effective democratic party system which presupposes that the final compromise will reflect the reasonable decision of a free electorate.

In fact, the basic assumption of democracy is the inevitability of differing views and the free operation of conflicting opinions. "The true democrat has a suspicion that he may not always be right," as W. Ivor Jennings remarked. Thus the opposition becomes the most important part of the parliament; its members are "critics by profession." It is not enough that Her Majesty's Opposition be highly respected by the ruling majority, but often its fruitful ideas are accepted—and, indeed, this is a wise course for the party in power to follow if it wants to remain there. Its political alternative represents not only the looming "Shadow Cabinet" but also an active participant in actual control.

The open forum of parliament becomes the clearinghouse for the policies that a state should follow. The political parties are the proper engine of such continuous plebiscite. They make the voters choose at least the lesser of two evils, thus forcing political differentiations into a few major channels. Yet important as such machinery of political concentration may be, the political services of the parties do not stop at that. What is even more essential, parties transform the private citizen himself. They make him a *zoon politikon;* they integrate him into the group. Every party has to present to the individual voter and to his powerful special-interest groups a picture of the community as an entity. It must constantly remind the citizens of this collective whole, adjust his wants to the needs of the community, and, if necessary, even ask sacrifices from him in the name of the community. Nor can even the so-called "class parties," which call upon only a specific part of the population, renounce this essential function. The outstanding example of such a class program, the *Communist Manifesto,* justifies its position with the claim that the united proletariat will represent the overwhelming majority and that its dictatorship will lead to a dissolution of all classes and therewith to the liberation of society as a whole. This second function differentiates the political party from a pressure group. Its specific interests must be fitted into the framework of the national collective. Wherever the policy-making parties do not succeed in this primary task, the modern state is in danger of deteriorating into a neofeudalism of powerful interest groups.

If the party in a democracy fulfils these two first functions of organizing the chaotic public will and educating the private citizen to political responsibility, then it can also lay claim to a third duty: *to represent the connecting link between government and public opinion.* Since democracies are pyramids built from below, the connection between leaders and followers becomes a necessity in the two-way traffic of democracy. It is the major function of the party to keep these lines of communication open and clear. Such a task makes the parties, if not the rulers, at least the controlling agencies of government in a representative democracy.

This crucial position is even more emphasized by the fourth function of a democratic party: *the selection of leaders.* Here as everywhere in a democracy, it is the competitive scheme, the choice between at least two oligarchies, which guarantees the quality of its leadership. Of course, such a selection presupposes an enlightened public, one qualified to make the right choice, and an intellectual climate appropriate to the functioning of democratic parties. Wherever these preconditions no longer prevail, the crisis of democracy is in the offing.

The crisis elements of democratic parties can be well perceived in the rise of dictatorial movements. In fact, dictatorial organizations often grow up within the democratic party system itself. They constitute a state within the state, alienated from its basic principles. And yet their rise is the expression of a basic lack within the society. They can recruit followers because there are those who no longer regard themselves as a part of the predominant society that does not seem to answer their essential desires and needs. No doubt every functioning group has and can bear some "outsiders" in its midst. So long as they do not represent a considerable number, they do not constitute a serious threat to the existing order. If, however, they succeed in recruiting an appreciable following, then the democratic process enters a critical stage. The rise of dictatorial parties within modern states is a storm signal for the democratic party system. From now on, the argument between parties concerns fundamentals and a fight over ultimate issues. For these integrated political groups compromise becomes increasingly difficult, and so does any coalition with another party.

The main purpose of the fully developed totalitarian parties becomes the fight ·for a new political order, for a new society. Speaking a different language and living according to a different set of values, the partisans have to be segregated from the political and social body of the ruling class and society, so the party leaders decree. Otherwise the partisans may be enchanted and taken in by the old order, the destruction of which is the essential purpose of the "guarantors" of the new morrow.

With the rise of the dictatorial party, its competitors in politics necessarily become more inflexible too. Struggle assumes the quality of a religious war; the only possible outcome for any contestant seems to be overwhelming victory or ultimate annihilation.

Such a situation explains the revolutionary functions of a dictatorial party before its seizure of power: it is, above all, the *revolutionary vanguard* of the future state.

The functions of the dictatorial parties in power, outwardly at least, do not appear to be different from the four features of their democratic counterparts. They, too, have to organize the chaotic public will and integrate the individual into the group; they equally have to represent the connecting link between government and public opinion and, above all, guarantee the selection of leaders. Yet as their concepts of leaders and followers differ diametrically from democratic ideals, the meaning of these functions changes fundamentally. Organization of the chaotic will is fulfilled by a "monolithic control"; integration of the individual means "enforcement of conformity"; and, though these tasks are often directed by a "Ministry of Education and Enlightenment," the maintenance of communication between state and society is assured by a mere one-way propaganda stream from above. True, dictatorships also have to concern themselves with "public opinion." They must listen to the "voice of the people," especially since this is muted under the tyrant's rule. Thus the party serves through its secret agencies as a necessary listening post. Through such diverse services this leviathan apparatus, which claims at the outset to be the party to end all parties, becomes in fact the key instrument of modern totalitarianism.

All three functions, if successfully administered, secure the fourth and crucial purpose: the selection of leaders. Yet it is especially on this level of the creation, preservation, and extension of the ruling elite that the basic differences between the party systems become obvious.

Lenin's fight at the turn of the century for a small centralized revolutionary elite, as opposed to the Mensheviks' idea of a loose democratic mass organization, laid the foundation for a disciplined castelike order. He thus anticipated what revolutionary parties experienced a generation later when they had to choose between thoroughly revolutionist cadres and a mass following.

Only in a "revolutionary situation"—i.e., when complete victory or the prospect of impending success brings a rush of adherents to the revolutionary cause—is it possible for such a radical party to win and to hold the masses. Revolutionary parties reckoning with a long struggle can count on only a small elite of unrelenting fighters who do not care for rewards today and who are ready to make the revolution their life's calling. Masses are in need of visible rewards. If they cannot reap the fruits now —or at least have reasonable expectation of doing so in the near future—they will leave the ranks. This fact explains the extraordinary fluctuation in membership to be observed in radical parties everywhere. The Fascist followers of yesterday are turning up today as communism's most reliable fighters; and the reverse may be true tomorrow. Whoever delivers the spoils has the confidence of the fluctuating masses; but if he cannot do so by tomorrow, another liberator will be sought out.

How different from the rank-and-file reaction are the attitudes of the vanguard and the core members of the established movement, taking their orders from the central party organization, whether it means robbing a bank, organizing a party cell, or conceiving a new program. The revolutionary intellectual in his great flight into a future morrow and the revolutionary "wire-puller" in his minute work, far apart though they be, have one thing in common: they do not expect rewards in this world. They have given their lives to the party, which in return becomes their own life. Discipline is the password of the movement. Said Lenin in 1900: "We must train men and women who will devote to the revolution not merely their spare evenings but the whole of their lives." This is the clarion call to the totalitarian party. It can appeal to the professional revolutionary at all times; yet to the masses it may be meaningful only during a revolutionary situation.

The Continental Communist parties in the interwar period opened their ranks to the masses partly because of their mistaken misapprehension of what they deemed a revolutionary situation (which had passed by 1920). They did not fare too well. In Soviet Russia, of course, they could offer their followers the spoils of the victor. In fact, many people joined the Bolshevik party for such reasons alone, and the early purges of the Soviet regime were partly to free the party from those "opportunists" (and more often from those whose services were originally useful but which now could be performed by newly recruited "reliable" followers).

The radical parties in the non-Communist countries did not have to eliminate "job-hunters" because there were no jobs to be distributed. As quickly as the prospects of revolutionary changes attracted the driftwood of a political reserve army, so did this army move quickly on to new shores which seemed more promising. The fate of the Communist parties outside Russia in the interwar period hinged on the dilemma between their revolutionary character and their aspirations for mass following, between their uncompromising attitude as a party which did not want to sell the revolution for a "mess of pottage" and the necessity of offering substantial results at once because the masses would not be satisfied with a promised millennium. They wanted higher wages, social security, political recognition—visible signs of success today. Thus they left the party that was preparing for a revolution not yet in sight.

A mass party cannot survive without foreseeable success. Its final fate becomes a race against time. The surprising staying power of the Communist

parties in western Europe since 1945 seems to contradict such a statement; yet, as Charles Micaud's analysis convincingly shows, the left-wing radicals have learned some lessons from their earlier failures and have defined more realistically the function and place of the totalitarian party in what they regard as the preparatory stage of an oncoming revolution. In fact, the continued appeal of communism in France and Italy, despite the Marshall Plan and NATO, serves as a warning to the democratic powers in areas where they have not yet succeeded in reintegrating large segments of their national community. It is the claim of the Communist movements that they can give their followers a feeling of belonging, an active faith, and a promising direction for the future when the party will possess the whole community and seize the power of the state.

## III. TOWARD A CLASSIFICATION OF PARTIES

Since political parties are mainly concerned with the control of governmental power, the most obvious differentiation would be to distinguish the *in-group* from the *out-group*. Indeed, such a classification may point at some fundamental traits of political strategy and emphasize the advantage of a two-party system for clear-cut confrontation. It would divide the "haves" and the "have-nots" in politics. Thus the insider at the controls would be often identified with the status quo, the conservative tendencies, while the challenging outsider would usually be the party of change and reform.

One may even go further and recognize in these two opposing camps a classification which has been frequently applied by Continental writers as the possessor's *party of patronage* versus the defiant's *party of principles* and thereby indicate the danger points of the two parties: the corruption of the "ins" by power and the irresponsible dogmatism of the "outs."

In a wider comparative approach, the degree of proximity to power may also explain interesting variations in national party systems. Wherever parties are called upon for political decision-making, as in the Anglo-American democracies, they may well emphasize the day-by-day *expediency interests*. On the other hand, in nations where the parties have played only a subordinate role or where they are purposely kept from political key positions by the government, as was the case during the greater part of German history, parties may easily retreat to the fundamental principles of an all-inclusive "faith movement" (*Weltanschauungs-* or *Glaubens-Parteien*).

These different national positions may also suggest a division of parties of *platform* and of *pro-*

*gram.* One may, however, observe that such a strict cleavage has become less significant in recent decades. The more the German parties have been drawn into responsible politics, especially in the contemporary attempt at a democratic government, the more they are forced to make daily decisions along lines of concrete interests. Contrariwise, the Western democracies have been increasingly confronted with fundamental issues of international reorientation, national planning, and individual soul-searching—all of which demand a basic ideological outlook. This interesting *rapprochement* of seemingly contradictory systems will have far-reaching consequences and deserves our most careful consideration. At this point we must mention that the traditional lines of demarcation between the parties of expedient interests and those of fundamental principles have been blurred.

In the light of these developments another classification is losing its sharp contours, the suggestive division of *parties of personages* versus *parties of programs.* Although this dichotomy has reappeared today, but in a different version, in the contrast between dictatorial and democratic rule, between personal and institutional government—parties of personages are of the past. Max Weber's three stages of party development from aristocratic cliques to party of notables to plebiscitarian democracy point to a general trend in the Western world. The British party growth is a case in point, as Samuel Beer's careful study clearly shows. On the Continent, leaving aside preliminary aristocratic factions, the early period of parliamentary development, with its emphasis on local representation, was characterized by notables (*Honoratioren*) giving their name and decisive mark to political groups (as in the German parliament of 1848, the center and right-wing factions in the French Third Republic, and in pre-Fascist Italy). Yet today, when nation-wide public issues of class, religion, nationality, and international affairs constitute the dividing line of political parties, their leadership is forced to comply with the over-all program. Thus the parties became nationalized even in such traditionally decentralized structures as the United States, as E. E. Schattschneider's chapter pointedly describes (though personalities may still be crucial in making or breaking a party's hold on a' nation, as the recent presidential elections in the United States abundantly testified).

The reality of modern politics represents a much more complex picture than is suggested by the simple array of insiders and outsiders, of parties of patronage and parties of principles, of expediency interests and Weltanschauung, of personages and programs. Such precise but utterly imaginary partitions fail to reveal the inner dynamics and tensions of a functioning democracy. In fact, it is the inexhaustible mixture of all these elements that comprises the life of modern political parties—and perhaps escapes any rigid classification.

A more modest attempt at systematization simply follows the number of contestants in the political field and speaks of one-, two-, or multiparty systems. But some important facts of political organization and control can be derived from such a classification.

A careful analysis of the causes and consequences of the two-party system versus the multiparty regime must probe into the historical circumstances, social structures, and institutional arrangements which underlie the divergent national political settings. While it is generally agreed that a two-party rule promises greater efficiency for the democratic process, as the British and American cases prove, it is equally obvious that such a political setting cannot be easily transplanted into national communities which do not meet its preconditions and which therefore, by no mere oversight or accident, possess a different political organization.

Historical precedents may suggest the following favorable circumstances for a two-party development: social homogeneity, political continuity, an early sanction of responsible political parties striving for political control, and their orientation at one elective office (the United States presidency, the British premiership) as the desired prize.

Wherever fundamental cleavages in social structure evolve and continue to exist because of differences in nationalities, regions, religion, or class which are often fostered by outside influences like *irredenta* movements and revolutionary internationals; wherever political revolutions coincide with great social transformations, as in France, central and eastern Europe, and the Near and Far East; wherever a controlling elite, through the divide-and-rule device, prevents parties from fulfilling their genuinely political functions of presenting clear-cut policy alternatives, as in Bismarck's strategies, for example; wherever the political machinery of a state diffuses the electorate's division by numerous choices—wherever any or all of these complicating factors enter the national political scene, a multiparty system finds its *raison d'être.* Obviously, it reflects in its more numerous groupings a fuller and more exacting picture of the peculiar features of a stratified society than a two-party system could ever present.

Once established, these different party systems have far-reaching consequences for the voting process and even more so for governmental decision-making. So far as elections go, in a two-party system both contenders will naturally compete for the shifting voter in the middle. Politics, therefore, will gravitate toward the center and the free-floating electoral bloc which is decisive for the winning or holding of a majority. The spectacle of a programmatic *rapprochement,* despite heated electoral campaigns, of the two main parties is not simply a trick of conniving politicians but a natural outcome of a party system that reflects a relatively stable order.

The double party has been called "a convenient system for contented peoples" who are agreed upon the general principles of the constitution and the policies of the government and feel not too intensely about measures over which they disagree. The fundamental cleavage over the slave issue broke for a time the efficacy of the American two-party system. The double party structure of modern England presupposed the reconciliation of the British Tories with the House of Hanover. Once the Glorious Revolution with its political institutions was recognized, they in turn could absorb the shock and major changes of the following social revolutions within their unchallenged political framework. Thus the miracle of British democracy in its combination of stability and progress was guaranteed. Once effectively established as a political institution, the two-party system reinforces and often perpetuates the trend toward conformity.

A multiparty system does not possess this unifying and centralizing order. On the contrary, yielding to its inability to produce a majority party in elections, its factions concentrate on the centrifugal forces of special-interest groups and may easily be directed at peripheral forces. Such diffusion of power, often emphasized by special electoral systems such as proportional representation (putting at high premium the true mirroring of all shades of public opinion), does not hold great promise for effective policy formation.

Policy-making in a two-party system is no doubt facilitated by its certain majorities and consequently its unmistakable party responsibilities. Yet even within the frame of the two major parties, a hidden multiparty system may often be detected with intra-party splits and factions or third parties, which may at times affect the crucial balance and enforce a break, new combinations, or compromises at the political front. In these critical moments the direct mandate of the people may be blurred by the parliamentary struggle for majorities until the voice of the electorate can be heard again.

What is exceptional in a two-party setting, however, becomes the rule under the procedures of a pluriparty system. By its very nature, it must transfer crucial decisions from a much-divided electorate to the parliament. This representative body in turn must content itself with a government by the formation of a coalition, attaining, after extended bickering, the compromise which in the two-party system is largely the voter's business to achieve within his own mind and political wisdom.

Even such a sketchy outline makes it obvious how much the character and policies of parties are defined by this formal division between two-party and multiparty systems. A classification along this line, therefore, proves to be quite suggestive and essential.

The differences are even more fundamental in the comparison of the one-party rule with the two-party and multiparty organizations. The character of the totalitarian rule indicates that a one-party system is a contradiction in terms. For clarity's sake it might be better to assign to this important contemporary phenomenon a different name, such as "political order." Modern usage, however, has coined the concept of the one-party state, and, if only for reasons of propagandistic appeal, the terminology has been accepted on the daily political fronts, both national and international. This being the case, one might recognize in the opposition of the one party versus the two and multiparties the fundamental cleavage of our time: *dictatorship versus democracy*. Along this dividing line all basic tenets of modern parties must be redefined: their structure and strategy, their leadership, their apparatus, their following, their techniques of mass communication, their national policies, and their international ties. Through the organization and practices of these contrasting party systems, in turn, the two great contenders over political control in our society stand fully revealed. The essence of democratic and dictatorial rule is embodied in the daily life of their parties.

Essential though this sharp hiatus is for a classification of modern parties, such a crude black-and-white comparison cannot suffice for a substantial analysis of the political processes in our time. It leaves too much unsaid and unexplained: the shaded differentiation between existing political orders along the line of democracy and dictatorship, the twilight zones of their correlations, the conditions under which a transition from one to the other is facilitated, the inner complexities of the functioning institutions in both systems, and the shifting position occupied, in recent decades, by the modern parties in relation to the individual and the community at large.

The detailed analysis of dictatorial parties shows to what extent democracy is not only a symbol of aggression but also a claimed property of modern totalitarianism. The organization and incorporation of the people become the overwhelming concern of the seemingly independent autocracies. On the other hand, the effective democratic party has also radically changed its character and role in modern society, although this fact may not yet be fully recognized by its adherents.

Perhaps it is altogether impossible to try to put into systematic categories such an intricate and constantly shifting political process—but, at best, one might conceive a set of "emergent concepts" which would be highly significant. If one dared to measure at this point the long-range trends of party development, one might arrive at the following conclusions.

Modern parties have steadily enlarged their scope and power within the political community and have consequently changed their own functions and character. In place of a *party of individual representation,* our contemporary society increasingly shows a *party of social integration.*

This shift must be seen within the context of our changing society and its underlying philosophy. Three major stages can be observed in its development. Modern parties originated with the drive of a rising, self-conscious middle class that fought for liberation from the shackles of a feudal society and for representation to check monarchical absolutism. While the French Revolution officially proclaimed the end of this first phase of modern social development, the successful emancipation of rational man from the bonds of the *ancien régime* and its caste system proved to be only a transitional second stage. The individual, set free, was soon striving at reintegration into a new society. In fact, since the middle of the nineteenth century diverse claims for such a new orientation have been raised, promising to stop the fragmentation of a laissez faire society. The first and lasting challenge of rising socialism, the emergence and appeal of political irrationalism, and an awakening social liberalism gave contrasting answers to this key issue of our century. The dislocations caused by the sweeping industrialization, radical urbanization, and international migration, by world wars and total revolutions, gave substance to a planned search for a new social order. We are still in the midst of this third phase. It constitutes the crisis of modern society.

It is against this background of crisis that a new concept of party is evolving. Its emergence and persistence, in fact, may well depend on the momentous character of social crisis. The well-balanced communities of the Scandinavian states and the Anglo-American world seem to be least affected by this new type, while it has found its most complete expression within nations in the grip of revolutions. The islands of social equilibrium, however, have shrunk, and the party of integration has no doubt become a salient feature of our contemporary landscape.

The *party of individual representation* is characteristic of a society with a restricted political domain and only a limited degree of participation. Its membership activity is, for all practical purposes, limited to balloting, and the party organization (if existent at all) is dormant between election periods. Its main function is the selection of representatives, who, once chosen, are possessed of an absolutely "free mandate" and are in every respect responsible only to their own consciences. This conception of an ephemeral party as a mere electoral committee does not correspond to the political reality and practice of the modern mass democracy, a fact which in many countries has been recognized (though often most reluctantly) in the crucial controversy over party discipline and even in numerous court decisions codifying party regulations, responsibilities, and prerogatives. The fundamental concept of party, however, has hardly been challenged within democratic thinking.

Under the cover of such a persistent framework and rarely perceived even by circumspect political observers, a new type of party has emerged —the *party of integration.* The claim with which this party approaches its adherents is incomparably greater than that of the party of individual representation. It demands not only permanent dues-paying membership (which may be found to a smaller extent within the loose party of representation too) but, above all, an increasing influence over all spheres of the individual's daily life.

The first example of such a new party was presented by the Continental Socialists. Their organization has been jokingly characterized as extending from the cradle to the grave, from the workers' infant-care association to the atheists' cremation society; yet such a description articulates the intrinsic difference from the liberal party of representation, with its principle of "free recruitment" among a socially uncommitted, free-floating electorate (the bulk of which, in reality, may not be so independent). The following of the new movement is, indeed, much more clearly circumscribed by its permanent membership, the definite class alignment of its voting population, and its far-flung participation in over-all social affairs. The party can count on its adherents; it has taken over a good part of their social existence.

Despite such extensive organization and intensified ties of its partisans, the Socialist party (and in an even more limited way the Catholic movement and other democratic parties of integration) include only a small active core among its wider circle of mere dues-paying members and its even greater number of mere voters. In fact, this differentiation is at the base of the much-disputed "oligarchical" tendencies of modern mass parties which permit a relatively small group to decide the political fate of the disinterested and apathetic majority. Still, what is important is that the party in modern mass democracies has generally taken on an ever increasing area of commitments and responsibilities assuring the individual's share in society and incorporating him into the community. This is no mere usurpation of power by the politicians but the natural consequence of the extension of the public domain and the constantly increasing governmental functions in a reintegrated twentieth-century society.

In this sense the phenomenon of the *party of democratic integration* has become a matter of record. This fact makes it the more imperative to recognize its basic variance from the *party of total integration,* which has found its prototype in bolshevism, fascism, and National Socialism. This all-inclusive party demands the citizen's unconditional surrender. It denies not only the relative freedom of choice among the voters and followers but also any possibility of coalition and compromise among parties. It can perceive nothing but total seizure and exercise of power, undisputed acceptance of the party line, and monolithic rule. The rise of this absolutist police state decrees the end of democracy, of constitutionalism, of communal self-government, of Western man and his inalienable rights, of political parties.

This radical juxtaposition should forewarn the responsible student of modern mass society against the threat of party petrifaction, but such a mortal peril cannot be met simply by a denial of the extended functions of modern parties and of their radically changing character—for the choice is not between the absolute state and the absolute individual or between autocracy or anarchy, as the great simplifiers and political demagogues make us believe. On the contrary, constructive thinking must concentrate on the much more difficult and urgent task of devising political institutions that allow for a new adjustment between the integrated society and the free individual. It is within such a realistic delineation of the fundamental prerequisites, present-day responsibilities, and necessary safeguards of a democratic society that the sociology of modern parties must be re-examined.

## IV. SOCIOLOGY OF POLITICAL PARTIES

The study of the sociology of political parties has been completely dominated by Robert Michels' iron law of the oligarchical tendencies of social movements which he expounded with intense single-mindedness more than a generation ago in his *Political Parties*. While a standard work without doubt, it has shared the fate of so many classics— to be widely quoted and rarely read. Unfortunately, little empirical research has been done in the field of political sociology either in defining Michels' underlying assumptions or even in testing the validity of his thesis. In fact, it has become almost an undisputed axiom.

The first prerequisite for a more accurate appraisal of the intricate web of social relations within modern parties is an exacting theoretical framework. Without it, all the concrete investigations in the area will be meaningless, undirected, and just so much ballast in the scholar's bark. At this point only a few crucial concepts, issues, and hypotheses can be presented that may be suggestive for a proper orientation of future research. Key terms such as "leaders" and "followers," "participation" and "apparatus," need renewed clarification and a realistic differentiation in respect to the divergent political systems. Only an age corroded by the demagogical simplifiers of modern dictatorship could postulate the idea of a leaderless democracy. Only a naïve countermovement of overconfident

democrats could overlook the weighty and often dangerous part played by aroused masses in present-day autocracies.

There are leaders and masses in democracies, just as in dictatorships. Leadership is a prominent theme of any political order. Yet every period, every society, every political system, establishes a different interrelation between leaders and followers. What is therefore important is to recognize clearly the divergent character, function, selection, and mobility, which vary in accordance with the whole structure of the prevalent political order. This social conditioning of modern leadership serves as a key to an understanding of the difference between democracies and dictatorships in our day.

Although differing greatly in time and space, two main types of political leadership can be distinguished: *institutional* and *personal*. These are types roughly corresponding to the contrasting political systems, democracy and dictatorship. The pre-eminent elements of leadership in a democracy are institutional. This fact, of course, leads to a difference in democratic leadership according to varying institutional structures. The unlike character of the British prime minister, the French president of the council, and the United States president are a reflection of different institutional setups of these democratic governments and their respective party systems. This institutional character defines the personal qualities of democratic authority, its functions, its rise to eminence, its continuation, and its fluctuation and limitations in power. Deference, which is no doubt a basic desideratum of any leadership, derives largely from the leader's skills, the extent of his knowledge, judgment, and foresight, his strength of conviction, his policies, his ability to attain social cohesion and to give direction to social forces. Balance of mind, distaste for violence of expression, a faculty for spreading conciliation on all sides, become highly valued qualities of democratic leadership. One should add, to enlarge upon Bagehot's famed remark, that the leader must be "an uncommon man of common opinions," which he articulates, intensifies, directs, and realizes through workable channels. This faculty of expressing the people's will points to a certain demagogical feature even in democratic leadership which is necessitated by the mass character of modern society. The pre-eminent elements of democratic authority, however, are institutional.

Dictatorial leadership is personal. Here again will be found variations due to national traditions, historical circumstances, and personality patterns; but all modern dictators have this in common: they are anti-institutional. In fact, their very rise indicates the weakening or nonexistence of political institutions, of a ruling class, of an accepted code of rules, of a belief in a rational order. The modern dictator is the substitute for institutions in the mass age of political confusion and social disintegration.

He is, above all, the demagogue—the leader of the people, who, rising from the dark as an unknown soldier, breaks through society's institutional barriers. He does not stand for a positive program but only for himself. He is responsible to no man but to God and the nation (who are conveniently removed from any direct interference), and in his very irresponsibility he is revered by the emotional, rootless, and amorphous masses seeking mystery, devotion, and the miraculous. He is the wonder-performing *charismatic* leader whose charm of personality conceals conflicts of policy. The "state of the masses" is indeed the key to the acceptance of his myth.

Charismatic leadership and bureaucracy may well accompany each other. Even though it may seem inconsistent with the emotional dynamics of this personal ruler, his power rests on a strong party organization, an apparatus. In fact, the guardians of his machine, the "lieutenants," reveal the true character of the one-party system, its daily life, its divided rule, its inner tensions, its chance for survival and succession. Generally speaking, it is on this second level of political control that the multifarious functions of modern parties become apparent, the differences in degree and kind between the democratic and dictatorial parties are manifest, and the resilience, flexibility, and deep antagonisms of contemporary political organizations are tested.

*Bureaucratization* is a categorical fate of modern society, involving equally government, business, and political parties. This fact may be deplored for its social strains and its often serious consequences of hampering spontaneity and free play in human affairs; it is still an indisputable necessity inherent in an efficient, highly developed mass organization. It implies stratification and hierarchy of office, specialization and fragmentation of the citizen's role, centralization of government. It has become "the organizational weapon" of modern dictatorship. Yet its perils are not met by denying its existence or by warning of the inevitable destruction of the democratic fiber by the spider of administration. What must be stated carefully, however, are the manifold expressions it has found, the conditions under which this necessary phenomenon may choke the basic forces of a free society, and the safeguards which can and must be erected against such constriction today and tomorrow.

As a preliminary investigation, an account should be given of the multifarious organizational forms within the diverse parties around the globe; possibly a comparison with developments in the adjacent trade-unions, business organizations, pressure groups, and social agencies would prove fruitful too. On the basis of these rich findings one might well arrive at some major qualifications of Robert Michels' glittering generalizations. They not only might be found to be an overstatement of the undeniable existence of oligarchical, hierarchic, and centripetal trends in every society but might be matched by data confirming the equally omnipresent democratic, leveling, and centrifugal forces encountered even within present-day totalitarian orders.

What is more important, Michels' emphasis may reveal a deeply imbedded bias in favor of the predominant bureaucratic, authoritarian values of his time. In this sense the initially socialist opponent of the Wilhelminic empire proves to be the latter's true child, who by no mere accident turns Fascist as a man. Such social conditioning may also be recognized in the crown witness of his inquiry—the German Social Democratic party, which, not without some justification, had been called one of the most Prussian institutions in the Reich. An analysis of other political movements growing out of a different social climate, such as the British Labour party, might have led Michels to very different conclusions.

Here is a random list of the multi-factored determinants within the internal party organization which can help to define the conditions under which its complex relationship of leaders and followers may take a line different from that postulated by Michels.

First of all, variations in the character of those who are led are as important as those among those who lead, especially as the *concept of the masses* presents an even more elastic term. Leaving aside frequent moral connotations (such as "canaille," "the great unwashed," the "rebellious masses"), sharp distinctions should be made between the social variations of rural and urban groups, of scattered crowds and congregated mobs, of the latent and aroused masses, of the illiterate, numb, and untried and the educated, alert, skilled people. Different social classes invite a variety of stimuli and reactions. Political parties find an uneven appeal in various social strata, in accordance with their specific social experiences and historical conditions. Le Bon's influential school of crowd psychology, generalizing the experiences of the revolutionary upheavals in modern European capitals, identified the masses with the highly emotionalized and unstable character of the mob, thus stigmatizing mass action as devoid of individual self-control. While his simplifications still have currency in popular thinking, highly sophisticated social research is beginning to uncover the much more complex interplay between the rational and irrational elements of modern mass reaction. Its findings will give a more adequate evaluation of mass participation in modern political movements.

Next to the specific character of the rank and file, the people's role in politics will depend on the *size of organization*. The transition from aristocratic factions to modern mass parties no doubt necessitated the development of bureaucracies, as in any other large-scale organizations. All other factors being equal, this must diminish the individual member's potential in policy-making. Moreover, time, continuous effort, and skills are increasingly demanded for adequate legislative decision and subsequent administration. Naturally, these prerequisites lead to the predominance of the permanent and party professional over the political amateur. The problem of political organization, however, is not solved by abolishing the experts but by finding methods of checks and controls by an alert citizenry. Danger spots for a dynamic democracy appear where an incumbent party administration has a permanent hold on the organizational machine, absolute control over financial resources, and monopoly of the internal channels of communication, thus stifling the voicing of counterpropaganda and alternative solutions and the rise of a substitute elite. The concrete situation in each nation and movement will depend on the complex of balances between party leadership and its apparatus, between parliamentary representation and national party conferences, between the executive core and peripheral membership.

Strength or weakness of the central authorities depends also on the *functions* to be performed. The single function of electioneering in the party of liberal representation will easily leave the power in the hands of "notables," just as trade-unions with an exclusive orientation toward labor contracts will not encourage wider membership participation. Not only do diffuse functions call for diverse leaders (efficient administrators and popular agitators, feudal confidants of the No. 1 man and reliable representatives of the interest groups, powerful masters of violence and political bosses, "ambassadors of the people," and informal holders of effective party patronage), but their consequent contradictions and controversies also offer the adherents alternative choices and increased influences. Even, and especially, the seemingly monolithic rule of modern dictatorships in their claim to total controls had to engage a multiple leadership that caused persistent tensions among the lieutenants, the inefficiency of secretly competing hierarchies within the party, and final disintegration of arbitrary government under the stress of supreme crisis. The failure of fascism and National Socialism might well be ascribed to the lack of open competition, of circulation of elites, and of free mass participation.

The *degree of participation* is a further key to the leader-followers relationship in political parties. Here again a preliminary exercise in definition is needed to clarify a politically charged and often purposely equivocal vocabulary. Ambiguity has become the secret weapon of modern autocrats. They will pride themselves on extending community enterprises as a genuine test of their "people's democracy." True, active involvement of a great number of party members can serve as a powerful counteracting force to oligarchical rule, yet democracy is not guaranteed by mere participation. If this means controlled and manipulated mass direction through the dictator's triple threat of all-embracing institutions, all-consuming fears, and an all-pervading propaganda, it can in fact become the most potent instrument of his lasting power. Indeed, so far as his rule aspires to a radical change in the societal structure, effective mass participation seems to be a prerequisite for the successful breaking of the traditional patterns, for channeling the people's discontent, and for preventing a counterrevolution. In this sense modern autocracies are still children of a democratic age; they are postdemocratic dictatorships, and, because of that, they outdemonstrate any popular government in masterplanned, minutely organized, mass meetings. Yet 100 per cent plebiscites are no demonstration of democracy, and true participation depends on more than "bread and circuses"; it demands political activation through free choice and decision. In order to assure such a democratic process it must, above all, keep its channels of communication clear and accessible to those who are ready to attend to their citizens' rights and duties.

A realistic appraisal of functioning democracies must, of course, take account of variations in popular participation in accordance with innate abilities, acquired skills, available time, and, above all, personal desires and aspirations. Negatively, the degree of apathy is indeed a most powerful and measurable factor in the failure of effective democracies. It is not the least conditioned by the promise of rewards in the sharing of power, although a careful analysis will also have to consider differentiations in popular participation in democracies without simplifying and unrealistic assumptions of equal sharing for *all* citizens in *all* actions at *all* times. The role of the expert, of the administrator, of the responsible policy-maker, will need a fresh evaluation.

The morale of the group depends largely on the extent of participation of its members. The degree of *fluctuation* in leadership, as enunciated by Mosca and Pareto in the suggestive theory of the *"circulation of elites,"* is a visible indication of the democratic chances of the party members. It gives a measure of the extent to which the controlling positions are open to free competition or monopolized by a closed group. It should also offer proof of the stability and longevity of the ruling class, although only isolated studies like Pontus Fahlbeck's classic on the Swedish aristocracy and similar works by Schott, Furlan, and Savorgnan on Continental development have so far presented the kind of exact material necessary for comprehensive comparative analyses.

Equally, if not more, important for democratic vitality is the party's ability to absorb and assimilate new social strata into the ruling class. Closely connected with this key problem is the much neglected phenomenon of the *succession in generations.* Many political revolutions have originated in this natural break between different political ages; the continuity of a political system, on the other hand, can well be measured in terms of its ability to guarantee a smooth and steady transition. This test of political wisdom and viability becomes manifest in the diverse selection and training of future leaders (and the mechanisms by which leaders can be retired). These procedures offer the most conclusive clue to the aims, character, and flexibility of the different party systems.

The usual *apprenticeship* of democratic aspirants through institutional channels of parliament, local government, and party organization is a selective process which tests particular qualifications: the capacity for effective statement, for framing legislation, for mastery in parliamentary debate, for teamwork, co-operation, and successful compromise. It offers a severe training and a slow rise to power—too slow for some young men in a hurry, who join extra-parliamentary movements that seem to promise a short cut to victory. The institutional path attracts certain personality types who may be groomed preferably by a definite educational system and who are more easily found in specific professions. The availability of trained political participants and, to use Max Weber's terminology, of "dispensable occupations" (lawyers, journalists, educators), which allow for career interruptions with even possible gains in skills and connections by such a political experience, will assure the filling of the necessary leadership reservoir. Equally important for the free flow of talent into political channels is a follow-up, a mechanism by which leaders can be retired and/or used for further advanced assignments without loss of craft and prestige. The rigidity of certain parties (and even more so, of many trade-unions) is often due to their petrified leadership which has no exit but oblivion.

While it is undoubtedly true, as Lasswell has stated, that stability of rule varies inversely with the degree of organization of a counterelite, the inner corruption of a power group is equally accelerated by the absence of an alternative challenge. And since the weakness of authority is often more significant for the breakdown of a system than is the strength of the opposition, one may perceive some chance for the disintegration of a monolithic rule, even if it has succeeded in destroying all articulate resistance.

*Selection of leadership* in modern autocracies meets with certain difficulties, despite the fact that conscious, long-range efforts are made for its preparation and for the master's succession. There is no natural competition in parliament or elsewhere to groom the dictator's lieutenants. Favoritism plays an important part in the selection, and especially in the higher brackets of the political hierarchy the leader's personal choice may even bring nonparty members into the inner council. The main channel, however is the party machine. Being a "charter member" of the party (the old guards of the first

hour, the martyrs of the preceding "system's" prisons) is equivalent to a "safe" seat in a democratic parliament. These important qualities of the ardent fighters and trustworthy confidants may, however, at times become embarrassing after the seizure of power, and the "comrades of early and trying conspiracies" may be faced with purges and even the firing squad.

The composite structure of modern dictatorship in its all-embracing power requires varied types of leaders—demagogical, bureaucratic, militant, and feudal—and the party machine has to put forth the necessary material. This often discordant variety of functions creates, in fact, a hidden multiparty system within the monolithic regime, bringing about selection through partisan factions, victorious before the unpredictable court of the supreme potentate, where the sycophant wins a friendly hearing and qualified potential is discarded. Such arbitrary selection may in the end cost the dictator his effective rule, especially in a time of great trial, as the demise of fascism and National Socialism amply illustrates. As long as he lasts, the modern tyrant has, however, the audacity to bid for the perpetuation of his regime even beyond his life by usurping complete control over the mind of the nation's youth. This monopoly of training through state-controlled youth movements and a completely co-ordinated educational system may be modern dictatorship's most potent weapon. It is certainly too early to draw any definite conclusion as to whether it will succeed where its classical forerunners failed; yet certain prerequisites can be recorded.

Two preconditions for successful *perpetuation* of the dictatorial system seem to be indispensable: (1) the establishment of a well-functioning party machine and (2) the destruction or absorption of the traditional institutions. Success or failure will depend largely on the degree to which the system is internally consolidated. If the shots fired at Lenin in August, 1918, had killed him, the Soviet regime could easily have collapsed. When he did die in January, 1924, an integrated power system had grown up around him, and, after the short struggle between Stalin and Trotsky, the master of the party machine emerged as the victor. Similarly, the "heir apparent" of Stalin's regime had first been Kirov, and after his mysterious assassination Zhdanov took his place until he preceded his superior in death. If Khrushchev, following Malenkov, is destined to inherit Caesar's mantle, as has been widely assumed for a long time—the present transitional committee leadership notwithstanding— then the succession will adhere to the established procedures. The sequence of the list of "No. 2" men in Nazi Germany from Göring to Hess to Bormann indicated that Hitler followed similar succession plans. Apparently, Goebbels or Himmler never had a chance at the "line of succession" set down by Hitler. On the basis of our experience, which is extremely limited, we may surmise that the end of the political "glamour boys" of the revolution and the rise of the less conspicuous middle-of-the-road *apparatchik* may well describe the bureaucratizing pattern of dictatorial succession and—if it prove triumphant—the changing character of the revolutionary one-party regime.

# V. THE PARTY IN A PLURALISTIC SOCIETY

This preliminary discussion of the sociology of political movements shows that a full definition of modern parties must include a clear understanding of the society of which they are a part and which they express. The nature and ethos of the ruling elite (military, managerial, intellectual, racial, religious, industrial, commercial, peasant, or proletarian, as the case may be), the status differentiation and degree of mobility (class or caste structure), the prevalent value system, the inner cohesion or crisis character of a nation—the complex interplay of these heterogeneous factors can alone indicate the extent of oligarchical trends or democratic participation within a political community.

Even the one-party state, with its seeming monolithic control by its dominant clique, cannot escape the intricacies of competing agencies in a highly developed society if it wants to survive. The purposely pluralistic democratic state must establish an ever renewed balance of society's divergent forces in order to assign the parties their proper place and function.

In fact, a high degree of diversity seems to create a favorable climate for a functioning democracy if it protects itself against the perils of castelike petrifaction and if it allows for a free interplay of its innumerable associations. And the varied parties serve as their forum.

Dictatorships, on the other hand, flourish among amorphous masses. If the natural groupings are not already pulverized, modern autocrats have to create a monolithic atmosphere, within which independent individuality and autonomous group life are submerged under the one-party rule and a "classless society" decrees "equality" before the tyrants. The fatal transformations in modern society—wars, inflation, depressions, and revolutions—prepared the ground and recruited the crucial strata of a dispossessed middle class, a propertyless peasantry, a rootless unemployed, and pugnacious partisans and perennial soldiers of fortune. Such constitute the social raw material of the rising autocracy, which systematically dismantles all free agencies and reduces them to the level of enforced conformity. And this means the end of a functioning democratic party system.

The democratic process has to respect and integrate the numerous special interests within a live society. This creates the intricate and fascinating interrelations between *parties* and *pressure groups,* which are not identical and do not exclude each other; they coexist in continuous interdependence. Parties are not merely the sum of all pressure groups; nor can the public simply dismiss the interests' proper functions by muckraking exposés of lobby activities. For a long time parties and pressure groups have had a bad press, largely because of a mistaken classical approach, which judged politics from the isolated individual's point of view. Once the social group is recognized as a proper starting point, the balance between the representation of homogeneous pressure groups (seeking influence) and the decision-making activities of heterogeneous parties (seeking office and reconciling the diverse forces within the state) becomes a major theme of national politics.

The techniques of interrelations differ in time and space. Pressure groups may try to establish or conquer parties, as has been the case with a number of European parties with strict class alignments or straight nationality backing. They may play the role of a free-floating vote bloc, seeking out the highest bidder, as practiced in Anglo-American patterns; they may extend their influence through divided representation in different parties (*Querverbindungen*); or they may concentrate on minor parties, pressing their special interests.

Whatever their methods, the strength of the "invisible government," as William Allen White called this consequential agglomeration of more than a hundred thousand associations of all types in this country, should not be underestimated. Their power rests largely on their singleness of purpose and their great degree of centralization. This directed appeal to specific concerns has evoked a most active response from the people, as the effective mass organizations of the trade-unions and employers' organizations in the Western world testify, while a deep-seated skepticism concerning the political parties prevails. Unaccountable to the public at large, the economic pressure groups have often overshadowed the political parties and have, in fact, hindered them in their primary task of integrating the special interests into the framework of the national whole. A merely descriptive analysis of what is happening on the political scene is misleading. It seems to confirm the make-believe of politics as the sum total of pressure-group activities. Constructive leadership, while recognizing their claims, must guard against their aggressions and, in the knowledge of their essential role, must lift the demands of the specific interests to the level of national needs. This is where effective parties come in.

This crucial problem of rational integration is not solved by the creation of "economic parliaments." On the contrary, useful though such bodies may be as supplementary advisory councils for national legislation, wherever they are introduced in place of political parliaments, they decree the end of democracy. The "expert" character of occupational representatives limits their authority and naturally suggests the creation above them of a political apex which claims to represent the whole of the nation. Bismarck and Mussolini were not accidentally the champions of a chamber of corporations and the declared enemies of political parties. It is, indeed, through the network of political parties that the place and responsibilities of pressure groups must be circumscribed if the modern society is not to deteriorate into a neo-feudalism of powerful interest groups.

While the correlation of party and pressure groups decides the smooth flow of social forces, the political process is even more dependent on a proper delineation of *party* and *bureaucracy*. Here again the differences between democracy and dictatorship are obvious. It is equally true that the one-party state has in no way solved the dualism of the two forces; nor can democracies claim to have established an airtight distinction between the policy-making party government and the executive civil service. Theirs is a fluid relationship dependent on the continuous interplay of the agencies and, last but not least, on the incalculable informal contacts between the legislative and the executive branches.

The need for bureaucracy in the modern state is unquestionable, and so is the necessity for continuous checks on governmental agencies by the political parties in a democracy. How to combine the expert and the politician, administrative efficiency and democratic control, is a daily test of the ingenuity of political thinking. The British parliamentary rule of the responsible cabinet, the American presidential system, and the continuity of the French permanent civil service (vis-à-vis constant cabinet shifts in a multiparty system)—all suggest different solutions.

Leaving aside popular slogans of "the managerial revolution" and "the dictatorship of bureaucracy," one must recognize that policy formulation in the highly complex and time-pressured present-day state is done largely by the administrative bureaus, while the functions of the political organs are limited primarily to the control, articulation, and communication of public affairs. No simple formula can describe this intertwining process. Each nation has been trying in different fashions to adjust the tenuous relationship between bureaucracy and parties. Much spadework on this aspect of comparative administration is still needed to arrive at a fuller appreciation of possible solutions. To mention only a few outstanding problems: selection, training, ratings, and reforms of civil service; the extent and limitations of patronage appoint-

ments; the right of bureaucrats to participate in party politics and to accept political offices, parliamentary mandates, and cabinet positions; the actual influence of bureau chiefs and permanent undersecretaries in policy formation; the scope of delegated legislation; the administrative functions and control chances of political ministers; the changing attitudes of parties in power and in opposition to governmental agencies—all these much-discussed and controversial issues are indicative of the fact that it remains one of the major tasks of modern democracy to strike a new balance between executive and legislative power.

Confronted with such a challenge, the one-party regime finds itself in an insoluble conflict. The administration must be co-ordinated with the one and only political will and purged of all "undesirable" elements in a much more comprehensive fashion than the natural shift of political appointees indicates in the democratic range of government. (This "cleansing" from "party-book appointees," cynically termed a "restoration of civil service," is in fact a crude guise for securing promised rewards to "deserving partisans.") Yet the same dictators must show gratitude for the bureaucracy's service in bridging the old and the new order. The result is a discrepancy which reveals not only an inner party struggle between moderates and revolutionaries but the even more significant clash between state and party.

Dictatorial systems have varied in their attempts to meet these inherent contradictions. Fascist Italy alone went so far in at least posing the question of the self-dissolution of the Fascist party after its conquest of the state. This very suggestion may be proof of fascism's relative conservatism and state absolutism or of its utter failure to subdue Italy's bureaucracy.

Soviet Russia, on the other hand, decreed the complete abolition of the traditional bureaucracy; and the original Bolshevik theory even predicted the "withering-away" of the state altogether. In reality, Lenin outstripped Peter the Great, and Stalin outdid Ivan the Terrible, in establishing the mammoth totalitarian apparatus in a super-planned society. The results were wavering methods, continuous fluctuations between the radical purge of a managerial class and the creation of a huge amount of red tape, suspicion against the "experts," and unlimited power for the machine. The NEP, the calling of foreign specialists, the praise of the "shock workers" (Stakhanovites), the temporary independence of the Red army officers—all these measures, halfheartedly undertaken and repeatedly reversed, showed the indecision of the Soviet regime in respect to modern management and testified to the fatal failure of a party dictatorship to arrive at a *modus vivendi* with an efficient bureaucracy. Of course, the ruling party could also—and did, indeed —turn such a misfortune into an asset by making the resistant bureaucracy a welcome scapegoat for all the ills of the monolithic order.

The Nazis' seeming success in establishing a monolithic order turned out to be an even greater failure. More revolutionary than fascism and yet more loaded with traditional liabilities than bolshevism, Hitler's Germany tried a weird solution of an artificial separation of state bureaucracy and party machine—a "Dual State." This separation between the party and the state (the one free from official handicaps expressing the "boiling soul of the people," the other not responsible for this "spontaneous outburst") could be clearly played up in an intricate technique of legalizing revolutionary upheavals. It was a useful device to cover up irresponsible party action with "respectable" formal legislation and thus to calm legal-minded people. The master-plan to enroll the "neutral experts" in the strange combination of "arbitrariness and efficiency based on order" was the essence of the Third Reich. But it did not prevent continuous clashes between the two hierarchies of party and bureaucracy. The discrepancies were fully revealed in the critical years of the Nazis' war on the world. After the party's collapse the bureaucracy still had to pay for the insincerities of the "Dual State."

Another critical relationship, especially in dictatorial systems, is found between *party and armed forces*. Democratic parties, by definition, exclude the creation of private armies, recognize the monopoly of military force in the hands of the state, and exercise their power through ballots, not bullets. It is only in their resistance to modern aggressive movements that constitutional parties in Europe have half-heartedly considered the development of a para-military arm. These auxiliary forces, in fact, have not halted the attack against constitutional government but have only epitomized its loss in power and prestige.

The control of the armed forces is a question of survival for modern dictatorship. The military are usually the personification and last stronghold of traditional power, which must be crushed as the only serious threat to established totalitarianism. Moreover, their services are badly needed for a system directed toward war. This fact gives the professional soldier, especially in countries with a military tradition, a preferred position and a prestige far superior to that enjoyed in the "unsoldierly bourgeois democracies." In the beginning the promise of promotion to career-bound, ambitious young officers and the semblance of seeming independence quickly flatter them into submission. Experts are often politically blind and usually raise no objections to having the policy-makers pass on to them the watchword in return for their "neutral services." In most dictatorships, however, it does not take long, especially for the controlling military circles, to realize that their fundamentally rational institu-

tion is worlds apart from the irrational politics of the modern *condottiere* and his irregulars who cannot be held by the hard-and-fast rules of army discipline. They take the world by surprise and manifest the unpredictable daring of the amateur and restless adventurer. Partisan guerrilla warfare and total terror are their weapons, not the carefully calculated and purposely limited campaigns of the professional high command. There is no compromise possible between these two conflicting concepts of strategy in violence. The continuous clashes between the Nazi storm troopers and the Reichswehr, between the Fascist Blackshirts and the Italian army of Marshal Badoglio's brand, between the Soviet political commissars and Red army commanders, between the Peronisti and the Argentine army, all testify to the persistent difficulties of the one-party state in mastering the professional soldier. Success or failure entirely determines the striking power of the dictatorial regime and its persistence, for its militant character is at the roots of the modern totalitarian party.

The militant structure of the dictatorial party is indeed the strikingly novel element in modern political organization. From its beginnings it is, above all, a "fighting league," with its "shirt" movements to "protect" the peaceful meetings of the rising party, its punitive excursions against recalcitrant opponents, its strict hierarchical order and party discipline, its actual fighting of a civil war. Politics becomes a battle of two irreconcilable opponents who are out to win and thereby to destroy the nation's or the classes' arch-enemy.

This permanent revolution has to go on even after the state is conquered—opposition groups must be seized, the party must be kept in warlike preparedness and must be regularly purged. All this militancy at home is only a prelude to the march on the world of the revolutionary party. Every revolution which claims to be more than a mere change of government and which pretends to create a new social order must also stir up neighboring countries and awaken in them a spirit of deep unrest. This quasi-religious "missionarism" knows no frontiers and, with the services of world-shaking ideologies as a moving propaganda arm, tries to recruit soldiers of the new creed in an international civil war. This appeal brings into dramatic focus another element of the modern party—indeed its most critical feature—the international impact of political movements.

## VI. THE INTERNATIONALS OF PARTIES

Political parties, when fully unfolded, operate in three concentric circles. They are based on personal loyalties; they manifest themselves through numerous groupings within a nation; and they reach out beyond state boundaries with their ideologies and their organized "Internationals." There is no Communist monopoly on world-wide planning, spectacularly and noisily though the Third International (Comintern or Cominform, as the case may be) has claimed a unique and unchallengeable position in this global battle of the minds. The color scheme runs the whole gamut of the spectrum. In fact, the basic character of any party may well be determined by its international behavior.

Little reliable material is available on these international ties and reactions; and the less is known, the more make-believe, rumor and mystery enter the speculations of the troubled citizens. Yet in our time—when the frontiers between domestic and international affairs are blurred, and revolutionary upheavals, destroying the stability of a prevailing social structure, are reaching beyond national compounds—political parties have become international forces that must be studied, especially where they shun the broad daylight in their submerged activities and, like an iceberg, allow only a small portion of their power bloc to appear on the global surface.

These world-wide disturbances may be registered and measured through a threefold approach: (1) through an evaluation of prevailing political ideologies; (2) through an analysis of the changing social structures; and (3) through an appraisal of partisan strategies on an international plane.

In order to make them useful yardsticks in the present political labyrinth, ideologies must be reconsidered as to their real meaning. Such an examination will find that the accustomed classifications of political movements in terms of conservatism, liberalism, socialism, communism, etc., are misleading, to say the least. Not only have innumerable combinations (such as national bolshevism, liberal conservatism, conservative socialism, the peoples' democracy) confused the political fronts, but the fundamental concepts themselves have shifted their original meaning under the impact of a radically changing society. One may even doubt the simple contrast between right- and left-wing movements. Originally, "radical" groups, such as the Parti Radical Socialiste, have been pushed to the right under the pressure of newly appearing leftist movements. At the same time frequent attempts at bridging right- and left-wing radical organizations, insignificant though they may be in view of long-range developments, point at similar psychological attitudes even among deadly political opponents.

The proper recognition of these difficulties should not lead to the easy dismissal of the concept of ideology altogether, as is frequently suggested by shortsighted "realists" in politics. On the contrary, ideologies cannot be taken seriously enough in the vacuum of a spiritual crisis when the underlying unity of Christian European traditions is challenged by a counterchurch, when uncompromising conflicts along petrified political fronts are threatening, and when the drives for fundamental reorientation are of primary importance in the final lineup of the peoples—at least, wherever they still remain free to choose.

Ideologies are the key to an understanding of the long-range strategy behind the day-by-day tactics of political movements. The means of international tactics are subservient to the ends of the axiomatic political religion. In such a world setting ideologies have become the most powerful weapon in international politics, and even their ambiguity has proved to be a potent factor in the political orientation or misdirection of a confused world society.

This confusion is to a large extent due to the radical transformations of the major social classes, which naturally have transcended national frontiers. Shifting party lines the world over cannot be understood without a full realization of the crisis of the middle class. It represents as important a hiatus, especially in Western society, as formerly did the collapse of the feudal order which culminated in the French Revolution. The coinciding changes within the proletariat are equally remarkable, whether it takes a turn toward bourgeois-mindedness or toward further class isolation.

The awakening of the peasantry, dormant for centuries, is another factor that may have far-reaching repercussions. The hesitant beginnings and sporadic appearances of a green International deserve careful watching. Last but not least, the rising crucial strata of all dimensions, the unemployed, the dispossessed, the militant irregulars—all have become international types and, as such, influence in some comparable fashion the political fronts in all nations.

In fact, the internationals of all colors have based their strategies on certain expectations of supranational class behavior. The beginnings of an international Christian Democratic movement (whose support by adroit papal diplomacy and its popular arm, the Catholic Action, is difficult to appraise), the resurgence of world liberalism, neo-Fascist rumblings, the revival of the Socialist Second International, the gathering of latent forces among the erstwhile resistance movements, the first international party alignments at Strasbourg's Council of Europe—weak though all these attempts may still be, they can count on a certain response within different nations. These movements ought to be studied not only as potential powers of the future but also in their direct and indirect influence on national policy decisions at the present time. Political campaigns here and abroad have been deeply affected by their global connections. The strategy and outcome of the Italian elections of 1948 and 1952, the Papagos victory in Greece, the Saar vote, the United States presidential elections of 1952, the West German elections of 1953, and the British elections of May, 1955, might have been very different, had it not been for their international implications.

Even bolshevism, despite its watertight isolation, cannot escape the influence from without, especially if it wants to affect this outside world. In this light, the transition from the Comintern to the Cominform may reflect a shrewd and realistic reappraisal of the changing dynamics of modern society. This new strategy, while still insisting on Lenin's fundamental formula of class loyalty above national loyalty, seeks more than a mere proletarian base of recruitment and mobilizes instead— if only for short-run tactical purposes—all elements of unrest within the nations. Now the party appeals, above all, to powerful national ambitions. It is not altogether a new turn. Mao Tse-tung and Ulbricht may take their line from Borodin and Radek of a quarter of a century ago. Revolutionary activists of the war resistance, an awakened peasantry in the shadow of feudal southeastern Europe, China, and southeast Asia, and a deeply disillusioned middle class everywhere can be steered into a new "Fatherland Front" and might be united by the militant appeal of a grass-roots, partisan nationalism, by the fear of American "imperialism," and by the promise of "lasting peace." Indeed, peace becomes a most potent political weapon of Cominform propaganda in a war-weary world. But, while the new Communist combine of the U.S.S.R. with its ring of satellites, as compared with the old Comintern, seemingly allows for greater national autonomy and a more decentralized system of Red internationalism, its main purpose still remains the establishment of a strong arm of Soviet foreign policy. Wherever the new nationalism comes into conflict with Russian interests, it must be denounced in the name of the revolution as a nationalist deviation.

The world revolution has found a fatherland. It gives the Third International a tremendous striking power, which a revolutionary state does not hesitate to exploit unscrupulously. This very connection, however, creates all the liabilities under which communism as the international arm of Russian bolshevism suffers within every nation. The divided loyalty of its members has meant continuous setbacks to the Communist parties within other nations, purges among their leadership, and confusion for their following.

Red imperialism, by no mere accident, experiences increasing tensions within its own camp. Titoism is more than a peripheral phenomenon of an overexpanded superpower, although the fact of geography is not a minor item in this first defection from the Bolshevist creed. Geography may well be counted a deterrent to an extended defiance of Soviet rule among adjacent satellites which can be easily held under the sway of the Red army and of militant bolshevism. The "good neighbors" must present governments "friendly to the Soviet regime."

Indeed, in this age of *international civil war*— cold, lukewarm, or hot as it may be—between the superpower blocs of this bipolar world, political parties are aligned in the name of, or in opposition to, *revolution*. Commonly regarded as a mere internal upheaval, revolution has become a world phenomenon. Its significance is measured by its international effect. Radical upheavals, as all great revolutions are, must be played on an international stage. Every region has become sensitive to the developments of far-distant lands.

The very fact that areas far apart geographically and historically have been pushed together on this shrinking planet has created a revolution altogether different from the stereotypes found in story-books and even in more learned texts. The complexity of this new cataclysm must be fully comprehended in order to appraise the specific nature and aims, the spread and directions, of the contemporary upheaval.

Different ages and different revolutions have become strange contemporaries. They cannot be isolated in neat separate compartments—they fight, they influence, they imitate one another. The contemporary revolutions are inextricably mixed in structure and strategy, in patterns and politics. Still every era has its predominant type; the stronger revolution sets the style.

What is the character of the twentieth-century upheaval? It is neither an objective phenomenon outside human control, such as the interference of God or nature (in the definition of the Renaissance) within world affairs, nor is it the free, subjective human act of heroes standing up against and reversing the natural trend of objective phenomena, as the age of the barricades and the Romantic revolutions saw it. Now the "objective" march of events and the "subjective" deeds of heroic man are interwoven into a new revolution when "the time is ripe" for it and when dynamic leaders can articulate the "revolutionary situation" which otherwise may pass by. There is nothing accidental in its outbreak, no chance in its unfolding, no sudden whim in its success or failure. The modern revolution is a calculated, planned, long-range process and is executed almost to cold scientific exactness by the "professional revolutionaries." No longer can it trust to the appearance of the dynamic dilettante whom the spirit moves to enter meteor-like and to disappear when the excitement of the heroic battle is over. It summons the sober rationality of the patient expert. Organized political parties play a major role in preparing and continuing the permanent revolution. Like modern warfare, its outcome is often decided long before the actual declaration of hostilities. In fact, the carefully planned revolution may well be over but for the shouting at the time of the official outbreak, as the Czech coup of February, 1948, proved so tragically. Moreover, not a single soldier may be needed to move across national frontiers in order to win the major battles in this international civil war. A central revolutionary authority (under whatever name—Politbureau or Central Committee) can direct its orders across frontiers by remote control through the well-established revolutionary pipelines of the disciplined party and its organizational weapons.

Such an upheaval can be defeated by its opponents only if they recognize the changed character of modern revolutions and thus meet the long-range strategies of the Moscow manipulators by equally circumspect planning against the root causes of unrest—in time and with vigor.

The second feature of modern revolution—its confluence of different types of upheavals—is a case in question. Probably the most blatant example of this complex phenomenon is presented in southeast Asia and the Middle East today, where the democratic, the national, and the social revolutions coincide. While the first and the second kind have been the characteristic revolutionary expression of the great world in the nineteenth century, they are now finally evolving in the erstwhile colonial areas. Yet their belated appearance in the Far East, southeast Asia, the Near East, and southeastern Europe makes them contemporaries of the twentieth-century social revolution. And as in earlier upheavals a stronger nationalism had penetrated and conquered the weaker liberal forces, today the dynamic social revolutions easily take command of the budding democratic-national movements and direct them into the stream of the "coming world revolution." This may not be surprising in view of the difficult plight of these newcomers among nations (the effect of long-lasting foreign political and economic domination, of "imported" revolutions, of inexperienced leadership, and of a weak middle-class basis). Such a turn is quickly offered by the master-strategists of the Soviet revolution, who, in accordance with the Leninist-Stalinist theory of imperialism, attempt to co-ordinate both social revolt and colonial liberation and therewith raise the claim to revolutionary world leadership.

Marxism, which within a highly industrialized society has met with remarkable resistance among the "internal proletariat," to use Arnold Toynbee's suggestive phrase, may be more successful with the "external proletariat" of the poverty-stricken masses of agrarian feudalism in underdeveloped areas. (Incidentally, it is significant that Italy and France, least dynamic in their industrial development and still influenced by feudal traditions, have been the only Western powers where Soviet infiltration has made persistent and deep inroads.) Imperialism, until recently a mighty weapon in the hands of distant exploiters, may be turned by rising colonial peoples into an easy scapegoat for all the ills that have befallen them under imperial occupation. The dangerously vacillating game of passing demagogues, like Iran's Mossadegh or Egypt's Naguib and their fanatical "party gangs," must be seen against this sordid background of desperately impoverished economies. No doubt, revolutionary Marxism has been not without success in these areas of awakening rationalism, and this despite the fact that the drive for Westernization has been the clarion call for the "underdeveloped peoples," the U.S.S.R. included. The Point Four program is an attempt at mobilizing and recapturing the imagination of the colonial world and no less that of the United States, which, we must remember, was also born of revolution.

Late may be the hour in this great competition for the support of the new protagonists just passing the threshold of their conscious history. Time is of the essence; yet it may not be ours. "The meeting of the East and West" has been a head-on collision brought about by wars and revolutions. This naturally means cultural dislocations and social tensions. To transplant complex production methods into a primitive economy and to telescope centuries of slow European growth into a short span of one generation presages serious perplexities. To direct the highly excited and equally immature masses will demand responsible leadership. Yet this individual sense of duty to the greater community may well be strange to oriental traditions. Besides, a germane political elite—one which has grown up in rebellion against imperial rule—may not be ready to take on the unaccustomed and different functions of governing. A new generation of leaders will be needed and may be wanting.

The development of a responsible party system could well be the secret of a successful transition from colonialism to political self-rule. India and Pakistan, despite their political "childhood diseases," show certain promising signs. The relatively smooth surrender on the part of the British, especially in the last critical stages, may have something to do with it.

These are but a few of the burning issues faced by the awakening nations and no less by their aged contemporaries. The peoples meet, clash, and conciliate their interests in the moves of organized parties on the international plane everywhere. They are often not sure of their own stand. Prelude or postlude, the intricate choices before them reflect the confluence of different streams of revolution and their consequent confusion. Hesitation and doubt also reflect widespread uncertainties as to the true nature and direction of the revolution in our time. Above all, however, this revolution challenges our ingenuity to articulate workable programs, to organize functioning movements, and to put them to constructive action—weighty responsibilities which rest primarily with the peoples' great intermediaries: the political parties.

# A METHODOLOGICAL CRITIQUE
# OF DUVERGER'S *POLITICAL PARTIES*

## Aaron B. Wildavsky

The high reputation of Maurice Duverger's *Political Parties* rests, for the most part, on the seeming success with which he has achieved his ambitious objective, *i.e.,* to "sketch a preliminary general theory of parties."[1] In view of the increasingly widespread search for variable general theories in the field of political science, a searching review of a study which appears to offer such a theory would seem to be in order.

The primary purpose of this paper is to develop a critique of Duverger's methodology.[2] It is hoped that a more adequate formulation of the tasks facing the student of political parties may emerge from an analysis of the ways in which Duverger relates his concepts and data to the world of politicians and parties. Such an analysis requires no prior resolution of the controversy over the possibility of achieving "a science of politics"; this paper proceeds on the assumption that the pursuit of adequately supported generalizations is one of the most rewarding and compelling tasks of the student of politics.

Since many of the judgments reached here on Duverger's methodology are adversely critical, it should be emphasized that his book contains a wealth of astute investigations, findings, and commentary which merit close attention by students of politics. In terms of the narrower focus adopted here, however, the argument is that methodological inadequacies prevent Duverger from fulfilling, among other things, his stated objective of presenting a general theory of parties.

## I

In order to penetrate to the core of Duverger's methodology, it will be helpful if we list the steps he usually goes through in order to arrive at and justify his central propositions.[3] He proceeds as follows:

1. Through a process of historical evolution, a system, structure, or institution ("X") has come to be dominant, or is at least expected to be present.
2. "X" seems to correspond to "the nature of things." It is "natural."[4]
3. Factor "Y" is associated with X. Where X is, one usually finds Y.
4. Factor Y tends to lead to X. This is established as a working hypothesis.
5. There are exceptions which, however, do not invalidate the working hypothesis since they are the result of special conditions which may be explained through the introduction of other factors.
6. The experience of the countries in which the exceptions are found leads to one of two results:
   (a) The proposition is temporarily modified to include a smaller range of phenomena.
   (b) The exceptions are noted but said not to affect the substance of the original hypothesis.
7. It is eventually found that there are one or more other factors which combine with Y to produce X.
8. The question arises as to whether Y alone can produce X. The answer is both yes and no. Y leads toward X but this only expresses a "basic tendency" which "combines with many others which attenuate it, check it, or arrest it."[5]
9. After discussion of this proposition has been completed, the author continues to utilize the original proposition without qualification or reformulation.

Analysis of this whole procedure reveals four striking logical fallacies:

### A. The Historicist Fallacy

Here, freedom of analysis is limited because of the commitment to an evolutionary-determinist view that in various cultures there are common forces

Reprinted from *The Journal of Politics,* Vol. XXI (1959), pp. 303–318, by permission of the Southern Political Science Association.

The author is indebted to Nelson W. Polsby, Allan P. Sindler, and David B. Truman for numerous valuable suggestions.

operating which must inevitably pass through similar types of experiences. If it becomes obvious that there are deviations in the cycle, the author is reduced to *ad hoc* explanations in order to argue away the discrepancies. (See steps 1 and 2 for the fallacy and 5 through 7 for the consequence.)

## B. The Mystical Fallacy

This refers to the imposition on the data studied of one's personal belief that certain phenomena are "natural." This fallacy takes on a more extreme turn when it is joined to the eminently superstitious impression that phenomena occur in pairs. Either everything is forced into one of two major tendencies, or phenomena which do not conform to a particular dualism are treated as aberrations requiring special explanation. (See step 2 for the fallacy and 7 and 8 for the consequences.)

## C. The And-So Fallacy

According to Robert Merton, this is one "which in effect makes an abstract analysis immune to criticism or disproof by simply attributing all discrepancies between the hypothetical scheme and actual observations to "other factors in the situation." At times there are passing allusions to these factors without serious regard to the complex problems of really incorporating these many additional variables into a disciplined analysis."[6] (For the fallacy see steps 5 through 8.)

## D. The Misplaced Concreteness Fallacy

Merton has applied this term to situations "in which conclusions are dubious because one has failed to acknowledge what is being left out of the analysis and assumes that conclusions apply to the complex situation as it really is rather than to the relations of a few elements in it."[7] (See step 9.)

It is significant that all these fallacies center around the problem of dealing with phenomena that do not fit into a particular pattern. In fallacies A and B the non-coincidence is explained by the introduction of peripheral factors; in fallacy C the exceptions are acknowledged but do not alter the conclusions; and in fallacy D the exceptions are simply not acknowledged for purposes of the analysis.

The precise nature of these fallacies may be more sharply delineated by considering a set of related propositions in which they are found. On the principle of meeting Duverger where he least resembles a straw man, his most confident generalizations have been selected for study. On pages 215 and 216 he asserts,

None the less the two-party system seems to correspond to the nature of things, that is to say that po-

litical choice usually takes the form of a choice between two alternatives. . . . This is equivalent to saying that the centre does not exist in politics: there may well be a Centre party but there is no centre tendency, no centre doctrine. . . . The natural movement of societies tends toward the two party system; obviously it may be countered by tendencies in the opposite direction; these we shall attempt to define below.[8]

The author is immediately involved in both the mystical and historicist fallacies. He must treat multi-partism as a deviation from his arbitrarily selected norm—arbitrary because he has no indices which would enable him to be confident that there is a trend toward bi-partism.

At this point Duverger offers us the most sweeping and best supported generalization at his disposal:

The simple-majority single-ballot system favours the two-party system. Of all the hypotheses that have been defined in this book, this approaches the most nearly perhaps to a true sociological law. An almost complete correlation is observation between the simple-majority single-ballot system and the two-party system: dualist countries use the simple-majority vote and simple-majority vote countries are dualist. The exceptions are very rare and can generally be explained as the result of special conditions.[9]

Failure to incorporate these "special conditions" into the analysis leads to the and-so fallacy.

The difficulties created by the considerable number of exceptions to his "law" lead the author to temporarily restrict its scope. The case of Canada, he asserts

. . . in common with the examples provided by Sweden and Denmark, makes it possible to define the limits of the influence of the simple-majority single-ballot system: it tends to the creation of a two-party system inside the individual constituency; but the parties opposed may be different in different areas of the country. The simple-majority system therefore makes possible the creation of local parties or the retreat of national parties to local positions.[10]

Having restricted his hypothesis, Duverger broadens it again by explaining how local bi-partism is converted into national bi-partism. But in order to do this, he is unable to fall back upon his single factor, the electoral system, but must admit new elements outside the scope of his original proposition. He declares:

None the less, the increased centralization of organization within the parties and the consequent tendency to see political problems from the wider, national standpoint tend of themselves to project on to the entire country the localized two-party system brought about by the ballot procedure: however, the true effect of the simple-majority system is limited to local bi-partism.[11]

Thus an entirely new factor, centralized party organization, must be present before national bi-partism may be said to result from the simple-majority system. But even this statement is far too simple. The cart has been put before the horse. If this argument were followed to its conclusion it would have to account for increased party centralization on the basis of still other factors. It assumes that the parties are already national organizations and then, after the fact, argues that local parties tend to become national parties.

The set of propositions concludes with the following statement:

> The electoral system works in the direction of bipartism; it does not necessarily and absolutely lead to it in spite of all obstacles. The basic tendency combines with many others which attenuate it, check it, or arrest it. With these reserves we can nevertheless consider that dualism of parties is the "brazen law" (as Marx would have said) of the simple-majority single-ballot electoral system.[12]

Nonetheless, Duverger, wedded to the fallacy of misplaced concreteness, refers to his "sociological law" without regard to the critical limitations he has recognized as restricting its applicability.

"Brazen law" would appear to be an apt description of one which admits of so many possible exceptions. While the author is justified in stressing the tenuous nature of his conclusions in a new and difficult field, he cannot avoid the responsibility of formulating them with sufficient exactness so that they can be fairly tested. At the very least, validation requires that Duverger state the possible conditions under which his hypothesis could theoretically be disproved—a difficult task since any one of the many possible exceptions he allows may be explained away as resulting from special circumstances.

## II

We have seen that Duverger's methodological fallacies involve him in extremely difficult situations, most of which concern the problem of accounting for the multitude of "exceptions" to his propositions. His fault does not lie in the inability to propound explanations to cover the exceptions (a task at which he is extremely creative), but in following methods of analysis which give rise to so many exceptions in the first place. There appear to be three fundamental reasons which help to explain why the "exceptions problem" is so acute.

The first reason is that Duverger's commitment to an evolutionary-deterministic theory makes it difficult for him to fulfill the requirements of scientific statement. He can rarely say that under "Y" conditions "X" will appear. Instead, he is often in the position of expecting a specific phenomenon to appear in the present historical stage, and must resort to factors outside the main scheme of analysis in order to account for the failure of reality to

measure up to his expectations. It is possible to become so enamored of a theoretical scheme that one fails to maintain adequate contact with the data.

A second major source of difficulty arises from Duverger's implicit rejection of a multi-causal approach. Perhaps the basic assumption underlying *Political Parties* is that political party phenomena can be largely explained through the independent use of three variables: party structures, party systems (the number of parties), and the electoral system. "Other factors" such as social and economic structure, national history, culture, institutional traditions, geography, climate, and so on are either rejected, neglected, or relegated to peripheral roles. In a way, Duverger is like the proverbial atheist in the foxhole *i.e.,* he does not call for outside help until he gets into trouble. He utilizes his single causes for as long as they are at all serviceable. It is only when they prove incapable of encompassing the many-sided face of reality that he brings in any number of other factors to help him out of the difficulties created by his method.[13]

As a consequence of his methodological errors, Duverger is led to disregard a serious search for other "causes." This may be illustrated by presenting the bare outline of a different approach to the previously considered problem of accounting for the existence of bi-partism. The first step would be to free oneself of the notion that the two-party system is "natural," an action which directs one's attention to a more searching look at the data. One salient fact is that the two-party systems in America and Great Britain are, for the most part, alliances of predominantly one-party areas.

The next task would be to attempt to explain why some areas give preponderant support to one party while others more evenly divide their allegiance. The type of ballot which is common to both one and two-party areas cannot provide the explanation. One possibility might be that one-party areas evidence a considerably higher degree of homogeneity in respect to a specified list of factors than two-party areas. It would then be necessary to attempt to construct a series of indices which would provide an accurate means of determining the level at which diversity or homogeneity in regard to these factors produce one or two-party systems. One might speculate, for example, that the degree of one-partism might depend upon the historical, cultural, racial, and other conditions under which the notion of an opposition party is legitimitized or made socially permissible. Without going any further it becomes apparent that no single-factor explanation is likely to prove adequate.

Lastly, the difficulties inherent in single-factor analysis are compounded by the implicit use of a key single-factor—social class behavior—which, on his own terms, Duverger cannot adopt. According to his own statement,

Party systems are the product of many complex factors, some peculiar to individual countries, others general. Amongst the first may be cited tradition and history, social and economic structure, religious beliefs, racial composition, national rivalries, and so on. . . . Among the factors of general application the electoral regime will be particularly studied in this book.[14]

If social and economic structures are peculiar to individual countries, then there are no possible general theoretical structures which can accomodate these factors. If one abandons the assumption that party systems are in some significant way dependent upon these factors, one must largely confine oneself to comparing surface elements such as the type of ballot, the number of parties, and the type of organization. Despite his frequent use of class terminology, Duverger has chosen the latter alternative.

Yet, while his own assumptions are such as to prohibit transnational generalizations, Duverger's lengthy discussion of oligarchy in government, and the rationale behind many of his other propositions, implicitly presuppose the world-wide uniformity of class behavior. Two typical quotations will serve to illustrate the point:

The choice of the branch by Socialist parties was perfectly natural. They were the first to try and organize the masses, to give them a political education, and to recruit from them the working-class elites. The branch corresponds to this triple requirement. In contrast to the caucus, the middle-class organ of political expression, it seemed the normal organ of political expression for the masses. . . . The middle class, whether it be upper, lower, or intermediate, is not fond of collective action; moreover it thinks (and here it is wrong) . . . that it does not need the teaching given at branch meetings. . . .[15]

The deepest significance of political parties is that they tend to the creation of new elites, and this restores to the notion of representation its true meaning, the only real one. All government is by nature oligarchic but the origins and the training of the oligarchs may be very different and these determine their actions.[16]

If social, economic, historical, and racial factors are unique to each country, then the class structure, dependent at least on some of these factors, will be different in each country, and so will the "origins and training of the oligarchs" that "determine their actions." Without special knowledge of each country it becomes impossible to predict what the behavior or psychology of a social class might be like, or how its oligarchs will act.

It is undoubtedly difficult to resist the temptation of concentrating on materials that are easily accessible and manipulated to the detriment of others which may be equally, if not more, significant. Perhaps Duverger meant to say not that social and economic factors were unique, but rather that he was then unable to describe them.

## III

*Political Parties* is divided into two parts. Part one is devoted to Party Structure and part two to Party Systems. It is therefore possible to construct two classificatory systems which will accommodate many of the propositions in each part. Classification I (Types of Party Structure) is based on Duverger's division of parties into three structural types—the cadre, mass, and devotee parties. Classification II (Party and Electoral Systems) is based on the virtually complete coincidence, in Duverger's work, between countries with both a two-party system and a simple-majority ballot on the one hand, and those having a multi-party system with either proportional representation (PR) or the second-ballot simple-majority system on the other. ". . . [T]he party system and the electoral system," Duverger declares, "are two realities that are indissolubly linked and even difficult sometimes to separate by analysis. . . ."[17] Both classifications are composed of a cluster of elements, representing propositions, which form a definable pattern. The classifications are presented in Tables 1 and 2.

Duverger describes the essential nature of his work in the following terms:

Our schema [referring to classification I] remains, moreover, very approximate and vague: it describes tendencies rather than any clear-cut distinction. More exactly, it is based upon a coincidence between several categories of individual differences, relating to the basic party elements, their general articulation, the organization of membership, the degrees and kind of participation, the nomination of leaders, the part played by parliamentary representatives, and so on. The essential aim of the investigation that follows lies in defining these basic distinctions with the maximum precision.[18]

Typical propositions of this kind are the following: ". . . [T]he essential fact is the general coincidence in practice of the caucus system with weak articulation, of the branch system with strong articulation, and of the cell and militia systems with very strong articulation."[19] Or, ". . . [P]arties founded on branches are more centralized than those founded on caucuses."[20] In this manner each element in the classification may, directly or indirectly, be related to the others.

It would be safe to say that on the basis of his research Duverger has concluded that the various elements in a particular classification are associated with one another. When one is found in a particular place and time, so is the other. There is some question in my mind, however, as to whether he wishes the reader also to infer a causal connection between the elements. Since an attempt to demonstrate causality would often involve him in serious, if not insoluble, difficulties, we shall assume that only an association of the elements is intended.[21]

Several critical questions emerge at this point. Are these correlations, in fact, high and positive? And are the classifications derived from them useful for the comparative study of political parties? Do we have a unified description of the comparative functioning of political parties or two disparate, essentially unconnected ones? What is it that is being compared?

Any proposed general theory of political parties embodied in a classificatory system must meet a number of requirements. Intimate knowledge of this theory should enable the possessor to anticipate what he will find in a specified system of political parties. Yet Duverger's classifications are so narrow that they do not even apply to parties which have long been the subject of inquiry by political scientists.[22]

The British Conservative Party, for example, is

## TABLE 1—Types of Party Systems: Classification I

| Type of party: | Cadre Party | Mass Party | Devotee Party | |
| --- | --- | --- | --- | --- |
| Basic organizational units | Caucus | Branch | Cell | Militia |
| Class nature of membership | Middle-class | Working class | Working class | Middle class |
| Ideological direction | Conservative and center | Socialist | Communist | Fascist |
| Articulation | Weak | Strong | Very strong | |
| Centralization | Weak | Strong | Very strong | |
| Discipline | Weak | Strong | Very strong | |
| Leadership | Oligarchic | Very oligarchic | Authoritarian | |
| Elites | Traditional | Developed by party | Developed by party | |
| Number of members | Small | Very large | Large | |
| Enthusiasm of members | Low | High | Very high | |
| Range of activity | Strictly political | Entire political and community life | Entire political, personal, and community life | |
| Duration of activity | Seasonal | All year | All year | |
| Importance of doctrine | Low | High | Very high | Low |

## TABLE 2—Party and Electoral Systems: Classification II

| The number of parties and the type of ballot: | Two-party system favors simple majority system and vice versa | Multi-party system favors PR and vice versa | Multi-party system favors second-ballot system and vice versa |
| --- | --- | --- | --- |
| Influence upon the number of parties | Changes 3 to 2, retains 2 | Retains multi-partism or increases number | Retains multi-partism |
| Growth of minor parties | Hinders | Aids | Aids |
| Frequency of alliances | Rare | Common | Common |
| Sensitivity to sudden, deep changes in opinion | Low | High | High |
| Distortion of electoral opinion as reflected in national legislature | High | Low | High |
| Political differences | Decreased | Increased | Indeterminate |
| Degree of demagogy | Low | High | High |
| Influence of extra-parliamentary party over candidates | High or low | High with list voting | Low if there are small constituencies |
| Antithesis of opinion | Largely coincident | Mutually exclusive | Mutually exclusive |
| Influence upon geographic location of opinion | Accentuates local differences | Strengthens national uniformity | Indeterminate |

far too centralized and disciplined to fall under the heading of a cadre party, far too democratic to be a devotee party, and far too middle-class in composition to qualify as a mass party. American parties, while they have mass memberships of a sort and generally meet in branches, reveal many of the characteristics of cadre parties. But Carmine De-Sapio is hardly a member of a "traditional" elite and not all party organizations recruit their candidates from "outstanding people." The Soviet Communist Party, although undoubtedly a devotee party, draws less than half its membership from the "working class."

A second requirement of a theory of political parties is that it account for the occurrence and frequency of the range of phenomena which it covers. Under what circumstances do they appear or fail to appear? Yet all we are told about the cadre, mass, and devotee parties is that they represent different historical stages and grew out of the development of mass suffrage.[23] Among other things, this fails to explain the contemporaneous existence of these three types of party, or why suffrage reform did not bring a mass party to the United States, or why the Bolsheviks were able to create a devotee party before a mass party existed.

The essential problem is that Duverger does not present us with indices by which a trend of any sort could be established. When he sees a trend this means that things look to him as if they will turn out in a certain way, always allowing for exceptions, although he does not offer an explicit statement of probabilities.

Finally, a general theory of political parties must permit the making of distinctions between institutions and practices which have identical or similar labels and yet manifest significantly different behaviors. Does the term "political party" describe the same types of behavior in every country? Unfortunately, Duverger's classifications hide these differences instead of revealing them. The Spanish Falange and the Soviet Communist Party are both single parties which do not permit an organized opposition; but once having said this, the differences between them begin to loom larger than the similarities. Australia, Denmark and France all have multi-party systems, but the Australian and Danish versions resemble the British two-party system far more than they do the French.

It is difficult, indeed, to apply Duverger's typology as a whole to any particular party system. If we compare classifications I and II, we find two systems of classification, both dealing with political party phenomena, neither of which appears connected to the other nor in contradiction to the other. Essentially, they just talk right past each other. There are numerous exceptions, as we have seen, to most of the elements within each separate classification. These exceptions build up to a multi-tude of deviations for the classification as a whole. Each classification thus becomes merely a collection of elements, sometimes, in some instances, found together, with no particularly compelling reason evident for believing they belong in the same place. Instead of extending the range of application, an attempt to put the two classifications together would actually narrow it by increasing the number of departures from reality. The end result would bear little resemblance to living political parties. It may be that Duverger intended to use his classifications for purposes other than those which have been mentioned here. If so, he has neglected to tell us what they are.

Duverger has most clearly stated and defended his approach in the following passage:

> This work starts from a basic contradiction: it is at the present time impossible to give a valid description of the comparative functioning of political parties; yet it is essential to do so. We find ourselves in a vicious circle: a general theory of parties will eventually be constructed only upon the preliminary work of many profound studies; but these studies cannot be truly profound so long as there exists no general theory of parties. For Nature answers only when questioned and we do not yet know what questions the subject demands. . . . The aim of this book is to break out of the circle and to sketch a preliminary general theory of parties, vague, conjectural, and of necessity approximate, which may yet serve as a basis and guide for detailed studies.[24]

Few would dispute the advisability of guiding future studies by reference to a viable general theory of parties, even though it might not yet be fully formed and might have less precision than we would like. But if this theory proves illusory or inapplicable to the "real world," such a strategy is likely to divert attention from the complex to the simple, and thus lead to less rather than greater profundity. The thesis of this paper has been that Duverger's methodological errors make it inadvisable to use *Political Parties* "as a basis and guide for detailed studies."[25]

## IV

In *Political Parties,* Maurice Duverger raises fundamental questions of methodology and theory in the study of political parties, and perhaps other political institutions as well. A cardinal virtue of his work has been to direct attention to a vital query—what is the best way to study political parties? Specifically, what factors ought to receive primary consideration in the attempt to derive significant generalizations about political parties?

The contribution which this paper can hope to make is, at best, largely a negative one. *Political*

*Parties* has had to be analyzed on its own terms because of the apparent lack of any superior theory or typology of political parties with which to compare it. Nor is it now possible to present a list of factors which, if properly utilized, would necessarily lead to the development of such a theory. Although it might be wise to study political parties as part of the pattern of the larger society in which they are implicated, there could certainly be no guarantee that the pattern of each society would not turn out to be unique. Such a conclusion might suggest that political parties need to be studied not according to their surface forms, but according to their consequences for the societies of which they are a part. It may be that uniformities are to be found in the functions performed rather than in the party institutions themselves. But until promise is dignified by performance we cannot be certain that this approach would succeed where others have failed.

That always pertinent query, "Where do we go from here?" cannot be answered in this paper except as the elimination of some alternatives helps to channel a fruitful inquiry. All that may legitimately be said here is that there are certain basic requirements of a theory and/or typology of political parties; that the commission of various types of methodological fallacies prevents these requirements from being met; and that the utilization of surface factors such as the number of parties, the type of ballot, and the type of party structure do not appear to provide the kind of propositions which would aid in the development of such a theory.

## NOTES

1. Maurice Duverger, *Political Parties, Their Organization and Activity in the Modern State,* translated by Barbara and Robert North (London, New York, 1954) p. xiii. Duverger notes on page xvii that "for this first edition in English I have completely revised and, where possible, brought up to date the text and figures of the original edition published in France in 1951."

2. For a detailed rebuttal of many of the substantive conclusions reached by Duverger, see G. E. Lavau, *Partis politiques et réalités sociales: Contribution à une étude réaliste des partis politiques* (Paris, 1953). There is a preface by Maurice Duverger. Whereas Lavau denies the possibility of a general theory of parties, this paper is directed toward elucidating the requirements which such a theory would have to meet.

3. A proposition is here defined as a statement involving two or more variables which advances some description of reality that is, theoretically, at least, capable of verification.

4. Duverger, *op. cit.,* p. 215.

5. *Ibid.,* p. 228.

6. P. F. Lazarsfeld and R. K. Merton, "Friendship as a Social Process," in M. Berger, T. Abel, and C. Page (eds.), *Freedom and Control in Modern Society* (New York, 1954), pp. 61–62. Merton is credited with these comments.

7. *Ibid.,* p. 62.

8. The passages quoted above have been carefully checked against the original French edition of the book in order to make certain that the translation was faithful to the text.

9. Duverger, *op. cit.,* p. 217. (Italics in the original.)

10. *Ibid.,* p. 223. Duverger inserts a footnote after the word "constituency" which reads: "Except for freak candidates with no chance of success. In Canada, out of 848 candidates in 1949, 159 achieved a combined total of only 6.9% of the poll."

11. *Ibid.* At best, however, Duverger's law argues for the discouragement of local multi-partism rather than necessarily for the maintenance of local bi-partism. Communities with a wide range of similar demographic characteristics may well find sufficient political expression through a single party.

12. *Ibid.,* p. 228.

13. The attractions of a streamlined theory in which all puzzling phenomena can be explained by reference to a single factor are undoubtedly great. Such a theory would have a certain boldness and *élan* regrettably lacking in more complex and mundane formulations. But if only a multi-causal approach will account for the data, either the explanation will prove unsatisfactory or other factors will have to be introduced, so to speak, through the back door. A great deal depends upon whether one looks upon "other factors" as life-preservers or part of everyday equipment.

14. Duverger, *op. cit.,* pp. 203–204. *Political Parties* is divided into two books.

15. *Ibid.,* pp. 25–26.

16. *Ibid.,* p. 425.

17. *Ibid.,* p. 204.

18. *Ibid.,* p. 3.

19. *Ibid.,* p. 47.

20. *Ibid.,* p. 23.

21. Duverger's method may be represented in abstract form as follows: X is associated with Y. How do we know? Because Y occurs when X does (at the same time, in the same place). How do we know? Because Y is associated with X.

22. Deliberately omitted from this brief list are, in Duverger's words, the "[s]everal types of parties [which] remain outside this general schema; first of all the Catholic and Christian Democrat parties, which occupy a position more or less midway between the old parties and the Socialist parties; next the Labour Parties, constituted on a basis of Trade Union and Co-operative Societies, according to a pattern of 'indirect structure' which will require special analyses; the Agrarian parties, whose diversity of organization is very great and whose role remains limited to a few countries; and lastly, the archaic and pre-historic types of party that will not be discussed here, and that are to be met within certain countries in the East, in the Middle East, in Africa, and in Latin America. . . ." Duverger, *op. cit.,* p. 3. The necessity of a special typology of direct and indirect structure reduces the usefulness of the general schema.

23. See Duverger, *ibid.,* pp. xxiii-xxxvii and pp. 1–3.

24. *Ibid.,* p. xiii.

25. For a view fundamentally opposed to the conclusions in this paper, see Engelmann's estimate that "Duverger's method is highly useful for analytical and comparative purposes. . . . Comparison and theory are not the same; but, in attempting to give us a theory, Duverger does give us excellent tools for comparison.

His systematic treatment of party systems and especially of party structures [is] the pilot work for future stasiological [political party] studies." Frederick C. Engelmann, "A Critique of Recent Writings on Political Parties." *Journal of Politics,* XIX (August, 1957), p. 433. See also the relevant literature cited in his article.

# THE PARTY IN MASS SOCIETY

## Otto Kirchheimer

Comparative politics as a discipline has been content too long with mere juxtapositions of isolated governmental systems. This critical view is shared by numerous students who, either individually or in teams, have applied considerable energy and resources in recent years to the drawing of blueprints for a truly comparative approach. To map out blueprints is one thing, and to put them into effect another; the latter—to judge from a recent symposium, *Modern Political Parties,* explicitly subtitled *Approaches to Comparative Politics*[1]—turns out to be a more difficult enterprise. Aiming at outlining a comparative framework, Professor Neumann and his highly qualified collaborators have presented findings on a great number of parties on both sides of our contemporary ideological and institutional curtain. Their survey, partly brilliant and inspiring, and partly disappointingly sketchy, follows throughout the traditional technique of presentation by countries or groups of countries. The reader is reminded of a *roman-fleuve* when watching the seemingly unending parade of problem categories and ideological or institutional relationships which, according to Professor Neumann's interesting concluding chapter, must be elucidated if party ways and operations are to be adequately understood. However, a *roman-fleuve,* even though it may have its advantages as a model, easily becomes an end in itself if it is not drawn to an intellectual center of gravity. The absence of such a center of gravity regrettably impairs the usefulness of Professor Neumann's summation. What remains is a comprehensive catalog of all applicable nomenclatures, with ample warnings against less fruitful approaches, and an account of all combinations of factors effectively determining

integration or disintegration of party systems. Surely, some of the outlined correlations must be more meaningful than others for a typology of parties in the modern era. Should it not be possible to arrive at a modicum of generalizations of the parties' role without instantly subjecting such judgments to qualifications or synchronizing discordant and asynchronous factual situations?

To some extent the job has been simplified, since by now most observers agree that the political systems of preindustrial society must be clearly distinguished from those of our own industrialized world. Reflecting two different stages of social and economic development, this points to rather obvious conclusions. More complex problems arise from the distinction between totalitarian and democratic systems, which Neumann—before entering the inevitable qualification—terms "the fundamental cleavage of our time."[2] But then again, some of the totalitarian "political cultures"—to borrow a concept coined by Almond[3] and meant to encompass both action and ideology—are characteristic of societies in transition from an earlier preindustrial stage to a fully developed industrial civilization. There ancient practices of despotism blend with paraphernalia of systems based on present-day patterns of technology and communication. Other totalitarian "political cultures" display, in varying degrees, traits of industrial society; the latter's impact on both material civilization and the mind of the twentieth-century individual has had an equal share in the rise of the two undeniably modern political systems: mass democracy and totalitarianism. Segregated in academic routine, both would more profitably be studied as interlinked manifestations of mass society, as Neumann at least sets out to do.

Everybody agrees that the role of the state has undergone considerable change. This crucial fact

Reprinted from *World Politics,* Vol. X (October, 1957–July, 1958), pp. 289–294, with permission of the publishers.

calls, nonetheless, for added emphasis. While it is true that democratic mass society may offer the individual vastly enhanced means of judicial defense, the functions of the democratic system of government—in accordance with the people's radically changed expectations—have become almost as all-embracing as those of the totalitarian state. The democratic government also taxes, defends, educates, and plans; it sets up the framework of man's material and—often beyond the call of duty—his intellectual existence. Cumulation of functions has an inevitable counterpart in centralized decision-making; deliberative assemblies are reduced to ill-defined positions, exposed to and threatened by the need for unifying administrative and political action, even where concentration of authority is not hastened by specific ideological preferences or hostilities.

Though the pace is not uniform, this development is not restricted to countries, like Italy or France, which have been affected by the clash of totalitarian and democratic structures. A recent instructive Belgian discussion by administrators, political practitioners, and university professors, *Aspects du régime parlementaire belge,*[4] emphasized the workings of phenomena detrimental to effective legislative action and budgetary controls; this "gliding," which so often turns parliamentary participation in the establishment of the budget into a "mere formality," was described as all-pervasive. Interaction of government and parties, which brings together decision-makers and engineers of consensus, can dispense with the need for the intercession of parliament. French experience may even lead to the conclusion that party control of political decisions is weakened rather than strengthened when decision-making is filtered through the agency of parliamentary bodies.

This tends to bear out Neumann's thesis that the party in modern mass democracy has been taking over an ever-increasing area of commitments and responsibilities. Regrettably, however, Neumann fails to analyze the major patterns of government-party interactions. With respect to both party structures and party-government interplay, there is a substantial difference between parties that initiate, purvey, and receive services and obligations while government agencies are confined to purely technical functions, and parties that merely strive to impose alternative claims on governmental bodies that retain an appreciable range of discretion in the adjudication and balancing of conflicting claims. At this point the ways of mass democracy diverge from those of totalitarian systems. The totalitarian party composes and adjudicates, or, if need be, suppresses conflicting claims according to program and goals; once a decision is rendered, an all-out effort will be made to get administrative implementation. Failure to implement decisions may on occasion be merely deplored as the result of untoward circum-

stances or "objective" weaknesses, but it will be punished as treason and/or cause a reversal of policy whenever it assumes the proportions of concerted action on the part of the governed. Conversely, mass democracy separates the political formula—outcome of party competition and pressure—from the executive decision. The parties lay siege to the government, but in the process of execution the government and its corps of technicians and administrators—*pouvoir minoritaire*, in Maurice Hauriou's parlance—filter and neutralize the political formula, making it objective. In the event of any discrepancy between the actual result and the parties' notion of what is desirable, the parties remain free to renew their assault and call out their shock troops—organized interests—or, less frequently and less vigorously, their foot soldiers—the distant electorate.

Will the administration give in, and, if so, at what point? There still remains here an area of uncertainty and choice. Moreover, there is the often emphasized fact of interparty competition, be it the traditional clash of pro-government and opposition forces or a tug-of-war inside a coalition of two or more parties. These facts preserve a certain distance between party and government, and prevent their freedom-obliterating amalgamation. The role of democratic mass parties as purveyors of material services for their supporters has dwindled considerably, and they no longer perform a paramount part as custodians of ideological traditions.[5] Instead, they—among others—register claims and press or arrange for priorities. It would be erroneous, though, to view them as automatic transmission-belts between popular will and governmental action; democratic mass parties as a rule retain some freedom of choice, although its extent varies from case to case. This freedom is bound to be the greater, the more variegated the gamut of group interests and the weaker the citizens' penchant for political as distinct from social action within the framework of modern mass society's welfare state.

Political signals emanating from the "people," spellbound by mass-media persuasion that is not primarily of political origin, are largely inconclusive and frequently inchoate. The voter may cease to connect the casting of his ballot with any political action. One then encounters the "protest party," which symbolizes attitudes of the hour rather than patterns of action to be realized in a foreseeable future, or the most extreme case of an "integration party," which espouses a given political system to the point of shedding its identity as an autonomous grouping of men pursuing specific objectives. Neither is a sufficient vehicle of democratic self-determination; both the uncontrollable influence of outstanding individuals and the danger zone of relationships between political leadership and the military, which Professor Neumann sees as the structural hazards of totalitarian societies, involve generalized questions of equilibrium in democratic mass societies as well. Structural hazards in the democratic system come to light whenever and wherever the political parties—this unique link between the mass society and its executive and administrative staffs—lose vitality and sense of mission. To perform its part a political party needs an atmosphere of constant approval and/or indignation from the ranks no less than it needs a dynamic contest with the bureaucracy and the military for mutual recognition and acceptance. It will succumb to paralysis when doomed to deal continually with an unresponsive clientele and overambitious administrative and army personnel.

The endurance potential of a mass party finds its expression in the degree of spontaneity that pervades the relationship between followers and "apparatus." For the totalitarian mass party the gulf opens with the seizure of governmental power, when the visions of its combative days are banished from the workaday reality of governing. Prior to the actual exercise of governmental power, spontaneity is an inestimable asset, even when carefully bridled for the sake of tactical maneuverability. Once the party is enthroned, spontaneity becomes ambiguous. Thorough bureaucratization of the party machine, as described by Joachim Schultz, in *Der Funktionär in der Einheitspartei*,[6] in respect of East Germany's governing "Socialist Unity Party," is essential for enforcing conformity in thought processes and adjustment to omnipresent controls. Estrangement from the people is manifestly common to all ruling Communist parties, if not necessarily to all of their former Fascist rivals. Under these conditions, rigid surveillance of the party rank and file may well be the basic condition of survival in a thoroughly hostile environment. On the other hand, spontaneity of action in the party's relation with the masses is urged. It is a fixed element of official ideology; it permeates the party's stereotyped jargon. The party cannot renounce it as a yardstick for the officeholder's performance, even though it may be fully aware of the degree of self-deception involved.

If spontaneity is doomed as an attribute of a totalitarian revolutionary party in power, what about the democratic mass party? Can it discard spontaneity, and rely solely on rational appraisal of interests and support from institutional backers, the services of the machine, and the election-day performance of the voter? Can politics be taken, in the manner suggested by Tingsten from Swedish experience,[7] as a kind of applied statistics, where elections serve as a census and political preferences are recorded with that same air of indifferent compliance with which one would state age, occupation, or civil status? If politics were nothing but the rational ordering of calculable claims of a limited number of participants of fairly well-known disposi-

tions and propensities, and if the rule of nonsubstitutability of functions formulated by Almond for the Anglo-American political culture amounted to more than an interesting though rather problematic hypothesis, spontaneity would indeed have but a tiny place in the political arena. But so long as there is strife between societies and so long as the effects of such strife limit the chance of a rational ordering of domestic concerns, democratic mass parties are confronted with the crucial choice either of abdicating in the face of perilous alternatives or of mustering spontaneous, possibly unrewarded, support sufficient for the attainment of specific objectives emerging from intended, organized, and continuously sustained political action.

Against this background, what are the prospects of comparative studies? Specific institutional problems—what the comparative blueprinters, following Robert K. Merton's terminology, are apt to call narrow-gauge problems—such as election procedures or the potentialities of courts in regard to safeguarding freedom or federalism, involve too many variables attendant on national structures and specific situations to permit conclusive inferences from comparative inquiry. George Lavau illustrated the point in his convincing criticism[8] of Maurice Duverger's endeavor[9] to link various national peculiarities in political organization and action to differences in electoral systems; and any author grappling with Duverger's systematization in the light of his own national political configuration will add his basket of qualifications and exceptions, underscoring the intellectual challenge of Duverger's approach but also the scarcity of results it may yield.

Outside the pale of traditional institutional devices there is the world of mass communication, with the action of political parties a substantial component. Here the needs and drives of society constantly blaze new trails that are only to a minor extent within the reach of regulatory action. While the remnants of political internationals languish, modern industrial society, this terrible *simplificateur,* creates global institutions for both expressing and manipulating mass aspirations. Is this the beginning or the end of comparative study? A great deal remains to be learned at the international level about preindustrial societies. In confronting the wide range of political formulae offered by more modern societies, it is likely that, remnants of former societal structures notwithstanding, we shall be dealing increasingly with a variety of manifestations of *one* societal structure. This would call for a critical analysis of what this society requires to satisfy the vital needs of the inhabitants, and—a quite different story—how such requirements are met in its everyday functioning.

## NOTES

1. Sigmund Neumann, ed., *Modern Political Parties: Approaches to Comparative Politics,* Chicago, University of Chicago Press, 1956.

2. *Ibid.,* p. 403.

3. Gabriel A. Almond, "Comparative Political Systems," *Journal of Politics,* XVIII, No. 3 (August, 1956), pp. 396 ff.

4. G. Ciselet, *et al., Aspects du régime parlementaire belge,* Brussels, Les Editions de la Librairie Encyclopédique, 1956.

5. See my remarks in "The Waning of Opposition in Parliamentary Regimes," *Social Research,* XXIV, No. 2 (Summer, 1957), p. 127.

6. Joachim Schultz, *Der Funktionär in der Einheitspartei: Kaderpolitik und Bürokratisierung in der SED* (Schriften des Instituts für Politische Wissenschaft, Vol. 8), Stuttgart und Düsseldorf, Ring Verlag, 1956.

7. H. Tingsten, "Stability and Vitality in Swedish Democracy," *Political Quarterly,* XXVI, No 2 (April–June, 1955), pp. 146–158.

8. G. E. Lavau, *Partis politiques et réalités sociales,* Cahiers de la Fondation Nationale des Sciences Politiques, No. 38, Paris, 1953.

9. Maurice Duverger, *Les partis politiques,* Paris, 1951.

# A CRITIQUE OF RECENT WRITINGS ON POLITICAL PARTIES

## Frederick C. Engelmann

Stasiology, the science of political parties,[1] has advanced greatly during the present decade. Before 1951, writings in this field had been confined largely to histories of parties, accounts of their electoral fortunes, and discussions of their programs and ideologies. Only two works by Western scholars, both written early in this century, stood out as significant works in analytical stasiology: M. I. Ostrogorski's *Democracy and the Organization of Political Parties*[2] and Robert Michels' *Political Parties: A Sociological Study of the Oligarchical Tendencies of Modern Democracy.*[3]

The development of analytical stasiology was propelled by the appearance, in 1951, of Maurice Duverger's *Les partis politiques.*[4] This work with its categorization of party organizations and party systems, the critiques elicited by the book, and monographs that developed alongside, most of them independently of Duverger's effort, caused Sigmund Neumann to write, in 1954: "Only of late, and at last, has the role of the political party entered the center of our professional concern."[5] Neumann himself took the latest step toward a systematic stasiology with his *Modern Political Parties.*[6]

Reprinted from *The Journal of Politics,* Vol. XIX (1959), pp. 423–440, by permission of the Southern Political Science Association.

Research for this study was aided by a grant from the Alfred University Research Foundation.

Although this progress has been remarkable, it has been made the subject of much criticism and self-criticism by political scientists. Duverger presents his book with much diffidence:

> The reader is . . . asked never to forget the highly conjectural nature of most of the conclusions formulated in this book. . . . In fifty years' time perhaps it will be possible to describe the real working of political parties.[7]

> The development of the science of political parties . . . will no doubt lead to the revision of many of the patterns we have traced.[8]

Neumann calls his theoretical chapter in *Modern Political Parties* "a tentative sketch of some persistent themes for a comparative analysis . . . nothing but preliminary propositions for further study, particularly in its attempt at a definition of modern political parties."[9] As recently as 1954, Alfred Diamant, who had earlier called for a basic theoretical framework for the study of political parties,[10] was justified (as, indeed, he would be justified today) in asking "whether, or to what extent, there can be comparative study of political parties if the literature about parties in the various countries, and by the scholars most competent to do these basic studies, does not provide comparable data and concepts."[11]

The recent achievements in the field of stasiology

will be assessed in the ensuing pages. No effort will be made to answer what is without doubt the most challenging question: Is a science of political parties possible? This question, left unresolved in the monumental controversy between Duverger and G. E. Lavau,[12] can be answered, if at all, only in conjunction with the major question: Is a science of politics possible? The present study will attempt to answer the following, more modest, questions:

1. What has been studied by stasiologists?

2. What approaches taken in these studies have actually furthered our systematic and analytical knowledge of political parties?

3. What, if any, are some obvious lacunae in stasiological studies?

These questions will be answered from recent (and in some cases not so recent) writings on political parties.

In this study, the consideration of writings on political parties will be limited in three ways. First, only writings on parties with democratic objectives will be considered. The present writer agrees with F. A. Hermens (and, by implication, disagrees with Duverger) that political parties, as we know them, are "instruments of democratic government," and cannot, therefore, be studied along with dictatorial parties in a meaningful, comparative way.[13] Second, American writings on political parties will be omitted from consideration if they are textbooks of primarily descriptive character, or if they are normative studies on the subject of party government.[14] Third, since parties are agencies concerned with the capture of power in political society, the emphasis in this study will be on writings that deal with the distribution of power within parties, and with the influence of parties on societal power; other writings in the field will only be dealt with incidentally.[15]

I

The pre-Duverger era in stasiology has been called the "political-biography-cum-political-ideology" phase.[16] This classification takes care of four questions which were asked by the pre-1951 writers on political parties:

1. What is the life story of a particular political movement?

2. Who are the personalities who give (or, more often, gave) impetus to particular political movements?

3. What are the basic views regarding the proper nature of political society which are held by these movements, and in the name of which these movements operate?

4. What are the specific programs espoused by particular political movements in particular fields at particular times?

More or less closely allied questions to which many of these writers addressed themselves were:

5. How do (or again, more often, did) parties interact in particular countries?

6. How are electoral battles fought by parties in particular countries, and what was the outcome of these battles?

Those who attempted to answer some of these questions—whether in writing on one party or on the parties of one country—usually published their findings in articles or in sections of general works.[17] By and large, more attention was paid to the dictatorial parties, both communist and fascist, in part, no doubt, because these parties seemed to influence the course of history more directly than did their democratic cousins. The writers did not seem to feel that stasiology was anything more than an aspect, albeit an important one, of political history. Their recounting of the political fortunes of leaders and of the electoral fortunes of parties was history; so were their descriptions of doctrines held by parties and of party programs and policies. Their work was important; many of the facts they reported might not have become part of our body of knowledge, had it not been for their efforts. Yet these writers could only supply the empirical elements for a general and systematic study; such a systematic study itself was beyond their scope, and presumably beyond their interest, whether or not they would have considered it feasible. But two early writers, who chose democratic parties for their investigations, submitted those parties to an analysis which, in addition to being without parallel until recent years, enabled the authors to undertake at least some degree of generalization and systematization. These writers were Ostrogorski and Michels.

Both of these early greats analyzed political parties with an identical purpose. This purpose was to study the compatibility of the organization of political parties with democracy. Both, incidentally, found the parties they studied defective as instruments of democratic control of government. Ostrogorski, who examined the extra-parliamentary organization of British and American parties at the end of the nineteenth century, made this discovery largely because of his particular atomistic notion of democracy.[18] Michels based his negative findings on the avowed democratic purposes of the continental social democratic parties which he studied.[19] But the chief stasiological significance of the work of these two writers lies not so much in their discussion of the democratic adequacy of political parties, but in their analysis of these parties. For the first time, there was a clear cognizance of the fact that here were organizations which were worth studying in their role as organizations, that there was intrinsic importance in the internal structure of these organizations, especially in the relations between leaders and followers, and that knowledge of the situs of power and of power relations within these organizations was relevant to an understanding of politics in general. Both writers asked the basic questions:

1. How does the actual structure of political parties differ from their formal structure?

2. Who runs political parties, and by what means is their leadership exercised?

But their work differs from that of traditional stasiologists not only because the two writers asked questions about party organization and about the distribution of power within political parties. Their approach was novel also in that it constituted a conscious effort to move from the particular to the general.

Ostrogorski does not claim to present us with any law that governs political parties. It is evident, however, that he considers his findings about British and American parties to be relevant for other situations where broad masses of the population are (or will be) drawn into the political process. He does not intend to present us with historical uniqueness; rather, he is interested in showing the consequences of rapid democratization, and the nature of the party as a vehicle of such rapid democratization—phenomena for which he claims great similarity in two quite different political societies with divergent systems of government. In Ostrogorski's work there is investigation into new and different fields, and the recounting of this investigation is important; but even more important is the fact that here is information which brings at least the possibility of an understanding of political parties everywhere.

With Michels, the desire to generalize was more pronounced. While his investigation was restricted to social democratic parties, he imposed no geographic limits on his study. Michels observes the mass organizations of these social democratic parties, and he is struck by the differentiation within them between leaders and followers, differentiation caused by such phenomena as the need for organization for electoral battles, the absence of any mass desire to run the parties, and the leaders' enjoyment of their own positions, which makes them desirous of perpetuating their positions. These phenomena, and corroborating data, which have been collected with zeal and then selected with care, convince Michels that there is an "iron law of oligarchy," a law with application to all democratic political parties: Parties everywhere are run by a small group in their own interests. Therefore, Michels argues, they are doomed as instruments of democratic government.

Not many of the stasiologists who followed Michels shared his judgment that political parties ought to be directed by their mass membership; most of them preserved an objective neutrality on the subject of intra-party democracy. But the iron law continued to be potent even when\it was stripped of its value base. Its validity was often assumed for no better reason than that no democratic party is run either by one absolute leader or by each individual adherent, and that all are, therefore, presumably oligarchies.[20] While this assumption makes the iron law universal, it also robs it of most of its meaning. Clearly, a systematic, comparative stasiology needed to develop beyond Michels' iron law.

It seems strange that modern political scientists, occupied as they are with studies of political institutions and processes, should have let decades go by without challenging Ostrogorski and Michels or, obversely, without showing much interest in developing further these writers' analyses of parties. There was, to be sure, recognition of the special quality of the work of the two men; many stasiologists gave expression to the notion that the two were responsible for all, or most, of the then-existing insights into the study of parties.[21] Meanwhile, stasiology was developed mainly by authors of general texts in political science: Herman Finer subjected political parties, especially democratic ones, to fairly close and stimulating analysis;[22] and Ernest Barker showed, in broad outline, the role of political parties in the policy-making structure of parliamentary government.[23] Only a handful of writers paid close attention to the internal organization of political parties in specifically stasiological works. Among them were Eugene Varga, the Soviet social scientist, who analyzed the strengths and weaknesses of social democratic parties in a work that was designed to be a report to the Third International;[24] and Sigmund Neumann, who analyzed German political parties in 1932.[25]

By 1950, it was apparent that there was no systematically developed study of political parties to match corresponding achievement in such fields as public administration and international relations. One year later, the publication of Duverger's *Les partis politiques* brought political parties among the systematically studied fields of political science.

## II

When Maurice Duverger took up the task of writing the first work on parties to combine analysis and systematic treatment, he found himself faced with this vicious circle:

> . . . a general theory of parties will eventually be constructed only upon the preliminary work of many profound studies; but these studies cannot be truly profound so long as there exists no general theory of parties . . . how can one refer to general questions when for the most part they are still undefined?[26]

His purpose was "to break out of the circle and to sketch a preliminary general theory of parties, vague, conjectural, and of necessity approximate, which may yet serve as a basis and guide for detailed studies."[27] He set out to do this in three ways:

by defining practical methods of investigation, some original and some adapted from earlier ones; by attempting "to draw up a general plan of the field of study by compiling a balance sheet of all the essential questions and by coordinating them one with another so as to bring out their interdependence and their individual importance," and by formulating "on the basis of preliminary evidence as complete, varied, and extensive as possible, but still of necessity fragmentary and inadequate, . . . hypotheses capable of guiding the future research which will one day permit the formulation of authentic sociological laws." He promised a constant endeavor to classify and systematize, in an effort "to transpose into political science the technique of the 'working model'" and thereby "to restore to favour . . . the methodical use of hypothesis in science." The value of these models or "coherent aggregates, more or less proximate in character," Duverger tells us, is "to inspire and to guide further detailed studies aimed at verifying them or, more probably, at destroying them."[28]

Duverger's search for "sociological laws" in the field of stasiology was not new; Michels had set out to do the same thing. The innovation in Duverger's approach was his use of the working model. He attempts to use the working model not so much in studying the social composition or the ideologies of parties, though he considers both important; rather, he promises to construct hypothetical "proximate aggregates" in order to study "party institutions and their place in the State."[29] The last two areas form, indeed, the subject matter of Duverger's book: party structure and party systems. His study of party systems encompasses not only one-, two-, and multi-party systems, but also such items as party strength, party alliances, the nomination of public officials, and the relation of parties and forms of government. The essence of Duverger's theory of party systems is their relation to electoral systems.[30] It is expressed in the following formulae: "The simple-majority single-ballot system favors the two-party system"[31] and "the simple-majority system with second ballot and proportional representation favor multi-partism."[32]

This attempt by Duverger to theorize about party systems was soon subjected to G. E. Lavau's criticism. Lavau feels that human affairs must be studied at the level of the individual phenomenon, which is unique in history.[33] This assertion makes him, of course, doubt the validity not only of theoretical stasiology, but of all social science. But even if one assumes the possibility of a general theory of political parties, Duverger's effort to develop a theory of party systems is particularly vulnerable. In his attack, Lavau points to the "reversibility of fundamental theses" and claims that Duverger could have done as good a job proving "that multi-partism causes proportional representation and bipartism the plurality system," or "that

political instability results from war and invasion and stability from opposite situations."[34] Lavau would, it seems, expect Duverger to abandon the attempt to classify party systems in general comparative political terms. Whether or not the attempt is in fact hopeless, it must be admitted that it has not as yet been made to general satisfaction.[35]

Duverger's other major effort is the classification of party structures. His treatment of party organization differs from that of Ostrogorski and Michels. Unlike these two predecessors, Duverger is not trying to prove a point. His purpose is systematic classification, and he goes at this with scientific neutrality. He studies both democratic and dictatorial parties, and he imposes no geographic limits on his data, though his information on parties in the United States is inadequate. The product of his organizational analysis consists of such useful categories as direct and indirect parties; caucus-, branch-, cell-, and militia-type basic organizational elements; cadre and mass parties; and electors, supporters, and militants. Michels' differentiae regarding leaders are enriched by the addition of new ones regarding the relation between party leaders and parliamentary representatives. Furthermore, the useful concept of the membership ratio[36] is introduced.

Duverger's method is highly useful for analytical and comparative purposes. Samuel Beer has judged its significance in these words:

No small part of the promise of his method is that it is truly comparative and raises the modest hope that we may be able to make some progress toward systematic generalizations widely applicable to party behavior in different countries.[37]

But it may well be, as Lavau insists, that this promise is hampered by too facile a reliance on structural factors.[38] It also remains true that Duverger does not keep his initial methodological promise;[39] instead of a continuous testing of a hypothetical working model, we get sound and methodical classification. Comparison and theory are not the same; but, in attempting to give us a theory, Duverger does give us excellent tools for comparison. His systematic treatment of party systems and especially of party structures establishes *Les partis politiques* as the pilot work for further stasiological studies.

Since 1951, there has been an acceleration in these studies. However, this increased pace is not solely due to Duverger, since a number of studies had been begun prior to the publication of *Les partis politiques*. It may be that post-war "normalcy" allowed political scientists to interest themselves in the relatively placid subject of democratic political parties. For whatever reason, we have recent studies of the party systems (involving, incidentally, careful studies of party organization) of the United Kingdom,[40] France,[41] Germany,[42]

Sweden,[43] Australia,[44] and the Canadian province of Alberta.[45] Of these studies, R. T. McKenzie's *British Political Parties,* with its close analysis of the internal organization and power structure of the Conservative and Labour parties, and its criticism of Ostrogorski and Michels in terms of the British parliamentary system, constitutes the most significant stasiological advance.

By 1956, the stage was set for a coordinated effort in general comparative stasiology. This effort was made with the publication, under Sigmund Neumann's editorship, of *Modern Political Parties.*[46] The major stasiological advances of the work are made in Neumann's concluding article, "Toward a Comparative Study of Political Parties."[47] Here we find, for the first time in a stasiological work, a tentative, generally applicable definition of political parties.[48] Neumann also categorizes the functions of both democratic and dictatorial parties,[49] and he suggests a fairly complex classification of parties based on ideological, sociological, and party-system considerations.[50] The sociology of parties, in turn, is subjected to further analysis with stasiological significance. The only claim Neumann makes for his effort is that he ventures "a tentative sketch of some persistent themes for a comparative analysis,"[51] and comparison is the keynote of the book. The coverage is not only inclusive, but it is also systematic. Facts are included not, as sometimes in Duverger and always in Michels, because they fit an hypothesis, but because they inform us about a particular party or party system; they are presented for their own sake.

Much of the material, both in the contributions and in Neumann's synthesis, deals with matters which, while essential to history and social science, are peripheral to stasiology proper. Included here are observations about the nexus of politics and other institutions, agencies, and groups, and Neumann's interesting addition, the suggested study of internationals of parties. Neumann's approach to party sociology, broader than Duverger's, differs from Michels' in that it is objective and neutral; it is therefore more useful than Michels' approach.

Neumann's attempt to classify political parties is less rigorous than Duverger's. Some of the rigor is lost through Neumann's introduction of sociological and ideological criteria, which are added to the structural and party-system criteria of Duverger. While the classification is thus broader, it is also beset with imprecisions and overlaps. There is, however, one set of categories which is of sufficient precision for use by the systematic student of parties: the categories of parties of individual representation and of social integration.

Neumann, who has sympathy with both the historical approach of Lavau and the social-science approach of Duverger, does not make, and thus cannot be held to keep, a theoretical promise as bold as Duverger's. But even though Neumann makes no effort to give us a complete stasiological system, his feat of coordinating what is known about various parties and party systems is remarkable. He has succeeded in getting a group of noteworthy, though necessarily dissimilar, contributors to compile a most significant and useful catalogue of parties and party systems. The prominence of these contributors indicates that stasiology is at last coming of age. The time is now ripe for stasiologists to apply Duverger's definite categories, and possibly even his theoretical promise, to the spadework of Neumann and his contributors.

This work could be undertaken now because stasiologists have, in recent years, succeeded in putting the study of party structures on a solid basis. This is the area where, thanks primarily to Duverger but also to others,[52] there have been the most successful recent developments in stasiology. But so far, the emphasis has been almost solely on the anatomy of political parties. Processes that determine organizational policies within parties have been studied, but investigations into the intra-party procedures that lead to the making of public policy have been few and far between. The next section of this study, while giving an account of these physiological writings, will point to the need for a greater concern with policy-making processes within democratic political parties.

III

There is an apparent neglect by stasiologists of intra-party processes that lead to the making of public policy. Ostrogorski had, to be sure, paid some, though scant, attention to the formation of policy issues within both the Liberal and the Conservative caucuses.[53] Duverger, however, pays no attention at all to such policy formation, and neither do most of Neumann's contributors.[54] The making of public policy within political parties has remained a stasiological lacuna. There are at least three reasons for this occurrence: (1) Some have felt that the role of parties in the making of public policy is unimportant. (2) The nature of public policy-making within parties varies with both party and governmental systems and tends to be complex and confusing. (3) Since the electoral functions of parties have been quite properly emphasized more than the others, discussions of public policy-making within parties have tended to turn into value-based discussions of intra-party democracy (*i.e.,* usually, discussions of the right of electoral aides to help determine the policies of elected public officials).

The first reason is of limited importance, since relatively few students of democratic policy-making processes maintain that the making of policy is nothing but an interaction of interest groups with governmental institutions, with political parties performing only brokerage services in the nominating process.[55] But clearly the second, the complexity of the nature of public policy-making within parties, continues. The formation of such policy not only varies with the number of parties and the nature of legislative-executive relations, but it may also be indistinguishable from the formation of public policy which takes place without definite involvement of political parties.

Under a *bona fide* multi-party system, where no party is likely to attain a legislative majority, the formation of public policy *within* political parties lacks finality, since policies, in order to be enacted, must be formed by negotiations *among* parties, and usually among their representatives in the legislature or in the executive. Only under a two-party system, where one party can attain a majority and therefore the sole responsibility of government, can definitive public policy be made within a political party. Here again, only a cabinet system seems capable of giving the government party the complete unity of responsibility necessary for the enactment of policy in the form in which it has been planned within the party. Under separation of powers, there is no such unity of responsibility, and parties may never be able to plan consistent policies with any hope of enacting them according to plan.

Historically, the unity of the governing party in a parliamentary system derives from the system itself, and not from the nature of the parties. In a parliamentary country like the United Kingdom, particularly, it is frequently emphasized that policy-making is the function of Her Majesty's Government, while the role of the party is to nominate parliamentary candidates and to organize the electorate in order to elect the candidates. This assertion suggests the third reason why studies of public policy formation within the political parties are not held to be of central importance. It is assumed that policy is and ought to be made by the cabinet. Under this assumption, any participation of the extra-parliamentary party in the making of public policy is nothing but a meddling with the Queen's Government by irresponsible and largely uninformed groups.

The present writer sees no need to establish a dichotomy between parties and government under the parliamentary system. Such a dichotomy can be avoided when it is realized that, in the twentieth century, the cabinet and the parliamentary party, as well as the electoral organization, make up the political party.[56] While the cabinet derives its central position in the British system from the Crown power with which it is vested, it acts primarily as a party agency, which interacts with other party agencies,[57] despite its paramount constitutional and traditional position. Policy formation in the United Kingdom is therefore greatly illuminated when it is studied with the focus on party, as has been done by R. T. McKenzie. The crucial importance

of the formation of public policy within political parties will be established once the term "party" is used in its full dimension. The classic statement of this full dimension is by Ernest Barker, who sees parties not only as formulators of issues to be presented to the electorate, but who shows clearly also their continuing role in governmental policy-making.[58] Democratic government cannot be understood fully before the processes through which parties participate in the making of public policy are subjected to thorough analysis.

The past few years have seen at least some progress toward such an analysis. McKenzie's painstaking effort to give a full picture of the distribution of power within the two major British parties involves much more than an analysis of their anatomy. In fact, his lively discussion of the interaction of leader, parliamentary party, mass organization, and central office,[59] gives his work the makings of a pilot study in party policy-making.

So far, McKenzie's work is unique in scope. However, other recent books are at least partly devoted to a discussion of the internal policy-making processes, both organizational and public, of parties. Both Wildenmann[60] and von der Heydte-Sacherl[61] contribute to our understanding of the physiology of contemporary German parties. Goetz Roth devotes an entire monograph to a very important aspect of party physiology, the role of parties in the formation of governments.[62] Macpherson's work on the peculiarities of Alberta politics contains a thorough discussion of the interaction of cabinet, legislative caucus, provincial party convention, and constituency organization in the formation of policy of the United Farmers of Alberta.[63] A thorough and detailed discussion of policy-making is part of Raymond Fusilier's *Le parti socialiste suédois: son organisation*.[64] Policy formation within political parties has also been considered in a few recent articles.[65] Thus, we are just beginning to have the kind of empirical investigations which will eventually permit generalizations about the role of political parties in the making of public policy.

Such generalizations will be useful only when they are based on some clear and distinct classification. For all party systems and all forms of democratic governmental organization, the internal public policy-making processes of parties will have to be distinguished from processes of inter-party policy-making, and both will have to be categorized. Discrete categories will have to be set up for two-party systems and multi-party systems, and for parliamentary and presidential forms of government. Public as well as organizational policy-making within political parties will have to be analyzed and synthesized with sufficient precision to have it ready for use by stasiologists when they tackle the job of constructing a definitive general theory of political parties.

Political parties are not only essential mobilizers of the electorate and selectors of candidates for public office; they also form an integral link in the chain of democratic policy-making. For a comprehensive understanding of democratic policy-making processes, we need to be adequately informed about the part played in these processes by political parties. Our understanding of the anatomy of parties has been immeasurably enriched in recent years. We now need process studies, similar to the recent successful ones in the fields of public administration and legislation, in order to develop and refine our understanding of stasiological physiology.

## IV

The significance of the recent developments in stasiology is qualitative as well as quantitative. Not only have we witnessed in recent years the appearance of *Les partis politiques* and *Modern Political Parties,* and of an increasing number of monographs and articles on parties; there has also been a noteworthy change in emphasis and approach. The recent writings are clear evidence that stasiology is no longer restricted to political-biography-cum-political-ideology, with an occasional sprinkling of Ostrogorski and Michels. Contemporary stasiology, based on the study of party structure and party systems, is power-centered and power-directed. It emphasizes the aspects of party which matter in the making of decisions within political societies. Such an emphasis has brought about the collection of empirical elements that are capable of assuring for theoretical stasiology a validity which equals that of other aspects of a theory of public policy-making.

## NOTES

1. The term "stasiology," derived from the Greek "stasis," meaning faction, was suggested by Maurice Duverger in *Political Parties,* translated by Barbara and Robert North (New York, 1954), p. 422.
2. Two vols., translated by F. Clarke (New York, 1902).
3. Translated by Eden and Cedar Paul (New York, 1949).
4. (Paris, 1951) Further references will be to the English translation (see n. 1).
5. "Toward a Theory of Political Parties," *World Politics,* VI (July, 1954), 549–563. The development was particularly rapid in Great Britain. There had been no treatise on the British parties since Ostrogorski. Within three years, the following works appeared: Sydney Bailey (ed.), *Political Parties and the Party*

*System in Britain* (New York, 1952); Ivor Bulmer-Thomas, *The Party System in Great Britain* (London, 1953); and R. T. McKenzie, *British Political Parties* (New York, 1955).
6. (Chicago, 1956) While the work is a collection of monographs on individual party systems, edited by Neumann, the editor wrote a significant concluding chapter, "Toward a Comparative Study of Political Parties," pp. 395–421 [Reprinted on pp. 351–367 of this volume].
7. *Op. cit.,* p. xiv.
8. *Ibid.,* p. 422.
9. P. 6.
10. Review of A. Joseph Berlau, *The German Social Democratic Party, 1914–1921* (New York, 1949), in *The Western Political Quarterly,* V (December, 1950), 639.
11. Review of Ludwig Bergstraesser, *Geschichte der politischen Parteien in Deutschland,* 7th rev. ed. (Munich, 1952), in *The Journal of Politics,* XVI (May, 1954), 377.
12. G. E. Lavau, *Partis politiques et réalités sociales* (Paris, 1953), pp. 5–46, 163–165. See also S. E. Finer, review of Duverger, *op. cit.,* in *Political Studies,* II (October, 1954), 273; and C. A. Micaud, review of Lavau, *op. cit.,* in *The Journal of Politics,* XVI (November, 1954), 729.
13. Review of Duverger, *op. cit.,* in *The Review of Politics,* XIV (October, 1952), 559. See also Austin Ranney and Willmoore Kendall, *Democracy and the American Party System* (New York, 1956), pp. 84–87. Neumann seems, at times, to agree; see *Modern Political Parties,* pp. 395–396.
14. During the first half of this century, American political scientists far outstripped Europeans in the production of stasiological writings. Some of them continued Ostrogorski's work of probing into the nature of American bossism. Among their writings, we find Harold Zink, *City Bosses in the United States* (Durham, N. C., 1930); H. F. Gosnell, *Machine Politics: Chicago Model* (Chicago, 1937); J. T. Salter, *Boss Rule* (New York, 1935); and Charles E. Merriam, *Chicago: A More Intimate View of Urban Politics* (New York, 1929). Most American writers, however, devoted their stasiological efforts to the compilation of textbooks on United States parties, elections, and pressure groups. The number of these books is legion. Among them, we find Charles E. Merriam and H. F. Gosnell, *The American Party System,* 4th ed. (New York, 1949); R. C. Brooks, *Political Parties and Electoral Problems,* 3rd ed. (New York, 1933); Howard R. Penniman, *Sait's American Parties and Elections,* 5th ed. (New York, 1952); P. O. Ray, *Introduction to Political Parties and Practical Politics,* 3rd ed. (New York, 1924); H. R. Bruce, *American Parties and Politics,* 3rd ed. (New York, 1936); V. O. Key, Jr., *Politics, Parties and Pressure Groups,* 3rd ed. (New York, 1952); Peter H. Odegard and E. A. Helms, *American Politics,* 2nd ed. (New York, 1947); Dayton D. McKean, *Party and Pressure Politics* (New York, 1949); and Hugh A. Bone, *American Politics and the Party System,* 2nd ed. (New York, 1955). These textbooks contain valuable information on party organization, but the formal aspects of such organization are often overstressed. Significant works dealing with the role of parties in American society are A. N. Holcombe, *The Political Parties of Today* (New York, 1924), and *The New Party Politics* (New York,

1933); and E. P. Herring, *The Politics of Democracy* (New York, 1940). E. E. Schattschneider, more than anyone else, set out to bare the true power picture within American parties; the emphasis in his provocative *Party Government* (New York, 1942), in the subsequent *The Struggle for Party Government* (College Park, Md., 1948), and in his article in Neumann, *op. cit.,* is, however, on the desirability of introducing responsible party government to the United States. This latter emphasis inspired the report "Toward a More Responsible Two-Party System," in *The American Political Science Review,* XLIV (Part 2, September, 1950), by the American Political Science Association's Committee on Political Parties, of which Schattschneider was chairman. There are three recent remarkable stasiological works, each *sui generis,* by American writers. They are, V. O. Key's *Southern Politics in State and Nation* (New York, 1949), which contains not only interesting political history and biography, but also analytical chapters; Ranney and Kendall's *Democracy and the American Party System* (see n. 13), which combines the textbook approach with general stasiological analysis and a critique of the party-government thesis; and V. O. Key's *American State Politics* (New York, 1956), the first thorough work on this subject.

15. The writer does not assume the responsibility of presenting a complete bibliography of political parties. There is no functionally integrated party bibliography. The two extant bibliographies use the country-by-country approach, and are only loosely coordinated. The first, now quite out of date, is part of the article "Political Parties" in *Encyclopedia of the Social Sciences* (New York, 1933), Vol. XI, pp. 636–639. The second is found in Neumann, *op. cit.,* pp. 425–446. This bibliography is remarkably extensive, though its considerable value would have been enhanced had the various authors followed the same pattern of organization. They also give no indication of a common notion regarding the limits of the field of stasiology.

16. By Diamant, in *The Journal of Politics* (see n. 11).

17. Among the notable exceptions are André Siegfried, *Tableau des partis en France* (Paris, 1930); Warner Moss, *Political Parties in the Irish Free State* (New York, 1933); and Dean E. McHenry, *His Majesty's Opposition* (Berkeley and Los Angeles, 1940). Significant sections on political parties can be found in James Bryce, *Modern Democracies,* 2 vols. (New York, 1921), and in *Encyclopedia of the Social Sciences,* Vol. XI, pp. 589–639.

18. See the brilliant analysis of Ostrogorski, *op. cit.,* in Austin Ranney, *The Doctrine of Responsible Party Government* (Urbana, Ill., 1954), esp. pp. 113–119, 128–133.

19. *Op. cit., passim.*

20. This argument is made cogently by W. J. M. Mackenzie in "Mr. McKenzie on the British Parties," *Political Studies,* III (June, 1955), pp. 157–159.

21. This is not to say that some credit was not given to such scholars as Lord Bryce and A. Lawrence Lowell. However, the specifically stasiological nature of the work of Ostrogorski and Michels caused them to be mentioned more frequently.

22. *The Theory and Practice of Modern Government,* rev. ed. (New York, 1949), Part 3, *passim.*

23. *Reflections on Government* (London, 1942), pp. 38–41, 81–94.

24. *Die sozialdemokratischen Parteien* (Hamburg, 1926).

25. *Die deutschen Parteien* (Berlin, 1932).

26. Duverger, *op. cit.,* p. xiii.

27. *Idem.*

28. *Ibid.,* pp. xiii-xiv.

29. *Ibid.,* p. xv.

30. *Ibid.,* pp. 216–228, 239–255.

31. *Ibid.,* p. 217.

32. *Ibid.,* p. 239.

33. See n. 12.

34. *Op. cit.,* p. 11 (author's translation).

35. An interesting addition to the study of party systems is the concept of the quasi-party system. *Cf.* C. B. Macpherson, *Democracy in Alberta* (Toronto, 1953), ch. 8, esp. pp. 237–239.

36. "The relation of the number of members to the number of electors." Duverger, *op. cit.,* p. 94.

37. "Les Partis Politiques," *The Western Political Quarterly,* VI (September, 1953), 514.

38. *Op. cit.,* pp. 8–9.

39. See Hermens, *loc. cit.,* p. 558, and Diamant, review of Duverger, *op. cit.,* in *The Journal of Politics,* XIV (November, 1952), 732.

40. Bailey, *op. cit.;* Bulmer-Thomas, *op. cit;* McKenzie, *op. cit.*

41. Philip Williams, *Politics in Post-War France* (New York, 1954).

42. Rudolph Wildenmann, *Partei und Fraktion* (Meisenheim am Glan, 1954); Friedrich August Freiherr von der Heydte and Karl Sacherl, *Soziologie der deutschen Parteien* (Munich, 1955).

43. Dankwart A. Rustow, *The Politics of Compromise* (Princeton, 1955).

44. Louise Overacker, *The Australian Party System* (New Haven, 1952).

45. Macpherson, *op. cit.* Along with these books should be mentioned Vol. X of *Occidente* (March–April, 1954), containing the following articles: Greeme Moodie, "Political Parties in America," 106–136; D. E. Butler, "Some Notes on the Nature of British Political Parties," 137–157; Philip Williams, "The French Party System," 158–183; and Giuliano Pischel, "I partiti politici italiani, oggi," 184–212. Ranney and Kendall's *Democracy and the American Party System* (n. 13) contains a valuable discussion of comparative stasiology (chs. 5 and 6).

46. The contributors, in addition to Neumann are: Frederick C. Barghoorn, Samuel H. Beer, Gwendolen M. Carter, Andrew Gyorgy, Charles A. Micaud, Felix Oppenheim, Dankwart A. Rustow, Robert A. Scalapino, and E. E. Schattschneider.

47. Neumann, *op. cit.,* pp. 395–421.

48. ". . . the articulate organization of society's active political agents, those who are concerned with the control of governmental power and who compete for popular support with another group or groups holding divergent views. . . . the great intermediary which links social forces and ideologies to official governmental institutions and relates them to political action within the larger political community." *Ibid.,* p. 396. Ranney and Kendall's definition, written in the same year and intended to apply to all democratic political parties, is, "Political parties are autonomous organized groups that make nominations and contest elections in the hope of eventually gaining and exercising control of the personnel and policies of government." *Op. cit.,* p. 85.

49. Neumann, *op. cit.*, pp. 396–400.

50. *Ibid.*, pp. 400–405.

51. *Ibid.*, p. 6.

52. Including, in addition to Neumann and some of his contributors, R. T. McKenzie, Philip Williams, Wildenmann, and von der Heydte.

53. *Op. cit.*, Vol. I, pp. 509–514, 523–529.

54. Beer is a notable exception. See Neumann, *op. cit.*, pp. 30–32, 51–53.

55. This notion was, and to some extent still is, wide-spread in the United States, possibly because of a *de facto* absence of responsible party government.

56. McKenzie realizes this fully, but the emphasis of his book seems to introduce the dichotomy in places (*e.g., op. cit.*, pp. 587–588).

57. The present writer, while emphasizing intra-party policy-making in this discussion, is of course mindful of the equally crucial importance of the interaction between the two parties in the making of public policy.

58. *Op. cit.*, pp. 37–43, 47–48, 53–54, 57–58.

59. *Op. cit., passim.*

60. *Op. cit.*, pp. 160–163.

61. *Op. cit.*, pp. 212–217, 220. This work contains also very valuable basic stasiological material.

62. *Fraktion und Regierungsbildung* (Meisenheim am Glan, 1953).

63. *Op. cit.*, pp. 62–92. Party policy-making is also discussed incidentally in S. M. Lipset's *Agrarian Socialism* (Berkeley and Los Angeles, 1950), which is an excellent sociological study of the C.C.F. in Saskatchewan.

64. (Paris, 1954) pp. 158–161, 175, 181–182, 186–191.

65. Samuel Beer, "The Conservative Party of Great Britain," *The Journal of Politics,* XIV (February, 1952), 65–71; Anthony T. Bouscaren, "The M.R.P. in French Governments, 1848–1951," *The Journal of Politics,* XIV (February, 1952), 104–105; Ivor Bulmer-Thomas, "How Conservative Policy is Formed," *The Political Quarterly,* XLIV (April, 1953), 190–203; James M. Burns, "The Parliamentary Labor Party in Great Britain," *The American Political Science Review,* XLIV (December, 1950), 856–858, 869–871; D. E. Butler, "Some Notes on the Nature of British Political Parties," *Occidente,* X (March–April, 1954), 148–152, and "American Myths about British Parties," *Virginia Quarterly Review,* XXXI (Winter, 1955), 52–56; Frederick C. Engelmann, "Membership Participation in Policy-Making in the C.C.F.," *The Canadian Journal of Economics and Political Science,* XXII (May, 1956), 161–173; R. N. Kelson, "The New Zealand National Party," *Political Science,* VI (Wellington, N. Z., September, 1954), 23, 30–32; Louise Overacker, "The Australian Labor Party," *The American Political Science Review,* XLIII (August, 1949), 696–702, and "The New Zealand Labor Party," *The American Political Science Review,* XLIX (September, 1955), 724–731; and Philip M. Williams, "The French Party System," *Occidente,* X (March–April, 1954), 166–169.

VI

# VI Pressure and Interest Groups

# Introduction:

# GROUP THEORY AND THE COMPARATIVE STUDY OF PRESSURE GROUPS

## Harry Eckstein

> "I was about to say," pursued Mrs. Wilfer,
> who clearly had not the the faintest idea of saying anything more:
> "that when I use the term attractions, I do so
> with the qualification that I do not mean it in any way whatever."
> —CHARLES DICKENS, *Our Mutual Friend*

## I

One of the many reasons that writers on comparative politics nowadays attach less importance to formal procedures and institutions than in the past is their discovery, in many cases very recent, of the great importance of "informal" politics, especially the politics of pressure groups. Only a few years ago, studies of political groups could have been considered the special hobbyhorse of the avant-garde in comparative politics. For instance, shortly after its organization, the Social Science Research Council's Committee on Comparative Politics—always the vanguard of the revolutionary movement in comparative political studies—decided to concentrate its main efforts on the study of political groups in various countries. This decision was taken, as far as one can gather, not only because of the clear discrepancy in quality and quantity between studies of American political groups and those of other countries, but also because of the belief that important old political mysteries could be cleared up and new ones discovered by the analysis of group politics. Partly in response to the Committee's prodding, partly through the efforts of independent writers, a large number of books and articles on pressure groups in foreign countries has, in fact, appeared in recent years. To be sure, other subjects have in the meantime come to be emphasized by frontier-minded writers in comparative politics. Studies of political "socialization" (in the psychological, not economic, sense of the term) and modernization may indeed be the newest wave of the future in the field; but

it is probably safe to assume that studies of group politics, now that the ice has most decidedly been broken, will continue to play a very important role in comparative politics research.

At any rate, one may hope so, for, despite the recent popularity of the subject, only a good start has been made so far in seeking out pressure-group data on a broad scale, and hardly even that in treating such data theoretically: formulating general hypotheses about them and putting the hypotheses to the test of rigorous comparison. As yet, for example, we have available few general notions about pressure groups, even inadequate or erroneous ones, to rank with, say, Hermens' theory about the effects of electoral systems on representative government. Certainly there is no single theoretical problem concerning pressure groups on which the present essay can focus, because present research in comparative politics also focuses mainly on the problem. The great majority of studies of pressure groups in foreign countries that have recently appeared have hardly even been comparative in character, in any meaningful sense of the term. They have dealt only with particular foreign pressure groups or the larger constellation of pressure groups in a particular country. Nevertheless, it is now at least possible, provided only that a few confessions of ignorance are made first, to include the subject of pressure groups in a reader of the present sort; and certainly the materials necessary for more systematic comparative studies are now being accumulated, in great contrast to the past.

Only one thing is really surprising about this, and that is the recency of the development. After all, the so-called "group theory" of politics has been in existence now for over half a century; the undoubted founder of the theory, Arthur F. Bentley, published his *Process of Government* in 1908. Since then, the largest possible claims have been made for the theory. It has been one of the very few notions in political science for which the status of a truly general theory has been claimed— the status of a simple formulation that can account for nearly all the phenomena of government. Only perhaps Marxists and elite theorists have made similar claims in the recent history of political science. Let us begin, then, by sketching the nature of group theory, and examining the validity of the enormous theoretical claims made for it, before considering how it is related to the comparative study of pressure groups.

## II

Like most theories of politics that are both grandiose and simple, group theory raises a massive number of complex issues. For detailed treatments of these issues, readers must be referred to works dealing intensively with group theory as such.[1] Here only the essentials are sketched, for the object is not to delineate all the philosophical nuances of group theory, but to relate it to comparative politics. For that purpose, it may be best to begin with a concise and stripped-down version of the theory, of the sort supplied by Hagan in a recent collaborative volume, *Approaches to the Study of Politics*.

"The purpose of [my] paper," says Hagan, near its beginning, "is to suggest a descriptive system which, properly understood and employed, can be as useful—*and* as uniting—for political scientists as the supply-and-demand categories are for the economists. The descriptive system I propose is generally known as the 'group concept,' and is most simply stated thus: values are authoritatively allocated in a society through the processes of the conflict of groups." Hagan here echoes, in language vigorous enough, the even more vigorous language of Bentley: "When the groups are stated, everything is stated. When I say everything, I mean everything." And again, "the whole of social life in all its phases can be stated in . . . groups of active men."

Without inquiring into the complicated methodological and semantic reasons underlying Bentley's position (or the ways in which he attempted to state everything there is to state, at least about government, in terms of groups), let us consider the essential bases of Hagan's assertion; in the main, they are derived from Bentley's thought in any case. Hagan's starting point, clearly, is the definition of the central concern of political science presented in David Easton's *The Political System*

—that political science analyzes the authoritative allocation of values in society, just as the central concern of economics—the problem that defines the field—is the allocation of scarce goods. Hagan's own concern begins where this definition of political science leaves off; he wants to know *how* values are authoritatively allocated for a society. He is certainly not the first political scientist to have that interest, but he is thoroughly dissatisfied with the manner in which most other political scientists have attempted to satisfy their interest in the subject, above all with the descriptive categories they have used. The descriptive apparatus he himself was taught, he points out, consisted basically of five concepts. There was, in the first place, the notion of a legal system (presumably, formal-legal rules). And then one talked, using Pendleton Herring's language, of interests, ideas, institutions, and individuals, or the same things in a less alliterative language. In the study of politics one tried to discover some sort of "working union" between these things: how they interacted and cohered to produce public policy and administration.

This may seem sensible enough. The trouble is, says Hagan, that all the concepts are hopelessly imprecise, so much so that it is left to every reader to read his own meanings into them. "How does an interest," he asks, "differ from an idea and how do you tell when one is operating rather than the other? The same questions can be made [sic] about the other two categories: the institution and the individual. The answers will be just as ambiguous." What he proposes instead is to regard politics (in Easton's sense) and everything that goes into politics, including the "four I's," in terms of group conflict, thus defining all the elements of politics from a common point of view and, allegedly, stating them less ambiguously. Thus, ideas are to be regarded as "the talking and writing facet" of group conflict, institutions as the "customary modes of acting" in group conflict, and individuals as the "physiological entities" engaged in group conflict. The idea of "interest" is perhaps a bit more difficult when understood in these terms. To grasp what "interests" are to Hagan, we must understand first what he means by the most fundamental concept that he uses, the very idea of the group.

The important point to realize is that Hagan, like Bentley before him, does not think of groups as if they were "real" entities in a certain sense: entities with a life of their own, almost like individuals—entities possessing boundaries that clearly demarcate them from one another, or entities with formal organization, legal existence, constitutions, charters, treasuries, officers, meeting places, and the like. In "group theory" the idea of the group is entirely an analytical construct. It does, of course, refer to concrete things in the real world, even if not to things we would call groups in conventional, or any other, language. By a group, Hagan and Bentley mean any mass of human activity tending in a common direction, hence, by a political group, a mass of activity tending in a common political direction. From this standpoint, the physiological entities we call individuals belong to as many political groups as they participate in political activities; so do the associations and persistent interactions of individuals; and various associations and interactions, individual citizens and officials, may all constitute a single (analytical) political group. The activity *is* the group. That is the vital point. It is also what group theorists mean by "interest," for when we say that an "interest" exists, we can only mean, they argue, that activities toward a common goal take place. In the world of scientific political analyses there is nothing but activity toward goals, and all the terminology of political science is descriptive language for bundles of such activity.

Boldly stated, the group theory of politics may therefore be summarized as follows: Politics is the process by which social values are authoritatively allocated; this is done by decisions; the decisions are produced by activities; each activity is not something separate from every other, but masses of activity have common tendencies in regard to decisions; these masses of activity are groups; so the struggle between groups (or interests) determines what decisions are taken.

That is really all there is to the theory—at least in gist. To be sure, Hagan takes a dozen or so closely printed pages to present and justify this view of politics, and Bentley, for all his concise sentences, a whole book. But the group theory is expressly meant to be a very simple theory, and if one strips it of all nonessentials, it can be reduced, without any distortion, to the proportions it has above.

Once the essential character of the theory has been sketched, the next question which would seem to arise is what it has to do with the comparative study of pressure groups. It should be apparent from its outlines that the theory is not concerned solely, or even primarily, with the masses of activity we generally call "pressure groups." Certainly, in asserting that all politics is group conflict, the group theory of politics says nothing so simple, or meaningful, as that all political decisions are decided by the conflict of organized pressure groups, so that one can, for analytical purposes, either forget about other elements of politics (like parties, officials, formal institutions, and unorganized interests) or regard them only as the pawns of the organized pressures.

What we conventionally call "pressure groups" is only one term, and not necessarily the most important, in the total universe of groups. There are many other masses of politically significant activity. Bentley, for example, deals expressly with

the special role of political leaders, including party leaders, as well as with unorganized opinion, formal-legal institutions and rules, and parties; and what we usually have in mind when we talk about pressure groups (organized vested interests and politically active voluntary organizations: reform organizations, occupational organizations, religious affiliation, and the like) is given by him, except for remarks in passing, only a part of a single chapter. Indeed, Bentley refers to such groups as "semi-political groups," possibly because of their involvement (unlike parties) in nonpolitical activities, possibly because their political objectives are nearly always confined to obtaining favorable decisions rather than the control of decision-making offices as such—but possibly also because such groups seem somehow more peripheral to politics than other constellations of activity.

So also for other group theorists. When we look at their conceptual equipment, we always find in it such terms as "potential groups" or "latent interests" (as yet unorganized interests), "majority groups" (the public acting in its capacity as electorate), "official groups" (holders of formal offices, including even the judiciary), and the like. What happens in group theory is not that pressure groups somehow displace all the other elements of politics, but that they become a term coequal to them in analysis and that all the analytical elements of politics are regarded from the point of view of the same frame of reference. Pressure groups are an essential part of the group schema, but only a part.

Yet this very fact furnishes a good reason for associating group theory specifically with the study of pressure groups. At the very least, in group theory pressure groups are regarded as a universal, perhaps an inevitable, certainly analytically important, element of the process of government; and that opens the door to pressure-group study as such, and incidentally to still more emphatic assertions about the significance of pressure groups than we find in the leading group theorists. If nothing else, group theory deprives the formal structures of government and the "fully political" organizations—parties, for example—of any right to special treatment and emphasis in the concerns of political scientists. In its original form, it, so to speak, legitimized the concern with "semi-political" groups in political science.

What is more, the whole influence of the theory has been in the direction of pressure-group analysis. For better or worse, many political scientists in fact took the group theorists to be saying something they took pains not to say; they confused the concept of the group in group theory with the more conventional meanings attached to the term in their own minds. This was certainly a gross misunderstanding, but the group theorists themselves were not without blame in the matter. In their actual analyses, if not their conceptual and methodological disquisitions, they seemed as much preoccupied with pressure groups in the conventional sense as their misinterpreters.

For example, while David B. Truman's *The Governmental Process* is subtitled *Political Interests and Public Opinion* (note: *and* public opinion), and while it makes the catholic points about latent interests and majority interests, its substantive parts are concerned almost entirely with the play of organized special interest groups. Three chapters are given to matters concerning their internal structure, eight to their tactics of influence, one to their origins and growth, and only a couple of sections in a couple of chapters to the conceptual complexities of group theory.

This is not meant to be a criticism of Truman, by any means. The work of Bentley himself explains such an emphasis, even if it does not justify it, for Bentley was also far more concerned in practice with pressure groups in the conventional sense than he admits to being in theory. His whole book can be regarded, without great distortion, as an essay in muckraking, no less than as an early attack on taking too seriously the legal forms and the political ideas that men profess (rather than the acts they perform), or as an early attempt to rid political science of its "spooks" (ideas, and feelings as causal forces) and make it concentrate on measurable observables. The latter are indeed Bentley's main professed objects; indeed, his book is a perfect example of how the quest for rigor in political science is related to the development of an interest in nonformal aspects of politics.

More often than not, however, Bentley supports these objects with examples of the activities of the "interests," in the best muckraking manner. "Interest" in the technical sense of group theory merges easily, even in his own work, into "vested interest" or "organized interest" in the sense of everyday speech. He talks about logrolling in Congress, about the influence of saloon interests and breweries, on one hand, and of opposing financial interests, on the other, upon a decision to set saloon license fees in Chicago at a certain level, and about the hard-and-fast interests behind certain kinds of executive decisions (tariffs, reactions to strikes). He never pretends that the organized vested interests are all. He expressly denies it, even in his examples; but their activities suit his book too well to be given as small a place among his data as they occupy in his theories, for in nothing else can one see so clearly the feebleness of the formal-legal approach to political study and the inadvisability of taking professed ideas and feelings at face value.

These arguments do not, of course, alter the fact that the identification of group theory with pressure-group analysis is a basic misinterpretation of the theory, however much they may explain how that misinterpretation occurred. Yet there is a certain sense even in the misinterpretation—perhaps better,

a sense in which the misinterpretation is preferable to the original theory. The reason is that it is difficult to see what "group theory" means, let alone why anyone should want to use it, if it is taken in the sense of the more sophisticated group theorists rather than their more simple-minded misinterpreters. And for this in turn there are several reasons.

In the first place, it is difficult to see that "group theory" is really a theory, in any sensible meaning of the term (hence the quotation marks). Unlike theories of supply and demand, for example, it does not relate any variables to one another, nor specify any possible relation between variables. For that reason also it does not "explain" anything in reality. It links no causes and effects; it specifies no formal relations (equations, for example) to which actual phenomena tend to correspond. Nothing in it can be correlated, nothing depicted on a two-dimensional or multidimensional graph. Indeed, one can see why group theory has little claim to being considered a theory not only when comparing it with the highly systematic and formal theories of economics, but even in comparison to generalizations like those of Hermens about electoral systems. At least, these generalizations do relate variables and tell us how they are supposed to be related, and that surely is the minimum that must be done by a "theory." Hermens may be wrong, but he *is* theoretical.

Not only must generalizations relate variables in order to be considered theories; they must also relate them in such a manner that the generalizations can be tested. In other words, it must be possible (at least conceivable) that the theory could be falsified, for when one tests a theory, one does not merely show that it is supported by certain data (most theories are), but rather that data contradicting it cannot be found despite diligent searches by one method or another. Theories that are in principle unfalsifiable are either absurd or, more likely, logical truisms: statements that either say nothing about the concrete world at all or are true by definition. And the statements of "group theory" are surely not falsifiable by any means whatever. If we say that politics involves the making of decisions, that decisions are made as a result of group conflict, that groups are the same thing as interests, and that both groups and interests are masses of activity, then we say merely that politics is activity. How could such a statement possibly be falsified?

We may wish to imply that political scientists ought to pay attention to informal aspects of political activity; but not even the discovery that a decision has been made entirely by officials occupying formal positions and acting in strict accordance with legal rules, without responding to any external pressures, would invalidate the theory, for such activity is activity too. In fact, not even the discovery that a decision has been made without conflict among masses of activity—that it results from universal agreement, for example—could falsify the theory, since the absence of struggle in that case accounts for the decision quite as much as the preponderant masses of activity account for decisions in others. The lack of any group conflict can simply be considered merely one extreme of the possible constellations of political forces, while mutually nullifying masses of activity, preventing any decision-making at all, can be considered the other.

But if "group theory" is not theory, then what is it and what is its use? The answer must be that it is a language for discussing political phenomena in terms of which some future theory might conceivably be stated. That indeed is what modern group theorists really think it is. They tend to talk more about the "group concept" than "group theory"; or they may, in the manner of Hagan, say that it is "descriptive theory," not "explanatory theory." In either case, they mean that it is a way one can talk about politics, not that it explains political events.

A new language that differs from both conventional and other kinds of technical language must, of course, be justified, and there are only two things that can justify it: that it is more precise than other languages for the same phenomena and that it can give rise to better theoretical formulations—formulations less ambiguous and less liable to be falsified. Does "group theory" then provide a particularly precise and unambiguous terminology? One may certainly doubt it. It could even be argued that it makes political science terminology less rather than more precise. To take merely the most conspicuous example, group theory uses three terms that all mean the same thing: groups, interests, and activities. Surely that is confusing—and the history of misunderstanding of the theory bears the point out. What is worse, it may even be dishonest. One might say simply that politics is decision-making as a result of activities that generally tend in different directions. As we have seen, one would be saying exactly the same thing as that politics involves the allocation of values through group conflict, a statement that seems to be saying something precise, arguable, and testable, while the simpler statement obviously says nothing at all. Could one not suspect with some reason that where the second statement is preferred, it is chosen just because it seems to say something it does not say in fact?

We can make our point, however, without alleging anything about the conscious or unconscious motives of group theorists; after all, has not Bentley himself warned us against analytical "spooks"? At the very least, group theory uses terms repulsive to usage and common sense. It says things that can already be said in language not repulsive to one or the other. The word "group" itself, for ex-

ample, has a pretty definite meaning in common sense and even more definite meanings in social science (where it may mean formally organized aggregates of individuals, or individuals who frequently interact, or individuals whose actions are interdependent, and so on). None of these meanings is used in group theory.

Nothing, moreover, seems to be gained by saying group when one means activity, if activity, in the conventional sense of the term, is what the term denotes. And where is the gain in saying "physiological entities engaged in political activities" rather than "individuals," or "customary modes of activity" rather than "institutions," or "writing and talking facets of activity" rather than "ideas"? One set of expressions is merely a *substitute* for the other and thus no more precise than they. Nor does the first set of expressions raise analytical problems different from the second. If, in one case, we want to know what significance is to be attached to particular individuals in political processes, in the other we want to know just as much about the significance of certain "physiological entities" (organizers and demogogues, for example), and there is no difference between one question and the other. None of the problems of traditional political science is abolished or changed by group language; problems about the effects of ideas, formal-legal processes and institutions or the environment of politics are merely restated. And so also for the elements of politics; not a single traditional element of political science is eliminated and no new ones are added. Only the language is altered.

If group language does nothing more than restate nongroup language, then how could it give rise to better theory? Certainly, Bentley's claim to have discovered a conception of politics that makes possible measurement in political science—a basis for political arithmetic—cannot be sustained. Phenomena stated in group language are no more measurable than phenomena stated in any other language—that is, if they are just the same phenomena. The history of studies done by group theorists certainly bears this out. At any rate, if group theory does provide a basis for political arithmetic, no one has yet proceeded from the verbal basis to the arithmetic itself. As for Bentley's injunction that we should stick to the observable facts and not allow ourselves to be misled by verbal professions and psychological *Gespenster,* by legal fictions and empty formal rules, surely that is just as possible (and difficult) without a universal group language as with it.

In the final analysis, then, what group theory accomplishes is nothing more or less than to call our attention to the "real forces" in political processes and to the need for better definitions and operations for dealing with these forces. Not least, it directs attention to those many semi-political groups of men who interact with fully political groups of men, in ways sometimes improvised and sometimes institutionalized, sometimes for purposes of special interest and sometimes for the general good—the world of "pressure politics" that everywhere supplements and takes place within the world of official and party politics. In that sense, the misinterpreters of group theory (those who, in Dowling's terms, have made it into "rhetorique" rather than "arithmetique") have, for the wrong reasons perhaps, gone right to the heart of its true utility. Even if one takes the group theorists to argue that everything in politics is governed by the actions of pressure groups, one improves in a certain sense the original "theory." At least, then, one says something which, however false, is certainly neither trivial nor, necessarily, absurd.

## III

Group theory, as the more faithful followers of Bentley understand it, is mainly a subject for verbal hair-splitting; group theory, as Bentley's misinterpreters represent it, is eminently a subject for comparative politics. In the first form it tends more to forestall than to inspire comparative inquiry, partly because it engenders so much argument about abstract definitions and partly because it gives the impression that the most general theory of group politics is already known prior to inquiry (even if that is not what group theorists intend). In the second form, however, it gives one immediately an important problem on which to focus comparative inquiry. Do pressure groups really play an all-important role in every polity (at any rate in representative systems)? Does one omit little or nothing of significance from an account of a political decision, no matter what or where taken, when one has described the forces exerted on it by "semi-political groups"? Or, if this is too patently unlikely a possibility even to consider, do pressure groups tend to play particularly crucial roles in some polities, or in regard to some decisions, rather than others? And what conditions determine the significance of pressure groups in different polities or in regard to different decisions?

These questions, of course, are not all one wants to ask in comparative studies of pressure groups. A great many other problems, substantive and procedural, need to be solved in such studies. For example, certain problems arise in regard to terminology: how are different kinds of pressure groups to be distinguished and labeled? Pressure groups, it goes without saying, are not all alike. Some represent, so to speak, vested interests: the interests of particular social groupings having some sort of objective characteristic in common, such as occupation, wealth, status, religion, color, locality, army service, and the like; others represent motley individuals who are simply agreed on some particular policy or set of policies regardless of their objective characteristics. Some are mainly self-regarding, some are mainly other-regarding, in their purposes. Some have a single purpose; others pursue complicated programs. Some are large-scale, formal, bureaucratized organizations; others are small, or informal, or without a bureaucratic structure. Some persist over long periods of time; others are ephemeral. The ordering of all this complicated detail through a clear and discriminating technical vocabulary is obviously a difficult task; but, like other forms of classification, it is an essential one. After all, one of the most crucial questions one can ask about pressure politics concerns the conditions under which one pattern of groups characterizes a system of pressure politics rather than another, while another important question concerns the chances of success of the different kinds of groups under different circumstances.

Another set of questions arises about the way pressure groups act in political systems: for example, what forms their activities tend to take, how intensely they are involved in politics, and how effectively they press for or against policy. Some groups concentrate their efforts mainly on the electorate by means of publicity and propaganda campaigns; others concentrate on legislatures; still others on the executive or parties. What then determines their choice of one principal object of pressure rather than another? Some groups are intensely involved in politics (in the sense of giving primacy to their political activities and pursuing them with a great expenditure of energy, funds, and manpower), while others are not. What forces determine that? Some groups frequently achieve their goals, while others often fail to achieve theirs. Why?

Finally, one wants to know something about the functional impact of pressure politics upon particular polities or policies, or polities and policies in general. Do pressure groups help to maintain or tend to undermine political systems? Do they frustrate or aid the achievement of the goals of policy? Are they salutary in some forms but not others, helps or hindrances in realizing good government or the adequate representation of public opinions?

In the present state of comparative pressure-group studies, most of these questions are still little more than questions; answers for them, adequate or inadequate, have hardly even been suggested. The selection by Almond reprinted in this section, reporting upon a planning session of the Social Science Research Council's Committee on Comparative Politics in 1957, shows to what extent inquiry into the comparative study of pressure groups is still in the programmatic stage, the stage of research design, while that by La Palombara gives some idea of the extent to which even the simplest and most basic difficulties arising in comparative research into pressure politics are still being thrashed out. The selection by Eckstein, on the other hand, does present many generalizations relevant to the questions sketched above, but these were put forward as a framework for the study of a single case of pressure politics—the role of the British Medical Association, particularly in relation to the National Health Service—and have not yet been put to the test of comparative inquiry.

From this standpoint, it would probably be advisable to stop here with the questions and not even to attempt to suggest any answers to them. One of the questions, however, we might speculate upon further, if only because it is the question most clearly derived from the main subject of this introduction—"group theory"—and its not unhappy misinterpretations. What is the general significance of pressure politics in representative government, and what conditions decide its degree of significance in particular political systems?

Although comparative research into pressure politics has as yet yielded very little in comparison with what it ought to yield, there are two things at least of which we can be sure. One is that pressure groups are active in all representative systems, and the other is that they are more active (as well as more successful) in some systems than in others. These two points are not much to be sure of, and hardly surprising, but they give rise to some knotty and interesting problems about the conditions determining different degrees of pressure-group activity. At least some tentative solutions of these problems can be offered on the basis of presently available research.

On the simplest and most basic level, the significance of pressure politics would seem to be a function of the degree to which a society is modernized: *modernization increases the significance of pressure groups in the political process.* It does so certainly in regard to the numbers of groups active in politics. The increasing differentiation of functions has been considered, at least since Durkheim, one of the cardinal features, indeed the most essential, of social development. This functional differentiation in its very nature fragments society into large numbers of groupings and tends to break the hold on social life of the primary kinship and locality groupings. It thus makes possible a social organization based upon large numbers of voluntary associations, either connected with the differentiated functions of society or simply consisting of individuals liberated from the constraints of family, clan, or tribe.

Perhaps this tendency is not important, however. Perhaps one should not assess the significance of pressure groups from the standpoint of crude numbers, but on the basis of whether or not the differentiated groupings of society are also active as pressure groups in its political system and with significant effects. A relatively undeveloped society will almost certainly have fewer differentiated groupings than a more developed one, but can we really say that its pressure-group life is insignificant if all the groupings are active, and intensely active, in national politics? Probably not; but the matter is not quite so simple, for there are other aspects of social development that make for intense and more significant pressure-group politics. One is the fact that modernization increases organizational capabilities in addition to functional differentiation and does so through a variety of factors: better communications for one and the development of bureaucratic forms of authority and administration for another.

In all highly developed societies in which voluntary association is possible, we find not only large numbers of social groupings and associations, but groupings and associations with well-articulated structures, large masses of members, wealthy treasuries, specialized administrators, and well-functioning channels of communications; these things make for power. Moreover, modernization also "disenchants" authority, to use Max Weber's term. Authority becomes less rooted in tradition, less sacred, distant, and awesome, while policy becomes more rationally calculated and changeable. These things also increase the willingness and capabilities of social groups to play a role in politics.

This generalization about the connections between modernization and pressure-group politics is not, however, enough. The significance of pressure-group politics varies a good deal among societies that are not very different from the standpoint of modernization. This variation obviously makes it necessary to look for further determinants with which to supplement the undoubtedly basic factor of social development. At least three such determinants are suggested by a simple fact that the comparative study of pressure groups, even in its presently modest form, has uncovered: pressure groups, while long active and significant in the major Western countries, have become particularly active and significant in the postwar political systems, especially in Britain, France, and Germany.

One rather obvious reason for this development is the growth of the social service state—of positive government regulating, planning, directing, or entirely drawing into itself all sorts of social activities. This trend has given social groups a greater stake in policies and therefore mobilized them to a much greater extent, while making government itself increasingly dependent on the collaboration and advice, technical or otherwise, of the groups. Another reason is the fact that disagreement about large and fundamental political issues that mobilize and integrate large masses of opinion has waned in the postwar West. (It has certainly done so in Germany, to a smaller extent in Britain, where there was less fundamental political conflict to start with, and according to some writers, even in France.) Furthermore, the pressure group is a formation more appropriate than parties or movements for expressing those particular views on small and largely technical administrative issues that become dominant in highly consensual societies. Both of these points—that the significance of pressure groups is a function of the policies of a government and that it is a function of the degree of political consensus in a society—are argued at somewhat greater length in the selection by Eckstein reprinted in this section and need only be adumbrated here.

One further suggestion, however, should be added to them. The significance of pressure groups may reflect the structure of a government no less than its policy or underlying political culture. More specifically, it seems to be relatively great in highly pluralistic structures of government and relatively small in highly monolithic ones. One of the widespread trends in modern representative government has been the increasing dispersion of decision-making power. In this respect, separation-of-powers systems, with their formal dispersion of governmental functions, had a head start on parliamentary systems, with their formal fusion of functions ·(which incidentally might help explain why pressure-group studies are American in origin).

The idea of a fusion of powers in the more advanced parliamentary democracies has become nothing more than a structural fiction; certainly it is more of a fiction now than in the past. No one can really think any longer, in this age of massive government, that the British cabinet, say, tightly controls all decisions, even major decisions. The universe of modern British decision-making is so complicated, so widely dispersed that it practically defies description. A role is played in it by the Prime Minister in his personal capacity, by special cliques of cabinet ministers, individual ministers either in or not in the Cabinet, Cabinet committees, subcommittees of Cabinet committees, other ministerial committees, the civil servants of particular departments, interdepartmental committees of civil servants, mixed committees of officials and ministers and informal groups of one, the other or both —not to mention the occasional Member of Parliament, or committee of Members, or committee of the parliamentary parties, who can exert some force in policy-making. Each and every one of these roles in the decision-making structure can be not merely active but crucial at one time or another, in connection with one decision or another. This dispersion of authority is typical of all complex modern representative governments, even of those which have strong and pretentious executive leadership, like the leadership of de Gaulle and Adenauer. A modern Bismarck could no more monopolize even the important decisions of government than could a modern Attlee, or an Eisenhower.

The relevance of this point to pressure-group analysis is, of course, that a pluralistic structure of government offers far greater opportunities of access to decision-making, and effective participation in it, than a monolithic one. It is relatively easy in such a structure of government for groups to establish special clientele relations with politicians or officials especially concerned with their interests, easy for them to get a hearing of any sort, easy to find some individual or group in government who can effectively hinder and delay decisions or can even prevent them from being taken altogether. In pluralistic structures of government, little closed universes of politicians, officials, and interest-group representatives, concerned with some particular aspect of policy, tend to develop, and groups need less to compete with one another for the favors of some integrated central decision-making structure. At the very least, this situation encourages the lesser interest and purpose groups in society to act in politics, along with the great and powerful interests and thus "politicalizes" almost the whole group structure of society.

## IV

These remarks should indicate at least how much there is to argue and how much to test by comparative study when one descends from the heady abstractions of "group theory" to the real quandaries of pressure-group analysis. Little, however, can as yet be added by way of reading to the materials reprinted in this part. Readers should certainly consult Samuel H. Beer, "Group Representation in Britain and the United States," *The Annals,* September, 1958, a pioneering, influential, but in scope very limited essay; and Henry Ehrmann, *Interest Groups on Four Continents* (1959), a broader work, consisting, however, mainly of particular country studies and little general theoretical material.

At present, the student of comparative pressure groups must still make the best he can of materials dealing mainly with pressure groups in particular political systems. Even so, little is available to him in English. For Britain, S. E. Finer, *Anonymous Empire* (1958), may be specially recommended and also a more recent work by Allen Potter, *Organized Groups in British National Politics* (1961), which gives a still more comprehensive and detailed account. For France, nothing in English rivals Jean Meynaud's *Les groupes de pressions en France* (1958), though Henry Ehrmann, *Organized Business in France* (1958), is useful, as is Val Lorwin, *The French Labor Movement* (1954). For Germany, only articles are available in English, the best of them probably Gabriel Almond, "The Political Attitudes of German Business," *World Politics,* January, 1956; the important works on the subject by Breitling, Eschenburg, Kaiser, and Reigrotzki have not been translated. Finally, a very broad, but generally very cursory, view of pressure groups in many different contexts can be obtained from a symposium in *The Annals*, "Unofficial Government, Pressure Groups and Lobbies," issued in September, 1958. (Readers should note also the relevant articles in the section on non-Western areas in this book.)

## NOTES

1. The main works in which group theory is expounded are: Arthur F. Bentley, *The Process of Gov-*ernment (1908); David B. Truman, *The Governmental Process* (1953); Earl Latham, *The Group Basis of Politics* (1952); and Charles B. Hagan, "The Group in a Political Science," in *Approaches to the Study of Politics,* ed. by Roland Young (1958). For critical essays on the theory, see, among many others, Peter H. Odegard, "A Group Basis of Politics: A New Name for an Old Myth," *Western Political Quarterly,* September, 1958; Stanley Rothman, "Systematic Political Theory: Observations on the Group Approach," *American Political Science Review,* March, 1960; Bernard Crick, *The American Science of Politics* (1959), Chapter VII; three articles (by R. E. Dowling, Myron Q. Hale, and Robert T. Golembiewski) jointly entitled "Bentley Revisited," *American Political Science Review,* December, 1960; and Harry Eckstein, *Pressure Group Politics* (1960), Chapter VII.

# A COMPARATIVE STUDY OF INTEREST GROUPS AND THE POLITICAL PROCESS

Gabriel A. Almond

The first research planning session of the Committee on Comparative Politics of the Social Science Research Council was held on April 5–10, 1957 at the Center for Advanced Study of the Behavior Sciences at Stanford, California. The participants included some of the recipients of SSRC grants for field studies of political groups, as well as a number of other scholars planning field research on these problems.[1] The purpose of the Committee in sponsoring planning sessions among its grantees and other interested scholars is to enhance the cumulative value of research efforts now under way or planned for the near future. As a result of the SSRC program, as well as of a number of other organized and individual efforts, we can anticipate in a few years an extensive monographic literature dealing with political groups and processes in a great many foreign countries and a variety of different culture areas. Systematic information on this scale may not only fill in "areas of ignorance," but offers an opportunity for significant advances in the general theory of politics. Our present theories of interest groups, political parties, and public opinion are based on American and to

Reprinted from *The American Political Science Review,* Vol. LII, No. 1 (March, 1958), pp. 270–282; permission of The American Political Science Association.

a lesser extent European experience. We can now look forward to a situation in the near future in which theories of interest groups, parties, and public opinion can be built up on the basis of a rich collection of intensive studies.

The likelihood of a significant theoretical product resulting from this fairly large group of individual efforts may be enhanced by the discussion of hypotheses and research approaches prior to field work, as well as by the pooling and exchanging of information and hypotheses during the course of research and the subsequent analysis. The purpose of the five-day planning session at Palo Alto was to explore the possibilities of agreement about research objectives and methods, and to codify the conclusions of the participants in the form of a research program statement. The planning session proceeded by plenary discussions and the presentation of specific reports by work groups concerned with special problems. The conclusions reached in the general discussions and the reports of the work groups are summarized in the present statement. The topics discussed during the session were as follows: (1) the general objectives of the comparative study of interest groups; (2) general description of the interest group system; (3) the selection of specific interest groups; (4) interest groups and public opinion; (5) interest groups and political parties; (6) interest groups and the legislature; (7) interest groups and the bureaucracy; and (8) the inclusion of non-Western countries in the comparative study.

## I. THE GENERAL OBJECTIVES

Comparative analyses of political institutions have thus far been confined to formal governmental institutions, and to political party and electoral systems. Dissatisfaction with these formal comparisons is widespread in view of the generally appreciated fact that formally similar governmental and party systems often function in radically different ways. And the search for explanation of the formally similar but differently functioning political systems has turned to vague residual categories such as "social structure," "national character," "consensus" or its absence, and "public opinion." In Duverger's study of political parties he concluded:

The development of parties has burst the bonds of the old political categories inspired by Aristotle and Montesquieu. The classic contrast between parliamentary, presidential, and National Convention regimes can henceforth no longer serve as the pivot for modern constitutional law. Kemalist Turkey, Soviet Russia, and Hitler Germany were profoundly similar because each was a single-party state, although the first practised the National Convention regime, the second a semi-parliamentary regime, and the third a semi-presidential regime. In spite of their common attachment to the parliamentary regime, Great Britain and the Dominions, under a two-party system, are profoundly dissimilar from Continental countries under a multi-partist system, and in certain respects are much closer to the United States in spite of its presidential regime. In fact the distinction between single-party, two-party, and multi-party systems tends to become the fundamental mode of classifying contemporary regimes[2]

In Duverger's subsequent remarks it becomes clear that even his distinctions between single-party, two-party and multi-party systems are inadequate as principles of explanation of the functioning of political systems. He and other scholars have noted the fact that the multi-party systems of France and Italy differ from those of the Scandinavian and Low Countries, and that the one-party system of Spain is rather different from those of Russia and Nazi Germany. To understand the differences between the multi-party systems of France and Italy and those of the Scandinavian countries we would have to look "below" the levels of the party systems into the "interest group" systems of these countries and into basic popular attitudes toward political authority, partisanship, and interest—their "political cultures" in other words. The differences between the one-party regimes of countries such

as the Soviet Union and Nazi Germany on the one hand and Spain on the other are to be accounted for largely by the different goals and practices of the groups controlling the authoritative governmental institutions.

In our search for types of polities and the principles governing their behavior it would be a mistake simply to go one or two steps beyond Duverger, and say not the party system, but the interest groups and political culture ". . . become the fundamental mode of classifying contemporary regimes." The mistake arises out of the search for some single "crucial institution" or principle of explanation. In other words we turn to the comparative study of interest groups not with the hope that these rather than parties or governmental institutions will yield *the principles* of discrimination between types of political systems, but rather with the expectation that the systematic examination of interest groups in their complex interrelations with public opinion, political parties and formal governmental institutions will enable us to differentiate more accurately between political systems as *wholes*. In other words, the growing concern among scholars with interest groups and public opinion is the consequence of a search for a more complete and systematic conception of the political process as a whole, rather than a search for an approach which is an *alternative* to the present emphasis on formal governmental institutions.

As Truman[3] and other scholars have pointed out, interest groups may be articulate or inarticulate, manifest or latent, formally organized, or simply a condition of like-mindedness and informal communication about issues. A comparison of Western and non-Western political systems brings out sharply the "latency" of the typical non-Western political system in contrast to the overtness of Western politics.[4] How different are the problems of public policy-making in a society where there are no effective mechanisms for the articulation of political demands, from one in which there is an elaborate set of structures for the formulation of demands, and the transmission of these demands into the party and governmental systems? The kinds of interest groups which are present in a society, the specificity or diffuseness of their demands, their conceptions of the political arena and of the "rules of the game," the ethos which they bring with them into the political process—these are the "raw materials" of politics—the unaggregated demands—which some set of mechanisms must transform into political personnel and public policy.

These general observations about interest groups not only suggest their importance as a subject of study, but set certain specifications in research design if the maximum value of a comparative study is to be attained. A good research job on interest groups in a particular country which may make possible meaningful comparisons with other countries, must examine the interest group system in its relations with the social structure and culture on the one hand and the other parts of the political structure on the other. In identifying the interest group system in any particular country this broad functional approach will prevent us from identifying interest groups with any particular kind of structure. The function of articulating and transmitting group interests may be performed in one system typically by the well organized and bureaucratized "pressure groups" familiar in the West, or it may be performed in another system typically through an informal and intermittent process of communication between and among class and status groups such as large landholders or businessmen, and cliques of bureaucrats and/or army officers. If it is possible to state the theme of the comparative study in the form of a single question it might be: What form does the articulation of political interests take in various societies, and how are these interests transmitted to other parts of the political and governmental structure, and translated into choices of political personnel and public policy?

## II. THE GENERAL DESCRIPTION OF THE INTEREST GROUP SYSTEM

It was the general conclusion of the planning session that each of the participants in the comparative study would attempt a general survey of the system of interest groups in his country, describing the kinds of interest groups which are present, their membership size in relation to potential, their financial resources, activities, patterns of coalition and interaction among them, and internal patterns of organization and decision-making. The usefulness of such a descriptive census was defended on the ground that many of the most significant differences among interest group systems will come out sharply through such description. Thus, three of the distinguishing characteristics of American interest groups—the large number of civic and ethnic interest groups, and the relatively high degree of membership participation in decision-making within interest groups—would come out clearly in such a comparative description. A comparison of the structure, the membership and the financial resources of the trade unions on the European continent will tell us a great deal about the differences between the political systems of France and Italy as compared with Germany, the United Kingdom, the Low Countries, and the Scandinavian countries. The predominance of functionally specific, bureaucratized, associational types of

interest groups in the West, and of kinship groups, status groups, and of informal cliques in the non-Western areas is one of the most crucial distinctions between these types of political systems. Again the clearer distinction between the functions of parties and interest groups in the United States, the United Kingdom and the Commonwealth, than obtains on the European continent and the non-Western areas, is a major clue to the special properties of Anglo-American politics.

The planning session was in full agreement on the desirability of such a general survey and appraisal of the interest group system as a whole. At the same time the discussion pointed up clearly the radically different conditions of research in the areas represented which might make such a general survey a full-time problem in one area, and an easier task in another. For example, in a country such as Germany, the high degree of formal organization of interest groups, the availability of directories, of interest group publications, and of monographic studies by German scholars, would make such a survey a relatively simple problem and quite consistent with a major allocation of research time to the characteristics and functioning of a limited number of selected groups. In India on the other hand even an attempt at an accurate survey of the kinds and characteristics of interest groups might very well constitute a full-time research operation. Even on the European continent the search for comprehensiveness of coverage and accuracy of detail in some countries might seriously conflict with other research purposes.

A review of the range of problems which might confront the participants in the comparative study in making such general surveys and appraisals led the group to the conclusion that these would in every case be ranked as a research goal, secondary to the more intensive analyses of the characteristics of specific, selected interest groups. They would be carried on primarily as a by-product of the documentary research and interviewing programs of the participants. It was recognized that this would make some of these general appraisals less well documented and more speculative than others. It was also agreed that the general descriptive material gained from such surveys, and the general hypotheses about the characteristics of interest group systems as wholes, would be reported by each participant in the form of a general introductory chapter or chapters in his monographic report. It was also agreed that these general appraisal chapters would be exchanged by the participants as early as possible in order to have included in the individual country studies propositions about similarities and differences between the interest groups of the particular country studied and those of the other countries.

## III. THE SELECTION OF
## SPECIFIC INTEREST GROUPS

While all the participants in the planning session had expressed the intention of studying interest groups in their particular countries, considerable variation emerged in the kind of group or groups which had been selected for emphasis. The original preferences were based on prior research interests and the salience of particular kinds of groups in the countries studied. The planning session brought out the point that while the choice of group or groups differed from one country to the next, all the studies had in common a concern with the political function of articulating and transmitting demands into the political process. The different choices of types of groups was largely due to the fact that different kinds of interest groups performed these functions in the various countries. Thus in the Western European countries, the job of translating the interests of different segments of the society into political demands, and bringing these demands to bear in the policy-making process was largely performed by the trade union movements, the agricultural federations, business groups and trade associations, and church groups of one kind or another. On the other hand, in Asia, the Middle East and Latin America two major classes of interest groups were in operation, one typical of the more modern, industrialized and westernized sectors of these societies, and the other typical of that part of the society less affected by change. Hence, a study of interest groups in the non-Western countries would have to sample both the older and the newer types of structures. It would have to look into the activities of the emerging trade union, business, and student movements in the modernized, primarily urban parts of these societies, and the status groups, kinship and lineage, religious and ethnic groups of the village and the countryside. The problem of interest group research in these areas is not only that of describing the characteristics and functioning of these two types of interest group systems, but also examining their relations with one another.

In the course of the discussions it was agreed that, while each participant might give greater emphasis to research on a particular class of groups, some attention would be given to the activities of the other significant groups. The argument here was that a study which, for example, concentrated on the political activities of trade unions would be incomplete without some attention to business groups and trade associations, agricultural organizations, and religious groups. Hence, those concerned with the European countries agreed that some attention would be paid to each of the major classes of interests. Specific decisions about the allocation

of emphasis and methods would have to be made by the researcher in the field, in the light of the availability of information, the relative importance of these groups, and his special interests. Those concerned with the non-Western areas agreed on the desirability of sampling the "modern, urban" type of interest groups, the interests operating within governmental agencies including the army, and the traditional groupings. Here again the specific selections would have to take into account the special characteristics of the political system in the area, as well as the conditions of research.

The general conclusion was that by being concerned with the "function" of interest in the political process, rather than certain kinds of structures, and by being concerned with sampling the interest group universe, a significant step toward comparability and cumulativeness of theory would be accomplished.

## IV. INTEREST GROUPS
## AND PUBLIC OPINION[5]

One of the most challenging opportunities presented by the comparative study was that of systematically introducing public opinion data into the study of political interests. One of the central problems in interest group theory is the relation between manifest and latent interest. To what extent can organized, overt interests be taken as reflecting the interest tendencies of the general population? The phenomena of the mob in non-Western countries, of riots in totalitarian countries, of "Caesarism," "Poujadism," and "incivisme" in the European area suggest that popular attitudes and tendencies are a separable factor in the political process, the properties of which cannot be inferred from the existing organized tendencies and from electoral behavior. Any characterization of a political system would be incomplete if it was confined solely to a description of current organizational patterns and processes. Latent interest may not only result in future changes in organization and process, it establishes an atmosphere which affects the contemporary operations of the political process.

It was agreed that the relations between interest groups and public opinion would be an important dimension of the comparative study. One of the main, but by no means the only, source of information about public opinion, would be the accumulations of public opinion data available in many of the European countries. In the course of the discussions of the kinds of polling material which were available it became clear that while there was much that might be useful there was relatively little that dealt directly with the problems of legitimacy and consensus, that is, popular attitudes toward governmental authority, and the attitudes of groups in the population toward one another. Thus, certain basic hypotheses about the relations between the condition of political opinion and the functioning of political systems in the European area had never been directly investigated, but were now in the form of inferences from the behavior of groups and institutions. The question put before the session was: Would it be possible through a survey of comparative political opinion to establish (1) that the British political process with its moderate interest groups, and its effectively functioning two-party system, is related to a homogeneous, secular, and loyal public opinion; (2) that the French and Italian political processes with their fragmented party and interest group systems, are related to fragmented, only partly secularized, and largely alienated political cultures; and (3) that the political systems of the Scandinavian and Low Countries with their "working multi-party systems," and their relatively moderate interest group systems were related to political communities in which the "consensual bond" was stronger than in France and Italy, and in which the great majority of the population viewed governmental authority as having a useful and constructive function in relation to their interests?

All the participants agreed to examine the accumulations of public opinion data in their countries and to use whatever information they could get from these sources on attitudes toward interest, party, and state. In addition they agreed to consult and advise in the planning and execution of a comparative opinion survey which might deal more directly with these phenomena, if such a survey should be undertaken as a part of the program.

A second aspect of the relations between interest groups and public opinion was discussed, the propaganda and information activities of interest groups. The ways in which interest groups conceive of their audiences, and the ways in which they represent their interests to the public should throw light on the functioning of the political system as a whole. For example, French business associations are different from the American in that they do not engage openly and on a large scale in public "informational" activities. This may reflect a general condition of fragmentation in political communication in France, a condition of distrust and alienation among interests. The general proposition was advanced that certain patterns of interest communications activity are associated with certain basic conditions of the political community.

It was agreed that the "public relations" of interest groups would be examined with the following questions in mind:

1. How does the interest group conceive of its audience?

2. How is the public relations function organized and what is the magnitude of the public relations effort?

3. How are interest groups related to the specialized communications system of the society (e.g., press, radio, educational system and the like)?

## V. INTEREST GROUPS AND POLITICAL PARTIES[6]

In the discussions and conferences of the Committee on Comparative Politics over the last three years, and in papers prepared by Committee members and other participants in the Committee's work, the broad outlines of a theory of comparative political systems has slowly developed.[7] In part, this theory has been concerned with the development of models of the various forms of the political process in existence today. During the planning sessions in Palo Alto these models were again discussed; they influenced much of the research design which is reported below. It may be useful to summarize these characterizations of the Anglo-American systems, the varieties of non-Western political systems, the French-Italian "crisis" system, and the "working multi-party" systems of the Scandinavian and the Low Countries.

In the Anglo-American type of political system the functions of political parties and interest groups are sharply differentiated. Interest groups articulate political demands in the society, seek support for these demands among other groups by advocacy and bargaining, and attempt to transform these demands into authoritative public policy by influencing the choice of political personnel, and the various processes of public policy-making and enforcement. Political parties tend to be free of ideological rigidity, and are aggregative, i.e., seek to form the largest possible interest group coalitions by offering acceptable choices of political personnel and public policy. Both the interest group systems and the party systems are differentiated, bureaucratized, and autonomous. Each unit in the party and interest group systems comes into the "market," so to speak, with an adjustive bargaining ethos. Furthermore, the party system stands between the interest group system and the authoritative policy-making agencies and screens them from the particularistic and disintegrative impact of special interests. The party system aggregates interests and transforms them into a relatively small number of alternative general policies. Thus this set of relationships between the party system and the interest group system enables choice among general policies to take place in the legislature, and assures that the bureaucracy will tend to function as a neutral instrument of the political agencies.

We might take as our second type a model summarizing the properties of the political systems which are to be found in Asia, the Middle East and Latin America in which neither parties nor interest groups are fully differentiated. Associational interest groups such as trade unions and business associations may exist in the urban Westernized parts of the society, but in the village and the countryside interest organization takes the form of lineage, caste, status, class and religious groups, which transmit political demands to the other parts of the political structure by means of informal communication. In one version of this class of systems parties tend to be *ad hoc* coalitions without permanent bureaucracies, and without grass roots organization. They exist primarily in election periods and in effect cease to exist in the intervals between. Given such weak and non-aggregative party systems the capacity of the legislatures to formulate alternative policy choices may be seriously impaired, as is their capacity to control the bureaucracies. In many of these political systems the significant political groups are neither the parties, nor the associational interest groups, but elements or cliques within the bureaucracy, and the army; and cliques, informal groupings and powerful families formed within such non-associational interests as religious communities, the large landowners, the business community, and the like. The political process consists of the informal communication and flow of influence between these informally organized interests, and groups within the bureaucracy and the army.

The instabilities of this type of political system arise out of the fact that the agencies for the articulation, communication, and aggregation of interests are incomplete and unrepresentative, as well as out of the fact that the demands transmitted into the political system from interest groups are vague, diffuse, and of radically unlike content and intensity. Latent interests, lacking overt and organized channels of expression may suddenly break into the political arena. The information available to influential groups and individuals about the expectations and attitudes of the various interests in the society cannot be complete or accurate. Hence, calculation is impossible, and the flow of political interaction involves under-reaction and over-reaction, violence and apathy, alternations of periods of political latency, with sudden and violent shifts in power.

Given the basic instability of this general class of political systems, authoritarian stabilizations are a frequent event. Indeed, in many of them the developmental pattern is one of a shift from an unstable pluralism to authoritarianism, and then back again, or a shift from the authoritarianism of one clique to that of another. Authoritarianism may be based on control of the army either by a clique of army officers, or a clique of bureaucrats controlling the army, or by a coalition of both. Still another pattern is one in which the desire on the part of a controlling group to secure its own power

and destroy opposition, or to mobilize the society for industrialization and national expansion, leads to the formation of an authoritarian party which actually penetrates the countryside. In some cases as in Turkey and in India the objectives of the ruling groups and of the dominant party are tutelary. That is, the function of the party is not only control and mobilization, but also political acculturation, the preparation of the ground for the emergence of a Western-type party system with a coherent, responsible, and loyal opposition.

Thus, it should be quite clear that there are many kinds of non-Western political systems. They all appear to have in common (1) a fragmented political culture as a consequence of Westernization, in many cases added on to an indigenous cultural heterogeneity, (2) poor political communications and a high degree of interest latency which renders political calculation difficult if not impossible, and (3) a party system which is incapable of aggregating and synthesizing interest demands into a small number of political alternatives either of personnel or of public policy. On a scale of political differentiation one would have to say that certain kinds of structures such as associational interest groups, the mass media of communication, and the kind of party system common in the West and essential for the functioning of a modern mass-suffrage parliamentary system, are present at best in only a limited degree. On a scale of functional specialization one would have to say that in the absence of fully developed associational interest groups, party systems, and modern media of communication, the functions of interest articulation, aggregation, communication and transmission are largely performed by bureaucratic or army cliques, traditional structures such as lineage or status groupings, and by mobs, street demonstrations and the like, which serve as one of the agencies by means of which latent interests are articulated and transmitted.

A third type of political system is exemplified by France and Italy and by the Germany of the Weimar Republic. Contemporary Germany appears to be moving in the direction of an autonomous interest group system and an aggregative two-party system; toward the Anglo-American model, in other words. In the French and Italian political systems parties and interest groups are organized and bureaucratized, but they are not autonomous systems. They interpenetrate one another and consequently fail to realize the two-stage pattern of the political process characteristic of the English and American systems. There are some parties which more or less control interest groups (*e.g.,* the Communist party and the Communist-dominated trade unions, and to a lesser extent the Socialist parties and the Socialist trade unions). There are some interest groups which more or less control other interest groups and parties (*e.g.,* the Church, the Catholic trade unions, and the Catholic parties, business interest groups, and the center and right wing parties, and the like).

When parties control interest groups they inhibit the capacity of interest groups to formulate pragmatic specific demands; they impart a political-ideological content to interest group activity. When interest groups control parties they inhibit the capacity of the party to combine specific interests into programs with wider appeal. What reaches the legislative process from the interest groups and through the political parties thus are the "raw," unaggregated demands of specific interests, or the diffuse, uncompromising, or revolutionary tendencies of the Church and the movements of the extreme right or left. Since no interest group is large enough to have a majority, and the party system cannot aggregate different interests into a stable majority and a coherent opposition, the electoral and legislative processes fail to provide alternative, effective choices. The result is a legislature penetrated by relatively narrow interests and uncompromising ideological tendencies, a legislature which can be used as an arena for propaganda, or for the protection of special interests, by veto or otherwise, but not for the effective and timely formulation and support of large policy decisions. And without a strong legislature, special interests and ideological tendencies penetrate the bureaucracy, and undermine its neutral, instrumental character.

A fourth type of political system is exemplified by the Scandinavian and Low Countries. These systems appear to differ from the French and Italian in two respects. First, the party systems tend to be aggregative (e.g., the Scandinavian Socialist and Catholic parties). Second, the relations between parties and interests appear to be more consensual, which makes stable majority and opposition coalitions possible. Thus, though the party systems fail to aggregate interests as thoroughly as in the British case, the public policy-making function of the legislature is not undermined to the same extent as in the French and Italian cases. What appears to happen in the Scandinavian and the Low Countries is that the function of interest aggregation and general policy formulation occurs at both the party and parliamentary levels. The parties are partly aggregative of interests, but "majority-minority" aggregation takes place finally in the coalition-making process in the legislature. This coalition-making process may be organized by parties in the formation of cabinets and the enactment of legislation or it may take the form of interest coalitions organized around issues of public policy. The capacity for stable majority-minority party coalitions and for relatively flexible issue-oriented interest coalitions is dependent upon the existence of a basic political consensus which affects both parties and interest groups. These appear to

be the properties of the so-called "working multi-party systems."[8]

These simplified models of political systems represent some of the general theory of political groups shared by the participants in the planning session. It represents a set of hypotheses about the characteristics and consequences of the main types of interest group systems to be found in the countries in which field research is planned. The problem of research tactics, of how to test, elaborate, and develop our theories further remains to be specified.

The discussion stressed that the relation between political parties and interest groups could be viewed as a continuum with substantial autonomy at one limit and sub- and super-ordination at the other. The relationship patterns which exist in historical political systems always involve two-way flows of influence, which differ from one another in the dominant direction of the flow and the different patterns which are occasioned by different kinds of issues. Thus the extreme case of the Communist party—Communist trade union dominance still involves a flow of information and influence from trade union to party, but the dominant direction of the flow is from party to trade union. In the case of the church and Catholic parties the flow of influence varies from country to country, and even among regions within countries. In addition, in certain areas of policy Catholic parties may be relatively free of church influence, or may even influence the church to take a position consistent with or supportive of that of the party. In Germany, for example, the fact that the CDU has both Protestant and Catholic support seriously limits the power of the Catholic church to intervene in party policy-making. In other legislative fields, the freedom of Catholic parties may be sharply circumscribed by a rigid church position, as in the field of educational subsidies and the like. In other policy areas, e.g., social-economic, there may be more give and take in the relations between church and Catholic party.

These considerations suggested that analysis of the flow of influence between parties and interest groups would require not only an examination of the interconnections through financing, interlocking memberships and directorates, sharing of ideological beliefs and the like, but would also require a judicious use of case study methods to discover the way in which different kinds of legislative issues affected the flow and pattern of influence between interest groups and parties.

It was generally agreed that a first task in analyzing parties and interest group relationships would involve a study of the history of these organizations and of their interrelations. In some cases parties formed or were influential in the forming of interest groups (e.g., the Communists and the "Red Unions," the Socialists and the Force Ouvrière); in many others interest groups formed or influenced the formation of parties (*e.g.,* some labor parties by trade unions, Catholic parties by the Church and/or elements of Catholic Action, and agrarian parties by agrarian interest groups). Whatever the history of the relationship may be, it will provide an important body of evidence on the relationship between the two and changes in the relationship through time.

A second major research task would involve a careful analysis of the structure, internal politics, activities, and ideologies of specific interest groups and parties as they relate to the flow of influence.

1. What is the relative financial strength of interest group and party? To what extent does the interest group finance the party, or *vice versa?* What is the special pattern of election financing?

2. What is their relative manpower potential? *E.g.,* does the party depend on the interest group for personnel during elections as is the case for Catholic and labor parties, or does it have a manpower reserve of its own?

3. What is the relative effectiveness of the grass roots organizations of parties and interest groups? *E.g.,* is the party organized primarily at the center and dependent on interest groups for the penetration of local areas, or does the party have an autonomous local organization of its own?

4. To what extent is there overlapping in membership and officers as between interest group and party?

5. What are the factional and ideological characteristics of interest groups and parties, and how do they affect the pattern of influence?

## VI. INTEREST GROUPS AND THE LEGISLATIVE PROCESS[9]

Interest groups tend to seek out the important points of access in the legislative process; the points where legislative policy is initiated, and where revision, vetoing, and favorable action are possible. Hence, the constitutional separation and distribution of powers, legislative organization and procedure, the characteristics of the electoral system and the parliamentary party organization, set the problem of interest group access in the legislative process. Thus, the American system of federalism, and separation of powers, creates a different interest group "target structure" than does the British parliamentary-cabinet system. The American federal system produces a party structure with its center of gravity at the state level. This kind of decentralized party organization limits the possibilities of congressional party discipline and hence opens the legislative process to interest group penetration. The susceptibility of the legislature to interest group penetration is enhanced by the Amer-

ican single-member district electoral system which frequently exposes the legislator to the effective pressure of interests which may be especially concentrated in his constituency. In addition, the American separation of powers system grants a powerful and independent role in legislation to both the House and Senate. And since relatively large collegial bodies are, other things being equal, less able to aggregate interests and protect themselves against interest penetration than Cabinet-dominated parliaments, this aspect of American constitutional structure contributes significantly to interest group action in the legislative process. If we consider this constitutional and statutory structure on the one hand, and the economic, regional, ethnic, and religious composition of the American population on the other, it is hardly surprising that the penetration of the legislative process by interest groups in the United States is greater than in the United Kingdom. There, a unitary constitution, and a Cabinet-dominated parliament make possible a disciplined parliamentary party system which protects the legislative process from effective interest group penetration. The main targets of interest groups are the upper levels of the parliamentary and extra-parliamentary party structure where power is concentrated, and the bureaucracy. And because of the cohesion of the party system and the concentration of legislative power in the Cabinet, the impact of any single interest group—with the exception of the trade unions—is quite limited.

France presents yet another problem of interest group access. In the United States aggregation and synthesis of interests is performed by the party system and a powerful presidency responsible to a national constituency. France has neither a powerful executive nor an aggregative party system. A culturally and politically fragmented society choosing its legislators by means of proportional representation produces a legislature capable of producing only weak and unstable coalitions. The standing committees of the *Assemblée* are in many cases colonized by powerful interests.[10] The net effect of this situation is a legislative process which can only rarely enact significant "national-interest" legislation, but which regularly and characteristically protects and subsidizes special interests. Still a fourth type of legislative interest group pattern is to be found in the Scandinavian countries where a stronger executive and a more aggregative party system limits the impact of interest groups in the legislative process.

These characteristics of constitutional, legislative, and party structures affect not only the tactics of interest groups, but the very goals and objectives which they can reasonably attain. A disciplined party system and a powerful executive forces interest groups to direct their energies to the upper levels of the executive and the bureaucracy where only moderate claims, well supported with technical information, become possible. A non-aggregative and undisciplined party system as in France opens up the legislative process to covert interest group domination of legislative committees and agencies, or to propagandistic interest group maneuvers of which "Poujadism" is only an extreme instance.

These hypotheses about patterns of interest-group-legislative relations in the European area suggest the importance of a careful analysis of the functioning of the constitutional, legislative, electoral, and party systems as they relate to interest group access. In other words, the aim of research in interest-group-legislative relations will be to determine the extent to which the parliamentary parties, or extra-parliamentary legislative institutions such as the American Presidency, are able to maintain independence of interest groups and relative freedom to legislate or influence legislation (a) by combining several interest groups in their support, and (b) by establishing and maintaining the discipline of the parliamentary party as a means of withstanding interest group pressures.

The discussions in the planning session turned on the question of how to test these hypotheses economically and effectively. It was agreed that research here would concentrate on four problems.

1. The first of these is the analysis of the "target structure" itself. This would involve an examination of the distribution and location of legislative power as between the parliament, the executive, and the bureaucracy; the internal organization and procedure of the parliament; the organization and operations of the party system in the parliament; and the effect of the electoral system on the party system and on the position of the individual parliamentarian. This phase of research would also include an examination of the various devices for formal interest group representation such as "economic councils" and advisory committees and groups of one kind or another.

2. Closely related to this first task is a study of how interest groups perceive and appraise the "target structure" of the legislative process. Such analysis would bring out significant differences between the interest groups in particular countries as well as between countries. If our general impressions are correct we would expect to find that British interest groups would share the same picture of legislative reality, and that it would tend to be a relatively accurate picture. In France, we would expect to find quite different conceptions of constitutional and legislative reality among interest groups. Thus, the different pictures of constitutional reality characteristic of the Church and the Communist trade unions would be the consequence of basically different ideological presuppositions and political experience. The C.G.T. would view the

French legislative process as incapable of realizing working class objectives. Consequently, their primary objective *vis-à-vis* the French Constitution would be to immobilize it, and to destroy it. The Church, on the other hand, would view the French legislative process as more amenable to pressure through access to the M.R.P. and right-wing parties, and through sympathetic elements in the bureaucracy. In many non-Western countries we would expect to find relatively new and inexperienced interest groups with highly inaccurate or vague pictures of political reality.

3. A third task involves study of the objectives of interest groups in the legislative process. Thus, in the United Kingdom we would expect to find interest groups entertaining moderate, secular objectives in the legislative process; in France we would expect to find interest groups seeking extreme, incompatible, and rigid objectives; in non-Western countries we would expect to find many interest groups seeking "expressive" rather than "instrumental" objectives.

4. A fourth area of study is of the means or techniques employed by interest groups to attain their objectives—what we might call the interest group style. Here, we would be concerned with whether or not the techniques are overt or covert, whether propaganda, negotiation, bribery, or demonstration and riot are the preferred means. In the United Kingdom we would expect to find an overt style, with propaganda, negotiation, and bargaining the favored means of interest groups. In France, we should find that much interest group activity is covert, and that demonstration and bribery occur with some frequency. In many non-Western countries the style of interest groups may be largely covert, and the techniques heavily on the riot, demonstration, and bribery side.

## VII. INTEREST GROUPS AND THE BUREAUCRACY[11]

The ideal of a neutral, instrumental bureaucracy, responsible to the political arm, comes closest to being realized in political systems where the political culture tends to be secular and rational, and where the functions of political choice—that is, the articulation and aggregation of interests and the making of public policy—are performed by specialized agencies. If the interest group system fails to articulate and communicate the demands of significant sectors of the population, or if the political demands which it transmits are irreconcilable, then the capacity of the party system to aggregate and to compromise demands and facilitate political choice in the legislative process is undermined. If the parliament and the "political executive" fail to perform the functions of interest articulation and aggregation, then the problem gravitates to the bureaucracy, and its capacity for neutral, responsible administration is weakened. Under these circumstances the bureaucracy tends to be multifunctional. It articulates and aggregates interests, makes public policy and administers it. To be sure the so-called "neutral bureaucracies" in the West do these same things, but only to a limited extent and under control, and in situations where there are effective political agencies outside the bureaucracy.

For purposes of the planning session four types of interest group-bureaucracy relationships were discussed. The first of these is illustrated by the situation in the United Kingdom where moderate interest groups, representative of the significant interest tendencies in the population, are aggregated by disciplined parties. Both of these conditions make possible an effective organization of the legislative process, and an effective political control over the bureaucracy. The second is illustrated by the Scandinavian countries where aggregation of interest is less thorough-going than in the United Kingdom. In the Scandinavian countries aggregation occurs both in the party system and in the coalition-making process in the parliaments. Nevertheless an effective parliamentary process makes possible a neutral, instrumental bureaucracy. The third type is illustrated by the situation in France where effective aggregation of interests and policy making does not occur in the party system, the parliament or the bureaucracy. The net result is a political system in which the agencies of political choice fail to function, and in which basic policy decisions cannot be made. It tends to be a government of "protection and maintenance" in which the effective agencies are the interest groups and the bureaucracy. The bureaucracy cannot be a neutral, responsible instrument under these circumstances. It is "colonized" by interest groups, and penetrated by incompatible ideological tendencies.

The non-Western areas present a variety of interest-group-bureaucracy relationships. In one quite common pattern parties and associational interest groups are only in their beginnings, and the political process operates primarily within the bureaucracy itself. The bureaucracy is a congeries of interests—family, religious, status, class, professional, ideological, and the like. A bureaucratic or army clique makes informal coalitions of these interests and maintains contact through them with their counterparts outside the bureaucracy. The political process may take the form of an unstable pluralism, or in a second variety, a particular clique or individual may establish authoritarian control and operate with the backing of the army. Another non-Western pattern is one in which an authoritarian party is formed, one of its main functions being to mobilize groups in the society, articulate their interests and

bring them to the support of the ruling groups. If the tendency of the authoritarian leadership is conservative, then traditional interests—status, economic, religious—will have favored access to the bureaucracy. If the tendency is toward modernization then urban, professional, industrial and labor interests may have favored access to the bureaucracy, and the traditional interests may be in a disadvantaged position.

The planning sessions agreed on the following specifications for research on interest group-bureaucracy relationships.

1. Each study would have to appraise the substantive areas of economic and social life affected by the bureaucracy. This would indicate the kinds of interests which were being affected by bureaucratic activity, and the ways in which they are being affected.

2. Each study would have to examine the organizational and influence pattern of the bureaucracy. To what extent and by what means is the bureaucracy controlled by extra-bureaucratic agencies such as the cabinet and/or the parliament? To what extent is the bureaucracy internally cohesive and subject to central control? Or put the other way around, to what extent are specific agencies and sub-agencies independent? Needless to say both the external political, and internal control patterns would set some of the problems of access of interest groups to the bureaucracy.

3. What are the characteristics of the members of the bureaucracy—particularly its higher echelons? From what social groups are they recruited? What are the training patterns, and what kinds of skills do they possess? What are their ideological and partisan characteristics? All of these attributes would affect their susceptibility to interest group pressures.

4. What are the goals and tactics of the various interest groups vis-à-vis the bureaucracy? Are they primarily concerned with gaining specific family, status group, class, or professional advantages, or do they advocate diffuse ideological objectives, or both? What methods of influence do interest groups employ in relation to the bureaucracy? Is bribery or violence a common pattern? Or is propaganda, negotiation, and the provision of information about the consequences of bureaucratic action for specific interests the typical pattern?

5. To what extent do interest groups actually penetrate the bureaucracy? Here we are not only concerned with formal provision for interest group representation in specific agencies in advisory capacities, or with the special relations between administrative agencies and their particular constituencies (e.g., labor ministries, economic ministries, agriculture ministries, and the like), but also with the direct control over specific bureaucratic functions, in other words the "colonization" of the bureaucracy by interest groups.

## VIII. COMPARISON OF WESTERN AND NON-WESTERN INTEREST GROUPS[12]

One of the most challenging questions confronting the planning sessions was the problem of comparing Western and non-Western political systems. Are they so different in culture and practice as to constitute basically different political species? Was the approach of political science scholarship in the study of Western and non-Western politics so different as to rule out effective collaboration? Did the group participating in the discussions and planning field studies share a common theory of politics which would make collaboration possible? The discussions led to the conclusion that Western and non-Western political systems have much in common, and that the particular group of scholars present shared a common approach and theory of politics.

The basis of this common outlook might be called the "functional" approach. The participants in the comparative study agreed that they were concerned with the functions of political choice, and with the wave in which these functions were performed in different societies. Every independent society makes political choices, *i.e.,* broad policy decisions which are backed up by severe sanctions. In making and enforcing these political decisions all societies have some way of articulating and communicating political demands, aggregating these demands, translating them into choices of political personnel and public policy, executing these decisions in specific cases, and testing the appropriateness of these specific actions. In studying interest groups comparatively the participants in the study are primarily concerned with the structures, institutions and processes by means of which these functions are accomplished. Research conclusions as to which structures and processes perform which functions in different societies, and how they perform them, will provide the basic materials for comparative analysis.

Not only are these functions performed in all independent political systems—Western and non-Western—but the structures and processes which perform them in both areas overlap to a considerable extent. The West is more like the non-West than we sometimes think. Even in the most differentiated and specialized political systems in the West, such interest groups as families, status groups, and religious communities affect the political process. And in most of the non-Western countries—however "underdeveloped"—the beginnings of functionally specialized political parties, and associational interest groups such as trade unions and trade associations, may be found. Even in the field of political communication the highly elaborated mass communication systems of Western societies should not obscure the fact that informal and face-to-face communication is still a political factor of enormous importance.

In still another respect Western and non-Western systems are alike. While it is true in general that Western political structures are more specialized than the non-Western, there is much "multi-functionalism" in the West. Thus in a country such as France political parties and interest groups are not sharply differentiated from one another. And in all countries the structural specialization of policy-making and administration is by no means complete, nor can it ever be complete. If it is peculiar to non-Western countries that bureaucracies are penetrated by interest groups and ideological tendencies, this situation differs only in degree from the Western pattern where rationality, responsibility, and neutrality are only partially realized at best.

The comparative study of interest groups will include a number of cases in Asia and Latin America. In particular it is anticipated that there will be studies of Malaya, Burma, India, and Indonesia in Asia; and of Brazil, Mexico, Cuba, and Peru in Latin America. The non-Western specialists at the planning session agreed to follow much the same pattern as the European specialists. This would include a general appraisal of the kinds of interest groups to be found in these countries, their composition, size, goals, methods of influence, and the like. It would also include more detailed investigations of selected interest groups. These intensive studies are likely to include trade unions, peasant groups, student groups, religious and tribal or ethnic groups. Some attention would be paid to the "mob" as an "anomic" interest group phenomenon, resulting from lack of effective access of some social groupings to politics, and generally poor political communications.

The planning session at Palo Alto was followed by another held in June, 1957 at Michigan State University for a number of scholars about to undertake research on political groups in Latin America. A third is planned for the late Spring in 1958 for recipients of grants for field research on political groups during the present year. By setting common questions and discussing common approaches the Committee on Comparative Politics hopes to introduce greater coherence in the research efforts under way. More recently it has begun to plan a series of comparative analyses which will draw the findings of these and other research efforts together.

## NOTES

1. The personnel of the session and the areas represented were as follows: France, Henry Ehrmann, University of Colorado; United Kingdom, Leon Epstein, University of Wisconsin; Germany, Sigmund Neumann, Wesleyan University and Gabriel A. Almond, Prince-

ton University; Italy, Joseph La Palombara, Michigan State University; Belgium, Val Lorwin, University of Oregon; Spain, Juan Linz, University of California (Berkeley); Burma, Lucian W. Pye, Massachusetts Institute of Technology; India, Myron Weiner, University of Chicago; Latin America, George Blanksten, Northwestern University and Bryce Wood, Social Science Research Council.

2. Maurice Duverger, *Political Parties* (New York, 1954), pp. 392–93.

3. David B. Truman, *The Governmental Process* (New York, 1951), pp. 14 ff.

4. Lucian W. Pye, *Guerrilla Communism in Malaya* (Princeton, N.J., 1956), pp. 346 ff.

5. This discussion was led by Seymour M. Lipset of the University of California and Gabriel A. Almond, Princeton University.

6. The report on this topic was presented by Sigmund Neumann of Wesleyan University and Val Lorwin of the University of Oregon.

7. Kahin, Pauker, Pye, "Comparative Politics of Non-Western Countries," *American Political Science Review* (Dec., 1955), pp. 1022 ff.; Almond, Cole, Macridis, "A Suggested Research Strategy in Western European Government and Politics," *ibid.,* pp. 1042 ff.; Almond, "Comparative Political Systems," *Journal of Politics* (August, 1956), pp. 391 ff.; Francis X. Sutton,

"Social Theory and Comparative Politics," (unpublished paper); Samuel H. Beer, "Pressure Groups and Parties in Britain," *American Political Science Review* (March, 1956), pp. 1 ff.; Dankwart Rustow, *Politics and Westernization in the Near East,* Center of International Studies, Princeton University, March, 1956; Rustow, "New Horizons for Comparative Politics," *World Politics* (July, 1957); Sigmund Neumann, "Comparative Politics, A Half Century Appraisal," *Journal of Politics* (August, 1957); Gabriel Almond and Myron Weiner, "A Comparative Approach to the Study of Political Groups," Agenda Paper for the Dobbs Ferry Seminar of the Committee on Comparative Politics, June, 1956.

8. See Dankwart Rustow, "Scandinavia: Working Multiparty Systems," in Sigmund Neumann (Ed.), *Modern Political Parties* (Chicago, 1956), pp. 169 ff.

9. The report to the planning session on this topic was presented by Leon Epstein and Henry Ehrmann.

10. Henry W. Ehrmann, *Organized Business in France* (Princeton, Princeton University Press, 1957), ch. V.

11. The report on this topic was presented by Juan Linz and Joseph La Palombara.

12. Reports on this problem were presented by Myron Weiner, Lucian Pye, George Blanksten, and Bryce Wood.

# THE DETERMINANTS
# OF PRESSURE GROUP POLITICS

## Harry Eckstein

## PROBLEMS

Case studies never "prove" anything; their purpose is to illustrate generalizations which are established otherwise, or to direct attention towards such generalizations. Since this is a case study of the political activities of the British Medical Association it may be well to state at the outset the broad principles it illustrates. These principles are formulated in answer to three questions:

a. What are the determinants of the *form* of pressure group politics in various political systems? What factors determine the principal channels and means through which pressure groups act on gov-

ernment and the character of the relations between the groups and organs of government?

b. What are the determinants of the *intensity* and *scope* of pressure group politics? "Intensity" here refers to the fervour and persistence with which groups pursue their political objectives as well as to the relative importance of political activities in their affairs; "scope," to the number and variety of groups engaged in politics.

c. What determines the *effectiveness* of pressure groups? From what principal sources do they derive their power *vis-à-vis* other pressure groups and the more formal elements of the decision-making structure, such as parties, legislature, and bureaucracy?

At the end of the study certain other theoretical questions generally raised in pressure group studies are discussed, but the questions listed above are the main problems of the study.

Reprinted from Harry Eckstein, *Pressure Group Politics* (Stanford: Stanford University Press, 1960), pp. 15–39.

# DETERMINANTS OF THE FORM OF PRESSURE GROUP POLITICS

## Channels

By the "form" of pressure group activities I mean, first, the channels of action on which such groups concentrate. The most important, and the most obvious, determinant of the selection of channels for pressure group activity, in any political system, is the *structure* of the decision-making processes which pressure groups seek to influence. Interest groups (or any other groups) become pressure groups because they want to obtain favourable policy decisions or administrative dispositions; hence, obviously, they must adjust their activities to the processes by which decisions and dispositions are made. To cite a very simple example: in Great Britain the National Union of Teachers is one of the larger and more active pressure groups on the national level, while in the United States teachers' groups play only a minor role, if any, in national politics;[1] the reason is simply that British educational policies are made and administered by the national government, while in the American federal system this is not the case, except only in the most indirect sense. But this is perhaps too simple an example. Pressure groups tend to adjust the form of their activities not so much to the formal (constitutional) structure of governments as to the distribution of effective power within a governmental apparatus, and this is often something very different from formal structure; in the competition for influence they cannot afford to be deceived by political myths. Hence their activities are themselves one of the more reliable guides to the loci of effective power in any political system, whenever the "political formula" of the system—as Lasswell and Kaplan call it[2]—does not indicate the loci correctly.

Not only the structure of the decision-making process but also the decisions which emerge from it—the *activities* of government—influence the predominant channels of pressure group politics, and this just because decisions have a reciprocal effect on the structures that make them. The most obvious example is the devolution of decision-making powers from legislatures to bureaucracies in this age of the social service state, both through the direct delegation of legislative powers and the indirect influence which bureaucrats enjoy over decisions still formally taken by legislatures.

Finally, the dominant channels of pressure group politics may be determined by certain *attitudes,* the most obviously important being attitudes toward pressure groups themselves. Where, for example, the pursuit of corporate interests by political means is normatively reproved—where "liberal" individualist assumptions[3] are deeply ingrained—pressure groups are likely to work through more inconspicuous channels and with more unobtrusive means than where corporate politics are normatively tolerated. But even attitudes not directly concerned with pressure groups may, indirectly, affect the form of their activities, at any rate if the attitudes have a bearing on the distribution of effective decision-making power. For example, a broad consensus on major policies—the sort of policies usually made by cabinets and legislatures—will tend to shift the major arena of political conflict, hence the major efforts of pressure groups, toward the administrative departments.

Basically, it is always the interplay of governmental structure, activities and attitudes which determines the form of pressure group politics (in the sense of channels of participation) in a given society. These factors may, of course, pull in different directions. Usually, however, they do not—chiefly (1) because the attitudes which bear directly upon a society's structure of decision-making (constitutional myths) and the attitudes which bear upon it indirectly (e.g., attitudes underlying governmental activities) tend to be integrated, and (2) because the activities of government and non-"constitutional" attitudes (such as attitudes on policy) generally have an important bearing on the decision-making structure itself. In Great Britain, at any rate, all three factors pull in a single direction: toward the concentration of pressure group activities on the administrative departments.

Pressure is concentrated upon the executive in Britain, first, because of the logic of cabinet government in a political system having two highly disciplined parties; such a system simply precludes any consistently successful exertion of influence through members of Parliament, or, less obviously perhaps, through the political parties.[4] Secondly, pressure is focused on the executive because the broad scope and technical character of contemporary social and economic policies has led to a considerable shift of functions to the bureaucracy; not only that, but the decision-making powers usually exercised by administrative departments are, generally speaking, of much more immediate and greater interest to British interest groups than the kinds of decisions made in Cabinet and Parliament.[5] Attitudes, finally, lead in the same direction. There does not exist in Britain any profound prejudice against corporate politics, against the organization of opinion by "interested" groups; this makes possible extraordinarily free, easy, open and intimate relations between public officials and lobbyists (using that term in a purely descriptive sense).[6] Attitudes in Britain also tend to shift pressure toward the executive in more direct and obvious ways: for example, because the lack of inhibitions upon delegating legislation gives to the administrative departments powers which legislatures more jealous of their functions than the British Parliament are likely to exercise themselves:[7] and because there has in fact existed in Britain a consensus on general policy, shifting political conflict to matters of technique and detail, that is, matters generally dealt with by administrative departments.[8]

All this, of course, applies to pressure groups only in a general sense—to predominant and characteristic modes of pressure group activity rather than the activities of every particular pressure group. Whether any particular pressure group will concentrate on the executive or some other part of the governmental machinery and political apparatus of a society depends on certain factors additional to the broad variables I have sketched. For example, the power base of the group certainly plays a role in the matter. A group which commands a large number of votes will tend, other things being equal, to exert pressure on elected members of the decision-making structure; a wealthy group on party organizations; a group in command of specialized knowledge on the specialists in the governmental structure, chiefly the bureaucrats. But, to repeat, this is so *ceteris paribus,* not under all circumstances. It is very likely to be the case, for example, where there exists a relatively even distribution of power among representatives, party oligarchy and bureaucracy; or it may be the case where the group has only one power base which can be effectively brought to bear only in one direction. Both these cases, however, are unusual. In the ordinary instance, speaking metaphorically, the power base of the group will do little more than deflect the momentum of its pressure off the idealized path prescribed by governmental structure, activity and relevant attitudes. The ultimate aim of pressure groups is always to bring power to bear where it will produce intended consequences, and this makes the power structure of government a more decisive desideratum than the power base of the group—granted that in unitary political systems like the British fewer alternatives for exerting effective pressure tend to present themselves than in polycentric systems like the American, and that in the latter, consequently, the power base of the group plays a more significant role in determining pressure group behaviour. Even in a system like the British, however, the direction of pressure may be seriously deflected, in special cases, from the executive departments. A group which simply does not have ready access to an executive department—which has no close clientele relationship with such a department—may be driven willy-nilly to seek its aims through other channels; so may a group which stands in a close relationship with a very weak department, when it wants a policy involving the interests of stronger departments; so also may a group pressing for a decision on some very controversial issue involving intense public opinion or high party politics, the sort of issues decided only at the very highest levels. These factors also work in the other direction. Where groups tend to press mainly on the legislature, the existence of close clientele relations with an executive department, or the fact that a group's business is not politically significant, may induce it to steer clear of parliamentary channels. But all these exceptions and modifications are just that, exceptions and modifications; they do not affect the general validity of the main point.

One should add that the factors which induce pressure groups to use certain channels of influence also have effects upon their internal organization and the means they use to exert political pressure. Pressure groups tend somehow to resemble the organizations they seek to influence. Take two examples, one American, the other British. Not only does the American federal system guide political pressure into certain channels, as in the case of teachers' organizations, but it impedes the formation of national associations as such. The American Bar Association, for instance, has a very small membership and was relatively late in getting under way compared to state and local legal associations. Why? Simply because training and admission to the profession—the two political concerns which most often lead to the formation and growth of professional associations—are controlled by state governments, not the federal government.[9] In broader terms, the formal dispersion of authority in government inhibits the concentration of membership in voluntary organizations, a fact with far-reaching consequences, because the "density" of members affects many aspects of a pressure group's activities (such as its political effectiveness and the extent to which it can participate in genuine negotiations with public authorities).[10] In Britain we can see equally clearly the effect of informal governmental power relations on the organization and tactics of pressure groups. As long as Parliament held the centre of the political stage—as long, that is to say, as political conflicts centred on parliamentary policies—interest groups tended not only to act chiefly through "interested" MPs but to be ephemeral, one-purpose organizations, chiefly concerned with raising a large volume of public support for important legislative changes. Nowadays, however, they possess much greater continuity and engage in a much wider variety of political activities, for their interests are being constantly affected by governmental actions. The public campaign has been replaced largely by informal and unostentatious contacts between officials, and interest groups themselves have become increasingly bureaucratized (in short, more and more like the government departments with which they deal), for only bureaucratic structure is appropriate to the kinds of negotiations groups nowadays must carry on to realize their interests. The changing pattern of policy is not alone responsible for this. The shift of power from Parliament to the Cabinet and from the Cabinet to the administrative departments is equally important. These shifts have not been simple adjustments to new policies but are the results of many other factors, such as the professionalization of the civil service and the development of large, disciplined, national parties (paralleled by the development of large, national interest group organizations in place of the much greater decentralization of vested interest organizations in the nineteenth century). The striking correspondence of governmental organization and the internal organizations of pressure groups in most countries may of course be the result of a still more basic factor: deeply established "constitutional" attitudes (an aspect of what Bentley called the "habit background" of societies) which dictate forms of organization and power relations ·(structures of authority) not only in government but also in voluntary associations. For the present purpose, however, it is sufficient to point out the similarity and to suggest that it is a product both of social norms and calculations as to where and how group pressure can be exerted most effectively.

There is then a two-fold relation between the channels of pressure group activity on one hand and structure of government, pattern of policy and political attitudes on the other: structure, policy and attitudes decide the channels pressure groups will use predominantly to exert influence, and the nature of these channels in turn affects pressure group organization and tactics.

## Consultations and Negotiations

By "form" of pressure group politics, I do not mean channels of influence only but also the kinds of relations which predominate among groups and governmental bodies. Leaving aside the intimacy and easiness of these relations (which has already been touched upon), we may distinguish here between polar extremes, consultations and negotiations, granting that most concrete relations involve both to some extent. Negotiations take place when a governmental body makes a decision hinge upon the actual approval of organizations interested in it, giving the organizations a veto over the decision; consultations occur when the views of the organizations are solicited and taken into account but not considered to be in any sense decisive. What decides whether one relationship or the other plays a significant role in government-group relations? The determining factors again are structure, policies and attitudes.

Structure is important because genuine negotiations can take place only if governmental decision-making processes and patterns of action within pressure groups are of a certain kind. Above all, those who speak for the public authority and those who speak for the interest group must be able to commit those whom they represent; otherwise their deliberations will have only a kind of consultative value, whatever their intentions. Negotiations, then, demand the concentration of authority on both

sides, as well as the vesting of considerable discretionary authority in the negotiators. Indeed, the latter presupposes the former. Genuine negotiations between governmental bodies and pressure groups are not likely to take place when a decision must be obtained from a large number of bodies before it has force—as in the American separation-of-powers system—so that decisions are made in effect by negotiations among governmental bodies themselves; and how can there be any negotiations when the negotiators have no discretion, no room to manoeuvre, to make concessions, to meet unexpected gambits and pressures? From both standpoints, an effective cabinet system like the British clearly permits negotiations more easily than a balance-of-power system like the American. It is also necessary, of course, that there should be on the side of the group a formal organization that can speak for most of the members, rather than many competing organizations, or organizations unable to mobilize a sizeable majority of group members. This also is the case in Britain more often than in America.

Policies and attitudes in Britain reinforce the tendency of governmental and group structure to produce negotiations as the dominant form of pressure group politics. The policies of the social service state, for example, demand technical knowledge which, frequently, the members of some interest groups (doctors, for example) are best able to supply. In any case, they often require the positive co-operation of interest groups if they are to be effectively carried out; and what is more natural than to give the groups a direct voice of some sort both in the formulation and administration of policies which cannot be administered without their support?

Among attitudes making for negotiations between government and pressure groups in Britain three are of particular significance. One is the widespread belief (in this case both in Britain and America) that technical experts (practitioners) have some singular competence even in regard to the social policies and administrative forms that touch upon their fields of practice, competence which politicians and bureaucrats do not possess. The second (certainly without an American counterpart) is the persistent "corporatism" in British social attitudes, the still lingering anti-individualist bias which Beer has labelled the "Old Whig Theory of Representation";[11] by this is meant a conception of society as consisting primarily not of individuals but of sub-societies, groups having traditions and occupational and other characteristics in common. Where Lockean liberalism is the dominant political myth, decisions of government are supposed to be the result of conversations, as it were, between individuals (electorate) and sovereign (state); the intervention of groups is considered inherently pernicious or at best something merely to be tolerated.[12] Where corporatistic attitudes persist, on the other hand, functional representation—that is, the representation of corporations (in the sociological, not legal, sense of the term) rather than individuals—is not only tolerated but insisted upon; governments tend to be regarded not as sovereigns in the Austinian sense but, in the pluralistic sense, as corporations among many other kinds of corporations. Hence the frequent normative insistence on negotiations between government and "voluntary" associations on matters of policy; in Britain, at any rate, a policy regulating, say, farmers, embarked upon without close conversations between government and farm organizations, would be considered to be only on the margins of legitimacy, whether highly technical in character or not. Indeed, close conversations are not enough. Note, for example, that in the debate on the second reading of the National Health Service Bill of 1946—the stage at which the most general policy considerations raised by a bill are discussed—the opposition hinged its case upon a motion alleging the failure of the Ministry of Health to *negotiate* the proposed Service with the medical profession; this despite the fact that plenty of talks (consultations) between the Ministry and the profession had taken place and that technical details were not at issue. And to the survival of the Old-Whig Theory of Representation we may add the concomitant survival of what might be called the Old-Tory Theory of Authority: the tendency both in British government and British voluntary associations to delegate inordinately wide powers to leaders and spokesmen, to ratify decisions taken by leaders almost as a matter of form, which affords such leaders a wide range of manoeuvre when they come face to face in negotiations.[13]

Consultations and negotiations are not, of course, the only "practices" through which pressure groups act upon government. In fact, these two concepts may be useful for characterizing pressure group activities only in political systems which have two, not in the least universal, characteristics: a high degree of differentiation between pressure groups, parties and formal decision-making offices, and relatively great ease of access by pressure groups to the formal decision-making offices. Where these conditions do not exist, pressure group activity will inevitably assume other forms. In multi-party systems, where parties and pressure groups are not sharply differentiated (that is to say, where many parties are pressure groups that merely call themselves parties and sometimes behave like parties) decisions will often be made, not by negotiations between pressure groups and formal decision-making officers, but by negotiations among the pressure groups themselves. In such countries, the basic assertion on which contemporary "group theorists" in political science have built their model—that politics is "the allocation of social values through group conflict"—comes much closer to a full description of political decision-making than it does in countries where political parties perform their integrating function effectively and where the formal structure of decision-making represents something more than the myths of the dominant groups in institutionalized form. On the other extreme, where groups are effectively segregated out of the formal political process—prevented from having access to formal offices—the chief form of pressure group politics will be intrigue, or violence; perhaps, however, it would be better in this case to speak of the cessation of politics rather than of a particular form of it.

## DETERMINANTS OF SCOPE AND INTENSITY

To discover the factors on which depend the scope and intensity of pressure group activity, it is necessary to bear in mind just what sort of political activity pressure group politics is. As I define it[14] pressure group politics has certain peculiar characteristics which are very important. On one hand, it involves the *political* promotion of interests and values, that is, the attempt to realize aspirations through governmental decision-making; on the other, it involves something less than an attempt by the group to become itself the government, or even to seize for itself certain political offices which are vitally concerned with its goals. That, at any rate, is how we generally differentiate pressure groups from parties, or political movements, or purely political "associations" (like the parliamentary associations which antedate the advent of mass parties in Great Britain). Moreover, pressure groups, normally, are not solely engaged in political activities; even in the case of "promotional" groups (groups seeking to achieve not their own interests but what they conceive to be broader social values) political activities rarely exhaust the full range of activities of the group. Pressure group politics, then, represents something less than the full "politicalization" of groups and something more than utter "depoliticalization"; it constitutes an intermediate level of activity between the political and the apolitical. In accounting for the growth and development of pressure group activity, therefore, we must simultaneously account for two things which are, at first sight, nearly paradoxical: how groups come to seek the political promotion of certain of their goals, yet are kept from attempting to promote them by the capture of authoritative offices or from pursuing politically all their objectives. I shall concentrate on the first of these problems, the political mobilization of groups; the second is of less immediate concern to the present case-study, although I shall touch upon it at the end of the section.

## The Political Mobilization of Groups: Policy

As governmental structure is the most obvious determinant of the form of pressure group activities, so the activities of governments are the most obvious determinants of their entrance into politics. British pressure groups have been so much discussed recently[15] for the simple reason that welfare state policies have, so to speak, generated such groups in large number (that is, transformed groups into "pressure groups"), or, where they already existed, intensified the pressures they exert. This is clearly due to the fact that private associations now have much more to gain or lose from governmental decisions than in the past: farmers their incomes, doctors the conditions in which they practice, businessmen a host of matters, from capital issues to raw materials.[16] The state in Britain today disposes directly of 40 per cent of the national income; and that fact speaks for itself. We may regard political systems as amalgams of potential and actual pressure groups: groups which from a political standpoint are merely "categoric" groups and groups which have actually been drawn into politics, chiefly through the impact of public policies, either policies actually adopted or policies which are "threatened." In short, we can usefully stand Bentley on his head to supplement Bentley right side up; if interaction among politically active groups produces policy, policy in turn creates politically active groups.[17]

There is also, however, a connection between the mobilization of pressure groups and governmental structure, and a further connection between the former and political attitudes, though neither may be quite so manifest as the influence of policy.

## Attitudes

Attitudes influence the scope and intensity of pressure group politics not only because they determine policy but also because pressure groups generally require some sort of legitimation before they come into play in the political process. The obstacle to legitimacy may be internal or external, so to speak; it may arise either from the convictions of group members or that of non-members, particularly if the latter occupy positions of power, that the political promotion of the group's collective interests is somehow illegitimate. Trade unions, for example, play a more significant political role today than in the nineteenth century, both in Britain and the United States, not only because they are larger and better managed, but also because they are more widely accepted and because they themselves are more reconciled to action within the operative political system. To consult with trade union leaders is no longer tantamount to conspiracy; nor do trade union leaders any longer regard political participation in democratic government as a kind of class treason, or as a trespass upon alien domain. Of course, the legitimacy of a group is not absolutely decisive in determining whether it will play a political role or not. Conspiracies do occur where negotiations are prohibited, but the difficulties in such cases are so great that "illegitimate" groups may find it desirable to leave politics alone, or impossible to find channels through which to act. The attitudes which legitimate pressure groups or deny them legitimacy usually constitute the fundamental political ethos of a society, such as the long prevalent liberal belief that economic actors should act upon each other through the spontaneously adjusting mechanics of the market rather than through the political process.[18]

Legitimacy in this case need not mean legitimacy in regard to political action only; a group may be prevented from taking an intense part in politics by much more general attitudes: for example, a prejudice against corporate organization as such. S. H. Beer has pointed out[19] that the major occupational interests—business, labour, and agriculture—are far more thoroughly and monolithically organized in Britain than in the United States and related this fact to the profound influence of liberal "atomism" in America and the survival of the older corporatistic theory of society in Britain. These differences in organization are marked by differences in the groups' involvement in politics and administration. The sub-groups of larger societies may, however, have significantly different attitudes toward organization as well as political action itself. Thus, while it is true, broadly speaking, that British attitudes are more corporatistic than American attitudes—and that, as a result, British pressure groups "even if compared with American examples . . . are numerous, massive, well-organized and highly effective"[20]—it is also true that British professional groups resist corporation as much as, if not more than, their American counterparts. The British Medical Association, for example, has not until very recently (when special factors compelling corporatization have been at work) managed to outstrip the Americal Medical Association in proportion of doctors enrolled in it. That is just one facet of a much broader behaviour pattern; another facet of this pattern is the resistance of the British medical profession to all corporate forms of practice, in partnerships, group practices and especially health centres. Both reflect a profound bias against association which, in the American case, is much stronger in the realm of economic affairs, the area in which the liberal atomistic model of society was most rigidly applied in the United States. But such inhibitions against corporatization may be overcome. In medicine, for example, contemporary scientific development has made isolated practice almost obsolete, and this undoubtedly has had an effect on the willingness of British doctors to participate in corporate activities, both strictly professional and not strictly professional, however much some of the old biases may linger.

Attitudes may determine the intensity of group politics in still another way. Even when they permit intense political activity by a group, they may keep that activity from assuming certain forms, i.e., limit the group's range of political activities. Some groups which play a legitimate role in government may be prevented, by normative attitudes no less than considerations of expediency, from openly associating themselves with a political party or taking a part in electoral campaigns;[21] again, certain groups such as professional associations—may have deep inhibitions against anything that smacks of trade unionism (any sort of bargaining, for example); still others may be prevented by their internal ethics from using certain instruments of pressure, such as strikes and boycotts, or certain kinds of publicity—although changes in the situation of the group may also change such attitudes, as they may change attitudes toward corporatization and political action themselves.

### Structure

Of the three basic determinants of pressure group behaviour which I have stressed, perhaps the least manifest determinant of their political mobilization is governmental structure; nevertheless, it also plays a role. Key, for example, argues that a two-party system stimulates the formation of pressure groups because special interests cannot find consistent champions in any party which must continuously appeal to a great many interests.[22] That, however, strikes me as an over-simplification. The parties in a two-party system may themselves be composed of wings and sub-groups which consistently espouse certain interests, making them, as Key himself has pointed out, more like multi-party systems in fact than they seem in form.[23] This is certainly true of American parties. It may also apply to British parties, for both Labour and the Tories include certain enduring sub-groups which stand for special, chiefly economic interests. The point that should be made surely is that two-party systems do not encourage all interest groups to seek political channels outside of the parties but only groups having certain characteristics;[24] and rather than maintaining that multi-party systems discourage the formation of organized pressure groups because the parties themselves are freely available to special interests, one should argue that (just because of this) many "parties" in such systems are themselves pressure groups in disguise, but pressure groups more fully politicalized than those we find in two-party systems.

Somewhat more persuasive is Truman's argument that certain groups are likely to pursue their goals through politics when the structure of government gives them important advantages over others and when they are in a relatively weak position on the "market," that is, in spontaneous adjustment to other groups. His chief case in point is that of American farmers who have a relatively weak bargaining position on the market but are over-represented in both state and national legislatures.[25] Rural areas in many other countries tend to be over-represented too, which may help to explain the relatively great readiness of farm groups everywhere to seek out government interference in their market relations.

This argument may, however, be stated much more broadly: governmental structure affects the scope and intensity of pressure group activity chiefly because expectations of success govern the political mobilization of groups, and whether or not a group can be successfully influential is determined at least partly by the structure of the government on which it acts. Undoubtedly there are factors which enhance a group's chances of political success under any circumstances, but the weight of these factors tends to vary according to the structure of decision-making in which they are brought to bear. This point will be discussed further below, in connection with a more general analysis of the conditions which determine the effectiveness of pressure groups. It ought to be noted here, however, that governmental structure may determine not only the influence of particular pressure groups (and therefore whether or not they will actually organize for politics) but also whether pressure groups in general can effectively translate their demands into policies (and therefore whether or not large numbers of them will be active, or whether political activity will play a large role in their affairs). I have in mind here the difference between systems like British cabinet government, which are highly effective in making decisions, and systems like the American or highly fragmented parliamentary systems, which seem more effective in frustrating them. The first kind of system is more likely to induce the political mobilization of groups than the second, if only because government offers them a reasonable chance of action—any sort of action; although, of course, everything depends in this case on whether groups actually want decisions to be made or to keep them from being taken. In the latter case, systems like the American clearly offer the greater chances, so that the distinction between active and inactive governments ought not perhaps to be made in terms of their effects on the political mobilization of groups as such, but in terms of the kinds of groups and aspirations they tend to involve in political affairs. In terms of sheer quantity of political activity one would certainly be hard put to find a significant difference between British and American pressure groups, but this does not preclude significant differences of other sorts.

## Inhibitions on Political Mobilization

If certain attitudes, elements of governmental structure, and the impact of governmental policy, adopted and threatened, account for the political mobilization of groups, what inhibits them from mobilizing on a full scale once they decide to become politically involved? Clearly, the relevant factors are the ways in which groups define their goals and evaluate their chances in the political arena, and the extent to which an existing governmental apparatus appears capable of satisfying their demands without being changed or captured. Each of these considerations, however, requires some elaboration.

There are conditions when government itself, not the detailed products of government, is the primary concern of politics, most clearly of all when new states are in the building or old forms of government widely discredited. Such conditions are obviously inhospitable to pressure group politics, for they awaken much more profound political concerns. Intensive pressure group politics then presupposes as its most fundamental condition a stable and widely accepted political apparatus— political consensus. To "press" upon a government is itself, in a way, a form of commitment to it; profoundly disaffected groups will rarely stoop to sully themselves by dealing with an abominated system. This accounts for the curious impression one gets in societies widely committed to their governments both of intense politics and political apathy; intense politics, because the society seems split into a myriad groupings, loosely, if at all, associated, all busily seeking to exert influence, to capture opinion, to enlist decision-makers; political apathy, because no fundamental issues are ever raised and people seem remarkably uninterested in what looms, in other societies, as decisive political activity: elections, for example. The simple reason for this apparent paradox is, of course, that political activities do not possess decisiveness intrinsically but only in terms of what people want to be decided: if the chief political question is one of the very location of formal power, then elections (or violence) become decisive; if political questions involve less fundamental issues—the detailed uses to which formal power is to be put—then influence-wielding, i.e. pressure group politics, becomes decisive. Consensus does not imply the cessation of politics, but it does imply a shift of political concern to issues best dealt with through the unobtrusive interplay of semi-politicalized groups; in "consensual" systems, therefore, fully politicalized groups will perform certain routine functions but only rarely absorb primary allegiances. Lack of consensus in a society will make almost every group join fully politicalized organizations, or try to become themselves such organizations, or wash their hands of politics altogether. Politics will become no concern of theirs, or all of their concern. Whether it will be the first or the second depends on contingent characteristics of the group and the situation under which it has to operate: its size, the extent to which an existing political state of affairs threatens it, the repressive power of existing governments, and the extent to which its aims can be achieved outside of politics.

Whether groups will define their goals as being fully political or, as do pressure groups, only partially political may depend also on still more fundamental characteristics of a society. A high degree of pressure group activity presupposes logically a high degree of social differentiation. It is difficult to envisage intensive pressure group politics in relatively primitive societies, not only because basic political questions loom relatively large in them these days, but also because the vast multiplicity of criss-crossing groups existing in more advanced societies does not exist (at least to the same extent) in the less advanced. Group politics in such societies tend therefore to define goals of very wide concern, and associations tend to absorb wide segments of society; in such a situation group politics becomes almost by definition social politics.[26] The communications system of a society also plays a fundamental role, at any rate in deciding the very possibility of association as a preliminary to political mobilization. But apart from such absolutely fundamental and obvious (perhaps tautological) conditions, the extent of politicalization of groups is primarily a reflection of the degree of consensus among them. In that sense, the existence of a multiplicity of pressure groups is a sign of health in the political organism, not, as the muckrakers thought, a symptom of disease.

Within consensual systems, however, different groups have different propensities to act in politics, depending on contingencies like those operating in non-consensual systems. Very large groups and very wealthy groups may be encouraged to play a direct role in party-political conflict, as do British trade unions—although one gets the impression nowadays that their identification with Labour is a cultural lag from days of more profound political disagreements, and that they yearn (many at any rate) for looser forms of political engagement. Stable two-party systems also discourage full political involvement,[27] although such party systems may themselves be, at bottom, products of consensus. Finally, groups may become disenchanted in the process of pressure politics if the resolution of group conflicts is consistently against their interests—if, in the political market, their power to compete is small, due to their objective characteristics or the structure of government on which they act. In that case, however, they are more likely to become fully alienated from the political system rather than fully involved in it.

In any case, the market of political competition tends to become so widely disjointed in highly consensual systems that almost any groups can get "satisfactions" out of it; that is to say, groups which are relatively weak in absolute terms (in size, wealth, prestige, etc.) may, due to wide agreement, simply not have to confront significant opposition in their political affairs. Despite that, however, calculations of the chances of a group's effectiveness help to decide not only whether the group becomes politically active at all, but also the extent to which it carries its political activity. What then determines the effectiveness of pressure groups?

## DETERMINANTS OF EFFECTIVENESS

Factors determining the effectiveness of pressure groups may be classified under three headings: (a) attributes of the pressure groups themselves; (b) attributes of the activities of government; (c) attributes of the governmental decision-making structure. Perhaps operative attitudes constitute a fourth category, since the ability of a group to mobilize opinion certainly enhances its chances of success in any political system in which opinion matters; but that is obvious and needs no elaboration.[28]

### Group Characteristics

Certain characteristics of groups are likely to determine decisively their effectiveness under almost any pattern of policies or structure of government (popular government, of course): for example, physical resources, size, organizational cohesiveness, and political skills. Physical resources means wealth, first and foremost: wealth to contribute to party treasuries, wealth for "buying" the goodwill of influential persons, wealth with which to advertise and circularize, and so forth. Other resources, of course, are useful too; for example, the possession by a group of a journal or newspaper, especially a popular newspaper, or (in a rather different sense of the term "resource") the fact that it has members in influential positions. Among useful resources must be included also the prestige of the group: the capital of public support, so to speak, which it can command regardless of the substantive policies it espouses. Certain groups possess not merely legitimacy to participate in decision-making processes, but also a sort of special privilege to determine the outcome of these processes; this is true especially of groups possessing technical competence in fields where there is a wide gulf between the professional and the layman, although any high

status and prestige can usually be converted into political profit, if only through the day-to-day influence of "opinion leaders."

The size of the group may itself be reckoned among its resources, although brute size is never likely to be of crucial account. Rather we should speak of the politically effective size of a group: its ability to make its quantitative weight felt. This is partly a matter of the other resources it commands—its wealth, prestige, whether it has easy access to public opinion and to influential persons—but still other considerations enter the equation as well. One of these is organizational cohesiveness, and this is a function of a great many variables. Does the group possess any formal organization at all? Is the membership split among a large number of such organizations or concentrated in an omnibus organization? Is membership perfunctory or the result of genuine commitment to the formal organization? Do members in fact participate in organizational affairs? Are their personal interactions frequent and persistent? Do they have important conflicting loyalties outside the group? Are their interests really compatible? Can the leaders mobilize disciplined and loyal legions in times of crisis? The answers to these questions will determine whether membership statistics can in fact be translated into influence.[29]

Among the skills which enable groups to achieve their political objectives we must therefore reckon the internal political and administrative skills of their leaders. Some groups, to be sure, are more cohesive than others in their very nature: if, for example, they have no cultural or ideological inhibitions against close association (unlike businessmen in a truly "liberal" society, or doctors in a country having a deep tradition of individual practice, as in Britain); if their members do have largely identical, at any rate easily comparable, interests; if they are concentrated in small areas; if status considerations or the nature of the members' work lead to social as well as occupational identification among the members.[30] But here, as in everything else, art can guide and support nature.

The nature of the objectives sought by a group may also be a determinant of effectiveness, but chiefly because this factor affects the other internal group characteristics mentioned. I have in mind here primarily the difference between groups agitating for their own corporate interests and groups dedicated to social causes not necessarily arising out of their members' self-interest—"interest groups" as against "promotional groups," as S. E. Finer calls them. The former generally have a more disciplined membership, more affluent treasuries, tighter bureaucratic organization, a more permanent and indeed also more active clientele. Their officers tend to acquire great skill in propaganda and negotiations, and they frequently have their own private channels of propaganda—journals and press departments, for example.

## Policy

As there are many kinds of resources which constitute political capital, so there are many kinds of organizational forms and political skills which may be turned to account in the decision-making process; *which* is likely to exercise a decisive influence depends largely on the setting in which the group functions. Generals cut a wider swath in war or cold war than in peace; groups that want money spent have a relatively hard task in times of inflation and retrenchment. The pattern of policies enforced in a political system is an important determinant of the effectiveness of pressure groups simply because it is one of the situational elements which selects among the objective attributes of groups those which are of special political account. Take two examples. A policy may demand, in its formulation or administration, some skill or knowledge over which members of a special group have, or are believed to have, a monopoly; this is increasingly the case in the age of the social service state. Again, it may be impossible to carry out a policy without some sort of active support by the group; what use, for instance, is an agricultural policy without cooperative farmers? In either case, the pressure group concerned may not get exactly what it wants, but the need for knowledge and cooperation at least acts as a limit on what can be imposed upon it; usually, of course, the group's influence is much more positive than that.

Policy may also impinge upon the effectiveness of groups in another way: by affecting their size and the resources they command. When a group is subjected to public regulation and control its members are more likely to join organizations which press the group's interests. They are more likely to contribute to group treasuries; to tolerate specialization of leadership and administration in their organizations; to sublimate differences of interest and attitude for the sake of common ends, and to respond in a disciplined way to group decisions. Policy, in short, may make it easier to mobilize the potential power of groups by accelerating tendencies toward corporatization and by making for greater cohesiveness within the organized groups.[31]

## Governmental Structure

Finally, the effectiveness of pressure groups is also determined to some extent by governmental structure. There is, for example, a great difference between systems in which power is concentrated and those in which it is dispersed. In American government, groups can ordinarily get what they want, at any rate if they want something important, only by obtaining favourable decisions from a large number of bodies: legislatures, legislative committees, executive officers; this, as has been repeatedly pointed out, favours defensive pressure groups, those that want to maintain the *status quo,* by promoting delay and inaction as such.[32] But while under effective cabinet government it is much easier to obtain positive decisions at all levels, from Parliament to the lowliest interdepartmental committee, such systems inhibit many manipulative activities familiar in systems where power is widely dispersed (senatorial courtesy, for example) which give minor groups useful entrées into politics and means for getting "positive" decisions.[33]

On a somewhat lower level of generalization, the influence of pressure groups may also be affected by electoral systems. Under proportional representation sheer weight of numbers is likely to be a matter of importance, while under the single-member system the distribution of members will be an important factor determining the "effective size" of a group; a group the members of which are strategically posted in a large number of doubtful constituencies will be able to exercise influence disproportionate to its size in simple quantitative terms. So also will a group which derives special advantages from distributive anomalies in an electoral system; a case in point are American farmers, who are benefited not only by the over-representation of agricultural districts in the House of Representatives, but even more by the peculiar system used to elect the Senate. The National Farmers Union of England and Wales failed in its original aim to play a role like that of the American farm bloc in British politics, partly because of the existence of two highly disciplined parties in Great Britain, but partly also because the British electoral system never favoured farmers as much as the American system.

Third, there is a relationship between the effectiveness of pressure groups and the character of the administrative structure upon which they act. A close "clientele relationship" between group and administrative department always tends to give the group important advantages over others, if only by obtaining for it a permanent spokesman within the structure of government; it has been argued, for example, that in America the air lines have important political advantages over other public carriers because they have a public regulatory agency all to themselves (the Civil Aeronautics Board) while the other carriers all come under the jurisdiction of the Interstate Commerce Commission, within which there is consequently a stiff, often self-defeating, struggle for power. Much depends also on the power which a given administrative department can exert on behalf of its clients within the executive structure. Administrative systems are not merely tools for executing policy, but are themselves structures of power; they influence (often make) policy, and within them different departments carry different degrees of weight, depending on the political positions of their heads, the broadness and significance of their functions, and their traditions. In British government, there certainly is a world of difference between important departments like the Treasury, Supply, and the Board of Trade on one hand and Education and Pensions on the other. Whether a pressure group can carry great weight in government obviously depends on the power of the agency through which its weight is exerted, as indeed do also certain aspects of the form of its activities—for example, the extent to which its relations with government have the character of genuine negotiations; normally a President of the Board of Trade can negotiate far more easily than a Minister of Education, if to negotiate means to take decisions by bargaining with pressure groups. Finally, we should add to clientele relations between groups and departments, clientele relations between groups and legislative committees. Similar considerations apply, although the absence of specializing standing legislative committees make this point inapplicable to the country with which this case-study deals.

## SUMMARY

To sum up the argument in very general terms, pressure group politics in its various aspects is a function of three main variables: the pattern of policy, the structure of decision-making both in government and voluntary associations, and the attitudes—broadly speaking, the "political culture" —of the society concerned. Each affects the form, the intensity and scope, and the effectiveness of pressure group politics, although in each case the significance of the variables differs—structure, for example, being especially important in determining the form of pressure group politics, policy especially important in determining its scope and intensity.

## NOTES

1. V. O. Key, Jr., *Politics, Parties and Pressure Groups* (Thomas Y. Crowell Co., New York, sec. ed. 1947) does not even mention them. David B. Truman's encyclopaedic *The Governmental Process* (Knopf, New York, 1951) mentions the National Education Association (p. 452), but does not bother to describe its activities.

2. Harold D. Lasswell and Abraham Kaplan, *Power and Society,* Routledge, London, 1950, p. 126 ff.

3. The term "liberal" is used in accordance with S. H. Beer, "The Representation of Interests in British Government," *APSR,* Sept., 1957, pp. 628 ff.

4. This is not to say that pressure on MPs is absolutely pointless. After all, they can ask parliamentary questions, press for adjournment debates, put down motions and amendments, make private representations to ministers and officials (i.e., use their prestige as MPs or their connections in the party), and exert influence within the party organizations. The very fact that pressure groups still find it profitable to "retain" MPs indicates that Parliament is not yet entirely a dead letter in the structure of effective authority in Britain. (See, for example, S. H. Beer, "Pressure Groups and Parties in Britain," *APSR,* March 1956, pp. 5-6; and S. E. Finer, "The Political Power of Private Capital," Part II, *The Sociol. Review,* July, 1956, p. 8. A comprehensive account of the parliamentary activities of British pressure groups may be found in the recently published work by J. D. Stewart, *British Pressure Groups,* Oxford Univ. Press, 1958.)

Pressure is also exerted to some extent through the political parties. Everyone knows that the Labour Party is in a sense an association of pressure groups: trade unions, co-operative societies and certain ideological societies. So is the Conservative Party; such business organizations as the Federation of British Industries, the National Union of Manufacturers, and the Economic League may not be affiliated but are certainly aligned with the Tories, and there is considerable overlapping on the local level between committees of the Conservative and Unionist Associations and committees of trade associations. (S. E. Finer, *op. cit.,* pp. 6-12.) Nevertheless, parties also play a relatively minor role as channels of influence. They exist primarily to win elections: hence only groups having considerable wealth to contribute to party treasuries or a considerable membership strategically located in doubtful constituencies can hope to act successfully through them. At the same time, no party can really afford, for electoral reasons, to affiliate itself too openly and consistently with special interests; nor is it wise for any interest group to identify itself too closely with any party, since the party may only be in power occasionally—as the National Farmers Union, after a long alignment with the Conservatives, seems now to have learned. These considerations operate with special force in a real two-party system. In such a system the support of any special interest is likely to be of small importance to the parties, while, from the standpoint of interest groups, a given political party is more likely to be excluded from influence upon policy than in multi-party systems. The oscillation of power in two-party systems militates against any one-sided party alignments by pressure groups; hence the tendency of British pressure groups to assume a pose of political neutrality, even when they are clearly biased in favour of one party or the other.

Nevertheless, it is an index of the structure of effective power in Britain that pressure groups do concern themselves rather more with parties than the legislature. It is also an index of the structure of effective power within British parties that pressure groups concentrate their activities on the parliamentary parties and, to a smaller extent, the central offices (i.e., bureaucracies) of the parties, rather than on theoretically more powerful bodies in the party organization. (See H. Eckstein, "The British Political System," in *Patterns of Government: The Major Political Systems of Europe,* eds. Beer and Ulam, New York, 1958, Ch. 12.)

5. Farmers, for example, are likely to be rather more interested in the annual price reviews than in broad agricultural policies, doctors more interested in conditions of service under the Health Service than in general medical policy. That, at any rate, is what the behaviour of the National Farmers Union and British Medical Association suggests.

6. See Beer, "Pressure Groups," p. 6 ff.

7. In Britain, after all, the process of delegating legislation hardly involves delegation in any real sense, but rather a shift of responsibility from ministers as leaders of Parliament to ministers as heads of administration. Hence the staggering number of statutory instruments in this age of the social service state and party government—from 174 general legislative "rules" made by government departments in 1900, to around 400 annually in the 1920's, to well over 1,000 since 1945, exceeding 1,500 in 1948. (See Sir Ivor Jennings, *Parliament,* 2nd ed., CUP, 1957, pp. 498-99.) British Acts tend nowadays to be mere frameworks for legislation. Of the 80 sections of the National Health Service Act, for example, half require subordinate legislation, and these sections concern all the more important aspects of the service, such as administrative organization and conditions of service; in the three years following passage of the act just under 150 statutory instruments were made under its provisions. (See *Butterworth's Annotated Legislation Service,* 1950, code [26], issue no. 283.) In the USA such blanket delegations of legislative responsibility are far less likely, if only because a real shift of power from the legislature to the executive is involved.

8. For a fuller discussion of this point, see Beer, "Pressure Groups," Part III. The arguments sketched above should not be interpreted to mean that British pressure groups concentrate solely on the executive, nor that pressure groups in other countries, e.g., the United States, do not also have close relations with the executive. Truman's *The Governmental Process,* Ch. 14, presents a wide range of data regarding the relations between pressure groups and the American executives, as do many other works, including Key, *Politics, Parties and Pressure Groups,* Avery Leiserson, *Administrative Regulation: A Study in Representation of Interests* (Chicago, 1942), E. P. Herring, *Public Administration and The Public Interest* (London: McGraw-Hill, 1936), C. H. Monsees, *Industry-Government Cooperation* (Washington, 1944) and E. W. First, *Industry and Labor Advisory Committees in the National Defense Advisory Commission and the Office of Production Management* (Washington, 1946). The difference lies in the degree of concentration, in the power wielded by pressure groups through their influence at the administrative level, the intimacy of their relations with administrators, and the extent to which they participate in decision-making or merely render advice.

It might be argued that this concentration of pressure group activity on the executive is not really a reflection of the distribution of power among the formal organs of government in Britain. Finer, for example, seems to take a slightly different line (in *Anonymous Empire,* pp. 21-22). He feels that the preponderance of contacts between pressure groups and departments is partly a matter of simple good manners, partly due to the wisdom of finding out whether something wanted is already authorized or not, and partly due to the desirability of keeping in the good graces of persons with whom close contact is required in the implementation of policy and who may make things difficult on the legislative level, whether they monopolize the legislative power or not. Of course, in all societies it is good manners to consult parties interested in or involved in decisions; still, in Britain, it is a particularly flagrant breach of etiquette if policies are made without close consultations between government and associations. As to legal uncertainties, one might argue simply that they are so very great in Britain because so much recent legislation has left details to be filled in by the departments, not because ministerial will as such is more important than parliamentary will as such. Add the fact that the large range of consensus in Britain keeps most political bickering within the range of administrative detail and prevents violent—or "important"—political controversies from arising, and one might draw the following conclusion: the bulk of pressure group activity does take place at the departmental level; but it is not qualitatively important, however considerable in quantity; and it tells us nothing about the distribution of power between Parliament and Ministry for that should be measured only by taking account of really controversial questions of general policy.

This conclusion is not unreasonable; but I think that a slightly different view is more reasonable. Whether Parliament plays a very significant role in serious controversies or not (I think not), the fact remains that the bulk of the work of government is done on the executive level, precisely because of consensus, skeletal legislation, and certain constitutional and normative attitudes. Serious controversies, at least compared with other countries, simply are few and far between, and that is one of the reasons for the predominance of the executive in Britain—although only one. The predominance of skeletal legislation is not due solely to circumstances (e.g., technical legislation) but also reflects the power of the executive, which likes to have a relatively free hand. And why should groups be so anxious not to get on the wrong side of the departments if the departments did not have crucial powers over affairs affecting the groups? In other words, even if one cannot quite maintain that the executive dominates the legislature in each and every case, from the standpoint of pressure group politics the centre of power does lie with the departments, and clearly so. If there is an argument against the interpretation I suggest here it is, therefore, that it is over-generalized if applied indiscriminately to the whole of British politics, rather than the restricted area relevant to this study.

Other studies which bear out my point are Self and Storing, "The Farmers and the State," *Political Quarterly,* vol. 29, no. 1, pp. 19-20 and PEP, *Industrial Trade Associations,* London, Allen & Unwin, 1951, p. 87.

9. Truman, *The Governmental Process,* p. 95.

10. Elaborated below, pp. 411-12.

11. Beer, "Representation of Interests," p. 614 ff.

12. For the best discussion of the origin and development of these attitudes, see Otto Gierke, *Natural Law and the Theory of Society,* Cambridge U. Press, 1934.

13. All this assumes that negotiations are in fact an important form of pressure group politics in Britain.

But Stewart denies that the distinction between consultations and negotiations has much value in the case of British pressure groups. Why? Because, says Stewart, the decisions of a Minister are always subject to Parliament, preventing him from entering into binding agreements. (Stewart, *British Pressure Groups,* p. 22.) This, I suggest, is taking constitutional myths too seriously. Ministers undoubtedly find it convenient to leave themselves loopholes in negotiations with pressure groups by making agreements "subject to the approval of Parliament." But ordinarily, once a Minister had made a decision, it is, for all practical purposes, final. Parliament reviews few departmental decisions in the first place, and those it reviews it generally rubber-stamps. The Cabinet reviews few more departmental policies, unless important interdepartmental disputes are involved. The most effective limitations on the powers of Ministers arise out of such interdepartmental relations; generally, however, Ministers, when negotiating with pressure groups, will also be negotiating with other interested departments, so that agreements reached with the pressure group will be cleared in advance.

14. See Preface, pp. 9 ff., of Harry Eckstein, *Pressure Group Politics,* Stanford, 1960.

15. For a list of publications on the subject, see Finer, *Anonymous Empire,* p. 148. Add Jennings, *Parliament,* esp. Ch. II, sec. 4 and Ch. VII, sec. 1 and 2.

16. How much such groups stand to gain or lose emerges most strikingly in the pioneering *Report of the Committee on Intermediaries,* Cmd. 7094 of 1950. The Appendices, in which the relations between government departments and private individuals or associations are listed, are particularly revealing. Note especially the stupendous variety of activities for which permission and means (licenses, allocations, etc) have had to be obtained from government departments. With the relaxation of controls since the immediate post-war period, departmental supervision over private activities has declined, but not much.

17. V. O. Key cites a quaint example: in 1862 the United States Congress levied a tax of one dollar per barrel on beer; shortly afterwards the Brewers' Association was created to exercise, according to the preamble of its constitution, "a proper influence in the legislative and public administration." Many manufacturers' associations were also organized in response to the first feeble attempts to regulate their activities. See Key, *Politics, Parties and Pressure Groups,* p. 177, and other works there cited. See also Truman, *The Governmental Process,* Ch. 4, *passim.*

The extension (or contemplated extension) of government policy is not, of course, the only factor which tends to draw groups into politics. Perhaps equally important is the desire to obtain legislation in order to impede rival groups or to regulate relations within the groups, e.g., the promotion by trade associations of retail price maintenance legislation or by professional associations of licensing regulations. Nor should one think of policies creating pressure groups in a sort of one-one relationship. Much depends on the objective characteristics and internal norms of the groups affected by the policies.

18. This point may be only of historical interest in Britain and the United States today, since modern democratic attitudes legitimate almost all groups. (One can think of exceptions—for example, groups supposed to be instruments of the state, such as the military—although these usually have their private bureaucratic channels of influence, apart from influence by conspiracy.) But in the past many groups—economic, religious, racial—have been more or less effectively excluded from any political participation by virtue of dominant social norms. Many also have had qualms about becoming tainted with politics: the British Medical Association itself is a case in point. Throughout the nineteenth century it tried, almost desperately, to remain purely a professional association, to the point of provoking outright mutiny by politically-minded doctors. (See H. Eckstein, "The Politics of the British Medical Association," *Pol. Quarterly,* vol. XXVI, no. 4, p. 345.) It is hardly necessary to mention revolutionary, e.g., syndicalist, groups as a case in point from a totally different perspective.

Not only groups but also their interests require legitimation; indeed, *felt* interests may be themselves functions of the value structure of a society. (See John Plamenatz, "Interests," *Political Studies,* February, 1954.) Attitudes may therefore restrict group politics either by ruling out all political activities by the groups or by prohibiting activities of certain kinds or in pursuit of certain goals.

19. In "Group Representation in British and American Democracy," *The Annals,* September, 1958, *passim.*

20. Beer, "Pressure Groups and Parties in Britain," p. 1.

21. Note, for example, that the British Legion stopped its efforts to influence elections when threatened with the withdrawal of royal patronage because of its forays into party politics. See Graham Wootton, "Ex-Servicemen in Politics," *Pol. Quarterly,* vol. 29, no. 1, pp. 34-5.

22. Key, *Politics, Parties and Pressure Groups,* p. 177.

23. *Ibid.,* Ch. 10, *passim.*

24. See note 2.

25. Truman, *The Governmental Process,* pp. 87 ff. and 107.

26. "Primitive" here is not meant as a synonym for non-western or industrially underdeveloped. It stands, in Durkheim's sense, for a low level of social differentiation, and there are many ways in which societies may be differentiated. But the economic division of labour being one of them, economic underdevelopment is at least a loose and imperfect synonym for the term.

27. See note 4 above.

28. Truman identifies three factors which determine the extent to which a group achieves "effective access" to the institutions of government: "(1) factors relating to a group's strategic position in society; (2) factors associated with the internal characteristics of groups; and (3) factors peculiar to the governmental institutions themselves." (Truman, *The Governmental Process,* p. 506.) (1) and (2) are grouped under (a) above; the determining role of public policy is not considered by Truman, at any rate not as explicitly as the other factors.

29. A fuller discussion of most of these points is given in Truman, *The Governmental Process,* part II, *passim.*

30. Note, for example, the decisive role of the printers' high status among manual workers and of the peculiar nature of their work in producing solidarity and comradeship in the International Typographical Union. Lipset, et al., *Trade Union Democracy,* 1957.

31. This is not to say that policy is the only factor affecting the corporatization and cohesiveness of interest groups. When different countries follow similar policies in regard to some interest, we often find the interest corporatized to a different extent and with a different degree of intensity; we may therefore suspect that deeper cultural factors also play an important role in determining what I have called the "effective size" of interest groups. Take agriculture in Britain and the United States. Undoubtedly British control over agriculture under the Agriculture Acts is more intense than is the case in America, but the difference is hardly so great as to account, on the face of it, for the very large differences in farmers' organizations in the two countries. The British National Farmers' Union includes some 90 per cent of those eligible to join it and has almost a complete monopoly over agricultural group organization; in the United States there are three major groups and some minor ones, having a total membership of only some 30 per cent of those eligible. What can account for this, if not certain deep cultural attitudes toward organization? (See Beer, "Group Representation," p. 134.) However, *within* the two societies, that is, when other factors tend to be equal, one can trace the effects of policy on the corporate size and cohesiveness of pressure groups. Note, for example, the great growth of the American Farm Bureau Federation as a result of agricultural policy during World War I, the depression, and the World War II and post-war periods. (Truman, *Governmental Process*, pp. 90-92.) The impact of these policies has been greater on the Federation than the other two major farmers' organizations, the National Grange and the Farmers' Union, but this is just because of the closer association between the Federation and government. In Britain, the growth of the NFU in response to the increasing involvement of government in farming is even more marked.

32. See Truman, *The Governmental Process*, p. 519, and Gabriel Almond, *The American People and Foreign Policy*, New York, 1950, pp. 144-45.

33. These points are usually made to contrast cabinet systems and separation of power systems, but they apply equally to coalition *v.* single-party governments, i.e., unstable *v.* stable parliamentary systems. In regard to the opportunities it offers to pressure groups, both to gain access to decision-making bodies and to realize their objectives, French government is probably more like American than British government.

# THE UTILITY AND LIMITATIONS
# OF INTEREST GROUP THEORY
# IN NON-AMERICAN FIELD SITUATIONS

Joseph LaPalombara

Among some American scholars . . . there exists the tendency to consider that schemes used in the United States for the analysis of political reality are perfectly adequate, except for some slight modification, for the study of political questions in the countries of Western Europe. . . . But it is enough to make a few concrete observations to understand the vanity and the dangers of such a position. Nothing will free European specialists in political science from the obligation to engage in an original methodological effort. In our discipline, analytical and, more logically, explicative schemes must be strictly adapted to the realities studied. Once this effort will have been made in each country, then one will be able to proceed to real and exact comparative studies. Without doubt, much time will pass before really satisfying results are obtained, but which is the sector of human understanding the construction of which has not demanded the efforts of several generations?[1]

Reprinted from *The Journal of Politics*, Vol. XXII (1960), pp. 29–49, by permission of the Southern Political Science Association.

This is a revised version of a paper delivered at the 1959 Annual Meeting of the Midwest Conference of Political Scientists. The field research reported here was made possible by a generous grant from the Committee on Comparative Politics of the Social Science Research Council.

Thus concludes Jean Meynaud in an article on French interest groups written for Italian consumption. It is not the first time that he has questioned whether the conceptual apparatus that has evolved in connection with American studies of interest groups is validly or usefully transferable to French or other European settings. Indeed, while he is quick to recognize that European political scientists might well follow some of their Anglo-Saxon colleagues in the exploration of the role of interest groups in Continental political systems, he is nevertheless skeptical about some of the claims made for the interest-group focus as the key to the systematic understanding of political systems any-where.

Meynaud's caveats appear at a time when European scholars in increasing numbers are "discovering" interest groups in places where, according to the folklore of an older political science, they were supposed to be either non-existent or minor phenomena when contrasted to their role in the American political process. Many of these "discoveries" have obviously been encouraged by American scholars who use European countries as research sites.[2] In recent years, however, they have been joined by Jean Meynaud, and by such other thoughtful scholars as Samuel Finer, Philip Williams, Mattei Dogan, Giovanni Sartori, Stanley Hoffman, and a host of others. In other words, interest group studies, like American jazz and wash-and-wear suits, are now fashionable abroad. And Meynaud's concern,[3] if I interpret it correctly, is that European scholars may accept *uncritically* not only the utility of the group focus in research but also the theoretical notions and methodological habits that have evolved in the United States in connection with it.

I shall argue in this paper that (1) except at a level of abstraction that renders it both useless and dangerous for empirical research, a general interest group theory does not exist, and (2) it is necessary to examine comparatively some middle-range propositions about interest groups in order to ascertain if the interest-group focus has any utility at all for the construction of a general theory of politics.

Regarding my first point, I would note that the literature in the United States is replete with more or less operational propositions, more or less normative statements about groups and their implications for a viable democratic political system, more or less useful concepts regarding groups, and more or less impressive empirical data regarding various aspects of group organization and behavior.

It might be objected by some that the work of Arthur F. Bentley adds up to a general theory, or that it becomes one when viewed alongside the work of Truman, Gross, and others who claim Bentley as an intellectual fountainhead. My own view is that Bentley never moved beyond his quite legitimate philosophical and epistemological concerns, and that many of his disciples have either over-simplified his "theory" or, what is worse, have created a fair amount of confusion in their efforts to elaborate and to operationalize what Bentley had in mind.[4] Efforts of the latter variety have unquestionable utility when they caution us about the ubiquitious tendency to reify the groups that we observe, to endow them with personalities, to give them life and a soul. Or we are helped by similar efforts that compel the researcher to view the group not as a collection of individuals with identifiable boundaries, but simply (simply?) as a way of conceptualizing the behavior of many individuals interacting.[5]

Much more damaging to political science—and, as I shall point out, much more dangerous for European scholars—is the oversimplification of Bentley's or any other conceptual scheme for which the interest-group is central. What Oliver Garceau has rightly dubbed simplistic group theory involves a view of public policy as the resultant of a parallelogram of organized pressure group forces. This is the theory that holds that all political behavior is group behavior, that the individual *qua* individual cannot participate in the political process, that political institutions are essentially the arena of group conflict or struggle, that this struggle itself is the raw material of the political process, that the struggle takes place in terms of basic and often material interests that are glossed over by the ideological or other verbiage of the group representatives, and so on.[6]

As Garceau aptly points out, the trouble with this "theory" is that the data from the field do not confirm it. And often it will not help to introduce the concepts of "potential," "latent," or "reference" groups to account for that portion of a legislator's, an adminstrator's, or an adjudicator's behavior that cannot be explained by the model. The policy process, as I have researched it in Italy, does not respond to the kind of explication of phenomena toward which most of group "theory" is directed. Nor will it suffice to observe that I may not have penetrated deeply enough to the really basic interests and interest groups that were involved in the evolution of a particular policy. Efforts to do this lead to a fantastic unstructuring of the situation under observation, in which the hapless researcher pursues an infinite regression of "less-than-basic" interests. Aside from the fact that some European researchers may experience the disillusionment with the ideal of rationalistic democracy that occurred among American scholars when the "fourth (or fifth, or sixth) branch of government" was discovered here, there exists the danger that the simplistic interest group theory is in a sense tailor-made for some of the gross, superficial characteristics of European societies. Some of the inarticulated ideological premises in American social science theory (and certainly in much of the interest group approach) are clearly of a Marxist character.[7] In societies in which class consciousness is strong, in which the idea of class conflict is widely accepted, in which political decisions are often viewed as the articulation of the interests of minority groups in the societies, simple group theory will have a strong appeal. The fact, for example, that pluralism has not had strong support in societies on the Continent is partially an explanation for the belated discovery of the interest group; but the lack of a strong pluralistic tradition will not prevent scholars and others in these same societies from seeing in interest group "theory" a vindication of some of the generalizations of Karl Marx.[8]

One reaction to Meynaud's caveat, then, is that there exists no genuine general theory of interest groups that need concern him. But because there does exist simplistic group theory—the kind that involves either an over-simplified projection of Marxist notions or a fancy elaboration of the dictum that man is a social animal—Meynaud is correct in doubting its applicability to European societies. For the facts show that such "theories" are not valid for the United States either.[9]

My second point is that Meynaud's concern should not lead us completely to eschew the kinds of comparative research out of which an integrated group theory might sometime emerge. This is not to say that one must lead from the assumption that a complete theory of the group will materialize or that, if it does, it will become in fact a general theory of politics or of political systems. As Gabriel Almond points out:

. . . we turn to the comparative study of interest groups not with the hope that these rather than parties or governmental institutions will yield *the principles* of discrimination between types of political systems, but rather with the expectation that the systematic examination of interest groups in their complex interrelations with public opinion, political parties and formal governmental institutions will enable us to differentiate more accurately between political systems as *wholes*. In other words the growing concern among scholars with interest groups and public opinion is the consequence of a search for a more complete and systematic conception of the political process as a whole, rather than a search for an approach which is an *alternative* to the present emphasis on *formal governmental* institutions.[10]

I would argue, therefore, that if some low-level (or middle-range) group theory does exist in the United States, if there are some concepts that have been used successfully here, if we can present a roll call of propositions that can be tested empirically, there is every reason why at least some European scholars should proceed to trace in other societies the research excursions that have occurred across the Atlantic. This is exactly what those of us who have participated in the SSRC-sponsored studies on pressure groups in Western and non-Western systems have attempted to do, and with some fruitful results. Unless I am greatly mistaken, Jean Meynaud agrees on this score; certainly several of his articles, as well as his recent book, suggest that his conceptual debt to American pressure-group "theorists" and researchers is very great, indeed.[11]

When I suggest that it is legitimate, even essential, that American conceptual baggage be carted to Europe (and to other parts of the world as well),[12] I do not mean that it will necessarily provide the key to our understanding political systems comparatively or, indeed, that the kinds of concepts and propositions that have "worked" in the United States will be equally useful abroad. As a matter of fact, I am increasingly skeptical not merely about the applicability of the interest group approach in non-American settings but also about whether the group framework of analysis, when taken alone, is the most valid approach to political behavior in any society,[13] including the United States.

It is precisely because we do not know very much about the validity of the interest group approach, because we do not yet have a general group theory or know if one is viable empirically, that we should insist that some of our notions be tested in political systems other than that of the United States. If we discover, not *a priori* but as the result of empirical, tightly organized research, that propositions about interest groups in politics do not in fact apply to other political systems, we have won a major skirmish in the campaign to sharpen our capacities as political and social scientists. Such an approach does not mean that European scholars should shrink from the original effort demanded by Meynaud; in their own work these men can be of great assistance in the business of challenging some of our assumptions and therefore of clarifying the very question that is central to any science, and that is, to what degree are theoretical statements and the empirical research findings growing out of them universally applicable.

## II

Perhaps I can best illustrate the utility of the position I have assumed by reporting some of the findings of my recent field research experience in Italy. Along with several other scholars supported by the SSRC Committee on Comparative Politics, I ventured abroad to look extensively and, in a more limited way, intensively at the interest group phenomenon in a foreign culture. The concepts, propositions and limited theory that governed my research were gleaned from writings that are familiar to all of us.[14] My intention was to accumulate empirical data that would suggest whether this particular approach would give meaningful results in Italy; whether, that is, the interest group approach would lead me to a more accurate understanding of Italian political institutions and behavior than would, say, a study of the Italian legislature, executive or constitutional decisions.

Because we are still analyzing the data accumulated, I cannot yet answer this question with a high degree of confidence. However, my impression is this: that while the interest group approach, if carefully used, permits the orderly classification of data regarding the behavior of many central actors in the political process, it falls short of providing a satisfactory *explanation* for the patterns of action and the policy outcomes that one encounters in the Italian political system. I should say more—and I have implied it earlier in this paper. The interest group approach at its highest level of generality tends to lead the researcher to offer explanations of behavior that are stretched beyond the point of minimal credibility, or it may create in him cynicism regarding, say, the behavior of public officials who seem not to be acting according to the requisites of the interest group model. Or, as Garceau says, "the search for . . . a complete theory of the group basis of politics may be stretching too far for theoretical elegance at the sacrifice of immediate convenience as an analytical tool."[15]

I would caution, therefore, that any attempt to explicate political behavior within the general framework of interest group "theory" is likely to be misleading and fruitless. If, instead, we conceive of the interest group approach as an analytical tool or as a system of describing certain (but not all!)[16] aspects of the political process, the approach has utility, both in the sense of supporting some American empirical findings and of raising questions about the cross-cultural applicability of classification schemes, propositions and concepts that have grown up around interest group research.

Before illustrating some of the problems and results of my field research, it may be appropriate to say something more about the setting within which the research was conducted and the methods utilized for the collection of data. I owe much to Gabriel Almond's article on political cultures as a convenient way of conceptualizing about and describing in broad detail the setting in which Italian interest groups are compelled to act.[17] In Almond's terms, Italy manifests an uneven development of her several political cultures. The society is notoriously fragmented; several political sub-cultures exist of which the major ones are those identified with Catholicism, a secular middle class, and a modernizing and innovating class. Each of these sub-cultures is atomized still further along ideological lines; each tends to have a total and highly articulated design for society as a whole and therefore for the political institutions within it. Although there are some peripheral points at which the views of the sub-cultures tend to merge, these are clearly exceptional; these major groupings are not compatible with each other. The sociologists would say about the society that it is not well integrated; the political scientists might speak of a low degree of consensus when measured, say, against the standard of the United States or Great Britain.

It is of vital importance to understand that formal interest groups in Italy frequently organize *within* these sub-cultures; very few of them cut across subcultural lines, even when the logic of a common economic interest would appear to compel such unification. For their own purposes, Communist-inspired or dominated groups often call for such unity of action and organization, but they are almost always repelled. Even within each of the sub-cultures, the groups are further fragmented. It is not uncommon, for example, to find Communist, Catholic, Socialist, Liberal, Republican, and Neo-Fascist rough equivalents of the American League of Women Voters. Or, within the Catholic sub-culture, one can discern functional groups that separate the wealthy from the poor, radical workers from conservative workers, agricultural day laborers from tenant farmers, from small property-holding farmers, and so on. In a context such as this, it is difficult to isolate what may be the "basic" or "fundamental" interests around which the groups are organized.

All of which results in an enormous proliferation of groups—of countless interest groups in a society where they have gone almost completely unnoticed by political scientists. In Rome alone we were able to identify some 3,000 formal national groups from which we drew both our mailed-questionnaire and interview samples. Of course, as our questionnaire responses show, most of the formal groups are only sporadically involved in the political process. Nevertheless, it is noteworthy that not more than a handful of the groups responding to our questionnaire indicated patterns of action that categorically excluded political intervention. For the rest, intervention ranged all the way from an occasional memorandum to a parliamentary committee or administrative agency to frequent and regularized contacts with political party and public officials in every branch of government.

This fragmented nature of Italian society is responsible, I believe, for the relatively important role that violence, and the threat of it, play in the general tactics utilized by interest groups in support of their demands. The group leaders who were queried on this phenomenon tended to see their activities as part of a basic struggle among the sub-cultures to impose hegemony over each other. For these leaders, domination by the opposition was generally taken to mean not merely difficult access to the key centers of policy making, but outright denial of any access at all to the group members of the sub-cultures not in power. As it turns out, this judgment is definitely not exaggerated; for the group leaders themselves freely indicate that, wherever and whenever possible, they seek utterly to exclude their opponents from the policy making areas. In a setting such as this, the threat or use of violence may be the only logical recourse open to a frustrated interest group.

Given this kind of general setting, it would be foolhardy to try to speak with authority about the characteristic patterns of interest group action in all sectors of Italian politics. My field effort focused primarily on the interaction between interest groups and the Italian bureaucracy, and the research was limited to a small number of groups and just a few administrative agencies. Special attention was given to *Confindustria* (Italy's equivalent of the N.A.M.), the trade unions, and Catholic Action in its various organizational manifestations. Their relationships to the Ministries of Industry and Commerce and of Labor and Social Security were intensively explored. Information was obtained through the following devices:

1. Content analyses of the major publications of the three groups over periods ranging from 10 to 50 years.

2. Mailed questionnaires to 129 formal groups. The questionnaires elicited information about internal organization, membership, leadership and intervention in the political process. Sixty-eight groups responded.

3. Analyses of newspapers and other periodical literature dealing with the three groups, the issues in which they were openly involved, and the bureaucratic agencies and personalities with whom they interacted.

4. Informal discussions with approximately 100 informants or "knowledgeables" from the fields of government, business, organized labor and the professions.

5. Three-hour focused interviews conducted with 125 group leaders, bureaucrats, party officials and selected members of the legislature.

Perhaps the most frustrating general finding of this study is that, except on the basis of highly unreliable impressions, it is impossible to measure the *relative influence* that groups exert over administrative decisions. The methods employed yielded essentially unsatisfactory results. For example, when respondents (group leaders and public administrators) are asked to differentiate among groups in terms of the power exercised in various administrative agencies, not very impressive results are obtained. For one thing the concept "power" (or "influence") is not easy to define, and, even after the interviewer suggests a definition, he cannot be certain that the respondents adhere to a specific denotation in their evaluations. The most that one can get from analyzing interview materials is a rough classification of responses. Thus, when the agency in question was a sub-division of the Ministry of Industry and Commerce, we obtained this pattern of response:

1. Bureaucrats in administrative agencies other than the ministry identify the unions as weak, Catholic Action as relatively strong, and the power of *Confindustria* as overwhelming.

2. Communist and Socialist trade union leaders describe themselves as weak (but see below!), the Catholic unions as just a little stronger, *Confindustria* as strong, and the power of Catholic Action as overwhelming.

3. Catholic trade unionists view themselves as

stronger than the Communists and Catholic Action, but weaker than *Confindustria*.

4. Other group leaders and political officials generally identify the unions as weak, Catholic Action as strong, and *Confindustria* as overwhelmingly powerful.

5. Bureaucrats in the ministry involved identify only Catholic Action and the Catholic unions as in a position "to interfere" with orderly bureaucratic processes.

6. *Confindustria* leaders describe themselves as weak, identify the Communist unions as similarly situated and ascribe overwhelming power to the Catholic unions and to Catholic Action.

Interestingly, group leaders tend to argue with the interviewer that their organizations are weak, but only to a certain point. That is, the articulation of weakness to the outsider tends to cease whenever the respondent is probed on the reactions of group members to such a situation. Thus Communist trade unionists insist that, even in the Ministry of Industry, things are not completely black for them. The only exception to this pattern worth mentioning is a leader of the Christian Democratic Association of Direct Cultivators, who describes his organization as a pressure group, claims that it wields enormous power and boasts that 62 Christian Democratic deputies owe their election to it.

Similar patterns of subjective evaluation are obtained regarding a long series of questions pertaining to the relative power of groups in administrative agencies. Only to a very limited extent do the replies of the various categories of respondents tend to vary as the focus of attention shifts from one bureaucratic agency to another. Out of the total responses emerges, first, widespread recognition that organized groups do seek to intervene in the administrative process, and second, the tendency of many respondents (both group leaders and bureaucrats) to ascribe dominant influence to Catholic Action and to *Confindustria*.

The difficulty with such ascription is that it is not at all corroborated by other measures. For example, we attempted to identify over a time the positions of the various groups regarding a series of issues that came before the administrative agencies, and to gauge whether the final decision (where we could identify one) corresponded to one position or another. This analysis shows that on almost every major issue in which it expressed itself over several years *Confindustria* was defeated by the groups with which it competes.

The same analysis conducted for Catholic Action, however, raises enormous difficulties. The organization is so vast, so subdivided into many smaller units, some of which compete among themselves, that it is difficult to know when one has isolated a consistent Catholic Action position. But even here, the current and historical data can be marshalled in support of the proposition that, as far as administrative decisions go, Catholic Action does suffer defeats and, in any case, probably enjoys much less influence than Italians generally ascribe to it.

One might conclude at this point that the subjective evaluations were simply in error and that the second type of measure is more reliable. We think not, and for several reasons. First, it is apparent that group representatives often overstate their demands. This is invariably the case with their public demands, if interview responses mean anything. Thus, it is difficult to know exactly what the interest group really wanted, or expected to get. Second, it is also evident that how these groups fare in any of the administrative agencies will tend to vary with the nature of the issue involved, and, alas, with a host of other intervening variables such as the temper of the Minister of the Treasury, the political deals that may be evolving in the legislature, the struggles within the dominant party, the unlikely alliances between Communist and Christian political leaders, to name only a few about which we have any information at all. Third, a focus on issues that engenders controversy and open opposition tends to lead one away from the many matters that are regularly handled quietly and on a routine basis. The way in which such less controversial issues are disposed of may reflect differing degrees of influence of the very groups about which we are attempting to make a total judgment. And last, this kind of analysis cannot shed any significant light unless a very careful accounting is given of the role of the bureaucrats themselves in these controversies.

Frankly, then, I come away from this experience with the feeling that we can describe relative group influence only in gross and therefore possibly misleading terms. For example, it is my impression that one of the very weakest interest groups in Italy today is *Confindustria,* about whose alleged enormous prowess millions of words have been printed in Italy. I believe that a complete analysis of our data will eventually bear out my assertion, and I recognize that, in making it, I am open to the criticism that I speak of relative group strength on the basis of pure impression. We know enough, in any event, to caution that it is not sufficient to support a claim of group influence in administration to show that an interest group maintains certain relations with the bureaucracy. It is the existence of these relationships between group leader and bureaucrats that has led some theorists to comment on the power of groups over bureaucratic decisions. Let us examine some of these relationships as they apply to Italy.

For example, it is sometimes suggested that the growth of the welfare state—or of economic planning—has intensified the contacts between group representatives and public administrators, especially in those administrative sectors that deal with economic regulation and welfare services. As Samuel Beer articulates it:

> . . . the structure of the welfare state and the controlled economy associates pressure groups more closely with the administration and makes pressure groups more concerned with the decisions made at the administrative level.[18]

Perhaps such a shift in the locus of interest group activity has occurred at the time and for the reason suggested. However, it is also possible that the welfare state has brought many new groups into existence and that the intensity of group activity in general has increased in all branches and at all levels of government. The kind of shift in emphasis probably began historically when delegated legislation became a major phenomenon, and as groups discovered that administrators have discretion in the implementation of legislative policies, notwithstanding what the juridical scholars may say.

Nor is it to be assumed that the nature of a group's interest will determine where it will concentrate its efforts to intervene in the political or governmental process. In Italy it is not clear that groups with strong economic interests gravitate toward the bureaucracy and groups with strong ideological content toward the legislature, as some writers expect. To be sure, Communist and Socialist groups are generally more visible in the legislature. Their leaders tell us, however, that this is not so much a matter of choice as it is the result of their not finding adequate access in administrative agencies where both management groups sporadically and Catholic groups always and with great determination seek to freeze them out.

With the industrialist and employer associations, on the other hand, there is an apparent preference for the administrative arena. Again, however, our findings show that the unwillingness of these group leaders to appear "in public" is largely a result of the trauma they suffered when the Fascist regime they so openly supported disintegrated. Italy's industrialists, for example, have carried this political shyness to the point where *Confindustria* has only three members in the national legislature who openly speak on behalf of the confederation. *Confindustria* leaders complain bitterly about their disadvantage alongside other organized groups with strong direct legislative representation. However, *Confindustria's* incredibly amateurish and abortive attempt to reenter the legislature in the elections of 1958 will cause both group leaders and the industrialists they represent to retreat once more into the more reassuring, even if not exclusively preferred labyrinth of Italian bureaucracy.

Because they are the easiest to identify, large-scale interest groups appear to dominate the Italian bureaucratic scene. Yet, we find that, with most of the administrators we interviewed, the peak associations are of less importance than the more specialized groups that the associations confederate. Thus, members of the Ministry of Industry are more concerned, they say, with, for example, the National Association of Automotive Industries or the National Association of Transport, than they are with *Confindustria* in which both organizations have membership. Similarly, Ministry of Labor bureaucrats show greater concern about the needs and demands of, say, the National Federation of Portworkers or the National Federation of Metal-mechanical Workers, than they do for the confederations in which these units have membership. This is true notwithstanding that the constitutions of almost all confederating associations stipulate that they and not the member units will carry on negotiations with governmental agencies or with other groups.

It is this identification between the governmental and the interest group specialists that leads Meynaud to suggest that the more recent and specialized ministries (labor, industry, commerce, *etc.*) are likely to be more susceptible to group pressures than older ministries such as war, the interior, and foreign affairs. There is no questioning the existence of this identification in the Italian ministries of industry and labor; respondents on both the interest group and bureaucratic sides articulated at great length about the advantages of dealing with persons who speak one's same professional language, who "really understand" the nature of the problems to which both sides address themselves. Supportive evidence for this point is also suggested by the fact that the most proletarian of trade unions will go to great lengths to insure that their representatives to bureaucratic agencies be university graduates whose status (and, perhaps, socio-economic background) is equal to that of the public administrators with whom the groups must deal.

I will defer until later the inferences that we might draw from patterns such as this. Here I wish particularly to add that we conducted a few interviews in the ministries of the interior and of foreign affairs specifically for the purpose of probing the relative susceptibility of the administrators there to group pressures. We also raised this issue with many of our "knowledgeables." Needless to say, we found that these ministries, too, have their clienteles, even highly specialized ones such as the National Association of Municipal Authorities that interact regularly with Ministry of the Interior officials, and all sorts of interest groups (European federation, protection of emigrants, *etc.*) that are in regular contact with the Ministry of Foreign Affairs. These group representatives, too, tend to speak specialized languages that relate to the activities of the public administrators with whom they are in contact. On the basis of our limited findings, I would suggest that hasty conclusions about the newer and more specialized ministries

be avoided.[19] It may well be that the proposition is valid for Italy. But it is also possible that not enough attention has been paid the older agencies where, superficially, it may appear that the major functional interest groups are inactive.

We also discovered in Italy a vast network of quasi-corporative relationships between certain interest groups and the administrative agencies. Similar arrangements exist in France and Great Britain,[20] and the practice has been described as providing the privileged groups with built-in access to critical points in the administrative decision-making process. In many of Italy's ministries, group representation is accorded on advisory committees that are expected to aid the minister and other top-level administrators in the formulation of general policy. Additionally, some groups have representation on specialized committees that set prices for consumers goods and scarce natural resources, for gas and electricity, and so on. Other similar agencies consult on matters of foreign commerce, including import-export priorities and regulations. There is no doubt of the intrinsic importance of the activities engaged in by these special committees. *Confindustria,* for example, maintains a card file on all of its leaders and members who hold positions on such committees, both nationally and locally. *Confindustria* leaders are quick to explain that such representation provides an excellent way for the agencies involved to hear the opinions of the parties affected by policy, as well as a way of assuring that the administrators will not succumb to the demands of a single interest group.

In general, representation on these ministerial committees is accorded to the industrial, agricultural and labor associations in the country, with the exception that Communist and Socialist groups in any of the areas have been barred for some years notwithstanding that in several sectors they have the largest organizations. Needless to say, the leaders of these groups complain about this. Interestingly, so did about half of the bureaucrats who were queried on this point. They generally offer as an explanation of their position the view that the representation is meaningless, and possibly harmful to the bureaucracy when it involves representatives of groups that recruit a small minority of the total organized persons in a particular area. This is especially the case where administrative regulation of the groups is the central function of the agency. Not having the regulated individuals represented when, in theory, they are supposed to be results in considerable difficulty for the bureaucrats.

What is one to say about this kind of group representation? In one or two areas, notably the Interministerial Committee on Prices, administrative bias in favor of the industrial representatives and their organizations has been so blatant as to result in the refusal of trade union and other group representatives to attend meetings. However, we have found this to be a glaring exception. For most of the other committees, we found each group represented articulating the view that the other groups were unduly advantaged, that the administrators were playing favorites, that it was really a hopeless task to try to deal rationally with the Italian bureaucracy.

This suggests that, perhaps, no group is dominant. It also indicates that corporative representation cuts two ways for the interest groups. On the one hand, they have ready access to the agencies and they can make their demands heard. They also have inside information that permits them to·handle more readily and expertly than unrepresented groups administrative matters that concern or affect them. On the other hand, the fact that they accept representation means that they share part of the responsibility for the policies that evolve. According to most respondents, such representation generally results in the making of more moderate demands than might otherwise be the case. In several instances we find that the group representatives to some of these committees are under great cross pressure and that, often, they tend to side with the administrative agency against their own groups!

This leads me to emphasize what may, perhaps, be well known to all who have looked in on pressure group behavior in administrative settings, and that is that administrative officials are anything but passive actors in the so-called group process. Instead, we often find them competing with group representatives in order to press a point of view that is unsupported by any of the formal groups that interact with the agency.

At times these bureaucrats reveal an amazing capacity for manipulation. For example, one of the officials in the Ministry of Industry has close personal relationships with several of *Confindustria's* leaders. During his interview, he indicated that not a day goes by without his talking with his contacts in *Confindustria* and with officials of the trade or industrial associations that relate to the activities of his division. He added that he never makes a major decision without consulting with representatives of these organizations. Yet, when probed about these contacts, it became apparent that the administrator was engaged in this activity as a means of getting commitments to his policies or, as he put it, as a means of preventing the groups from causing trouble later. When we interviewed the group of representatives about their relations with the agency, they described the public official as a "very difficult" person to deal with but also as someone who knew what he was doing and who generally "got things done."

This story could be repeated for most of the administrators who were interviewed in our study. The fact that the bureaucrats speak the same language as do the group representatives, that they

may have the same kinds of university degrees and come from the same social stratum of the society seems not to justify the conclusion that the administrators are prey to the demands of special interests.

I am not trying to force the judgment here that Italian administrative agencies are invulnerable to the pressures of special interests. Our study will spotlight, for example, many of the structural weaknesses of Italian bureaucracy which tend to make the administrators overly dependent on some of their clientele groups. The almost complete lack of research facilities and activities in the ministries is one of these structural shortcomings. Administrators frequently complain that they must rely for statistical and other information on which policy must be based on the research activities of the unions, *Confindustria* or Catholic Action. Even when the memoranda containing research "findings" are suspect, the administrators often have no way of demonstrating this. At best, and this is a very limited practice in the ministries we observed, the bureaucrat might go out of his way to solicit other memoranda from groups that clearly compete with the organizations from which their statistical and other technical data usually come. The thing that struck me was that administrators complained, almost to a man, about this dependence.

## III

Much of what we have found fits not so much the interest group "theory" of politics as it does the kind of propositions about organizational behavior that have been expounded by Simon, Selznik and others. To be sure, there are points at which elements of interest group "theory" writ large enter the writings of Simon. However, much value would seem to lie with a research focus that is institutionally circumscribed and which seeks to delineate, or at least to outline, the major behavioral contours that are likely to be associated with the institution or organization itself. Thus, when examining bureaucracy and bureaucratic behavior there is no need for following the proclivities, say, of the neo-Bentleyans who would make the bureaucracy an arena for group conflict and the bureaucrat a mere pawn in the "process of government." One can conceptualize about characteristics regarding *all* large-scale organizations insofar as they must reach decisions and implement them, without regard to whether the actors in them are the objects of interest group strategies.

Our data clearly point up the fact that a person who enters a bureaucratic agency is to some degree socialized by it; that is, he takes on some of the values of the administrative agency itself. This identification with his agency, as well as the ideal requirements of the role he occupies, will in some measure curb what might otherwise be a tendency to become an instrument of interest group desires and manipulations.

The bureaucrat also tends to develop certain skills that permit him in turn to manipulate the interest groups, and to play them off against each other for his own purposes. It is for this reason that administrators often welcome group clienteles and, where such do not exist, will seek to create them.[21]

Understanding this, the general interest group "theorists" will observe that, in these instances, the administrative agencies are not merely arenas but an integral part of the battle; the administrators, not merely mediators but participants (in interest group terms) in the struggle to have one's own values or views predominate. But we need not posit the bureaucracy, or any single unit or individual within it, as a competing interest group in order to recognize and explicate the bureaucrat's role in the governmental process. Certainly we could do more research than we have in the direction of exploring the possibility of the highly individualized art of administrative decision-making.[22] Such research is doomed to foredrawn conclusions, however, if our conceptual apparatus makes even the suspicion of such behavior unthinkable and the holder of such a view appear to be hopelessly naive.

In our field interviews, I was impressed by the frequency with which the bureaucrats interviewed sought to explain their policy positions or behavior in terms of a "national interest" or a "general welfare." To be sure, such responses were never accepted at face value, but in many instances (too many to ascribe merely to a chance factor) probing failed to turn up the reference or other group interests that the administrators were serving in the name of a mythical national interest. This failure raises for us, as it has for others who have studied the administrative process, perplexing questions not simply about administrative behavior but about the concept of the "public interest," its meaning, its role and its susceptibility to empirical analysis.[23]

One way out of difficulties such as this is to speak of the administration as using the "community," the consumer, his fellow administrators, or all those living or dead with whom he feels allied as a reference group. I am increasingly suspicious of such convenient escape hatches. Procedures such as this loom not so much as scientific insights but as self-fulfilling prophesies—or as the kind of cynicism that I touched on earlier. They also point up once more the possibility that simplistic interest group "theory," in seeking to account for all political behavior, may not be useful in providing satisfactory explanations for any political behavior in particular. It is to the latter that the field researcher's attention must be directed, and, for the time

being at least, only limited propositions about groups appear to have any utility at all.

## NOTES

1. Jean Meynaud, "I gruppi d'interesse in Francia," *Studi politici,* IV (Florence, July–September, 1957), 433–434.

2. This is not the place to inventory the American studies I have in mind. However, it is worth recalling that Samuel Beer, Henry Ehrmann, Val Lorwin, Gabriel Almond, and Leon Epstein, to name but a few who come to mind, have been instrumental in turning both American and foreign scholarly attention to the importance of interest group organization and behaviour in British and Continental politics.

3. A concern more profoundly shared by Professor Giovanni Sartori, of the University of Florence, and provocatively articulated in his recent "Gruppi di pressione o gruppi di interesse? Una discussione sul neo-pluralismo," *Il mulino,* LXXXVII (Bologna, January, 1959), 7-42. *Cf.* Earl Latham, "The Group Basis of Politics: Notes for a Theory," *American Political Science Review,* XLVI (June, 1952), 380 ff.

4. One of my colleagues, Joseph Schlesinger, observes that the vague and mystical group notions of Bentley have often been borrowed to lend an aura of respectability to research on interest groups conducted essentially in the tradition of the journalistic muckrakers or the "inside dopesters." That the mantle of Bentley's or anyone else's "general group theory" does not really fit is unimportant; it does make the interest group scholar *feel* less naked.

5. This is the burden of Charles B. Hagan, "The Group in a Political Science," in *Approaches to the Study of Politics* (Evanston, 1958), pp. 38–51.

6. Garceau's essay on this point is required reading: "Interest Group Theory in Political Research," *Annals of the American Academy of Social and Political Science,* CCCXIX (September, 1958), 104–112. Charles Hagan points out that interests other than the material ones (*e.g.,* family, friendship, patriotism) are also included as important by the interest group adherents. This may be true, but I also recall that Bentley had some harsh words about interests that masquerade behind Fourth-of-July orations.

7. The contribution of pluralism to the growth of group analysis is recognized. Not as recognized—or articulated—is the contribution of Marxist thought to modern sociology and, indeed, to the assumption of the neo-pluralists.

8. It should be noted that the latent Marxian analogy involves two dangers for the interest-group researcher. The first is that he may conceptualize about the "group struggle" in terms of a more or less rigid economic determinism. The second (and prior!) danger is that he may take as a given exactly what should be the central *question* of his inquiry—that the political process is epitomized by group-oriented behavior, that groups conflict and compete in an effort to influence policy, and that policy and political change is the outcome of essentially this kind of behavioral input.

9. Garceau, *op. cit., passim.*

10. Gabriel Almond, *A Comparative Study of Interest Groups and the Political Process.* Mimeographed by the Social Science Research Council (New York, April, 1957), p. 5.

11. See his "Essai d'analyse de l'influence des groupes d'intérèt," *Revue economique* (Paris, No. 2, 1957), 3-46; and *Les groupes de pression en France* (Paris, 1958).

12. One very interesting excursus of the type I have in mind is Myron Weiner's "Interest Groups in India," a paper delivered at the 1958 Annual Meeting of the American Political Science Association, St. Louis, Missouri, September 4-6, 1958.

13. For example, in many instances the focus on interest groups seems not to differ in substance from previous emphasis placed on more formal institutions of government such as the legislature or the executive. Macrocosmic group analysis, as well as theoretical endeavors in the interest group area, seem to create much impressionistic folklore about the nature of groups and their relationship to the political process. Much is written, but little research is conducted, on the obvious problem of *demonstrating* how certain variables regarding interest groups, the political culture, or the character of political institutions and policy makers affect the political process.

14. A first statement of my research prospectus is reported in "On the French and Italian Bureaucracies" (with J. T. Dorsey), *PROD,* I (September, 1957), 35-40. I might add that the literature is overrun with "middle-range" propositions regarding interest groups and the political process. Here are a few:

A. A group's influence *vis-à-vis* its competitors will vary with the proportion of the total membership in its specialized area that it is able to organize.

B. Although formal organization is not essential to an interest group, all other things being equal, organization is in itself an independent variable affecting the degree of success a group can have in influencing decisions or policies.

C. A group's ability to intervene efficaciously in governmental decisions affecting it varies directly with the nature of the group's access to decisional information.

D. Bureaucratic agencies differ in the degree to which they are penetrable by organized groups. Responsiveness to group demands will be maximized in those agencies that are newer and more functionally specialized.

E. All other things being equal, decision makers will favor those group representatives or negotiators who evidence life experiences (social origin, social class, education, *etc.*) similar to those of the decision makers.

F. Interest groups will be ineffective in the degree to which the concept of the "public interest" is a strongly held myth by the governmental decision makers.

G. Interest groups will be more active in public administrative areas in those countries displaying the highest degree of delegated legislation.

H. The administrative role, as such, limits the influence of interest groups because, like all roles, it involves required, permitted and forbidden behavior.

I. The power of any sample of politically active groups (on any given series of issues) will vary with (a) the political "styles" of the groups, (b) the reference groups of the bureaucrats, and (c) the structure and processes of the bureaucracy.

15. Garceau, *op. cit.,* p. 106.

16. On this point, note Samuel Beer's comment that the exclusive use of group theory would constitute an unsatisfactory conceptual framework for the analysis of British politics. "Pressure Groups and Parties in Britain," *American Political Science Review,* L (March, 1956), 2.

17. "Comparative Political Systems," in H. Eulau, S. J. Eldersveld, and M. Janowitz, *Political Behavior* (New York, 1956), pp. 34-42.

18. Beer, *op. cit.,* 15. Similarly, Meynaud, "Essai d'analyse de l'influence des groupes d'intérèt," *op. cit.,* 24.

19. Jean Meynaud's remarks on the differing susceptibility of administrative agencies to group demands are contained in his "Les groupes d'intérèt et l'administration en France," *Revue française de science politique,* VII (Paris, July–September, 1957), 573-593.

20. See *ibid.,* 584 ff. and Beer, *op. cit.,* 6.

21. See H. Simon, D. Smithburg, and V. Thompson, *Public Administration* (New York, 1950), pp. 461-465, and H. Simon, *Administrative Behavior* (New York, 1947), Ch. 10.

22. Alfred DeGrazia attacks the "individual behavior" notions of political science, sociology and social-psychology in his "Nature and Prospects of Political Interest Groups," *Annals of the American Academy of Social and Political Science,* CCCIXX (September, 1958), 113-122, especially pp. 113-117. Although DeGrazia rejects simplistic group theory, his comments about groups are essentially Bentleyan. The second part of this article contains some extremely provocative comments on democracy, old and new.

Another important source worth consulting on this point is Norton E. Long, "Public Policy and Administration: The Goals of Rationality and Responsibility," *Public Administration Review,* XIV (Winter, 1954), 22-31, especially pp. 25-30.

23. On the problem of "the public interest" in administrative decision-making, the reader should consult the article by my colleague, Glendon A. Schubert, Jr., "'The Public Interest' in Administrative Decision-Making: Theorem, Theosophy or Theory?" *American Political Science Review,* LI (June, 1957), 346-368. Schubert reviews both critically and caustically various abortive attempts to define the concept operationally. He also notes "the bland optimism" with which some writers "contemplate the impact of the group struggle upon public policy." Although he, too, seems committed to the idea that decision-making is epitomized by governmental accommodation of conflicting interests, his model of "administrative due process" would seek to account for administrative behavior that cannot be explicated by simplistic group "theory."

# VII

# VII   Totalitarianism and Autocracy

# INTRODUCTION

Harry Eckstein and David E. Apter

"Fascism," according to Benito Mussolini, "is organized, centralized, authoritarian democracy." Some of the Communists call their governments People's Democracies. The Nazis, despite their contempt for the historic institutions of popular government, brandished popular symbols like *Freiheit* and *Volksgemeinschaft*—freedom and "community."

At first glance these appear to be typical examples of totalitarian Newspeak, but are these formulations really so dishonest? The very fact that totalitarianism and populistic democracy are both emanations of modern life should keep one from dismissing them out of hand.

We wish to raise here the problem of the relations between totalitarianism on one hand and democracy and autocracy on the other.[1] Should one regard totalitarianism as a particularly virulent form of autocracy—a form of rule as old as government itself—and thus as the very opposite of democracy, or as a kind of democracy: democracy corrupted, perhaps, or democracy extended beyond tolerable limits? Or would it be better to regard totalitarianism as a synthesis of two opposites, the form that autocracy must take once democratic norms have become widely accepted and democratic structures widely established? Or is it really *sui generis,* something that has nothing at all in common with other kinds of government?

This is not just a question of definition. On our answer depends the way we answer many other, more manifestly important questions—questions about the origins of totalitarian regimes, about the requisites necessary to keep them in existence, and about their internal dynamics.

## II

The reasons for regarding totalitarianism as virulent, or perfected, autocracy are manifest. Autocracies are highly centralized and hierarchical governments, the scope of their rule is generally wide, and they permit little opposition. Putting the same points differently: autocracies are governments that permit little personal freedom, little organizational autonomy (either in government or society), and little legitimate political competition. These, obviously, are characteristics of totalitarianism as well, and with a vengeance. We could certainly say (it *has* been said) that totalitarianism simply magnifies the elements of autocracy to their farthest limits—that it is a form of rule in which all governmental structures are hierarchically integrated, all human relations subsumed to government, and all legitimate political activity mobilized to support the governmental structure.

Totalitarianism does differ from autocracy in degree—but so does democracy. Democracies never tolerate all forms of competition and autonomy; they always involve some degree of hierarchy, integration, and control and some autonomy on the part of rulers. The point is, of course, that differences in degree do sometimes constitute differences in kind. Above all, there are qualitative differences between much or little of something and all or nothing of it. Take a simple example. It has been argued that there is only a difference in degree among various weapons of destruction, from the bow and arrow to nuclear weapons—a great difference in degree, to be sure, but a quantitative difference just the same. Perhaps so. But imagine a weapon so powerful that it must destroy the users as well as the intended victims. Such a weapon is surely of a kind different from all others, for hardly any difference exists between possessing such a weapon and not possessing any weapons at all. Whether one has no arms to use or whether the arms one has cannot be used makes little difference; in either case, one is defenseless.[2] Thus, the zero point and totality point of destructive power both differ profoundly from all the intermediate levels; they resemble one another more than anything in between them.

The analogy applies to forms of rule: totalitarianism is unique precisely because it is total. However paradoxical it may seem, it resembles *anarchy* more than any form of government. In both democracy and autocracy it makes sense to speak of government, since government is somehow distinct from society; it governs society. But in both anarchy and totalitarianism the dividing line between government and society has disappeared, not just been shifted. Even the mythology and symbolism of totalitarianism intimates this. In Nazi ideology the difference between the German state and the German "people" (*Volk*) vanished, and in Communist philosophy an organic connection is made between total dictatorship and the total withering of the state. The more subtle critics of totalitarianism have seen this too. In *Animal Farm* Orwell depicted an autocratic system, but in *1984* he depicted a totalitarian one. The society of *1984* is characterized by the obliteration of privacy and autonomy much more than by despotic rule, as symbolized by the very nebulousness of Orwell's rulers in *1984*.

The essence of totalitarianism, then, is that it annihilates all boundaries between the state and the groupings of society, even the state and individual personality. At any rate, that is the intention of totalitarians. Of course, their ideal is hard to realize. No doubt there are "islands of separateness" in any actual totalitarian society;[3] but the whole thrust of the system is directed at the integration of these "islands" into the flat homogeneity, the totality, of totalitarian life. The attempt itself gives totalitarianism a distinctive mold. Certainly no other social order (except only perhaps for Calvin's Geneva, which may well be considered an early totalitarian society) has tried to integrate so many aspects of human existence: family life, friendship, courtship, education, work, leisure, production, exchange, worship, status, art, manners, travel, dress—even that final assertion of human privacy, death.

Some of the most deeply puzzling aspects of totalitarian behavior become less mystifying when we think of totalitarianism as something which embraces and tends to obliterate all autonomous elements of society and personality. How else make sense of the abject willingness of tough old Bolsheviks, not visibly suffering from physical torture or drugging, to destroy themselves in conformity with party will in the great Stalin purges? What but the submergence of personality in totalitarian life can account for this? Recall the last plea before the judges of Bukharin, an old Bolshevik and leading Marxist philosopher:

I shall now speak of myself, of the reasons for my repentance. Of course it must be admitted that incriminating evidence plays a very large part. For three months I refused to say anything. Then I began to testify. Why? Because while in prison I made a re-evaluation of my entire past. For when you ask yourself: "If you must die, what are you dying for?"—an absolutely black vacuity suddenly arises before you with startling vividness. There was nothing to die for, if one wanted to die unrepented. And, on the contrary, everything positive that glistens in the Soviet Union acquires new dimensions in a man's mind. This in the end disarmed

me completely and led me to bend my knees before the Party and the country.[4]

Broken in spirit, no longer convinced of his moral rightness in resisting Stalinism, Bukharin bowed to the larger, to him more glorious, claims of the totalitarian society. As Leites has put it, when the oppositionist "believed in the correctness of his (Stalin's) line, he had to ward off feelings of guilt for being in opposition at all. When Stalin's line came to seem less incorrect, his (the accused's) guilt became intense and may even have colored the memory of his previous misgivings."[5] And guilt, of all feelings, is uniquely personal. We do not often feel it in regard to political views, not even if we are convinced majoritarians finding ourselves in a minority position. To feel guilt about political ideas is the ultimate indication of a fusion of politics and personality.

The executioners give one the same impression as the executed. If the Eichmann trial has made anything apparent, it is that Eichmann was not a sadistic monster, indulging a personal bloodlust in the extermination camps. Nor was he merely a model clerk, obedient for the sake of the rewards of obedience. His outstanding characteristic surely was (and remained) his remarkable impersonality, his submersion of self into Nazism to the point that he seems not to have had any private feelings, neither lust nor anger, nor guilt and repentance. He, of all people, was the epitome of totalitarian man: a functional cell in an all-embracing organism—the very model of Hannah Arendt's "inanimate man."[6] After all, even Stalin's victims were still men enough to feel guilty.

The attempt to bring about the complete identity of state, society, and individual underlies the minutiae of totalitarian life no less than its enormities. Totalitarian leaders are incredibly fussy about all sorts of inconsequential aspects of life—like the most anxious and demanding of parents; and this is precisely because they, like demanding parents, want to shape human material in their own image, to create a totally renovated man (*l'uomo nuovo,* in one of Mussolini's pet phrases). In Italy, the aim was to create men "less likeable and more ruthless," men "serious, efficient, hard and militaristic"—in short, as different as possible from the Italians as the Fascists themselves saw them. The Nazis dreamed of men obsessed with obedience, willing to carry out orders "even when it is unjust for them to do so." And in the Soviet Union men are to have "a socialistic attitude to labor and social property, industriousness and discipline, trueness to Party idea and principle, and an understanding of the paramount importance of social interests (over personal interests)."

In the attempt to shape such men nothing is too inconsequential to order and regulate. Like those fanatic patriots who, at the height of the French Revolution, wore only patriotic clothes, attended only patriotic plays, took part only in patriotic rites, ate only patriotic food, and slept only in patriotic beds, totalitarian men are meant to eat, sleep, and breathe totalitarianism. Fascist plays dealt mainly with Roman nobility and heroism and Fascist films with party ceremonies, army parades, maneuvers, battleships, and bombers; the Nazis too were subjected to unending exhibitions of heroics; Soviet men get stiff doses of "socially useful music" and socialist morality plays, in which dedicated proletarians triumph over careerists, conspirators and saboteurs. The Fascists ruled out formal dress; Hitler railed at "dandified fashionableness"; the Russian Communists used ostentatiously to wear boiler suits (the Chinese still do) and to hound the *stilyagi,* the stylish and casual in dress. Fascists were urged to develop a "terse and abrupt manner of speaking and writing," and to salute rather than shake hands; Nazis were told never to indulge in "idle chatter"; Russians have been urged upon the highest authority not to smoke or spit. Spontaneous humor is frowned upon by them all—indeed if anything is typical of all totalitarians it is their grim distaste for fun. The Chinese—shades of Calvin!—counsel against all lightheartedness, the Russians encourage serious satires in which class enemies are unmasked, the Fascists at one time even forbade Mickey Mouse cartoons. What could explain such a fantastic preoccupation with trivialities except a conception of life in which trivialities simply do not exist (or are not permitted)—in which the highest purposes of state and least concerns of personal life have become indistinguishable?[7]

## III

We prefer to talk about totalitarian societies rather than totalitarian governments or totalitarian states. "Government" and "state" denote specialized structures within society alongside of other specialized structures, all of which enjoy some autonomy from one another. The term "state," in fact, came into currency when political authority first became formally differentiated from economic privilege, social status, and religious ministry. It denotes a legal and administrative structure regulating society but not coterminous with it. This specialized structure is still intact in autocracies. Totalitarianism, however, does imply its withering away, though not quite in the sense Marx had in mind. One can think of it, metaphorically anyway, as the end of a dialectical process in which the antitheses are differentiation and integration. In the beginning, men are integrated in all-embracing, but mild and small-scale, traditional societies; there is much horizontal and little vertical differentiation of human life. Through increasing vertical (or functional) differentiation, larger networks of coordinated so-

cial relations (that is to say, more horizontal integration) become possible: large-scale states, markets, and national armies. In the end, horizontal and vertical integration are combined in the all-embracing, large-scale society—totalitarian society.

Such a society requires the convergence of many conditions and preconditions. It becomes possible only when certain ideas become conjoined with certain technical capabilities and social conditions, and that conjunction of ideas and forces became possible only in the twentieth century.

The first requirement of totalitarianism might be called the idea of "sovereignty." This idea, established between the sixteenth and eighteenth centuries, is in fact a complex of three notions. It implies, first, the emancipation of authority from traditional and divine law, substituting for the concrete checks upon rulers of autonomous churches and judicial systems the much more ephemeral limitations of the ruler's reason. It also implies the centralization of political authority in relatively large units: the "state" is no longer required to share political authority with various competitive, intermediate social corporations. The many crisscrossing, petty authorities of society (feudal, municipal, ecclesiastic, economic) are eliminated, and a grand authority develops in their place. Finally, the idea of sovereignty implies the autonomy of this grand authority from still grander authorities, supranational (indeed potentially universal) powers like church and empire. These three notions are separable, yet all of a piece in the peculiar circumstances of postmedieval Europe. Because of the lack of certain technical capabilities, universal centralization was hardly feasible at that time. Any kind of large-scale political centralization required an attack on the traditionalistic and religious ideas that supported structures competitive with political rulers and prevented a "rationalistic" approach to coordination.

The realization of the idea of sovereignty was the work of absolute monarchy. Royal absolutism, however, was still worlds apart from totalitarianism. Not only did the absolute monarchies lack certain technical capabilities needed to achieve the full political integration of society; not only did the persistence of particularistic (that is, hereditary) norms of political recruitment prevent the full rationalization of political life; more important still, absolutism rigidly separated the ruler from the ruled, in both thought and practice. The absolute monarchies ruled society; they did not claim to represent, or incorporate, it. Louis XIV could say that he was the state, but never that he was the nation. This dichotomization of ruler and subject acts as a large hindrance to power no less than responsibility, for it logically implies a kind of dual autonomy in society—the ruler in his sphere, others in theirs. At the very least, it deprives truly absolute rule of a truly absolute justification: that it is self-imposed.

The work of breaking down the separation of ruler and ruled was done by democratic thought, by the idea of *popular* sovereignty. The identification of the two is certainly the master-idea of modern democracy. This idea is two edged: it obviously enlarges greatly the potential scope of the ruler's accountability, but provides as well a most persuasive rationale for the unlimited exercise of power. All that is necessary now to justify total rule is some basis for claiming that the ruler's will is really that of his subjects: a plebiscite, perhaps, or some other show of accord between rulers and populace, or some theory of the inherent interests of "the people" that requires a totally repressive onslaught on their "enemies." "Beginning with perfect liberty," said Dostoievski, "one always ends with perfect despotism"; or anarchy equals totalitarianism. Perhaps not always, but Dostoievski is right at least to the extent that total despotism would be inconceivable without ideas premised on the desirability of total self-rule.

Nowhere is the identification of ruler and ruled made plainer than in Rousseau's *Social Contract,* and nowhere are there clearer intimations of the possibilities of despotism when the ideas of popular rule and sovereignty are joined. It is fitting, therefore, that the first concerted attempts to turn democracy to the account of absolutism should have been made in France. Perhaps the very first example is furnished by the French Revolutionary Government of 1793, but even more instructive is the example of Bonapartism, particularly the dictatorship of Louis Napoleon (1852–1871).

Louis Napoleon characterized his regime as rule "in basis democratic, in organization hierarchic." It would be difficult to imagine a more suitable formula for his aspirations, if not achievements—unless it be Mussolini's equally pungent, equally incongruent, definition of fascism. Bonapartism was certainly the first regime to work out an institutional structure for "democratic authoritarianism." The regime was based on plebiscitary elections, but took great care to avoid awkward electoral results. It used a certain amount of judicious rigging, it used propaganda and education to manufacture support and it used censorship and repression to discourage opposition. It tried to mobilize genuine popular sympathy by a great show of liberalism, by the exploitation of revolutionary symbols and the parading of nationalist sentiments. Coupled with these attempts to legitimize the regime as an artifact of popular sovereignty was the development of an efficient and loyal military and administrative establishment, at least a fairly well-developed machinery for coordinating social life.

Bonapartism thus portended totalitarianism, but it also fell short of its full realization. It certainly did not extend government to embrace all social and personal life. At least one important traditional structure remained fully intact under it (namely, the Church, with which both Bonapartes reached a somewhat surprising *modus vivendi*). The Bonapartes also used much of the traditional military and administrative structures, despite their attempts to overhaul them and make them more serviceable instruments. They made no concerted attempt to turn the economic patterns of society wholly to the account of the regime's purposes; while exploiting the higher bourgeoisie, they also allowed themselves to be exploited by it. Nor did they attempt to mobilize in service of the state the many elements of life remote from government—family life, the arts, informal associations among men. Life under Bonapartism was not all that different from life before or after; in the final analysis, it differed more on the governmental than the social plane.

One cannot help feeling that this imperfect anticipation of totalitarianism by Bonapartism was due to the absence, or insufficient development, of two conditions—conditions as essential to totalitarian life as the joining of absolutist and populistic ideas. One involves the technical capacity to coordinate the life of a society; totalitarian coordination requires a level of organizational and coercive skill and a development of communications not yet achieved in mid-nineteenth century societies. The other is a certain ideological vigor to give point to the whole enterprise of total coordination and to reconcile men to its enormous costs; this condition can probably be derived only from a messianic social vision, and Bonapartism lacked such a vision.

Perhaps a third important ingredient for the concoction of totalitarianism was lacking as well. Totalitarianism needs great destructive as well as reconstructive power to come into existence under any circumstances; but, obviously, the amount of power it requires depends upon the viability of the social structures totalitarians must reshape and the extent to which their subjects lend themselves to reconstruction. In other words, the more the intermediary structures of society are intact (the less need men have for new integrative social forms) the less likely is totalitarianism. Perhaps the France of the Bonapartes was, from this standpoint, simply unripe for totalitarianism, even if the Bonapartes had been able to muster the skill, force, and élan necessary to produce it.

All this allows us to state more comprehensively the conditions and preconditions on which totalitarianism depends. Totalitarianism would be inconceivable without the idea of sovereignty, which centralizes, makes autonomous, and rationalizes the exercise of governmental authority. It would be equally inconceivable without the idea of populistic democracy, which annihilates the disjuncture of sovereign and subject. It requires great destructive capacities, not merely for getting rid of individual opponents but, much more important, for shattering potentially obstructive networks of social relations: in short, for separating men from their pretotalitarian associations, isolating them, and thus making them available for reintegration. This task is greatly facilitated if the pretotalitarian structures are already greatly impaired. (Indeed, one is tempted to consider some weakening of these structures not merely an advantage to totalitarians but a requisite for totalitarianism too. No destructive power might be great enough to annihilate the structures otherwise, and an adequate nucleus of totalitarian extremists might never come into being where the various structures of nontotalitarian society are strong and cohesive. Kornhauser's *Politics of Mass Society* has much to say on this.) A concomitant of the requirement of great destructive power is great reconstructive power, and this implies two things: first, a great capacity to "resocialize," or re-educate, people, to implant in them new orientations—values, cognitions, and tendencies to respond to symbols; second, a great capacity to coordinate by direct controls structures artificially imposed upon society, the integration of which, in whole or part, can be left in only small degree to norms of conduct internalized in individuals. Finally, totalitarianism needs a potent mystique—something that will supply the great psychic energy required to eradicate and totally to reconstruct social structures and personalities.

Once all this is understood, it is much easier to explain why totalitarianism is something completely modern, something only foreshadowed before the twentieth century. More than that, almost *everything* we think of as peculiarly modern seems to contribute to its possibility and likelihood: the decline of tradition and rise of rational modes of behavior, the sovereign nation-state, nationalism, mass democracy, mass education, highly developed science and technology, even modern capitalism, industrialism, and high rates of social mobility.

Erich Fromm relates the rise of totalitarianism to the burdens of freedom in a society without traditional guidelines (to the "fear of freedom"). Certainly, the crumbling of old authorities in modern life can be linked to the craving for new directions in life and new communities that totalitarian movements and their utopias satisfy. Mass education may be necessary to the existence of an informed democratic citizenry, but is at the same time an indispensable tool for socializing men on a grand scale into totalitarian society. Science and technology provide indispensable means for coordination and control and for indoctrinating those who can no longer be caught by the educational network. Providing leisure, they also liberate men from the sort of deep absorption in their occupations that would make them unavailable for political manipulation. High rates of social mobility tend to weaken the primary and secondary ties of society, from family and neighborhood relations to the oc-

cupational group or friendly society. Industrialism, as many great social thinkers (Durkheim, Weber, Tönnies, among others) have pointed out, weakens men's sense of identity and community and makes them vulnerable to the bearers of new identities and modes of communities. Nationalism provides one source of strong psychological drives that totalitarian movements can exploit. Capitalist society develops material resources, organizational skills, and mobile individuals, all of which totalitarians can use, even to the detriment of capitalist systems. The desire for capitalism—at any rate, for the industrialization it first produced—may provide the animus necessary to totalitarianism; so also may revulsion against capitalism in the shape of socialist utopian visions.

These arguments not only tell us why totalitarianism is an artifact of modern life, but they also establish yet another link between totalitarianism and democracy. The plain fact is that most of the requisites of mass democracy are also requisites of totalitarianism: widely diffused education, for example, or a highly developed technology (especially communications), a mobile society, rational modes of conduct, sufficient leisure for political participation, and considerable organizational skill (for example, in the management of parties and other organs of political participation and competition). Perhaps only those elements of modern life which make for intensity in politics are functional to totalitarianism and dysfunctional in democracies. There is even a link here, however, since democracy provides many means by which demagogues, visionaries, and symbol manipulators can whip up totalitarian enthusiasm. This link in turn suggests that modernized societies face a poignant dilemma in their politics: either successful democracy *or* totalitarianism, but no real possibilities short of one or the other. Certainly this view gains plausibility from a fact mentioned at the beginning: many of the totalitarian systems were preceded by democratization, often very rapid and thorough in nature.

At the same time, the connection between totalitarianism and modern life can tell us why some societies achieve totalitarianism at relatively little cost and in a relatively short time, while others pay a much higher price over a much longer period. One could hazard the hypothesis that the more modernized a society, the less the cost that has to be paid for totalitarianism and the shorter the time in which it can be realized (although totalitarianism always presupposes some substantial degree of modernization). Highly developed Germany took to totalitarianism with frightening speed and relatively little cost in coercion—though the costs of totalitarianism, even at their least, are always repellently high. Less developed Italy paid a lower cost in peace and life, but never attained anything like the German level of totalitarianism. Russia took much longer than Germany to achieve a large measure of totalitarian coordination (perhaps as much as twenty years) and paid for it an atrocious price in repression. The price China has had to pay seems to be equally terrifying; and the time span required, despite the availability of past experience, seems to be just as long.

## IV

There are other ways of depicting the nature of totalitarianism than the one presented in this Introduction, some of which are illustrated in the readings. One can think of it, for example (as do Friedrich and Brzesinski), as a large combination of elements, some or all of which are also characteristic of other governmental systems, though never in the totalitarian combination. (The elements they single out are official "ideology" containing a utopian and chiliastic claim, the existence of a single, hierarchical mass party, terroristic police controls, a monopoly of effective mass communication, a near-complete monopoly of means of effective armed combat, and central economic control and direction.)[8] Or one can select one or another particular element of totalitarianism as its distinctive characteristic: its revolutionary adaptation to environment (that is, the desire to carry out, not piecemeal, but total, social transformation, inside and outside a particular society), its unprecedented hierarchy, or its use of party as a means simultaneously for stirring up enthusiasm, for indoctrination, for providing intelligence to the rulers, and for coordinating all governmental and social activities.

All these elements provide illuminating and useful ways to look at totalitarianism, but all of them seem to us to acquire a fuller meaning when viewed in terms of the characterization we have developed. All are facets of the desire to create homogenized, depersonalized men in a totally coordinated society —a society so integrated that to be excluded (as Jews were in Germany or kulaks in Russia) is tantamount to having no right to exist at all, while to be included robs one of the right to an autonomous life. One facet of totalitarianism may provide its instrumental means (that is, the totalitarian party), another its legitimation and psychic energy (utopian ideology), while still others may be the economic, educational, or military expressions of total coordination; but the whole is somehow greater than the sum of the parts.

Autocracies can be made to fall into place by this characterization too. If totalitarianism is characterized by a vision of total social coordination and a high degree of success in bringing it about, autocracy may be defined as authoritarian rule that falls in any way short of the vision and a long way short of its realization. One can also characterize different types of autocracy in terms of the particular reasons for their falling short of the totalitarian extreme. There is the autocracy of men who lack vision and psychic drive, the autocracy of men who lack technical means for more, the autocracy of men who are committed to the autonomy of certain nongovernmental structures, and the autocracy of traditionalists who disdain rational attitudes toward life or cherish traditional privileges. Plenty of examples of each can be found in the contemporary world, and even more in past history.

## V

Because both totalitarianism and democracy are children of modern life, the undoubtedly great growth of autocracy in the new states need not unduly alarm us. Certainly it is less than realistic to be sorrowful or angry at the lack of full-fledged democracy in the developing nations, their one-party systems, military oligarchies, and father-figure rulers. Autocracy in relatively underdeveloped areas may be regarded not only as inevitable, but even as functionally desirable from certain important points of view. Men are not natural democrats, any more than they are natural totalitarians. Their governments grow from functional needs that their environment imposes, not from their souls; and they always grow out of very limited sets of possibilities. Most of the world's governments have been nondemocratic just for that reason.

Consider Europe in the feudal period, for example. It was attacked from the south by the Moors, suffered incursions from the Norsemen in the north and west, and from the east was invaded by Magyar tribesmen. In a Europe suffering from a general breakdown in internal order, the critical concerns of the societies of the day could scarcely have been those of democracy, even if its virtues had been familiar. Rather, the manor-fief developed as a kind of nuclear unit, personal in its relationships, easily allied with others for defense, capable of self-sufficiency. To a remarkable degree it was geared to its own protection. Kinship and nobility, chivalry and personal fealty created social solidarity that (despite rigid hierarchy, some capriciousness in the exercise of power, intrigue, and a contempt for human life) provided a successful response to the threats that were its daily burden. An intimate sort of autocracy was the essence of feudal life, and out of autocratic rule came protection and organization.

So also the political forms of the new states grow out of their conditions and tasks. Peaceful recurrent political competition is hardly feasible where the very basis for community still wants creating; without a sense of community with one's opponents, political competition is war. Indeed, in some new states even literacy is so low that the very problem of identifying parties on ballots poses difficulties. Nor is it easy to instill democratic norms into men only recently separated from (perhaps still caught in) the intimate authoritarian nets of tribalism or the alien authoritarianism of colonial rulers.

Whether rapid economic change requires autocratic rule is another matter. Democracy would seem to be a system of government peculiarly adapted to the problem of innovation. Permitting the peaceful succession of one set of leaders after another, group competition to determine whose views will for the moment prevail, a certain attitude of mind that welcomes piecemeal innovation—all these are characteristic of the democratic outlook, but these very attitudes are difficult to achieve in periods of major upheaval. Hence, even if one could prove that democratic attitudes are particularly suitable in innovating societies, the demonstration might be beside the point. Where there is a strong conscious dedication to particular innovations, even the realization that democracy lends itself well to innovation in a general sense would hardly win it many adherents. In any case, it makes little sense to say that many new states have *chosen* the autocratic road to development, if they really had no choice.

For those who abominate totalitarianism more than they love democracy, there is, then, something infinitely reassuring in the greatly imperfect autocracies of the contemporary world. Were they more capable of democracy, they would probably also come much closer to totalitarianism.

Yet one may suspect that a lethal brew is being concocted in some of these autocracies. They are deeply dedicated to the idea of sovereignty. They claim also to be systems of popular sovereignty and like to brandish democratic norms. Sekou Touré writes that some people

. . . are astonished to discover that, in Guinea, there is only one party, a national party: the P.D.G. It must be emphatically asserted that political unity is not a final objective; it is only a means of creating and sustaining a progressive movement, a means taken to serve the general interest.

One can read into this the notion that the single party state is only an interim measure on the way to competitive democracy, or that it is necessary to create that all-embracing general will which is the hallmark of totalitarian democracy. And Touré goes on to say that unity

. . . can be developed, can effectively serve the national cause only so far as it means unity of action by all the populations mobilized in a dynamic manner in support of positive objectives and dedicated to the constant reinforcement of the democratic character of the evolution of our country. We can say immediately that the life of a society, a community, a nation is not fundamentally regulated by laws, decrees, and decisions. The life of

a society is regulated by habits, customs, historical traditions and the necessities of its maintenance and its development.[9]

This statement raises some questions to be answered. For if mobilization of the community, unregulated by law, results in a change of those customs of which Touré speaks, then the disciplined single party state becomes a permanent feature of the new society. What may begin as a means to an end may become the end itself.

There is a great difference between totalitarianism and autocracy. In the new nations, however, where all problems are characteristically political, where matters of ethnicity, language, religion, family, and the rest all acquire a political quality, where rulers attempt with great verve to mobilize society in pursuit of large and remote goals to which there is fanatic commitment, it is possible to see the rudimentary, technologically inhibited, elements of totalitarianism. And the technologies of these societies are developing. They build roads, acquire radio sets and mass newspapers, and develop organizational skills and networks of coordination. At the same time, they uproot men from their traditional ties, mobilize them, and make them receptive to new ways, cosmologies, and social panaceas. What will be the outcome of all this?

This question is not meant to spread alarm. The signs do not point exclusively in one direction. Rule by the army in Burma has not prevented a restoration of democracy. In Turkey a similar possibility presents itself. Other autocracies, such as Pakistan and Sudan, two countries in which the army rules in the name of the people, all point to the genuine possibility of democratic reform. Even in Spain, despite efforts by the Falange to induce a full-blown transformation of society by forced means, many continue to go about their affairs while paying lip service to the state.

In history nothing is fixed, but one must also realize that at particular points in history very few things may be possible. If we are right, the pathos of modern political life lies not in the spread of autocracy and the disappointment of those once strong beliefs in the universal possibility of democracy. Rather, it lies in the constantly more restricted, as well as more dramatically contradictory, choices open in political life. A world that presents a choice between successful democracy and stark totalitarianism is not an altogether tragic world, but one in which it is certainly not very comfortable to live.


VI

The selections included here cover most of the important ideas that have been used in the comparative study of autocracy and totalitarianism. The symbolic, personality, and emotional side has, however, been given less representation here than it deserves. A considerable literature devoted to the psychological aspects of totalitarianism and, indeed, personalistic rule by dictators ought to be referred to. Fromm's *Escape from Freedom*, Adorno and associates' *The Authoritarian Personality*, Shils's and Janowitz' "Cohesion and Disintegration in the Wehrmacht in World War II" in *Public Opinion Quarterly* (1948) have all become minor classics. There is also, of course, a very large literature dealing with the phenomenon of the Moscow trials, the most interesting from a psychoanalytical point of view being Nathan Leites' *Ritual of Liquidation*. On autocracy there is a vast literature going back many generations. Perhaps the wisest summaries of autocracies are found in Ernest Barkers' two books, *Principles of Social and Political Theory* and *Reflections on Government*. A more recent effort to gain insight into modern mass society and the conditions that lead to autocracy and totalitarianism is Kornhauser, *The Politics of Mass Society*.

## NOTES

1. For the present purpose we use the terms "democracy" and "autocracy" simply to denote governments by rulers accountable to the ruled and rulers who are not. "Autocrats" are self-ruling rulers; "democrats" exercise delegated, hence, revocable authority.

2. In the second case, one can, of course, do one thing that cannot be done in the first—commit murder plus suicide; but suicide is hardly sound defense.

3. See Carl J. Friedrich and Zbiginew K. Brzezinski, *Totalitarian Dictatorship and Autocracy*, Cambridge, Mass.: Harvard University Press, 1956, Part IV.

4. Quoted in W. B. Walsh, *Readings in Russian History* (Syracuse, N. Y.: Syracuse University Press, 1950).

5. See Nathan Leites and Elsa Bernaut, *Ritual of Liquidation* (New York: The Free Press of Glencoe, 1954).

6. See Hannah Arendt, *The Origins of Totalitarianism*, New York: Harcourt, Brace and World, 1958, p. 441.

7. These data come from various sources, including W. Ebenstein, *Fascist Italy*, New York, 1939; Dante L. Germino, *The Italian Fascist Party in Power*, Minneapolis, 1959; Raymond A. Bauer, *The New Man in Soviet Psychology*, Cambridge, Mass., 1952; Wright Miller, *Russians as People*, New York, 1961; *The Great Soviet Encyclopedia; The Nazi Primer* (Harwood Childs, transl.), New York, 1938; and Robert Guillain, *600 Million Chinese*, New York, 1957. One of the best compilations of such data is in an unpublished paper by A. K. Sleght, "Totalitarian Man: An Essay on the Possible."

8. Friedrich and Brzezinski, *op. cit.*, pp. 9–10.

9. Sekou Touré, *Towards Full Re-Africanization*, Paris, Presence Africaine, 1959, p. 15.

*Totalitarianism*

# A CLASSLESS SOCIETY ✓

## Hannah Arendt

### 1. THE MASSES

In view of the unparalleled misery which totalitarian regimes have meant to their people—horror to many and unhappiness to all—

it is painful to realize that they are always preceded by mass movements and that they "command and rest upon mass support"[1] up to the end. Hitler's rise to power was legal in terms of majority rule and neither he nor Stalin could have maintained the leadership of large populations, survived many interior and exterior crises, and braved the numerous dangers of the relentless intraparty struggles if they had not had the confidence of the masses. The widespread belief that Hitler was simply an agent of German industrialists and that Stalin was victorious in the succession struggle after Lenin's death only through a sinister conspiracy are both legends[2] which can be refuted by many facts but above all by the leaders' indisputable popularity. Nor can their popularity be attributed to the victory of masterful and lying propaganda over ignorance and stupidity. For the propaganda of totalitarian movements which precede and accompany totalitarian regimes is invariably as frank as it is mendacious, and would-be totalitarian rulers usually start their careers by boasting of their past crimes and carefully outlining their future ones. The Nazis "were convinced that evil-doing in our time has a morbid force of attraction,"[3] Bolshevik assurances inside and outside Russia that they do not recognize ordinary moral standards have become a mainstay of Communist propaganda, and experience has proved time and again that the propaganda value of evil deeds and general contempt for moral standards is independent of mere self-interest, supposedly the most powerful psychological factor in politics.

The attraction of evil and crime for the mob mentality is nothing new. It has always been true that the mob will greet "deeds of violence with the admiring remark: it may be mean but it is very clever."[4] The disturbing factor in the success of totalitarianism is rather the true selflessness of its adherents: it may be understandable that a Nazi or Bolshevik will not be shaken in his conviction by crimes against people who do not belong to the movement or are even hostile to it; but the amazing fact is that neither is he likely to waver when the monster begins to devour its own children and not even if he becomes a victim of persecution himself, if he is framed and condemned, if he is purged from the party and sent to a forced-labor or a concentration camp. On the contrary, to the wonder of the whole civilized world, he may even be willing to help in his own persecution and frame his own death sentence if only his status as a member of the movement is not touched.[5] It would be naïve to consider this stubbornness of conviction which outlives all actual experiences and cancels all immediate self-interest a simple expression of fervent idealism. Idealism, foolish or heroic, always springs from some individual decision and conviction and is subject to experience and argument.[6] The fanaticism of a member of a totalitarian movement whom neither experience nor argument can reach is based, on the contrary, on a conformism and identification for which not even torture is an experience and through whose stupor not even the fear of death can pierce.

The totalitarian movements aim at and succeed in organizing masses—not classes, like the old interest parties of the Continental nation-states; not citizens with opinions about, and interests in, the handling of public affairs, like the parties of Anglo-Saxon countries. While all political groups depend upon proportionate strength, the totalitarian movements depend on the sheer force of numbers to such an extent that totalitarian regimes seem impossible, even under otherwise favorable circumstances, in countries with relatively small populations.[7] After the first World War, a deeply anti-democratic, prodictatorial wave of semitotalitarian and totalitarian movements swept Europe; Fascist movements spread from Italy to nearly all Central and Eastern European countries (the Czech part of Czechoslovakia was one of the notable exceptions); yet even Mussolini, who was so fond of the term "totalitarian state," did not attempt to establish a full-fledged totalitarian regime[8] and contented himself with dictatorship and one-party rule. Similar nontotalitarian dictatorships sprang up in pre-war Rumania, Poland, the Baltic States, Hungary, Portugal and Franco Spain. The Nazis, who had an unfailing instinct for such differences, used to comment contemptuously on the shortcomings of their Fascist allies while their genuine admiration for the Bolshevik regime in Russia (and the Communist Party in Germany) was matched and checked only by their contempt for Eastern European races.[9] The point is that in all these smaller European countries nontotalitarian dictatorships were preceded by totalitarian movements, so that it appeared that totalitarianism was too ambitious an aim, that although it had served well enough to organize the masses until the movement seized power, the absolute size of the country then forced the would-be totalitarian ruler of masses into the more familiar patterns of class or party dictatorship. The truth is that these countries simply did not control enough human material to allow for total domination and its inherent great losses in population.[10] Without much hope for the conquest of more heavily populated territories, the tyrants in these small countries were forced into a certain old-fashioned moderation lest they lose whatever people they had to rule. This is also why Nazism, up to the outbreak of the war and its expansion over Europe, lagged so far behind its Russian counterpart in consistency and ruthlessness;[11] even the German people were not numerous enough to allow for the full development of this newest form of government. (Conversely, the chances for totalitarian rule are frighteningly good in the lands of traditional Oriental despotism, in India and China, where there is almost inexhaustible material to feed the power-accumulating and man-destroying machinery of total domination, and where, moreover, the mass man's typical feeling of superfluousness—an entirely new phenomenon in Europe, the concomitant of mass unemployment and the population growth of the last 150 years—has been prevalent for centuries in the contempt for the value of human life.) Moderation or less murderous methods of rule were hardly attributable to the governments' fear of popular rebellion;

depopulation in their own country was a much more serious threat. Only where great masses are superfluous or can be spared without disastrous results of depopulation is totalitarian rule, as distinguished from a totalitarian movement, at all possible.

Totalitarian movements are possible wherever there are masses who for one reason or another have acquired the appetite for political organization. Masses are not held together by a consciousness of common interest and they lack that specific class articulateness which is expressed in determined, limited, and obtainable goals. The term masses applies only where we deal with people who either because of sheer numbers, or indifference, or a combination of both, cannot be integrated into any organization based on common interest, into political parties or municipal governments or professional organizations or trade unions. Potentially, they exist in every country and form the majority of those large numbers of neutral, politically indifferent people who never join a party and hardly ever go to the polls.

It was characteristic of the Nazi movement in Germany and of the Communist movements in Europe after 1930[12] that they recruited their members from this mass of apparently indifferent people whom all other parties had given up as too apathetic or too stupid for their attention. The result was that the majority of their membership consisted of people who never before had appeared on the political scene. This permitted the introduction of entirely new methods into political propaganda, and indifference to the arguments of political opponents; these movements not only placed themselves outside and against the party system as a whole, they found a membership that had never been reached, never been "spoiled" by the party system. Therefore they did not need to refute opposing arguments and consistently preferred methods which ended in death rather than persuasion, which spelled terror rather than conviction. They presented disagreements as invariably originating in deep natural, social, or psychological sources beyond the control of the individual and therefore beyond the power of reason. This would have been a shortcoming only if they had sincerely entered into competition with other parties; it was not if they were sure of dealing with people who had reason to be equally hostile to all parties.

The success of totalitarian movements among the masses meant the end of two illusions of democratically ruled countries in general and of European nation-states and their party system in particular. The first was that the people in its majority had taken an active part in government and that each individual was in sympathy with one's own or somebody else's party. On the contrary, the movements showed that the politically neutral and indifferent masses could easily be the majority in a democratically ruled country, that therefore a democracy could function according to rules which are actively recognized by only a minority. The second democratic illusion exploded by the totalitarian movements was that these politically indifferent masses did not matter, that they were truly neutral and constituted no more than the inarticulate backward setting for the political life of the nation. Now they made apparent what no other organ of public opinion had ever been able to show, namely, that democratic government had rested as much on the silent approbation and tolerance of the indifferent and inarticulate sections of the people as on the articulate and visible institutions and organizations of the country. Thus when the totalitarian movements invaded Parliament with their contempt for parliamentary government, they merely appeared inconsistent: actually, they succeeded in convincing the people at large that parliamentary majorities were spurious and did not necessarily correspond to the realities of the country, thereby undermining the self-respect and the confidence of governments which also believed in majority rule rather than in their constitutions.

It has frequently been pointed out that totalitarian movements use and abuse democratic freedoms in order to abolish them. This is not just devilish cleverness on the part of the leaders or childish stupidity on the part of the masses. Democratic freedoms may be based on the equality of all citizens before the law; yet they acquire their meaning and function organically only where the citizens belong to and are represented by groups or form a social and political hierarchy. The breakdown of the class system, the only social and political stratification of the European nation-states, certainly was "one of the most dramatic events in recent German history"[13] and as favorable to the rise of Nazism as the absence of social stratification in Russia's immense rural population (this "great flaccid body destitute of political education, almost inaccessible to ideas capable of ennobling action"[14]) was to the Bolshevik overthrow of the democratic Kerensky government. Conditions in pre-Hitler Germany are indicative of the dangers implicit in the development of the Western part of the world since, with the end of the second World War, the same dramatic event of a breakdown of the class system repeated itself in almost all European countries, while events in Russia clearly indicate the direction which the inevitable revolutionary changes in Asia may take. Practically speaking, it will make little difference whether totalitarian movements adopt the pattern of Nazism or Bolshevism, organize the masses in the name of race or class, pretend to follow the laws of life and nature or of dialectics and economics.

Indifference to public affairs, neutrality on political issues, are in themselves no sufficient cause for the rise of totalitarian movements. The competitive and acquisitive society of the bourgeoisie had produced apathy and even hostility toward public life not only, and not even primarily, in the social strata which were exploited and excluded from active participation in the rule of the country, but first of all in its own class. The long period of false modesty, when the bourgeoisie was content with being the dominating class in society without aspiring to political rule, which it gladly left to the aristocracy, was followed by the imperialist era, during which the bourgeoisie grew increasingly hostile to existing national institutions and began to claim and to organize itself for the exercise of political power. Both the early apathy and the later demand for monopolistic dictatorial direction of the nation's foreign affairs had their roots in a way and philosophy of life so insistently and exclusively centered on the individual's success or failure in ruthless competition that a citizen's duties and responsibilities could only be felt to be a needless drain on his limited time and energy. These bourgeois attitudes are very useful for those forms of dictatorship in which a "strong man" takes upon himself the troublesome responsibility for the conduct of public affairs; they are a positive hindrance to totalitarian movements which can tolerate bourgeois individualism no more than any other kind of individualism. The apathetic sections of a bourgeois-dominated society, no matter how unwilling they may be to assume the responsibilities of citizens, keep their personalities intact if only because without them they could hardly expect to survive the competitive struggle for life.

The decisive differences between nineteenth-century mob organizations and twentieth-century mass movements are difficult to perceive because the modern totalitarian leaders do not differ much in psychology and mentality from the earlier mob leaders, whose moral standards and political devices so closely resembled those of the bourgeoisie. Yet, insofar as individualism characterized the bourgeoisie's as well as the mob's attitude to life, the totalitarian movements can rightly claim that they were the first truly antibourgeois parties: none of their nineteenth-century predecessors, neither the Society of the 10th of December which helped Louis Napoleon into power, the butcher brigades of the Dreyfus Affair, the Black Hundreds of the Russian pogroms, nor the pan-movements, ever involved their members to the point of complete loss of individual claims and ambition, or had ever realized that an organization could succeed in extinguishing individual identity permanently and not just for the moment of collective heroic action.

The relationship between the bourgeois-dominated class society and the masses which emerged from its breakdown is not the same as the relationship between the bourgeoisie and the mob which

was a by-product of capitalist production. The masses share with the mob only one characteristic, namely, that both stand outside all social ramifications and normal political representation. The masses do not inherit, as the mob does—albeit in a perverted form—the standards and attitudes of the dominating class, but reflect and somehow pervert the standards and attitudes toward public affairs of all classes. The standards of the mass man were determined not only and not even primarily by the specific class to which he had once belonged, but rather by all-pervasive influences and convictions which were tacitly and inarticulately shared by all classes of society alike.

Membership in a class, although looser and never as inevitably determined by social origin as in the orders and estates of feudal society, was generally by birth, and only extraordinary gifts or luck could change it. Social status was decisive for the individual's participation in politics, and except in cases of national emergency when he was supposed to act only as a *national,* regardless of his class or party membership, he never was directly confronted with public affairs or felt directly responsible for their conduct. The rise of a class to greater importance in the community was always accompanied by the education and training of a certain number of its members for politics as a job, for paid (or, if they could afford it, unpaid) service in the government and representation of the class in Parliament. That the majority of people remained outside all party or other political organization was not important to anyone, and no truer for one particular class than another. In other words, membership in a class, its limited group obligations and traditional attitudes toward government, prevented the growth of a citizenry that felt individually and personally responsible for the rule of the country. This apolitical character of the nation-state's populations came to light only when the class system broke down and carried with it the whole fabric of visible and invisible threads which bound the people to the body politic.

The breakdown of the class system meant automatically the breakdown of the party system, chiefly because these parties, being interest parties, could no longer represent class interests. Their continuance was of some importance to the members of former classes who hoped against hope to regain their old social status and who stuck together not because they had common interests any longer but because they hoped to restore them. The parties, consequently, became more and more psychological and ideological in their propaganda, more and more apologetic and nostalgic in their political approach. They had lost, moreover, without being aware of it, those neutral supporters who had never been interested in politics because they felt that parties existed to take care of their interests. So that the first signs of the breakdown of the Continental party system were not the desertion of old party members, but the failure to recruit members from the younger generation, and the loss of the silent consent and support of the unorganized masses who suddenly shed their apathy and went wherever they saw an opportunity to voice their new violent opposition.

The fall of protecting class walls transformed the slumbering majorities behind all parties into one great unorganized, structureless mass of furious individuals who had nothing in common except their vague apprehension that the hopes of party members were doomed, that, consequently, the most respected, articulate and representative members of the community were fools and that all the powers that be were not so much evil as they were equally stupid and fraudulent. It was of no great consequence for the birth of this new terrifying negative solidarity that the unemployed worker hated the status quo and the powers that be in the form of the Social Democratic Party, the expropriated small property owner in the form of a centrist or rightist party, and former members of the middle and upper classes in the form of the traditional extreme right. The number of this mass of generally dissatisfied and desperate men increased rapidly in Germany and Austria after the first World War, when inflation and unemployment added to the disrupting consequences of military defeat; they existed in great proportion in all the succession states, and they have supported the extreme movements in France and Italy since the second World War.

In this atmosphere of the breakdown of class society the psychology of the European mass man developed. The fact that with monotonous but abstract uniformity the same fate had befallen a mass of individuals did not prevent their judging themselves in terms of individual failure or the world in terms of specific injustice. This self-centered bitterness, however, although repeated again and again in individual isolation, was not a common bond despite its tendency to extinguish individual differences, because it was based on no common interest, economic or social or political. Self-centeredness, therefore, went hand in hand with a decisive weakening of the instinct for self-preservation. Selflessness in the sense that oneself does not matter, the feeling of being dispensable, was no longer the expression of individual idealism but a mass phenomenon. The old adage that the poor and oppressed have nothing to lose but their chains no longer applied to the mass men, for they lost much more than the chains of misery when they lost interest in their own well-being: the source of all the worries and cares which make human life troublesome and anguished was gone. Compared with their nonmaterialism, a Christian monk looks like a man absorbed in worldly affairs. Himmler,

who knew so well the mentality of those whom he organized, described not only his SS-men, but the large strata from which he recruited them, when he said they were not interested in "everyday problems" but only "in ideological questions of importance for decades and centuries, so that the man . . . knows he is working for a great task which occurs but once in 2,000 years."[15] The gigantic massing of individuals produced a mentality which, like Cecil Rhodes some forty years before, thought in continents and felt in centuries.

Eminent European scholars and statesmen had predicted, from the early nineteenth century onward, the rise of the mass man and the coming of a mass age. A whole literature on mass behavior and mass psychology had demonstrated and popularized the wisdom, so familiar to the ancients, of the affinity between democracy and dictatorship, between mob rule and tyranny. They had prepared certain politically conscious and overconscious sections of the Western educated world for the emergence of demagogues, for gullibility, superstition, and brutality. Yet, while all these predictions in a sense came true, they lost much of their significance in view of such unexpected and unpredicted phenomena as the radical loss of self-interest,[16] the cynical or bored indifference in the face of death or other personal catastrophes, the passionate inclination toward the most abstract notions as guides for life, and the general contempt for even the most obvious rules of common sense.

The masses, contrary to prediction, did not result from growing equality of condition, from the spread of general education and its inevitable lowering of standards and popularization of content. (America, the classical land of equality of condition and of general education with all its shortcomings, knows less of the modern psychology of masses than perhaps any other country in the world.) It soon became apparent that highly cultured people were particularly attracted to mass movements and that, generally, highly differentiated individualism and sophistication did not prevent, indeed sometimes encouraged, the self-abandonment into the mass for which mass movements provided. Since the obvious fact that individualization and cultivation do not prevent the formation of mass attitudes was so unexpected, it has frequently been blamed upon the morbidity or nihilism of the modern intelligentsia, upon a supposedly typical intellectual self-hatred, upon the spirit's "hostility to life" and antagonism to vitality. Yet, the much-slandered intellectuals were only the most illustrative example and the most articulate spokesmen for a much more general phenomenon. Social atomization and extreme individualization preceded the mass movements which, much more easily and earlier than they did the sociable, nonindividualistic members of the traditional parties, attracted the completely unorganized, the typical "non-joiners," who for individualistic reasons always had refused to recognize social links or obligations.

The truth is that the masses grew out of the fragments of a highly atomized society whose competitive structure and concomitant loneliness of the individual had been held in check only through membership in a class. The chief characteristic of the mass man is not brutality and backwardness, but his isolation and lack of normal social relationships. Coming from the classridden society of the nation-state, whose cracks had been cemented with nationalist sentiment, it is only natural that these masses, in the first helplessness of their new experience, have tended toward an especially violent nationalism, to which mass leaders have yielded against their own instincts and purposes for purely demagogic reasons.[17]

Neither tribal nationalism nor rebellious nihilism is characteristic of or ideologically appropriate to the masses as they were to the mob. But the most gifted mass leaders of our time have still risen from the mob rather than from the masses.[18] Hitler's biography reads like a textbook example in this respect, and the point about Stalin is that he comes from the conspiratory apparatus of the Bolshevik party with its specific mixture of outcasts and revolutionaries. Hitler's early party, almost exclusively composed of misfits, failures, and adventurers, indeed represented the "armed bohemians" who were only the reverse side of bourgeois society and whom, consequently, the German bourgeoisie should have been able to use successfully for its own purposes. Actually, the bourgeoisie was as much taken in by the Nazis as was the Roehm-Schleicher faction in the Reichswehr,[19] which also thought that Hitler, whom they had used as a stoolpigeon, or the SA, which they had used for militaristic propaganda and paramilitary training, would act as their agents and remain under their control.[20] Both considered the Nazi movement in their own terms, in terms of the political philosophy of the mob,[21] and overlooked the independent, spontaneous support given the new mob leaders by masses as well as the mob leaders' genuine talents for creating new forms of organization. The mob as leaders of these masses was no longer the agent of the bourgeoisie or of anyone else except the masses.

That totalitarian movements depended less on the structurelessness of a mass society than on the specific conditions of an atomized and individualized mass, can best be seen in a comparison of Nazism and Bolshevism which began in their respective countries under very different circumstances. To change Lenin's revolutionary dictatorship into full totalitarian rule, Stalin had first to create artificially that atomized society which had been prepared for the Nazis in Germany by historical circumstances.

The October Revolution's amazingly easy victory occurred in a country where a despotic and centralized bureaucracy governed a structureless mass population which neither the remnants of the rural feudal orders nor the weak, nascent urban capitalist classes had organized. When Lenin said that nowhere in the world would it have been so easy to win power and so difficult to keep it, he was aware not only of the weakness of the Russian working class, but of anarchic social conditions in general, which favored sudden changes. Without the instincts of a mass leader—he was no orator and had a passion for public admission and analysis of his own errors which is against the rules of even ordinary demagogy—Lenin seized at once upon all the possible differentiations, social, national, professional, that might bring some structure into the population, and he seemed convinced that in such stratification lay the salvation of the revolution. He legalized the anarchic expropriation of the landowners by the rural masses and established thereby for the first and probably last time in Russia that emancipated peasant class which, since the French Revolution, had been the firmest supporter of the Western nation-states. He tried to strengthen the working class by encouraging independent trade unions. He tolerated the timid appearance of a new middle class which resulted from the NEP policy after the end of the civil war. He introduced further distinguishing features by organizing, and sometimes inventing, as many nationalities as possible, furthering national consciousness and awareness of historical and cultural differences even among the most primitive tribes in the Soviet Union. It seems clear that in these purely practical political matters Lenin followed his great instincts for statesmanship rather than his Marxist convictions; his policy, at any rate, proves that he was more frightened by the absence of social and other structure than by the possible development of centrifugal tendencies in the newly emancipated nationalities or even by the growth of a new bourgeoisie out of the newly established middle and peasant classes. There is no doubt that Lenin suffered his greatest defeat when, with the outbreak of the civil war, the supreme power that he originally planned to concentrate in the Soviets definitely passed into the hands of the party bureaucracy; but even this development, tragic as it was for the course of the revolution, would not necessarily have led to totalitarianism. A one-party dictatorship added only one more class to the already developing social stratification of the country, i.e., bureaucracy, which, according to socialist critics of the revolution, "possessed the State as private property" (Marx).[22] At the moment of Lenin's death the roads were still open. The formation of workers, peasants, and middle classes need not necessarily have led to the class struggle which had been characteristic of European capitalism. Agriculture could still be developed on a collective, co-operative, or private basis, and the national economy was still to follow a socialist, state-capitalist, or a free-enterprise pattern. None of these alternatives would have automatically destroyed the new structure of the country.

All these new classes and nationalities were in Stalin's way when he began to prepare the country for totalitarian government. In order to fabricate an atomized and structureless mass, he had first to liquidate the remnants of power in the Soviets which, as the chief organ of national representation, still played a certain role and prevented absolute rule by the party hierarchy. Therefore he first undermined the national Soviets through the introduction of Bolshevik cells from which alone the higher functionaries to the central committees were appointed.[23] By 1930, the last traces of former communal institutions had disappeared and had been replaced by a firmly centralized party bureaucracy whose tendencies toward Russification were not too different from those of the Czarist regime, except that the new bureaucrats were no longer afraid of literacy.

The Bolshevik government then proceeded to the liquidation of classes and started, for ideological and propaganda reasons, with the property-owning classes, the new middle class in the cities, and the peasants in the country. Because of the combination of numbers and property, the peasants up to then had been potentially the most powerful class in the Union; their liquidation, consequently, was more thorough and more cruel than that of any other group and was carried through by artificial famine and deportation under the pretext of expropriation of the kulaks and collectivization.[24] The liquidation of the middle and peasant classes was completed in the early thirties; those who were not among the many millions of dead or the millions of deported slave laborers had learned "who is master here," had realized that their lives and the lives of their families depended not upon their fellow-citizens but exclusively on the whims of the government which they faced in complete loneliness without any help whatsoever from the group to which they happened to belong.[25]

The next class to be liquidated as a group were the workers. As a class they were much weaker and offered much less resistance than the peasants because their spontaneous expropriation of factory owners during the revolution, unlike the peasants' expropriation of landowners, had been frustrated at once by the government which confiscated the factories as state property under the pretext that the state belonged to the proletariat in any event. The Stakhanov system, adopted in the early thirties,

broke up all solidarity and class consciousness among the workers, first by the ferocious competition and second by the temporary solidification of a Stakhanovite aristocracy whose social distance from the ordinary worker naturally "was felt more acutely than the distance between the workers and the management."[26] This process was completed in 1938 with the introduction of the labor book which transformed the whole Russian worker class officially into a gigantic forced-labor force.

On top of these measures came the liquidation of that bureaucracy which had helped to carry out the previous liquidation measures. It took Stalin about two years, from 1936 to 1938, to rid himself of the whole administrative and military aristocracy of the Soviet society; nearly all offices, factories, economic and cultural bodies, government, party, and military bureaus came into new hands, when "nearly half the administrative personnel, party and nonparty, had been swept out," and more than 50 per cent of all party members and "at least eight million more" were liquidated.[27] Again the introduction of an interior passport, on which all departures from one city to another have to be registered and authorized, completed the destruction of the party bureaucracy as a class.[28]

None of these immense sacrifices in human life was motivated by a *raison d'état* in the old sense of the term. None of the liquidated social strata was hostile to the regime or likely to become hostile in the foreseeable future. Active organized opposition had ceased to exist by 1930 when Stalin, in his speech to the sixteenth Party Congress, outlawed the rightist and leftist deviations inside the Party, and even these feeble oppositions had hardly been able to base themselves on any of the existing classes.[29] Dictatorial terror—distinguished from totalitarian terror insofar as it threatens only authentic opponents but not harmless citizens without political opinions—had been grim enough to suffocate all political life, open or clandestine, even before Lenin's death. Intervention from abroad, which might ally itself with one of the dissatisfied sections in the population, was no longer a danger when, by 1930, the Soviet regime had been recognized by a majority of governments and concluded commercial and other international agreements with many countries. (Nor did Stalin's government eliminate such a possibility as far as the people themselves were concerned: we know now that Hitler, if he had been an ordinary conqueror and not a rival totalitarian ruler, might have had an extraordinary chance to win for his cause at least the people of the Ukraine.)

If the liquidation of classes made no political sense, it was positively disastrous for the Soviet economy. The consequences of the artificial famine in 1933 were felt for years throughout the country; the introduction of the Stakhanov system in 1935, with its arbitrary speed-up of individual output and its complete disregard of the necessities for team-work in industrial production, resulted in a "chaotic imbalance" of the young industry.[30] The liquidation of the bureaucracy, that is, of the class of factory managers and engineers, finally deprived industrial enterprises of what little experience and know-how the new Russian technical intelligentsia had been able to acquire.

Equality of condition among their subjects has been one of the foremost concerns of despotism and tyrannies since ancient times, yet such equalization is not sufficient for totalitarian rule because it leaves more or less intact certain nonpolitical communal bonds between the subjects, such as family ties and common cultural interests. If totalitarianism takes its own claim seriously, it must come to the point where it has "to finish once and for all with the neutrality of chess," that is, with the autonomous existence of any activity whatsoever. The lovers of "chess for the sake of chess," aptly compared by their liquidator with the lovers of "art for art's sake,"[31] and not yet absolutely atomized elements in a mass society whose completely heterogeneous uniformity is one of the primary conditions for totalitarianism. From the point of view of totalitarian rulers, a society devoted to chess for the sake of chess is only in degree different and less dangerous than a class of farmers for the sake of farming.

Mass atomization in Soviet society was achieved by the skillful use of repeated purges which invariably precede actual group liquidation. In order to destroy all social and family ties, the purges are conducted in such a way as to threaten with the same fate the defendant and all his ordinary relations, from mere acquaintances up to his closest friends and relatives. The consequence of this simple and ingenious device is that as soon as a man is accused, his former friends are transformed immediately into his bitterest enemies; in order to save their own skins, they volunteer information and rush in with denunciations to corroborate the nonexistent evidence against him; this obviously is the only way to prove their own trustworthiness. Retrospectively, they will try to prove that their acquaintance or friendship with the accused was only a pretext for spying on him and revealing him as a saboteur, a Trotskyite, a foreign spy, or a Fascist. Merit being "gauged" by the number of your denunciations of close comrades,[32] it is obvious that the most elementary caution demands that one avoid all intimate contacts, if possible—not in order to prevent discovery of one's secret thoughts, but rather to eliminate, in the almost certain case of future trouble, all persons who might have not only an ordinary cheap interest in your denunciation but an irresistible need to bring about your ruin simply because they are in danger of their own lives.[33] In the last analysis, it has been through the development of this device to its farthest and most fantastic extremes that Bolshevik

rulers have succeeded in creating an atomized and individualized society the like of which we have never seen before and which events or catastrophes alone would hardly have brought about.

Totalitarian movements are mass organizations of atomized, isolated individuals. Compared with all other parties and movements, their most conspicuous external characteristic is their demand for total, unrestricted, unconditional, and unalterable loyalty of the individual member. This demand is made by the leaders of totalitarian movements even before they seize power. It usually precedes the total organization of the country under their actual rule and it follows from the claim of their ideologies that their organization will encompass, in due course, the entire human race. Where, however, totalitarian rule has not been prepared by a totalitarian movement (and this, in distinction to Nazi Germany, was the case in Russia), the movement has to be organized afterward and the conditions for its growth have artificially to be created in order to make total loyalty—the psychological basis for total domination—at all possible. Such loyalty can be expected only from the completely isolated human being who, without any other social ties to family, friends, comrades, or even mere acquaintances, derives his sense of having a place in the world only from his belonging to a movement, his membership in the party.

Total loyalty is possible only when fidelity is emptied of all concrete content, from which changes of mind might naturally arise. The totalitarian movements, each in its own way, have done their utmost to get rid of the party programs which specified concrete content and which they inherited from earlier, nontotalitarian stages of development. No matter how radically they might have been phrased, every definite political goal which does not simply assert or circumscribe the claim to world rule, every political program which deals with issues more specific than "ideological questions of importance for centuries" is an obstruction to totalitarianism. Hitler's greatest achievement in the organization of the Nazi movement, which he gradually built up from the obscure crackpot membership of a typically nationalistic little party, was that he unburdened the movement of the party's earlier program, not by changing or officially abolishing it, but simply by refusing to talk about it or discuss its points, whose relative moderateness of content and phraseology were very soon outdated.[34] Stalin's task in this as in other respects was much more formidable; the socialist program of the Bolshevik party was a much more troublesome burden[35] than the 25 points of an amateur economist and a crackpot politician.[36] But Stalin achieved eventually, after having abolished the factions of the Russian party, the same result through the constant zigzag of the Communist Party lines, and the constant reinterpretation and application of Marxism which voided the doctrine of all its content because it was no longer possible to predict what course or action it would inspire. The fact that the most perfect education in Marxism and Leninism was no guide whatsoever for political behavior—that, on the contrary, one could follow the party line only if one repeated each morning what Stalin had announced the night before—naturally resulted in the same state of mind, the same concentrated obedience, undivided by any attempt to understand what one was doing, that Himmler's ingenious watchword for his SS-men expressed: "My honor is my loyalty."[37]

Lack of or ignoring of a party program is by itself not necessarily a sign of totalitarianism. The first to consider programs and platforms as needless scraps of paper and embarrassing promises, inconsistent with the style and impetus of a movement, was Mussolini with his Fascist philosophy of activism and inspiration through the historical moment itself.[38] Mere lust for power combined with contempt for "talkative" articulation of what they intend to do with it is characteristic of all mob leaders, but does not come up to the standards of totalitarianism. The true goal of Fascism was only to seize power and establish the Fascist "elite" as uncontested ruler over the country; totalitarianism's aspiration to total domination eliminates the distance between the ruler and the ruled population. "National Socialism has never demanded a new state form but has always demanded a reformation of the individual German,"[39] or, as Hitler put it very early, the "conquest of the German soul."[40] In other words, the ultimate goal of the dictatorial party aiming at one-party rule, *i.e.,* the seizure of power and the occupation of the state machinery, is for the totalitarian movement only a transitory stage in its total expansion into the population, an important turning point in its development, a welcome addition to, but neither the beginning nor the climax, of its power.

## II. THE TEMPORARY ALLIANCE BETWEEN THE MOB AND THE ELITE

What is more disturbing to our peace of mind than the unconditional loyalty of members of totalitarian movements, and the popular support of totalitarian regimes, is the unquestionable attraction these movements exert on the elite, and not only on the mob elements in society. It would be rash indeed to discount, because of artistic vagaries or scholarly naïveté, the terrifying roster of distinguished men whom totalitarianism can count among its sympathizers, fellow-travelers, and inscribed party members.

This attraction for the elite is as important a clue to the understanding of totalitarian movements (though hardly of totalitarian regimes) as their more obvious connection with the mob. It indicates the specific atmosphere, the general climate in which the rise of totalitarianism takes place. It should be remembered that the leaders of totalitarian movements and their sympathizers are, so to speak, older than the masses which they organize so that chronologically speaking the masses do not have to wait helplessly for the rise of their own leaders in the midst of a decaying class society, of which they are the most outstanding product.[41] Those who voluntarily left society before the "wreckage of classes"[42] had come about, along with the mob, which was an earlier by-product of the rule of the bourgeoisie, stand ready to welcome them. The present totalitarian rulers and the leaders of totalitarian movements still bear the characteristic traits of the mob, whose psychology and political philosophy are fairly well known; what will happen once the authentic mass man takes over, we do not know yet, although it may be a fair guess that he will have more in common with the meticulous, calculated correctness of Himmler than with the hysterical fanaticism of Hitler, will more resemble the stubborn dullness of Molotov than the sensual vindictive cruelty of Stalin.[43]

In this respect, the situation after the second World War in Europe does not differ essentially from that after the first; just as in the twenties the ideologies of Fascism, Bolshevism, and Nazism were formulated and the movements led by the so-called front generation, by those who had been brought up and still remembered distinctly the times before the war, so the present general political and intellectual climate of postwar totalitarianism is being determined by a generation which knew intimately the time and life which preceded the present. This is specifically true for France, where the breakdown of the class system came after the second instead of after the first War. Like the mob men and the adventurers of the imperialist era, the leaders of totalitarian movements have in common with their intellectual sympathizers the fact that both had been outside the class and national system of respectable European society even before this system broke down.

This breakdown, when the smugness of spurious respectability gave way to anarchic despair, seemed the first great opportunity for the elite as well as the mob. This is obvious for the new mass leaders whose careers reproduce the features of earlier mob leaders: failure in professional and social life, perversion and disaster in private life. The fact that their lives prior to their political careers had been failures naïvely held against them by the more respectable leaders of the old parties, was the strongest factor in their mass appeal. It seemed to prove that individually they embodied the mass destiny of the time and that their desire to sacrifice everything for the movement, their assurance of devotion to those who had been struck by catastrophe, their determination never to be tempted back into the security of normal life, and their contempt for respectability were quite sincere and not just inspired by passing ambitions.

The postwar elite, on the other hand, was only slightly younger than the generation which had let itself be used and abused by imperialism for the sake of glorious careers outside of respectability, as gamblers and spies and adventurers, as knights in shining armor and dragon-killers. They shared with Lawrence of Arabia the yearning for "losing their selves" and the violent disgust with all existing standards, with every power that be. If they still remembered the "golden age of security," they also remembered how they had hated it and how real their enthusiams had been at the outbreak of the first World War. Not only Hitler and not only the failures thanked God on their knees when mobilization swept Europe in 1914.[44] They did not even have to reproach themselves with having been an easy prey for chauvinist propaganda or lying explanations about the purely defensive character of the war. The elite went to war with an exultant hope that everything they knew, the whole culture and texture of life might go down in its "storms of steel" (Ernst Juenger). In the carefully chosen words of Thomas Mann, war was "chastisement" and "purification"; "war in itself rather than victories, inspired the poet." Or in the words of a student of the time, "what counts is always the readiness to make a sacrifice, not the object for which the sacrifice is made"; or in the words of a young worker, "it doesn't matter whether one lives a few years longer or not. One would like to have something to show for one's life."[45] And long before one of Nazism's intellectual sympathizers announced, "When I hear the word culture, I draw my revolver," poets had proclaimed their disgust with "rubbish culture" and called poetically on "ye Barbarians, Scythians, Negroes, Indians, to trample it down."[46]

Simply to brand as outbursts of nihilism this violent dissatisfaction with the pre-war age and subsequent attempts at restoring it (from Nietzsche and Sorel to Pareto, from Rimbaud and T. E. Lawrence to Juenger, Brecht, and Malraux, from Bakunin and Nechayev to Alexander Blok) is to overlook how justified disgust can be in a society wholly permeated with the ideological outlook and moral standards of the bourgeoisie. Yet it is also true that the "front generation," in marked contrast to their own chosen spiritual fathers, were completely absorbed by their desire to see the ruin of this whole world of fake security, fake culture, and fake life. This desire was so great that it outweighed in impact and articulateness all earlier attempts at a "transformation of values," such as Nietzsche

had attempted, or a reorganization of political life as indicated in Sorel's writings, or a revival of human authenticity in Bakunin, or a passionate love of life in the purity of exotic adventures in Rimbaud. Destruction without mitigation, chaos and ruin as such assumed the dignity of supreme values.[47]

The genuineness of these feelings can be seen in the fact that very few of this generation were cured of their war enthusiasm by actual experience of its horrors. The survivors of the trenches did not become pacifists. They cherished an experience which, they thought, might serve to separate them definitely from the hated surroundings of respectability. They clung to their memories of four years of life in the trenches as though they constituted an objective criterion for the establishment of a new elite. Nor did they yield to the temptation to idealize this past; on the contrary, the worshipers of war were the first to concede that war in the era of machines could not possibly breed virtues like chivalry, courage, honor, and manliness,[48] that it imposed on men nothing but the experience of bare destruction together with the humiliation of being only small cogs in the majestic wheel of slaughter.

This generation remembered the war as the great prelude to the breakdown of classes and their transformation into masses. War, with its constant murderous arbitrariness, became the symbol for death, the "great equalizer"[49] and therefore the true father of a new world order. The passion for equality and justice, the longing to transcend narrow and meaningless class lines, to abandon stupid privileges and prejudices, seemed to find in war a way out of the old condescending attitudes of pity for the oppressed and disinherited. In times of growing misery and individual helplessness, it seems as difficult to resist pity when it grows into an all-devouring passion as it is not to resent its very boundlessness, which seems to kill human dignity with a more deadly certainty than misery itself.

In the early years of his career, when a restoration of the European status quo was still the most serious threat to the ambitions of the mob,[50] Hitler appealed almost exclusively to these sentiments of the front generation. The peculiar selflessness of the mass man appeared here as yearning for anonymity, for being just a number and functioning only as a cog, for every transformation, in brief, which would wipe out the spurious identifications with specific types of predetermined functions within society. War had been experienced as that "mightiest of all mass actions" which obliterated individual differences so that even suffering, which traditionally had marked off individuals through unique unexchangeable destinies, could now be interpreted as "an instrument of historical progress."[51] Nor did national distinctions limit the masses into which the postwar elite wished to be

immersed. The first World War, somewhat paradoxically, had almost extinguished genuine national
feelings in Europe where, between the wars, it was
far more important to have belonged to the generation of the trenches, no matter on which side, than
to be a German or a Frenchman.[52] The Nazis based
their whole propaganda on this indistinct comradeship, this "community of fate," and won over a
great number of veteran organizations in all European countries, thereby proving how meaningless
national slogans had become even in the ranks of
the so-called Right, which used them for their
connotation of violence rather than for their specific national content.

No single element in this general intellectual
climate in postwar Europe was very new. Bakunin
had already confessed, "I do not want to be *I*,
I want to be *We*,"[53] and Nechayev had preached
the evangel of the "doomed man" with "no personal interests, no affairs, no sentiments, attachments, property, not even a name of his own."[54]
The antihumanist, antiliberal, anti-individualist, and
anticultural instincts of the front generation, their
brilliant and witty praise of violence, power, and
cruelty, was preceded by the awkward and pompous
"scientific" proofs of the imperialist elite that a
struggle of all against all is the law of the universe,
that expansion is a psychological necessity, before
it is a political device, and that man has to behave
by such universal laws.[55] What was new in the
writings of the front generation was their high
literary standard and great depth of passion. The
postwar writers no longer needed the scientific
demonstrations of genetics, and they made little if
any use of the collected works of Gobineau or
Houston Stewart Chamberlain, which belonged already to the cultural household of the philistines.
They read not Darwin but the Marquis de Sade.[56]
If they believed at all in universal laws, they did not
particularly care to conform to them. To them,
violence, power, cruelty, were the supreme capacities of men who had definitely lost their place in
the universe and were much too proud to long for
a power theory that would safely bring them back
and reintegrate them into the world. They were
satisfied with blind partisanship in anything that
respectable society had banned, regardless of theory
or content, and they elevated cruelty to a major
virtue because it contradicted "every value of the
Christian and humanitarian and liberal tradition."[57]

If we compare this generation with nineteenth-
century ideologists, with whose theories they sometimes seem to have so much in common, their chief
distinction is their greater authenticity and passion.
They had been more deeply touched by misery,
they were more concerned with the perplexities and
more deadly hurt by hypocrisy than all the apostles
of good will and brotherhood had been. And they
could no longer escape into exotic lands, could
no longer afford to be dragon-slayers among strange

and exciting people. There was no escape from the
daily routine of misery, meekness, frustration, and
resentment embellished by a fake culture of educated talk; no conformity to the customs of fairy-
tale lands could possibly save them from the rising
nausea that this combination continuously inspired.

This inability to escape into the wide world,
this feeling of being caught again and again in the
trappings of society—so different from the conditions which had formed the imperialist character—
added a constant strain and the yearning for violence to the older passion for anonymity and losing
oneself. Without the possibility of a radical change
of role and character, such as the identification
with the Arab national movement or the rites of an
Indian village, the self-willed immersion in the
suprahuman forces of destruction seemed to be a
salvation from the automatic identification with
pre-established functions in society and their utter
banality, and at the same time to help destroy the
functioning itself. These people felt attracted to
the pronounced activism of totalitarian movements,
to their curious and only seemingly contradictory
insistence on both the primacy of sheer action and
the overwhelming force of sheer necessity. This
mixture corresponded precisely to the war experience of the "front generation," to the experience of
constant activity within the framework of overwhelming fatality.

Activism, moreover, seemed to provide new answers to the old and troublesome question, "Who
am I?" which always appears with redoubled persistence in times of crisis. If society insisted, "You
are what you appear to be," postwar activism
replied: "You are what you have done"—for instance the man who for the first time had crossed
the Atlantic in an airplane (as in Brecht's *Lind-
bergh Flug*)—an answer which after the second
World War was repeated and slightly varied by
Sartre's "You are your life" (in *Huis Clos*). The
pertinence of these answers lies less in their validity
as redefinitions of personal identity than in their
usefulness for an eventual escape from social
identification, from the multiplicity of interchangeable roles and functions which society had imposed.
The point was to do something, heroic or criminal, which was unpredictable and undetermined
by anybody else.

The pronounced activism of the totalitarian
movements, their preference for terrorism over all
other forms of political activity, attracted the intellectual elite and the mob alike, precisely because
this terrorism was so utterly different from that of
the earlier revolutionary societies. It was no longer
a matter of calculated policy which saw in terrorist
acts the only means to eliminate certain outstanding personalities who, because of their policies or
position, had become the symbol of oppression.
What proved so attractive was that terrorism had
become a kind of philosophy through which to ex-

press frustration, resentment, and blind hatred, a kind of political expressionism which used bombs to express oneself, which watched delightedly the publicity given to resounding deeds and was absolutely willing to pay the price of life for having succeeded in forcing the recognition of one's existence on the normal strata of society. It was still the same spirit and the same game which made Goebbels, long before the eventual defeat of Nazi Germany, announce with obvious delight that the Nazis, in case of defeat, would know how to slam the door behind them and not to be forgotten for centuries.

Yet it is here if anywhere that a valid criterion may be found for distinguishing the elite from the mob in the pretotalitarian atmosphere. What the mob wanted, and what Goebbels expressed with great precision, was access to history even at the price of destruction. Goebbels' sincere conviction that "the greatest happiness that a contemporary can experience today" is either to be a genius or to serve one,[58] was typical of the mob but neither of the masses nor the sympathizing elite. The latter, on the contrary, took anonymity seriously to the point of seriously denying the existence of genius; all the art theories of the twenties tried desperately to prove that the excellent is the product of skill, craftsmanship, logic, and the realization of the potentialities of the material.[59] The mob, and not the elite, was charmed by the "radiant power of fame" (Stefan Zweig) and accepted enthusiastically the genius idolatry of the late bourgeois world. In this the mob of the twentieth century followed faithfully the pattern of earlier parvenus who also had discovered the fact that bourgeois society would rather open its doors to the fascinating "abnormal," the genius, the homosexual, or the Jew, than to simple merit. The elite's contempt for the genius and its yearning for anonymity was still witness of a spirit which neither the masses nor the mob were in a position to understand, and which, in the words of Robespierre, strove to assert the grandeur of man against the pettiness of the great.

This difference between the elite and the mob notwithstanding, there is no doubt that the elite was pleased whenever the underworld frightened respectable society into accepting it on an equal footing. The members of the elite did not object at all to paying a price, the destruction of civilization, for the fun of seeing how those who had been excluded unjustly in the past forced their way into it. They were not particularly outraged at the monstrous forgeries in historiography of which all totalitarian regimes are guilty and which announce themselves clearly enough in totalitarian propaganda. They had convinced themselves that traditional historiography was a forgery in any case, since it had excluded the underprivileged and oppressed from the memory of mankind. Those who were

rejected by their own time were usually forgotten by history, and insult added to injury had troubled all sensitive consciences ever since faith in a hereafter where the last would be the first had disappeared. Injustices in the past as well as the present became intolerable when there was no longer any hope that the scales of justice eventually would be set right. Marx's great attempt to rewrite world history in terms of class struggles fascinated even those who did not believe in the correctness of his thesis, because of his original intention to find a device by which to force the destinies of those excluded from official history into the memory of posterity.

The temporary alliance between the elite and the mob rested largely on this genuine delight with which the former watched the latter destroy respectability. This could be achieved when the German steel barons were forced to deal with and to receive socially Hitler the housepainter and self-admitted former derelict, as it could be with the crude and vulgar forgeries perpetrated by the totalitarian movements in all fields of intellectual life, insofar as they gathered all the subterranean, non-respectable elements of European history into one consistent picture. From this viewpoint it was rather gratifying to see that Bolshevism and Nazism began even to eliminate those sources of their own ideologies which had already won some recognition in academic or other official quarters. Not Marx's dialectical materialism, but the conspiracy of 300 families; not the pompous scientificality of Gobineau and Chamberlain, but the "Protocols of the Elders of Zion"; not the traceable influence of the Catholic Church and the role played by anticlericalism in Latin countries, but the backstairs literature about the Jesuits and the Freemasons became the inspiration for the rewriters of history. The object of the most varied and variable constructions was always to reveal official history as a joke, to demonstrate a sphere of secret influences of which the visible, traceable, and known historical reality was only the outward façade erected explicitly to fool the people.

To this aversion of the intellectual elite for official historiography, to its conviction that history, which was forgery anyway, might as well be the playground of crackpots, must be added the terrible, demoralizing fascination in the possibility that gigantic lies and monstrous falsehoods can eventually be established as unquestioned facts, that man may be free to change his own past at will, and that the difference between truth and falsehood may cease to be objective and become a mere matter of power and cleverness, of "pressure and infinite repetition."[60] Not Stalin's and Hitler's skill in the art of lying but the fact that they were able to organize the masses into a collective unit to back up their lies with impressive magnificence, exerted the fascination. Simple forgeries from the viewpoint of scholarship appeared to receive the sanction of history itself when the whole marching reality of the movements stood behind them and pretended to draw from them the necessary inspiration for action.

The attraction which the totalitarian movements exert on the elite, so long as and wherever they have not seized power, has been perplexing because the patently vulgar and arbitrary, positive doctrines of totalitarianism are more conspicuous to the outsider and mere observer than the general mood which pervades the pretotalitarian atmosphere. These doctrines were so much at variance with generally accepted intellectual, cultural, and moral standards that one could conclude that only an inherent fundamental shortcoming of character in the intellectual, *"la trahison des clercs"* (J. Benda), or a perverse self-hatred of the spirit, accounted for the delight with which the elite accepted the "ideas" of the mob. What the spokesmen of humanism and liberalism usually overlook, in their bitter disappointment and their unfamiliarity with the more general experiences of the time, is that an atmosphere in which all traditional values and propositions had evaporated (after the nineteenth-century ideologies had refuted each other and exhausted their vital appeal) in a sense made it easier to accept patently absurd propositions than the old truths which had become pious banalities, precisely because nobody could be expected to take the absurdities seriously. Vulgarity with its cynical dismissal of respected standards and accepted theories carried with it a frank admission of the worst and a disregard for all pretenses which was easily mistaken for courage and a new style of life. In the growing prevalence of mob attitudes and convictions—which were actually the attitudes and convictions of the bourgeoisie cleansed of hypocrisy—those who traditionally hated the bourgeoisie and had voluntarily left respectable society saw only the lack of hypocrisy and respectability, not the content itself.[61]

Since the bourgeoisie claimed to be the guardian of Western traditions and confounded all moral issues by parading publicly virtues which it not only did not possess in private and business life, but actually held in contempt, it seemed revolutionary to admit cruelty, disregard of human values, and general amorality, because this at least destroyed the duplicity upon which the existing society seemed to rest. What a temptation to flaunt extreme attitudes in the hypocritical twilight of double moral standards, to wear publicly the mask of cruelty if everybody was patently inconsiderate and pretended to be gentle, to parade wickedness in a world, not of wickedness, but of meanness! The intellectual elite of the twenties who knew little of the earlier connections between mob and bourgeoisie was certain that the old game of *épater le bourgeois* could be played to perfection if one started to shock society with an ironically exaggerated picture of its own behavior.

At that time, nobody anticipated that the true victims of this irony would be the elite rather than the bourgeoisie. The avant-garde did not know they were running their heads not against walls but against open doors, that a unanimous success would belie their claim to being a revolutionary minority, and would prove that they were about to express a new mass spirit or the spirit of the time. Particularly significant in this respect was the reception given Brecht's *Dreigroschenoper* in pre-Hitler Germany. The play presented gangsters as respectable businessmen and respectable businessmen as gangsters. The irony was somewhat lost when respectable businessmen in the audience considered this a deep insight into the ways of the world and when the mob welcomed it as an artistic sanction of gangsterism. The theme song in the play, *"Erstens kommt das Fressen, und dann kommt die Moral,"* was greeted with frantic applause by exactly everybody, though for different reasons. The mob applauded because it took the statement literally; the bourgeoisie applauded because it had been fooled by its own hypocrisy for so long that it had grown tired of the tension and found deep wisdom in the expression of the banality by which it lived; the elite applauded because the unveiling of hypocrisy was such superior and wonderful fun. The effect of the work was exactly the opposite of what Brecht had sought by it. The bourgeoisie could no longer be shocked; it welcomed the exposure of its hidden philosophy, whose popularity proved they had been right all along, so that the only political result of Brecht's "revolution" was to encourage everyone to discard the uncomfortable mask of hypocrisy and to accept openly the standards of the mob.

A reaction similar in its ambiguity was aroused some ten years later in France by Céline's *Bagatelles pour un Massacre,* in which he proposed to massacre all the Jews. André Gide was publicly delighted in the pages of the *Nouvelle Revue Française,* not of course because he wanted to kill the Jews of France, but because he rejoiced in the blunt admission of such a desire and in the fascinating contradiction between Céline's bluntness and the hypocritical politeness which surrounded the Jewish question in all respectable quarters. How irresistible the desire for the unmasking of hypocrisy was among the elite can be gauged by the fact that such delight could not even be spoiled by Hitler's very real persecution of the Jews, which at the time of Céline's writing was already in full swing. Yet aversion against the philosemitism of the liberals had much more to do with this reaction than hatred of Jews. A similar frame of mind explains the remarkable fact that Hitler's and Stalin's widely publicized opinions about art and their persecution of modern artists have never been able to destroy the attraction which the totalitarian movements had for avant-garde artists; this shows the elite's lack of a sense of reality, together with its perverted selflessness, both of which resemble only too closely the fictitious world and the absence of self-interest among the masses. It was the great opportunity of the totalitarian movements, and the reason why a temporary alliance between the intellectual elite and the mob could come about, that in an elementary and undifferentiated way their problems had become the same and foreshadowed the problems and mentality of the masses.

Closely related to the attraction which the mob's lack of hypocrisy and the masses' lack of self-interest exerted on the elite, was the equally irresistible appeal of the totalitarian movements' spurious claim to have abolished the separation between private and public life and to have restored a mysterious irrational wholeness in man. Since Balzac revealed the private lives of the public figures of French society and since Ibsen's dramatization of the "Pillars of Society" had conquered the Continental theater, the issue of double morality was one of the main topics for tragedies, comedies, and novels. Double morality as practiced by the bourgeoisie became the outstanding sign of that *esprit de sérieux,* which is always pompous and never sincere. This division between private and public or social life had nothing to do with the justified separation between the personal and public spheres, but was rather the psychological reflection of the nineteenth-century struggle between *bourgeois* and *citoyen,* between the man who judged and used all public institutions by the yardstick of his private interests and the responsible citizen who was concerned with public affairs as the affairs of all. In this connection, the liberals' political philosophy, according to which the mere sum of individual interests adds up to the miracle of the common good, appeared to be only a rationalization of the recklessness with which private interests were pressed regardless of the common good.

Against the class spirit of the Continental parties, which had always admitted they represented certain interests, and against the "opportunism" resulting from their conception of themselves as only parts of a total, the totalitarian movements asserted their "superiority" in that they carried a *Weltanschauung* by which they would take possession of man as a whole.[62] In this claim to totality the mob leaders of the movements again formulated and only reversed the bourgeoisie's own political philosophy. The bourgeois class, having made its way through social pressure and, frequently, through an economic blackmail of political institutions, always believed that the public and visible organs of power were directed by their own secret, nonpublic interests and influence. In this sense, the bourgeoisie's political philosophy was always "totalitarian"; it always assumed an identity of politics, economics and society, in which political institutions served only as the façade for private interests. The bourgeoisie's double standard, its differentiation between public and private life, were a concession to the nation-state which had desperately tried to keep the two spheres apart.

What appealed to the elite was radicalism as such. Marx's hopeful predictions that the state would wither away and a classless society emerge were no longer radical, no longer Messianic enough. If Berdyaev is right in stating that "Russian revolutionaries . . . had always been totalitarian," then the attraction which Soviet Russia exerted almost equally on Nazi and Communist intellectual fellow-travelers lay precisely in the fact that in Russia the revolution was a religion and a philosophy, not merely a conflict concerned with the social and political side of life."[63] The truth was that the transformation of classes into masses and the breakdown of the prestige and authority of political institutions had brought to Western European countries conditions which resembled those prevalent in Russia, so that it was no accident that revolutionaries also began to take on the typically Russian revolutionary fanaticism which looked forward, not to a change in social or political conditions, but to the radical destruction of every existing creed, value, and institution. The mob merely took advantage of this new mood and brought about a short-lived alliance of revolutionaries and criminals, which also had been present in many revolutionary sects in Czarist Russia but conspicuously absent from the European scene.

The disturbing alliance between the mob and the elite, and the curious coincidence of their aspirations, had their origin in the fact that these strata had been the first to be eliminated from the structure of the nation-state and the framework of class society. They found each other so easily, if only temporarily, because they both sensed that they represented the fate of the time, that they were followed by unending masses, that sooner or later the majority of European peoples might be with them—as they thought, ready to make their revolution.

It turned out that they were both mistaken. The mob, the underworld of the bourgeois class, hoped that the helpless masses would help them into power, would support them when they attempted to forward their private interests, that they would be able simply to replace the older strata of bourgeois society and to instill into it the more enterprising spirit of the underworld. Yet totalitarianism in power learned quickly that enterprising spirit was not restricted to the mob strata of the population, and that in any event such initiative could only be a threat to the total domination of man. Absence of scruple, on the other hand, was not restricted to the mob either and, in any event, could be taught in a relatively short time. For the ruthless machines of domination and extermination, the masses of co-ordinated philistines provided much better material and were capable of even greater crimes than so-called professional criminals, provided only that these crimes were well organized and assumed the appearance of routine jobs.

It is not fortuitous, then, that the few protests against the Nazis' mass atrocities against the Jews and Eastern European peoples were voiced not by the military men nor by any other part of the co-ordinated masses of respectable philistines, but precisely by those early comrades of Hitler who were typical representatives of the mob.[64] Nor was Himmler, the most powerful man in Germany after 1936, one of those "armed bohemians" (Heiden) whose features were distressingly similar to those of the intellectual elite. Himmler was himself "more normal," that is, more of a philistine, than any of the original leaders of the Nazi movement.[65] He was not a bohemian like Goebbels, or a sex criminal like Streicher, or a crackpot like Rosenberg, or a fanatic like Hitler, or an adventurer like Goering. He proved his supreme ability for organizing the masses into total domination by assuming that most people are neither bohemians, fanatics, adventurers, sex maniacs, crackpots, nor social failures, but first and foremost job holders and good family men.

The philistine's retirement into private life, his single-minded devotion to matters of family and career was the last, and already degenerated, product of the bourgeoisie's belief in the primacy of private interest. The philistine is the bourgeois isolated from his own class, the atomized individual who is produced by the breakdown of the bourgeois class itself. The mass man whom Himmler organized for the greatest mass crimes ever committed in history bore the features of the philistine rather than of the mob man, and was the bourgeois who in the midst of the ruins of his world worried about nothing so much as his private security, was ready to sacrifice everything—belief, honor, dignity—on the slightest provocation. Nothing proved easier to destroy than the privacy and private morality of people who thought of nothing but safeguarding their private lives. After a few years of power and systematic co-ordination, the Nazis could rightly announce: "The only person who is still a private individual in Germany is somebody who is asleep."[66]

In all fairness to those among the elite, on the other hand, who at one time or another have let themselves be seduced by totalitarian movements, and who sometimes, because of their intellectual abilities, are even accused of having inspired totalitarianism, it must be stated that what these desperate men of the twentieth century did or did not do had no influence on totalitarianism whatsoever,

although it did play some part in earlier, successful, attempts of the movements to force the outside world to take their doctrines seriously. Wherever totalitarian movements seized power, this whole group of sympathizers was shaken off even before the regimes proceeded toward their greatest crimes. Intellectual, spiritual, and artistic initiative is as dangerous to totalitarianism as the gangster initiative of the mob, and both are more dangerous than mere political opposition. The consistent persecution of every higher form of intellectual activity by the new mass leaders springs from more than their natural resentment against everything they cannot understand. Total domination does not allow for free initiative in any field of life, for any activity that is not entirely predictable. Totalitarianism in power invariably replaces all first-rate talents, regardless of their sympathies, with those crackpots and fools whose lack of intelligence and creativity is still the best guarantee of their loyalty.[67]

## NOTES

1. See the illuminating remarks of Carlton J. H. Hayes on "The Novelty of Totalitarianism in the History of Western Civilization," in *Symposium on the Totalitarian State,* 1939. Proceedings of the American Philosophical Society, Philadelphia, 1940, Vol. LXXXII.

2. The illusion that Hitler was simply a creature of industrialists and high finance has been dispelled by Konrad Heiden, *Der Führer. Hitler's Rise to Power,* Boston, 1944: "The German economy did not raise up Hitler. He is no creature of money; to be sure, he did approach big capital—though as a blackmailer, not as a lackey. But in that spring day of confidence [*i.e.,* from 1925-1929], there was nothing to be had from capital by blackmail" (p. 264).—For Stalin's career, Boris Souvarine, *Stalin. A Critical Survey of Bolshevism,* New York, 1939, is still a standard work. Isaac Deutscher, *Stalin: A Political Biography,* New York and London, 1949, is indispensable for its rich documentary material and great insight into the internal struggles of the Bolshevik party; it suffers from an interpretation which likens Stalin to—Cromwell, Napoleon, and Robespierre.

3. Franz Borkenau, *The Totalitarian Enemy,* London, 1940, p. 231.

4. Quoted from the German edition of the "Protocols of the Elders of Zion," *Die Zionistischen Protokolle mit einem Vor- und Nachwort von Theodor Fritsch,* 1924, p. 29.

5. This, to be sure, is a specialty of the Russian brand of totalitarianism. It is interesting to note that in the early trial of foreign engineers in the Soviet Union, Communist sympathies were already used as an argument for self-accusation: "All the time the authorities insisted on my admitting having committed acts of sabotage I had never done. I refused. I was told: 'If you are in favour of the Soviet Government, as you pretend you are, prove it by your actions; the Government needs

your confession.' " Reported by Anton Ciliga, *The Russian Enigma,* London, 1940, p. 153.

A theoretical justification for this behavior was given by Trotsky: "We can only be right with and by the Party, for history has provided no other way of being in the right. The English have a saying, 'My country, right or wrong.' . . . We have much better historical justification in saying whether it is right or wrong in certain individual concrete cases, it is my party" (Souvarine, *op. cit.,* p. 361).

On the other hand, the Red Army officers who did not belong to the movement had to be tried behind closed doors.

6. The Nazi author Andreas Pfenning explicitly rejects the notion that the SA were fighting for an "ideal" or were prompted by an "idealistic experience." Their "basic experience came into existence in the course of the struggle." "Gemeinschaft und Staatswissenschaft," in *Zeitschrift für die gesamte Staatswissenschaft,* Band 96. Translation quoted from Ernst Fraenkel, *The Dual State,* New York and London, 1941, p. 192.

7. The Moscow-dominated Eastern European governments rule for the sake of Moscow and act as agents of the Comintern; they are examples of the spread of the Moscow-directed totalitarian movement, not of native developments. The only exception seems to be Tito of Yugoslavia, who may have broken with Moscow because he realized that the Russian-inspired methods would cost him a heavy percentage of Yugoslavia's population.

8. Proof of the nontotalitarian nature of the Fascist dictatorship is the surprisingly small number and the comparatively mild sentences meted out to political offenders. During the particularly active years from 1926 to 1932, the special tribunals for political offenders pronounced seven death sentences, 257 sentences of 10 or more years imprisonment, 1,360 under 10 years, and sentenced many more to exile; 12,000, moreover, were arrested and found innocent, a procedure quite inconceivable under conditions of Nazi or Bolshevik terror. See E. Kohn-Bramstedt, *Dictatorship and Political Police. The Technique of Control by Fear,* London, 1945, pp. 51 ff.

9. Nazi political theorists have always emphatically stated that "Mussolini's 'ethical state' and Hitler's 'ideological state' [*Weltanschauungsstaat*] cannot be mentioned in the same breath" (Gottfried Neesse, "Die verfassungsrechtliche Gestaltung der Ein-Partei," in *Zeitschrift für die gesamte Staatswissenschaft,* 1938, Band 98).

Goebbels on the difference between Fascism and National Socialism: "[Fascism] is . . . nothing like National Socialism. While the latter goes deep down to the roots, Fascism is only a superficial thing" (*The Goebbels Diaries (1942-1943),* ed. by Louis Lochner, New York, 1948, p. 71. "[The Duce] is not a revolutionary like the Führer or Stalin. He is so bound to his own Italian people that he lacks the broad qualities of a worldwide revolutionary and insurrectionist" (*ibid.,* p. 468).

Himmler expressed the same opinion in a speech delivered in 1943 at a Conference of Commanding Officers: "Fascism and National Socialism are two fundamentally different things, . . . there is absolutely no comparison between Fascism and National Socialism as spiritual, ideological movements." See Kohn-Bramstedt, *op. cit.,* Appendix A.

Hitler recognized in the early twenties the affinity between the Nazi and the Communist movements: "In our movement the two extremes come together: the Communists from the Left and the officers and the students from the Right. These two have always been the most active elements. . . . The Communists were the idealists of Socialism. . . ." See Heiden, *op. cit.,* p. 147. Roehm, the chief of the SA, only repeated a current opinion when he wrote in the late twenties: "Many things are between us and the Communists, but we respect the sincerity of their conviction and their willingness to bring sacrifices for their own cause, and this unites us with them" (Ernst Roehm, *Die Geschichte eines Hochverräters,* 1933, Volksausgabe, p. 273).

During the last war, the Nazis more readily recognized the Russians as their peers than any other nation. Hitler, speaking in May, 1943, at a conference of the Reichsleiter and Gauleiter, "began with the fact that in this war bourgeoisie and revolutionary states are facing each other. It has been an easy thing for us to knock out the bourgeois states, for they were quite inferior to us in their upbringing and attitude. Countries with an ideology have an edge on bourgeois states. . . . [In the East] we met an opponent who also sponsors an ideology, even though a wrong one. . . ." (*Goebbels Diaries,* p. 355).—This estimate was based on ideological not on military considerations. Gottfried Neesse, *Partei und Staat,* 1936, gave the official version of the movement's struggle for power when he wrote: "For us the united front of the *system* extends from the German National People's Party [*i.e.,* the extreme Right] to the Social Democrats. The Communist Party was an enemy outside of the *system.* During the first months of 1933, therefore, when the doom of the *system* was already sealed, we still had to fight a decisive battle against the Communist Party" (p. 76).

10. The following information reported by Souvarine, *op. cit.,* p. 669, seems to be an outstanding illustration: "According to W. Krivitsky, whose excellent confidential source of information is the GPU: 'Instead of the 171 million inhabitants calculated for 1937, only 145 million were found; thus nearly 30 million people in the USSR are missing.' " And this, it should be kept in mind, occurred after the dekulakization of the early thirties which had cost an estimated 8 million of human lives. See *Communism in Action.* U.S. Government, Washington, 1946, p. 140.

11. F. Borkenau said in 1940, that is, before the Nazis had shown their "consistency" in racism: "In ideological matters Russia is by far the more consistent of the two" (*op. cit.,* p. 28).

12. F. Borkenau describes the situation correctly: "The Communists had only very modest success when they tried to win influence among the masses of the working class; their mass basis, therefore, if they had it at all, moved more and more away from the proletariat" ("Die neue Komintern," in *Der Monat,* Berlin, 1949, Heft 4).

13. William Ebenstein, *The Nazi State,* New York, 1943, p. 247.

14. As Maxim Gorky had described them. See Souvarine, *op. cit.,* p. 290.

15. Heinrich Himmler's speech on "Organization and Obligation of the SS and the Police," published in *National-politischer Lehrgang der Wehrmacht vom 15.-23. Januar 1937.* Translation quoted from *Nazi Conspiracy and Aggression.* Office of the United States Chief of Counsel for the Prosecution of Axis Criminality. U.S. Government, Washington, 1946, IV, 616 ff.

16. Gustave Lebon, *La Psychologie des Foules,* 1895, mentions the peculiar selflessness of the masses. See chapter ii, paragraph 5.

17. The founders of the Nazi party referred to it occasionally even before Hitler took over as a "party of the Left." An incident which occurred after the parliamentary elections of 1932 is also interesting: "Gregor Strasser bitterly pointed out to his Leader that before the elections the National Socialists in the Reichstag might have formed a majority with the Center; now this possibility was ended, the two parties were less than half of parliament; . . . But with the Communists they still had a majority, Hitler replied; no one can govern against us" (Heiden, *op. cit.,* pp. 94 and 495 respectively).

18. Compare Carlton J. H. Hayes, *op. cit.,* who does not differentiate between the mob and the masses, thinks that totalitarian dictators "have come from the masses rather than from the classes."

19. This is the central theory of K. Heiden, whose analyses of the Nazi movement are still outstanding. "From the wreckage of dead classes arises the new class of intellectuals, and at the head march the most ruthless, those with the least to lose, hence the strongest: the armed bohemians, to whom war is home and civil war fatherland" (*op. cit.,* p. 100).

20. The plot between Reichswehr General Schleicher and Roehm, the chief of the SA, consisted of a plan to bring all paramilitary formations under the military authority of the Reichswehr, which at once would have added millions to the German army. This, of course, would inevitably have led to a military dictatorship. In June, 1934, Hitler liquidated Roehm and Schleicher. The initial negotiations were started with the full knowledge of Hitler who used Roehm's connections with the Reichswehr to deceive German military circles about his real intentions. In April, 1932, Roehm testified in one of Hitler's lawsuits that the SA's military status had the full understanding of the Reichswehr. See David Riesman, "Democracy and Defamation," in *Columbia Law Review,* 1942, p. 1101, note 68. For documentary evidence of the Roehm-Schleicher plan, see *Nazi Conspiracy,* V, 456 ff. See also Heiden, *op. cit.,* p. 450.

Roehm himself proudly reports his negotiations with Schleicher, which according to him were started in 1931. Schleicher had promised to put the SA under the command of the Reichswehr officers in case of an emergency. See *Die Memoiren des Stabschefs Roehm,* Saarbrücken, 1934, p. 170.

21. Roehm's autobiography especially is a veritable classic in this kind of literature.

22. The following is the estimate of Rakovsky, writing in 1930 from his exile in Siberia: "Under our eyes has formed and is being formed a great class of directors which has its internal subdivisions and which increases through calculated co-option and direct or indirect nominations. . . . The element which unites this original class is a form, also original of private property, to wit, the State power." This clearly has become the standard explanation of the left-wing critics of the Soviet Union. Quoted from Souvarine, *op. cit.,* p. 564.

23. In 1927, 90 per cent of the village Soviets and 75 per cent of their chairmen were non-party members; the executive committees of the counties were made up of 50 per cent party members and 50 per cent non-party members, while in the Central Committee 75 per cent of the delegates were party members. See the article on "Bolshevism" by Maurice Dodd in the *Encyclopedia of Social Sciences.*

How the party members of the Soviets, by voting "in conformity with the instructions they received from the permanent official of the Party," destroyed the Soviet system from within is described in detail in A. Rosenberg, *A History of Bolshevism,* London, 1934, chapter vi.

24. Victor Kravchenko, *I Chose Freedom, The Personal and Political Life of a Soviet Official,* New York, 1946, contains interesting information about the artificiality of the Russian famine in the early thirties: "When the first of the new grain was being delivered to the granary near the railroad station, I made a discovery. . . . Cached in the brick structure were thousands of pounds of the previous year's grain collections. These were the State reserves for the district ordered by the government, their very existence hidden from the starving population. . . . Subsequently I came to know that in many other parts of the country the government hoarded huge reserves while peasants in those very regions died of hunger" (pp. 128-129).

25. Kravchenko, *op. cit.,* p. 130, reports an explanation given by the secretary of the regional party committee which admits the political purpose of the famine: "A ruthless struggle is going on between the peasantry and our regime. It's a struggle to the death. This year was a test of our strength and their endurance. It took a famine to show them who is master here. It has cost millions of lives. . . . We've won the war."

26. *Ibid.,* p. 191.

27. *Ibid.,* pp. 278 and 303.

28. The party card was originally the most coveted treasure of a Communist in the Soviet Union. In 1938, the "new rule was put into effect: Thereafter a Communist wishing to leave one city . . . to settle in another —even if the change were on orders from above—had fisrt to wait for a formal decision by the City Committee" (*ibid.,* p. 306).

29. Stalin's Report to the Sixteenth Congress denounced the deviations as the "reflection of the resistance of the peasant and petty bourgeois classes in the ranks of the Party. (See *Leninism,* 1933, Vol. II, chapter iii.) Against this attack the opposition was curiously defenseless because they too, and especially Trotsky, were "always anxious to discover a struggle of classes behind the struggles of cliques" (Souvarine, *op. cit.,* p. 440).

30. Kravchenko, *op. cit.,* p. 187.

31. Souvarine, *op. cit.,* p. 575.

32. Kravchenko, *op. cit.,* p. 212.

33. See Kravchenko's description of party purges, *op. cit.*

34. Hitler stated in *Mein Kampf* (2 vols., 1st German ed., 1925 and 1927, respectively. Unexpurgated translation, New York, 1939) that it was better to have an antiquated program than to allow a discussion of program (Book II, chapter v.). Soon he was to proclaim publicly: "Once we take over the government, the program will come of itself. . . . The first thing must be an inconceivable wave of propaganda. That is a political action which would have little to do with the other problems of the moment." See Heiden, *op. cit.,* p. 203.

35. Souvarine, in our opinion wrongly, suggests that Lenin had already abolished the role of a party pro-

gram: "Nothing could show more clearly the non-existence of Bolshevism as a doctrine except in Lenin's brain; every Bolshevik left to himself wandered from "the line" of his fraction . . . for these men were bound together by their temperament and by the ascendancy of Lenin rather than by ideas" (*op. cit.*, p. 85).

36. Gottfried Feder's Program of the Nazi Party with its famous 25 points has played a greater role in the literature about the movement than in the movement itself.

37. The impact of the watchword, formulated by Himmler himself, is difficult to render. Its German equivalent: *"Meine Ehre heisst Treue,"* indicates an absolute devotion and obedience which transcends the meaning of mere discipline or personal faithfulness. *Nazi Conspiracy,* whose translations of German documents and Nazi literature are indispensable source material but, unfortunately, are very uneven, renders the SS watchword: "My honor signifies faithfulness" (V. 346).

38. Mussolini was probably the first party leader who consciously rejected a formal program and replaced it with inspired leadership and action alone. Behind this act lay the notion that the actuality of the moment itself was the chief element of inspiration, which would only be hampered by a party program. The philosophy of Italian Fascism has been expressed by Gentile's "actualism" rather than by Sorel's "myths." Compare also the article "Fascism" in the *Encyclopedia of Social Sciences.* The Program of 1921 was formulated when the movement had been in existence two years and contained, for the most part, its nationalist philosophy.

39. Ernst Bayer, *Die SA,* Berlin, 1938. Translation quoted from *Nazi Conspiracy,* IV, 783.

40. *Mein Kampf,* Book I, chapter xi. See also, for example, Dieter Schwarz, *Angriffe auf die nationalsozialistische Weltanschauung,* Aus dem Schwarzen Korps, No. 2, 1936, who answers the obvious criticism that National Socialists after their rise to power continued to talk about "a struggle": "National Socialism as an ideology [*Weltanschauung*] will not abandon its struggle until . . . the way of life of each individual German has been shaped by its fundamental values and these are realized every day anew."

41. See Hayes' remarks quoted above, note 18.

42. Heiden, see note 19.

43. See the frequently quoted anecdote, originally reported by Souvarine, *op. cit.,* p. 485: "One summer night in 1923, opening his heart to Dzerzhinsky and Kamenev, Stalin is supposed to have said: 'To choose one's victim, to prepare one's plans minutely, to slake an implacable vengeance, and then to go to bed . . . There is nothing sweeter in the world.'" It is obvious that such traits are not necessarily those of a man who plans the murder of many millions of people.

44. See Hitler's description of his reaction to the outbreak of the first World War in *Mein Kampf,* Book I, chapter v.

45. See the collection of material on the "inner chronicle of the first World War" by Hanna Hafkesbrink, *Unknown Germany,* New Haven, 1948, pp. 45, 81, 43, respectively. The great value of this collection for the imponderables of historical atmosphere makes the lack of similar studies for France, England, and Italy all the more deplorable.

46. *Ibid.,* pp. 20-21.

47. This started with a feeling of complete alienation from normal life. Wrote Rudolf Binding for instance: "More and more we are to be counted among the dead, among the estranged—because the greatness of the occurrence estranges and separates us— rather than among the banished whose return is possible" (*ibid.,* p. 160). A curious reminiscence of the front generation's elite claim can still be found in Himmler's account of how he finally hit upon his "form of selection" for the reorganization of the SS: ". . . the most severe selection procedure is brought about by war, the struggle for life and death. In this procedure the value of blood is shown through achievement. . . . War, however, is an exceptional circumstance, and a way had to be found to make selections in peace time" (*op. cit.*).

48. See for instance, Ernst Juenger, *The Storm of Steel,* London, 1929.

49. Hafkesbrink, *op. cit.,* p. 156.

50. Heiden, *op. cit.,* shows how consistently Hitler sided with catastrophe in the early days of the movement, how he feared a possible recovery of Germany. "Half a dozen times [*i.e.,* during the Ruhrputsch], in different terms, he declared to his storm troops that Germany was going under. 'Our job is to insure the success of our movement'" (p. 167)—a success which at that moment depended upon the collapse of the fight in the Ruhr.

51. Hafkesbrink, *op. cit.,* pp. 156-157.

52. This feeling was already widespread during the war when Rudolf Binding wrote: "[This war] is not to be compared with a campaign. For there one leader pits his will against that of another. But in this War both the adversaries lie on the ground, and only the War has its will" (*ibid.,* p. 67).

53. Bakunin in a letter written on February 7, 1870. See Max Nomad, *Apostles of Revolution,* Boston, 1939, p. 180.

54. The "Catechism of the Revolutionist" was either written by Bakunin himself or by his disciple Nechayev. For the question of authorship and translation of the complete text, see Nomad, *op. cit.,* pp. 227 ff. In any event, the "system of complete disregard for any tenets of simple decency and fairness in [the revolutionist's] attitude towards other human beings . . . went down in Russian revolutionary history under the name of 'Nechayevshchina'" (*ibid.,* p. 224).

55. Outstanding among these political theorists of imperialism is Ernest Seillière, *Mysticisme et Domination. Essais de Critique Impérialiste,* 1913. See also Cargill Sprietsma, *We Imperialists. Notes on Ernest Seillière's Philosophy of Imperialism,* New York, 1931; G. Monod in *La Revue Historique,* January, 1912; and Louis Estève, *Une nouvelle Psychologie de l'Impérialisme. Ernest Seillière,* 1913.

56. In France, since 1930, the Marquis de Sade has become one of the favored authors of the literary avant-garde. Jean Paulhan, in his Introduction to a new edition of Sade's *Les Infortunes de la Vertu,* Paris, 1946, remarks: "When I see so many writers today consciously trying to deny artifice and the literary game for the sake of the inexpressible [*un évènement indicible*] . . . , anxiously looking for the sublime in the infamous, for the great in the subversive . . . , I ask myself . . . if our modern literature, in those parts which appear to us most vital—or at any rate most aggressive—has not turned entirely toward the past, and if it was not precisely Sade who deter-

mined it." See also Georges Bataille, "Le Secret de Sade," in *La Critique,* Tome III, Nos. 15–16, 17, 1947.

57. Borkenau, *op. cit.,* p. 138.

58. Goebbels, *op. cit.,* p. 139.

59. The art theories of the Bauhaus were characteristic in this respect. See also Bertold Brecht's remarks on the theater, *Gesammelte Werke,* London, 1938.

60. On the falsification of history, see Kravchenko, *op. cit.,* pp. 304 ff.

61. The following passage by Roehm is typical of the feeling of almost the whole younger generation and not only of an elite: "Hypocrisy and Pharisaism rule. They are the most conspicuous characteristics of society today. . . . Nothing could be more lying than the so-called morals of society." These boys "don't find their way in the philistine world of bourgeois double morals and don't know any longer how to distinguish between truth and error" (*Die Geschichte eines Hochverräters,* pp. 267 and 269). The homosexuality of these circles was also at least partially an expression of their protest against society.

62. The role of the *Weltanschauung* in the formation of the Nazi movement has been stressed many times by Hitler himself. In *Mein Kampf,* it is interesting to note that he pretends to have understood the necessity of basing a party on a *Weltanschauung* through the superiority of the Marxist parties. Book II, chapter i: "*Weltanschauung* and Party."

63. Nicolai Berdyaev, *The Origin of Russian Communism,* 1937, pp. 124–125.

64. There is, for instance, the curious intervention of Wilhelm Kube, General Commissar in Minsk and one of the oldest members of the Party, who in 1941 *i.e.,* at the beginning of the mass murder, wrote to his chief: "I certainly am tough and willing to co-operate in the solution of the Jewish question, but people who have been brought up in our culture are, after all, different from the local bestial hordes. Are we to assign the task of slaughtering them to the Lithuanians and Letts who are discriminated against even by the indigenous population? I could not do it. I ask you to give me clear-cut instructions to take care of the matter in the most humane way for the sake of the prestige of our Reich and our Party." This letter is published in Max Weinreich, *Hitler's Professors,* New York, 1946, pp. 153–154. Kube's intervention was quickly overruled, yet an almost identical attempt to save the lives of Danish Jews, made by W. Best, the Reich's plenipotentiary in Denmark, and a well-known Nazi, was more successful. See *Nazi Conspiracy,* V, 2.

Similarly Alfred Rosenberg, who had preached the inferiority of the Slav peoples, obviously never realized that his theories might one day mean their liquidation. Charged with the administration of the Ukraine, he wrote outraged reports about conditions there during the fall of 1942 after he had tried earlier to get direct intervention from Hitler himself. See *Nazi Conspiracy,* III, 83 ff., and IV, 62.

There are of course some exceptions to this rule. The man who saved Paris from destruction was General von Choltitz who, however, still "feared that he would be deprived of his command as he had not executed his orders" even though he knew that the "war

had been lost for several years." That he would have had the courage to resist the order "to turn Paris into a mass of ruins" without the energetic support of a Nazi of old standing, Otto Abetz, the Ambassador to France, appears dubious according to his own testimony during the trial of Abetz in Paris. See New York *Times,* July 21, 1949.

65. An Englishman, Stephen H. Roberts, *The House That Hitler Built,* London, 1939, describes Himmler as "a man of exquisite courtesy and still interested in the simple things of life. He has none of the pose of those Nazis who act as demigods. . . . No man looks less like his job than this police dictator of Germany, and I am convinced that nobody I met in Germany is more normal. . . ." (pp. 89–90)—This reminds one in a curious way of the remark of Stalin's mother, who according to Bolshevik propaganda said of him: "An exemplary son. I wish everybody were like him" (Souvarine, *op. cit.,* p. 656).

66. The remark was made by Robert Ley. See Kohn-Bramstedt, *op. cit.,* p. 178.

67. Bolshevik policy, in this respect surprisingly consistent, is well known and hardly needs further comment. Picasso, to take the most famous instance, is not liked in Russia even though he has become a Communist. It is possible that André Gide's sudden reversal of attitude after seeing the Bolshevik reality in Soviet Russia (*Retour de l'URSS*) in 1936, definitely convinced Stalin of the uselessness of creative artists even as fellow-travelers. Nazi policy was distinguished from Bolshevik measures only insofar as it did not yet kill its first-rate talents.

It would be worthwhile to study in detail the careers of those comparatively few German scholars who went beyond mere co-operation and volunteered their services because they were convinced Nazis. (Weinreich, *op. cit.,* the only available study, and misleading because he does not distinguish between professors who adopted the Nazi creed and those who owed their careers exclusively to the regime, omits the earlier careers of the concerned scholars and thus indiscriminately puts well-known men of great achievement into the same category as crackpots.) Most interesting is the example of the jurist Carl Schmitt, whose very ingenious theories about the end of democracy and legal government still make arresting reading; as early as the middle thirties, he was replaced by the Nazis' own brand of political and legal theorists, such as Hans Frank, the later governor of Poland, Gottfried Neesse, and Reinhard Hoehn. The last to fall into disgrace was the historian Walter Frank, who had been a convinced antisemite and member of the Nazi party before it came to power, and who, in 1933, became director of the newly founded Reichsinstitut für Geschichte des Neuen Deutschlands with its famous Forschungsabteilung Judenfrage, and editor of the nine-volume *Forschungen zur Judenfrage* (1937–1944). In the early forties, Frank had to cede his position and influence to the notorious Alfred Rosenberg, whose *Der Mythos des 20. Jahrhunderts* certainly shows no aspiration whatsoever to "scholarship." Frank clearly was mistrusted for no other reason than that he was not a charlatan.

# THE RISE OF TOTALITARIAN DEMOCRACY

## J. L. Talmon

This study is an attempt to show that concurrently with the liberal type of democracy there emerged from the same premises in the eighteenth century a trend towards what we propose to call the totalitarian type of democracy. These two currents have existed side by side ever since the eighteenth century. The tension between them has constituted an important chapter in modern history, and has now become the most vital issue of our time.

It would of course be an exaggeration to suggest that the whole of the period can be summed up in terms of this conflict. Nevertheless it was always present, although usually confused and obscured by other issues, which may have seemed clearer to contemporaries, but viewed from the standpoint of the present day seem incidental and even trivial. Indeed, from the vantage point of the mid-twentieth century the history of the last hundred and fifty years looks like a systematic preparation for the headlong collision between empirical and liberal democracy on the one hand, and totalitarian Messianic democracy on the other, in which the world crisis of to-day consists.

## 1. THE TWO TYPES OF DEMOCRACY, LIBERAL AND TOTALITARIAN

The essential difference between the two schools of democratic thought as they have evolved is not, as is often alleged, in the affirmation of the value of liberty by one, and its denial by the other. It is in their different attitudes to politics. The liberal approach assumes politics to be a matter of trial and error, and regards political systems as pragmatic contrivances of human ingenuity and spontaneity. It also recognizes a variety of levels of personal and collective endeavour, which are altogether outside the sphere of politics.

Reprinted by permission of the publishers from J. L. Talmon, *The Origins of Totalitarian Democracy* (New York: Beacon Press), pp. 1-11. British rights (London: Martin Secker & Warburg, Ltd.).

The totalitarian democratic school, on the other hand, is based upon the assumption of a sole and exclusive truth in politics. It may be called political Messianism in the sense that it postulates a preordained, harmonious and perfect scheme of things, to which men are irresistibly driven, and at which they are bound to arrive. It recognizes ultimately only one plane of existence, the political. It widens the scope of politics to embrace the whole of human existence. It treats all human thought and action as having social significance, and therefore as falling within the orbit of political action. Its political ideas are not a set of pragmatic precepts or a body of devices applicable to a special branch of human endeavour. They are an integral part of an all-embracing and coherent philosophy. Politics is defined as the art of applying this philosophy to the organization of society, and the final purpose of politics is only achieved when this philosophy reigns supreme over all fields of life.

Both schools affirm the supreme value of liberty. But whereas one finds the essence of freedom in spontaneity and the absence of coercion, the other believes it to be realized only in the pursuit and attainment of an absolute collective purpose. It is outside our scope to decide whether liberal democracy has the faith that totalitarian democracy claims to have in final aims. What is beyond dispute is that the final aims of liberal democracy have not the same concrete character. They are conceived in rather negative terms, and the use of force for their realization is considered as an evil. Liberal democrats believe that in the absence of coercion men and society may one day reach through a process of trial and error a state of ideal harmony. In the case of totalitarian democracy, this state is precisely defined, and is treated as a matter of immediate urgency, a challenge for direct action, an imminent event.

The problem that arises for totalitarian democracy, and which is one of the main subjects of this study, may be called the paradox of freedom. Is human freedom compatible with an exclusive pattern of social existence, even if this pattern aims at the maximum of social justice and security? The paradox of totalitarian democracy is in its insistence that they are compatible. The purpose it proclaims is never presented as an absolute idea, external and prior to man. It is thought to be immanent in man's reason and will, to constitute the fullest satisfaction of his true interest, and to be the guarantee of his freedom. This is the reason why the extreme forms of popular sovereignty became the essential concomitant of this absolute purpose. From the difficulty of reconciling freedom with the idea of an absolute purpose spring all the particular problems and antinomies of totalitarian democracy. This difficulty could only be resolved by thinking not in terms of men as they are, but as they were meant to be, and would be, given the proper conditions. In so far as they are at variance with the absolute ideal they can be ignored, coerced or intimidated into conforming, without any real violation of the democratic principle being involved. In the proper conditions, it is held, the conflict between spontaneity and duty would disappear, and with it the need for coercion. The practical question is, of course, whether constraint will disappear because all have learned to act in harmony, or because all opponents have been eliminated.

## 2. THE EIGHTEENTH-CENTURY ORIGINS OF POLITICAL MESSIANISM: THE SCHISM

Enough has been said already to indicate that totalitarian democracy will be treated in these pages as an integral part of the Western tradition. It is vital to add that much of the totalitarian democratic attitude was contained in the original and general eighteenth-century pattern of thought. The branching out of the two types of democracy from the common stem took place only after the common beliefs had been tested in the ordeal of the French Revolution.

From the point of view of this study the most important change that occurred in the eighteenth century was the peculiar state of mind which achieved dominance in the second part of the century. Men were gripped by the idea that the conditions, a product of faith, time and custom, in which they and their forefathers had been living, were unnatural and had all to be replaced by deliberately planned uniform patterns, which would be natural and rational.

This was the result of the decline of the traditional order in Europe: religion lost its intellectual as well as its emotional hold; hierarchical feudalism disintegrated under the impact of social and economic factors; and the older conception of society based on status came to be replaced by the idea of the abstract, individual man.

The rationalist idea substituted social utility for tradition as the main criterion of social institutions and values. It also suggested a form of social determinism, to which men are irresistibly driven, and which they are bound to accept one day. It thus postulated a single valid system, which would come into existence when everything not accounted for by reason and utility had been removed. This idea was, of course, bound to clash with the inveterate irrationality of man's ways, his likings and attachments.

The decline of religious authority implied the liberation of man's conscience, but it also implied something else. Religious ethics had to be speedily replaced by secular, social morality. With the rejection of the Church, and of transcendental justice, the State remained the sole source and sanction of morality. This was a matter of great importance, at a time when politics were considered indistinguishable from ethics.

The decline of the idea of status consequent on the rise of individualism spelt the doom of privilege, but also contained totalitarian potentialities. If, as will be argued in this essay, empiricisim is the ally of freedom, and the doctrinaire spirit is the friend of totalitarianism, the idea of man as an abstraction, independent of the historic groups to which he belongs, is likely to become a powerful vehicle of totalitarianism.

These three currents merged into the idea of a homogeneous society, in which men live upon one exclusive plane of existence. There were no longer to be different levels of social life, such as the temporal and the transcendental, or membership of a class and citizenship. The only recognized standard of judgment was to be social utility, as expressed in the idea of the general good, which was spoken of as if it were a visible and tangible objective. The whole of virtue was summed up as conformity to the rationalist, natural pattern. In the past it was possible for the State to regard many things as matters for God and the Church alone. The new State could recognize no such limitations. Formerly, men lived in groups. A man had to belong to some group, and could belong to several at the same time. Now there was to be only one framework for all activity: the nation. The eighteenth century never distinguished clearly between the sphere of personal self-expression and that of social action. The privacy of creative experience and feeling, which is the salt of freedom, was in due course to be swamped by the pressure of the permanently assembled people, vibrating with one collective emotion. The fact that eighteenth-century thinkers were ardent prophets of liberty and the rights of man is so much taken for granted that it scarcely needs to be mentioned. But what must be emphasized is the intense preoccupation of the eighteenth century with the idea of virtue, which was nothing if not conformity to the hoped-for pattern of social harmony. They refused to envisage the conflict between liberty and virtue as inevitable. On the contrary, the inevitable equation of liberty with virtue and reason was the most cherished article of their faith. When the eighteenth-century secular religion came face to face with this conflict, the result was the great schism. Liberal democracy flinched from the spectre of force, and fell back upon the trial-and-error philosophy. Totalitarian Messianism hardened into an exclusive doctrine represented by a vanguard of the enlightened, who justified themselves in the use of coercion against those who refused to be free and virtuous.

The other cause for this fissure, certainly no less important, was the question of property. The original impulse of political Messianism was not economic, but ethical and political. However radical in their theoretical premises, most eighteenth-century thinkers shrunk from applying the principle of total renovation to the sphere of economics and property. It was however extremely difficult to theorize about a rational harmonious social order, with contradictions resolved, anti-social impulses checked, and man's desire for happiness satisfied, while leaving the field of economic endeavour to be dominated by established facts and interests, man's acquisitive spirit and chance. Eighteenth-century thinkers became thus involved in grave inconsistencies, which they attempted to cover with all kinds of devices. The most remarkable of these certainly was the Physiocratic combination of absolutism in politics with the laissez-faire theory in economics, which claimed that the free, unhampered economic pursuits of men would set themselves into a harmonious pattern, in accordance with the laws of demand and supply. But before the eighteenth century had come to an end, the inner logic of political Messianism, precipitated by the Revolutionary upheaval, its hopes, its lessons and its disappointments, converted the secular religion of the eighteenth century from a mainly ethical into a social and economic doctrine, based on ethical premises. The postulate of salvation, implied in the idea of the natural order, came to signify to the masses stirred by the Revolution a message of social salvation before all. And so the objective ideal of social harmony gave place to the yearnings and strivings of a class; the principle of virtuous liberty to the passion for security. The possessing classes, surprised and frightened by the social dynamism of the idea of the natural order, hastened to shake off the philosophy which they had earlier so eagerly embraced as a weapon in their struggle against feudal privilege. The Fourth Estate seized it from their hands, and filled it with new meaning. And so the ideology of the rising bourgeoisie was transformed into that of the proletariat.

The object of this book is to examine the stages through which the social ideals of the eighteenth century were transformed—on one side—into totalitarian democracy. These stages are taken to be three: the eighteenth-century postulate, the Jacobin improvisation, and the Babouvist crystallization; all leading up to the emergence of economic communism on the one hand, and to the synthesis of popular sovereignty and single-party dictatorship on the other. The three stages constitute the three parts into which this study is divided. The evolution of the liberal type of democracy is outside its scope.

Modern totalitarian democracy is a dictatorship resting on popular enthusiasm, and is thus completely different from absolute power wielded by a divine-right King, or by a usurping tyrant. In so far as it is a dictatorship based on ideology and the enthusiasm of the masses, it is the outcome, as will be shown, of the synthesis between the eighteenth-century idea of the natural order and the Rousseauist idea of popular fulfilment and self-expression. By means of this synthesis rationalism was made into a passionate faith. Rousseau's "general will," an ambiguous concept, sometimes conceived as valid *a priori,* sometimes as immanent in the will of man, exclusive and implying unanimity, became the driving force of totalitarian democracy, and the source of all its contradictions and antinomies. These are to be examined in detail.

## 3. TOTALITARIANISM OF THE RIGHT AND TOTALITARIANISM OF THE LEFT

The emphasis of this theory is always upon Man. And here is the distinguishing mark between totalitarianism of the Left, with which this study is concerned, and totalitarianism of the Right. While the starting-point of totalitarianism of the Left has been and ultimately still is man, his reason and salvation, that of the Right totalitarian schools has been the collective entity, the State, the nation, or the race. The former trend remains essentially individualist, atomistic and rationalist even when it raises the class or party to the level of absolute ends. These are, after all, only mechanically formed groups. Totalitarians of the Right operate solely with historic, racial and organic entities, concepts altogether alien to individualism and rationalism. That is why totalitarian ideologies of the Left always are inclined to assume the character of a universal creed, a tendency which totalitarianism of the Right altogether lacks. For reason is a unifying force, presupposing mankind to be the sum total of individual reasoning beings. Totalitarianism of the Right implies the negation of such a unity as well as a denial of the universality of human values. It represents a special form of pragmatism. Without raising the question of the absolute significance of the professed tenets, it aspires to a mode of existence, in which the faculties of man may—in a deliberately limited circumference of space, time and numbers—be stirred, asserted and realized so as to enable him to have what is nowadays called a wholly satisfying experience in a collective *élan,* quickened by mass emotion and the impact of impressive exploits; in brief, the myth.

The second vital difference between the two types of totalitarianism is to be found in their divergent conceptions of human nature. The Left proclaims the essential goodness and perfectibility of human nature. The Right declares man to be weak and corrupt. Both may preach the necessity of coercion. The Right teaches the necessity of force as a permanent way of maintaining order among poor and unruly creatures, and training them to act in a manner alien to their mediocre nature. Totalitarianism of the Left, when resorting to force, does so in the conviction that force is used only in order to quicken the pace of man's progress to perfection and social harmony. It is thus legitimate to use the term democracy in reference to totalitarianism of the Left. The term could not be applied to totalitarianism of the Right.

It may be said that these are distinctions that make little difference, especially where results are concerned. It may further be maintained that whatever their original premises were, totalitarian parties and régimes of the Left have invariably tended to degenerate into soulless power machines, whose lip service to the original tenets is mere hypocrisy. Now, this is a question not only of academic interest, but of much practical importance. Even if we accept this diagnosis of the nature of Left totalitarianism when triumphant, are we to attribute its degeneration to the inevitable process of corrosion which an idea undergoes when power falls into the hands of its adherents? Or should we seek the reason for it deeper, namely in the very essence of the contradiction between ideological absolutism and individualism, inherent in modern political Messianism? When the deeds of men in power belie their words, are they to be called hypocrites and cynics or are they victims of an intellectual delusion?

Here is one of the questions to be investigated. This essay is not concerned with the problem of power as such, only with that of power in relation to consciousness. The objective forces favouring the concentration of power and the subordination of the individual to a power machine, such as modern methods of production and the *arcana imperii* offered by modern technical developments, are outside the scope of this work. The political tactics of totalitarian parties and systems, or the blueprints of social positivist philosophies for the human hive, will be considered not for their own sake, but in their bearing on man's awareness and beliefs. What is vital for the present investigation is the human element: the thrill of fulfilment experienced by the

believers in a modern Messianic movement, which makes them experience submission as deliverance; the process that goes on in the minds of the leaders, whether in soliloquy or in public discussion, when faced with the question of whether their acts are the self-expression of the Cause or their own wilful deeds; the stubborn faith that as a result of proper social arrangements and education, the conflict between spontaneity and the objective pattern will ultimately be resolved by the acceptance of the latter, without any sense of coercion.

## 4. SECULAR AND RELIGIOUS MESSIANISM

The modern secular religion of totalitarian democracy has had unbroken continuity as a sociological force for over a hundred and fifty years. Both aspects, its continuity and its character as a sociological force, need stressing. These two essential features permit us to ignore the isolated literary ventures into Utopia in the earlier centuries, without denying the influence of Plato, Thomas More, or Campanella upon men like Rousseau, Diderot, Mably, or Saint-Just and Buonarroti. If one were in search of antecedents, one would also have to turn to the various outbursts of chiliasm in the Middle Ages and in the Reformation, especially to the extreme wing of the Puritan Revolution in seventeenth-century England. The coexistence of liberal democracy and revolutionary Messianism in modern times could legitimately be compared to the relationship between the official Church and the eschatological revolutionary current in Christianity during the ages of faith. Always flowing beneath the surface of official society, the Christian revolutionary current burst forth from time to time in the form of movements of evangelical poverty, heretical sects, and social-religious revolts. Like the two major trends of the modern era, the Church and the rebels against it derived their ideas from the same source. The heterodox groups were, however, too ardent in their literal interpretation of God's word. They refused to come to terms with the flesh and the kingdom of this world, and were unwilling to confine the ideal of a society of saints to the exclusively transcendental plane.

There were, however, vital differences between the chiliastic movements of the earlier centuries and modern political Messianism. The former were only sporadic occurrences, although the tension from which they sprang was always latent. A flame burst forth and was soon totally extinguished, or rendered harmless to society at large. The crisis might leave behind a sect. The myth might survive and perhaps rekindle a spark in some remote place and at some later date. Society as a whole went on much as before, although not quite free from the fear and mental discomfort left by the conflagration, and not wholly immune to the influence of the new sect.

There was however a fundamental principle in pre-eighteenth-century chiliasm that made it impossible for it to play the part of modern political Messianism. It was its religious essence. This explains why the Messianic movements or spasms of the earlier type invariably ended by breaking away from society, and forming sects based upon voluntary adherence and community of experience. Modern Messianism has always aimed at a revolution in society as a whole. The driving power of the sects was the Word of God, and the hope of achieving salvation by facing God alone and directly, without the aid of intermediary powers or submission to them, whether spiritual or temporal, and yet as part of a society of equal saints. This ideal is not unlike the modern expectation of a society of men absolutely free and equal, and yet acting in spontaneous and perfect accord. In spite of this superficial similarity, the differences between the two attitudes are fundamental. Although the Christian revolutionaries fought for the individual's freedom to interpret God's word, their sovereign was not man, but God. They aimed at personal salvation and an egalitarian society based on the Law of Nature, because they had it from God that there lies salvation, and believed that obedience to God is the condition of human freedom. The point of reference of modern Messianism, on the other hand, is man's reason and will, and its aim happiness on earth, achieved by a social transformation. The point of reference is temporal, but the claims are absolute. It is thus a remarkable fact that the Christian revolutionaries, with few exceptions, notably Calvin's Geneva and Anabaptist Münster, shrunk from the use of force to impose their own pattern, in spite of their belief in its divine source and authority, while secular Messianism, starting with a point of reference in time, has developed a fanatical resolve to make its doctrine rule absolutely and everywhere. The reasons are not far to seek.

Even if the Monistic principle of religious Messianism had succeeded in dominating and reshaping society the result would still have been fundamentally different from the situation created by modern political "absolutism." Society might have been forbidden the compromises which are made possible by the Orthodox distinction between the kingdom of God and the earthly State, and as a consequence social and political arrangements might have lost much of their flexibility. The sweep towards the enforcement of an exclusive pattern would nevertheless have been hampered, if not by the thought of the fallibility of man, at least by the consciousness that life on earth is not a closed circle, but has its continuation and conclusion in eternity. Secular Messianic Monism is subject to no such restraints. It demands that the whole account be settled here and now.

The extreme wing of English Puritanism at the time of the Cromwellian Revolution still bore the full imprint of religious eschatology. It had already acquired modern features however. It combined extreme individualism with social radicalism and a totalitarian temperament. Nevertheless this movement, far from initiating the continuous current of modern political Messianism, remained from the European point of view an isolated episode. It was apparently quite unknown to the early representatives of the movement under discussion. While eighteenth-century French thinkers and revolutionary leaders were alive to the political lessons of the "official" Cromwellian Revolution as a deterrent against military dictatorship, and a writer like Harrington was respected as a master, it is doubtful whether the more radical aspects of the English evolution were much known or exercised any influence in France before the nineteenth century. The strongest influence on the fathers of totalitarian democracy was that of antiquity, interpreted in their own way. Their myth of antiquity was the image of liberty equated with virtue. The citizen of Sparta or Rome was proudly free, yet a marvel of ascetic discipline. He was an equal member of the sovereign nation, and at the same time had no life or interests outside the collective tissue.

## 5. QUESTIONS OF METHOD

Objections may be urged against the view that political Messianism as a postulate preceded the compact set of social and economic ideas with which it has come to be associated. It may be said that it is wrong to treat Messianism as a substance that can be divorced from its attributes; to consider it altogether apart from the events which produced it, the instruments which have been used to promote it, and the concrete aims and policies of the men who represented it at any given moment. Such a procedure, it may be said, presupposes an almost mystical agency active in history. It is important to answer this objection not less for its philosophical significance than for the question of method it raises.

What this study is concerned with is a state of mind, a way of feeling, a disposition, a pattern of mental, emotional and behaviouristic elements, best compared to the set of attitudes engendered by a religion. Whatever may be said about the significance of the economic or other factors in the shaping of beliefs, it can hardly be denied that the all-embracing attitudes of this kind, once crystallized, are the real substance of history. The concrete elements of history, the acts of politicians, the aspirations of people, the ideas, values, preferences and prejudices of an age, are the outward manifestations of its religion in the widest sense.

# TOTALITARIAN DICTATORSHIP AND AUTOCRACY

## Carl J. Friedrich and Zbigniew K. Brzezinski

### THE GENERAL CHARACTERISTICS OF TOTALITARIAN DICTATORSHIP

Everybody talks about totalitarian dictatorships and about totalitarianism. They are said to be tyrannies, despotisms, absolutisms. And yet, the greatest uncertainty surrounds the most elementary aspects of this form of government. One flatters it, actually, when one calls a dictatorship of this kind a tyranny or a despotism. The autocratic regimes of the past were not nearly as ghastly as the totalitarian dictatorships of our time. Yet, one also maligns totalitarian dictatorship by these descriptions, for, whereas tyranny was conducted, according to the definition of Aristotle, for the benefit of the tyrant, it is not very realistic to make that kind of egoism the basis of an interpretation of totalitarian dictatorship.

The truth of the matter seems to be that totalitarian dictatorship is a logical extension of certain traits of our modern industrial society (oftentimes called "capitalism"). It is our purpose to trace the main aspects of this novel kind of government and thereby lay out the pattern for the later more detailed treatment. We also propose to indicate by way of contrast how and why totalitarian dictatorships differ from autocracies of the past. Though actually neither a tyranny nor a despotism, totalitarian dictatorship is apparently linked to both in certain important ways, or at least there are significant similarities which justify putting all of these regimes into one common category. This category might properly be suggested to be that of "autocracy."

There have been many types of autocracy in the history of government. The several forms of

despotism, often associated with the deification of the ruler characteristic of the Orient, the tyranny of the Greek cities and their replicas in Renaissance Italy, and the absolutist monarchies of modern Europe, are among the more familiar patterns of autocracy. In all these systems, the truly distinguishing feature is that the ruler is not responsible to anyone else for what he does; he is the *autos,* who himself wields power; that is to say, he makes the decisions and reaps the fruits of them. The logical opposite of autocracy, therefore, would be any rule in which another, an *heteros,* shared the power through the fact that the ruler is responsible to him or them. In the modern West, it has become customary to speak of such systems as responsible or constitutional governments.[1] Among these, constitutional democracy has become the predominant type, though there have been constitutional monarchies, aristocracies, and theocracies in the past.

Since any pattern of responsibility must be expressed in rules of some kind, which together constitute the "constitution," and, as rules are properly speaking a kind of legal norm, it has been customary since Plato and Aristotle to stress the role of law and to distinguish political systems according to whether or not they are characterized by the subordination of the political rulers to law. From this viewpoint, an autocracy is any political system in which the rulers are insufficiently, or not at all, subject to antecedent and enforceable rules of law—enforceable, that is, by other authorities who share the government and who have sufficient power to compel the law-breaking rulers to submit to the law.

This problem of the control of the rulers by the law must be distinguished from the problem of the role of law in a given society. All human societies, communities, and groups of any sort have some kind of law, and the totalitarian dictatorships of our time are characterized by a vast amount of "legislation," necessitated by the requirements of a technically industrialized economy and of the masses of dependent operators involved in such a society.[2] Similarly the Roman empire saw an increase, not a decline, in the detailed complexity of its legal system during the very period when it was becoming more and more autocratic. This autocracy eventually reached the point of deifying the emperor, while the detailed development of the legal system continued. Long before this time, all enforceable control of the ruler had vanished and the responsibility of which the Republic had been so proud had completely disappeared. The will of the emperor was the ultimate source of all law. This conception was expressed in a number of celebrated phrases which eventually became the basis of the doctrine of sovereignty that provided the rationalization for the autocracy of absolute monarchs in the seventeenth century.

Autocratic legalism, however, must not be confused with the totalitarian distortion of the notion of law in what is spoken of as the "laws of movement." These are presumably "laws of nature" or "laws of history" (but history understood as a part of nature); they contain an existential, rather than a normative, judgment. The interrelation of existential and normative law has been a central problem in the long history of the law of nature.[3] The totalitarian ideology tends to dissolve the normative in the existential realm, and to consider all ordinary laws merely as expressions of laws of nature and history. "All history is the history of class struggles," for example, would be such a law in terms of which the positive legal order must be structured; it provides the standard by which to measure positive laws, to interpret and if necessary to alter and break them. All laws become fluid when they are treated merely as the emanation of such laws of movement, and their very multiplicity testifies to their normative weakness.[4] Such fluidity makes them incapable of serving as standards of responsible conduct, since every violation can be argued away by the rulers as merely an adaptation to the higher laws of movement. A similar difficulty attached to the law of nature when it was to serve as a restraint upon absolute rulers, who in the past were allowed to contravene it in case "reason of state" required it.

Thus, as far as this characteristic absence of responsibility is concerned, totalitarian dictatorship resembles earlier forms of autocracy. But it is our contention in this volume that totalitarian dictatorship is historically unique and *sui generis*. It is also our conclusion from all the facts available to us that fascist and communist totalitarian dictatorships are basically alike, or at any rate more nearly like each other than like any other system of government, including earlier forms of autocracy. These two theses are closely linked and must be examined together. They are also linked to a third, that totalitarian dictatorship as it actually developed was not intended by those who created it—Mussolini talked of it, but meant something different—but

resulted from the political situations in which the anticonstitutionalist and antidemocratic revolutionary movements and their leaders found themselves. Let us take the third of these points first, treating the second and first afterward.

The fascist and communist systems evolved in response to a series of unprecedented crises, and they have shown a continuous, though intermittent, tendency to become more "totalitarian." There is no present reason to conclude that the existing totalitarian systems will disappear as a result of internal evolution, though this possibility cannot be excluded. The two totalitarian governments which have perished thus far have perished as the result of wars in which they had become involved with outside powers, but this does not mean that the Soviet Union necessarily will. We do not presuppose that totalitarian societies are fixed and static entities, but, on the contrary, that they have undergone and continue to undergo a steady evolution, presumably involving both growth and deterioration.

In terms of historical perspective, three points might be added. First, certain autocracies in the past have shown extraordinary capacity for survival. Not only the Roman but also several Oriental empires lasted for hundreds of years, at least as systems they did, though the dynasties changed.[5] By contrast, the tyrannies of the Greek city states were usually short-lived, as Aristotle noted. Second, such autocracies have as a rule perished in consequence of foreign invasions. Third, their autocratic features have usually been intensified over long periods, the reason being that violence is readily available for dealing with the tensions and breakdowns that occur. In short, some of these autocracies were not stable, but lasting.

To the uncertainties about the end correspond the controversies about the beginning of totalitarian dictatorship. The debate about the causes or origins of totalitarianism has run all the way from a primitive bad-man theory[6] to the "moral crisis of our time" kind of argument. A detailed inspection of the available evidence suggests that virtually every one of the factors which has been offered by itself as an explanation of the origin of totalitarian dictatorship has played its role. For example, in the case of Germany—Hitler's moral and personal defects, weaknesses in the German constitutional tradition, certain traits involved in the German "national character," the Versailles Treaty and its aftermath, the economic crisis and the "contradictions" of an aging capitalism, the "threat" of communism, the decline of Christianity and of such other spiritual moorings as the belief in the reason and the reasonableness of man—all have played a role in the total configuration of factors contributing to the over-all result. As in the case of other broad developments in history, only a multiple-factor analysis will do. But at the present time, we cannot fully explain the rise of totalitarian dictatorship. All we can do is to explain it partially by identifying some of the antecedent and concomitant conditions. Broadly speaking, totalitarian dictatorship is a new development; there has never been anything quite like it before.

Now concerning the second point, it is very important to explain somewhat at the outset why the totalitarian dictatorships, communist and fascist, are *basically alike*. What does this mean? In the first place, it means that they are *not wholly alike*. Popular and journalistic interpretation has oscillated between two extremes; some have said that the communist and fascist dictatorships are wholly alike, others that they are not at all alike. The latter view was the prevailing one during the popular-front days in Europe as well as in "liberal" circles in the United States. It was even more popular during the Second World War, especially among Allied propagandists. Besides, it was and is the official Soviet and Hitler party line. It is only natural that these regimes, conceiving of themselves as bitter enemies, dedicated to the task of liquidating each other, should take the view that they have nothing in common. This happened before in history. When the Protestants and Catholics were fighting each other during the religious wars of the sixteenth and seventeenth centuries, they very commonly denied to each other the name of "Christians," and argued about each other that they were not "true churches." Actually, and from the viewpoint of the sectarians whom they both persecuted, they were indeed that.

The other view, that communist and fascist dictatorships are wholly alike, is presently favored in the United States and in Western Europe to an increasing extent. Yet they are obviously not wholly alike. For example, they differ in their proclaimed purposes and intentions. Everyone knows that the communists say they seek the world revolution of the proletariat, while the fascists proclaimed their determination to establish the world dominance of a particular nation or people, or at least their imperial predominance in a region, as in the case of the Italian Fascists. The communist and fascist dictatorships differ also in their historical antecedents: the fascist movements have arisen in reaction to the communist challenge and have offered themselves to a frightened middle class as the saviors from the communist danger. As we shall have occasion to show in the chapters which follow, there are many other differences which do not allow us to speak of the communist and fascist totalitarian dictatorships as wholly alike, but which suggest that they are sufficiently alike to class them together and contrast them not only with constitutional systems, but also with former types of autocracy.

Before we turn to these common features, however, there is another difference which used to be emphasized by many who wanted "to do business with Hitler" or who admired Mussolini and therefore argued that, far from being wholly like the communist dictatorship, the fascist regimes must really be seen as merely authoritarian forms of constitutional systems. It is indeed true that more of the institutions of the preceding liberal and constitutional society survived in the Italian Fascist than in the Russian Communist society. But this is due in part to the fact that no liberal, constitutional society preceded Soviet Communism. The promising period of the Duma came to naught as a result of the war and the disintegration of tsarism, while the Kerensky interlude was far too brief and to superficial to become meaningful for the future. In Czechoslovakia and in the Soviet Zone of Germany (German Democratic Republic) we find precisely such institutions. as universities, churches, and schools surviving. It is likely that, were a communist dictatorship to be established in Great Britain or France, the situation would be similar, and that here even more such institutions of the liberal era would continue to operate for a considerable initial period at least. Precisely this argument has been advanced by such British radicals as Sidney and Beatrice Webb. The tendency of isolated fragments of the preceding state of society to survive has been a significant source of misinterpretation of the fascist totalitarian society, especially in the case of Italy. In the twenties, Italian totalitarianism was very commonly misinterpreted as being "merely" an authoritarian form of middle class rule, with the trains running on time, and the beggars off the street.[7] In the case of Germany, this sort of misinterpretation took a slightly different form. In the thirties, various authors tried to interpret German totalitarianism as either "the end phase of capitalism" or as "militarist imperialism."[8] These interpretations stress the continuance of a "capitalist" economy whose leaders are represented as dominating the regime. The facts as we know them do not correspond to this view. For one who sympathized with socialism or communism it was very tempting to try and depict the totalitarian dictatorship of Hitler as nothing but a capitalist society and therefore totally at variance with the "new civilization" that was arising in the Soviet Union. These few remarks have suggested, it is hoped, why it may be wrong to consider the totalitarian dictatorships under discussion as either wholly alike or basically different. Why they are basically alike remains to be shown, and to this key argument we now turn.

The basic features or traits which we suggest as generally recognized to be common to totalitarian dictatorships are six in number. The "syndrome," or pattern of interrelated traits, of the totalitarian dictatorship consists of an ideology, a single party typically led by one man, a terroristic police, a communications monopoly, a weapons monopoly, and a centrally directed economy. Of these, the last two are also found in constitutional systems: Socialist Britain had a centrally directed economy, and all modern states possess a weapons monopoly.

Whether these latter suggest a "trend" toward totalitarianism is a question which will be discussed in the last chapter [of *Totalitarian Dictatorship and Autocracy*].

These six basic features, which we think constitute the character of totalitarian dictatorship, form a cluster of interrelated traits, intertwined and mutually supporting each other, as usual in "organic" systems.[9] They should therefore not be considered in isolation or be made the focal point of comparisons, such as "Caesar developed a terroristic secret police, therefore he was the first totalitarian dictator," or "the Catholic Church has practised ideological thought control, therefore. . . ."

The totalitarian dictatorships all possess the following:

1. An official ideology, consisting of an official body of doctrine covering all vital aspects of man's existence to which everyone living in that society is supposed to adhere, at least passively; this ideology is characteristically focused and projected toward a perfect final state of mankind, that is to say, it contains a chiliastic claim, based upon a radical rejection of the existing society and conquest of the world for the new one.

2. A single mass party led typically by one man, the "dictator," and consisting of a relatively small percentage of the total population (up to 10 per cent) of men and women, a hard core of them passionately and unquestioningly dedicated to the ideology and prepared to assist in every way in promoting its general acceptance, such a party being hierarchically, oligarchically organized, and typically either superior to, or completely intertwined with the bureaucratic government organization.

3. A system of terroristic police control, supporting but also supervising the party for its leaders, and characteristically directed not only against demonstrable "enemies" of the regime, but against arbitrarily selected classes of the population; the terror of the secret policy systematically exploiting modern science, and more especially scientific psychology.

4. A technologically conditioned near-complete monopoly of control, in the hands of the party and its subservient cadres, of all means of effective mass communication, such as the press, radio, motion pictures.

5. A similarly technologically conditioned near-complete monopoly of control (in the same hands) of all means of effective armed combat.

6. A central control and direction of the entire economy through the bureaucratic co-ordination of its formerly independent corporate entities, typically including most other associations and group activities.

The enumeration of these six traits or trait clusters is not meant to suggest that there might not be others, now insufficiently recognized, but that these are universally acknowledged to be the features of totalitarian dictatorship to which the writings of students of the most varied backgrounds, including totalitarian writers, bear witness.

Within this broad pattern of similarities, there are many significant variations to which the analysis of this book will give detailed attention. To offer a few random illustrations, at present the party zealots play less of a role in the Soviet Union than the party bureaucrats, as contrasted with an earlier stage; the ideology of the Soviet Union is more specifically committed to certain assumptions, because of its Marx-Engels bible, than that of Italian or German fascism, where ideology was formulated by the leader of the party himself; the corporate entities of the fascist economy remained in private hands, as far as property claims are concerned, whereas they become public property in the Soviet Union.

Let us now turn to our first point, namely, that these systems are historically "unique"; that is to say, that no government like totalitarian dictatorship has ever before existed, even though it bears a resemblance to autocracies of the past. It may be interesting to consider briefly some data which show that the six traits we have just identified are to a large extent lacking in historically known autocratic regimes.[10] Neither the Oriental despotisms of the more remote past, nor the absolute monarchies of modern Europe, neither the tyrannies of the ancient Greek cities, nor the Roman Empire, nor yet the tyrannies of the city states of the Italian Renaissance and the Bonapartist military dictatorships of the last century exhibit this design, this combination of features, though they may possess one or another of its constituent traits. For example, efforts have often been made to organize some kind of secret police, but they have not been even horse-and-buggy affairs compared with the terror of the Gestapo or of the OGPU (MVD today). Similarly, there have been both military and propagandistic concentrations of power and control, but the limits of technology prevented any thoroughgoing development along totalitarian lines. It is very evident, we trust, that the six distinctive features here sketched, and to be developed in what follows, sharply differentiate contemporary totalitarian dictatorships from past autocratic regimes. Certainly neither the Roman emperor nor the absolute monarch sought or needed a party to support him nor an ideology in the modern party sense, and the same is obviously true of oriental despots. The tyrants of Greece and Italy may have had a party—that of the Medicis in Florence was called *lo stato*—but they had no ideology to speak of. And, of course, all of these autocratic regimes were far removed from the very distinctive features which are rooted in modern technology, from the terror to the centrally directed economy.

Something more should perhaps be added on the subject of technology. This technological aspect of totalitarianism is, of course, particularly striking in the matter of weapons and communications, but it is involved also in the secret police terror, depending as it does upon technically enhanced possibilities of supervision and control of the movement of persons. In addition, the centrally directed economy presupposes the reporting, cataloging, and calculating devices provided by modern technology. In short, four of the six traits are technologically conditioned. To envisage what this technological advance means in terms of political control, one has to think only of the weapons field. The Constitution of the United States guarantees to every citizen the "right to bear arms" (Fourth Amendment). In the days of the minutemen, this was a very important right, and the freedom of the citizen was indeed symbolized by the gun over the hearth, as it is in Switzerland to this day. But who can "bear" such arms as a tank, a bomber, or a flame-thrower, let alone an atom bomb? The citizen as an individual, and indeed in larger groups, is simply defenseless against the overwhelming technological superiority of those who can centralize in their hands the means with which to wield these modern arms and thereby physically to coerce the mass of the citizenry. Similar observations are easy to make regarding the press, the radio, and so forth. "Freedom" does not have the same potential, resting as it did upon individual effort, which it had a hundred and fifty years ago. With few exceptions, the trend of technological advance implies the trend toward greater and greater size of organization. In the perspective of these four traits, therefore, totalitarian societies appear to be merely exaggerations, but nonetheless logical exaggerations, of the technological state of modern society.

The same cannot be said with respect to the first two distinctive features of totalitarian dictatorships, for neither ideology nor party have any significant relation to the state of technology. (This may not be strictly true, since the mass conversion continually attempted by totalitarian propaganda through its effective use of the communications monopoly could not be carried through without it.) However, the party, its leader(s), and the ideology link the totalitarian dictatorship to modern democracy. It is the perversion of democracy. Not only did Hitler, Mussolini, and Lenin build typical parties within a constitutional, if not a democratic, context but the connection is plain between the stress on ideology and the role which platforms and other types of ideological goal-formation play in democratic parties. To be sure, totalitarian parties developed a pronounced authoritarian pattern while organizing themselves into effective revolutionary instruments of action; but, at the same time, its leaders, beginning with Marx and Engels, saw themselves as constituting the vanguard of the democratic movement of their day, and Stalin always talked of the Soviet totalitarian society as the "perfect democ-

racy"; Hitler and Mussolini[11] made similar statements. Both the world brotherhood of the proletariat and the folk community were conceived of as supplanting the class divisions of past societies by a complete harmony—the classless society of the socialist tradition.

Not only the party but also its ideology harkens back to the democratic context within which the totalitarian movements arose. Ideology, generally, but more especially totalitarian ideology, involves a high degree of convictional certainty. As has been indicated, totalitarian ideology consists of an official doctrine which radically rejects the pre-existing society in terms of a chiliastic proposal for a new one. As such it contains strongly utopian elements, some kind of notion of a paradise on earth. This utopian and chiliastic outlook of totalitarian ideologies gives them a pseudoreligious quality. In fact, they often elicit in the less critical followers a depth of conviction and a fervor of devotion usually found only among persons inspired by a transcendent faith. Whether these aspects of totalitarian ideologies bear some sort of relationship to the religions which they seek to replace is arguable. Marx denounced religion as "the opium of the people." It would seem that this is rather an appropriate way of describing totalitarian ideologies. In place of the more or less sane platforms of regular political parties, critical of the existing state of affairs in a limited way, totalitarian ideologies are perversions of such programs. They substitute faith for reason, magic exhortation for scientific knowledge. And yet, it must be recognized that there is enough of these same elements in the operations of democratic parties to attest to the relation between them and their perverted decendants, the totalitarian movements. That is why these movements must be seen and analyzed in their relationship to the democracy which they seek to supplant.

In summary, these regimes could have arisen only within the context of mass democracy and modern technology. In a conclusion we propose to consider the problem of stages of totalitarian development and to consider the possibility of projecting such developmental models into the future.

## THE STAGES OF DEVELOPMENT
## AND THE FUTURE
## OF TOTALITARIAN DICTATORSHIP

In much of the foregoing discussion, there have been some implicit notions about the stages or phases of totalitarian development. From time to time, explicit statements have been made regarding them. At the very outset, we suggested that totalitarian dictatorship does not come into existence by a "seizure of power," as is assumed in so much of the literature regarding the subject. What is seized is the control of the existing government, customarily referred to as the state, and a dictatorship is set up in order to realize the totalitarian ideology of the party movement which has "seized the power." But the total transformation of the existing society that this ideology calls for quickly runs into numerous and formidable obstacles. The series of critical situations thus created give rise to the swift enlargement of power, and the totalitarian radicalization of the means of control; in the course of this process the totalitarian dictatorship comes into being.

In view of this gradual emergence of the totalitarian features of these dictatorships, it is evident that these totalitarian systems were not the result of intentional action.[12] True, the total character of the ideology led to a dim appreciation of the difficulties, and a corresponding ideological acceptance of force and violence. The acceptance of violence also carried with it the acceptance of fraud, and more especially propagandistic fraud on a large scale, as a more special form of violence, namely, that done to mind and sentiment. But force, fraud, and violence have always been features of organized government, and they do not constitute by themselves the distinctive totalitarian operation. This operation we have defined in terms of a syndrome of interrelated traits or model features, the emergence of which signalizes the consummation of the totalitarian evolution. It is easy to identify these features, once they have come into full play: Italy, Germany, Russia—they all had emerged by about 1936 as totalitarian dictatorships; China and a considerable number of satellites have followed suit in the years since the Second World War. All these exhibit the six traits we have identified as characteristic: a total ideology, a single mass party, a terroristic secret police, a monopoly of mass communication, a monopoly of weapons, and a centrally directed planned economy.

The collapse of two of these totalitarian dictatorships occurred as a result of war and foreign invasion. If we study these wars, we find that they were the natural consequence of the ideologies of these particular dictatorships. Demonstrably, the ideologies themselves, with their glorification of violence, were at least in part responsible for the grave errors in judgment which launched the leadership into their belligerency. Other difficulties contributed to the defeat; some of these are once again definitely traceable to ideological and other defects of these regimes. More particularly the concentration of all power in a single man's hands, when combined with the absence of any sort of continuing critical evaluation of governmental operations, greatly enhanced the probability of erroneous judgments with fateful consequences.

But the end of these particular regimes, linked as they were to some specific features of their ideology, must not mislead one into readily assuming the early demise of totalitarianism. One need not go so far as to envision with George Orwell a world which in 1984 will be divided between three warring sets of totalitarians in order to appreciate the possibly lasting qualities of totalitarian dictatorship. More particularly the inroads of totalitarianism into the Orient, where despotic forms of government have been the rule for thousands of years, ought to give one pause, and prevent any too optimistic estimate of the totalitarians' lack of capacity for survival. We noted at the outset that autocratic regimes have often lasted for centuries, even when their oppressive practices became ever more pronounced. Therefore the mere maturing of the totalitarian autocracy into regularized patterns of organized violence need not spell their destruction; quite the contrary. Hence, since the end of totalitarian dictatorship is purely a matter of speculation to which we may return at the end of this discussion, let us start with its beginning.

As we just noted and indicated at various points in our study, the totalitarian dictatorship in our meaning of the term emerges some time after the seizure of power by the leaders of the movement that had developed in support of the ideology. The typical sequence is therefore that of ideology, movement, party, government. The point of time when the totalitarian government emerges may be reasonably fixed and delimited. It is that point at which the leadership sees itself obliged to employ open and legally unadorned violence for maintaining itself, most particularly against internal opposition due to ideological dissensions arising from within the movement's own ranks. In the Soviet Union, this point is marked by Stalin's liquidation of his erstwhile colleagues in the USSR's leadership and more particularly by his epochal struggle with Trotsky. In Nazi Germany, Hitler's bloody suppression of Roehm and his followers represents this totalitarian "break-through." In Mussolini's Italy, the Matteotti murder and its sequel are one turning point, the attack on Abyssinia another. In China, the totalitarian government seems to have emerged full-fledged, which is due to the fact that a kind of dictatorial government had been in existence for a considerable time prior to the Communists' establishment of control over all of China, namely, in those provinces that they had controlled and developed in their war against the Japanese. But even here, the true totalitarian maturation may be fixed at the point where the urge of any competitors to Mao Tse-Tung's absolute dictatorial control occurred.

The development in the Eastern European satellites of the USSR follows a definite pattern, too, culminating in the totalitarian breakthrough some time after the seizure of control by the Communists. However, in these regimes it may be claimed that the establishment of a totalitarian dictatorship was definitely willed at the outset. We do not know for sure, and there are indications that at least the local leadership had some illusions expressed in notions about the more democratic form which the Communist regimes would take in Poland, Czechoslovakia, and Hungary. But it is likely that the Soviet leaders had definite plans for the structuring of the society concerned in their own image, to become "people's democracies" in their own parlance, totalitarian dictatorships in ours. This inference is supported at least in part by the remarkable parallelism in the development of all these regimes. On the other hand, highly authoritative voices from within the Soviet Union took a line which makes it conceivable that the Soviet leadership itself was uncertain, and only "crossed the Rubicon" toward the totalitarian breakthrough in the light of the actual situational need. Thus we read, in an article by E. S. Varga, "The social order of these states differs from all states known to us so far. It is something completely new in the history of mankind."[13] A. Leontiev even went so far as to claim that neither Marx nor Lenin foresaw or could foresee such a form of state, the reason being that these regimes were organized in response to a specific and novel historical situation.[14] But whether intentional or not, here too the totalitarian features came into existence not immediately upon the seizure of power, but some time afterward, and regularly in connection with the purging of dissident elements in their own ranks, presumably men who had questioned the need for setting up a regime in the image of the Soviet Union.

In a recent study[15] it has been possible to show that the totalitarian dictatorship in the satellites developed in accordance with a definite pattern. The spark which set off the totalitarian break-through was the defection of Tito from the Cominform. It highlighted, as in the corresponding situations in older totalitarian systems, the dangers inherent in the survival of potential centers of dissent from the Soviet-controlled Communist movement. It brought on the total dominance of the several societies by the Russian-directed Communist Parties, except of course in Jugoslavia, where it enabled the anti-USSR group of the Communist Party to establish totalitarian predominance.[16]

If one inquires how this break-through was conditioned, one finds two antecedent stages in these regimes. During the first, the totalitarian movement achieved a key position within an as-yet nontotalitarian political environment. It therefore entered into coalitions with other parties to form a government. It was maintained that this represented a novel and unique form of democracy, unlike the USSR, and that its political task was to liquidate the old ruling class, and to seize control of the major instruments of power: the resistance movements, trade unions and other associations, the armed forces, land reform and socialization, and the key ministries such as Interior, Justice, Com-

munications, and Education which would yield control of the police and courts, as well as mass communication and propaganda. It is evident that this pattern corresponds to the features characteristic of a totalitarian dictatorship as we have analyzed it. Hence it is hardly surprising that in the second stage, the government is definitely molded in the image of the totalitarian dictatorship. Hence the pretense that these regimes were novel and unique was dropped and their kinship with the USSR as a model for building the communist society frankly proclaimed, as well as their dependence upon Soviet political and military support readily acknowledged. During this phase, opposition was destroyed and dissenters purged from the party coalitions. Opposition leaders fled or were liquidated, while their parties were either reduced to impotence or dissolved. During this process, the Soviet Union itself shifted gradually from moderation and tolerance toward tight control and intransigence, preparing the ground for actual total control at the point of the break-through.

The reason for sketching these recent developments in the satellites is that they throw some light on the evolution of totalitarian dictatorship in the major countries. For without drawing sharp lines we find the coalition with nontotalitarian parties in Italy and Germany, the compromise with remaining bourgeois and "rich" peasants' groups in Russia, as well as Hitler's and Mussolini's "deals" with "Big Business," with the churches, and so on, and an insistent emphasis on the democratic features of the new regime. If it was stressed later in the discussions on the satellites that their "road to socialism" was easier than had been that of the Soviet Union, there was an element of truth in such an assertion; for the lack of a "model" had indeed been a striking feature of the development of totalitarian dictatorship in the Soviet Union, as we have stressed at the outset. The lack of such a model cannot be claimed with quite the same justification in the case of the Fascists and Nazis; for while they doctrinally rejected the Soviet Union altogether, there is a good deal of evidence that they followed its example in a number of respects concerning vital features of the totalitarian system. When they instituted the secret police and the monopoly of propaganda, the corresponding transformation of education, and the organizing of the youth, and finally the central planning, and when they developed the technique of a rigidly hierarchical party apparatus, the Fascists followed essentially Soviet models. To what extent this was a matter of conscious imitation does not seem very important, since these features are inherent in the dynamics of the totalitarian movement. It may, however, be well to trace this "phasing" through some of its distinctive component fields, more especially ideology, party, and secret police. This sketch provides a summary of what has been discussed in greater detail before.

We saw when discussing ideology that the radical change which a totalitarian ideology demands necessarily occasions adjustments and adaptations to reality and its situational needs when an attempt is made to "realize" such an ideology. The totalitarian revolutionaries are, in this respect, in no different situation than have been other revolutionaries before them. In the French revolution, especially, the violent controversies over the ideological "meaning" of the revolution led to the *Terreur*. But since the ideology lacked that pseudo-scientific ingredient which has enabled the Communist and Fascist totalitarians to insist on the "mercilessness of the dialectics" (Stalin) and the "ice-cold reasoning" (Hitler), a totalitarian ideology did not develop. Whether its exponents are convinced or merely pretending, the totalitarian ideology requires that it be maintained even while it is being "corrupted." It is at this point, when the inner contradictions of the totalitarian ideology become evident, that the totalitarian break-through occurs. For since there is no longer any possibility of maintaining the logicality of the ideology on logical grounds, total violence must be deployed in order to do so.

In the development of the party, which is closely related to this ideological evolution, an analogous process takes place. In the original movement, when the party fights for success against an hostile environment, all the leader's authority, or a very large part of it, springs from the genuine comradeship which unites the effective participants. After the seizure of power, this relationship continues to operate, but—due to the new situation confronting the leadership with the vast tasks of a government that aspires to accomplish a total change and reconstruction of society—it becomes rapidly bureaucratized. Not only the government but the party is transformed into an increasingly formalized hierarchy. As is always the case, the *apparat* acquires its own weight and operates according to its inherent laws of large-scale bureaucracy. At the point of the totalitarian break-through, purges of former "comrades" reveal that it is no longer a matter of "belonging" to a movement, but one of submission to autocratic decisions which determine a person's right to belong to the party.

Hand in hand with this development goes that of the secret police. In order to become the instrument of total terror which the police system is in a matured totalitarian system, it must acquire the requisite knowledge of its human material, the potential victims of its terroristic activity. Centers of possible opposition have to be identified, techniques of espionage and counterespionage have to be developed, courts and similar judicial procedures of a nontotalitarian past have to be subjected to effective control. Experience and observation show that the time required for these tasks varies. In the Soviet Union, the tsarist secret police provided a ready starting point, and hence the Soviets got under way in this field with their Cheka very quickly. The entrenched liberal tradition in Italy allowed the Fascists to organize the secret police effectively only in 1926, and it took another two years before it really "got hold" of the situation. The Nazis, although anxious to clamp down at once, did not perfect their secret police system until well after the Blood Purge of 1934, when Himmler first emerged as the key figure in the manipulation of this essential totalitarian ingredient.

It is at the point at which the totalitarian break through occurs that the total planning of the economy imposes itself. For it is at this point that the social life of the society has become so largely disorganized that nothing short of central direction will do. In a sense, this total planning is the sign of the culmination of the process. In Soviet Russia, it is the year 1928, in Nazi Germany that of 1936, while in Italy it comes with the instituting of the corporative set-up in 1934 (it had been grandiloquently announced in 1930), though perhaps the Ethiopian war was even more decisive. It is not important in this connection to what the planning effort amounts; it will vary in significance in inverse proportion to the economic autonomy of the country concerned. The crucial point is that this total planning imposes itself as the inescapable consequence of the totalitarian evolution in the economic field. It is therefore not surprising that plans should have sprouted all over the satellite region, and that even Red China should have produced a "plan," announced in 1952 and starting in 1953, even though many of the essentials of planning are absent in that vast and unorganized country, where not even the statistical basis for planning exists, actually.

If we view these several factors or determinants in combination, we find that roughly speaking the totalitarian break-through occurs sometime after the seizure of power, depending upon the various conditions, both favorable and unfavorable. What can be said about the projection of totalitarian dictatorships into the future? We exclude here the problems raised by the possibility of a world-wide conflict between totalitarian and nontotalitarian regimes; such a war, while possible, is too speculative in its military and political implications to allow reasonable reflections. But the internal evolution of the totalitarian dictatorships, given some species of peaceful coexistence, allows for some projection on the basis of past experience.

One possibility should be excluded, except in the satellites: that is the likelihood of an overthrow of these regimes by revolutionary action from within. Our entire analysis of totalitarianism suggests that it is improbable that such a "revolution" will be undertaken, let alone succeed.[17] The records of the resistance in the several totalitarian regimes which have collapsed reinforce this conclusion. When the characteristic techniques of a terroristic police and of mass propaganda are added to the monopoly of weapons which all modern governments enjoy, the prospect of such a revolutionary overthrow becomes practically nil. This may be true, though one doubts that, "even if opposition were less savagely repressed, the people of the totalitarian countries, no matter how badly off or how dissatisfied they are, would not want to engage in any large-scale struggle—they seem to feel that disorder, chaos, and destruction would make them even worse off."[18] The doubt is suggested by the events of June 17, 1953, in the Soviet Zone of Occupation (German Democratic Republic), and those of June 1956 in the Polish province of Poznan. But the dismal failure of these upheavals unfortunately confirms the conclusion that revolution is not likely to succeed even if it is begun.

What then is going to be the course of totalitarian development? If one extrapolates from the past course of evolution, it seems most likely that the totalitarian dictatorships will continue to become more total, even though the rate of intensification may slow down. This view is questioned by those who expect the requirements of the bureaucratic organization to assert themselves and to lead to a less violent form of autocratic regime.[19] In this connection, it is argued that the technological needs of an advancing industrial civilization will also play a decisive role. There is the possibility here of an inherent conflict between industrialization and totalitarian dictatorship, through the rise of a class of managers and technicians, who, when they allied themselves with the military, might wish to abandon the ideology and the party and thus bring the totalitarian dictatorship to an end. This development is conceivable, but not very likely. It may be doubted that such managers and technicians have any imaginable conception of the ground upon which the legitimacy and hence the authority of their continuing power might be built.[20]

One feature of the probable future course that can be predicted with some confidence is related to totalitarian foreign policy. In the past, when tensions and partial breakdowns in autocratic systems increased, the employment of violence likewise increased in order to solve these tensions. As part of this general pattern, autocratic organizations have tended to turn to violent aggression as a way of solving their difficulties. In totalitarian regimes, it appears that ideology plays a greater role in this respect. In the case of the Nazi regime, one of the initial decisions after the seizure of power was to gear the national economy to a large-scale war preparation. Internal developments, as well as actual strength, were largely ignored by the dictator. In the case of the Soviet Union, there is no doubt that the Soviet leaders have tended to emphasize international relaxation at times of internal difficulties. This was as true in the days of the "Popular Front" as it is in the era of "the spirit of Geneva." At the

same time, however, the ideological doctrine of class war can be utilized to develop aggressive belligerency in subject populations throughout the world. The Soviet regime, by maintaining a sham sense of identity with these populations, can abet their revolutionary efforts and exploit them politically.

The degree of direct Soviet involvement in such "revolutions" varies; in some areas, as in Europe, such upheavals were in fact created by Soviet armies; in others, as in Asia, the communists have merely exploited and channeled a stormy situation. When the United States military strength blocked further Soviet advance in Europe, Stalin, in response to this, intensified the totalitarianization of the captive nations, and encouraged the Chinese Communists in their revolutionary activity. It seems likely that in the future the Chinese Communists will continue, on the Soviet pattern, to encourage revolutionary movements in Asia and to give them ideological and institutional backing. The Soviet Union, especially since the "spirit of Geneva" formally limits the opportunity for direct action, will continue to attempt to exploit the current relaxation to undermine the military barriers built up against it in Europe and to mobilize some of the sympathy existing for the USSR in European intellectual circles.[21] There is also no doubt that areas of conflict and unrest in the Middle East will provide the Soviet Union with ample opportunities for political maneuvers to set in motion a revolutionary chain of events. And all of this will be carried on without direct clash with the still preponderant military might of the United States, while at home energetic efforts will be pursued to solve the agricultural and related problems.

It therefore appears as we have observed, that the Nazi and Fascist regimes, drawn into a policy of war, on the traditional pattern, by the ideological blindness of their leaders, committed themselves in advance to an open conflict the outcome of which was more than doubtful. Except for a very few areas, such as Austria, their opportunities for creating revolutionary upheavals which they could exploit were limited. The Communists, launching a broad economic and social revolution at home, can combine these domestic measures with a foreign expansion, short of war. It is therefore rather unlikely that they would launch a major and open campaign of aggression because of internal difficulties. They accept such difficulties as part of the revolutionary process. Their refined, yet often brutal, system of controls dooms any effective resistance in advance. The possibility of open war will increase, however, as the Communists gain in military preponderance.

Whether it is possible, in terms of a developmental construct, to forecast the probable course of totalitarian evolution seems more doubtful. We prefer the simple extrapolation of recent trends, and the estimate of broader potentials in terms of long-range observations of autocratic regimes throughout history.[22] Considered in such terms, the prospect of totalitarian dictatorship seems unclear. Leaving aside the possibility of liquidation by war, there might conceivably be internal transformation. "It is possible," as one highly qualified observer said, "that the 'wave' of totalitarianism has reached its high water mark. And it may well be that in the not too distant future it will start rolling back."[23] It may be. But if one such totalitarianism disappeared, others may appear to take its place, due to the endemic conditions which have given rise to them. Totalitarian dictatorship, a novel form of autocracy, more inimical to human dignity than autocracies in the past, appears to be a highly dynamic form of government which is still in the process of evolving. Whether it will, in the long run, prove to be a viable form of social and political organization remains to be seen. Nonetheless, large portions of mankind may have to pass through its crucible, before becoming ready, if they survive the ordeal, for more complex forms of political organization.

# NOTES

1. The term *heterocracy* has never been suggested though as it is the genuine logical alternative to *autocracy* there is something to be said for it, in order to escape the common connotations surrounding the term "constitutional government."

2. Ernest Fraenkel, *The Dual State—A Contribution to the Theory of Dictatorship*, New York, 1941, *passim*.

3. C. J. Friedrich, *Die Philosophie des Rechts in historischer Perspektive*, Heidelberg, 1955, chapter 8.

4. Hannah Arendt, "Ideology and Terror: A Novel Form of Government," *Review of Politics*, 15:309 ff. (1953). The antecedents in earlier discussions of the law of nature are inadequately recognized, since Miss Arendt takes only the normative (scholastic) law of nature into account.

5. *Ibid.*, pp. 303 ff. In this interesting paper, Miss Arendt advances the thesis that it is not merely the utopian nature of the ideology, but its alleged logicality, that leads to the terror. Based on a "scientific" law of movement, these ideologies are "literally the logic of an idea" which is carried through with "icecold reasoning" (Hitler) or with the "mercilessness of dialectics" or the "irresistible force of logic" (Stalin). We believe the point Miss Arendt makes to be a significant aspect of totalitarian ideology, but not to have the broad importance she attributes to it.

6. Alan Bullock, *Hitler—A Study in Tyranny*, London, 1952, *passim*.

7. G. A. Borgese, *Goliath, the March of Fascism*, New York, 1937, pp. 271–344. For a bitter criticism of this tendency, see Emil Ludwig's *Mussolini* (119), p. 231.

8. Franz Neumann, *Behemoth*, New York, 1942.

Also Maxine B. Sweezey, *The Structure of the Nazi Economy*, Cambridge, Mass., 1941, and R. A. Brady, *The Spirit and Structure of German Fascism*, New York, 1937. Neumann's analysis is much the ablest of the three. The "imperialist" interpretation ties in with Thorstein Veblen's earlier analysis of German and Japanese militarism and imperialism.

9. Livon Bertalanffy, *General System Theory: A New Approach to the Unity of Science*, 1951. A system is characterized by three features: it consists of several parts that are quite distinct and different from each other; these parts bear a defined functional relation to each other; and typically the destruction of some of these parts (the essential ones) entails the destruction of the system as a whole. Such systems may be composed of physical entities, of animated beings, or of thoughts. A social or cultural or political system is typically a combination of all three.

10. Autocratic regimes, as defined above, should be clearly distinguished from the broader category of "authoritarian" regimes of which some of them form a subdivision. Thus both monarchy and tyranny may be said to have been authoritarian, but the difference has long been decisive.

11. A. Tasca, *Nascita e avvento del Fascismo*, Rome, 1950. Mussolini's attitude toward democracy was ambivalent. Fascist theory was much more frankly elitist than Nazi ideology.

12. Theodor Heuss, *Hitler's Weg—Eine historische-politische Studie über den Nationalsozialismus*, Stuttgart, 1932.

13. E. S. Varga, "Demokratiya Novogo Tipa," *Mirovoe Khoziaistvo i Mirovaya Politika*, 1947, p. 3.

14. A. Leontiev, "Ekonomischeskie Osnovy Novoy Demokratii," *Planovoie Khozjaistvo*, no. 4 (1947), p. 69.

15. Richard J. Medalie, "The Stages of Totalitarian Development in Eastern Europe," *Public Policy*, Volume VII, Cambridge, Mass., 1956. Earlier Hugh Seton-Watson attempted to generalize upon the more conventional subject of the "seizure of power." See his *The East European Revolution*, second ed., New York, 1952. We benefited greatly from Medalie's discussion of these phenomena.

16. A. Gyorgy, in C. J. Friedrich, ed., *Totalitarianism*, Cambridge, Mass., 1954, pp. 381 ff., does not share this view and argued that neither ideologically, nor in relation to the secret police, has the totalitarian nature of these regimes been established, but the evidence he adduces is unconvincing.

17. P. Kecskemeti, in *ibid.*, pp. 345–360, where the decline of the revolution as a form of political action has been argued persuasively on purely observational ground. The reason for revolution becoming "an extinct political form" appears to be the weapons monopoly.

18. *Ibid.*, p. 359.

19. Barrington Moore, *Terror and Progress USSR*, Cambridge, Mass., 1954, *passim*. This view has been for some time espoused by George F. Kennan and others.

20. Z. Brzezinski, "Totalitarianism and Rationality," *American Political Science Review*, 3 (50), September, 1956.

21. See Raymond Aron, *L'opium des intellectuels*, Paris, 1955.

22. H. D. Lasswell, in Friedrich, ed., *Totalitarian-*

*ism, op. cit.,* pp. 153 ff., deems the emergence of a world of one or more "garrison states" as probable. In the course of his analysis he qualified his former concept of the garrison state and introduced that of a garrison police state that is, in effect, a totalitarian

dictatorship. The only alternative he allowed was that of a world federation of constitutional democracies; the continuation of something like the present situation he did not include among his alternatives.

23. P. Kecskemeti, in *ibid.,* p. 360.

# THE TOTALITARIAN MYSTIQUE: SOME IMPRESSIONS OF THE DYNAMICS OF TOTALITARIAN SOCIETY

## Alex Inkeles

Two broad approaches bulk large in the efforts made to understand modern totalitarianism. Perhaps most prominent, certainly most extensive, are those analyses which assign a central role to such formal ideologies as Marxism-Leninism. A rather different approach holds that modern totalitarianism may be understood primarily in terms of the drive for absolute power. The difference between the action of the modern totalitarian and that of earlier seekers after power is generally seen by those taking this position as lying in the thoroughness and effectiveness of the technical means of control both necessary to and possible for the ruler of a modern industrial society. This paper seeks to add another explanatory principle to these, on the grounds that there are important dimensions of totalitarian social organization which cannot adequately be explained solely in terms of formal ideology and power seeking, used either separately or jointly as explanatory principles. In addition, this paper seeks to extend our grasp of totalitarianism by concentrating on totalitarian society, which has been relatively neglected, rather than on totalitarian politics, which have previously been the prime focus of analysis. To these ends I present below a series of what appear to me general characteristics of the totalitarian elites' approach to society, as well as several illustrations of the pattern of *social* action which is manifested by them when they come to power.

Specifically, it is posited here that the totalitarian

leader is a particular type of individual in that he is characterized by a distinctive approach to problems of social organization. This approach is assumed to manifest itself regardless of the particular content of the totalitarian's formal ideology—although it may be that only certain kinds of formal ideology will appeal to him. This element of the totalitarian "character" is not conceived of as replacing the power drive, but rather as distinguishing the totalitarian from other individuals who also seek power, even absolute power.

I have used the term "mystique" to represent the combination of elements which make up the totalitarian's distinctive approach to social organization. Although the several elements which constitute this orientation are individually discussed below, a word of explanation about the general term "mystique" is in order here. The term is used to express the idea that the totalitarian, despite extensive rationalization of his position through the citation of purported biological or historical fact, is convinced that he has *directly* perceived some immanent law of social development. This law is seen as relatively overriding, and its implication is bound eventually to be manifested. Consequently, the totalitarian's knowledge of the law is seen by him both as dictating necessary action on his part, and as guaranteeing the "correctness" of that action. Further, although the point is not developed in this paper, I believe that only a certain psychological type is likely to have such conceptions. To my mind this common psychological characteristic accounts for a significant amount of the similarity in the pattern and tone of totalitarian action programs, even when this action starts from different formal ideological premises and occurs in radically different socio-cultural environments. In other words, the totali-

Reprinted by permission of the publishers from Carl J. Friedrich (ed.), *Totalitarianism: Proceedings of a Conference Held at the American Academy of Arts and Sciences* (Cambridge, Mass.: Harvard University Press, 1954), pp. 87–107. Copyright, 1954, by the President and Fellows of Harvard College.

tarian mystique is presented not as a quality of the totalitarian society, but as a quality of the totalitarian *leader* who imposes his conception on the society in which he comes to power.

Thus the mystique posited in this paper is not meant to replace formal ideology or power seeking as bases for explaining totalitarianism, nor is it meant to stand above them as having a "higher" explanatory potential. Like them it has its limitations as an explanatory principle, and in my opinion could not alone adequately explain the facts of totalitarian social organization. The concept of the totalitarian mystique is offered simply as a supplement to explanations based on the role of ideology and of power seeking, and it is the central focus in this paper only because I feel it to have been neglected. The task of assessing the relative importance of formal ideology, power seeking, and the mystique in the development and functioning of totalitarian social structures is beyond the scope of this paper. I must, therefore, limit myself to the comment that I assume the mystique to have its greatest importance and widest influence in the early decades of the establishment of a totalitarian society, and to operate largely as a "residue," although an important one, in the actions of the "second generation" of totalitarian leaders.

The principles and characteristics presented here are aspects of an ideal type in the sense in which Max Weber used the term. Consequently, although the model which underlies the ideal type is the Soviet social system, I will proceed largely without reference to many of the specific and distinctive institutional features of Soviet society. Indeed, the central aim of this statement is to suggest a mode of analysis which can encompass totalitarian systems as divergent in their concrete institutional structure as the Communist and Nazi systems, which most closely approximate the ideal type; Fascist Italy, which only imperfectly approximated it; and Franco Spain, which fits the model in only a few crucial respects.

It should perhaps go without saying that the principles and operating characteristics of totalitarian social organization presented here are highly tentative. Further, they are not meant to be in any sense complete or exhaustive, but are selected as simply illustrative of the results given by the general mode of analysis adopted here.

## SOME BASIC PRINCIPLES OF TOTALITARIAN SOCIAL ORGANIZATION

### 1. The Principle of the Precedence of the Totalitarian Mystique

It is proposed here that the most distinctive and basic determinant governing the structuring and operation of totalitarian society is the principle that certain essentially mystically derived, relatively abstract goals and imperatives must stand above and take precedence over considerations of human welfare, of personal and group interest, comfort, and gratification, and of stable and calculable patterns of social relations. This orientation is usually characterized as the principle of "the subordination of the individual to the state." While that statement goes far in exposing the central feature of totalitarianism, it fails to deal with several important dimensions of the problem.

Totalitarianism does not merely subordinate the *individual* to "the state," but it also, indeed preëminently, subordinates human *associations,* the organizations and institutions which man creates to meet his social needs. Neglect of the prime importance that totalitarianism gives to the subordination of institutions as such, may lead to neglect of some of the most important structural features of totalitarian social organization. Traditional liberalism, because of its emphasis on the individual, his rights and needs, naturally tends to see first in totalitarianism its direct impact on the individual, in particular his subordination to state purposes. But totalitarianism, in contrast to liberalism and pluralism, leaps over the individual to give full recognition and weight to the role of social institutions in the structure and functioning of society. It recognizes that one of the important aspects of social organization in the large-scale society is that the individual is related to the total social system primarily through the institutional networks in which he is enmeshed. And it has therefore given special and primary emphasis to the subordination of the traditional human associations, the organizations and institutions, of which the individual is a member. This becomes the *chief* tool for its ultimate subordination of the individual to the state. Totalitarianism recognizes that so long as certain of its crucial membership units are not themselves subordinated to the demands of the central authority, the individual himself may to that degree be immune to full subordination.

The second difficulty I would like to note in the formula that defines totalitarianism as a system in which the individual is subordinated to the state lies in its emphasis on "the state." To stop at this point is to assume that it is indeed the state in and of itself which is the ultimate goal toward which the totalitarian is oriented. Further, since the final concern of the state is with power, there is a tendency in contemporary political analysis to assume rather facilely that the prime interest of the totalitarian is in *power* per se. It should not be forgotten that in the last analysis all participants in politics are interested in power, yet many are far from totalitarians. Indeed, although those who are interested in power as an ultimate end may become dictators, not all dictators are totalitarians. The significant question, of course, is "power for what?" It is in the *ends* for which he seeks power that the crucial characteristic of the totalitarian emerges.

I submit that it is not power in and of itself which motivates the totalitarian, but power sought for some specific "higher purpose." In other words, the totalitarian sees the state as predominantly an instrument of another purpose, a mere vessel which he gives content. It is precisely this which makes him so great a threat to established institutions and freedom—that he has no real respect for the state as such, for the state as an institution with legitimacy and purpose in and of itself. Paradoxically, it is rather the non-totalitarian who accepts the state as sufficient unto its own purpose of governing, of allocating authority, and of regulating relations among men. The characteristic of the totalitarian is that he sees the state as an institution with no right to existence in itself, but rather as a mere tool serving the attainment of some higher goal which is above the state. It is essentially the imperatives of this higher law which spell the doom of "the rule of law."

Invariably this higher goal involves some mystique, some principle above man, some force that responds to laws of its own and that merely requires the state as the instrument through which it may work out its inner imperatives. The mystique may be the dialectal laws of history and of social development for the Marxist, the destiny of the nation and race for the Hitlerian, or the ideal of the true Christian society for Franco. In each case the totalitarian fortifies himself with—indeed loses himelf in—this mystique. It is the fulfillment of the higher law, the mystical imperative, which he sees himself placed on earth to achieve. The state is of course the most obvious and indeed indispensable instrument for effecting this purpose. But in the last analysis what dominates the totalitarian is his compulsion to make man and social development conform to the dictates of his particular perception of higher law. It is not the state as such he values, nor its power per se, but the use he can put them to in order to make man conform to the dictates of the higher law. The totalitarian subordinates not only the individual—in the end he subverts the state itself.

This is not to say that the totalitarian may not in time become so involved in the state as the instrument of his mission that state power becomes an "autonomous" goal. Neither is it to deny that given sufficient time men come into leadership in totalitarian societies whose main training and preoccupation has been with the state as an instrument of power per se and as an end in itself. But it is submitted here that in both of these cases the original dedication to a mystical goal will continue to exercise substantial influence, and an understanding of the behavior of the totalitarian leader will not be fully accessible if it neglects to account for this principle.

I recognize that this view runs counter to many, perhaps most current interpretations of modern totalitarianism. I suspect it will be particularly objected to because it does not make full allowance for the cynical manipulative propensities of totalitarian rulers. Lest there be serious misunderstanding, therefore, permit me to stress that I do not minimize the cynicism and the manipulativeness of totalitarians. Indeed I suspect the world has never seen cynicism and manipulation to surpass theirs. The questions are what makes them cynical and what are they cynical about? The mystique dictates their morality, indeed it stands above ordinary human morality and places its adherent outside the demands normally to be made of a man and leader. Hence the totalitarian may be cynical about and manipulate "law," "loyalty," "truth," "honesty," and so on. For as long as he manipulates these in the service of the mystique, his action is beyond question—it is law, truth, honesty, loyalty, unto itself.

In our efforts to understand the behavior of the totalitarian we have become so disillusioned from his evident and obvious disregard for "principle," as we commonly understand it, that we have been driven to the theory that the mainspring of his behavior is raw, immoral power seeking by whatever means are available. But the man who is interested in power only as an end in itself can be counted on to make predominantly rational calculations about the balance of forces as they affect his chances to secure and hold power. He therefore can, to some extent, be controlled and manipulated by the action of others within a total power field. The lasting and profound danger to our liberty and freedom, I submit, lies in the fact that the full-blown totalitarian such as Lenin, Hitler, or Stalin is *not* interested in power alone. Frequently he appears to respond first to the imperative of his mystique, and the mystique is by nature arational. It does not defer to the rational calculus of power. Indeed its threat lies in the fact that it may drive the totalitarian leader to run risks in response to the demands of a higher law, of a mystical calculus which seeks to break through the earth-bound rational calculus of power.

Such an orientation is, unfortunately, much less subject to control and manipulation from without through a mere shifting of the balance within the total world field of forces. Therein lies the permanent threat of totalitarianism to world peace. There is no threat to others greater than the pursuit by rational means of an essentially irrational goal—it is just this combination on the level of the individual personality which makes the psychopath so dangerous. Magnified to the $n$th degree as a pattern of state policy, it is dangerous beyond measure.

## 2. The Principle of Monolithic Social Organization

One branch of modern sociology and anthropology is characterized by its emphasis on structural-functional analysis. This assumes that the discrete institutions and institutional complexes in any society are intimately interrelated and interdependent, so that the structure and operation of any given institutional pattern has important implications for other institutions and for the structure as a whole. In brief, society is seen as an institutional *system*. It is rather striking that without giving explicit formulation to this concept, totalitarian movements and leaders reflect a similar set of assumptions.

Our image of the totalitarian leader as motivated primarily by the desire for power has tended to encourage us to neglect what the totalitarian leader *does* with his power by way of remaking the society he comes to control. The weight given to the principle of power alone as an end in itself has also frequently caused us either facilely to assume the preservation of power as the prime motivation for almost every major program of social change undertaken by the totalitarian dictator, or to attribute many of the actions of the dictator to caprice, to paranoia, or some similar deviant personality manifestation in the dictator. Much of this "residual category" type of explanation can be avoided if there is full recognition of the extent to which the dictator and his lieutenants in modern totalitarian society are oriented to the assumption that every element of the social system, no matter how minor, has implications for the structure as a whole. It is this assumption which prompts the close examination of *every* institution, *every* pattern of behavior, to test its relevance for the whole.

Clearly, if the subordination of the individual cannot be complete without the subordination of his associations, then it follows further that *absolute* subordination of the individual requires absolute subordination of *all* the human associations which form the web of society. But it is not on these grounds alone that the totalitarian exempts no organization from being measured against his Procrustean rule. The mystique implies a plan of the good society. It provides a single metric for all forms of human organization. The totalitarian rejects outright the principle which inheres in the formula "render unto Caesar the things which are Caesar's." He accepts no distinction between the sacred and the profane, the public and the private, in social life. The demands of the mystique determine what decision shall be taken in regard to any particular institution, but all institutions are equally subject to review.

Take, for example, the attack on the family and the church in the early decades of Soviet rule. What rational balance sheet of power would have led a group of leaders who were concerned first and foremost with preserving their power to attempt that particular diversion of energy with its obvious consequences of social resentment and popular hostility? Surely this cannot be understood unless we see the extent to which the Soviet leaders had a mental image of the society their particular mystique demanded be created, an image in which traditional "bourgeois" family life and widespread religious belief and practice were seen as inadmissible because they did not fit the pattern of the future society to which "history" was giving birth. To them it was axiomatic that the "new man" of this society, the rational, socially motivated, scientific man of the future, could not be expected ever to arise were he to be raised in the atmosphere of the traditional family and in the presence of the other worldly values of religion.

This is not to deny that the regime did not also see a direct challenge to the new authority in the parents' influence on their children in the old family structure. Similarly, it must be recognized that the Church had a substantial amount of real control over people's loyalties and actions. But it can hardly be argued that the Soviet leaders were ignorant of the probable impact on their own power which would result from attacking these institutions, *relative* to the probable effects of a *laissez faire* attitude. For the totalitarian there is a design, and everything which exists must serve a function in fulfilling this design. The totalitarian is a social teleologist. But this is teleology stood upon its head, because the design inheres not in what is, but in what must be brought to exist. Not the calculus of power alone, therefore, but equally the Communist totalitarian's opposition to any suggestion of pluralism in society, and his devotion to the mystique of the planned and integrated monolithic society, must be considered for a full understanding of these early action programs of the Soviet leaders.

## 3. The Principle of Elite Leadership

We generally think of totalitarian leadership in terms of the principle of dictatorship—that is, absolute one-man rule based on the ability to seize and hold power without regard to traditional right, popular consensus, or the rule of law. We tend to look on the men immediately around this dictatorial leader as essentially henchmen utilized by him for his purpose of controlling the society, and motivated on their part by the desire to secure the share in power which he offers them. We are prone, further, to think that the totalitarian dictator looks on the organization or party which he builds and heads as a simple and necessary instrument for effecting his rule. In brief, as far as *political* organization is concerned, we incline to equate the totalitarian dictator with the non-totalitarian dictator.

As in the case of the formula for totalitarian society as one subordinating the individual to the state, there is a great deal of validity in this characterization. But this description of the totalitarian dictator equally neglects to emphasize certain essential dimensions of the situation which I believe may be an aid in attaining fuller understanding of totalitarian society.

Consider again our first-stated principle of the subordination of men and their associations to a mystical general social law. One may fruitfully view the dictatorial leader as the man who sees himself as the essential *instrument* of the particular mystique to which he is addicted. He conceives of himself as having been placed on earth for the specific purpose of seeing that the imperatives of the mystique are met, and considers that his life lacks meaning unless he consecrates himself to that purpose. Thus Hitler is, from this point of view, seen as regarding himself as destined by fate (a theme that runs through his autobiography) to secure the fulfillment of the historic destiny of the German race, and Lenin as viewing his life as unfulfilled unless he served as the midwife of history in assuring the revolutionary birth of the new Communist society.

On the basis of this assumption, the lieutenants of the dictator may be seen in a new light, for there emerge requirements for these positions which go beyond mere adaptability to the dictator's power goals. Two such requirements are most prominent.

First, the cohorts of the dictator are obliged themselves to have a substantial awareness of and commitment to the mystical commandments. Unless they do they cannot be expected to serve efficiently in the cause of working out the destiny dictated by fate, history, the laws of social development, or the imperatives of "Christian" civilization. The orders given to those high in command and responsibility cannot be more than general directives, which they must know how to implement. Large amounts of initiative are inevitably left to them no matter how centralized the structure of authority. If then they are to act "meaningfully," "correctly," they must understand the general purposes and direction of the total program. They must understand the mystical law.

Second, the totalitarian dictator's cohorts must be above the usual demands of the human spirit in this world. Most important, they must be above the things of this world in their ability to turn a deaf ear to the groans of their fellow men. Their consecration is not to man, but to the mystical law which they seek to fulfill. If they be moved by the hopes, the fears, and especially the pains of their fellow men, or be slowed in the execution of duty by the hatred of those fellow men, then they lack the quali-

ties essential in a disciple of the leader. The sufferings of ordinary human beings are but temptations designed to deflect the elect from the pursuit of the true goal. Note the statement of Stalin: "The Party is no true Party if it limits its activities to *a mere registration of the suffering* and thoughts of the proletarian masses . . . if it cannot rise superior to the transient interests of the proletariat." Thus the totalitarian, following Ulysses, lashes himself to the mast of his mystique and stops his sailors' ears with wax against the cries of the popular sirens, lest the ship of the revolution be swept up in the current of decadent bourgeois sentimentality and founder on the rock of compromise.

As with the lieutenants so with the rank and file of the movement, even if in lesser degree. It is not enough that they be willing soldiers who carry out orders precisely. They too must have some understanding of the mystique, some vision, however simple, of the overriding law of which they are the instrument. And like the leaders, they too must be able to resist the human pressures of their fellow men, to stop their ears to their cries, to "push on the masses from without." They must excel not so much in their propensity for self-sacrifice as in their ability to remain unblenched at the sacrifice of those all around them. No one is wholly, fully, one with the party and its cause until he in fact or in reasonable facsimile has smashed against a wall the head of a baby of racially inferior stock or denounced a close comrade to the secret police. Such unholy acts of consecration are the most important rites of passage into full status in the totalitarian movement. One wonders, further, whether or not this demand of the mystique does not figure prominently as an element in the logic of the purges, for so often their victims seem to be sacrificed not so much for what they have done as for what they have not done. They are cast out not for bashing in the wrong heads, but for not bashing in enough heads. They are tried not so much for acting incorrectly, but for inaction which is taken as a sign of waning devotion and doubt in the mystique. The terror is most merciless with those of its agents who have blanched at the execution of the mystical imperative.

## 4. The Principle of Contamination

The preceding section has already hinted at the last of the general principles I shall discuss: the principle of inner contamination, or what might be termed the virus theory of social pathology. It is a characteristic of totalitarian leaders that they see every social movement as having within it the seeds of its own destruction, and that they are ridden by fear that within their own movement and social organization there is such a potentially destructive foreign body which must be wholly and violently expunged—it is not enough to build antibodies against it—lest it cripple its host society from within. For Hitler it was the Jews and all other forms of "race mixture," whether of blood, of physical contact, or of ideas, which he saw as opening up the possibility of the disintegration of his particular mystical structure. For the Soviet Bolshevik it is the taint of capitalist thought remnants, or of various forms of "deviation." And I suppose that for Franco it is any sign of "socialism" or "anticlericalism."

When the inner taint is "discovered," there is no solution but to cut out the infected part, root and branch, to destroy the tainted carrier himself lest he soon infect all. Furthermore, the taint may be manifested not only in people, but by institutional forms, ideas, and systems of ideas. Once the taint is recognized in them, the threat of contamination of the whole organism requires the absolute elimination of these types of carrier as well. By its nature, however, this taint, this cancer which can in no time spread to the whole organism and precipitate its breakup and decay, is not wholly specific and concrete. It has a specific and concrete original source in most cases, but it is not limited to that specific source. Jewishness, bourgeois-capitalist sentiments, lack of "vigilance," atheist or protestant heresies, may appear anywhere in the total social organism. Even the healthiest and greatest may some day be discovered to be tainted.

Here again one is led to consideration of the phenomenon of the totalitarian purge, which seems to be underlain by and to derive its intensity from essentially irrational compulsion. The terror may be an instrument of power designed to stimulate fear, and through fear obedience, in the common people. But the *purge* under Hitler as under Stalin struck mainly at the faithful, indeed in large measure at the inner circle and those immediately concentric to it. Is not the threat of contamination all the more anxiety-provoking the closer to home the dreaded taint is thought to be found?

# SOME OPERATING CHARACTERISTICS OF TOTALITARIAN SOCIAL ORGANIZATION

We turn now to a consideration of some illustrative patterns of social action which characterize the implementation of totalitarian goals in the society in which the totalitarian leader and his organization have seized power. Although these action patterns may be directly derived from the general principles already described, no systematic effort to relate them will be attempted. Further, it is hoped that for the purposes of the present discussion they will be considered each as standing on its own merits relative to the general principles and to the other patterns.

## 1. The Subversions of Independent Associations and Loci of Power

Among the earliest actions of the totalitarian in command of state power there seems always to be the effort to destroy or convert to new purposes all existing independent associations and other potential loci of socio-political and economic power. The most prominent of these are other political parties, certain ethnic or socio-economic class groups, and selected major economic organizations, but regularly attention is also given to trade unions, universities, professional associations, national recreational associations such as those for sport, and certain religious organizations or sects. Furthermore, although these are the more massive and prominent human associations, the list is not limited to these. Rather it will extend as far as those small and intimate, universally present associations, the family and the friendship group.

Almost without fail each and all will at least be subjected to examination and evaluation. Some will be destroyed outright, others will be "remade" in a new mold, still others will be freshly created to meet the needs of the totalitarian leaders. Which ones are marked for any given course of action will, of course, vary with the totalitarian movement, its program, proclivities, and sensitivities, as determined by its particular mystique. But when the examination is complete, only those associations will remain which fit the required pattern, or can be made to fit. The rest will be ruthlessly expunged, and where necessary their membership will likewise be destroyed or dispersed.

Why is this pattern so widespread and the program of action so thorough and drastic? If we take the dissolution of all political parties save that of the totalitarian leader, or the subversion of the trade unions into instruments of state policy, the explanation seems obvious enough. The totalitarian leader seeks for power, indeed for absolute power, and hence he cannot permit the existence of any group with which he must in any sense "share" power. Further, the totalitarian leader is characterized by fear, hence he must seek out and destroy or emasculate real or potential challengers to his power. But as one moves away from the obvious power-potential associations like political parties and trade unions to the universities and the sports clubs, and still further to the family, the theory of power as the wellspring of action cannot fully satisfy the demands of the situation. Indeed one may even doubt how adequately the theory of power alone explains even the destruction of other political parties and the subversion of the trade unions. Is not some essential element missing?

I would suggest that the subversion of the independent association is governed not alone, nor indeed primarily, by considerations of power, but rather by the demands of the totalitarian mystique. The mystique is a higher law, a universal principle, an incontrovertible truth. Further, it is the essence of the totalitarian orientation that it assumes one truth, one law, one interest, and hence only one program. How then shall there be independent political parties? Parties stand for programs, they express political truths, they represent interests. To permit more than one political party, that one which is the expression of the mystique, is to admit the existence of other truths which require other programs, other interests which belie the central and only valid interest. To tolerate these expressions signifies lack of faith in the absolute law, indeed a direct challenge to it. It is to sanction blasphemy.

In addition the mystique implies a plan, a model of the true society, a blueprint for the working out of the principles of the mystical law. Hence, for each association there is a place and a function in the society of the future, and a role to be played in bringing that society into being. All that are permitted to live must assume their appropriate place and begin to exercise their function. All those for which there is no place or function are dross to be cast off. And the principle of contamination comes into operation here, for if there be associations for which there is no place or function, clearly they were not *meant* to be and are in some sense evil. Being evil they may infect the rest of the system, taint and contaminate. Hence those institutions which have been in the Marxist sense "outlived," must be expunged, cut out root and all like the cancerous growths which they are.

## 2. The Nationalization of Affect

The totalitarian society is not spartan in its orientation to human emotion and feeling. It does not seek to suppress the expression of affect. Love and hate, desire and ambition, all have their place. But the totalitarian society permits the expression of affect only for specific purposes and in the last analysis only for one purpose, the purpose of meeting the requirements of the mystique and of insuring the working out of the basic law of society.

It is only "private," personal emotion, particularly sadness and depression, that is frowned upon and indeed suspected. Frowned upon because man has only so much emotional energy, and what he expends for private ends he does not have to contribute toward working out the imperatives of the mystique. Thus, when Lenin indicates his opposition to sexual excess he does so not on moral grounds nor on the basis of some principle like that of the golden mean, but rather because this energy could be better applied to fighting the battles of the revolution! You do not have children

for the pleasure they give you, but so that Hitler and Mussolini may have more workers and soldiers to effect the high purposes for which they were put on the earth. Friendship is not important for the gratification it gives, but because comrades may join forces in carrying out the greater task of all.

## 3. The Communalization of Communication

The means of mass communication are an obvious instrument of power in modern society, and their immediate seizure and monopolization by the totalitarian movement which has assumed command should require no special comment. But it is perhaps a neglected fact that the exclusive concern of the ever-present and ironically named ministry of information is not with the transmission of orders, instructions, and other communications intimately relating to the exercise of power. Rather it is to an amazing degree engaged in the business of disseminating and inculcating the articles of faith, in spreading abroad the mystique and seeking to win allegiance to it. It concentrates not so much on commanding obedience to orders, as on winning converts, strengthening the faith and consecration of the common man to the sacred goals —or at least to the humble part assigned him in the program for achieving those goals. The Soviet press spreads the common man's Marxism-Leninism-Stalinism and features the elaborate iconography of its saints. Hitler's press devoted itself to the task of making convinced racists of the last German, consecrating all to the greater glory and fulfillment of the *Herrenvolk*.

But perhaps more important than what totalitarianism does to mass communication is what it does to private communication. Mass communication receives a new content, but remains mass, whereas private communication is transformed and ceases to be private. No matter what the context, on the street talking to a stranger or in the intimacy of one's home, one must say only the right thing. And one must say it as publicly as possible. Private communication becomes suspect, for to speak privately implies the desire to speak without being overheard by others. And the wish not to be overheard suggests that one is saying forbidden things —for if they were not forbidden, blasphemous things, would you not be proud to say them aloud for all to hear? In the end, even silence becomes suspect, for it may mean an unwillingness to reiterate the catechism which the mystique requires all to intone, and hence mark one out as an alien, a non-believer, and a potential source of contamination. Thus, private communication becomes public communication, and along with mass communication is subverted to fulfilling the imperatives of the mystique. Communication is communalized.

## 4. The "Stratification" of the Arts

In thinking of the common totalitarian incursion into art we usually recognize that everywhere the totalitarian classifies art into two broadly defined groups of the acceptable and the unacceptable. Any given piece of art is defined as good or bad in so far as it is German or racially mixed art, bourgeois idealistic art or socialist realism, decadent or progressive, and so on. But what makes it so? The actual characteristics of "good" art, whatever the precise label, tend to be much the same in all modern totalitarian societies regardless of differences in the specific content of the mystique. Such art must be concrete rather than abstract, directly representational, "wholesome" rather than dealing with "unpleasant" subjects, light in color rather than dark in shade and tone, "social" rather than predominantly "private" in subject matter, and "cheerful" rather than somber or "depressing."

These characteristics of the totalitarian orientation to art are widely recognized and have been frequently commented on. The policy is usually explained on much the same grounds as the totalitarian's seizure and subversion of the media of mass communication. According to this theory, art is simply another instrument used by the totalitarian to affect his absolute rule. It is reduced by the totalitarian to propaganda, for it is only as propaganda that art becomes a useful instrument of power much like the media of mass communication. Further, according to this theory, since art is treated primarily as an instrument of communication, a means for mobilizing people to serve the purposes of the state, it must be understandable to those being communicated with. Hence, it is reduced to the level of taste of the common man.

While I do not challenge this formulation, I would like here again to attempt to go beyond it. I submit that the degradation of the arts under totalitarianism has only a tenuous connection with matters of taste and is not predominantly due to the effort to insure communicability.

That this is the case is all too apparent in the Soviet Union, where it appears that however simple in taste the officially approved plays and novels are, they do *not* appeal to the tastes of the average Soviet reader—who indeed seems to avoid official art and to prefer to snatch such reading from the classics as he can get. Furthermore, I do not think that what is officially approved necessarily has too much to do with the taste of the elite either. Although I cannot support this, I have the distinct impression that Andrei Zhdanov, the arbiter of Soviet literature during his lifetime, had no more "taste" for the novels he approved and praised than for those he rejected and excoriated during the literary purges. Indeed the essence of the totali-

tarian approach to art is that taste, including the taste of the totalitarian leader, is *irrelevant* to its evaluation. He praises not what he likes aesthetically, but what he approves as serving his mystique. Consider for a moment Mr. Zhdanov's infamous commentary on the Leningrad writers. The writer, said Mr. Zhdanov, is "on the forward line of the ideological front," and a successful work of art "may be compared with a battle won or with a great victory on the economic front." The significance of a work of art derives from its status "as a means of bringing about social reform." In Mr. Zhdanov's diatribe there is hardly a word said about taste, good or bad.

But if the business of art is not to satisfy tastes, what then is its function? Its function is to serve the mystique. Literature must express the mystique, it must show what will be when the totalitarian's particular image of the "good society" has come to pass. Thus, Mr. Zhdanov notes that just as the feudal and later the bourgeois period of full flowering "could create art and literature that asserted the establishment of the new order and, sang its praises," just so "it goes without saying that our [Soviet] literature . . . must reflect the new socialist order that represents the embodiment of all that is best in the history of human civilization culture."

This gives a new meaning to the representational character normally attributed to totalitarian art. Such art is not obliged to be, as it is so often thought to be, representational in the sense that photography is representational. For photography represents what was in the past or what is now; it shows things as they are. Photography may, of course, be used to distort true images. But even the best tricks of photography cannot accomplish the task which Zhdanov assigns to art, namely "to show our people not only as they are today but to glance into their future *and to show them as they shall be tomorrow.*" In addition, photography cannot tell you what "not" to be, yet Soviet literature "while disclosing his future . . . must at the same time show our people what they should *not* be like, we must scourge the survivals of yesterday. . . ." Thus, the arts for the totalitarian are not really representational, photographic, realistic. Paradoxically enough they are the essence of the symbolic. But they symbolize only what is yet to be. They must expose the future and show a glimpse of what the mystique holds in store, what the kingdom of heaven on earth will look like when the totalitarian leader has finally fulfilled his glorious mission.

Further, the totalitarian leader is not prepared to rest here. Unlike the ordinary dictator he is unwilling to ignore the existence of "bad" art so long as he can be assured of getting enough of the "good" art. On the contrary, the totalitarian seeks the elimination, the physical destruction of the bad art, no matter how much of the good art he can get and no matter how limited the circulation of the bad art. Indeed, it is not enough to say that he does not encourage the bad art. He actually proscribes not merely its circulation but its very *creation*. Even when the artist produces it in the privacy of his studio, for his own eyes alone, indeed even if he destroys it soon after its creation, the artist may not produce bad art. Why is this so? Is this too to be understood as simply another example of the extremity and absoluteness of the totalitarian's thirst for power? I think not.

Art, being expressive, is linked to affect. If it is produced privately for private viewing, it violates the principles of the nationalization of affect and the communalization of communication. The expression of the artist which is undertaken primarily for private reasons is equated with that sexual energy which Lenin could not bear to see lost to the greater glory and advancement of the higher cause, to the working out of the mystical law of social development. Such expression, by virtue of being private, is, in addition, suspect. No less than in the case of conversation, the fact of its being private hints that it is a-communal, and more likely that it is anti-communal; else why should the artist seek to hide it? Finally, the war on private art is determined by the more general principle of contamination. Private art, by definition corrupt art because it does not serve the cause, holds out by its mere existence the threat that it will infect and contaminate other art. It poses a double threat, for it may sneak into the public art of the artists who create it, and it may be seen by others and contaminate their taste for the acceptable public art.

## 5. The Institutionalization of Anxiety

The terror is probably the most revolting and dehumanizing feature of totalitarianism, and it wins this dubious distinction from a field of by no means mild competitors from the Augean stable of totalitarianism. It is therefore right and proper that it should have received so much attention, and that we should have tried so hard to understand it. Yet even in this most discussed field there is an important dimension of the problem which from the point of view of social structure we have perhaps given inadequate attention. Our discussions of the terror tend to focus primarily on its methods as directly applied to its physical victims, and to the victims themselves. In human terms these are of course the aspects of the terror which most urgently command our attention. But have we not in our disgust for the terrorist and our compassion for his immediate victim neglected to give adequate attention to the important functions which terror performs for the totalitarian social order in its effects on those fortunate enough never to become immediate victims?

Terror is tremendously important in an immediate and practical way to the totalitarian for handling those who are a problem for him, or who he believes could potentially become problems. The latter are those who come under the formula of prophylactic arrest, which Mr. Gliksman discusses in his contribution to this symposium. But prophylaxis through arrest is only one dimension of the prophylactic function of terror. Attention must be given to the importance of the prophylactic virtues of terror in dealing with the *non*-arrested.

I am suggesting that the terror is as important for handling those whom the regime regards as relatively solid citizens as it is for dealing with those whom the totalitarian wishes to eliminate or put out of circulation for varying periods. In other words terror is a means for institutionalizing and channeling anxiety. Its purpose is to create in every man a deep sense of insecurity. This insecurity is not merely fear, a state in which the expectation of harm has a specific referent, but rather is anxiety in the technical sense. That is, the individual who anticipates being harmed does not really know for what he will be harmed, but merely has a vague feeling that he will indeed be harmed because of "something" he may have done or not done.

Anxiety, if properly harnessed and given focus, can be a powerful force. The regime seeks to create in every man the nagging fear that he may have done something wrong, that he may have left something undone, that he may have said some impermissible thing. It is an important part of the pattern that he be unable ever to find out with certainty whether he actually did err or not, or if he did, exactly what it was that he did wrong. In this light the studied caprice of the terror in its impact on its actual victims may be seen in a new light. The non-victim, looking at the actual victim, can never find out why the victim was victimized, because there are different and contradictory reasons for different victims, or *there may have been no reason at all*.

The non-victim thus becomes the prisoner of a vague uncertainty which nags him. It is this nagging uncertainty in the non-victim which the terror seeks to create. For it is a powerful force in making every man doubly watch his every step. It is prophylactic in the extreme. It will make the citizen properly compulsive about saying the correct things in public and saying them loud for all to hear, or, almost as good, it will teach him to say nothing in public. It will wake him in the middle of the night to go back to his office to do his sums over again, to redraw his blueprint and then redraw it again, to edit and then edit again the article he is writing, to check and then recheck and then check his machine again. Anxiety demands relief, and compulsive reiteration of action is one of the most common human patterns for the handling of anxiety. It is this compulsive conformity which the totalitarian regime wants. It gets it as a derived benefit from the influence of the terror on the non-victim, who puzzles over the reasons for the treatment of the victim. Anxiety has been institutionalized.

# ENVIRONMENTAL CONTROLS AND THE IMPOVERISHMENT OF THOUGHT

## Else Frenkel-Brunswik

### THE ROLE OF PSYCHOLOGY IN THE STUDY OF TOTALITARIANISM

It is conceivable that in the study of certain social and political movements, especially the more matter-of-fact or rational ones, psychology will have little to say. Thus psychology may not play an obvious or prominent role in the explanation of the formation and structure of the American Constitution. But in the elucidation of inherently compensatory and distortive social systems such as totalitarian the picture could not be made complete without the aid of psychology.

To be sure, totalitarianism originates in the structure of society as a whole and this structure is shaped in the ultimate analysis by historical, economic, and political forces. Since all these factors depend on psychological process for their mediation it is obvious that psychological dynamics may play into the resulting course of events. Especially as soon as we shift our view from the origin of political institutions to the manner of their functioning, and particularly to the influence they exert upon the cognitive and social behavior of the individuals and groups that make up the concrete instruments of their execution, it becomes clear that totalitarianism, almost by definition, undertakes to permeate and to indoctrinate every area of individual or collective life. An inquiry into the complete cycle must therefore consider both the structure of the social institutions and the different ways in which the political and social organization is experienced by, and incorporated within, the individual.[1]

Although in authoritarian systems promises concerning economic and social amelioration seem to play an outstanding role, there are strong reasons to believe that it is not these promises which exercise the most potent psychological appeal. For those who have fallen within the grasp of totalitarianism, rational argument is over-shadowed by the image of an all-powerful, superhuman leader whose aura of strength, superiority, and glory afford surcease from feelings of isolation, frustration, and helplessness and whose doctrines provide an absolute and all-embracing answer to the conflicts and confusions of life and relief from the burdens of self-determination. These solutions, presented in a dogmatic, apodictic, and often inarticulate and unintelligible way, are formulated for the explicit purpose of by-passing the processes of reasonable consideration and of finding their mark in those emotional and instinctual processes which prompt to precipitant action. Reason, deliberation, and a many-sided orientation toward objects, situations, or toward life itself then appear as irrelevant and thus as morbid. Beyond and above material advantages offered, there is provided a style of thought and of life, a systematic outlook, an ideology.

This ideology delineates not only the required political attitudes but implies by force of psychological necessity the attitudes toward authority in general, and the conceptions of family, of work, of sex roles;[2] upon some scrutiny it seems that there hardly remains a corner of thought or activity that completely escapes its reach.

Here, again, we must call upon historic, economic, and political factors to explain the conditions under which people are rendered helpless and develop a longing for total surrender and a craving for absolute and definite solutions. The same factors may provide an explanation of why certain groups within a population, as for instance the lower middle-class in Germany, are especially susceptible to totalitarian ideology. The marginality of this group and the discrepancy between its social aspirations and its actual socio-economic position have been frequently mentioned in this context. But looking beyond the socio-economic factors concerned, it is psychology which is instrumental in discerning the particular psychic needs to which totalitarian ideology appeals and in identifying the strong emotive reactions which lead to a partially voluntary renunciation not only of critical faculties but in the end of self-interest as well, and to a readiness for self-sacrifice or even for self-destruction.

Although the ideology as such also must be conceived as originating in the total structure and history of a given society, it is its psychological function which provides an explanation of why dictators are able to elicit spontaneous and genuine followings over and above the adherence they ever could achieve by compulsion, and why those who follow do not become disillusioned in the face of material promises which are never fulfilled. We may perhaps expand psychologically upon the frequently used phrase that the function of totalitarianism is comparable to that of a religion.[3] Totalitarianism seems to create the illusion that merely embracing its ideology confers a kind of magical participation in the source of all power and thus provides absolute salvation and protection.[4] The analysis of magical thinking with its characteristic confusions of subject and reality and of reality and symbol has been one of the prime concerns of recent psychology, especially in areas bordering on anthropological and evolutionary or developmental considerations.[5] Only by recourse to magic involvement can we hope to account for the fact that individual freedom is cheerfully relinquished by many and that the most contradictory statements —such as the Nazi's promise of socialism to the masses and their promise to industry that capitalism would be saved—are taken in stride. The function of the ideology more than compensates for the lack of a realistic program. This is one of the reasons why fascistic movements must depend as much as they do on elaborate ideologies.

This system of ideas as expressed in an ideology is not, as Marx would have it, merely a superstructure or an epiphenomenon; it is the formative force which molds and shapes into total subjection those whom it touches. These ideologies not only appeal skillfully to the so-called higher moral forces by their reference to glory, superiority, honor, and other virtues: they also provide outlets and give permission for the release of "lower" needs, especially aggression, under the pretext of subordinating these needs to the exercise of moral indignation. Though it is of course beyond doubt that opportunistic reasons are of considerable significance in the totalitarian appeal, especially as far as adequate instrumentality and adequate means-end relationships are concerned, much of the behavior, especially on the part of the genuinely enthusiastic branch of the followership, must be viewed as irrational.[6] In the face of the concrete psychological evidence which is continually accumulating, and some of which is to be surveyed below, it would be extremely difficult to shut one's eyes to the fact that irrationality, distortion of perception, and the projections of hostility and of other thwarted tendencies enter the social and political scene as a major component. In turn this irrationality, although more prominent under certain specified historical and socio-economic conditions, cannot be explained within the framework of these conditions alone but must be viewed, in addition, from a psychological point of view.

In the present paper an attempt is made to throw light on the psychological mechanisms by which the totalitarian outlook is transmitted and the role it plays in the adjustment balance of the individual. Our findings show a parallelism between the social and political organization of totalitarianism and the structure and functioning of individuals who are susceptible to this ideology. Thus we will find in statistical samples of such individuals a more or less pronounced preponderance of mechanization, standardization, stereotypy, dehumanization of social contacts, piece-meal functioning, rigidity, intolerance of ambiguity and a need for absolutes, lack of individuation and spontaneity, a self-deceptive profession of exalted ideals, and a combination of over-realism with bizarre and magic thinking as well as of "irrationality with manipulative opportunism."[7] All these are features inherent in the system of totalitarian ideologies. Not only do we find statistically significant relationships between political attitudes and personality makeup, but our understanding of social and political beliefs and of religious and ethical ideologies is deepened when these factors are woven into the matrix of the total individual. That these attitudes are also woven into the pattern of society is more widely stressed and is more generally accepted than are the relationships of these attitudes to the seemingly more remote intimate aspects of our lives.[8] The time seems to have come to establish a proper balance by stressing personality structure along with social behavior as important links in the societal network. An analysis of the psychological processes involved will increase our understanding and possible control of totalitarianism, as long as we remain aware that this avenue of approach is by no means the only one and that totalitarianism, like every social movement, is multi-determined. This fact, however, does not require that every single investigator deal with and control all the factors involved. Such a quest for completeness would be but an invitation to dilettantism.

Since the eradication of independent and critical judgment lies at the very core of totalitarianism, we shall concentrate on this theme. But we hope at the same time to throw light on other psychological aspects of totalitarianism. We shall draw on the resources of academic psychology, with its emphasis on perception and cognition and the adaptive processes in general, as well as on those of social psychology, with its emphasis on social attitudes and their relationship to social institutions, and last but not least on those of depth psychology, which has sharpened our eyes to the underlying pattern of the emotive and instinctual life and has helped us to differentiate the "official" façade from the "dynamic" realities of social behavior.

In order to expand our knowledge concerning distortive interference with thought processes, our group at the University of California undertook to study the cognitive approach of a sample of children and adolescents (age ten years and older) growing up in American homes.[9] We proceeded through direct observation and by experiment, using as our subjects those who had previously been found to have either a relatively extreme democratic or a relatively extreme totalitarian outlook. The susceptibility to totalitarian ideas turned out to be correlated with the outlook of, and the home regime exercised by, the parents, who had been interviewed separately from the children. These data were collected during and shortly after the last war. Many of the parents selected on the basis of their susceptibility to totalitarian ideas expressed more or less veiled sympathies for the existing dictatorships in Germany or Italy, or at least they made some attempts to vindicate these regimes.

Choice of the approach via personality is especially called for when objective social structure is taken for granted as a common background for an investigation aiming primarily at the finding of differences in the appeal various aspects of one and the same civilization—here the American—exert upon varying personalities. In a society as complex as ours, we find contradictory social institutions and political currents. Psychological factors must be called in to help explain selectivity and choice between alternative ideologies. Although our studies are concerned with American samples, the universality of the authoritarian personality type will emerge by the comparison of our findings with the views of the leading Nazi psychologist, E. R. Jaensch, who explicitly extolled rigidity, lack of adaptability, and anti-intellectualism—all features which develop in the wake of totalitarianism and which we too found prominently displayed in individuals in this country who are susceptible to totalitarian ideas.

For a number of years my students and I collected materials on perception, reasoning, and imagination and related them to the types of upbringing to which our subjects were exposed. The intimidating, punitive, and paralyzing influence of an overdisciplined, totalitarian, home atmosphere seems to have effects upon the thinking and creativity of the growing child analogous to those which are apparent under totalitarian social and political regimes. We came to realize that situations encountered within the family unit and the special destinies of early experiences stemming from these situations contribute in large measure to the way social institutions are experienced, integrated, and selectively responded to. This may be especially true in countries where such choices are actually open to the individual. A consideration of the responses to threats in childhood seems to reveal much about the ways in which people react to threats in adult life, though such intensive experiences in later life are undoubtedly in themselves capable of superseding both earlier influences and the individual predispositions to a certain extent. It seems that external pressures of a traumatic character, be they past or be they presently imposed, are likely not only to bring authoritarian personalities to the fore but to reinforce authoritarian trends in individuals who otherwise would remain democratic-minded.

Our finding that harsh discipline at home inhibits and paralyzes the thought processes of growing children does not necessarily imply a direct or exclusive causal relationship between family structure and the rise of totalitarianism. Although in Germany a long history of authoritarian regimes is mirrored in, and undoubtedly reinforced by, authoritarian family and school structures, totalitarianism may well arise in countries with more permissive family atmospheres. Anxiety-inducing social and political situations such as economic depression or war can bring to the fore irrational elements and feelings of helplessness, and thus create susceptibility to totalitarianism regardless of how democratic the family situation might have been. What we mainly want to achieve by reference to the family atmosphere of our authoritarian subjects is to demonstrate in slow-motion the effects of threats upon thinking and thus to understand better the analogous processes in the social and political area.

## SUBMISSION TO AUTHORITY, DOGMA, AND CONVENTION

Before we proceed to a more detailed discussion of the thought patterns, in the cognitive area proper, of the individuals susceptible to totalitarian ideas, let us sketch briefly the way in which preconceived and stereotypical categorizations determined by authority, dogma, and convention permeate their general social outlook. The materials reveal a hierarchical rather than equalitarian conception of human relationships characterized primarily by an admiration for the strong and contempt for the weak. There is a tendency for total, unquestioning, albeit ambivalent, surrender to every manner of authority—be it a political leader, a superior in business or army, a teacher, a parent, or, as we will see, even a perceptual stimulus. The same rigid and compulsive conformity is exercised toward socially accepted standards of behavior—even though the standards may sometimes be unwritten and those of a small "ingroup"—and this conformity is accompanied by an unrealistic and punitive condemnation of those who deviate from such norms.

This compulsive conformity with its all-or-none character differs in several ways from genuine and constructive conformity. First, it is excessive since it compensates for feelings of marginality and the attendant fear of becoming an outcast, and since it often serves the function of covering up the resentment—unconscious as this resentment may be —toward the social system as a whole. The lack of a genuine incorporation of the values of society accounts for the rigidity of the conformity; at the same time it accounts for a certain unreliability, the readiness to shift allegiance altogether to other authorities and other standards. The adherence to the letter rather than to the spirit of the social institutions, which further characterizes the compulsive conformist, issues from his distortion and simplification of the system of norms and commands in the direction of what one may call unidimensional interpretation.

Along the lines just listed the ingroup is glorified while the outgroup is rejected *in toto*. External criteria rather than intrinsic values are prevalent in these dichotomies. In order to be able to maintain the image of oneself and of one's group as strong and at the same time as virtuous, fear, weakness, passivity, and aggressive feelings against authoritative ingroup figures are repressed. Lack of insight and differentiation in the emotional area result in the impoverishment of interpersonal relations and in projection of the unaccepted tendencies into the environment. Thus the other ones—and especially outgroups—are apt to be seen not only as basically weak and impotent but also as immoral, hostile, and depraved, and as imbued, therefore, with all the secondary power and strength such forces of darkness may be able to impart. In the wake of this there follows an attempt to compensate for the ensuing general distrust of people and pervasive cynicism by an overcredulity towards a few chosen leaders.

In the evaluation of the self[10] the authoritarian person is prone to emphasize such morally overpitched traits as "will power" and an iron determination in overcoming the handicaps and vicissitudes of a struggle for existence, the hardships of which are perceived in the image of unmitigated brutality. Energy, decisiveness, "ruggedness," and "toughness" tend to be particularly prominent in the ego-ideal of the men in this group. There is evidence in our material that the display of a rough masculine façade serves to a considerable extent as a compensation for a basic self-contempt and

intimidatedness and for the ensuing tendency toward passivity and dependence.

The ostentatious stress which, according to the findings in *The Authoritarian Personality,* is placed by the ethnocentric person upon sincerity, honesty, courage, and self-control, along with his tendency toward self-glorification, must be evaluated in the light of certain earlier results based on a comparison of verbally espoused ideals with actual behavior.[11] It was found that emphasis on favorable traits, of the type just mentioned, in one's "official" self-image or self-ideal tends to go with objective weakness rather than strength in the particular area concerned. One of the most significant findings concerning the authoritarian personality is the fact that the explicit self-image is in exactly the same contradiction to the one revealed by a more objective evaluation by the expert as had been found in the earlier study just referred to.

In line with repressions and the lack of insight we also find in authoritarian individuals a break in the experienced continuity between childhood-self and present-self. Subjects in this group tend to display a reluctance to make spontaneous reference to their lives as developmental units. They also tend to refrain from going into judicious socio-psychological explanations of the self as well as of others or of society in general.

The stereotypical approach to social and ethical challenges with all its inherent inhibitions carries over into such related, more specific areas as the conception of sex roles, parental roles, and so forth. At least on the surface there is an emphasis on aggression and "toughness" and a disparagement of tenderness and softness ("sissiness") in the masculine ideal, and an emphasis on submissiveness, docility, and "sweetness" in the feminine ideal professed by the authoritarian of either sex. The possibility of trespassing from one syndrome to the other is explicitly excluded. Rigid defenses are erected against cross-sexual tendencies, leading to a "rigid and exaggerated conception of masculinity and femininity"[12] at the ideological level, albeit with frequent break-throughs of these repressed tendencies on the action level.

There is rigid categorization in terms of clearly delineated norms even if this should imply the acceptance of restrictions and disadvantages for one's own sex group.

Aside from strength *vs.* weakness, virtue *vs.* vice, badness *vs.* goodness, masculinity *vs.* femininity, such dichotomies involve cleanliness *vs.* dirtiness and a host of other pairs of opposites vaguely related to the basic juxtapositions. In each case the cleavage between the opposite attributes tends to be considered mutually exclusive, absolute, natural and eternal. In this manner, there is a general tendency toward prejudgments on the basis of rigid set or dogma. Such an approach does not provide sufficient space for an independent variability or evaluation of facts nor for learning to use one's own experiences. It is in this manner that human relations become shallow and externalized.

In the individual children whom we have studied the total outlook, just described, seems to a very appreciable extent to have its root in the home. However, as mentioned above, we do not imply that this is the only or the decisive source of such attitudes; it is necessary to keep in mind that social conditions and institutions have a direct bearing on the family structure. Second, political institutions influence personality formation directly, especially if they are forcefully imposed with the help of all-inclusive ideologies as is the case in totalitarian regimes. In this context we must not forget that although at the action level Hitler may have contributed to the weakening of the family by placing loyalty to the state over loyalty to the family, at the ideological level he made use of the family as a potential instrument in the execution of totalitarianism by advocating as a model of a man one who is a good soldier-father and as an ideal woman one who fulfills her child-rearing functions.

It is primarily the fact that the home discipline in authoritarian homes is experienced as overwhelming, unintelligible and arbitrary, demanding at the same time total surrender, which makes for a parallelism with totalitarian political and social organizations. The parallel becomes even more evident if we consider that the child, by virtue of his objective weakness and dependence, is entirely at the mercy of the parental authorities and must find some way to cope with this situation. In our study we found that parents in the authoritarian group frequently feel threatened in their social and economic status, and that they try to counteract their feelings of marginality by an archaic and frequently unverbalized need for importance. It is noteworthy that what seems to matter is not so much the actual status on the socio-economic ladder nor the objective marginality within a certain class that seems decisive in this respect; but rather the subjective way these conditions are experienced and allowed to build up to certain vaguely conceived aspirations. Recent data further suggest that the status-concern of individuals susceptible to totalitarianism is quite different from a realistic attempt to improve their position by concerted effort and adequate means-goal instrumentality. More often, we find their aspirations to take the form of an unspecific expectation of being helped by sudden changes in the external situation or by an imaginary person who is strong and powerful.

Authoritarian disciplinary rules seem to have their chief origin in this vaguely anticipatory yet inefficient state of social unrest on the part of the parents rather than in the developmental needs of the child. The parents expect the child to learn quickly certain external, rigid, and superficial rules and social taboos. At the same time they are im-

patient, demanding a quick execution of commands which leaves no time for finer discriminations and in the end creates an atmosphere comparable to acute physical danger. The rules to be enforced are largely nonfunctional caricatures of our social institutions based on a misunderstanding of their ultimate intent; in many ways one may even speak of a defiance of culture by external conformity. In any case, the rules are bound to be beyond the scope and understanding of the child. Compelling the child to obey the rules which he is thus unable to internalize may be considered as one of the major interferences with the development of a clear-cut personal identity. The authoritarian form of discipline is thus "ego-destructive" in that it prevents the development of self-reliance and independence. The child, being stripped of his individuality, is made to feel weak, helpless, worthless, or even depraved.

Parents and parental figures, such as teachers or other authorities, acquire a threatening, distant, and forbidding quality. Disciplining, controlling, and keeping one in line is considered to be their major role. A systematic inquiry into the children's conceptions of ideal parents has shown that authoritarian children tend to consider strictness and harshness as some of the prime attributes of ideal parents. Next to this, another desirable quality of the ideal parent stressed by children in this group is that of delivering material goods. By contrast, the more democratic-minded children are given to stress primarily companionship, and understanding, and demonstration of love as the function of ideal parents.

It seems to be largely fear and dependency which discourage the child in the authoritarian home from conscious criticism and which lead to an unquestioning acceptance of punishment and to an identification with the punishing authority. This identification often goes as far as an ostentatious glorification of the parents. As we have learned from psychoanalysis, however, repressions of hostility cannot be achieved without at least creating emotional ambivalence. Thus the same children who seem most unquestioningly to accept parental authority have frequently been found to harbor an underlying resentment and to feel victimized without being fully aware of this fact. The existing surface conformity without genuine integration expresses itself in a stereotypical approach devoid of genuine affect. The description of the parents elicited by interview questions is characterized by the use of exaggerated clichés rather than by expressions of genuine feelings. The range of responses is rather narrow and without the variations commonly found in descriptions of real people. Only the more palpable, crude, and concrete aspects are mentioned.

The rigidification of the child's personality originally induced by the stress on self-negating submission and on the repression of non-acceptable tendencies not only leads to stereotypy; eventually the inherent pattern of conflict may result in a more or less open break between the different layers of personality, and in a loss of control of instinctual tendencies by the individual. This contrasts rather sharply with the greater fluidity of transition and intercommunication between the different personality strata which is typical of the child in the more permissive home. This is not to say that we necessarily find a minimum of guidance and direction in the homes of those of our children and adolescents who exhibit the syndrome of liberalism of personality structure and social outlook most markedly. On the contrary, guidance is essential, especially when it is combined with acceptance and understanding and thus strengthens the moral functions of the children and helps them to overcome their impulses toward selfishness and aggression.

## PATTERNS OF PERCEPTION
## AND THOUGHT:
## INTOLERANCE OF AMBIGUITY

The emotional makeup and the rigidity of defense, lack of insight, and narrowness of the ego of the authoritarian personality as just described carries over even into the purely cognitive domain. Here too, ready-made clichés tend to take the place of realistic spontaneous reactions. This is one of the findings of experiments on perception, memory, and thinking in liberal and authoritarian children[13] which have been conducted with the purpose of investigating the pervasiveness of ways of functioning within the authoritarian personality. The shift from the social and emotional to cognitive area has the added advantage of removing us from the controversial social issues under consideration. So long as we remain under the potential spell of certain preconceived notions, the evaluation of what is reality-adequate or reality-inadequate may be difficult. The fascist may accuse the liberal, and the liberal the fascist, of distorting reality.

In one of the experiments a story—conceived as a clear-cut piece of reality—was presented to children of distinctly authoritarian and of distinctly liberal outlook. The story began with the portrayal of a number of different children and proceeded to a description of their behavior toward a newcomer in terms of aggressiveness *vs.* protectiveness. In retelling the story, authoritarian children tended toward a restriction of scope by concentrating on certain single phrases and details; or else they tended to stray away from the original altogether so that in extreme cases there was almost no relation to the material presented. In other words, there was either a clinging to the original elements with little freedom and distance—a "stimulus-boundness" in

the sense of the psychiatrist, Kurt Goldstein[14]—or else a farreaching neglect of the stimulus in favor of purely subjective fantasies. In this manner a rigid, cautious, segmentary approach seems to go well with one that is disintegrated and chaotic. One and the same child sometimes manifests both patterns in alternation or in all kinds of bizarre combinations. Both of these ways of responding result in any avoidance of uncertainty, one by fixation to, and the other by breaking away from, the given realities.

Another result of this experiment was that the authoritarian children tended to recall a higher ratio of undesirable over desirable features in the characters involved. This result is in line with another of our empirical findings, that is, a general overemphasis on negative, hostile, and catastrophic features in stories given by authoritarian-minded subjects in responses to indirect, so-called "projective" tests involving "thematic apperceptions" of still pictures.[15]

In democratic-minded children the average ratio of undesirable to desirable features recalled was closer to the ratio in the original story than was the case in authoritarian children, indicating greater faithfulness to the "reality" presented. In addition there is some tendency toward remembering the friendly features better than the unfriendly ones. This is in line with other evidence from liberal subjects revealing the operation of a mechanism of "denial" of aggression and violence, that is, a certain naïveté or ostrich policy toward evil.

Some of the trends reported above become especially apparent in an experiment on perception. When presented with pictures of familiar objects and then with similar but ambiguous or unfamiliar stimuli, authoritarian children tended to cling to the name of the original object and in other ways to respond but slowly to the changing of the stimuli. There was a marked reluctance to give up what had seemed certain, and a tendency not to see what did not harmonize with the first set, as well as a shying away from transitional solutions. Once broken, this rigid perseveration was usually followed either by a spell of haphazard, reckless guessing or by a complete blockage. Situations possessing inherent uncertainties or otherwise lacking in firmness seem thus bewildering and disturbing to the authoritarian child even if there is no particular emotional involvement. In most of the other verbal productions there is a similar pattern of either restrictiveness or flow of sterile rumination. Assumptions once made, even though proved faulty and out of keeping with reality, tend to be repeated over and over and not to be corrected in the face of new evidence.

The conclusion suggests itself that all this constitutes an effort to counteract, in the cognitive sphere, the excessive underlying emotional ambivalence induced by environmental overcontrol. The resulting syndrome I have proposed to call "intolerance of ambiguity." A rigid cognitive superstructure in which everything opaque and complex is avoided as much as possible is superimposed upon the conflict-ridden emotional under-structure. In effect, this merely duplicates slavery to authority rather than remedying it. Now there is slavery not only to the authority of the other person; there also is slavery to the authority of the stimulus. In other words, the attitude toward a perceptual stimulus or a cognitive task mirrors the attitude toward authority.

The following aspects of intolerance of ambiguity may be specified: tendency toward unqualified black-white and either-or solutions, oversimplified dichotomizing, stereotypy, perseveration and mechanical repetition of sets and of faulty hypotheses, premature "closure" and preference for symmetry, regularity, and definiteness in the sense of "good" (or *prägnant*) form as defined by Gestalt psychology,[16] achieved either by diffuse globality or by overemphasis on concrete detail; compartmentalization, piecemeal approach, stimulus-boundness; quest for unqualified certainty as accomplished by pedantic narrowing of meanings, by stress on familiarity, by inaccessibility to new experience, or by a segmentary randomness and an absolutizing of those aspects of reality which have been preserved; satisfaction with subjective yet unimaginative, overconcrete or overgeneralized solutions. Totalitarian propaganda takes advantage of this syndrome by the use of vague generalities combined with reference to unessential concrete detail. The opposite attitude, "tolerance of ambiguity," embraces the many-sidedness, complexity, and differentiation which is an essential aspect of the creative process; it has nothing to do with confusion or inarticulate vagueness, in fact, it is in diametrical opposition to these latter features.

The fact that specific manifestations of intolerance of ambiguity tend to reoccur within an individual in contexts seemingly far removed from each other is best brought out by a synoptic analysis of corresponding segments in the protocols of individual cases. Thus, one of the boy subjects in our study showed a great deal of conformity and compliance toward parents and authorities with an occasional breaking through of fits of rage and explosive aggression. This was reflected in the various perceptual and thinking experiments by a generally cautious, restricted, and conservative attitude toward the stimulus with an occasional shift toward disintegrated, random behavior when the strain of coping with the task became too great. Other case studies reveal that some of the authoritarian children perform well on some relatively simple or routine perceptual and cognitive tasks— on tasks which do not require imagination or freedom from stimulus-boundness—in spite of the fact that there are signs of rigidity in their performance;

here we are reminded of the frequently noted technological abilities of the Nazis.

The subtle but profound distortion of reality in the course of the elimination of ambiguities is in the last analysis precipitated by the fact that stereotypical categorizations can never do justice to all the possible aspects of reality. So long as a culture provides socially accepted outlets for suppressed impulses, smooth functioning and fair adjustment can be achieved within the given framework. But the adjustment of the authoritarian-minded person depends on conditions that are comparatively narrowly circumscribed. Whenever differentiation and adaptability to change are required, this adjustment will run the risk of breaking down. Basically, therefore, the various forms of rigidity and of avoidance of ambiguity, directed as they are toward a simplified mastery of the environment, turn out to be maladaptive in the end.

Dramatized, concrete, and at the same time global, diffuse, and undifferentiated types of thinking are, of course, characteristic of certain early developmental stages as such. However, the atmosphere of the home and the more specific expectations of the parents regarding the child's behavior determine whether such primitive reactions become fixated, or whether progress toward higher developmental stages can take place. For the latter course, a reduction of fear, greater relaxation, acceptance of and tolerance for insecurity and weakness in and by the child are necessary. Realism, originality and imaginative cognitive penetration presuppose some such advance in general psychological maturity.

## CLOSENESS OF OPPOSITES
## AS A PRINCIPLE
## OF PERSONALITY ORGANIZATION

In spite of the rather consistent recurrence of common elements in various areas, there is no obvious or simple "unity of style" in the authoritarian personality. This is due at least in part to the many repressions and to the break between the consciousness and unconscious levels as discovered and explored by depth psychology.[17] In the sense of the above brief exposition, the authoritarian person has been found to combine within himself rigid perseverative behavior with an overfluid, haphazard, disintegrated, random approach; compulsive overcaution with the tendency toward impulsive shortcuts to action; chaos and confusion with orderly oversimplification in terms of black-white solutions and stereotypy; isolation with fusion; lack of differentiation with the mixing of elements which do not belong together; extreme concreteness with extreme generality; cynicism with gullibility; overrealism with irrationality; self-glorification with self-contempt; submission to powerful authorities with resentment against them; and stress on masculinity with a tendency toward feminine passivity.

The seeming paradox given by these coexistences is resolved when one considers the fact, hinted at previously in this paper, that a personality thrown out of balance in one direction usually requires counterbalancing in the opposite direction. Elsewhere I have spoken of the "closeness of opposites" as an essential feature of authoritarian personality organization. Indeed, the authoritarian personality may be characterized as consistently inconsistent, or as consistently self-conflicting. In elaborating on tolerance of ambiguity it became evident that lack of distance and too much distance to culture, parents, and other stimulus configurations are more closely related to each other than is either of these opposites to what may be termed "medium distance" from these environmental realities. The nonauthoritarian personality avoids undue reduction of existing complexities and retains balance by maintaining a flexible type of conformity and order. A kind of self-reconciled consistency is thus achieved which manages the inconsistencies of reality at the conscious level rather than allowing them to invade the unconscious and to be lived out by devious means of tension-reduction and by displacement of aggression upon substitute targets.

Although most of our authoritarian adolescents tend to follow the self-conflicting pattern described above, we are able to distinguish subvarieties in whom one or the other side prevails. In one there is a prevalence of control, rigidity, caution, and order as far as overt behavior is concerned, while the chaotic side becomes manifest only under stress; in the other there is a predominance of chaos, fusion, and impulsive action while the ideal of control and rigid order remains to a large extent confined to the symbolic level of consciously accepted values.

## EXPLICIT ESPOUSAL OF RIGIDITY IN THE NAZI PERSONALITY IDEAL

While to us the authoritarian pattern of personality semed impoverished and closed to new experiences, many of the features which from the standpoint of adjustment to physical or social realities must be described as negative were listed among the desirable attributes of an ideal type of personality by E. R. Jaensch of Marburg. Jaensch is probably the most articulate and brilliant exponent of the Nazi ideology so far as professional psychological contributions to this field are concerned. He was the Hitler-appointed permanent President of the German Psychological Association until his death in 1940. He formulated a comprehensive valuative personality typology on the thousands of pages he published during the last years of his life. An analysis of his writings reveals some important aspects of the most markedly fascistic version of German thinking. Exposure of his self-contradictions and rectification of his errors is important in view of the fact that his writings carry a great deal of sweep and persuasive power, hardly diminished by the endless repetitions and confusions with which they are encumbered. His misuse and distortion of basic categories and facts, his subtle mixture of insight and confabulation will continue to have a great appeal to a frame of mind by no means dead with the military defeat of Nazism. Jaensch's most comprehensive publications on the subject bear the following characteristic title, in translation: "The Antitype: Psychological-Anthropological Foundations of German Culture Philosophy Based on What We Must Overcome."[18] This antitype (*Gegentypus*) is seen as the enemy of the national German movement and the incorporation of all that is evil.

The antitype is characterized primarily by tendencies toward loosening (*Auflockerung*) and dissolving (*Auflösung;* hence also the term "lytic type"). The antitype is also called the S-type since he allegedly often manifests synesthesia, the well-known phenomenon of color-hearing or tone-seeing. Jaensch sees in this latter phenomenon a lack of clear-cut and rigid evaluation of, and submission to, the stimulus on the part of the perceptual response.

Passages from Jaensch's *Der Gegentypus,* presented in my own literal translation, will illustrate his notions of the antitype. It should be stressed at this point that Jaensch is notorious for his neglect of even the most elementary principles of statistical scrutiny. Many of his statements concerning interrelationships of traits are downright incorrect, while others are merely unsubstantiated.

We begin with a quotation referring to perception:

> His spatial perceptions are unstable, loosened up, even dissolved. Normally the objects of the external world are given to the psychophysical organism of man in a univocally determined spatial order. (Each object in the external world creates an image on the retina of our eye. . . . To the points of the retina correspond firmly and univocally determined locations in visual space or, as this is usually expressed, the spatial values of the retina are fixed.) This fixed—more precisely we should say relatively fixed—coördination between its stimulus configuration and perceptual Gestalt is disrupted in the case of the S-type (p. 37).

In this quotation, Jaensch considers his ideal German type as giving unambiguous reactions to stimuli, a feature which he confuses with receptiveness and precision. This desideratum of a one-to-one relationship between stimulus and response directly contradicts the findings of modern psychology, especially those of the so-called Gestalt psychology, which experimentally demonstrated the universal multiple determination of our perceptual responses by a variety of factors, some of them constellational and some attitudinal or temporal. It is for the stress on spontaneous perceptual "restructuring" and on its crucial role in problem-solving and in scientific or artistic creativity that Jaensch has declared the orientation of Gestalt psychology to be "morbid." The glorification of rigid stimulus-response relationships by Jaensch and his assertion of their predominance in the ideal Nazi type fits well with the fact that what we have called intolerance of ambiguity is predominant in our authoritarian children.

Rigid control, perseveration, and avoidance of differences also are an integral part of Jaensch's ideal of discipline. To him, one of the most gratifying experiences is the feeling of "equality of palpable, physical characteristics . . . [wearing a] uniform, marching in step and column" (p. 337). The antitype is criticized for his aspiration to some measure of being different in developing his individuality.

All this ties in with a questionable notion of masculinity. As we have found in our authoritarian subjects, emphasis on an exaggerated ideal of "toughness" goes with repression and rejection of feminine traits in men, and with contempt for women. There is hardly any mention of women in the presentation of Jaensch; when there is, usually some affinity between women and the antitype is construed. According to Jaensch, the struggle between firmness and lack of firmness, between stability and what he calls "lability," is identical with the struggle between the masculine and its opposite, disparagingly labeled the "effeminate."

All-important to Jaensch is the evaluation of the antitype as to his aptitude for military service, considered by him one of the highest values:

The pronounced lytic type is . . . an "anti-type" not only from the standpoint of our German national movement but also from that of military psychology. He is the one of whom the army must beware most, the extremely unsoldierly type. . . . Since he lacks all firmness the lytic type is always more or less unvirile . . . far removed from a heroic conception of life (pp. 38ff.).

The intellect, as such, is considered a nonvirile element in this latter sense. The antitype is said to have an inclination toward the playful, aesthetic and intellectual. We have actually found this inclination to be present in our liberal-minded subjects but have found little reason for looking askance at it. Again, Jaensch confuses two essentially disparate and incompatible features, the looseness or arbitrary license, on the one hand, and the loosening of rigid fixations that defines genuine mastery of the stimulus at the level of essentials, on the other. So he comes to think that "liberalism" of any kind —"liberalism of knowledge, of perception, of art, etc." (p. 44)—is identical with a libertine lack of

firmness and stability of the personality. And he assumes liberalism—along with "adaptability" in general (see below)—to be degenerative, immoral, and dangerous for society.

Prominent in Jaensch's version of anti-intraceptiveness and antiintellectualism is his attitude toward scientific theorizing. Theory is seen by Jaensch not in its positive function as a detour to better understanding of reality but rather as a subjectivistic leading-away from reality. (It is possible to trace such overemphasis on nearness to reality to an underlying tendency to escape from reality.) Concerning the particular case of relativity theory in physics Jaensch has this to say:

The struggle conducted by the physicists Lenard and Stark in an attempt to dislodge the theory of Einstein by establishing a more concretely oriented "German Physics" can be understood only from this point of view. It is the struggle for consideration of reality in natural science and against the . . . inclination to dissolve all reality into theory (pp. 46, 49).

It will be remembered that more recently Soviet writers have attacked Einstein from an antitheoretical standpoint very similar to that of the Nazis, accusing him of an "idealistic" orientation in his physics.

Systematic espousal of rigid environmental controls by totalitarian regimes thus seems not only to stifle imagination and to prevent the acquisition of the theoretical skills so necessary for the comprehension of reality but even to lead to glorification of this defect and to its being turned into a propagandistic weapon. In tricks of this kind lie one of the seeds of self-destruction inherent in totalitarian systems.

The way in which intolerance of ambiguity and anti-intellectualism tie in with racial theory is revealingly illustrated by the following quotation from Jaensch. In the case of racial mixture,

. . . nature has to leave . . . everything uncertain and in suspense. . . . The individual at birth may be endowed with nothing fixed and certain, just with the uncertainty, indeterminability, and changeability which will enable him to adjust to each of the various conditions of life. . . . The opposite is true if an individual possesses only ancestors who from time immemorial have lived in the North German space and within its population. . . . The characteristics necessary for this life therefore may be safely placed in his cradle as innate, fixed, and univocally determined features (pp. 230 ff.).

Jaensch further states that in the case of bloodmixture, which he considers an "abnormal state of affairs," adaptability must be increased since "the entire conduct of life and the total existence is entrusted to intelligence alone"; and he adds condemningly that "among all the higher mental functions intelligence is the most flexible and adaptable." In discussing adaptability, Jaensch further points out that the antitype, when engaged in psychology and anthropology, is prone to think in terms of environment, education, intellectual influences, and reason while his ideal type will refer to such factors as blood, soil, and heredity.

The Jews are considered the purest though by no means the only representative of the S-type, and this Jaensch attempts to relate to racial mixture:

According to Hans F. K. Gunther, the Jews do not constitute a primary race but rather a highly complex racial mixture. This may be taken as an explanation for the fact that they tend so much toward the dissolving type, and that they play such an outstanding role in the development of a dissolution culture (p. 22).

Racial pollution is connected in the mind of Jaensch with physical pollution by germs: "Already in studying adults we were impressed by the fact that bodily illness, especially tuberculosis, is found most frequently in the group representing the S-type" (p. 22). Fear of germs and of spread of contagious disease has in our California material been found to be a prominent preoccupation of the authoritarian personality syndrome. According to psychoanalytic theory, the idea of pollution and contamination with germs is related to sexual thoughts. And indeed Jaensch, somewhat fantastically, proceeds to say:

Since some kind of a connection between tuberculosis and schizophrenia is established on the basis of the development and the symptomatology of the two diseases, and since, on the other hand, the connection between schizophrenia and an affliction of the genital sphere seems highly probable, it seems to follow that we should pay more attention than hitherto to the hidden effects of camouflaged tuberculosis, infections (and mixed infections) in the genital sphere when approaching the problem of schizophrenia (p. 460).

Our above considerations are by no means limited to Jaensch. It is well known that Hitler thought of blood-mixture as the sole cause of the decline and death of cultures. Equally well known is the exaggerated fear of syphilis—"syphilidophobia" as labeled in psychiatry—in the writings of the leading Nazis, and the connection they see between this infection and sexual intercourse between what they consider different races. Like Hitler, Jaensch thinks of the Nazi movement as "a biological movement, a recuperative movement, with the purpose of guiding humanity or at least our own people out of the vestibule of the psychiatric clinic" (p. 461).

Jaensch's programatic quest for firmness, for absence of ambiguity, and for definiteness is in strange contrast with the fact that his own writings are endless, full of needless repetitions, speculative intricacies, and bizarre if sometimes shrewd and subtle observations. It seems that Jaensch is struggling for a way out of his own and his culture's unbearable complexity. Reportedly Jaensch was well aware of the presence of "antitypical" features in himself; apparently it is the projections of these features which he fights in his image of the antitype.

In his conceptions of mental health as being mainly a matter of vitality and physical vigor Jaensch somewhat resembles Nietzsche whom he often quotes as his master. It is interesting to note that he joins forces with Nietzsche, another sick man, when he says: "The struggle against the hollowed-out and diseased Christianity (of the antitype) . . . was at the climax of this unfortunate epoch already carried on by Nietzsche. . . . Today we shall carry it on by action" (p. 511).

Just as in our empirical findings on authoritarian children, the stimulus-boundness ascribed by Jaensch to his ideal German personality type all too soon reveals its affinity to confusion, chaos, and to a missing-out on essential aspects of reality-adaptation. The Nazi tendencies to expansion were unrealistic, to say the least, and so was their gross distortion of the personality of the enemy, as, for example, their view of the American as unsoldierly and effeminate. In this manner the refusal to face masculinity-femininity conflicts or other alleged or real difficulties or shortcomings in oneself turns out to lead to a personalized, "projective" view of other nationalities and of the outside world, resulting in a general distortion of reality and eventually in self-destruction.

## SOCIAL AND POLITICAL OUTLOOK

The political irradiations of the personality pattern as found in the authoritarian individual and as idealized by Jaensch are grave. The feeling of unworthiness and the resulting anxiety implanted into the individual in an authoritarian atmosphere prevent him from squarely facing his weaknesses, shortcomings, and conflicts, and prompt him to project into his social environment—that is, to "externalize"—what he considers "evil." Evil then is fought outside rather than inside. There is, as we have seen, a striving for compensatory feelings of superiority as afforded by the condemnation of others, especially of outgroups. Images of social groups are thus dramatized and conceived as either altogether good or altogether bad, and social realities appear as oversimplified and excessively clear-cut structures.

Under an authoritarian regime—may this be a state or the home—the hostilities against the given authority must be repressed and the helplessness of the individual is exploited. This fact must be considered a strong reinforcing agent for the "anti-weakness attitude" which in our material was found to be a further attribute of the authoritarian personality and an accompaniment of his positive if superficial identification with the strong. Sympathy for the weak cannot develop where there is ingrained fear of weakness and where the weak furnishes the only practical target of aggression. It is this same fear which makes for a shying away from responsibility and from the facing of one's own guilt, for the rejection of individuals, groups and nations different from oneself, and for magic expectations of, and magic dependence on, strong leaders and "fate." Blind trust in the potency of fate frequently leads to the development of elaborate systems of superstition. It is primarily the "strength" of the leader and the fact of force in general which reaches the authoritarian individual. He pays very little attention to the political program as such but follows the lure of a few slogans incorporating the dichotomies discussed above in the context of intolerance of ambiguity. Such persons could not possibly at the same time be accessible to democratic values.

The authoritarian person may sometimes be kept in check by authorities, who take over for them the regulatory functions of conscience and reality testing. This need for permanent reinforcement tends to persist and is likely to become an entrenched state of affairs. The preferred authority is the one who promises most in terms of material goods, who offers an ideology as a means of orientation and self-confidence, and who grants permission for more or less unbridled release of the suppressed hostile tendencies in certain specified directions. It is in this manner that the combination of over-realism and irrationality finds its expression in the political scene.

Since, as we have seen, there is ample underlying resentment against authorities on the part of the authoritarian-minded follower, we find a tendency toward easy exchange of such authorities. The combination of surface conformity with lack of internalization and integration explains the apparently paradoxical fact that we often find the rigid conformist flooded by repressed unsublimated and unmodified tendencies which threaten the brittle and tenuously maintained superstructure. Out of anxiety this individual adheres to the familiar and unquestioningly accepts the customs of his society; out of the same anxiety, however, he readily turns against this very society, the values of which he has never espoused with more than a divided heart. This is but one of the vicious circles inherent in a personalization of the social and political scene.

Under an authoritarian regime, the conception of society must become as unpsychological and ahistorical as is that of one's own life. Since continuities can be perceived only when there are no repressive breaks and no taboos on the application of freely searching social or psychological concepts and theories, the authoritarian individual tends to expain individual actions or social events in terms of incidental factors or of superstition and magic forces.

The feelings of social and economic marginality which we found to be predominant in the home atmosphere of our authoritarian subjects suggests a further parallel between certain results of our studies and the rise of fascism, especially the rise of Nazism in Germany.

Another comparison may be based on the fact that differentiation, articulation, spontaneity and autonomy are in an authoritarian home or state taken away not only from the individual; these characteristics are also lost so far as the organization of society as a whole is concerned. Both the individual and the society in which he lives are transformed into an amorphous aggregate with a superimposed strong leadership.[19] In our California studies we have tried to supply details on the impoverishment of the individual personality that forms the counterpart to the impoverishment of the social institutions under authoritarian rule. Under this aspect it is primarily the lack of integration and individuation which compels the authoritarian individual to use all kinds of stereotypes, clichés, and ideologies as crutches and substitutes for personal opinion and as an antidote against underlying confusion.

## THE ROLE OF REASON

In spite of the great hopes which the eighteenth and nineteenth centuries placed upon reason and progress, we are faced today with an eruption of the irrational and with a skepticism concerning reason and science. In part, the abandonment of the critical and independent faculties of man is voluntary. Were the expectations concerning the dynamic force of reason unrealistic? Has the rational approach been overrated and did modern civilization nourish an illusion? Is mankind governed, perhaps, by altogether different forces? I think these questions must partially be answered in the affirmative. It is certainly true that in the era of Enlightenment an overly simple conception of human motivation was entertained. We have learned from Freud that the unconscious and irrational factors are of great importance in the formation of personality. We know today that they also influence the social and political attitudes, at least of some individuals. Under irrational factors Freud includes tendencies toward destruction and excessive dependence along with derivatives of infantile sex attitudes, such as Oedipal residues, especially if unconscious and displaced; further included are magic, archaic, and primitive patterns of thought and action. Over and above these irrational factors which are rooted in the history of the individual, Freud[20] as well as some sociologists, among them LeBon[21] and Mannheim, have stressed the irrational factors which derive from the participation in groups. Total identification with the masses and the collective often leads to the renunciation of individual responsibility, to a reduction of intellectual ability, to an increase of cruelty, and a lack of moderation. Unless some measure of individuation is achieved, there can be no constructive group membership.

Both Durkheim and Weber have emphasized that the foundation of society lies in fundamentally nonrational moral or religious qualities. In contrast with the irrational factors just mentioned Durkheim[22] stresses such factors as respect for normative rules and moral obligation. Although Weber[23] elaborated on the rationalism of Western civilization, he was much concerned with the problem of the nonrational meaning of life; he made the well-known assumption that within Protestantism religious feelings, interests and experiences have led from the preoccupation with salvation to an ascetic puritanism and the emphasis on exemplary earthly life based on work, self-reliance, rational planning, and virtue. It was also Weber who predicted that there will be a reaction to the rationalism of the nineteenth century. Pareto, Sorel, and Nietzsche thought they had to abandon—with varying degrees of despair—the hopes that the masses will be open to reason.

Freud, on the other hand, while far from underestimating the power of irrational tendencies, was not discouraged. He never relented in supporting the struggle for greater awareness and mastery of the unconscious. His famous saying that the voice of the intellect, "though low, does not stop until it is heard," is one of the many expressions of his belief that some day reason will prevail. Further relevant in this context is the realization that for the establishment of genuinely ethical behavior it is not enough to make the instincts conscious and integrated so as to render them modifiable. Ethical behavior can be achieved only if both the so-called id-tendencies and the frequently overlooked, likewise unconscious sadistic, primitive, and unadaptable superego-tendencies, clothed as they are in moralism and the condemnation and exclusion of others, are replaced by more reasonable moral judgments.

In some respects the authoritarian children of our study were found to display a severity of moral standards reminiscent of the primitive superego tendencies just referred to. Thus, in answering the question of what type of punishment should be imposed for different types of misdemeanor, children in this group tended to demand cruel and extreme retaliation for the slightest infractions. We know today that sheer repression and denial of evil does not assure its being overcome and that such devices are detrimental rather than constructive for genuinely socialized behavior. The avoidance of conscious guilt-feelings and of related kinds of suffering is achieved by projection of the unaccepted impulses onto others, especially outgroups, and by unquestioning loyalty to a questionable ideal or leader on whom the moral demands of the conscience are projected and at whose disposal the individual has placed himself. The authoritarian individual does not generally succeed in making the maturational step from repressive fear of authority to an internalized social conscience. It is the repressed, latent forces which are most likely to be projected onto the political and social scene. Especially in the authoritarian personality, rational control extends to a relatively small sector of the personality only and the repressed impulses lurk close to the surface, ready to break through at any appropriate occasion. Totalitarianism and its political and social propaganda machinery attempt to appeal primarily to these impulses, reinforcing them at the same time. In order to effectively counteract the potential chaos resulting from these impulses, such slogans as that of Goebbels, "cleanliness and orderliness are the foundation of life," were at the same time promoted.

For the clarification of the interplay of impulses and their eventual mastery we owe much to psychoanalysis with its stress on the importance of awareness, integration, rationality, coöperativeness, and maturity. However, psychoanalysis has often been misunderstood; by virtue of such misunderstanding it has contributed, along with other theoretical systems, to a swinging of the pendulum from the traditional blind faith and belief in reason to an overextended relativism and tendency toward unmasking of motives. A number of misunderstandings has arisen through the widespread tacit notion that if something is bad, its opposite must be good. Thus, the idea has been promoted in many homes and in some educational systems and political circles that in order to avoid authoritarianism, all authority must be forsworn. Against this ultramodern view it must be held that total permissiveness would verge upon anarchy. Respect for the authority of outstanding individuals and institutions is an essential aspect of a healthy society. It does not as such lead to total surrender to, nor to an absolute glorification of, the given leaders. This is especially true if leadership is limited to specialized fields or to special functions.

We must further stress that rationality does not imply amorality and freedom from obligation. On the contrary, genuine ethical behavior involves a comprehension of the issues involved, a facing of all uncertainties, conflicts and one's own guilt, and a readiness to accept the anguish involved in such an open confrontation. Irrationality and the tendency toward destruction of self and of others, on the other hand, are often combined with a short-range over-realism and an orientation toward immediate material benefits.

Furthermore, the avoidance of the quest for

certainty does not imply cynicism and morbid doubt. On the contrary, in the authoritarian personality the need for absolutes turns out to be combined with basic disbelief and general distrust. In this sense the obvious function of the philosophical outlook which at the present time dominates Germany in general, and her philosophy and psychology in particular, that is, existentialism, is that of emphasizing—to a generation plagued by the deepest doubts about the value of living— the worthwhileness of anything that exists by virtue of the sheer fact of its existence. Nazi rigidity and intolerance of ambiguity has here given way, in a remarkably close succession of opposites, to the extreme relativism which is at the core of existentialism.

Many modern writers seem resigned to the fact that only what is irrational, absolute, and dogmatic can really incite people and motivate them to action, whereas the rational, many-sided approach is seen as inherently inhibitory and as leading to a barren and sterile conception of life. Against this we must hold that virility of a nation does not seem to be grounded in blind fanaticism, militant aggressiveness, and short-cuts to action. The "official" optimism often characteristic of such an outlook disguises only thinly an underlying despair. Our findings show that individuals who are more open to reason and facts are in general those who have a more differentiated internal life and deeper and more reliable—though often relatively calm— emotions. They are also those who, although less fanatic and less compulsive, show more consistency, conviction, and dedication in their principles and ideals. But the fact remains that the extreme and obvious positions lend themselves more readily to verbal formulation and thus give the false impression of solving some of the eternal perplexities. Very concrete as well as very general formulations can be put into the service of such definite and unqualified statements. In the task of a positive formation of democratic outlook and values, we must face the difficulties intrinsic in the complexities, ambiguities, flexibilities, and less fetching logicalities of the social realities.

Examples of apodictic and nonrational systems are given by both the race doctrine of Nazi Germany and the dialectical materialism of Soviet Russia. Though the two differ in the particulars of their bizarreness, both offer an essentially unscientific, metaphysical, all-inclusive *Weltanschauung* which has the appearance of definiteness, but is unrelated to fact. There is empirical evidence that individuals susceptible to totalitarianism manifest more disturbance in their empirical and rational thinking than they do in the area of pure logic; furthermore, metaphysical systems do not prevent the acquisition of technological skills which constitute a domain by themselves. However, totalitarian states stifle free inquiry not only in the social sciences and in psychology, but even in physics, at least so far as theory construction is concerned. We have witnessed this in the reaction to Einstein on the part of both Nazi Germany and Soviet Russia. An interesting problem is posed by the question how long a society can exist in which there is a certain mastery of technology but in which the social, political, and human outlook is impoverished to the point of dogmatic and distortive schemes.

Different countries vary thus to some degree in their readiness to tolerate ambiguity. As we have seen, this readiness relates not only to the structure of social and political institutions, but is also expressed in the philosophical and psychological outlook. For America, a long-range optimism seems justified to this writer. On the one hand, it must be granted that there are probable reinforcers of the authoritarian personality pattern in our culture. Among them we may list the following as the most important: presence of external threats; cultural emphasis on success and power; the necessity of proving oneself, if by no other means than by establishing social distance to those who are allegedly lower on the social scale; increasing standardization; increasing unintelligibility of political and social forces; presence of a powerful propaganda machinery used to manipulate public opinion; increasing difficulties in a genuine identification with society, resulting from the anonymity of big organizations and the ensuing isolation of the individual; some tendency toward a short-cut to action, toward externalization, and toward avoidance of introspection and contemplation. But it seems that these reinforcers of authoritarianism are more than counterbalanced by a long list of powerful rienforcers of tolerance for ambiguity and for liberalism in general: the democratic political tradition with its many-power check-and-balance system; the tradition of a pragmatic philosophy which, in contrast to the German philosophical tradition, is undogmatic and antimetaphysical; the general preference for scientific and rational explanations; the relative weakness of the tendencies toward oversystematization and fanaticism; the American "melting pot" ideal; the democratic tradition with its protective attitude toward the weak; the emphasis on individualism; the equalitarian relationships between children and parents, and between pupils and teachers; the readiness to criticize governmental as well as parental authorities; the increased choices offered by technological progress; the rising attempts to understand the social and economic processes in their inconsistencies and irrationalities; and the readiness and ability to accept tentativeness, conflict, and suspense.

The struggle between these opposing forces characterizes not only our civilization as a whole, but every single individual. How this struggle will end and which of these opposing trends will be victorious does by no means hinge solely on the number of mature and rational individuals, but on the interplay of political, social, and psychological phenomena in their entirety.

## NOTES

1. For the function of psychology in the study of political movements see also Else Frenkel-Brunswik, "Interaction of Psychological and Sociological Factors in Political Behavior," *American Political Science Review,* XLVI (1952).

2. The function of ideology in totalitarian systems has been emphasized by most students of totalitarianism. See especially Erich Fromm, *Escape from Freedom* (New York: Holt, Rinehart, Winston, 1941), and Karl Mannheim, *Ideology and Utopia* (New York: Harcourt, Brace and World, 1949).

3. See especially Sigmund Neumann, *Permanent Revolution: The Total State in a World at War* (New York: Harper, 1942).

4. The propensity toward magic thinking and superstition in individuals susceptible to totalitarianism has been empirically demonstrated. See T. W. Adorno, Else Frenkel-Brunswik, Daniel J. Levinson, and R. Nevitt Sanford, *The Authoritarian Personality* (New York: Harper, 1950), and Else Frenkel-Brunswik, "A Study of Prejudice in Children," *Human Relations,* I (1948).

5. Heinz Werner, *Comparative Psychology of Mental Development* (rev. ed.; Chicago: Follett, 1948).

6. The quality of irrationality has been stressed by many investigators of totalitarianism. See especially Fromm, *Escape,* and Mannheim, *Ideology.*

7. See the present writer's paper on "Interaction of Psychological and Sociological Factors," p. 45.

8. Harold D. Lasswell, *Psychopathology and Politics* (Chicago, 1930), should be singled out as a pioneer study in relating political attitudes to personal life histories.

9. Brief surveys of the plan and of some of the major results of the project involved, the California Study of Social Discrimination in Youth, were given by the present writer in "A Study of Prejudice in Children," and in "Patterns of Social and Cognitive Outlook in Children and Parents," *American Journal of Orthopsychiatry,* XXI (1951). This project is part of

the activities of the Institute of Child Welfare of the University of California. The separate project on *The Authoritarian Personality,* cited above, had dealt with adult subjects only and did not involve a study of the conception of social roles at the ideological level, of purely cognitive processes, nor did it involve a direct observation of the subjects' families. The present paper concentrates on the aspects just listed.

10. For more extensive discussion of the attitude toward the self, toward sex roles, and toward parents and other figures of authority see the present writer's chapters x, xi, and xii in *The Authoritarian Personality,* and the material on adolescents referred to above, note 9.

11. See also Else Frenkel-Brunswik, "Mechanisms of Self-Deception," *Journal of Social Psychology,* X (1939).

12. See the present writer's "A Study of Prejudice in Children," p. 299; on the same page the reader will find verbatim passages from the protocols of authoritarian and democratic-minded adolescents concerning their notions of masculine and feminine ideals.

13. Concerning the problems and results discussed in this section see Else Frenkel-Brunswik, "Intolerance of Ambiguity as an Emotional and Perceptual Personality Variable," *Journal of Personality,* XVIII (1949).

14. Kurt Goldstein, "The Significance of Psychological Research in Schizophrenia," in S. S. Tomkins (ed.), *Contemporary Psychopathology* (Harvard University Press, 1943). See also Kurt Goldstein and Martin Scheerer, "Abstract and Concrete Behavior," *Psychol. Monog.,* LIII (1941), no. 239.

15. For a description of the Thematic Apperception Test see H. A. Murray and workers at the Harvard Psychological Clinic, *Explorations in Personality* (New York: Oxford University Press, 1938), pp. 530–545.

16. Kurt Koffka, *Principles of Gestalt Psychology* (New York: Harcourt, Brace and World, 1935).

17. Sigmund Freud, "Instincts and Their Vicissitudes" (1915). In *Collected Papers,* vol. IV (London: Hogarth, 1925).

18. Erich Jaensch, *Der Gegentypus* (Leipzig: Barth, 1938).

19. Emil Lederer, *State of the Masses* (New York: Norton, 1940).

20. Sigmund Freud, *Group Psychology and the Analysis of the Ego,* translated by J. Strachey (New York: 1949).

21. Gustave LeBon, *The Crowd: A Study of the Popular Mind* (1895). Translation, London: Unwin, 1920.

22. Emile Durkheim, *The Rules of Sociological Method,* translation, edited by G. E. C. Catlin (New York: Free Press, 1950).

23. Max Weber, *The Protestant Ethic and the Spirit of Capitalism* (New York: Scribner, 1930).

# CRACKS IN THE MONOLITH: POSSIBILITIES AND PATTERNS OF DISINTEGRATION IN TOTALITARIAN SYSTEMS

Karl W. Deutsch

Is there a pathology peculiar to totalitarian systems? Are there, that is to say, specific ways in which established totalitarian governments or cultures tend to be destroyed, divided, or otherwise basically changed by their own inner development?

Are there, in particular, any recurrent tendencies to stagnation or division, to schisms, heresies, or secessions—social, regional, or ideological—*which can be traced to the fundamental structure of totalitarian government,* and which could be tested, at least in principle, against available data from concrete cases? If so, what inferences for policy expectations and research programs in the free countries could be derived from them?

All that will be offered in this paper in answer to these questions will be a scheme of analysis drawn from the theory of communication and control, and to some extent from the theory of organization, and brought to bear on a problem in political thought, so that it may be confronted with data from history and from comparative political research. To gather these data in detail, to use them to test the specific theory, and to modify the theory in their light will of necessity have to be the task of later work.

## SOME CHARACTERISTICS OF TOTALITARIANISM

Before we even approach the questions we just asked, we must first pause briefly to deal with a preliminary one. Is there a "totalitarianism" in the abstract, or as an ideal type, somewhat in Max Weber's sense, or are there only particular totalitarian systems?[1] In this paper it will be answered tentatively that there are particular totalitarian systems which are comparable among each other to the extent to which they have certain limited performance characteristics in common.[2]

The three most important of these characteristics are perhaps extreme *mobilization of effort, unity of command,* and effective *power of enforcement.* These three characteristics, perhaps more than any others, make totalitarian systems perform differently from other systems of social and political decision-making. Their loss is conspicuous whenever totalitarian governments succumb to stagnation or disintegration.

Totalitarianism characteristically involves the extreme mobilization of the efforts and resources of population under its government. "In a democracy," runs a well-known joke, "everything that is not forbidden is permitted; under an authoritarian regime, everything that is not permitted is forbidden; under totalitarianism, everything that is not forbidden is compulsory." The citizen of a totalitarian state or culture has no time and no possessions that he could truly call his own. His free time after working hours should be spent digging victory gardens, or volunteering for a work brigade, or attending party meetings, or in some other activity or campaign prescribed by the regime. His home and goods, if any, must likewise be devoted to the cause. Ideally, he is expected to be unceasingly active, with all his time and all his resources.

As with the individual, so with the country. Nothing must be held back, and none may withhold themselves. Whatever the avowed purpose of the cause or the regime, it must now be served and pushed forward "with all thy heart and all thy strength," "unstintingly and unflinchingly," "not sparing our own blood or treasure," "without mental reservation or evasion," "rejoicing to be damned for the glory of God." As the old inscription of the Hanseatic sailors had it, *navigare necesse est, vivere non.*

This is the language of enthusiasm. Every phrase just cited can occur and indeed has occurred, in a non-totalitarian context. In a non-totalitarian setting, however, such total commitment, even if it should be demanded, remains transitory, or it remains limited to some particular sphere of activity, or to some particular group of people. The more totalitarian a culture or regime becomes, the more permanent and all embracing become its demands for mobilization and commitment,[3] and the more thoroughly are they reinforced by the two other characteristics of totalitarianism; singleness of command and a significant probability of enforcement.

The term "singleness of command" is used in two different meanings. It may mean that all commands in the system originate from a single source, or are at least controlled by a single source, whether or not these commands are consistent among themselves. Or the term may mean that all commands in a system are consistent among themselves, whether they originate from a single source or from several sources. It is singleness in this latter sense of mutual consistency of commands which is essential for the operation of a totalitarian system.

The third characteristic, the probability of enforcement, requires the existence of sufficient power to enforce all decisions within the totalitarian system, and to prevent all effective interference from outside; although it does not necessarily require sufficient power to achieve some avowed external goal of the regime.

Each of the three characteristics or functions which we have listed—mobilization of resources, singleness of command, and power of enforcement—is dependent on some underlying conditions without which it cannot be maintained.

## THE EMBARASSMENT OF PREVIOUS COMMITMENTS

Thus the mobilization of resources required by totalitarianism presupposes that these resources have already been freed from previous commitments, both from commitments of custom and from commitments imposed by previous political systems or even by earlier stages or policies of the totalitarian regime itself. Totalitarianism thus must destroy previous custom, even where its spokesmen may profess to defend it. Its leaders must divert resources, manpower, and attention from past institutions, even where these institutions are supposed to be preserved. Finally, totalitarianism must take away resources and attention from its

own past policies and past demands of consistency wherever these past policies or past commitments threaten to cut down the range of resources available to it presently for recommitment.

Changes in the previous political line, or in the old guard of decision-making personnel, are therefore not peripheral or accidental in totalitarian regimes, but seem likely to recur. As soon as the new commitments of resources mobilized by totalitarianism tend to become permanent, these resources are no longer completely available to the totalitarian regime. The more permanent and irrevocable the commitment of its resources, the less totalitarian in the long run must a regime become. Either, that is to say, its resources become frozen in commitments to an unusual strategy for an improbable goal—in which case the regime loses much of its capacity to maneuver and to learn, and thus to preserve itself, and risks stagnation or destruction—or else its resources become ever more firmly committed to patterns of activity which are quite capable of being carried on repetitively and within the limits of a self-preserving and self-maintaining society. In this event, the totalitarian regime begins to erode into an increasingly traditional society. In either case a totalitarian regime is to some extent threatened by the permanence of its own memories and of its own traditions. Either these traditions force it to persist in some ever more unrewarding strategy or pattern of behavior, or else they turn into a new network of customs and established expectations which increasingly limit the range of decisions still open to the totalitarian command.

In order to maintain the mobilization of its resources, a totalitarian regime needs therefore some machinery, formal or informal, to counteract the hardening of its own abstract traditions or professed ideologies, such as creeds, dogmas, philosophies, political doctrines, and the like, and it needs similar machinery to counteract the hardening of its own past preferences for particular geographical centers or particular groups of personnel. Traditions of doctrine, as well as preferences for geographical centers or for sociological groups of personnel, can easily become matters of heresy in totalitarian systems; but it is one of the paradoxes of totalitarianism that excessive orthodoxy in one of these three matters may have anti-totalitarian consequences and expose the die-hard orthodox partisan of the regime to some of the same penalties which threaten the heretic.

## THE PROBLEM OF CONSISTENCY OF COMMANDS

The second function, unity of command and of intelligence, requires some machinery either to insure a single source of decision, or a set of arrangements or devices to insure consistency of decisions among several sources. A single source of decisions is in effect an arrangement by which all important incoming information available to the system is channeled to a point where it can be confronted with data recalled from a single integrated memory pool. The outcome of the interaction of these collected data from the outside world and the data recalled from an integrated set of memory facilities are then the current decisions of the system.[4]

In its extreme or "ideal type" form, a totalitarian decision system would need to have five properties:

1. *Transitivity,*[5] that is, the property that each decision was either clearly superior or clearly subordinate to some other decision, and that no sequence of such hierarchically ordered decisions could be circular.

2. *Rigor,* that is, uniqueness of outcome of each step at all the relevant stages of decision-making below the top.

3. *Awareness of intake* and facilities for its simultaneous inspection, that is, arrangements to make sure that all important items of incoming information are confronted with each other and with data recalled from the memory facilities of the system; this involves the labeling of important items of incoming information by means of secondary symbols attached to them, and it involves the bringing together of these items for simultaneous inspection.

4. *Self-awareness,* or the internal intelligence function, that is, arrangements to make sure that information about internal changes within the system itself are brought to bear on the system's current decisions; there must be symbols for the constituent sub-assemblies, organizations, resources, or personnel of the system itself, which are processed and brought to the memory facilities of the system in such a manner that the system "knows" what is going on within its own organization, and is capable of acting on this information.

5. *Learning capacity,* that is, the ability to recombine items of incoming information with items recalled from memory in new patterns, so as to produce new combinations of symbols sufficient to survey, test, or devise new strategies of behavior, as well as the ability to produce new combinations of actual physical resources and manpower in such a way that the new strategies can actually be put into action; systems with this capacity will have the power to initiate new courses of behavior.

Actually existing totalitarian systems of government may well be deficient in any or all of these respects. Yet to the extent that they are so deficient, they will be less effective as totalitarian systems, and their chances for survival or expansion may be correspondingly lessened.

## THE DEPENDENCE ON COMPLIANCE

The third characteristic of totalitarian government, the enforcement of decisions, depends to a large extent on the compliance habits of the population. Compliance and enforcement are interdependent; they reinforce each other, and the varying proportions in which they do so, form as it were a a continuous spectrum. At one end of this spectrum, we could imagine a situation where everybody obeys habitually all commands or decisions of the totalitarian regime, and no enforcement is necessary; at the other end of this spectrum, we could imagine a situation where nobody obeys voluntarily any decision of the totalitarian system, and everybody has to be compelled to obey at pistol point, or under conditions of literally ever-present threat and ever-present supervision.

In the first of these cases, enforcement would be extremely cheap and, in fact, unnecessary; in the second, it would be prohibitively expensive, and in fact no government could be carried on on such a basis. Even the behavior of an occupying army in wartime in enemy territory falls far short of this standard; even there, many of its orders are obeyed more or less habitually by an unwilling population in situations where immediate supervision is not practicable. If the occupying army had to put a soldier behind every man, woman, and child of the local population, it would be extremely difficult for the army to keep sufficient numbers of its men detached from such occupation duties to continue with further military operations. Somewhere in the middle between these extremes of universal compliance and ubiquitous enforcement is the range of effective government. There a majority of individuals in a majority of situations obeys the decisions of the government more or less from habit without any need for immediate supervision. Yet the probability of supervision and detection, though possibly small, is still large enough to strengthen and reinforce the habits of obedience; and the habits of obedience, in most individuals and in most situations, are widespread and strong enough to make enforcement in the exceptional situations both practical and probable in its success. The higher the probability of voluntary compliance among the population, the greater therefore is the probability of enforcement in the exceptional cases. This will be so particularly if the enforcement facilities of the government are supported by voluntary efforts of the population in giving information, and in rendering voluntary assistance to the police and the troops of the government in case of necessity, as in the mobilization of a militia, the activities of guerillas, or the case of a posse of deputy sheriffs.

These considerations apply to totalitarianism as they apply to all types of government, but in their application to totalitarianism they again suggest a paradox. Totalitarian power is strong only if it does not have to be used too often. If totalitarian power must be used at all times against the entire population, it is unlikely to remain powerful for long. Since totalitarian regimes require more power for dealing with their subjects than do other types of government, such regimes stand in greater need of widespread and dependable compliance habits among their people; more than that, they need to be able to count on the active support of at least significant parts of the population in case of need.[6]

What are the sources of such compliance and support? As under all systems of government, they cover a whole range of social and psychological motives. At one extreme, we find mere passive acquiescence to the acts or commands of a government for which its subjects have no shred of sympathy but which they are too apathetic, too exhausted, or too disillusioned to resist. Further up the scale, we may find individuals supporting the government, still without any liking for its institutions or policies, but for what its current supporters may consider reasons of their own cold self-interest. Such men may support a government in the belief of using it for their own ends, as an instrument to procure some advantage to themselves or to inflict some damage on their enemies.

Still further up the scale of political support, we may find persons looking upon the government as in some manner an extension of themselves, or upon themselves as an extension of the government. Here we find self-identification and ego-involvement: the triumphs and successes of the government—or the state, the flag, the nation—are felt as personal triumphs by its subjects; its defeats are experienced as personal dishonor or misfortune; the prestige of the regime, the ideology, the state, the nation have become criteria for the self-respect of the individual subjects or citizens who have made this identification. Such ego-involvement need not necessarily involve considerations of general morality or religion, and thus in one sense what Freudians call the "superego." The ardent patriot may be well aware that his government's action is immoral: "Our country!" ran Stephen Decatur's toast: "In her intercourse with foreign nations may she be always in the right; but our country, right or wrong." Men with such views prefer, sometimes quite wittingly, their symbol or group identification to their conscience. They find it easier to transgress against their general morals than against their collective self-esteem. Or else they may accept the theory of Machiavelli and his successors: the doctrine of the double morality, one applying to relations among individuals, based on honesty and peaceable dealings, the other applying to relations among states, governments, or peoples, and based on force, deceit, and fear.[7]

Finally, at the extreme top of the scale of political support, we find those persons who have identified obedience and support to their government not merely with their self-esteem but also with their general beliefs and convictions of morality and even of religion. Here we find the men—so often satirized by George Bernard Shaw—who always succeed in believing sincerely that the commands of Providence coincide exactly with the currently proclaimed "interests" of their state and the current policies of its rulers. Here we find, too, the men who sense that there is a tension between blind and complete support for all policies of a government and the highest commands of morality and religion, but who have decided to resolve this tension in favor of the deification of the political institution and its symbols.

Totalitarianism clearly endeavors to elicit wherever possible this most complete type of political support in which each individual unites a state-made self-respect with a state-made morality and a state-made religion for the support of the regime. This state of affairs, however, is not easily achieved. As most students of the learning process know, loyalty taught through indoctrination, through what men are told by their rulers, does not go very deep. It is by their own experiences and actions that men learn most thoroughly. It is by what they themselves can tell their government, and do within its framework, and elicit a response to their own questions or appeals, that they learn to feel at home in it and to identify themselves with it. To elicit full identification and loyalty, therefore, a government must be to a considerable extent accessible and predictable.[8] It must be accessible to the questions, problems, needs, desires, and communications of its subjects; its office must be accessible to personnel recruited from their ranks; the minds of its decision-makers must remain open to the hopes, fears, and wishes of the population; and their commands and actions must be predictable in their impact on the lives and fortunes of its citizens. Any government under which life becomes unpredictable in some really important matters—even a democracy in an extreme economic depression—becomes suspect as arbitrary and may become feared and resented as alien or tyrannical. The well-known substitution of "they" for "we" in people's conversational references to their government may well occur in such situations.[9]

Totalitarian governments need at least the appearance of accessibility and predictability if they are to hold the active support of a large portion of their subjects. But the accessibility of a government interferes with its need to hold down the burden on the time and attention of its decision-making personnel, and we have seen that totalitarian regimes may be already prone to overload their central decision-making institutions. Predictability, in turn, implies the commitment of manpower and resources to the repetition of previous patterns of behavior which now have become expected, or to the carrying out of policies which have been previously promised. Totalitarian regimes thus need to elicit identification from their subjects while tending to produce feelings of alienation among them. The more predictable and expectable a government becomes, the less totalitarian is it likely to remain; and the more totalitarian a government remains, the less likely it is in the long run to retain the active support of its population. Obviously, these inherent conflicts in the basis of the political support of totalitarian regimes can be sustained for considerable periods of time; but as these periods lengthen into generations the fate of most totalitarian regimes should become increasingly dubious. In order to function, the power machinery of totalitarianism requires the voluntary support and active help of a significant part of the population; but this very dependence upon the habitual and voluntary support of a relatively large part of the people makes it more difficult for any totalitarian regime to preserve itself for two other conditions for its own functioning: its unity of command and its freedom from previous commitments.

Each of the three major characteristics of totalitarianism thus gives rise to a peculiar set of difficulties. The totalitarian mobilization of resources, human and material, depends on a freedom from previous commitments which is constantly threatened, not only by the possibility of a relapse of the population into apathy or resentment, but also by the previous political, organizational, or ideological commitments of the totalitarian regime itself. The totalitarian unity of command and the consistency of decision-making depends on a unity of memories and a coördination of information processes, which is constantly threatened by the tendency toward a diversification of memories, on the one hand, and the danger of overloading the undiversified centralized decision-making facilities on the other. The enforcement function, finally, of totalitarianism is threatened by its dependence on at least limited popular support, and by the tendency toward a downward migration of power which is inherent in most hierarchial systems of command.

Some of the weaknesses peculiar to centralized decision-making and to hierarchies of power may now be discussed somewhat further.

## THE LIMITED CAPACITY OF CENTRALIZED DECISION-MAKING

The conflict between centralization and delegation of decisions is fundamental in many systems of government, but it is perhaps most critical in totalitarianism. Centralization of decisions means, essentially, that responses to incoming items of information are made in terms of data recalled from a single pool of memories, such as the memories carried in the head of a single man, the decision-maker; such a single decision-maker may of course consult other individuals and their memories, but these memories are then data which are to be used or rejected in terms of the data which his own memory is supplying to himself. Where the range of memories carried by a single individual is no longer large enough for the type of decision-making needed, the single decision-maker or theater commander may be replaced by a central committee of some sort. In this case incoming messages of major importance are brought to the attention of all committee members who all recall from their individual memories pertinent data for suggesting a response. These suggestions are then discussed and in effect simultaneously inspected in the course of the discussion of the committee, and the "sense of the meeting," or the collective decision, may emerge. It is possible, of course, that a particular committee member carries most influence in the committee, and the borderline is fluid between decisions made essentially in terms of the memories carried in the head of a single individual, and decisions made in terms of the memories and agreements of a whole committee.

All centralized facilities for decision-making, however, committees as well as individuals, can only give attention to a very limited number of items for decisions at the same time, and can therefore be very easily overloaded. The distributive attention of individuals is notoriously limited, and so is the amount of business any committee can transact within a given time. Julius Caesar has been renowned for his legendary exploit of dictating seven letters at one and the same time; and chess masters who can play forty games simultaneously are objects of admiration. Major military decision systems or political decision systems, on the contrary, may easily require decisions of many hundreds of problems in substantially the same interval of time.

A simple example of the difficulties involved can be found in the problem of the plotting room of an anti-aircraft defense center in a city under air attack; by means of a number of ingenious arrangements, it may be possible there to represent at one and the same time the attack of several hundred enemy aircraft and to make decisions about how to oppose most effectively every one of them. Nevertheless, the decision-making capacity of even a very good anti-aircraft plotting center is quantitatively limited. These quantitative limitations become particularly sharp and painful when the question arises of how to defend a warship against aerial attack. Here the attacking enemy aircraft can be represented on radar screens but the number of tracks symbolizing attacking aircraft may very soon become too large for the decision-making capacity of any single individual; it is possible from this point of view to saturate not merely the physical, but rather the intellectual or cognitive defenses of the ship. Just as a massed attack of aircraft coming simultaneously from many different directions may overload the capacities of a directing center for anti-aircraft defense, so the amount of problems requiring urgent decision may overload the decision-making capacities of a government.[10]

Moreover, the more absolute, dictatorial, or totalitarian such a government is, the more likely it is to politicize, that is, to make subject to decisions, an ever larger sphere of life, and therefore the more likely it is to be thus overloaded with decisions with which it can no longer cope, except at the price of either intolerable delays or an increasing probability of potentially critical mistakes.

The answer to this problem of the overloading of centralized decision-making facilities has been, of course, decentralization. Classes of decisions have been delegated to sub-assemblies of the system, where they are made in terms of separate pools of memories. These subordinate decision centers with their subordinate facilities for the storing of data may in turn be controlled more or less closely from some common decision-making center. Such control, however, is apt to be incomplete. Once the subordinate centers have been delegated some authority, and once they have been given their own facilities for storing memories, these subordinate centers and memory pools will in the future receive only part of their input from the supreme government. A significant part of their future experience will be local, in terms of their own peculiar local, regional, or functional situations, or in terms of their own probabilities of internal recombinations, their own ideas, preferences, customs, or habits of behavior, as they may evolve from the internal workings of their own smaller system. The more imperfect the facilities for the pooling of experience among all the subordinate centers—and all pooling of such experience is necessarily imperfect to some extent—the faster will be this increase of the share of diversified memories and diversified experiences in each subordinate organization.

The result will be a steady drift to a peripheralization and pluralization of the centers of decision. In the long run there is thus perhaps inherent in every totalitarian system of government a tendency either toward overloading of its central facilities for the making of decisions, or toward an automatic corrosion of its original centralized structure and its disintegration into increasingly separate parts.

## THE INSTABILITY OF
## HIERARCHICAL POWER

The difficulties that militate against the viability of any permanent system of totalitarian centraliza-

tion are paralleled, in a sense, by the difficulties in the way of any permanent hierarchical distribution of power. A hierarchy of power requires that all power should be located at the apex of a pyramid, and that all power should lead downward in terms of a transitive chain of command, transmitting orders from the single power holder or the few power holders at the top to the many soldiers or policemen at the bottom. However, every such pyramid of power is inherently unstable. To maintain transitivity it must be steered by orders coming from the apex. Yet the shortest communication routes to all relevant sub-centers and sub-assemblies of power is not from the apex, but from some location farther down, let us say one, two, or three tiers farther down in the chain of command, according to the size of the pyramid and the speed with which the number of power holders increases from each layer of authority to the next lower one.[11] In all such pyramids, the Prime Minister, Shogun, Grand Viziers, Major Domus, or Police Chief, is closer to the real deposits of power than the king or prince whom such an official is supposed to serve. Power may very well then migrate from the king or dictator to some of his subordinates; it may migrate from the marshals and generals in the army of some small dictatorship to the brigadier-generals or colonels, or in a small country even to the captains or sergeants. The lower an officer or official is in such a pyramid of power, the closer he is to the ultimate facilities of power, the common soldiers or policemen, provided only that he succeeds in organizing for himself the support of a sufficient number of his peers on his own level.

If several strata of power holders in a hierarchy of command, such as, say, generals, colonels, and captains, may be thought of as potential competitors for power, then the stratum most likely to emerge victorious may well be that which best fulfills the interplay of two conditions:

1. Among its rivals, it is sufficiently low in the hierarchy to be "close to the people," or at least to the soldiery.

2. It is still high enough in the hierarchy to have sufficiently small numbers so as to facilitate the effective organization of a proportion of its members sufficient to isolate all higher levels in the chain of command.

Power may thus migrate from the apex a small way down the pyramid; if so, the old apex may shrink to a ceremonial shadow of its past, or may disappear altogether. In effect, a new, somewhat lower apex then has come into being; and the pyramid of power has been made somewhat less steep. But the new apex is again located above the point of shortest communication with the entire pyramid. Again it is liable to be challenged and superseded by a shift of power to the incumbents of the central strategic positions on some lower level; and the pyramid of power may remain unstable through several repetitions of this process. Theoretically, this process might stop when power has shifted so far down the hierarchy and the pyramid of command has become so broad and blunt that the remaining distance between the last apex of the pyramid and the point of shortest communication is no longer significant.

At this stage, however, the center of command may find itself again overloaded with the flood of current decisions to be made. After all, the reducing of this burdensome volume of decisions—through suitable screening, delegation, and selection of matters to be decided at different levels of command— had been one of the primary advantages of the original pyramid of power. Some of the conditions for reducing the burden of communication and decision-making are thus the opposite of the conditions for preserving the stability of power. The steeper the pyramid, and the more numerous the intermediate layers between the bottom and the top, the less is the danger of overloading the information-processing and decision-making capacities of the men or groups at the apex. The blunter the pyramid and the fewer screens or layers of delegated authority between bottom and top, on the other hand, the greater is the danger of such overloading. Since it takes less communicative and decision-making capacity to seize power at a favorable opportunity than it takes to exercise such totalitarian power for longer periods, it may well follow that the problem of the pure power pyramid—the pursuit and location of power per se in a transitive chain of command—has none but unstable solutions.

## TOTALITARIANISM AND SOME LIMITATIONS OF TECHNOLOGY

Thus far we have listed a number of weaknesses and conflicts inherent in the working of totalitarian systems and making for their eventual stagnation, disintegration, or corrosion. But have all these tendencies not been overbalanced by the impact of new technological developments which might increase the power of dictatorial governments far beyond all precedent and all previous political and social limits?

Will not the future development of microphones and television cameras supply every totalitarian regime with cheap and ever-present spies, just as the development of tanks and airplanes has supplied them with weapons which can be concentrated in the hands of a few, and as barbed wire has supplied them with facilities for inexpensive concentration camps?

Several reasons seem to suggest that no presently indicated development of technology is likely to increase significantly the stability or cohesion of totalitarian regimes. In a world of rival powers, the concentration of effective weapons in the hands of a trusted few men is a luxury no great power can afford. Throughout all advances in military technology, governments have become more dependent, not less, on the support of millions of their citizens. Armies, navies, air forces, tank corps, civil defense and production organizations all require hundreds of thousands or millions of persons in their ranks, and the day of the quasi-aristocratic war, carried on by small groups of highly skilled professionals, seems even farther away than at the time of its early prophets in the 1920's.

To the extent, on the other hand, that decisive instruments of military power should become concentrated in the hands of a few specialists, some additional positions would be created for the power struggle within the totalitarian regime. None of the potential rivalries between the political leadership, the propagandists, the administrators, the army, the police, and any other major power group—rivalries of the kind instanced by the executions of Soviet Marshal Tukhachevsky and Soviet Police Chief Yagoda in the 1930's at the behest of the Politburo —could be wholly abolished by any technological development. The problems of mobilizing mass support for national military strength, and of insuring unity of command and cohesion among the different parts of the regime, are all essentially political in nature. They are fraught with the hopes and fears, the expectations and motives of individuals. They involve, therefore, all the difficulties of totalitarian regimes which were discussed earlier; and no increase in the gadgetry of violence will solve them.

If totalitarianism can expect no decisive aid from the technology of violence, neither can it expect such aid from any improvements in the gadgetry of supervision or persuasion. Electronic devices can be used to improve the reception and transmission of information in these processes, but they can do little or nothing to facilitate its use and thus its ultimate effectiveness. Even if supervisory television devices and microphones were to be installed in the home of every citizen, the totalitarian state would still have to find the huge numbers of officials necessary to look at and listen to the vast amounts of information thus obtained—a difficulty from which the dictatorial government in George Orwell's nightmare world of 1984 seems to have been conveniently free.[12] Anyone who has tried to wade through several hundred pages of the transcript of a tape recording of a conference will have at least an inkling of the quantitative problem involved. Human greed cannot be listened to with understanding at very much higher speed than it can be spoken, and the talk and gossip of even one person's lifetime may well require something resembling half a lifetime's listening on the part of some luckless policeman.

The introduction of universal electronic super-vision, even were it technologically feasible, would drown the totalitarian regime in an ocean of trivi-alities, and the addition of automatic transcription devices would merely convert their output of trivial noise into a flood of paper. Political supervision is a feedback process in which incoming information must be responded to in terms of behavior that reaches back to the citizen or subject. It thus con-sists in its essence in the paying of attention and the exercise of judgment and neither of these func-tions can be mechanized with any equipment likely to exist for the rest of this century or longer.

Similar considerations apply to the problem of persuasion. As noted earlier, persuasion is not a one-way process, except on the simplest levels of advertising designed to change none but very minor habits of its addressees. More deep-reaching per-suasion requires again listening, responsiveness, and the creation of learning situations. None of these functions can be readily mechanized by presently indicated technological developments.

Finally, electronic devices may speed the trans-mission of orders and reports, and exchange of information among top-ranking personnel of the regime, and facilitate to some extent the pooling of information essential to maintain unity of com-mand. However, while radio during World War II could transmit reports from the German armies in Russia to Adolf Hitler's headquarters, no electronic device could force the Führer or his staff to make intelligent use of them. Television conferences may leave men as self-centered, quarrelsome, or antag-onistic to each other as did simpler methods of communication. Some of the most bitter conflicts in both Germany and Russia occurred among groups or leaders living and working relatively near to each other.

The heart of the matter is perhaps in the tend-ency of economic and technological progress thus far to increase the decision load of governments as fast or at a faster rate than the means of govern-ments to cope with them. By "decision load" is meant the total volume of social and political de-cisions to be made, and the extent and number of their probable consequences to be taken into ac-count, by a given organization within a given time. Because of this growth in the decision load of governments, the business of governing has become harder instead of easier during the last fifty years, just as driving an automobile through rush-hour traffic has become harder, and this growth in the decision burden has been greatest in the case of totalitarian regimes. Confronted with such pressures and demands, their crucial difficulty is still in the limited capacity of the individual human mind to pay sufficient attention to a large number of other individuals and to learn significantly from the whole range of their memories and preferences. All these are matters of the give and take of human learning

and human communication, and in all these mat-ters so crucial in resisting disintegration, totalitar-ianism as such is not stronger, and may well be weaker, than democracy.

## TOTALITARIAN POLICIES
## TO RESIST DISINTEGRATION

If the trends and conflicts making for the loosen-ing or dissolution of totalitarian regimes are not counteracted effectively by technological develop-ments, we may well ask how any totalitarian govern-ments have managed to maintain themselves for longer periods of time. Perhaps the persistence of totalitarian governments or movements, and of so-cial institutions having at least some totalitarian features, over several decades or even several generations, may be due in part to their develop-ment of a whole series of resources for the main-tenance of the unity of command. Such unity of command, or consistency of decisions, depends to a large extent upon the unity of consistency of the memories, both of factual data and of operating preferences, in terms of which all such decisions must be made. The problem of maintaining unity of command is thus essentially that of maintaining a sufficient unity of memories, and it is by providing for a larger share of relatively uniform memories, and of relatively uniform processes for adding new but uniform, or at least compatible experiences, that totalitarian governments or movements have attempted to persist over larger expanses of space and over longer periods of time.

The first and most obvious method of totalitarian regimes to maintain unity among their subjects and subordinate organizations consists, of course, in setting them a common goal. It is such a goal in terms of which totalitarianism carries out its at-tempts to bring about the mobilization of all ma-terial and human resources which is so characteristic for its workings. Since the totalitarian goal is by definition overriding, its imposition resolves many, though not all, possible conflicts with established habits of procedure, or even with lesser policies of the regime.

Such unification through an overriding goal which is then to be sought spontaneously by all loyal subjects of the government is based on the hidden assumption that the government knows, and that its subjects can know easily, just which actions will in fact bring the country nearer to the goal, or will in fact promote the best interests of the regime, nation, or ideology. This totalitarian assumption often proves unwarranted. As the inhabitants of the ruined cities of Germany have had occasion to find out, the usefulness of Nazi policies to the Ger-man people had been greatly overrated. Yet without certain and easily available knowledge of how to promote in fact the proclaimed goal, the united striving for a common purpose is likely to degenerate into endless wrangling over means and methods, made only more bitter by the total devotion and intolerant zeal which totalitarianism enjoins upon all its followers.

Another method of promoting unity might consist in standardizing common rules of procedure for the finding of facts and the making of decisions, either in addition to the stating of goals, or even in place of them. The Koran of Mohammed, the Corpus Juris of Justinian, the Corpus of Canon Law and the Code Napoleon are all examples of pre-totalitarian or in some cases perhaps proto-totalitarian attempts to insure the unity of far-flung or long-lasting organizations or regimes. All of the codes listed have been successful in some measure, although their success has at times been greater, and their life span longer, than that of the regimes which gave them birth. No such codes were lastingly established by the totalitarian regimes of Italy and Germany. Whether the growing body of Soviet law shows any signs of playing a similar unifying role in the eventual development of Russian society might well be an interesting question for research.

A more far-reaching attempt to insure effective unity of memories consists in the imposition of a common ideology. Such an ideology may be couched in secular or in religious terms. In either case it includes not only common statements of value, common assertions of supposed fact and some common rules of procedure in decision-making, but it also contains often a common epistemology, at least by implication. Its inherents are told which kinds of knowledge, which sources, and which methods of gaining it, are to be trusted and which ones are to be shunned., With common goals, common procedural values, common memories, and common methods for screening and acquiring new information, the probability of maintaining consistency among future decisions and commands is greatly enhanced, even if these decisions have to be made by individuals cut off from communication with each other.

Despite the potential effectiveness of ideologies, most people are more likely to respond to personal contacts than to abstract thoughts or even to colorful symbols. Totalitarian regimes, like other governments, may attempt to maintain their unity by creating a common pool of leading or decision-making personnel—perhaps in the form of a common political party—or of particular institutions, formal or informal, for the training and rotation of leaders. They may make a point of drawing to the capital leading personnel from potentially doubtful outlying districts, somewhat as the Nazis brought wittingly or unwittingly an unusual number of Catholics and Bavarians to Berlin, or as the Soviets put some Georgians, Armenians, and Jews on their central decision-making bodies. They may

send their officials from one district to another, so as to maintain the unity of a service corps among them even at the expense of making more casual and distant their relations to the population among whom these officials reside during any particular tour of duty; or they may even command their officials to do two potentially contradictory things at one and the same time: to retain absolute loyalty to the common center and yet to develop numerous deep and intimate contacts with the people among whom they work as in the case of model Communist Party workers extolled in Soviet literature.

Perhaps the most effective way of insuring a community of memories is one over which totalitarian regimes have only very limited control. It is the community of memories that derives from the possession of a common universe of experiences as they are produced by a new way of life, a new fundamental pattern of culture, a new economic system, or a new religion. To the extent that a totalitarian regime becomes established in the course of such a fundamental rearrangement of society, and to the extent that it draws its personnel from those who share in the common ensemble of continuing new experiences resulting from that fundamental change, it can count on at least one significant degree of similarity or uniformity in the outlook both of its decision-making personnel and of its underlying populations, not only in the central regions of its territory but throughout the areas over which the full effects of the fundamental social changes have become extended.

What is perhaps even more important, a totalitarian regime that has arisen in the course of such a fundamental change can count on the unifying effect of the antagonism of the populations and groups of personnel among whom these changes have become accepted against the outside world which has remained skeptical or hostile to the new dispensation. Foreign threats to the totalitarian regime appeal then readily as threats to the new way of life, the new gospel of salvation, or the new institutions of society, and even the remaining domestic opponents of the regime appear in the eyes of the converted population as aliens or infidels.

The contrast between the two types of totalitarianism becomes reinforced by the differences between the psychological and educational techniques employed by each regime. The main emphasis of Nazism was on hardness, will and action; on obedience and command; and on the subordination or annihilation of inferior races. Nazi theories of learning were rudimentary; inventiveness and creativity were considered biological rather than psychological categories. Little if anything in the Nazi education encouraged listening to other people. The circular flow of information from the led to the leaders and from the leaders to the led was to be replaced by a one-way arrangement of commands coming from the top down. In the Nazi world the loudspeaker thus outgrew the microphone and the mouth the ear; and the result seems to have been a gradually increasing bias throughout the system against discovery and against learning.

The Soviet rulers, too, like all dictators, have been eyeing rather warily the human capacity for new discoveries and new social learning, but instead of ignoring it, or trying to stifle most of it outright as the Nazis did, the Soviets have tried to control this capacity and use it for their purposes. Soviet literature in education, psychology, science, and the arts constantly urges individuals to display resourcefulness, initiative, and creativity, while at the same time insisting that they should keep closer to permitted patterns. This double insistence cannot but burden the individuals concerned with a good deal of constant strain and tension; and, to the extent that genuine learning capacity and initiative can survive and grow under such strained circumstances, they may well in the long run contribute their share toward the undermining of the conformity that is essential for the continuation of the totalitarian regime. The strains and stresses inherent in these aspects of Soviet life, terrible as they are for many of the individuals concerned, are occurring on a higher level of complexity and are leaving a wider range of resources available to the regime than did the comparable educational and psychological practices in fascist countries. These differences do not make the Soviet dictatorship less of an opponent of democracy and of the Western world; rather they make it a more formidable one.


## SOME TENTATIVE PROSPECTS

Considerations of this kind bring us back to the problem of assessing the capabilities and performance characteristics of different governments and types of government. In many cases, the communicating of information and the reaching of decisions may be as vital to the survival of governments as the functioning of the nervous system would be to the survival of some complex organism. Governments, of course, are not organisms, and the metaphor should not be pushed too far. Even so, different political systems may be profitably compared in terms of the performance of their "nerves of government," and particularly in terms of their ability to maintain political cohesion and unity of decision-making under conditions of social, political or economic strain. Applied to existing governments, an analysis of this kind reveals major differences between totalitarian and democratic governments in general, as well as between different types of totalitarian regimes, and perhaps between different kinds of democratic policies and institutions.[13]

At this stage, any inference from our survey of the patterns of disintegration of totalitarian systems must be tentative and provisional. Thus qualified, they will be indicated here, at the risk that readers will call obvious those findings which fit in with their views, while calling unsound those which do not. Both strictures may turn out to be correct; yet perhaps it may be hoped that they will be imposed only after some careful testing. If treated thus as inferences to be tested, rather than as conclusions to be believed, the following suggestions may yet fulfill some useful function.

1. Totalitarianism is by no means immune from processes of disintegration; on the contrary, many of the dictatorial techniques which are intended to combat schism or disintegration may in fact tend to accelerate and intensify these very processes.

2. The basic processes of political integration and disintegration occur on a more fundamental level than that of mere political, military, or police techniques, or of government-run propaganda. This is even more true in the occurrence of schisms and secessions of supra-national philosophies or ideologies. Research on the probability of a future split—for instance, between the Communist regimes of Russia and China—might most profitably be aimed at these more fundamental levels.

3. Although there are significant analogies in the behavior of different totalitarian systems, the aims of particular totalitarian regimes may make a considerable difference to their ability to maintain cohesion for a longer period of time. The same seems true of the nature of the underlying social changes in the course of which a totalitarian regime may become established; and further considerable differences may be due to the specific practices and institutions by which particular totalitarian regimes may attempt to combat their own automatic drift toward pluralization and disintegration.

4. For all these reasons, no schematic predictions can be made concerning a general probability of all totalitarian regimes to split up or disintegrate within a short period of time. In particular, a number of important performance characteristics of Russian Soviet totalitarianism, on the one hand, and of German Nazi totalitarianism on the other, differ radically from each other. What imperfect data we have surveyed seem to suggest that the Soviet dictatorship in Russia still disposes of substantial resources to stave off its own disintegration or pluralization for a considerable time.

5. These considerations apply, however, only to time scales of about twenty to fifty years. Most of the major economic and social changes in history which were violent enough to give rise to regimes with some totalitarian features were substantially completed within a period of the order of fifty years, and with the slowing down of the rate of major changes there has usually followed a period of pluralization and a dwindling of totalitarian expansiveness. If similar considerations should apply

to the totalitarian regimes of Russia and China, which established themselves in consequence of revolutions which disrupted the *status quo* in these countries as early as 1911 and 1917, respectively, then we might well expect the 1970's or 1980's to bring a slowing of the expansive pressure from these two regimes, or a growing divergence of policies between them, or among some of their constituent regions, or some combination of all these changes, leading in either case to a diminution in "classic" patterns of totalitarian behavior.

6. In the meantime, the free countries of the world cannot rely on the disintegration of Soviet-type regimes to rid them of their present opponents; nor does there seem to be much evidence that any propaganda or underground activities short of all-out war could influence the course of events behind the Iron Curtain decisively in favor of freedom. Even the political results of an all-out war against totalitarianism might be hazardous to predict, quite apart from its probable atomic devastation, so long as even the final results of our "reëducation" of the German and Japanese people are by no means clear. The prospects seem to indicate, therefore, a period of prolonged tension until at least the 1980's, followed perhaps then, with luck, by a slackening of pressure.

7. Throughout this period it will be essential to maintain the political, economic and moral strength of the free world. This involves the maintenance of adequate military strength for defense, and the protection of the territories of the democratic countries. In the long run, such Western power will be not very much aided by centering our whole attention on the task of confining the Communist regimes to a particular line or perimeter drawn somewhere on the map of Asia, nor by borrowing doubtful strength for the cause of the democracies from a motley crew of minor totalitarian regimes who detest our ideals but offer us support for pay. Rather the essential strength of the free world in all likelihood will have to come from the genuinely free countries within it, and our best defense during the next thirty years may well consist in the strengthening of the free world from the ground up and from the inside out, through the growth and strengthening of centers and core areas of genuine freedom.

In geographic terms, this might mean particularly the strengthening of the English-speaking countries, the democracies of Western Europe, and on the Asiatic continent perhaps India and Pakistan. Within these areas, and in terms of politics and economics, as well as of our whole cultural, moral and spiritual climate, it might mean the insistence on the continuing growth of freedom and democracy in all their dimensions.

## NOTES

1. Terms such as "total state" were used by some spokesmen of the Fascist regime in Italy and the Nazi government in Germany in referring to some of their own political institutions since the late 1930's. Since then, opponents of Communism and Fascism have gradually popularized the term "totalitarian" as a means to emphasize certain similarities between fascist and Communist one-party governments.

2. For some discussions of totalitarianism, see Sigmund Neumann, *Permanent Revolution: The Total State in a World at War* (New York: Harper, 1942; Hans Kohn, "Fascism and Communism—A Comparative Study," in *Revolution and Dictatorships* (Cambridge: Harvard University Press, 1939), pp. 179–199; Hannah Arendt, *The Origins of Totalitarianism* (New York: Harcourt, Brace and World, 1951); and the excellent account of the use of the concept of the "total state" in the rivalry between state and party bureaucracies in Germany and Italy, in Franz Neumann, *Behemoth: The Structure and Practice of National Socialism* (New York: Oxford University Press, 1942), pp. 47–82.

3. For some suggestive observations on the growing psychological readiness for totalitarian mobilization, see Ernst Jünger, *Die totale Mobilmachung* (2nd ed.; Berlin: Junker, 1934), esp. pp. 10–18, 29–31. See also Hans Kohn, *Force or Reason: Issues of the Twentieth Century* (Cambridge: Harvard University Press, 1937), pp. 35–38, 132–133.

4. For a further discussion of the theory of communication and decision-making used in this section, see Norbert Wiener, *The Human Use of Human Beings: Cybernetics and Society* (Boston: Houghton Mifflin, 1950); and Karl W. Deutsch, "Communication Models in Social Science," *Public Opinion Quarterly,* XVI, No. 3, Fall 1952, pp. 356–380; and "Communication Theory and Social Science," *American Journal of Orthopsychiatry,* XXII, No. 3, pp. 469–483.

5. Cf. John von Neumann and Oskar Morgenstern, *Theory of Games and Economic Behavior* (2nd ed.; Princeton: Princeton University Press, 1947), pp. 38–39.

6. A comparison of the relation of compliance habits and enforcement probabilities in different countries was included in the checklist for comparative political studies, suggested by the Research Seminar on Comparative Politics of the Social Science Research Council. On the work of this seminar, and its implicit suggestions for the study of totalitarianism, see Roy C. Macridis, "Comparative Politics: Method and Research," *Social Science Research Council Items,* VI, No. 4, December 1952, pp. 45–49.

7. For the general problem of such a split between personal and political morality, see Gerhart Ritter, *Die Dämonie der Macht* (6th ed.; Munich: Leibniz Verlag, 1948). On the extreme reliance of National Socialism on this split and the resulting use of *arcana dominationis,* see Franz Neumann, pp. 464–467.

8. On the relationship between unpredictability and alienation, see Karl Mannheim, *Man and Society in the Age of Reconstruction* (New York: Harcourt, Brace and World, 1948); and Karl W. Deutsch, *Nationalism*

*and Social Communication* (New York: John Wiley and Massachusetts Institute of Technology Press, 1953).

9. E. H. Carr, *Conditions of Peace* (New York: Macmillan, 1943), pp. 36–37.

10. On possible strategic uses of this overload problem, see K. W. Deutsch, "Game Theory in Politics: Some Applications of Games Theory to International Relations."

11. Suggestive small group experiments on the relation between the location of power and the shortness of communication lines have been carried out by Alexander Bavelas and associates at Massachusetts Institute of Technology.

12. George Orwell, *1984* (New York: Harcourt, Brace and World, 1949).

13. A brief survey of some of the unifying or unity-maintaining techniques and policies of the totalitarian regimes of Soviet Russia and Nazi Germany was presented to the Conference on Totalitarianism of the American Academy of Arts and Sciences as part of the present paper. The length of this survey precluded its inclusion here without disturbing the balance of this book; and it may be published in due time elsewhere. Some of its findings, however, have been used in the section which follows here; and the indulgence of the reader is asked for omitting references to specific policies and cases, which were presented to the Conference.

# DIFFERENT ROADS TO SOCIALISM

## Paul E. Zinner

The twin and inseparable problems of the pattern of internal evolution of the Communist-dominated countries in Eastern Europe and the precise nature of their relationship to the Soviet Union have been in the forefront of interest ever since 1944 when—with Soviet support—Communist Parties began to bid for power in Eastern Europe. At first the evolutionary pattern of the East European "people's democracies" was interpreted by local Communists as following a path of "national exclusiveness" in accordance with the traditions and particular conditions prevailing in any given country. Early notions of "national exclusiveness" were aided and abetted by a number of outstanding Soviet scholars, e.g., the late I. P. Trainin, E. S. Varga, and L. A. Leontiev. Varga characterized the emerging people's democratic states as representing a "social order" which "differs from all hitherto known to us."[1] Trainin saw the people's democracies as hybrid regimes combining features of the proletarian (Soviet) and bourgeois type of "democracy" but being really at variance with both.[2]

The concept of people's democracy, not fully worked out to be sure, as that of a "third" or "different" type of social system was justified by Lenin's dictum on the distinctness of the evolutionary pattern of various countries, the "different roads to socialism."

In 1948, following the completion of the seizure of power in Eastern Europe (the coup in Czechoslovakia in February, 1948) and the first break in the outward solidarity of the Communist countries (Yugoslavia's expulsion from the Cominform in June, 1948), an abrupt and drastic revision in the concept of people's democracy took place. To some extent the revision was forecast at the founding meeting of the Cominform in September, 1947. While Andrei Zhdanov, the chief Soviet spokesman at the meeting (the other was G. M. Malenkov), stressed that "the Soviet Union unswervingly holds the position that political and economic relations between states must be built exclusively on the basis of equality of the Parties and mutual respect for their sovereign rights,"[3] he also made it clear that the Soviet Union did not choose to abandon its task of guiding and instructing foreign Communists and that the East European Communists would do well to avail themselves of the rich experience which the Soviet Union had accumulated on its road to socialism.

The new theory of people's democracy was clearly enunciated by Georgi Dimitrov, leader of the Bulgarian Workers Party (Communist), in December, 1948, when he said that "in accordance with the Marxist-Leninist view, the Soviet regime and the people's democratic regime are two forms of one and the same power . . . i.e., the proletarian dictatorship."[4]

Reprinted from Paul E. Zinner (ed.), *National Communism and Popular Revolt in Eastern Europe* (New York: Columbia University Press, 1956), pp. 3–8, by permission of the publishers.

From then on the essential, or substantive, identity of the Soviet and people's democratic systems was stressed by Communist theoreticians and political leaders as well. The emulation of the Soviet pattern was supported by Lenin's dictum concerning the applicability of "bolshevik experience" anywhere at any time.[5]

The essence of the new theory and its practical implications were summarized by Klement Gottwald, leader of the Czechoslovak Communist Party, in the following terms:[6]

Lenin's teachings on the international applicability of the Bolshevik experience extends to the construction of socialist society as well.

It is, of course, natural that on our road to socialism, as in the other people's democracies, there should have been significant differences compared with the Soviet Union. It would have been stupid and dangerous dogmatism had we not observed these differences after 1945. On the contrary, because we observed them and exploited them we won our victory over the bourgeoisie in 1948.

On the other hand it would be criminal stupidity if we wanted to conserve some of these "differences" which were only of temporary nature and progressively tend to disappear.

Ever greater utilization of Soviet experiences and thus ever closer approximation of the Soviet example, this is one of the main laws of development of the people's democratic countries. Therefore every additional step along this line . . . marks . . . significant progress toward socialism. . . . Conversely, retaining the lower transitional forms and presenting them as unchanging "norms" . . . and rejecting Soviet examples and experiences finally leads to the denial and overturn of the very substance of people's democracy and to the restoration of capitalism.

Indeed, the development of the people's democratic regimes of Eastern Europe from 1948 to 1953 was marked by ever closer imitation of Soviet political, economic, and cultural organization and practice, and subordination of national aims to those of the "socialist camp" as formulated by the Soviet leadership.

While Stalin's death in March, 1953, did not bring any explicit reformulation of the notion of people's democracy in its wake, the relaxation of internal pressures in the Soviet Union was extended to the people's democracies as well. The response of these countries to the policies of the "new course"—associated with the premiership of G. M. Malenkov in the USSR from March, 1953, to February, 1955, and characterized, among other things, by greater attention to the needs of consumers—was not uniform. Hungary mapped out a fairly ambitious program of changes. Others, like Poland and Czechoslovakia, moved more cautiously. Simultaneously with these developments, intellectuals and students began to grope for greater freedom of expression. In this respect, Hungary and Poland showed the most pronounced signs of ferment. The very fact that differences in individual country responses to the new situation were discernible might have been interpreted as an indication of possibilities for national initiative and departure, at least within certain limits, from a rigidly held pattern of behavior.

In the spring of 1955 the Soviet leadership of Party (Khrushchev) and Government (Bulganin) bid to restore friendly relations with Tito's Yugoslavia. The gesture, emphasized by the fact that the Soviet leaders journeyed to Belgrade for the purpose, carried with it implications of a possible acceptance and approval of a degree of national independence under Communist rule, less subordination to the direction of Moscow, and experimentation with indigenous variations in social organization within the framework of "socialist construction." The question was not whether the East European people's democracies would be accorded a status identical with Tito's Yugoslavia, but rather on what terms the differences between Tito and the Kremlin could be made up, and to what extent and in what form the patching up of these differences would modify the relationship between the people's democracies and Moscow.

The "Declaration of the Governments of the Union of Soviet Socialist Republics and the Federal People's Republic of Yugoslavia" issued in Belgrade on June 2, 1955,[7] stated as one of the principles from which the two governments proceeded to examine the questions of reciprocal concern: "mutual respect and non-interference in one another's internal affairs for whatever reason, whether of an economic, political, or ideological nature, inasmuch as questions of internal organization, difference of social systems, and difference in the concrete forms of socialist development are exclusively the concern of the peoples of the respective countries."

One of the aims of future contact, according to the Declaration, was "to assist and facilitate cooperation between public organizations of the two countries through the establishment of contacts, exchange of socialist experience, and free exchange of opinions." This stipulation pertained especially to contacts between the Communist Parties of the two countries. It was not followed by tangible results until June, 1956, when, on the occasion of Tito's return visit to Moscow, a "Declaration on Relations between the Yugoslav League of Communists and the Communist Party of the Soviet Union" was issued.[8]

In the wake of the Belgrade Declaration of 1955 signs of possible adjustment in the relations between the Soviet Union and the people's democracies came to light. The most important of these was in a *Pravda* editorial appraising the findings of a plenary session of the Communist Party's Central Committee which "heard and discussed a report by Comrade N. S. Khrushchev, on the results of the Soviet-Yugoslav talks."[9]

The course and results of the Soviet-Yugoslav talks [said *Pravda*] vividly express the foreign policy worked out by our Party and based on the firm principles of Leninism and on respect for the sovereignty and equality of all countries, large and small.

"Our experience," taught V. I. Lenin, "has formed in us the deep conviction that only tremendous attentiveness to the interests of the various nations eliminates the ground for conflicts, removes mutual distrusts, removes fear of any intrigues, and creates trust, particularly among workers and peasants speaking different languages, without which any peaceful relations between peoples and any successful development at all of everything which is valuable in modern civilization are absolutely impossible."

It is precisely tremendous attentiveness to the interests of various nations which is a most important feature of socialist internationalism, radically hostile to any manifestations of bourgeois ideology, including nationalism.

Soviet Communists consider it their sacred duty to set an example of the practice of the principles of socialist internationalism, as befits representatives of a multinational socialist country in which the national question has been solved consistently on the basis of Marxist-Leninist theory.

Relations between the Soviet Union and the people's democracies are built upon the granite foundation of socialist internationalism. The Communist Party has always willingly shared and still shares its wealth of experience with all fraternal parties, and at the same time Soviet Communists are called upon to study assiduously and imitate all that is advanced to be found in the people's democracies in the sphere of management of the national economy, achievements of science, technology, and so on.

All nations will arrive at socialism, Lenin pointed out; that is inevitable, but not all will arrive there in exactly the same way. Each one will introduce its own features into this or that form of democracy, into this or that form of dictatorship of the proletariat, into this or that rate of socialist transformation of different aspects of social life.

The historical experience in the Soviet Union and of the people's democracies shows that, given unity in the chief fundamental matter of ensuring the victory of socialism, various ways and means may be used in different countries to solve the specific problems of socialist construction, depending upon historical and national features.

The question of "different roads to socialism" was next treated by *Kommunist,* the CPSU's theoretical journal (No. 14, September, 1955). Shortly afterward the tenets of the discussion were taken up by *Nowe Drogi,* the theoretical journal of the Polish United Workers Party (PUWP) (October, 1955). Under the title "For an Increase of Our Creative Effort and Ideological Work," the Polish journal said, among other things: "We have paid too little attention to that which is innate in our movement, in our historical road, in our methods of construction, in our struggle and slogans, to that which arises from the specific conditions in the development of our country and from our historical past. . . ." At the same time, *Nowe Drogi* sought to guard against misunderstanding of the meaning of national "specificity." It attacked "harmful confusion and ideological chaos . . . nihilistic tendencies to disregard the achievements . . . of the past ten years, particularly in the field of culture and morality," and censured "tendencies to revise our ideological principles, attempts at an allegedly creative 'supplementation' of Marxism . . . concepts of liberalism, solidarism, relativism, cultural autonomy . . . an autonomy conceived as being independent of the class struggle, of politics, and of the leading role of the Party."

## NOTES

1. See E. S. Varga, "Democracies of a New Type," *Mirovoye Khoziaistvo i Mirovaia Politika,* 1947, No. 3, pp. 3–14. See also Samuel L. Sharp, "New Democracy: A Soviet Interpretation," *American Perspective,* Vol. I, No. 6 (November, 1947).

2. I. P. Trainin, "Democracy of a Special Type," *Sovetskoye Gosudarstvo i Pravo,* 1947, No. 1, pp. 1–15, and No. 3, pp. 1–14.

3. See *For a Lasting Peace, for a People's Democracy,* organ of the Cominform, November 10, 1947. See also A. Ulam, *Titoism and the Cominform,* Harvard University Press, 1952, pp. 39–68.

4. Dimitrov's remarks were reprinted in the Cominform journal, January 1, 1949, and in *Pravda,* December 21 and December 27, 1948.

5. See, for example, P. F. Yudin, "On the Path of Transition to Socialism in the People's Democracies," *Voprosy Filosofii,* 1949, No. 1, pp. 40–59; B. S. Mankovsky, "Class Essence of the People's Democratic State," *Sovetskoye Gosudarstvo i Pravo,* 1949, No. 6, pp. 7–17; N. P. Farberov, *Gosudarstvennoye Pravo Stran Narodnoi Demokratii* (Public Law in the States of People's Democracy), Moscow, 1949. See also H. Gordon Skilling, " 'People's Democracy' in Soviet Theory," *Soviet Studies,* III, No. 1 (July, 1951), 16–33, and III, No. 2 (October, 1951), 131–149.

6. *Rude Pravo,* January 22, 1953.

7. *Review of International Affairs* (Belgrade), VI, No. 124 (June 1, 1955), 1, 2.

8. See Document 2 in this chapter.

9. See *Pravda,* July 16, 1955, also a full translation of the editorial in *The Current Digest of the Soviet Press,* VII, No. 26 (August 10, 1955), 3.

# THE ORGANIZATION OF
# THE COMMUNIST CAMP

Zbigniew K. Brzezinski

The Communist camp is composed of twelve states: the Soviet Union, China, Poland, Czechoslovakia, East Germany, Rumania, Hungary, Bulgaria, North Korea, North Vietnam, Albania, Mongolia. Jointly, the Communist-ruled states account for about 38 per cent of the world's population, 24.2 per cent of the world's area, and approximately one-third of the world's industrial output. During Stalin's lifetime the Communist bloc operated essentially through a relatively simple subordination of the various units to the dictator's will, generally expressed by indirect methods of police and party control. This somewhat informal organization reflected in part the old dictator's specific political style; in part it was a function of the relatively immature stage of the bloc's development. As a result, the "maturation" of the bloc coincided with the difficult post-Stalin period of transition within the USSR and was marked by major upheavals and tensions. By 1958–1959, however, the crisis had subsided, and a new and more complex image of the bloc became apparent. While the Soviet Union continued to exercise leadership, acknowledged at the November, 1957, conference of the Communist parties and buttressed by Soviet international and technological prestige, the camp had developed more elaborate mechanisms and processes of cohesion that also contributed to its unity. Some of them dated back to the Stalinist days, but were now infused with new vitality. Others emerged during the post-Stalin phase.

For analytical purposes, these mechanisms are treated in this article under two general headings: formal institutional aspects, including the multilateral and bilateral framework of the camp; and the dynamic aspects, including the various processes of unity, such as party contacts, contributions to the inter-party ideological organ, patterns of

Reprinted from *World Politics,* Vol. XIII, No. 2 (January, 1961), pp. 175–209, by permission of the author and the publishers.

trade, and cultural contacts. The focus of the study is on the organization of the camp, and not on the relations or conflicts within it.[1] A concise but inclusive treatment is provided of the various institutions and emerging processes that buttress and/or increase the political unity of the camp and organize the relations among its members. In the concluding pages, some of the broader implications of the changing character of the camp are discussed.

## I. FORMAL INSTITUTIONAL ASPECTS

The formal institutional ties both for maintaining unity and for defining relations among the Communist states have become much more prominent since Stalin's death. They may be examined in terms of the following four general categories: multilateral ties, bilateral political treaties, bilateral economic agreements, and cultural pacts.

At the present time there is no multilateral party organization resembling the Comintern or the Cominform. These organizations, discredited by Stalinism, have not been resuscitated, although efforts have been made to replace them by frequent *ad hoc* multilateral meetings of party chiefs and by a theoretical inter-party journal, both of which are discussed in part II of this study. The two most important multilateral organs binding some of the Communist states together are the Warsaw Treaty Organization (WTO) and the Council for Economic Mutual Assistance (CEMA). There is, however, no organ officially including all the Communist states. It is symptomatic of the post-Stalin diversity in the orbit that efforts to create a new supra-party bloc organ were resisted by some of the leaderships in and out of the bloc, and that the unity of the bloc has had to be promoted through the utilization of institutions which existed prior to 1956. In recent years both the WTO and CEMA have increased in importance as agencies for the articulation of common purposes and for the isolation and eventual subordination of those Communist leaders who were suspect of being unduly influenced by their own national perspective in the shaping of policy.

The WTO is both a political and a military organization. Established formally on May 14, 1955, under the Treaty of Friendship, Cooperation, and Mutual Assistance, it is composed of eight of the twelve Communist States, with China "associated" but not a member, and North Korea, North Vietnam, and Mongolia remaining outside of the pact. It is thus primarily a European organization, serving externally as a counter to NATO, internally as the formal device for the perpetuation of close ties between the Soviet Union and its European satellites. In fact, to this day it constitutes the single most important formal commitment binding the European Communist states to the USSR, officially limiting their scope for independent action by precluding their participation in other alliance systems (Art. 7).

The founding meeting of the WTO provided for a Political Consultative Committee which was empowered to establish supplementary multilateral organs. The Committee exercised this power in its January 1956 Prague meeting by setting up a regular secretariat, with representatives from member states, and a standing commission for foreign policy co-ordination.[2] The meeting also decided that the Committee was to meet not less than twice yearly. However, when Khrushchev addressed the next consecutive meeting, he had to concede that "more than two years have passed since the Political Consultative Committee last met in Prague in 1956."[3] Since the Committee did not convene again until February 1960, it appears that the 1956 decision has lapsed. Two hypothetical explanations may account for this: the resistance of the Poles to such meetings; or (what is more likely, since the Poles could hardly prevent them) the unwillingness of the Soviet Union to push the development of the WTO too far lest it become a genuine consultative organ.

At the present time, meetings of the Political Consultative Committee serve primarily as forums for the articulation of a common stand on important international issues and, in effect, for implicitly delegating the USSR to be the spokesman of the bloc in dealing with the West.[4] The May, 1958, session was primarily devoted to an analysis of the international situation, with special emphasis on the program which the Soviet leaders would submit at a summit meeting with the Western powers. Particular stress was put on troop reductions within the bloc as proof of the bloc's stability and peaceful intentions. The 1960 meeting in effect served to endorse the position which the Soviet leadership was to adopt at the expected May, 1960, summit

meeting, with the only discordant note coming from the Chinese observer, who attended the meetings in keeping with China's status as "associated" with the WTO (see part II).

Judging from the three sessions—the second and third lasting merely one day—it appears that the Political Consultative Committee does not serve as an active policy-making agency, comparable to some of the multilateral meetings of party chiefs, noted in part II. The political importance of the WTO is that it (1) provides a formal framework binding the various states together, (2) supplies the juridical basis for limiting the exercise of their sovereignty, and (3) serves as a useful forum for the articulation of unanimity, expressing ritualistically the bloc's support of Soviet foreign policy initiatives. It is significant that one of the charges most often cited against Imre Nagy was that he violated the unity of the bloc through his unilateral decision to leave the Warsaw Pact.

The essentially static, restrictive function of the WTO is evident also in its military aspects. The original agreement provided for a Unified Command of the armed forces of the signatories, and, indeed, the signing of the treaty was followed immediately by a communiqué announcing that a joint command had been set up. Soviet Marshal I. S. Konev was appointed commander-in-chief, another Soviet officer became joint chief of staff, and the command headquarters was to be situated in Moscow. Defense Ministers of the participating states have attended ostentatiously the three sessions of the Political Consultative Committee and Marshal Konev (recently replaced by Marshal Grechko) delivered reports to these sessions on the military situation. Probably some strategic "division of labor" has also been made. However, to the extent that it can be determined, this exhausts the military aspects of the WTO. The international military command has not been set up. The various states have not delegated their ranking officers to serve on it, nor have liaison officers been appointed. In this case, the Soviet Union's fear of arousing new anti-Soviet sentiments was combined with its desire not to share Soviet military secrets with its allies. Since the uprisings of 1956, the stationing of Soviet troops in East Europe has been regularized by bilateral agreements which used the Warsaw Treaty as their point of reference (see below), but they could have easily been concluded independently of such a treaty.

A much more active, positive role is played by the multilateral Council for Economic Mutual Assistance (CEMA), originally set up in January, 1949, but activated only after Stalin's death, and particularly after the disruptive events of October–November, 1956. The founding members were the USSR, Poland, Czechoslovakia, Hungary, Rumania, and Bulgaria. Subsequently they were joined by East Germany and Albania. These states together have about 300 million inhabitants, or 11 per cent of the world's population. They cover about 17 per cent of the world's surface and produce nearly 30 per cent of the world's industrial output. Although not members, China, Mongolia, North Korea, and North Vietnam have in recent years been sending observers to the Council's sessions.[5] In its initial stage, CEMA resembled the Warsaw Pact: primarily restrictive in purpose, it was designed to keep the European Communist states out of the Marshall Plan.[6] Following its founding session, CEMA held only two more plenary meetings during Stalin's lifetime: one in August, 1949, and a secret session, presumably sometime after the outbreak of the Korean War. During this early period, the organization concentrated primarily on redirecting the trade of its members toward each other and it may be surmised that it co-ordinated the development of their armaments industries during the Korean War. After Stalin's death, plenary sessions became more regular and increasingly more important. At first primarily formal gatherings, they gradually developed into working sessions at which common decisions were formulated.[7]

Formally, all members of CEMA are equal and all decisions must be unanimous. This provision, however, is meaningless if the relative economic strengths of the various participants are considered. Indeed, given the often conflicting interests of the various members, it is difficult to conceive how CEMA could operate if this provision were adhered to rigidly. The preponderant economic superiority of the Soviet Union in all instances serves as the determining factor, although this does not mean that the Council is merely a rubber stamp. On such issues as Polish coal, specialization, and prices, vigorous disputes have developed. Formally, the decisions of CEMA are not binding until approved by subsequent bilateral or multilateral formal agreements between the parties involved.

The steady growth of CEMA's bureaucratic machinery has been a concomitant of its increasingly active integrative role. It is headed by a permanent secretariat, located in Moscow, currently directed by a Soviet chairman and Polish and Czech deputy chairmen, with representatives from each of the participating states. The secretariat is paralleled by a conference of deputies whose task is to maintain consultation among the member states while the Council is not in session. The sessions of the Council rotate among the capitals of the participating states, to underline the equality of CEMA's members. In addition, there are thirteen permanent, specialized, multilateral commissions, each for a major branch of the economy (subdivided into even more specialized subcommissions) and each located in the capital of the country with the predominant interest in that particular branch.[8] On an average, the commissions meet approximately twice a year.

At the present time, CEMA is doubtless the single most important organ for actively shaping policies designed to promote the camp's unity.[9] In the difficult post-1956 period, it provided a sorely needed forum for multilateral consultation from which the Poles could not absent themselves,[10] and in the subsequent period of stabilization it has been the source of numerous policies designed to mold a "world socialist market" as the basis for the camp's political and ideological unity.[11] Khrushchev underlined the importance attached to this work when he remarked that

Extensive co-operation in all spheres of economic, social, political, and cultural life is developing among the sovereign countries of the socialist camp. Speaking of the future, it seems to me that the further development of the socialist countries will in all probability proceed along the lines of consolidation of the single-world socialist economic system. The economic barriers which divided our countries under capitalism will fall one after another. The common economic basis of world socialism will grow stronger, eventually making the question of borders a pointless one.[12]

Two other multilateral bloc organizations should be briefly mentioned. The first of these is the Danube Commission set up in August, 1948,[13] which includes the Soviet Union, Bulgaria, Czechoslovakia, Hungary, Rumania, and Yugoslavia. Its purpose is to ensure normal navigation on the Danube as an international waterway. The Paris peace conference of 1946 provided for such an organization, but the United States, the United Kingdom, and France refused to sign the August, 1948, agreement on the grounds that it violated the provisions and intentions of the Paris agreement. The Danube Commission held its first session in November 1949 and since then has met twice a year, usually in June and December—failing, however, to meet in December, 1956. Since the Commission from the very start contained a participant from outside the bloc, it cannot be viewed as primarily an institution for the promotion of the bloc's political unity. However, during the Stalinist phase it did serve, under Soviet directorship, as an agency for the promotion of Soviet bloc objectives in the campaign against Yugoslavia. (The May–June, 1951, and the December, 1952, sessions were preoccupied with mutual recriminations.) A major change took place shortly after Stalin's death: the Soviets manifested an increasing willingness to pass control over to the Danubian powers; also, since June, 1956, the European Economic Commission has been participating in the sessions as an observer, and since June, 1957, both Austria and the German Federal Republic have attended as experts. As a result, the Danubian Commission has increasingly become an international technical agency, not restricted to the camp alone. Its technical character makes it similar to such organizations as, for instance, the Organization of Co-operation of the Socialist Countries in the field of communications, set up on Soviet initiative by the 1957 conference of ministers of communications of all the "socialist" countries.[14]

The other multilateral Communist organization to be noted here is the Institute for Nuclear Research set up in March, 1956. In part, its establishment reflected the internal pressures on the Soviet Union to share its nuclear monopoly with its allies. The original founding agreement was signed by all the Communist states save North Vietnam, which joined in September of the same year. The agreement appears to have been the outgrowth of the Soviet decision of January 7, 1955,[15] to undertake collaborative research efforts with China, Poland, Czechoslovakia, Rumania, and East Germany, countries which supplied the USSR with uranium and which could be expected to entertain scientific ambitions. Curiously, however, Hungary did not appear on the list, even though it was known to be an extractor of uranium. The January, 1955, decision was followed by a series of bilateral agreements concluded by the USSR and the aforementioned states in April, 1955, providing for the supply to these states of limited quantities of fissionable material, experimental accelerators, and atomic piles, relevant equipment, and documentation.[16] This was followed shortly by an identical agreement with Hungary in June, 1955. (Possibly Nagy's fall from power eliminated doubts that might have existed earlier in Moscow.)

The preceding agreement laid the basis for the March, 1956, conference of eleven Communist states which resulted in the creation of the Joint Institute for Nuclear Research. The Institute was located at Dubno, just north of Moscow; it was to be headed by a director and two assistant directors. In practice, the former has always been a Soviet scientist, while the latter have represented the participating states. Dues for the maintenance of the Institute were apportioned among the participating states on a graduated basis. The Institute was subdivided into specialized laboratories, each apparently also headed by a Soviet scientist. Thus, by and large, effective Soviet control has been maintained even though the Soviet Union did meet at least part way the desire of the other bloc members to share in nuclear development and to acquire the basis for training cadres of their own. Over 100 non-Soviet scientific workers were said to be working in Dubno in 1959, with the Czechs being the most numerous.[17] The Institute as a multinational organization can be seen as combining elements of control with some adjustment to the demands of the members of the bloc.

This multilateral framework is buttressed by a web of bilateral agreements. Of these, the most important are the friendship and mutual aid agreements. They are usually directed against a specific outside threat—either Germany or Japan, and their possible allies—and they contain pledges of mutual support. In that sense, an effort is made to relate the alliance to a concrete danger, activating deeply felt anti-German or anti-Japanese popular feelings existing within some of the Communist-ruled states. However, it would be specious to argue that a treaty of friendship and mutual assistance between, let us say, Rumania and the Soviet Union represents a meaningful partnership. Rather, the treaty is essentially a cloak for a relationship of political subservience, with the juridical fiction of equality serving both to mask this relationship and to perpetuate it.[18] Quite another matter is the Soviet-Chinese treaty of alliance. Here, the two contracting partners have in effect formalized a relationship of alliance and have expressed it in terms which impose meaningful obligations on both sides.

The Soviet Union has entered into friendship and mutual aid treaties with all but three of the Communist states—East Germany, North Vietnam, and North Korea, all divided nations. It seems likely that the Soviet Union does not wish to create a juridical situation which could impede the unification of these nations under Communist auspices, and premature ties might possibly constitute such an impediment. Furthermore, in the past at least, the Soviet Union may have considered the possibility that ties of alliance could involve the Soviet Union in local conflicts which might easily erupt (or be provoked) between the opposing sides of the divided nations. However, it is likely that in the foreseeable future the Soviet Union will conclude treaties with these states so as to eliminate an anomalous distinction between them and the other members of the camp, a distinction increasingly less necessary with the apparent consolidation of the outer limits of the camp. East German membership in the WTO and attendance of its sessions by North Vietnamese and North Korean observers would seem to augur this. At this stage, the East European states, while bound to one another by treaties of mutual aid and friendship, do not have such treaties with any of the Asian states; rather, the expedient of the vaguer friendship and co-operation treaty has been used. Symptomatic of certain political affinities noted in part II, China has concluded such friendship and co-operation agreements only with East Germany (December 25, 1955) and Czechoslovakia (March 27, 1957).[19]

All of the mutual aid treaties were concluded by 1950—i.e., in Stalin's lifetime. It is noteworthy that the treaties did not provide a juridical basis for the stationing of Soviet troops on the territory of the members of the camp. A provision for Soviet bases abroad was contained in the multilateral WTO, and even that agreement was very general in its wording. In a way, therefore, the most substantive bilateral political agreements concluded among the Communist states were those which for the first time formalized and rendered explicit the basis for the presence of Soviet troops on the soil of the other Communist-ruled states.

The model for such agreements was the Polish-Soviet treaty of December 17, 1956 (ratified by both parties in February, 1957), concerning the status of Soviet troops "temporarily" stationed in Poland. This treaty reflected the new situation created by the changes that took place in Poland in October, 1956, and was designed to meet long-standing Polish grievances. The political foundation for it was laid by the agreement reached by the Soviet and Polish government and party leaders in a conference held in Moscow in mid-November, and expressed by the joint declaration of November 18, alleviating many past Soviet abuses and explicitly defining the principles which govern the status of Soviet troops in Poland. The declaration imposed severe restrictions on any unilateral Soviet activity, explicitly prohibited the use of Soviet troops for political purposes in Poland, enjoined the Soviet command to co-ordinate their disposal, transportation, and numbers with the wishes of the Polish government, and made their personnel and dependents subject to Polish law. These provisions were reaffirmed in the formal treaty and a mixed Polish-Soviet commission was established to settle any disputes that may arise.[20]

The Soviet-Polish treaty, while perpetuating Soviet military presence in Poland, marked a definite step forward for Poland and the negotiation of this treaty did involve a measure of bargaining and definite Soviet concessions. Even the subsequent consolidation of Soviet influence within the bloc, which necessarily gave the Soviet Union new opportunities for exerting pressures (any formal limitations notwithstanding), did not undo this arrangement. Furthermore, the concessions won by Poland could not be denied to the other, more loyal Communist states. As a result, a mere three weeks after the signing of the Polish-Soviet treaty, a Soviet-East German declaration (of January 7, 1957) announced that a formal agreement regularizing the presence of Soviet troops on German soil would soon be concluded. Such an arrangement had been prefigured by the Soviet-East German treaty of September 20, 1955, defining the relations between the two countries, and granting East Germany "full freedom" as a sovereign state. However, it seems clear that it was the change in Soviet-Polish relations which prompted the execution of this commitment, and on March 12, 1957, a formal agreement was signed between the USSR and the DDR (East Germany), regularizing the presence of Soviet troops in East Germany.[21] Similar agreements were concluded shortly thereafter with Hungary (the March 28, 1957, joint Soviet-Hungarian political declaration laid the basis for it, and the formal agreement was signed on May 27, 1957),[22] and with Rumania on April 15, 1957.[23] The Rumanian and Hungarian agreements were similar to the one concluded with Poland, except that they did not cede control to these states over entry and exit of Soviet forces. The agreement with East Germany was even more restricted, in that it did not involve the restrictions cited in the Polish case, although asserting East German "sovereignty." The greater concessions made to the Poles reflected the relatively involuntary character of the Soviet adjustments.

Insofar as Poland and Hungary are concerned, the joint Polish-Soviet and Hungarian-Soviet governmental and party declarations of November 18, 1956, and March 28, 1957, respectively, represent the most important bilateral agreements concluded within the bloc. The first of these made it possible for the Polish Communist leadership to remain within the bloc while pursuing policies of relative domestic autonomy, some of which were at the time obviously displeasing to the Soviets. Nonetheless, the granting of compensation for past Soviet economic exploitation, the withdrawal of Soviet overseers from Poland, the acceptance by the Soviets of the Gomulka regime, and the restrictions imposed on the Soviet troops in Poland all were substantive measures designed to normalize and improve Polish-Soviet Communist relations.[24] In the case of Hungary, the March 28 declaration was also designed to improve Soviet-Hungarian relations and involved economic concessions and promises of aid. However, unlike the Polish case, the declaration was much more a unilateral effort on the part of the Soviet government to improve the domestic position of a satellite regime recently imposed on the population by the force of Soviet arms, than an agreement between two states. Nonetheless, it did involve a step forward for the Hungarians as well, especially when compared with the earlier period. Generally speaking, the agreements subsequent to October–November, 1956, can be seen as reflecting a recognition on the part of the Soviet leaders of the need to regularize the semi-colonial pattern of relations prevailing between the Soviet Union and most of the other Communist states. An expression of this recognition was the declaration issued by the Soviet Union (and prompted directly by the Hungarian revolution) on October 30, 1956, promising to liquidate the most obnoxious aspects of the Stalinist pattern of Soviet-satellite relations.[25]

Bilateral trade treaties also serve to unify the camp and are meant to create a common and enduring interest in its preservation. Since about 1957 these treaties have been designed to express in more detail and in a binding manner the recommendations of CEMA. Given over-all state control of the economy, such treaties govern the totality of trade among its members, and since most of the foreign trade of the Communist states takes place within the camp (see Table 6, part II), these agreements have an important bearing on the future livelihood and development of the signators. In recent years, there has been a veritable flood of statistics on the volume, composition, direction, etc., of trade between and among the Communist states, and there have been many valuable discussions of the degree of discrimination practiced by the Soviet Union against its weaker neighbors. There can be no doubt that such relations in the past did favor the Soviet Union and there is some evidence that they continue to do so. However, since 1956, the Soviet Union has become more actively engaged in issuing credit to the bloc states, and this has offset some of the still-prevailing discrimination and, at the same time, has constituted an important bond.[26] There is no need to cover the same ground here. Insofar as the trade agreements are concerned, it should be noted that they are usually concluded for relatively long-term periods, varying from two to seven years. In the early stages of the bloc, annual trade agreements were favored, since long-term planning co-ordination had not yet been effected.[27]

The long-term agreements include a protocol valid for one year, providing a much more detailed breakdown of items to be traded. The protocol is usually renegotiated for subsequent single years and sometimes a price adjustment is made. In some cases, the agreements also outline a longer-range "perspective," sketching out the anticipated volume of trade over a longer period than the actual agreement; on occasion the agreements envisage co-ordination of capital investment and co-operation in production, as well as credits.[28] This enables the contracting parties to plan several years ahead and to remain reasonably confident both of their supply and of their external markets. This is particularly important to states, like Poland, which are just developing certain branches of their industry—for instance, ship-building—and which would find it difficult to compete on the world market against the more advanced industrial states. However, at the same time the dependence of the more industrially developed Communist states (Czechoslovakia and East Germany) on Soviet supplies of raw materials, and of the less developed states (e.g., China) on Soviet machinery, is even further intensified by such long-term commitments.[29] A corollary of these trade agreements is an extensive exchange of scientific knowledge and scientific cadres,[30] and there have been numerous bilateral arrangements between the various national institutes and academies as well as the bilateral commissions for scientific-technical collaboration established not only between the Soviet Union and the other Communist states, but among the People's Democracies as well.

The final link in the formal web of ties that deserves brief mention is provided by the cultural agreements concluded between the Communist states. Since art, culture, and science are subject to state control under the Communist system, all cultural contacts between the various members of the camp must be regulated through official and formal channels. During Stalin's lifetime, however, such contacts were very much limited and only began to develop with the gradual lifting of the internal iron curtains by which the old dictator had isolated each Communist state. Thus, although European Communist states concluded cultural collaboration treaties with one another and also with China quite early in the history of the bloc (1947–1948, except for China and East Germany, which concluded such treaties in 1951 and 1952, respectively), cultural contacts remained essentially dormant until the middle 1950's.[31]

The Soviet Union displayed ostentatious contempt for such arrangements, and refrained (with only one exception[32]) from concluding such cultural collaboration agreements until the mid-1950's. This abstinence, however, did not prevent the Soviet Union from concluding a whole series of limited agreements with the members of the bloc, providing for the training of their citizens in Soviet institutions of higher learning, for "co-operation" in radio programing and subsequently also in television, and finally for collaboration between their respective Academies of Science. It was only in the wake of the attack on Stalin and within the context of very hurried efforts to improve and normalize Soviet relations that the Soviet Union concluded cultural collaboration agreements with all the Communist states.[33] These agreements provided for expanded contacts in education, art, music, literature, the theater, films, press, radio, television, sports, and even tourism. In effect, they were meant to establish a broad social basis for contacts with "the first country of socialism," hitherto sealed off hermetically. In all but four cases, the agreements were to run for five years; in the case of Mongolia, half-absorbed by the USSR, and of Soviet-controlled Korea and what was still Rakosi's Hungary, they covered ten years; and in the case of Vietnam, only three. In an effort to remove obvious discrimination, in the course of 1956–1957 the Soviet Union set up friendship societies with China, Bulgaria, etc., to match analogous friendship societies with the Soviet Union which had existed in the other states since the late 1940's. During 1957–1958 friendship societies also were established among all the Communist states.

The fact that these formal institutional aspects have in the majority of cases been developed or given substance in the post-Stalin phase of the camp's history is not without meaning. It would seem to suggest that these various devices, in spite of their original propagandistic purposes, have become more important to the Communist, and particularly the Soviet, leaders as instruments for the preservation and expression of their camp's unity. Indeed, as if to underscore this development, the old word "camp" (*lager* in Russian) now has a new equivalent: *sodruzhestvo* or, roughly, "commonwealth."[34] This in itself suggests a degree of maturation within the bloc, its growth from a relatively simple, informal combination of personal dictatorship and "big nation" imperialism, to a more complex pattern which preserves the privileged position of the dominant state but expresses this relationship through a more formal institutionalized set of arrangements.

## II. DYNAMIC ASPECTS

The formal institutional aspects provide a broad framework for the organization of the unity of the Communist camp. This unity, however, is given content by the continuous interaction of its members, resolving conflicts, shaping policies, developing close trade contacts, engaging in exchanges and, of course, responding to the demands of the camp's most powerful state. This section will consider the various forms which these processes of unity take within the camp, often revealing the degree of cohesion that exists between the various groups of member states. Again, it is to be noted, Soviet power, the dependence of most of these states on the USSR, and the common ideological outlook of their regimes are taken for granted.

The most important dynamic aspect of the camp's unity is provided by frequent contacts between the top leaders of the various ruling parties. This practice is a relatively recent development and involves an important change in the political style of the bloc.[35] During Stalin's domination, contacts between party leaders were rare and usually involved bilateral dealings with the Soviet leaders. In recent years, however, and particularly since October–November, 1956 (which can be considered as a sort of watershed in the bloc's history), relatively frequent bilateral and multilateral consultations between the party leaders have taken place. Even more important, Soviet leaders journey frequently to the other Communist states and necessarily have become much more conscious of the problems that the other ruling parties face. While not all of these meetings are of actual policy-making importance, they do help to keep the various party leaders better informed about current difficulties and they invariably involve a measure of discussion. Since at such meetings the Soviet leadership can muster the overwhelming support of the other regimes, the multilateral meeting is a useful forum for articulating common principles and for forcing recalcitrant parties (until about 1958, the Polish; more recently, the Chinese) into declarations of unity. The most recent example of this was provided during the Rumanian Party Congress in June 1960, when the Chinese were in effect faced with the choice of endorsing the Soviet line or being isolated through open disagreement.

The most important policy meetings—i.e, meetings at which positions and principles were actually hammered out—took place in the wake of the 1956 crisis. These involved, as already noted, many Polish-Soviet meetings, meetings between the Chinese and the various ruling European parties, meetings between the more orthodox ruling parties, such as the East German, Czechoslovak, and Bulgarian, and multilateral conferences initiated by the November, 1957, Moscow meeting. The relative surface stabilization of the bloc during 1958–1960 did not diminish the policy importance of subsequent party meetings, and certainly not their informational-declarative value. Soviet-Chinese and Soviet-Polish meetings in 1958 and 1959 dealt with (not merely dictated) important domestic and external issues, while meetings of leaders of the other ruling parties among themselves and with the Soviets and the Chinese defined common stands on such issues as revisionism, collectivization, and foreign policy matters. The party congresses held in the USSR, East Germany, Bulgaria, Poland, Hungary, and Czechoslovakia, as well as the Chinese tenth-anniversary celebration, also created opportunities for frequent top-level multilateral meetings. In addition, as noted earlier, the Communist chiefs were brought together on the occasion of some of the CEMA and WTO sessions. All of these multilateral meetings took place after the November, 1957, meeting, which overcame the Polish objections to multilateral gatherings.[36]

Tables 1 and 2 indicate the pattern and the intensity of party meetings at the Politburo level within the bloc. A few observations derived from them might be relevant here. Until the November, 1957, Moscow meeting, the top CPSU leaders did not engage in extensive travels, but instead played host to frequent delegations from abroad. (It is to be remembered that during this period there was an intense conflict within the Soviet leadership.) At that time Moscow was visited by the top leaders of every Communist state, with some of them coming several times: Kadar three times, Gomulka twice, Zhivkov twice, Siroky twice. Of the thirty-one Politburo-level meetings attended by the Soviet leaders between November, 1956, and November, 1957, twenty-five were held at home (see Table 2). In the course of this "stabilization" period, Budapest, East Berlin, and Prague were also focal points for such top-level activity (twenty-one home meetings, as compared with only two in Warsaw). In general, worthy of note is the somewhat relatively higher incidence of meetings of East German–Bulgarian–Czechoslovak representatives, whose parties enjoy a neo-Stalinist reputation.

By way of contrast, in the post-1956 "stabilization" phase, the Chinese party was quite active externally, more so than in the subsequent post-1957 period. (A Chinese Politburo delegation was sent twice to tour Eastern Europe in an attempt to resolve the existing differences between some of the

### TABLE 1—Politburo-Level Multilateral and Bilateral Meetings of Delegations in the Periods November, 1956-November, 1957, and 1958-1959*

|  | COUNTRY MAKING THE VISITS | | | | | | | |
|---|---|---|---|---|---|---|---|---|
| *Country Visited* | *USSR* | *China* | *Poland* | *Czech.* | *E. Germany* | *Rumania* | *Hungary* | *Bulgaria* |
| USSR |  | 5–3 | 5–5 | 3–5 | 2–5 | 2–4 | 5–4 | 3–5 |
| China | 2–2 |  | 1–1 | 1–1 | 0–2 | 0–1 | 0–2 | 1–1 |
| Poland | 0–5 | 1–1 |  | 0–1 | 1–2 | 0–1 | 0–2 | 0–2 |
| Czechoslovakia | 1–1 | 1–1 | 1–1 |  | 1–2 | 0–2 | 0–2 | 1–2 |
| E. Germany | 2–2 | 1–1 | 1–1 | 1–2 |  | 1–1 | 0–3 | 0–2 |
| Rumania | 0–1 | 1–0 | 0–1 | 1–0 |  |  | 0–1 | 1–0 |
| Hungary | 1–3 | 1–1 | 0–3 | 2–1 | 2–1 | 2–1 |  | 2–1 |
| Bulgaria | 0–2 | 1–1 | 0–2 | 0–1 | 1–1 | 1–1 | 0–2 |  |

\* The table probably shows the minimum figures, since doubtless many unannounced meetings were held. The first figure in each box represents meetings held in a given country between November 1, 1956, and November 15, 1957; the second figure represents the meetings held in 1958-1959. E.g., China was visited by Politburo-level East European and the Soviet regimes.) Soviet delegates twice in the first period and twice in the second; on the other hand, the Soviet Union was visited by the Chinese five times in the first period and three times in the second. Thus the total Soviet-Chinese meetings amount to twelve (four times in China, eight times in the USSR); see Table 2.

During this phase, Sino-Soviet contacts were most frequent, presumably reflecting a common concern with the prevailing instability within the bloc. In the post-1957 period, the initiative passed into Soviet hands. Soviet activity increased greatly, and Khrushchev undertook a series of personal visits to all the Communist capitals (something which Stalin never did). After the November, 1957, conference, which marked Gomulka's formal subservience to the principle of camp unity, Polish-Soviet meetings became frequent and Polish activity within the bloc increased greatly. It should be noted, however, that although more than half of the meetings registered in the tables involved first secretaries of the ruling parties, until October, 1960, Gomulka and Novotny had never exchanged formal visits (which presumably had something to do with the latter's behavior in October, 1956).

Every meeting normally concludes with a statement of principles, reaffirming a common ideological commitment and warning against various dangers to Communist unity. These meetings also serve to symbolize the equality that is formally said to prevail within the Communist camp. At the same time such gatherings provide their participants with convenient arenas for the exercise of subtle pressure. Thus the 1957 meetings were used by the East Germans, the Czechs, and the Bulgarians to assert the fundamental importance of Soviet leadership within the camp and to scourge revisionism. Similarly, in 1959 the Chinese tenth-anniversary meeting gave these party leaders an opportunity to praise effusively the Chinese domestic program and the relatively Stalinist ideological stand of the Chinese, thereby quietly indicating their hope that the other party leaderships would follow suit. The Moscow session of the WTO in February, 1960, presented

### TABLE 2—Total Meetings between Politburo Delegations in the Periods November, 1956-November, 1957, 1958-1959, and Both Combined*

|  | *USSR* | *China* | *Poland* | *Czech.* | *E. Germany* | *Rumania* | *Hungary* | *Bulgaria* |
|---|---|---|---|---|---|---|---|---|
| USSR |  |  |  |  |  |  |  |  |
| China | 7–5 = 12 |  |  |  |  |  |  |  |
| Poland | 5–10 = 15 | 2–2 = 4 |  |  |  |  |  |  |
| Czechoslovakia | 4–6 = 10 | 2–2 = 4 | 1–2 = 3 |  |  |  |  |  |
| E. Germany | 4–7 = 11 | 1–3 = 4 | 2–3 = 5 | 2–4 = 6 |  |  |  |  |
| Rumania | 2–5 = 7 | 1–1 = 2 | 0–2 = 2 | 1–1 = 2 | 1–1 = 2 |  |  |  |
| Hungary | 6–7 = 13 | 1–3 = 4 | 0–5 = 5 | 2–3 = 5 | 2–4 = 6 | 2–2 = 4 |  |  |
| Bulgaria | 3–7 = 10 | 2–2 = 4 | 0–4 = 4 | 1–3 = 4 | 1–3 = 4 | 2–1 = 3 | 2–3 = 5 |  |
| Total meetings with bloc | *USSR* | *China* | *Poland* | *Czech.* | *E. Germ.* | *Rumania* | *Hungary* |  |
| Politburo delegations | 31–47 = 78 | 16–18 = 34 | 10–28 = 38 | 13–21 = 34 | 13–25 = 38 | 9–13 = 22 | 15–27 = 42 | 11–23 = 34 |
| Of these: |  |  |  |  |  |  |  |  |
| At home | 25–31 | 5–10 | 2–14 | 5–10 | 6–12 | 3–2 | 10–11 | 3–10 |
| Abroad | 6–16 | 11–8 | 8–14 | 8–11 | 7–13 | 6–11 | 5–16 | 8–13 |

\* The first figure in each column refers to the period November, 1956-November, 1957; the second to 1958-1959; the third to the two combined. Thus the Soviets and the Chinese met seven times during the first period and five during the second, for a total of twelve.

the Chinese delegate with a chance to assure the other party leaders that the dangers of war are still acute and that the camp ought to avoid excessive reliance on "peaceful coexistence."[37] These top-level unity meetings thus involve important doses of "esoteric communication," which would not have been possible in Stalin's day.[38]

The top-level contacts, although frequent, still operate on an *ad hoc* basis. In 1957 there was some pressure from the Soviets and the other centralist leaders (East German, Czechoslovak) to re-establish some regular, institutionalized channel of inter-party contacts. Owing to the resistance of some parties (primarily the Polish, and possibly the Chinese also) this proposal was not implemented. Rather, two substitute methods were developed. First, the Soviet Union began to rely primarily on experienced party leaders, usually of a rank equivalent to a republican or *oblast'* first secretary, as its ambassadors to the other Communist states. In this way, Moscow assured itself of a degree of continuous party contact on a responsible level, subject directly to the CPSU Central Committee's department for dealing with bloc affairs.

Secondly, according to a decision reached at the November, 1957, conference, an inter-party political-ideological magazine was established. Its editorial offices were located in hyper-loyal Prague and a high-ranking CPSU specialist in international Communist affairs, A. Rumyantsev, was appointed as its head. It was entitled the *World Marxist Review* in its English edition, and *Problems of Peace*

*and Socialism* in its Russian edition. (The editions include the twelve languages of the bloc and seven others: English, French, Spanish, Italian, Dutch, Swedish, and Japanese.) Although distribution of the review is not restricted to the bloc, it was clear from the outset that one of its tasks would be the consolidation of a common ideological-political line for the bloc. Precisely because of that it was hailed by the East Germans[39] and met with silence in Warsaw.

Since publication of its first issue in September, 1958, the magazine has appeared once a month. Although it does not seem to have lived up to expectations as the vital organ for the crystallization of ideological and political unity in the bloc, it is the only inter-party publication on ideological-political matters, and in some ways a successor to the Cominform journal, *For a Lasting Peace, For a People's Democracy*. Apart from occasional editorials, it usually contains several major feature articles dealing with sundry problems of foreign policy, ideology, economy, or bloc affairs. A second section, which appears irregularly, is devoted to shorter "exchanges of views" between the various Communist parties. The third section contains brief notes on party activities.

An examination of twenty-six issues (September, 1958–October, 1960) shows that the magazine's contributors are by no means restricted to the bloc alone. The proportion of bloc contributions is highest among the major feature articles—95 out of 191; in the briefer "exchange of views" category,

**TABLE 3—Feature Articles in "World Marxist Review," September, 1958-October, 1960***
**(Total Number of Articles, 191; Soviet Bloc Contributions, 95)**

| Countries | Articles by Bloc | EXTERNAL ISSUES | | | | BLOC ISSUES | | | DOMESTIC ISSUES | | |
|---|---|---|---|---|---|---|---|---|---|---|---|
| | | For. Pol. Gen. | For. Pol. Nat'l. | Econ. Issues | Ideol. Issues | Polit. Issues | Ideol. Issues | Econ. Issues | Polit. Issues | Ideol. Issues | Ec. & Soc. Issues |
| Albania | — | | | | | | | | | | |
| Bulgaria | 7 | | | | 1 | | 1 | | 1 | 1 | 3 |
| China | 6 | | | | | | | | 1 | 2 | 3 |
| Czecho. | 15 | 1 | | 2 | 2 | | 2 | 3 | 2 | 1 | 2 |
| E. Germany | 11 | | 2 | | 1 | 3 | | | 2 | 1 | 2 |
| Hungary | 6 | | | | 1 | | | | 3 | 1 | 1 |
| Mongolia | — | | | | | | | | | | |
| N. Korea | 3 | | 1 | | | | | | | | 2 |
| N. Vietnam | 2 | | | | | | | | | | 2 |
| Poland | 8 | 2 | 1 | | | | | 1 | 1 | 1 | 2 |
| Rumania | 3 | 1 | | | | | | | 2 | | |
| USSR | 34 | 7 | 1 | 3 | 7 | | 3 | 3 | 3 | | 7 |
| TOTAL | 95 | 11 | 5 | 5 | 12 | 3 | 6 | 7 | 15 | 7 | 24 |

* (1) Not included are unsigned articles of indeterminate character as well as editorials. Included is one supplement on economic development in the bloc. (2) Arbitrary or borderline categorizations include several articles on purely cultural developments (e.g., an article in the April, 1960, issue, "A Playwright on Lenin"); such articles have been included under the heading of economic and social issues. An article on science and space, in the October, 1960, issue, which focuses on the scientific achievements of the USSR and briefly compares them with those of the United States, has been listed under the domestic social-economic heading. An article by G. Obichkin, "Lenin and the Party" (May, 1960), dealing with Lenin's theory of the party, has been included under external ideological issues—USSR, on the assumption that it is valid for all CP's, not just for those of the bloc. Otto Kuusinen's article, "Perspectives of Monopoly Capital" (April, 1960), is also listed under external ideological issues—USSR, on the grounds that the topic is more than purely economic.

**TABLE 4—Exchange of Views in "World Marxist Review," September, 1958-October, 1960\***
**(Total Number of Articles, 157; Soviet Bloc Contributions, 52)**

| Countries | Articles by Bloc | EXTERNAL ISSUES | | | BLOC ISSUES | | | DOMESTIC ISSUES | |
|---|---|---|---|---|---|---|---|---|---|
| | | For. Pol. Gen. | For. Pol. Nat'l. | Econ. Issues | Ideol. Issues | Pol. & Ideol. Issues | Econ. Issues | Pol. & Ideol. Issues | Ec. & Soc. Issues |
| Albania | 2 | | | | | 1 | | 1 | |
| Bulgaria | 4 | | | | | 2 | | 2 | |
| China | 5 | | | | | 1 | | 3 | 1 |
| Czecho. | 3 | | | | 1 | 1 | 1 | | |
| E. Germany | 13 | 1 | | 7 | 1 | 1 | | 2 | 1 |
| Hungary | 3 | | | | | 1 | | 1 | 1 |
| Mongolia | 1 | | | | | 1 | | | |
| N. Korea | — | | | | | | | | |
| N. Vietnam | 2 | | | | | 1 | | | |
| Poland | 3 | | | | | 1 | 1 | 1 | |
| Rumania | 4 | | | | 1 | 1 | 1 | 1 | |
| USSR | 12 | 4 | | 4 | | 1 | 1 | 1 | 1 |
| TOTAL | 52 | 5 | | 11 | 3 | 12 | 4 | 13 | 4 |

\* Under this heading is included not only a section labeled "Exchange of Views," which is usually a forum on such questions as "What Are the Changes in the Structure of the Working Class?" (May and September, 1960), but also a monthly feature entitled "Communications and Comment," reports on international congresses, and an occasional feature called "Pages from History." Items were excluded if their authorship could not be determined.

the proportion is 52 out of 157; in the short news items, 59 out of 238. However, given the origins of the magazine and the fact that it is presently the only open inter-party forum, it is an important and revealing source of information concerning inter-party dynamics within the bloc. Tables 3, 4, and 5 provide a breakdown of the various contributions from the parties belonging to the Communist camp.

The tables seem to warrant the following conclusions insofar as the camp is concerned:

1. Not unexpectedly, the leading role in the magazine is played by the CPSU.

2. More striking perhaps, however, is the domination of the magazine by three parties—the Soviet, the Czech, and the East German. Of the 95 major bloc contributions, they account for 60; of the 52 "exchange of views" in the second table, the Soviets and Germans alone account for 25; of the 59 informational items, the three parties account for 25.

3. It is also noteworthy that these three parties monopolize almost entirely the serious discussion of bloc affairs and dominate heavily most of the comments on external issues.

4. By the way of contrast, the contributors from the other ruling parties seem to restrict themselves to their own domestic problems.

5. Very striking is the limited participation of the Chinese party: in feature articles, it is less than that of Czechoslovakia, East Germany, or Bulgaria, and no greater than that of Hungary; its share in the other categories is similar.

6. Not less striking is the small total of contributions from the Asian countries: instead of contributing roughly one-third (four countries out of twelve), they contributed little more than one-ninth of the camp's feature articles, one-sixth of the "exchange of views" contributions, and one-eighth of the activities items. This seems to have a further implication: insofar as the camp is concerned, the journal is primarily an organ of Soviet orthodoxy, designed to articulate on *major issues* the line developed by the Soviet leaders and their most devoted lieutenants, the East Germans and the Czechs. The other parties either shun the magazine or are pushed into a relatively narrow, domestically oriented background. This "in-group" seems to parallel the one noted in regard to leadership contacts.

Little can be said without access to classified data concerning the dynamic side of military relations within the bloc. However, certain facts do

**TABLE 5—Articles Headed "In the Communist and Workers' Parties," in "World Marxist Review," September, 1958-October, 1960 (Total Number of Articles, 238; Soviet Bloc Contributions, 59)**

| | |
|---|---|
| Albania | 4 |
| Bulgaria | 4 |
| China | 3 |
| Czechoslovakia | 8 |
| East Germany | 7 |
| Hungary | 8 |
| Mongolia | 2 |
| North Korea | 3 |
| North Vietnam | — |
| Poland | 8 |
| Rumania | 2 |
| USSR | 10 |

stand out. Since 1956, the Soviet Union has striven to remove the most overbearing aspects of its military domination of Eastern Europe, a domination to which the Soviet leaders had to admit during the critical days of October, 1956.[40] With the recall of most of the Soviet advisers (Hungary excepted), and with the highly publicized treaties governing the presence of Soviet troops in other Communist states, the most glaring irritants were removed. At the same time, the Soviet Union ensured the availability to its forces of certain strategic areas: e.g., Polish and Rumanian ports as well as frontal positions in East Germany and Hungary. However, these adjustments do not amount to close co-operation and/or military integration. In fact, it would appear that on the military level, the Soviets, possibly anxious to protect their military secrets and hypersensitive to security matters, prefer to avoid tight military integration. Apart from providing some of the satellites with the technical information necessary for the production of Soviet-type weapons (thereby alleviating delivery pressures on the USSR), and general standardization of weapons within the camp, military co-operation tends to operate primarily at the top political-military levels, through exchange of visits and a general definition of broad strategic tasks, but without real military integration or frequent and regular joint maneuvers of the various Communist forces.

The Soviets' determination to protect their military preponderance within the bloc is particularly evident with respect to nuclear weapons. Unwillingness to share them has been expressed through such maneuvers as the scheme for an atom-free Asia (coolly received by the Chinese) and by continuing equivocation in response to requests for greater nuclear assistance from the other "socialist" states, particularly China. It was presumably with this in mind that, according to Radio Peking of June 8, 1960, a Chinese leader, Liu Chang-sheng, made this veiled criticism of the Soviet stand:

We hold that the utmost efforts must be made to reach agreement on the banning of nuclear weapons and to prevent the outbreak of a nuclear war in the world. Soviet mastery of nuclear weapons has now deprived U.S. imperialism of its monopoly of such weapons. The Soviet Union and the other socialist countries should continue to develop their lead in the sphere of atomic energy and, at the same time, the people throughout the world should wage a more extensive struggle against imperialism and against nuclear weapons. Only in these circumstances can such agreement be reached.

In other words, the best way to get a nuclear ban would be to share nuclear weapons with China and the other Communist-ruled states.

With respect to the matter of diplomatic relations among the Communist states, considerable regularization is to be noted. In the course of 1957–1958, the Soviet Union concluded a whole series of consular conventions with the other members of the bloc, defining consular competence and clarifying such still outstanding issues as dual-citizenship, problems of mutual legal aid, and civil, criminal, and familial legal issues.[41] However, the Soviet Union still retained its traditional reticence concerning the opening of foreign consulates on Soviet soil; the Poles, for instance, were unsuccessful in their efforts to increase their consular representation in the Soviet Union. At the higher diplomatic level, as noted earlier, the trend in the Soviet case has been toward the appointment of party officials as ambassadors to the other Communist states.[42] However, this does not necessarily mean that the ambassadorial role has actually increased. In some cases, such appointments were made in the wake of the domestic disgrace of the individual concerned (e.g., Molotov and Pervukhin), and in general it may be seen as part of a trend to improve inter-party contacts through the development of a sense of *partiinost* in common dealings, while leaving the determination of more important issues to higher-level party meetings which, as already observed, have become relatively frequent. In this connection, quite suggestive is the increase in the frequency of Soviet ambassadorial shifts in those states which during Stalin's time were almost ruled by the Soviet ambassador. During the Stalinist phase six Soviet ambassadors in Hungary, Poland, Rumania, and East Germany, served a total of twenty-six years, or roughly four and a half years for each appointment. In the post-Stalin phase, twelve ambassadors served out twenty-six years, or just over two years each. Apart from domestic Soviet factors involved in such changes, one may well suspect that the relative decrease in the role of the Soviet ambassador as the direct superior of the domestic leaders of the countries involved may have had something to do with this.

These various high-level forms of relations testify to a steadily intensified contact between the ruling regimes. The number of visits of various ministers, deputy ministers, regional party secretaries, assembly deputies, technical and scientific delegations, youth activists, etc., runs virtually into the hundreds.[43] These, too, compare notes and sometimes engage in subtle communications.[44] Recent years have also seen a marked increase in personal contacts among the several Communist states, something not possible during Stalin's era. The gradual development of tourism means that each year tens of thousands of private citizens of one Communist country visit other Communist countries. (In 1959, for instance, about 60,000 Bulgarians, 70,000 Czechs, and 70,000 Poles traveled within the orbit.[45]) However, in this respect some striking differences among the various states have to be noted. Of the Poles, almost as many visit non-Communist as Communist states, whereas in the case of the other bloc members the total going west is at the most one-fourth (Czechoslovakia) and usually less. Furthermore, the greatest exchange of tourists seems to be among East Germany, Czechoslovakia, and Bulgaria; this is easily explainable in terms of Bulgaria being a genuine tourist attraction, but other considerations would appear to be involved in the case of the large number of Czechs or Bulgarians visiting East Germany, but not, for instance, Poland. Among the many other forms of intensified contacts, one should also note an increasing student exchange, especially between the USSR and China,[46] special conferences of bloc scholars,[47] collaboration agreements between the several national academies of science (e.g., the December, 1957, and January, 1958, scientific and technological agreements between the respective Chinese and Soviet institutions), and circulation of bloc literature and newspapers (particularly Soviet) among the various states. For instance, the year 1959 saw meetings of the orbit's publishers, economists, film producers, even circus directors. The film producers decided, inter alia, to emphasize partiinost in their productions, close ties with reality, and "the unmasking of revisionism in aesthetics."[48] All of these measures are designed to foster a sense of community, a sense of common identity in "the camp of socialism."

The extensive efforts to promote unity, so lacking during the Stalinist phase of the camp's development, has two further aspects which deserve mention. The first is the matter of trade, the second that of the literature of unity. The importance of close trade ties as a factor of interdependence was recognized much earlier than the need for co-ordinated planning and for the activization of the dormant institutions of CEMA. However, with specialization, trade has assumed an even more important role in shaping a "socialist world market," distinct from the capitalist world and fully self-sufficient. Table 6 shows not only the degree to which trade patterns have been channeled primarily within the bloc, but also the intensity of trade among the various Communist states. In addition

to the obvious point that trade with the USSR is of central importance to all of the states, whatever the level of their economic development, it would appear that China depends also to a great extent on supplies from East Germany and Czechoslovakia, thus paralleling the particular ideological affinities of these regimes for one another. While it would be incorrect to claim that there is a causal relationship between trade patterns and ideological orientations, it is a fact that states like East Germany and Czechoslovakia, which entertain a centralistic conception of the bloc, do happen to play an important role in the general economic life of that bloc. Their economic strength thus buttresses their political orientation and gives them greater influence in such organs as CEMA.

In general, in the eyes of the Communist leaderships, the emerging economic interdependence is said to have not only economic but great political and ideological significance. It is quite evident that in the thinking of the Soviet leaders, the consolidation and growth of a "socialist world market," and eventually its preponderance over the "capitalist" market, is one of the determining factors shaping the present epoch.[49] The economic growth and integration of the camp are thus becoming central factors in the Communist perspective on world affairs.

The final aspect to be registered involves the literature of unity that is mushrooming within the bloc and particularly in the USSR. By this is not meant the trite, propagandistic, and largely sterile treatments of the often illusory advantages for the various Communist-ruled countries of friendship with the Soviet Union. Such publications have been available for a long time. In the last two or three years, however, there have been signs that more serious thought is being given in the various states, and particularly in the USSR, to what might be called the problematics of the Communist camp. Apparently it became evident to all concerned that the emergence of a series of Communist states created problems and issues which had specific characteristics and which could not be answered

### TABLE 6—Intra-Bloc Trade Patterns*
### (in Per Cent of Total)

| Countries | BULGARIA | | CHINA | | CZECH. | | E. GERMANY | |
|---|---|---|---|---|---|---|---|---|
| | 1957 | 1958 | 1957 | 1958 | 1957 | 1958 | 1957 | 1958 |
| Bulgaria | | | .04 | | 3.0 | 2.7 | 1.9 | 2.1 |
| China | 1.0 | 2.5 | | | 5.0 | 7.0 | 6.0 | 9.4 |
| Czech. | 11.5 | 10.5 | 5.7 | 5.7 | | | 7.6 | 11.3 |
| E. Germany | 8.0 | 9.3 | 7.5 | 6.6 | 10.1 | 11.0 | | |
| Hungary | 2.6 | 2.4 | 2.2 | 2.7 | 5.4 | 5.8 | 3.6 | 4.3 |
| Poland | 3.5 | 4.9 | 3.2 | 3.2 | 10.0 | 11.0 | 7.4 | 10.4 |
| Rumania | 1.8 | 1.5 | | | 2.3 | 2.1 | 1.8 | 2.0 |
| USSR | 52.0 | 53.3 | 50.0 | | 34.0 | 33.1 | 45.0 | 43.0 |
| Total share intra-bloc trade | 85.0 | 85.9 | 75.0 | 75.0 | 69.8 | 72.7 | 73.3 | 82.5 |

* Read down for the trade of any particular country.

by the standard political, ideological, and economic literature written primarily for Soviet domestic consumption. Furthermore, it became evident that the experience of the other ruling parties often raised issues which could be disturbing to the CPSU membership.

As a result, by 1958 and 1959 even important Soviet publications appeared to be drafted with at least one ear cocked toward possible bloc reactions and domestic echoes of bloc problems. The recently published *Istoriia KPSS,* or the most up-to-date formal statement of the ideology, *Osnovy Marksizma-Leninizma,* edited by O. V. Kuusinen, not only were clearly intended for domestic Soviet consumption but attempted to address themselves to problems that face the other ruling parties. The realization that Stalin had erred in insisting that almost every aspect of Soviet experience was relevant to "the construction of socialism" elsewhere meant that serious thought could be given to the task of defining which parts of this experience were and were not relevant. The efforts of the CPSU's new official history to define the universal laws of "socialist construction" was a response to this need.[50] Similarly, Kuusinen's book was in large part an attempt to provide an up-to-date, authoritative, and serious statement of the doctrine, refuting both the revisionist and the dogmatist views penetrating some of the ruling parties, including the CPSU.[51]

In addition, within the last two years a spate of books devoted to bloc affairs has been published in the USSR.[52] As the partial listing below suggests, their primary emphasis appears to be on the theme of economic collaboration and on the emergence of a "socialist world market." Occasionally they contain useful comparative materials on the economic development of the various Communist-ruled states and on the stages of their "socialist construction." There are, in addition, two other kinds of general treatment: volumes primarily devoted to the negative task of rooting out "revisionist" tendencies within the ruling parties,[53] and more

general political-ideological discussions of the camp's affairs. The latter category supplies perhaps the more interesting examples of the developing literature of unity. One may cite, for instance, the symposium sponsored by the Philosophy Institute of the Academy of Sciences, entitled *The Commonwealth of Socialist Countries (Sodruzhestvo Stran Sotsializma).* This 300-page book addresses itself to such issues as the generalities and specifics of the building of communism, the impact of the October Soviet revolution on the development of the concept of People's Democracy (a matter which was once actively discussed in the bloc), a discussion of the peculiarities of building socialism in China, etc.[54] While often simplistically dogmatic in its approach (this is particularly true of a chapter dealing with "proletarian internationalism" in relations between the Communist states), such literature is a modest step forward in the direction of at least recognizing some of the problems involved in building "socialism" on the basis of a common ideology but within the context of several societies, ranging from the technologically most advanced to the most primitive.[55]

## III. SOME CONCLUSIONS

Insofar as the organization of the Communist camp is concerned, recent years have seen concrete efforts in the direction of (1) the regularization of relations among its members; and (2) the intensification of such relations. Many of the earlier sources of tension were due to the essentially informal and indirect system of Stalinist controls, to the blurred lines between central authority and domestic autonomy, to the air-tight compartmentalization of the camp's members, each surrounded by an iron curtain and beholden only to Moscow. The regularization of these relations, and their concomitant intensification, have been designed to reduce the number of tension points, and to liquidate

### TABLE 6—Intra-Bloc Trade Patterns (Cont'd.)
### (in Per Cent of Total)

|  | HUNGARY | | POLAND | | RUMANIA | | USSR | |
|---|---|---|---|---|---|---|---|---|
|  | 1957 | 1958 | 1957 | 1958 | 1957 | 1958 | 1957 | 1958 |
| Bulgaria | 1.8 | 1.5 | 1.2 | 1.6 | 2.5 | | 4.5 | 4.7 |
| China | 5.2 | 6.9 | 3.7 | 4.7 | 4.2 | | 15.4 | 17.5 |
| Czech. | 13.9 | 13.1 | 6.2 | 7.3 | 6.7 | | 11.2 | 11.1 |
| E. Germany | 11.0 | 11.0 | 13.0 | 11.5 | 7.5 | | 19.5 | 18.7 |
| Hungary | | | 2.4 | 2.7 | 3.3 | | 4.3 | 4.1 |
| Poland | 4.9 | 5.1 | | | 4.2 | | 8.3 | 7.4 |
| Rumania | 2.5 | 2.3 | 1.5 | 1.1 | | | 5.3 | 5.6 |
| USSR | 29.5 | 27.0 | 30.6 | 26.2 | 47.6 | | | |
| Total share intra-bloc trade | 70.2 | 66.3 | 58.6 | 55.1 | 76.0 | | 68.5 | 69.1 |

the earlier ambiguities in the division of power between the center and its dependencies and/or allies. While foreign affairs, military affairs, and ideology still remain primarily in the Soviet domain (excepting the special case of China), a limited measure of autonomy in regard to the tempo and specific character of domestic social and economic policies is gradually developing insofar as the other Communist states are concerned. Although the Soviet Union yielded to this development with hesitation and often painfully, the regularization of relations and their simultaneous intensification were both necessities dictated by this concession and responses to the new situation. Most of the organizational aspects of the promotion of unity treated in the preceding pages became important only in the last few years.

This greater emphasis on the organizational aspects of the camp has certain implications for its general character. For one thing, since its unity now involves much more conscious effort on the part of the various ruling elites than was the case earlier, one can note something which could not have occurred in Stalin's day—namely, the appearance, albeit still very timid, of constellations or "in-groups" within the camp. On a number of important issues, it would appear that the East German and Czechoslovak leaderships share similar approaches, and quite often they seem to enjoy Bulgarian support. (This corresponds to some of the factual evidence noted in part II of this study.) Furthermore, on occasions they have displayed more sympathy for some of the Chinese attitudes, both on ideology and on foreign policy. For the time being, the Poles, the Rumanians, and the Hungarians have been closer to the Soviets with respect to international affairs, even though the Czechs and the East Germans are relied upon by Moscow to promote the internal line of bloc unity.[56]

Finally, the regularization and intensification of relations within the camp, and the abandonment of the relatively informal Stalinist pattern, have revealed a striking differentiation in the formal institutional structure of the camp insofar as the Asian group of Communist states is involved. They are not in the formal alliance system nor in CEMA, and their contacts with the other parties appear to be less intense. Furthermore, since much of the Soviet hope for the future political and ideological unity of the camp is based on the present drive for closer economic interdependence, an autarkic Chinese development means that in the years to come Chinese unity with the rest of the camp will rest almost entirely on the ideological-political plane. While this is not tantamount to disunity, it does reflect a somewhat less homogeneous reality than the Communist leaders would have the world believe.

This leads to two further points. The history of the camp can now be evenly divided into the Stalinist and the post-Stalinist periods, each lasting about seven years. From a historical standpoint, these are very short phases indeed. What is striking, however, is the difference between them. In the first place, the camp no longer seems as monolithic and as invulnerable to change as during Stalin's lifetime. Because of that, the alternative to it seems less likely to be violent upheavals. Today, in some ways the camp is better equipped to absorb the strains which occur in any multinational organization, and particularly in one dominated by a single national group. By suppressing such tensions through terror, accompanied also by economic exploitation, Stalin created the preconditions for a revolutionary situation. This no longer appears to be the case. On the other hand, because of the greater elasticity which now absorbs the strains and prevents an explosion erupting from stored-up frustration, the danger of a gradual erosion of the camp's ideological unity seems greater than ever before. Even the small measure of diversity which now exists, even the formal steps taken to regularize and improve relations, can gradually become impediments to the maintenance of the Leninist-Stalinist type of internal organizational discipline, so necessary to the unity of a camp founded on a doctrinaire ideology. This is particularly the case since the camp is still undergoing evolutionary change requiring a continuous adjustment of the ideology to varying and often conflicting national circumstances. Furthermore, to the degree that the Soviet leadership finds it necessary to mobilize the support of other Communist regimes in opposition to some Chinese stands,[57] the relationship of political power between Moscow and the other capitals becomes increasingly less asymmetrical.

Secondly, it seems fair to note that the camp in its first phase was in effect a national empire, centrally directed and run largely to the advantage of the dominant Soviet party. In some ways, if one for a minute overlooks the ideological elements, it was much like the Roman or French or English empire in their earlier days. Precisely because of that, it did not require elaborate machinery. The present development within the camp is increasingly transforming it into an international Communist empire, dominated by various Communist elites, bound together, to be sure, by Soviet power but also by common interests and aspirations. While united in their efforts and in their vested interest in keeping their ideologically oriented empire together and their populations suppressed, they increasingly find it necessary to express their unity through various organizational devices. The need for such organizational devices is felt to be particularly great because in the current Communist thinking "socialist" and subsequently even Communist countries will continue to exist as separate entities until a world-wide Communist society emerges.[58] During this transitional, but probably lengthy period, unity between the ruling parties is to be cemented through continuing efforts to develop ever closer political and economic ties among the countries ruled by them. To the extent that such ties do establish normative principles (if only in theory), particularly the principle of equality and independence, they will gradually consolidate the transition from a national to an international empire. By preserving state forms but emptying them gradually of their content, the ultimate hope is to surmount the traditional forces of nationalism and to create in effect an interlocking supra-society. While many obstacles still remain and others may arise, particularly with the further development of China, the West would do well not to underestimate the importance of the organizational development of the Communist camp.

## NOTES

1. The article takes it for granted that the bloc depends on Soviet power for its unity, that Soviet primacy and military dominance are essential to its survival, and that a common ideology helps to maintain a sense of mutual purpose. It also takes for granted the fact that strains exist within the camp and that forces are at work which challenge its unity. With all these as given, the study seeks to describe and discuss the structure of the camp's unity, which is essential if common purposes and policies are to be positively articulated and executed.

2. *Izvestia,* January 29, 1956.

3. *Izvestia,* May 27, 1958.

4. This does not, however, exclude a certain division of labor in dealing with the outside world: e.g., the Polish initiative in the form of the Rapacki Plan; the East German scheme for a Baltic Peace Zone; the Rumanian-Bulgarian plan for a Balkan treaty, etc.

5. China since 1956; North Korea since 1957; North Vietnam and Mongolia since 1958. See the excellent treatment, "The Role of the Comecon," *East Europe* (New York), VIII, No. 11 (November, 1959), pp. 3–11, which describes more fully the operations and organization of CEMA.

6. See Imre Nagy, *On Communism,* New York, 1957, p. 189, for a concise statement of the essentially negative role of CEMA.

7. For a description of the CEMA organization and a discussion of its operation, see *East Europe,* VI, No. 11 (November, 1957), and IX, No. 4 (April, 1960). See also *Voprosy vneshnei politiki stran sotsialisticheskogo lageriia,* Moscow, 1958, pp. 21–23 (hereafter cited as *Voprosy vneshnei politiki).* The December, 1959, CEMA meeting took the important formal step of adopting a Charter and a Convention on Competence, Privileges, and Immunities, which was said to contain "provisions that are generally accepted in international practice." For fuller treatment, see *Vneshanaia torgovlia* (Moscow), No. 2 (February, 1960).

8. Although ostensibly an international organization open to other nations, CEMA operations are shrouded in secrecy. On a recent trip to the bloc, this writer was denied permission to visit its Moscow offices, while Sofia officials even denied the existence of a CEMA commission in Sofia. For a list of these commissions, see *East Europe,* IX, No. 4 (April, 1960), p. 4. For a somewhat more recent treatment, see *Tygodnik Powszechny* (Krakow), February 28, 1960. For an interesting account of the operations of one such commission, see I. Pramov, "For Some Results of Co-operation in the Field of Rural Economy between the Countries Participating in the Council of Economic Mutual Assistance," *Mezhdunarodnyi Sel'skokhoziaistvennyi Zhurnal* (Sofia), No. 4 (1958).

9. This is openly admitted by Communist commentators—e.g., V. Kaigl, "Co-operation with the Countries of the Socialist Camp Is One of the Main Conditions for the Completion of Socialist Building of the CSR," *Nova Mysl* (Prague), June, 1958, who says: "Apart from political and ideological aspects, economic shortcomings helped to a considerable degree in the upsurge of bourgeois nationalism and revisionism in the fall of 1956. Following these experiences, the Communist and worker's parties in the member states of the Council drew the only right conclusion, namely, to strengthen the unity of the socialist camp *through increased economic unity,* and through a higher standard of its planning. The Council of Mutual Economic Assistance decided at its eighth planning session in June, 1957, to work out co-ordinated, long-term plans for the development of national economies of the member states covering the period until 1975. The foundation of this co-ordination is to be the mutually heightened approved specialization of the individual countries which would make them into a *truly homogeneous, economic unit"* (italics added).

10. See my study, *The Soviet Bloc: Unity and Conflict,* Cambridge, Mass., 1960, chap. 12.

11. E.g., a multilateral payment scheme was set up in 1959, plans were developed for statistical analyses of national incomes, the problem of pricing was tackled, etc. For more detailed treatment, see A. Zauberman, "Economic Integration: Problems and Prospects," *Problems of Communism* (July-August 1959); H. Mendershausen, "Terms of Trade between the Soviet Union and Smaller Communist Countries, 1955–1957," *Review of Economics and Statistics,* XLI, No. 2 (May, 1959), pp. 106–18; O. Hoeffding, *Recent Efforts toward Coordinated Economic Planning in the Soviet Bloc,* The RAND Corporation, 1959; and S. J. Zyzniewski, "Economic Perspectives in Eastern Europe," *Political Science Quarterly,* LXXVI, No. 2 (June, 1960), pp. 201–28. That the problem of pricing has been a source of major difficulty in interbloc planning has been openly admitted by Communist economists. See, for instance, M. Cizkovsky, "A New Stage in the Cooperation between the Countries of the Socialist Camp," *Rude Pravo* (Prague), March 5, 1959; or V. Ciernansky, "Prices in Trading with Foreign Countries," *Predvoj* (Prague), June 11, 1959; or *Voprosy ekonomiki,* No. 2 (1960), for a discussion of the prevailing pricing system within the bloc. The most recent CEMA venture is a huge oil pipeline, linking the oilfields of the middle Volga basin to Poland, East Germany, Czechoslovakia, and Hungary. Construction

began in the summer of 1960 and is to be finished in 1963.

12. *Pravda,* March 27, 1959. Presumably a further step in ·that direction would involve the co-ordination of investment policies of the member states. See Gomulka's criticisms of CEMA's failure to do so in *Trybuna Ludu* (Warsaw), June 21, 1960.

13. *Izvestia,* August 19, 1948. For a recent discussion, see David T. Cattell, "The Politics of the Danube Commission under Soviet Control," *American Slavic and East European Review,* XIX, No. 3 (October, 1960), pp. 380–95.

14. *Svet Sovietu* (Prague), No. 24 (1959).

15. *Pravda,* January 8, 1955.

16. The agreements are listed in R. Slusser and J. Triska, *A Calendar of Soviet Treaties, 1917–1957,* Stanford, 1959, pp. 326–27. For fuller treatment, see George Modelski, *Atomic Energy in the Communist Bloc,* New York, 1959.

17. V. Svanev, "Science and Technology in the Multi-National Family of Scientists," *Pravda* (Bratislava), January 10, 1959.

18. For a fuller discussion, see P. S. Wandycz, "The Soviet System of Alliances in East Central Europe," *Journal of Central European Affairs,* XVI, No. 2 (July 1956), pp. 177-84; E. Korovin, *Nerushimaia druzhba narodov SSSR i narodno-demokraticheskikh stran,* Moscow, 1955; *Voprosy vneshnei politiki, op. cit.;* and Brzezinski, *The Soviet Bloc, op. cit.,* for listings with dates.

19. Czechoslovakia also concluded such a treaty with Outer Mongolia on April 9, 1957. I am indebted to Dr. Tao-tai Hsia of the Library of Congress for the information about China. Chinese sources include *Chung hua jen min kung ho kuo t'iao yueh chi* (Ministry of Foreign Affairs, Peking), Vols. I-VIII, 1949-1959; *Jen min shou ts'e* (Peking), 1955-1959.

20. See *Pravda,* November 19, 1956; *ibid.,* December 18, 1956.

21. *Izvestia,* March 14, 1957.

22. *Ibid.,* May 28, 1957.

23. *Ibid.,* April 17, 1957.

24. For extended treatment, see Brzezinski, *The Soviet Bloc, op. cit.*

25. See *Pravda,* October 31, 1956.

26. See Mendershausen, *op. cit.;* Hoeffding, *op. cit.;* Zauberman, *op. cit.;* J. Wszelaki, *Communist Economic Strategy: The Role of East Central Europe,* Washington, D.C., 1959. For some figures concerning Soviet credit in the crisis period of 1956–1957, see M. Choluj, "Soviet Credit Aid to Socialist Countries," *Predvoj* (Prague), November 7, 1957, in which the figure of 5,776 million rubles is cited as being granted to Eastern Europe by the Soviet Union between December, 1955, and February, 1957, 58 per cent of which went to Poland, Hungary, and Yugoslavia. *Vneshnaia torgovlia* has also provided some data.

27. See G. Radulescu, "Ten Years of Comecon Activity," *Rominia Libera,* April 29, 1959, for a partial list of long-term Rumanian agreements; *Izvestia,* November 20, 1955, for aspects of Soviet-Mongolian agreements of 1950–1954 and 1955–1957. See also Slusser and Triska, *op. cit.,* for list of Soviet trade agreements; and J. Dolina, "Poland's Foreign Trade Agreements," *Polish Review* (New York), Autumn, 1956, and Winter–Spring, 1958, for the most complete listing, including brief statements of major provisions.

28. E.g., the Czech-Polish agreement for 1961–1965, signed May 17, 1958; see *Rude Pravo,* May 15, 1958. For Soviet-Czech agreements, see *Pravda,* January 15, 1957, and October 16, 1958; and *Izvestia,* March 7, 1959.

29. A good example of this dependence was provided by the panic caused in these capitals by the recent and unconfirmed report to the effect that the Soviet Union would severely cut down its delivery of raw materials to Poland, East Germany, and Czechoslovakia in 1965 (see *New York Times,* April 4, 1960, for a report from Warsaw that at the February, 1960, CEMA meeting, the Soviet Union indicated that it no longer wished to deliver unprocessed raw materials).

30. For statistics, see N. I. Ivanov, *Razvitie ekonomicheskikh sviazei evropeiskikh stran narodnoi demokratii,* Moscow, 1959 (hereafter cited as *Razvitie*).

31. For instance, when the vice-president of the Rumanian Institute for Cultural Relations with Foreign Countries contributed a commemorative article to a Polish newspaper on the occasion of the tenth anniversary of Rumanian-Polish cultural relations, everything he cited dated back to the pre-1939 period (O. Livezeau, "Ten Years of Co-operation," *Zycie Warszawy,* February 28, 1958; see also Imre Nagy, *op. cit.,* p. 240).

32. Mongolia, agreement of February 27, 1946.

33. At the same time the Soviet Union hastened to return to some of the European Communist-ruled states a portion of the art treasures which it had seized in the course of various hostilities. For instance, on June 12, 1956, *Pravda* announced that the Soviet government was returning to Rumania art treasures held in the USSR since World War I; on July 8, 1956, *Izvestia* announced the return of Polish art treasures, seized by the USSR during World War II. Insofar as cultural co-operation agreements are concerned, they were signed in the following sequence: with Rumania—April 7, 1956; East Germany—April 26; Bulgaria—April 28; Albania—May 3; Hungary—June 28; Poland—June 30; China—July 5; North Korea—September 5; Czechoslovakia—January 12, 1957; North Vietnam—February 15, 1957; also a renewal of the ten-year agreement with Mongolia on April 24, 1956.

34. See Kurt L. London, "The 'Socialist Commonwealth of Nations,'" *Orbis,* III, No. 4 (Winter, 1960), pp. 424–42, for a detailed analytical treatment of the origins of the new term and of its broader implications.

35. A recent Soviet volume devoted to the foreign policy of the bloc (*Voprosy vneshnei politiki, op. cit.*) states: "A form of developing and tightening the unity of the socialist nations, in addition to concluding bilateral and multilateral agreements, are the meetings and the consultations between the leaders of the socialist countries" (p. 9).

36. In the period November, 1957–March, 1960, there appear to have been no less than ten multilateral meetings attended either by the first secretaries and/or Politburo members of the ruling parties, not counting the two more restricted top-level multilateral meetings in January, 1957 (the five-party meeting in Budapest, and the Soviet-Chinese-Hungarian meeting in Moscow).

37. A full text of the vigorous statement by a Chinese observer, significantly ignored by the Soviet and East European press, is contained in *East Europe,* IX, No. 3 (March, 1960).

38. This communication takes the form either of

reiteration of certain key and meaningful formulas or of ostentatious omission of certain key concepts. Thus, for instance, the repetition of the formula "proletarian internationalism" as the basic principle guiding relations between the Communist states was directed against the Poles' emphasis on the need to respect their own road to socialism; similarly, the insistence on hailing Soviet leadership was meant to combat the concept of full equality of Communist states. Repeated attacks on revisionism (and silence on dogmatism) were directed against those parties and party members who were pressing for anti-Stalinist reforms. Similarly, attacks on dogmatism were often aimed at the USSR and, in 1959-1960, at China. The recent Chinese emphasis on the innately aggressive character of imperialism, as shown by Lenin, is a form of subtle pressure against those Communist leaders who are willing to concede that war is not inevitable even while capitalism still exists. Finally, exaggerated praise for the policies of one party can be a form of pressure against another; e.g., praise of China can be directed at the USSR, or praise of Bulgaria for rapidly collectivizing can be aimed at Poland, etc.

39. *Neues Deutschland* (East Berlin), November 30, 1957.

40. "In the process of the rise of the new systems and the deep revolutionary changes in social relations, there have been many difficulties, unresolved problems, and downright mistakes in the mutual relations among the socialist countries—violations and errors which demeaned the principle of equality in the relations among the socialist states" (from the October 30, 1956, declaration by the government of the USSR).

41. See Slusser and Triska, *op. cit.*

42. On the basis of recent listings, nine out of eleven Soviet ambassadors to Communist-ruled states appear to have been former senior party functionaries. During Stalin's lifetime, they appeared to come primarily from among the technical-police groups that staffed Molotov's Foreign Ministry.

43. E.g., in 1957, the USSR sent out 1,116 such delegations; in the first half of 1958, 587. In the same periods, Czechoslovakia sent out 503 and 250; Poland 472 and 263, etc. More than half of these, however, were technical and sports groups. See Ivanov, *Razvitie, op. cit.*, pp. 112-13, for data on exchanges of specialists.

44. For instance, the head of the Polish parliamentary delegation to Rumania emphasized in his account of the meetings with Rumanian parliamentarians the fact that the Rumanians expressed great interest in the ratio of governmental decrees to legislative acts in post-1956 Poland. When he told them that for seventy-six parliamentary acts passed in Poland in 1958, there was only one governmental decree, the Rumanians admitted that in their case the ratio was almost reversed, but said they were also struggling for a change (*Zycie Warszawy*, October 16, 1958).

45. *Lidova Demokracie* (Prague), January 7, 1959; *Rude Pravo* (Prague), February 10, 1959; for the most complete treatment, *East Europe*, VIII, No. 7 (July 1959).

46. For Sino-Soviet student exchanges, see M. S. Kapitsa, *Sovetsko-Kitaiskie otnosheniia*, Moscow, 1958, p. 379. However, the Soviet Union is not actively engaged in sending its students abroad; in 1958 there were, for instance, 1,040 Czechoslovak students in the USSR and only 124 Soviet students in the CSR (*Svo-*

*bodne Slovo*, Prague, July 19, 1958). Similarly, in Poland the largest number of foreign students from within the bloc came from the Asian countries (*Zycie Warszawy*, October 8, 1958).

47. For instance, see J. Kowalski, "At the International Conference of Historians of the Communist Movement," *Nowe Drogi* (Warsaw), January, 1958, for an account of the three conferences held for party historians of the bloc.

48. G. A. Mozhaev, *Mezhdunarodnye Kulturnye Sviazi SSSR*, Moscow, 1959.

49. This theme is often repeated by Khrushchev. See also E. Varga, "The Capitalism of the 20th Century," *Kommunist*, No. 17 (November, 1959), and particularly his prognosis for the next ten to fifteen years. Probably the most elaborate and sophisticated development of the expected international and political consequences of the growth of a "socialist world market" is contained in T. Lychowski, *Stosunki Ekonomiczne Miedzy Krajami o Roznych Ustrojach*, Warsaw, 1957, pp. 590-605, where he argues that the existence of such a market will profoundly alter the present pattern of relations between the industrialized Western nations and the developing nations.

50. *Istoriia Kommunisticheskoi Partii Sovetskogo Soiuza*, Moscow, 1959, especially pp. 672–74.

51. To this writer, Kuusinen's volume is the most important Soviet attempt to define Communist ideology since Stalin's statement in 1952. Clearly meant to be a guide to international communism on all political-ideological aspects, including such matters as patterns of the socialist revolution, the issue of war, and the nature of a Communist society, the volume is particularly striking in its de-emphasis of the Chinese experience. While primarily relying on Marx-Engels-Lenin for doctrinal citations, it cites Mao Tse-tung only twice in the course of 750 pages; Khrushchev, by way of contrast, is cited sixteen times, but Stalin also only twice.

52. E.g., N. I. Ivanov, *Razvitie Ekonomiki Stran Narodnoi Demokratii*, Moscow, 1958; A. K. Kozik, ed., *Ekonomicheskoie sotrudnichestvo i vzaimopomoshch mezhdu Sovetskim Soiuzom I Evropeiskimi Stranami Narodnoi Demokratii*, Moscow, 1958; Ivanov, *Razvitie, op. cit.*; *Voprosy vneshnei politiki, op. cit.*; *Sodruzhestvo Stran Sotsializma*, Moscow, 1958; O. Butenko, *Osnovnye cherty sovremennogo revizionizma*, Moscow, 1959; *Protiv sovremennogo revizionizma*, Moscow, 1959; D. D. Bytakov, ed., *Finansy Stran Narodnoi Demokratii*, Moscow, 1959. In addition to these general works, there is an increasing number of books dealing with specific problems of individual Communist states—e.g., V. Zhamin, *Sel'skoe khoziaistvo Kitaia*, Moscow, 1959; *Problemy novoi sistemy planirovaniia i finansirovaniia cheskoslovatskoi promyshlennosti*, Moscow, 1959; and many others. This reawakened interest in the "problematics" of bloc affairs harks back to the 1946–1949 period, during which time there were many active discussions and publications pertaining particularly to the question of the nature of "People's Democracy" and its relationship to Marxist-Leninist doctrine. Such centers as the Institute of World Economy and International Relations, or the Institute of International Relations, seem to be particularly interested.

53. E.g., Butenko, *op. cit.*, or *Protiv sovremennogo revizionizma, op. cit.*

54. Its lead article was contributed by M. B. Mitin, member of the Academy of Sciences and of the Central

Committee of the CPSU, in the past a Soviet delegate to the Bulgarian and Hungarian Party congresses and, last but not least, in 1955 the editor of the Cominform journal, *For a Lasting Peace, For a People's Democracy*. A more recent example is the recently published volume, *Obshche zakonomernosti perekhoda k Sotsializmu i osobennosti ikh proiavleniia v raznykh stranakh*, Moscow, 1960.

55. Literature of this broader sort has also been making its appearance in the satellite states, although perhaps even more timidly. One may cite, for example, *Mezinarodni delba prace v socialisticke svetove soustave*, Prague, 1958; G. Tsonkov, *Obshchoto i spetsifichnoto v razvitieto na sotsialisticheskata revoliutsiia*, Sofia, 1959; or the more general work by T. Lychowski cited in note 49.

56. As one highly placed East European Communist said to the writer: "You have your mad dogs of capitalism [paraphrasing a Stalinist statement]—namely, Adenauer; we have our mad dogs of Communism—the East Germans and the Czechs."

57. For a recent treatment of Sino-Soviet differences, see D. Zagoria, "Strains in the Sino-Soviet Alliance," *Problems of Communism* (May–June, 1960). For the argument that the Sino-Soviet alliance involves a dynamic relationship of "divergent unity," see this writer's "The Pattern and Limits of the Sino-Soviet Dispute," *ibid.* (September–October, 1960). For a discussion of the problematics of ideological "relativization" and then "erosion," see Z. K. Brzezinski, "Communist Ideology and International Affairs," *Journal of Conflict Resolution*, IV, No. 3 (September, 1960), pp. 266–91.

58. The fullest and most recent Soviet ideological statement, the thick volume *Osnovy Marksizma-Leninizma*, Moscow, 1959, edited by O. V. Kuusinen, speaks of economic co-operation among Communist countries (not just "socialist") as preliminary to the eventual emergence of a single global "Commonwealth" (pp. 749–51). It is interesting to note that the new "socialist" constitution of Czechoslovakia (which is said to be no longer a People's Democracy) states in chapter I, article 1, that "The Czechoslovak Republic belongs to the world socialist system . . ." as a matter of constitutional law.

# *Autocracy*

# THE SYSTEM OF THE SINGLE-PARTY STATE

Ernest Barker

## 1. THE ORIGINS, THE DIFFERENT FORMS, AND THE COMMON CHARACTERISTICS OF THE SYSTEM OF THE SINGLE PARTY

The present conjuncture of tendencies has already produced, in a number of European countries, the new political phenomenon of the single party. The political party has been torn from its natural context in the system of democratic institutions in which it originated; it has ceased to be an organ which serves the sovereign purpose of democracy by preparing a "case" and vindicating it in discussion against other and similar (if also different) "cases"; and it has suffered a triple

Reprinted from Ernest Barker, *Reflections on Government* (Oxford: The Clarendon Press, 1942), pp. 284-311, by permission of the publishers.

change. It has been adjusted to the new cult of heroism; it has been turned into the mirror or focus of the new self-consciousness of national society; it has been made the planner or director of a newly nationalized system of economics. The new style of party (which is the negation of party in the old sense, because it claims to be total, and recognizes no other case than its own) belongs to the present century.[1] We may even go further and say that it has arisen, established itself, and flourished in the period since the war of 1914–18. In its immediate origins—though its ultimate roots go deeper—it is the reflection, or the perpetuation, of the nation at war. Just as the nation at war sends into the field a national army of some two or three millions of men, so, in the time of a troubled peace, some of the nations continued to deploy a national party of some two or three millions of adherents. In Italy and Germany ex-servicemen were active in the formation of such a party. In both countries the party, true to the core of its immediate origins, assumed a form of military uniform: in both the party ultimately became a new sort of militia, standing side by side with the regular army of the nation. The Russian Communist party, it is true, originally showed a different character; and it did so not only at the time of its triumphant emergence at the end of 1917, but also for a decade, or more, of its subsequent history. It began, not in a mood of war, but in a mood of reaction against war. Nor was it, in its origins, based on a cult or profession of nationalism. On the contrary it acknowledged, and even professed to foster and extend, the rights of national minorities within its borders; and outside its borders it even sought to become àn international party, not limiting its doctrines, or its adherents, to any national soil, but making the world its province and uniting, under its banner, all the workers of the world. The spirit of this original pacificism and this original internationalism is not dead; but the more Russian Communism has established itself as a particular and peculiar way of Russian national life, which appeals to the proper pride of all who share in that life, and the more it has felt itself confronted by opposition or threats to that peculiar way, the more has the Russian Communist party been drawn into the military and national trend of the analogous single parties in other countries. If it is not a uniformed party, and if it has no party militia, it is a uniform party which can now formally describe itself, in the new Russian Constitution of 1936, by the military style of a "vanguard"; and it is a party which needs no party militia only because the regular Red Army (not inherited from any previous régime, but newly constituted to defend the new régime) is itself indoctrinated and imbued with the principles of the party.

The system of the single party is a system which may take different forms. The Russian form is peculiar in more than one respect. In Russia the whole of the political system has been recast and remoulded by the party, and brought into conformity with its doctrines. The party is under no necessity of establishing any relations, or any form of concordat, with old and inherited military and political institutions; it has no need to claim formal rights in regard to other institutions, and it has no incentive to estabilsh "paramilitary" or "parapolitical" organizations by their side. In Russia, again, the whole of the social system has been similarly recast and remoulded by the party. The direction and planning of the economic structure is total: there is no grafting of new party ideas of corporativism or autarky on a previous stock: there is simply a totally new economic structure, built by the party, or at any rate built in accordance with the ideas of the party. In Italy and in Germany the eruption of the single party has been more complicated and less engulfing. The single party has supervened on an existing political constitution and an existing social system. It has sought to superimpose itself on the former, while retaining many of its institutions and methods: it has not, as yet, totally altered the latter.

But the analogies of form and character are perhaps greater than the differences. The single party, in each case, is allied with the ideas of the heroic age and the heroic leader. The whole of the party, in each case, professes a "vocation of leadership" in the nation, for which it finds the example and the inspiration in the single leader, who leads his "following" of leaders. The single party, again, professes to be, in each case, the focus and the power-house of the general pulsation of a whole self-conscious society. It centralizes in itself all voluntary social activities (among them the leisure activities of adults, and the activities of youth movements for the training of juvenile life); and these voluntary social activities, so centralized, are henceforth coloured by the character of the party, turned by its alchemy into something more than social, and made to assume a quality which is predominantly political. (It is in this sense that the new Russian Constitution of 1936 describes the Communist Party as "the nucleus of all organizations.") Finally, in each case, the single party becomes the planner and director of the national economic structure, either (as in Russia) in the light of its own original objectives, or (as in Italy) in the light of objectives which it proceeds to extemporize after its initial triumph. The objectives may range from communism to corporativism; they may range, again, according to the state and posture of foreign affairs, from ideas of a peace economy, intended to secure some form of internal solidarity, to ideas of a war economy intended to secure external security by State control of production in the interest of national defence. In any case there will be control and direction: in any case (with martial ideas of the heroic age, and missionary ideas of extending a doctrine, both generally prevalent) there will be a tendency towards the economy of war.

In spite of all these analogies of form and character, it is still possible, and indeed it is tempting, to think of "a conflict of ideologies" between the different varieties of the single-party State. Each of these single parties has its different single doctrine; and each of these doctrines (like the doctrines of the religious confessions in earlier days) tends to be pushed to the point of conflict with other doctrines. It is particularly tempting to think of a conflict between the doctrine of Communism and the doctrines (different in themselves, but united in opposition to that doctrine) of the other varieties of the single-party State. But it is also possible, and it is perhaps just, as well as possible, to think of the "harmony of ideologies" between all the different varieties. This harmony begins to appear as soon as we reflect on the relation of all the varieties of the single-party State to the form of State in which parties are still plural; where discussion between the different parties is still practised; and where parliaments still act as the meeting-ground of parties and the forum of discussion. Divided among themselves by their different doctrines, the single-party States are also divided, as a group, from the form of State which has no single party or doctrine—unless it be the doctrine that there is not, and should not be in matters political or in any other "matters of the mind," a compulsory single doctrine. Not that this deeper division is a division leading more surely to war. On the contrary war, if war should come, is as likely to be war between different single-doctrine States as between a single-doctrine State (or States) and a State (or States) professing no such doctrine.[2]

## 2. THE SPIRIT OF THE SINGLE PARTY: TOTALITARIANISM AND TRIALISM

The single party is already, in its nature, a supersession of parliament and the general system of parliamentary democracy. It does not, indeed, expressly abolish parliamentary institutions. It simply makes them otiose. In effect, it substitutes a new and vaster parliament—a parliament of millions, the whole body of its adherents—for the old parliament of a few hundreds. The substitution is so simple, and so thorough, that the old parliament may be left in existence as a harmless, if also useless, survival. It is even possible that, as in Russia, the single party may call into existence a new parliament, under the style of the Supreme Council, or again that, as in Italy, it may first add a new council of corporations to the old chamber of parliamentary deputies, and then recast the old chamber by making it a piebald body, partly recruited from the new council and partly from the party itself. The fact remains that the single party is itself the essential parliament. But it is a parliament of a new style. It may conduct some form of discussion within its own ranks, among its own members, under the terms and subject to the limits of its own doctrine. But it is not a true organ of national discussion, and still less is it an organ in a general system of national discussion which includes other organs as well as itself. Unlike an ordinary parliament, it does not conduct a public discussion, open to all the world, which serves as a vent for all trends of opinion and a winnowing fan to separate the chaff from the wheat in each trend. The single party, by its nature, must present an apparent front of unity; and the discussions within its ranks, when they touch the raw nerve of real difference, will be conducted in secret and fought out in the dark. This constitutes a deep and genuine difference between the State of a single party and the State of a plurality of parties. The one may seem divided, and even distracted: the other seems to be one and undivided. But the division of the one is the public and open division which leaves a central core of unity: the unity of the other is a screen which hides both the secret differences of the single party and the suppressed opinions of the dissidents.

Unlike an ordinary parliament, again, the parliament constituted by the adherents of a single party has no other organ of discussion by its side. If the old parliament is otiose when the new style of parliament appears and grasps the reins, the same is true of the electorate, which ceases to be an organ of discussion and becomes an instrument of registration; and it may even be said to be true of the cabinet, now no longer actively engaged in a joint formation of policy and its joint defence against the opposition, but swayed by the party leader and merged in the general party. A new system of politics emerges under these conditions. It may be called a system of unitarianism, because it depends on a single party which is not confronted by other parties in parliament or the nation, nor limited by the effective action of a real electorate or a genuine cabinet. It may also be called, and for the same reason, a system of totalitarianism. Any single authority is by its nature total. Having no other authority at its side, with which it must divide the exercise of power, it will equally leave no possible object (or subject) of power untouched: having no partners in power, it will leave no loopholes and no exemptions from power. It is for this reason that the system of single-party government is led to engulf—to absorb, or at any rate regulate—churches, trade unions, institutions of education, charitable organizations, and every form and phase of the activity of the community's life.

But while this new system of politics may be called a system of unitarianism, or a system of totalitarianism, it may also be called—from another point of view—a system of trialism. If we hold that the party stands at the centre of the common life, reaching out on the one hand into the State (which is the political structure of the army, the civil administration, and the general government), and reaching out on the other into the People or *Volk* (which is the social-economic structure of professions, occupations, and general social groups), then we may say that there are three things in the new system; but, having said that, we are bound at once to add that the three are one in the central party, which at once animates the State and inspires the People or *Volk*. This is the view which is expressed by Dr. Carl Schmitt in his pamphlet, published in 1933, on the theme of *Staat, Bewegung, Volk*.[3]

In his view the "liberal-democratic" State is essentially a system—or rather an anarchy—of unresolved dualisms. There is the dualism of "State and the Individual," which may also be called, when we take into account the social groups formed (or supposed to be formed) by numbers of individuals, a dualism of "State and Society." There is the dualism of legislature and executive expressed in the idea and practice of a division of powers. There is the dualism of law and politics, which pits a fixed body of static rules—and with it, and behind it, the judges—against the dynamic movement of political life and political exigencies. Particularly important is the dualism of the State and the individual, or, as it is also called, of State and society. In form—but only in form—it opposes the "rights" of the individual, or the "free play" of society, to the claims of the State. In reality it creates a gulf between the operation of a paralysed State and the dark activities of vigorous and powerful parties which use the cover of individual rights and social liberty to pursue their own sinister interests. Neither the State nor the individual can flourish under these conditions. The State is threatened, or even captured, by dark and irresponsible powers: the individual is coerced by the drill and discipline of the very forces which profess to be acting in his name. The result is a plurality of irresponsible tyrannies, usurping the prerogatives of the State and defeating the rights of the individual.[4]

To dualism of this order, reduced to such desperate straits, Dr. Schmitt opposes the saving grace of trialism. Under the system of trialism the anarchical multitude of irresponsible parties disappears. A single party, eliminating the rest, assumes an open control. It establishes itself in the centre: it becomes the bridge and the reconciler of State and People: a system of resolved trialism (one may almost say trinitarianism) takes the place of a system of unresolved dualism. The division between executive and legislature is ended by the unity of party spirit and the unity of common leadership: the gulf between law and politics is filled by the moving of the party and the doctrines of the party (the doctrine of a common leadership and loyalty, and the doctrine of the common inspiration of a common blood) into the gulf. The essence of the new unity is thus a new system of party: a party conceived as an "order" or an "elite," to distinguish it from the political parties of the old liberal State: a party which "carries" State and People, and which, while it recruits itself from all sections of the People, is in itself exclusive (or "shut") and hierarchically led.[5]

The party, so conceived and so organized, on the one hand "occupies the key positions in the official organization of the State," and, on the other, "penetrates, in a corresponding manner," the social-economic structure (with its professions and occupations) in which the People lives its daily life.[6] It constitutes the community typical of the twentieth century—not only in National Socialist Germany, but also (if in a different way) in Fascist Italy; and not only in Germany and Italy, but also in Soviet Russia, where "a trialistic system of State, party, and labour, has been attempted as the total expression of political and social reality."[7] The new or triple community thus constituted by the single party is not only the typical fact of our times: it also corresponds to the great traditions of political theory which were established by Hegel.[8] It is the synthesis which Hegel sought; and for all its trialism it is the perfect expression of unity. "Distinct but not divided, connected but not coagulated, the three great fly-wheels must run side by side, each according to its own internal law, but all in the unison of the political whole which is carried by the movement of the party."[9]

Unity is thus the transcendent note behind the system of trialism. The unity of the community, expressed in and vindicated by the single party which carries the community in both of its manifestations (as a State and as a People), is the essential thing. This unity is prior to law. Before law can exist as an actual body of substantive rules (and not merely as a formal idea), the prior condition is a full assurance of political unity. Only on the basis of uncontested political decisions (proceeding from the single and uncontested party) can the actual development of substantive law begin to proceed.[10] But law is not only affected by being made secondary to the cause of political unity; secondary, therefore, to the single party which expresses and vindicates that cause; secondary, in the last resort, to the single leadership which inspires and controls that party. It is also affected in another way. It loses any specific legislative organ of creation: it loses any independent judicial organ of interpretation. The principle of leadership, which is the essential expression of the cause of unity, abolishes any separation of executive and legislative powers, and vests the executive power with the initiative of all legislation.[11] In Germany, as in Italy and in Russia, the same trialistic type of State involves the same consequence of the repudiation of division of powers. The very judicature must be trained and tuned to unity; and the man entrusted with the interpretation of the law of his community must be steeped in its particular spirit and penetrated by its particular doctrine.[12] Law is always the law of a particular community; and its only true interpreter is he who is rooted and grounded in the reality of belonging to his people and his race.[13] "Every political unity needs a consistent internal logic of its institutions and rules. It needs a unitary idea of form, which shapes every part of the public life without exception or intermission. In this sense there is no normal State which is not total."[14]

## 3. PARTY IN SINGLE-PARTY STATES AND PARTY IN STATES OF THE PARLIAMENTARY TYPE

The system of the single-party State, in the form in which it is described and defended by Dr. Schmitt, is a system common to a number of countries. Russia, Italy, and Germany are all agreed in acting through a single party, which in turn acts upon both State and society, and holds them together in a common allegiance to its principles and its control. But there are obvious differences between these countries, as well as a formal agreement. Their agreement is largely negative. They all reject the ideas and the institutions of parliamentary democracy—the idea of discussion, which presupposes the idea of toleration: the institutions (dependent on these ideas) of a party system which embraces more than a single party, of an electorate which chooses between and among several parties, of a parliament which is composed of a number of parties, and of a government or cabinet which is successively constituted by different parties according to the electoral verdict and the parliamentary majority. They reject, again, the system of developed differentiation on which the ideas and institutions of parliamentary democracy are based. As they go back to an earlier heroic age, so they also go back to an earlier age of undifferentiated homogeneity, prior to the present stage of political evolution. They seek to obliterate or to transcend the distinction between State and society, seeking to fuse the two in the common life and the common inspiration of the single party. This is a return to the old Greek city-State, in which State and community were still one and undivided: it is a return, from another point of view, to the thought of the sixteenth century, in which it was assumed, by a similar identification, that the people of a single "region" must be a single Church as well as a single State. And just as the distinction between State and society, which is one of the conquests of modern civilization, is thus obliterated or transcended, so the distinctions within the State, which have been gradually achieved in the process of human development, are similarly removed. The legislative and the executive power are blended in a practice, open or implicit, of total leadership: the law of the constitution, like the rest of law, is merged in the merger of the two powers;[15] and even the judge is drawn, like the legislature, in the train of the party and its chief.

In negation, then, the single-party States present a common front to the States which follow the practice of parliamentary democracy. It is when they begin to affirm that they also begin to diverge. We may consider their affirmations from two different points of view. Some of them turn on matters of method—on the formal position of the party in the State and the social system, or on the formal position of the leader in the party. Others (and they are obviously the more important) turn on matters of end or aim—on the social elements dominant in the different single-party States, and the social and political objectives which the different single parties accordingly use their position of dominance to achieve.

But before we turn to the divergent affirmations of the single-party States, we may pause to consider the general problem of the relation between States of this type and States of the parliamentary type. It may be asked whether the part which is played by party in the two types of States is, after all, fundamentally different. In States of the parliamentary type party may be regarded as a conduit between society and the State. The party system gathers, at one end, the different currents of social opinion into the definite and recognized channels of party; and it then releases them, at the other end, to turn the wheels of the State, partly by providing and inspiring the party government which moves the wheels, and partly by providing and inspiring a party opposition which balances the government. In this sense States of the parliamentary type may also be called trialistic. They do not, after all, institute a dualism of State and society; they provide a channel or conduit between them; which enables the one to act on the other and, more particularly, enables society to act on the State. States of the single-party type are only doing what States of the parliamentary type have already done before; but they are doing it to a far less extent and with a difference of degree which constitutes, after all, a difference of kind. They begin by blocking up all the channels between State and society except one. The single channel thus left, just because it is single, becomes something more than a channel. It becomes the fountain-head—the original and the only moving power. Instead of responding to social movement and receiving social impulses, it works back on society as a controlling force, which determines what society shall be and what it shall say and do. Instead of carrying social impulses into the State, it carries only itself—or, so far as it carries any social impulse, it carries only the impulse which it has itself determined. It thus stands between State and society not as a mediator, but as a controller. The one channel holds the original and only waters of life, which flow down on either hand into State and society. Society becomes a stagnant uniformity, receiving waters which cannot drain away, and with no original inward springs in itself.[16] The State becomes a single revolving wheel, without compensation or balance—a great mill-wheel, turning in isolation, into which one water incessantly pours from a single "lead."

There is thus, when all is said, a difference of

kind between the single-party State and the State of the parliamentary type. The fact that there is party in both, and that, in both, party stands related to the State on one side and society on the other, does not obliterate the other and more important fact that party is a very different thing in the one from what it is in the other, and that it stands related to State and society in a very different way. In the one type of State the distinction between society and State remains (though they are kept in connection and interaction): in the other the distinction between them is blurred or confused by the party, which dominates and controls them both alike. In the one type there is a distinction within the State, not only in the form of division between different powers of government, but also in the form of compensation and balance between the government party and the opposition party: in the other this distinction, in both of its forms, is gone. In the one type toleration, discussion and compromise are involved by the fact of a varied society with many currents of opinion, all flowing freely through the various channels provided by different parties, and all acting within and upon the State into which they flow; in the other a compulsorily uniform society, flowing perforce in a single channel, issues in a State which is equally uniform.

## 4. DIFFERENCES BETWEEN SINGLE-PARTY STATES IN MATTERS OF METHOD: THE RELATION OF PARTY AND STATE AND THE FACTOR OF LEADERSHIP

But there are also differences among the States of the single-party type—differences both of method and of aim. The differences of method are less deep and less characteristic; but they have their importance. There are differences, first of all, in regard to the relation of the single party to the social system. In Russia the single party has entirely recast society, introducing an organization (exactly parallel with its own organization) of trade unions in the sphere of production, and co-operative societies in the sphere of consumption, which constitutes a society multiform in appearance if uniform in spirit.[17] In Italy the single party has stamped on Italian society—but stamped less deeply and pervasively—a form of corporativism which leaves it still largely what it was. In Germany the single party has been content, in the main, with introducing its principle of "leader" and "following" into the social order, turning the employer into the adventurous leader and the employed into faithful followers. But the difference between the attitudes of the different single parties to the social system is really more than a difference of method:

it involves a difference of aim; and it can only be properly considered in connection with aims.

More purely a matter of method is the difference between the attitudes of the different single parties to the State. In Russia the Communist party, though it is mentioned in one of the sections of the constitution of 1936 as the vanguard of the toilers and the leading nucleus of all their organizations, stands generally in the background. It is not included in the constitution of the State as one of its formal elements: it has no formal rights: whatever it does, it does *de facto,* in virtue of the influence which it exercises, or through the presence of its individual members on the governing bodies of the State, but not in virtue of any *de jure* power with which it is legally vested. In Italy the position is different. The party is formally recognized by law, and vested with formal powers by law. Its Grand Council, from 1928 to 1938, had the legal right of presenting the whole list of parliamentary candidates for approbation to the whole of the national electorate; and since 1938 its National Council (a different body) has been legally included as part of the new Chamber of Fasci and Corporations. More important, the Grand Council has also the legal right of offering advice on all questions of a constitutional character.[18] In Germany the National Socialist party is perhaps more formally connected with the State than the Russian Communist party, but it is certainly less formally connected with it than the Italian Fascist party. It is secured a legal monopoly by a law of July, 1933, prohibiting the formation of other parties: under a law of December, 1933, for securing the unity of the party and the State, it is vested with the position of a corporate public-law body (analogous, for example, to our English municipal corporations); and by the same law the deputy of the party leader, and the chief of staff of the party militia, are made *ex officio* members of the Government. On the whole, however, the National Socialist party in Germany, like the Communist party in Russia, acts *de facto* rather than *de jure*: it is a permeating influence in the State rather than a formal organ of the State. Originally, perhaps, it was less powerful than the Russian single party, in that it had to reckon with an old and surviving army tradition and with the old and surviving tradition of the German civil service; but even before 1939 the Army had been brought into line with the party, and a Civil Service Act of 1937 had already given the party a large measure of control over the recruitment of the civil service.[19]

Another difference of method between the different States of the single-party type turns on the position of the party leader, and on the importance assigned to the factor of leadership in the constitution of the party and thereby in the constitution of the State. In Germany the factor of leadership is so prominent that it may almost be called the core not only of the constitution of the party, but also of its doctrine. Racialism, or the doctrine of the necessary identity of the community in kind and "blood," is indeed another essential doctrine; but in some presentations of the party belief and practice it is evident that racialism is regarded as a consequence and corollary of leadership. In Dr. Schmitt's view, for example, the primary idea is that of "the immediate fact and real presence" of leadership; and it is on the basis of this idea that there ensues the further idea of racial unity, or identity of kind, uniting the body of followers both to one another and to their leader, and thus providing the leader with the homogeneous and loyal following which he essentially requires.[20] But whether or no we assign a position of logical priority to the idea of leadership, it is evident that the fact of leadership is the primary fact in the National Socialist party and the National Socialist State. "Leader" is the essential title of the head of the State: leadership runs through the constitution of the party, the constitution of the State, and the constitution of economic society.

The factor of leadership is less overtly present in Fascist Italy. It is there: it appears on the very walls, where the word "Duce" is ubiquitous; the leader of the party is the "head of the government," and the head of the government dominates every power and every sphere of the action of the State. But leadership here is more of a fact than a doctrine; and while party is more formally inscribed in the Italian State than it is in the German, the principle of leadership is less formally inscribed as the central and permeating principle of the whole community than it is in Germany. In the State there is still a King as well as a Duce; and in economic society the general principle is that of corporativism (in the sense of a conjunction of employers and employed in each branch or category of production) rather than that of leadership.

In Russia the principle of leadership is even less formally inscribed than in Italy. This is not to say that leadership is not actually present and active. The memory of autocracy is a long memory in Russia. But the modern autocrat of all the Russias goes by the simple title of secretary of the party;[21] and the institutions of the State present a plethora of other authorities. There is the elected Supreme Council; there is the Presidium which it elects in turn from its members; there is also the Council of People's Commissars, which the Supreme Council equally "forms by its choice." Among these authorities the Supreme Council is defined as "the supreme organ of State power"; but over and above the Supreme Council, which is only an "organ" or agent of power, there stand the soviets of the workers' deputies, to which the essence of power itself is formally and finally ascribed. In the Russian State there is thus a large apparatus of political

authorities, professing a democratic character or origin, which surrounds the hidden leader; and Russian society, in its trade unions and other unions of producers, and in its co-operative societies of consumers, presents (or professes to present) a similar apparatus of democratic social authorities. We may add that the Communist party itself, in its own internal constitution, is similarly constituted: it is built up from below by election, and presents (or professes to present) its own apparatus of democratic party authorities, parallel to the similar political and social authorities.

Form and fact often differ in the actual working of political and social systems. The problem of Russia is the problem of discovering the facts of political and social *direction* behind the forms of political and social *election*. There can be no doubt (it is frankly admitted, and indeed asserted, by its own members) that the direction, or "directives," of the party determine the action which is actually taken in the institutions of the State and the parallel institutions of society. But though the directives of the party determine the action of the political and social authorities, a doubt may still be raised whether the direction of the secretary determines the directives of the party, and whether a single central leadership is an essential factor of the nature and action of the party.[22] Remembering the deification of the dead Lenin, and the cult of his living successor, we may resolve the doubt in the affirmative. But the fact remains that the actuality of leadership, and even the actual cult of the actual leader for the time being, are something different from the vindication of the "leader principle" as the pivot of the general life of the community. They are pragmatic facts rather than moving and stirring theories.

## 5. AGREEMENTS AND DIFFERENCES BETWEEN SINGLE-PARTY STATES IN MATTERS OF SUBSTANCE: COMMON CULTIVATION OF YOUTH; COMMON RELEASE OF A NATIONAL TREND; VARIETIES OF SOCIAL BASIS

From differences of method we may turn to differences of substance—differences in the ends or aims pursued by the different single-party States. The ends or aims of a party determine the character and the class of the adherents whom it recruits; but it is also true, conversely, that the character and the class of the adherents whom it seeks to recruit affect the objects and the programme of a party. In any case our view of the ends and aims of the great single parties may be more concrete, and more living, if we start from the human material on which they draw, and which they seek to attract. A number of factors would appear to be operative in determining the recruitment of these parties. One is the factor of age, or the nature of the age-group and the character of the generation to which appeal is made. Another is the factor of class, or the nature of the social group and the character of the economic aspirations which parties seek to enlist. A third factor, which is concerned not with cross-sections of age or class, but with the long continuous line of national development, is the factor of the national trend and the dominant national longing. The party which can discover and release this trend is at once on the way to become the single party of the nation. An age-group or a social group may be particularly powerful; but it is always confronted by other age-groups or other social groups. A party which not only appeals to some age-group or some social group, but also discovers and releases a national trend or longing will soon find itself, or make itself, unhampered by rivalry.

In the matter of age and the generations the different new single parties are not divided. They all began in revolution; and the appeal of revolution is always an appeal to youth. Whether we regard the ardours of revolution, or whether we regard its material basis (the capture of power and position from the clinging hands of their old possessors), we come to the same result. The old possessors of power may be attacked on many counts: they may be denounced as unpatriotic or unprogressive, as Jewish or capitalistic, as selfish place-hunters or secret traitors; but it is always one of the counts, even if it is a hidden count, that they simply block the path of the new and rising generation. All the new single parties—and not least the National Socialist party—have cleared the way for youth.[23] One of their striking features, when once they have established their power, is the organized provision which they proceed to make for the enlisting of youth. In Italy the juvenile auxiliaries of the Fascist party ran four deep, from the Young Fascists and the Avanguardisti down to the Balilla and Pre-Balilla: in Russia (where the Communists themselves number at most three millions) there are five millions of young Comsomols, and six millions of younger Pioneers and still younger "Little Octobrists": in Germany the Hitler youth, if less graded and differentiated, is a similar ally of the National Socialist party.

No doubt the appeal to youth, in this form, is the natural policy of a single party, necessarily compelled to make provision for the perpetuation of itself in the unique position which it has achieved. The closed party, not open to every applicant, must train and test the young who, in their day, will be candidates for admission. Nor can the single party, by its very nature, leave the young untutored and undrilled, exposed to educational influences which might inbue them with alien ideas and a foreign tradition. If it is to perpetuate its régime, it must not only isolate its adult opponents in a sort of sanitary detention (as the medieval Church sought to isolate heretics): it must also indoctrinate the fluid mind of the adolescent with its own orthodoxy. Alike in the interests of its own recruitment and in the interest of the consolidation of the régime which it has established, it must bend youth to itself and its needs.

But in bending youth to itself, it is also bending itself to youth. Springing from an *élan* and revolt of youth, it devotes a large measure of its attention to youth. It seeks to satisfy their aspirations, their heroic longings, and their material desires for career and advancement. If the long competition of democracies—the slow selective influence of protracted debate, both within the parties and between the parties—often tends to leave leadership with older statesmen, the single-party State (at any rate apart from its leader) is more ready to renew its youth. It sheds its elder statesmen even before they have become elderly. Perhaps the interest of the leader leads him to prefer younger and newer colleagues less likely to rival his prestige. But apart from any such possible interest there is always a looking to youth and a tendency to bid for the support of the coming generation. In a state of multiple parties each party naturally seeks to attract the vote of the neutrals, and the neutrals are generally men and women of middle years, who have lost youthful ardours and allegiances. In the single-party State there are no neutrals; and the vote and support which are naturally sought are those of the one residuary factor—the young.[24]

The factor of age, however, hardly serves to differentiate the various forms of the single party and the single-party States. It may be more pronounced in one than another; but it distinguishes them all, if in different degrees, from States of the multi-party and parliamentary type. It gives them all an impetus towards rapid action; towards a new-planned future; toward the cult of a new heroic age and its new heroic virtues; towards the passionate asseverance of some doctrine, apprehended with the ardour and the insistency of youth. Far more important, when we come to the differences of the single parties, is the factor of social class —the nature of the social group which forms the nucleus of the party, and the character of the social aspirations which inspire its policy.

We need not be believers in the doctrine of class war, or in the philosophy of economic determinism which is associated with it, if we recognize the importance of this factor. But we have equally to recognize that it is only one factor among others, with which it is so curiously intertwined that we shall find it difficult or even impossible to disengage it for separate study. We can hardly measure it, therefore, in itself, or estimate its specific and particular influence. The factor of social class will be intertwined, for example, with what may be called the political (or perhaps better the national) factor—with a desire for some greater measure of internal unification, or for some greater share of external prestige and position; and though this desire may be particularly conscious of itself in a particular class, and be particularly expressed by a particular party connected with that class, it will also be generally present in the general feeling of all classes. Here class runs into the nation, and the nation runs back into class; and here, too, we touch that third factor—the factor, as it was previously termed, of the national trend and the dominant national longing —which, like the factor of social class with which it is intertwined, can never be treated in entire separation because it is never entirely separate. A national trend and longing obviously lies behind both the Fascist and the National Socialist movement; and if it is less obvious in the background of the Russian Communist movement, it may still be said that the Russian desire for leadership of a general crusade of all workers is only a new form of that old and general national desire which once made Russia the general champion of all the Orthodox Churches.

Another reflection, which goes even deeper, may also be added. Just as the factor of social class is intertwined with the political factor of the national trend, so it is also intertwined with the intellectual factor of international thought. In other words, the idea of class and the existence of class consciousness tend to be closely connected with the general movement of thought and ideas on that international plane on which thoughts and ideas naturally move. It is difficult, for example, to disengage the factor of general and international Marxist thought from the factor of social class in any consideration of Russia. It may be said, of course, that Marxism would never have been accepted in Russia if there had not been a proletarian class which turned to Marxism. But it may also be said, and that not in a paradox, that there would never have been a proletarian class in Russia—a class conscious of itself, and ready to form a party (and eventually a State) out of itself—unless Marxist thoughts had turned to Russia, diffused itself in Russia, and created a self-conscious proletariat in Russia by virtue of its diffusion.[25] If social class can issue in thought appropriate to itself, it is also true that thought can issue in social class, and may create the consciousness and active operation of class. In the tangled skein of human affairs there is no first origin of everything else; and as we pick at the knot we are driven to confess that it is tied of a number of strings.

## 6. THE SOCIAL INTERPRETATION OF THE SINGLE-PARTY SYSTEM, AND THE LIMITS OF SUCH INTERPRETATION

But the factor of social class, even if it is tangled with national and international factors, is none the less a factor of the first order of importance. There was a period—a period which lasted, at any rate in form, down to 1914—in which old dynastic States appeared to determine the destinies of Central and Eastern Europe, alike in Germany, in Russia, and in Austria-Hungary. The monarch, with his army and his staff of civilian officials, seemed to stand above the play of society; to reconcile and to harmonize its conflicting elements; to impose the order of his peace. This was the theory of Hegel; and facts could be held to warrant the theory. It is true that, from 1848 onwards, parliamentary institutions began to appear in the dynastic states; it is true again that, under the shelter of those institutions, parties also began to appear—some based on a social interest, some on a religious basis, and some on political ideas of national minorities and their proper rights. The dynastic States thus seemed to acquire two centres of gravity—the dynasty itself, with its army and its officials; and the parliament with its parties. But the dynastic centre (in the broad sense in which it included the army and the civilian officials as well as the monarch himself) remained the real centre, determining the nature of social cohesion, and manipulating parliament and parties to suit its purposes. The war then brought the dynastic States, as allies or as enemies, into contact with the democratic States of Western Europe. The dynastic States collapsed. It was the natural, but it was also the illogical, expectation of the victors that the dynastic States would be succeeded by parliamentary States in the image of themselves—States in which the conflicting elements of society would attain a voluntary adjustment by the parliamentary method of discussion and compromise. What the dynastic States had done from above, and as it were transcendentally, would now be done from below, by the immanent power of a national society homogeneous enough to reconcile for itself its conflicting elements, and sufficiently skilled to do so through the organs and by the methods of parliamentary government.

This was a large and, as we now know, an unwarranted expectation. What actually happened was something different. The linchpin had gone; and in its absence society, which it had held together in some sort of system, fell apart into its different elements. There was not sufficient homogeneity to attain any voluntary adjustment; and parliaments, which might have been the organs of such an adjustment if homogeneity had only been present, were set an impossible task. The vacuum created by the disappearance of the dynastic State was not and could not be filled by a parliamentary State: it remained a vacuum. The parties which had existed in the old dynastic States were not used to the practice of active co-operation in working a parliamentary system. Never enjoying real power or genuine responsibility, which always sobers and moderates, they had been used to hot conflicts with one another, varied by the manipulations and manoeuvres of a governing authority which stood above them all, but was ready to enlist and use now one and now another of them for its own purposes. When the governing authority was removed, they stood face to face, with one habit of co-operation among themselves, and with no higher authority now present to draw or force them into co-operation with itself. In these conditions national heterogeneity and an acute division of parties were the dominant facts; and either accentuated the other. A distracted society, which had lost its old centre, made parties still more divided: divided parties, destitute even of the unity once provided for them by the action of the old governing authority, made society still more heterogeneous. Social classes and social interests had a clear field; and the only way in which a system of social cohesion could be achieved was either a return to the old dynastic State, or a movement forward in the direction of a single party, sustained by a dominant class, which would end the clash by its victory. The third way—the way of the sovereignty of parliament, and of the co-operation of parties in working a parliamentary system—was blocked.

In Germany the vacuum (filled, but filled in vain, by the Weimar Constitution) lasted from the end of 1918 to the beginning of 1933. In Russia the vacuum was of brief duration: the collapse of the dynastic State was followed, after some few months of parliamentarianism, by the rapid triumph of a single party sustained by a single dominant class. In the old Austrian Empire the dynastic State not only collapsed, but also dissolved. In some parts into which it dissolved (such as Czechoslovakia) the sense of a new-found nationality—at any rate among the Czechs—was strong enough to keep the new State together, and to give it, until it was overpowered by external force, the homogeneity which could serve as the basis of parliamentary institutions and the parliamentary method of discussion. In others (such as Austria) parliamentary institutions were tried, but in the absence of social cohesion failed, and were replaced by a modified and moderate form of the system of a single party. Poland, constituted from fragments of all the three dynastic Empires, first tried, and then, un-

der Pilsudski, gradually shed, a parliamentary system; and in the event, on the eve and under the shadow of war, a virtual system of the single party had already begun to emerge.

Italy followed a line of development peculiar to herself. She had not been the home of a dynastic State: there had been no collapse: a system of parliamentary institutions had been working since the *Statuto* of 1848, and was still in active existence when the dynastic systems crashed. It had weathered the task of war: it had weathered, though more precariously, the task of making peace, but only on terms which failed to satisfy the national sense of sacrifice and the national desire for prestige. The general considerations which apply to the great States of Central and Eastern Europe do not apply to Italy. Here a parliamentary State, with a history at least as long as that of the Third French Republic, converted itself during the years between 1919 and 1922 into a State of the single-party type. The factor of social class, was, no doubt, operative in producing the change. The system of parliamentary government, never strong, and never deeply rooted, was confronted by new claims and new movements of the working classes. They were movements with which it is possible that it might have dealt successfully, if the new and rising party of the Fascists had agreed either to co-operate with the government or to oppose the government on the lines of parliamentary opposition. It did not agree. The very fact that it did not agree, and that it preferred and was allowed to take the line of solitary action by the use of its armed squadrons, proves of itself that independent social factors were emerging, and that the old parliamentary State, if it had not collapsed, was collapsing. Fascism was both a cause and a symptom of that collapse. Whether it was provoked by the new and threatening movements of the working classes, or whether it was in itself no more than one of those movements, which rapidly swung to the other side in the course of its evolution, it attested the dissolution of the old form of State, and it showed that control was passing into the hands of independent social combinations, destined to struggle with one another until one of them became the victor.

The struggle proved to be brief; but it was only brief because the Fascist party depended on something besides the support of a social class or an alliance of social classes. It enlisted and it expressed a political trend and a national longing: it drew the support of all who believed that a more united and a greater Italy mattered more than anything else. The period in which it transcended, or professed to transcend, a policy of reliance on any social class was the period in which it marched to victory. When after its victory it began to take stock, and to construct a philosophy of ends and aims, its philosophy began with the assertion of national unity and national prestige, and it proceeded, on that basis, to the assertion of an ideal of corporativism which aimed at linking together both employees and employers under the aegis and the direction of a highly national State. It may be argued, therefore, that the rise of Fascism, though it began in social struggles and the clash of social factors, was in the last resort, and in the main, due to specifically political factors. One form of State was substituted for another, during a social crisis which might otherwise have been readily surmounted, because the old form had failed to satisfy a national desire which the new form promised to fulfil.

We may thus conclude that the development of Italy, though it shows some similarities to that of Central and Eastern Europe, was in its essence different. There had not been a dissolution of a dynastic régime, followed by a parliamentary régime which failed, for want of the necessary temper, to hold society together on a new basis of mutual self-accommodation, and was therefore forced to yield to the domination of a single party. There had been a long, if never very strong, régime of parliamentary government, which, confronted by a period of social difficulties, proved inadequate to deal with them because they were complicated by political difficulties arising from injured national pride and unsatisfied national desire. The party which expressed this pride and this desire triumphed; and in its triumph it ejected the régime of parliamentary government, not so much because it had failed to hold society together, as because it had failed to carry the long process of the national *risorgimento* to the expected goal. True, the new party soon developed, and sought to realize, a new doctrine of social cohesion. But it is also true that the new doctrine has some of the marks of an after-thought; and in any case the goal of political unity and political expansion has determined the essential action of Italian Fascism.

But if a distinction may thus be drawn between the development of Italy and that of Central and Eastern Europe, there is still a close parallel between them—and more especially between the development of Germany and that of Italy. In Germany, too, the political factor, from the end of 1918 onwards, was indissolubly mixed with the social. Whatever the new system of parliamentary government might have achieved if it had been confronted only by social problems (and the odds were perhaps against it even on that assumption), the fact remains that it was also confronted, from the very first, by the political problems of injured national pride and unsatisfied national desire. The National Socialist party has always been national as well as social. Perhaps the only distinction that can safely be drawn between Germany and Italy is that in Germany the social difficulties, even if they were mixed with political problems, were graver than they were in Italy. In Germany a new and untried system of parliamentarianism, succeeding to an older and different system under the dangerous auspices of defeat, had to deal with a society dislocated by a sudden change affecting all its range and the whole of its nature. If, under these conditions, there was social turmoil, and if, out of that turmoil, a social combination emerged which sought to impose its will on society as a new form of peace, the upheaval was not surprising, even if it was aided and hastened by other than social factors. Still less need we be surprised by the upheaval of a new social class in Russian society, which had been still more dislocated by the fall of the old dynastic State, and had even less chance to give any trial to the parliamentary State. If the key of social interpretation cannot unlock all the secrets of the growth of Italian Fascism, it is more powerful in explaining the similar—and yet different—developments which have taken place outside Italy.

But it is nowhere the only key; and though we must allow that the factor of social class has played a leading part in creating the system of the single party, we must also allow that this part has been played on a peculiar scene, that it has been played in combination with other actors, and that the actor who played the leading part has not always revealed his features clearly. The scene has been peculiar, because social forces and interests have been free to act in a political vacuum caused by the crash of old dynasties or the atrophy of an old parliament. There has been a combination of actors, because the action of social class has been mixed with the action partly of national trends and partly (at any rate so far as Russia is concerned) of international ideas. The features of the social class which has played the part have not always been clearly revealed, partly because, in all countries and at all times, the outlines of social class are never clear-cut or definite, and partly because, in the particular countries and times concerned, the outlines of class have been more than usually blurred by disturbances and dislocations. (In Germany, for example, the effects of deflation and general unrest were shown, during the years immediately succeeding the end of the last war, in a rising and sinking of social position which confused the whole system of classes.) It is difficult, therefore, to describe the social significance and the class basis of the systems of the single party. But the difficulty of description will not excuse us from recognizing the existence of such significance and such a basis.

In each of the countries concerned the emergence of a single party represents, to a large degree, the uprising and triumph of a social class or combination of classes. That is a feature common to all. But the class or combination of classes emerging varies from country to country; and to discover the essence of each case we must discover the particular nature of the emergent class or combination of classes. We are thus confronted by the simple question: "So far as a social class has captured the government and annexed the State, by the formation and the victory of a single party, what has been the nature of that class in each of the three main single-party States?"

In Russia the emergent class—originally a small minority class, which then proceeded to make itself first a majority and eventually the whole—was the industrial urban proletariat. In Germany no simple answer will meet the case. But it may be said that the National Socialist party, while claiming to be a party of the workers, drew its origin mainly from the ranks of the lower middle class in town and country; that it was swollen, as it grew, by the adherence of wealthy elements in industry and commerce; and that it eventually became the vehicle or (as the Germans say) the "bearer" of a national trend of Folk-memory and Folk-pride which proved itself to be stronger than class or the sentiment of class. In Italy too no simple answer is possible. But here again it may be said that the Fascist party, while it too claimed in its infancy to be a party of labour, similarly drew its origin mainly from the ranks of a middle class which was frightened by the prospect of loss of social position; that it similarly became, in its growth, a party of wealthier elements; and that it also became, above everything else, a party which served as the vehicle or bearer of a national trend towards unification and a national desire for expansion. Both Germany and Italy thus illustrate the mixture or intertwining of factors which we have already had reason to notice. But in both the origin was the eruption of the middle class, and especially, perhaps, the lower middle class (alarmed, but yet ambitious; bourgeois in its sentiment, but yet professing to be anti-bourgeois and even revolutionary in the new culture which it sought to establish); and this original eruption has continued to leave its mark. The new Russia, whatever else it may be or become, can hardly be called middle-class. The new Germany and the new Italy, whatever the glories of blood and State they seek to achieve, retain that character.

The old aristocracy, now banished from the scene in so many countries, had its signal defects. But it had also its merits—a cosmopolitan sense; a feeling for the values of literature and art, and even for the truths of pure science; a capacity (at its best) for unselfish public service. The eruption of the middle class in Germany and Italy has left a legacy of what may be called a middle-class temper: an instinct for getting on and making a career; a tendency towards conformity to type; a passion for security rather than liberty. It is true that the middle class has come under the influence of a national trend and become the bearer of an ardent nationalism; but it is also true that this nationalism,

if in one sense more powerful than its bearer, has in another sense been subjected to the character and colour of the class by which it is borne. It has become less of a cherished ideal and more of an imposed convention. Revolutionary and anti-bourgeois in its own conception, the new elite is none the less resolved to be, and to force others to be, respectable—respectable, indeed, "from a national point of view," but still respectable.

## NOTES

1. The Russian Communist party is the oldest; and it may be said to have begun in 1900, though it did not assume the role of a single party till the end of 1917. The Italian Fascist party began in the spring of 1919 and became a single party after the march on Rome in the autumn of 1922, or, at any rate, after the suppression of any opposition in 1925. The German National Socialist party began in 1920 and became a single party in 1933.

2. It will be obvious to the reader that these words were written before 1939. I have left them as they stood.

3. See especially the second part of the pamphlet, entitled *Die Dreigliederung der politischen Einheit,* pp. 11-22.

4. It would take the argument too far afield to discuss, at this point, the justice of Dr. Schmitt's analysis of the working of the Weimar Constitution, as it is here expressed. But it is just to observe that, while he speaks of the liberal-democratic State of the nineteenth century, he is really concerned only with one form of that State, the German, and with that only as it existed in the twentieth century, from 1918 to 1933. (He himself remarks, and remarks very justly, that "behind the façade of the dualistically interpreted liberal *Verfassungsstaat,* the German State, even in the liberal nineteenth century, remained a State of the army and the official, and therefore a *Verwaltungsstaat.*") It is perhaps also permissible to add that, so far as party was hypertrophied in the German liberal-democratic State of 1918-33, this was perhaps due to the hypertrophy of the idea of the State, which affected and exaggerated parties. So insistent was the ubiquitous idea of the State that even the party groups, formed in the social area, tended to become States, and to employ the drill and discipline of a State. In England we tend to make the State itself a sort of club and to extend the methods of the club into the management of the State. In Germany, it may be said, there is a tendency to make even a club into a sort of State and to extend the methods of the State into the management of clubs.

5. Schmitt, *op. cit.,* p. 13.

6. *Ibid.,* pp. 17, 20-21.

7. *Ibid.,* p. 13.

8. *Ibid.,* p. 13. Later, however (pp. 31-2), Dr. Schmitt argues that "Hegel died" on 30 January 1933, when the National Socialist party came into power. Hegel had been content with a *Beamtenstaat* in which the army and the officials had taken upon themselves the duty of "carrying" the State. He had identified the historic fact

of this type of State with the philosophical idea of a realm of objective reason (p. 29). Hegel was transcended when a party took on its shoulders the duty of "carrying" the State—and not only the State, but also the People.

9. *Ibid.*, p. 32. I find it difficult to see the machine which is here suggested, but I have done my best to translate the passage literally.

10. *Ibid.*, p. 15. It is thus a mistake to substitute justice for political leadership (p. 40): leadership comes first, and justice adjusts itself to its primacy.

11. *Ibid.*, pp. 10, 35.

12. *Ibid.*, p. 44.

13. *Ibid.*, p. 45.

14. *Ibid.*, p. 33. The conception of the position of the Church in the community, which Dr. Schmitt is thus led to entertain, is simple. If a Church does not itself raise any totalitarian claim, it may "find its place in the third sphere"—that of the social-economic structure—under the control of the total claim of the party and the party State.

15. Russia, however, appears to form an exception, by virtue of her promulgation (alone among single-party States) of a new constitution, in 1936, which can only be amended by a special majority of the legislature, and which guarantees in one of its chapters (Chap. X) the basic rights of citizens. Moreover, if we take the constitution as operative and as being a fact and not only a statement, we must admit that Russia has not only promulgated a separate law of the constitution: she has also enunciated, in that law, a distinction between the legislative and the executive (under which the former is declared to be "the supreme organ of State power"), and a distinction between the judicature and the other powers.

16. The lines of Wordsworth occurred to me after I had written the words "stagnant uniformity." Perhaps I read too much into them; but they have for me a deep significance:

A fen
Of stagnant waters: altar, . . . pen,
Fireside, the heroic wealth of hall and bower,
Have forfeited their ancient . . . dower
Of *inward* happiness.

17. It may be said, as it is said by the Webbs, that the Russian community is more than triple: it is sextuple. Besides the State and the party, there are also four forms of society—the form composed of the trade unions of wage-earning producers employed by the State; the form composed of unions of agricultural owner-producers; the form composed of unions of industrial owner-producers; and the form composed of co-op-erative societies of consumers. In effect, however, the four forms of society (which is purely and only *economic* society) are only different expressions of a single uniform scheme.

18. Under a statute of 1928 (on the constitution and attributes of the Grand Council) the advice of the Grand Council is formally necessary for any constitutional law, along with the approval of the Senate and Deputies; and a law of 30 December 1930 accordingly enacted a new form for the promulgation of any such law, which records the advice of the Council (and the approval of the Parliament) before proceeding to the Royal sanction.

19. We may also add that under a law of January, 1934, for the ordering of national labour, the head of the National Socialist cell in any industrial enterprise has the legal right to join with the "leader" of the enterprise (the employer) in drawing up the list of the members of the Works Council (*Vertrauensrat*).

20. Dr. Schmitt, *op. cit.*, p. 42.

21. More exactly, he is the Secretary of the Central Committee of the party (a body of some seventy members); and he is also a leading member of the Polit-bureau, a standing sub-committee of the Central Committee which is the inner core of its activity. (By a recent development the Secretary is now also Premier.)

22. See the Webbs, *Soviet Communism,* Vol. I, pp. 431-40, where this doubt is discussed. Repudiating the idea that the Secretary is a dictator, they describe him as "a national leader . . . persistently boosted . . . generally admired . . . and irremovable against his will."

23. *Giovenezza* and *Jugend* may almost be said to be key-words in Italy and Germany. But we must also take into account the feeling of national rejuvenation. It is the whole nation, as one body, apart from its members or a section of its members, which is, or rather thinks itself, young. It is a body of *enfants de la patrie,* as the French sang in 1792.

24. The passage of time has already produced, in Russia, a new generation which has known nothing but Communism and the teaching of Communism. If time should operate similarly in other single-party States, the factor of age may operate less. But under the conditions of the single-party State it will always be there.

25. It may be urged in reply that Marx was himself the product and the inevitable voice of a social class and a social interest. But even if it be admitted that the thought of Marx was produced by the social conditions of Western Europe, it still remains true that his thought was one of the factors which helped to produce the idea of class and the existence of class-consciousness in Russia.

# POLITICS AND PSYCHE IN THE VICIOUS CIRCLE

## Daniel Lerner

Political leadership in any society needs a base in some social class, from which it can recruit its cadres. The modern West established a base in the mobile, continuously self-reconstituting middle classes. The military junta in Egypt has sought to create some such base rapidly. The Western model has not been feasible so far, but neither has the Soviet model. Proletarian democracy is hardly viable in a society lacking a proletariat: the Workers in the Egyptian sample bear the marks of genuine proletarians, but they are few in number. Nor is agrarian democracy: the impoverished, illiterate fellahin take more strength from the leadership than they can give and each effort to align this inert mass for political action is fraught with great risks. This is another version of Nasser's "crisis of the millstones." Every leadership seeking to modernize a traditional society rapidly faces this dilemma—in Egypt the distance between the horns is widened by the extraordinary gap between pretension and performance, between claims and capacities.

This gap led the Egyptian intelligentsia into extremist alarums and concealments which suggest, in Professor E. A. Speiser's phrase, "the nervousness of one whistling in the dark."[1] Uncertainty as to their identity, their function, their future obscured clear vision of themselves in the future world and increased their remoteness from the Egyptian masses. Their ambivalence foreshadowed the zigzag course of Egyptian policy since the military coup of July 23, 1952. When the original interviews were made, the Free Officers (*Zubat al-Ahrar*) were a clandestine organization of quite junior officers who mainly produced some muted echoes of the nationalist clamor. Now they rule Egypt as the Revolutionary Command Council (R.C.C.). They have brought Egypt's problems to a dramatic focus at the center of the world arena. But their course has been erratic, their goal remains undefined, and their future path obscure.

The junta's course has been zigzag largely because the difficulties of modernizing Egypt are real; perhaps no other Arab land represents quite so unfavorable a net ratio of population to resources. But they lacked clarity on an important question that preceded any program: which set of problems ought to have priority—their own need for a stable elite to bolster their national leadership, or rapid movement toward the Good Society promised as the fruit of independence? Before their revolution, the junta had perceived national independence and social justice as reciprocal functions. Once in power, they learned that the two were badly out of phase. Their attention fluctuated from one to the other, and their policies were improvised responses to unavoidable pressures.

The shifts in the junta's policy are exhibited in the autobiographical accounts published by their two successive chiefs—General Naguib and Colonel Nasser. These leaders, like their contemporaries, acquired early familiarity with the conflicts experienced by persons who observe their ancient world being flooded with new and impotent desires. Nasser writes of his school years:

Waves of thoughts and ideas came over us while we were not yet developed enough to evaluate them. We were still living mentally in the captivity of the 13th century. . . . Our minds tried to catch up with the caravan of human progress, although we were five centuries or more behind. The pace was fearful and the journey was exhausting.[2]

The goal was modernity on the Western model, designed in Britain. This shaped the junta's quest for a usable political identity in the early phase. But it *assumed* an inevitable correlation between the national and social revolutions. The Egyptian nation was to find itself by driving the foreigner out and bringing the good life in. The equation was simultaneous. Nationalism meant a free and equal homeland—free of the British and equal for the Egyptians.

Hence, their focus of attention was domestic. Events outside Egypt seemed unreal; only the homeland was vivid and present. Even the 1948 war

Reprinted from Daniel Lerner, *The Passing of Traditional Society: Modernizing the Middle East* (New York: The Free Press of Glencoe, 1958), by permission of the author and the publishers.

against Israel bears, in Nasser's account, the extraordinary title: "Egypt Was the Center of Our Dreams." It begins with this remarkable sentence, considering Israel's current role as devil in Egyptian imagery: "When I now try to recall the details of our experience in Palestine, I find a curious thing: we were fighting in Palestine, but our dreams were centered in Egypt." (p. 21)

The junta, in that early phase, conceived their revolutionary role in Robin Hood terms. Armed with the long bow of primitive Marxism, they would equalize the homeland by taking from the rich and giving to the poor. But they soon learned that their brave new land reform, while high-minded, was conceived in innocence. With a maximum of one million acres for potential development, of which but 5,000 acres are actually under cultivation, such an enterprise as the Liberation (*Tahrir*) Province is notable mainly for its heuristic intent. Dr. Warriner, a sympathetic expert, concluded: "No reform, even if it went much further than the present measure, could provide land for all in this congested country, or could increase employment in agriculture."[3]

As the staggering burden of real needs was borne in on them, the R.C.C. began to feel oppressed by their slow progress and sought other solutions elsewhere. The focus of effort shifted from home economics to world politics, and the junta acquired a new official vision of the future. This entailed a reallocation of ideological priorities and the communication revolution in Egypt took a new turn. The historic shift, personified by the two main actors in the drama, can be summarized in three phases: Naguib primacy, transition, Nasser control.

## PHASE 1: THE NAGUIB TECHNIQUE— VOX POPULI

The issue between Naguib and Nasser turned, indeed, upon the process which is the theme of this chapter—the use of public communication as an instrument of social change. The conflict is dramatized in their respective autobiographical reflections on the revolution. Naguib summarized the case thus:

I shall not enumerate my specific differences with the Council here. It is enough, I think, for me to say that most of them revolved around what Abd el Nasser has called the "philosophy" of the revolution. Perhaps, since neither of us are philosophers, it would be better to call it the "psychology" of the revolution. Abd el Nasser believed, with all the bravado of a man of thirty-six, that we could afford to alienate every segment of Egyptian public opinion, if necessary, in order to achieve our goals. I believed, with all the prudence of a man of fifty-three, that we would need as much popular support as we could possibly retain. . . . It remains for the course of history to determine which of us was right.[4]

Naguib hinged the long-term success of the revolution, from the start, to popular acceptance. In these terms he explains why the junior officers sought his leadership before attempting the coup:

I was known to every man in the Army and could count on its support; my reputation was above reproach; and my personality was such as to appeal to the Egyptian people. (p. 33)

It was his function to win them "the popular following necessary to succeed." (p. 14)

The management of public communication can be decisive for the style of modern governance. Naguib and Nasser disagreed, fundamentally, on who constituted the relevant public and what was the proper scope of their participation.

### Naguib

I did my best to make it a persuasive rather than a coercive dictatorship. . . . I travelled throughout the country listening patiently to everyone's complaints. I encouraged people to petition the Government to redress their grievances and I personally saw to it that thousands of grievances were redressed. I spoke to the people in their own language, and in my speeches, most of which were extemporaneous, I confined myself to the use of simple phrases and expressions that they could understand. That no attempt has yet been made on my life, I think, is proof that my approach to the Egyptian people was correct. (pp. 191–192)

### Nasser

We were deluged with petitions and complaints by the thousand and hundreds of thousands. . . . There was a confirmed individual egotism. The word "I" was on every tongue. . . . I realized that [our task] would be accomplished at the expense of popularity. We had to be blunt, outspoken, armed with reason whenever we addressed the people. Our predecessors were skilled in deluding people and telling them what they liked to hear. How easy it is to appeal to people's emotions and how difficult to appeal to their reason. . . . We could have smothered the public with resounding words compounded of delusion and fancy. . . . But was this the mission with which Fate had entrusted us? (pp. 35, 36, 72–73)

A governing body cannot long endure with its public face chronically divided between a smile and a scowl. Naguib was retired and replaced by Nasser. But the populace was disturbed and their demonstrations, doubtless abetted by the Communists and Muslim Brothers, who foresaw ampler scope for themselves under Naguib's tolerance than under Nasser's austerity, impelled the junta to restore him. But the differences were profound, not easily reconciled, and the restoration was short-lived. Again Naguib was retired and Nasser advanced. The official R.C.C. statement of the issue was broadcast by the Minister of National Guidance, Major Salah Salem, on February 26, 1954, over E.S.B.

This is a revealing document on the use of mass media. Dealing with the "psychological crises from which Naguib continued to suffer," the statement said:

When I assumed the post of Director of the E.S.B. in October last in order to reorganize it I had to face tragedies every day. For the President . . . used to contact E.S.B. officials . . . to give them direct orders to repeat broadcasts of his speeches several times. Even the news bulletin could not be broadcast before it was checked by him and before he personally recorded his contacts, visits and meetings.

During his trip to Nubia he used to give direct orders to the Deputy Director of the E.S.B. and other officials to change the programmes and to repeat the speeches delivered by him there several times, so much so that the public had become disgusted and abstained from switching on their radio sets. This was contradictory to the orders issued by me to the chiefs of sections in the E.S.B. not to make any changes in the programmes except in certain serious cases. These chiefs often complained to him that they were at a loss as to which order they should obey. Two senior officials of the E.S.B. had to feign illness in order to avoid the consequences of such contradictory orders.

One day in December last when I was facing the Sudanese election campaign alone I felt near a nervous breakdown as a result of Naguib's contradictory orders from Nubia and his insistence on punishing officials who failed to carry them out to the letter, although most of such orders could not possibly be carried out for material and technical reasons.

I remember, for example, on the Prophet's Birthday he asked me to repeat three broadcasts, of which one lasted for 76 minutes, the second 30 minutes, and the third 45 minutes. This was the day on which we had to broadcast the Prophet's birthday celebrations. I gave orders for two of his broadcasts to be postponed to the next day. The same evening, however, the Deputy Director of the E.S.B. received a telegram from General Naguib demanding punishment of those who had not obeyed his orders.

One day, I could stand this state of affairs no longer and went along to tell my comrades on the Revolutionary Council all about them. They asked me to keep on trying to improve the E.S.B. As this did not solve my problems I finished up by going along to the Military jail at Bab al-Hadid and asking for a cell where my friends found me in the evening and called on me to stand up to the situation.

As I had control of the press, I recall too that General Naguib used to send delegates to the newspapers and ask them to publish photographs, statements and special articles. Any editor, reporter or official can confirm my statement.

Very often I was obliged to censor certain of his statements which contradicted decisions taken by the Revolutionary Council. One day I had to suppress the title of an article which he sent to al-Ahram for publication on the front page. This was an article by John Gunther entitled "The Smiling Dictator of Egypt."

He telephoned me and insisted that this title appear. I tried in vain to dissuade him as we could not permit a newspaper to call Naguib a dictator at the very moment that Churchill was making the same charge in the Commons. He refused and I had to ask the Editor-in-Chief of al-Ahram to publish the article as it had been sent by General Naguib.

I defy any Editor or reporter to mention any one member of the Revolutionary Council who has asked for his photograph or a special article to be published.

The chief editor of al-Ahram even got in touch with the Chief Censor and said that he could not as a patriot publish a statement that Naguib was a dictator. I told him to do as he was ordered by the President. . . .

You ask why we made him into a symbol of confidence and to this I reply that we never wished to create symbols as in the olden days. No member of the Revolutionary Council is permitted to praise any of his colleagues. Some of them were even angry with me when they were praised in the press. Personally I am convinced that the public was wrong, for it should never place all its hopes in any one person, but should concentrate on principles only.[5]

## PHASE 2: TRANSITION—
## WHAT PRICE PERSUASION?

Nasser and his youthful colleagues were deeply shaken by the implications of Naguib's bid for mass popularity. In words begin responsibilities; a communication network implies a power structure. The democratic use of power requires communication from below as well as from above. Discussion and decision tend, in a participant society, to implicate each other. It is unnecessary to persuade those whose views can be assumed or ignored; it can be fatal to ignore or coerce those whose consent must be gained. Naguib's courtship of the vox populi implied a politics of mass participation which seemed dangerous to the R.C.C. To Nasser, the masses that had "come in endless droves" through the revolutionary breach already appeared "dark and ominous."

Nasser preferred the military image of an orderly "advance" led by a vanguard and followed by masses that would "fall in behind in serried ranks." The principle of a "smiling dictatorship" was more risky than the impersonal politics of a proper "chain of command." The Egyptian masses were not "ready" for mass participation, hence a politics of persuasion was premature. Nasser's account of his disillusionment by the Egyptian mass is candid:

Before July 23rd, I had imagined that the whole nation was ready and prepared, waiting for nothing but a vanguard to lead the charge against the battlements, whereupon it would fall in behind in serried ranks, ready for the sacred advance towards the great objective. . . . but how different is the reality from the dream! The masses that came were disunited, divided groups of stragglers. The sacred advance was stalled, and the picture that emerged on that day looked dark and ominous; it boded danger. . . . We were not yet ready. So we set about seeking the views of leaders of opinion and the experience of those who were experienced. Unfortunately we were not able to obtain very much. (pp. 32–34)

In turning from the mass to seek "the views of leaders of opinion," the R.C.C. shifted its priority to the formation of a usable elite. In good military fashion, they sought to recruit the cadres which could then train the line regiments. Their task was to create a fresh coalition out of aggressive elements in the old elite and the newer group of Transitionals. They turned first to the radical intellectuals—the symbol-manipulators who can give direction to the forward movement of a revolutionary program. Since the orthodox intelligentsia often will not or cannot fill this role, revolutionary leadership usually turns to the secular intellectuals located at more "mobile" positions in the universities or mass media. But we have seen how ambivalent the secular intelligentsia of Egypt had become; and the literature of political sociology suggests how treacherous their political alliances in any country can be.[6] Nasser experienced the symptoms at first hand:

I remember visiting once one of our universities where I called the professors together and sat with them in order to benefit from their scholastic experience. Many of them spoke before me and at great length. It was unfortunate that none of them advanced any ideas; instead, each confined himself to advancing himself to me, pointing out his unique fitness for making miracles. Each of them kept glancing at me with the look of one who preferred me to all the treasures of earth and heaven. (p. 37)

His sense of deception by the fawning professors was matched in other elite circles, among which he singles out for special mention "large landholders . . . the politicians of the old regime . . . many government officials." (pp. 74–75) This deprived him of any solid base among the existing elites of enlightenment, wealth and power. So Nasser came to the crucial decision that, faced with masses whose deeds could be "dark and ominous" and without an efficient elite to count on, his mission "would be accomplished at the expense of popularity."

Small wonder, then, that Nasser, a Puritanical man with exacting moral standards, should have formed his Revolutionary Command Council exclusively with fellow Army officers of equal dedication:

The situation demanded the existence of a force set in one cohesive framework, far removed from the conflict between individuals and classes, and drawn from the heart of the people: a force composed of men able to trust each other; a force with enough material strength at its disposal to guarantee a swift and decisive action. These conditions could be met only by the Army. (p. 42)

But a scowling dictatorship is not necessarily more efficient, and is probably less durable, than a smiling dictatorship. To run a revolution takes more than an austere mien; and other than military perspectives are needed to run a civil society. Atatürk had symbolized this by changing his public portrait from military uniform to white tie and tails. More recent military *coups d'état* in the Arab area—the prewar seven in Iraq (1936–1941) and the postwar four in Syria (1949–1952)—have also shown that recruitment from a broader social base soon becomes essential. Professor Majid Khadduri, keen student of the military role, suggests why:

At best the reform program of the military was eclectic; it included various ideas and proposals that had become popular among the people, but these were never integrated or worked out by specialists as to the ways and means of carrying them out. Thus in Egypt, the army has been advocating land reform by limiting landownership to a legal maximum of 200 acres and encouraging small holdings; but in advocating this appealing program, which has become very popular among the masses, the military do not seem to realize that improving the economic condition of the nation would be dependent on new means of increasing agricultural production for an already overpopulated country rather than on redistributing the land among a larger number of people.[7]

Confronted with apparently insuperable short-term problems of social organization and economic development at home, Nasser overlapped them to stake the Egyptian future upon his skill at long-term play in the world political game. He shifted public attention from land-reform to Czechoslovak arms and Suez tolls. Thereafter, he no longer detailed the program for an Egypt of social justice but sketched the portrait for an Egypt of surpassing greatness.

Naguib had chosen, for the closing theme of his book, this sentence:

The revolt of the Arab peoples, after all, is but a belated reflection of the revolt of the Western peoples that began with the revolutions in the United States and France. . . . the sort of federation that I envision would begin like Benelux and end like Switzerland. (pp. 273, 262)

For Nasser this has become a parochial view of the Egyptian future. In *his* current aspiration, Egypt figures as the patron spirit of a nascent Africa, as the vital center of an Arab circle, as the prime ministry of an Islamic World Parliament. His vision has wandered far from the homeland. As his sketch of the Egyptian future closes, Nasser's new reveries are playing political arithmetic with

. . . the 80 million Muslims in Indonesia, and the 50 million in China, and the millions in Malaya, Siam, and Burma, and the nearly 100 million in the Middle East, and the 40 million in the Soviet Union, together with the other millions in far-flung parts of the world—when I consider these hundreds of millions united by a single creed, I emerge with a sense of the tremendous possibilities which we might realize through the cooperation of all these Muslims. (p. 113)

What had happened to Nasser?

## PHASE 3: THE NASSER SYNDROME

The shift from home democracy to global imperialism appears at first to be an aberration. This sort of talk from a man of modest mien does not seem serious. For the Muslim millions of the world are no more "united by a single creed" than, say, the Catholics of Mongolia and the Baptists of Mississippi. But there is psychic meaning in political visions, even when aberrant.

Nasser has gone the way of total politization—the distinctive mark of totalitarianism in our century. Wielding inadequate power to enact rapidly their designs, such leaders have yoked all values to their grand quest for more power. Nasser has perceived how the "dark and ominous" mass, which so depressed him when it had to be served, can be made to serve him—and through him, so runs the rationale, ultimately serve its own "higher ends." Such thinking has come to seem a viable political strategy in the era of mass communications. Now it appears feasible to shape mass emotion to a large political purpose. Nasser's new communication strategy shows in the burst of activity given, under his guidance, to the "Voice of the Arabs" and to the "Arab News Agency." Also in his new readiness to exploit, politically, the pieties of the pilgrimage to Mecca:

Journalists of the world should hasten to cover the Pilgrimage, not because it is a traditional ritual affording interesting reports for the reading public, but because of its function as a periodic political conference in which the envoys of the Islamic states . . . lay down in this Islamic world-parliament the broad lines of their national policies and their pledges of mutual cooperation from one year to another. (p. 112)

Utter politization underlies such efforts to fuse modern parliamentarianism with the ancient theocracy of Islam in a global fantasy. It suggests why a once austere leader, contemptuous of public opinion, is beguiled by chimera that will attract the "journalists of the world." More than political calculation is at work here. The naive candor of Nasser's "philosophy" stems from the conviction that his vision is clever—and righteous. He seems, at times, to be still fighting the battle of his youth: to show the hated imperialist from the West that he is just as strong and much more virtuous than his conqueror. He writes:

Sometimes when I re-read the pages of our history, I feel a tearing grief . . . we were the victims of a tyrannous feudalism which did nothing for us except suck the lifeblood from our veins. Nay, even worse—it robbed us of all sense of strength and honor. It left in the depths of our souls a complex which we will have to fight for a long time to overcome. (p. 63)

This is the sense of shame before their conquerors which has scarred the Egyptian leaders and marred their conception of right role and proper place. Naguib, a simpler person than Nasser, speaks of the same "complex" somewhat more bluntly:

I was ashamed of the low esteem in which Egyptians were held by Britons and other foreigners, and I was determined to show our cynical rulers that something could and would be done about it. (pp. 19-20)

These statements explicate the feelings so widespread among the intelligentsia interviewed in 1951 —viz., the schoolteacher who, although he believed "England is the greatest country," would nevertheless "feel ashamed [to live there] because they would look at me as a master looks at his slave."

The difference is that Nasser makes Egyptian policy, and the year is 1958. The battle for independence is done and won. The British Empire is gone—from Cairo, from Suez, and now even from the Sudan. To persist in shaping the world to the ambivalent imagery of youth, among ex-colonials as among ex-imperialists, may in the long run serve pathology better than policy. Seeking to compensate the fantasy life for damages inflicted in a no longer relevant past obscures the lines to a realistic political future. The new Constitution, announced by Nasser on January 16, 1956, documents the excesses of ambivalent nationalism. It proclaims Egypt to be an Islamic and Arab state under a republican and democratic form of government. But this combination of all desirable identities is, at the moment, sheer fantasy. To proclaim Egypt a democratic republic ignores. but does not alter, the fact that it is a military dictatorship. To proclaim Egypt formally an Arab nation (for the first time in history) leaves unaltered the fact that Egyptians are ethnically *not* Arabs. To proclaim that "the Arab nation" now "extends from the Atlantic Ocean to the Persian Gulf" overlooks current reality in order to prophesy a massive rearrangement of the present facts of life.

Whether this is "rational prophecy," of the sort described by Max Weber, remains to be seen. But we shall be better prepared for observation by understanding the psychopolitical model which the "Nasser syndrome" seeks to diffuse. Ambivalence is still the recurrent theme in the unfinished script of the Egyptian drama. But release through aggression is the approved new posture defined by Colonel Nasser. His role on the world stage provides the living model to his countrymen. Only optimists in the West interpret his seizure of Suez, for example, in such petty terms as canal tolls. The press and radio of Egypt, as indeed of all Arab lands, celebrate a more basic meaning—exalting the Self by humiliating the West. Nasser is aware, however, that avenging past nightmares can become a dangerous self-indulgence. Hence he speaks of:

... the crisis of the millstones—a revolution which obliges us to unite in one phalanx and *forget the past,* and another revolution which demands that we restore lost dignity to our moral values by *not forgetting the past.* . . . One revolution makes it obligatory that we unite and *love one another;* the other brings dissension upon us against our desires, causing us to *hate each other.* (pp. 44, 41)

Ambivalent affect and erratic policy will continue, probably, until Egyptians agree to do one effectively—to forget or not forget, to love or hate —instead of struggling to do both simultaneously. Meanwhile, Nasser has accepted total engagement with the "dark and ominous" mass and has undertaken to cope with the heavy emotional requirements of mass communication. Now, no longer hesitant to acknowledge his dictatorship, he often smiles in public.

## NOTES

1. E. A. Speiser, *The U.S. and the Near East* (1947), p. 144.

2. Gamal Abdul Nasser, *Egypt's Liberation: The Philosophy of the Revolution* (1955), pp. 67–68. Further page references to this book are given after each quotation.

3. D. Warriner, *Land Reform and Development in the Middle East* (1957), p. 48.

4. Mohammed Naguib, *Egypt's Destiny* (1955), pp. 215–216. Further page references to this book are given after each quotation.

5. Text quoted from *Egyptian Mail,* No. 10993-268 (February 27, 1954), pp. 1, 4.

6. The classic short essay and long bibliography is Robert Michel's "Intellectuals," in the *Encyclopedia of the Social Sciences.* On Egypt, see W. C. Smith in S. N. Fisher (ed.), *Social Forces in the Middle East* (1955).

7. Majid Khadduri, "The Army Officer," in Fisher (ed.), *ibid.,* p. 178. Also his "Role of the Military in Middle East Politics," *American Political Science Review,* XLVII, 2 (June, 1953), pp. 511–524.

# VIII

# VIII  *Political Change*

# INTRODUCTION

## David E. Apter

### I

Barker comments that what makes the state natural for Aristotle "is the fact that, however it came into existence, it is as it stands the satisfaction of an immanent impulse in human nature towards moral perfection—an immanent impulse which drives men upwards, through various forms of society, into the final political form."[1] Most of us probably share this view. Upon it rests our basic optimism about politics. Even in cynical moods, when the idea of progress is in doubt, there remains a pervasive hope that an immanent impulse will drive us towards moral perfection. Without some such faith, all hope for political man would disappear.

Whether or not such a view is accepted, it raises a fundamental problem. What are the arrangements whereby men express their moral aspirations, and, more particularly, what political form expresses them best? Such a concern may be divided into two parts. One involves existing political arrangements. The other, which is the subject of the present section, centers around the problem of change.

The major forms of political development involve not only historical transformations in political arrangements, but in political values as well. History is punctuated with trial and error. At times great changes occur within the existing framework of social order. At other times there is a breakdown in social life.

## II. EVOLUTIONARY CHANGE AND POLITICAL DEVELOPMENT

"Political evolution" is the term that best expresses the countless changes in outlook and political arrangements that can be absorbed without a breakdown in social life. It may have its discontinuities—for example, evolution with respect to representative government in England had its Chartist Movement and its struggles over the passage of the Reform Acts—but mainly it takes place within the context of the existing community, which in turn is both strengthened and modified by change.

Evolution, although less dramatic than its alternative, revolution, is also more demanding from an analytical point of view. The two forms of change are obviously related. To examine evolutionary change, we analyze the receptivity of institutions with respect to their flexibility. In the West this concern has been shaped by our interest in representative government and constitutional democracy. We view democracy as a system that institutionalizes a framework that allows change to go on, but in an orderly fashion. We recognize that democracy inhibits change and makes it less epic. It is necessary to denature change in order to render it compatible with what already exists. Where it can not be so rendered, it becomes dangerous. Indeed, one cornerstone of our faith in the wisdom of democracy as a political form is that while never quite a match for the social and political problems facing it, democracy nevertheless remains the most satisfactory method of responding to changing wants and needs.

Much of the Western democratic world has shown a remarkable ability to absorb change. Early notions of democracy were founded on simplistic ideas of progress, with social life centered in the intimate and relatively serene atmosphere of rural and small town life. From such beginnings democracies have shown themselves capable of absorbing vast increases in population as well as a remarkable degree of urbanization, the rise of industrial economies, and an increasingly intricate set of political institutions. In spite of its inadequacies, democracy has achieved more adequate distribution of rights and obligations along with the expansion of goods and services in an increasingly advanced technological setting. Such changes have not destroyed the ability of our democratic societies to provide for the orderly transition of governments and men and the circulation of elites with a minimum of violence and bloodshed. There are obvious exceptions to this condition. France provides an example of periodic failures in democracy. In Germany and Italy also democracy once failed—and may again; but Belgium, the Netherlands, the Scandinavian countries, Great Britain, the United States, and the older dominions are all examples of democratic stability and peaceful or evolutionary change in which politics, no matter how turbulent, have not given way to full-scale revolution.

Notwithstanding democratic successes in providing a suitable framework for development, peaceful change is, of course, not the same thing as democracy. There have been long periods of political and social evolution in nondemocratic nations when revolutions have been absent. For over a thousand years, China, a monarchy, did not have a revolution, although there were changes in dynasties. The Revolution of 1911, which brought about the end of the Manchu Dynasty, resulted from the inability of China to absorb those patterns of commercial and social innovations that had begun to penetrate from the West a generation earlier.

Japan, in contrast, was able to absorb those same innovations, while requiring alterations in the political structure that made it more powerful. Indeed, the growth of militarism in Japan can be regarded as one means whereby innovation and change were regulated in accordance with traditions and social institutions that already prevailed. Militarism rendered innovation less dangerous to the moral order —an order that governments are always destined to protect as part of their *raison d'être*.

What can we learn from the comparative study of political change? Most obviously there are added to those political techniques available at any given time new ones that can, with suitable adaptation to fit local conditions, be employed in a variety of countries. One of the most complex and interesting of these has been, in modern times, the growth of bureaucracies. Another has been the use of planning bodies and fiscal controls in government. These and others reflect a larger developmental tendency, that of the enlarged role of government in contemporary society.

This latter point has been of major concern precisely because of the crucial role that government plays in regulating all other forms of change. Industrial and health regulations and administration, education and scientific research, urban relocation and financial aid to towns, and the processing of government business—all are aspects of the problem of political change. Techniques of government that are novel and fresh, emerging as responses to larger problems, also need to be absorbed and digested; and accordingly the problem of big government is part of the problem of political development.

Political development then is a specific response to wider changes in social life, but political development is not simply a reflex of society. Government always has a dynamic of its own, and comparative studies of change need always to reflect the impact of government upon society. The functioning of the one always affects the workings of the other.

This problem can be seen most clearly under two kinds of circumstances. One is when the community poses problems for government of such magnitude that rather drastic alterations in government policy are required if a breakdown of order is not to occur. The Hapsburg monarchy in the old Austrian-Hungarian Empire provides an example of how inadequate governmental policy prepared the way for disasters on the battlefield that destroyed the Empire. A similar example is Tsarist Russia. History is strewn with such cases. More modern examples are afforded by Kuomintang China and several Latin American countries. Indeed, preserving order in the face of grave social problems while attempting to reform governments whose normal actions are hampered by inefficiency and widespread corruption is a key policy problem for the United States in its dealings with many overseas nations. Moreover, such problems cannot be handled purely at the governmental level. The political effects of social and economic development also become an essential part of the problem. In many nations undergoing rapid change, everything is political, and that is the heart of the problem.

There is another special difficulty of political development in new governments. Not only is there a question of the form and spirit, the techniques and mechanisms that seem appropriate, but the basic authority of the state must also be agreed upon in principle by the citizens of new polities. How to make authority legitimate, that is, how to create the constitutional framework and give it meaning, is one important matter for comparative analysts to examine. With undigested views stemming from many political philosophies and opinions, political leaders of the new states tend to be eclectic and experimental and at the same time miss many of the more subtle interconnections between governmental acts and forms, between public participation and responsibility. In the search for alternatives in public policy and government structure, they miss those connections of outlook and practice that enable particular political mechanisms to be successful in one case and fail in another.

How can evolutionary change and political development be studied? Several alternative efforts have emerged in contemporary comparative studies. One approach treats government along with other factors in a development situation and tries to correlate the speed of development by determining the progress made in each dimension. Without doubt Deutsch's concept of social mobilization remains the most successful attempt to correlate basic variables involved in the total development process. Whether or not his major thesis is basically correct cannot be verified by his variables. He says, for example, that:

Other things assumed equal, the stage of rapid social mobilization may be expected therefore to promote the consolidation of states whose peoples already share the same language, culture, and major social institutions;

while the same process may tend to strain or destroy the unity of states whose population is already divided into several groups with different languages or cultures of basic ways of life.[2]

This statement can be regarded only as an interesting proposition, since it is quite possible that those states with the least identity of language and culture will be drawn together in the development process. Guinea in West Africa is a case in point. Our purpose, however, is not to argue with Deutsch but rather to point out that his method of correlating such factors as population, literates, per capita income, and urban population is one means of examining political development. Others who have tried to work along these lines are Lyle Shannon and S. M. Lipset.

The great difficulty with the use of such variables is that they assume that certain key indicators, most characteristic of the development process in the West, will turn out to have the same significance in the developing areas. These theorists have a tendency to view political development as a fairly uniform process, and in this they have been aided by economists who by and large tend toward the same view.

The alternative is to be found in such efforts as Shils' "Political Development in the New States."[3] In Shils' work there is recognition of the need to sketch the main characteristics of social and political organization first to see what over-all similarities exist between political processes. Only in this way can the more statistical approaches be brought into the specific context of institutional change. Efforts such as the Almond-Coleman scheme of functional analysis[4] attempt to bring the two approaches together within the context of developmental, or process, theory.

Two other efforts that attempt to handle political development by bringing together structural variables with more general basic data are Lerner's *Passing of the Traditional Society* and Apter's *The Political Kingdom in Uganda*.[5] The former deals directly with the effect of modern communications upon the formation of new roles, while the latter provides a framework for studying comparative political development. All these approaches represent different kinds of efforts to make sense out of the processes of political development and evolutionary change.

There are times, of course, when the community can no longer absorb innovation. There may be structural weaknesses in both society and government that result in a weakening of their moral fiber. Political institutions fall into disrepute. Society either becomes subject to a widespread malaise, a kind of anomie, or it seeks more drastic solutions to its problems. Such drastic solutions, especially when they represent a profound rupture in political continuity, are normally revolutionary.

## III. REVOLUTIONARY CHANGE

We often speak of the "industrial revolution" or the "Copernican revolution" or even the "technological revolution." This use of the term "revolution" is a way of conveying how drastic have been the consequences of the events characterizing the period. Such terms, however, go beyond what we ordinarily mean to imply by the word "revolution." In this view, revolution is a drastic alteration in the values and polity of a nation characterized by internal violence.

There are violent internal conflicts that result in changes of regime. These changes are fundamental to the extent that they incorporate new values and polities. Fundamental revolutions in our terms thus have a strong normative element, a measure of political messianism, and a moral urgency lacking in lesser revolutions.

What are some of the characteristics of revolution? When do they begin and end? How do they differ from armed insurrection? All these questions have concerned scholars who examine the process of change and, more particularly, rapid change. In this view, Latin America has had few fundamental revolutions. Perón's in Argentina and Castro's in Cuba are exceptions, since they violently incorporated certain fundamental changes in polity and values, particularly in Cuba. Similarly, in Central America, the revolutionary case is Mexico. Other "revolutions" in Latin America have been more ephemeral.

One indication of the significance of a revolution is whether or not its tenets are serviceable elsewhere. To be fundamental, a revolution needs to have broad consequences. Fundamental revolutions engender further revolutions. Indeed, the Mexican and the Cuban revolutions have had far-reaching implications in Latin America. In this, they follow in the traditions of two others, the French and the Russian.

Revolutionary change does have certain general characteristics. Tocqueville, writing about the French Revolution, observed that:

During revolutions of long duration, it is easy to mistake the signs indicating the approach of great turning points; for these signs vary with the different periods. They even change their character as the revolution advances.

In the beginning public opinion is excited, lively, intolerant, presumptuous and mobile; at the end it is stolid and sad. After having tolerated nothing, there seems to be nothing it will not endure. But submission is accompanied by resentment, irritation increases, suspicion becomes more inveterate, and hatred grows in the midst of obedience. The nation has no longer, as in the beginning of the Revolution, sufficient energy to push a government towards the precipice, yet everyone enjoys the spectacle of its fall.[6]

For Tocqueville, major revolutions represented transformations in the beliefs by which men live. There is nothing casual about them; they are not simply seizures of government by armed men or insurrection. Revolutions are profound alterations of social and political life. They are caused by a basic disease in the body politic; and when the crisis is reached, the result is a breakdown of authority. Laws and orders, rights and obligations are dissolved. Conflict is not confined to members of the old regime versus the revolutionaries but extends to struggles between revolutionaries.

Revolutions, as Edwards suggests, have a characteristic syndrome. There is, first, public restlessness, a generalized kind of striving not easily satisfied. Second, vice, immorality, and moral malaise bite deep into society. Third, frustration becomes pervasive. Life is now, according to Edwards, repressed, unsatisfying, and increasingly intolerable. These are telltale warnings of the danger of revolution.[7]

So much for the character of revolution. What were some of the great ones? In recent times they include the English Revolution, extending roughly from the decapitation of Charles I to the restoration of the monarchy; the French Revolution, which is far easier to indicate in its beginnings than in its end; the American Revolution, which was, on the whole, the least revolutionary of the major revolutions; and finally, the Russian. So powerful have these revolutions been that they remain a seedbed for other and subsequent movements that, if not revolutions in themselves, have been carried forward by revolutionary antecedents.

Not all revolutions are progressive. Hitler's rise to power, as Mussolini's before him, resulted in some earthshaking events. The sorry spectacle of millions of Germans, regimented, uniformed, and muzzled, channeling their passion for order into devotion for an absurd man with a toothbrush mustache is a phenomenon that later generations will find difficult to understand. The posturing and grimaces of Mussolini were no less ridiculous. These revolutions were truly revolutionary in that they established a new standard of right and wrong, a new pattern of authority to maintain the standard, and a new moral language to express the standard.

The fascist revolutions, as well as those of Argentina, Cuba, and Mexico, were momentous, yet they were not perhaps "fundamental." They lacked the moral imperatives of the English, the American, the French, and the Russian. Like the Communist revolution in China, their contribution to human thought and feeling is not very great. In evaluation or revolution it is important to separate the technique of insurrection from the contributions of revolution.

Revolutions vary considerably in their causes. General dissatisfaction with a government can never, of course, be pinned down to a single factor. Some, however, were more concerned with economic problems, others ethnic, still others religious. Indeed, early revolutions, like the Christian conquest of ancient Rome, had as the basis of their moral impetus new moral values. Christianity and Islam inspired men to a host of revolutionary actions that unfolded in many countries and over many years.

The most recent of the fundamental revolutions is the Marxist, of which the Soviet Union is merely one aspect.[8] The elaboration of revolutionary change leading to a higher stage of society was the Marxist utilization of the French Jacobin tradition. By integrating it with Hegelian dialectics and Ricardian economic theories, social and political revolution was made into a feature of progress and of changes between epochs. Engels, Marx's friend and collaborator, claimed that it was

. . . Marx who had first discovered the great law of motion of history, the law according to which all historical struggles, whether they proceed in the political, religious, philosophical or some other ideological domain, are in fact only the more or less clear expression of struggles of social classes, and that the existence and thereby collisions, too, of these classes are in turn conditioned by the degree of development of their economic position, by the mode of their production and by the form of exchange resulting from it. This law . . . has the same significance for history as the law of the transformation of energy has for natural science. . . .[9]

This view, to a greater or less degree, was shared by others in the revolutionary tradition. Some were less concerned with the "scientific" notion of revolutionary progress but were rather interested in the mystique of revolution. Revolutionary activity did not need to show a unilinear line of progress toward a higher order. Rather, its liberating effect could derive from violence, a shaking loose from past inhibitions and institutions. The syndicalist view of revolution departed from the Marxist because of doubt in Marx's prophetic accuracy. Hence, it was necessary to create new ethical conditions for violence. Sorel's *Reflections on Violence* is just such an effort. Sorel put the issue as follows:

The Marxian theory of revolution supposes that capitalism, while it is still in full swing, will be struck to the heart when—having attained complete industrial efficiency—it has finally achieved its historical mission, and whilst the economic system is still a progressive one. Marx does not seem to have asked himself what would happen if the economic system were on the down grade; he never dreamt of the possibility of a revolution which would take a return to the past, or even social conservation, as its ideal.[10]

Revolutionary thought did not remain limited to the socialist tradition. After World War I, in Germany, Italy, Portugal, Spain, Roumania, Bulgaria, and, for a time, in Greece, revolutions of the right occurred. Sometimes these had "social conservation" as the ideal, as in the more Catholic of the fascist revolutions. Sometimes there was a frank return to an atavistic past, as in the case of fascist Italy or Nazi Germany. Violence was seen as freedom from decadence. War and destruction were regarded as the proper symbols of freedom. Discipline and regimentation became the artifacts of achievement. Hence what the Jacobins and Marx had unleashed as progressive revolution helped to install tyrannies of the left and the right as the immediate progeny of revolution itself.

If revolutionary traditions are striking and even fearsome, the evolutionary view is certainly unheroic and mundane. It is more rational in the sense that rationality comes about through criticism and understanding by individuals. As Popper points out, if it is the case that authoritarianism and rationalism are antithetical to one another, then "reason, like science, grows by way of mutual criticism; the only reasonable way of 'planning' its growth is to develop those institutions that safeguard the freedom of this criticism, that is to say, the freedom of thought."[11]

Revolutions do not, characteristically, establish such institutions but rather suppress them. In that sense, neither revolutions in the name of science (the Marxist), or revolutions in the name of violence (the fascist), conform to a rational ideal, however much they try to "rationalize" their societies. The true revolutionary sees in violence either a regrettable but necessary adventure into the future or seeks the romanticism of danger, the excitement of destruction, the power of fear.

A sense of destiny is thus characteristic of revolutionaries, whether through a class, as among the Marxists, or a national state, as among National Socialists. Such a sense of destiny does more than serve a pragmatic end. In the end it validates the revolution. It presses its claim for a new society as the basis for a new authority. In a word, it tries to supplant the existing system of authority with a new legitimacy, the right of revolutionary power.

We have said that fundamental revolutions have a moral aspect to them—whether they are retrograde or progressive, whether they are deistic and rationalistic, as in the French Revolution,[12] secular and anticlerical as in the Russian, or mystical and pagan as in the fascist and Nazi revolutions. None is complete without a pantheon of saints and devils, heroes and villains, dogmas and heresies by means of which it establishes the rights of the revolution, its historic drive. After it has won power, it uses these to eliminate the remnants of the former society.

## IV

Representative democracy, when it flourishes properly, is one alternative to revolution, since the organs of government reflect, through policy, the changing needs of a population that manifest themselves in the mechanisms of popular government. The evolutionary tradition, whether of the left or the right, is based first on the concept of representative government.

What is so intriguing about this concept is that most representative governments were themselves born in revolution. The point is that a difference exists between what might be called "radical" and "liberal" revolutions. The former tries to restructure and alter almost all the features of social life, that is, to modify values, attitudes and institutions according to some set of goals. To gain these ends, radical revolutions need to politicize all aspects of community existence. Nothing escapes surveillance. Liberal revolutions, on the contrary, accept the main values, attitudes, and institutions of the community but regard the government as imperfect. A revolution for constitutional government gives power to the people to make those laws pleasing to the majority. Government policy, based on recurrent majorities, reflects diverse groupings engaged in a coalitional competition by means of the party system and elections. Thus, if there are internal problems in the society, these will be reflected in the political mechanisms. Public policy will be directed to their elimination. If there are failures in this regard, then the representative system must be tinkered with and amended in order to more perfectly reflect the public humor.

Are the differences in radical and liberal revolutions simply matters of degree? In part they are. In part, too, they reflect differences in conception. Radical revolutions may act in the name of the public, but in the long run the public is their obstacle. Participation in politics is tolerated only within narrow limits laid down by party or government, so that visible exercise of governmental authority is its most pronounced characteristic. Radical revolutions have great difficulty in retiring old revolutionaries. The revolutionary movement tends to "eat its young." This was noted by Trotsky, who called it the "Thermidorian reaction" and held that it was characteristic of the French, Russian, Italian, and German radical revolutions. And of course in the end the Thermidor destroyed Trotsky himself.[13]

One consequence of these revolutions is found in the decline of colonialism, itself a momentous period of change in human affairs. Decolonization has not been revolutionary. Rather, it has been the carrying forward of those revolutionary ideas contained in all the major revolutions listed above; those defining individual liberty as in the English Revolution, political democracy and representative institutions as in the French and the American, economic progress and drastic social change as in the Russian. One finds the ideological progeny of these revolutions scattered throughout the rhetoric and thought of nationalist leaders in Asia and Africa.

Today, the Western world watches its revolutionary chickens come home to roost in the new nations. The need to shape and sort out political arrangements makes the process of peaceful political evolution dangerous. The new nations come into the world without the original sin that taints the West and the East, but they are also eclectic, brash, and ignorant in many ways in spite of a pronounced humanism. They are out to claim their rightful inheritances. They will soon dominate in the United Nations. Meanwhile, they stumble in efforts to straighten out their affairs, to attack the discontinuities within their own societies. This is political development in the raw, a process full of dangers to all. Yet there is no substitute for it. Planning through borrowed techniques, applying ideas eclectically, using force, refusing to be judged, the "third world," as it is often called, raises up new problems for comparative politics. Is Jaspers right when he says that former colonies "are still largely incapable of freedom"? The answer will depend upon the political development of the new nations. They have the same potentialities for persecution and tyranny as the older ones. Whether they will safeguard both individual and social freedom remains to be seen. Unfortunately, few governments have been able to establish both simultaneously.

## V

Two interesting studies of the role of revolution that appear in biographies of well-known revolutionaries are *The Political Philosophy of Bakunin: Scientific Anarchism* (New York: The Free Press, 1953, edited by G. P. Maximoff), and C. A. Sainte-Beuve's *P. J. Proudhon, sa vie et sa correspondance* (Paris: Ancienne Librairie Schleicher, 1947). Providing a good background for the growth of the Jacobin tradition and its origins in the French Revolution is J. L. Talmon's *The Origins of Totalitarian Democracy* (London: Secker and Warburg, 1955). Providing the link between the left syndicalist tradition of revolution and the national socialist varieties is Georges Sorel's *Reflections on Violence* (New York: The Free Press, 1950).

The largest single list of works on revolution stems from the Marxist library. Perhaps the most interesting of these, aside from the Communist Manifesto, which is itself a tract, a kind of *Mein Kampf* of the left rather than a basic work, are two: Marx's *The Eighteenth Brumaire of Louis Bonaparte* (New York: International Publishers, n.d.) and Lenin's *State and Revolution* (New York: International Publishers, 1932).

In this section are reprinted some of the major comparative works dealing with revolution. The first selection by Brinton is an effort to comprehend the theoretical implications of revolutions and their implications with respect to the problem of

rapid change. An obvious omission here, not to be minimized because the author was so much a participant, is Trotsky's classic, *The History of the Russian Revolution,* probably the best analysis of a revolution to be found in the literature. So rich and detailed is this work, however, that it is difficult to remove a section of it for separate treatment in a Reader. Nor is it strictly speaking a comparative study, however many references to other revolutions or passages useful for broader studies it may contain.

Much of the general literature on political change now relates to the new nations. These show such remarkable contrasts and discontinuities that they are a most useful source of research and knowledge about the more general processes of change, as well as very particular ones. Moreover, it is becoming more common to compare recent change in new nations with other historical periods. Several very recent studies of change include Deutsch's *Nationalism and Social Communication,* Lipset's *Political Man,* and the final chapter of Almond and Coleman's *The Politics of the Developing Areas.* These are attempts to utilize "hard data" with respect to indicators of change.

Despite the interest in the politics of development, there is still no over-all comparative study that can combine the analysis of process with that of structure. The Almond and Coleman volume is a step in that direction and therefore merits special attention. There have also been a few behavioral studies that lend themselves to comparative treatment. Indeed, L. Doob's *Becoming More Civilized* is one of the rare efforts by a psychologist to discuss the process of modernization from the point of view of the individual. As Herbert Hyman points out in the opening chapter of his book, *Political Socialization,* the wide variety of contributions that psychologists could give to the comparative study of adaptation to modernization are yet to be made. Pye's pioneering efforts to fill that gap are to be found in a variety of his works, and his forthcoming analysis of Burmese politics will have wide significance.

There is current research underway by anthropologists and psychologists that will have implications for the analysis of politics, perhaps the most important of which deals with socialization and is being conducted by D. Campbell and R. LeVine. The prospective research is outlined in the *Journal of Conflict Resolution,* March, 1961. At the University of California at Los Angeles work on the social background of elites in Jamaica is underway under the direction of Professor Wendell Bell, and a similar project has been undertaken for East and Central African political leadership by Professors James S. Coleman of the University of California at Los Angeles and Carl Rosberg of the University of California at Berkeley.

We mention these studies because the analysis of political development is itself underdeveloped. What has been undertaken so far is a blocking out of certain key variables, but all the critical interstices of analysis remain to be explored. How do political values and ideas change? What new mechanisms for handling government business have made their appearance? Indeed, is the new industrial revolution accompanied by a new managerial revolution? To what extent is political development merely a reflection of that?

Some of the more important books and articles available on the subject of political development, in addition to those indicated above, include E. Banfield, *The Moral Basis of a Backward Society;* the M.I.T. document prepared for the Senate Foreign Relations Committee, "The Objectives of United States Economic Assistance Programs"; and B. Hoselitz (ed.), *The Progress of Underdeveloped Areas.* We put these three in a group because they get at very different but equally relevant aspects of the development process.

Another interesting group includes Carter and Brown (eds.), *Transition in Africa: Studies in Political Adaptation;* Max Gluckman, *Custom and Conflict in Africa;* and L. A. Fallers, *Bantu Bureaucracy.* All these deal with political aspects of change in Africa.

Another useful cluster of books dealing with development includes P. T. Bauer and B. S. Yamey, *The Economics of Underdeveloped Countries;* W. A. Lewis, *The Theory of Economic Growth;* and H. Leibenstein, *Economic Backwardness and Economic Growth: Studies in the Theory of Economic Development.* In this connection a useful book is W. W. Rostow, *The Stages of Economic Growth: A Non-Communist Manifesto.* A good analysis of development processes is also to be found in Neil Smelser's *Social Change in the Industrial Revolution: An Application of Theory to the British Cotton Industry.*

A curious although provocative book is E. E. Hagen, *On the Theory of Social Change.* This is a book which is concerned with creativity and innovations in economic and social development. For a contrast, however, see also Ursula Hicks, *Development from Below.* In addition, there is a recent book which surveys the major problems of social change—R. Braibanti and J. J. Spengler (eds.), *Tradition, Values, and Socio-Economic Development.*

There are, of course, many works devoted to the particular study of development within a given country. Morroe Berger's *Bureaucracy and Society in Modern Egypt* is one of the best of these. Another valuable book is Philip Woodruff, *The Men Who Ruled India.* Although not comparative in their treatment, they nevertheless have implications for comparative analysis. Our theories for making such comparisons are still weak and also need some development. These and other related materials show that there is ferment on the intellectual side of the development process. The works of Pye, Shils, and Coleman would alone testify to that. And there are many others.

## NOTES

1. See E. Barker, Introduction, *The Politics of Aristotle* (Oxford: The Clarendon Press, 1948), p. xlix.

2. See Karl W. Deutsch, "Social Mobilization and Political Development," *American Political Science Review,* LV, No. 3 (September, 1961), p. 501.

3. See E. A. Shils, "Political Development in the New States" in *Comparative Studies in History and Society,* July, 1960.

4. Almond and Coleman, *The Politics of Developing Areas* (Princeton: Princeton University Press, 1960).

5. See D. Lerner, *The Passing of the Traditional Society* (New York: The Free Press, 1959), and D. Apter, *The Political Kingdom in Uganda* (Princeton: Princeton University Press, 1961).

6. See Alexis de Tocqueville, *The European Revolution and Correspondence with Gobineau* (New York: Doubleday Anchor Books, 1959), p. 123.

7. See L. P. Edwards, *The Natural History of Revolution.*

8. In an extremely interesting passage, Wilfred Cantwell Smith writes,

"The Marxist movement we may take as the largest, most resolute, organized, explicit attempt in man's development thus far to construct a good society, to control historical development and to realize within it a dream of what life for the human community should be. It is distinguished from the religions, of course, by its exclusive concern with this mundane world. It is distinguished also from Western humanisms, from the impulsion instanced in secular liberalism and in the American and French revolutions, by its intense and all-inclusive articulation, its total concentration on this one ambition. It puts every last egg in the historical basket; nothing whatever matters but the kind of history that it is sure will, and is determined shall, evolve. In its view there is no meaning, no value, and in the end no reality to human life other than its meaning as an item in the on-going historical process, as a contributor or obstacle to the kind of history that is to obtain tomorrow. It is as a means to an end, or in any case in relation to that end, an end that is given within and by history, that in Marxism the human person has significance; and this is his only significance, for himself and for others." *Islam in Modern History* (New York: Mentor Books, 1959), p. 31.

9. See Frederick Engels, Preface to Marx, *The Eighteenth Brumaire of Louis Bonaparte* (New York: International Publishers, n.d.), p. 10.

10. G. Sorel, *Reflections on Violence* (New York: The Free Press, 1950), p. 107.

11. See Karl Popper, *The Open Society and Its Enemies* (London: Routledge and Kegan Paul Ltd., 1945), Vol. II, p. 214.

12. Tocqueville said that the French Revolution "was made by a system of general ideas, forming a single body of doctrine, a kind of political gospel where every idea resembles a dogma." *Op. cit.,* p. 101.

13. See L. Trotsky, *The Revolution Betrayed* (New York: Doubleday, 1937), Chapter V.

# THE ANATOMY OF REVOLUTION

Crane Brinton

## THE OLD REGIMES

### I. The Diagnosis of Preliminary Signs

From France, which has long carried out a kind of linguistic Free Trade, comes the phrase "old regime." Applied to the history of France, it covers the society of the last two-thirds of the eighteenth century, the generation or two preceding the revolution of 1789. We may reasonably extend its use to describe the varied societies out of which our revolutions emerged. Following our conceptual scheme, we shall look in these societies for something like a revolutionary prodrome, for a set of preliminary signs of the coming revolution.

Such a search must not be undertaken without one important caution. Disorder in some sense appears to be endemic in all societies, and certainly in our Western society. The historian turned diagnostician can find evidences of disorders and discontents in almost any society he chooses to study. If a stable, or healthy, society is defined as one in which there are no expressions of discontent with the government or with existing institutions, in which no laws are ever broken, then there are no stable or healthy societies. Not even the totalitarian state, one suspects, can live up to this standard. Our normal or healthy society, then, will not be one in which there are no criticisms of the government or the ruling class, no gloomy sermons on the moral decay of the times, no Utopian dreams of a better world around the corner, no strikes, no lockouts, no unemployment, no crime waves, no New Deals. All we can expect of what we may call a healthy society is that there should be no striking excess of this sort of thing, and perhaps also that most people should behave as if they felt that, with all its faults, the society were a going concern. Then we may look about for the kind of signs just described—discontents expressed in words or deeds —and try to estimate their seriousness. We shall, of course, very soon find that we are dealing with a large number of variables, that for given societies studied in their old regimes these variables combine variously and in different proportions, and that in some cases certain variables are apparently absent altogether or nearly so. We are surely unlikely to find in all the cases we study one clear, omnipresent symptom, so that we could say: when you find x or y in a society, you know that a revolution is a month, or a year, or a decade, or any time in the future. On the contrary, symptoms are apt to be many, and by no means neatly combined in a pattern. We shall be lucky if, to borrow another medical term, they form a recognizable syndrome.

### II. Structural Weaknesses, Economic and Political

As good children of our age, we are bound to start any such study as this with the economic situation. All of us, no matter how little sympathy we may have with organized communism, betray the extent of Marx's influence in the social studies— and of the influences that influenced Marx—by the naturalness with which we ask the question: "What had economic interests to do with it all?" Now it is incontestable that in all four of the societies we are studying the years preceding the outbreak of revolution witnessed unusually serious economic, or at least financial, difficulties of a special kind. The first two Stuarts were in perpetual conflict with their parliaments over taxes, and the years just before 1640 resounded with complaints about Ship Money, benevolences, tonnage and poundage and other terms now strange to us, but once capable of making a hero of a very rich Buckinghamshire gentleman named John Hampden, who was financially quite able to pay much larger taxes than he did. Americans need not be reminded of the part trouble over taxation played in the years just before the shot fired at Concord defied all the laws of acoustics. "No taxation without representation" may be rejected by all up-to-date historians as in itself an adequate explanation of the beginnings of the American revolution, but the fact remains that it was in the 1770's a slogan capable of exciting our fathers to action. In 1789 the French Estates-General, the calling of which precipitated the revolution, was made unavoidable by the bad financial state of the government. Official France in 1789 was financially in as unhappy a way as, until our own times, one would have believed it possible for a government to be. In Russia in 1917 financial collapse did not perhaps stand out so prominently because the Czarist regime had achieved an all-round collapse in all fields of governmental activity, from war to village administration. But three years of war had put such a strain on Russian finances that, even with the support of the Allies, high prices and scarcity were by 1917 most obvious factors in the general tension.

Yet in all of these societies, it is the *government* that is in financial difficulties, not the societies themselves. To put the matter negatively, our revolutions did not occur in societies economically backward, nor in societies undergoing widespread economic misery or depression. You will not find in these societies of the old regime anything like unusually widespread economic want. In a specific instance, of course, the standard against which want or depression is measured must be the standard of living more or less acceptable to a given group at a given time. What satisfied an English peasant in 1640 would be misery and want for an Iowa farmer of 1938. It is possible that certain groups in a society may be in unusual want even though statistically that abstraction "society as a whole" is enjoying an increasing—and almost equally abstract —"national income." Nevertheless, when national income is rapidly increasing, someone does get the benefit. We must look more carefully at our four societies in this respect.

France in 1789 was a very striking example of a rich society with an impoverished government. The eighteenth century had begun to collect statistics about itself, and though these would not satisfy a modern economist they enable us to be very certain about the increasing prosperity of eighteenth-century France. Any series of indices—foreign trade, population growth, building, manufactures, agricultural production—will show a general upward trend all through the eighteenth century. Here are a few examples: wastelands all over France were being brought under the plow and in the *élection* of Melun alone in two years from 1783 to 1785 uncultivated land was reduced from 14,500 to 10,000 *arpents;* Rouen in 1787 produced annually cotton cloth worth fifty millions of *livres,* having at least doubled its production in a generation; French trade with North Africa (the Barbary Coast) increased from about 1,000,000 *livres* in 1740 to 6,216,000 *livres* in 1788; the total French foreign trade had in 1787 increased nearly 100,000,000 *livres* in the dozen years since the death of Louis XV in 1774.

Even in our imperfect statistics we can distinguish short-term cyclical variations, and it seems clear that in some respects, notably in the wheat harvest, 1788–89 was a bad year. It was, however, by no means a deep trough year like 1932 for this country. If business men in eighteenth-century France had kept charts and made graphs, the lines would have mounted with gratifying consistency through most of the period preceding the French revolution. Now this prosperity was certainly most unevenly shared. The people who got the lion's share of it seem to have been the merchants, bankers, business men, lawyers, peasants who ran their own farms as businesses; the middle class, as we have come to call it. It was precisely these prosperous people who in the 1780's were loudest against the government, most reluctant to save it by paying taxes.

In America, of course, with an empty continent available for the distressed, general economic conditions in the eighteenth century show increasing wealth and population, with economic distress a purely relative matter. There can be no talk of starvation, of grinding poverty in the New England of the Stamp Act. Even the minor fluctuations of the business cycle fail to coincide with the revolution, and the early years of the 1770's were distinctly years of prosperity. There were economic stresses and strains in colonial America, as we shall soon see, but no class ground down with poverty.

Nor is it easy to argue that early Stuart England was less prosperous than late Tudor England had been. There is rather evidence that, especially in the years of personal government which preceded the Long Parliament, England was notably prosperous. Ramsay Muir writes that "England had never known a more steady or more widely diffused prosperity and the burden of taxation was less than in any other country. The coming revolution was certainly not due to economic distress." Even in the Russia of 1917, apart from the shocking breakdown of the machinery of government under war-strain, the productive capacity of society as a whole was certainly greater than at any other time in Russian history; and to take again the long view, the economic graphs had all been mounting for Russia as a whole in the late nineteenth and early twentieth centuries, and the progress in trade and production since the abortive revolution of 1905 had been notable.

Our revolutions, then, clearly were not born in societies economically retrograde; on the contrary, they took place in societies economically progressive. This does not, of course, mean that no groups within these societies cherished grievances mainly economic in character. Two main foci for economic motives of discontent seem to stand out. First, and much the less important, is the actual misery of certain groups in a given society. No doubt in all our societies, even in America, there was a sort of submarginal group of poor people whose release from certain forms of restraint is a very important feature of revolution itself. But in studying the preliminary signs of revolution, these people are not very important. French republican historians have long insisted on the importance of the bad harvest of 1788, the cold winter of 1788–89, and the consequent sufferings of the poor. Bread was relatively dear in that spring when the Estates-General first assembled. There was apparently a tightening up of business conditions in America in 1774–75, but certainly nothing like widespread distress or unemployment. The local sufferings of Boston, considerable under the Port Bill, were really a part of the revolution itself, and not a sign. The winter of 1916–17 was certainly a bad one in Russia, with food rationing in all the cities.

The important thing to note, however, is that French and Russian history are filled with famines, plagues, bad harvests, sometimes local, sometimes national in sweep, many of which were accompanied by sporadic rioting, but in each case only one by revolution. In neither the English nor the American revolution do we find even this degree of localized want or famine. Clearly, then, the economic distress of the underprivileged, though it may well accompany a revolutionary situation, is not one of the symptoms we need dwell upon. This the subtler Marxists themselves recognize, and Trotsky has written: "In reality, the mere existence of privations is not enough to cause an insurrection; if it were, the masses would always be in revolt."

Of much greater importance is the existence among a group, or groups, of a feeling that prevailing conditions limit or hinder their economic activity. We are especially aware of this element in our American revolution, and Professor A. M. Schlesinger has shown how the prosperous merchants, their immediate interests damaged by the new imperial policy of the British government, led an agitation against the legislation of 1764 and 1765 and helped stir up a discontent among the less well-to-do which these merchants later found a bit embarrassing. No doubt, too, that many of the firm spots in the very uneven and wavering policy of the British government—the Stamp Act and subsequent disorders, the announced intention of enforcing the Navigation Act, and so on—did have momentary ill effects on business, did throw men out of work. The currency question was of course mismanaged in a day when common sense did not very effectively supplement ignorance of economic processes. The colonies were always lacking in specie, and business enterprise suffered from this lack. Paper money, to which recourse was inevitable, was also an inevitable source of further quarrels between governors and governed.

The working of economic motives to revolt among possessing classes normally inclined to support existing institutions is especially clear among the aristocrats of tidewater Virginia. Largely de-

pendent on a single crop, tobacco, used to a high standard of living, increasingly indebted to London bankers, many of the planters hoped to recoup their fortunes in the western lands they regarded as clearly belonging to Virginia. George Washington's own involvements in western land speculations make one of the favorite topics of the debunkers. By the Quebec Act of 1774, however, the British government took the trans-Allegheny lands north of the Ohio from Virginia and other claimant colonies, and incorporated them with Canada. This act gave a grievance to others besides the planter-speculator. The closing of this frontier was also an offense to a class perhaps normally more inclined to revolt—the restless woodsmen and fur traders, and the only slightly less restless small pioneer farmers who had already occupied the Appalachian valleys, and were ready to pour over into the Kentucky and Ohio country. The Quebec Act in itself does not, of course, explain the American revolution; but taken with a long series of other acts, the Stamp Act, the Navigation Act, the Molasses Act, it accounts for the feeling so evident among active and ambitious groups in America that British rule was an unnecessary and incalculable restraint, an obstacle to their full success in life.

In France the years preceding 1789 are marked by a series of measures which antagonized different groups. With striking awkwardness, the government offered with one hand what it withdrew with the other. Tax-reform efforts, never carried through, offended privileged groups without pleasing the unprivileged. Turgot's attempted introduction of *laissez-faire* into labor relations offended all the vested interests of the old guilds. The famous tariff reduction treaty with England in 1786 directly affected French textiles for the worse, increased unemployment in Normandy and other regions, and gave the employer class a grievance against the government. So, too, in seventeenth-century England, there is no doubt that the attempt to revive obsolete forms of taxation seemed to London or Bristol merchants a threat to their rising prosperity and importance.

Thus we see that certain economic grievances—usually not in the form of economic distress, but rather a feeling on the part of some of the chief enterprising groups that their opportunities for getting on in this world are unduly limited by political arrangements—would seem to be one of the symptoms of revolution. These feelings must, of course, be raised to an effective social pitch by propaganda, pressure-group action, public meetings, and preferably a few good dramatic riots, like the Boston Tea Party. As we shall see, these grievances, however close they are to the pocketbook, must be made respectable, must touch the soul. What is really but a restraint on a rising and already successful group, or on several such groups, must appear as rank injustice towards everyone in the society. Men may revolt partly or even mainly because they are hindered, or, to use Dr. George Pettee's expressive word, *cramped;* but to the world —and, save for a very few hypocrites, also to themselves—they must appear *wronged.* Revolutions cannot do without the word "justice."

All this, however, is rather less than what the Marxists seem to mean when they talk about the revolutions of the seventeenth, eighteenth, and nineteenth centuries as deliberately the work of a class-conscious bourgeoisie. Not having the benefit of the writings of Marx to go by, nor indeed those of the still little known Adam Smith, even eighteenth-century revolutionists and discontented spirits used a very non-economic vocabulary. Of course the Marxist, aided by Freud, can reply neatly that economic motivation drove these bourgeois at an un- or subconscious level. The trouble with this, from the point of view of the person brought up in the conventions of professional historical research, is that the subconscious never, or rarely, writes documents or makes speeches. If we confine ourselves to what these bourgeois said and did, we find plenty of evidence that separate groups—the American merchants, for instance—felt specific economic grievances, but no signs that bourgeois, entrepreneurs, business men, were aware that as a class their interests in free economic expansion were blocked by existing "feudal" arrangements. Indeed in France a great many business men were more annoyed by the semi-free trade treaty of 1786 with England than by any other governmental step. Certainly one finds no trace of men in England or America or France saying: "Organized feudalism is preventing the triumph of middle-class capitalism. Let us rise against it." Nor, as a matter of fact, were there in these countries just before the revolutions any serious *economic* barriers to prevent the clever lad, even in the lower classes, from making money if he possessed the money-making gifts. Dozens of careers —a Pâris-Duverney, an Edmund Burke, a John Law, a John Hancock—show this. Certainly one cannot deny that class antagonisms existed in these countries; but so far as we can judge, these class antagonisms do not seem to have a clear and simple economic basis. In twentieth-century Russia, of course, these antagonisms were expressed in the language of economics, even though here we shall probably also find that human sentiments as well as human interests are involved.

To sum up so far, if we look at economic life in these societies in the years preceding revolution, we note first that they have been on the whole prosperous; second, that their governments are chronically short of money—shorter, that is, than most governments usually are; third, that certain groups feel that governmental policies are against their particular economic interests; fourth, that, except in Russia, class economic interests are not openly advanced in propaganda as a motive for attempting to overturn existing political and social arrangements. It is interesting to note here that Professor R. B. Merriman, in a study of six seventeenth-century revolutions in England, France, the Netherlands, Spain, Portugal, and Naples, finds that they all had in common a financial origin, all began as protests against taxation.

If now we turn from the stresses and strains of economic life to the actual workings of the machinery of government, we find a much clearer situation. Here, again, we must not posit a normal condition in which this machinery works perfectly. Government here on earth is at best a rough and ready thing, and the governed will always find something to grumble about, from favoritism in distributing low-number automobile license plates to post-office pen points. But there are obviously degrees of governmental inefficiency, and degrees of patience on the part of the governed. In our four societies the governments seem to have been relatively inefficient, and the governed relatively impatient.

Indeed, the near-bankruptcy of a government in a prosperous society might be regarded as good *a priori* evidence of its inefficiency, at least in the old days when governments undertook few social or "socialized" services. France in 1789 is a striking example of a society the government of which simply no longer works well. For generations French kings and their ministers had fought the particularistic tendencies of the provinces to get out of the control of Paris by devising a whole series of agencies of centralization, which may be said in a sense to run from the *missi dominici* of Charlemagne to the *intendants* of Richelieu and Louis XIV. Almost as if they had been Anglo-Saxon, however, they destroyed very little of the old in the process, so that France in 1789 was like an attic stuffed full of all kinds of old furniture—including some fine new chairs that just wouldn't fit in the living room. We need not go too deeply into the details of the situation, which can perhaps be summed up graphically by saying that in the sense in which you could make a map of the United States showing all our administrative areas—townships, counties, states—you could not possibly make *one* map of the administrative areas of old France. Even the confusion added to an administrative map of the United States by the various, and relatively new, federal commissions, bureaus, agencies, administrations, does not begin to equal that of France in 1789. You would need at least half a dozen maps to show the criss-cross units of *paroisse, seigneurie, baillage, sénéchaussée, généralité, gouvernement, pays d'état et d'élection, les cinq grosses fermes, pays de grande et de petite gabelle*—and this is but a beginning.

There is told about Louis XV one of those revealing anecdotes the actual historical truth of which is unimportant, since they reflect contemporary opinion of a concrete condition. Traveling in the provinces, his majesty saw that a town hall or some such building in which he was to be received had a leaky roof. "Ah, if I were only a minister, I'd have that fixed," he remarked. A government of which such a tale could be told was perhaps despotic, but most certainly inefficient. In general, it would seem the inefficiency is more readily recognized by those who suffer from it than is the despotism.

The incompetence of the English government under the first two Stuarts is much less clear, but one can safely say that the central government was not as well run, especially under James I, as it had been under Elizabeth. What is most striking in the English situation is the total inadequacy to modern government of a tax system based on the modest needs of a feudal central government. For the government of James I was beginning to be a modern government, to undertake certain elementary social services, and to rest on a bureaucracy and an army that had to be paid in cash. The chronic need for money which confronted James I and Charles I was by no means a result of riotous living and courtly extravagance, but was for the most part brought on by expenses no modern government could have avoided. And yet their income was on the whole determined and collected by old-fashioned medieval methods. At any rate it is clear that the Stuarts needed money; but their attempts to fill their coffers were awkward, hand-to-mouth expedients that brought them into sharp quarrels with the only people from whom they could collect money—the gentry and the middle class. Their struggles with Parliament threw the whole machinery of English government out of gear.

In America the failure of the machinery was a double one. First, the central colonial administration in Westminster had been allowed to grow in the hit-or-miss fashion Anglophiles have long regarded as the height of political wisdom. In this crisis, however, muddling through clearly was not enough. The attempted reform in colonial administration after the Seven Years' War only made matters worse, as did Turgot's attempted reforms in France, since it was carried out in a series of advances and retreats, cajolings and menaces, blowings-hot and blowings-cold. Second, within most of the colonies the machinery of government had never been properly adjusted to the frontier. The newer western regions of many colonies complained that representation, courts, administrative areas, were rigged in favor of the older seaboard settlements.

The breakdown of Czarist administration is now so much a commonplace that one is tempted to suspect that it has been a bit exaggerated. Looking at the decades preceding 1917—for in all these countries we have been considering the background of the revolutions and not their actual outbreaks—it seems possible to maintain that the government of Russia in peacetime, at least, was perhaps a bit more of a going concern than the other governments

we have been studying. From Catherine the Great to Stolypin a great deal of actual improvement can be seen in Russian government. But one thing is clear from the hundred years preceding 1914. Russia could not organize herself for war, and failure in war had, especially in 1905, brought with it a partial collapse of the machinery of internal administration. We must be very careful here to stick to facts and to avoid judgments which have so insinuated themselves into our awareness of Russia that we regard them as facts. It may be that there is some wild oriental element in the Russian soul that makes Russians both incompetent and submissive politically, subject, however, to fits of alcoholic rebellion. This soul is certainly very hard to observe scientifically; and even in literature one may hesitate to label Dostoevski more Russian than Turgenev, who seems far from wild, oriental, drunken or mystic. For our purposes, it is sufficient to note that the Russian *governmental* breakdown, clear in 1917 or even 1916, was by no means clear, say in 1912.

Finally, one of the most evident uniformities we can record is the effort made in each of our societies to reform the machinery of government. Nothing can be more erroneous than the picture of the old regime as an unregenerate tyranny, sweeping to its end in a climax of despotic indifference to the clamor of its abused subjects. Charles I was working to "modernize" his government, to introduce into England some of the efficient methods of the French. Strafford is in some ways but an unlucky Richelieu. George III and his ministers were trying very hard to pull together the scattered organs of British colonial government. Indeed, it was this attempt at reform, this desire to work out a new colonial "system," that gave the revolutionary movement in America a start. In both France and Russia, there is a series of attempted reforms, associated with names like Turgot, Malesherbes, Necker, and Stolypin. It is true that these reforms were incomplete, that they were repealed or nullified by sabotage on the part of the privileged. But they are on the record, an essential part of the process that issued in revolution in these countries.

### III. The Desertion of the Intellectuals

So far we have fixed our attention on the machinery of economic and political life, and have tried to distinguish signs of any approaching breakdown. Let us now turn to the state of mind—or better, feeling—of various groups within these societies. First we may ask the question, does the disorganization of the government find a counterpart in the organization of its opponents? We shall have later to deal with what are nowadays well known as "pressure groups," men and women organized in societies with special aims, societies which bring all sorts of pressure—from propaganda and lobbying to terrorism—to the attaining of their aims. Such societies in one form or another are apparently a constituent part of all modern states and the mere fact of their existence cannot be taken as a symptom of revolution, or we should have to regard the A.S.P.C.A. or anti-billboard associations as signs of a coming second American revolution. There seems to be no simple and sole test to determine when and under what conditions the existence of pressure groups may be taken as a symptom of approaching political instability. The pre-revolutionary decades in our four societies do show, however, an intensity of action on the part of pressure groups, an action more and more directed as time goes on towards the radical alteration of existing government. Certain groups, indeed, begin to go beyond lobbying and propaganda, begin to plan and organize direct action, or at least a supplanting of the government in some dramatic way.

In America the merchant's committees organized to resist measures for imperial control did a great deal of quite modern pressure-group work, from straight propaganda to stirring up popular demonstrations and to intercolonial co-operation through resolutions, conferences, and so on. They form the prelude to those efficient revolutionary cells, the correspondence committees Sam Adams handled so well in the 1770's. Similar organizations are to be found lower down the social scale, where they edge over into boisterous tavern parties. In many of the colonies, the legislatures could be used for pressure-group work against the imperial government in a way not possible in the other societies we are studying. The New England town meeting provided a ready-made framework for this kind of agitation.

In France, the work of Cochin has shown how what he calls the *sociétés de pensée,* informal groups gathered together to discuss the great work of the Enlightenment, gradually turned to political agitation and finally helped steer elections to the Estates-General of 1789. Though the official school of historians in the Third Republic has always distrusted such notions, it is difficult for an outsider not to feel that Cochin has put his finger on the essential form of group action which turned mere talk and speculation into revolutionary political work. Freemasonry, even French Republican historians admit, had a place in the preparation of the revolution. Masonic activity in eighteenth-century France was clearly no dark plot, but it certainly was far from being purely social, recreational, or educational. Almost all the ambitious nobles and bankers, almost all the intellectuals were freemasons. Even at the time, clerical conservatives were shocked at what they considered the subversive aspects of freemasonry.

In Russia, societies of all degrees of hostility to things as they were had long flourished. Nihilists, anarchists, socialists of all stripes, liberals, westernizers, and anti-westernizers, expressed themselves in various ways from bomb-throwing to voting at Duma elections. One gathers from a consideration of the last years of the Czarist regime that the diversity and cross-purposes of its opponents did much to keep that regime in the saddle. Certainly the Russian revolution had plenty of advance publicity, and the role of pressure groups in its preparation is singularly clear.

England here is a less clear case. Nevertheless there are definite indications of systematic opposition of merchants and some of the gentry to measures like Ship Money, and the parliamentary majorities which were rolled up against Charles after the period of personal government were the product of embryo pressure groups, as a glance at the very prolific pamphlet literature of the time will show. Moreover, the English revolution was the last of the great social overturns within the active domination of specifically Christian ideas. In a sense, the pressure groups most obvious in seventeenth-century England are simply the Puritan churches, and especially the churches called Independent. Their very existence was as much a menace to Charles as was that of the Bolshevik party to Nicholas.

It must be noted that some of these pressure groups, the American merchant's committees, the French *sociétés de pensée* and freemasons, for instance, would not in the heyday of their action have admitted they were working for a revolution, certainly not for a violent revolution. What perhaps separates them from pressure groups like the A.S.P.C.A. or anti-billboard associations—which we can surely agree are not to be taken as symptomatic of revolution—is their basic aim at a radical change in important political processes. Thus the American merchants were really aiming to reverse the whole new imperial policy of Westminister; the French who prepared the elections to the Third Estate were aiming at a new "constitution" for France. On the other hand, some of the Russian organizations were from the very start violently revolutionary; but these were not the important elements in the Russian situation from 1905 to 1917, any more than the antinomians or anarchistic religious sects were in England before 1639.

There were, then, pressure groups with purposes more or less revolutionary in all these societies. Their activity is seen against a background of political and moral discussion which in these societies seems particularly intense. We come now to a symptom of revolution well brought out in Mr. Lyford P. Edwards's *Natural History of Revolution,* and there described as the "transfer of the allegiance of the intellectuals." Although the word "desertion" has perhaps unfortunate moral overtones, the shorter phrase "desertion of the intellectuals" is so much more convenient that we propose to use it, rather than the longer one, in this study.

We must, however, be clear as to what we are

talking about before we attempt to use the desertion of the intellectuals as a symptom. Intellectuals we may define without undue worry over preciseness as the writers, teachers, and preachers. Further subdivision into the small group of leaders who initiate, or at least stand prominently in the public eye, and the larger group who grind over material they get from the leaders, is not of major importance here. What is important, and somewhat puzzling, is the general position of the intellectuals in our Western society since the Middle Ages. Clearly we must not posit agreement among its intellectuals before we decide that a given society is reasonably stable. Even in the thirteenth century, in which so many of our contemporary thinkers find an enviable unanimity as to fundamentals of belief, the amount of bickering among the intellectuals was in reality very considerable. There were rebels and prophets aplenty throughout the Middle Ages. In modern times we expect the intellectuals to disagree. Moreover, for a number of reasons, writers, teachers, and preachers are to a large degree committed by their function to take a critical attitude towards the daily routine of human affairs. Lacking experience of action under the burden of responsibility, they do not learn how little *new* action is usually possible or effective. An intellectual as satisfied with the world as with himself would simply not be an intellectual.

Here, as so often in the social sciences, and indeed in the natural sciences, we are dealing with a question where quantitative and qualitative differences shade most confusingly one into the other. Quantitatively, we may say that in a society markedly unstable there seem to be absolutely more intellectuals, at any rate comparatively more intellectuals, bitterly attacking existing institutions and desirous of a considerable alteration in society, business, and government. Purely metaphorically, we may compare intellectuals of this sort to the white corpuscles, guardians of the bloodstream; but there can be an excess of white corpuscles, and when this happens you have a diseased condition.

Qualitatively, we may discern a difference of attitude, partly, no doubt, produced by the numbers and unity of these intellectuals in attack, but partly produced by a subtler reality. Victorian England, for instance, was a society in equilibrium, an equilibrium now in retrospect a bit unstable, but still an equilibrium. Here Carlyle upbraided a generation addicted to Morison's Pills instead of to heroes. Mill worried uncomfortably over the tyranny of the majority, Matthew Arnold found England short of sweetness and light, Newman sought at Rome an antidote for the poison of English liberalism, Morris urged his countrymen to break up machines and return to the comforts of the Middle Ages, and even Tennyson was worried over his failure to attain to anything more useful than a high, vague, and philosophical discontent. Many,

though by no means all, Victorian intellectuals were in disagreement among themselves, united apparently in nothing but a profound dislike for their environment. If, however, you look at them carefully you will find a curious agreement that not too much is to be done right away to remedy matters. It is not, as we are told so often of the scholastic intellectuals of the Middle Ages, that these Victorians were in agreement on fundamental metaphysical and theological assumptions. They weren't in any such agreement. It is rather that they were in agreement about the less dignified but in some ways more important routines and habits of daily life, and they did not expect the government to change such matters.

The difference between the intellectual atmosphere of a group like the Victorians, writers who cannot be said as a whole to have deserted, and a group which has deserted, will be clear in a moment if we look at that famous group in eighteenth-century France which stood at the center of the great Enlightenment. One has first the impression of immense numbers of intellectuals, great and small, all studying matters political and sociological, all convinced that the world, and especially France, needs making over from the tiniest and more insignificant details to the most general moral and legal principles. Any of the textbooks will give you the roll—Voltaire, Rousseau, Diderot, Raynal, d'Holbach, Volney, Helvétius, d'Alembert, Condorcet, Bernardin de St. Pierre, Beaumarchais—rebels all, men leveling their wit against Church and State or seeking in Nature a perfection that ought to be in France. You will hardly find active literary conservatives like Sam Johnson or Sir Walter Scott, nor even literary neutrals, men pursuing in letters a beauty or an understanding quite outside politics.

Literature in late eighteenth-century France is overwhelmingly sociological. If you look in the yellowing remains of French eighteenth-century journalism, if you try to reconstruct the chatter of salons and clubs, you will find the same chorus of complaints and criticisms of existing institutions, the same search for Nature's simple plan of perfection in politics. There is both a bitterness and a completeness in this chorus of complaint that you will not find in Victorian complaints. Statistically, one might establish the fact that there were proportionately more intellectuals "against the government" in eighteenth-century France than in nineteenth-century England. But the difference goes beyond statistics, and into what we have called the qualitative difference. The French have a tone, at once more bitter and more hopeful, quite different from the Victorians. That this is not altogether a national difference will be clear to anyone reading the pamphlet literature of the age of Milton. Then the English intellectuals had deserted, as they had not under Victoria.

Russia, too, is a clear example of this desertion of the intellectuals. There is certainly much more than political propaganda in the series of novelists who have made Russian literature a part of the education of us all. But there is unmistakably political and social criticism of Czarist Russia even in the work of the most Olympian of them, Turgenev. And the impression one gets from even a cursory view of Russian intellectual life in the nineteenth and early twentieth centuries is unmistakable; to write, teach, or preach in those days meant being against the government. There are exceptions, and degrees of opposition, but the above statement would probably be accepted even by present-day Russian exiles.

America is not so neat an instance. In Boston, for instance, in the 1760's and 70's, a good many of the kind of people we are discussing—intellectuals will have to do—were as firmly as such people are now against so un-Bostonian an activity as sedition. It is clear that Harvard was by no means unanimous against the Crown, let alone in favor of the democratic machinations of her distinguished alumnus, Sam Adams. But if the literary and journalistic output in the colonies between 1750 and 1775—and even if we include the sermons—could be statistically assigned as either for or against the actual policies of the imperial government, there seems little doubt as to the very considerable balance against these policies. The Enlightenment, especially through Locke and Montesquieu, had come to the American colonies. The natural and inalienable rights of man were in this country, as in Europe, concepts introduced by intellectuals.

England may seem at first sight an exception to the desertion of the intellectuals. Lovelace, Suckling, even Donne seem hardly preoccupied with sociology. Yet at a second glance it is quite clear the English literature under the first two Stuarts is far from being the chorus of loyal praise it was in the days of Queen Bess. A glance into Professor Grierson's *Cross Currents in English Literature in the Seventeenth Century* will show how much that literature was a dissolvent of the merry England of the Renaissance. Even more important is the fact that in those days there were no real newspapers, and the pamphlet took their place. Now the pamphlet literature of the early seventeenth century in England, quantitatively enormous, even by modern standards, is almost wholly preoccupied with religion or politics—better, religion *and* politics—about as good an example of the desertion of the intellectuals as could be found. Indeed, as Professor Gooch has written, in the reign of James I "proclamation followed proclamation against the sale of 'Seditious and Puritan books,' and there was 'much talk of libels and dangerous writings.'"

To what do these intellectuals desert? To another and better world than that of the corrupt and inefficient old regimes. From a thousand pens and voices there are built up in the years before the revolution actually breaks out what one must now fashionably call the foundations of the revolutionary myth—or folklore, or symbols, or ideology. Some such better world of the ideal is contrasted with this immediate and imperfect world in all the ethical and religious systems under which Western men have lived, and notably in Christianity. It is not quite accurate to assert that for medieval Christianity the other, ideal world is safely put off to heaven. Yet it is clear that with the Reformation and the Renaissance men began to think more earnestly about bringing part of heaven, at any rate, to this earth. What differentiates this ideal world of the revolutionaries from the better world as conceived by more pedestrian persons is a flaming sense of the immediacy of the ideal, a feeling that there is something in all men better than their present fate, a conviction that what is, not only ought not, but need not, be.

We shall later meet these revolutionary ideals in their fully developed forms. Here we need only notice that in the writings and preachings of the English Puritans—and to a lesser extent the constitutional lawyers—in those of the eighteenth-century *philosophes,* in those of the nineteenth- and twentieth-century Marxists, the evil, and indeed illegitimate existing regime is very effectively contrasted with the good, and indeed inevitable, rule of right to come. In England, America, and in France, the essential principle to which men appealed against present conditions was Nature, with its clear and simple laws. Ship Money in England, Stamp Act in America, patents of nobility in France, were all contrary to the law of Nature. Even in England and America, where there was also much appeal to rights to be found in Magna Charta or the common law, the final appeal was always to a law of Nature "engraved in the hearts of men." As the Puritan Henry Parker wrote in England, the common courts were "furnished only with rules of particular justice, which rules being too narrow for so capacious a subject [the relation of Crown to People] we must refer to those that the original laws of Nature hold out to us." By the eighteenth century this kind of language had become almost universal among intellectuals. That Nature always counseled what the intellectuals in revolt wanted is an observation we must in these days feel bound to make. It seems likely, however, that for most of those who appealed to her Nature was as definite and explicit as God had once been, and as dialectical materialism was to be.

For the Russian writers and agitators of the Czarist regime, Nature did not play so prominent a part. Not that Nature is lacking in the pages of Tolstoy and his follows, and the contrast between "artificial" society and "natural" instincts was not disdained even in Socialist propaganda. But the official ideology of most of the Russian radicals was Marxism, and Marxism finds that the existence of capitalists, the rule of the bourgeoisie, is altogether natural. Only, its destruction by the proletariat is also natural, and this destruction is determined by forces quite beyond capitalistic control. The inevitable march of economic forces would then for the Marxists accomplish what the English Puritan expected from God and the French *philosophe* from Nature and Reason. The essential thing all these pre-revolutionary agitators have in common, the essential ingredient, intellectually at least, in the revolutionary myth, is this abstract, all-powerful force, this perfect ally.

One special point is here worth our attention for a moment. Not only does God, Nature, or dialectical materialism make the victory of the present under-dog certain. The present upper-dog can be shown—perhaps for propaganda purposes *must* be shown—to have acquired his preponderance by an accident, or a particularly dirty trick, while God or Nature was temporarily off duty. Thus in the English revolution the royalists and indeed the gentry as a whole were labeled "Normans," descendants of a group of foreign invaders with no right to English soil. John Lilburne, the Leveller, goes so far as to assert that the whole common law was a badge of slavery imposed upon the free people of England by the Norman Conquest. American hatred of absentee British government hardly needed such artificial fanning. The French were told by no less a person than Siéyès that all their trouble came from the usurpations of the Franks over a thousand years ago. French noblemen in 1789 were descendants of barbarous Germans, while French commoners were descendants of civilized Gauls and Romans. Revolution was but restoring the conditions of A.D. 450. Marxism explained the exploiting class without recourse to such pseudo-historical notions. And yet there is plenty of reference in Russian revolutionary agitation to the usurpation of land by the nobles, to their Varangian, or Tartar, or Western, or at any rate foreign origins.

Finally, a great deal of energy has been expended on the question as to whether this revolutionary ideology "causes" revolutionary action, or whether it is merely a sort of superfluous decoration with which the revolutionists cover their real acts and real motives. Most of this discussion is in the highest degree futile, since it is based on a crude notion of causation altogether untenable in fruitful scientific work beyond a very simple level. There is no more point disputing whether Rousseau made the French revolution or the French revolution made Rousseau than in disputing whether egg or chicken came first. We note that in our pre-revolutionary societies the kind of discontents, the specific difficulties about economic, social and political conditions that hard-boiled moderns focus on are invariably accompanied by a very great deal of writing

and talking about ideals, about a better world, about some very abstract forces tending to bring about that better world. It is, indeed, the *expression* of ideas, rather than particular ideas—which may vary enormously in different revolutions—that makes the uniformity. We find that ideas are always a part of the pre-revolutionary situation, and we are quite content to let it go at that. No ideas, no revolution. This does not mean that ideas cause revolutions. It merely means that they form part of the mutually dependent variables we are studying.

## IV. Classes and Class Antagonisms

Certain groups in our four societies of the old regimes nourished feelings of dislike, mixed or unmixed with contempt, for other groups. If we avoid the narrow economic connotations of the term, we may call these groups classes; if we realize the struggle was not simply one between two contending classes, feudal vs. bourgeois or bourgeois vs. proletariat, we may even speak of class struggles. This type of struggle in one form or another seems as endemic as many other kinds of violence in the stablest of Western societies. Here again we must not postulate for the normal society with which we contrast our pre-revolutionary societies, a lying down together of the lion and the lamb. But even so, it will soon appear that these class hatreds are stepped up, exacerbated in a noticeable degree in the old regimes. Class distinctions are seen, not as barriers the clever, brave, or ambitious can cross, but as unnatural and unjust privileges, established by wicked men against the express intention of Almighty God, Nature, or Science. These class struggles are by no means simple duels; there are groups within groups, currents within currents. We must try and analyze some of these currents.

In the first place, what may be called the ruling class seems in all four of our societies to be divided and inept. By ruling class we understand, it may be too generously, the people who run things, the people in the public eye—the politicians, the important civil servants, the bankers, the men of affairs, the great landowning nobles, the officers, the priesthood, perhaps even some of the intellectuals. Formal nobility of the blood has in the Western world usually been a much too narrow test of membership in a ruling class. Even in early modern times, the ruling class was something like what we have outlined above, the minority of men and women who seemed to lead dramatic lives, about whom the more exciting scandals arose, who set the fashion, who had wealth, position, or at least reputation, who, in short, ruled. Indeed, in a socially stable society it seems likely that the great masses of poor and middling folk, as also the obscure and unsuccessful people who by birth and training might seem to be in the ruling class, really accept the leadership of those at the top of the social pyramid, and dream rather of *joining* them than of *dislodging* them.

Now the ruling classes in our societies seem, and not simply *a posteriori* because they were in fact overthrown, to have been unsuccessful in fulfilling their functions. It is unlikely that short of Sparta or Prussia the simpler military virtues alone are enough for a ruling class. Such a class ought not, however, to shrink from the use of force to maintain itself, and it ought not to value wit and originality in its own members too highly. Wit, at any rate, it can usually hire adequately enough from other sources. A mixture of the military virtues, of respect for established ways of thinking and behaving, and of willingness to compromise, is probably an adequate rough approximation of the qualities of a successful ruling class—qualities clearly possessed by the Romans of Punic War times, and the English of the eighteenth century, though the latter failed in relations with America.

When numerous and influential members of such a class begin to believe that they hold power unjustly, or that all men are brothers, equal in the eyes of eternal justice, or that the beliefs they were brought up on are silly, or that "after us the deluge," they are not likely to resist successfully any serious attacks on their social, economic and political position. The subject of the decadence of a ruling class, and the relation of this decadence to revolution, is a fascinating and, like so much of sociology, a relatively unexplored subject. We can here do no more than suggest that this decadence is not necessarily a "moral" decadence if by "moral" you mean what a good evangelical Christian means by that word. Successful ruling classes have not infrequently been quite addicted to cruel sports, drinking, gambling, adultery, and other similar pursuits which we should no doubt all agree to condemn. It is a reasonable assertion that the virtuous Lafayette was a much clearer sign of the unfitness of the French aristocracy to rule than were Pompadour or even Du Barry.

The Russians here provide us with a *locus classicus*. To judge from what appears of them in print, Russian aristocrats for decades before 1917 had been in the habit of bemoaning the futility of life, the backwardness of Russia, the Slavic sorrows of their condition. No doubt this is an exaggeration. But clearly many of the Russian ruling classes had an uneasy feeling that their privileges would not last. Many of them, like Tolstoy, went over to the other side. Others turned liberal, and began that process of granting concessions here and withdrawing them there that we have already noticed in France. Even in court circles, it was quite the fashion by 1916 to ridicule the Czar and his intimates. As Protopopov, a hated Czarist minister, writes:

Even the very highest classes became *frondeurs* before the revolution; in the grand salons and clubs the policy of the government received harsh and unfriendly criticism. The relations which had been formed in the Czar's family were analyzed and talked over. Little anecdotes were passed about the head of the state. Verses were composed. Many grand dukes openly attended these meetings. . . . A sense of the danger of this sport did not awaken until the last moment.

Finally, when those of them who had positions of political power did use force, they used it sporadically and inefficiently. We shall have more to say about this general problem of the use of force when we come to the first stages of actual revolution. In this connection it will be sufficient that the Russian ruling classes, in spite of their celebrated Asiatic background, were by the late nineteenth century more than half ashamed to use force, and therefore used it badly, so that on the whole those on whom force was inflicted were stimulated rather than repressed. The line in actual practice of government between force and persuasion is a subtle one, not to be drawn by formulas, by "science" or textbooks, but by men skilled in the art of ruling. One of the best signs of the unfitness of the ruling class to rule is the absence of this skill among its members. And this absence is recorded in history in the cumulated minor disturbances and discontents which precede revolution.

Russia remains the classic instance of an inept ruling class, but France is almost as good a case. The salons in which the old regime was torn apart—verbally, of course—were presided over by noblewomen and attended by noblemen. Princes of the blood royal became freemasons, and if they did not quite plot the overthrow of all decency, as witch-hunters like Mrs. Nesta Webster seem to think, at least sought to improve themselves out of their privileges and rank. Perhaps nowhere better than in France is to be seen one of the concomitants of the kind of disintegration of the ruling class we have been discussing. This is the deliberate espousal by members of the ruling class of the cause of discontented or repressed classes—upperdogs voluntarily turning under-dogs. It is not altogether cynical to hazard the guess that this is sometimes an indication that there is about to be a reversal in the position of the dogs. Lafayette is in some ways a good example of this kind of upperdog, since he seems to have been an unintelligent and ambitious man, whose course was largely determined by fashion. Lafayette tried to do what his own circle would most admire, and since he could not dance well—and his circle admired good dancing—he went to fight for freedom in America, which was also something his circle admired. But ruling classes cannot profitably fight for freedom—freedom, that is, for the other fellow.

In America this decadence of a ruling class is not a prominent symptom of the coming revolution. Our native ruling class was still young, still in the process of formation, and seen as a class exhibited none of the ineptness we have noted in Russia and France. But of course a large part of our ruling class espoused the American revolution, which is probably one of the reasons why our revolution stopped short of a full-blooded Reign of Terror. As far as the ruling class in England at the time of our revolution is concerned, it was very far from being capable of a resolute course towards America. It managed to hold on in England in the eighteenth and nineteenth centuries, but only by granting concessions to the middle classes, concessions which its French counterpart refused to grant. Many of these Englishmen were, however, anything but defenders of the established order as regards relations with America. Fox, Burke, the Whigs in general, sided with the Americans even after 1775, and their attitude unquestionably helped give the rebellious Americans heart.

Even in seventeenth-century England this sort of symptom is to be discerned. In the English aristocracy of Jacobean times there is not, of course, exactly the same mixture of weariness, doubt, humanitarian hopes, and irresponsibility we have found in Russia or in France. Yet most of these elements can be found in the group later known as Cavaliers. Picturesque, romantic, appealing though the Cavaliers seem to us now in literature and tradition, it would be hard to maintain that they displayed the solidarity and balance necessary to a ruling class. And the Cavalier legend is not wholly a product of the years after the Great Rebellion. The Cavaliers were romantic even to themselves, and in a harsh world of Puritans and money-making had already begun that search for a golden past so characteristic of the émigrés of later revolutions. Nor are the enlightened or inspired, the Lafayettes or the Tolstoys, altogether lacking in the English ruling classes of the time. Even though you accept the nineteenth-century evaluation of the English as always hard-headed, practical, compromise-loving, you will do well to recall that a Tudor gentleman gave the word "Utopia" to political thought, and that Harrington's famous Utopia, *Oceana,* is a seventeenth-century product.

Still, what conceals from us the extent to which many able and ambitious English gentlemen had deserted the established order in early Stuart times is that they deserted, not as did Lafayette, to America and the abstract rights of man, but to God and the way of salvation. Puritanism, in one or another of its many forms, proved attractive not merely to humble men, nor even to traders and bankers, but to many of the gentry and the nobility. Do not forget that Cromwell himself was a gentleman. Finally, what we may call the politico-legal opposition to the first two Stuarts—though separation of political and religious for that time is purely a matter of analysis, the two being inextricably mixed in the feelings of contemporaries—this po-

litico-legal opposition was, as far as leadership went, almost wholly recruited from gentry and nobility. Men like Hampden and Essex resemble Washington in that they are essentially conservatives driven to rebellion by the ineptness of their immediate rulers; they are not, like Lafayette, sentimental deserters of their class.

Except perhaps in America, we find the ruling classes in the old regimes markedly divided, markedly unsuited to fulfill the functions of a ruling class. Some have joined the intellectuals and deserted the established order, have indeed often become leaders in the crusade for a new order; others have turned rebels, less because of hope for the future than because of boredom with the present; others have gone soft, or indifferent, or cynical. Many, possibly even most of the rank-and-file of the ruling classes, the English squire, the French and Russian country nobleman, retained the simple faith in themselves and their position which is apparently necessary to a ruling class. But the tone of life in the upper classes was not set by such as these. Fashion had deserted with the intellectuals. The sober virtues, the whole complex series of value-judgments which guards a privileged class from itself and others, all these were out of fashion at Whitehall, at Versailles, at the old court of St. Petersburg. *Esprit de corps* is a subtle thing, difficult, indeed impossible, to analyze with the methods of the chemist or the statistician. The intricate balance of sentiments and habits which hold men together in any such group as those we have been discussing may be altered by changes apparently insignificant, and extremely difficult to trace. But the fact of the alteration is clear. The very wit, refinement, the cultural graces so evident in what we know of the Cavaliers, the French aristocrats of Versailles and the salons, the Russian upper classes of the ballet, the opera, the novel, are signs of the decadence, not necessarily moral, but certainly political, of a ruling class.

Nor is it possible, even for those who find the simple forms of the economic interpretation of history inadequate and misleading, to deny that in three of our societies—England, France, and Russia—there are clear signs that the ruling classes were in a very shaky economic position. In each case there had been a notable rise in the standards of living of the nobility and gentry; finer houses, finer clothes, the luxuries brought by the decorative arts, by sculpture, painting, and music all cost a great deal of money, and were not in a purely economic sense good investments. Though the prohibitions against a gentleman's making money in business were by no means as absolute, even in France, as they sometimes appear in textbooks of history, it is a fact that most gentlemen had neither the gifts nor the training for such money-making. Most of them lived from agricultural rents, which could not be stretched to meet their rising costs, and from pensions, sinecures, and other aids from the government, which were at least as inelastic. Notably for the French and Russian upper classes, it is clear that some of the discontent which undermined their *esprit de corps* at the outbreak of the revolution had its origin in their economic difficulties.

So much for the upper or ruling classes. The classes immediately beneath them in the social structure display in England, France, and Russia, and to a lesser degree in America, a more than ordinary dislike for their superiors. Here once more we are confronted with the problem of what is normal in class relationships in Western societies. The view that in a normal society there are no class antagonisms is as much to be rejected as the Marxist view that in such societies—at least up to the present—the class struggle has been unceasingly and equally bitter and ferocious. A picture of our Old South, for instance, which sees contented, well-fed slaves, prosperous artisans and traders with no dislike for their gentlemanly patrons, a serene plantation aristocracy nobly patriarchal, is plain nonsense; but so, too, is one which sees only smoldering discontent among the slaves, envy and hatred among poor whites, pride and fear among the planters. Men in Western societies have never been free, equal, and brothers; there has always been political, social, and economic inequality among groups within these societies, groups we commonly call classes. The existence of antagonisms among classes is a fact, however much it may be to the interest of the ruling class to deny it. But the various antagonisms, by no means purely economic, which set class against class are in a normal society subordinated to other concerns, wider or narrower, cut across by other conflicts, subdued by other interests. At any rate they are not concentrated, embittered, strengthened by an almost unanimous support from the intellectuals, as we shall find they were in the old regimes we are studying.

In England, where we have usually been taught to believe that class hatreds were minimized by the good relations between country gentlemen and villagers, by the absorption of younger sons of the nobility in the middle classes, by some English sense of solidarity and decency, the seventeenth century saw a bitter class struggle. The following quotation from Mrs. Lucy Hutchinson is not only a fair specimen of the feelings of a middle-class Puritan towards the nobility; it can stand as a sample of the kind of intense, and always highly moral, atmosphere of such class antagonisms in other prerevolutionary societies:

The court of the King [James I] was a nursery of lust and intemperance . . . the nobility of the land was utterly debased. . . . The generality of the gentry of the land soon learned the court fashion, and every great house in the country soon became a sty of uncleanness. Then began murder, incest, adultery, drunkenness, swearing, fornication, and all sorts of ribaldry to be countenanced vices because they held such conformity to the court example.

Or, more gently:

> courtesy,
> Which oft is sooner found in lowly sheds
> With smoky rafters, than in tapst'ry halls
> And courts of princes, where it first was nam'd
> And yet is most pretended.

This was not written by an eighteenth-century disciple of Rousseau, but by John Milton.

We need hardly labor the point that both the French and the Russian middle classes hated, and envied, and felt morally superior to their aristocracies, and that their writings are filled with passages indicative of the strength and spread of these sentiments. At fourteen years Manon Phlipon, later as Madame Roland something more than Egeria to the Girondin party, told her mother after a week spent with a lady of the suite of the Dauphiness, "Another few days and I shall detest these people so much that I shan't be able to control my hatred." And to her mother's question as to what harm these aristocrats did her she answered, "It's just feeling the injustice, thinking every moment about the absurdity of it all." The higher the French bourgeois rose, the closer he came in his way of life to the aristocracy, the more vividly in some respects he felt the gap which separated him from his neighbor with four quarters of nobility. "It wasn't the taxes," wrote Rivarol in his memoirs,

. . . nor the *lettres de cachet,* nor all the other abuses of authority; it wasn't the vexations of the *intendants,* nor the ruinous delays of justice which most irritated the nation; it was the prejudice of nobility. What proves this is that it was the bourgeois, the men of letters, the financiers, in fine all those who were envious of the nobility, who raised against the nobility the petty bourgeois of the towns and the peasants in the country.

How far the lower classes or the proletariat really were stirred against their betters in these societies is not wholly clear, save perhaps in Russia. In England there can be little doubt that the more prosperous artisan classes in the big cities, and in regions like East Anglia the peasantry, were won over to Puritanism; and this meant hostility to the Anglican upper classes. Mixed inextricably with the religious fervor and phrases of the pamphlet literature is a great deal of social hatred, which later came out fully as the revolution moved towards its radical extreme. The French peasantry in many, perhaps most regions, showed by acts in 1789 that they hated their absentee landlords, or the institutions of land tenure, but conclusive evidence that this hatred was much stronger and more universal than it had been for several hundred years has not yet been produced. We cannot be sure whether they hated individuals or a status. Certainly the old notion, evident even in the work of Taine, that the French peasantry were in 1789 smarting under a sharpened double oppression from government and from *seigneurs,* is at least a revolutionary myth rather than an historical fact. A great deal of work remains to be done in the objective study of the actual sentiments of suppressed or oppressed classes at the bottom of the social scale.

The Russian proletariat, at least in the cities, had certainly been exposed to several generations of Marxist propaganda, and had acquired, so far as its elite goes, a sense of mission against nobles and middle class alike. As the first manifesto of the Social Democratic party, issued in 1898 before the split between Mensheviks and Bolsheviks, put it:

> The farther one goes to the East of Europe the weaker, baser and more cowardly becomes the bourgeoisie and the larger cultural and political tasks fall to the lot of the proletariat. On its strong shoulders the Russian working class must bear and will bear the cause of conquering political liberty. This is necessary, but only as the first step toward the achievement of the great historic mission of the proletariat: the creation of a social order in which there will be no place for the exploitation of man by man. The Russian proletariat will cast off from itself the yoke of the autocracy in order with all the greater energy to continue the struggle with capitalism and with the bourgeoisie until the final victory of socialism.

Just how the Russian peasants felt towards classes above them is a difficult problem. We may assume a good deal of variety, as also in eighteenth-century France, depending on local conditions, the character of the landlord, the prosperity of the peasants themselves. There is some indication that by the twentieth century one can risk the generalization: the more prosperous the peasants, the more discontented. But here, as throughout the range of our study, trustworthy materials of one kind are scarce: neither historians nor sociologists have paid sufficient systematic attention to the *sentiments* towards other groups which seem to prevail in a given social group or class.

We have noted the ineptness of the ruling classes, and the existence among the middle and parts of the lower of more than normally strong sentiments hostile to the ruling classes. It remains to consider how far these class lines were rigid, how far, in particular, the "career open to talents" existed in these societies. One might well argue *a priori* that in Western societies any approach to a rigid caste-system which would bar the possibility of rise to the able but low-born, any stoppage of what Pareto calls the *circulation of the elites,* would be a very important preliminary symptom of revolution. Able men do seem to get born in the humblest ranks, and an accumulation of able and discontented men would provide splendid natural leaders for groups restive and ready for revolt. Yet this test

of the career open to talents is one of the hardest to apply to our societies. The normal standard for a Western society is here very difficult indeed to sketch, even as roughly as we have done for our other variables.

One might start with a characteristic American assumption, and say that in this country at least we have full freedom of opportunity. Very well, let us take at random some self-made contemporaries— Babe Ruth, Henry Ford, Rudy Vallée, Sinclair Lewis. It would be comforting to be able to say confidently that in the societies of the old regimes these able men would have been kept down by hard-and-fast caste lines, condemned to obscurity or to revolt. Unfortunately, it would not be true. We must not, indeed, be indecently sure about such hypothetical matters. The professional athlete as such could probably not have attained in any other society than our own the wealth Mr. Ruth has nor as much honor—public attention, if you prefer— save perhaps in the Rome of the gladiators. Yet in early feudal society sheer physical strength might have won him knighthood, and even in later societies noble patronage might have carried him far. Mr. Ford may be taken as the entrepreneur-inventor, and though one doubts whether any other society than our own would have made him a national hero, it is likely that in eighteenth-century France or in twentieth-century Russia he could have secured substantial financial success. Mr. Vallée is the man who amuses, and Western society has usually rewarded adequately, and sometimes highly, those who could amuse it. Perhaps aristocracies have never quite concealed their contempt and democracies have made no attempt to conceal their admiration for those who amused them. Yet actors, musicians, jesters, and their like seem not, in spite of the example of Figaro, to have been greatly irked by their social status in the past. Certainly the French eighteenth century was kind enough to them, even economically. As for Mr. Lewis, he would presumably have been in his element among the *philosophes,* and with proper national and racial adjustments, among the Gorkys and the Chekhovs. He would have made proportionately quite as much money, and have been even more honored.

We are dealing with very subtle variables of human sentiments. At all times and in all societies, probably, some men feel that they have abilities which are denied free play by existing social, political, and economic restrictions. Some men always feel balked, cramped, kept-down, and some of them really are. Probably in societies on the eve of revolution there are very large numbers of such men. Yet it is very difficult to put one's finger on those kinds of activity, those fields of distinction, where this restraint is most felt. Here as elsewhere the given situation is always a complex of restraints, no one or two or three of which would, without additional elements of disturbance, be anything but a quite normal social fact. Moreover, there are other elements besides restraint. Men conditioned to loyalty may put up with great hardships. Fact and feeling seem to vary independently. Thus in Western society there has always been—say in comparison with Hindu caste-society—a very high degree of the "career open to talents." The circulation of the elites has always gone on. We can here but glance at our societies and see whether there were any special limitations to that circulation in the years prior to the revolution.

In eighteenth-century France, the way to wealth and fame was open practically unrestricted to business men, adventurers, adventuresses, actors, artists, writers—to Pâris-Duverney, to Cagliostro, to Mme. Du Barry, to Talma, to Watteau, to Voltaire. The way to political power was much harder, though the Abbé Dubois, an apothecary's son could attain its highest peak. On the whole, substantial political power, the power of making programs and policies, was open to the courtier talents even more than to noble birth; administrative power was almost entirely in the hands of the *noblesse de robe,* an hereditary, conscientious, and not incapable bureaucracy. Social position, the highest honors, we are frequently told, went only to those who could show four quarters of nobility. Certainly a privileged nobility did exist, and was disliked in the abstract by many a bourgeois who had no concrete experience of it. Twentieth-century Russia is in many ways a close parallel in these respects. A privileged nobility topped the social system, and closed the very highest social honor to plebeian talent. This class was disliked and bitterly disliked by those who saw it from the outside; and no doubt many of its individual members were insufferably haughty, overbearing, dissolute, vain, empty-headed, and the rest, just as if they had come from the pages of *A Tale of Two Cities.* Yet the way to fame and fortune was far from closed in pre-revolutionary Russia, with new industries rising, with an active theoretical, ballet, and musical life, with university and administrative positions open to ambitious and able young men even from the villages. Rasputin you may perhaps regard as an unhealthy example of the career open to talents, but you can hardly deny that the Siberian monk reached the top.

One clue to this problem of the circulation of the elite may lie in a stoppage of that circulation in a particular and very delicate spot, such as the professions, and especially the "intellectual" professions; that is, among people especially liable to the feeling of frustration, of being excluded from good things. One is struck in studying French society in the years just preceding the revolution with a kind of jam in the stream of bright young men descending on Paris to write and talk their way to fortune. Mercier in his *Tableau de Paris* tells how every sunny day young men may be seen on the quays, washing and drying their only shirts, ruffled and lacy symbol of high social status. There are also in Russia signs of pressure in competition in the ranks of what we should call "white-collar men," intellectuals, bureaucrats, clerks, and the like. We know that a similar stoppage in the society of the Weimar Republic had a great deal to do with the Nazi revolution of 1933. This symptom is, like most others that indicate strong social tensions, nearly lacking in eighteenth-century America, and extremely difficult to trace, partly for lack of proper historical materials, in the English revolution. Naturally enough, a stoppage in the circulation of the elite into journalism, literature, and such professions is likely to be rapidly reflected in the desertion of the intellectuals.

Finally, social antagonisms seem to be at their strongest when a class has attained to wealth, but is, or feels itself, shut out from the highest social distinction, and from positions of evident and open political power. This, broadly speaking, does describe the situation of the Calvinist gentry and merchants in seventeenth-century England, the colonial aristocracy and merchants of America, at least in relation to the British ruling class, the French bourgeois of the eighteenth and the Russian bourgeois of the nineteenth centuries. Individuals in each society might rise from ranks even lower than the middle class, and surmount all these barriers. Even as a class, the bourgeoisie in all four societies really had a determining voice in major political decisions even before the revolutions. But the countries were "run" by other, and privileged, beings, and from the highest social distinctions the bourgeoisie as a class were hopelessly excluded. Moreover, this exclusion was symbolized, manifested continuously in all but the most remote rural districts. Long before Marx, long before Harrington's *Oceana,* practical men knew that political power and social distinction are the handmaids of economic power. Where wealth cannot buy everything—everything of this world, at any rate—you have a fairly reliable preliminary sign of revolution.

## V. Summary

In summing up, the most striking thing we must note is that all of these preliminary signs—government deficits, complaints over taxation, governmental favoring of one set of economic interests over another, administrative entanglements and confusions, desertion of the intellectuals, loss of self-confidence among many members of the ruling class, conversion of many members of that class to the belief that their privileges are unjust or harmful to society, the intensification of social antagonisms, the stoppage at certain points (usually in the professions, the arts, perhaps the white-collar jobs generally) of the career open to talents, the separation of economic power from political power and social distinction—some, if not most of these signs may be found in almost any modern society at any time. With the wisdom of hindsight, we can now say that in four, or at least in three, of our societies these— and no doubt other signs we have omitted to consider—existed in some unusual combination and intensities before revolution ensued. But clearly we must infer from what we have just done that in its earlier stages diagnosis of revolution is extremely difficult, and certainly cannot be reduced to a neat formula, a recipe, a set of rules. This is also true of the diagnosis of human illnesses. The best diagnosticians, we are told on good authority, could not possibly analyze out and put into formal logical sequence all the steps they take in the clinical diagnosis of disease.

We are not, however, left altogether helpless before some mystic gift for short-term prophecy in the successful diagnostician. His methods are not those of magic, but rather the gift for making what is, until familiarity has made it easy, the difficult and rarely explicit synthesis of past experience and present observation into a successful generalization—or hunch if you prefer. And we can in this instance hazard something further as to signs of revolution in our four societies. In all of them, and especially in France and in Russia, there is as the actual outbreak of revolution approaches increasing talk about revolution, increasing consciousness of social tension, increasing "cramp" and irritation. Prophets of evil there always are, and we need not lay much stress on any specific prediction of a given revolution, such as the Marquis d'Argenson made forty years before the French revolution. But when such fears—or hopes—become something like common property, when they are, to use a very aged metaphor to which the invention of the radio has given an ironic twist, in the air, then it is fairly safe to take this general sentiment as a pretty conclusive sign of revolution. Even then, however, we have a sign difficult to use. For people never seem to expect revolution for themselves, but only for their children. The actual revolution is always a surprise. This is true even for Russia, where the revolution had long been in the air.

It must, however, be really in the air, and not simply in the mouths of professional seers or timid conservatives. It must, above all, go beyond the intellectuals. For, valuable as the desertion of the intellectuals is as a sign if found with others, as part of a syndrome, in itself alone this desertion proves nothing. After all, one of the great functions of the intellectuals in Western society has always been to shake ordinary mortals out of their unthinking optimism, and Cassandra has perhaps as much claim as Plato to be founder of a great academic tradition. But Cassandra's successors have not quite achieved her unhappy infallibility.

## TYPES OF REVOLUTIONISTS

### I. The Clichés

It would clearly be helpful in our inquiry if we could at this point isolate the revolutionist as a type. To pursue our analogy of the fever, may it not be that certain individuals act as "carriers," and that they can be classified, labeled, described in economic and sociological terms as well as in those of psychology or common sense? This is at any rate a lead which seems worth following.

There are, however, several ways in which such a pursuit might lead us astray. We must beware of regarding revolutionists, and revolutionary leaders in particular, as literally bearing disease germs of revolution. Here as throughout this study, our conceptual scheme must never be allowed to lead us into fantasy. It must be a convenience, not an obsession. We must more than ever avoid using terms of praise or dispraise, which lurk in every corner of this particular field. For the simple word "revolutionist" is likely to call up in the minds of most of us a relatively uncritical personification, the sort of loose change of daily intercourse that serves us well enough to get on with "poet" or "professor" or "Frenchman."

Even the subtlest thinker, the most delicate and conscientious artist in words, has to come down in daily life to something very close to the clichés that serve the man in the street. You and I, of course, do not picture poets as long-haired, delicate, bohemian and tubercular, nor professors as impractical, absent-minded, kindly and bearded, nor Frenchmen as polite, dapper, wax-mustached, ladies' men. But we cannot go into Proustian intricacies with ourselves when we use such words, nor can we use them as rigorously as a scientific systematist. We get along with them as best we may, adjusting them roughly to our experience and our sentiments.

Now what "revolutionist" means at this level to various persons and various groups is in itself an important element in a full sociology of revolutions. What all sorts of people feel about revolution is perhaps most easily studied in the clichés which arise out of words like "revolutionist" and "revolutionary," or their more concrete parallels, "Jacobin," "Bolshevik," "red," and the like. We cannot attempt such a study here, but we must look a bit further into a few of these clichés, if only as a warning and a contrast.

Probably for most Americans in the fourth decade of the twentieth century the word "revolutionist" carries unpleasant overtones. At the level of the Hearst papers or the Macfadden publications, a revolutionist appears as a seedy, wild-eyed, unshaven, loud-mouthed person, given to soapbox oratory and plotting against the government, ready for, and yet afraid of, violence. Even at slightly more sophisticated levels, one suspects many of our countrymen feel much the same about revolutionists, or at any rate are convinced that they are pronouncedly queer people, failures under pre-revolutionary conditions, sufferers from inferiority complexes, envious of their betters, or just downright ornery, "agin the government" on principle and by disposition. Other and more favorable pictures of the revolutionist no doubt arise in other minds. To judge by some of our proletarian writers —not themselves proletarians—the revolutionist is a sturdy, broad-shouldered steelworker, uncorrupted by the falsities the bourgeois call education, but well-versed in Marx and Lenin, strong, kindly, a warrier-spirit with just a redeeming touch of Shelley about him.

Now the social uses of beliefs of this sort are plain enough. In an old bourgeois society like the United States, sentiments hostile to revolutionists are probably important factors in maintaining social stability. Revolutionists were all right in 1776, but not in 1938. Any society that is a going concern must apparently contain large numbers of people who feel this way about revolutionists. Even in Russia, where memories of violent revolution are still fresh, a concerted effort is being made by the government to discredit living, flesh-and-blood revolutionists. Revolution was all right in 1917, but not in 1938. On the other side, it is clear that radicals and extremists who think of revolutionists as fine fellows, as heroes and martyrs, are also aiding in their own social discipline, strengthening themselves for the fray.

The social scientist, however, cannot let the matter rest here. He must attempt an objective classification of revolutionists, as complicated as his data about them makes necessary. We can say with confidence that even a hasty review of the four revolutions with which we are concerned is very far from confirming either set of clichés we have outlined. And notably, since the derogatory set is commoner in this country, such a review by no means confirms the notion that our revolutionists were seedy, loud-mouthed, bomb-throwing failures in the old regimes. If we include, as we must, those who took the first steps in revolution as well as those who ruled in the reign of terror, our type becomes still less simple.

Let us take a random list of names as they come to mind: Hampden, Sir Harry Vane, John Milton, Sam Adams, John Hancock, Washington, Thomas Paine, Lafayette, Marat, Talleyrand, Hébert, Miliukov, Konavalov, Kerensky, Chicherin, Lenin. All are revolutionists; all opposed constituted authority with force of arms. The list includes great nobles, gentlemen, merchants, journalists, a professor of history, a political boss, a ward-heeler. It includes several very rich men and one or two poor men. It includes many who would by conventional Christian standards seem to have been good men; and it includes several who would by such standards seem to have been very wicked men. It includes some who were important people in their pre-revolutionary days, some who were quite unknown, and two, perhaps three, who were apparent failures in life until the revolution gave them a chance to rise. Surely it is no easy task to find a least common denominator for a list like this.

No doubt we shall be aided by making a distinction between the men who dominate in the early stages of a revolution—on the whole the moderates—and those who dominate in the crisis stage —on the whole the extremists. But it will not do to say that only our extremists are real revolutionists. After all, even George Washington seems to have taken an oath of loyalty to the British Crown, and his breaking that oath would have been treason had the American revolution failed. We have been taught by Whig historians to believe that Essex and Pym were defending the sacred laws of England, and that therefore they weren't real revolutionists. This was not, by any means, the current opinion in Europe in the 1640's, where the Parliamentarians were regarded as shocking rebels against their king; and monarchy was in seventeenth-century Europe as solidly rooted in the sentiments which give force to law as the American Constitution seems rooted with us in this country at the present time. No, we must list the moderates among our revolutionists, even though they were defending the higher law against the lower, and weren't just nasty anarchists and rebels.

## II. *Economic and Social Position: Rank and File*

One of the most useful approaches to the problem of the personnel of revolutionary movements is from the relatively objective indications of the economic and social status of those who take part in the uprising. Now it is very difficult to find out much about the rank and file of the revolutionists. Like the private soldier in war, the ordinary revolutionist is inarticulate and nameless. For the French revolution, however, some such study is not impossible. In the surviving records of the Jacobin Clubs, which served as centers of revolutionary action, and resemble both the Russian soviets and the American corresponding committees, we have a large number of lists of members—imperfect, of course, but still lists. Some years ago the present writer made a study of these lists, and, aided by tax-rolls and other documents in French local archives, was able to arrive at certain rough statistical generalizations about these revolutionists. Some of these generalizations must be here summarized from the author's *The Jacobins: A Study in the New History*.

In general, it is possible to arrive at some statisti-

cal approximation of the social and economic positions of these Jacobin revolutionists in pre-revolutionary France. There are tax-rolls extant for
various years between 1785 and 1790, and on these
many of the Jacobins can be found, with the sums
they were assessed at. As these were direct taxes
not too far out of proportion to income, it is possible thus to get a rough estimate of Jacobin wealth.
Occupations are usually given, and this is a useful
indication of social position. Finally, it is also possible to study certain clubs at specific moments in
the revolution, so that a sample can be taken during
the early or moderate period, and another during
the later rule of the extremists. Here, briefly, are
some of the results.

For twelve clubs, with a total membership of
5,405 over the whole course of the revolution,
1789–95, in both its moderate and its violent
phases: 62 per cent of the members were middle
class, 28 per cent working class, 10 percent peasants. For twelve clubs in the moderate period,
1789–92, with a membership of 4,037: 66 per
cent were middle class, 26 per cent working class,
8 per cent peasants. For forty-two clubs in the violent period, 1793–95, with a membership of 8,062:
57 per cent were middle class, 32 per cent working
class, 11 per cent peasants. The tax-rolls confirm
what occupational and social classification suggests.
In eight clubs considered over the whole period of
revolution, club members paid an average tax of
32.12 *livres,* where the average tax for all male
citizens of the towns considered was 17.02 *livres;*
in twenty-six clubs considered in the violent period
only, club members paid 19.94 *livres,* male citizens
14.45 *livres.* Thus, though there was certainly a
tendency for the clubs to be recruited in the violent
period from social strata a bit lower, on the whole
one is forced to the conclusion that "the Jacobin
was neither a nobleman nor a beggar, but almost
anything in between. The Jacobins represent a complete cross-section of their communities."

Other relatively objective indices help us a bit. It
was often possible to list the ages of members of the
clubs during the revolution. As far as the rank and
file of these clubs went, the notion that revolutionists are recruited from the young and irresponsible was not borne out. For ten clubs the
average age varied from 38.3 years to 45.4 years,
and for all ten together came to 41.8 years. These
were clearly not foolhardy youngsters. Nor were
they footloose itinerants, shock troops imported
from revolutionary urban centers like Paris. Out of
2,949 members of fifteen clubs, only 378, or 13
per cent, had moved into the towns since the outbreak of trouble in 1789. The actual membership
of the clubs varied as the revolutionary movement
grew more and more extreme—or in modern terms,
went more and more to the Left. Many moderates
emigrated or were guillotined, many disreputable
extremists, often though by no means always from

the lower classes, only "made" the clubs later on.
Yet in six clubs with a total membership from 1789
to 1795 of 3,028, something over 31 per cent
managed to stay on the books for the whole period,
to have been successfully good monarchists, good
Girondists, good Montagnards. It is not true that
the personality of these clubs became dominantly
lower or working class after the fall of the monarchy in 1792, nor even that their newer recruits
were largely from the proletariat. And it is quite
clear that these people are not on the whole failures
in their earlier environment; rather they represent
the abler, more ambitious and successful of the
inhabitants of a given town. It is as if our Rotarians
today were revolutionists.

A similar statistical study could probably not be
made for the English revolution since lists corresponding to the Jacobin membership lists are not
available. The material certainly exists for such a
study of the actual membership of the soviets in,
say, the crucial year 1917, but it would have to be
put together from scattered sources available only
in Russia. We know a good deal about the membership of our own American revolutionary groups,
from merchants' committees and corresponding
committees to continental congresses. Even for the
English revolution we have enough scattered material to permit some generalizations about the
personnel of the movement.

In the early stages of the English revolution
there can be no doubt about the respectability and
economic prosperity of the men who backed Parliament. Baxter, somewhat exaggeratedly, but with a
kernel of truth, writes that when the Great Rebellion broke out "it was the moderate Conformists
and Episcopal Protestants who had long been crying of Innovations, Arminianism, Popery, Monopolies, illegal taxes and the danger of arbitrary government, who raised the war." The merchants of
London, Bristol and other towns, great lords, small
landowning gentry, all rose in sedition against their
king. Even in what we may call the extremist or
crisis period of the English revolution, which begins
in 1646 or 1647 when the tension between the New
Model Army and the Presbyterians becomes acute,
your revolutionists are very far from riffraff. Even
Baxter reports of that army—which was to the
English revolution what the Jacobins were to the
French and the Bolsheviks to the Russian revolutions—that "abundance of the common troopers
and many of the officers I found to be honest, sober,
orthodox men, and others tractable, ready to hear
the truth, and of upright intentions." An historian
has estimated that when the New Model "took the
field in 1645, of its thirty-seven chief officers, nine
were of noble, twenty-one of gentle birth, and only
seven not gentlemen by birth." The English lower
classes, or at least the more proletarian elements
as opposed to independent artisans, on the whole
stood aloof from the conflict. Even the wilder sec-

tarians seem to have been recruited from humble, but by no means poverty-stricken people, men who had taught themselves to follow the theological disputes, men on the whole representing the more active and ambitious of their class. The poorer peasants, especially in the North and West, actually sided with the King and against the revolutionists.

In America we have already pointed out the well-known fact that it was the merchants who first organized opposition to the Crown. This opposition was echoed by many planters in the southern coastal plain, and by many very respectable yeomen farmers of the Piedmont. It is quite true that there are numerous signs of the pretty active participation of what a good conservative would regard as the dregs of the population. The Boston Sons of Liberty, who performed most of the actual work of violence there, were recruited from workingmen and actually met habitually in the counting-room of a distillery. The Tories, whom it is now more fashionable to call Loyalists, naturally saw their opponents as a pretty shabby lot. Hutchinson writes of the Boston town meeting that it is

. . . constituted of the lowest class of the people under the influence of a few of the higher class, but of intemperate and furious dispositions and of desperate fortunes. Men of property and the best character have deserted these meetings; where they are sure of being affronted.

Actually the line between Tory and Whig is a very irregular one, depending on much besides economic status, as can be seen from the late J. F. Jameson's *The American Revolution Considered as a Social Movement.* If the rich gentlemen of "Tory Row" in Cambridge sided with the Crown, there were plenty of sober, respectable farmers, merchants, and lawyers, who turned revolutionist. Such men were likely to be shocked at the doings of wild young apprentices in the Sons of Liberty, but this did not necessarily turn them to the British side, though it made them critical of the Congress. A good sign of the respectability of revolution is the adhesion of the clergy, which save for the Episcopalians was in most colonies general. As a disgruntled Tory put it,

The high sons of liberty include the ministers of the gospel, who instead of preaching to their flocks meekness, sobriety, attention to their different employments, and a steady obedience to the laws of Britain, belch from the pulpits liberty, independence, and a steady perseverance in endeavoring to shake off their allegiance to the mother country. The independent ministers have been . . . the instigators and abettors of every persecution and conspiracy.

To sum up we shall have to agree with Jameson that the strength of the revolutionary movement in the long run lay with the plain people—not with the mob or "rabble," for American society was rural and not urban—but with country artisans, small farmers, and frontiersmen. But we shall also have to agree with Alexander Graydon that "the opposition to the claims of Britain originated with the better sort: it was truly aristocratical in its commencement."

The February revolution in Russia seems to have been welcomed by all classes save the most conservative of conservatives—a few army officers, a few members of the Court and the old nobility. No one knows who made the February revolution, but there can be no doubt as to its popularity. Almost everyone, liberal noble, banker, industrialist, lawyer, doctor, civil servant, *kulak,* and workingman, was glad to co-operate in giving the Czarist regime its final blow. Even the Bolsheviks, whose sudden victory in the October revolution of 1917 makes the time-scheme of the Russian revolution so very different from those of the English and French revolutions, were by no means what confirmed haters of revolution call riffraff, rabble, "the masses." They seem to have been recruited chiefly from the more enterprising, able, and skilled workingmen in the factories of Petrograd, Moscow, and specialized industrial centers like Ivanovo-Vosnessensk or the Don basin. Their most important leaders were largely drawn from the middle class. One might perhaps argue that the Kadets, led by Miliukov, were so early discouraged that they may not be counted as a revolutionary party. But the Mensheviks and S-R (Socialist-Revolutionary) party, later scorned as "Compromisists" by triumphant Bolshevik historians, are most certainly revolutionary elements. The Mensheviks may have been mostly intellectuals, but the S-R were also recruited from the prosperous peasants, from the people who ran the co-operatives, from small shopkeepers and the like.

## III. Economic and Social Position: Leaders

Hitherto we have been considering the main bodies of the revolutionists, and have found that on the whole they by no means represent the dregs of society, even in the great proletarian uprising, and that they commonly include members of almost every social and economic group in a given society, except possibly the very top of the social pyramid. And yet the Essexes, Washingtons, and Lafayettes are very close to the top. Even in Russia, Brusilov, a distinguished Czarist general, lived to serve the Soviet government in the 1920 drive on Warsaw.

Let us now see what we can make of the leaders, judging them first by the comparatively objective standards of their social origins and economic status. With the Jacobins the present writer was able to make some study of the purely local leaders, the men who normally don't get into history. From the careers of dozens of these subalterns of revolution, a conclusion seemed clear:

The leaders are substantially of the same social standing as the rank and file. Possibly there are, among the leaders during the Terror, more men who seem definitely, in 1789, failures, or at least at odds with their environment. Yet the proportion of these village Marats is not striking.

As for the national leaders in the French revolution, they are, judged by these standards, a varied lot. In the years 1789–92 they include noblemen like the King's cousin, the Duke of Orléans, Mirabeau, the Lameths, Lafayette; lawyers in vast numbers, from well-known Parisian lawyers like Camus to obscure but thoroughly respectable provincial lawyers like young Robespierre from Arras (who had once written his name de Robespierre), or rising barristers like Danton, come to Paris from a peasant background in Champagne; men of science like the astronomer Bailly, the chemist Lavoisier, and the mathematician Monge; and, nursed by the new power of the press, journalists like Marat and Desmoulins, publicists like Brissot, provincial bourgeois of Chartres, and Condorcet, a marquis and a *philosophe*. After 1792, extremely few new leaders came to the top. The men who ran France in 1793-94 were, perhaps, somewhat less refined or distinguished than the hopeful intellectuals of Mme. Roland's circle; and they would have seemed very barbarous at Versailles in 1788. They were not, however, of very different social origins from the men who really ran old France—the literate bourgeoisie from which were ultimately recruited the bureaucracy.

Of the striking respectability and excellent social standing of the men who signed our Declaration of Independence most Americans are fully aware. Of its fifty-six signers thirty-three held college degrees and only about four had little or no formal education. There were five doctors, eleven merchants, four farmers, twenty-two lawyers, three ministers. Twelve were sons of ministers. Nearly all were affluent. Sam Adams, who seems among the more disreputable of our leaders, came from a merchant family of some means, and graduated from Harvard in 1740, where he was listed fifth out of twenty-two in those mysterious lists which before Professor S. E. Morison's researches we all thought directly measured social standing. Even the Tories, though they flung words like "rabble" about very freely, could consistently reproach the revolutionary leaders with nothing worse in this respect than being amateurs in the art of governing.

From shopkeepers, tradesmen, and attorneys they are become statesmen and legislators. . . . Almost every individual of the governing party in America fills at present, in his own fancy, a station not only superior to what he had ever filled before, but to what he had ever expected to fill,

writes a conservative, or moderate, in the *Middlesex Journal* for April 6, 1776.

We need not go into the social origins of the leaders of the moderates in the English revolution. They are clearly among the highest in the land. The immoderates present an interesting spectacle, a mixture of gentlemen of good breeding, of self-educated careerists and of humble men inspired by a fury as yet divine, as yet without benefit of psychoanalysis. Cromwell himself, of course, was an East Anglian country gentleman, whose family tree ramified into a good deal of the new wealth originating in Tudor confiscations. Ireton, who became his son-in-law, was of similar antecedents, as were many other Independent leaders in old and new England. Ludlow the regicide was a son of Sir Henry Ludlow of Wiltshire, and went to Trinity, Cambridge. Even John Lilburne the Leveller is described as "of good family" dating back to the fourteenth century, and seems to have been typical of the lesser gentry whose sons not infrequently passed over into trade. We know little of the social origins of such men as Winstanley the Digger or Edward Sexby, a soldier of Cromwell's regiment who appears later as a kind of international agent of republicanism. Robert Everard, with Winstanley a leader of the curious communistic group known as the Diggers, was a captain in the army and is described as a "gentleman of liberal education." John Rogers the Millenarian was the son of an Anglican clergyman and a Royalist.

Russia presents a case more nearly parallel to our other countries in respect to the social origins of the leaders of her revolution than might at first sight seem likely in a proletarian revolution. Perhaps the moderates in Russia held power so briefly and so uncomfortably that they hardly count. Kadets like Miliukov, a historian of good family, Tereschenko, a Kiev sugar millionaire, the Octobrist Guchkov, a wealthy Moscow merchant, and poor old Prince Lvov remind us of the rich Puritan lords and merchants of the English revolution, the well-born Feuillants of the French revolution. The Menshevik and Social-Revolutionary leaders were mostly intellectuals, petty officials, trade union and co-operative leaders; some of their most eloquent orators came from Georgia, "the Gironde of the Russian revolution." Kerensky was a radical lawyer of provincial bureaucratic stock from the little Volga town of Simbirsk, now called Ulianovsk, in memory of a greater one than Kerensky who also hailed from Simbirsk. As a matter of fact, V. I. Ulianov, better known by his revolutionary name of Lenin, came from exactly the same social class as Kerensky. His father was an inspector of schools at Simbirsk, a position of much more social standing in bureaucratic Czarist Russia than it would seem to us to be —very definitely in the superior bourgeoisie.

The other Bolshevik leaders are a varied lot: intellectual Jews like Trotsky (born Bronstein) and Kamenev (born Rosenfield), both educated men, by no means typical Ghetto Jews; Felix Dzerzhinsky,

THE ANATOMY OF REVOLUTION

of noble Polish-Lithuanian stock; Sverdlov, by training a chemist; Kalinin, whom one might call a professional peasant; Stalin (born Djugashvili) of Georgian peasant-artisan stock, destined by his mother for the priesthood, and actually for some time a student in a seminary; Chicherin, of stock sufficiently aristocratic to hold himself at least as well-born as Lord Curzon; Antonov-Ovseënko, Red Army leader with the fine bourgeois inheritance of a hyphenated name. The negotiations at Brest-Litovsk, however, afford a neat synopsis of Bolshevik leadership and proof of its non-proletarian character. When the first Russian delegation was sent to that town to meet the Germans it included as samples of the proletarian achievements of the revolution one specimen each of sailor, worker, and peasant. The peasant is said, no doubt by malicious enemies of the working class, to have distinguished himself chiefly by his interest in the liquor supply. When, however, the negotiations really got going after a recess, the Russians dropped their ornamental sailor, worker, and peasant, and were represented by men of course not the social equals of the high-born Germans opposite them, but, one suspects, their cultural superiors—Joffe, Kamenev, Pokrovsky, Karakhan—and by a somewhat neurotic lady-Bolshevik, Mme. Bitzenko, who had won her spurs by shooting a Czarist official in the bad old days. But, of course, even orthodox Marxism admits that the proletariat cannot lift itself by its own bootstraps, and that its leaders must therefore come from classes sufficiently privileged to have had an education fitting them to interpret the subtleties of Marxist theology.

Finally, the inexperience, the "newness," of the revolutionary leaders has generally been exaggerated in our textbooks. They had, especially in Russia, a long training in the direction of dissenting and persecuted little societies, the revolutionary groups. And revolutionists as a group are so much like any other human beings that to learn the art of leading them is to have gone a long way in political apprenticeship. Even in France, the members of the National Assembly were not as politically innocent as they are supposed to have been. Many had had business experience, or had been diplomatists, or civil servants, or had taken part in local politics in provinces which had their own estates. All of them were used to the politics of pressure groups. These revolutionary leaders are mostly far from academic, unworldly, pure theorists; they do not step suddenly from the cloister to the council hall. Their training may have subtly unfitted them for leading a stable society; but that is another, and at present insoluble, problem. They are certainly fitted for leadership in an unstable society.

We have, then, found that both rank and file and leaders of active revolutionary groups cannot be catalogued neatly as coming from any one social or economic group. They are not even strikingly,

precociously, young. Their leaders are usually in middle age, the thirties and forties, and thus younger than most of the politically prominent in stable societies, which naturally incline to the rule of the old. But the St. Justs and the Bonapartes, the boys in their twenties, are the exception, not the rule. The leadership of the Russian revolution which, with the distortion that comes from contemporaneousness, we are likely to regard as the most "radical," was on the average the oldest in years of all our revolutions. The revolutionists tend to represent a fairly complete cross-section of their communities, with a sprinkling of the very highest ranks of their societies—men like Lafayette, for instance, whom Mr. Lothrop Stoddard calls "misguided superiors"—and, as far as the active ruling groups go, extremely few of the submerged, downtrodden, lowest ranks. This is as true of the Bolsheviks as of the Puritans and the Jacobins. Bums, hoboes, the mob, the rabble, the riffraff, may be recruited to do the street-fighting and the manor-burning of revolutions, but they emphatically do not make, do not run, revolutions—not even proletarian revolutions.

## IV. Character and Disposition

We now face a much more difficult task, one where our information is neither so objective nor so readily catalogued as our information about the social and economic status of revolutionists. This is the problem—psychological at bottom—of seeing how far these revolutionists belong to types which are normally viewed by John Jones as queer, eccentric, or downright mad. Now one might quite justifiably argue *a priori* that a wholly contented man could not possibly be a revolutionist. But the trouble is that there are so many ways of being discontented, as well as contented, on this earth. Indeed, the cruder Marxists, and the cruder classical economists, make an almost identical error: they both assume that economics deals exhaustively with whatever makes men happy or miserable. Men have many incentives to action which the economist, limited to the study of men's rational actions, simply cannot include in his work. They observably do a great deal that simply makes no sense at all, if we assume them to be guided *wholly* by any conceivable rational economic motive: near-starving in the British Museum to write *Das Kapital,* for instance, or seizing deserts under the comforting illusion that trade follows the flag, or making the world quite safe for democracy. Yet clearly a man who takes part in a revolution before it is demonstrably successful—and after it is successful it may perhaps be said to have ceased to be a revolution anyway—is a discontented man, or at least a man shrewd enough to estimate that there are enough discontented men to be forged into a group that can make a revolution. We must make some effort to study the nature of such discontents as seen in individuals.

For here the method of statistical study of large groups of revolutionists, like the Jacobins, will not work. At most these rank and file are names, with profession and perhaps some other indication of social status. Modern interest in social history and the common man has indeed made available a certain number of old diaries and letters of common men, and the Russian revolution has done its best to keep alive the memory of worker this of the Putilov factory or sailor that of the *Aurora*. Trotsky himself is very eloquent about the role of these heroic workers, sailors, and peasants in his *History of the Russian Revolution,* yet he manages to spend as much of his time on the great names as if he were a mere bourgeois historian. We have, of course, the blanket denunciations—they are hardly descriptions—of one side by another. These are much too emotional as a rule to have any evidential value, except as to the intensity of emotions evoked during revolutions. Even in our own presumably mild revolution one notes a Tory who is reported to have said, "It would be a joy to ride through American blood to the hubs of my chariot wheels." Of course these American Tories thought the revolutionists were wild radicals, scheming inferiors, jealous rabble. On the other hand, most of us who were brought up without benefit of the new history were taught in school to regard the Tories as just straight villains, traitors, morally reprehensible people without economic, social, or indeed any characteristics that separated them from such villains of fiction as Simon Legree. So in the French revolution, each side accused the other of all sorts of moral failings, but rarely got down to effective details of daily life.

If we cannot for these reasons do much with the political and social psychology of large groups of revolutionists, we can at least look over some of the leaders, hoping that the list we decide upon will not be too unrepresentative. Here at least we can count upon quite a bit of biographical information. Thanks to those admirable works, the *Dictionary of National Biography* and the *Dictionary of American Biography,* we can even sample some of the lesser leaders, the noncommissioned officers of revolutions. The French are now at work on their biographical dictionary, which promises to be even more scholarly than its Anglo-Saxon prototypes, but as it has only just conquered the letter "A" it is not of much use to us. Russia is very difficult indeed from this point of view; there are plenty of brilliant comments on Lenin, Trotsky, and Stalin, but they are also very contradictory. On the lesser figures there is not much trustworthy biographical writing available in the Western languages, nor for that matter in Russian. We may note here, however, that the extraordinary proliferation of assumed names in the Russian revolution probably does not stem with most of these pseudonymous heroes from any feelings of shame for a criminal or disgraceful past. Their crimes were no doubt many, but crimes only against Czarist oppression. Perhaps there was originally some mildly melodramatic notion that these aliases were useful against the Czarist police, but soon they became a mere fashion, a revolutionary fad.

At this point there is some danger of our falling into a dreary catalogue. At the risk of seeming to turn aside from strictly scientific systematizing, we shall have to group our facts as we go along under certain human types of characters. This is a process which has been done successfully by a great many shrewd observers of human behavior, from Theophrastus through Molière to Sainte-Beuve and Bagehot. It is perhaps in some respects a more useful way of classifying men than formal psychology or formal sociology has yet worked out. These are not, one hopes, imaginary characters. If they are one-tenth as real as Alceste or the Penurious Man they are more real than anyone the average sociologist ever dealt with.

We may begin with the gentleman-revolutionist, whom Mr. Lothrop Stoddard calls the "misguided superior," the man born on top, but perversely unwilling to stay there. He is by no means a simple person, and indeed sometimes manages to combine an astonishing number of revolutionary traits. It must be admitted that with many of these misguided superiors in our four societies, dislike for the ways of their class is apparently partly motivated by their inability to succeed in certain activities honored in that class. You need not be a debunking historian to admit that Lafayette revolted against the Court of Louis XVI and Marie Antoinette partly because he cut so awkward a figure there. Liberty, fortunately, did not need to be courted in a minuet. We must not seem to be cynical in these matters. Lafayette's love of liberty was no doubt morally a far better thing than if he had loved place, pension, or mistress. But we must infer from his actions that he had very early realized that nothing short of a love of liberty would get him very far. And so today, when you find in one of our colleges a well-nurtured youth turned Communist, you can be almost certain that he is not captain of the football team nor secretary of Chi Phi Digamma. He may indeed be Phi Beta Kappa. This condition we need not here either applaud or condemn, but simply note.

It would, however, be cynical—and hence quite unscientific—to deny that many of these misguided superiors are also moved by what we shall have to call sincere idealism. Their own social group comes to seem to them dissolute, or dull, or cruel, or heartless. They see the possibilities of a better world. They are influenced by the writings of the intellectuals, who have begun their desertion of the established order. They come to struggle for

God's kingdom on this earth. They are usually, of course, uncomfortable on this earth, but for a whole lot of reasons, many of which cannot be simply dismissed as being in the province of the psychiatrist. Shelley, who never actually got a chance at revolution outside poetry, is a familiar example of this sensitive, and often neurotic, type. Dzerzhinsky, the Polish aristocrat who gave life to the terrible Cheka, was a delicate and sincere fanatic. The Marquis de St. Huruge, who figures disreputably in the disorders and street-fighting of the French revolution, was apparently pretty crazy, and not even a gentleman. Condorcet, also a marquis, was a gentleman and scholar, and if he had a good deal of the vanity that goes naturally enough with both, and very little of the sense that sometimes goes with either, was at heart a kind and sensitive man.

Others desert their class and join the revolution for the ignoble but sometimes socially very useful reason that they think the signs point to the victory of the revolution. Sometimes these men are like Mirabeau, rather shady characters who have for some time compromised themselves by irregular lives. Sometimes they are men like Talleyrand, careful, sensible men whose main desire is to keep in a position of honor and affluence, and who have no sense of loyalty to abstract notions of right and wrong. And, of course, in the early stages of our revolutions, even the Russian, plenty of rich and influential men of no extraordinary intelligence or stupidity joined the revolution because the revolution was fashionable, and an apparent success. Often these men, who had not been directly in political power, were flattered by the prospect of political power—men like the Duc d'Orléans or Bailly or Tereschenko or Konovalov. But they were essentially fairly ordinary human beings, no fitter subjects for hagiography—Christian, Freudian, or Marxist—than you or I.

If we leave the superiors, those who belong by birth or upbringing to the ruling classes, and who yet side with revolt, and turn to leaders who come from classes below the ruling one, we shall find the same very great variety of what we must tritely call human nature. We shall find fools, scoundrels, idealists, professional agitators, diplomatists, lunatics, cowards, and heroes.

Now it would be useless to deny that among those who come to the top in the troubled times of revolution are many who probably never would have been heard of in normal times. Some of these were certainly failures in the old society, men who were unable to attain the objects of their ambition. In spite of all that an able defender like Professor L. R. Gottschalk has written to prove Marat's learning and respectability, it is still true that on the whole the *Friend of the People* was not a success before the revolution. Marat was a self-educated man of humble stock, with a habit

of presenting himself with academic degrees and honorary distinctions his biographers—and even his contemporaries—were not always able to confirm. He tried very hard to storm the Parnassus of the *philosophes,* but was never admitted. Like most enlightened eighteenth-century men of letters, he dabbled in natural science, and emerged with a variant of the old phlogiston theory of combustion, the originality and truth of which were not properly appreciated by his jealous contemporaries. Lavoisier and the "new chemistry" were triumphing in the 1780's, and Marat failed to recognize the meaning of the revolution in this science.

When the Estates-General met in 1789 he was a disappointed intellectual, a man who had failed of acceptance by that little band of writers and talkers who in late eighteenth-century France perhaps enjoyed more unalloyed admiration from the public than such folk have ever enjoyed. No Frenchman could at that epoch have coined a term like "brain-trust"; but if he had it would have carried no such ironic overtones of scorn as it does in twentieth-century America. Marat, rejected by these admired leaders of opinion, was in 1789 full to the brim with envy and hatred of everything established and esteemed in France. Soon revolutionary journalism was to give him an ample outlet. He became the watch-dog of the revolution—a mad watch-dog, always in his *l'Ami du Peuple* at work scenting plots against the people, always hating those in power, even when they were of his own party, always crying for blood and revenge. A most unpleasant fellow, no doubt. Whether he was a more unpleasant one than certain journalists of normal and unrevolutionary twentieth-century America, it is hard to say. Journalism was very new in France in 1790, and people expected a good deal. Marat at least had one excuse. He was suffering from an incurable skin disease which gave to his life an almost unbearable nervous tension.

Yet the failures are by no means all of the relatively simple type of Marat. Sam Adams was certainly a failure when judged by the standards of thrifty, sober New England. He had no money sense whatever, ran through a small inheritance, was constantly in debt; let his wife and children get along as they could while he organized his famous caucus and committees of correspondence. He is by no means a figure for the copybooks. Yet Adams could do certain things extremely well, and if these things were not in the 1770's as financially rewarding as they are now, Adams at least reaped less tangible rewards in his own time—and he did become governor of Massachusetts. Adams's gifts, of course, as they are deftly analyzed in Mr. J. C. Miller's recent study, are those of the expert propagandist and organizer. It is hard to believe that today the advertising business would leave a man of his parts undiscovered and unrewarded.

Thomas Paine, who managed to involve himself

in two revolutions, the American and the French, is still another revolutionist who amounted to very little before the revolution. When he sailed for America in 1774 he was thirty-eight, certainly no longer a young man. He came from East-Anglian Quaker artisan stock, and had picked up an eighteenth-century education, chiefly in the sciences and in the philosophy of the Enlightenment, while pursuing half a dozen different occupations from privateering to stay-making and shopkeeping. He had made an unsuccessful marriage, been in and out of the excise service twice, acquired a reputation as the town "atheist" of Lewes in Sussex, and had led an unsuccessful and somewhat premature attempt at lobbying in the interest of his fellow-excisemen. This attempt, which resulted in his second and final dismissal from the service, also brought him to the attention of Benjamin Franklin, who encouraged him to emigrate. But Paine arrived in Philadelphia like many another European, an unsuccessful man looking for a new start. The revolution gave it to him, and *Common Sense* made him a distinguished publicist. Paine was the professional radical, the crusading journalist, the religious rationalist, a man who in quiet times could hardly have been more than another Bradlaugh, another Ingersoll.

On the other hand, revolution not infrequently brings to the top men of very practical abilities, men of the kind that even cautious and hard-headed conservatives must recognize as worthy of respect. Such men may have lived in obscurity simply because they had not been disturbed; or they may have been the victims of some such stoppage in the circulation of the élite, the career open to talents, as we noted in a previous chapter. Cromwell is a classic example of a man who might have remained a simple country gentleman with an undistinguished career in the House of Commons had it not been for the Puritan revolution. Of Washington himself a similar generalization can be made. We shall come back again to this question of the soundness of revolutionary leadership.

So far we have said nothing of the men of blood, of Carrier and the *noyades* of Nantes, of Collot d'Herbois and the *mitraillades* of Lyons, of those to us nameless agents of the Cheka whose work made the French Reign of Terror seem mild in comparison, or of those English agents of the so-called Cromwellian settlement of Ireland who for long-time effectiveness perhaps hold the record among Terrorists. We shall later come to the problem of terroristic methods during the crisis period of our revolutions. Here we are simply interested in pointing out that among the personnel of the revolutionists are a number of men who have been singled out by posterity as examples of the kind of monster that comes to the surface in revolutions. No one can deny the fact of such emergence, nor the fact that such men can hardly be understood save with the help of criminology and abnormal psychology.

Carrier himself is a perfectly good example of these men. However much Republican apologists may try to soften down the melodramatic accounts his enemies have left of his activities at Nantes, the fact remains that he did so speed up the revolutionary courts that it became much easier to drown convicted persons in batches in the river Loire than to wait for the slow-moving guillotine. Carrier was a provincial lawyer who had got himself elected to the Convention by joining his local club and repeating the stock phrases of the Enlightenment. He was sent as a representative on mission to Nantes, and there power seems to have gone to his head. Moreover, Nantes was on the edge of the always dangerous Vendée, and Carrier may well have been driven to cleaning up his enemies in a group by fear of conspiracy against his own life. He certainly put up a bold front, swaggered about town, gave entertainments, talked big, and left behind him festering hatreds that brought his downfall and condemnation to death after the Terror was over.

Carrier reminds one of Mr. James T. Farrell's gangsters. There is the bravado, the consciousness of life lived at the level of melodrama, the new, crude sense of power, the constant haunting fear of reprisals, the childish immediacy of purpose. What one does not find in Carrier is a specific pathological love of bloodshed, a diseased mind of the sort linked with the name of the Marquis de Sade. Indeed, this latter kind of insanity is more often found among the jailers, thugs, and hangers-on of revolution than among its leaders, even leaders at the level of Carrier. And of course to many people the most revolting acts in general are the acts of revolutionary mobs—the September massacres at Paris in 1792, for instance, which are very closely paralleled by the history of lynching in America. Here there crop up some of the most shocking instances of human cruelty; but they are by no means specifically to be associated with revolutions. Pogroms and lynchings are at least as bad. Revolutions and mobs are not interchangeable terms; you can and usually do have one without the other. The kind of cruelty more properly associated with revolutions is the cruelty—to some people more revolting than the cruelty of mobs—of judicial murders done in cold blood, and on principle.

There is another type commonly, but erroneously, held to come to the top in revolutions. This is the crack-brained schemer, the fantastic doctrinaire, the man who has a crazy gadget which will bring Utopia. Briefly, perhaps, in the honeymoon stage the lunatic fringe has its innings, and in the English revolution rather more than its innings, at least in print. But revolutions are a serious business, not to be distracted by eccentricities. Once the line of revolutionary orthodoxy is established—and though as we shall see it is a grim and rigid line, it is not a crazy and aberrant one—once this orthodoxy is established the lunatics, mild or serious, are pretty well kept down. There are Marxist revolutions, natural rights revolutions, but none for the Single Tax, Social Credit, Theosophy, or Extra Sensory Perception. It is only your very stable societies, like Victorian England, that can afford to turn a Hyde Park over to the lunatic fringe. Even if you think Cromwell, Washington, Robespierre, Napoleon, Lenin, and Stalin all belong to this lunatic fringe, you will have to admit that in their day of power they clamped down pretty hard on other and discordant lunatics.

Nor is it possible to isolate a revolutionary type labeled "criminal," "degenerate," and neatly conforming to some anthropometric standards. Attempts to do this sort of thing have certainly been made. There are probably those who hold that revolutionists have a fixed cephalic index, or that they are predominantly dark-haired. Certainly there are many revolutionists who, like Carrier, behave as criminals behave in stable societies; but the proportion of such revolutionists does not seem extraordinarily high.

A more characteristic revolutionary type is the disputatious, contrary-minded person who loves to stand out from the crowd of conformists. Indeed, one of our revolutionary groups, the English Puritans, was filled with this especially rugged anarchism. Not only do individuals stand out in this respect; the group as a whole sets itself off deliberately from the great and the fashionable. As a social historian has written:

Whatever was in fashion is what the Puritan would not wear. When ruffs were in vogue, he wore a large falling band; when pickadillies [ruffs] were out of request [1638], and wide falling bands of delicate lawn edged with fine lace came in, he wore a very small band. Fashionable shoes were wide at the toe; his were sharp. Fashionable stockings were, as a rule, of any color except black; his were black. His garters were short, and, before all, his hair was short. Even at the end of Elizabeth's reign, short hair was a mark of Puritanism.

The type is seen most clearly, however, in certain individuals. John Lilburne, the English Leveller, is virtue incarnate and uncomfortable. He seems to have come of a family of rugged individuals, for his father, a gentleman of Durham, is said to have been the last Englishman to have recourse to the feudal right to ask for judgment through ordeal by combat in a civil suit. John was steadily addicted to contention, and attacked Presbyterians and Independents as bitterly as he had earlier attacked the Court. Indeed, as an historian has written,

Lilburne was tried in almost every court in the kingdom, under varying conditions, during a period of some twenty years, for libels on the Government of the day, King, Parliament, Commonwealth, and Protector. One of the first duties that devolved upon the judges of the Commonwealth was to deal with this gentleman.

Yet he seems to have preserved a good deal of social pride along with that intellectual and spiritual pride which is one of the marks of the English Puritan. On trial in 1653, he told his judge, a self-made man of artisan background who had risen with Cromwell, that "it was fitter for him [the judge] to sell thimbles and bodkins than to sit in judgment on a person so much his superior." Henry Marten, the regicide, who ought to have been a good judge of such matters, said that if the world were emptied of all but John Lilburne, Lilburne would quarrel with John and John would quarrel with Lilburne. Lilburne's pamphlets are full of the self-righteousness of those who fight always for the right, and who seem to take delight in the uncomfortable position to which the poet later assigned the right—"Right forever on the scaffold, wrong forever on the throne." We are close to the martyrs.

Lilburne's motives were no doubt of the highest. He believed in absolute democracy, and his platform of manhood suffrage, biennial parliaments, religious toleration, equality before the law, was one day to secure pretty complete acceptance in England. But in 1645 only a very doctrinaire person, only a fanatic, could have held this platform possible of immediate realization. Lilburne was not only a disputatious man, a courter of martyrdom; he was what the world commonly calls an idealist, and suggests a consideration of a type which occurs very frequently in these revolutions. It does not seem altogether wise to single out any one type as the perfect revolutionist, but if you must have such a type, then you will do well to consider, not the embittered failure, not the envious upstart, not the bloodthirsty lunatic, but the idealist. Idealists, of course, are in our own times the cement of a stable, normal society. It is good for us all that there should be men of noble aspirations, men who have put behind them the dross of this world for the pure word, for the idea and the ideal as the noblest philosophers have known them. But in normal times such idealists do not seem, at least in Western society, to occupy positions of power and responsibility. In normal times today we look up to our idealists, and occasionally give them prizes and honorary degrees, but we do not choose them to rule over us. We notably refuse to let them make our foreign policies.

Indeed, one of the distinguishing marks of a revolution is this: that in revolutionary times the idealist at last gets a chance to try and realize his ideals. Revolutions are full of men who hold very high standards of human conduct, the kind of standards which have for several thousand years been described by some word or phrase which has the overtones that "idealistic" has for us today. There is no need for us to worry over the metaphysical, nor even the semantic, implications of the term. We all know an idealist when we see one, and certainly when we hear one.

Robespierre would have been an idealist in any society. There is a familiar story of how the young Robespierre resigned a judgeship rather than inflict the death penalty, which ran counter to his humanitarian eighteenth-century upbringing. Historians have pretty well destroyed that story, as they have so many others from the cherry tree to Alfred and the cakes. But, except in the very narrowest and least useful senses of the word, such stories are in many important ways usually "true." This story about Robespierre suggests that he was a good child of the Enlightenment. One need only read some of his speeches, full of the simplicities, the moral aphorisms, the aspirations of that innocent age, to realize that he was quite capable of resigning, or buying, a judgeship rather than abandon his ideals. He would, indeed, kill for his ideals.

Those ideals, as they got formed by 1793, may seem to us somewhat less than heroic, and they were certainly bolstered by a good deal of personal ambition and sheer vanity in Robespierre. But there they were: Robespierre wanted a France where there should be neither rich nor poor, where men should not gamble, nor get drunk, nor commit adultery, nor cheat, nor rob, nor kill—where, in short, there would be neither petty nor grand vices—a France ruled by upright and intelligent men elected by the universal suffrage of the people, men wholly without greed or love of office, and delightedly stepping down at yearly intervals to give place to their successors, a France at peace with herself and the world—but surely this is enough? Robespierre's personal rectitude is now hardly questioned even by historians hostile to what he stood for; in his own day, and especially immediately after his fall, he was accused of almost every possible crime and moral delinquency. He seems actually not even to have had any of the fashionable vices—no drink, no gaming, no women. Modern historians claim to have evidence that for a brief time in Paris he kept a mistress. If he did, one supposes it must have been out of motives of fancied hygiene; or possibly for a few weeks the country lawyer had ideas of living as did the fashionable Parisians. The Robespierre of the Terror, however, had certainly put such ideas behind him, and was, as the Incorruptible, a living symbol of the Republic of Virtue in his public and private life.

Now this idealist type is by no means simple. Cromwell should clearly not be listed primarily under this category, and yet there is something of the puritanical "seeker" in Cromwell, something that makes his tortuous policy—indeed his double-dealing—very hard to understand if you insist on seeing human beings as logically consistent wholes. Both Lenin and Trotsky are strange compounds of idealism and realism. This coupling of idealism and realism does not mean simply that they both on occasion could use realistic methods to attain ends dictated by their ideals. Robespierre, Cromwell, Gladstone, or Woodrow Wilson could do that. It means that they were also capable of pursuing realistic immediate ends. Lenin, of course, was a very skillful propagandist and organizer, with a great deal of what we shall have to call executive ability. But, at least in 1917, he seems to have thought that world-wide revolution was just around the corner, and that absolute economic equality could be introduced immediately in Russia. The New Economic Policy of 1921 is a clear indication that Lenin would not pursue his ideals to the bitter end of defeat and martyrdom.

Trotsky has one of the best critical minds of any Marxist, is even capable, at moments, of a kind of skepticism about his own aims. The Civil War of 1917–21 in Russia gave convincing proof of his abilities both as an orator and as an executive under pressure. Yet the Trotsky of the exile years seems to be howling for the moon, which is one definition, perhaps too unkind, of idealism. Had Trotsky remained in power he might indeed have made peace with bureaucracy, inequality, socialism-in-one-country, Thermidorean decadence, and all the other evils he now associates with the name of Stalin. And yet it seems not unlikely that this intransigeance of Trotsky's, this insistence on bringing heaven immediately to earth, this unwillingness to accommodate his aims to human weakness, or if you like, to human nature, help to explain why he did not last in post-revolutionary Russia.

Sentimental idealism was of course distinctly out of fashion in the Russia of 1917. The harsh realities, or at any rate the harsh *formulas,* of Marxist Socialism had replaced the naïve hopes with which the French revolution had set out to make this a better world. In both Lenin and Trotsky you can trace this desire to seem to be hard-boiled, and it will not do to imply that they did not in some ways succeed. There is one pure idealist among the Russian leaders, however, one who presents us with still another variant of the type. That is Lunacharsky, long Commissar for Education, the artist and man of culture of the movement. Lunacharsky, in spite of his past as a revolutionary agitator, was unquestionably a softie. He possessed the ability to talk movingly about life and education and art, and carried over into a century where it seemed a little strange something of Rousseau or of *Paul and Virginia.* The world should be grateful to him, however, for he helped greatly to prevent the wholesale destruction of works of art identified offhand with a dissolute capitalistic past.

There is, finally, the man almost wholly of words, the man who can hold crowds spellbound, the revolutionary orator. He may be listed as an idealist, because although part of his role is to egg the crowd on to acts of violence, he is even more typically the soother, the preacher, the ritual-maker, the man who holds the crowd together. In this role his words need hardly have any meaning at all, but commonly they can be analyzed out into pleasant aspirations and utterances. Much of Robespierre comes under this head, as do Patrick Henry, Vergniaud, Tseretelli. The type, of course, exists in all normal societies, and is usually esteemed. Zinoviev seems in the Russian revolution to have borne some such role. Lenin realized how useful Zinoviev was as an orator and even as a kind of Petrograd boss, but he seems to have had a pretty complete contempt for his sense and intelligence.

## V. Summary

To sum up, it should by now be clear that it takes almost as many kinds of men and women to make a revolution as to make a world. It is probable that, especially in their crisis periods, our revolutions threw up into positions of prominence and even of responsibility men of the kind who would in normal or healthy societies not attain similar positions. Notably, great revolutions would appear to put idealists in possession of power they do not ordinarily have. They would seem also to give scope for special talents, such as Marat had, for yellow journalism and muck-raking of a very lively sort. They certainly create a number of empty places to fill, and give an opportunity to clever young men who may also be unscrupulous. They probably insure a bit more public attention, for a while at least, to the chronic rebel and complainer, as well as to the lunatic fringe of peddlers of social and political nostrums.

But they do not re-create mankind, nor do they even make use of a completely new and hitherto suppressed set of men and women. In all four of our revolutions, even in the Russian revolution, the rank and file was composed of quite ordinary men and women, probably a bit superior to their less active fellows in energy and willingness to experiment, and in the English, American, and French

revolutions, even in their crisis periods, people of substantial property. These revolutionists were not in general afflicted with anything the psychiatrist could be called in about. They were certainly not riffraff, scoundrels, scum of the earth. They were not even worms turning. Nor were their leaders by any means an inferior lot suddenly elevated to positions of power which they could not worthily occupy. There is no question that in the turmoil of revolutions a good many scoundrels rise to the top —though they can also rise to the top without benefit of revolution, as a glance at some of the phases of either the Grant or the Harding administrations should amply prove. But the level of ability, of ability in an almost technical sense, the ability to handle men and to administer a complex social system, the level of ability suggested by names like Hampden, Pym, Cromwell, Washington, John Adams, Hamilton, Jefferson, Mirabeau, Talleyrand, Carnot, Cambon, Danton, Lenin, Trotsky, Stalin, is certainly very high.

All this by no means amounts to asserting the paradox that there are no real differences between revolutions and ordinary times. On the contrary, especially in their crisis periods, revolutions are like nothing else on earth. But you cannot altogether explain the differences between societies in revolution and societies in equilibrium by suggesting that a whole new crew operates during a revolution; by saying, if you dislike a particular revolution and all its works, that the scoundrels and the bums put it over on the good souls; or if you happen to like and approve a particular revolution, that the heroes and sages turned out the corrupt old gang. It just isn't as simple as all that. Since on the whole the evidence would seem to show that revolutionists are more or less a cross-section of common humanity, an explanation for the undoubted fact that during certain phases of a revolution they behave in a way we should not expect such people to behave, must be sought in changes worked on them by the conditions they live under, by their revolutionary environment.

# SOCIAL MOBILIZATION
# AND POLITICAL DEVELOPMENT

## Karl W. Deutsch

Social mobilization is a name given to an over-all process of change, which happens to substantial parts of the population in countries which are moving from traditional to modern ways of life. It denotes a concept which brackets together a number of more specific processes of change, such as changes of residence, of occupation, of social setting, of face-to-face associates, of institutions, roles, and ways of acting, of experiences and expectations, and finally of personal memories, habits and needs, including the need for new patterns of group affiliation and new images of personal identity. Singly, and even more in their cumulative impact, these changes tend to influence and sometimes to transform political behavior.

The concept of social mobilization is not merely a short way of referring to the collection of changes just listed, including any extensions of this list. It implies that these processes tend to go together in certain historical situations and stages of economic development; that these situations are identifiable and recurrent, in their essentials, from one country to another; and that they are relevant for politics. Each of these points will be taken up in the course of this paper.

Social mobilization, let us repeat, is something that happens to large numbers of people in areas which undergo modernization, i.e., where advanced, non-traditional practices in culture, technology, and economic life are introduced and accepted on a considerable scale. It is not identical, therefore, with this process of modernization as a whole,[1] but it deals with one of its major aspects, or better, with a recurrent cluster among its consequences. These consequences, once they occur on a substantial scale, influence in turn the further process of modernization. Thus, what can be treated for a short time span as a consequence of the modernization process, appears over a longer period as one of its continuing aspects and as a significant cause, in the well known pattern of feedback or circular causation.

Viewed over a longer time perspective, such as several decades, the concept of social mobilization suggests that several of the changes subsumed under it will tend to go together in terms of recurrent association, well above anything to be expected from mere chance. Thus, any one of the forms of social mobilization, such as the entry into market relations and a money economy (and hence away from subsistence farming and barter) should be expected to be accompanied or followed by a significant rise in the frequency of impersonal contacts, or in exposure to mass media of communication, or in changes of residence, or in political or quasi-political participation. The implication of the concept is thus to assert an empirical fact—that of significantly frequent association—and this assertion can be empirically tested.

This notion of social mobilization was perceived early in intuitive terms, as a historical recollection or a poetic image. It was based on the historical experiences of the French levée en masse in 1793 and of the German "total mobilization" of 1914–18, described dramatically in terms of its social and emotional impact by many German writers, including notably Ernst Jünger. A somewhat related image was that of the long-term and world-wide process of "fundamental democratization," discussed in some of the writings of Karl Mannheim.[2] All these images suggest a breaking away from old commit-

Reprinted from *The American Political Science Review*, Vol. LV, No. 3 (September, 1961), pp. 493-514, by permission of The American Political Science Association.

A draft version of this paper was presented at the meeting of the Committee on Comparative Politics, of the Social Science Research Council, Gould House, Dobbs Ferry, N.Y., June 10, 1959. An earlier version of this text is appearing in *Zeitschrift für Politik* (Köln, Germany).

Further work on this paper was supported in part by the Carnegie Corporation, and I am indebted for assistance in statistical application to Charles L. Taylor and Alex Weilenmann.

ments to traditional ways of living, and a moving into new situations, where new patterns of behavior are relevant and needed, and where new commitments may have to be made.

Social mobilization can be defined, therefore, as the process in which major clusters of old social, economic and psychological commitments are eroded or broken and people become available for new patterns of socialization and behavior. As Edward Shils has rightly pointed out,[3] the original images of "mobilization" and of Mannheim's "fundamental democratization" imply two distinct stages of the process: (1) the stage of uprooting or breaking away from old settings, habits and commitments; and (2) the induction of the mobilized persons into some relatively stable new patterns of group membership, organization and commitment. In this fashion, soldiers are mobilized *from* their homes and families and mobilized *into* the army in which they then serve. Similarly, Mannheim suggests an image of large numbers of people moving away *from* a life of local isolation, traditionalism and political apathy, and moving *into* a different life or broader and deeper involvement in the vast complexities of modern life, including potential and actual involvement in mass politics.

It is a task of political theory to make this image more specific; to bring it into a form in which it can be verified by evidence; and to develop the problem to a point where the question "how?" can be supplemented usefully by the question "how much?" In its intuitive form, the concept of social mobilization already carried with it some images of growing numbers and rising curves. In so far as the constituent processes of social mobilization can be measured and described quantitatively in terms of such curves, it may be interesting to learn how fast the curves rise, whether they show any turning points, or whether they cross any thresholds beyond which the processes they depict have different side effects from those that went before. Notable among these side effects are any that bear on the performance of political systems and upon the stability and capabilities of governments.[4]

# I. AN ANALYTICAL FORMULATION

Let $M$ stand for the generalized process of social mobilization, and let us think of it as representing the general propensity or availability of persons for recommitment. In this sense, $M$ could be measured by the average probability that any person, say between fifteen and sixty-five years old, would have undergone, or could be expected to undergo during his lifetime, a substantial change from old ways of living to new ones.

In order to define this change more precisely, it is necessary to make three assumptions: (1) there are different forms of social recommitment relevant for politics; (2) these forms tend to be associated with each other; and (3) these forms tend to reinforce each other in their effects. Two further points may be noted for investigation: (4) each of these forms may have a threshold at which some of its effects may change substantially; and (5) some or all of these thresholds, though not identical in quantitative terms, may be significantly related to each other.

For these constituent processes of social mobilization we may then choose the symbols $m_1$, $m_2$, $m_3$, . . . , $m_n$. Thus we may call $m_1$ the exposure to aspects of modern life through demonstrations of machinery, buildings, installations, consumer goods, show windows, rumor, governmental, medical or military practices, as well as through mass media of communication. Then $m_2$ may stand for a narrower concept, exposure to these mass media alone. And $m_3$ may stand for change of residence; $m_4$ for urbanization; $m_5$ for change from agricultural occupations; $m_6$ for literacy; $m_7$ for per capita income; and so on.

Our $m_1$ could then stand for the percentage of the population that had been exposed in any substantial way to significant aspects of modern life; $m_2$ for the percentage of those exposed to mass media, *i.e.*, the mass media audience; $m_3$ for the percentage of the inhabitants who have changed their locality of residence (or their district, province or state); $m_4$ for the percentage of the total population living in towns; $m_5$ for the percentage of those in non-agricultural occupations among the total of those gainfully occupied; $m_6$ for the percentage of literates; $m_7$ could be measured simply by net national product, or alternatively by gross national product in dollars per capita. At this stage in the compilation of evidence the exact choice of indicators and definitions must be considerably influenced by the availability of statistical data. In many cases it may be most satisfactory to use the data and definitions published by the United Nations, in such volumes as the *United Nations Demographic Year Book,* the *United Nations World Social Survey,* the *United Nations Statistical Year Book,* and a host of more specialized UN publications.[5]

In a modern, highly developed and fully mobilized country $m_7$ should be above $600 gross national product per capita; $m_1$, $m_2$, and $m_6$ should all be well above 90 per cent; $m_4$ and $m_5$ should be above 50 per cent, even in countries producing large agricultural surpluses beyond their domestic consumption; and even $m_3$, the change of residence, seems to be higher than 50 per cent in such a country as the United States. In an extremely underdeveloped country, such as Ethiopia, $m_7$ is well below $100 and the remaining indicators may be near 5 per cent or even lower.

In the course of economic development, as countries are becoming somewhat less like Ethiopia and somewhat more like the United States, all these indicators tend to change in the same direction, even though they do not change at the same rate. They exhibit therefore to some extent a characteristic which Paul Lazarsfeld has termed the "interchangeability of indicators"; if one (or even several) of these indicators should be missing it could be replaced in many cases by the remaining ones, or by other indicators similarly chosen, and the general level and direction of the underlying social process would still remain clear.[6] This characteristic holds, however, only as a first approximation. The lags and discrepancies between the different indicators can reveal much of interest to the student of politics, and some of these discrepancies will be discussed below.

The first and main thing about social mobilization is, however, that it does assume a single underlying process of which particular indicators represent only particular aspects; that these indicators are correlated and to a limited extent interchangeable; and that this complex of processes of social change is significantly correlated with major changes in politics.

The overall index of social mobilization, $M$, is a second order index; it measures the correlation between the first order indices $m_1 \ldots m_n$. It should express, furthermore, the probability that the $(n + 1)$th index will be similarly correlated with its predecessors, regardless of how large a number $n$ might be, provided only that the index itself was appropriately chosen. Differently put, to assert that social mobilization is a "real" process, at certain times and in certain countries, is to assert that there exists for these cases a large and potentially unlimited number of possible measurements and indicators, all correlated with each other and testifying by their number and by the strength of their correlation to the reality of the underlying phenomenon.

In practice, of course, the range of available measurements and indicators is likely to be limited, and ordinarily there should be no need to compile for any particular time and country even all those data that could be found. On the contrary, one's usual aim will be economy: to get the greatest amount of useful information from the smallest body of data. The seven indicators of social mobilization listed above as $m_1$ to $m_7$ should quite suffice, in most cases, to give a fairly good first picture of the situation. They were chosen in part on grounds of availability and convenience, but also because they are less closely correlated, and hence less completely interchangeable, than some other indices might be.

Each of the seven processes chosen could itself be measured by several different indicators, but in each case these subindicators are apt to be very closely correlated and almost completely interchangeable. Literacy, for instance, can be measured as a percentage of the population above fifteen or above ten, or above seven years of age; it could be defined as the ability to recognize a few words, or to read consecutively, or to write. Each of these particular definitions would yield a different numerical answer, but so long as the same definition was used for each country, or for each period within the same country, each of these yardsticks would reveal much the same state of affairs. If applied to Morocco between 1920 and 1950, *e.g.*, each of these tests would have shown how the number of literate Moroccans began to outgrow the number of literate Frenchmen in that country, with obvious implications for its political future.

Similarly, urbanization could be measured in terms of the population of all localities of more than 2,000 or more than 5,000, or more than 20,000, or 50,000 inhabitants; or it could be measured, less satisfactorily, in terms of the population of all those localities that had a charter or a city form of government. Each of these criteria of measurement would have revealed the same process of large-scale urban growth in Finland between 1870 and 1920, for instance, or in India between 1900 and 1940, which had such far-reaching effects on political life in these countries. A recent unpublished study by Frederick E. Tibbetts 3d suggests once again the close interchangeability of different indicators of urban growth in Canada, as they bear upon the problems of assimilation and differentiation among the French-speaking and English-speaking population of that country. Urbanization, Tibbetts finds, has outstripped in recent decades the learning of English among French-Canadians; he finds among urban residents, and generally in nonagricultural occupations, a growing number of persons who speak no other language but French. The political significance of this development, which was largely concentrated in the province of Quebec, is highlighted by his observation that in 1951 Quebec (omitting Montreal), with 21 per cent of the total population of Canada, had only 4 and 7 per cent, respectively, of the veterans of World Wars I and II.[7]

Among the seven major indicators of social mobilization proposed in this paper, the correlations between economic development and literacy are less complete and the discrepancies more revealing. Ethiopia and Burma both have per capita gross national products of about $50, but Ethiopia has less than 5 per cent literates and is politically stable; Burma reports over 45 per cent literates and is not.[8] Of the states of India, Kerala, with one of the highest rates of literacy, elected a Communist government in the late 1950s.

It may thus be useful to seek answers to two kinds of questions: (1) how good is the correlation between the seven main indicators and (2) how interesting are the variant cases? As regards the first question, it has already been pointed out that the numerical values of the seven main indicators will not be identical. However if we think of each of these indicators as forming a separate scale, on which each country could rank anywhere from, say, the top fifth to the bottom fifth, then we could measure the extent to which the rankings of a country on each of these indicator scales are correlated. From general impressions of the data, I should surmise that these rank order correlations should have coefficients of correlation of about 0.6 to 0.8, accounting on the average for perhaps one-half of the observed variation. As regards the second question, each of the cases showing substantial discrepancies between some of the main indicators will have to be studied separately, but the examples of Burma and Kerala, just mentioned, suggest that such cases may well repay investigation, and that the comparison of indicators may serve political scientists as a crude but perhaps useful research device.

For a somewhat more refined study the notion of two thresholds may be introduced. The first of these is the threshold of significance, $S$, that is, the numerical value below which no significant departure from the customary workings of a traditional society can be detected and no significant disturbance appears to be created in its unchanged functioning. For each of the particular indicators, $m_1$ through $m_7$, we should expect to find a corresponding particular threshold of significance, $s_1$ through $s_7$; and our concept of social mobilization should imply that, once several major indicators move to or beyond this threshold of significance, the remaining indicators should also be at or above their respective levels of significance. The probability that this will be in fact the case should indicate once again what degree of reality, if any, may be inherent in the concept of social mobilization as an over-all process.

The second threshold would be that of criticality for significant changes in the side effects, actual or apparent, of the process of social mobilization. At what level of each of the indicators we listed above do such changes in social or political side effects appear?

The indicator of literacy may serve as an example. It has often been remarked that even a considerable advance in literacy, say from 10 per cent to 60 per cent of the population above fifteen years of age, does not seem to be correlated with any significant change in the birthrate, if one compares literacy and birthrate levels of a large number of countries in the 1950s. At the level of 80 per cent literacy, however, there appears a conspicuous change: for the same collection of countries, not one with a literacy rate above 80 per cent has a birthrate above 3 per cent a year.[9] As a provisional hypothesis for further testing, one might conjecture that a literacy rate of more than 80 per cent might indicate such an advanced and thoroughgoing stage of social mobilization and modernization as to influence even those intimate patterns of family life that find their expression in the birthrate of a country. Obviously such a hypothesis would require other evidence for confirmation, but even in its quite tentative stage it may illustrate our point. If it were true, then the 80 per cent level would be a threshold of criticality on the particular scale of literacy as an indicator of social mobilization.

Since we called the indicator of literacy $m_6$, we might write $c_6$ for the particular threshold of criticality on that scale and put it as equal to 80 per cent. It would then be a matter for further investigation to find out whether other critical changes also occur near the passing of the 80 per cent literacy level. If so, $c_6$ might turn out to be the main threshold of criticality for this indicator. If important side effects should show critical changes at different literacy levels, we might have to assume several thresholds of criticality, which we might write $c_6'$, $c_6''$, and so on.

Other indicators might well have their own thresholds of criticality at other percentage points on their particular scales. It might turn out, for instance, that most of the countries with more than 80 per cent literacy were also more than, say, 40 per cent urban, and that the apparent side effects observable above the 80 per cent literacy mark were also observable above the 40 per cent level on the urbanization scale. If such different but correlated thresholds of criticality could be found for all of our seven indicators, then the concept of social mobilization could be expressed as a probability that, if for some country $n$ different indicators should show values equal to or greater than their respective critical levels, then any relevant $(n+1)$th indicator also would turn out to be at or above its own critical threshold.

Much of what has been said thus far may be summarized in concise notation. If we write $P$ as the conventional symbol for probability, $M_S$ as the symbol for the overall process of social mobilization in regard to the thresholds of significance, and $M_C$ as the symbol for the same process in regard to the thresholds of criticality, then we may write the general concept of social mobilization briefly as follows:

(1) $M_S = P$ (if $m_n \leq s_n$, then $m_{n+1} \leq s_{n+1}$)

or briefly,

(1a) $M_S = P (m_n \leq s_n)$

and

(2) $M_C = P$ (if $m_n \leq c_n$, then $m_{n+1} \leq c_{n+1}$)

or briefly,

(2a) $M_C = (m_n \leq c_n)$

and perhaps also

(3) $M = P (M_S = M_C)$

None of these shorthand formulas should require further comment here. They merely summarize what has been said at greater length in the preceding pages. Readers who find such formulations uncongenial may skip them, therefore, without loss, so long as they have followed the verbal argument.

## II. SOME IMPLICATIONS FOR THE POLITICS OF DEVELOPMENT

In whatever country it occurs, social mobilization brings with it an expansion of the politically relevant strata of the population. These politically relevant strata are a broader group than the elite: they include all those persons who must be taken into account in politics. Dock workers and trade union members in Ghana, Nigeria, or the United States, for instance, are not necessarily members of the elites of these countries, but they are quite likely to count for something in their political life. In the developing countries of Asia, Africa and parts of Latin America, the political process usually does not include the mass of isolated, subsistence-farming, tradition-bound, and politically apathetic villagers, but it does include increasingly the growing numbers of city dwellers, market farmers, users of money, wage earners, radio listeners and literates in town and country. The growth in the numbers of these people produces mounting pressures for the transformation of political practices and institutions; and since this future growth can be estimated at least to some extent on the basis of trends and data from the recent past, some of the expectable growth in political pressures—we may call it the potential level of political tensions—can likewise be estimated.

Social mobilization also brings about a change in the quality of politics, by changing the range of human needs that impinge upon the political process. As people are uprooted from their physical and intellectual isolation in their immediate localities, from their old habits and traditions, and often from their old patterns of occupation and places of residence, they experience drastic changes in their needs. They may now come to need provisions for housing and employment, for social security against illness and old age, for medical care against the health hazards of their crowded new dwellings and places of work and the risk of accidents with unfamiliar machinery. They may need succor against the risks of cyclical or seasonal unemployment, against oppressive charges of rent or interest, and against sharp fluctuations in the prices of the main commodities which they must sell or buy. They need instruction for themselves and education for their children. They need, in short, a wide range and large amounts of new government services.

These needs ordinarily cannot be met by tradi-tional types of government, inherited from a pre-commercial and preindustrial age. Maharajahs, sultans, sheikhs, and chieftains all are quite unlikely to cope with these new problems, and traditional rule by land-owning oligarchies or long established religious bodies most often is apt to prove equally disappointing in the face of the new needs. Most of the attempts to change the characteristics of the traditional ruling families—perhaps by supplying them with foreign advisers or by having their children study in some foreign country—are likely to remain superficial in their effects, overshadowed by mounting pressures for more thoroughgoing changes.

In developing countries of today, however, the increasingly ineffective and unpopular traditional authorities cannot be replaced successfully by their historic successors in the Western world, the classic institutions of eighteenth and nineteenth century liberalism and laissez-faire. For the uprooted, impoverished and disoriented masses produced by social mobilization, it is surely untrue that that government is best that governs least. They are far more likely to need a direct transition from traditional government to the essentials of a modern welfare state. The developing countries of Asia, Africa, and parts of Latin America may have to accomplish, therefore, within a few decades a process of political change which in the history of Western Europe and North America took at least as many generations; and they may have to accomplish this accelerated change almost in the manner of a jump, omitting as impractical some of the historic stages of transition through a period of near laissez-faire that occurred in the West.

The growing need for new and old government services usually implies persistent political pressures for an increased scope of government and a greater relative size of the government sector in the national economy. In the mid-1950s, the total government budget—national, regional and local—tended to amount to roughly 10 per cent of the gross national product in the very poor and poorly mobilized countries with annual per capita gross national products at or below $100. For highly developed and highly mobilized countries, such as those with per capita gross national products at or above $900, the corresponding proportion of the total government sector was about 30 per cent. If one drew only the crudest and most provisional inference from these figures, one might expect something like a 2.5 per cent shift of national income into the government sector for every $100 gain in per capita gross national product in the course of economic development. It might be more plausible, however, to expect a somewhat more rapid expansion of the government sector during the earlier stages of economic development, but the elucidation of this entire problem—with all its obvious political implications—would require and reward a great deal more research.

The relationship between the total process of social mobilization and the growth of the national income, it should be recalled here, is by no means symmetrical. Sustained income growth is very unlikely without social mobilization, but a good deal of social mobilization may be going on even in the absence of per capita income growth, such as occurs in countries with poor resources or investment policies, and with rapid population growth. In such cases, social mobilization still would generate pressures for an expansion of government services and hence of the government sector, even in a relatively stagnant or conceivably retrograde economy. Stopping or reversing in such cases the expansion of government or the process of social mobilization behind it—even if this could be done—hardly would make matters much better. The more attractive course for such countries might rather be to use the capabilities of their expanding governments so as to bring about improvements in their resources and investment policies, and an eventual resumption of economic growth. To what extent this has been, or could be, brought about in cases of this kind, would make another fascinating topic for study.

The figures just given apply, of course, only to non-Communist countries; the inclusion of Communist states would make the average in each class of government sectors higher. It would be interesting to investigate, however, whether and to what extent the tendency toward the relative expansion of the government sector in the course of social mobilization applies also, *mutatis mutandis,* to the Communist countries.

A greater scope of governmental services and functions requires ordinarily an increase in the capabilities of government. Usually it requires an increase in the numbers and training of governmental personnel, an increase in governmental offices and institutions, and a significant improvement in administrative organization and efficiency. A rapid process of social mobilization thus tends to generate major pressures for political and administrative reform. Such reforms may include notably both a quantitative expansion of the bureaucracy and its qualitative improvement in the direction of a competent civil service—even though these two objectives at times may clash.

Similar to its impact on this specific area of government, social mobilization tends to generate also pressures for a more general transformation of the political elite. It tends to generate pressures for a broadening and partial transformation of elite functions, of elite recruitment, and of elite communications. On all these counts, the old elites of traditional chiefs, village headmen, and local notables are likely to prove ever more inadequate; and political leadership may tend to shift to the new

political elite of party or quasi-party organizations, formal and informal, legal or illegal, but always led by the new "marginal men" who have been exposed more or less thoroughly to the impact of modern education and urban life.

Something similar applies to elite communications. The more broadly recruited elites must communicate among themselves, and they must do so more often impersonally and over greater distances. They must resort more often to writing and to paper work. At the same time they must direct a greater part of their communications output at the new political strata; this puts a premium on oratory and journalism, and on skill in the use of all mass media of communication. At the same time rapid social mobilization causes a critical problem in the communications intake of elites. It confronts them with the ever present risk of losing touch with the newly mobilized social strata which until recently still did not count in politics. Prime Minister Nehru's reluctance to take into account the strength and intensity of Mahratti sentiment in the language conflict of Bombay in the 1950s and his general tendency since the mid-1930s to underestimate the strength of communal and linguistic sentiment in India suggest the seriousness of this problem even for major democratic leaders.

The increasing numbers of the mobilized population, and the greater scope and urgency of their needs for political decisions and governmental services, tend to translate themselves, albeit with a time lag, into increased political participation. This may express itself informally through greater numbers of people taking part in crowds and riots, in meetings and demonstrations, in strikes and uprisings, or, less dramatically, as members of a growing audience for political communications, written or by radio, or finally as members of a growing host of organizations. While many of these organizations are ostensibly non-political, such as improvement societies, study circles, singing clubs, gymnastic societies, agricultural and commercial associations, fraternal orders, workmen's benefit societies, and the like, they nevertheless tend to acquire a political tinge, particularly in countries where more open outlets for political activities are not available. But even where there are established political parties and elections, a network of seemingly nonpolitical or marginally political organizations serves an important political function by providing a dependable social setting for the individuals who have been partly or wholly uprooted or alienated from their traditional communities. Such organizations may serve at the same time as marshalling grounds for the entry of these persons into political life.

Where people have the right to vote, the effects of social mobilization are likely to be reflected in the electoral statistics. This process finds its expression both through a tendency towards a higher voting participation of those already enfranchised and through an extension of the franchise itself to additional groups of the population. Often the increase in participation amongst those who already have the right to vote precedes the enfranchisement of new classes of voters, particularly in countries where the broadening of the franchise is occurring gradually. Thus in Norway between 1830 and 1860, voting participation remained near the level of about 10 per cent of the adult male population; in the 1870s and 1880s this participation rose rapidly among the enfranchised voters, followed by extensions of the franchise, until by the year 1900, 40 per cent of the Norwegian men were actually voting. This process was accompanied by a transformation of Norwegian politics, the rise to power of the radical peasant party *Venstre,* and a shift from the earlier acceptance of the existing Swedish-Norwegian Union to rising demands for full Norwegian independence.[10] These political changes had been preceded or accompanied by a rise in several of the usual indicators of social mobilization among the Norwegian people.

Another aspect of the process of social mobilization is the shift of emphasis away from the parochialism and internationalism of many traditional cultures to a preoccupation with the supralocal but far less than worldwide unit of the territorial, and eventually national, state.

An as yet unpublished study of American communications before the American Revolution, which has been carried on by Richard Merritt, shows how during the years 1735–1775 in the colonial newspapers the percentage of American or all-colonial symbols rose from about 10 to about 40 per cent, at the cost, in the main, of a decline in the share of symbols referring to places or events in the world outside the colonies and Britain, while Britain's share in American news attention remained relatively unchanged. Within the group of American symbols, the main increase occurred among those which referred to America or to the colonies as a whole, rather than among those referring to particular colonies or sections.[11]

More recent experiences in some of the "development countries" also suggest a more rapid rise of attention devoted to national topics than of that given to world affairs, on the one hand, and to purely local matters, on the other. This, however, is at present largely an impression. The nature and extent of attention shifts in mass media, as well as in popular attitudes, in the course of social mobilization is a matter for research that should be as promising as it is needed.[12]

Some data on the flow of domestic and foreign mails point in a similar direction. Of five development countries for which data are readily available the ratio of domestic to foreign mail rose substantially in four—Egypt, Iran, Nigeria, and Turkey —from 1913 to 1946–51; the fifth, Indonesia, was an exception but was the scene of internal unrest and protracted warfare against the Dutch during much of the latter period. The trend for Egypt, Iran, Nigeria, and Turkey is confirmed in each case by data for the intermediate period 1928–34, which are also intermediate, in each case, between the low domestic-foreign mail ratio for 1913 and the high ratios for 1946–51. Many additional development countries—including the Gold Coast (now Ghana), the Belgian Congo, Malaya, French Morocco, Kenya-Uganda, Tanganyika, Mozambique, and Malaya —for which data were found only for the 1928–34 to 1946–51 comparison, show upward trends in their ratios of domestic to foreign mail.[13] Here again, a relatively moderate investment in the further collection and study of data might lead to interesting results.

According to some data from another recent study, a further side effect of social mobilization and economic development might possibly be first a substantial expansion, and then a lesser but significant reduction, of the share of the international trade sector in the national economy. Thus, in the course of British development, the proportion of total foreign trade (including trade to British overseas possessions) rose from an average of 20 per cent in 1830–40 to a peak of 60 per cent in 1870–79, remained close to that level until 1913, but declined subsequently and stood at less than 40 per cent in 1959. Similarly, the proportion of foreign trade to national income rose in Germany from about 28 per cent in 1802–1830 to a peak of 45 per cent in 1870–79, declined to 35 per cent in 1900–1909, and by 1957 had recovered, for the much smaller German Federal Republic, to only 42 per cent. In Japan, the early proportion of foreign trade to national income was 15 per cent in 1885–89, rising to peaks of 41 per cent in 1915–19 and 40 per cent in 1925–29; but by 1957 it stood at only 31 per cent. Data for Denmark, Norway, France and Argentina give a similar picture, while the same foreign-trade-to-national-income ratio in the United States fell, with minor fluctuations, from 23 per cent in 1799 to less than 9 per cent in 1958.[14] Here again the evidence is incomplete and partly contradictory, and the tentative interpretation, indicated at the beginning of this paragraph, still stands in need of confirmation and perhaps modification through additional research.

The problem of the ratio of the sector of internationally oriented economic activities relative to total national income—and thus indirectly the problem of the political power potential of internationally exposed or involved interest groups *vis-à-vis* the rest of the community—leads us to the problem of the size of states and of the scale of effective political communities. As we have seen, the process of social mobilization generates strong pressures towards increasing the capabilities of government, by increasing the volume and range of demands made upon the government and administration, and by widening the scope of politics and the membership of the politically relevant strata. The same process increases the frequency and the critical importance of direct communications between government and governed. It thus necessarily increases the importance of the language, the media, and the channels through which these communications are carried on.

Other things assumed equal, the stage of rapid social mobilization may be expected, therefore, to promote the consolidation of states whose peoples already share the same language, culture, and major social institutions; while the same process may tend to strain or destroy the unity of states whose population is already divided into several groups with different languages or cultures or basic ways of life. By the same token, social mobilization may tend to promote the merging of several smaller states, or political units such as cantons, principalities, sultanates or tribal areas, whose populations already share substantially the same language, culture and social system; and it may tend to inhibit, or at least to make more difficult, the merging of states or political units whose populations or ruling personnel differ substantially in regard to any of these matters. Social mobilization may thus assist to some extent in the consolidation of the United Arab Republic, but raise increasing problems for the politics and administration of multilingual India—problems which the federal government of India may have to meet or overcome by a series of creative adjustments.[15]

In the last analysis, however, the problem of the scale of states goes beyond the effects of language, culture, or institutions, important as all these are. In the period of rapid social mobilization, the acceptable sale of a political unit will tend to depend eventually upon its performance. If a government fails to meet the increasing burdens put upon it by the process of social mobilization, a growing proportion of the population is likely to become alienated and disaffected from the state, even if the same language, culture and basic social institutions were shared originally throughout the entire state territory by rulers and ruled alike. The secession of the United States and of Ireland from the British Empire, and of the Netherlands and of Switzerland from the German Empire may serve in part as examples. At bottom, the popular acceptance of a government in a period of social mobilization is most of all a matter of its capabilities and the manner in which they are used—that is, essentially a matter of its responsiveness to the felt needs of its population. If it proves persistently incapable or unresponsive, some or many of its subjects will cease to identify themselves with it psychologically; it will be reduced to ruling by force where it can no longer rule by display, example and persuasion; and if political alternatives to it appear, it will be replaced eventually by other political units, larger or smaller in extent, which at least promise to respond more effectively to the needs and expectations of their peoples.

In practice the results of social mobilization often have tended to increase the size of the state, well beyond the old tribal areas, petty principalities, or similar districts of the traditional era, while increasing the direct contact between government and governed far beyond the levels of the sociologically superficial and often half-shadowy empire of the past.

This growth in the size of modern states, capable of coping with the results of social mobilization, is counteracted and eventually inhibited, however, as their size increases, by their tendency to increasing preoccupation with their own internal affairs. There is considerable evidence for this trend toward a self-limitation in the growth of states through a decline in the attention, resources and responsiveness available for coping with the implicit needs and explicit messages of the next marginal unit of population and territory on the verge of being included in the expanding state.[16]

The remarks in this section may have sufficed to illustrate, though by no means to exhaust, the significance of the process of social mobilization in the economic and political development of countries. The main usefulness of the concept, however, should lie in the possibility of quantitative study which it offers. How much social mobilization, as measured by our seven indicators, has been occurring in some country per year or per decade during some period of its history, or during recent times? And what is the meaning of the differences between the rates at which some of the constituent subprocesses of social mobilization may have been going on? Although specific data will have to be found separately for each country, it should be possible to sketch a general quantitative model to show some of the interrelations and their possible significance.

## III. A QUANTITATIVE MODEL OF THE SOCIAL MOBILIZATION PROCESS

For a quantitative description, it is convenient to express our first six indicators not in terms of the total percentage of the population which is literate, or exposed to modern life, etc., but in terms only of that average annual percentage of the total population which has been added to, or subtracted from, the total share of the population in that category. If for some country our indicator showed, say, 40 per cent exposed to significant aspects of modern life in 1940, and 60 per cent so exposed in 1950, the average annual percentage shift, $dm_1$ would be 2 per cent. The seventh indicator, per capita increase, may be broken up into two elements and written as the annual percentage of the total income added, $dm_7$ and the annual percentage of population growth, $p$.

Adopting these conventions, we may use in this model, for purposes of illustration, crudely estimated magnitudes from various collections of data. If we add indicators for the increase in voting participation, and in linguistic, cultural or political assimilation, we may write for a case of fairly rapid social mobilization a small table of the sort shown in Table 1. The case represented by this table is an imaginary one, but the different rates of subprocesses of social mobilization are not necessarily unrealistic, and neither are the consequences suggested by this model, for the stability of the government in any country to which these or similar assumptions would apply.

Before discussing these consequences more explicitly, it should be made clear that the annual rates of change are likely to be realistic, at most, only for countries during the rapid middle stages of the process of social mobilization and economic development—say, for a range of between 10 to 80 per cent literacy and for analogous ranges of other indicators of economic development. In the earliest stages, the annual percentages of the population shifting into a more mobilized state are apt to be much smaller, and in the late stages of the process something like a "ceiling effect" may be expected to appear—once 80 or 90 per cent of the population have become literate, any further annual gains in the percentage of literates in the population are likely to be small.

Within the middle stages of development, however, which are appropriate to the assumptions of the model, a cumulative strain on political stability may be expected. All the rates of change in group I tend to make for increased demands or burdens upon the government, and all of them have median values above 1 per cent per year. The rates of change in group II are related to the capabilities of the government for coping with these burdens, but the median values of all these rates, with only one exception, are well below 1 per cent. If it were not for this exception—the assumed 5 per cent annual increase in national income—one would have to predict from the model an annual shift of perhaps 1 per cent or more of the population into the category of at least partly socially mobilized but largely unassimilated and dissatisfied people.

If one assumes, in accordance with this model, an annual entry of 2.75 per cent of the population into the mass media audience and a shift of only 0.6 per cent into non-agricultural employment, then the expectable increase in the numbers of not adequately reemployed new members of the mass media audience might be as high as 2.15 per cent of the population per year, or more than one-fifth of the population within a decade. This might be the proportion of people newly participating in their imagination in the new opportunities and attractions of modern life, while still being denied most or all of these new opportunities in fact—something which should be a fairly effective prescription for accumulating political trouble. The spread of more effective methods of production and perhaps of improved patterns of land tenure, rural credit, and other betterments within the agricultural sector could do something to counteract this tendency; but short of major and sustained efforts at such agricultural improvements the dangerous gap between the fast-growing, mass media audience and the slow-growing circle of more adequately employed and

**TABLE 1—A Hypothetical Example of a Country Undergoing Rapid Social Mobilization: Rates of Change**

| SYMBOL OF INDICATOR | | DESCRIPTION | AVERAGE ANNUAL % OF TOTAL POPULATION OR INCOME ADDED TO CATEGORY | |
|---|---|---|---|---|
| | | | Range | Median |
| Group I: | $dm_1$ | Shift into any substantial exposure to modernity, incl. rumors, demonstrations of machinery or merchandise, etc. | 2.0 to 4.0 | 3.0 |
| | $dm_2$ | Shift into mass media audience (radio, movies, posters, press) | 1.5 to 4.0 | 2.75 |
| | $dm_8$ | Increase in voting participation | 0.2 to 4.0 | 2.1 |
| | $dm_6$ | Increase in literacy | 1.0 to 1.4 | 1.2 |
| | $dm_3$ | Change of locality of residence | 1.0 to 1.5 | 1.25 |
| | $p$ | Population growth | (1.9 to 3.3) | (2.6) |
| Group II: | $dm_5$ | Occupational shift out of agriculture | 0.4 to 1.0 | 0.7 |
| | $dm_4$ | Change from rural to urban residence | 0.1 to 1.2 | 0.5 |
| | $a$ | Linguistic, cultural or political assimilation | —0.5 to 1.0 | 0.25 |
| | $dy$ | Income growth | (2.0 to 8.0) | (5.0) |
| | $dm_7$ | Income growth per capita | — | (2.3) |

NOTE: Figures in parentheses refer to percentage increases against the previous year, and thus are not strictly comparable to percentage shifts among sub-categories of the total population. A shift of 1.2 per cent of all adults into the category of literates, for instance, would refer to the total adult population, including the part just added by population aging; etc.

equipped persons is likely to remain and to increase.

If linguistic, cultural or political assimilation—that is, the more or less permanent change of stable habits of language, culture, legitimacy and loyalty—is also a relevant problem in the country concerned, then the lag of the slow assimilation rate, put at only 0.25 per cent per year in our model, behind the far more rapid mobilization rates of 0.5 to 3.0 per cent for the various subprocesses in our model, might be even larger for some of them, and potentially more serious.

Table 2 shows some of the implications of our model for a hypothetical country of 10 million population, $100 per capita income, a principal language spoken by 35 per cent of its inhabitants, and a relatively low degree of social mobilization in 1950. Conditions somewhat similar to these can in fact be found in several countries in Africa and Asia. Table 2 then shows the expectable state of affairs for our imaginary country in 1960 and 1970, if we assume the rates of change given in our model, as set forth in Table 1, and their persistence over twenty years. As can be seen from Table 2, the cumulative effects of these changes from 1950 to 1960 will appear still moderate, but by 1970 these effects will have become so great that many of the political institutions and practices of 1950 might be no longer applicable to the new conditions.

As Table 2 shows, a major transformation of the underlying political and social structure of a country could occur—and could pose a potential threat to the stability of any insufficiently reform-minded government there—even during a period of substantially rising per capita income.

To be sure, many of these political and social difficulties could be assuaged with the help of the benefits potentially available through the 5 per cent increase in total national income, which was assumed for our model. Such a 5 per cent growth rate of total income is not necessarily unrealistic. It is close to the average of 5.3 per cent, found by Paul Studenski in a recent survey of data from a large number of non-Communist countries.[17] Since the rate of population growth, assumed for the model, was 2.6 per cent—which is well above the world average in recent years—the average per capita income might be expected to rise by slightly more than 2 per cent per year.[18] These additional amounts of available income might well go at least some part of the way to meet the new popular needs and expectations aroused by the mobilization process, if the income can be devoted to consumption and price levels remain stable. But any increments of income will also be needed for savings (in addition to loans and grants from abroad) to permit a high rate of investment and an adequate rate of expansion of opportunities for education, employment and consumption for the growing numbers of the mobilized population.

These beneficial consequences could only be expected, however, if we assume that an adequate share of the increase in income would go directly or indirectly to the newly mobilized groups and strata of the population. Unfortunately, no assumption of this kind would be realistic for many of the developing countries of Asia and Africa.

It would be far more realistic to assume that in most of these countries the top 10 per cent of income receivers are getting about 50 per cent of the total national income, if not more. If we assume further, as seems not implausible, that in the absence of specific social reforms the increase in income will be distributed among the various strata of the population roughly in proportion to the present share of each group in the total national income, then we may expect that the richest 10 per cent of the people will get about 50 per cent of the additional income produced by income growth. At the same time, since these richest 10 per cent are not likely to be much more fertile than the rest of the population, they are likely to get only 10 per cent of the population increase; and they will, therefore, on the average

**TABLE 2—A Hypothetical Example of a Country Undergoing Rapid Social Mobilization: Assumed Levels for 1950 and Expectable Levels for 1960 and 1970**

| SYMBOL OF INDICATOR | | DESCRIPTION | PER CENT OF TOTAL POPULATION | | |
|---|---|---|---|---|---|
| | | | 1950 | 1960 | 1970 |
| Group I: | $m_1$ | Population exposed to modernity | 35 | 65 | 95 |
| | $m_2$ | Mass media audience | 20 | 47.5 | 75 |
| | $m_8$ | Actual voting participation | 20 | 41 | 62 |
| | $m_6$ | Literates | 15 | 27 | 39 |
| | $m_3$ | Persons who changed locality of residence since birth | 10 | 22.5 | 35 |
| | $P$ | Total population (millions) | (10) | (12.9) | (16.7) |
| Group II: | $m_5$ | Population in non-agricultural occupations | 18 | 25 | 32 |
| | $m_4$ | Urban population | 15 | 20 | 25 |
| | $A$ | Linguistically assimilated population | 35 | 37.5 | 40 |
| | $Y$ | Total income (million $) | (1000) | (1629) | (2653) |
| | $m_7$ | Per capita income ($) | (100) | (126) | (159) |

NOTE: Figures in parentheses refer to absolute numbers, not percentages. Because of rounding, calculations are approximate.

not only get richer in absolute terms, but they will also retain the full extent of their relative lead over the rest of the population; and so they will increase in absolute terms the gap in income that separates them from the mass of their countrymen. Under the same assumptions, however, we should expect that the poorest nine-tenths of the population will get only one-tenth of the total income gain, but that they will get up to nine-tenths of the entire population growth; and that on the average these poorest 90 per cent of the people will remain in relative terms as far below the level of the rich one-tenth as ever. The fact that the poorer majority will have become slightly richer in absolute terms may then in the main increase their awareness of the wide gap between their living standards and those of their rulers; and it might at the same time increase their ability to take political action.

Differently put, if for the entire country the *average* per capita income was assumed to rise, we must now add that under the assumptions stated, the "social gap"—the gap between the incomes of the poorest 90 per cent and those of the top 10 per cent—may well be expected to increase. Political stability, however, may well be more affected by changes in the income gap than by changes in the average which in this respect might be little more than a statistical abstraction. Our model would lead us to expect, therefore, on the whole the danger of a significant deterioration of political stability in any development country to which its assumptions might apply. Since these assumptions were chosen with an eye to making them parallel, as far as possible, to the more rapid among the actual rates found in countries of this type, the expectations of rising political tensions in countries undergoing rapid social mobilization may not be unrealistic.

To rely upon automatic developments in economic and political life in those countries of the Free World to which the assumptions of our model apply, would be to court mounting instability, the overthrow of existing governments and their replacement by no less unstable successors, or else their eventual absorption into the Communist bloc. Deliberate political and economic intervention into the social mobilization process, on the other hand, might open up some more hopeful perspectives. Such intervention should not aim at retarding economic and social development, in the manner of the policies of the regime of Prince Metternich in Austria during much of the first half of the nineteenth century. Those policies of slowing down social mobilization and economic development in the main only diminished the capabilities of the government, paved the way to domestic failures and international defeats and were followed over the course of three generations by the persistent backwardness and ultimate destruction of the state. A more promising policy might have to be, on the contrary, one of

active intervention in favor of more rapid and more balanced growth; a somewhat more even distribution of income, related more closely to rewards for productive contributions rather than for status and inheritance; the more productive investment of available resources; and a sustained growth in the political and administrative capabilities of government and of ever wider strata of the population.

The crude model outlined above may have some modest usefulness in surveying and presenting in quantitative terms some of the magnitudes and rates of change that would be relevant for understanding the basic problems of such a more constructive policy in developing countries.[19] Somewhat as the economic models of the late Lord Keynes drew attention to the need of keeping the national rates of spending and investment in a country in balance with the national propensity to save, so it may become possible some day for political scientists to suggest in what areas, in what respects, and to what extent the efforts of government will have to be kept abreast of the burdens generated by the processes of social mobilization. The first steps toward this distant goal might be taken through research which would replace the hypothetical figures of the model by actual data from specific countries, so that the model could be tested, revised, and advanced nearer toward application.

Any cooperation which social scientists and other students of cultural, political, and economic development and change could extend to this effort—by improving the design of the model or by suggesting more precise or refined definitions of some of its categories, or by furnishing specific data—would be very much appreciated.

# APPENDIX. A GLANCE AT ACTUAL CASES: PARTIAL DATA FOR NINETEEN COUNTRIES

(with the assistance of Charles L. Taylor and Alex Weilenmann)

The following data, presented in Tables 3-5, have been compiled or computed, respectively, in order to illustrate the possibility, in principle, of the kind of analysis proposed in the main body of this paper, and to demonstrate the availability of enough actual data to get such work at least started.

For certain categories—such as voting participation, immigration and internal migration, linguistic and cultural assimilation, and the inequality of income distribution—not enough data were readily available to permit even the simple type of tabulation presented here. Even for the data that we have collected, the gaps in such countries as Ghana, Ni-

**TABLE 3-A—Selected Indices of Social Mobilization for Nineteen Countries: Aggregate Levels**

| Country | (1) GNP per capita (1955) US $ | (2) GNP (1955) million US $ | (3) Population (1953, 1958) 1,000 | (4) Radio audience % | (5) Newspaper readers % | (6) Literates % | (7) Work force in non-agric. occupations % | (8) Urban Population % |
|---|---|---|---|---|---|---|---|---|
| Venezuela | 762 | 4,400 | 5,440 | 12.8 ('48) | — | 43.5 ('41) | 50 ('41) | 39 ('41) |
| | | | 6,320 | 48.9 ('57) | 30.6 ('56) | 51.0 ('50) | 59 ('50) | 50 ('50) |
| Argentina | 374 | 7,150 | 18,400 | 51.2 ('50) | — | 64.9 ('14) | 75 ('47) | 53 ('14) |
| | | | 20,248 | 65.0 ('59) | 54.0 ('58) | 86.7 ('47) | 77 ('55) | 63 ('47) |
| Cuba | 361 | 2,180 | 5,829 | 42.7 ('49) | — | 71.8 ('31) | 59 ('43) | 50 ('43) |
| | | | 6,466 | 59.3 ('59) | 38.7 ('56) | 76.4 ('53) | 58 ('53) | 57 ('53) |
| Colombia | 330 | 4,180 | 12,111 | 17.6 ('50) | — | 55.8 ('38) | 28 ('38) | 29 ('38) |
| | | | 13,522 | 24.7 ('56) | 17.7 ('58) | 61.5 ('51) | 46 ('51) | 36 ('51) |
| Turkey | 276 | 6,463 | 22,850 | 4.8 ('48) | — | 20.9 ('35) | 18 ('35) | 24 ('40) |
| | | | 25,932 | 17.6 ('59) | 9.6 ('52) | 34.3 ('50) | 23 ('55) | 25 ('50) |
| Brazil | 262 | 15,315 | 55,772 | 19.2 ('50) | — | 43.3 ('40) | 33 ('40) | 31 ('40) |
| | | | 65,725 | 25.5 ('58) | 18.9 ('57) | 48.4 ('50) | 42 ('50) | 37 ('50) |
| Philippines | 201 | 4,400 | 21,211 | 1.6 ('49) | — | 48.8 ('39) | 27 ('39) | 23 ('39) |
| | | | 24,010 | 5.2 ('57) | 5.7 ('56) | 61.3 ('48) | 43 ('58) | 24 ('48) |
| Mexico | 187 | 5,548 | 28,056 | 11.4 ('48) | — | 48.4 ('40)[a] | 35 ('40) | 35 ('40) |
| | | | 32,348 | 34.6 ('58) | 14.4 ('52) | 56.8 ('50)[a] | 42 ('58) | 43 ('50) |
| Chile | 180 | 1,220 | 6,437 | 36.9 ('49) | — | 71.8 ('40) | 65 ('40) | 52 ('40)[b] |
| | | | 7,298 | 38.4 ('58) | 22.2 ('52) | 80.6 ('52) | 70 ('52) | 60 ('52)[b] |
| Guatemala | 179 | 580 | 3,058 | 2.8 ('50) | — | 34.6 ('40)[a] | 29 ('40) | 27 ('21) |
| | | | 3,546 | 4.6 ('54) | 6.6 ('58) | 29.7 ('50)[a] | 32 ('50) | 32 ('50) |

## TABLE 3-A—Selected Indices of Social Mobilization for Nineteen Countries: Aggregate Levels (Cont'd.)

| Country | (1) GNP per capita (1955) US $ | (2) GNP (1955) million US $ | (3) Population (1953, 1958) 1,000 | (4) Radio audience % | (5) Newspaper readers % | (6) Literates % | (7) Work force in non-agric. occupations % | (8) Urban Population % |
|---|---|---|---|---|---|---|---|---|
| Honduras | 137 | 228 | 1,556 / 1,828 | 5.9 ('48) / 7.2 ('57) | — / 7.5 ('57) | 32.6 ('35)[a] / 35.2 ('50)[a] | 17 ('50) / 16 ('56) | 29 ('45) / 31 ('50) |
| Ghana | 135 | 624 | 4,478 / 4,836 | 0.8 ('48) / 8.9 ('59) | — / 11.4 ('58) | 20–25 ('50) | — / — | — / — |
| Egypt | 133 | 3,065 | 22,003 / 24,781 | 4.8 ('49) / 13.2 ('57) | — / 7.5 ('52) | 14.8 ('37) / 22.1 ('47) | 29 ('37) / 36 ('47) | 25 ('37) / 30 ('47) |
| Thailand | 100 | 2,050 | 19,556 / 21,474 | 0.5 ('50) / 1.6 ('58) | — / 1.2 ('52) | 52.0 ('47) / 64.0 ('56) | 11 ('37) / 12 ('54) | — / 10 ('47) |
| Republic of the Congo (Leopoldville) | 98 | 1,639 | 12,154 / 13,559 | 0.2 ('48) / 1.0 ('59) | — / 0.9 ('57) | 35–40 ('50) / — | — / 15 ('55) | 16 ('47) |
| India | 72 | 27,400 | 372,623 / 397,390 | 0.3 ('48) / 1.6 ('59) | — / 2.7 ('58) | 9.1 ('31)[c] / 15.1 ('41)[c] / 19.9 ('51) | 29 ('51) / 30 ('55) | 11 ('31)[c] / 13 ('41)[c] / 17 ('51) |
| Nigeria | 70 | 2,250 | 30,104 / 33,052 | 0.2 ('48) / 1.0 ('58) | — / 2.4 ('58) | 11.5 ('52/3) | 26 ('31) | 4 ('31) / 5 ('52) |
| Pakistan | 56 | 4,560 | 80,039 / 85,635 | 0.3 ('50) / 1.2 ('58) | — / 2.7 ('54) | 9.1 ('31)[c] / 15.1 ('41)[c] / 13.5 ('51)[a] | 24 ('51) / 35 ('54/6) | 11 ('31)[c] / 13 ('41)[c] / 11 ('51) |
| Burma | 52 | 1,012 | 19,272 / 20,255 | 0.2 ('48) / 0.5 ('56) | — / 2.4 ('52) | 40.2 ('31) / 57.3 ('54) | 32 ('31) / 30 ('55) | 10 ('31) / — |

a. Unequal age groups (see Notes below, Column 6).
b. Variation of definition of "urban" (see Notes below, Column 8).
c. Applies to pre-partition India, i.e., to India and Pakistan together.
Further notes to Tables 3-5 begin on p. 599.

**TABLE 3B—Selected Indices of Social Mobilization for Nineteen Countries: Aggregate Levels: Projected for 1945 and 1955**

| Country | | (4) Radio Audience % | (6) Literates % | (7) Work force in non-agric. occupations % | (8) Urban population % | (9) Exposure to modernity % |
|---|---|---|---|---|---|---|
| Venezuela | '45 | 1 | 47 | 54 | 44 | 63 |
| | '55 | 41 | 55 | 64 | 56 | 75 |
| Argentina | '45 | 44 | 85 | 74 | 62 | >95 |
| | '55 | 59 | 92 | 77 | 65 | >95 |
| Cuba | '45 | 36 | 75 | 59 | 51 | 83 |
| | '55 | 52 | 77 | 58 | 58 | 84 |
| Colombia | '45 | 12 | 59 | 38 | 33 | 60 |
| | '55 | 22 | 63 | 52 | 38 | 72 |
| Turkey | '45 | 1 | 30 | 21 | 24 | 34 |
| | '55 | 13 | 39 | 23 | 26 | 40 |
| Brazil | '45 | 15 | 46 | 37 | 34 | 52 |
| | '55 | 23 | 51 | 46 | 40 | 61 |
| Philippines | '45 | 0 | 57 | 32 | 24 | 56 |
| | '55 | 4 | 71 | 41 | 25 | 70 |
| Mexico | '45 | 4 | 52 | 37 | 39 | 57 |
| | '55 | 28 | 61 | 41 | 37 | 64 |
| Chile | '45 | 36 | 75 | 67 | 56 | 89 |
| | '55 | 38 | 83 | 71 | 62 | >95 |
| Guatemala | '45 | 1 | 32 | 31 | 31 | 40 |
| | '55 | 5 | 27 | 34 | 33 | 42 |
| Honduras | '45 | 6 | 35 | 18 | 29 | 40 |
| | '55 | 7 | 36 | 16 | 33 | 43 |
| Ghana | '45 | 0 | — | — | — | — |
| | '55 | 6 | — | — | — | 21[b] (1950/58) |
| Egypt | '45 | 1 | 20 | 35 | 29 | 40 |
| | '55 | 11 | 28 | 42 | 34 | 47 |
| Thailand | '45 | 0 | 49 | 12 | — | 38 |
| | '55 | 1 | 63 | 12 | — | 47 |
| Republic of the Congo (Leopoldville) | '45 | 0 | — | — | — | — |
| | '55 | 1 | — | — | — | 33[b] (1947/50) |
| India | '45 | 0 | 18[a] | 27 | 14[a] | 28[c] |
| | '55 | 1 | 24[a] | 30 | 16[a] | 34[c] |
| Nigeria | '45 | 0 | — | — | 5 | — |
| | '55 | 1 | — | — | 5 | 23[b] (1931/53) |
| Pakistan | '45 | 0 | 18[a] | 11 | 14[a] | 20[c] |
| | '55 | 1 | 24[a] | 35 | 16[a] | 37[c] |
| Burma | '45 | 0 | 50 | 31 | — | 50 |
| | '55 | 0 | 58 | 30 | — | 55 |

Data in Columns 4, 6, 7, 8, based on corresponding data in Tables III-A and IV-A.

Data in Column 9 are 125% of means of the two highest figures in each of the other columns. (See Notes.)

a. Pre-partition India.

b. Based on the two highest data for country in Table III-A.

c. No distinction made between pre-partition India and India and Pakistan respectively.

**TABLE 4-A—Selected Indices of Social Mobilization for Nineteen Countries: Shifts and Rates of Growth**

| Country | LEVEL (1) Per capita GNP (1955) US $ | AVERAGE ANNUAL RATES OF GROWTH (2) Total GDP (1954-58) % | (3) Population (1953-58) % | (4) Per capita GDP (1954-58) % | (5) Radio audience % | AVERAGE ANNUAL SHIFTS (6) Literate population % | (7) Work force in non-agric. occupations % | (8) Urban population % | (9)* Population exposed to modernity % |
|---|---|---|---|---|---|---|---|---|---|
| Venezuela | 762 | (8.8) | (3.0) | (7.5) | 4.0 (1948–57) | 0.8 (1941–50) | 1.0 (1941–50) | 1.2 (1941–50) | 1.2 / 3.2 / 2.2 |
| Argentina | 374 | (2.4) | (1.9) | (0.5) | 1.5 (1950–59) | 0.7 (1914–47) | 0.3 (1947–55) | 0.3 (1914–47) | 0.0 / 1.4 / 0.7 |
| Cuba | 361 | (3)ª (1957–60) | (1.9) | (1.1)ᵉ (1957–60) | 1.7 (1949–59) | 0.2 (1931–53) | —0.1 (1943–53) | 0.7 (1943–53) | 0.1 / 1.5 / 0.8 |
| Colombia | 330 | (3.1) | (2.2) | (0.8) | 1.2 (1950–56) | 0.4 (1938–51) | 1.4 (1938–51) | 0.6 (1938–51) | 1.2 / 1.6 / 1.4 |
| Turkey | 276 | (8.1) | (2.7) | (5.2) | 1.2 (1948–59) | 0.9 (1935–50) | 0.3 (1935–55) | 0.1 (1945–50) | 0.6 / 1.3 / 1.0 |
| Brazil | 262 | (6.4) | (2.4) | (4.0) | 0.8 (1950–58) | 0.5 (1940–50) | 0.8 (1940–50) | 0.5 (1940–50) | 0.9 / 1.0 / 1.0 |
| Philippines | 201 | (4.8) | (2.5) | (2.2) | 0.5 (1949–57) | 1.4 (1939–48) | 0.8 (1939–58) | 0.1 (1939–48) | 1.4 / 1.4 / 1.4 |
| Mexico | 187 | (4)ª (1957–60) | (2.9) | (1.1)ᵉ (1957–60) | 2.3 (1948–58) | 0.8ᵉ (1940–50) | 0.4 (1940–58) | 0.8 (1940–50) | 0.7 / 1.9 / 1.3 |
| Chile | 180 | (2.0) | (2.5) | (—0.6) | 0.2 (1949–58) | 0.7 (1940–52) | 0.4 (1940–52) | 0.7ᶠ (1940–52) | 0.6 / 0.9 / 0.8 |

| Country | | | | | | | | Column 9 | | |
|---|---|---|---|---|---|---|---|---|---|---|
| Guatemala | 179 | (8.3) | (3.0) | (5.2) | 0.4 (1950–54) | −0.5[e] (1940–50) | 0.3 (1940–50) | 0.2 (1921–50) | 0.2 | 0.4 | 0.3 |
| Honduras | 137 | (6.6) (1954–57) | (3.3) | (3.2) (1954–57) | 0.1 (1948–57) | 0.2[e] (1935–50) | −0.2 (1950–56) | 0.4 (1945–50) | 0.3 | 0.4 | 0.4 |
| Ghana | 135 | (3)[a] (1957–60) | (1.6) | (1.4)[c] (1957–60) | 0.7 (1948–59) | — | — | — | — | 0.9 | — |
| Egypt | 133 | (2.1) (1954–56) | (2.4) | (−0.3) (1954–56) | 1.0 (1949–57) | 0.7 (1937–47) | 0.7 (1937–47) | 0.5 (1937–47) | 0.7 | 1.0 | 0.8 |
| Thailand | 100 | (3.1)[b] (1950–54) | (1.9) | (1.2)[d] (1950–54) | 0.1 (1950–58) | 1.3 (1947–56) | 0.1 (1937–54) | — | 0.9 | 0.9 | 0.9 |
| Rep. of the Congo (Leopoldville) | 98 | (1.7) | (2.2) | (−0.8) | 0.1 (1948–59) | — | — | — | — | 0.1 | — |
| India | 72 | (3.3) | (1.3) | (1.9) | 0.1 (1948–59) | 0.6[g] (1931–41) | 0.3 (1951–55) | 0.2[g] (1931–41) | 0.6[h] | 0.6[h] | 0.6 |
| Nigeria | 70 | (4)[a] (1957–60) | (1.9) | (2.1)[c] (1957–60) | 0.1 (1948–58) | — | — | 0.0 (1931–52) | — | 0.1 | — |
| Pakistan | 56 | (1.8)[b] (1950–54) | (1.4) | (0.4)[d] (1950–54) | 0.1 (1950–58) | 0.6[g] (1931–41) | 2.8 (1951–54/6) | 0.2[g] (1931–41) | 1.7[h] | 2.1[h] | 1.9 |
| Burma | 52 | (3.8) | (1.0) | (2.8) | 0.0 (1948–56) | 0.7 (1931–54) | −0.1 (1931–55) | — | 0.5 | 0.4 | 0.4 |

* In each box of Column 9, the first figure is based on the levels in Table III-B, Column 9; the second figure is based on the two largest shifts for country (Columns 5–8, this table), and the third figure is the average of the two preceding figures in the box. (See Notes to Table IV-A, Column 9).

a. Growth in GNP.
b. Growth in national income.
c. Growth in per capita income.
e. Based on unequal age groups. (See Notes to Table III-A, Column 6.)
f. Variation in definition of "urban." (See Notes to Table III-A, Column 8.)
g. Applies to pre-partition India, i.e., to India and Pakistan together.
h. No distinction made between pre-partition India and India and Pakistan respectively.

### TABLE 4-B—Selected Indices of Social Mobilization for Nineteen Countries: Averages in Shifts and Rates of Growth

| Range (acc'd. to per capita GNP) US $ | AVERAGE LEVEL (1) Per capita GNP (1955) US $ | AVERAGE ANNUAL RATES OF GROWTH (2) Total GDP # % | (3) Total population % | (4) GDP per capita % | AVERAGE ANNUAL SHIFTS (5) Radio audience % | (6) Literate population % | (7) Population engaged in non-agricultural occupations % | (8) Urban population % | (9)† Population exposed to modernity % |
|---|---|---|---|---|---|---|---|---|---|
| 400 + (N=1) | 762 | (8.8) | (3.0) | (7.5) | 4.0 | 0.8 | 1.0 | 1.2 | 1.2 / 3.2 / 2.2 |
| 300–399 (N=3) | 355 | (2.8) | (2.0) | (0.8) | 1.5 | 0.4 | 0.5 | 0.5 | 0.4 / 1.5 / 1.0 |
| 200–299 (N=3) | 246 | (6.4) | (2.5) | (3.8) | 0.8 | 0.9 | 0.6 | 0.2 | 1.0 / 1.2 / 1.1 |
| 100–199 (N=7) | 150 | (4.1) | (2.5) | (1.6) | 0.7 | 0.5 (N=6) | 0.3 (N=6) | 0.5 (N=5) | 0.6 (N=6) / 0.9 / 0.8 |
| 50–99 (N=5) | 70 | (2.9) | (1.6) | (1.3) | 0.1 | 0.6* (N=2) | 1.0 (N=3) | 0.1* (N=2) | 0.9 (N=3) / 0.7 / 0.8 |
| Total 50–750 (N=19) | 209 | (4.2) | (2.2) | (2.0) | 0.8 | 0.6* (N=15) | 0.6 (N=16) | 0.4* (N=14) | 0.7 (N=16) / 1.1 / 0.9 |

These averages are entirely based on data of Table IV-A.

* Data for pre-partition India were used only once in calculating the average.

# GDP = gross domestic product.

† In Column 9, in each box, the first figure is the average of shifts based on highest levels, the second figure is the average of shifts based on largest shifts, and the third figure is the average of the first two. (See Table IV-A and Notes to Table IV-A, Column 9.)

**TABLE 5—Selected Indices of Social Mobilization for Nineteen Countries:
Projected Minimum Levels in 1960, 1970**

| Country | (1) Radio audience % | | (2) Literates % | | (3) Percentage of economically active population in non-agricultural occupations % | | (4) Urban population % | | (5) Exposure to modernity % | |
|---|---|---|---|---|---|---|---|---|---|---|
| | 1960 | 1970 | 1960 | 1970 | 1960 | 1970 | 1960 | 1970 | 1960 | 1970 |
| Venezuela | 61 | >95 | 59 | 67 | 69 | 79 | 62 | 74 | 86 | 95 |
| Argentina | 67 | 82 | >95 | >95 | 79 | 82 | 67 | 70 | 95 | 95 |
| Cuba | 61 | 78 | 78 | 80 | 57 | 56 | 60 | 65 | 87 | 93 |
| Colombia | 30 | 42 | 65 | 69 | 59 | 73 | 41 | 47 | 79 | 93 |
| Turkey | 19 | 31 | 43 | 52 | 24 | 27 | 26 | 27 | 45 | 55 |
| Brazil | 27 | 35 | 53 | 58 | 50 | 58 | 42 | 47 | 66 | 76 |
| Philippines | 7 | 12 | 78 | 92 | 45 | 53 | 25 | 26 | 77 | 91 |
| Mexico | 39 | 62 | 65 | 73 | 43 | 47 | 51 | 59 | 70 | 83 |
| Chile | 39 | 41 | 86 | 93 | 73 | 77 | 66 | 73 | 95 | 95 |
| Guatemala | 7 | 11 | 25 | 20 | 35 | 38 | 34 | 36 | 44 | 47 |
| Honduras | 8 | 9 | 37 | 39 | 15 | 13 | 35 | 39 | 45 | 49 |
| Ghana | 10 | 17 | — | — | — | — | — | — | — | — |
| Egypt | 16 | 26 | 31 | 38 | 45 | 52 | 37 | 42 | 51 | 59 |
| Thailand | 2 | 3 | 69 | 82 | 13 | 14 | — | — | 52 | 61 |
| Rep. of the Congo (Leopoldville) | 1 | 2 | — | — | — | — | — | — | — | — |
| India | 2 | 3 | 26* | 32* | 32 | 35 | 17* | 19* | 37 | 43 |
| Nigeria | 1 | 2 | — | — | — | — | 5 | 6 | — | — |
| Pakistan | 1 | 2 | 26* | 32* | 49 | 77 | 17* | 19* | 46 | 65 |
| Burma | 1 | 1 | 62 | 69 | 30 | 29 | — | — | 57 | 61 |

\* On basis of pre-partition India.

## NOTES TO TABLE 3-A

Table 3-A gives the level of economic and social indices at the beginning and end of a period for each of the 19 countries. Gaps in the available data render it at present impossible to find data for equal periods for all of the indices of any one country. To compensate somewhat for this difficulty, projected levels for the same two years (1945 and 1955) have been computed in Table 3-B by applying the average annual shifts of Table 4-A to the levels given in this table.

The present state of comparative international statistics is such that the table contains several weaknesses which are discussed below:

*Columns 1 and 2.* Per capita gross national products in United States dollars for 1955, and gross national products for 1955 were compiled by the Research Center in Economic Development and Cultural Change, University of Chicago, and reported in *Foreign Aid Program,* 85th Congress, 1957, Senate Document 52, pp. 239 f.

*Column 3.* Mid-year population estimates for 1953 and 1958 were taken from United Nations, Statistical Office and Department of Economic and Social Affairs, *Demographic Yearbook, 1959* (New York, 1959), pp. 109 ff.

*Column 4.* Column 4 gives the percentage of the population exposed to radio broadcasting. The figures were arrived at on the assumption of 4 listeners for each radio receiver. This factor of 4 seems to be justified by the fact that countries which can with good reason be considered to have reached a level of saturation in numbers of radio receivers show approximately 4 persons per radio receiver. The outstanding exception is the United States, with 1.2 persons per radio receiver. Canada has 3.6, Western Germany 4.2, the Netherlands 4.3, Norway, 3.8, Sweden 3.0, Switzerland 4.1, and the United Kingdom 3.7 persons per receiver set (these figures, for 1952 to 1955, are based on data given in UNESCO, *World Communications: Press, Radio, Film, Television,* Paris, 1956). The factor of 4 is further substantiated by a sample poll of persons above 18 years of age in the German Federal Republic, in which 92% said they listened to radio (see Noelle, Elisabeth, and Erich Peter Neumann, editors, *Jahrbuch der oeffentlichen Meinung, 1947–1955,* 2d rev. ed., Allensbach am Bodensee, Verlag fuer Demoskopie, 1956, p. 62) a percentage that corresponds roughly to four times the number of radio receivers per 100.

*Sources.* The numbers of radio receivers for the years indicated were taken from United Nations, Statistical Office and Department of Economic and Social Affairs, *Statistical Yearbook, 1960* (New York, 1960), pp. 608f. The percentages were calculated on the basis of the population figures given for the corresponding years in United Nations, Statistical Office, *Monthly Bulletin of Statistics,* Vol. XIV, no. 12 (New York, December 1960). For Thailand, 1950, the percentage of radio receivers was taken directly from United Nations, Bureau of Social Affairs, *Report on the World Social Situation* (New York, 1957), p. 90; and the

1958 population figure for Nigeria was taken from the United Nations *Demographic Yearbook, 1959*.

*Column 5.* This column shows the percentage of the population exposed to daily newspapers. The figures are the result of multiplying the number of daily newspaper copies per 100 persons by a factor of 3. This factor seems justified by the fact that the number of daily newspaper copies in well advanced countries is approximately one third of the total population figure (United States 34.5%, Federal Republic of Germany 31.2%, Norway 39.2%, the Netherlands 25.9%, Switzerland 30.8%; figures based on UNESCO, *World Communications*). Professor Wilbur Schramm also uses the factor of 3 in his "Data on Mass Communications in 90 Countries" (Stanford University, 1957, mimeographed).

*Column 5.* Only the circulation of daily newspapers has been considered, even though various kinds of periodicals, such as illustrated weeklies and monthlies of general interest, may enjoy greater popularity than newspapers in many countries. Also, popular illustrated magazines may reach isolated and hard-to-reach places more readily than daily newspapers are likely to. Total exposure to the press is thus somewhat understated.

It was found feasible to give figures for only one year; this column does not therefore appear in the following tables.

*Source.* The United Nations *Statistical Yearbook, 1960*, pp. 206f., gives the estimated number of daily newspaper copies per 1000 of population. The *Yearbook* defines a daily newspaper "for the purposes of this table as a publication containing general news and appearing at least four times a week." It points out: "In interpreting the data, it should be borne in mind that in different countries the size of a daily newspaper may range from a single sheet to 50 or even more pages."

*Column 6.* Comparable international statistics on literacy are still difficult to obtain. In their enumerations, countries differ with respect to the age group of the population to be considered and to the definition of literacy or illiteracy. Not only do countries differ among each other, but a country may change definitions from one census to another. Most sources used for this column endeavor to give literary (or illiteracy) figures based on defining literates as persons able to read and write. The degree of this ability may again vary from country to country (see UNESCO, *Progress of Literacy in Various Countries*, Paris, 1953). An attempt has been made to find or compute data in such a way that the same age limits apply to both years for each country; exceptions are duly indicated. The data in such exceptional cases are still deemed valid for our purposes. In 15 cases in which corresponding calculations have been made, the difference between the percentages of literates in the population of 10 years of age and over and that in the population of 15 years of age and over averages 0.9% and ranges from 0.1% to 2.6%. For the purposes of this analysis, these magnitudes are negligible, particularly regarding average shifts per year.

*Column 6.* The high literacy rates reported for such countries as Burma and Thailand include to a large, though diminishing, extent men who have received traditional training in Buddhist monasteries and are not necessarily involved in the process of social mobilization.

Several sources used for this column give percentage of illiterates. To find the percentage of literates, the former was subtracted from 100%. In some cases, this method may count a small percentage of "unknowns" as literate, and thus very slightly overstate the number of literates.

*Sources and age groups by countries and years:*
(Abbreviations used and summary of sources)

*DY 1948*—United Nations, Statistical Office and Department of Economic and Social Affairs, *Demographic Yearbook, 1948* (New York, 1948), pp. 204 ff., gives numbers of illiterates and of total population in several age groups, by country (*e.g.,* 10 years and over, and 10 to 15 years);

*DY 1955*—United Nations, Statistical Office and Department of Economic and Social Affairs, *Demographic Yearbook, 1955* (New York, 1955), pp. 436 ff., lists total population, number of literates and percentage of literates in several age groups, by country;

*StY 1957*—United Nations, Statistical Office and Department of Economic and Social Affairs, *Statistical Yearbook, 1957* (New York, 1957), pp. 599 ff., lists percentage of illiterates and total population in several age groups, by country;

*UN Report*—United Nations, *Report on the World Social Situation*, pp. 79 ff., lists percentage of literates;

*Progress*—UNESCO, *Progress of Literacy in Various Countries*, gives percentage of illiterates;

*BFF*—UNESCO, *Basic Facts and Figures: International Statistics Relating to Education, Culture and Communications, 1959* (Paris, 1960), pp. 27 ff., gives percentage of illiterates.)

*Venezuela:* 1941: *DY 1948*, age group 15 years and over computed from age groups 10 and over and 10–14; 1950; *DY 1955*, age group 15 years and over computed from age groups 7 and over and 7–14.

*Argentina:* 1914 and 1947: *Progress*, age group 14 years and over.

*Cuba:* 1931: *Progress*, age group 10 years and over; 1953; *StY 1957*, age group 10 years and over.

*Colombia:* 1938: *DY 1948*, age group 10 years and over; 1951; *StY 1957*, age group 10 years and over.

*Turkey:* 1935: *DY 1948*, age group 10 years and over; 1950: *DY 1955*, age group 10 years and over.

*Brazil:* 1940: *DY 1948*, age group 10 years and over; 1950: *DY 1955*, age group 10 years and over.

*Philippines:* 1939 and 1948: *Progress*, age group 10 years and over.

*Mexico:* 1940: *DY 1948*, age group 10 years and over; 1950: *UN Report*, age group 6 years and over.

*Chile:* 1940: *DY 1948*, age group 10 years and over; 1952: *StY 1957*, age group 10 years and over.

*Guatemala:* 1940: *DY 1948*, age group 7 years and over; 1950: *DY 1955*, age group 10 years and over.

*Honduras:* 1935: *Progress*, age group 15 years and over; 1950: *UN Report*, age group 10 years and over.

*Ghana:* 1950: *UN Report*, estimate, age group 15 years and over.

*Egypt:* 1937: *DY 1948*, age group 10 years and over; 1947; *DY 1955*, age group 10 years and over.

*Thailand:* 1947: *DY 1955*, age group 15 years and over computed from age groups 10 years and over and 10–14; 1956: *BFF,* age group 15 years and over.

*Congo:* 1950: *UN Report,* estimate, age group 15 years and over.

*Pre-partition India:* 1931: *Progress,* age group 10 years and over; 1941: Davis, Kingsley, *The Population of India and Pakistan* (Princeton, Princeton University Press, 1951), p. 151, Table 70, quoted in Karl W. Deutsch, *Nationalism and Social Communication,* p. 201, age group 10 years and over, based on a sample and correction factor.

*India:* 1951: *DY 1955,* age group 10 years and over, based on 10% of census returns.

*Nigeria:* 1952/53: *UN Report,* age group 15 years and over.

*Pakistan:* 1951: *UN Report,* all ages, including semi-literates (13.5%). Another figure, 18.9%, excluding aliens and the population of the Frontier Regions, is given in *Pakistan—1959–1960* (Karachi, Pakistan Publications, October 1960), p. 89. Both data are reported to be based on the 1951 census.

*Burma:* 1931: *Progress,* age group 10 years and over; 1954: *StY 1957,* age group 10 years and over.

*Column 7.* The percentages of economically active population engaged in non-agricultural occupations (*i.e.,* those other than agriculture, forestry, fishing and hunting) were taken from Food and Agricultural Organization, *Production Yearbook, 1959* (Rome, 1960), pp. 19 ff., except those for Guatemala (1950), Honduras (1950), and Pakistan (1951) which were calculated from International Labour Office, *Yearbook of Labour Statistics, 1960* (Geneva, 1960), pp. 14 ff.; Cuba (1943) which was calculated from the 1947/8 edition of the same publication, pp. 10f.; and Argentina (1955), India (1955) and Burma (1955) which were taken from United States Senate, *Foreign Aid Program,* op. cit., p. 243.

*Column 8.* Urban data were reported in United Nations, Statistical Office and Department of Economic and Social Affairs, *Demographic Yearbook, 1952* (New York, 1952), pp. 168 ff., and United Nations, *Demographic Yearbook, 1955,* op. cit., pp. 185 ff. Those for Nigeria were taken from United Nations, Department of Economic and Social Affairs, *Economic Survey of Africa Since 1950* (New York, 1955), p. 14; and for Cuba (1953) from *UN Report, 1957,* p. 172.

Definitions of "urban" vary widely from country to country, but an attempt has been made to see that the definition remained the same for both dates used in calculations for each country. For Chile, this was not possible. In 1940, "urban" included cities and towns of 1000 or more inhabitants and administrative centers of less than 1000 population. In 1952, the definition was population centers which had definite urban characteristics contributed by certain public and municipal services. It would seem, however, that these two definitions are close enough for our purposes.

A higher 1950 urban population (almost 54%) is given for Venezuela in *UN Report, 1957,* p. 172; if we had used it, it would have made the mobilization rates for Venezuela still somewhat higher.

## NOTES TO TABLE 3-B

To be in a better position to compare the available data all indices of social mobilization (Columns 4 and 5–8) have been adjusted to the same two years (1945 and 1955), by applying the annual average shifts of Table 4-A to the corresponding levels given in Table 3-A. It is thereby assumed that shifts did not change significantly over the relevant years. While most of the adjustments involve only a few years, the risk of possible slight distortions had to be taken in cases in which a longer period was involved.

As we have only one level for newspaper readers, Column 5 does not appear in this table.

*Column 9.* The persons exposed to modernity are those who have in one way or another come into contact with aspects of modern life. Since hardly enough surveys in this respect have been made in the countries under consideration, the percentage of the population exposed to modernity must be estimated indirectly. It is initially assumed for the purpose of this table that (1) exposure to modernity includes any one of our indices (Columns 4–8) in addition to other, more informal exposures such as markets, travel, rumor, etc.; (2) the sector of the population in a smaller percentage index is entirely included in the sector of a higher percentage so that the exposed population groups form concentric circles—*e.g.,* all of the newspaper readers would be exposed to radio, and all of the radio listeners would be literate, but that some literates would not listen to radio, etc., (3) the largest sector is that exposed to any form of modernity, and (4) 20% of the population exposed to modernity are unaccounted for in Columns 4 to 8, because the groups indicated there do not overlap completely, and because of less formal ways of exposure. As has been pointed out in the introduction to this Appendix, however, in order to discount to some extent the effects of any single indicator that seems too far out of line with the rest, the procedure followed to estimate the percentage of the population exposed to modernity has been to increase the average of the two highest of the indices for each country and year by 25 per cent. This method reduces the impact of a single indicator with weak correlation to other indicators to such a degree that the percentage of persons exposed to modernity appears to be smaller than that of some other population sector in cases in which the correlation of single index is extremely weak (*cf.* Philippines, Thailand, Pakistan, Burma).

In actual fact, we have good reason to suppose that these assumptions understate in general the total extent of exposure. It is quite likely that some of the population sectors overlap only to a lesser degree. This can particularly be expected in countries with balanced low levels of social mobilization.

Calculated percentages exceeding 95% are assumed to behave differently. They are merely listed as being over 95%.

## NOTES TO TABLE 4-A

*Column 1.* See notes to Table 3-A, Column 1.
*Column 2.* Average annual rates of growth in gross domestic product for the years 1954–1958 were reported in United Nations, Statistical Office and Department of Economic and Social Affairs, *Yearbook of National Account Statistics, 1960* (New York, 1961), pp. 265 ff.

Data for Cuba, Mexico, Ghana and Nigeria are average annual rates of growth in gross national product for 1957–1960, and were taken from P. N. Rosenstein-Rodan, "International Aid for Underdeveloped Countries" (multilithed, Cambridge, Mass., M.I.T., August, 1960), pp. 3 ff.

Data for Thailand and Pakistan are average annual rates of growth in national income for 1950–1954, and were taken from Paul Studenski, *The Income of Nations: Theory, Measurement and Analysis: Past and Present* (New York, New York University Press, 1958), pp. 229f.

According to the sources, all rates are based on constant prices.

*Column 3.* The rates of population growth are the geometric means of the differences between the mid-year estimates of populations in 1953 and 1958. They were taken from the United Nations *Demographic Yearbook, 1959*, pp. 109 ff.

*Column 4.* Average annual rates of growth in per capita gross domestic product in constant prices for 1954–1958 were taken from United Nations, *Yearbook of National Account Statistics, 1960*, pp. 265 ff. Data for Cuba, Mexico, Ghana, Thailand, Nigeria and Pakistan were calculated on the basis of columns 2 and 3 of this table.

*Columns 5–8.* While Columns 2, 3 and 4 show average percentage rates of growth per year, Columns 5 to 8, and 9, represent average annual percentage shifts, *i.e.,* that average annual percentage of the population which has been added to, or subtracted from, the total share of the population in that particular category. Thus, these percentages were obtained by dividing the difference between the pair of levels in Table 3-A by the proper number of years (see explanation of Table 1, above). Since the figures in these four columns are entirely based on the data in Columns 4 and 6 to 8 in Table 3-A, the notes and the sources for Table 3-A and for its respective columns apply also to Columns 5 to 8 of Table 4-A.

Since we have the percentage of newspaper readers for only one year (Column 5, Table 3-A), shifts into the exposure to newspapers have had to be omitted.

*Column 9.* Shifts in the population exposed to modernity were calculated in three different ways.

The first figure in each box is based on the levels of modernity given in Column 9 of Table 3-B, and calculated in the same way as the shifts of Columns 5 to 8. For a discussion of the assumptions made, see Notes to that Table, Column 9.

The second figure in each box is based on the average of the two fastest growing indicators, as expressed by the percentage shifts in Columns 5 to 8. The underlying assumptions in this case are similar to those set forth for Column 9 in Table 3-B. It is again assumed that the shift into the aggregate of all groups involved in at least one process of social mobilization should grow faster than shifts into any of the particular processes. If two or more sectors of the population did not overlap at all, yet each index was an expression of modernity, the shifts into each of these sectors would have to be added to obtain a basis for the calculation of the shift into modernity, and the fastest shift would constitute a minimum. A conservative estimate of the percentage shift into exposure to modernity, taking into account informal exposures, has been to take the average of the two highest of the percentage shifts in Columns 5 to 8, and increase it by 25%.

The first method here used may perhaps best be applied to countries that already have very high levels of minimal exposure to modernity. The second figure may be more representative of the shift to minimal exposure in low-range countries, and of the shift to more intense mobilization in more advanced ones.

The third figure in each box is the average of the first two figures.

## NOTES TO TABLE 5

The projections, for 1960 and 1970, are based on the levels of Table 3 and on the shifts of Table 4-A. For Column 9, the median shifts (third figure in each box of Column 9, Table 4-A) have been used in computing the projections of the exposure to modernity.

It is assumed that the average annual shifts will continue to hold. In actual fact, we have good reason to believe that shifts will grow as the countries develop and that these projections represent minima. Since results of the censuses taken around 1960 will soon be available, the reader will be able to check our projections for that year.

Calculated figures close to 100% are assumed to behave differently and are listed as being over 95% (>95).

---

geria, and Congo illustrate the need for more research.

Moreover, the data being presented on the basis of the figures that appear in United Nations publications and similar sources make no attempt to estimate the margins of error to which they may be subject, or the differences in significance which a particular indicator of social mobilization may have in the cultural context of certain countries, in contrast with its significance in others. The high literacy rates reported for Burma and Thailand, *e.g.,* include a substantial proportion of literates trained through traditional monastic institutions. These rates show only a weak correlation to other indicators of modernity for those same countries, while the high literacy rates for Chile by contrast, refer to the effect of a more modern type of school system and are far better correlated to other indicators.

We have tried to take some account of these matters by basing estimates of over-all exposure to modernity not on the highest single indicator but on the average of the two highest indicators for each country, so as to discount to some extent the effects of any single indicator that seems too far out of line with the rest. Despite these precautions, the figures in projection offered here represent at best a crude beginning intended to stimulate far more thorough and critical statistical work, and its critical evaluation by experts on each of the countries and areas concerned.

For discussion of specific data and sources, see the Notes following the tables.

# NOTES

1. For broader discussions of the modernization process, see Rupert Emerson, *From Empire to Nation* (Cambridge, Harvard University Press, 1960); Harold D. Lasswell, *The World Revolution of Our Time* (Stanford University Press, 1951); and Gabriel A. Almond and James S. Coleman, eds., *The Politics of the Developing Areas* (Princeton, Princeton University Press, 1960). *Cf.* also Daniel Lerner, *The Passing of Traditional Society* (New York, Free Press, 1958), and Lerner, "Communication Systems and Social Systems: A Statistical Exploration in History and Policy," *Behavioral Science,* Vol. 2 (October, 1957), pp. 266–275; Fred Riggs, "Bureaucracy in Transitional Societies: Politics, Economic Development and Administration," American Political Science Association Annual Meeting, September, 1959, multigraphed; Dankwart Rustow, *Politics and Westernization in the Near East* (Center of International Studies, Princeton University, 1956); and Lyle Shannon, "Is Level of Development Related to Capacity for Self-Government?" *American Journal of Economics and Sociology,* Vol. 17 (July, 1958), pp. 367–381, and Shannon, "Socio-Economic Development and Political Status," *Social Problems,* Vol. 7 (Fall, 1959), pp. 157–169.

2. Karl Mannheim, *Man and Society in an Age of Reconstruction* (New York, 1940).

3. Edward Shils, at the Social Science Research Council Conference on Comparative Politics, above, asterisked note.

4. For a broader discussion of quantitative indicators, bearing on problems of this kind, see Karl W. Deutsch, "Toward an Inventory of Basic Trends and Patterns in Comparative and International Politics," *American Political Science Review,* Vol. 54 (March, 1960), p. 34.

5. *Cf.* the pamphlets issued by the Statistical Office of the United Nations, Statistical Papers, Series K, No. 1, "Survey of Social Statistics," (Sales No.: 1954. XVII. 8), New York, 1954, and Statistical Papers, Series M, No. 11, Rev. 1, "List of Statistical Series Collected by International Organizations," (Sales No.: 1955. XVII. 6), New York, 1955. For somewhat earlier data, see also W. S. Woytinsky and E. S. Woytinsky, *World Commerce and Governments: Trends and Outlook* (New York, The Twentieth Century Fund, 1955), and *World Population and Production: Trends and Outlook* (New York, The Twentieth Century Fund, 1953).

6. See Hortense Horwitz and Elias Smith, "The Interchangeability of Socio-Economic Indices," in Paul F. Lazarsfeld and Morris Rosenberg, *The Language of Social Research* (New York, Free Press, 1955), pp. 73–77.

7. Frederick E. Tibbetts, 3d, "The Cycles of Canadian Nationalism," Yale University, typescript, 1959, pp. 24, 26–31. For details of the Finnish and Indian cases referred to above, see K. W. Deutsch, *Nationalism and Social Communication* (New York, 1953), pp. 102–11, 170–82, 197–204.

8. Note, however, the comment on Burmese literacy, in the Appendix to this article, below.

9. Rosemary Klineberg, "Correlation of Literacy Rates with 1956 Birth Rates," Fletcher School of Law and Diplomacy, 1959, unpublished.

10. See Raymond Lindgren, *Norway-Sweden: Union, Disunion, Reunion* (Princeton, Princeton University Press, 1959); and K. W. Deutsch, *et al., Political Community and the North Atlantic Area* (Princeton University Press, 1957).

11. Richard Merritt's monograph, "Symbols of American Nationalism, 1735–1775," which is to cover eventually one or more newspapers from Massachusetts, New York, Pennsylvania, and Virginia, respectively, will be published in due course.

12. For examples of pioneering contributions of this kind, see the series of Hoover Institute Studies by Harold Lasswell, Ithiel Pool, Daniel Lerner, and others, and particularly Pool, *The Prestige Papers* (Stanford, Stanford University Press, 1951).

13. See charts 1, 3, and 4 in Karl W. Deutsch, "Shifts in the Balance of Communication Flows: A Problem of Measurement in International Relations," *Public Opinion Quarterly,* Vol. 20 (Spring, 1956), pp. 152–155, based on data of the Universal Postal Union.

14. See Karl W. Deutsch and Alexander Eckstein, "National Industrialization and the Declining Share of the International Economic Sector, 1890–1957," *World Politics,* Vol. 13 (January, 1961) pp. 267–299. See also Simon Kuznets, *Six Lectures on Economic Growth* (New York, Free Press, 1959), esp. the section on "The Problem of Size" and "Trends in Foreign Trade Ratios," pp. 89–107.

15. For more detailed arguments, see Deutsch, *Nationalism and Social Communication,* and Deutsch, *et al., Political Community and the North Atlantic Area;* see also the discussions in Ernst B. Haas, "Regionalism, Functionalism and Universal Organization," *World Politics,* Vol. 8, (January, 1956), and "The Challenge of Regionalism," *International Organization,* Vol. 12 (1958), pp. 440–458; and in Stanley Hoffmann, *Contemporary Theory in International Relations* (Englewood Cliffs, N.J., Prentice-Hall, 1960), pp. 223–40.

16. *Cf.* Karl W. Deutsch, "The Propensity to International Transactions," *Political Studies,* Vol. 8 (June, 1960), pp. 147–155.

17. *Cf.* Paul Studenski, *The Income of Nations* (New York, New York University Press, 1958), p. 249; *cf.* also pp. 244–250.

18. *Cf.* United Nations, Department of Social and Economic Affairs, Population Studies No. 28, "The Future Growth of World Population" (New York, 1958), and United Nations, Bureau of Social Affairs, *Report of the World Social Situation* (Sales No.: 1957. IV. 3) (New York, 1957), p. 5

19. For other highly relevant approaches to these problems, see Almond and Coleman, eds., *The Politics of the Developing Areas,* esp. the discussion by Almond on pp. 58–64. The problem of rates of change and their acceleration is discussed explicitly by Coleman, *ibid.,* pp. 536–558. While this work presented extensive data on levels of development, it did not take the further step of using explicit quantitative rates of change, which would be needed for the type of dynamic and probabilistic models that seem implicit in the long-range predictions of the authors, as set forth on pp. 58–64, 535–544.

# THE END OF COLONIALISM

## Karl Jaspers

The present world situation is the result of four centuries of European expansion, which has united mankind as a factual unit of communication. Today hardly anything can happen anywhere without concerning everybody. In the paper we read every day of events the world over.

This unity of communication, technologically based and now intensified to the highest degree by airplanes and radio waves, is the premise of mutual knowledge, of understanding and participation, of revulsion and hatred, or of co-operation. Whether it will grow into a world communion of the human spirit, and how this might look, is an unanswered question. It depends on a spiritual and moral choice: whether mutually exclusive human possibilities are divided by a gulf that must lead to mutual rejection and a desire to destroy what is foreign, or whether men are united by a rational spirit in which all can meet without having to surrender the differences of their ways of life and faith. The question will not be answered by experience; it will be decided by the human beings who will work for one or the other. There is an uneasy readiness for unity in all nations. It has been demonstrated; it has also been denied. That mankind has one root and one goal, that true human beings are linked by something that transcends even mortal conflicts—this is a faith which can indeed be buried only along with rational humanity itself.

Since 1914, the flow of emigration has come to an abrupt stop. The event crept up on us, at first without attracting attention. The world is no longer open; all at once, everything has been jarred within bounds. There is no more running away. There are no distant opportunities either for the individual or for the overflow of populations. At first, this damming-up causes confusion everywhere, as water recoils in eddies if it cannot flow on.

The time is past when men knew themselves sur-

rounded by a wide world—which most of them dreaded, but which meant liberty because it beckoned to the daring. Now, Earth has been distributed. There is no more freedom to move.

Globally speaking, this freedom of movement had been a Western prerogative. Even America soon banned the immigration of Chinese and Japanese, when she had too many of them. Now such bans are common. All countries, large and small, select and choose in each case whom they will allow to immigrate.

Since the globe has been divided up, all men must make do in the space they are born with. If there is to be peace, the territorial status quo must be respected. The slogan of a "nation without space" confers no right; it simply means war. If the division of Earth is not acknowledged, there seems to be no alternative but war—wars of extermination or forced migration.

The present division of territories is the result of past history and largely accidental. Some nations have vast land masses with rich resources—America, Russia, China; others have little room. With the jolt that put an end to expansion, the situation of that moment proved highly favorable to some and most unfavorable to others. Each insists on the possession of his own territory. External population pressures due to unequal increase justify no claim to land in less populated areas. Australia did not admit any Japanese; Russia closes her Asian border against immigration from China. Any seizure of land means war.

How did the age of European expansion differ from all previous conquests, migrations, and colonial movements? Western expansion spread to *all* non-Western peoples; it was a conquest of the globe. But this entire globe was held to be fair prey, as beyond the pale of European laws and mores. An abyss lay between Europe and the world: in Europe there was a common ethos, a community in biblical religion, a legal order fixed in a host of treaties and partitions; outside Europe were unoccupied lands that belonged to no one—to no European, that is—and thus invited pillage, occupation, settlement, and exploitation by anyone who wished and dared.

This expansion could succeed because resistance to the superior weapons of European technology was impossible, even for the highly civilized nations of Asia. These nations lived in their large but, in global terms, limited spaces, regarding their world as the world of mankind, utterly ignorant of the violence that was unleashed against them. And the superiority of the Europeans was further enhanced by the sum of their rational skills.

This colonization ushered in an age of horror for all the peoples on Earth. A spirit of greed, ruthlessness, and tyranny became general. If Europeans happened to meet in this no man's land of the whole non-European Earth, they started fighting as fiercely over the booty as they had fought the original inhabitants. They were at peace in Europe, but abroad they waged an informal war without beginning or end, often in such obscurity that no news of it reached Europe. On Spitsbergen, for example, many graves still testify to nameless battles fought by the Dutch and the British while their countries were at peace—symbols in a far-off place of the atmosphere of lawlessness and rapacity which the Europeans spread around the globe. This colonial process was perhaps most pitiless in North America, where the native population was exterminated over the centuries. Today, a few Indian remnants are kept there on reservations, as in a game preserve; and masses of Negro slaves were imported.

Decisive for this colonial age was the fact that Europeans did not regard non-Europeans as human beings like themselves. The biblical view of the unity of the race held good in theory, but in practice the foreign peoples were not only not equal, they were without any rights whatever. Only Christians had the rights of men. The others, the savages, were, at best, human beings whose conversion to the Christian faith—that is, to one of the contending Christian sects—and consequent salvation was a Christian duty. Otherwise, if not wiped out, they were objects of exploitation. No authority with political power kept the Europeans from forcing these people to do their bidding, or from killing them outright.

Later, the non-Europeans became objects of research. A distinction was made between "savages" and "semicivilized nations." But all of them and their products, including the glorious art of China, were objects of knowledge; their place, as late as the beginning of this century, was in ethnological museums. They were degraded. And correspondingly, world history was seen as the continuous history of the West.

The consequence of this colonial process of four centuries was a hatred of Europeans by all other nations on Earth. It was inevitable, since they were deemed inferior races, since the spirit of their native cultures was slighted, since their exposure to ruinous technology kept them for a long time in humiliating impotence. For generations this hatred has been bred into them. They have become rightly sensitive, so much so that today the slightest reminder of their past will rekindle their indignation. A basic reality of mankind's present existence is this open or hidden hate of Westerners—both Europeans and Americans—in all who are not Westerners.

People wonder why in Asia, for instance, "nationalism" is a much stronger force than in Europe. But there the same word "nationalism" has quite a different meaning. The nationalism of the great Asian nations is based on a real racial difference between them and the Westerners, all of whom are akin, from the Americans to the Russians. It is rooted, further, in their entire culture, essentially different in its age-old-heritage; the Indian, Chinese, and Japanese worlds are spiritually much closer to each other, linked by historical events, mainly by the spread of Buddhism, than all of them are to the West. Finally, this nationalism derives from feelings of inferiority in the reluctant acquisition of Western technology and thought, combined with feelings of superiority in their own religiously and philosophically grounded way of life.

These people have been awakened from the comparative quiet of many centuries of misery and many centuries of beautiful and joyous living. They have been swept into the movement of a technological age which they feel to be foreign to themselves. They may seem happy as children over their technical successes, but they are deeply unhappy at the same time. And this evil, too, is due to the West that indirectly forced them to turn to technology as a condition of their self-preservation. In the end, the West also taught them the nationalist way of thinking. They use Western concepts to justify its application to their own very different reality. Thus their nationalism has something inappropriate and brittle about it, but unlike its Western counterpart it is bound up with dark, elemental drives.

Now, after centuries in which it seemed impossible for non-European nations to have any importance of their own, this era has all but abruptly ended. As recently as 1900, the British Empire seemed unshakable. Other nations had their colonies in its shadow. After a German diplomat was murdered in Peking by the secret society of the Boxers, England, Germany, Russia, America, and other countries intervened with a joint expeditionary force under British leadership—a military operation without any risk to themselves. Kaiser Wilhelm II dispatched his troops from Germany with orders to "give no quarter and take no prisoners." The British field commander's order, "The Germans into the line!" caused rejoicing in Germany. It was the last demonstration of a fundamental colonialism spawned by the arrogance of Western powers.

But the tide had already begun to turn. One had been obliged to ask Japan to join in the act of violence against China. In 1895, in her war against

China, Japan had surprised the Westerners; she was the first foreign power to prove herself by the adoption of European military and organizational techniques. In 1904–5, this same Japan inflicted a disastrous defeat on Russia. A mighty empire of the white race, half-European, one of the world's great powers, succumbed to an Asian nation, which had to be recognized now as a great power itself.

What had happened? At first, the whites were like gods, because they possessed the miracle of technology. Or else they seemed—to the Chinese, for example—barbarians without an inkling of the depth, truth, and beauty of human culture and joy of living. But the prestige of their invincibility paralyzed nations even where only glimpses of it appeared. British world dominion was a bluff, says Liddell Hart, a Briton. But if it was a bluff, it ceased working when England and France brought millions of Indians and Africans to Europe, as soldiers in their war against Germany. The result was a tremendous increase in the self-assurance of the non-Europeans. "We can do this, too," they were bound to think, especially in view of the war of whites against whites.

For the peoples of the globe, subjected to European technology, the question was whether to go down as important objects of oppression or to adopt this technology for their own self-preservation. Today, they have all more or less gone the way of Japan. They have claimed their freedom from the West and, with some exceptions, have achieved it. But the independence they won is still in the process of consolidation. In the areas of the so-called underdeveloped countries, European technology and production methods are yet to be established.

The age of colonialism is at an end. Europe's rule of the world is shattered, her world position in ruins, her pre-eminence a thing of the past, her own future gravely imperiled. What will happen? If the world's population grows from two billion to three billion and more; if the Westerners, already outnumbered, continue to fall behind; if the vast colored masses, possessing most of the world's areas and the bulk of its resources, become the technological equals of the West—will this human majority, not yet free from the hatred begotten by four centuries, not turn against the West? Is there a chance for a community of all nations?

With the collapse of colonial rule, technology has conquered the world and made history, for the first time, world history. Is this a triumph of the European mind—not only in science and technology but in its thinking processes, in Anglo-Saxon enlightenment, in Marxism, in nationalist oratory, in the whole rationale of organization, of planning, of calculating? A common knowledge and know-how covers the world. Whether received with the delight of children who suddenly discover an undreamed-of skill or with the reluctance of one who adopts what he feels will lead to his destruction—it is always the same irresistible development of the technological age.

It is no European triumph. What came into the world by means of Europe, historically speaking, is valid in itself, independently of its origin. It is not a unique culture but the property of man as such, of man as a rational being. It is identically transferable. Where it has once been acquired, it can, with more or less talent, be cultivated—whether for mere use, for participation in further scientific research, or for technical inventions. The necessary talent is no basic trait or permanent condition of nations. For example, the number of patent applications is today a sort of yardstick of national inventiveness, and it varies enormously. In the nineteenth century, France marched in the van of progress, but today new French patents are scarce, and we find the highest number in America. Among the men active in the immensely difficult construction of the American atom bomb were a large number of European immigrants from Germany, Italy, and Hungary. What we have in common is the technological age of history; the talent for it is scattered at random and attracted by challenges and opportunities. It no longer belongs to a few privileged nations. In Russia and Japan, for instance, discoveries and inventions have reached the universal level of human ability.

But this common element does not unite. Science and technology are equally well understood and practiced, but they are employed no less as weapons than as bonds. A common, identical understanding of the atom bomb does not prevent us from making these bombs for the purpose of destroying one another. Peace can come only from bonds that link, not only intellect with intellect, but man with man.

Peaceful union presupposes understanding. The possibilities of such universal understanding must grow, the more all human kinds can meet in reality. The image of man changes where it is no longer harnessed in narrow blinders and deprived of means of comparison. The unity of mankind can come to clear and steady consciousness only by the actual experience of diversity.

We have so far neglected this aspect in our description of the colonial age, because in past centuries it has been almost ineffective. But though futile in the process at large, things that bespoke the good will of individual Westerners, at least, happened even in the course of colonization. Not a few were moved by the humanity of the "natives," by their moral and religious depth—especially in China and India. In dealing with them, they came to a loving, thorough understanding of the spiritual life of these nations. They turned to scientific investigation of their languages, their creations, their lives, much as humanism had once taken up the study of Antiquity. They not only fought the injustices done to these nations but opened ways of communication for human heritages meeting on the same level, and thus they brought new wealth to the West as well. Their reports and translations of foreign works taught Europeans to know these extraordinary phenomena. The Jesuits in China, for example, acquired their understanding of Chinese thought and faith in order to infuse the natives with biblical thought; but this understanding led to their great achievement of communicating the Chinese reality to the West. Their aim was to make possible a new source of religious life in China, but their reports became the basis of European thinking about China by such men as Leibniz, Voltaire, and Hegel. The consequences over the centuries and the needs of today both follow this line of love and understanding. For communication does not begin until understanding goes beyond the insipidity of average rational thought, to the historic essence.

We cannot say that such communication is now taking place the world over. For today the substance of great traditions is steadily dwindling here as well as in Asia. The age of technology makes questionable what we live by; it uproots us, and it does so all around the globe. And to the great Asian cultures it does it more violently, since they lack the transitional period in which the West was producing the technological world—a world that now, finished and overpowering, engulfs people whom their past culture has neither prepared for nor disposed toward it.

We human beings meet each other less and less on the ground of our respective faiths, more and more in the common uprooting vortex of our existence. Technology with its consequences is initially ruinous for all age-old traditional ways of life.

A common concern, therefore, unites the nations today: can technology be subordinated as a tool? As yet no one knows how. Will the deeper source, dried up at first, well up again with new vigor, in new forms; will it master technology and convert it into the mere management of life? We see no sign of this, but we must expect it if we are conscious of our human roots. Or will technology become absolute and destroy man—a notion easy to throw out but impossible to think through?

We are looking for outlines of political thought that would aim, in the breathing spell before the threatening end, at two inseparable objectives: true humanity and the preservation of existence. Let us try to draft such a kind of new politics for our situation at the end of the colonial age. It will be governed by two basic, closely related problems.

One concerns *liberation and self-preservation*. Peace can be served only by truth, not by lies in points of principle. From the Western point of view,

honesty requires, first, the actual and unqualified liberation of all colonial areas, and second, in view of the dangers arising therefrom, the accompanying defensive self-preservation of the West.

As to the first, there is no more stopping the non-European peoples' march to freedom. It is futile to maintain domination anywhere, in any past forms, with no matter how many concessions. The withdrawal from all colonial areas demands a simultaneous reversal of the colonial idea into its opposite, a will to leave the existence of others to their own responsibility.

As to the second, the vast dangers arising from racial hatred; from shortsighted, confused actions of the liberated; from their frequent incompetence in making their way in the technological age; from the incalculable consequences of the violence they employ toward each other—these dangers can be met only by a defensive union of the West. This calls for substantial economic sacrifices, for giving up ingrained feelings of national power, and for a transformation of technological, economic, and social ways of life. Only thus can we preserve ourselves reliably and non-aggressively.

The second problem concerns the direction *toward a world order*. In liberation and self-preservation, the prevailing mood is still one of hostility. The final stage of peace cannot be mere juxtaposition, cannot involve constant threats and the constant danger of explosions. The grand objective of politics must be a world order—starting out, to be sure, from the given states, territories, and power relationships. We must envision possible ways, as well as seemingly insuperable obstacles, to such an order.

Both aspects of the new politics are problems of mankind. They outrank all special national problems and pervade all politics not thoughtlessly confined to local interests of the moment. Yet both, today, differ from the analogous conceptions of past ages. They are not to be imagined after the pattern of the former European community; they must come into being in the framework of the one, globe-wide humanity, not in the framework of a European world. We cannot seek order by means of the communion of any single faith, only by means of a future communion of reason. Therefore, this new world order cannot be symbolized either by an idea of empire or by the idea of a universal church. These could only be deceptive stage props of a global despotism. If freedom is to be saved— that is to say, if man is to be saved—he will have to keep struggling for himself in a process of self-education that can never end. What remains—in constant danger, based on historical premises, never lastingly terminable—will be an unstable situation that must always be realized and secured again.

A fundamental fact is that the conflict between

the West and its former colonies cuts across another conflict: between Russia and the West, between totalitarianism and freedom. Both Russia and America support anticolonialism. Russia foments hatred and offers herself and her communism as useful allies, but America also offers herself and her freedom. Neither is acting unselfishly, for they vie for influence abroad. Each stresses her anti-colonialism and accuses the other of colonialism; each wants to increase her own power and to contain the other's. It is in the shadow of this struggle over the vast formerly colonial areas that we must see the possibilities of liberation and self-preservation. On the one hand, the interplay of the two conflicts—West versus former colonies, and America versus Russia—promotes the rapid but still quite external liberation of all colored nations; but, on the other hand, it beclouds the liberation issue that might otherwise be clear.

Descriptions of the colonial age sound either like indictments or like vindications. In view of this whole four-hundred-year process that made the European technological era a global era, and thus made the world one and let history become world history, indictments and vindications seem rather inappropriate, unless we speak in terms of original sin. Still, it was we of the West who wrought this evil.

Particular indictments and vindications always bear on common human traits. Terrible, merciless, treacherous actions mark the history of China and India no less than ours. Indeed, it is to the credit of Europe that in her case self-criticism of colonial activities set in early and persisted. Nor was it quite ineffective. The motives of the Europeans active in colonialism were varied: adventure; love of danger and violence, of discovery and exploration; missionary zeal; self-sacrifice in the service of God; greed; the search, on foreign soil, for a freedom suppressed at home; or the will to create new political forms. This great process was a terrible outbreak of human passions. But its greatness lies on the dreadful side of world history, beyond good and evil. No one intended this dreadful greatness; no one may cite it either for vindication or complaint.

We may doubt the desirability of freeing peoples who have never known inner political freedom. Their liberation has thrown mankind into chaos. Were not all nations happier—as far as men can be happy—before the end of colonial rule? Was the world peace about 1900, the world communion under British dominance, not a great and singular moment in world history? Yet we are deceiving ourselves if we give in to this idea. If the Westerners' political wisdom and moral purity had entitled them to rule and educate mankind until their guidance, respecting the spiritual roots of others, would have nurtured the slow growth of world-wide political freedom—then such colonial rule would have been preferable. But the West, in its actual conduct, has been no better or politically wiser than the great Asian civilizations, even though individual thinkers and statesmen realized what was happening and tried to do better—as the British, at times, did in India. In fact, the combination of common human cruelty, of negligence and sloth, of the enjoyment of fruits reaped by adventurers, of ambiguous administration and imperialistic ambition—the combination of these blazed a trail unfit to be the high road of humanity. For a moment, the West had a task. It failed. The results are final.

Yet the non-Westerners are no better. Those who have obtained freedom from us are men, not angels. The freedom that all but fell into their laps in the technological age—thanks, above all, to Anglo-Saxon initiative—confronts them with a task which they must now solve for themselves. No one can guide or teach them. They have forgotten their own traditional wisdom—and again it is frightening how much they seem like the natural prey of totalitarian rule. But not inevitably.

As yet, no one blames us for our most dubious achievement: having dragged down all mankind to a technological fate. What is resented is not technology but dependence upon the white man; his technological world, and all that it implies, is exactly what all seem to want. On grounds of religious tradition, some nations were initially averse and later reluctant, but now all accept with enthusiasm. It is like a conquest—not by human beings, not by a foreign culture, not by Europeans, but by the thing itself which belongs to man as an intellectual being, to all men alike, challenging all to make of it what they can.

The liberation of nations from colonial rule is governed not only by an elemental urge for independence but by ideas introduced by colonization itself. In liberating themselves, they continue what colonial rule began. Without England, for example, there would today be no large, unified India with rudiments of common education, of a common law, and of industrial development. Everywhere intellectuals educated in or by the West are leading the way. The nations themselves are still largely in the dreamlike hold of newly questioned traditions. But no country seeks to return to its condition before colonial rule. China and India deal with their historic susbtance—the very thing that so greatly distinguishes them in our eyes—as if it were of no account.

To achieve world peace, to reduce the hatred which more than half of mankind harbors against the West, it is essential for the West to acknowledge honestly and unreservedly that colonialism is finished. We must think through the consequences of this situation and outline the principles of the resulting political actions. That is easy to say, but for Westerners, and for all others, it is hard to find the right and effective way to peace in the world chaos left behind by colonialism—and this world peace alone can save us from the atom bomb.

The first step is a great renunciation. The Western powers must withdraw to their own territories. They must grant others the full independence they seek. In large measure this has already been done. Where it has not yet been done, there is constant unrest—in the Near East, in North Africa, in the African territories. The renunciation must be simultaneously political and economic, to establish political and economic relations on a new basis of free reciprocity. Why and to what end is this renunciation necessary for world peace?

First: expansion has come to an end because the world has been distributed. As the globe at large has no more free space, the self-restriction of all to their own territories must follow.

Second: people resent not only the political power of the West but its economic power. Their experience with this strikes them, often justly, as exploitation, oppression, fraud. Taxation seems like tribute to them, the procurement of raw materials from their territories, with the help of freely hired and paid native labor, like robbery and enslavement. Economic thinking, tied to legal warrants and calculable sureties, is foreign to them. This attitude is fostered by transferring Marxist notions of the entrepreneur-worker relationship to that of colonial powers and natives. The existence of this attitude is a powerful fact, a fact surmountable only if the liberated will have their own experience of freedom, and if the economic ethics of a technologically unified world will draw upon a new source for the binding force of equality.

Third: granting that all achievements of the colonial powers—of the British in India, the Dutch in Indonesia, the Germans in their former African colonies and in Chinese Kiao-Chou—testified to technological skill and economic efficiency and benefited the natives, they still were not motivated by the natives' interest, even if this was subsequently considered. The motives were self-interest and delight in achievement as such, and these have no absolute value that would justify placing them above everything else. We must restore the true hierarchy of values, which technological and economic progress has obscured for both colonial powers and natives.

Withdrawal to one's own territory has taken economic sacrifices and will take more. Moreover, its inescapable consequence is a change in the principle of the industrial age. In this age industry lived by expansion, by the extension of markets, by the steadily increased procurement of raw materials wherever they were made cheapest by organized Western exploitation, and by the export of capital for the establishment of enterprises abroad. The result of all this was direct or indirect economic

expropriation, secured by the power of governments assuming the protection of business transactions and agreements. Now, external expansion must yield to inner intensification.

If this alone can pave the way to world peace, the greatest sacrifices would be minor in comparison with the alternative. The new principle, which seems absurd to our economic and technological thinking, must at least be thought through. This is a matter for the energies of economic analysis—which is not my field—in conjunction with a new moral will.

It takes free will to keep the inevitable from taking a ruinous course; it cannot be done in the framework of past economic thought alone. If European expansion conditioned nineteenth-century economic life, the end of this expansion requires a change in economic life. If economic development must turn about, from expansion to intensification, we need a new economic ethics.

Domestically, we must not regard problems such as economic balance and world peace as soluble by institutions, by certain laws, by any contrived nostrum; the reform of a non-expansive, internally intensified economy will probably be very radical. And in foreign policy the renunciation of colonialism calls for private enterprise abroad to be controlled by the renouncing nations; they can no longer allow their citizens to contract freely for the uncontrolled exploitation of the natural resources of formerly colonial areas. In fact, economies can no longer be separated from politics. The method of winning global economic success without accepting political responsibility, of economic domination and political "neutrality"— "dollar imperialism"—has become illusory. The actual way of uniting politics and economics is daily being settled in practice, but still in rather murky fashion. Full clarity about this basic problem of both politics and economics remains to be achieved in intellectual conflict.

It is an illusion to consider foreign raw materials as vital to the free world. There is no doubt, in view of present dependence, that serious economic crises would result from the failure of this supply; but although the present tendency is to identify special interests with requisites of life, even grave impediments to our economic existence do not affect the absolute necessities. The end of expansion is the destiny and turning point of our economy. Whether the limit is the globe or half the globe, the principle is the same.

True, it is foolish and imprudent to let raw materials lie unused. Men are understandably reluctant to renounce anything under pressure of unreasonable political forces; they are right in considering the whole business absurd. But world peace comes first. And if we prepare for it and do not violate its temporary and permanent conditions, renunciation need not at all mean a rupture of relations and a permanent loss of the use of the raw materials. We cannot tell what will be possible under conditions of world peace and a new political ethics. If business interests were tempered and controlled instead of being absolute, our relations with the formerly colonial world could freely develop once more, without expansion, and mutual access to raw materials would be re-established around the world.

We in the free world must not be deceived any longer by allegedly inviolable economic demands. From Germany's World War I claim that "the German economy could not exist without the Briey Basin" (a claim then backed by many leading economists), to Eden's proclamation of the Suez Canal as "Britain's life-line," or the present thesis that "Europe absolutely needs Middle Eastern oil" —the kernel of truth in these and similar statements is always only a need to solve a serious economic problem or, perhaps, to surmount a seemingly disastrous situation. We have surmounted worse situations. We must find the will and the way in the co-operation of all nations of the free world. This co-operation, and great sacrifices—of glory, of prestige, of sovereignty, of material comfort, of privilege—are premises of survival. If they are forced upon us by events, the situation will be far more disastrous than if we reflect calmly, in time, and muster the *élan* of doing freely, in time, what we recognize as unavoidable.

We now condemn in public what has always been done and is still being done: capital investment abroad, in risky but lucrative ventures under the protection of the home government; dealing with natives ignorant of the mechanism of economic calculation; employing native labor, paying them wages, and raising their standards of living, but so as to make their lives empty and their pleasures meaningless because the substance of their tradition succumbs to the deceptive glamor of technological civilization. We thought we could educate the nations, as the British—often with the best intentions—did in India on a large scale. But essentially they could bring only book learning, techniques, organization, administration, law—the things whereby, thanks to England, an Indian empire can now, for the time being, do without England. But nations want to teach themselves; they do not want to be taught. They want to deal with the new technology and economy on their own initiative, out of their inherited substance.

Even with colonialism at an end, those nations can never return to their previous state. Along with Western technology they have come to know Western thought—usually in garbled or misunderstood form—and to take up Western amusements on their lowest level. Men molded by the new civilizing patterns run to a basic agnosticism—unconsciously due, in Asians, to Buddhist and Hinduist attitudes which the intellectuals among them deny as substantive beliefs. They cling to traditional rites and modes of conduct but like to accept nihilistic ways of thinking as truth. This means, however, that the modern intellectual struggle for the meaning of life, for the image of man, for insight into Transcendence, has become world-wide. It is just beginning, and it takes freedom of communication to carry it on.

It is false to take Western civilization for the only true one, to regard technological progress, material prosperity, and a high standard of living by themselves as happiness. Abandonment of the colonialist spirit means tolerance for other possibilities of life. There is really no need to bring the whole world to our technological civilization, as supposedly the only one. This is what happens now and will probably go on happening, owing as much to its universal appeal—for all want to be part of it—as to the greed of private or public enterprise everywhere, among all races and nations.

International trade in the technological age requires observance of generally recognized rules. Everyone wants this trade, even the totalitarians who lift their iron curtains for this purpose, under state control. The reduction of colonialism and the great renunciation, the West's withdrawal to its own territories, means neither a break in relations nor a refusal to trade; but the first requirement of pure and honest relations is the freedom of the former subjects of colonial rule. Even if we know that material hardship, perhaps a misery greater than ever, will be the first consequence of their desire for freedom, this is no reason to force ourselves upon them. It seems that the natives everywhere gather their own experiences; they cannot believe what they have not experienced themselves, and not until then will they seek co-operation on their own initiative.

After the reduction of colonialism, therefore, the great question is how international trade can be carried on. The old way—now to treat others as people like ourselves, now to despise and suppress and trick them—can no longer be taken for granted. But the idea of their meeting us in a generally human business spirit, measured by the standards of the honest trader and engineer, is as false today as the notion that the West had, in most instances, met them in this spirit.

Put more precisely, the great question is what conditions would permit agreements to be made in good faith and equally well understood by both parties, so that the benefit would be equal not only in fact but in purpose.

Agreements require the same spirit in both partners. Both must know what they are doing and must have the will to keep their promises. Agreements made in any other spirit are not really agreements; they are disguises to conceal either superior power or an impotence that yields but seeks to gain by cunning. He who does not know, or does not want, real agreement is abusing the form; he secretly takes it for an act of violence or fraud and is subsequently ready to break the agreement. Without a common spirit of contractual fidelity, there can be no real agreements and no trade relations, least of all in the technological age. If there is to be trade, it cannot rest only on trust in the business spirit. It needs guarantees envisioning compulsion or other safeguards; but the weaker side feels that this constitutes coercion and enslavement. The native populations have not entered into commerce on their own initiative; it has come over them. They are rightly distrustful, feeling fettered without knowing how. The West distrusts them as well—and just as rightly, having found out that agreements are not kept.

In consequence of the nations' desire for freedom, previous treaties—which such native powers as Egypt, Indonesia, Iran, etc., break or cancel at will, anyway—are now either liquidated or freely re-established on new, consciously phrased premises. The rejection of violence as a means for their enforcement presupposes a spiritual and moral-political development of the natives. There is no telling how it will come about—except for this: peace has no chance if we maintain the old fictions. Reality tells us that agreements can be made only with exact guarantees of reciprocity, without deceit, for mutual benefit. The premise of mutual reliability means—if faith is genuine—a simultaneous stipulation of the consequences of a breach of faith. If this is not possible, neither is honest trade; but it is better for peace to have no trade than to have dishonest agreements. Nations are right to call for freedom, but only if they can freely help themselves and can turn license into freedom under law. Else the call would mean: "You must free us—but you must also keep giving us the means to use our freedom as we please, without sharing in the hard work and orderly life of the technological age."

At the outset, reality puts quite a different face on the nations' high and just claim to independence and self-education. The terrible misery, malnutrition, and starvation in many parts of the world cry out for help, but the immediate material help from the West, rendered in Christian charity, is never more than a drop in the bucket. It is most admirable and often gives the few beneficiaries a chance to live; it bespeaks a helpful turn of mind; it is good that it exists—but it does not change the total misery anywhere. Nor is the cry of people's acute distress the cry of their governments, which would like to treat the distress as their own business and feel humiliated by outside help.

What the governments demand is not less; it is more. They want economic help with their development as a whole, in line with the freeworld principle of "aid to underdeveloped countries."

Gifts have also been made to "developed" countries. In the postwar emergency, America helped Europe through the Marshall Plan. This was "pump priming" to get the economy started again; the point was to help the recipients to help themselves. Such aid worked wonders in some cases, but the effects varied greatly, even among the nations of Europe.

Aid to "underdeveloped" countries is another matter. It is supposed to push them into the age of technology, although their way of life has not prepared them for the thinking and working style of this age. Economic help is futile if the premises of its use are lacking. It is not only pernicious for competing Western oil companies to lavish millions of dollars on Oriental despots, just because the oil they can do nothing with happens to lie beneath their soil; it is pernicious also to render "economic aid" where it remains a gift and is not transformed into spontaneous work. Such aid falls into a bottomless pit and serves only to make the recipient nations greedier. Material help to the "underdeveloped" is senseless if they do not want it as a spark for self-help. We must leave them room to live in their own way, to starve, to be born in masses, and to perish. They have the right to be free, but they do not have the right to expand beyond their borders. The abolition of colonialism cuts both ways, and the distribution of the globe has drawn the lines.

The present world situation often shows both the "underdeveloped" and the "helpers" in a strange light. The underdeveloped demand independence, sovereignty, and freedom in disposing of the help given to them. They want no strings attached to it. But they demand it as their right—credit, capital investments, supplies of arms and machinery, help for their hungry. When it is forthcoming, they are not thankful but suspicious of encroachments upon their independence; and if it is not forthcoming, they are indignant—it is a denial of their due, a hostile act. As for the nationalization —that is, expropriation—of capital investments, this is their sovereign right. They feel that what Western technology has produced, with enormous effort, is theirs even though they have taken no part in the effort. Being wooed by the two superpowers of the free and totalitarian worlds, they want thanks for their willingness to accept gifts.

Of course, the underdeveloped are not all alike; this general description is unfair to each single one of them. But they have this in common: they cannot help themselves in the new technological world they are coming to know; they are familiar with the problems of hunger and overpopulation; they more or less lack the Westerners' working ethics and initiative; and they have neither experience with nor a will to domestic political freedom.

Nor do the "helpers" present a better picture. They are self-serving; their help is not primarily meant to help at all. They give it to win sympathy for themselves, to influence the recipients against the other great power. They want to create economic dependencies for their own economic benefit—to assure themselves of oil, for example. Or, in regard to the natives' political development, they think that all men could become instantly democratic and manage their affairs by majority vote. Deluding themselves about the vast problems of their own democracy, without an inkling of the hand-to-mouth existence of the masses, they presume all men to be naturally fit for immediate political freedom and the modern life of skilled workers in highly developed industries. And if their expectations are disappointed, they consider violence justified.

Let us restate the implications of the required renunciation. We must give up all forms of struggle, whether political, military, or economic, for territories which are not at one with the West historically and by the will of their people. This retreat must be unconditional. But the free world, despite its constant losses, has not yet managed this fundamental decision to confine itself to what clearly belongs to it.

We must permit others to live in ways that differ from ours but have meaning to them. For the sake of world peace, we must put up with any way of life that stays within a nation's borders. If a nation is incompetent and lazy, tends to idleness and playful self-indulgence, we must let it be as one possibly true form of humanity. We must not seek to rule, to exploit, or to destroy it. Everyone has a right to be materially wretched; things may grow in him that competence can never understand. But those who live in misery must bear the consequences.

We do not segregate them. Though prudence compels us to start from the solidarity of free nations rather than from the abstraction of an entirety of all human bodies politic, this solidarity is open to all. Yet it is bound to premises grown and obtained in history. The solidarity of a part of mankind, united for self-preservation but not for conquest, can be reliable only if every member lives contractually and truly in a community of mutual trust. No one may join who has not proved himself; no one is forced to join against his will.

Freedom is the most-used word of our time. What it is seems obvious to all. Every country, every people, every individual wants to be free; the whole world seems as one in claiming and asserting freedom. Yet there is nothing more obscure, more ambiguous, more abused.

A few words on political freedom:

It is historically manifold, and nowhere quite reliable. We find it in ancient English liberty, in Dutch and Swiss liberty, in the liberty of the French Revolution, in that of the Scandinavian states, even in that of Bismarck's pseudo-constitutional Germany, and in American liberty. There is no such thing as universal freedom; there are only its his-

torical metamorphoses. It is not yet freedom when a so-called democratic structure is imposed, as a matter of form, on a population that knows nothing of freedom and is merely ruled in its name by despotic, if not totalitarian, methods in our technological age.

Political freedom is not identical with, but essential to, Western freedom. Where political freedom is forsaken, we feel that freedom as such, Europe, and the West are forsaken as well. Europe is rooted in the idea of freedom. Europe is where the reality of the present rests upon the inner voice of thirty centuries, where men, despite all divergencies, are linked by this age-old common past.

We may object: How is world peace to come if so many nations are still unable to create their own free political life? We may ask: What is to become of the millions without substance, of the victims of the technological age, while we of the West are about to lose our own substance? The answer is that neither we nor any others have the world in hand. We must see what the formally liberated want and will do. We cannot coerce them, because freedom cannot be coerced. We must wait to see what responsibilities they will encounter and accept.

All this would be simple and unequivocal if there were no totalitarian Russia. The free world is dealing with the former colonies under pressure of the Russian menace, and we must reckon with the possibility that the non-Western peoples may throw themselves into the Russians' arms. But we can successfully fight this only by not fighting, by being ready for a free partnership, if anyone meets us in freedom, good will, and veracity.

The great mass of former colonial subjects are now objects of competition. The great powers vie for permission to give presents to the small ones, and the small ones let them, expecting to remain free. Even the tiniest of them plays Russia against America; we do not hear about the reverse, but it may well be going on in secret. The situation becomes a menace to all.

America rightly fears that the former colonies will fall to Russia if their wishes are not met. So she keeps yielding. Mighty America bows to the most brazen challenges as if she were weaker than any Oriental puppet; and indeed, the combination of warlike acts and peaceful gestures on the part of totalitarianism is steadily reducing the possessions and prestige of the free world. Treaties are broken on a vast scale, and the West acquiesces, at America's urging, so as not to risk a world war. The totalitarians, on the other hand, insist on the letter of their agreements wherever they have set foot, and they do not shrink from extreme terrorism.

The nations of the free world give up positions and grant sovereignty where they used to rule—always expecting thus to gain a more loyal allegiance. The opposite usually happens. The method seems proper, as an inescapable reversal of past colonialist conduct; but it becomes illusory if Russia—in other forms, under other names, and by stirring up the anticolonialist hatred of the colored —seeks a rule that will be more terrible than any past colonial one. The nations knew the old colonialism for four hundred years; it is a ghost now, but they still see it as reality. Russian rule is unknown except in areas living under Russian terror. England withdrew from Jordan when the Jordanian government demanded it, but what happened in Hungary in October, 1956, seems to have made no impression outside the Western world. What has not been felt does not work on the imagination.

Colonialism has by no means given way to universal national independence and freedom. The former colonies are still largely incapable of freedom. We see them sink into chaos, as in Indonesia; and it is possible and may be probable that India—still a unit, thanks to British patterns—will follow up its original partition with Pakistan by disintegrating into the many senselessly and aimlessly embroiled dominions of her previous history. Colonial memories backed by the Marxist rejection of the capitalist world make the method of free communication and free enterprise seem like oppression to most nations. To them, the new form of rule which threatens to replace colonialism is not an experience but a welcomed paradise, a utopian order which will turn out to be terror only in reality. The totalitarians cloak their ambitions in charges of colonialism and use "liberation" to make the colored peoples gradually but wholly dependent upon themselves. The charge of imperialism cloaks their own new way of pursuing world domination. It is curious that today it does not help to speak of Russian imperialism or Russian colonialism; the world outside the West simply does not believe it.

We talk of a struggle for the "vacuum" between Russia and America—a vacuum that includes the bulk of the globe. The question arises: What risks must the Western world run of Asian, African, and American nations turning to Russia if their demands are refused?

1. The world situation may look as if the globe-wide colonial struggles of the Western powers were continuing by different methods, such as "aid to underdeveloped countries." In this, the West is at an obvious disadvantage. Its propaganda of freedom is felt to be propaganda for the well-known old colonialist attitudes, while the totalitarian Marxist propaganda appears to be a confidence-inspiring promise. The West can have a chance only if its traditional colonialist motivations are really and completely given up, if its renunciation of colonialism is sincere enough to be convincing. In deceit and coercion Russia is superior, not only because she has no scruples, but chiefly because of her unified political leadership, in contrast to the lack of solidarity among the Western powers.

The Western notion of keeping totalitarianism out of Asia and Africa by economic aid, given under free-enterprise ethics, may be a political mistake. For these economic ethics will always make the recipients feel that they are taken advantage of, while communism attracts them as a vague paradise, unknown and blindly desired. If this is the case, all aid would in the long run strengthen them only for further progress toward communism, until they succumb to totalitarian rule and the jail door slams shut. The West, deceived by short-term curbs on Russian influence, would be actually arming its enemies. Totalitarian gains cannot be halted by means of aid that is not given in a common spirit—least of all by subsidizing political adventurers and princes who in a crisis will not hesitate to sell out to the Russians, or whose people, in league with the Russians, will kick them out.

2. The question, in every case, is whether states and nations that are still free have an honest desire to be protected from totalitarian conquest by Western powers that have honestly renounced colonialism. The only weapon against Russian interference is non-interference. Only if honest Western readiness meets with an equally honest will to mutual protection—as apparently in Turkey's case —can aid really be helpful, and then only should arms be supplied. The readiness must be free from any trace of imposing oneself. The risk that the bulk of mankind will join the totalitarian terror against the free world is inescapable.

3. The freedom of wavering between East and West, playing one side against the other, is a fiction that has a certain reality only at this moment of transition. The seesaw politics found all over the world today is the cunning of the unscrupulous, with Tito as its seemingly successful model. In the long run, this very wavering means the beginning of totalitarianism.

4. The danger cannot be averted by continuous concessions on the part of the West. Nations cannot be spared the experience of Russian oppression by submission to their blackmail, but only by their own insight that would lead to true co-operation with the insight of the free West. What matters is the freedom of relations between the West and the former colonies. Where this has been achieved by nations aware of the Russian menace, no anxious opportunism should consider yielding, at the expense of such nations, to the demands of other, ambiguous nations.

5. The "struggle" can succeed only without a struggle—that is to say, by the example of free communication. First, the West would have to change; only our credible, non-aggressive will to co-operate rather than dominate can be convincing. Our success is questionable, but unquestionably we have reason to fear the billions of others— especially as we Westerners, until we have become

what we should be, cannot deal with them as we should.

6. Political freedom as a form of government is of European origin, founded in Greek and Roman reality and thought, and in the German concept of co-operation. This form of government has means and forms that seem translatable like science and technology—the parliamentary system, for example, the separation of powers, and so on. If so, they would not be bound to the West but accessible to all men. It is not enough, however, to translate them intellectually, like technology; they need a deeper grounding in man himself, a basis which to us seems generally human but may not be that at all. We must wait and see what the non-Westerners will do. They can develop their freedom only by self-education in view of the free world; we cannot educate them except by making ourselves into an example. We can only be ready for them, if they want us.

Must the liberated be caught in the snare of totalitarianism? Must they experience what they will then for a long time—forever, perhaps—be unable to throw off? Is it certain that they will travel this road? No, although for many it is probable.

Although the risk of Russian expansion is today inevitable, it is reduced by reliable and unequivocal ties with the nations whose own free will prompts them to seek solidarity with the West. It is further reduced by our readiness for mutual economic reinforcement, by free agreements based on respect for the sanctity of agreements, wherever there is a clear will to that end. The risk of Russian expansion is reduced, finally, by the attraction of the free Western way of life, provided it becomes purer, more honest, and more homogeneous among the Western nations than it is now.

Some day, perhaps, when they have experienced Russian oppression, the spirit of the Asians will turn against it. A day may come when the Russians appear to them as Westerners worse than any they have ever known. Then the Chinese threat might finally cause Russia to seek an alliance with the West. But all this is still far from the realm of real political reflection.

We conclude: in the nations' own interest, in the course of our self-preservation, in view of the world peace that is our responsibility—under all these aspects—there is no avoiding the risk that the liberated will be caught up in Russia's totalitarian machinery, used and consumed like Russia's own population. This risk is a necessary concomitant to the honest reversal of colonialism. But the demand is and remains the same: Liberate! If the totalitarians seem to the peoples in question to be doing this, while obviously doing nothing of the kind, only the freedom of the affected can decide which view they wish to take.

How can we cope with the risk? Only in the solidarity of self-preservation. The risk is justifiable on one condition only: the West must realize its determination to preserve itself by standing firmly together. We shall either fail to achieve solidarity and be destroyed, or we shall run the essentially inevitable risk together. Our self-preservation can be successful only if the nations of the West—Europe, America, and all the rest that are free not as a mere matter of form but in the moral-political consciousness of their population—join voluntarily, firmly, and in time.

Solidarity must now pervade all political motivations. It can be kept firm by the terrible threat to us all; this uncomfortable knowledge, compelling foresight and sacrifice, must not be concealed. Wishful thinking, neutralism—whose blindness and lack of convictions make it as contemptible as treachery—and fatalism are destructive of solidarity.

For us Westerners, there is no way but radical renunciation of world dominion and simultaneous, absolutely reliable unity. Unless we take this road, the world will go down in chaos and totalitarianism or else it will perish by the bomb.

As yet, solidarity has not been achieved. It is disturbing—in fact, in view of the world situation, it is almost incredible—that it seems still so distant. Everyone talks about it, but the slightest demand for sacrifice is enough to thwart any attempt. We have no right to spoil solidarity in fact by clinging to remnants of old domination—as Great Britain and France, above all, are still doing. Half-measures, in old-style politics and in calling for a new kind, plunge the West into the political and intellectual confusion which the Russians exploit with great success. In short, we seem to be rushing headlong toward self-annihilation—in the activities of traditional diplomacy, in dissident politics, in indecision, and in the irresponsibility of a decaying democracy, where every self-will, every opinion, every interest and privilege claims its absolute right, at home as well as in the democracies' dealings with one another. If they want to save their freedom, they must make themselves responsible for it. Only thus can democracy become real and worth saving.

Let us examine some phenomena which indicate that this has not happened yet.

The fact that totalitarianism kills freedom has by no means entered the minds of all. Many Western intellectuals go in for fuzzy, neutralist thinking. The presence of totalitarian influences, rudiments, and trail blazers in the Western world shows that the loss of freedom in totalitarianism is a generally human possibility apart from the Russian blueprint.

Further: nationalism has a right to survive in Europe only in distinct ways of life, in traditional views, in language, spirit, and education; as a power principle of states it has not only lost its reason for being but works against Western unity. European frontiers ought to turn more and more into boundaries of Europe's administrative areas. There are some great individual "Europeans," but their field is thought, not politics. Our hopes still rest in personalities only, notably from the small nations; in the larger European countries the old nationalism appears indestructible. The nation, its interests, its position in the world are foremost in everyone's mind, and Europe comes later. There are countless examples. Churchill, for instance, when he resumed as Prime Minister, seemed to have forgotten his marvelous Zurich speech of 1946, ending in the call, "Europe arise!" And after Eden's political and military failure in the Suez crisis revealed the British position and power as they really are, the new Prime Minister, Harold Macmillan, could say, "Great Britain has been great, is great, and will remain great." Nor were the statesmen alone led by national pride: in the summer of 1956, after Nasser's coup, enthusiastic crowds in British ports watched the fleet sail for the Mediterranean.

Finally: political unification can be secured only by a mutual limitation of sovereignty among all Western nations. This alone would make their position impregnable to any possible attack, totalitarian or otherwise. But their solidarity is still feeble. It is frightening to observe Russia's success in increasing her power by the ancient maxim of "divide and rule," used by every unscrupulous conqueror. The present success of this policy is purely the fault of the West, of the free nations' pursuit of their own selfish interests—eventually to the grotesque extent of America, because of Egypt, teaming up with Russia, ordering Britain and France to withdraw from Suez, allowing Bulganin to threaten their capitals with atom bombs, and thus making them yield. A Russo-American alliance prevailed over free nations, and Eisenhower proudly declared that America, for the first time, had made herself independent of British and French Asian policies! Let us admit: it was the most foolish and the most disgraceful moment of contemporary Western politics.

True, Britain and France, in their political confusion and imprudence, were at least as much to blame for the rupture of solidarity, for they ignored the tacit, morally and politically justified hegemonic position which the greatest power in the free world inevitably holds in regard to foreign policy decisions. Solidarity requires that no one act in foreign affairs without a previous understanding with America, and America has an analogous obligation to the smaller powers: she must consider the real, non-fictitious interests of the several free nations but subordinate them to the total interest of common self-preservation. Global policy cannot be made by majority votes. Solidarity demands compliance. In case of disagreement at any given moment, America must prevail even if she is wrong. Yet such hegemonic solidarity can endure only in a relationship of mutual loyalty among unequal partners—realized by consulting, reasoning together, pointing out, listening to arguments, visualizing the over-all situation, and assessing special motives and wishes. Without such loyalty—which at some time will exact hard renunciations from everyone—freedom must fail and prove inferior to the centrally directed will of the great totalitarian power.

The centralization of terror that is possible in the technological age stands against the league of free nations. In the free world, therefore, all depends on faith in the mutual alliance, while in the totalitarian world the suspicions of all against all are forced to co-operate by iron bonds. But faith, a premise of free-world survival, demands—without being able to enforce it—that no government conspire on behalf of its own interests with powers outside the alliance. Their utterly invulnerable solidarity should be the cardinal principle of the free nations. Individually they ought to shun no sacrifice; any sacrifice is better than the loss of everyone's freedom —which otherwise would in the end be shown up as a freedom not worth protecting and preserving. The people whose freedom has grown from their history, and they alone, are responsible for the consequences to all of mankind if this freedom should be lost.

To sum up: unless Europe and all of the West can be firmly united in time, Europe will be overrun and America lost in short order. At the right moment we ought to see something as radical as Churchill proposed in 1940 for a part of Europe: all Englishmen and all Frenchmen were at one stroke to be citizens of one state, with equal rights, to preserve themselves against the totalitarian Germany of Hitler. We need not extend this particular proposal to the entire West, but some such union must be deemed urgent by anyone who does not blink the facts. With weapons technology as it is, there will be no time after the outbreak of hostilities to make up for previous neglect—as the Anglo-Saxon countries used to do in the past, at sacrifices far exceeding those that would have been advisable beforehand. Today these sacrifices would be futile. We shall only be saved by foresight and by acting upon it. The democracies will have lost the moral right to their freedom if they waste its use on ephemera.

History shows us a great example of foresight in Themistocles. He advised the Athenians to use all income from their mines at Laurium to build a fleet on a par with the Persian colossus in the East, which would surely attack Greece one day. His simple foresight, and the material sacrifice made by the prudent Athenians, saved Greece and Western freedom ten years later, when the attack was launched with all the might of the huge empire.

How shall we preserve ourselves in the rising tide of chaos? Today a single totalitarian power has built up an immense war machine and is strengthening it daily, exploiting its whole population according to plans which a few men can make in a totalitarian state and force upon the ignorant remainder. Against this, nations can remain free only if their freedom enables them, out of prudence, to make the sacrifices of material goods, living standards, cheap pleasures, which terror can compel elsewhere —if the statesman, under much more complex conditions, can emulate Themistocles and convince the people themselves.

World peace is now threatened only by totalitarianism. Hitler, aware of his superiority in armaments, recklessly unleashed war in 1939; Russia raped the Baltic countries, Poland, Hungary, and others, and provoked the Korean and Indochinese wars. If men are not blackmailed into choosing slavery, peace can be saved only by a sufficiently vigorous self-defense of the free world, to deter totalitarian attack and initiate developments that may end in a natural world peace. Self-defense involves risks; we cannot foresee the reaction of the others, whom we now call "the vacuum." But their reactions will also depend on our actions. We must reckon with the possibility that almost all of them may topple into totalitarianism. We cannot prevent this by force, only by persuasion. In this sphere, our only weapon is non-violence, combined with readiness to co-operate in the common spirit of freedom and veracity for our objectives as free men.

The West, like all mankind, has the only non-violent weapon at its disposal: the truth. The conflict of the two worlds is one between falsehood and truth—but while totalitarianism rests upon the principle of falsehood and thus grows mighty, the free world is not truthful enough and thus grows weak.

The power of truth is incalculable, but between freedom and totalitarianism it will be decisive. To preserve itself, the free world must make itself more truthful by ceaseless self-education—a hard task that cannot be planned. Easier, but equally necessary, is a much more active public enlightenment about facts and right thinking. Today the energy behind planned totalitarian lies still exceeds the energy devoted by the intellectuals of the West

to the constant, clear exposition of facts. In daily newscasts, in the papers, in other writings, the untruthfulness of the totalitarian world, its deception of others and its self-entanglement in its own lies, should not be unmasked only now and then—which is done—but shown up time and again, in ever new instances, and more simply manifested to all. Even the Eastern literary defenders of Marxist thought draw more strength from the heritage of philosophy than their Western opponents—who believe they know it all, ignore the power of philosophical thinking, and refuse to bother.

Non-violence presupposes the strongest possible armament against possible aggression by the totalitarian war machine. The maxim, "Attack is the best defense," does not apply to the battle for the vacuum, or to the case of an opponent armed to the teeth and seemingly about to strike. Today's maxim says: Reliable unity, solidarity in arming for defense and in dealing with both the totalitarians and the nations of the vacuum, and community in sacrifice—these alone can make up a body that will be capable of self-preservation, though even the biggest of its parts would be lost if it would depend upon itself.

Self-preservation in our own realm forbids even the slightest offensive action to enlarge this realm. It is only in case of attack—including totalitarian violence against the very smallest allied nation— that it would rebound as a powerful offense by all means. This peaceful attitude, aimed only at self-preservation and truly not at expansion, does not permit a shift from "containment" to "rolling back" —except by agreements that would bring about an understanding between totalitarian Russia and the free world about nations of Western character and origin, such as Hungary, Poland, East Germany. If the free nations are true to their own selves, they will not wish to be guilty of using the atom bomb and initiating the annihilation of mankind—which means that they will go in for powerful conventional rearmament, inevitably lowering their standards of living. The next question is whether the self-preservation of freedom also requires readiness for the total sacrifice in which mankind might perish.

# POLITICAL INSTABILITY
# IN THE NEW STATES OF ASIA

Michael Brecher

## INTRODUCTION

Government in contemporary Asia has taken many forms—constitutional monarchy, absolute monarchy, republic, military régime, and Communism. In practice, too, there has been diversity, with three general types of political system—democracy, Communist dictatorship, and non-Communist authoritarianism.

"Democracy" in this context refers to a political system based on the Western model, more precisely, the Anglo-American models. Its principal components are a parliamentary or congressional form of government; a representative legislature; periodic secret elections based on universal adult suffrage; the rule of law, guarded by an independent judiciary, individual rights effectively guaranteed, such as freedom of speech, press, assembly, religion, and organization; respect for minority views and protection of minority rights—religious, ethnic, political, cultural and economic; and more than one political party competing for influence and power, with circulation in the political élite. A system so defined may be found, with deviations from the pure model, in India, Japan, the Philippines, and Malaya and, more precariously, in Ceylon.

The Soviet, or Communist, model is evident in three Asian governments—China, North Korea, and North Viet Nam. There, a constitutional façade masks the monopoly of power in the hands of the Communist (or Workers') Party. State organs are subordinate to the party; the legislature is hand-picked; elections are unfree, that is, without any choice; the courts lack tenure or independence; individual rights are subject to party-government decision and revision; minority rights may or may not be protected, depending upon the needs and plans of the party; and the political process is frozen under one-party control, a domination exercised by a variety of techniques involving persuasion and coercion.

This is an original article, printed for the first time.

All other Asian states reveal some form of authoritarianism. It may be mild, as in Pakistan since 1958, or severe, as in South Viet Nam under Ngo Dinh Diem since 1955 and in South Korea under Synghman Rhee. It may be military rule, as in Thailand, South Korea, Burma and Pakistan in 1958–62; civilian dictatorship, as in South Viet Nam; an uneasy blend of civil-military control, as in Indonesia; or absolute monarchy, as in Afghanistan, Nepal, and Cambodia. In all these cases, the indexes of democracy are absent in whole or in part. In some, the disregard for civil liberties is as great as in Communist lands, and the instruments of control are no less oppressive. In most, the Army has become a major political force, either exercising power directly (Thailand, South Korea, and Burma) or standing in the wings ready to seize control from a faltering civil authority and acting as guardian of the political order (e.g., Pakistan and Indonesia). In none of these states, however, is authoritarianism total; this is one vital distinction between Communist governments and those of "the middle zone." Another difference is the commitment in principle to democracy, though this commitment has lessened in recent years; but even among those who seek alternative paths to a stable political system, there is acceptance of the idea of change in the political élite, protection for individual and minority rights, the notion of choice by the governed as to who shall be the governors, and other components of democracy. Because of these commitments and the possibility of change in the political system, these authoritarian régimes are potentially closer to the substance of Democracy than to the rigid, closed political system of Communism. For the present, however, they remain almost as far removed from democracy as is Communism; and many are less welfare-oriented than either of the polar models.

All three types of political system in Asia today are "Western" in the sense that they are legacies of the Western epoch in Asian history. Democracy is the direct intrusion of colonial rulers, Communism is the product of Western ideas and the example of a non-Asian state, and the "middle zone" of authoritarianism uses Western-derived techniques and political forms to maintain power. No system is tradition-oriented, although some current experiments, notably in Pakistan and Indonesia, draw inspiration partly from the pre-Western period of their history.

One further introductory comment is in order. The three types do not correspond to the three major colonial empires—British, French, and Dutch —nor can they be correlated with former colonial areas and independent Asian states. All former British colonies began as "democracies," but Pakistan and Burma turned to authoritarianism. In former French dependencies there are examples of Communism and civilian dictatorship, along with absolute monarchy; and in the former Dutch Indies, non-Communist authoritarianism holds sway. Among the few Asian states that escaped direct Western domination, all three models are evident —Democracy in Japan, Communism in China, and military rule in Thailand.

## POLITICAL INSTABILITY: THE RECORD

The dominant feature of politics in the new states of Asia is instability. The range is wide, from near-constant flux in Pakistan and Indonesia to relative calm in India. But no new Asian state has been free from threats to a stable political order. The record is emphatic on this theme.

### Pakistan

In the first eleven years of statehood Pakistan had four Governors-General (and President) and eight cabinets. If one excludes the lengthy tenure of the first Prime Minister, Liaquat Ali Khan, there was an average of one cabinet a year. The turnover in the provinces was almost as rapid—six Governors of the Punjab and six of the North West Frontier Province between 1947 and 1955 and seven Chief Ministers of Sind during the same period. On three occasions the normal process of constitutional government broke down in the provinces and Governor's rule was imposed—in the Punjab from 1949 to 1951, in Sind from 1951 to 1953, and in East Bengal in 1954–5. Despite sincere intentions and frequent pledges, no national election was ever held, the members of the Constituent Assembly (which doubled as a legislature) having been elected to provincial legislatures *before* independence. Three provincial elections were held; but two were marred by official interference and bias, and the third, in East Bengal in 1954, was followed almost at once by severe disorders and Governor's rule.

Political instability in Pakistan appears in bold relief when one glances at the sequence of leadership at the center. The first year was dominated by the creator of Pakistan, Mohammed Ali Jinnah, who held three key posts simultaneously—Governor-General, President of the Moslem League, and President of the Constituent Assembly. His death in 1948 was a severe blow to the new state. Fortunately, his principal lieutenant, Liaquat Ali Khan, remained as Prime Minister, to whose office Jinnah's power as Governor-General was now effectively transferred. A moderate, religious Bengali leader, Kwaja Nazimuddin, succeeded to the Governor-Generalship. Another blow befell Pakistan in September, 1951, with the assassination of Liaquat. Thereafter, the vacuum of leadership was never adequately filled. Nazimuddin stepped down to the Prime Ministership; and an able career civil servant, Ghulam Mohammed, became Governor-General. Another crisis occurred in 1953, with severe religious riots in the Punjab, proposed concessions to *mullah* control over the Constitution, and a serious food shortage. Without awaiting a vote of nonconfidence in the Assembly, the Governor-General dismissed Nazimuddin and appointed another Bengali, Mohammed Ali of Bogra, as Prime Minister.

Perhaps the gravest constitutional crisis took place eighteen months later, in the autumn of 1954. An attempt to curb the powers of the Governor-General led to his abrupt dismissal of the (first) Constituent Assembly, the nullification of its enactments since 1947, and the formation of a "cabinet of talents" under the discredited Mohammed Ali. A test before the Supreme Court vindicated Ghulam Mohammed's action, but it insisted that a new Assembly be formed. The cause of stability and respect for authority were not enhanced. In the meantime, too, the election in East Bengal had swept the Moslem League Ministry from power with a resounding victory for a leftist United Front, seeking greater autonomy for Bengal. A month after the election, however, widespread riots led to the dismissal of the United Front and the imposition of Governor's rule.

To satisfy the Bengali demand for equality with the western region and to calm Punjabi fears of Bengali domination through a larger population, Ghulam Mohammed forced through the "One Unit Scheme," creating the province of West Pakistan to replace the mélange of provinces and tribal areas. He then induced the formation of a new Constituent Assembly, indirectly elected and with equal representation for East and West Pakistan. All the old Assembly's laws were revalidated, and a constitution for the Islamic Republic of Pakistan was finally passed in March, 1956.

By that time, a paralyzed Ghulam Mohammed was replaced by "strong man" Iskander Mirza as Governor-General, later Acting President. Like Jinnah and his immediate predecessor, the new head of state played an active role in politics; indeed, he manipulated politicians and parties to suit his whim. Thus, he backed Dr. Khan Saheb of the Frontier Province in his newly-formed Republican Party, which held power in the province of West Pakistan. He also helped to bring another civil servant, Chaudhri Mohammed Ali, to the Prime Ministership in the summer of 1955. A year later, the Bengali leader of the *Awami* (People's) League, H. S. Suhrawardy, became Prime Minister. A clash between President and Prime Minister led to the latter's dismissal without a vote of nonconfidence, a measure of the adherence of Pakistani leaders to constitutional processes. The President then appointed I. I. Chundrigar as Prime Minister in 1957; within a fortnight, still another pliant politician, Firoz Khan Noon, succeeded to the post.

The dismal game of Pakistani political chairs came to an end in October, 1958, when President Mirza abrogated the constitution, imposed martial law, dismissed the central and provincial governments, and outlawed political parties. Within three weeks Mirza himself was ousted by General (later Field Marshal) Mohammed Ayub Khan, Commander-in Chief of the Army. The experiment in parliamentary government, bedeviled from the outset, had come to an end and with it the chronic instability of Pakistan's political life. The "club" of 150 men who controlled politics for eleven years and made a mockery of democracy were swept aside, a few into jail, many barred from public life for a long time. The military took power and rejected the British system as unworkable in the Pakistani environment.

There is no better description of Pakistan's prolonged crisis of instability and political malaise than that contained in General Ayub Khan's statement of October 8, 1958:[1]

. . . there was no alternative to it [the imposition of martial law] except the disintegration and complete ruination of the country. . . . These chaotic conditions . . . have been brought about by self-seekers who in the garb of political leaders have ravaged the country or tried to barter it away for personal gains. . . . Their aim is nothing but self-aggrandizement or thirst for power. Meanwhile weak and irresolute Governments looked on with masterly inactivity and cowardice and allowed things to drift and deteriorate and discipline to go to pieces.
Ever since the death of the Quaid-e-Azam [Great Leader, referring to Jinnah] and Mr. Liaquat Ali Khan, politicians started a free-for-all type of fighting in which no holds were barred. They waged ceaseless and bitter war against each other regardless of the ill-effects on the country, just to whet their appetites and satisfy their base motives. There has been no limit to the depth of their baseness, chicanery, deceit and degradation. Having nothing constructive to offer, they used provincial feelings, sectarian, religious and racial differences to set a Pakistani against a Pakistani. . . . The country and people could go to the dogs as far as they were concerned. . . .

The result is total administrative, economic, political and moral chaos in the country. . . .

The General was an interested party, but no objective observer of Pakistani politics during the first decade would disagree with this harsh critique.[2]

### Indonesia

The crisis of instability was no less severe in the successor to the Dutch Indies. There were seven cabinets from 1949 to 1958, when "Democracy" gave way to "guided democracy." Violence has been endemic, starting with the acquisition of weapons from the departing Japanese in 1945 and the lengthy war of independence against the Dutch. Banditry has never been stamped out, nor has guerilla war, beginning with a force led by Dutch Captain "Turk" Westerling in 1949. A fanatic, orthodox Moslem group, Dar-ul-Islam, has never ceased terrorist activities in West Java in support of a theocratic state. The main area of disorder has been the "outer islands." There, regional loyalties and the fear of "Javanese imperialism" have led to four major insurrections: in the Moluccas, Macassar, and Amboina on two occasions, in 1950–51 and 1954–55; in Sumatra in 1956–57; and a complex series of revolts in Sumatra, Borneo, and the Celebes in 1958–60.

In the political arena, too, fragmentation has been the keynote. Dozens of groups engaged in the struggle for power. Three parties held the center of the stage—the Nationalists, the Masjumi, and the Communists—but none was strong enough to establish a firm majority. Coalition cabinets, the bane of political order in other states of Asia and the West, accentuated the problem. Only in one respect, perhaps, was Indonesia more fortunate than Pakistan; the leading symbol of Indonesian nationalism, Sukarno, has been President throughout the transition period, offsetting in part the elements of disruption. Even he, however, has been unable to create a stable polity.

The measure of Indonesia's political flux and uncertainty may be gauged in the sequence of cabinets. Vice-President Hatta served briefly as Prime Minister immediately after independence. There followed a series of coalitions. First, the Moslem party, the Masjumi, dominated the cabinet under Mohammed Natsir, leader of its liberal wing, in 1950–51 and under Sukiman, a prominent conservative, in 1951–52. Another short-lived cabinet was headed by moderate Premier Wipolo in 1952–53. Then came the Nationalists, under Sastroamidjojo, with Presidential support, from 1953 to 1955. The Masjumi remained aloof, but parliamentary support was assured by Communist backing—forthcoming because of the strong neutralist line of the Nationalists, culminating in the Bandung Conference.

Real power, then as before, was in the hands of Sukarno.

A turning point in the unsuccessful quest for stability was the general election of 1955, the only genuine national poll in Indonesia's history. (Members of the Provisional Parliament [1949-55] had been appointed in proportion to the estimated strength of the various parties at the time of independence.) The results did not augur well for the future, for fragmentation was now solidly entrenched. The Nationalists and Masjumi each won fifty-seven seats, a more conservative Muslim Teachers Party forty-five, and the Communists thirty-nine. Once more, a coalition was necessary. Both Moslem parties rejected Sukarno's proposal to include the Communists; but they joined the Nationalists, again under Sastroamidjojo, in a new cabinet formed in the spring of 1956.

Tension mounted during the next year—between Sukarno and Vice-President Hatta, between Java and the "outer islands," and among the political parties. Hatta finally resigned in December, 1956, over the issues of growing Communist influence, the President's "guided democracy" plan, and excessive Javanese control. At that time, too, army commanders in north Sumatra led a revolt against the center. It was this continuous evidence of dissension, and perhaps his admiration for the monolithic solidarity of China, that led Sukarno to challenge the parliamentary system itself.

The President's assault gathered momentum after Hatta's resignation. The essence of his argument was contained in a speech early in 1957:[3]

I have finally come to the conclusion that the cause [of political instability] lies in our practicing a system not suited to our specific requirements, in our indiscriminate adoption of every feature of the system that is known as western democracy. . . . The principles of western democracy . . . incorporate the concept of an active opposition. . . . By accepting this concept we have come to think in a manner that is alien to the Indonesian way of life [where decisions were traditionally arrived at by consensus].

To overcome the dissensions of the parliamentary system, Sukarno proposed and succeeded in creating a National Council to "guide"—that is direct —the cabinet on major policy issues. Parliament would remain and so would the cabinet, but ultimate power would be vested in the Council. A forty-three-member Council was installed in July, 1957; all parties and the armed forces were represented. Thereafter, the façade of parliamentary government remained, but its substance was destroyed. Even the form itself was eliminated in 1959; and the following year, Sukarno used his decree powers to restore the first, and provisional constitution of 1945, which gave the President vast authority. In Pakistan, then, a decade of instability led to military rule; in Indonesia, civilian government remained, but democracy was destroyed, and the army acquired considerable power, virtually an equal partner of Sukarno in his "guided democracy."[4]

Other illustrations of instability in the new states of Asia may be treated more briefly.

## Burma

The symptoms of disorder in Burma were flagrant, and the survival of the Union was in grave doubt for a decade. The crisis began in August, 1947, on the eve of independence, when General Aung San, leader of the nationalist movement, the Anti-Fascist People's Freedom League (AFPFL), and six cabinet colleagues were assassinated by a rival group. The danger of chaos was overcome by the closing of nationalist ranks under the leadership of U Nu.

The gravest challenge came from open rebellion by various groups. Most serious was the revolt of the Karens, a militant minority of a million who sought an independent state. Two bands of Communists, White Flag (Stalinist) and Red Flag (Trotskyite), also defied the central government; so did a segment of the wartime underground People's Volunteer Organization (PVO), and extremists of other minorities such as the Chins and Kachins. Indeed, during most of the 1950's, the writ of the Union Government extended only to Rangoon and its immediate surroundings. Gradually, the Communists were reduced to insignificance, the PVO personnel were amnestied, and the Karens were given acceptable assurances of autonomy. During the process of consolidation the army grew in prestige, as did its leader, General Ne Win.

The political process itself was much more tranquil. The AFPFL was a coalition of many interests —the Socialist Party, the Karen League, and Congresses of the Kachins, the Chins, and the hill people. With the Communists in revolt, and the extreme Right virtually nonexistent, there was no one to challenge the AFPFL at the polls. Thus, in the 1951 elections, it won 220 of 250 seats in the dominant lower house, the upper house being the Council of Nationalities. In 1956, its majority was reduced to 169 out of 250; but the real danger to the party, and the crisis it precipitated, came from within.

The split became ominous in 1957–58, with Socialist and Peasant Organization members of the ruling party voting on opposite sides in the house. Violence occurred, and with it an open struggle for the party machine. Prime Minister U Nu, backed by the Peasants' Organization, sought to retain his weakened position by strange tactics—an offer of statehood to dissident Arakanese and Mons, a pledge of amnesty to Communist rebels in the hope of winning support from the leftist National Front in Parliament, and the dismissal of treason charges against two M.P.'s so that they could vote! He thereby secured a narrow vote of confidence, but the rot had gone too far. In October, 1958, the Army took over direct authority—at the request of U Nu—and General Ne Win became Prime Minister. The Army promised to restore civilian rule after the residue of corruption was swept away; and so it did, in February, 1960, when new elections returned U Nu to power as head of the "clean" faction of the AFPFL. The Army remains in the background—as guardian of "Democracy." This rare example of self-abnegation was short-lived, however. In March, 1962, Ne Win and the Army acted in accord with time-honored patterns; they seized power in a coup d'etat, imposed martial law, outlawed parties, and put an end to the British-type political system in Burma.[5]

## Ceylon

No country in Asia seemed to have better prospects for a stable democracy than the island dominion. A peaceful road to independence, a high literacy rate (65 per cent), and a Westernized élite with experience in government all augured well for the future. Indeed, the early years were relatively tranquil. The conservative United National Party won a substantial majority in the elections of 1947 and 1952. There were many opposition groups, including two Trotskyite parties and one Communist party, and two Tamil parties; but none threatened UNP control. Until the mid-1950's, Ceylon seemed an exception to the pattern of Asian instability.

Beneath the surface, however, new political forces and problems were gathering strength, notably a new rural élite of Buddhist monks, village teachers, and Ayurvedic doctors, all highly nationalistic, especially towards the fermenting problems of language and the Tamils. A growing demand for "one national language" to replace English angered the large Tamil minority, two million out of a total of ten million. The cry of "Sinhalese only" was championed by S.W.R.D. Bandaranaike and his leftist Sri Lanka Freedom Party. The tradition-oriented rural élite rallied to this party, and the UNP was swept from power in the elections of 1956. Bandaranaike took fifty-one of the ninety-five seats; but his victory ushered in a period of intense lawlessness in the country—widespread strikes organized by the far Left parties, especially in Colombo, and riots by the supporters and opponents of "Sinhalese only." The clashes in 1956 and 1958 led to a thousand dead and many more injured, with widespread arson, looting, and assault. Only martial law restored order in the summer of 1958. The tension remained, as economic discontent added fuel to the flames. In the autumn of 1959, the Prime Minister was assassinated by a Buddhist monk.

New elections in March, 1960, were inconclusive; soon after, however, fresh elections brought the slain Prime Minister's widow to power with a bare majority, the first woman head of government in the world. Once more, severe Tamil-Sinhalese riots occurred, as the date for the imposition of one national language drew near. By 1961, the hopes for a model democracy had faded into history; Ceylon had joined the ranks of troubled Asian lands.[6]

## Laos

Nowhere is politics as confused and unsettled as in this remote, land-locked kingdom. The French protectorate was terminated by the Geneva Agreements of 1954, but the years of independence have seen constant violence and tension. Even before independence, civil war raged between the Royal Laotian Government and the pro-Communist Pathet Lao (Free Laos) movement, which occupied the two northern provinces. A precarious truce and, for a brief period, an uneasy coalition of the rivals was maintained by the International Control Commission. By 1959, however, the coalition was sundered, the Pathet Lao leader was imprisoned, and outside Powers had openly intervened. The United States backed the Royal Government, while China and Viet Nam backed the Pathet Lao.

Disorder has been permanent since the late summer of 1959. First came an intensification of the civil war and Royal Government charges of massive Chinese and North Viet Namese intervention. A UN Security Council inquiry mission found no direct evidence, and tension declined. Early in 1960, a leftist paratrooper, Captain (later General) Kong Le, led a rebellion that was supported by neutralist Premier Souvanna Phouma; the Pathet Lao was brought back into the cabinet. Then came a right-wing coup that replaced the Prime Minister with Prince Boun Oom. Souvanna Phouma fled to Cambodia, his régime still recognized by Moscow, Peking, and Hanoi. Then, in the autumn of 1960, the civil war became ominous, as the Soviet Union airlifted supplies and weapons on a large scale, with the United States retaliating. The danger of another Korea was grave.

The struggle on the battlefield moved rapidly in favor of the Pathet Lao; by the time a truce was arranged in the spring of 1961, almost two-thirds of Laotian territory was under its control. A fourteen-power conference in Geneva finally reached agreement in July, 1962, on the basis of a neutralized Laos. Within Laos itself, prolonged negotiations led to a delicately balanced coalition of right-wing, neutralist, and Pathet Lao factions under the premiership of Prince Souvanna Phouma. There remains a Gilbertian quality to Laos today, with the threat of grave political instability ever present.[7]

## South Viet Nam

Non-Communist Viet Nam is more stable than Laos today, but only at the price of authoritarian rule. In the early years, 1954–55, it seemed doubt-ful whether the Saigon regime would survive. In-deed, only decisive action by Ngo Dinh Diem—backed by the United States—prevented utter chaos. In succession, Diem destroyed the bandit Binh Xuyen, who controlled the Saigon police, asserted control over the army, reduced the Hoa Hao sect to insignificance, and eliminated the Cao Dai as an autonomous force. Finally, he deposed Emperor Bao Dai in a "popular" referendum and became Chief of State. Within eighteen months of Geneva, Diem was master of the South. Then, lip service was paid to the forms of democracy by having a Con-stituent Assembly enact a new constitution. For all practical purposes, Diem is dictator of South Viet Nam, aided by a small coterie, mainly of close relatives; nothing is done without his—or their—approval.

It would be wrong to assume, however, that South Viet Nam is stable and secure. Parts of the country are heavily infiltrated by the Viet Cong, Communists working with the North. By assiduous guerilla warfare, they have killed thousands, includ-ing many village officials, thereby disrupting admin-istration and tax collection in the rural areas. Some 2,500 dead on both sides in the civil war was the estimate in the first seven months of 1961. Saigon itself is virtually surrounded by Communist guerilas, and few will venture forth after dark. Moreover, discontent with rigid Diem family rule bursts out periodically, the most recent crisis being in Novem-ber, 1960. Three battalions of paratroops sur-rounded the presidential palace and demanded re-forms, including free speech and a new (military) cabinet. The revolt was suppressed, but the régime nearly toppled. Thus, the surface of South Viet Nam is stable; but fear and dictatorship prevail, and dis-ruptive forces are within, growing steadily. Without massive U.S. aid, it is likely that chaos—or Com-munist control—would ensue.[8]

Enough examples have been cited to demonstrate a pattern of political instability in the new states of Asia. There are some notable exceptions—India, Malaya, and the Philippines; but even they are not free from grave threats to political order.

## India

India is the most stable of the new Asian states. The Congress Party has held power in Delhi and in all but one of the states since 1947. Three gen-eral elections and five state contests have been free from disruption, violence, and corruption. The Army is clearly subordinate to the civil authority, the judiciary is independent, political parties are free to organize and persuade, but threats to law and order have been suppressed. Social and eco-nomic reforms have been effected within a stable framework. At no time has the existing political system been in danger of being swept away.

Yet there have been acts of disorder and sources of instability in India. The coming of six million refugees posed serious problems to the new govern-ment—as it did in neighboring Pakistan. Both Kerala in the south and Orissa in the east and Punjab in the north had to be placed under Presi-dent's rule on various occasions because of tension and deadlock in the political arena. Fasting has triggered off disorder frequently, notably in Andhra in 1952. Regional loyalties and linguistic passions have caused widespread violence and destruction, as in Bombay during the States' Reorganization period in 1956 and in Assam in 1960. Students are often in revolt against authority, major strikes are not uncommon, and a Communist-led revolt in Hyderabad caused havoc and disorder from 1948 to 1950. The latest challenge to stability was the Sikh demand for a separate state within India. In short, India has not escaped the political illness afflicting all Asian states. The difference has been in the capacity of the Government to withstand the challenges and the commitment to democracy. In both spheres, India has been a notable success, but symptoms of disquiet are widespread beneath the surface of Indian politics.[9]

## The Philippines

May also be regarded as a stable democracy. Its constitution is modeled on that of the United States, and its political process has also drawn much from the former colonial ruler. There have been six elections to the presidency, not without malpractice, but leading to orderly transfers of power to the winner. Parties have been less im-portant than in British-type patterns of politics, resembling rather those of America. The consti-tutional order has been firmly established but not entirely serene. Indeed, for almost a decade after the coming of independence in 1946, Manila was confronted with a challenge from the Communist-led Hukbalahap movement. This began as an anti-Japanese army based on the peasantry and mushroomed into a broad political organization for land reform and basic political change. In the early years it held effective control over parts of central Luzon. Guerrilla war continued until 1955, and the threat was only overcome by the one outstanding Philippine leader of recent times, Ramon Magsay-say. Apart from the Huk threat, Philippine politics have been relatively tranquil.[10]

## Malaya

The Federation of Malaya was the last Asian state to achieve independence, in 1957. Too little time has elapsed to judge the success of democracy and the degree of stability, though on both counts the evidence is favorable. Yet it should be noted that a Communist rebellion wreaked havoc in Malaya from 1948 to 1957 and has not been totally eradicated. The continued presence of Commonwealth troops has shored up Malaya's internal security; the threat still remains below the surface.[11]

## CAUSES OF INSTABILITY

Almost all the new states of Asia inherited the forms of democracy. All but a few set out to build a political order of the Western type. The key motive seems to have been psychological—the belief of the nationalist élites that only by working a constitutional democracy would their claim to equal status with the former rulers be recognized. It was also the line of least resistance, for many had a full-blown system to ease the transition. Nationalist leaders had absorbed the idea, as well as the assumed superiority, of democracy. There was no appeal in the traditional political system; by temperament, philosophy, and experience they were committed to democracy, whether of the British, American, French, or Dutch variety.

Whatever the stimuli, most failed: within a decade of independence the elaborate framework of constitutional democracy has been dismantled in much of South and Southeast Asia or was robbed of content. A glance at the record has shown the environment of that area to be unreceptive on the whole to that bold experiment. Many of the states have adopted some form of authoritarian rule. Most striking, perhaps, has been the rise of the officer corps to prominence—so much so that it achieved direct authority in Burma, Pakistan, and South Korea, and a crucial position in Indonesia, South Viet Nam, and Laos. Only India, Malaya, and the Philippines (and Ceylon with reservations) remain in the "democratic column." Finally, the record suggests widespread instability in the region, both in states that have "fallen from democratic grace" (one of the causes of the "fall") and those which persist with the task of political adaptation. It is to the reasons for these related developments that we may now turn: the causes of instability in the region as a whole, the causes of the failure of democracy, and an explanation for the growth of army influence. This discussion will be supplemented by a sketch of obstacles to stability and democracy in specific countries.

## GENERAL CAUSES OF INSTABILITY

### Poverty

The sources of instability in the new states of Asia are varied and complex. Perhaps the most disquieting—because it is certain to remain on the Asian scene indefinitely—is widespread poverty. People who live at the margin of subsistence are either indifferent or hostile to government, and in Asia there are hundreds of millions who are underfed, disease-ridden, and uneducated. Their reaction will range from passivity to overt anger; if aroused, they will blame those in power for their ills, frequently resorting to riots and demonstrations against authority. Certainly, they cannot be expected to act as "responsible citizens" sympathetic to order and the delicate process of constitutional democracy. Where they have been receptive, special factors intrude—tradition or faith in a charismatic leader or a nationalist movement committed to democracy or enough material improvement to induce patience and faith in the future. Nevertheless, it remains true for most of the new Asian states that all-pervasive poverty undermines government of any kind. It is a persistent cause of instability and makes democracy well-nigh impossible to practice.

### Antipathy to Government

To this cause must be added a tradition of antipathy to government, an attitude born of untold centuries of fear and resentment of the power of Authority. Asia's peasants, about 75 per cent of her population, have long identified government with the tax collector and the oppressor, the friend and protector of moneylender and landlord. Regimes came and went, but government remained. Foreign or native, it performed the same functions, made the same demands, imposed the same onerous obligations. Since their conditions of life did not change very much, Asia's masses did differentiate one set of rulers from another. When independence came, it brought another change of tax collector—and often an oppressor. In most states of the region it did not bring a perceptible improvement in the peasant's standard of living. Why then should he change his time-honored distrust or antipathy to those in power? It was hard to maintain stability in the transition period, much more difficult to build the delicate mechanism of democratic process. In short, the new regimes lacked a broad base of support in the crucial early years.

### Oppositionism

Even within the political élite hostility to Government was widespread. This was a legacy of the struggle for independence, when almost everything done by the colonial ruler was deemed evil. It was natural to carry this attitude of oppositionism, or negativism, over to the post-colonial period, especially among those out of power. In most of the new states, then, obstruction became the norm of political behavior, partly because it had brought results in the past and partly because it was familiar. The notion of a loyal opposition, one of the most significant in the democratic process, was unknown among almost all nationalist movements in Asia. Thus, both the groups now in power and those outside found the idea unappealing; all opposition seemed treason and all Government seemed immoral. In most states elections were a farce and were so regarded by rivals for power. This tended to place a premium on extraconstitutional means of achieving power, the *coup d'état,* civil war and the like. Hence violence occurred frequently in the politics of the new Asian states. Weak and untried regimes could hardly flourish in this environment. Many faced permanent crisis and were toppled. Instability became the rule and democracy an illusion.

### Tradition of Autocracy

There was, too, an unreal quality to the democratic experiment. Asian politics had a long tradition of autocracy, whether monarchical or military, native or foreign. Government was stern as well as distant, harsh, and unused to criticism, even after the coming of the West and even after democratic forms were introduced. Government by decree and ukase, by police power and threat of punishment, was the recognized pattern. In some colonial areas, like Indonesia and Indo-China, autocratic rule remained to the very end, despite the constitutional façade. In others, like British and American colonies, the beginnings of democratic practice were apparent in the decade or two before the transfer of power; but the crucial fact remained that democracy was a sharp break with tradition.

### Limited Experience with Democracy

This is, perhaps, another way of saying that the peoples of Asia had limited experience with democracy. The middle class were familiar with its form and substance, although few had held positions of responsibility before independence. To the peasantry, however, both the idea and the institutions of democracy were alien; their contact with government was limited to the district official and an occasional glimpse of a visiting dignitary. No less important, in this connection, was the gap between the small Westernized élite, the carrier of the new idea, and the masses. Most nationalist leaders spoke a Western language, dressed in Western clothes, and behaved like the foreigner. Indeed, they stood suspended between their own culture and that of the West; some, as Nehru remarked about himself, were "a queer mixture of the East and the West, out of place everywhere, at home nowhere." To the extent that they became Westernized, they became alien in their own societies. No wonder, then, that the masses looked askance at their political

innovation if they looked at all. In short, the bulk of the population were accustomed to autocracy, while a minority considered democracy superior but had inadequate preparation in the art of constitutional government—two further reasons for the political crisis in the new states.

### Habits of Violence

There were other disturbing legacies of the recent past. One was the upheaval of war and revolution and the habit of violence formed during the years 1940–45. Political armies date to the Japanese conquest, and states like Burma, Malaya, and Indonesia have paid a heavy price. Even more serious was the attitude to politics born of that tumultuous era, with the stress on force to achieve goals. This attitude alone undermined the precarious stability of many successor states.

### Shortage of Civil Servants

Another residue was the shortage of trained civil servants to fill the needs of welfare states. Only in India, Pakistan, Ceylon, and Malaya was an adequate "steel frame" left by the departing colonial power. Elsewhere the new governments had to depend upon a handful of their own people and a host of unqualified political appointees. All this occurred against a background of rising expectations for material improvement, imposing even heavier burdens on state administration. With few exceptions the challenge was not met. Bureaucracies floundered amidst the enormous strain of transition, building a welfare state, planning the economy, and maintaining law and order in the face of dissension, rebellion, and violence. The outcome could not have been different in some Asian states, given the paucity of competent, relatively honest administrators. Even where a substantial body of civil servants was available, there was much friction with nationalist politicians, who identified them with the colonial regime. In this respect, too, instability may be traced partly to the impact of colonialism.

### Small Middle Class

More broadly conceived, it was the inadequacy of trained manpower in a host of spheres that made the creation of a stable order more difficult. These countries also suffered from the small size of the middle class. In the West, this class has been the strongest proponent of political democracy; and this system has been successful only in countries with a substantial middle class (though some states so endowed are models of autocracy). In the new states of Asia the urban population was relatively small, and the literate, aware, comfortable middle class was tiny even in terms of these islands of progress surrounded by a sea of tradition-bound peasants. The fact that this class was apart from the mass and was Western in outlook only aggravated the problem of political innovation—the creation of a democratic system on flimsy foundations of the colonial era.

## Leadership

The presence and quality of leadership has played a role in the quest for stability. Nehru survives and is deeply committed to democracy; he also helps to unify the myriad of groups and interests in Indian society. Pakistan was less fortunate. Jinnah died a year after independence, and Liaquat Ali was assassinated three years later; the resulting vacuum was not filled until 1958. In Burma, Aung San was removed from the scene even before the transfer, amidst turmoil and dissension. Other lands have been less favored with outstanding men, and in still others democracy has been expendable, as with Sukarno in Indonesia, or held in contempt, as with Ngo Dinh Diem in Viet Nam.[12]

## Party

The presence of an efficient, popular mass party has also influenced the degree of stability. In India, the Congress played a vital role, supporting the new régime, educating the masses in the benefits of democracy, and linking the middle class of the cities with the peasantry. No other party in Asia was successful in these roles. Indeed, most political parties in the new states were ill-prepared for responsible self-government, let alone constitutional democracy. For one thing, they were movements, not parties; that is, they brought diverse, often conflicting, interest groups under the umbrella of a "national movement" struggling for independence. None succeeded in shedding the trait of heterogeneity, not even the Indian National Congress; but it had compensating features enabling it to exercise power responsibility. These movements were held together by the common aim of independence; but few had a positive social and economic program, certainly not the Moslem League in Pakistan, the United National Party in Ceylon, the Alliance in Malaya, nor the Nationalist Party in Indonesia, while the AFPFL in Burma never freed itself of the mélange character attending its birth in the midst of war.

Political parties also contributed to instability through their ignoble behavior. Almost all "national movements" ceased to aggregate and articulate interests after independence. Rather, they degenerated into *factional strife* and *corruption*. The lure of power overcame scruples. Politicians switched loyalties frequently. More important, they lost touch with the masses, with the result that the political "game" became utterly divorced from society as a whole and devoid of content and mean-

ing. Cabinets changed frequently, but the same men in different combinations reappeared. The club was very small and functioned in a vacuum. Only when elections were held was there any pretense of concern for real issues and the people's welfare. The frequency of political turnover, the glaring gap between politicians and people, the widespread corruption and nepotism—all these undermined respect for democracy or, indeed, for any Government.

## Social Heterogeneity

The new states of Asia have also been troubled with the problem of social heterogeneity. All have large and vocal minorities who undermine internal unity. They may be religious groups, such as the Hindus of East Pakistan or the Moslems and the Sikhs in India. They may be ethnic or national in character, like the Tamils in Ceylon, the Indians in Burma and Malaya, or the Chinese all over Southeast Asia. They may be linguistic or cultural or regional units, such as the dozen non-Hindu language groups in India or the Karens, Kachins, and Chins in Burma. Whatever their distinctive trait, these minorities are often unassimilable and, at best, are sources of irritation and instability.

Reference has already been made to the lengthy Karen revolt in Burma that delayed political stability for a decade. In Ceylon, the corrosive influence of the Tamil-Sinhalese clash was no less severe and threatens the very unity of the island. Here is a well-organized minority, related to a giant neighbor who feels a sense of responsibility for their welfare. Ceylon has sought a mass of repatriation or withdrawal of recent immigrants to Ceylon from India. Delhi has steadily objected, as has the Tamil community itself. Since 1949, when a special discriminatory Ceylon citizenship bill was passed, until today, the tension has been high, frequently boiling over into violence like the riots of 1956, 1958, and 1960. The clash has rent the new state asunder, particularly as it became enmeshed with the question of language. Until the question is resolved, or reduced to manageable proportions, the stability of Ceylon will be fragile and the political system combustible.

The abrupt discriminatory action against Chinese traders in the Indonesian countryside in 1960 illustrates the precarious and resented economic role of that minority all over the region. It also suggests that some states will take advantage of exposed minorities for other ends. In Malaya, the position of the Chinese is stronger, yet more corrosive. Indeed, it is the overwhelming Chinese community in Singapore that keeps the island colony apart from the Federation of Malaya. In more general terms, the Chinese minority in half a dozen states of the area is a challenge to political stability made more difficult by the presence of a powerful interested mainland Chinese regime.[13] In India, according to some observers, the presence of fourteen distinct language groups represents a major threat of political Balkanization in the coming decades.[14] Even if this speculation is alarmist, it remains true that the reorganization of the Indian States in 1956 unleashed disruptive forces and left deep scars among some minorities—witness the Sikh agitation to the present day. Viewed in terms of the quest for stability, these illustrations reveal local loyalties that transcend a "national" identity. When to these are added tribal, caste, family, and communal attachments, often more purposeful than attachment to "the nation," the problem of stability seems overwhelming.

### Lack of Tolerance

Some of the obstacles to democracy in Asia were noted earlier. One of the more important is an apparent clash between its principle of tolerance and the aims of the new states. An active, free opposition is essential to democracy, but democracy is a slow and divisive technique of decision-making. To the Asian élites time is short, and the crucial need is a strong government to achieve unity and modernize their antiquated economies. The gap has seemed wider with the passage of time, and democracy has been a natural scapegoat for the slow pace of progress.

It remains to note the most common explanation: Asian states do not possess the classic conditions of democracy—a high level of literacy, a general level of prosperity well above subsistence, social homogeneity, a strong and large middle class, and a lengthy period of peace. These conditions have obtained in the established Western democracies. They are also to be found in some Western autocracies. It is also true that none is found in India, where democracy has most successfully been transplanted. All that may be said is that the presence of these conditions is likely to make democracy successful and that their absence, in whole or in part, increases the magnitude of the task. A more rigid correlation seems unwarranted at this stage of the political evolution of Asia and of the West.[15]

It was this complex of factors that led to the twin phenomena of recent Asian politics—the decline of democracy and the upsurge of army influence; the climax was reached in 1958. To state it succinctly, the military rode to power on the crest of a wave of despair with civilian government in general and democracy in particular. Much had been promised by the nationalist politicians, and relatively little had been achieved. The spectacle of corruption and inefficiency did not endear democracy to those who pondered the future, either the middle class or the army, but the latter had distinct assets.

The army was, in most of the new states, the only disciplined and organized group capable of ensuring stability and continuity. Moreover, it had a reservoir of educated men, in predominantly illiterate societies, men who are aware of the enormous problems on the road to a modern state. It is likely to be less corrupt than civilians in power, and it has an élan to move the society and economy. For many intellectuals in Asia the army became the savior; some officers also saw their role in this light. In any event, the army has become a vital political force.[16]

## SPECIFIC CAUSES OF INSTABILITY

### Pakistan

All the sources of instability in the region as a whole were present in Pakistan—and then some. Indeed, here is an outstanding example of the political crisis in the new states of Asia, especially the decline and fall of democracy.

Poverty is intense in the "Land of the Pure" with an annual per capita income of about $60. Illiteracy is awesome, upwards of 75 per cent. The middle class is small, comprising civil servants, members of the liberal professions, the officer corps, and the infant business community in the cities. Peasant antipathy to government was profound, the legacy of millenia of oppression; the British *Raj* did not alter this basic attitude. Autocracy was woven into the fabric of life; democracy seemed alien to all but a few. Moreover, the Moslems of the subcontinent were late in accepting Western education, so that even for the Moslem élite constitutional democracy was a novel system; the authoritarianism of Islam in politics did not make them more receptive. Even though the British were the most advanced in preparing their subjects for self-government, few Moslems had adequate experience in this sphere.

The severity of the struggle for Pakistan placed a premium on "unity, discipline, and faith"—in Jinnah's (and the Moslem League's) leadership. Indeed, for some years after independence, criticism of the League was termed treason by the Prime Minister. After independence, too, the attitude of negativism persisted in the political community, particularly among those out of power. The vacuum in leadership has already been noted. The fact that no one of stature followed Jinnah and Liaquat Ali Kahn brought grave consequences: the "national movement," that is, the Moslem League, suffered irreparably, its decline beginning in the early fifties. The completion of a constitution was delayed, and friction between East and West Pakistan was exacerbated.

Pakistan did not fare better with her parties.

None but the Moslem League had nationwide influence; both the Awami League and the Krisak Sramik Party were East wing in origin and scope, the Republican Party, West wing. More serious was the rot of corruption invading the Moslem League, ultimately poisoning the political system beyond cure. Nowhere in Asia was the spectacle of political degeneracy so evident to the public—politicians crossing the floor of the House for personal gain, factionalism run amuck, the head of state manipulating men and parties, even the killing of the Deputy Speaker of the East Pakistan Assembly. No wonder that few tears were shed when Ayub Khan cast the parties to oblivion in 1958.

Pakistan was also troubled by a large minority—the twelve million Hindus of East Bengal, who were difficult to assimilate in an "Islamic State." Moreover, they seemed to hold a balance-of-power position between the Moslems of the two wings; the controversy over separate and joint electorates centered on Hindu electoral influence. They were also a source of tension between Pakistan and Hindu India, a continuation of the communal discord that contributed much to the Partition in 1947. The great migration of Hindus to West Bengal in 1950 and the continuous trickle thereafter (a total of three million have reportedly left East Pakistan) testify to the persistent discord arising from the presence of this minority. Finally, among the elements in the general formula, Pakistan suffered from the pitifully few experienced civil servants available at the time of independence. Most Moslems in the I.C.S. opted for Pakistan, but there were no more than a hundred in the middle or senior ranks. This shortcoming was magnified manyfold by the enormity of the burdens imposed on the state at its birth. It is also worth noting that the operative principle of tolerance in democracy is not shared by Islam in its attitude to unbelievers. Like all other new states of the region, Pakistan did not have the "classic conditions of Democracy."

There were also special problems in Pakistan. Perhaps the foremost was geographic separation, with 1,100 miles of Indian territory between the two wings; physical contact is possible only by air across India or the lengthy sea route around the southern tip of the sub-continent. The gap is accentuated by the fact that 54 per cent of the population live in East Pakistan while the political élite, the army, industry, and the "national movement" are centered in the West. Closely related was the friction between the two wings, arising out of the tendency of the Eastablishment in Karachi to treat East Pakistan as a subordinate area. This was further aggravated by still another barrier, the ethnic differentiation of the people in the two wings. There are differences in language, customs, dress, diet, in fact, in everything but the two pillars of Pakistan, a common faith, Islam, and fear of Indian (Hindu) domination. Among other effects of East-West tension was the nine-year delay in completing the new constitution, itself a continuing source of discord. Another reason for the delay was the deep cleavage between secular and religious groups over the appropriate political system for a Moslem Pakistan; the rift was never healed.

From the outset, Pakistan was faced with herculean tasks: the absorption of six million refugees from India, mostly peasants and unskilled workers; the flight of six million Hindus and Sikhs, including the majority of professional men and skilled workers; the creation of an administration in Karachi, with few competent civil servants and no physical plant; the outbreak of war over Kashmir and prolonged tension with India; and the forging of a meaningful link between East and West, that is, the creation of one state out of two territories and one nation out of two peoples. Throughout its history, there have been strong centrifugal pulls, as regional, tribal, and familial loyalties were asserted. Indeed, in the light of this array of handicaps and problems, the wonder is not that Pakistan failed to establish a stable democracy but that it survived at all.[17]

## Indonesia

The plight of the former Dutch Indies was no less severe than that of Pakistan—in poverty and illiteracy, in the traditions of autocracy and antipathy to government, in negativism, in party factionalism and corruption, in the paucity of trained administrators, and in other residues of the colonial era. There is no need for more elaborate recapitulation of these barriers to stability. It is rather with the few special factors that we are concerned. First is the widespread habit of violence, a much greater source of disorder in Indonesia than in Pakistan. Law and order, the first requisite of a stable polity, has never been firmly established; but most important has been the attitude to political change bred by the absence of law and order and the military role in the winning of independence. The democratic process cannot easily flourish in this environment.

Indonesia has been favored with individual leaders of stature, men like Sukarno, Mohammed Hatta, and Soetan Sjahrir, the outstanding Socialist intellectual. Yet these and others have not performed the vital roles of Nehru in India or Jinnah and Liaquat Ali for a few years in Pakistan. Sjahrir's influence waned with the decline of his party. Hatta broke with Sukarno. And the President himself, for all his fiery talk and dynamic personality, has not been an unmixed political blessing.

Symbol of unity and nationalism, Sukarno has alienated many in the "outer islands" by excessive centralization. He has interfered constantly in the parliamentary process, making and breaking cabinets. He has shown himself more interested in prestige abroad than the solution of grave problems at home, indeed, more concerned with words than deeds. Certainly he undermined the democratic experiment by an authoritarian bent and later destroyed the constitutional order. Nor has he encouraged or permitted the rise of younger men to leadership.

Perhaps the gravest cause of instability in Indonesia has been the clash between the forces of centralization (Java) and those of genuine federalism (many on the "outer islands"). This has sparked the four major rebellions, each further weakening the respect for democracy and stability of any kind. They also caused serious economic dislocation, aggravated the friction between Sukarno and Hatta, and brought the army to prominence, notably General Nasution. Poor communications within each island and between them has accentuated the "natural" tendency to throw off central control and hinder unification. The fissiparous tendencies have been strengthened by powerful regional loyalties, some overriding "Indonesian" identity, and a corresponding desire for autonomy, for greater freedom from Javanese control. Such aspirations have not met with respect by Sukarno and his followers.

The political order itself suffered from a multiplicity of parties, more precisely, the lack of one party with a clear majority. The necessity for coalition Governments and the widespread corruption of politicians led to declining prestige for the process as a whole. One should also mention the clash between the religious and secular forces, represented by the Masjumi and the Nationalists-Communists, respectively; though not as serious as in Pakistan, it was a corrosive factor. Taken together with the long-term components, these provide insight into the crisis which led to the abandonment of democracy.[18]

### Burma

The reasons for instability in Burma are not essentially different from those applying to Pakistan and Indonesia; the basic, enduring elements are noticeable there too. Especially noteworthy is the habit of violence. Not only did it decapitate the AFPFL leadership just before independence; it also was evident in the plethora of rebellions, political and ethnic, from 1948 to 1957. The presence of substantial minorities, not easily assimilable, has made the road to stability even more arduous; the one million Karens were extraordinarily influential in this respect. The assassination of six leaders was a grievous blow. The political elite had never been large. And U Nu, gentle and devout Buddhist though he may be, lacked the forceful quality of Aung San, so necessary during widespread revolt.

Nor did Burma have sufficient qualified civil servants, whose task was made more onerous by the physical destruction of the early years.

The AFPFL had a monopoly of political power for a decade. Considering the magnitude of the challenge, its record was not unimpressive. Over the years, however, corruption and factionalism reached alarming proportions, as noted earlier. With them came declining respect for parties and the democratic process, culminating in the "fall from democratic grace," first in 1958, and more ominously in 1962. Traditional politics has gone into disrepute.[19]

## THE WAY OUT

The year 1958 was a turning point in modern Asian history, the climax to political crisis in the new states. In different terms, it was the year of retreat from democracy and the rise of the military to power in Pakistan and Burma, with Indonesia and Ceylon perched at the brink. These twin developments should not occasion surprise, in the light of the foregoing analysis. Indeed, they were part of a sweeping process embracing the Middle East, Africa, Asia, and even part of Western Europe: in half a year, generals took control of the governments of seven countries—Iraq, Lebanon, the Sudan, Pakistan, Burma and Thailand, and France; by the end of 1958, they headed sixteen governments in the non-Communist world. What is striking is the effort to find a way out of the crisis, the experiments with new techniques to fill the gap between Western political forms and the Asian milieu.

Various Asian leaders spoke out boldly in criticism of Western democracy—Sukarno of Indonesia, Ayub Khan of Pakistan, Bandaranaike of Ceylon, and Narayan of India. The common theme was its alien character or, to use Sukarno's mystical phrase, it was "not in harmony with the soul of the Indonesian nation." All decried the party bickering and dissension and saw the parliamentary process as the basic cause of instability verging on disintegration. Yet all felt the need to retain the spirit of democracy, perhaps because this device gave the sanction of respectability to their deviations from the pure model, hence the formal link —Sukarno's "Guided Democracy," Ayub Khan's "Basic Democracy," Bandaranaike's "substance of democracy," and Narayan's "partyless democracy." No wonder that people everywhere are confused as to the meaning of this political concept.

All who sought an alternative to Anglo-American democracy would probably share Ayub Khan's direct, soldierly formulation of the way out:[20]

Pakistan must have democracy. The question then is: what type of democracy? The answer need not be sought in the theories and practices of other people alone. On the contrary, it must be found from within the book of Pakistan itself.

To my mind, there are four prerequisites for the success of any democratic system in a country like Pakistan:

1. It should be simple to understand, easy to work and cheap to sustain.

2. It should put to the voter only such questions as he can answer in the light of his own personal knowledge and understanding, without external prompting.

3. It should ensure the effective participation of all citizens in the affairs of the country up to the level of their mental horizon and intellectual calibre.

4. It should be able to produce reasonably strong and stable governments.

Such was the rationale behind "Basic Democracy," the most impressive political innovation in the new states of Asia.[21]

In essence, "Basic Democracy" is a system of local government with a mixture of elected and appointed representatives. There is a heavy reliance on civil servants for leadership and a marked similarity with local government forms during the last half century of British rule. A five-tiered structure was created by the *Basic Democracies Order 1959*, promulgated on the first anniversary of the military seizure of power. Both East and West Pakistan would have a hierarchy of Councils, as follows:

|  | Percentage Elected |
|---|---|
| Development Advisory Council | 16 2/3% |
| Division Council | 25 |
| District Council | 25 |
| Tahsil or Thana Council | 50 |
| Union Council | 66 2/3 |

This sliding scale of electees, all *indirectly* elected at the higher levels, is in accord with Ayub's view that a political system must be so structured in highly illiterate societies as to be close to the common man, who understands only local issues and knows only local candidates and is therefore qualified to elect representatives only to local bodies.

The Union Council is the most important organ in the system. There are about eight thousand in the entire country, each serving a group of villages with a combined population of approximately ten thousand. Each Union Council has an average of ten elected members. In addition, a number no more than half as many as the elected members are appointed by the district officer to ensure adequate representation of all interests. The typical Union Council, then, consists of ten elected and five appointed members; these elect the Chairman of the Council. Town and Union Committees in urban areas are constituted the same way. The term of office is five years, but members may

be removed for misconduct or excessive absence, appointees by the district officer and electees by a majority of the next higher Council. Funds are limited but may be raised by a special tax on adult males for public works; the bulk is provided by the provincial government.

The functions of the Union Councils are theoretically wide. They may supervise village police, assist government revenue officers, and exercise responsibility for agriculture, industry, and community development; the latter is the most important, to be coordinated with Development Advisory Committees. Control over the Union Councils is vested in the "Controlling Authority," that is, the Deputy Commissioner. He may countermand any action, suspend the execution of any resolution, or require the council to do his bidding; he may also take any action outside of the Council to achieve the ends of the Order. Indeed, these powers of overseer are remarkably similar to those of the Viceroy and the Governors in the 1935 Government of India Act. The intent is to prevent demagogic control of the Councils, but the provisions give great power to the civil servants.

The next higher body, the *Tahsil* Council, called the *Thana* Council in East Pakistan, consists of all chairmen of Union Councils and Town Committees and an equal number appointed by the district officer; thus, half the members are indirect electees; the Chairman, ex officio, is the *tahsil* or *thana* officer. This body has only two functions, neither initiating—to coordinate the activities of the lower organs and to implement the decisions of the District Council.

The District Council is composed of the Chairmen of the *Tahsil* Councils, Chairmen of Municipal Bodies, Vice-Presidents of Cantonment Boards, and representatives of government departments in the area—that is official members—and an equal number appointed by the Commissioner. Half of the latter must be Chairmen of Union Councils; thus, one-fourth of the membership are indirect electees. The functions of the District Council are both compulsory and optional. In the former category are the provision and maintenance of schools, libraries, and hospitals and responsibility for agriculture and community development. This body is also expected to coordinate the activities of all Councils in the district.

Next in the hierarchy is the Divisional Council, consisting of Chairmen of District Councils, representatives of government departments, cities, and Cantonment Boards (50 per cent of the total) and appointees, of whom half must be Chairmen of Union Councils. Here, too, 25 per cent are indirect electees; the chairman is the Commissioner. This is primarily a coordinating agency, but it may also review activities and make recommendations regarding development to the capstone of the structure, the Development Advisory Councils. On this highest body are heads of government departments in the province (50 per cent of the total) and appointees of the President, of whom one-third are Chairmen of Union Councils; indirect electees are, then, only one-sixth of the total. Its functions are purely advisory, the supreme counsel for the Governor in the developmental field.

A formal link between "Basic Democracy" and economic development has been forged. Village Agricultural and Industrial Development (AID) has become the National Development Organization (NDO), and its chain of command now coincides with the areas covered by the various Councils. The two can now work hand in hand to generate enthusiasm in nation-building activities—one of the prime motives of "Basic Democracy."

The first elections to the Union Councils took place in December–January, 1959–60. Candidates' expenditure was limited to Rs. 200 ($40). Discussion was confined to the quality of candidates, each of whom ran on an "individual ticket." No candidate was allowed to criticize the system of "Basic Democracy" or foreign policy or to raise religious issues or regional discontents. The contests were mild in tone. Many candidates withdrew, a substantial number being elected by acclamation. Perhaps 50 per cent of the electors cast their ballot; some eighty thousand "Basic Democrats" were elected to eight thousand Councils. In mid-February, 1960, a referendum was held among the "Basic Democrats" on the question, "Do you have confidence in President Ayub Khan?" The result was a foregone certainty.

A few days later, a Constitution Commission was formed, with clearly defined terms of reference—a guide to Ayub's political thought: to take account of the genius of the people, the general standard of education and political judgment, the need of sustained development, and the effect of recent changes; and to submit constitutional proposals to achieve a democracy adaptable to the changed circumstances and based on the Islamic principles of justice, equality, and tolerance, the consolidation of national unity, and a firm and stable system of government. The Commission reported in May, 1961, and the new Constitution was promulgated in March, 1962.

Suffice it to note some of the salient features.[22] The tone is highly authoritarian, with a pronounced Gaullist influence. Indeed, the most apt term to describe the new political system of Pakistan is "presidentialism" or "presidential democracy." All executive authority, including broad ordinance and emergency powers, is vested in the President of the Republic, who is elected (indirectly) for a five-year term by an electoral college of eighty thousand, equally divided between the two wings—an extension of the principle of "basic democracy." The President has vast appointive powers—judges, army commanders, the Attorney-General, the Audi-

tor-General, provincial Governors, members of the Advisory Council of Islamic Ideology, etc. Moreover, all military and civil servants hold office during his "pleasure." A similar, wide-ranging power is vested in his provincial counterpart and appointee, the Governor, who doubles as de facto chief minister. The President is responsible only to the electoral college. He may (but need not) appoint a cabinet of advisors. Nor is there judicial review of executive action or legislation.

To these powers of the President is added a significant role in the legislative process. The Constitution provides for a unicameral National Assembly (150 members divided equally between East and West wings, with six seats reserved for women) and two provincial assemblies (155 seats each, of which five are reserved for women). These assemblies have the authority to frame and pass bills. The President may withhold assent and resubmit the bill. The Assembly can overcome his veto by a two-thirds majority of total members; and he, in turn, has the authority to refer the bill to a referendum by the electoral college. In short, it is virtually impossible to enact a bill without the President's support, especially since parties are not allowed in the Assembly. This procedure for resolving a conflict between President and Assembly obtains for all bills, even proposed amendments to the Constitution. The President may be removed by a vote of three-fourths of the total membership of the Assembly, but if less than half the membership supports the impeachment motion those who gave notice must resign from the Assembly.

It is, of course, still too early to assess the new political system. The first elections to the National Assembly, in May, 1962, witnessed the return of many prominent figures of the ancien régime. As if to suggest continuity with that discredited system, Tamizuddin Khan, Speaker of the first Constituent Assembly, was unanimously elected Speaker of the new National Assembly, the second most important post in the state. Already there have been rumblings against the ban on political parties, and informal groups have been formed in the Assembly. This much is clear, however. This is Ayub Khan's constitution—in form and susbtance. As the preamble notes, ". . . I, Field Marshal Mohammed Ayub Khan . . . do hereby enact this Constitution." And the principle of limited popular participation in politics is duly enshrined, along with the bias against professional politicians and the old élite.

Of "Basic Democracy" a few themes have become evident. The Union Council is the key body, but it is too much under the domination of civil servants and is unlikely to attract the most talented members of the community. The District Magistrate and Commissioner possess vast powers under the scheme which may well throttle whatever democratic tendencies exist. The scheme has potentialities for economic development, effective, grass roots local government, and even social progress—but it is *not* democracy. There is little popular control over the Councils and none over the government; as compensation, it is more rooted in tradition and is simple to manage, two important assets for Asians seeking alternative political systems to Western democracy. Already, the King of Nepal has declared his intention to introduce a form of "Basic Democracy" into his backward land. General Pak Chung Hi, military dictator of South Korea, has also pledged a Pakistan-style "Guided Democracy." And Jaya Prakash Narayan, former Indian Socialist leader and a possible successor to Nehru, has expressed admiration for the Pakistani experiment. Others may follow suit.

An alternative path to stability is being followed by China—"People's Democracy," or *"New Democracy,"* to use Mao Tse-tung's phrase.[23] In reality, this is a Soviet-style Communist dictatorship, with a parallel pyramid of state and party authority and a fusion of personnel and functions at the top. This structure is perhaps best portrayed in tabular form:

the party.[24] Indeed, this curtailment reached its peak in the one innovation of "New Democracy," the "people's Communes."[25]

This institution may be viewed in two settings—as the final stage in the program of total collectivization of agriculture or as an outgrowth of changes in economic and administrative organization. Either analysis would be accurate; both elements were involved. Commune-ization began in the summer of 1958 and by the end of that year it embraced all of rural China, some twenty-six thousand communes for five hundred million peasants. At the outset, the degree of deprivation was oppressive —even to observers from other Communist lands: from dawn to dusk and even beyond life was rigidly regulated; nurseries for children, community mess halls, and barracks only accentuated the loss of individuality. Later, this process was reversed, and the powers of the Commune were considerably reduced. By 1961, the commune fervor appeared to have vanished, as did the commune in its original monastic form.

The commune was a multipurpose unit, really a

| Party Apparatus | Government Organization | |
|---|---|---|
| Party Chairman | Chairman of the Chinese People's Republic | |
| Politbureau and its | Supreme State Conference | |
| Standing Committee | | |
| Central Committee | State Council | Standing Committee |
| | (Cabinet) | of National |
| | | People's Congress |
| National Party Congress | National People's Congress | |

Until 1959, Mao held all the key positions —Chairman of the Party, the Politbureau and its Standing Committee, the Central Committee, and the National Party Congress; he was also Chairman of the Republic, the Supreme State Conference, and the National People's Congress. His state posts have been taken over by Liu Shao ch'i, but decision-making remains concentrated in the Big Five of Chinese Communism—Mao Tse-tung, Liu Shao ch'i, Chou En-lai, Chu Teh, and Ch'en Yün. All five are members of the Standing Committee of the Politbureau and the Supreme State Conference; Mao retains his party leadership, Liu the governmental posts, Chou En-lai is head of the State Council, Chu Teh is Chairman of the Standing Committee of the People's Congress or Parliament, and Ch'en Yün is in charge of economic planning.

As in the Soviet Union, Parliament is a rubber-stamp body; so too is the Party Congress. Elections to both bodies are empty ritual; and the political process is an intraparty phenomenon, governed by the principle of democratic centralism. Authoritarian direction from higher bodies, ultimately the inner élite, is the manner of decision-making on all matters of public, and often private, concern. The judiciary is simply another arm of the party. Individual freedoms exist, if at all, only at the whim of

four-fold entity—economic, political, military, and social. In area, it was equated with the traditional *hsiang,* or district, with an average of twenty thousand persons, though some had as many as fifty thousand. Each commune comprised about twelve former "higher agricultural cooperatives," that is, collectives; these were now Production Brigades; they, in turn, were divided into Production Teams of a dozen families each.

The commune was a complete, self-sufficient economic unit with trade and credit organs, tax powers, and production quotas. It was also a military category, a division in the nation's militia, with compulsory military training for all adults. The governing body was an "elected" Administrative Council, dominated unobtrusively by Communist Party members. Its functions were all-pervasive—to control economic, educational, and military aspects of life within the commune. At first, control was highly centralized, but experience led to gradual devolution of authority. By comparison with the traditional collective, the commune was much larger in area and population, broader in scope, and more rigid in control. The attempt was to create a self-sufficient rural city, somewhat like the Soviet experimental Agrotown. The result was hailed by the Chinese as a "leap forward" to the ideal society, condemned by anti-Communists as an "ant heap," and criticized by other Communists, notably Soviet leaders, as impractical. In the context of the quest for stability, the commune offered an alternative road to the ideologically uncommitted states of South and Southeast Asia, especially in 1959, when Peking made grandiose claims of economic progress during the first year of the commune. When these figures were drastically downgraded, the attraction of the commune—and the political system of which it is a dramatic symbol—declined among the onlookers in the region.[26]

Amid the experiments with "Basic Democracy" and "New Democracy," a few Asian states persisted in the effort to apply and adapt the original, Western form of democracy. India is the outstanding example, a model of this system, as Pakistan and China are of the competing types. A sketch of the system as it works in India is therefore appropriate here.

Three years of careful deliberations led to the Constitution of India in 1950. It is the longest and most comprehensive written constitution in the world, with 395 articles and eight schedules. One of its striking features is the continuity with British-Indian practice—some 250 articles were taken from the 1935 Government of India Act. Another is the total absence of distinctively Indian ideas. Indeed, the Indian Constitution is a mélange of Western ideas and practices. From Britain came the parliamentary form of government. The federal idea owes much to the United States and Australia. From Eire came the inspiration for Part IV, the Directive Principles of State Policy, an expression of the goals of the "fathers" of the Constitution. From the United States was derived the idea of a detailed list of fundamental rights that comprise Part III.

The new India is a Sovereign Democratic Republic and a Union of States. Although federal in form, it is markedly unitary in spirit. This is evident from the division of powers among the three lists —Union, States, and Concurrent—the control over and distribution of finances, the organization of administrative services, the right of Parliament to alter the territory of States, and, most important, the imposing array of emergency powers vested in the central government.

In form, functions, and powers, the Indian Cabinet follows the established British model. The executive power of the Union is vested in the President, who is "aided and advised" by a Council of Ministers (Cabinet) headed by a Prime Minister. The President appoints the Prime Minister—by convention, the leader of that party which commands a majority in the Lower House of Parliament—and, upon his advice, all other members of the Cabinet. Ministers retain office "during the pleasure of the President," but the Cabinet is responsible to the Lower House; that is, it remains in office as long it it maintains the "confidence" of the legislature. As in Cabinet systems elsewhere, the Indian Cabinet drafts and presents the government's legislative program and conducts the business of the Union.

There have been five Indian Cabinets since 1947, all headed by Jawaharlal Nehru and all composed largely of Congressmen. At no time has the Government been in danger from a vote of "no confidence," for the Congress has had an overwhelming majority in Parliament thus far. Thus, the Cabinet system in India has been very stable. Yet, there is evidence that the Cabinet has not always functioned smoothly: there have been nine major resignations since Independence; five concerned economic issues, two Indo-Pakistani relations, one States' Reorganization, and one the Mundhra Affair, India's great scandal.

Cabinet procedure is similar to British-type Cabinets elsewhere. There are a number of Standing Committees, notably on Finance, Defence, and External Affairs. Discussion seems to be frank and free at Cabinet meetings. Nehru is the outstanding figure, as befits his office and his status in the Congress and the country at large. A few Ministers venture beyond the items under their jurisdiction; Nehru's interest extends to all issues. The Prime Minister has great skill in winning his colleagues to his view on most issues by persuasion without offending them. Where there is disagreement, the outcome depends on how strongly Nehru feels. If he is firm, his colleagues give way because of respect for his leadership. On the whole, the Indian Cabinet has performed its functions very well, as steering committee of Parliament and executive of the Union.

Some see India's Parliament as a training ground for democracy in Asia. Others view it as a façade behind which Nehru and the Congress wield absolute power. At first glance, the parliamentary process seems artificial because one party has had a preponderant majority since 1947 and could push through any legislation with ease. The opposition parties have never comprised much more than 25 per cent of the membership in the House and were often mutually hostile. It is also true that Parliament is not the center of power and decision-making in India; this function is performed by the Congress caucus and ultimately by Nehru and the party's High Command. Nevertheless, Parliament has a vital role. It provides a forum for the ventilation of grievances and the debate of public policy. It also helps to educate public opinion.

In the broadest sense, Parliament is a symbol of the experiment in democracy and an instrument to educate those who will wield power in the future. It is also a unifying force among different groups and is the leveler in a country that has not yet fully accepted the notion of equality. In time there may develop a habit of looking to Parliament to solve disputes and to reduce the divisions in Indian society, but much depends on the progress of economic betterment. Democratic processes are not yet rooted in Indian soil. If India fails to achieve economic development by consent—it now seems well on the road to success—Parliament there, as elsewhere in Asia, will suffer a mortal blow.

Thus far, the election record has been impressive, as noted earlier. All seven contests were efficiently conducted by an independent Election Commission. There were very few cases of corruption, despite an electorate of 173 million in 1951–52, 193 million in the second general election of 1957 and 205 million in 1962. Perhaps the most encouraging feature was the response of the electorate: 60 per cent voted in the first election and slightly more in 1957 and 1962. Nor was there a stampede in favor of the Congress, comparable to the near-total support for "the party" in totalitarian states. Although it won an overwhelming majority of the seats in all three general elections, the Congress received less than 50 per cent of the popular vote. The achievement of free, impartial, and periodic elections in India is especially impressive in the light of the high rate of illiteracy, the unfamiliarity of many candidates, officials, and voters with the nuances of electioneering, and the temptations to the governing party to tamper with the conduct of the Election Commission, as almost everywhere else in the new states.

The record of Indian democracy has also been favorable in the judicial sphere. The courts have retained their independence despite pressures, and the Rule of Law has been well established. So too have civil liberties, although the picture is not stainless: a Preventive Detention Act has been in force since the Communist rebellion of 1948–50, and the Government has wide-ranging powers of detention of suspected threats to stability; fortunately, they have been used with restraint over the years. Apart from this blemish, individual rights are as well protected as in most Western democracies. On the basis of the first fifteen years, the Indian experiment in democracy may, indeed, be judged a striking success.

The widespread collapse of democracy in the new states is not surprising. In fact, the only surprise is that it has succeeded at all. The quest for stability remains unfulfilled, with the three competing systems now showing their wares throughout South and Southeast Asia—democracy, "Basic (or Guided) Democracy," and "New Democracy." The outcome of this competition will have consequences far beyond that region and its peoples.

## NOTES

1. Text is in *Dawn* (Karachi), October 9, 1958.
2. Pakistan's politics before the military coup are ably dissected in K. Callard, *Pakistan: A Political Study* (London 1957), and *Political Forces in Pakistan 1947–1959* (New York 1959); Mushtaq Ahmad *Government and Politics in Pakistan* (Karachi, 1959); and K. B. Sayeed, "Collapse of Parliamentary Democracy in Pakistan," *Middle East Journal,* Autumn 1959, pp. 389–406, and *Pakistan: The Formative Phase* (Karachi 1960).

See also: Leonard Binder, *Religion and Politics in Pakistan* (Berkeley 1961), Parts Two and Three; G. W. Choudhury, *Constitutional Development in Pakistan* (London 1959); Herbert Feldman, *A Constitution for Pakistan* (Karachi, 1956); Sir Ivor Jennings, *Constitutional Problems in Pakistan* (Cambridge, 1957), pp. 3–75; W. C. Smith, *Islam in Modern History* (Princeton 1957), Ch. V; Richard D. Lambert, "Factors in Bengali Regionalism in Pakistan," *Far Eastern Survey,* XXVIII, April, 1959, pp. 49–58; K. J. Newman, "Pakistan's Preventive Autocracy and Its Causes," *Pacific Affairs,* XXXII, No. 1, March, 1959, pp. 18–33.

3. Quoted in George McT. Kahin (ed.), *Major Governments of Asia* (Ithaca, 1958), pp. 565–66.
4. See George McT. Kahin, "Indonesia" in *Major Governments of Asia,* Chapters XXI–XXIII, for a good, succinct analysis of that state's political travail.

See also: Louis Fischer, *The Story of Indonesia* (New York, 1959), Part II; Miriam S. Budiardjo, "The Provisional Parliament of Indonesia," *Far Eastern Survey,* XXV, February, 1956, pp. 17–23; Herbert Feith, *The Indonesian Elections of 1955* (Ithaca, 1957) and *The Wilopo Cabinet, 1952–1953* (Ithaca, 1958); John D. Legge, *Problems of Regional Autonomy in Contemporary Indonesia* (Ithaca, 1957); Guy J. Pauker, "The Role of Political Organizations in Indonesia," *Far Eastern Survey,* XXVII, September, 1958, pp. 129–42; Roeslan Abdulgani, "Indonesia's National Council: The First Year," *Far Eastern Survey,* XXVII, July, 1958, pp. 97–104; Irene Tinker and Millidge Walker, "Indonesia's Panacea: 1959 Model," *Far Eastern Survey,* XXVIII, December, 1959, pp. 177–82; Justus M. Van der Kroef, "Instability in Indonesia," *Far Eastern Survey,* XXVI, April, 1957, pp. 49–62, and "Disunited Indonesia," *Far Eastern Survey,* XXVII, April, 1958, pp. 49–63 and *ibid.,* May, 1958, pp. 73–80.

5. The most comprehensive and thoughtful analysis of Burmese politics since independence is Hugh Tinker, *The Union of Burma,* 3rd ed. (London, 1961). See also Josef Silverstein, "Burma," in George McT. Kahin, (ed.), *Governments and Politics of Southeast Asia* (Ithaca, 1959), Chapters VI, VII.

On the crisis of 1958, see John H. Badgley, "Burma's Political Crisis," *Pacific Affairs,* XXXI, December, 1958, pp. 336–51, and Frank N. Trager, "The Political Split in Burma," *Far Eastern Survey,* XXVII, October, 1958, pp. 145–55.

For an analysis of the Army *coup* in 1962, see Richard Butwell, "The Four Failures of U Nu's Second Premiership," *Asian Survey,* II No. 1, March, 1962, pp. 3–11.

See also Richard Butwell, "The New Political Outlook in Burma," *Far Eastern Survey,* XXIX, February, 1960, pp. 21–27; Richard Butwell, and Fred von der Mehden, "The 1960 Election in Burma," *Pacific Affairs,* XXXIII, June, 1960, pp. 144–57; Alan Gledhill, "The Burmese Constitution," *Indian Yearbook of International Affairs* (Madras, 1954), II, pp. 214–24; and Josef Silverstein, "Politics, Parties and National Elections in Burma," *Far Eastern Survey,* XXV, December, 1956, pp. 177–84, and "The Federal Dilemma in Burma," *ibid.,* XXVIII, July, 1959, pp. 97–105.

6. The most valuable and thorough treatment of Ceylon's politics since independence is Howard W. Wriggins, *Ceylon: Dilemmas of a New Nation* (Princeton, 1960).

See also Sir Ivor Jennings, *The Dominion of Ceylon* (London, 1952); S. Namasivayam, *Parliamentary Government in Ceylon 1948-1958* (Colombo, 1959); Tarzie Vittachi, *Emergency '58* (London, 1958); D. K. Rangnekar, "The Nationalist Revolution in Ceylon," *Pacific Affairs,* XXXIII, No. 4, December, 1960, pp. 361-74; Calvin A. Woodward, "The Trotskyite Movement in Ceylon," *World Politics,* XIV No. 2, January, 1962, pp. 307-21.

7. See Bernard B. Fall, "The International Relations of Laos," *Pacific Affairs,* XXX No. 1, March, 1957, pp. 22-34, and "The Laos Tangle," *International Journal,* XVI No. 2, Spring, 1961, pp. 138-57; and Robert Gilkey, "Laos: Politics, Elections and Foreign Aid," *Far Eastern Survey,* XXVII, June, 1958, pp. 89-94.

For the negotiations at Geneva and among the three princes, from April 1961 to July 1962, the best source is the *New York Times.*

8. See Wells C. Klein, and Marjorie Weiner, "Vietnam" in Kahin (ed.), *Governments and Politics of Southeast Asia,* Chapter XIX, and Richard W. Lindholm (ed.), *Viet Nam: The First Five Years* (East Lansing, 1959); Francis J. Corley, "The President in the Constitution of the Republic of Viet-Nam," *Pacific Affairs,* XXXIV No. 2, Summer, 1961, pp. 165-74; John T. Dorsey, Jr., "South Viet Nam in Perspective," *Far Eastern Survey,* XXVII, December, 1958, pp. 177-82; Bernard B. Fall, "South Viet-Nam's Internal Problems," *Pacific Affairs,* XXXI No. 3, September, 1958, pp. 241-60; Wesley R. Fishel, "Political Realities in Vietnam," *Asian Survey,* I No. 2, April, 1961, pp. 15-23; Roy Jumper, "Mandarin Bureaucracy and Politics in South Viet Nam," *Pacific Affairs,* XXX No. 1, March, 1957, pp. 47-58; Robert G. Scigliano, "Political Parties in South Viet Nam under the Republic," *Pacific Affairs,* XXXIII No. 4, December, 1960, pp. 327-46; U. S. Senate Committee on Foreign Relations: *Situation in Viet Nam,* (Washington, D.C., 1960), 2 Parts.

9. For analyses of Indian politics since independence, see Michael Brecher, *Nehru: A Political Biography* (London, 1959), Chapters XV-XVIII; W. H. Morris-Jones, *Parliament in India* (Philadelphia, 1957), especially Chapters 1, 2, 4, 7; Norman D. Palmer, *The Indian Political System,* (Boston, 1961), Chapters 5–10; and Richard L. Park and Irene Tinker (eds.), *Leadership and Political Institutions in India* (Princeton, 1959), Parts 3–6.

See also Margaret W. Fisher and Joan V. Bondurant, *The Indian Experience with Democratic Elections* (Berkeley, 1956); M. V. Pylee, *Constitutional Government in India* (Bombay, 1960); Myron Weiner, *Party Politics in India* (Princeton, 1957), Chapters 1, 2, 8, 9, 11, 12; Lloyd I. Rudolph

and Susanne Hoeber: "The Political Role of India's Caste Associations," *Pacific Affairs,* XXXIII No. 1, March, 1960, pp. 5–22; M. Singer, H. C. Hart, M. Weiner and L. I. Rudolph, "Urban Politics in a Plural Society: A Symposium," *Journal of Asian Studies,* XX, No. 3, May, 1961, pp. 265–97; and Myron Weiner, "India's Third General Elections," *Asian Survey,* II No. 3, May, 1962, pp. 3–18.

10. See David Wurfel, "The Philippines," in G. McT. Kahin (ed.), *Governments and Politics of Southeast Asia,* Chapter 24. See also Willard H. Elsbree, "The Philippines," in Rupert Emerson, *Representative Government in Southeast Asia,* (Cambridge, Mass., 1955), pp. 82–117; Robert Aura Smith, *Philippine Freedom, 1946–1958* (New York, 1958), Chapters 4–8; and David Wurfel, "The Philippine Elections: Support for Democracy," *Asian Survey,* II No. 3, May, 1962, pp. 25–37.

11. See J. Norman Parmer, "Malaya and Singapore" in G. McT. Kahin (ed.), *Governments and Politics of Southeast Asia,* Chapters 14–16.

See also Charles Gamba, "Labour and Labour Parties in Malaya," *Pacific Affairs,* XXXI No. 2, June, 1958, pp. 117–30; J. Norman Parmer, "Constitutional Change in Malaya's Plural Society," *Far Eastern Survey,* XXVI October, 1957, pp. 145–52; and T. E. Smith, "The Malayan Elections of 1959," *Pacific Affairs,* XXXIII No. 1, March, 1960, pp. 38–47.

12. See M. Brecher: *Nehru, op. cit.,* Chapters I, XX; Hector Bolitho, *Jinnah: Creator of Pakistan* (London, 1954); Hugh Tinker, "Nu, The Serene Statesman," *Pacific Affairs,* XXX, June, 1957, pp. 120–37; Leslie H. Palmier, "Sukarno, the Nationalist," *Pacific Affairs,* XXX, June, 1957, pp. 101–19; and Vera Micheles Dean, *Builders of Emerging Nations* (New York, 1961), Part I, p. 3.

13. See Victor Purcell, *The Chinese in Southeast Asia* (Cambridge, 1951).

14. Selig S. Harrison, *India: The Most Dangerous Decades* (Princeton, 1960).

15. R. Emerson, "The Erosion of Democracy," *Journal of Asian Studies,* XX No. 1, November, 1960, pp. 1–8.

16. For a sympathetic view of the role of the officer corps in the New States, see Guy J. Pauker, "Southeast Asia as a Problem Area in the Next Decade," *World Politics,* XI No. 3, April, 1959, pp. 325–45. See also H. Tinker, "Climacteric in Asia," *International Journal,* XV, Winter, 1959, pp. 14–24, and United States Foreign Policy: *Asia* (Conlon Report to Senate Foreign Relations Committee), 1959, pp. 31–36, 45–53, 55–62.

17. See Charles Burton Marshall, "Reflections on a Revolution in Pakistan," *Foreign Affairs,* 37 No. 2, January, 1959, pp. 247–56, and the items in note 2 above.

18. Cf. the sources in note 4 above.

19. Cf. the sources in note 5 above.

20. In *Foreign Affairs,* 38, No. 4, July, 1960, as quoted in *Pakistan News Digest,* Karachi, July 1, 1960.

21. See Harry J. Friedman, "Pakistan's Experiment in Basic Democracies," *Pacific Affairs,* XXXIII, June, 1960, pp. 107–125, and "Notes on Pakistan's Basic Democracies," *Asian Survey,* I No. 10, December, 1961, pp. 19–24; and K. B. Sayeed, "Pakistan's Basic Democracy," *Middle East Journal,* XV, Summer, 1961, pp. 249–63.

22. Cf. *The Constitution of the Republic of Pakistan* (Government of Pakistan Press, Karachi, 1962).

23. *On New Democracy* (1940), in *Selected Works of Mao Tse-tung* (London, 1954), Vol. 3, pp. 106–156.

24. The most objective study of Communist China's governmental structure is S. B. Thomas, *Government and Administration in Communist China,* 2nd rev. ed. (New York, 1955).

See also Chao Kuo-Chun: "The National Constitution of Communist China," *Far Eastern Survey,* XXIII, October, 1954, pp. 145–51; and "Leadership in the Chinese Communist Party," in Howard L. Boorman (ed.), "Contemporary China and the Chinese," *The Annals,* January 1959, pp. 40–50; Harold C. Hinton, "China," in Kahin (ed.), *Major Governments of Asia,* pp. 52–96; H. Arthur Steiner, "Ideology and Politics in Communist China," in Boorman: *op. cit.,* pp. 29–39; and Yu-nan Chang: "The Chinese Communist State System under the Constitution of 1954," *Journal of Politics,* August, 1956, pp. 520–46.

25. See G. F. Hudson, A. V. Sherman, and A. Zauberman, *The Chinese Communes* (London, 1960); Audrey Donnithorne, "Background to the People's Communes: Changes in China's Economic Organization in 1958," *Pacific Affairs,* XXXII, December, 1959, pp. 339–53; D. E. T. Luard, "The Urban Communes," *The China Quarterly,* No. 3, July–September, 1960, pp. 74–79; R. MacFarquhar, "Communist China's Intra-Party Dispute," *Pacific Affairs,* XXXI, December, 1958, pp. 323–35.

26. See Chu-yuan Cheng, "The Changing Pattern of Rural Communes in Communist China," *Asian Survey,* I No. 9, November, 1961, pp. 3–9; Harold C. Hinton, "Intra-Party Politics and Economic Policy in Communist China," *World Politics,* XII No. 4, July, 1960, pp. 509–524; Theodore Shabad, "China's Year of the 'Great Leap Forward'," *Far Eastern Survey,* XXVIII, June, 1959, pp. 89–96 and July, 1959, pp. 105–109, and "China's 'Leap Forward' Reconsidered," *Ibid.,* October, 1959, pp. 156–58.

# THE EROSION OF DEMOCRACY
# IN THE NEW STATES

Rupert Emerson

$O$f the many democracies which have been born in the past century and a half, only a handful have survived. In the past years the casualties have been peculiarly heavy among the former dependencies of the West for the simple reason that these were the countries which were currently embarking on democratic experiments. The fragile mechanism of representative democracy which almost all of them adopted proved shortly to be unfitted to the needs and capabilities of most of them. In thus at least temporarily abandoning their democratic institutions the ex-colonies were demonstrating no singular weakness or instability but were following in what has been by far the more common experience of mankind.

Simon Bolivar, liberating Venezuela was prophetic of the way the world has generally gone:

It is a terrible truth that it costs more strength to

Reprinted by permission of the publishers from Rupert Emerson, *From Empire to Nation,* Chapter XV, pp. 271–292. Cambridge, Mass.: Harvard University Press, Copyright, 1960, by The President and Fellows of Harvard College.

maintain freedom than to endure the weight of tyranny. Many nations, past and present, have borne that yoke; few have made use of the happy moments of freedom and have preferred to relapse with all speed into their errors.[1]

And when he spoke of the people of the American hemisphere as having been purely passive for centuries with no political existence—"absent from the universe in all that related to the science of government"—he spoke for many other peoples around the globe as well.

The story which has repeated itself over and over is that peoples have set out on the democratic path with revolutionary enthusiasm, but before long they have lost their way and settled back into authoritarian or dictatorial regimes. The real success of democracy has been confined to some of the peoples living in or stemming from Western Europe: the British, the Irish, the Belgians and Dutch, the Scandinavians, the Swiss, more dubiously the French, and overseas, the peoples of the United States and the older British Dominions. With these central exceptions each of the successive waves of democratic experimentation has ended in over-all failure. The revolt against European rule in Latin America in the nineteenth century brought into being an array of democracies whose record has been spotty and untrustworthy at best. The drive for self-determination which followed the defeat of the autocracies in World War I stimulated the emergence of democratic institutions in Central and Eastern Europe, but after a few years Czechoslovakia was the sole democratic survivor. Among the non-colonial Asian and African countries which tried out new political forms, only Japan, China, and Turkey could at any time have been seriously counted in the democratic ranks, and none of these three could be cited as a model of democratic behavior. The statistical odds against the survival of democracy outside the small circle of Western European peoples and their descendants overseas seem overwhelming.

For the non-European peoples it is, in the large, the former colonies of the West which have made the nearest approach to democracy, despite the serious defections which have recently taken place. The faith of their leaders in democracy was shown at the outset in the style of constitutions which they created; in a few countries, headed by India and the Philippines, these constitutions have so far maintained themselves as living realities; and even where democracy has gone into eclipse, as in Pakistan and Burma, the new rulers have pledged themselves to let it shine forth again promptly with a new splendor. Whether and when and by whom these pledges will be redeemed is a different matter. It must also be recorded that a ground swell of protest against the assumption that Western-style parliamentary institutions are appropriate for non-European peoples has been increasingly evident.

The push toward democracy which Western colonialism has often given is not limited solely to Asia and Africa. In the Caribbean the democratic structure and stability of the dependencies of the United States, Britain, France, and the Netherlands stand out sharply against the dictatorial tendencies and political inconstancy of neighboring independent countries and indeed of Latin America as a whole. Puerto Rico, demographically akin to other Spanish-settled countries of the area, has, in its new Commonwealth guise, become a paragon of democratic advance as contrasted with the next-door Dominican Republic and Haiti. In the postwar surge of colonial reform the French Territories were converted into Departments of France, while the Dutch dependencies secured far-reaching self-government in association with the Netherlands. The British West Indies, having tried out representative institutions on an individual basis, have now moved on to a federal parliamentary structure. In estimating the current state of political development in these Caribbean territories it is, of course, a fact to be taken into the reckoning that none of them is currently independent, nor is independence contemplated for any other than those in the British orbit. How steadfastly they would maintain their present democratic posture as sovereign states can only be a matter of conjecture.

The contrast which still exists between colonial and non-colonial countries serves to confirm the presumption that a new look at Western colonialism and its contribution to the world is in order. From a number of standpoints colonialism is an intolerable evil, and its character as evil is attested by the passionate unanimity with which all colonial peoples seek to escape from it. Yet the effects which it has had in shaping the peoples on whom it has been imposed cannot be dismissed as solely bad.

The most striking and unexpected tribute to Western colonial practice came from Charles T. O. King, Liberian Ambassador to the United States. When Vice-President Nixon journeyed to the inaugural ceremonies for Ghana, reporters who accompanied him noted that Liberia was still largely primitive while the former Gold Coast was relatively well developed. Iconoclastically attacking all the truths concerning colonialism as oppression and exploitation which the liberals and the left have accepted as sacred and self-evident, the Ambassador explained that independent Liberia's backwardness stemmed from the fact it had never had the advantages of colonialism:

> It is the difference between the home of a man who has had to accomplish everything by his own sweat and toil and that of a man who has enjoyed a large inheritance. . . . The United States did not care about a colony on the coast of Africa, and we were left alone and struggling to vegetate in the midst of developing European colonies.[2]

Not without a parallel to Adam Smith's dictum that the worst of all governments for a colony was government by a company, it might be argued that areas of the world, such as China and the Middle East, which have fallen victim to imperialism but have had no, or no effective, colonial regime imposed upon them have had the worst of the deal. The distortions arising from Western penetration are present, but not the positive contributions toward adjustment which colonialism has it within its power to make, even though it has by no means always made them. The stability of the states that emerged from the Indian Empire persuaded Bernard Lewis that the imperial peace was not without its merits:

> But there is little that can be said in defense of the half-hearted, pussy-footing imperialism encountered by most of the peoples of the Middle East—an imperialism of interference without responsibility which would neither create nor permit stable and orderly governments.[3]

Also drawing on India's example, Barbara Ward suggested that:

China's ordeal was worse than India's, for India gained a hundred years of orderly administration and inherited in 1947 a functioning state and civil service, whereas China was left to drift like a sailless junk, its old equipment destroyed by the West but with no new machinery installed.[4]

A further illustration of the disadvantages of non-colonial imperialism might be found in the intervention of the United States in the affairs of the independent Central American and Caribbean republics in the opening decades of this century. Here likewise was interference without acceptance of responsibility, and the results which it produced were not unlike those in the Middle East. The relatively smooth functioning of the representative institutions of the Philippines, which was subjected to American colonial rule, contrasts favorably with the dictatorships and revolutions of Cuba which was spared it.

Depending on one's point of view, it may be counted among the virtues of colonialism that it has served in various ways to predispose the colonial peoples toward democratic political systems, or counted among its vices since it exposed peoples to the hazards of trying to live with institutions alien to their past. At all events we have good reason to question how deeply democratic conceptions and practices have penetrated and how long-lasting their effects can be expected to be. Already the contrast between the colonial and the non-colonial countries is fading. Once independence has been achieved the special forces and circumstances of colonialism cease to be operative, and the further the remove from colonialism the more attenuated the effects must be. In consequence, the ex-colonies find themselves in the same situation as the states which retained their independence; and one by one they have begun to drift away from the democratic standards they had originally set for themselves.

At the same time the non-colonial states are continuing, generally at an accelerated pace, their processes of adaptation to the modern world, of which one significant feature is "a high rate of recruitment of new elements into political activity" as a result of social and economic change.[5] Revolutionary innovations are taking place in the relations between the few at the top, the small but growing middle class, and the many at the bottom. Government will continue in most instances not to be *by* the people, but, recognizing the necessities of an era of "fundamental democratization," it must increasingly create the popular impression that it is *for* the people and responsive to their needs. In net effect, the two sets of countries whose recent history led them by divergent routes are now moving toward a common middle position.

As far as the former colonies are concerned, by far the most striking evidence of this shift is the open or only slightly concealed abandonment of the representative parliamentary institutions which came into being with the transition to independence. 1958 was the year of the great collapse. Within a few weeks of each other, Pakistan, Burma, and the Sudan surrendered their civilian governments into the hands of the military who in varying degree abrogated constitutions, postponed elections, and abolished or sidetracked political parties. In the Middle East, where Egypt and Syria had already made the transition, the revolution in Iraq installed a general in power, setting in motion the abortive American and British military interventions in Lebanon and Jordan, and Lebanon elected the chief of its army to the presidency. Ceylon was having its considerable troubles, and Indonesia, plagued by revolution and political feuding, retained only the remnants of parliamentary rule under the watchful eye of the military. In Ghana, Nkrumah and his associates ruled with a strong hand, cavalierly overriding the usual rights of the opposition. Guinea, thrust suddenly into independence, explicitly endorsed the one-party system and summed up its one party in the person of Sékou Touré.

The reasons for the erosion of democracy are not far to seek. Basically they are common to the new states even though the turn of events in each of them derives from a special set of circumstances which has produced distinctive results. The position of Ne Win in Burma cannot be equated with that of Mohammed Ayub Khan in Pakistan, nor can either of these two be identified with Abdul Karim Kassem in Iraq. Chief of Staff Nasution has not seized power in Indonesia, although he has a large say in the governing of the country, and in Ghana the army has played no political role—its loyalty to the new regime, it has been said, being guaranteed by the fact that its officer corps remains largely British. Yet, when all the differences are taken into account, many common elements stand out.

One among them is the lack of national unity which in virtually all the new countries threatens disruption and is met by enforced centralization. Nationalism is the dominant creed but the nations are still far from being consolidated. Of Pakistan it has been written that "no recollection of history and concord" binds the two wings, separated by a thousand miles of India;[6] in Burma inchoate civil wars have challenged the hold of the government since independence; and in Indonesia great stretches of territory remain under the control of Darul Islam, the Revolutionary Government which proclaimed its existence in 1958, and other dissident groups.

One country which has so far retained its democratic institutions despite great internal diversity is Malaya. Here, on the basis of what has happened elsewhere, the gloom-seeking prophet was and perhaps still is, entitled to assume that radical discord must soon bring open civil strife or strong man rule or both, but the governing coalition, the Alliance, has been able to hold the leading Malay, Chinese, and Indian parties together within the constitutional framework. The country has been independent, however, only since 1957, and the precedents suggest that the momentum derived from the colonial period and the *élan* coming from winning independence take a longer time than this to run down.

In addition to the lack of national unity, the most basic explanation for the failure of democracy in so many of the new states is the almost universal absence of what have been assumed to be the preconditions for its success. Although argument still rages as to precisely what these may be, the usually accepted list includes such items as mass literacy, relatively high living standards, a sizable and stable middle class, a sense of social equality, and a tradition both of tolerance and of individual self-reliance.[7] In virtually no instance are these conditions met in the colonial countries whose independence had led them into democracy. Instead these countries are characterized by peasant masses living at the subsistence level, overwhelmingly illiterate, unacquainted not only with the great world but even with their own country, accustomed to a high degree of social stratification, and with slight middle classes often strongly alien in composition. The representative government which emerges can be no stronger than the society which it represents.

Furthermore, the democratic institutions which were adopted were the work of the relatively small group which had come to significant acquaintance with the West. They were the product neither of the mass of the people, who inevitably had little understanding of them, nor of the evolutionary development of the society as a whole. Although social mobilization has been in full swing, the sudden universal enfranchisement of the peoples of Asian and African states differed sharply from the gradual adaptation to changing circumstances in the West where there was often a rough coincidence between the rise of new elements to economic and social consequence and their access to the ballot box. It is an immense added complication that while the democracies which came into being in the nineteenth and earlier twentieth centuries were concerned with the management of relatively simple political and economic systems in a still spacious world, the newly rising peoples seek full-scale social welfare states with most complicated mechanisms, plus the extra complexity of the drive for social and economic development, in a terrifying world of population explosion, superpowers, and nuclear weapons.

The increase in the numbers of those who were drawn into some measure of political participation did not necessarily enhance the prospects of democratic achievement. Poverty-ridden people in a climate of rising expectations are not likely to make their first concern the preservation of political forms and liberties whose meaning is obscure to them and whose promise may appear of less significance than other prospects held out to them. If democracy fails to produce results with adequate speed and if the politicians who manipulate the machinery come to be seen as self-interested and corrupt, the masses cannot be counted on to rise to the defense of unfamiliar political machineries.

The people at large lack not only the democratic tradition but also the more basic tradition of standing up to do battle for their rights against the remote and superior authorities which have through the ages pushed them around. Government, save at the local level where it was usually interwoven with old-established ties of family and status, has almost always been something imposed from above. What Gertrude Bell wrote of the Ottoman Empire half a century ago holds true for many other peoples:

> The government was still, to the bulk of the population, a higher power, disconnected from those upon whom it exercised its will. You might complain of its lack of understanding just as you cursed the hailstorm that destroyed your crops, but you were in no way answerable for it, nor would you attempt to control or advise it, any more than you would offer advice to the hail cloud.[8]

Sporadically the people have risen in revolt against abuses felt to be intolerable or at the urging of some popular leader, but little has come their way to imbue them with the sense that they are possessors of human rights and fundamental freedoms which they are entitled and able to defend. The democratic constitutions of the post-independence period have been almost as much imposed on them from above as any of the previous regimes, and in many instances it is probable that the people would feel more at home with a government which tells them what to do than one in which they must exercise freedom of choice.[9] Nasser, writing of the philosophy of the Egyptian revolution, has spoken of the pain and bitterness which tore his heart when he found that the leaders must continue to command because the "majestic masses" which should have joined in the hallowed march to the great end actually brought sloth and inertia and not the needed zeal and ardor.

If the newly enfranchised masses are uncertain defenders of the democratic institutions with which they have been endowed, what of the nationalist elites to whom the institutions owe their being? These elites are composed of men for the most part committed to the proposition that a radical democratization of their societies is in order, but their ability to live up to their proclaimed creed has already been demonstrated to be highly dubious. Even assuming that they or reasonably like-minded successors retain their hold, with what confidence can it be predicted that they will survive the temptation, baited by the insidious corruptions of power, to see themselves as a distinctive corps with closed ranks. A Burmese newspaper editor wrote of the leaders of the dominant political party in Burma that they have "a 'Messiah' complex by which they can justify deviations from democracy with the excuse that they must remain in power for the good of the country."[10]

The tendency of the nationalist parties and movements to be built around dominant personalities rather than on programs or ideologies has often been noted. The emergence of Fascism, the virtual deification of Stalin in the U.S.S.R., the return of de Gaulle to supreme power in France, the abundant Latin American experience, and even the wartime preëminence of Churchill and Roosevelt, among many other examples, make it absurd to regard this emphasis on personal leadership as in any way a peculiarly Oriental or African aberration. Its occurrence elsewhere, however, does not obscure the apparent need of the newly rising peoples to have a single personal focus of loyalty, symbolic of national unity: Gandhi and then Nehru in India, Jinnah in Pakistan, Quezon and Magsaysay in the Philippines, Ngo Dinh Diem in Vietnam, Nasser in Egypt, Nkrumah in Ghana, and Sékou Touré in Guinea, to suggest only a few.

This personalization of loyalties and movements must be attributed in large part to the lack of political experience and sophistication of the mass of the people who require the personal figure of a leader to bring political abstractions down to the level of comprehensible reality. Another part may perhaps be linked to the general phenomenon of centralization of power in time of national crisis, as in the growth in stature of the American presidency in wartime. On such grounds it is not difficult to explain why the role of the leader should have expanded in Asian and African countries as they came to the critical struggles for independence, national consolidation, and economic development. It remains to be established, however, that leaders who have felt the intoxication of embodying the national will can be trusted to surrender its formulation to the people at large when the critical years are passed. The record of other parts of the world does not encourage the belief that the proclaimed adherence of such leaders to democratic principles is any guarantee that these principles will not be abandoned as the revolutionary tide ebbs and the attractions of power and privilege become greater.

The simple human inclination for those who have power to hold on to it is bolstered in Asia and Africa by the age-old assumption that the few at the top are rightfully masters of the people. "Most educated Asians," E. O. Reischauer has remarked, "simply take it for granted that they will be leaders."[11] The gap in awareness of the modern world between the Western-oriented elite and the largely unreformed mass furnishes additional justification for the exclusion of the mass from any effective share in political life. Until the gap is greatly lessened the claim of the educated few to manage the affairs of the society is as good—and

as bad—as that of the colonial administrators who preceded them, with the one great difference that they operate within and not outside the national fold. The white man's burden thus finds its counterpart in the contention that those who know best should be the custodians of power.

This is an ancient dilemma, and one which Rousseau confronted in proposing the democratic concept of the general will as the source of law:

How can a blind multitude, which often does not know what it wills, because it rarely knows what is good for it, carry out for itself so great and difficult an enterprise as a system of legislation? Of itself the people wills always the good, but of itself it by no means always sees it. The general will is always in the right, but the judgment which guides it is not always enlightened. . . . This makes a legislator necessary.[12]

In the Asian and African setting it can occasion no great surprise when the Legislator, willing the good of which his people are unaware, takes over from the struggling infant democracies, as he has so often taken over elsewhere. The Communists offer one version in their people's democracies: the dictatorship of the proletariat, exercised by the Party which is controlled by the one or the collective few at the top. Other versions range from some variant of Fascism through military rule to a more traditionalistic reassertion of older ways, and include always the possibility of mere degeneration into rule by a governing clique uninspired by any loftier ideology than clinging to its privileged position. As a species these are more akin to the Asian and African experience than are the parliamentary systems imported from the West.

The erosion of democracy in the new states has taken two characteristic forms: the seizure of power by the military and the turn to a one-party system. Whichever way the dice come up, a common feature is that politicians and political parties are denounced as corrupt, self-interested, and divisive betrayers of the public interest. Politics itself becomes an evil word, and Western-style democracy is publicly discredited by its fruits, or the lack of them. In contrast, the military or the single party are billed as representing the creative and unified national force which is needed to promote the common good and rescue the country from the disintegration with which the politicians and their parties threaten it. Thus Sukarno, himself a politician of note, sought to make the abolition of parties a feature of his guided democracy and portrayed Eastern democracy as "democracy accompanied by leadership"; and *Dawn* in Karachi hailed General Ayub Khan's coming to power as the end of a long winter:

The trees of our economic, social, and moral lives— withered and shrivelled by blasts of greed, corruption, self-seeking, and intrigue—are now beginning to blossom again into tender green leaves to herald the awakening of a glad and fruitful spring.[13]

The taking over of the government by the military in a number of the new states follows a pattern well established in other parts of the world. Although no dependency possesses significant armed forces of its own, as soon as it becomes its own master it moves to build them up as an essential symbol of sovereign manhood. Once the forces are available, the power they wield makes it exceedingly difficult for them to avoid playing a political role if any serious weakness develops in the civilian government. Where the civilian authorities stand firm as in India and the Philippines, or where a strong individual commands the scene as does Ngo Dinh Diem in Vietnam, the military can be kept within their proper sphere, but leading elements in the officers corps are almost certain to swing into action if the country seems threatened by corruption, administrative ineptitude, party or factional strife, or subversion. The wonder is not that the military have intervened as often as they have, but rather that they have so often stayed their hand. The presumption must be that we will see more and not fewer regimes dominated by the military in the years ahead as more governments are brought into being which are inadequate to the tasks confronting them.

Whether or not democracy is held to vanish when the military establish their control over the government or when a single party establishes a monopoly of power is a matter of definition. In Western terms democracy has gone by the board when a group of officers seizes the government, pushes the constitution aside, and abolishes or suspends parties and elections. The counterclaim has, however, been made, as, for example, on behalf of the government of Pakistan, that, since the basic concept of democracy is rule by consent, where a government has popular support it is by definition a democracy regardless of its structure.[14] This is a claim to be rejected. A government controlled by the military may be doing an admirable and necessary job, as in attacking corruption, undertaking land reform in West Pakistan, or cleaning up Rangoon, but it is debasing the currency of political terminology to call it a democracy, even though it has the honest intention of creating conditions under which democratic institutions can be restored.

A better case, or at least a different one, can be made for the regimes which have implicitly or explicitly adopted the one-party system—a single party which in most instances furnishes the vehicle for control by the one strong man at the center. The two most significant arguments, often blended together into one, are that Asia and Africa have their own democratic forms which differ from the parliamentary institutions of the West, and that, although representative bodies continue in existence, the need for national unity is too great to allow a dispersion of forces.

Increasingly it has been contended in recent years that the Western assumption of the majority's right to overrule a dissident minority after a period of debate does violence to conceptions basic to non-Western peoples. Although the Asian and African societies differ vastly among themselves in their patterns of customary action, their native inclination is generally toward extensive and unhurried deliberation aimed at an ultimate consensus. The gradual discovery of areas of agreement is the significant feature and not the ability to come to a speedy resolution of issues by counting heads. For the Chinese and other peoples among whom neither majority rule nor representative government had any traditional roots, the voice of the elders, the wise, and the specially qualified was entitled to extra or even decisive weight. As a symbol of the lack of relation between the concept of parliamentary opposition and the nature of West African decision-making, it has been asserted that "the word 'opposition' can only be translated into the majority of Ghanaian languages as 'enemy' (in the wars and bloodshed sense of the term)."[15]

The controversy has come to center in considerable part about the question of an opposition. A strong case can be made for the proposition that it is precisely the existence of an opposition which determines whether or not there is democracy. Only if an opposition party is available and is equipped with the rights essential to its free functioning can the ordinary citizen have any assurance that he is being presented with the facts and alternatives on which informed judgments can be based. Without the existence of an opposition he is inevitably forced to rely largely on the information which comes to him from the government and the governing party and to vote for the single slate of candidates officially laid before him. The freedom of choice which democracy implies is effectively denied him.

This conception of the role of the opposition has come under heavy attack. As one of the most articulate spokesman for a type of democracy with roots in local tradition Sukarno declared in 1957 that it was the adoption of the Western concept of an active opposition which gave rise to Indonesia's difficulties and brought people to think in a manner alien to the Indonesian way of life. Defeated in his proposal that parties be abolished, he asked for the representation of all parties in the cabinet and even more urgently advocated a program for the direct representation in the central councils of a wide array of social groupings, including the armed forces. These doctrines represented no recent conversion derived from his visit to Communist countries. As early as June 1, 1945, in the speech in which he outlined the *Pantjasila*, the five principles of the Indonesian state, he expressed his distrust of the Western democracy which left the capitalists as bosses in Europe and America, and announced the need for a consultative body "which, together with the community, will be able to give effect to two principles, *political justice and social justice*."[16] He has also never concealed his conviction that his role as president is actively to ensure the success of the Indonesian revolution.

In Africa south of the Sahara the one-party system has of late been endorsed in a number of quarters, following precedents well established in Egypt, Tunisia and Morocco. Although Kwame Nkrumah has not accepted the principle of a single party, he has asserted that

Even a system based on social justice and a democratic constitution may need backing up, during the period following independence, by emergency measures of a totalitarian kind. Without discipline, true freedom cannot survive.[17]

In the drive for independence Nkrumah opened himself to charges of a high-handed and demagogic manipulation of power both personally and through the Convention People's Party, a party which has been described as a "Tammany-type machine with a nationalist ideology . . . composed of a militant elect who dominate and spearhead the nationalist movement." But David Apter, who so characterized the C.P.P., further contended that it was the charismatic leadership of Nkrumah which at least temporarily "endowed the structure of parliamentary government with legitimacy."[18]

After assuming power in independent Ghana, Nkrumah took a course which left the backers of democracy breathless but not without hope. Great attention was focused on himself, as in putting his image on coins and erecting a more than life-size statue of himself in Accra; the normal powers of government were stretched to secure the expulsion or suppression of elements of the opposition; and yet much of the democratic constitutional machinery remained at least temporarily intact. One American observer found that Nkrumah favored benevolent dictatorship and that neither he nor his associates had any liking for the parliamentary system except for the provisional use they could make of it and the unchecked power which it gave the dominant party,[19] but others saw no more resort to extraordinary measures than a critical situation called for.

In Nigeria, where each region has tended to develop a single party of its own, a more drastic attack was made on democracy by one Chike Obi, M.Sc. (London), Ph.D. (Cambridge), a mathematician at Ibadan's University College and founder of the politically inconsequential Dynamic Party. In his view the right question to ask was:

What type of self-government has any chance within a short time to succeed in persuading the illiterate, ignorant, lazy, individualistic and undisciplined natives of Nigeria to make a great physical and mental sacrifice in military and labour camps for the defense of their country and the common good?

Since a people so described is obviously unready to make use of democratic freedoms, Obi saw salvation only in a planned and regimented Kemalism which would ensure that political power came to those "who will make the unavoidable dictatorship as benevolent and as short as possible."[20]

The vesting of a monopoly of power in a single party has found growing favor in both theory and practice in the present and former French territories of sub-Saharan Africa as they have moved to independence or more extensive self-government within the new French Community. In independent Guinea, Sékou Touré has accorded his Democratic Party, reaching out into the country through thousands of local committees, a monopolistic position and has declared that "Guinea cannot permit herself to disperse her forces, her energy, her will in political dualism."[21] In the Ivory Coast, Houphouet-Boigny, representing the right-wing of French African politics, has developed a one-party rule approximately as all-embracing as that of the more left-wing Touré in Guinea. The antiquity of this system in Africa is demonstrated in nearby Liberia where the True Whigs, continuously in power since 1878, are the only party and where President Tubman, in office since 1943, piled up 530,566 votes to his opponent's 55 in the presidential election of May, 1959.

The single-party thesis was extolled by some of the spokesmen for French African territories at the Conference on Representative Government and National Progress held at Ibadan in March 1959. The flavor of their position can be garnered from a paper entitled "In the Phase of National Construction the Fusion of Parties Becomes a Categorical Imperative" which was presented to the conference by Alexandre Adande of Dahomey. Calling for prompt and bold action, he stressed the need for a unity not hampered by sterile sectarianism. Although he saw some people playing into the hands of a hard-pressed imperialism by raising the scarecrows of dictatorship, fascism, and totalitarianism, he contended that there should be no servile copying of European multiparty regimes.

Beneath its "idealistic" appearance, every political party actually represents a definite class or definite economic interest which it must defend in parliament. The result of this is a squabbling among selfish oppositions that has nothing in common with the true and exclusive interest of the nation . . . they stop at nothing: lies, demagogy, compromise, corruption. . . . We have nothing to do with these poisons.[22]

This one-party philosophy was given the blessing of Guinea's Minister to Ghana who was reported as having spoken passionately in favor of "a united and democratic party without opposition," which would contain all the nationalists, maintain representative institutions, and encourage wide popular discussion. In good elitist fashion he asserted that the people must not be confused by a multiplicity of parties, at least in the first years of independence.[23]

According to the usual single-party schemes, differences of opinion would be fully aired within the party, but once a party decision was reached, the Communist principle of democratic centralism would be applied.

In the former Asian colonies the trend has been somewhat the same as in Africa, although, as in the Middle East, the role of the military has been greater. In India the Congress has retained so dominant a position as to be accused of running a one-party system, but other parties have been given free play and the general elections which have been held were models of democratic procedure. The Philippines of Quezon's days had little in the way of party diversity, and Burma came close to being a one-party state under the sway of the AFPFL until that organization split in the spring of 1958, starting the series of events which brought Ne Win to power in the fall. In Vietnam and Korea opposition parties have had no encouragement to challenge the hold of the parties supporting the established regimes. Serious doubts about the desirability of Western parliamentary government for Ceylon have also been raised by Prime Minister Bandaranaike, although, oddly enough, his charge against the British parliamentary system was not that it encouraged the disruptive forces of the opposition but that it opened the door to cabinet dictatorship. In its place he proposed a series of executive committees, to one or another of which every member of parliament would belong—a plan drawn from one of Ceylon's colonial constitutions.[24]

The breakdown of Western representative institutions in so many countries has inevitably led to a renewed searching of souls both in Asia and Africa and in the West. The good sense of the West in proposing such institutions for underdeveloped non-Western peoples and of the nationalists in insisting on them in the first rounds of independence has been called in question.

What we are witnessing is the failure of a series of experiments in grafting an alien form of government on peoples whose background and circumstances are totally dissimilar from those among whom it originated, and who were, on virtually every count, demonstrably ill-prepared to make it work. The first phase of the post-colonial reaction to colonialism involved the copying of the institutions of the imperial West. The failure of those institutions and its aftermath constitute a second phase which may be expected to bring political systems more nearly akin to the experience, capabilities, and present needs of the Asian and African peoples. What the inarticulate masses wanted from the revolutions through which they were passing—insofar as they wanted anything other than to be left alone in peace—was presumably not constitutional democracy or parliamentary government, but

economic and social advance under their own leaders within a framework of national unity and strength. Where the representative institutions could plausibly be accused of failing to move toward these goals, their overthrow would be accepted with indifference or even enthusiasm.

The rise of the strong man to power when governments are unstable and times are troubled is an age-old phenomenon. If he has to look for other sources of support than the armed forces, the single party is a convenient instrument for him in an era when the masses must be taken into political account. Even if the large assumption be made that democracy of a more or less Western variety is ultimately the best of all forms of government for all peoples, it is still not difficult to put together a case for the strong man in the present circumstances of most of the non-European world.

The peoples of the West advanced toward democracy by very slow and gradual stages which included long periods of rule by absolute monarchs and despots, benevolent or otherwise. The achievement of ordered societies, reasonably in agreement on those basic elements of social cohesion necessary for the functioning of democracy and well started on the path of economic development, was in good part the product of the firm authoritarian rule which bridged the transition from the Middle Ages to the contemporary world.

For a backward people precariously moving out from under colonialism into independence with all the problems of economic development still ahead of them, it is highly doubtful that the sovereign remedy is a full-scale installment of democracy as the latter has evolved in advanced and prosperous Western societies. Democracy implies far-reaching freedoms, and an opposition; but the prime requirement is not for more freedoms but for discipline and hard work, not for opposition but for a national consolidation of all forces and talents. This is all the more true in countries such as Nigeria or Malaya where the opposition is likely to be made up of parties formed on tribal, racial, or religious lines, deepening inner divisions at a time when the essential need is strong and unified management. The achievement of coherent national unity can properly be set as the first goal since it is an indispensable condition for internal order and security and for representative government as well. The premature exercise of an overabundant democracy, laying its stress on the rights of the opposition, can destroy the foundations on which a successful democracy may later be built. In a speech answering critics of his country's alleged departures from acceptable constitutional practices, Nkrumah asserted that Africa would stand by its own version of democracy, but added: "As a new and young government, our first responsibility has been to preserve the independence and security of our state."[25]

One issue habitually recurs. The swing away from

democracy is justified in the name of democracy: powers vested in the people are removed from the people in order that they may later be restored for more effective use. Unquestionably a wise and effective authoritarian regime could do much in the way of establishing the preconditions which would make democracy viable in areas where it now is not, but that authoritarianism would either realize its potentialities for development or be prepared to relinquish its powers into popular hands is very far from being proved. An expert on Southeast Asia reported in 1959 that instability and disintegration has progressed so far in that region that Communism was bound to win, unless the military took over. In the officer corps he found men who are "the product of an unusual process of natural selection," devoted to their countries, committed to moral values, disciplined and yet accustomed to command, and progressively acquainted with the modern world.[26] That the military of the new states usually oppose Communism and also have much else to offer is undeniable, particularly when they are contrasted with corrupt and discordant civilian regimes, but can they be trusted to ward off corruption from their own ranks, to carry through development programs outside the range of their experience and training, and not to perpetuate themselves for selfish advantage? The historical record produces few affirmative answers to questions such as these.

A functioning democracy must rest upon a judicious mixture of two potentially antagonistic principles of individual and collective rights. Wherever nationalism is the main driving force, the collective principle is likely to ride roughshod over individuals and minorities whose counterclaims seem to threaten the solidarity of the nation. This, however, gives no clue as to how the collectivity is to be represented: specific content must be given to the national will, and those who formulate it must be singled out. Rousseau's *volonté générale,* only accidentally identified with the concrete wills of actual human beings, must somehow be brought down to earth. Whose voice speaks for the national will? The soul of the nation may reside in the simple peasants and workers who constitute the democratic majority, but their ignorance, and lack of experience render them, it is likely to be contended, unable to give it true expression. In their stead, an elite or a charismatic leader takes over as the emanation of the national will which, in the vocabulary of Rousseau, is the *real* will of the individuals although not one they can be trusted to discover for themselves. The nation is sovereign but the exercise of the sovereignty, so the argument runs, should for the good of the nation itself be entrusted to those who can use it rightly. By this time national democracy has been transmuted into nationalist autocracy; and it was down this road that the German people were stampeded into the disaster of Nazism. It is not my intention to predict that a comparable fate will befall any or all of the presently democratic Asian or African peoples, although some of their neighbors, if they have not already succumbed, are at the least dangerously close to it. The democratic tides still run strongly in the world, but it would be folly to ignore the fact that they have often been turned aside, as in the Communist version which combines the name of democracy with the reality of totalitarian control. How much credence may be given to the pessimistic tone of Guy Wint in his survey of British territories in Asia?

Easy come, easy go. The liberal civilization came more or less by chance from the association of the ancient world with Great Britain, and as easily it may go. It is perhaps simpler to turn Oriental man into an imitation Bolshevik, competent and ruthless, than into an imitation Western liberal.[27]

Save for a chosen few, democratic institutions have not been able to establish the conditions under which democracy could survive the buffetings of the world. It remains to be seen whether authoritarian rule can do better. Dynamic forces are in motion to bring the preconditions of democracy into being, and the drive toward social and economic development has its inescapable democratic implications. Even authoritarian regimes will have to take the people at large more into account than in the past and make use of plebiscitary symbols—the familiar frauds of an age which so frequently can neither take democracy nor leave it alone—but with no certainty that they will progress beyond symbolism. The best of all safeguards for the survival of democracy or for a return to it would be the mobilization of a populace vigilant to defend its rights and manage its own affairs. "Since the beginning of time," Adlai Stevenson has said, "governments have been mainly engaged in kicking people around. The astonishing achievement in modern times in the Western world is the idea that the citizens should do the kicking."[28] The future hangs on the question as to how many of the Asians and Africans will want to do the kicking when the chance comes their way.

## NOTES

1. Cited by C. Northcote Parkinson, *The Evolution of Political Thought* (Boston: Houghton Mifflin Co., 1958), p. 253. For the succeeding quotation, see A. C. Wilgus, ed., *South American Dictators* (Washington, D.C.: George Washington University Press, 1937), p. 24.

2. *The New York Times,* March 24, 1957. Mr. King acknowledged that Ghana had better roads, schools, harbor facilities, and a more highly developed industry, agriculture, and public revenue. John Gunther, ac-

knowledging the advantages of enlightened colonialism, reported that most educated Africans pay lip service to Liberia because of its independence, but inwardly despise it because it is regarded as a betrayal of what modern Africans stand for. *Inside Africa,* p. 847. He added (p. 860) that it is a striking phenomenon that three of Africa's independent states—Ethiopia, Libya, and Liberia—should be the poorest and most backward on the continent, much poorer than most colonial areas.

3. "Democracy in the Middle East—Its State and Prospects," *Middle Eastern Affairs,* vol. VI, no. 4 (April 1955), p. 105.

4. *The Interplay of East and West* (New York: W. W. Norton & Co., 1957), p. 47. See also Herbert Lüthy, "The Passing of the European Order," *Encounter,* vol. IX, no. 5 (November 1957), p. 6.

5. George McT. Kahin, Guy J. Pauker, and Lucian W. Pye, "Comparative Politics of Non-Western Countries," *American Political Science Review,* vol. XLIX, no. 4 (December, 1955), p. 1024.

6. Charles Burton Marshall, "Reflections on a Revolution in Pakistan," *Foreign Affairs,* vol. XXXVII, no. 2 (January, 1959), p. 253.

7. See, Seymour Martin Lipset, "Some Social Requisites of Democracy: Economic Development and Political Legitimacy," *American Political Science Review,* vol. LIII, no. I (March, 1959), pp. 69–105.

8. Cited by Zeine N. Zeine, *Arab-Turkish Relations and the Emergence of Arab Nationalism* (Beirut: Khayat's, 1958), p. 91, n. 3.

9. O. Mannoni came to the conclusion that the majority of Madagascans, if left to themselves, would spontaneously recreate a feudal type of society: "They would lack the courage to face the terrors of a genuine liberation of the individual." *Prospero and Caliban: The Psychology of Colonization* (New York: Frederick A. Praeger, 1956), p. 65.

10. U Law Yone, "Burma's Socialist Democracy," *Atlantic Monthly,* vol. CCI, no. 2 (February 1958), p. 158.

11. *Wanted: An Asian Policy* (New York: Alfred A. Knopf, 1955), p. 165.

12. *The Social Contract,* book II, chap. vi.

13. *Dawn,* Nov. 1, 1958. For the preceding citation from Sukarno, see Gerald S. Maryanov, *Decentralization in Indonesia as a Political Problem,* Interim Reports Series of the Modern Indonesia Project (Ithaca: Department of Far Eastern Studies, Cornell University, 1958), pp. 49–50.

14. See the letter of the Press Attaché of the Pakistan Embassy, Washington, in the *Washington Post,* Jan. 30, 1959. This letter also asserted the maintenance of the rule of law and of civil administration by the new government.

15. J. H. Price, cited in Hansard Society for Parliamentary Government, *What Are the Problems of Parliamentary Government in West Africa?* (London: Hansard Society, 1958), p. 48.

16. *The Birth of Pantjasila,* 3rd ed. (Djakarta: Republic of Indonesia, Ministry of Information, 1958), p. 27.

17. *Ghana,* p. xvi. It takes little reading between the lines in Richard Wright's *Black Power* (New York: Harper & Brothers, 1954), to sense the danger to democracy in Nkrumah's methods; and Wright's concluding open letter to Nkrumah explicitly advocated a disciplined militarization of African life from above as a bridge to span the gap between tribal and industrialized ways of life.

18. *The Gold Coast in Transition,* pp. 202, 294. Nkrumah's biographer, Bankole Timothy, asserted that, because of fear of possible political rivalry, Nkrumah "surrounded himself with timeservers, job-hunters and sycophants; in other words, 'yes-men' who were out for personal favours." *Kwame Nkrumah,* p. 118. Timothy, who was later expelled from Ghana, maintained that "There is no doubt at all that Nkrumah's success has, to a large extent, been due to the co-operation of the unsophisticated masses; their gullibility, their hero-worship, and their capacity for following blindly." P. 172.

19. Henry L. Bretton, "Current Political Thought and Practice in Ghana," *American Political Science Review,* vol. LII, no. I (March, 1958), p. 52. Seeing Ghana as a new country of conflicting tribes without any cohesion and lacking all possibility of making a Western style of democracy work, Peregrine Worsthorne accused the British of making dictatorship inevitable there through the "monstrous folly" of imposing parliamentary government as a face-saving device to cover colonial retreat. "Trouble in the Air," *Encounter,* vol. XII, no. 5 (May, 1959), pp. 3–13.

20. *Our Struggle* (Yaba: John Okwesa & Co., 1955), pp. 30, 56. See *West Africa,* no. 2045 (June 23, 1956), p. 413 for a brief "Portrait" of Chike Obi. An earlier and more moderate version of elitism, asserting the rightful claim of the articulate minority to rule, was put forward by another Nigerian, Obafemi Awolo, later premier of Western Nigeria, in his *Path to Nigerian Freedom* (London: Faber and Faber, Ltd., 1947), p. 63.

21. Cited by Thomas F. Brady, *New York Times,* section 4, May 3, 1959. He has also stated: "The Party exercises a dictatorship, it is the dictatorship of the people." *Afrique Nouvelle* (Dakar), April 10, 1959.

22. Conference paper no. F/413, p. 2. The conference was held under the auspices of the Congress for Cultural Freedom in association with University College, Ibadan, Nigeria.

23. "Summary of Discussions," Ibadan Conference, paper no. F/415, p. 4.

24. *New York Times,* April 20, 1959.

25. Cited in *Ghana Today,* vol. II. no. 23 (Jan. 7, 1959), p. 4. Raymond Aron has remarked that the prime necessity is a working machinery of government. "Particularly in the new states what is first needed is not an opposition but a majority." *Manchester Guardian Weekly,* Oct. 23, 1958.

26. Guy J. Pauker, "Southeast Asia as a Problem Area in the Next Decade," *World Politics,* vol. XI, no. 3 (April, 1959), pp. 339–340.

27. *The British in Asia* (London: Faber and Faber, Ltd., 1947), p. 131.

28. "Party of the Second Party," *Harper's Magazine,* vol. CCXIII, no. 1269 (February, 1956), p. 32.

IX

# IX Non-Western Government and Politics

# INTRODUCTION

## David E. Apter

## I. BASIC PROBLEMS OF POLITICAL DEVELOPMENT

Among the new nations of the world a wide range of more or less undigested bits of Western practices have been fed into formerly dependent areas through colonial and imperial relationships. With independence, all the problems that have habitually plagued the West, whether political, social, or economic, have descended all at once on the new nations. In this sense there is a revolution underway in the developing areas—not the kind we discussed in our section on political development and change, but one that is more fundamental. It needs to fit together communities, political practices, and new beliefs. In the developing areas, if the two mutually antagonistic forces—one for change and the other for integration—cannot be resolved, the nations of Asia, Africa, and Latin America may plunge the world into chaos, for in an age of congealed cold war, such interstices of interest and pockets of political uncertainty can trigger a major explosion.

Some political leaders will respond to the effervescent and random hopes wrought by revolution and independence with a new puritanism and a militancy expressed in the development of elite structures that will control cleavage, brand factions as hostile, and build populism by expanding the government until, excessively politicized, the mushroom cloud hanging over the heads of the people is a political rather than a nuclear reactor. For them economic development is state development, and state development is government expansion and control. Nor is this trend antagonistic to populism. Quite the contrary, what more politically effective form of populism than the expansion of the polity by the proliferation of political opportunity through government?

Another possible reaction by political leaders of new governments is more likely in large than in small states. (Sheer size is an obvious organizational factor that is often neglected.) Systems must be built which, in order to maintain themselves intact, must service the past in some partial and acceptable manner and cater to diverse power clusters which are regionally based. Democracy may come in such systems less for reasons of positive acceptance of its desirability than because no single group is powerful enough to do away with others. A functional democracy is possible that is different from the populist forms. It is organized around multiple parties (regionally, linguistically, or ethnically strong) and a decentralized government, mainly federal or confederal in structure.

Between these two general patterns of organization of the governments of the new states, there are, of course, wide variations in political form and expression. None turn out to be faithful replicas of Westminister or the French National Assembly, as is, of course, to be expected. New institutions have been grafted on old ones, and the result is a kind of institutional indigestion; but the structural malintegration takes place against a still wider panorama of problems. The crucial problems common to all new nations result from social discontinuity, "cultural strain," and pragmatic problems of development, both political and economic. Under such circumstances, independence injects a very different kind of blood into the veins and arteries of government. Not only is the meaning of Western institutions altered, but it also is rare that government itself and the constitution are the legitimate expressions of the society. Anticolonialism also produces a generalized antiauthority reflex; and, in no small measure, nationalists inherit a nest of old grievances most of which do not lend themselves to comfortable reconciliation. Weakly legitimized new governments try to acquire public sanction in those problem areas where they are most on trial. Who can blame them if they try to eliminate a problem, not by resolving it, but by refusing to recognize it?

Two handicaps, cultural strain and weakly legitimized government, make the actions of new governments rather unpredictable. They also invite efforts on the part of political leaders, first, to become as strong as they can and, second, to alter prevailing institutional practices so as to make them more desirable to those in power. Contemporary leadership in the new nations is often highly personal and sometimes messianic, and such leadership is notoriously unstable. Hence, the building of single-party systems or personal parties with powerful bureaucratic support in the mdidle ranks is often the earmark of the organizational revolution in new nations. Without such an organizational revolution, political leaders would be unable to conserve political autonomy, make the best use of the country's resources, or produce a "political take-off" into an integrated machinery of administration and government.

Not only are modifications of Western practices inevitable in such conditions, but also are changes in the social meaning of political action. Several new governments may appear at loggerheads with one another, while in practice the party leaders running the governments may be old friends and warmly agreed on fundamental issues of nationalism. This was so, for example, in the case of Ghana and Togoland, two countries where the rhetoric used by the political leaders toward each other suggested a serious political rift. The same is true elsewhere. The point is that politics remains extremely fluid. Political roles have not yet crystallized.

There is, then, another aspect of politics in new nations that also results from the unlegitimized quality of government. Government is itself less binding upon its incumbents than in more established systems. Politicians are free to act in ways that turn on some wider racial or ideological membership, that is, African or Asian, Marxist or religious, as the case might be.

This freedom helps to introduce a quality of randomness in the actions and meanings of politics in new nations that accounts for many of the political surprises confronting observers. For example, a new nation like the Ivory Coast appears to be pro-French and relatively conservative in its political leadership. In practice, while giving fewer nods in the direction of Marxism, the organizational structure of the Ivory Coast is not dissimilar to that of Guinea, a country regarded with consternation by the West. Moreover, since the Ivory Coast's political leaders were once affiliated with the French Communist Party, it would take no great effort for them to identify with both Guinea and a more Marxist ideology once again.

Thus, the realities of building national polities and mending cultural cleavages helps promote a wider sense of common political situations, problems, and destinies transcending the arbitrary boundaries resulting from colonial rule—a fraternalism in spirit and an organizational mood that has built up a vague and emotional identification of new nations with one another and persists quite apart from potential conflicts that come to the fore. Bearing the brand of color, regarding themselves as the world's exploited, a set of *nations proletaires,* they feel that time can be made to work on their side

only if their organizational revolutions are successful.

Who are the leaders of these organizational revolutions? In the main they are well educated. They are products of the universities of the West. Among them are men of a rare worldliness, for example, Africans and Asians who may have been born Muslims, been educated in Catholic mission schools, and have become Communists in their student days in Paris or London, acquiring a universalism both compassionate and suspicious, passionate in its idealism, yet tough and cynical in its practical affairs.

There are as well political "teddy boys," whose hostilities and raw edges are produced by a well-deserved sense of inadequacy. Suffering from acute status sensitivity, they generally lack political convictions. Almost all political parties in new nations require them. They are the brokers between government leaders and the public. They live close to the bazaar and are the fixers and translators of politics. No party can do without them, and they normally exert great influence and control over party leaders, presenting them with the realities of power, preventing a more Olympian view from prevailing. Using the political teddy boys without being victimized by them is almost the prerequisite of successful leadership in a new nation. Such elements are certainly useful and important, not only because they remain close to the public, but also because their own responses to political decisions are likely to be similar to public reactions to government policy. They are thus essential links in the chain of polity that ends in a national state.

A third elite group commonly found in new states —the civil service—bears the inheritance of the earlier colonial system. Sometimes the devotion to service, the emphasis on efficiency, and the depersonalization of role so important to a civil servant drives the political teddy boys to distraction. Sometimes also these civil service values are to be found, not in the service at all, but in the military. The effect of this system of values is well known in the Sudan, in Pakistan, and for a time, in Burma. Where the civil service is based on highly competitive recruitment and continues practices modeled after former metropolitan traditions, its political importance in new nations is well beyond its counterpart in older ones, for it also becomes a preserve of values and the source of a conception of disinterested government that is the obverse of the personal politics of politicians seeking to establish legitimacy or of political teddy boys operating and mediating the areas of cultural strain.

There are other politically important groups. Trade unions, established and separatist churches, and other voluntary associations that have counterparts in the West have a critical significance in situations of cultural strain and weakly legitimized government. Often they are linked to some social nerve ending, some immemorial institution that can arouse a latent commitment on the part of people and produce chaos and trouble for political leaders. Voluntary associations thus have their own universe of discourse, their own symbolism of role and idea. Like the political brokers, they mediate between government and the social system at large.

Many such groups have historical links with the West. The "old boys' " associations in India or Pakistan or Nigeria represented both a source of nationalism and a strand of continuity. Members of university faculties in many new nations are carriers of intellectual freedom and discipline that may be strikingly out of step with the requirements of an organizational revolution. Trade unions, too, are utterly Western, although, in response to the organizational revolution, they sometimes change their pattern from that of an independent and free movement to that of a third force pitched midway between government and society. Often they show their alienation from Western trade unionism in the bitter condemnation of the International Confederation of Free Trade Unions.

All these are ingredients of the new blending and changing of institutions that are working their way out in the new nations. As older traditions reassert themselves and as modifications of colonial practice come into being, there is also a natural growth in alienation from the West and with it disdain— not enough to rob nationalists of their sense of struggle and victory, but sufficient to show toward the West a contempt born of familiarity. For behind it there also lies a fear that independence was won only because the colonial powers calculated that colonialism could be more efficient under a different guise and that the colonial political connection was no longer essential. The idea that the West left its colonial possessions only because it could rule them by other means spawns a continuation of the anticolonial reflex. Anticolonialism continues, and is even strengthened as scapegoats are sought for internal difficulties incurred after independence.

But not all is serious in the polities of new nations. Among the less messianic leaders there are some who regard politics as sheer fun. To add one's name to posterity is enjoyable and exhilarating. It heightens one's sensibilities and reactions. This aspect of politics in new nations is unfortunately not often scrutinized, perhaps because it is too obvious. As a result we fail to recognize that the new nations represent the last area of old-fashioned entrepreneurship left in the modern world. Like the economic entrepreneurs of old, the new political entrepreneurs have a buccaneering quality. Politics is adventure, a game of sorts, to them. Few political leaders feel that, on the reckoning of the people whom they lead, they might be called to answer for deeds casually done and maliciously performed. A strange sense of immunity hangs over most of the political leaders of the new nations. They exempt themselves from the normal judgments of men and politics. Not only do they feel that the bar of history will not judge them ill, but also that they are so many brands plucked from the burning. Theirs is a world of uncertainty and struggle, of unpredictable rewards and punishments, of political exemptions and rhetorical postures, of political intimacy with others and ruthlessness—all so far removed from the ordinary world of Western nations and their diplomats and politicians that even the most familiar similarities contain snares to the understanding and traps to interpretation.

How do such political entrepreneurs operate? They create organizational weapons that gather momentum from internal resources, their fuel is the hatred of colonialism and the love of development. Some rely on the state or the party. Others rely on the process of "natural" growth—diverse sources of spontaneity and development emerging from the countryside. Both approaches have their advantages and disadvantages. Both deserve further attention. What kind of politics emerges depends in no small measure upon the nature of the social and economic raw material that exists, the degree of cultural strain, and the institutional framework, antique and modern, which is the inheritance of a new nation. The sources of cultural strain and its implications for building effective politics will be our major concern here.

Cultural strain, weak legitimacy, and the qualities of leadership and group behavior in new nations are the main determinants of the future of new nations. Most important of these is the effect of cultural strain. Does it create deep fissures in the social body that can be papered over only by a weak constitutional device? Do severe social and economic conflicts follow lines of natural difference such as ethnic ones, so that one range of conflicts inevitably drags in others? This is the difficulty in the Republic of the Congo, where tribal differences, religious differences, and class conflict all follow precisely the same lines of cleavage. As a result, government was so weakly legitimized and short-lived that its restoration has been supremely difficult. And without legitimacy, leaders who seek to create an organizational revolution are greatly handicapped.

Cultural strain thus sets the task of government at their very widest. Creating the necessity for an organizational revolution, it might also make such a revolution impossible. Within this context, the actions of political entrepreneurs, whether leaders or brokers, whether securely entrenched or weakly established, can be seen as a constant probing for ways and means to consolidate power more effectively and to gain the benefits of independence.

## II. SOURCES OF CULTURAL STRAIN

Cultural strain may derive from family division, religious division, antitraditionalism, urban migration, ethnic competitiveness, racial compartmentalization, economic discrimination, reliance on political solutions, or any combination of these factors. They are all potential sources of cleavage and social tension, for they mirror fundamental differences in outlook and belief from which most new nations suffer in an extreme form. Indeed, the most distinguishing characteristics of new nations is the great range of divergencies incorporated by the casual lines drawn by the colonial political cartographers in another day.

### Family Division

Divisions within the family result in wider impacts upon personality than is the case with other, more ordinary, primary and secondary social groupings. The family is endowed with high solidary and affectual qualities. These qualities make the family a key agency of socialization. Basic divisions in the family, which arise from widespread lack of consensus in society at large, reflect themselves in a failing of the family to create stable roles and images of propriety, right conduct, and social responsibility.

Where the family can no longer perform the role of a basic orienting device, those molecules of stability which the family normally represents are themselves diminished. The normal schedule of desirable roles that is institutionalized through the family, its position, and the normal expectations it provides for its junior members is upset. Socialization is weakened when its function is shifted to other primary and secondary organizations. Political groups, clubs, schools and universities, and work associations can absorb only some of the socialization burden. The chief reason, however, that the family can do the socialization job so well is that the internalization of certain fundamental norms of right and propriety depends upon natural affection and the need for familial approval and makes the socialization process ultimately possible.

In contrast, secondary groupings cannot provide the emotional gratifications that lie behind socialization, unless they take on familial qualities. A political party, having personalized leadership, may be one alternative to the family in the socialization process, if the family becomes a scene of conflict and malintegration. Another alternative is a separatist religious movement. Either way, challenges to the scope of authority in the family make the task of social control by external means, political and social, much more difficult.

Family conflicts are not simply limited to socialization. They appear in conflicts over division of sexual roles—a common difficulty in Moslem countries, for example, and even worse where part of a country follows Moslem practice while another part does not.

Conflicts in the family are, of course, for the most part between generations. The younger elements are often in spiritual rebellion, not simply against their parents, but against what their parents represent in lost opportunity, acceptance of the past, and lack of vision. Indeed, there is much in common between the younger generations in new nations and second-generation Americans. Embarrassment over a way of life that is increasingly regarded as socially marginal is common in both cases.

Of course, the family continues to play a mediating role in all new nations. It is rare to find family, ethnicity, and tradition so strong that children are deliberately separated from the family and sent into differing areas and among differing tribal peoples to live. But this is happening in the case of Guinea. More commonly, the extended family, for example, may itself incorporate such a wide range of occupations and social groupings that it is a microcosm of the society, with a flexibility and a range of alternatives open to members wide enough that the family does not become a hindrance, but rather a help, in accommodation. Such situations are relatively frequent. Typically, however, as the family consists of traditionally oriented members, it will contain conflicts over tradition, ancestral religious factors, land, and the allocation of responsibilities. Where the family is pitched between traditionalism and modernity, it may involve other strains such as that between husband and wife, particularly if the former is better educated than the latter (a common occurrence because of the colonial practice of giving greater educational and occupational opportunities to men).

Whatever their source, conflicts in the family arouse and promote fundamental emotional disequilibrium, which has the effect of increasing hostility between members of a society, adding to the psychological intensity of all other cleavages and conflicts in a society. Most new nations have been traditionally "family centered." When the importance of the family diminishes, all other aspects of social life are profoundly affected.

### Religious Division

In most new nations there was a close and intimate connection between traditional religious practices and beliefs and the pre-colonial political systems. The colonial period was not only a point of entry for new and alien religious forms, but also involved the secularization of authority. Systems in which the legitimacy of government had in the past relied upon religious myths and beliefs were thus governed by colonial regimes whose claims to rule were based, first, on superior power, second, upon superior institutions, and third, upon efficiency and welfare. Independent governments coming into office may find that the withdrawal of the Europeans involves a sudden resurgence of traditional religious practice that may result in open religious conflicts, some of which had always smouldered under the surface, although others might be quite new. Meanwhile, the new governments try to incorporate a new system of political legitimacy that itself is not entirely dissimilar to religion. New gods are substituted for old ones, to be worshiped in the name of reason and modernity.

This religious aspect of nationhood is extremely important. The very symbol of nationhood and independence is birth, the supreme act of creativity. Such creative acts are endowed with a special mystical appeal. Inevitably the establishment of political legitimacy and the more usual conflicts over religion are intimately connected, especially as in many new nations we find a rebirth of religion through political ideals, often indeed in the name of modernity, secularism, and socialism.

Thus, the problem of religious division extends far beyond the competition between major religious groupings—Moslem, Hindu, Christian—and far beyond ordinary variations in values. The classic conflicts in the West, between the spiritual and secular spheres of life, is not what is at stake here, but rather competing spiritualities; the values of government and leadership, moral proprieties of state action—all these are involved in the religious sphere, no less than what we generally think of as religious matters. It is no accident that the language of nationalism is often the language of religious usage, and the "political kingdom" is both a claim to secular authority, and an ecclesiastical allusion, the one reinforcing the other.

## Antitraditionalism

Closely related to the problem of religious division, the problem of traditionalism lies athwart religious change. We can distinguish several different factors here. First, a good many old issues that were of political origin tend to renew themselves when seen as a fight over custom. These in turn may give meaning to a parochial society that itself has not yet accepted the idea of a larger polity or citizenship. Clan conflicts, arguments over custom, and the like all help to make the continuation of traditional life appear as the fundamental reality, with some modern forms and institutions regarded as more extraneous. Hostages to fortune, traditionalists have been badly used by contemporary political leaders. In Ghana or Eastern Nigeria, for example, traditionalists are viewed with dislike. The Accra Conference of December, 1958, branded "tribalism" as feudal and reactionary. The traditionalists, on the other hand, seek to preserve their power by absorbing "modernity" where possible. Sometimes they are extremely successful in this attempt, as has been shown by the political achievements of the Northern Nigerians or the Kabaka's government in Buganda.

Occasionally a new form of traditionalism appears. This is the traditionalism of the "establishment" versus the politicians. The more usual case of this occurs where the army or the civil service reflects the emphasis on a rational and efficient polity reminiscent of the colonial period. Often fed up with what becomes viewed as political vagrancy, the establishment sees the nation dissipating its energies and resources on inane political battles and steps in, just as, in a previous day, colonial officers would have done to insure "normalcy." This has happened in Burma, where, after restoring order and cleaning up the towns, the army turned the responsibilities for running the state back to the politicians. In Pakistan and the Sudan, where similar situations have occurred, there are few signs that the army is about to restore the politicians. In contrast, in Ghana the clash has resulted in threats by the politicians to "politicize" the civil service, that is, to introduce a spoils system.

The conflicts over traditionalism vary a good deal. One kind refers to the prescriptive quality of past culture as a necessary validation for current behavior, another to a form of institutional behavior characteristic of Western society. If politicians take on both as adversaries, they wind up by having to smash the first and make use of the second. Recent governments, such as that in Senegal, which seeks to transpose tradition and custom into an affirming philosophical credo under the ideology of *negritude,* utilizes the efficiency and workmanlike susceptibilities of the civil service to bring about a state of material grace (which can, in turn, be blessed by traditionalism).

## Urban Migration

The migration of rural people to towns always creates uncertainty. Consider the rural person who decides to leave the intimacy of his surroundings, the warmth of the hearth, and the security of ascertainable career prospects. He knows that the town is exciting, that his kinsmen will help him, and that the rhythm of life will be very different from that which he has known. His is the classic problem of the rural person becoming a townsman—a subject of a very large literature, both scientific and literary. But in new nations this is a particularly complex process. For one thing, there is rarely a sharp division between the rural and the urban area. Many cities in new nations have tightly enclosed rural centers, almost self-contained villages, existing within the town itself, organized around occupational and ethnic clusters. Stubborn differences in outlook and attitude may continue to prevail within the city, without its usual effects of atomization and homogenization. Indeed, many cities in new nations are dormitories for migrant populations rather than urban settlements in a real sense.

At the same time, this is a generational problem. Kinship and religious ties do tend to loosen in cities. Heterogeneous relationships between social groups are inevitable as children are thrown together in schools and as industry and commercial penetration make the town a center of economic and social dynamism. Where loyalties are being robbed of their particularism, the tendency is towards the opposite extreme, particularly among the young—toward atomism, separatism, and personal independence. This is the milieu which produces the political "street urchin," the broker, and the political entrepreneur. They find ready-made political groups in those protective associations, churches, trade unions, and tribal societies, which are characteristic of cities in new nations. Local urban followings propel them into national politics. The effect of town politics is a corrupting one, primarily because towns provide so many opportunities to politicians, with few requirements of accountability. Rarely are the dormitory towns bearers of culture, although they may give rise to senior social elites who are profoundly aware of their self-importance (as well as objects of envy and often fear).

Characteristically the towns in new nations have not experienced a sharp break between rural and urban life, but rather a blending of one into the other. One could be a townsman and have strong rural ties. One could be a villager and have close economic and social ties with the town. Suppliers of produce, for example, might have a family "outlet" for their produce in the market place. With rapid economic development, however, town and countryside begin to proceed in different directions. The towns accumulate Western products, attract talent, create wealth. The rural areas, in contrast, gain only in relative impoverishment. The result is a polarization of social life.

Several Communist countries have tried to correct this situation by creating such intervening institutions as "agrogrods," or rural cities. The Chinese commune system is an example of the effort to blend city and rural life. Otherwise, the cities rob the rural areas of both talented people and cultural spontaneity. In the West the suburban communities (as well as the extension of urban life well into the countryside), have been the countervailing force against such polarization, but this process requires great wealth and industrial capacity.

### Ethnic Competitiveness

Too often the ethnic factor is regarded as a somewhat romantic figment of the past, its passing viewed with regret, but what is termed "ethnicity" is not simply of residual interest—a quaint and historical antecedent in a new nation. Quite the contrary: ethnic formation is another form of nationhood. The still remaining primary attachment of many in new nations is not to the polity of the modern state, but to the polity of the ethnic group. Such ethnic attachments do not wither away with the formation of a national state. As a result many new countries experience bitter conflict between ethnic groups that challenges the new politics in demands for federal political arrangements and other claims to autonomy.

Where ethnicity is strong, few institutions can be immune to its effects. In the case of Indonesia, for example, it has proved most difficult to create a civil service free from ethnic conflict. Such conflict has manifested itself in political party affiliations of administrators, and brought competitive party politics inside the administration. A similar situation prevails in parts of former French Africa.

### Racial Compartmentalization

The problem of racial compartmentalization is most acute in those societies which have a substantial proportion of *white* settlers. Where there are other minority groups in important economic or social positions, such as the Chinese in Thailand, Sarawak, or Malaya, the problems have usually not been acute unless activated from "outside," as, for example, the recent effort of the Chinese government to exhort the Chinese community in Indonesia to resist relocation schemes favored by the Indonesian government.

Racial compartmentalization exists in any society where racial groups have a very high number of transactions within the racial group and very few outside the group. Thus, in South Africa, Kenya, or Southern Rhodesia, a European can live a full life without coming into contact with Africans or Asians except under highly regularized and, in a sense, "ritualized" ways. Perhaps only the roles of master and servant, or of merchant and consumer, are permissible forms of relations between one racial group and another. In these systems the problem of building a national society is analogous to that of early nineteenth-century England, where class rather than racial compartmentalization was the political problem. The arguments for and against the expansion of the franchise in nineteenth-century England are scarcely dissimilar from the debates over common versus communal roles and eligibility to vote that have been under way in East and Central Africa for the past ten years.

How to build a plural society is one problem posed by racial compartmentalization. How to prevent racial conflict from becoming class conflict is another. Where race, culture, and class combine in racial compartmentalization, the outlook for violence and turbulence becomes pronounced. We have only to regard South Africa to see this.[1]

The greatest difficulty with racial compartmentalization is that, once created, the nature of the relationship between the races becomes hardened and fixed so that any alteration of it is tantamount to a social revolution. Under such circumstances any increase in the transactions between racial communities only helps to confirm each in its prejudices.

Commonplace in Western studies of race relations is the idea that as members come to know one another their prejudices slowly begin to give way. Unfortunately this is not the case in plural societies. There is a difference between a racial *group* and a racial *community*. Once a community is built on grounds of race, it repels or tries to render impotent any threats to the stereotyped basis of its conceptions. For a racial *community* cannot dismiss race as trivial or irrelevant if it wishes to maintain its exclusiveness. Under such circumstances, increased contact between *communities* simply means greater prejudice. Either contact continues along ritualized grooves, or the situation becomes threatening. We see the effects of plural communities in Algeria and South Africa, to cite extreme examples. For new nations they are problems for which no satisfactory political solution has been found.

## Economic Discrimination

Economic discrimination tends to carry over its effects long after it is removed. It becomes part of the heritage of nationalists who, explaining backwardness as a consequence of Western exploitation, see in their country's inability to "catch up" with the West an extension of an earlier process. We have always tended, however, to regard economic discrimination as something practiced by Europeans against Africans or Asians, whether in the form of large expatriate firms or in the practices of colonialism, including debarment of native peoples from participation in the economy in all but the most subservient positions. This still goes on to some degree in many areas, but by and large both "social welfare colonialism" of the postwar period and effective organization by nationalists have made these forms of discrimination less significant, except in plural societies.

There is some danger that the nationalism of the 1940's, mainly Marxian in its overtones, should result in a reverse kind of economic discrimination. For example, it is quite possible that attitudes toward private investment, resulting from a previous period of aggressive capitalism, should lead politicians to deny any useful role to private investors. By so doing, they can easily make the burden for planning and state enterprise too great. The machinery of government may become clogged by the load it is expected to carry, instead of proceeding with the confidence and buoyancy that should accompany the development of a new nation.

Another reason that private enterprise is denigrated in new nations is related to the informal and unplanned manner of doing business that is the historical way of the West. When they were protected and controlled by strong colonial oligarchs with a commitment to service and efficiency under the later periods of social welfare colonialism, the colonial territories were in some measure safeguarded against the inroads of uncontrolled commerce. After independence the situation is radically different. In hordes arrive the speculators, the businessmen out to convince credulous politicians of the efficacy of their products, the visiting foreign missions, each with vague words of aid, hidden threats, and little in the way of concrete proposals. All the "patent medicine" dealers of the Western world are represented. They are willing to bribe and cheat to gain some comparative advantage for their employers. Few are ultimately effective in displacing the well entrenched and established foreign corporations. Hence, the intensity of the efforts to sequester commercial undertakings for themselves. In the process they inject into the atmosphere a kind of social poison of fear, suspicion, and hidden motives.

It is one thing to speak in lofty terms of private and public investment from the West. It is another to see many of the creatures spawned by "private enterprise" sitting in decrepit hotels, their own acts a testimonial of contempt for the peoples with whom they wish to establish commercial relations, often seeking, by political means and by playing on rivalries and interparty disputes, to win special favors for themselves. These practices reinforce the anti-colonial reflex and also encourages the puritanism of the socialist leaders, who, disturbed by the invasion of ragged and shady Westerners, fear they cannot always distinguish between this aspect of Western association and more superior aspects. In contrast, the limited contacts of the Soviet bloc countries have been models of constraint and sobriety. It is always easier to deal with a government-controlled corps of technicians. Strong government dealing with strong government seems often to provide the necessary order that is useful to the politicians of the new nations. It is all very well to speak of the need for liberalism, but in an intellectual concern for freedom in the new nations we tend to discount the impact of those elements in our own society which represent the worst expressions of liberalism and themselves would abuse it in the new nations.

## Emphasis on Political Solutions

It is characteristic of new nations that, having won their freedom through political action and having taken over from civil service oligarchies responsible for the major activities of social life and welfare, they should continue to view progress in purely political terms. Politics is at once a major means of social mobility and a source of power and prestige. Thus, government tends to become omnivorous. Indeed, in most new nations government depletes the intellectual resources of regions, towns, and villages, drawing men of ability towards the center and then pushing a few reluctant administrators outward again to handle administrative tasks.

Politics becomes itself society rather than only a part of it. This trend is a most important source of strain in new states, for it causes all social matters to become political. Education, development, and religion all become evaluated in political terms. Planners, politicians, and administrators begin to live by the competitive practices of power rather than an image of public well-being. There is great danger of the public itself being viewed as the greatest of all obstacles, and tension between rulers and ruled becomes acute. Most new nations are democracies and believe in majority rule; but, as Panikkar points out, the right of the majority to exact obedience runs into grave difficulties. The difficulties of new nations stem from the very factors we have been discussing and, if fundamental enough, lead politicians to prefer forms of government other than majority rule.[2]

## III. THE POLITICS OF NEW NATIONS

No matter what the ideology of political leaders, once they come to power, they discover the natural conservatism of cultures. Cultures are composed of more or less stable elements that do not easily change. Normally, political leaders in new nations develop from the more culturally marginal groups in the community. They are rebels against forces of tradition and custom that already prevail. Their task, once they attain office, is in the largest sense to create a new cultural community in which neither they nor their authority represents a marginal factor.

If they seek change for this reason, they also find that the cultural discontinuities that are characteristic of new nations and help to produce a marginal, aggressive group of political entrepreneurs are reflected in competitive social groupings that appear extremely parochial when viewed from above. Yet even the most tradition-minded and parochial in these groups expect change, particularly material change, as a consequence and benefit of independence. Political leaders are then caught in a dilemma. If they mobilize all the major social clusters in the society to create a grand push on the economic and political problems of the day, they find themselves in danger of getting embroiled in an angry collection of vested interests whose conflicts prejudice the future of the society. If they attack such groups with the object of smashing traditional culture and breaking down parochial discontinuities, they find that their public becomes the biggest obstacle to success.

The colonial heritage in which government was the major force for change, the tradition of planning itself (and no colonial territory did not have its five- or ten-year development scheme), and the political focus of nationalism all help to make government the mechanism by means of which all problems are to be solved. Burdens are shifted upwards within the system to the senior political leaders and administrators, with the result that their problems outstrip their abilities to solve them. If there are many sources of power, the fact that the political system is itself unconsolidated results in constitutional conflicts. Struggles over federal as distinct from unitary forms of government mirror the bitterness of ethnic and regional conflicts, which themselves disguise demands for special treatment or urgent attention. If there is a single source of power, that must be maintained in the face of competing factions in the nationalist party and of conflict between administrators and politicians or between army officials and politicians.

Because they inherit both cultural conservatism and an impossible burden of public expectations and overhopeful promises from independence, leaders of government in new nations seek a new framework of order and social discipline within which to make policy. Few of them are prepared for the astonishing transition that accompanies the shift in role from that of public protagonist to that of antagonist; few are prepared for that sudden loneliness and separation from the public that forms the natural gulf between ruler and ruled.[3]

Because of these difficulties, new nations need to consolidate their independence by establishing stable government. During the period of consolidation political leaders seek some license in being temporarily free from the ordinary vagaries of fickle political fortune. Most new nations have opposition groups which themselves developed in the colonial period. They have an antigovernment reflex born out of the fight against colonialism. Regarding the new government as they did the old, that is, as illegitimate, they weaken the constitutional bases of society.

Thus, there is dilemma for new nations. Their political leaders have inspired a vision of progress. To achieve progress requires social mobilization. Social mobilization requires direction, an organizational revolution that offends the natural conservatism of the public. Autocracy is thus intrinsic to a development situation in which political entrepreneurship is the source of change and government its director. Wherever we look we find these problems.

In Indonesia, in spite of a much vaunted intellectual elite, problems of regional, ethnic, and cultural differences are particularly great. The political framework remains unsteady. Sumatra is not completely subdued after its abortive attempt to free itself from Javanese control. The army and the civil service are divided between political party groupings. Extraparliamentary groups abound. Indeed, in the immediate postindependence period even tiny parties could arise and maintain a claim to have popular support merely on the basis of political bluff. Political bluff indeed became the order of the day. Extravagant claims of party membership and organization were placed in news bulletins and, where possible, in government publications. For example, the PRN (National People's Party), an organization with only a shadowy existence outside Djarkarta, wrote in a publication of the Ministry of Information that it had a membership of two million persons.[4]

Nor is Indonesia alone in suffering from the ethnic parochialism which continually jeopardizes national survival. Nigeria, which has just received independence, is scarcely firm on its consolidated national boundaries. Its three regional governments have agreed to a loose federal arrangement giving maximum autonomy to the region. They have simply postponed the day of reckoning between the populous Moslem North, the secular and aggressive East, and the middle-class and prosperous West. Conflicts over regional boundaries, minority rights and representation, and the role of traditional authorities accompanied even the peak period of nationalism in Nigeria. Independence has not resolved these problems. The prospect of internal conflict remains.

In the Congo the conflicts are rural versus urban, Catholic versus Socialist, and ethnic minorities versus ethnic majorities, divided on a provincial basis, plus a compartmentalized racial community of 40,-000 whites who controlled the economy and services of the whole country. The sad effect of such cleavages at present threatens to interject cold-war politics in Africa and has brought even the United Nations into contempt.

Where such differences are mirrored in competitive multiparty situations, very little political coherence is possible. Many of the discontinuities that multiparty systems reflect lead to rampant political party opportunism and national cynicism. Such circumstances led the Sudanese army to take over government from political parties. A not too different situation prevailed in Pakistan.

Repudiation of a shabby parochial and stifling multiparty system, relatively unconcerned with the growth and development of an effective viable society, characterized Burma as well. Sudan, Pakistan, and Burma have seen the army take over the nation and continue a paternalistic pattern of military administration not unlike the system of welfare colonialism that it replaced.

Even those nations where the economic prospects for development were favorable and the internal political temperature was relatively low have shown a decided need to restrict freedom in favor of consolidating the political structure. Ghana has imposed restrictive legislation, crippled the opposition, and become a managerial state in which trade unions, voluntary associations, and collective farms all help to serve the large purposes of national development. Moreover, Ghana serves both as a center of pan-Africanism and a model of political development for other new nations in Africa.

Guinea, which has joined with Ghana in a very loose association, has shown similar tendencies. Handicaps there were far greater than in the case of Ghana. When the French departed, they took the typewriters from the offices, pulled out the telephones from the public buildings, and stripped the country of virtually all movable equipment. Today, Guinea has Czechoslovakian typewriters, telephones, and other equipment. Bulgarian farm experts have replaced French agronomists. And Guinea has coalesced all political parties into the Democratic Party of Guinea. In practice as well as theory a one-party state prevails.

Nations such as Indonesia, India, and China are faced with all the problems listed above, plus the special difficulties imposed by population growth. The problems of Ghana, Nigeria, and Guinea look rather puny in contrast to China, where the population is increasing at the fantastic rate of 55,000 a day. With an annual rate of increase of 3.5 per cent, "barring major war or internal revolt, famine or epidemic, China could reach the billion mark within about three decades."[5]

In India, in spite of the fact that large-scale public corporations and private investment have worked together to develop the basic economy, the population is such that few net per capita gains can be registered. The frightening prospect there is that although the economy continues to gain, population increase is gaining even more rapidly.

China has an estimated population density of 149.5 per square mile. India has a density of 293 per square mile! In contrast, one of the most heavily populated countries in Africa—Nigeria—has a density of 87.7 per square mile. Former French West Africa had 9.7 per square mile.

Admittedly population statistics of this sort overlook a whole range of problems. For one thing, there can be pocket population problems in otherwise not densely populated areas. Soil fertility and resources greatly affect the meaning one can attach to these figures. But the undisguised problem of countries with fearful population growth is that the proportion of savings to investment needs to be appreciably higher to produce the same net gains as in nations without major population problems. Implicit in those areas with population problems is the need for drastic solutions if disaster is to be avoided. Since all the additional problems of other new nations also exist in countries with population difficulties the population problem is virtually crushing.

The normal condition of new nations is a desperate effort to solve such basic problems as these just mentioned. The great difficulty with the social mobilization process is that with increasing autocracy there is also a decline in the *information* available to political leaders. The public is afraid to express opposition. Vigorous opposition movements are regarded as disruptive. The emphasis is on unity, cooperation, and social transformation. The decision-making burden on government becomes more intense. There is less freedom for decentralized decision-making, and lesser figures become fearful of making decisions. Government gets a reduced "feedback" from the public. To insure support, it comes to rely on some measure of coercion. There is a decline in internal political pluralism, and a greater emphasis on achieving goals via a disciplined population.[6]

## IV. CONCLUSION

The various problems that appear in greater or lesser degree in all new nations can be summarized as follows:

1. Independence carries with it high expectations of material and social gains on the part of the public.

2. Political leaders are in danger of offending the public by trying to produce change.

3. Governments are not yet well institutionalized.

4. Unless governments take special steps to consolidate their tenure, they are more likely to become weak than strong.

There is a growing literature on the developing areas. Perhaps the most ambitious effort at comparison is Almond and Coleman's *Politics of the Developing Areas*. A more knowledgeable but less systematic effort is Rupert Emerson's *From Empire to Nation*. The effort by Daniel Lerner in *The Passing of Traditional Society* is directly comparative within the context of the Middle East. Perhaps the best recent analysis is Fatma Mansur, *Process of Independence*.

Other studies that, although examining cases, nevertheless are significant for comparative purposes are Skinner's *Leadership and Power in the Chinese Community in Thailand*, Pye's *Guerrilla Communism in Malaya*, Apters' two books, *The Gold Coast in Transition* and *The Political Kingdom in Uganda*, and Coleman's *Nigeria: Background to Nationalism*. These may be compared with the very different pattern of political development found in Japan. Two books on Japan stand out. One, Robert Bellah's *Tokugawa Religion*, although not a work in political science, is important to an understanding of the religious aspects of Japanese authority. The other is Scalapino's *Democracy and the Party Movement in Prewar Japan*.

These and other books are concerned with non-Western areas in a manner suitable for comparative analysis. Much remains to be done, however. There is nothing in the literature of non-Western systems to compare to the sweep and power of Schumpeter's *Capitalism, Socialism, and Democracy*. Earlier comparative studies that had a strong economic concern, such as Hobson's *Imperialism* or Schumpeter's *Imperialism and Social Classes,* the latter containing two extremely valuable studies, are nevertheless out of date.

There is, however, a kind of order imposed by the problems of non-Western areas. The first requirement imposed on scholars is basic information about them. The second is the arranging of that data so that we get a feeling for how each of these systems of political and social life fit together. The third is the comparison of the developing areas according to a defined set of important problems. The fourth involves the development of comparative methods which allow effective research on these problems. Finally, out of such efforts will come theories relevant to the problems defined and the opening up of new areas of inquiry, those which have wider implications for the analysis of change in our own country and our own time.

## NOTES

1. Europeans amount to 21 per cent of the population in South Africa. See *State of the Union,* Economic, Financial and Statistical Year Book for South Africa, Capetown, Culemborg, 1957, p. 37.

2. See K. M. Panikkar, *The Afro-Asian States and Their Problems* (London, Allen & Unwin, 1959), p. 19.

3. Indeed, in those systems where nationalist leaders were the most militant and popular, the transition is most sharp. If the gulf between leader and led becomes very large, political leaders reach out for a new means of identifying with the public. In such instances the great danger is that the party becomes the church. The church becomes the state. The state becomes the leader, and personal loyalty is to him. The leader establishes a faith and a dogma. The dogma gives meaning to the state. The party lays down the line of doctrinal infallibility. This is the establishment of a new theocracy. It is the source of messianic totalitarianism.

4. See Herbert Feith, *The Wilopo Cabinet, 1952–53; A Turning Point in Post-Revolutionary Indonesia* (Modern Indonesia Project, Cornell University, 1958), p. 28.

5. See Sripati Chandrawekhar, "The 'Human Inflation' of Red China" in the *New York Times Magazine,* Dec. 6, 1959.

6. Administrators pass upward only information pleasing to their leaders. The public disguises its reactions. Political leaders come to live in a world of uncertainty.

# THE NON-WESTERN POLITICAL PROCESS

Lucian W. Pye

The purpose of this article is to outline some of the dominant and distinctive characteristics of the non-Western political process. In recent years, both the student of comparative politics and the field worker in the newly emergent and economically underdeveloped countries have found it helpful to think in terms of a general category of non-Western politics.[1]

There are, of course, great differences among the non-Western societies. Indeed, in the past, comparative analysis was impeded by the appreciation of the rich diversity in the cultural traditions and the historical circumstances of the Western impact; students and researchers found it necessary to concentrate on particular cultures, and as a consequence attention was generally directed to the unique features of each society. Recently, however, attempts to set forth some of the characteristics common to the political life of countries experiencing profound social change have stimulated fruitful discussions among specialists on the different non-Western regions as well as among general students of comparative politics.

For this discussion to continue, it is necessary for specialists on the different areas to advance, in the form of rather bold and unqualified statements, generalized models of the political process common in non-Western societies.[2] Then, by examining the ways in which particular non-Western countries differ from the generalized models, it becomes possible to engage in significant comparative analysis.

1. *In non-Western societies the political sphere is not sharply differentiated from the spheres of social and personal relations.* Among the most powerful influences of the traditional order in any society in transition are those forces which impede the development of the distinct sphere of politics. In most non-Western societies, just as in traditional societies, the pattern of political relationship is largely determined by the pattern of social and personal relations. Power, prestige, and influence are based largely on social status. The political struggle tends to revolve around issues of prestige, influence, and even of personalities, and not primarily around questions of alternative courses of policy action.

The elite who dominate the national politics of most non-Western countries generally represent a remarkably homogeneous group in terms of educational experience and social background. Indeed, the path by which individuals are recruited into their political roles, where not dependent upon ascriptive considerations, is essentially an acculturation process. It is those who have become urbanized, have received the appropriate forms of education, and have demonstrated skill in establishing the necessary personal relations who are admitted to the ranks of the elite. Thus, there is in most non-Western societies a distinctive elite culture in which the criteria of performance are based largely on non-political considerations. To be politically effective in national politics, one must effectively pass through such a process of acculturation.

At the village level it is even more difficult to distinguish a distinct political sphere. The social status of the individual and his personal ties largely determine his political behavior and the range of his influence. The lack of a clear political sphere in such communities places severe limits on the effectiveness of those who come from the outside to perform a political role, be it that of an administrative agent of the national government or of a representative of a national party. Indeed, the success of such agents generally depends more on the manner in which they relate themselves to the social structure of the community than on the substance of their political views.

The fundamental framework of non-Western politics is a communal one, and all political behavior is strongly colored by considerations of communal identification. In the more conspicuous cases the larger communal groupings follow ethnic or religious lines. But behind these divisions there lie the smaller

Reprinted from *The Journal of Politics*, Vol. XX, by permission of The Southern Political Science Association.

This is a revised version of a paper presented at the annual meeting of the American Political Science Association on September 5–7, 1957.

but often more tightly knit social groupings that range from the powerful community of Westernized leaders to the social structure of each individual village.

This essentially communal framework of politics makes it extremely difficult for ideas to command influence in themselves. The response to any advocate of a particular point of view tends to be attuned more to his social position than to the content of of his views. Under these conditions it is inappropriate to conceive of an open market place where political ideas can freely compete on their own merits for support. Political discussion tends rather to assume the form of either intracommunal debate or one group justifying its position toward another.

The communal framework also sharply limits freedom in altering political allegiances. Any change in political identification generally requires a change in one's social and personal relationships; conversely, any change in social relations tends to result in a change in political identification. The fortunate village youth who receives a modern education tends to move to the city, establish himself in a new sub-society, and become associated with a political group that may in no way reflect the political views of his original community. Even among the national politicians in the city, shifts in political ties are generally accompanied by changes in social and personal associations.

2. *Political parties in non-Western societies tend to take on a world view and represent a way of life.* The lack of a clearly differentiated political sphere means that political associations or groups cannot be clearly oriented to a distinct political arena but tend to be oriented to some aspect of the communal framework of politics. In reflecting the communal base of politics, political parties tend to represent total ways of life. Attempts to organize parties in terms of particular political principles or limited policy objectives generally result either in failure or in the adoption of a broad ethic which soon obscures the initial objective. Usually political parties represent some sub-society or simply the personality of a particularly influential individual.

Even secular parties devoted to achieving national sovereignty have tended to develop their own unique world views. Indeed, successful parties tend to become social movements. The indigenous basis for political parties is usually regional, ethnic, or religious groupings, all of which stress considerations not usually emphasized in Western secular politics. When a party is merely the personal projection of an individual leader it is usually not just his explicitly political views but all facets of his personality which are significant in determining the character of the movement.

In the past, the tendency for political parties to adopt world views was in some instances strongly encouraged by the desire of traditional authoritarian governments or colonial regimes to suppress all explicitly political associations, and such associations found it expedient to adopt a religious cloak to hide the character of their activities. In time, however, the religious aspect came to have genuine significance in determining the character of the group and maintaining its continuity. This was the case with most of the secret societies common to traditional Chinese society. The same development also took place in French Indo-China, where political activity took the form of organizing quasi-religious sects. Both the Cao Dai and the Hoa Hao began as political movements masking as religions, and, although they never lost their political character, they found a basis of integration in their religious aspects.

The history of the secular nationalist movements reflects a similar tendency for parties essentially to represent ways of life. Even after independence the tendency remains strong because such parties are inclined to feel that they have a mission to change all aspects of life within their society. Indeed, such parties often conceive of themselves as representing a prototype of what their entire country will become in time. Members of such movements frequently believe that their attitudes and views on all subjects will become the commonly shared attitudes and views of the entire population. Those committed to modernizing their societies can see few aspects of life which must not be altered, while those more attached to tradition have equally broad concerns.

3. *The political process in non-Western societies is characterized by a prevalence of cliques.* The lack of a distinct political sphere and the tendency for political parties to have a world view together provide a framework within which the most structured units of decision-making tend to be personal cliques. Although general considerations of social status determine the broad outlines of power and influence, the particular pattern of political relationships at any time is largely determined by decisions made at the personal level. This is the case because the social structure in non-Western societies is characterized by functionally diffuse relationships; individuals and groups do not have sharply defined and highly specific functions and thus do not represent specific interests that distinguish them from other groupings. There is no clearly structured setting that can provide a focus for the more refined pattern of day-to-day political activities. Hence, in arriving at their expectations about the probable behavior of others, those involved in the political process must rely heavily upon judgments about personality and the particular relations of the various actors to each other. The pattern of personal associations provides one of the firmest guides for understanding and action within the political process. Personal cliques are likely to become the key units of decision-making in the political process of most non-Western societies.

Western observers often see the phenomenon of cliques as being symptomatic of immoral and de-viously motivated behavior. This may actually be the case. Considerations of motive, however, cannot explain either the prevalence of cliques in non-Western societies or their functions. It should also be noted that the fact that cliques are based on personal relations does not mean that there are no significant differences in their values and policy objectives. Since the members of a given clique are likely to have a common orientation toward politics, if their views were fully articulated they might appear as a distinct ideology that would be significantly different from those of the other factions.

In order to understand the workings of the political process in most non-Western countries it is necessary to analyze the character of the interclique reactions. To ignore the importance of cliques would be comparable to ignoring the role of interest groups and elections in analyzing the behavior of American Congressmen.

4. *The character of political loyalty in non-Western societies gives to the leadership of political groups a high degree of freedom in determining matters of strategy and tactics.* The communal framework of politics and the tendency for political parties to have world views means that political loyalty is governed more by a sense of identification with the concrete group than by identification with the professed policy goals of the group. The expectation is that the leaders will seek to maximize all the interests of all the members of the group and not just seek to advance particular policies or values.

So long as the leaders appear to be working in the interest of the group as a whole, they usually do not have to be concerned that the loyalties of the members will be tested by current decisions. Under such conditions, it is possible for leadership to become firmly institutionalized within the group without the particular leaders having to make any strong commitments to a specific set of principles or to a given political strategy.

Problems relating to the loyalty of the membership can generally be handled more effectively by decisions about intra-group relations than by decisions about the goals or external policies of the group. So long as harmonious relations exist within the group, it is generally possible for the leaders to make drastic changes in strategy. Indeed, it is not uncommon for the membership to feel that matters relating to external policy should be left solely to the leadership, and it may not disturb them that such decisions reflect mainly the idiosyncracies of their leaders.

5. *Opposition parties and aspiring elites tend to appear as revolutionary movements in non-Western politics.* Since the current leadership in non-Western countries generally conceives of itself as seeking to effect changes in all aspects of life, and since all the political associations tend to have world views, any prospective change in national leadership is likely to seem to have revolutionary implications. The fact that the ruling party in most non-Western countries identifies itself with an effort to bring about total change in the society makes it difficult to limit the sphere of political controversy. Issues are not likely to remain as isolated and specific questions but tend to become associated with fundamental questions about the destiny of the society.

In addition, the broad and diffuse interests of the ruling elites make it easy for them to maintain that they represent the interest of the entire nation. Those seeking power are thus often placed in the position of appearing to be, at best, obstructionists of progress and, at worst, enemies of the country. Competition is not between parties that represent different functional specific interests or between groups that claim greater administrative skills; rather, the struggle takes on some of the qualities of a conflict between differing ways of life.

This situation is important in explaining the failure of responsible opposition parties to develop in most non-Western countries. For example, the Congress Party in India has been able to identify itself with the destiny of the entire country to such a degree that the opposition parties find it difficult to avoid appearing either as enemies of India's progress or as groups seeking precisely the same objectives as Congress. Since the frustration of opposition groups encourages them to turn to extremist measures, they may in fact come to be revolutionary movements.

6. *The non-Western political process is characized by a lack of integration among the participants, and this situation is a function of the lack of a unified communications system in the society.* In most non-Western societies there is not a single general political process that is the focus of most political activities throughout the population; rather, there are several distinct and nearly unrelated political processes. The most conspicuous division is that between the dominant national politics of the more urban elements and the more traditional village level of politics. The conflicts that are central to the one may hardly appear in the other.

Those who participate, for example, in the political life of the village are not an integral part of the national politics, since they can act without regard to developments at the central level. Possibly even more significant is the fact that at the village level all the various village groups have their separate and autonomous political processes.

This situation is a reflection of, and is reinforced by, the communication system common to non-Western societies, where the media of mass communication generally reach only to elements of the urban population and to those who participate in the national political process. The vast majority of the people participate only in the traditional word-of-mouth communication system. Even when the media of mass communications do reach the village, through readers of newspapers or owners of radios, there is almost no "feedback" from the village level. The radio talks *to* the villagers but does not talk *with* them. The views of the vast majority of the population are not reflected in the mass media. Indeed, it is often the case that the Westerner has less difficulty than the majority of the indigenous population in understanding the intellectual and moral standards reflected in the media of mass communication, not only because these media are controlled by the more Westernized elements but also because the media may be consciously seeking to relate themselves more to the standards of the international systems of communication than to the local scene.

The lack of a unified communication system and the fact that the participants are not integrated into a common political process limit the types of political issues that can arise in non-Western societies. For example, although these are essentially agrarian societies in which industrial development is just beginning to take place, there has not yet appeared (in their politics) one of the issues basic to the history of Western politics: the clash between industry and agriculture, between town and countryside. Questions of agriculture usually arise in politics when the urbanized leaders advance plans for increasing production and developing village life. The values and concepts of the rural element are not effectively represented in the national political process largely because its fragmented character and the lack of a unified communications system leave the rural elements without a basis for mobilizing their combined strength and effectively advancing their demands on the government. It is possible that in time the rural masses, discovering that they have much in common, will find ways to mobilize their interests and so exert their full potential influence on the nation's political life. Such a development would drastically alter the national political character. In the meantime, however, the fragmented political process of the non-Western societies means that fundamentally agrarian countries will continue to have a form of national politics that is more urbanized than that commonly found in the industrial West. In many cases one city alone dominates the politics of an entire country.

7. *The non-Western political process is characterized by a high rate of recruitment of new elements to political roles.*[3] The spread of popular politics in traditional societies has meant a constant increase in the number of participants and the types of organizations involved in the political process. This development has been stimulated by the extraordinary rise in the urban population, which has greatly increased the number of people who have some understanding about, and feeling for, politics at the national level. A basic feature of the acculturation process which creates the sub-society of the elite is the development of attitudes common

to urban life. It is generally out of the rapid urban growth that there emerge the aspiring elites who demand to be heard. In almost all non-Western societies, there is a distinct strata of urban dwellers who are excluded from direct participation in national politics but whose existence affects the behavior of the current elite.

The more gradual reaching out of the mass media to the countryside has stimulated a broadening awareness that, although participation in the nation's political life is formally open to all, the rural elements actually have little access to the means of influence. In some places political parties, in seeking to reach the less urbanized elements, have opened up new channels for communicating with the powerful at the nation's center which may or may not be more effective than the old channels of the civil administration. In any case, the existence of multiple channels of contact with the national government tends to increase the number of people anxious to participate in national decision-making.

8. *The non-Western political process is characterized by sharp differences in the political orientation of the generations.* The process of social change in most non-Western societies results in a lack of continuity in the circumstances under which people are recruited to politics. Those who took part in the revolutionary movement against a colonial ruler are not necessarily regarded as indispensable leaders by the new generations; but their revolutionary role is still put forward as sufficient reason for their continued elite status. As a result, in some countries, as in Indonesia and Burma, groups that were not involved in the revolution feel that they are now being arbitrarily excluded from the inner circle of national politics. For these people, the current elite is claiming its status on the basis of ascriptive rather than achievement considerations.

This problem in non-Western societies is further complicated by demographic factors, for such societies are composed of rapidly growing populations that have a high birth rate. In Singapore, Malaya, and Burma, over half the population is under voting age, and the median age in most non-Western countries is in the low twenties. There is thus a constant pressure from the younger generation, whose demands for political influence conflict with the claims of current leaders who conceive of themselves as being still young and with many more years of active life ahead. In most of the newly independent countries, the initial tendency was for cabinet ministers and high officials to be in their thirties and forties, a condition which has colored the career expectations of the youth of succeeding generations, who now face frustration if they cannot achieve comparable status at the same age.

This telescoping of the generations has sharpened the clash of views so that intellectually there is an abnormal gap in political orientations, creating a potential for extreme reversal in policy, should the aspiring elites gain power. Ideas and symbols which are deeply felt by the current leaders, including those relating to the West, may have little meaning for a generation which has not experienced colonial rule.

9. *In non-Western societies there is little consensus as to the legitimate ends and means of political action.* The fundamental fact that non-Western societies are engrossed in a process of discontinuous social change precludes the possibility of a widely shared agreement as to the appropriate ends and means of political activities. In all the important non-Western countries, there are people who have assimilated Western culture to the point that their attitudes and concepts about politics differ little from those common in the West. At the other extreme there is the village peasant who has been little touched by Western influences. Living in different worlds, these individuals can hardly be expected to display a common approach toward political action.

The national leadership, recruited from people who have generally become highly urbanized, is in a position to set the standards for what may appear to be a widely shared consensus about politics. However, more often than not, this apparent national agreement is a reflection only of the distinct qualities of the elite sub-society. The mass of the population cannot fully appreciate the values and concepts which underlie the judgments of the elite and which guide its behavior.

The lack of a distinct political sphere increases the difficulties in achieving agreement about the legitimate scope and forms of political activities. The setting is not one in which political issues are relatively isolated and thus easily communicated and discussed. Instead, a knowledge of national politics requires an intimate acquaintance with the total social life of the elite. The fact that loyalty to the particular group rather than support of general principles is the key to most political behavior strengthens the tendency toward a distinct and individual rather than a shared orientation towards politics.

The situation is further complicated by the fact that, since most of the groupings within the political process represent total ways of life, few are concerned with limited and specific interests. The functionally diffuse character of most groups means that each tends to have its own approaches to political action in terms of both ends and means. Under these circumstances, the relationship of means to ends tends to be more organic than rational and functional. Indeed, in the gross behavior of the groups it is difficult to distinguish their primary goals from their operational measures. Consequently, the political actors in non-Western societies tend to demonstrate quite conspicuously the often-forgotten fact that people generally show greater imagination and ingenuity in discovering goals to match their means than in expanding their capabilities in order to reach distant goals.

Given the character of the groups, it is difficult to distinguish within the general political discourse of the society a distinction between discussions of desired objectives and analyses of appropriate means of political action.

10. *In non-Western societies the intensity and breadth of political discussion has little relationship to political decision-making.* Western observers are impressed with what they feel is a paradoxical situation in most non-Western countries: the masses seem to be apathetic toward political action and yet, considering the crude systems of communications, they are remarkably well informed about political events. Peasants and villagers often engage in lengthy discussions on matters related to the political world that lies outside their immediate lives, but they rarely seem prepared to translate the information they receive into action that might influence the course of national politics.

The villagers are often responding in the traditional manner to national politics. In most traditional societies, an important function of the elite was to provide entertainment and material for discussion for the common people; but discussions in villages and teashops could center on the activities of an official without creating the expectation that discussion should lead to action. Thus the contemporary world of elite politics provides a drama for the common people, just as in many traditional cultures the popular forms of literature and drama stressed court life and the world of officialdom.

A second explanation for this pattern of behavior is that one of the important factors in determining social status and prestige within the village or local community is often a command of information about the wider world; knowledge of developments in the sphere of national and even international politics has a value in itself. But skill in discussing political matters again does not raise any expectations of actual participation in the world of politics.

Finally, many of the common people in non-Western societies find it desirable to keep informed about political developments in order to be able to adapt their lives to any major changes. Since their lives have often been drastically disrupted by political events, they have come to believe it prudent to seek advance warning of any developments which might again affect their lives; but it has not necessarily encouraged them to believe that their actions might influence such developments.

11. *In the non-Western political process there is a high degree of substitutability of roles.*[4] It seems that in non-Western societies most politically relevant roles are not clearly differentiated but have a functionally diffuse rather than a functionally specific character. For example, the civil bureaucracy is not usually limited to the role of a politically

neutral instrument of public administration but may assume some of the functions of a political party or act as an interest group. Sometimes armies act as governments. Even within bureaucracies and governments, individuals may be formally called upon to perform several roles.

A shortage of competent personnel encourages such behavior either because one group may feel that the other is not performing its role in an effective manner or because the few skilled administrators are forced to take on concurrent assignments. However, the more fundamental reason for this phenomenon is that in societies just emerging from traditional status, it is not generally expected that any particular group or organization will limit itself to performing a clearly specified function. Under these conditions there usually are not sharply defined divisions of labor in any sphere of life. All groups tend to have considerable freedom in trying to maximize their general influence.

12. *In the non-Western political process there are relatively few explicitly organized interest groups with functionally specific roles.* Although there are often large numbers of informal associations in non-Western countries, such groups tend to adopt diffuse orientations that cover all phases of life in much the same manner as the political parties and cliques. It is the rare association that represents a limited and functionally specific interest. Organizations which in name and formal structure are modeled after Western interest groups, such as trade unions and chambers of commerce, generally do not have a clearly defined focus.

In many cases groups, such as trade unions and peasant associations that in form would appear to represent a specific interest, are in fact agents of the government or of a dominant party or movement. Their function is primarily to mobilize the support of a segment of the population for the purposes of the dominant group, and not primarily to represent the interests of their constituency.

In situations where the associations are autonomous, the tendency is for them to act as protective associations and not as pressure groups. That is, their activities are concentrated on protecting their members from the consequences of governmental decisions and the political power of others. They do not seek to apply pressure openly on the government in order to influence positively the formation of public policy.

This role of the protective association is generally a well developed one in traditional societies and in countries under colonial rule. Under such authoritarian circumstances, since informal associations could have little hope of affecting the formal law-making process, they tended to focus on the law-enforcing process. Success in obtaining preferential treatment for their membership did not require that they mobilize general popular support. On the contrary, activities directed to broadly articulating

their views were generally self-defeating. They were likely to be more successful if they worked quietly and informally to establish preferential relations with the policy-enforcing agents of the government. Under such conditions each association generally preferred to operate separately in order to gain special favors. The strategy of uniting in coalitions and alliances to present the appearance of making a popular demand on the government, as is common in an open democratic political process composed of pressure groups, would only weaken the position of all the informal associations in a traditional society, for it would represent a direct challenge to the existing governmental elite.

This approach to political activity common in traditional societies still lingers on in many non-Western societies. Informal associations tend to protect all the interests of their members in relations with the government. At the same time, many interests in the society are not explicitly organized. Although the process of social change is creating the basis for new interests, the formation of explicit interest groups rarely moves at the same pace. Often the new groups turn to the more traditional informal associations and only very gradually change their character. In other cases interest groups that fundamentally represent the newly developing aspects of the society perform according to the standards of the traditional groups.

From this brief discussion we may note that when interest groups act as protective associations, focusing on the law-enforcing process and seeking special treatment for their members, they are likely to avoid articulating publicly their goals and are likely to base their requests for special favors on particularistic rather than universalistic considerations. In appealing to policy-enforcement agents, prudence dictates the desirability of framing a request as an isolated demand; for any suggestion that a request constitutes a widespread demand, consistent with the general interest or the public good, would threaten the preserve of the law-makers, who were presumed to be unapproachable in most traditional societies.

We may sum up these observations by formulating a general hypothesis that would read: "Whenever the formally constituted law-makers are more distant from and more inaccessible to the general public than the law-enforcing agencies, the political process of the society will be characterized by a high degree of latency, and interests will be represented by informally organized groups seeking diffuse but particularistically defined goals which will not be broadly articulated nor claimed to be in the general interest." The corollary of this hypothesis would, of course, read: "Whenever the formally constituted law-makers are less distant from and more accessible to the general public than the law-enforcing agencies, the political process of the society will be open and manifest, and interests will

THE NON-WESTERN POLITICAL PROCESS

be represented by explicitly organized groups seeking specific but universalistically defined goals which will be broadly articulated and claimed to be in the general interest."

13. *In the non-Western political process the national leadership must appeal to an undifferentiated public.* The lack of explicitly organized interest groups and the fact that not all participants are continuously represented in the political process deprive the national leadership of any readily available means for calculating the relative distribution of attitudes and values throughout the society. The national politician cannot easily determine the relative power of those in favor of a particular measure and those opposed; he cannot readily estimate the amount of effort needed to gain the support of the doubtful elements.

It is usually only within the circle of the elite or within the administrative structure that the national leaders can distinguish specific points of view and the relative backing that each commands. In turning to the population as a whole, the leaders find that they have few guides as to how the public may be divided over particular issues. Thus, in seeking popular support, the politician cannot direct his appeal to the interests of particular groups. Unable to identify or intelligently discriminate among the various interests latent in the public, the political leader is inclined to resort to broad generalized statements rather than to adopt specific positions on concrete issues. This situation also means that, whether the question is one of national or of merely local import, the leadership must appear to be striving to mobilize the entire population.

The inability to speak to a differentiated public encourages a strong propensity toward skillful and highly emotional forms of political articulation on the part of non-Western leaders. Forced to reach for the broadest possible appeals, the political leader tends at times to concentrate heavily on nationalistic sentiments and to present himself as a representative of the nation as a whole rather than of particular interests within the society. This is one of the reasons why some leaders of non-Western countries are often seen paradoxically both as extreme nationalists and as men out of touch with the masses.

14. *The unstructured character of the non-Western political process encourages leaders to adopt more clearly defined positions on international issues than on domestic issues.* Confronted with an undifferentiated public, leaders of non-Western countries often find the international political process more clearly structured than the domestic political scene. Consequently, they can make more refined calculations as to the advantages in taking a definite position in world politics. This situation not only encourages the leaders of some non-Western countries to seek a role in world politics that is out of proportion to their nation's power, but it also allows such leaders to concentrate more on international than

on domestic affairs. It should also be noted that in adopting a supra-national role, the current leaders of non-Western countries can heighten the impression that their domestic opposition is an enemy of the national interest.

15. *In non-Western societies the affective or expressive aspect of politics tends to override the problem-solving or public-policy aspect of politics.* Traditional societies have generally developed to a very high order the affective and expressive aspects of politics. Pomp and ceremony are usually basic features of traditional politics, and those who are members of the ruling elite in such societies are generally expected to lead more interesting and exciting lives than those not involved in politics. In contrast, traditional societies have not usually emphasized politics as a means for solving social problems. Questions of policy in such societies are largely limited to providing certain minimum social and economic functions and maintaining the way of life of the elite.

Although in transitional societies there is generally a greater awareness of the potentialities of politics as a means of rationally solving social problems, the expressive aspects of politics usually continue to occupy a central place in determining the character of political behavior. The peculiar Western assumption that issues of public policy are the most important aspect of politics, and practically the only legitimate concern of those with power, is not always applicable to non-Western politics. Indeed, in most non-Western societies the general assumption is not that those with power are committed to searching out and solving problems, but rather that they are the fortunate participants in the central drama of life. Politics is supposed to be exciting and emotionally satisfying.

In part the stress on the affective or expressive aspect of politics is related to the fact that, in most non-Western countries, questions of personal loyalties and identification are recognized as providing the basic issues of politics and the bond between leader and follower is generally an emotional one. In fact, in many non-Western societies, it is considered highly improper and even immoral for people to make loyalty contingent upon their leaders' ability to solve problems of public policy.

In the many non-Western societies in which the problem of national integration is of central importance, the national leaders often feel they must emphasize the symbols and sentiments of national unity since substantive problems of policy may divide the people. It should be noted that the governmental power base of many non-Western leaders encourages them to employ symbols and slogans customarily associated with administrative policy in their efforts to strengthen national unity. The Western observer may assume that statements employing such symbols represent policy intentions when in fact their function is to create national loyalty and to condition the public to think more in policy terms.

16. *Charismatic leaders tend to prevail in non-Western politics.*[5] Max Weber, in highlighting the characteristics of charismatic authority, specifically related the emergence of charismatic personalities to situations in which the hold of tradition has been weakened. By implication, he suggested that societies experiencing cultural change provide an ideal setting for such leaders since a society in which there is confusion over values is more susceptible to a leader who conveys a sense of mission and appears to be God-sent.

The problem of political communication further reinforces the position of the charismatic leader. Since the population does not share the leadership's modes of reason or standards of judgment, it is difficult to communicate subtle points of view. Communication of emotions is not confronted with such barriers, especially if it is related to considerations of human character and personality. All groups within the population can feel confident of their abilities to judge the worth of a man for what he is, even though they cannot understand his mode of reasoning.

So long as a society has difficulties in communication, the charismatic leader possesses great advantage over his opponents, even though they may have greater ability in rational planning. However, the very lack of precision in the image that a charismatic leader casts, especially in relation to operational policy, does make it possible for opposition to develop as long as it does not directly challenge the leader's charisma. Various groups with different programs can claim that they are in fact seeking the same objectives as those of the leader. For example, in both Indonesia and Burma, the Communists have been able to make headway by simply claiming that they are not directly opposed to the goals of Sukarno and U Nu.

Charisma is likely to wear thin. A critical question in most non-Western societies that now have charismatic leaders is whether such leadership will in the meantime become institutionalized in the form of rational-legal practices. This was the pattern in Turkey under Kemal Ataturk. Or will the passing of the charismatic leader be followed by confusion and chaos? The critical factor seems to be whether or not the leader encourages the development of functionally specific groups within the society that can genuinely represent particular interests.

17. *The non-Western political process operates largely without benefit of political "brokers."* In most non-Western societies there seems to be no institutionalized role for carrying out the tasks of, first, clarifying and delimiting the distribution of demands and interests within the population, and, next, engaging in the bargaining operation necessary to accommodate and maximize the satisfaction of those demands and interests in a fashion consistent with the requirements of public policy and administration. In other words, there are no political "brokers."

In the Western view, the political broker is a prerequisite for a smoothly operating system of representative government. It is through his activities that, on the one hand, the problems of public policy and administration can be best explained to the masses in a way that is clearly related to their various specific interests and, on the other hand, that the diverse demands of the population can be articulated to the national leaders. This role in the West is performed by the influential members of the competing political parties and interest groups.

What is needed in most non-Western countries in order to have stable representative institutions are people who can perform the role that local party leaders did in introducing the various immigrant communities into American public life. Those party leaders, in their fashion, were able to provide channels through which the immigrant communities felt they could learn where their interests lay in national politics and through which the national leaders could discover the social concerns of the new citizens.

In most non-Western societies, the role of the political "broker" has been partially filled by those who perform a "mediator's" role, which consists largely of transmitting the views of the elite to the masses. Such "mediators" are people sufficiently acculturated to the elite society to understand its views but who still have contacts with the more traditional masses. In performing their role, they engage essentially in a public relations operation for the elite, and only to a marginal degree do they communicate to the elite the views of the public. They do not find it essential to identify and articulate the values of their public. Generally, since their influence depends upon their relations with the national leadership, they have not sought to develop an autonomous basis of power or to identify themselves with particular segments of the population as must the political "broker." As a consequence, they have not acted in a fashion that would stimulate the emergence of functionally specific interest groups.

## NOTES

1. For two excellent discussions of the implications for comparative politics of the current interest in non-Western political systems, see: Sigmund Neumann, "Comparative Politics: A Half-Century Appraisal," *Journal of Politics,* XIX (August, 1957), 269–290; and Dankwart A. Rustow, "New Horizons for Comparative

Politics," *World Politics,* IX (July, 1957), 530–549.

2. The picture of the non-Western political process contained in the following pages was strongly influenced by: George McT. Kahin, Guy J. Pauker, and Lucian W. Pye, "Comparative Politics in Non-Western Countries," *American Political Science Review,* XLIX (December, 1955), 1022–41; Gabriel A. Almond,

"Comparative Political Systems," *Journal of Politics,* XVIII (August, 1956), 391–409; Rustow, *op. cit.,* and also his *Politics and Westernization in the Near East,* Center of International Studies (Princeton, 1956).

3. Kahin, Pauker, and Pye, *loc. cit.,* p. 1024.

4. See Almond, *loc. cit.,* p. 30.

5. Kahin, Pauker, and Pye, *loc. cit.,* p. 1025.

# *Discontinuity and Politics in the Developing Areas*

# ETHNICITY AND NATIONAL INTEGRATION IN WEST AFRICA

Immanuel Wallerstein

Many writers on West Africa, whether academic or popular, assert that there is currently a conflict between tribalism and nationalism which threatens the stability of the new West African nations. In fact, the relationship between tribalism and nationalism is complex. Although ethnicity (tribalism) is in some respects dysfunctional for national integration (a prime objective of nationalist movements), it is also in some respects functional. Discussion of the presumed conflict might be clarified by discussing this hypothesis in some detail. Before doing so, it should be noted that we deliberately use the term ethnicity in preference to tribalism, and we shall preface our remarks by carefully defining our use of the term ethnicity.

In a traditional, rural setting, an individual is a member first of all of a family and then of a tribe.[1] The demands the tribe makes on him vary with the complexity of the tribal system of government,[2]

Reprinted from *Cahiers d'Études Africaines,* No. 3 (October, 1960), pp. 129–138, by permission of Immanuel Wallerstein, Assistant Professor, Department of Sociology, Columbia University, and *Cahiers d'Études Africaines,* published by the Centre d'Études Africaines, École Pratique des Hautes Études, Sorbonne.

Revised version of a paper delivered at the Annual Meeting of the American Sociological Society, 1959.

as does the degree to which family and tribal loyalties are distinct. To a large extent, however, family and tribal loyalties support each other harmoniously.

Under colonial rule, the social change brought about by European administrators and the process of urbanization has led to widespread shifts of loyalty. This process has been called "detribalization." Writers speaking of tribal loyalty often confuse three separate phenomena which it would be useful to distinguish: loyalty to the family; loyalty to the tribal community; and loyalty to the tribal government, or chief.[3] Often what a writer means by detribalization is simply a decline in chiefly authority. It does not necessarily follow that an individual who is no longer loyal to his chief has rejected as well the tribe as a community to which he owes certain duties and from which he expects a certain security.[4]

It may be objected that West Africans do not make a distinction between the tribal government and the tribal community. This is perhaps true in the rural areas but they do when they reach the city. For in the city they find that there are new sources of power and prestige which, for many persons, are more rewarding than the tribal government. Hence they tend to lose some of their respect for the authority of the chief. The tribe, however, still can play a useful, if partially new, function as an ethnic group. The *Gemeinschaft*-like community to which the individual belongs may no longer be exactly the same group as before; the methods of government are different; the role in the national social structure is different. This community, however, bears sufficient resemblance to the rural, traditional "tribe" that often the same term is used. In this discussion, however, we shall use "tribe" for the group in the rural areas, and ethnic group for the one in the towns.

Some writers have challenged the very existence of detribalization. Rouch, for example, says he finds instead "supertribalization" among the Zabrama and other immigrants to Ghana.[5] For as Mitchell has commented of another part of Africa: "People in rural areas are apt to take their tribe for granted, but when they come to the town their tribal membership assumes new importance."[6] This is, however, a false debate. We shall see that quite often the group from which the individual is "detribalized" (that is, the tribe to whose chief he no longer pays the same fealty) is not necessarily the same group into which he is "supertribalized" (that is, the ethnic group to which he feels strong bonds of attachment in the urban context).

Membership in an ethnic group is a matter of social definition, an interplay of the self-definition of members and the definition of other groups. The ethnic group seems to need a minimum size to function effectively, and hence to achieve social definition.[7] Now it may be that an individual who defined himself as being of a certain tribe in a rural area can find no others from his village in the city. He may simply redefine himself as a member of a new and larger group.[8] This group would normally correspond to some logical geographical or linguistic unit, but it may never have existed as a social entity before this act.

Indeed, this kind of redefinition is quite common. Two actions give such redefinition permanence and status. One is official government sanction, in the form of census categories,[9] or the recognition of "town chiefs"; the other is the formation of ethnic (tribal) associations which are described more accurately by the French term, *association d'originaires*. These associations are the principal form of ethnic (tribal) "government"[10] in West African towns today.

Some of these ethnic associations use clearly territorial bases of defining membership, despite the fact that they may consider their relationship with traditional chiefs as their *raison d'être*. For example, in the Ivory Coast, Amon d'Aby has described the process as follows:

L'un des phénomènes les plus curieux enregistrés en Côte d'Ivoire au lendemain de la Libération est la tendance très marquée des élites autochtones vers la création d'associations régionales. . . .

Ces associations groupent tous les habitants d'un cer- cle ou de plusieurs cercles réunis. Leur objet est non plus le sport et les récréations de toutes sortes comme les groupements anodins d'avant-guerre, mais le progrès du territoire de leur ressort. Elles ont le but d'apporter la collaboration des jeunes générations instruites aux vieilles générations représentées par les chefs coutumiers accrochés aux conceptions périmés, à une politique surannée.[11]

It should be observed that the administrative units in question (les cercles) are the creation of the colonial government, and have no necessary relationship to traditional groupings. Such ethnic associations, formed around non-traditional administrative units, are found throughout West Africa.[12] A presumably classic example of the significance of tribalism in West African affairs is the role which traditional Yoruba-Ibo rivalry has played in Nigerian politics. Yet, Dr. S. O. Biobaku has pointed out that the very use of the term "Yoruba" to refer to various peoples in Western Nigeria resulted largely from the influence of the Anglican mission in Abeokuta in the nineteenth century. The standard "Yoruba" language evolved by the mission was the new unifying factor. Hodgkin remarks:

Everyone recognizes that the notion of "being a Nigerian" is a new kind of conception. But it would seem that the notion of "being a Yoruba" is not very much older.[13]

Sometimes, the definition of the ethnic group may even be said to derive from a common occupation —indeed, even dress—rather than from a common language or traditional polity. For example, an Accra man often tends to designate all men (or at least all merchants) coming from savannah areas as "Hausamen," although many are not Hausa, as defined in traditional Hausa areas.[14] Similarly, the Abidjan resident may designate these same men as Dioula.[15] Such designations may originate in error, but many individuals from savannah areas take advantage of this confusion to merge themselves into this grouping. They go, for example to live in the *Sabon Zongo* (the Hausa residential area), and even often adopt Islam, to aid the assimilation.[16] They do so because, scorned by the dominant ethnic group of the town, they find security within a relatively stronger group (Hausa in Accra, Dioula in Abidjan, Bambara in Thiès), with whom they feel some broad cultural affinity. Indeed, assimilation to this stronger group may represent considerable advance in the prestige-scale for the individual.[17]

Thus we see that ethnic groups are defined in terms that are not necessarily traditional but are rather a function of the urban social situation. By ethnicity, we mean the feeling of loyalty to this new ethnic group of the towns. Epstein has urged us to distinguish between two senses of what he calls "tribalism": the intratribal, which is the "persistence of, or continued attachment to, tribal custom," and tribalism within the social structure, which is the "persistence of loyalties and values, which stem from a particular form of social organization."[18] This corresponds to the distinction we made above between loyalty to tribal government and loyalty to the tribal community. In using the term ethnicity, we are referring to this latter kind of loyalty. This distinction cannot be rigid. Individuals in West Africa move back and forth between city and rural area. Different loyalties may be activated in different contexts. But more and more, with increasing urbanization, loyalty to the ethnic community is coming to supersede loyalty to the tribal community and government. It is the relationship of this new ethnic loyalty to the emergent nation-state that we intend to explore here.

There are four principal ways in which ethnicity serves to aid national integration. First, ethnic groups tend to assume some of the functions of the extended family and hence they diminish the importance of kinship roles; two, ethnic groups serve as a mechanism of resocialization; three, ethnic groups help keep the class structure fluid, and so prevent the emergence of castes; fourth, ethnic groups serve as an outlet for political tensions.

First, in a modern nation-state, loyalties to ethnic groups interfere less with national integration than loyalties to the extended family. It is obvious that particularistic loyalties run counter to the most efficient allocation of occupational and political roles in a state. Such particularistic loyalties cannot be entirely eliminated. Medium-sized groups based on such loyalties perform certain functions —of furnishing social and psychological security— which cannot yet in West Africa be performed either by the government or by the nuclear family. In the towns, the ethnic group is to some extent replacing the extended family in performing these functions.

The role of the ethnic group in providing food and shelter to the unemployed, marriage and burial expenses, assistance in locating a job has been widely noted.[19] West African governments are not yet in a position to offer a really effective network of such services, because of lack of resources and personnel. Yet if these services would not be provided, widespread social unrest could be expected.

It is perhaps even more important that ethnic associations counter the isolation and anomy that uprooted rural immigrants feel in the city. Thus Balandier has noted in Brazzaville the early emergence of ethnic associations tends to indicate a high degree of uprootedness among the ethnic group, which tends to be found particularly in small minorities.[20]

But from the point of view of national integration is the ethnic group really more functional than the extended family? In the sense that the ethnic group, by extending the extended family, dilutes it, the answer is yes. The ties are particularistic and

diffuse, but less so and less strong than in the case of kinship groups. Furthermore, such a development provides a precedent for the principle of association on a non-kinship basis. It can be seen perhaps as a self-liquidating phase on the road to the emergence of the nuclear family.[21] Thus, it can be said with Parsons, that ethnic groups "constitute a focus of security beyond the family unit which is in some respects less dysfunctional for the society than community solidarity would be."[22]

The second function suggested was that of resocialization. The problem of instructing large numbers of persons in new normative patterns is a key one for nations undergoing rapid social change. There are few institutions which can perform this task. The formal educational system is limited in that it is a long-range process with small impact on the contemporary adult population. In addition, universal free education, though the objective of all West African governments at the present time, is not yet a reality in any of these countries. The occupational system only touches a small proportion of the population, and a certain amount of resocialization is a prerequisite to entry into it. The government is limited in services as well as in access to the individuals involved (short of totalitarian measures). The family is in many ways a bulwark of resistance to change.

The ethnic groups, touching almost all the urban population, can then be said to be a major means of resocialization. They aid this process in three ways. The ethnic group offers the individual a wide network of persons, often of very varying skills and positions, who are under some obligation to retrain him and guide him in the ways of urban life.

By means of ethnic contacts, the individual is recruited into many non-ethnic nationalist groupings. Apter found evidence of this in Ghana, where he observed a remarkable number of classificatory brothers and other relatives working together in the same party, kinship thus providing a "reliable organizational core in the nationalist movement."[23] Birmingham and Jahoda similarly suggest the hypothesis that kinship (read, ethnic) links mediated Ghana political affiliation.[24]

And lastly, members of the ethnic group seek to raise the status of the whole group, which in turn makes it more possible for the individual members to have the mobility and social contact which will speed the process of resocialization.[25]

The third function is the maintenance of a fluid class system. There is in West Africa, as there has been historically in the United States, some correlation between ethnic groups and social class, particularly at the lower rungs of the social ladder. Certain occupations are often reserved for certain ethnic groups.[26] This occurs very obviously because of the use of ethnic ties to obtain jobs and learn skills.

It would seem then that ethnicity contributes to rigid stratification. But this view neglects the normative context. One of the major values of contemporary West African nations is that of equality. Individuals may feel helpless to try to achieve this goal by their own efforts. Groups are less reticent, and as we mentioned before, its members usually seek to raise the status of the group. The continued expansion of the exchange economy means continued possibility of social mobility. As long as social mobility continues, this combination of belief in equality and the existence of ethnic groups striving to achieve it for themselves works to minimize any tendency towards caste-formation. This is crucial to obtain the allocation of roles within the occupational system on the basis of achievement, which is necessary for a modern economy. Thus, this is a self-reinforcing system wherein occupational mobility contributes to economic expansion, which contributes to urban migration, which contributes to the formation of ethnic associations and then to group upward mobility, which makes possible individual occupational mobility.

The fourth function we suggested was the ethnic groups serve as an outlet for political tensions. The process of creating a nation and legitimating new institutions gives rise to many tensions, especially when leaders cannot fulfill promises made. Gluckman's phrase, the "frailty in authority"[27] is particularly applicable for new nations not yet secure in the loyalty of their citizens. We observed before that ethnic groups offered social security because the government could not. Perhaps we might add that this arrangement would be desirable during a transitional period, even were it not necessary. If the state is involved in too large a proportion of the social action of the individual, it will be burdened by concentrated pressure and demands which it may not be able to meet. It may not yet have the underlying diffuse confidence of the population it would need to survive the non-fulfilment of these demands.[28] It may therefore be of some benefit to divert expectations from the state to other social groups.

The existence of ethnic groups performing "an important scapegoat function as targets for displaced aggression"[29] may permit individuals to challenge persons rather than the authority of the office these persons occupy. Complaints about the nationalist party in power are transformed into complaints about the ethnic group or groups presumably in power. This is a common phenomenon of West African politics, and as Gluckman suggests:

These rebellions, so far from destroying the established social order [read, new national governments] work so that they even support this order. They resolve the conflicts which the frailty in authority creates.[30]

Thus, in rejecting the men, they implicitly accept the system. Ethnic rivalries become rivalries for political power in a non-tribal setting.

The dysfunctional aspects of ethnicity for national integration are obvious. They are basically two. The first is that ethnic groups are still particularistic in their orientation and diffuse in their obligations, even if they are less so than the extended family. The ethnic roles are insufficiently segregated from the occupational and political roles because of the extensiveness of the ethnic group. Hence we have the resulting problems of nepotism and corruption.

The second problem, and one which worries African political leaders more, is separatism, which in various guises is a pervasive tendency in West Africa today.[31] Separatist moves may arise out of a dispute between élite elements over the direction of change. Or they may result from the scarcity of resources which causes the "richer" region to wish to contract out of the nation (e.g., Ashanti in Ghana, the Western Region in Nigeria, the Ivory Coast in the ex-federation of French West Africa). In either case, but especially the latter, appeals to ethnic sentiment can be made the primary weapon of the separatists.

In assessing the seriousness of ethnicity as dysfunctional, we must remember that ethnic roles are not the only ones West Africans play. They are increasingly bound up in other institutional networks which cut across ethnic lines. Furthermore, the situation may vary according to the number and size of ethnic groupings. A multiplicity of small groups is less worrisome, as Coleman reminds us, than those situations where there is one large, culturally strong group.[32]

The most important mechanism to reduce the conflict between ethnicity and national integration is the nationalist party. Almost all of the West African countries have seen the emergence of a single party which has led the nationalist struggle, is now in power, and dominates the local political scene.[33]

In the struggle against colonial rule, these parties forged a unity of Africans as Africans. To the extent that the party structure is well articulated (as, say, in Guinea) and is effective, both in terms of large-scale program and patronage, the party does much to contain separatist tendencies.

Linguistic integration can also contribute, and here European languages are important. It is significant that one of the Ghana government's first steps after independence was to reduce the number of years in which primary schooling would be in the vernacular. Instruction in English now begins in the second year. We might mention, too, that Islam and Christianity both play a role in reducing centrifugal tendencies.

Lastly, there is the current attempt to endow pan-Africanism with the emotional aura of anti-colonialism, the attempt to make Unity as much a slogan as Independence. Even if the objective of unity is not realized, it serves as a counterweight to ethnic separatism that may be very effective.

Thus we see that ethnicity plays a complex role in the contemporary West African scene. It illustrates the more general function of intermediate groups intercalated between the individual and the state, long ago discussed by Durkheim. It points at the same time to the difficulties of maintaining both consensus and unity if these intermediate groups exist.

## NOTES

1. A tribe is what Murdock calls a community, and he notes: "The community and the nuclear family are the only social groups that are genuinely universal. They occur in every known human society. . . ." (G. Murdock, *Social Structure,* New York, Macmillan, 1949, p. 79.)

2. Statements on the typologies of tribal organizations in Africa are to be found in: M. Fortes and E. Evans-Pritchard, ed., *African Political Systems,* Oxford, 1940;—J. Middleton and D. Tait, *Tribes without Rulers,* London, 1958;—D. Forde, "The Conditions of Social Development in West Africa," in *Civilisations,* III, No. 4, 1953, pp. 472–476.

3. We shall not discuss further the role of the family in West Africa today. We note here that it would be an oversimplification to suggest that family ties have drastically declined in the urban areas. In any case, the strength of family ties can vary independently of the strength of tribal ties.

4. There are, to be sure, cases where the two loyalties decline together, and there is consequently severe anomy. Failure to distinguish this case from one in which primarily loyalty to the chief alone diminishes can result in much confusion. See this comment by Mercier in which he tries to clarify this confusion: "C'est dans cette minorité [la population saisonnière] que l'on peut parler réellement de faits de *détribalisation,* au sens de pure dégradation du rôle des anciens cadres sociaux. Au contraire, nous avons vu que, dans la population permanente, *les structures de parenté et l'appartenance ethnique* jouaient un rôle considérable." (P. Mercier, "Aspects de la société africaine dans l'agglomération dakaroise: groupes familiaux et unités de voisinage," p. 39, in P. Mercier *et al.,* "L'Agglomération Dakaroise," in *Études sénégalaises,* No. 5, 1954.)

5. J. Rouch, "Migrations au Ghana," in *Journal de la Société des Africanistes* XXVI, No. I/2, 1956, pp. 163–164.

6. J. C. Mitchell, "Africans in Industrial Towns in Northern Rhodesia," in *H. R. H. The Duke of Edinburgh's Study Conference,* No. I, p. 5.

7. Mercier observes: "Il faut noter également que, moins un groupe ethnique est numériquement important dans la ville, plus la simple parenté tend à jouer le rôle de liens de parenté plus proches." (*Op. cit.,* p. 22.)

8. In Dakar, Mercier notes: "Un certain nombre de personnes qui étaient manifestement d'origine Lébou . . . se déclaraient cependant Wolof, preuve de la crise de l'ancien particularisme Lébou." (*Op. cit.,* p. 17.)

9. For example, G. Lasserre writes: "L'habitude est prise à Libreville de recenser ensemble Togolais et Dahoméens sous l'appellation de 'Popo.'" (*Libreville,* Paris, Armand Colin, 1958, p. 207.)

Epstein notes a similar phenomenon in the Northern Rhodesian Copperbelt towns, where one of the major ethnic groups, sanctioned by custom and by census, is the Nyasalanders. Nyasaland is a British-created territorial unit, but people from the Henga, Tonga, Tumbuka, and other tribes are by common consent grouped together as Nyasalanders. (A. L. Epstein, *Politics in an Urban African Community,* Manchester, Manchester University Press, 1958, p. 236.)

10. By government we mean here the mechanism whereby the norms and goals of the group are defined. There may or may not be an effective formal structure to enforce these norms.

11. F. Amon d'Aby, *La Côte d'Ivoire dans la cité africaine,* Paris, Larose, 1952, p. 36.

12. Similar phenomena were reported in other areas undergoing rapid social change. Lewis reports the growth in Somalia of a "tribalism founded on territorial ties [in] place of clanship," at least among the southern groups (I. M. Lewis, "Modern Political Movements in Somaliland, I," in *Africa,* XXVIII, July, 1958, p. 259). In the South Pacific, Mead observes: "Commentators on native life shook their heads, remarking that these natives were quite incapable of ever organizing beyond the narrowest tribal borders, overlooking the fact that terms like 'Solomons,' 'Sepiks' or 'Manus,' when applied in Rabaul, blanketed many tribal differences." (M. Mead, *New Lives for Old,* New York, Morrow, 1956, p. 79.)

The article by Max Gluckman, which appeared since this paper was delivered, makes the same point for British Central Africa. Cf. "Tribalism in British Central Africa," in *Cahiers d'Études Africaines,* I, Jan. 1960, pp. 55–70.

13. T. Hodgkin, "Letter to Dr. Biobaku," in *Odù,* No. 4, 1957, p. 42.

14. Rouch, *op. cit.,* p. 59.

15. A. Kobben, "Le planteur noir," in *Études éburnéennes,* V, 1956, p. 154.

16. The religious conversion is often very temporary. N'Goma observes: "L'Islam résiste mal à la transplantation des familles musulmanes de la ville à la campagne. On a remarqué que le citadin qui retourne à son groupement d'origine revient souvent au culte de la terre et des Esprits ancestraux." (A. N'Goma, "L'Islam noir," in T. Monod, ed., *Le Monde noir,* Présence africaine, No. 8–9, p. 342.) The motive for the original conversion may in part explain this rapid reconversion.

17. G. Savonnet observes in Thiès, Sénégal: "Le nom de Bambara est employé généralement pour désigner le Soudanais (qu'il soit Khassonké, Sarakollé, ou même Mossi). Ils acceptent d'autant plus volontiers cette dénomination que le Bambara (comme tout à l'heure le Wolof) fait figure de race évoluée par rapport à la leur propre." ("La Ville de Thiès," in *Études sénégalaises,* No. 6, 1955, p. 149.)

18. Epstein, *op. cit.,* p. 231.

19. Mercier notes: "Nombreux sont ceux qui, dans l'actuelle crise de chômage, ne peuvent se maintenir en ville que grâce à l'aide de leurs parents. Cela aboutit

à une forme spontanée d'assurance contre le chômage." (*Op. cit.,* p. 26.)

See also *passim,* K. A. Busia, *Report on a Social Survey of Sekondi-Takoradi,* Accra, Government Printer, 1950; I. Acquah, *Accra Survey,* London, University of London Press, 1958; O. Dollfus, "Conakry en 1951–1952. Etude humaine et économique," in *Études guinéennes,* X–XI, 1952, pp. 3–111; J. Lombard, "Cotonou, ville africaine," in *Études dahoméennes,* X, 1953.

20. G. Balandier, *Sociologie des Brazzavilles noires,* Paris, Armand Colin, 1955, p. 122.

21. Forde suggests that "This multiplicity of association, which is characteristic of the Westernization procedure, is likely to preclude the functional persistence of tribal organisations as autonomous units in the economic or political sphere." (*Op. cit.,* p. 485.)

22. T. Parsons, *The Social System,* New York, Free Press, 1951, p. 188.

23. D. Apter, *The Gold Coast in Transition,* Princeton, Princeton University Press, 1955, p. 127.

24. W. B. Birmingham and G. Jahoda, " A Pre-Election Survey in a Semi-Literate Society," in *Public Opinion Quarterly,* XIX, Summer, 1955, p. 152.

25. Glick explains the role of Chinese ethnic groups in Chinese assimilation into Hawaiian society in just these terms. (C. Glick, "The Relationship between Position and Status in the Assimilation of Chinese in Hawaii," in *American Journal of Sociology,* **XLVII,** September, 1952, pp. 667–679.)

26. P. Mercier, "Aspects des problèmes de stratification sociale dans l'Ouest Africain," in *Cahiers internationaux de sociologie,* XVII, 1954, pp. 47–55; Lombard, *op. cit.,* pp. 57–59.

27. M. Gluckman, *Custom and Conflict in Africa,* Oxford, Basil Blackwell, 1955, ch. 2.

28. Unless, of course, it compensate for lack of legitimation by increase of force as a mechanism of social control, which is the method used in Communist countries.

29. Parsons, *op. cit.,* p. 188.

30. Gluckman, *op. cit.,* p. 28.

31. Separatism, of course, arises as a problem only after a concept of a nation is created and at least partially internalized by a large number of the citizens.

32. J. S. Coleman, "The Character and Viability of African Political Systems," in W. Goldschmidt, ed., *The United States and Africa,* New York, The American Assembly, 1958, pp. 44–46.

33. There is normally room for only one truly nationalist party in a new nation. Other parties in West African countries, when they exist, tend to be formed on more particularistic (ethnic, religious, regional) bases.

# POLITICAL GROUPS IN LATIN AMERICA

## George I. Blanksten

I feel it necessary to begin with an attempt to define the term "political group" as used in this paper: it is a system of patterned or regular interaction among a number of individuals. The interaction is sufficiently patterned to permit the system to be viewed as a unit, and the action of the unit is directed toward some phase of the operation of government. Every political group has an interest. This is simply the central and continuing type of activity that gives the group its property as a system or a unit. Interest, then, is consistent with the

Reprinted from *The American Political Science Review,* Vol. LIII, No. 1 (March, 1959), pp. 106–127, by permission of The American Political Science Association.

A paper delivered at the 1958 Annual Meeting of the American Political Science Association, St. Louis, Missouri, September, 1958. Some of the material presented was developed in connection with my work with the SSRC Committee on Comparative Politics, to which I express my indebtedness.

observed pattern of interaction, and not contrary to it. "The interest and the group are the same phenomenon observed from slightly different positions, and an 'interest group' is a tautological expression. The interest is not a thing that exists apart from the activity or that controls activity."[1]

Let me add a few points regarding the relationship between the political group and its member individuals. If the group be regarded as the pattern of interaction among its members, then it follows that the group has an existence apart from that of the individuals associated with it. So a political group may have a history or a career of its own, distinguishable from those of the individuals participating in the interaction. Further, at any given time a single individual may take part in more groups than one; a person with such "overlapping memberships" may pursue different and, in some cases, contradictory interests.[2] Finally, the size of a group is not material here. No issue is raised by queries as to how large or small a political group may be. It is defined by the pattern of interaction, and not by the number of individuals contributing to it.

I

Two propositions about political groups should be obvious. First, the number of such groups functioning in a given political system is likely to be quite large. Second, a wide variety of types of groups exists, suggesting the feasibility of some system of classification. Several bases for classification are, of course, possible; let me advance one scheme here. Political groups may be regarded as (1) institutional, (2) associational, and (3) non-associational. Each of these categories, as used in the context of research in Latin American politics, calls for some discussion.

1. *Institutional* groups are formally constituted agencies, or segments of them, with established roles in a political system, roles usually recognized and generally accepted. It is useful to distinguish between two broad types of such institutional groups. One is the species which is formally and ostensibly assigned authoritative political functions—such as rule-making, rule-application, and rule-adjudication —and which performs them. In other words, formally established government is itself composed of a number of groups whose role it is to carry out political functions, and so some political groups can be studied in the examination of formal agencies of government. If to nothing else, American political scientists have been conventionally trained to direct their attention to such structures. Let me therefore pass by this category, pausing only to remark that, while we are still with the old familiar subject-matter of conventional political science—the formal structures of government—the group emphasis does imply a difference in the *manner* in which these agencies are studied. I plan to return to this proposition at a later point.

The second type of institutional political group needs to be examined more closely. This is the group which, while associated with a formal institution, performs a political function differing markedly from the established or ostensible role of the institution. The study of political groups of this type in Latin America is of high importance, and deserves priority among political inquiries in the area. Let me mention a few such institutional groups of this type in Latin America—not an exhaustive list, but rather a relatively small sample illustrative of one type of political organization to which the serious attention of research scholars is urgently invited.

The Roman Catholic Church is one of the major political groups of this sort in Latin America. Historically, Church and State were united in the Spanish tradition. This was true throughout the colonial period; indeed, the movement for separation of Church and State is, in a sense, a relatively recent development in the area. In most of the countries, the Church pursues political objectives, and in some of them its functions resemble those of a political party. Some Latin American political parties are essentially Church parties, as for example the Conservative parties of Colombia and Ecuador. Consider this statement by the Conservative Party of Ecuador of its *political* program:

Man is essentially a religious being and religion, consequently, is a natural phenomenon. . . . The end of man is God, whom he should serve and adore in order to enjoy after death the beatified possession of divinity. . . . The purpose of the state is to facilitate religious action so that its subjects will not lack the necessities of the spirit and will be able to obtain in the next life the happiness which can never be achieved in this.[3]

The power of the Church as a political group varies, of course, from country to country. It is perhaps strongest in Ecuador and weakest in Mexico, but there is no Latin American state in which the Church is not to be counted as a major political group.[4] It has, of course, been studied from several points of view, but published assessments of it in this capacity are rare.

Similarly, there are very few studies of the armed forces, particularly the armies, of Latin America as political groups. This is a curious indictment of political scientists interested in the area, since militarism has long been recognized as a fundamental characteristic of Latin American politics. "The last step in a military career is the presidency of the republic"[5] is a well-known and frequently practiced precept in the area. Rather than the defense of the community, the basic functions of the Latin American military lie in domestic politics. Everywhere high-ranking army officers are important politicians; everywhere the military influence provides a species of backdrop for politics. Generally this is more true of the armies than of the other armed services, although in a few of the countries—notably Argentina[6] and Paraguay—the navies also operate as significant political groups. Political studies of the Latin American armed services are sorely needed. Topics especially requiring investigation include the process of political clique-formation among military and naval officers, and the relationship between militarism and the class system. Certain military ranks—*e.g.,* major and lieutenant-colonel—appear to be of peculiarly critical political significance.

Few studies, again, have been made of bureaucracy in Latin America, and consequently little can be said of the roles of public workers as political groups. In some of the countries government work, like other types of occupations, is organized on the basis of part-time jobs. Moreover, few of the republics have developed effective merit systems of civil service, and a spoils system is generally characteristic of the area. These considerations suggest patterns of action differing from those to be found in Western Europe or the United States. Latin American government workers no doubt may be regarded as political groups. However, the current state of research on this problem does not permit evaluation at this time of their full significance.

2. Let me now turn to the *associational,* or second major category, of political groups. These are consciously organized associations which lie outside the formal structure of government and which nevertheless include the performance of political functions among their stated objectives. Generally speaking, associational groups carry out less authoritative functions than the institutional organizations. That is to say, this second category tends to concentrate its activity on such matters as political recruitment, interest articulation, interest aggregation, and —in some cases—political communication, rather than on more authoritative political functions such as rule-making, rule-application, and rule-adjudication.

Two chief types of associational groups may be distinguished. The differences are roughly similar to those, familiar to students of politics in the United States, between political parties and pressure groups. However, the distinction sought here is not quite the same as that. In the United States and in many of the countries of Western Europe, "political parties tend to be free of ideological rigidity, and are aggregative, that is, seek to form the largest possible interest group coalitions by offering acceptable choices of political personnel and public policy."[7] On the other hand, pressure groups in those same so-called "Western" systems "articulate political demands in the society, seek support for these demands among other groups by advocacy and bargaining, and attempt to transform these demands into authoritative public policy by influencing the choice of political personnel, and the various processes of public policy making and enforcement."[8] In many Latin American countries, particularly in those with the more underdeveloped economies—and, no doubt, in most of the so-called "non-Western" political systems—the dividing line does not fall in quite the same place. Political parties tend to be more non-aggregative than aggregative, and some of the functions of the other associational groups include activities usually restricted to political parties in the United States and in some of the Western European systems.

Despite the fact that political parties have long been included among the accepted concerns of political scientists, it remains a curious circumstance that very little research has been done on these organizations in Latin America. Indeed, only one political party in the area has been the object of a full-blown monographic study.[9] "The field is one which needs a vast amount of spade work of a primary sort and on top of that additional synthesis in order to put the raw materials in proper arrangement and perspective," Russell H. Fitzgibbon has said. "I commend the field of Latin-American political parties to a whole generation of prospective graduate students in political science."[10]

Not only the party systems, but also the parties themselves, are of various types in Latin America. Let me once again, therefore, undertake the task of classification. Although the existing literature of political science contains a number of fairly elaborate attempts at categorization, nothing more complicated is necessary for the present purpose than a simple dichotomy separating one-party systems from competitive party systems. Both types are to be found in Latin America.

The one-party system, of course, is the situation in which a single political party holds an effective monopoly of public power and controls access to government office. In some one-party systems, this may be provided for by law, other political parties being considered illegal or subversive; in another type of one-party system, other parties may exist legally but—for reasons largely unrelated to legal questions or government coercion—find themselves unable to challenge effectively the dominant party's hold on the system.

Thus conceived, two varieties of dominant parties hold power in the one-party systems of Latin America. One may be dubbed the "dictatorial" party. Where it exists, an official attempt is made to obscure the distinction between the party in power and the government of the country, and so to render opposition to the party virtually synonymous with treason against the state. By definition, then, the party in power being the only legal party, any others are not merely in opposition but in rebellion, open or covert. The best current Latin American illustration of this type of party is to be found in the Dominican Republic. Such a system has also operated in Venezuela. Paraguay's arrangement is a borderline case—other parties than the *Colorado* are theoretically legal, but the price of participating in them is often imprisonment or exile.

The other type of group holding power in a one-party system may be designated as the "dominant non-dictatorial" party. In this case, one party holds a monopoly of political power in the sense that it is victorious in virtually all elections, but other parties are legal and do exist. This is somewhat similar to the stereotype—but I beg you not to hold me responsible for its validity—of the "Solid South" or of northern rural areas in the United States. The leading Latin American case is in Mexico, where the Party of Revolutionary Institutions (PRI[11]) is without a serious rival. Other Mexican parties exist legally, but they exercise virtually no authority in government.[12] Uruguay's system may also be included here, if we agree with Fitzgibbon that it cannot be regarded as a two-party affair.[13] Further, it has been noted that the situation in Paraguay's case is borderline—if one Paraguayan foot is in the "dictatorial" party camp, the other is with the "dominant non-dictatorial" party.

Competitive party systems exist where two or more parties, none of them a dominant or "official" organization, contend among themselves. In general, there are two classes of competitive systems, multi-party and two-party arrangements.

A multi-party system contains three or more major political parties, normally making it impossible for any one of them to command a majority of the seats in a representative assembly. Politics in these systems frequently operates through coalitions or blocs involving two or more parties, and these understandings are designed to produce working majorities. Latin America's best illustration of a multi-party system is to be found in Chile, where there are at least six major political parties, none of which controls a legislative majority.[14] Multi-party arrangements also exist in Argentina, Bolivia, Brazil, Costa Rica, Cuba, Guatemala, Panama, and Peru.

Two-party systems contain two major political parties sufficiently matched in strength to permit their alternation in power. "Third" or "minor" parties are legal in these systems, but are rarely serious rivals at the polls of the two major parties. Thus conceived, two-party systems are rare in Latin America; indeed, they are rare outside the English-speaking world. The best Latin American illustration is to be found in Colombia, where the Conservative and Liberal Parties, roughly evenly matched, have historically alternated in power. Uruguay also has two major political parties— the Colorados and the Blancos—but there is some question as to whether this is a clear case of a two-party system. Fitzgibbon, for example, believes that, since the Colorados have been victorious in almost all national elections, it cannot be said that Uruguay's is a true two-party arrangement.[15]

Most of the major parties in the competitive systems of Latin America are what might be called traditional political parties. In general, they have two major characteristics. First, the issues which concern them have historically troubled Latin Americans as long-range political problems of their respective countries. Primarily, these issues have been the questions of land tenure and the temporal role of the Roman Catholic Church. Second, the traditional parties draw their membership, in terms of the class systems of Latin America, primarily from the upper classes; the other classes—often involving majorities of national populations—virtually are excluded from direct participation in these parties. The traditional parties may be roughly branded as conservative or liberal. Conservative parties generally defend the interests of the large land-owners and advocate an expanded temporal role for the Church, sometimes including union of Church and State. Conservative parties have been in power in most of the countries of Latin America during most of the years of their respective national histories. Representative conservative parties include the Conservative Party of Argentina, the Conservatives of Colombia, the Conservative Party of Ecuador, the Blanco Party of Uruguay, and COPEI of Venezuela. Liberal parties, on the other hand, have generally advocated some kind of land reform, separation of Church and State, and a general reduction in the temporal influence of the Church. Representative liberal parties are the Radical Party of Argentina, the Radicals of Chile, the Liberals of Colombia, the Radical-Liberal Party of Ecuador, and the Colorados of Uruguay.

The parties whch participate in the competitive systems of Latin America may be classed as pragmatic, ideological, and particularistic. Pragmatic parties are those which make no major ideological or philosophical demands upon their membership. Such parties are far more interested in commanding the votes than the minds of their followers, who may enter or leave the pragmatic groups without benefit of the trauma of ideological, philosophical, or religious conversion on such occasions.

Pragmatic parties may be broadly or narrowly based, depending on how large a sector of the politically articulate population the group appeals to. Perhaps Latin America's best illustrations of the broad-based pragmatic party are the Argentine Radical Party (UCR[16]) and the Chilean Radical Party. The UCR has endeavored with some success to appeal for the electoral support of organized labor, commercial and industrial interests, associations of university students, and professional and intellectual organizations. Indeed, under the leadership of Arturo Frondizi in the presidential election of 1958, the UCR, which had bitterly fought the Perón dictatorship (1946–1955), successfully campaigned for the votes of those who had formerly supported Perón! In Chile, the Radical Party has joined together university students, labor organizations, teachers' associations, and the smaller commercial and industrial interests.

Narrow-based pragmatic parties are more numerous in the area. In general, these are of two types —personalistic and ad hoc parties. Personalistic parties are an outgrowth of personalismo, a long-standing ingredient of Latin American politics. Personalismo may be defined as the tendency to follow or oppose a political leader on personality rather than ideological grounds, through personal, individual, and family motivations rather than because of an impersonal political idea or program. This historic attribute of the politics of the area has been noted by many students of Latin America. Pierson and Gil, for example, point to "the high value placed on the individual and personal leadership," promoting "a disposition to vote for the man rather than the party or the platform."[17] Another student has said: "From earliest days the Latin Americans

. . . have always been more interested in their public men than in their public policies. They have tended to follow colorful leaders, to the subordination of issues. . . . A picturesque demagogue is virtually assured a large following."[18]

Latin Americans like to say—and this exaggerates the situation—that "Every 'ism' is a somebody-ism." Personalist parties are "Somebody—ist" groups organized in support of the political ambitions of strong personal leaders. Paraguay has its *Franquista* Party, composed of the followers of General Rafael Franco;[19] Brazil had a *Querimista*[20] party; Ecuador a *Velasquista* organization, made up of the followers of Dr. José María Velasco Ibarra; and Uruguay a *Batllista* "faction," founded by the nineteenth-century statesman, José Batlle y Ordóñez. There is some evidence that personalist parties are currently declining in number and influence in Latin America.

Finally, there are *ad hoc* parties. These are fluid organizations created for the purpose of achieving short-range political objectives and disappearing when these ends have been accomplished or defeated. These parties are particularly important in the politics of Bolivia, Ecuador, and Paraguay. "In these times," a Bolivian wrote in 1942, "nothing is simpler than to found a political party. To form a political party only three people and one object are necessary: a president, a vice president, a secretary, and a rubber stamp. The party can get along even without the vice president and the secretary. . . . There have been cases in which the existence of only the rubber stamp has been sufficient."[21] Parties of this type are especially important in times of political instability and so-called revolution, times not infrequent in a number of the countries of Latin America.

Ideological parties are also to be counted among the actors in the competitive party systems of the area. Communist parties, for example, exist throughout the Americas. The most important Communist organizations are in Argentina; Bolivia, where the party has long been known as the Leftist Revolutionary Party (PIR[22]); Brazil; Chile; Cuba; Guatemala; and Mexico, where the group is called the Popular Party. Although the Mexican party system is not a competitive one, the Mexican Communists are nevertheless worth mentioning here. Despite indications that the party is small and weak from the standpoint of its influence upon domestic politics in Mexico, the Communist organization in that country does perform a noteworthy international function in serving as a point of liaison, and as an informational clearing-house, between European Communists and those of Central America and the Caribbean islands. Meetings of the Communist leaders of the smaller countries of Middle America are occasionally held in Mexico.[23]

Socialist parties also exist in virtually all of the countries of Latin America. The membership of these parties is generally dominated by middle-class intellectuals with a strong interest in Marxism. Despite their avowed interest in the problems of the working classes, the Socialists of Latin America have, in fact, developed little genuine influence with the masses. In country after country, the Socialists "have become increasingly doctrinaire, academic, and intellectualized."[24] Ray Josephs once remarked that "the Socialist weakness lies in addicton to theory and philosophy and what we might call their lack of practical, sound common sense."[25] It need hardly be added that Socialists have never been in power any appreciable length of time in any country of Latin America.

A number of Church-oriented parties are to be found in the area, and these too may be regarded as largely ideological parties. The best current illustrations are the Conservative parties of Colombia and Ecuador. Heavily Catholic in doctrinal orientation, Church parties have participated in most of the competitive systems of Latin America during the past century. Not since the regime of Gabriel García Borena in Ecuador (1859–1875) has a Church group been the dominant party in a one-party system. In that case, religious intolerance was revived, only practicing Catholics were permitted to be citizens of the country—then called the "Republic of the Sacred Heart"—and government was heavily authoritarian in character.[26]

Nationalist groups also may be counted among the ideological parties of Latin America. The typical Latin American nationalist party is narrow-based, addressing a concerted appeal to a small sector of the society in which it operates. Indeed, it is not unusual to find a given country in the area with two or more small nationalist parties functioning in rivalry relationships with each other. While anti-clerical nationalists are not unheard of—one such group once effectively employed "We are Ecuadorans, not Romans!" as its slogan— the nationalist parties more frequently embrace the Church, demand religious intolerance, oppose secularization, and attempt to eradicate foreign influence in their countries. Often such parties are active centers of anti-Semitism. In recent times the most important nationalist parties of Latin America—all of them narrow-based rather than comprehensive—have operated in Argentina, Bolivia, Paraguay, and Venezuela.

The area also has its share of Fascist parties. For many of these, "Fascist-like" or "quasi-Fascist" would probably be better designations, since they generally combine selected elements of Fascist ideology with enough indigenous Latin American ingredients to render the organizations difficult to equate with European Fascist parties. During World War II, most of them pressed pro-Axis foreign policy objectives in Latin America. Representative parties of this type are the *Peronista* Party of Argentina, the Nationalist Revolutionary Movement (MNR[27]) of Bolivia, the Integralist Party of Brazil, the *Nacista* Party of Chile, and the National Sinarquist Union of Mexico.

Also occupying a significant place on the roster of the area's ideological parties are the agrarian-populistic group. In Latin America, these have come to be called *Aprista* parties. They have two distinguishing characteristics. First, they seek far-reaching social and economic change, usually including radical land reform and the integration of the lower classes into the political process. Indeed, there is a greater percentage of lower-class adherents in the membership of *Aprista* groups than in any other type of Latin American party. Second, *Aprismo* is indigenous to the area. Such international connections as the movement has—and they are not many—are entirely within Latin America. The chief prototype of this class of political party is the celebrated *Aprista* Party or APRA of Peru. Other *Aprista* parties include *Acción Democrática* of Venezuela, the *Auténtico* Party of Cuba, the National Liberation Party of Costa Rica, and, in a sense, Mexico's PRI.[28]

Particularistic parties have on occasion appeared in the competitive systems of Latin America, although there is no clear illustration of the type operating in the area today. Such organizations, concerned in a separatist fashion with selected ethnic groups or regions and including some form of secession among statements of political objectives, have from time to time filled major roles in the Americas. Indeed, this is one of the reasons why what were once only eight Spanish colonies are now as many as eighteen independent states. In the historic past, particularist parties have been led by such personalities as General José Antonio Páez, who directed the secession of Venezuela from Gran Colombia; General Juan José Flores, who presided over the separation of Ecuador from the same entity; and Dr. Amador, prominent in the detachment of the isthmus of Panama from Colombia. Particularistic parties were also active in the reduction of the former Central American Confederation to its present five separate heirs. So far as the contemporary scene is concerned, although no major particularistic parties are functioning in the area, there are significant evidences of the presence of some of the ingredients of which such groups may be fashioned. In Brazil, for example, the two states of São Paulo and Minas Gerais, which had stubbornly opposed the regimes of President Getulio Vargas (1930–1945; 1951–1954), have fallen into a political collaboration against other sections of the country which approximates particularism. Again, in the countries where regionalism is a major political force—such as Peru, Ecuador, and Bolivia—there is a tendency for political parties to become regionally based. The record of the past

and the current scene combine to suggest that it might not be unreasonable to expect the reappearance of such organizations in the area from time to time in the future.

I attempted earlier to distinguish between two chief types of associational political groups, offering parties as the first of them. I turn now to the second type, roughly resembling what are called pressure groups in the United States. In Latin America these organizations perform some of the functions usually restricted in the "North American" system to political parties. Without presenting an exhaustive list I shall mention a number of them to illustrate their functions in the political systems of Latin America.

Associations of landowners, in one form or another, exist in all countries of the area. In view of the significant role of the land in the economy of Latin America and the predominance of feudal-like systems of land tenure, these groups are of high importance. In Argentina, for example, fewer than two thousand families' landholdings constitute a combined area greater than England, Belgium and the Netherlands put together; and statistics produced by some of the American republics indicate that approximately three-fourths of their respective land surfaces are owned by about two percent of their respective populations. Landowning groups wield political as well as economic power. The best-known landowners' association in the area is the Argentine Jockey Club; similar organizations operate in most of the other states.

Foreign companies function as political groups in some of the countries. In northern Latin America —particularly in the Caribbean area—United States corporations are prominent among these groups. Excellent illustrations can be found in the United Fruit Company as it operates in a number of the states of Central America, and in the influence of a number of oil companies in Venezuelan politics. In southern South America—Argentina, Uruguay, Paraguay, and Chile—British firms function in a similar fashion.

Labor organizations, though still small, are of growing importance as Latin American groups. The role of these organizations is expanding as industrialization begins to take hold in the area. From the standpoint of their functions as political groups, the most important labor organizations in the area are Argentina's CGT,[29] Chile's CTCH,[30] Cuba's CTC,[31] and Mexico's CTM.[32] Organized labor in Latin America is, in general, quite politically articulate, and its support has long been sought by Socialist parties.

Student associations are vigorously active groups in all of the countries involved. Hear this account of student life in the area: "The . . . university, traditionally, is a miniature battleground of national politics. Students strike, riot, and stage political demonstrations on the slightest provocation."[33] Politics "becomes a passion that invades and confuses everything. I myself remember many postponed examinations; many study hours disturbed; countless meetings, discussions, strikes—a whole year lost in them—elections that ended with gunfire. . . ."[34] As political groups, student associations are far more significant in Latin America than in the United States.

Professional associations should also be counted among the active groups of the area. Lawyers' associations are perhaps the oldest of these. With the growing economic development of Latin America, associations of engineers, still small, are of rising importance. Business groups are also small in the area. However, these may be expected to grow in significance as industrialization and economic development continue.

Veterans' associations, important in the United States, are of little significance as Latin American political groups, except in Bolivia and Paraguay. In both countries, organizations of veterans of the Chaco War (1928–1935) have become major pressure groups. In Bolivia, such a group served as the nucleus for the MNR party. In the absence of systematic studies, however, any explanatory statement at this point can be little more than conjecture. My guess—and it is only that—is that in most of Latin America such influence as veterans' groups might have had has been more than engulfed by the groups representing the armed services. International wars producing veterans are, after all, rare in contemporary Latin America; on the other hand, militarism and the military are ever-present.

3. Finally, some discussion of the *non-associational* category of political groups is in order. These are not formally or consciously organized. Indeed, they may be regarded more as latent or potential than as currently functioning political groups, for the non-associational variety is far less structured than the institutional and associational types. In Latin America, non-associational interests tend to coalesce around such symbols as class, status, ethnic groups, kinship and lineage, and regionalism.

The class systems are fairly rigid in most of the countries of the area. Classes, of course, are not formally or consciously organized groups; yet significant political interests arise from them. With some variations from country to country in Latin America, the typical class system is composed of three levels. The highest class is usually referred to as the creoles or "whites"; the middle group is known as the *mestizos* or, in some countries, *cholos;* and, in the countries with large Indian populations, these have constituted the lowest class. Scholars who have examined these classes in Latin America have devoted more attention to the creoles, and to the Indians, than they have to the *mestizos* or *cholos*.

The highest class—creoles or "whites"—are the most politically articulate of the three, and in most of the countries of the area their interests—the preservation of the systems of land tenure, the control of the Church and of the high military ranks, and the maintenance of a European rather than an indigenous cultural orientation—are the best-protected and espoused. Where commercialization and industrialization have taken hold, new interests are created, primarily among the "whites." In some of the countries, this has a divisive effect upon "white" interests, for land ownership is sometimes held to be threatened by commercialization and industrialization. Conscious of themselves as the ruling group in most of the countries of the area, the "whites" share an interest in the avoidance of true revolution and, in general, oppose political reforms believed to imperil their dominant position.

Less is known about the *mestizo* or *cholo*. A detribalized Indian but not yet a "white," the *mestizo* accounts for over 30% of the populations of some of the countries. He is not politically articulate, and rarely organizes. He is interested in working his way into the "white" group, and usually, in severing his ties with the Indians. The *mestizo* is frequently employed as an artisan or a tradesman. In some of the countries of the area, the *mestizo* is an important source of the labor supply. As a class, the *mestizos* no doubt have interests. But given the paucity of available data, little more can be said here regarding their non-associational interests without risking the hazards of a major excursion into the realm of speculation.

About the Indian, entire libraries have been written. Indian communities and villages are tightly organized, and the Indians feel strong loyalties to them, but the Indian class as a whole is not organized in any of the Latin American countries. In general, the Indians resist incursion upon their way of life by the "whites." They desire, as they frequently put it, to be left alone. They seek decentralized, loosely organized, or inefficiently administered government, so that the number of "white" government officials entering their communities bearing rules and regulations from the national capital will be held to a minimum. Having normally a deep love for their villages and communities, they strongly resist resettlement programs involving relocation of the lower classes. Typically, the Indian does not own much, if any, land. Many writers have argued that in Latin America the Indian problem is basically a land problem, and have urged land reform programs which would deliver holdings to Indian ownership.[35] The Indians, however, have rarely expressed this sentiment themselves, and have been slow to respond to land redistribution programs. Being quite inarticulate politically, they rarely communicate their desires to the "white" officials of the governments which rule them.

Interests also arise from the concept of status,

especially within the "white" groups. In colonial times the upper class was acrimoniously divided within itself, with the creoles—persons born in the colonies—pitted against the *peninsulares*—born in Europe—who enjoyed higher status. Indeed, this intra-class struggle was one of the factors giving alignment to some of the fighting during the wars of independence. Since then, the *peninsulares* have dropped from the Latin American class structure, but the concept of the "old families" or "good families" remains. These—when they can establish themselves as such—enjoy considerable prestige within the ruling class. Although the "whites" are at least as racially mixed as any other group in Latin American society, the "old families" are constantly engaged in heraldic research designed to demonstrate their unmixed Spanish descent. To be accepted as an "old" or "good" family is to be the aristocracy of the aristocracy. Families which have achieved this enviable position have a strong interest in preserving those elements of the system —particularly the older patterns of land tenure— that lend security to the prestige system, and in making it difficult for "new" families to become "old" and share the higher status.

Again, in view of the paucity of research on the *mestizo* or *cholo* group, little can be said here of the prestige patterns within that class. In general, however, the *mestizos* strive to become "whites."

Status is at least as important among the Indians as it is among the "whites." A significant difference, however, should be noted. Whereas those who acquire high prestige among the "whites" enjoy it on a national—and, in some cases, international— basis, status among the Indians has meaning only on a local village or community level. As in the case of the "whites," status among the Indians rests on ascriptive more than achievement considerations. Village elders, and their relatives, enjoy prestige, as do witch doctors and medicine men. To hold high status in the Indian community is to exercise some power—frequently of government —within it, and those who have this prestige are interested in preserving it and preventing its adulteration through too-easy access of other Indians to the status positions.[36]

Non-associational interests also arise among some ethnic groups in Latin America. For example, Negroes—numerous in the Caribbean island republics, and in some parts of Brazil—have developed strong interests though they emerge on an unorganized basis. So, too, have a number of the European immigrant groups, notably the Italians, Germans, Spaniards, and Jews. The European immigrant groups are normally more articulate than many of the indigenous groups, particularly the Indians and *mestizos,* and generally have developed interests, usually directed toward the preservation of their social and economic positions in society.

Patterns of kinships and lineage also produce systems of non-associational interest in Latin America. This is especially true among the "whites" and Indians; the *mestizos* again, for the time being at least, stand as an unknown quantity. Among the "whites," reference has already been made to the "old" or "good" families. High values are assigned to belonging to them, or if that is impossible, to being somehow related or connected to them. The extensive use made of, and the exaggerated importance given to, the famous letters of introduction among the "whites" have frequently reached the proportions of a joke. A letter of introduction from a well-known member of an established "good family" is, in many of the countries, indispensable to the candidate seeking employment or some other favor from government. "The municipal department had become a perfect teeming house of *recomendados*—persons for whom jobs had been found whether jobs were to be had or not," an observer has said of local politics among the "whites." "In the old days of the Deliberative Council, it used to be a standing joke that business offices could be wall-papered with the letters of introduction given to job applicants."[37] Although this particular reference is to local government, the practice is general.

Three generalizations can safely be made regarding the role of kinship and lineage among the Indians of Latin America. First, as a determiner of interest, it is even more basic in this class than among the "whites." Next, in many Indian groups, kinship and lineage are more centrally and directly related to politics and government than is true of the upper classes. Finally, in contrast to the situation among the "whites," this is important among the Indians on the local—village and community—level to the almost total exclusion of other levels of politics. Unfortunately, these are virtually the only generalizations on the subject that can be made with assurance. Practices in this field vary widely among the indigenous peoples of the area, for two major reasons. First, it is in many senses unrealistic to lump all of the Indian groups together and treat them as a unit. These people have differing cultures, languages, and social, economic, and political systems. Secondly, the extent to which "white" practices have penetrated Indian systems varies considerably, not only from country to country but also within many of the countries. Kinship and lineage functioned as a major determinant of political station and interest in the overwhelming majority of the indigenous Indian systems of Latin America. In some areas, where these systems have been relatively little interfered with by the "whites," this is still true. Indeed, instances exist in which Indian systems of village government continue to function undisturbed despite the fact that the "whites" have promulgated written constitutions providing for very different patterns of local government.[38] But there are cases—often in other regions of the same countries—where acculturation has taken the form of

Indian responses to "white" influences which have fundamentally altered, or even obliterated, the indigenous practices. A number of monographic studies of such cases in specific Indian communities have been published. Short of reporting these detailed findings, there is little alternative to stressing the importance of kinship and lineage and emphasizing that, as a rule, Indian groups are markedly less politically articulate than the upper class. Thus, this type of interest, while often more crucial in the lower classes, typically receives far less of a hearing when emanating from the Indians than from the "whites."

Non-associational interests also arise on regional bases. Regionalism is characteristically a major feature of the pattern of Latin American politics. It stems not only from the role of regional loyalties in Spanish culture, but also from the historic difficulty of transportation and communication across the mountains and through the jungles of Latin America. Living in a species of isolation from each other, the regions of Latin America have developed their own sets of interests. In Peru and Ecuador, for example, the regions known in each country as the "Coast" (located west of the Andes Mountains) are receptive to secularization and commercialization, fostering commercial and industrial interests; whereas, in both countries, the "Sierra" (lying between the eastern and western cordilleras of the Andes), less secularized, cultivates the interests of the landowners and the Church. In both countries, the sometimes bitter conflict of interests between these regions is a major element of the national political patterns. In Argentina, to cite another illustration, the interests of the landowners and the Church in the "interior" have historically been pitted against those of the secularized and far more commercialized metropolitan region of Greater Buenos Aires. A second major aspect of the regional base of non-associational interests arises from the process of urbanization. A number of the Latin American countries have had to cope with the problem of *la cabeza de Goliat* (Goliath's head): a giant metropolitan center (usually the capital city) rests on the dwarflike body of the rest of the country. In some cases as much as half the national population lives in the one large city. The secular, commercial, and sometimes industrial interests of the metropolis are in chronic conflict with those of the religious and quasi-feudal "interior." In Latin America, the major illustrations of this pattern are to be found in Argentina, Cuba, and Uruguay.

## II

My concluding task is to attempt to show that this sort of group analysis has some merit and may stimulate some productive new departures for politi- cal scientists interested in the field of comparative politics. Let me first enter two disclaimers: novelty is no guarantee of merit, and an interest in political groups is not new among American political scientists. Nevertheless, previous expressions of that interest have not, in general, included two elements significant here. One of these is the application of group analysis to foreign political systems, and the other is its use in comparative studies. Notwithstanding the regrettable tendency within our profession to regard "foreign governments," "comparative government," and "comparative politics" as synonymous terms, the study of political groups in foreign systems and in comparative analysis are two separate and distinct matters. Let me, then, turn my attention to the first of them. The bulk of the work —particularly the earlier work—done by "North American" political scientists in Latin America has generally involved, in one way or another, the description of formal structures of governments. It has often taken the form of translating the written constitutions of the various countries and abstracting or summarizing these legal provisions. This type of research has its uses, for some familiarity with constitutional forms is, if not necessary, at least helpful, in the analysis of other political problems. But while there are always new Latin American constitutions to be translated and summarized —and I will even concede that there is room, in the off years when no new constitutions are promulgated in the area, for the improvement of the translations and summaries of the older texts—this type of activity reaches the point of diminishing returns. Indeed, I will argue that we long ago arrived there.

It is, in short, necessary to work with more than the formal structures in Latin America. Again, this is not a new point. For some years Latin Americanists have been looking for non-constitutional materials. Seduced by the anthropologists, many of us have experimented with cultural approaches. We have become enamored of political styles arising from alien cultures. We have examined the class systems and made much of the "whites" while we neglected the *mestizos* in order to carry the torch for the downtrodden Indians, until it took a Moisés Sáenz to tell us that "in order to be fair to the Indian, it is not necessary to stick feathers in our hair or wield a war club."[39]

There are considerable advantages in examining political groups in Latin America as alternative non-constitutional materials. Beginning with the most unstructured considerations, I might start by pointing out that this is a major area of our ignorance in Latin American politics. We know virtually nothing about the area's political groups, and there is some virtue in our beginning to acquire that knowledge for its own sake.

On a little more structured level, it can also be said that research on political groups would help us to understand problems which have long concerned us in Latin American politics. Take the Argentine case as an example. I choose Argentina because it has long been regarded as one of the more important of the countries of the area and because much research has been done there; more articles and books have been published by "North American" scholars about that country than about most other Latin American states. On June 4, 1943, the Argentine government was overthrown in one of the area's most significant so-called "revolutions" of recent times. Who or what was directly responsible for the revolution? A political group: a clique of army officers known as GOU[40] or "colonels' clique." What was the GOU? Where did it come from? How did it operate? Nothing in all our research—none of the product of our long-standing interest in Argentina, nothing in all our scholarly articles and books—could suggest answers to such questions. So far as the existing political science was concerned, the Perón revolution came from nowhere.

If we agree that the Perón coup was one of the more significant political developments of our time in one of the most important countries in the area, how did it happen that the GOU took the area specialists by surprise? How does it happen that we have let militarism and the process of military clique-formation, one of the more basic characteristics of Latin American politics, go unstudied? Why is our ignorance so inclusive that it covers not only the military but most of the other political groups in Latin America? If it is argued that this is an unfair challenge, that as political scientists we have been trained to examine institutions rather than the amorphous entities embraced by the unfamiliar jargon of associational and non-associational groups, I reply that the GOU was an institutional group, part and parcel of the formal structure of government, and nothing so exotic as associational or non-associational.

How many more translations and summaries of Argentina's Constitution of 1853, as remarkable as that celebrated document may be, can we afford to make before we undertake the analysis of the political groups of that and other Latin American countries? Or, to put the question in another way, which route to the mainsprings of the area's politics is more fruitful for the scholar—to wait for GOU after mysterious GOU to ambush him, or to seize the initiative in seeking out these groups, tracking them even to associational and non-associational sources? No doubt this has policy implications as well, but they are not my concern at the moment. My point has been the relatively simple one that the study of political groups in Latin America would not only close considerable gaps in our knowledge of the area but also improve significantly our understanding of its politics.

This is among the less structured of the merits of the study of groups. To move to the arena of comparative analysis is to enter a more sophisticated level. Before taking that step, let me reiterate the high importance of the distinction between comparative politics and the study of foreign governments. In comparative analysis, as I understand it, an attempt is made, through precise study of two or more objects, to isolate and identify their similarities and differences. The techniques of comparative study may be, of course, of varying degrees of complexity. I have heard it claimed for some of the more complex modes of comparative analysis that through them similarities and differences may be not only isolated and identified but also explained. I am not myself convinced that the comparative method alone can do the explanatory job. Isolation, definition, and identification of properties can be handled in this way, but the task of explanation seems to require that the comparative method, where used, be assisted or supplemented by additional modes of analysis.

One of the constantly recurring problems in the comparative study of politics is the circumstance that in this field we generally deal with the so-called "macro" materials—that is, with large units or universes such as entire countries or political systems. In doing this, so far as precision is concerned, we are at a decided disadvantage in comparison with the scholar engaged in a "micro" analysis of a small unit which lends itself more rapidly to precise study. No doubt, this is one reason why much of what is called "comparative government" consists of roughly parallel descriptions of two or more "macro" systems, without benefit of comparative analysis. It is not easy—and some may think it impossible—to handle two or more systems in a fashion permitting them to be compared precisely. Countries, cultures, even systems of government, appear in many ways to be unique as large universes. Argentines behave differently from Cubans; even the task of comparing the Mexican congress with the Chilean national legislature presents formidable pitfalls.

One solution to this "macro" problem might involve a conceptualization permitting the abstracting of precisely defined components common to two or more large universes, components which could then be subjected to comparative analysis with some promise of precision. Political groups are among the forms such components might take. So it might be claimed for the introduction of political groups into comparative analysis that it has the advantage of furnishing a method of abstraction rendering political systems more precisely comparable, thereby making comparative analysis more manageable. Indeed, it could be argued that this method creates the possibility of comparative studies of large units which would be intrinsically incomparable in the absence of some such abstractive device.

Another potentially significant contribution of

the group emphasis to comparative politics lies in the examination of structures in terms of their political functions. Structural-functional analysis holds some promise of advancing comparative studies. Consider a relatively simple variation of it. If we were to devise a list of the functions performed in all political systems, such as political recruitment, communication, interest-articulation, interest-aggregation, rule-making, rule-application, and rule-adjudication, the group focus might serve to locate the structures performing each of these functions in the systems being compared. These structures, which are groups, might then be analyzed for their political functions.

Suppose, for example, a comparative analysis of the political systems of Chile, Mexico, and Paraguay. The national legislatures of these three countries are given similar names—"Congress" in Chile and Mexico, and "Chamber of Representatives" in Paraguay—by the constitutions, which contain a few additional similar stipulations about the legislatures. But the bases for comparative analysis end here. If, on the other hand, we seek the groups which perform the political functions common to the three systems, we might well be on more significant ground. For example, I suspect that much of the rule-making function is indeed performed in the Congress in Chile, but in the PRI, the dominant non-dictatorial party, in Mexico, and by a military clique within the Asunción garrison in Paraguay. If that is so, a comparative analysis of the Chilean Congress, the Mexican PRI, and the Paraguayan military should give us a far more significant result, and a deeper insight into the three political systems, than a comparison of the three national legislatures. Thus, the second branch of my case for the use of political groups in comparative analysis is the argument that it would not only give us greater precision but would also permit us to direct that accuracy to more important propositions about the actual functioning of political systems.

Further, the group emphasis may be expected to make a major contribution in a field of rapidly growing concern in comparative politics, the problems of underdeveloped areas. "Underdevelopment" or "underdevelopedness" has been chiefly an economic concept related primarily to technology. The proposition central to this concept can be demonstrated in comparing two models of economic systems, one "advanced" or "developed," and the other underdeveloped. In the "advanced" model, a given input into the productive process (capital, raw materials, man-hours of labor, etc.) is subjected to a given technology, from which a measurable production emerges. In the underdeveloped model, the same input may go into the productive process, but is subjected to a less efficient technology, and so results in a measurably lower level of production characterized by low standards of living. Owing largely to technological problems affecting the state

of their productive arts, the underdeveloped areas present us with a challenge.

These underdeveloped areas, of course, include much of Latin America. A major key to the problem lies in technological change, to raise the levels of production, and so the standards of living, in the underdeveloped areas. A number of public programs based on this solution are currently in operation. A modest sector of the foreign aid programs of the United States—variously known from administration to administration as technical assistance, "Point Four," and technical cooperation—has as its objective the stimulation of technological change in the underdeveloped areas. The technical assistance programs of the United Nations are similarly conceived. All of the Latin American countries participate in the foreign aid programs of the United States; some of these countries are also involved in United Nations technical assistance. Partly on account of these programs technological change and economic development should be counted among the more significant movements afoot in contemporary Latin America. In some of the countries—witness Brazil and Mexico—the rapidity of this change is little short of spectacular.

Thus far the economist has done the work for us. But the political scientist interested in Latin America—or any other underdeveloped area—cannot much longer neglect the major analytical task awaiting him there. It is widely assumed that there is some interplay between levels of economic development on the one hand and political systems on the other. It is believed that the politics of say, Bolivia, Haiti, and Paraguay are integrally tied to their underdeveloped economies, and that, as these change, so must their political systems. Again we have policy implications: many of the foreign aid programs of both the United States and the United Nations are based on the assumption that political change goes hand in hand with economic development, but others, in the name of prudence, take recipient institutions as they find them.

Yet all this is still in the realm of belief, of assumption, and even of faith. Apart from the rival slogans of private enterprise and socialism, we have not even the beginnings of a theory of the relations between economic levels and political systems. When the political scientist undertakes, as he must, the search for this theory, he will no doubt have recourse to comparative analysis. I do not claim foreknowledge of the direction this theory will take, but I think it reasonable to expect that again we will be dealing with political groups. I say this because I see one road to the remarriage of economics and politics for this purpose through the theory of interests. Economic development, technological change, and trends toward industrialization imply changes in employment patterns; these alter the distribution of interests. Interest theory is closely allied to group theory; indeed, they may be the same. I suggested early in this paper that every political group has an interest, which could be regarded as the central or continuing type of activity giving the group its property as a system or unit.[41] If such a formulation comes to underlie our understanding of the relationship between economic development and political change, the comparative analysis of groups might then unlock new doors not only to Latin American but also to other underdeveloped areas which, after all, embrace most of the people of the world.

These other areas bring me to the fourth element in my case for the comparative analysis of political groups, the problem of inter-area comparison. Specialists on an area like Latin America are in some danger of becoming the victims of inertia and other forces restricting them to that area alone. It is a danger because it is a form of imprisonment. We should not devote our careers to learning more about Latin America for the sole purpose of learning more about Latin America. Science seeks to generalize, and the more we can apply to other areas what we learn in Latin America, the greater the likely contribution to comparative politics and to political science as a whole.

Substantial obstacles make the practice of this preachment difficult. It is not easy to learn new languages or to develop, in working with the nuances of strange cultures, the skills that we have cultivated, and at some sacrifice, in Latin America. Yet sooner or later we should be prepared to do this. As political scientists in the confines of a single area, we do serious harm to ourselves as well as to our discipline. Actually, there are grounds for optimism on this score. In the last few years, scholars working in other foreign areas have made noteworthy progress toward inter-area comparison. But its difficulties are hard and real. This is another point at which we might make substantial strides through the comparative analysis of political groups. The formula here may be similar to what I have suggested above with respect to the "macro" problem of comparing large universes. In principle I see no serious methodological difference between applying this as between two or more countries in the same area, and as between two or more systems in different areas. If it is feasible to compare the Chilean Congress, the Mexican PRI, and the Paraguayan military, the theoretical task is not substantially different in comparing, say, the *Apristas* with *Mau-Mau* or the GOU with the Young Turks. My point is not merely that this can be done, but rather that, sooner or later, it must be done.

Further, we should realize that while in loosening our areal shackles in order to work in the underdeveloped areas at large we enter a wider field, this bigger, better, more comfortable, and more significant realm is still an intellectual prison. We will not be fully free until we can compare *all* political systems, inside and outside of the under-developed areas. It is in this light that we should view the recent work of the SSRC's Committee on Comparative Politics, which has proposed the curious dichotomy distinguishing "Western" from "non-Western" political systems. We can quarrel with this terminology—for my own part, I am not happy with it, particularly as it applies to Latin America —but to concentrate our attention on the terms is to miss the larger point. Some political systems are significantly more urbanized, secularized, commercialized, integrated and receptive to technological change than others, and we should be able to compare these extremes, whether we call them "Western" and "non-Western" or something else. Essentially, this would bring us back to the examination of political structures in terms of their functions. Where these political functions are performed in a "Western" (*i.e.,* secularized, integrated, etc.) fashion in one system and in a "non-Western" (*i.e.,* traditional, unintegrated, etc.) manner in another, we can study these systems by examining structures (*e.g.,* political groups) exercizing the functions. Once again, then, we find ourselves with the comparative analysis of political groups.

A final problem remains. This is the question of the extent to which comparative analysis is necessary to the development of general theory. There are those who argue that the comparative method can be—some even say ought to be—bypassed in the development of general theory. But to the extent that comparative analysis has a role to play in the achievement of this objective, we have the final component of my case for the comparative study of political groups. Two aspects of it need mention. First, this would give added point to our re-examination of the work of Bentley, Truman, and Latham. If comparative analysis of political groups is necessary to arrive at a general theory of groups, this is one element that has been missing from the existing literature on the study of groups and the basic justification for dusting off a book published in 1908 to say something new about it. In the second place, if comparative study is necessary to arrive at a general theory of politics, the comparative analysis of political groups carries still deeper significance. In the current stage in the development of political science it has become increasingly clear that the field of comparative government or comparative politics is not paying its own way in the discipline. If the field is to hold its own, it must contribute to political science as a whole; that is, comparative study must take part in the search for a general theory of politics. This is the fundamental element in the case—it may well be that, in the long run, this is the *entire* case—for the comparative analysis of political groups.

This may seem too ambitious an argument for the study of political groups in Latin America. Let me say in conclusion, however, that basically I have made only three claims in its defense. The first is that it would close important gaps in our knowledge of Latin America and thereby lead us to greater understanding of the mainsprings of its politics. In the second place, it would give a sharper edge to comparative political analysis, and so contribute to an improvement of the quality of research in the field of comparative politics by encouraging more meaningful comparisons of the Latin American systems with each other, and with "Western" and "non-Western" systems in other areas. Finally, the types of inquiry I have suggested here would stimulate a more significant contribution from the field of comparative politics to political science as a discipline. If this is indeed too ambitious a case, I hope to learn of a formula whereby the student of foreign politics may shrink from this ambition and at the same time enjoy a respectable role as a useful political scientist.

## NOTES

1. Charles B. Hagan, "The Group in a Political Science," in Roland A. Young (ed.), *Approaches to the Study of Politics* (Evanston: Northwestern University Press, 1958), pp. 38–51, particularly pp. 44–46.

2. See David B. Truman, *The Governmental Process* (New York, 1951), *passim*, especially ch. 2.

3. Jacinto Jijón y Caamaño, *Política Conservadora* (Riobamba: La Buena Prensa del Chimborazo, 1934), Vol. 1, pp. 26, 32.

4. See J. Lloyd Mecham, *Church and State in Latin America* (Chapel Hill: University of North Carolina Press, 1934).

5. Quoted in George I. Blanksten, *Ecuador: Constitutions and Caudillos* (Berkeley, 1951), p. 36.

6. See Blanksten, *Perón's Argentina* (Chicago, 1953), pp. 314–316; and Arthur P. Whitaker, *Argentine Upheaval* (New York, 1956), *passim*.

7. Gabriel A. Almond, "A Comparative Study of Interest Groups and the Political Process" (unpublished paper, Committee on Comparative Politics, Social Science Research Council, 1957), p. 20. See also Sigmund Neumann, *Modern Political Parties* (Chicago, 1956).

8. Almond, *op. cit.*, pp. 19–20.

9. Harry Kantor, *The Ideology and Program of the Peruvian Aprista Movement* (Berkeley, 1953).

10. Russell H. Fitzgibbon, "The Party Potpourri in Latin America," *Western Political Quarterly*, Vol. 10 (March, 1957), pp. 21–22.

11. After the initial letters of *Partido Revolucionario Institucional*.

12. See L. Vincent Padgett, "Mexico's One-Party System: A Re-evaluation," *American Political Science Review*, Vol. 41 (December, 1957), p. 995; Frank R. Brandenberg, "Mexico: An Experiment in One-Party Democracy" (Ph.D. thesis, University of Pennsylvania, 1955); and Robert E. Scott, "Mexico: Government in Transition" (Urbana, unpublished manuscript), particularly pp. 161–214.

13. See below, note 15.

14. See John Reese Stevenson, *The Chilean Popular Front* (Philadelphia: University of Pennsylvania Press, 1942).

15. Fitzgibbon, *op. cit.*, p. 18; see also his *Uruguay: Portrait of a Democracy* (New Brunswick: Rutgers University Press, 1954), especially pp. 137–152.

16. After the initial letters of *Unión Cívica Radical* (Radical Civic Union).

17. William W. Pierson and Federico G. Gil, *Governments of Latin America* (New York, 1957), p. 31.

18. Austin F. Macdonald, *Latin American Politics and Government* (New York, 2d ed. 1954), p. 2.

19. Not connected with Spain's Generalissimo Francisco Franco.

20. Literally, "we wantist," a popular abbreviation of "We want Vargas."

21. Luis Terán Gómez, *Los Partidos Políticos y su Acción Democrática* (La Paz: Editorial La Paz, 1942), pp. 60–61.

22. After the initial letters of *Partido Izquierdista Revolucionario*.

23. See Robert J. Alexander, *Communism in Latin America* (New Brunswick: Rutgers University Press, 1957).

24. Fitzgibbon, "The Party Potpourri in Latin America," *op. cit.*, p. 13.

25. Ray Josephs, *Argentine Diary* (New York: Random House, 1944), p. xxxiii.

26. See Richard Pattee, *Gabriel García Moreno y el Ecuador de su Tiempo* (Mexico City: Editorial Jus, 1944), *passim*.

27. After the initial letters of *Movimiento Nacionalista Revolucionario*.

28. See Kantor, *ibid.*; and Robert J. Alexander, "The Latin-American *Aprista* Parties," *Political Quarterly*, Vol. 20 (1949), pp. 236–247.

29. After the initial letters of *Confederación General del Trabajo* (General Confederation of Labor).

30. *Confederación de Trabajadores Chilenos* (Confederation of Chilean Workers).

31. *Confederación del Trabajo Cubano* (Confederation of Cuban Labor).

32. *Confederación de Trabajadores Mexicanos* (Confederation of Mexican Workers).

33. Ysabel F. Rennie, *The Argentine Republic* (New York: The Macmillan Company, 1945), p. 212.

34. Luis Guillermo Piazza, "There'll Always Be a Córdoba," *Americas* (January, 1950), p. 27.

35. See, for example, José Carlos Mariátegui, *Siete Ensayos de Interpretación de la Realidad Peruana* (Lima: Editorial Librería Peruana, 1934); W. Stanley Rycroft (ed.), *Indians of the High Andes* (New York, Committee on Cooperation in Latin America, 1946); Eyler N. Simpson, *The Ejido: Mexico's Way Out* (Chapel Hill: University of North Carolina Press, 1937); Moisés Sáenz, *Sobre el Indo Ectuatoriano* (Mexico City: Secretaría de Educación Pública, 1933); Sáenz, *The Peruvian Indian* (Washington: Strategic Index of the Americas, 1944); and Sáenz, *The Indian: Citizen of America* (Washington: Pan American Union, 1946).

36. See Aníbal Buitrón and John Collier, *The Awakening Valley* (Chicago: University of Chicago Press, 1950).

37. Ray Josephs, *op. cit.*, p. 26.

38. See, for example, Manning Nash, "Relaciones Políticas en Guatemala," in Jorge Luis Arriola (ed.),

*Integración Social en Guatemala* (Guatemala City: Seminario de Integración Social, 1956), pp. 137–156; and K. H. Silvert, *A Study in Government: Guatemala,* Part I (New Orleans: Middle American Research Institute: Tulane University, 1954), *passim, especially* pp. 62 ff.

39. Sáenz, *The Indian, Citizen of America,* p. 1.

40. These initials conveniently and interchangeably stood for *Grupo de Oficiales Unidos* (United Officers' group), and *¡Gobierno! ¡Orden! ¡Unidad!* (Government! Order! Unity!), the group's slogan.

41. See above, note 1.

# PROLEGOMENA TO THE COMPARATIVE STUDY OF MIDDLE EAST GOVERNMENTS

## Leonard Binder

Only the cold war has overshadowed the second most striking political phenomenon of the post World War II scene. The demise of imperial power over vast Asian and Middle Eastern territories and the rise of new independent states is in part the result of the transfer of power from Europe to the United States and the Soviet Union, and in part a distinct phenomenon. The politics of these new states have an increasing interest, partly because of their possible subversion to Communist allegiance, and partly because of the desire to assess the possibilities of successfully transplanting democracy. Emphasis on the danger of subversion intensifies interest in the political process in these non-western countries; but the context of these politics, *i.e.,* that which may be subverted, is the primary concern of the discipline of comparative government.

Political scientists have been among the last to extend the area of their research to non-western countries. They have been preceded by travelling diarists, students of comparative religion, archaeologists, historians, and latterly, anthropologists. From these sources much material, though of varied and uneven quality, exists to start with. A few political histories, fewer studies of various aspects of non-western politics, and still fewer studies of the constitutional development of these areas supplement these resources. Materials are scantiest for the Middle East.

Reprinted from *The American Political Science Review,* Vol. LI, No. 3 (September, 1957), pp. 651–668, by permission of The American Political Science Association.

Acknowledgement, entailing no responsibility, for corrections and suggestions is made herewith to my colleagues, Professor D. E. McHenry and Dr. R. Huckshorn.

## I

The attempt to extend the study of comparative government to the Middle East needs little excuse either from the point of view of the strategic interest in this region or, simply, of its attractiveness to the individual scholar; but it does pose certain problems. The first of these is the justification for the selection and definition of a geographical area to limit the field of inquiry. Theoretically the concepts of an academic discipline should be universally applicable. Against this sort of objection we must appeal to those elements of religious, ecological, and anthropological similarity which tend to give unity to the area.[1] Against the argument that all former colonial territories might make a better subject of comparison, one might answer that western imperialism only briefly, and often indirectly, touched the Middle East, and that Ottoman imperialism had a far greater influence.[2] A more positive argument, however, is that the Middle East is the only former colonial region which offers a vigorous ideological alternative to nationalism.[3] Elsewhere religion tends to reinforce nationalism. The opposition of fundamentalist[4] and traditional[5] Islam to nationalism gives a distinctive character to potential alterations or transformations of existing political institutions, whether they are traditional or borrowed from the west.

A second problem in the extension of the study of comparative government to the Middle East is the lack of developed data. Here one must balance the danger of prejudicing future research by premature generalizations against the risk of wasting much valuable effort in aimless pursuits. To be fruitful, the gathering of data must be based on some sort of preliminary hypotheses. So we must posit some hypotheses while remaining ready to discard them for new ones. This essay purposes both to discard and to posit anew.

To be discarded at the outset, as a basis of comparison, is the notion of stability. Aside from its vagueness, it is an inappropriate starting point because it is an effect and not a cause. Nor are existing institutions a sufficiently firm foundation for our study. They are often abruptly changed, and their functioning is frequently, if temporarily, interrupted. We cannot base our study on the differentiation between "modern" and traditional states either, for those that are modern have been traditional, and none that is traditional was ever modern. The comparative study of governments of the Middle East might better be based on the assumption that all of the states of the area are "tending" toward the modern; that the economic development which nearly all of them are experiencing, albeit often uncertainly, reinforces this tendency; and that the nation-state is the modern "type" rather than the democratic state. On these assumptions our study ought to be aimed at assessing the possibility of the creation of nation-states in the Middle East; and where the obstacles to that seem too great, at discovering the possible alternatives that might arise.

Institutional diversity and instability in the Middle East deprive us of the usual criteria of comparison. Even if we successfully describe the institutional constellation of the Middle East at any moment, we can be sure that it will not outlast a season or two. Even the classification of states as traditional, transitional, and modern is risky when we realize that a handful of really determined men might have moved the Yemen from the first category to the second,[6] or that Riza Shah's acceptance of the throne of Iran did not move Iran from the second to the first.[7] We must, therefore, supplement the study of existing institutions by probing into the changing social basis of the political order, and by attempting to construct model state-forms in which these institutions may eventually become fixed. Here argument must cease and exposition begin.

## II

*The changing concept of legitimacy in the Middle East* appears to provide the most fruitful approach to the contemporary study of comparative government in that region. It calls attention to the institutional instability of the area, and at the same time implies that newer and more stable forms of the state may be emerging. It also stresses the role of ideology in establishing and fixing institutional arrangements. Insofar as these arrangements can be scientifically related to certain economic and social prerequisites, the latter are crucial to our study.

The most superficial observation of Middle Eastern governments will reveal the absence of any common concept of legitimacy. Existing concepts vary all the way from that associated with the modern democratic state, with its constitution, parliament, and contractual accoutrements, to the medieval Imamate, with its traditional, prescriptive order, and its theocratic implications. Turkey lies at one end of the scale, and at the other possibly the Yemen. Turkey enjoys a two-party system, has a constitution providing for representative government, is a secular state, and has even adopted the Latin script. Above all, Turkey is a nation-state. Both Ottoman imperialism and Pan-Islam have been rejected, while, since the abolition of the Caliphate in 1924, a complete national historical myth has been elaborated and diffused through an expanding educational system.[8] The Yemen, on the other hand, retains a constitutional arrangement which is a thousand years old. The Imam Ahmad is the final court of appeal in both civil (decree) law and religious (shar'i) law. Though a Shi'i Imamate, this Zaidi state was so early established that its head is not accorded the later messianic aspects of divine guidance and personal infallibility. The Imam is elected by the dignitaries of the state because he is the most qualified of the descendants of 'Ali, the most able in interpreting the sacred law, and the most courageous in defending the state from external aggression.

Between these two extremes are many variations. Libya, for example, is a constitutional monarchy; but the king, himself, is the leader of the Sanusi brotherhood. Since the Sanusi have "arrived"— so to speak—they are no longer a reforming force. The dominant tendency is to run the government along the lines of a medieval sultanate. Iraq is also a constitutional monarchy, but there the dominant tendency is to rule through the outstanding political leaders of the parliament. The Lebanon is a republic, whose president is always a Christian and whose prime minister always a Sunni Muslim. Members of the Lebanese parliament are elected from confessional (communal) constituencies, reflecting, in a way, the traditional Ottoman millet system. Syria is also a republic, but Islam is established and the President must be a Muslim.[9] The Syrians, themselves, are not sure whether they seek to build a new nation of their own, to integrate all the original members of the Arab League into a single nation-state, or to develop a new Islamic-Arab state form. Their constitution reflects most of these conflicting ideas. Pakistan, though its inclusion in this discussion is questionable, is a democratic-republican-Islamic State. Its institutions are definitely comparable to those of the west, but its constitution has established the relationship between Islamic polity and the maintenance of the sacred law. The constitution of Iran provided for the establishment of a board of mujtahids[10] to pass upon the repugnancy of Majlis[11] legislation to the shari'a.[12]

As for political ideologies, theories of representative government and the rule of law exist side by side with those of the "pious sultan"[13] and the traditional dichotomy of qanun[14] and shari'a. Except for the incorrigible traditionalists, represented by the unregenerate "ulama" and the ruling elites of peripheral states,[15] nearly all accept the dogmas of representative government. Where parliamentarism has been tried and found wanting, it has been supplanted, for the time being, at least, by plebiscitary democracy. Most educated Muslims have reconciled democracy and Islam through the romantic device of identifying the Prophet's shura[16] with representative government. Secularism is associated with extremist nationalism or communism, though both are often camouflaged behind a rhetorical façade which rejects the shari'a as casuistry and finds in Islam only certain vague general principles of the brotherhood of believers, or the state's responsibility for social welfare.[17] Fundamentalists, while accepting the notion of representative government, reject democracy. For them it is not the will of the people that counts, but the will of God as revealed to His Prophet and correctly interpreted by wise and pious men learned in religious science.

The wide diversity of political institutions in this region is a phenomenon with a time as well as a space dimension. Diversity is found not only as between various countries, but also, over time, within the same country. This institutional change is not characterized by any regularity and so might better be known as instability, rather than development. It is often rapid, sometimes violent, and consists of alternations between parliamentary rule and military, nationalist or popular revolutions, without visible progress toward actual democracy or legitimacy.

The changes which have occurred in Turkey seem to be regular enough in the progress of that state from empire to nation. On the other hand the reforms of Ataturk were certainly rapidly introduced. The *coups* of 1908 and 1909 were not without violence, nor has it been absent from the enforcement of later reforms. These *coups* were repeated by Ataturk, and some of the illiberal tactics of his party are now being renewed by the incumbent Democratic Party.[18] Iraq and Syria both have suffered from chronic *coups d'état* on the part of the military, but authority, if not power, has always returned to the politicians in parliament. In both cases the military have remained disunited, and they have failed to win wide popular support. In Jordan, violence has attended the devolution of some power from the king to the Assembly. Egypt has undergone a series of constitutional changes, the last of which resulted from the *coup* within a *coup* of Nasir against Nagib. Parties have been abolished, but a return to parliamentarism has been promised.

Indeed part of the reason for Nagib's ouster was his desire to precipitate the return to parliamentarism before the rest of the military were ready for it. The Sudan and Libya have suddenly attained independence with all the paraphernalia of representative government. While the future of parliamentarism in both of these states remains somewhat obscure, it seems fair to surmise that Libya will have to go through a number of "repeat performances" before parliamentarism is well established. The Yemen came within an ace of experiencing a "liberal" revolution, while the Lebanon seems to have barely missed having a *coup* of its own. Iran had its revolution early in the twentieth century, followed by reaction, occupation, a *coup,* renewed constitutionalism, a period of nationalist *étatisme,* occupation again, an attempt to oust the Shah, and finally a royalist *coup.* Afghanistan had a small taste of liberal reform, followed by reaction. Pakistan has overcome a severe threat to its parliamentary regime, in which the military played a minor role. Saudi Arabia alone has experienced neither striking political change, nor the imminent threat of it. Syria's latest military *coup* is still enigmatic.

No clear pattern of democratic or constitutional development emerges from these facts. During the past fifty years or so populations have increased, industrial production has increased, agricultural land area has increased, the number of modern schools has increased, and communications have been greatly improved. But none of these changes has been of such magnitude, except possibly in Turkey, as to have provided a new socio-economic basis for a stable political system. During this period, nevertheless, nearly all the states of the Middle East have received written constitutions providing for representative government. Perhaps most significant is the fact that, while traditional institutions have sometimes persisted alongside modern ones, and while representative government has often been suspended, there is a definitely discernible trend to return to parliamentarism. On the other hand, the position of the traditional "sultan" in Jordan, Iraq, and Libya, and of the Shah of Iran has been fundamentally altered. The only successful dictatorship in the Middle East before Nasir was that of Ataturk, and he laid the foundation of Turkish nationalism.

The tendency toward according a lasting legitimacy to a parliament is clear; but that need not imply the derivation of legitimacy from the ideal of democracy or even democratic-nationalism. Parliaments have been imported from the outside, and nothing else has been devised to supplant them. But parliaments have not been popular or democratic or efficient; nor is it agreed whether parliaments are to represent the nation, the various confessions, economic interests, or whether they are simply to institutionalize a learned élite. For the present it seems that membership in parliament is not looked upon as a representative function, but rather as the privilege of a select group of notables. The legitimacy accorded a parliament of this nature may only be temporary. Either the basis of these parliaments must change, or a new institutional form may be expected to take their place.

All these institutional details, and changes in them, need to be put into some kind of conceptual framework. In order to understand change, certain points of reference must be fixed. These points, if they are to apply to all parts of the region, become less accurate as we approach the present; and they become alternatives when we extend them into the future.

## III

The political institutions of the Middle East are less important for what they are, than for what they were, and what they will be. At present they are simply changing, and the final issue is very much in doubt. We may be sure of one thing, and that is the continuing influence of earlier regional experience. Medieval institutions can accordingly form our first point of reference. The Middle East has not turned its back on Islam, and does not seem likely to do so.[19] Imperialism has produced the new intellectual pursuit of the competitive comparison of cultures. The world-wide ideological conflict has intensified the search for a middle way. Islam itself continues in vigorous proselytization, and with some success. Western historians have already infected Muslims with a fascination for their own glorious past, and the efforts of Muslim historians have been encouraged by the growing demand for new national historical myths. Even the traditional Islamic religious institution has shown vigor, and not a little political wisdom and restraint. Only Turkey has pursued a policy of vigorous secularization, and that, too, seems to have been more superficial than has been commonly assumed; and it has recently been somewhat relaxed.[20] The development of vigorous fundamentalist movements with obvious political intentions has encouraged the existing political élites to cooperate more and more with the ulama, who, themselves, have been undergoing a reform for some two centuries or so.

Our knowledge of past political and legal institutions in the Middle East is fairly good, and improving all the time. The Islamic legal, political, and administrative tradition was built upon that of the ancient Near Eastern empire, but much of its history is that of a struggle to "Islamicize" inherited institutions and traditions. At the height of the Abbasid Caliphate in the ninth century it may be said that a successful compromise had been achieved, but this cultural-political equilibrium was upset during the decline of the Caliphate and in the aftermath of the Mongol invasions. Islam as a religion won out, but as an explanation of civil polity it underwent changes of such magnitude that it is possible to say that the ancient Iranian tradition reasserted itself. On the other hand, it is important to note that this old tradition reappeared without the ancient unity of empire. The political forces which now asserted themselves were those of the Satraps; the empire was only partially reestablished by the Ottomans, with the notable exclusion of heterodox Iran. The unity imposed by the Ottomans did not lead to the re-emergence of the classical Islamic doctrine.

They accepted the traditional and recognized division of mankind into a variety of social orders: "men of the sword," "men of the pen," merchants, artisans, cultivators, *dimmis,* slaves. To each order were assigned its functions, and regulations were drawn up to ensure the proper carrying out of those functions, and that none should interfere with or infringe the functions or rights of others.[21]

In many cases the goverment did not deal directly with the individual members of these orders, but only with their appointed representatives. Rights and privileges, for most political purposes, were enjoyed only by virtue of the civil or religious status derived from such membership. This was the doctrine of ancient Iran, and so far was it successful, that even the ulama were incorporated and made part of this alien quasi-feudal system.

Out of the hegemony of the Satraps there developed three more or less stable empires, the Ottoman, the Safavid, and the Mughal. The imperial systems of each were similar; and they were all fairly efficient within the limitations of contemporary administrative techniques. The revival of the classical Islamic doctrine of the Caliphate coincides with the decline of each of these three imperial institutions. This decline spans both the eighteenth and nineteenth centuries; it was characterized only at the end by the encroachment of western power, and it was accompanied throughout by efforts at religious reform by the ulama. Finally, the Ottoman claim to the universal Caliphate was based on the literary discoveries of western scholars, the improvement of communications between the various parts of the Islamic world, the misinterpretation of the Caliphate as parallel to the Papacy, and the usefulness of this doctrine in the struggle of Abdul Hamid II to maintain his empire.

The result of this development has been the unwarranted belief that Islamic legal and political thought has remained stagnant at the point achieved about one thousand years ago. The fact of the revival has been mistaken for unbroken continuity, and the legitimate basis of earlier imperial government remains an enigma. Thus we find the Islamic world, while yet on the threshold of the modern period, questioning the legitimacy of its government, striving to purify its religion, and threatened with a renewal of the hegemony of the Satraps. The development of the modern Muslim state has been viewed by many Muslims as a step backward.

In sum, the elements to be stressed in this sketch of historical influences are the contrast between the idea of a universal empire and the actual breakup into satrapies; the re-emergence of this same problem in modern dress in modern times; the submergence of the theory of the "pious sultan" which might have legitimized Islamic nation-states; the institutional and traditional-theoretical roots of contemporary fundamentalism; and the fact that the revival of classical (Caliphate) theory has obscured the function and political interest of the ulama. The Islamic theory of the empires denies that feudalism existed in them; feudalism is therefore "alien." But improving historical knowledge makes it plain that the practice of the Islamic empires approximated feudalism, with the important exceptions of the roles of cities and the ulama. The theory has survived and the feudalistic practices have been attacked both by western innovations and by the religious revival. Muslim "modernists" would reject all Islamic influences, while fundamentalists would go back to an ideal imperial system that never actually existed.

The second point of reference is the impact of western influences upon the changing political systems of the Islamic east. This impact was particularly severe because it fell upon three empires in decline. From these special circumstances a kind of double reaction may be discerned: the first, and most obvious, is the relative ease with which western methods might be borrowed because of the increasing failure of traditional ways. The second type of reaction came from those who, knowingly or not, were destroying the old system in the hope of reforming it. They looked upon the western encroachment as a new trial of piety. Inevitably there developed many intermediate positions, maintained principally by the new and transformed classes produced by the changes of the last century or so.

For our purposes, the impact of the west took three major institutional forms: the new division of labor within the military; government concern with economic development and financial stability; and the anonymity of government itself. The net effect of these influences has been to enhance the importance, while transforming the function, of the military and administrative classes. New industrial and commercial classes have developed, and the old corporative groupings have begun to break down. Finally, the old imperial governmental forms have been demolished.

Of course, there are parts of the Middle East where this process has not yet taken place, but it is hard to believe that even the remote fastnesses of tradition can withstand the onslaught of twentieth-century forms. Even Afghanistan has accepted foreign technical and financial aid towards agricultural development; and its government has in recent years embarked upon a program of fostering Pakhtun nationalism both in the schools and among the tribes along Pakistan's north-west frontier. The Yemen was threatened with modernization through the efforts of emigrés who have been little affected in their sentiments by the restoration of the Imamate. The king of the Libyan Federation has suffered foreign air-bases to be constructed on its soil, and the Libyan people, living next to Egypt and Tunisia, cannot be expected to ignore the trumpeting of Middle Eastern nationalism. It seems inevitable that all must tread the same path of transformation, at least in some approximation of these three western influences.

The acceptance of western military organization, including the citizen army, and of western administrative organization, including the merit system, and of western industrial organization, including state capitalism, does not commit the Middle East on the central question of the nature of legitimate government. Many of the changes involved in the acceptance of these ideas and institutions were accomplished by the traditional sultans, others were imposed by external pressure, and some were the work of the military and administrative elites themselves. The principle of the anonymity of the state, and of its adjunct the rule of law in the form of logical, positive codes, has not yet been fully accepted. The military and civil services seem to favor such a change, but the industrial and commercial élites are at least ambivalent. To the urban lower classes this kind of government is incomprehensible, and devoid of that element of human charity which is often the only positive aspect of Middle Eastern government. The peasant has already suffered grievous loss by the application of western ideas of contract to his agricultural borrowing.

The third point of reference is that, without settling the question of legitimacy, western governmental institutions have been established throughout most of the Middle East. The reasons and historical circumstances behind each incident vary, but generally speaking parliaments have come into being to limit a sultan or to begin the process of the devolution of western imperial power. It is a matter of more than passing significance that parliamentary institutions, already accepted in the west, were simply transferred wholly grown to the Middle East. They were, and remain, an artificial legalism, and a continuing temptation to go outside the law. The two bases for the establishment of parliaments imply two not necessarily coordinate theories of legitimacy. The first of these is that associated with the idea of democracy institutionalized and modified in a representative assembly. The second is associated with the somewhat vaguer idea of national self-determination.

The total effect of the western impact, including the recent decline in western imperialism, has been to leave a residue of parliamentary institutions on the debris of traditional sultanates. These institutions, though welcome to the officials in most cases, are without any strong and stable social basis. With some interruption, these institutions have been maintained *faute de mieux,* but they are certainly shaky. Nationalism, while continuing to be expressed in these parliaments, often finds it difficult to work with them; while the parliaments themselves have been notably unable, and often unwilling, to extend the scope of democratic government.

Since no important theories of legitimacy have received general acceptance since the breakdown of the sultanates, idealistic attempts "to get things done" without parliaments have had to rely upon charismatic leadership. Such leadership can as well be adapted to an integral nationalism as to a plebiscitary democracy, but it is also, and perhaps ideally, suited to the government of a theocratic state. Less successful leaders than Ataturk have discredited military dictatorship as much as parliamentarism, so the stage may be set for trying a kind of theocratic dictatorship.

Those ulama who have continued in their reforming tradition of the eighteenth and nineteenth centuries are as suspicious of nationalism as they are of lay religious fundamentalism. However, the secularist tendencies of some nationalists have at times tended to drive the ulama toward the fundamentalists. The ulama are fairly immune to the democratic charms of parliaments, and they tend, like Plato, to put more faith in the abilities of a cooperative autocrat.

The fourth point of reference is the fact of economic development and change. It is important here in a special sense. We are concerned with how much, but also with how little. We are concerned with how fast, but also with how long and how frequent the interruptions may be.

In only a few Middle Eastern countries has economic development been so little as to have had no substantial effect on the distribution of social and political power. Again in only a few of them has the peculiar concentration of economic power in the hands of the sultan been maintained. In all the rest far-reaching economic change has occurred involving restriction on production, currency controls, state-capitalism, the diffusion of a money economy, and great outlays on public capital projects.

We still have much to learn about the political effects of economic change, in the Middle East as elsewhere, and especially when the question concerns the speed and sustained character of economic development in its relation to the development of democracy. There are, however, two things we can say that are relevant here. The first is that economic development will proceed in the Middle East; and the second is that this economic development will result in broadening the basis of politics in the region.

The most persistent form in which economic development takes place in the Middle East is the provision of the public capital prerequisites for development. A railroad, a bridge, a dam, a telegraph line will all outlast the temporary domestic upheaval or foreign boycott which dries up the flow of foreign capital and sends the factory worker back to the village. Sometimes these public capital projects are more closely tied to military projects, and then their effect upon communication and "social mobilization" is even more pronounced. This kind of development has already begun and so long as international communications remain at their present level, and so long as some states are considerably more developed than others, it will continue.

At some point in the future the economic development of various Middle Eastern countries may reach the point where a vigorous democratic nationalism may be reasonably expected to emerge. But there may be many obstacles to overcome; and it is possible that the political form of these states may become fixed long before that time. What possible forms may they take?

The fifth point of reference is the future form of the "typical" Middle Eastern state. We have already intimated that there are only two important genera which are competing for legitimization. The first is the nation-state, and the second may be called the Islamic-State.[22] Both terms are already in use in the Middle East, and sometimes in reference to the same state. Turkey even now may be considered a nation-state, while Pakistan calls itself an Islamic-State. Saudi Arabia, the Yemen, Morocco, and Afghanistan resemble the medieval Islamic-State of the "pious sultan." For our purposes neither of these terms can be referred to an actual state. Both are ideal constructs against which to judge political development. Middle Eastern states will tend toward one extreme or the other. The development of intermediate forms will be greatly hampered (a) by the force of the pent-up reaction against existing traditional sultanates, (b) by the lack of a mediator in the form of a legitimate political institution with legalized procedures in countries of erratic economic and political development, or (c) by the previous settlement of the issue. In Turkey, which seems to enjoy a firmly established form of government which may mediate between these two positions, economic development is most likely to continue to diffuse secularism and strengthen nationalism. Only Pakistan has provided in its constitution for a means whereby the Islamic-State may come into being; but Pakistan is a very special case.

## IV

Once we have established two alternative lines of development, and have eliminated for all academic purposes intermediate forms, we are no longer required to use them both. It will be sufficient if we take only one form for our fifth point of reference, understanding throughout that all obstacles to the progress of a Middle Eastern state in this direction will turn it toward the other pole.

Of the two it seems that our choice must fall upon the nation-state, for a number of reasons. First, the nation-state is most familiar to us. Second, the nation-state is the most widely accepted form in the world today, and so compels the use of its justifications in all international relations. Third, the forces of nationalism are in the ascendant throughout most of the Middle East. The Islamic-State is a tantalizing concept, for it exists nowhere, except possibly in Pakistan where the issue has not yet been fully resolved, and where it has failed of the ungrudging support of the religious classes. Only in Egypt has there been a powerful organization working for the establishment of an Islamic-State; but the Muslim Brotherhood has been crushed, at least for the time being. The Wahhabi and Sanusi movements in Saudi Arabia and Libya, respectively, belong to an earlier reform of traditional Islam. Both these movements fail to recognize the modernization of the state apparatus, but emphasize instead the religious views and performance of the Head of the state. Both movements have lost much of their vigor and social sense as a result of their comparative success, so that King Saud's government resembles a traditional sultanate, while that of King Idris would be similar but for the inconvenience of a legislative assembly imposed by the United Nations.

The type of Islamic-State which may arise as a real alternative to nationalism remains largely undefined, but some of its features can be specified. Such a state will declare the sovereignty of God as the foundation of the legitimacy of its government. The sovereignty of God is not merely nominal, for God has revealed His will through His Prophet. The law of the state will be based upon the qur'an (Koran) and the traditions of the Prophet, but it will reject the later consensi of the legal schools. The Head of the state will have the power of interpreting the sacred law in applying it to new situations. It is possible that legislation on some points by an assembly will be permitted. The Head of state and assembly will be elected, but there will

be only one party, or perhaps none at all. Candidates will not canvass for election, but they will be elected on the basis of their knowledge of the law, their piety, their respectability, and their *modern* knowledge. The composition of the assembly may reflect economic interests, but probably not geographical areas. The law will be a respecter of persons in regard to religious differences. Only Muslims will be able to hold policy-making positions, but non-Muslims will be permitted to live in accordance with their own personal status law. Private property will be safeguarded, but exceptionally large accumulations of wealth will be prohibited. Women will be excluded from public life, and secluded in the home whenever possible. The major domestic duty of the government will be to foster the good and suppress evil in encouraging the growth of a truly Muslim society.

As may be judged from this sketch, the romantic-fundamentalist groups agitating for the establishment of such a state are presently or potentially "power-aspiration" groups. Groups of this kind have had considerable appeal among the lower middle classes which are made up both of those less successful in the westernized sector of Muslim society and those whose intermediate position in the traditional social structure has been undermined by recent change. Before these groups can hope for success, they must win to their support either a much larger segment of the administrative and military élites, or many more individuals who have been frustrated by the inability of the existing political structure to satisfy their aspirations. The latter situation can only arise when the social basis of political life is considerably broadened. It is the narrow basis of political life in Saudi Arabia and Libya which makes all the difference between the political qualities of the old and new fundamentalism.

In the absence of any concrete example of the Islamic-State, and with only a highly theoretical statement of its law and but a vague notion of its political organization, it cannot serve efficiently as an ideal construct. Moreover, it does not grow out of the contemporary social and economic phenomena which have elsewhere produced the familiar form of the nation-state. Looked at in terms of the aspirations of most of the ruling elites of the Middle East, the Islamic-State could only come into being after the failure of the current effort to build nation-states. It seems, therefore, preferable to posit the nation-state as the model construct toward which the Middle East is moving.

The establishment of nation-states throughout the Middle East entails the final breakdown of the medieval corporations and the de-emphasis of the heretofore all-important religious distinctions. Wherever traditional institutions obtain, the newly rising middle classes will have to transform or overthrow them. The privileges and obligations of citizenship will have to be much more widespread. The obligation of the government in terms of popular health, welfare, and education, and in the creation of economic opportunity, will have to be fulfilled in more than mere declaratory fashion. Communication must improve to the point where the individual's horizon spreads beyond his immediate community, and appropriate national myths will have to be evolved to keep the individual's allegiance within the territorial bounds of the nation-state. The nation-state must also have sufficient power, and its leaders sufficient skill, to maintain its independence under all foreseeable circumstances short of a third world war.

Given certain prerequisites, all these things may be achieved in an orderly political environment capable of adjusting to and controlling a sustained economic development of an appropriate magnitude. The absence of optimum political and economic conditions, which we know to exist, will hamper and possibly permit the perversion of the development of nation-states. But even under optimum conditions certain difficulties may appear which cannot be overcome. These difficulties arise primarily from the manner in which the contemporary Middle East is politically demarcated.

Paradoxical though it may be, the primary legal and political sphere of the nation-state is territorial. Language, history, and religion may be the stuff of nationalism, but the nation-state remains heir to the territorial sovereignty of the monarchical states of pre-modern Europe. The territorial divisions of the Middle East were devised by European powers to meet their own needs and aspirations. Boundaries do not coincide with the areas of strongest potential national feeling in many cases, and yet they mark the limits of governmental effort toward the creation of nation-states. Arbitrary territorial divisions have not always hampered the development of nation-states elsewhere, when they were not evolved in a period of conscious nationalism. But arbitrary territorial divisions have created states which must be economically and militarily dependent on their neighbors.

The population-land ratio will also have much to do with the successful creation of nation-states in the Middle East. Economic development may be severely disturbed by either too low or too high a ratio. Underpopulation may make the maintenance of external security difficult, while the maldistribution of population and the existence of large tribal groups hinders social integration. Religious minorities, whether heterodox Muslims or non-Muslims, and linguistic minorities are other obvious obstacles to the creation of nation-states.

The unequal distribution of natural resources in the area will tend to encourage more rapid development in some, and may be an insurmountable obstacle to development in other states. The more advanced state may then attract the loyalties and cooperation of its neighbor's citizens.[23] Wide stretches of desert throughout the area will remain a barrier to rapid and efficient transport and communication. Territorial nationalism will have to compete with Pan-Islam and Pan-Arabism, which survive in the area under the confused guise of nationalist ideologies. Finally, there is always the possibility that intra-area conflict or external subversion may bring the effort to establish nation-states within the territorial states of the Middle East to an untimely end.

## V

The preceding observations enable us now to make a preliminary classification of the countries of the Middle East into three groupings in terms of their satisfaction of the prerequisites of the nation-state. The first grouping, comprising Turkey, Egypt, and Iran, comes very close to satisfying the conditions. The second grouping, comprising the states of the Fertile Crescent, is furthest away from fulfilling these conditions. The third grouping, comprising Saudi Arabia, Libya, the Yemen, and possibly Afghanistan, still retains elements of an earlier legitimacy.

The population of Turkey is largely homogeneous, with the Kurds forming the only significant minority. The Kurdish "problem" has long been largely eliminated by a twofold process of repression and assimilation; and since both Turks and Kurds are Sunnis, there has been no religious extension of political issues between them. For the present Turkey is somewhat underpopulated, but the trend is toward rapid growth. At the same time, with the support of American foreign aid programs, the improvement of communications and the provision of state capital for economic development have been steady over the last decade. In the thirty-five years since Ataturk's victory over the Greeks, nationalism has spread throughout the educational system, which has been modernized and expanded. The alphabet reform speeded the spread of literacy, which, in turn, has been fed by a new nationalist literary movement. A new national myth has been created by skipping back over the Islamic period to the legendary reports concerning the Turks of Central Asia. The dominant political elite has its roots in the westernized official classes of the Ottoman Empire, but they have found in the Turkish nation an adequate compensation for the loss of a reactionary Sultan and an unmanageable empire.

Egypt is also a country of homogeneous population. The Copts number barely 5 percent of the population, and are Arabic speaking too. There are only a few and unimportant nomadic tribes in

Egypt. The country is predominantly agricultural, and the overwhelming majority of the population is concentrated along the Nile. Among the consequences of this concentration are ease of communication and the necessity, realized by all, of centralized control. Egypt is, however, limited in agricultural resources, and suffers from a very adverse land-population ratio. The national myth of Egypt has been based upon the glories of the Pharaonic civilization quite as much as upon Arabic symbols. Even under Islam, Egypt long enjoyed an independent administration, and its ties to the Ottoman empire were loose to the point of insubordination. Given a stable political order and the skill and finances to overcome its population problem, there is little doubt that Egypt can emerge in the recognizable form of a western nation-state. Even if no transitional political system can persist, but if economic development proceeds, one might expect the same results. On the other hand, if economic development continues erratic, and if political decision-making remains haphazard or adventurous, the Muslim Brotherhood may yet arise more powerful than before.

Iran suffers from maldistribution of population, poor internal communications, and the decentralizing effects of large and powerful tribal groups. On the other hand, Iran is most favorably endowed for development as a nation-state. It has a large territory and a growing population, tremendous resources of petroleum and adequate resources of other minerals. The ideological, historical, and literary bases of Iranian nationalism are stronger than those of many a European state. Iran is a Shi'i state, and yet is ruled by a Shah who calls himself *Pahlavi,* referring to the rulers of ancient Parthia. Modern Iran has been an independent, unified empire for over four centuries. Like Turkey, it has a unique national language, and one which can boast of an exceptional poetic achievement crowned by a national epic which may be heard from the lips of many an illiterate Iranian. Had the government of Iran the will and the ability to invest the proceeds of its petroleum sales properly, it could most probably effect the social integration lacking in that country. The problem of Iran is, however, much greater than that of either Turkey or Egypt when seen from the standpoint of existing linguistic and racial homogeneity. On the other hand, the tribal and linguistic minorities may be swept up in a new vigorous nationalism, since there are few external attractions for them. The only serious competing nationalism is that of Soviet Azerbaijan, but here the USSR overplayed its hand in 1946, and this is not forgotten nor forgiven, In any case, once economic development gets under way the peasant classes should become far more important than the tribes.

In the Fertile Crescent, the Lebanon is an Arab state, but not a nation-state. The precarious balance of Christians and Muslims in the population is insti-tutionalized in the division of political offices and in the distribution of parliamentary constituencies. Though the Lebanese standard of living is higher than that of Syria, its economic position is precarious also. Its major sources of income are from the transit trade, the tourist trade, foreign receipts from emigrants, and an overworked agriculture. Its attempt to boast an historical connection with ancient Phoenicia is belied by the dominance of Arabic sentiment and the rigidity of confessional politics. The historical basis of its separate existence is French intervention on behalf of the Christians of the Levant. There is little likelihood that the Lebanon will ever become either a nation-state or an Islamic-State; but there is the danger that it may be incorporated in a Greater Syria.

The Hashemite Kingdom of Jordan was created in 1922 by the British government for reasons of British policy. Until recently it was ruled as a traditional sultanate, but with the annexation of Cis-Jordan the Kingdom acquired a new majority. This new majority was far more advanced than the sparse population of Trans-Jordan, and also politically frustrated. The only nationalism popular in Jordan is Pan-Arabism. Jordan, itself, has been economically sustained by subventions from the British government which it has lately sought to replace by similar grants from Egypt, Syria, and Saudi Arabia. Evidently this arrangement has not worked out very well, and now Jordan seems likely to become a client of the United States. The patronage of the greatest world power is bound to prolong the existence of even this most artificial of states, but sheer power does not suffice for every purpose. Recent events indicate that Jordanian independence cannot withstand the growth of nationalism within its own borders.

Syria and Iraq are alike in many ways. They are separated in the south by the Syrian desert, and they are joined in the north by the potentially rich agricultural area of the upper Euphrates. Both are underpopulated. Both have powerful nationalist and Pan-Arab movements. Both have important minority problems, but in both the Sunni Muslims are politically dominant. They share the problem of settling nomadic tribesmen, but Iraq's share is greater. Iraq has great resources of petroleum, and presently invests 70 percent of its royalties in a respectable economic development plan. Syria accommodates two Iraq petroleum pipelines at a considerable income. Both Syria and Iraq can look forward to a substantial expansion of their agricultural land area.

Iraq is ruled by a constitutional monarchy which has weathered over half a dozen *coups.* Syria is a republic when it is not ruled by a military dictator. To the extent that their national myths differ, Syria emphasizes the Umayyad Caliphate of Damascus, and Iraq emphasizes the Abbasid Caliphate, but the distinction is not crucial. The greatest obstacle to unity is the existence of two sets of political, military, and administrative élites. The unity of the Fertile Crescent is also opposed by both Egypt and Saudi Arabia for reasons of their own. In Syria, the ideal of Arab unity is enshrined in the 1950 constitution; and Iraqi statesmen pay similar homage to the Pan-Arabic aspiration.

Should the two states combine in the near future, it is obvious that Iraq, because of its resources, somewhat stabler politics, and powerful western support, would be dominant. If the two were united, a stable Sunni electoral majority would be created, the income from Iraqi petroleum could be shared and development thus equalized, the problem of trans-desert communications and the settlement of the tribes could be jointly dealt with, and the military security of both would be enhanced. Should they remain divided, it is difficult to imagine the ideological basis for separation, and even more difficult to conceive of a widely accepted legitimacy being granted these governments. At present neither Iraq nor Syria can claim complete nationalism. Possibly because of the prevalence of heterodoxy, neither country has a powerful fundamentalist movement, so that the prospect of the creation of an Islamic-State in the Fertile Crescent seems remote. The governments of Syria and Iraq may stumble for a long time before losing their opportunity of creating an Arab nation-state in the Fertile Crescent.

In the third grouping of states, still dominated by traditional political forces, one can only speculate as to the timing and source of political change. In Saudi Arabia one looks to the growing group of westernized administrators not belonging to the royal house, and to the employees of the Arabian-American Oil Company; in Libya one looks, perhaps, to the federal parliament; in the Yemen one looks to the Yemeni emigrants; in Afghanistan one looks to a handful of military and administrative officials. It is possible, if unlikely, however, that political change will come about peacefully in these countries; if so, they may avoid the growth of nationalism and hit upon some intermediate form. In all likelihood, developments in other parts of the Middle East will be so far advanced by the time these traditional governments are weakened that the nation-state will be the only logical solution.

Finally, a word about Pakistan, which is the only state claiming the title "Islamic." The present constitution of Pakistan enjoins the National Assembly to codify Islamic Law, and prohibits the Assembly from enacting any law repugnant to the qur'an and sunna. But the constitution seems to leave these matters to the final discretion of the legislators themselves, so that the Assembly may have as much of an effect on Islam as Islam may have on Pakistan. As a concrete application of the modern doctrine of the constitutive character of the consensus of *all* Muslims (not merely those specially qualified), this type of provision may be acceptable even in a national constitution.

## VI

In summary, while the potential development of Islamic-States or the possible elaboration of political forces committed to that model as a goal has been taken as a basis for demarcating the Middle East as an area to which the discipline of comparative government may be applied, these potentialities do not seem sufficient to justify an undifferentiated application to all parts of the area. Existing political institutions have been considered too weak a staff upon which to lean, while the changing concept of legitimacy has been stressed. The political process is crucial to the dynamics of the changes going on, but it has been deemed theoretically subordinate to the central problem of comparative government. The possibility of the success of Communism in the Middle East, outside of the framework of nationalism, has been ignored as unlikely in the foreseeable future, and the persistence of parliamentary institutions has been dealt with briefly.

Limited spheres of disciplinary application have been delineated on the basis of an argument from the impact of historical and economic forces upon diverse ideological, territorial, and institutional complexes. This argument turns on five points of reference: medieval institutions; the impact of western influences; the establishment of western institutions; economic development; and the future form of the Middle Eastern state. Finally, it is suggested that reasonable comparisons and the most valid estimates of similarity of development can be made regarding the following groups of states: (1) Turkey, Egypt, and Iran; (2) the Fertile Crescent countries; (3) those states whose political institutions are dominated by systems of traditional authority, especially Saudi Arabia, the Yemen, Libya, and Afghanistan. Morocco and the Sudan may fit into the second group. Pakistan offers special difficulties because of its geography and lengthier imperial experience, as do Tunisia and Algeria because of the presence of a large French minority in each of them. The presence of politically powerful fundamentalist groups and organizations of the traditional ulama in Indonesia may permit limited comparisons on the ideological level, but not much more.

## NOTES

1. R. Patai, "The Middle East as a Culture Area," *Middle East Journal*, Vol. 6 (Winter, 1952), pp. 1–21.

2. Even this influence was not uniform; see H. A. R. Gibb and H. Bowen, *Islamic Society and the West* (London, 1950), Vol. 1, Part I, p. 20.

3. The Middle East has been, and remains, an ambiguous term. For the purposes of this essay the applicability of the comparative method is the only limitation. Islam as a political ideology therefore provides a preliminary criterion of limitation. If this looseness is unacceptable, the "American" Near East plus the "British" Middle East may be substituted. These two usages include all the countries from Libya to Pakistan. While the State of Israel lies within these geographic limits, the comparability of its political institutions with those of its neighbors is at least enough in doubt to warrant its exclusion from the present discussion.

4. By fundamentalism is meant a reforming movement emanating from the romanticization of early Islam, but insisting upon strict adherence to Islamic law. Another variety of fundamentalism is the Wahhabi and related Sanusi types, which are of earlier origin and were mostly directed against mystic and primitivistic accretions to Islam.

5. *I.e.,* that of the "ulama," representing the whole of the accumulated legal and social tradition of Islam and stressing the related function of the ulama as a religious institution. The ulama "know" the law, hence are clergy.

6. See Royal Institute of International Affairs, *The Middle East: A Political and Economic Survey* (London, 2d ed., 1954), p. 104.

7. For a short period Iran was without a Shah, and throughout 1924–5 Riza was undecided whether to become President or Shah of Iran.

8. D. Rustow, *Politics and Westernization in the Near East,* Center of International Studies (Princeton, 1956), p. 14.

9. *Constitution of the Republic of Syria* (September 5, 1950), Preamble and Chapter I, Article 3, (1) and (2).

10. Shi'ite legists competent to interpret the law of Islam.

11. The Iranian parliament.

12. Islamic Law.

13. See H. A. R. Gibb, "Some Considerations of the Sunni Theory of the Caliphate," *Archives d'Histoire du Droit Orientale,* Tome III (Wetteren, 1948), p. 405.

14. Civil decree without religious sanction.

15. *I.e.,* peripheral to the historical Islamic empire: Afghanistan, the Yemen, Morocco, even Arabia.

16. A council of notables, with floating membership.

17. W. Z. Laqueur, *Communism and Nationalism in the Middle East* (New York, 1956), p. 167.

18. *E.g.,* suppression of opposition newspapers.

19. This view differs from that of Laqueur, *op. cit.,* p. 6.

20. See B. Lewis, "Islamic Revival in Turkey," *International Affairs,* Vol. 28 (January, 1952), pp. 38–48; L. V. Thomas, "Recent Developments in Turkish Islam," *The Middle East Journal,* Vol. 6 (Winter, 1952), pp. 22–40; and E. Marmorstein, "Religious Opposition to Nationalism in the Middle East," *International Affairs,* Vol. 28 (July, 1952), pp. 344–349.

21. Gibb and Bowen, *op. cit.,* p. 200.

22. Communist influences, though growing in the Middle East, seem most likely to manifest themselves within the framework of the nation-state. It may be assumed that the United States will actively resist the subversion of any of the "Northern Tier" states bordering on the USSR, *i.e.,* those most likely to imitate communist forms in such an eventuality.

23. See K. W. Deutsch, *The Political Community at the International Level,* Doubleday Short Studies (New York, 1954), p. 44.

# SINGLE-PARTY SYSTEMS IN WEST AFRICA

### Ruth Schachter

In this paper I propose to examine the tendency towards single-party systems in West Africa, particularly in relation to the social structure and the historical circumstances in which the parties emerged.[1] I shall therefore point up the distinction between "mass" and "patron" parties, and then consider the new single-party governments, most of them based on mass parties, in relation to the prospects of democracy in West Africa. My argument is

Reprinted from *The American Political Science Review* (June, 1961), pp. 294–307, by permission of The American Political Science Association.

that mass parties are created by African leaders out of the very liberating and egalitarian forces we in this country generally associate with democracy. Some of the mass parties encourage the growth of forces and institutions which may ultimately make possible the machinery of democratic systems familiar to us: as, for instance, competition for every citizen's vote by more than one organized team of candidates. At this stage of West African party history, it seems to me, the number of parties is far too simple a criterion upon which to decide whether or not a system is democratic.

General statements about parties in the new West

African States can be made only tentatively. Significant rights to vote and organize parties came to West Africa only after the Second World War. Since then formal institutional change has taken place at a rapid pace. The constitutional framework in which the parties grew changed continuously. The franchise expanded until it became universal, the powers of African elected representatives grew by stages from consultative to legislative and eventually to executive, and the locus of political power shifted from London or Paris to Africa. Even so basic a feature of a political system as its territorial and international frontiers occasionally altered. For example, Upper Volta was reconstituted as a separate territory in 1947; and some eleven years later the federation of French West Africa was dissolved and Ghana had absorbed British Togoland. The Mali Federation, born in 1959, dissolved before it was two years old. The general points evident from an examination of party history over less than twenty years may turn out to be of minor importance in a later perspective.

All these are reasons for caution. Nevertheless, the parties are among the oldest national political institutions in West Africa, wholly Africanized long before the governments or the civil services (which still are not). Hence parties give better guidelines to African politics than those formal institutions of government which were set up by French and British colonizers at least in part as a condition for their recent political withdrawal, and are being changed by Africans after independence.

The majority of the new West African sovereign nations are based on single parties, likely to dominate for some time whether or not opposition parties are allowed to exist alongside. Most of their governments are founded on mass parties: Ghana, Guinea, Ivory Coast, Mali (formerly Soudan), Senegal, Togo and—with qualifications—the Eastern and Western Regions in the Federation of Nigeria. Without the pressure these mass parties exerted on the French or British colonial authorities, it is doubtful whether the colonial era in West Africa would have ended quite so soon. Perhaps, indeed, the nationalist drive of these particular mass movements, linked with the rapid decline of European power, carried along towards independence in 1960 even those states in which mass parties have not yet emerged: the Northern Region of Nigeria, the Islamic Republic of Mauretania, and (with qualifications) Niger and Upper Volta, which are also single party systems, but based on parties of the "patron," "cadre," or "personality" types.[2] In Dahomey, however, government rests on an unstable alliance of parties, both of the mass and patron types, still regional and not territorial in scale.

Successive post-war electoral results in West Africa make obvious another clear trend: the only sharp changes in party majorities took place prior to independence, and were from patron to mass

party majority; never the reverse. An apparent exception was Ivory Coast, where the *Parti Démocratique de la Côte d'Ivoire* (PDCI) rode to power in 1946, immediately after Africans were able to organize parties legally. Between 1949 and 1952 it lost a series of elections and by-elections, but only because the French administration had tampered with the ballot. Officially, then, some candidates of the allied patron parties of Ivory Coast won, but the PDCI resumed its monopoly of offices as soon as the voters could register their choice freely once more.

## I. MASS AND PATRON PARTIES

The main distinction between mass and patron parties lies not in the social origins of aspiring national leaders, and not in the scale of party organizations. It lies rather in the reply to the questions: How are the national leaders related to the rest of the population, and on what groups and with what ideas and structures did they build their parties? The distinction is perhaps best seen first at the local branch level.

Mass parties generally sought the adherence of every single individual. They wanted to enroll each man, woman, and even child, and so they had to establish local branches with headquarters, regular meetings and elections for branch leaders. Examples are the *Parti Démocratique de la Côte d'Ivoire* or the *Parti Démocratique de Guinée* (PDG) of Guinea. The patron parties usually terminated their structure simply with the adherence of influential notables or patrons; these were mostly the officially recognized "chiefs" or their direct representatives. Examples are the *Union Nigérienne des Indépendants et Sympathisants* (UNIS)*[3] of Niger, the *Parti Progressiste Soudanais** (PSP *sic*), the *Bloc Africain de Guinée** (BAG) or, with qualifications, the *Northern People's Congress* (NPC) of Nigeria. Most patron parties did little to reach every individual in the community, and relied upon the "patrons" for their local influence. A defection from the local branch of a mass party rarely led to the disintegration of the branch. But the defection of a local notable from the patron party seriously weakened it in the locality.

Mass parties, such as the *Parti Démocratique de Guinée* of Guinea, the *Union Soudanaise* (US) of Mali, the *Convention People's Party* (CPP) of Ghana, the *Action Group of Nigeria*, the *Union Progressiste Sénégalaise* (UPS) of Senegal, the *National Council of Nigeria and the Cameroons* (NCNC), the *Parti Démocratique de la Côte d'Ivoire* of Ivory Coast, and the *Comité de l'Unité Togolaise* (CUT) of Togo counted their numbers in the hundreds of thousands. First organized around an anti-colonial platform, they claimed to "represent 'all the pople'; to embody the national will . . . "[4]

Several structural concepts elaborated by Duverger and applied to Moroccan parties by Rézette[5] can be usefully employed in connection with the tropical African parties. At least for a time, most mass parties were strongly articulated, relatively disciplined and called forth considerable direct participation from members, in varying degrees roughly indicated, in descending order, by the sequence of their listing above. The leaders of these parties emphasized organization partly because they opposed the established authorities and could not use established institutions. They usually created parallel women's and youth organizations. They published newspapers, set up central and regional headquarters, hired permanent staff, distributed membership cards, charged dues, and, especially before independence, synchronized activities and shared personnel with African trade unions. The more effective their organization, the more mass party leaders were in a position to implement their decisions. *Union Soudanaise* and *Parti Démocratique de Guinée* leaders, for example, regarded their mass parties as "weapons"[6] designed to achieve independence and economic development with the greatest speed possible.

In contrast, most patron parties—*Parti Progressiste Soudanais,** for instance, and *Union Nigérienne des Indépendants et Sympathisants*—were weakly articulated, comparatively undisciplined, with little if any direct membership participation. This difference in structure between mass and patron parties is one of several reasons why, though mass parties took the place of patron parties with a regularity suggesting a definite pattern, so far no mass party has ever been replaced by a rival in free election.

Closely related to structure was the pattern of authority within the party. Not all but some of the mass parties had both institutionalized and collective leadership, such as the *Union Progressiste Sénégalaise,* the *Action Group of Nigeria,* the *Union Soudanaise* and the *Parti Démocratique de Guinée.* Elections were fairly regular; officers gave some account of their stewardship to the members; discipline was given serious attention; a predetermined procedure was followed when important decisions were to be made. Patron parties, and a mass party such as the *Parti Démocratique de la Côte d'Ivoire* after 1950, had essentially personal leadership; leaders, either as individuals or as a group, made decisions and reconciled conflicts in ways unfettered by pre-arranged rules. The parties with institutionalized leadership could deal far more smoothly with the problems posed by renewal and succession.

For an understanding of the authority pattern within the parties a modified notion of charisma is sometimes useful,[7] provided it is not understood simply as "the polar opposite of formal and traditional bonds,"[8] or taken to mean the total "absence of any defined hierarchy."[9] Thus some, but not all, mass

party top-level leaders—Sékou Touré of the *Parti Démocratique de Guinée* and Mamadou Konaté (d. 1956) of the *Union Soudanaise*—enjoyed a type of charisma which was limited both by the constitutional procedure they themselves insisted upon within their mass parties, and by the power exercized to a greater or lesser extent by other groups and individuals within the party. Other leaders, particularly of patron parties—such as Fily Dabo Sissoko of the *Parti Progressiste Soudanais** and Sourou Migan Apithy of the *Parti Républicain du Dahomey** (PRD)—used their charisma comparatively unchecked by procedure, though limited by the power and influence of the "patrons." This was also true for some mass party leaders, such as Félix Houphouët-Boigny of the *Parti Démocratique de la Côte d'Ivoire.* Still other leaders, like Lamine Kaba of the Kankan region of Guinea, enjoyed charisma only within a locality considerably smaller than a territory. Their gift, usually recognized by only one ethnic group, came to be regarded as a threat to national party discipline. The notion of charisma, denoting extraordinary qualities ascribed to an individual, is a useful starting point for further investigation. But it is only a starting point; perhaps sharper than the idea Carlyle expressed with "Find in a country the Ablest Man . . . raise him to the supreme place . . . what he tells us to do must be precisely the wisest, fittest . . ."[10]

The distinction between mass and patron parties has implications beyond those already discussed—local branch organization, size of membership, patterns of authority, and structure. It illuminates also variations in social composition, methods and function. Before turning to these, however, we must look somewhat more closely at the total society in which West African parties sought support.

## II. MODERN AND TRADITIONAL ELEMENTS

The West African societies in which ten new sovereign states emerged between 1957 and 1960 were at an earlier stage of economic and social history than the retiring colonial powers. The specific figures are less reliable than the generalizations they are designed to illustrate. As a result of the reforms extended after the Second World War, the vote became universal in a society where—on very rough average—fifteen per cent could read or write, perhaps three per cent were regular wage earners, and another three per cent were employed away from their villages. Considerably more than half the people's efforts still went into subsistence activity outside the exchange economy.[11] In Europe, by contrast, the vote became general only after almost everyone was deeply involved in the market economy. Indeed, not even the middle classes could vote until after the emergence of the "commercial civilization from the feudal, the society based on contract from the society based on status."[12] Not so in West Africa. Although there is an educated elite—mainly clerks, teachers, nurses, doctors, lawyers, and low-level technicians—only Senegal, Ivory Coast, Ghana, and southern Nigeria have a growing minority of literate Africans self-employed in trade, transport, and farming for export.

Several hundred different ethnic groups make up the approximately sixty million inhabitants of the new West African nations. The educated minority is almost alone in seeing a clear interest in maintaining the present territorial frontiers, or in enlarging them, and in preventing tribal separatism from fragmenting the new nations. With a few exceptions, the existence of this elite, its size and even its distribution according to ethnic and geographic origins, were due to the forces of economic and social change accompanying the arrival of the Europeans in West Africa. Much more economic activity took place in the coastal and forest belt of West Africa, and the proportion of people educated from that region is far greater than from the savannah and *sahel* belts. This caused trouble both for parties and for nations. Northern Nigerians, Ghanaians, and Ivory Coasters, for example, resent having too many party organizers, too many civil servants, and too many government leaders come from the southern regions of their countries. Some seeds of the 1958 riots against Dahomeans in the Ivory Coast were planted before the war, when the French West African educational system trained an unusually high proportion of them.

The political facts of colonial rule, and then the democratic reforms extending over some two decades, sped up the process whereby the modern layer of African society acquired the lead politically, even though it was still so small a minority. The European powers enlarged the scale of West African political units from the many tribal to the present territorial ones. Together with their new technology they introduced or reinforced secular values such as equality and merit, weakened traditional religious sanctions, and overthrew kinship as the main determinant of rank. Although the British believed in indirect rule and the French in direct rule, in varying degrees they both undermined the secular authority of the pre-European authorities.

There were few areas in which the presence of the Europeans did not add yet another dimension to the already thorny issue of succession. Pre-war "native authorities," or members of the *commandement indigène*—the official "chiefs"—did not necessarily also have a traditional claim to high rank. These categories seem to have overlapped most in the savannah region of the western Sudan, where such historic pre-European empires as Mali and Ghana existed, and where in the nineteenth century the Europeans could not install their administrations until they had defeated the warrior-kings, Samory Touré and the sons of Hajj Umar Tall. The official "chiefs" were no regular mobile civil servants recruited by standards of merit; few were literate; they were for the most part stationed among their kinsmen. In time, these official "chiefs" constituted a new stratum of the population in the countryside, with a sense of corporate identity transcending the limits of their different ethnic groups. They were aware that the postwar reforms affected the "prestige of the chiefs, precedence, deportment, decoration, housing, salaries."[13]

This awareness developed farthest in Northern Nigeria, in Mali, Niger, and the plateau and savannah regions of Guinea. It became the basis for the more successful "patron" parties, including those now behind the single-party governments of Northern Nigeria, Niger, and Mauretania. In Mali and Guinea also, the patron parties which won in the postwar elections until defeated, in 1956, by the *Union Soudanaise* and the *Parti Démocratique de Guinée* mass parties respectively, were based on these "chiefs." It was therefore in these territories particularly that the struggle against the colonial power barely masked another struggle, most acute in the countryside, between traditionalists and modernizers. In Mali and Guinea the mass party leaders, as soon as they were in a position to do so, consolidated their electoral victory by doing away altogether with the official "chiefs" and replacing them with regular civil servants, assisted by elected village councils. In Niger and Northern Nigeria, however, the challenge to the "chiefs," though already offered by the respective opposition parties—*Sawaba* and the *Northern Elements Progressive Union* (NEPU)—has not yet been successful.

Even before the war educated Africans rather than traditional or official "chiefs" were increasingly sought out by their kinsmen to help them settle controversies with the Europeans and their laws. After the war, by the order in which they came as well as by their content, the reforms in West Africa helped the educated elite to assume the political initiative. (The recent history of the Congo illustrates, by contrast, the importance of this by-product of a reform phase preceding total independence.) In West Africa, most people took it for granted that Africans elected to postwar representative posts would know how to read and write in English or French—if only to talk to the Europeans who had promulgated the reforms. Moreover, in most territories the franchise was initially weighted in favor of those who were able to identify themselves in the records kept by the colonial power—which meant the literate and those earning money, mainly the people in the regular civil service, and only to a lesser degree those recognized as candidates for official "chief." The reforms gave the educated Africans legal channels for organizing the expulsion of the colonial power. They had reason to want to. Most of them lived in towns, saw Europeans often and were directly affected by the discrimination—racial, cultural, social and professional—which characterized the pre-war colonial system.

The postwar reforms strengthened the position of the educated elite further by synchronizing political developments in areas of unequal political pressure, and by forcing even those traditional leaders who could still count upon the following of their ethnic groups, as in Mauretania or Northern Nigeria, to select educated "front men" for the new elective offices. Moreover, because the reforms extended over approximately two decades before full independence came, aspiring leaders had time to build records as nationalists, to champion opposition causes in the countryside, to build parties, and so anchor their authority to some degree. Nationalism gave the educated elite a powerful theme: to make all Africans once again masters in their own land. With a few exceptions this educated elite, rather than the traditional aristocrats or official "chiefs," got the credit for expelling the European colonizers.

Major or minor parties, mass or patron, these educated men staffed them. They provided the candidates for the new government offices after the war, they took the seats in legislative assemblies, in cabinets, and public corporations; they filled the senior civil service posts. A majority of them were of the first generation in their families to read or write a language other than Arabic. They had been trained in schools designed to produce only subordinates for Europeans in that phase of colonial history when all senior posts were reserved for Europeans. Many were only primary school graduates; a minority—significantly larger in southern Ghana and Nigeria, which were richer, than in French-speaking Africa—went to secondary school. Only a tiny number graduated from universities.

Since most university places only opened up to West Africans after the war, few graduates were available to take the first offices. Nearly all of these had to content themselves with second-level posts, usually in the civil service. Some, indeed, were in the peculiar position of working under African ministers who were contemporaries, but who had failed the secondary school or college entrance examinations—which had left them free to take part in the crucial first years of postwar political activity, and so to become "founding fathers." The mass franchise, in effect, added yet another reason why, for the modern elite, the standards of success in the schools of the Europeans were often the reverse of the standards of success in African elections. Under the prewar conditions of total European control, the most educated generally acquired the highest of the subordinate offices open to Africans. But after the war, when the villagers acquired the vote and so became arbiters in the competition for power among members of the elite, those with only a primary school education often spoke the language of the

people and exhibited talents which appealed to the villagers.

While the state schools helped weaken ethnic and historic antagonisms, they also created new cleavages among the educated elite, which in some territories acquired some political significance. For example, in postwar Guinea most of those who had been prewar students in the dominant French West African secondary school, the École Normale William-Ponty, wanted to keep the only paying jobs open to them. These were invariably in the civil service and so they had little alternative, prior to 1956, but to go into "administrative" parties. Most of them joined one of the officially preferred regional patron parties. The mass party in Guinea, the *Parti Démocratique de Guinée,* was led by products of the lower state schools, who accused Ponty graduates of "betraying the masses," and called them "valets of the administration." In Gold Coast (now Ghana) also, political and educational cleavages were to some degree superimposed when the "Standard VII boys" joined a radical breakaway from the more highly educated leaders of the *United Gold Coast Convention** (UGCC) and built the *Convention People's Party.* In Ivory Coast by contrast, Ponty graduates took the lead both in the regional "patron" parties, and in the mass party—the *Parti Démocratique de la Côte d'Ivoire.* There Ponty graduates found alternatives to administrative employment in cocoa and coffee farming. Consequently in Ivory Coast political cleavages did not relate closely to differences in the diplomas achieved by members of the elite.

Apart from levels of education, differences of generation also made for cleavages among the elite, such as those which divided the Senegalese leaders of the *Bloc Démocratique Sénégalais** (BDS)[14] from the leaders of the Senegalese federation of the *Section Française de l'Intérnationale Ouvrière** (SFIO);[15] or the young organizers of the *Convention People's Party* from the older leaders of the *United Gold Coast Convention.** There are differences in ideology too: Marxist-inspired for the *Parti Démocratique de Guinée* and the *Union Soudanaise;* a blend of Catholic and socialist political doctrine for many leaders of the *Union Progressiste Sénégalaise.* These differences are sharpest in the minor parties organized by university trained graduates: dissident-Marxist for some leaders of the *Parti du Régroupement Africain* (PRA)—*Sénégal;* close to orthodox Communism for the leaders of the Senegalese *Parti Africain de l'Indépendance* (PAI); an Africanized version of Emmanuel Mounier's French Catholic social doctrine for those participating in the *Mouvement Africain de Libération Nationale* (MLN). There were also differences in status, distinguishing in Senegal, for example, the prewar privileged "citizens" in the SFIO* from the "subjects" in the *Bloc Démocratique Sénégalais;** the former had earlier access to education, more wealth often from the peanut trade, and higher jobs in the civil service.[16]

These differences within the modern elite were balanced, however, by a certain common outlook. They conceived of themselves as Africans rather than Malinke, for example. Their common experiences in schools, jobs, and in the money economy, in prewar town associations, and with colonial administration gave them a homogeneity. But no such common outlook linked all the elite to the mass of the population. Instead, a separation gradually developed, most marked among people several generations or several decades removed from the village, e.g., the "citizens" of Senegal or many of the French- or British-trained university graduates. Africans building parties to bridge this gulf after the war had to work with peoples mostly ignorant of French or English. Yet these were the languages expressing the modern constitutional decisions, including the decisions to introduce the universal franchise. Few had ever been to a large town and most had never lived in one; almost all handled money rarely and lived far from roads or railroads. The African organizer who came into a village to solicit votes was at the same time a transmitter of news of a modern world. This world was symbolized by the airport located perhaps fifty miles from the village, if the distance is reckoned in physical mileage; but several hundred years away if the distance is plotted against the timetable of European economic and social history.

Grass roots politics are different from national politics in most parts of the world, and particularly great in Africa. The educated elite are few in number and disproportionately distributed over even the most important of the many ethnic groups and regions of various types. The gap is large between the traditions which inspired the formal governments of the new nations and the pre-European institutions. To some extent most people continue to relate themselves to political parties through a "screen of kinship," a fact which made it necessary for all successful parties—mass or patron—to develop skill in "ethnic arithmetic" when selecting leaders and candidates. This skill is at the core of the new African parties' methods of approaching the important work of social integration.

## III. THE INTEGRATING FUNCTION

In illuminating the functions of the parties, the mass-patron distinction again has meaning. Patron parties fulfilled only the minimum tasks assigned to parties by the formal institutions; they integrated only the patrons. With the possible exception of the Northern People's Congress, these parties were interested in an individual only insofar as he happened to be included in the franchise; they provided candidates for election and the minimum machinery for

bringing the voter to the polls. They paid little attention to the function of political education, and barely explained the context of the postwar reforms to the population.

By contrast, the functions of mass parties were far more complex and varied. On occasion, before they acquired government responsibilities, mass parties disregarded—indeed replaced—the existing legal institutions. To the extent that for a time they substituted, or proposed to substitute, their structure for that of the state—that they developed their own ways of administering justice or of keeping order—these parties filled a revolutionary function. (Though in West Africa, unlike Cameroun or Algeria, none waged guerrilla war.) For some time the population considered them, far more than the legal institutions conceived in London or in Paris, to be legitimate. By agreeing to work at least partly within the postwar representative institutions, therefore, these parties legitimized the formal structure, rather than vice versa. Coincidentally, these parties acted as national "melting pots," educating people as Africans. Insofar as they provided a new social framework for people no longer firmly rooted in a stable ethnic tradition, they can be termed "parties of social integration."[17] They and their cultural affiliates were interested in everything from the cradle to the grave—in birth, initiation, religion, marriage, divorce, dancing, song, plays, feuds, debts, land, migration, death, public order—and not only in electoral success.

An analysis of the modern and traditional status and ethnic origins of national and local leaders shows how the mass parties performed this integrating function. This analysis is particularly important, since the achievement of independence in West Africa allowed shifts in the distribution of power not only between Europeans and Africans, but also within African society—between the modern and traditional elites, within each of these groups, and in the links connecting them with the mass of the population.

Perhaps the best approach is the relatively simple question—what group or sub-group predominated in the major parties? Trade unionists predominated within the Parti Démocratique de Guinée and were of great significance in the Union Soudanaise and the (outlawed) Sawaba mass party of Niger. African planters formed the Parti Démocratique de la Côte d'Ivoire, and people associated with the cocoa export trade were influential in the Action Group of Nigeria. The educated former "subjects" constructed the Bloc Démocratique Sénégalais* to challenge, in effect, the "citizen"-led socialists. All these dominant groups were in the modern categories of the population, a feature all mass parties had in common and shared with only those few "patron" parties that were based on a prewar town elite.

Who predominated in those patron parties resting on important village personalities? The distinction between mass and patron parties, in relation to local party structure, was less neat in fact than in definition. When first organizing, aspiring mass party leaders did not disdain to accept the backing of an important local personage—an official chief, a traditional aristocrat, a Muslim *marabout* or an animist sage. But partly because most mass parties were born after the war either as or out of anticolonial "congresses,"[18] locally important persons in West Africa connected with the colonial establishment usually held aloof until the mass party was itself becoming the establishment. Then many "shifted their rifles from one shoulder to the other."[19] Most important local personages without modern education who became identified with the mass parties during the height of the independence struggle— *la lutte anti-impérialiste*—had special reasons for lining up against the colonial administration, usually connected with a local quarrel over chieftaincy, prestige or property. Many rivals to the official "chiefs," at the village or regional level, joined the mass parties at an early stage. However, when such a personality became included locally within the mass party, the methods of the mass party worked to control his local influence, to make of him but one among many. There were, of course, variations in degree, related to mass party structure and to the type of tribal political organization.

Where there was an educated urban middle class, also identified both for cultural and economic reasons with the colonial power, its members hesitated too before becoming associated with the radical, anti-colonial mass parties, usually initiated by younger, less educated men, less acceptable to the Europeans. The clearest examples of this were in Senegal and in Gold Coast (Ghana). The prewar "subjects," shortly after they acquired the vote in 1945, broke from the "citizen"-dominated SFIO* of Senegal to organize their *Bloc Démocratique Sénégalais.** Similarly in Gold Coast the younger, more radical men broke from the *United Gold Coast Convention** to organize the *Convention People's Party.*

Thus in some areas, in spite of their many differences, a prewar town elite holding the highest positions permitted to Africans in the colonial system, and the official "chiefs" already conscious that the presence of the Europeans stabilized their position, made common cause in patron parties against mass party leaders. The lineup of "haves" against their "have not" challengers was evident in the epithets exchanged at election time. Urban patron party leaders called mass party leaders "vagrants" (Guinea), "veranda boys" (Ghana); in the countryside patrons underlined that their rivals were "slaves" or "strangers." Mass party leaders, for their part, hurled labels like "union of featherbedders" at the patron party leaders.

In varying degrees, the nationalist struggle helped stir up "loyalty" issues, national and local, fre-

quently with the result of providing yet another cause for disintegration in an already fragile society. For where they could, those lower on the traditional or modern social scale used the issue of nationalism to strengthen their own position through the mass parties. And those with privileges to lose, as in Niger or Nigeria, showed signs of preferring rule by the Europeans to rule by the *talakawa* (commoners in Hausa). Especially in the countryside, showing loyalty to the mass party when it was under pressure from the colonial power, was one way to compensate for a weak claim to belonging to the local ethnic group—for the immigrant *dioula* ("strangers") in Ivory Coast to show they were as loyal, for example, as the *originaires* who first came to the area.

With so few in the educated elite, and a subtle network of kinship connecting leaders and followers, it was logical that leaders of both mass and patron parties organized on a territorial scale should have gone through the first and simplest stage of "ethnic arithmetic": they kept a rough correspondence between the ethnic origins of leaders and followers. This correspondence is at least as important in Africa as in Boston or New York City politics. Defeating a patron party which has not been through this first stage was relatively easy for mass party leaders—as when, the *Bloc Démocratique Sénégalais** used "favorite sons" in the Casamance region of Senegal, to defeat the SFIO* which was locally (as well as territorially) dominated by Wolof and Lébou from Dakar or Saint-Louis. Leaders who tried to build national parties failed when they did not have among their ranks representatives of the most important ethnic groups. The Socialist party of Guinea was in this category. It grew from the Fulani club at the Ecole Normale William-Ponty and never really succeeded in broadening its ethnic base, even though it underwent several important changes, from an ethnic to a nationalist ideology. Too many of one ethnic group, too few of another, caused jealousies and difficulties for any party. The *Parti Démocratique de la Côte d'Ivoire* had relatively little trouble with ethnic separatism from the Baule, while the *Convention People's Party* had considerable difficulty with the Ashanti. These two ethnic groups, traditionally related, occupy similar historic and geographic positions in their respective states, produce most of the coffee and cocoa and so have the most wealth. The PDCI from the beginning had Baule associated with them through the person of their leader, Félix Houphouët-Boigny; while in Ghana the CPP started, and except in the revolutionary years 1949–1950 remained, without similar support among the Ashanti. They are conscious of losing power to southerners, and "young men" on occasion lament with their more conservative elders the present absolute reversal of Ashanti fortunes."[20]

While patron parties' leaders, once through this

first simple phase of "ethnic arithmetic," generally stopped their calculations there, the leaders of mass parties had taken that as a point of departure. They tried to use their party organizations in order to awaken a wider, national sense of community. They appealed to particular categories existing within or cutting across ethnic groups—a technique suitable to recruiting in a mobile, changing society. Youth and women were of course two such categories which mass parties emphasized heavily. As already noted, in many villages mass party organizers went to rivals of official "chiefs"; from these they discovered local grievances. They often appealed to rural underprivileged groups. For example, the *Parti Démocratique de Guinée* first gained a following in the Fouta Djallon plateau not among the Fulani majority, but rather among the "captives" living in the ancillary villages (*roundé*). They appealed to rural scribes, whose modern skills set them apart, and to those who had travelled, often "strangers" who were among the most recent immigrants to a flourishing agricultural area. In some areas they went to veterans—in Ghana, for example, and in Senegal. They sought out religious dissidents—Harrists in the Ivory Coast, Hamallists in Mali. In some areas they found Muslim proselytizers opposed by the "chief"—either because he was animist, or because though Muslim he nevertheless felt his secular position under attack. They found camel drivers, chauffeurs, transporters, and peddlers—such as the *dioula* traders of Western Upper Volta, Mali, Guinea, and Ivory Coast, or some "Hausa" traders of Ghana and Nigeria. (Many of these in fact came from families with a tradition as middlemen in the trans-Siberian trade before it declined under trans-Atlantic competition.) Finally, they appealed to those who earned money income for growing coffee, cocoa, peanuts or bananas, and had become restless with tradition; to young men who no longer listened to the old; and to women who made money trading in the marketplace. People responded to the mass party organizers' appeals against established authorities.

People in these non-ethnic social categories were still in a minority, to be sure; most of them had some roots in a tribal community and they too wanted party leaders of roughly similar origins to their own. Mass party leaders were well aware they needed associates who were kinsmen of those they sought as followers, even while many rejected the principle that ethnic considerations should enter into the selection of party office holders. Indeed, conflicts among ethnic groups were often sharper in mass than in patron parties, since mass parties made a continuous attempt to propagate modern values and diminish the weight of ethnic exclusiveness. For example, after their 1956 victories, both *Union Soudanaise* and *Parti Démocratique de Guinée* leaders developed the habit of deliberately scrambling the ethnic origins of party propagandists

and their audiences. Men from the Guinea coast campaigned in the forest and Fouta Djallon; men from Upper Guinea, on the coast. All these tactics had the purpose of encouraging people to relate themselves directly to the party.

Conflicts between modern and traditional leaders were also often sharper in mass than patron parties since most mass parties were egalitarian by policy. The traditional upperclass standing of Sékou Touré or Modibo Keïta, for example, was important because of the high popular esteem given to them. The *Parti Démocratique de Guinée* began to make headway among the Fulani after Diallo Sayfoulaye, the son of an important Fulani chief, "like La Fayette . . . left his privileges to join the democratic cause."[21] Félix Houphouët-Boigny, in the militant years of the *Parti Démocratique de la Côte d'Ivoire* before 1952, used his prestige as official chief, and not only as a doctor and wealthy planter, in order to entrench the PDCI in the countryside. On the whole, they used their nobility to preach equality.

The majority of the national and regional leadership in patron parties is of traditional upper-class status, while the majority of the mass party national and regional leadership is of commoner origin. But mass parties have a surprisingly large number of people with high traditional status as the top national party leaders. And patron parties have an exceptionally large number of prime ministers, or officials holding the first post in the modern institutions, with low traditional status. (Is this a method of chiefly control, reminiscent of their habit, at the turn of the century, of sending not their own but sons of slaves to the schools of the Europeans?) Alhaji Abubakar Tafawa Balewa, the Northern Nigerian designated by the *Northern People's Congress* to become Prime Minister of the Federation of Nigeria, is of low traditional status. So is Joseph Conombo, who until 1956 was deputy to the French National Assembly from Upper Volta, elected through a patron party based on the Mossi chiefs. So was Yacine Diallo (d. 1954), Guinea deputy to the French National Assembly representing the then dominant patron party alliance, and more specifically the Fulani chiefs. So is Hubert Maga, Prime Minister of Dahomey, who represented a regional patron party strong in Northern Dahomey. It is as if "princes" fear least the competition of "captives"; while villagers, first hearing equality preached, learn fastest from "princes."

Thus within mass parties, not only ethnic origins but also ethnic status continue to count, often causing more conflict precisely because mass party ideology usually ignores or challenges these differences. Yet men with high modern but low traditional qualifications—Ponty graduates of *griot*[22] descent, for example, lawyers descended of "captives"—were rarely put forward by local mass party branch members as candidates for elective office. In varying degrees, mass party national leaders usually maintained a continuous pressure in favor of such nominations, as of West Indians and other "strangers," to prove they believed in equality. (Precisely so as to be able to maintain this pressure, mass party leaders often preferred multi-member to single-member constituencies in legislative assembly elections. Where ten seats were to be filled, local branch members were more inclined to accept some candidates that national headquarters designated, than where only one seat was involved.) Though they tried much harder than patron party leaders, mass party leaders did not always succeed in avoiding institutionalizing ethnic differences. So in the long run, friction among ethnic groups in Ivory Coast may have been intensified by the *Parti Démocratique de la Côte d'Ivoire*'s decision to organize local branches on an ethnic, rather than a neighborhood principle. This distinguished the PDCI local structure from that of most other mass parties. The *Union Soudanaise,* the *Parti Démocratique de Guinée,* and the *Union Progressiste Sénégalaise,* for example, made strenuous efforts to mix ethnic groups at the local level—and did so at least to the extent that neighborhoods did. The PDCI decision was a recognition of the way people actually communicated in Ivory Coast, a concession to reality, unwillingly made by many educated leaders because they knew they might need to assemble their followers rapidly. It was challenged by a PDCI Congress resolution in 1959, as yet not implemented.[23]

The various methods used by mass and patron parties further illustrate the differences between them. Patron parties adopted methods respectful of established authority. They rarely called mass meetings and until 1957 generally avoided the techniques of protest, offered few if any personal services to supporters, and were little concerned with party symbols. The mass parties, prior to achieving government majorities, employed techniques related to their revolutionary, legitimizing, educational and social integration functions. Demonstrations, strikes, boycotts and occasional violence were revolutionary techniques. The parties paid considerable attention to the creation of new national symbols: insignias, colors, slogans, party cloth for women to wear. The *Action Group of Nigeria* even hired American public relations advisers. Mass party choices of symbols and slogans were based on sound insight into popular responses, and repetition is at the heart of African oratory, as of drumming and dance.[24] "Vote the elephant; he is wise and never forgets." The *Parti Démocratique de Guinée* and the *Parti Démocratique de la Côte d'Ivoire* painted the elephant on walls and roofs and streets and cars. In the savannah, however, the *Union Soudanaise* never made much of the fact that the elephant was its symbol also; for there *Union Soudanaise* opponents said with effect, "the elephant eats your crops and leaves you destitute." The *African Group of*

*Nigeria* adopted the palm tree as its symbol of the "life more abundant." Elaborating on the meaning of the *Bloc Démocratique Sénégalais** party colors, Léopold Senghor of Senegal wrote "Green is for the Muslim majority, the color of the Prophet's flag; green is for the Christian minority, the color of hope; green is for the animists, the symbol of youth and the irrepressible force of Black Africa."[25] And using the elimination of forced labor to their ends, aspiring mass party *Union Démocratique Nigérienne**[26] leaders of Niger, whose ballot carried the picture of a camel, warned people not to vote for the patron *Union Nigérienne des Indépendants et Sympathisants** party which had a yellow ballot bearing the picture of a stick and a basket. "Vote for the camel, and you will be as free as he," they said, well acquainted with that ornery beast. And they added, "The yellow ballot is a stick and a basket; if you vote for it forced labor will come back." The *Northern People's Congress* made *salama*—"peace"—its slogan. Prayers were often connected with party ceremonies, and so a libation was poured in connection with *Convention People's Party* and *Parti Démocratique de la Côte d'Ivoire* meetings, or the Fatiha (opening *sura* of the Koran) was intoned prior to some *Parti Démocratique de Guinée* meetings.

Personal oratory was one of the most effective educational techniques. Campaigning against the Guinea regional patron parties during 1954–6, Sékou Touré explained, "I am Diallo the shepherd from the Fouta, I am Mamba the planter from Nzerekore, Keïta the rice grower from Siguiri, Soumah the fisherman from the coast, I am African, I am every man." Both because they believed it, and because the "important people" in the countryside opposed them, most mass party organizers preached equality. "Vincent Auriol and Lamine both die if they go hungry." Or, "three men want to go to Bamako. The governor goes by plane, Mamba by bicycle, Yacine on foot. Who arrives first?" "The governor," shouts the crowd. "Next?" "Mamba." "Then?" "Yacine." In such dialogues leaders communicated the idea that the environment accounts for most human differences.

The identification of the mass party with the community before independence was emphasized not only by party sponsorship of dances, festivals, songs, receptions, by party organization of weddings or funerals, but also by the existence of an informal party social security system which resulted in support for indigent partisans, legal advice for imprisoned militants, payment of medical bills for the sick, food and housing for families of party widows or grass widows, as well as automatic hospitality for party-sponsored travellers. On occasion the mass party could count on free labor even for the construction of bridges, roads, and schools—on popular good will that the *Parti Démocratique de Guinée* and *Union Soudanaise* leaders termed human investment—*investissement humain*—and included in their inventory of economic resources.

## IV. DEMOCRACY AND THE SINGLE PARTY SYSTEM

The nationalist struggle strengthens the position of the educated elite in largely traditional societies and encourages the elite to knit into mass parties the forces for change and dissent both traditional and modern. There is not yet evidence to show that the trend from patron to mass party majority continues after independence. The distinctions between and among mass and patron parties turn on differences in degree, and some parties fall between the two categories. Is the *Parti Démocratique de la Côte d'Ivoire,* for example, losing its mass party characteristics and becoming a patron type? The efficiency of its organization has declined, as has its interest in social equality; there have been many signs of rising discontent; it has been increasingly unable to cope with ethnic separatist pressures. The *Northern People's Congress,* on the other hand, because of its growing emphasis on mass recruitment, may be moving towards the mass party type. Despite these transitional cases the distinction between types is useful.

It is useful in considering the now popular question: how far are the West African single-party systems democratic? I use "democratic" to mean, roughly, that decisions are made with general consent, according to established procedures, in harmony with such values as social equality, and under conditions in which opposition can be expressed. It is difficult to argue that West African single-party systems resting on patron parties are or are becoming democratic, notwithstanding variations in degree. Northern Nigeria has been mentioned. Least in Mauretania, somewhat more in Niger and Upper Volta, can significant evidence be found of general consent, of social equality as a value, or of opportunity to express opposition in the dominant party. The main opposition groups are outlawed. Of the single patron-party states it is easier to argue they are moving towards military dictatorship.

In the present phase of West African party history, there is more evidence that the single-party systems based on mass parties are moving towards democracy. There is, first, the element of widespread consent. During at least a brief period the territorial and party communities were indistinguishable; the mass party reflected the "general will." This was usually just prior to taking over responsibility for governing, but after using to advantage the fact of being in opposition. Discontent was the common denominator. Typical of the instructions national mass party leaders gave to local leaders were, "Go and talk to the peasants in the field."

"Tell Abdoulaye his daughter cannot be forced to marry the old chief." "Tell the peasants not to sell their crops at that ruinous price." "Defend Pango's palm trees against destruction by the administrator." "Speak up for Binta's right to cultivate the land the chief claims." While not all the questions were settled, villagers found a national platform in the mass party which they had never known. Mass party organizers sought out grievances, expressed them in the marketplace, coordinated them. They blamed European rule for forced labor, taxes, abuses of official "chiefs," racial discrimination, poverty. Out of these grievances they welded their massive demonstrations against colonial rule. Most patron party leaders were too linked with the established authorities to play this muckraking role.

Muckraking paid. Mass party membership was open to all, and practically all sought to acquire it. This characteristic of recruitment distinguished West African states based on mass parties from states based on single parties confining their membership —as most fascist or Communist parties do—to a selected group. The widespread influence and number of followers of the mass parties at their peak, their national character long before the institutions of government were controlled by Africans, their success in acquiring the credit for the national revolution—all these bore out the mass party claim to represent the entire population. This helps explain why many West African mass party leaders saw little contradiction between claiming to be democratic and insisting on the existence of only a single, mass-based party. It is the African version of that "sole and central power which governs the whole community, by its direct influence,"[27] which de Tocqueville observed in the nineteenth-century American idea of the state.

The prospect of democracy in West African mass party states is enhanced, second, by party organization and procedure. Mass parties, at their best, have developed the organization which can publicize and encourage the mass discussion of important issues. Local branches involve the many rather than honor the few, and mass party leaders try to use traditional organizations in order to reach individuals. They are often more effective than the civil service. Leaders are chosen by voting. In the thoroughly organized mass parties, institutionalized leadership was also collective. Set procedures were followed for the making of decisions and leaders were expected to report back. Thus the mass parties reenforced the African version of responsibility.

Mass parties strengthened democratic forces, in the third place, to the extent that they encouraged social equality. The modern elite, themselves in favor of such values as merit rather than birth as the determinant of rank, were in a stronger position in the mass party states. Moreover, most mass party leaders rose from lower positions both in the modern and the traditional social scale, and used their new power in favor of social equality. Though they had to employ both ethnic and status "arithmetic" to bridge the gap between the educated and the mass of the population, mass party leaders, unlike patron party leaders, did so in a manner to blur ethnic differences and weaken status differences.

The fourth contribution of mass parties to the prospects of democracy is setting conditions in which opposition is possible. Among the elite, there is enough consensus about the rules of the political game to make it possible for them to disagree without coming, too often, to blows. After all, in prewar Senegal, as in nineteenth-century Britain or present Southern Rhodesia and South Africa, the vote, and controversies among the several parties, remained confined to a few who spoke the same language and fought for similar interests. In the long run in Africa, restricting the franchise to a privileged few is a greater threat to democracy than the existence of but a single party. At the present stage of African social history, the mass party organization makes it possible for people to disagree within it, without necessarily triggering incidents endangering the rule of the elite and the stability of the state. Confining disagreements to the issues at hand is difficult in a society where only the members of an educated elite born of different ethnic groups are able to speak directly to each other in French or English. Even where the organization of a mass party is a "spider's web"[28] villagers often have different ideas than national leaders. Sékou Touré spoke of this to the Fifth Congress of the *Parti Démocratique de Guinée* in September, 1959:

. . . democracy, within our Party, is not a democracy of clan or family, but a basic democracy to which the entire population contributes directly and freely . . . the old forms of social democracy anchored in the villages often influence the party militants, who believe themselves authorized to violate the new individual forms prescribed within the PDG. Therefore at each new election for officers, dissensions arise within the Movement. This occurs because we have not yet accomplished our work.[29]

As long as kinship is an important link between the educated and their rural constituents divisions among the elite on such constitutional matters as federalism, independence, or the position of "chiefs," is often taken by their kinsmen as a signal for settling entirely unrelated traditional issues over land, women or water. This was one of the dynamic factors behind the Kumasi riots which accompanied the *Convention People's Party-National Liberation Movement*\* (NLM)[30] controversy about constitutional matters after 1956. A similar dynamic helped to explain the Ivory Coast incidents of 1949–51. In the relatively integrated societies of North America or Western Europe, pluralism is quite rightly counted among the democratic virtues. In Africa today, it is rather a vice.

These four points back up the argument that West African states based on dominant mass parties are moving towards democracy. West Africans justify their insistence on a single party on yet other grounds—that a national emergency exists. The struggle for independence is "not the concern of a day, a year, or an age; posterity are virtually involved in the contest. . . ."[31] These words of Tom Paine's reflect the African sense of history.[32] Africans argue the plural "party system under imperialist domination is synonymous with a sterile division that profits only those who want to see to it that their privileges continue."[33] This is the logic of a community at war, considering an *administratif* to be like a "quisling." Most Africans carry their sense of urgency into the post-independence era, and consider unity necessary in order rapidly to "install the apparatus of the State, at the service of economic development, of social and cultural development."[34]

While there is good evidence for the argument that West African states based on dominant mass parties are moving towards democracy, there is also evidence of forces moving against. How does a mass party continue to reflect the "general will" after independence? The full responsibilities of government have already brought out centrifugal forces—opposition within the mass parties from its youth, labor and traditionalist affiliates. Some officials have used their public office for personal gain. There have been signs of ethnic separatism, particularly on international frontiers. Rural friction intensified between "strangers" or *dioula* and the original owners of tribal lands. It appears, as Thomas Hodgkin claims, that the logical consequence of self-determination is anarchy. Yet perhaps even a greater threat to democracy is the fear of anarchy, making new African governments as quick to pass Preventive Detention Acts as the United States was to adopt the Alien and Sedition Acts in 1798.

What opportunity is there in the mass party states to express disagreement? This varies. *Within* the mass parties the greatest opportunity appears to exist in the best organized ones. So far discussion is widespread and frank—within the *Parti Démocratique de Guinée* and the *Union Soudanaise,* for example—and leaders have on many occasions been outvoted on important issues. Not only individual disagreement is possible under the party umbrella, but also organized disagreements by *tendances*—such as trade union, youth, student and cultural organizations, even the civil service. In the less highly organized mass party states, such as Ivory Coast, the Eastern Region of Nigeria, Senegal and Togo, these modern associations tend to be foci of opposition outside of the mass party, though not necessarily calling themselves parties.

The opportunity to express opposition through rival political parties also varies. In no West African mass party state is *all* organized opposition to the dominant party directly excluded by law, though specified parties or types of parties are outlawed in most states. It is excluded in effect, however, where it is a matter of doctrine to insist on the single party, the *parti unique,* and on its identity with both the popular will and with the state. It is less excluded where leaders justify the single party for empirical reasons as a *parti unifié,* making common cause in the present national emergency. Where single-party states are based on patron parties, opposition groups exist which are already or potentially mass parties; at least in Niger, Northern Nigeria, and to less extent Upper Volta these have considerable momentum behind them. But in mass party states, from among what groups has organized opposition come? There are "one-man shows" such as the *Union Démocratique et Sociale Africaine** of Guinea or the *Front de Libération Noire** of Ivory Coast; rump groups left over from mergers or reorganizations, like the postwar *Parti Socialiste Sénégalais** and the "expatriate" groups such as the *Parti de la Libération de la Côte d'Ivoire* in Guinea; these have simply curiosity value and generally exist only for a short time. Limited staying power also characterizes parties like the *Parti de Solidarité Sénégalaise,* built by disaffected "clan leaders" and other rural personalities. Numerous ethnic minor parties exist in the countryside, such as the *Union Dogon** of Mali, or the Socialists among the Bété of Ivory Coast. When ethnic parties are based on urban areas, their supporters usually belonged to the tribes which originally owned the land—the *Rassemblement Démocratique Sénégalais* among the Lébou of Dakar, for example.

Standing alone these ethnic parties have little potential on the national scene. But they might have in inter-state politics if, for example, Guinea leaders used as an instrument of pressure the loyalty to the *Parti Démocratique de Guinée* of ethnic groups living on the frontiers of Liberia or Sierra Leone. Or there might be a future in federal politics if well organized teams of educated leaders synchronized the discontent among minority groups—as the *Action Group of Nigeria* has done in the North and the *National Council of Nigeria and the Cameroons* has done in the West of the Federation. The political history both of Nigeria and the former French West African federation suggests that federalism adds to the prospects for organized opposition groups. Partly this is because the desire to control the federation offers mass party leaders dominant in one region incentives to seek support in another. Furthermore the desire to work together in a federation is a reason why leaders of the dominant party in one region may at least hesitate before repressing opponents having political support in another region.

Most significant are opposition groups among "young Turks," mainly town-dwellers differently educated or younger than the men leading the dominant parties: JUVENTO in Togo, *An Nahda al Watenia al Mauritania* (Party of the National Renaissance of Mauretania), *Parti du Regroupement Africain-Sénégal,* and the *Parti Africain de l'Indépendence* of Senegal. With the possible exception of the PAI, these avant-garde groups had no conscious elitist theory governing recruitment, but in practice their audience is still confined to the modern elite, to youth and student and trade union groups. Particularly when the party in power is of a mass type, most of these groups alternate between opposing it and joining it in order to constitute a "party within a party." These "young Turks" are nationalists and modernizers. They have little appetite for ethnic, separatist opposition of the type loosely allied in the *United Party* of Ghana.

The "young Turks" constitute the actual or potential national, not ethnic, opposition. They might be joined, eventually, by breakaway groups from among the "founding fathers."[35] As long as the elite is small, the civil service is likely to absorb the most newly educated strata of the elite—and dominant parties will brook no partisan opposition from within the civil services. On economic development depends the growth of the modern strata of African society in large enough numbers, and spread evenly enough across ethnic groups, to permit opposition party leaders to calculate in ethnic and status "arithmetic." The chance of opposition groups eventually displacing in elections the dominant mass parties in the single-party states, may increase as the "national emergency" ends. Independence is mostly acquired. Now in West Africa, unity for economic development is the order of the day.

There are, in the mass party states of West Africa, obstacles to the growth of democracy, as in most other parts of the world. But on balance, to a much greater extent than the colonial governments which they succeeded, the mass party states rest on popular consent, strengthen procedures and institutions on a scale essential for accomplishing the tasks of the modern democratic state, reflect egalitarian values and leave room for the expression of opposition. So far, the mass party states have used to good effect the emphasis on "union, a word like friendship, goodness, an abstract thing having no face, raising no concrete image in the mind. It goes into all sauces; it accommodates itself to irreconcilables."[36]

## NOTES

1. Evidence for this paper was gathered during field trips to West Africa, and is to be published in my *Parties of French-Speaking West Africa.* I am most grateful to Jeffrey Butler, Thomas Hodgkin, Richard Sklar and Immanuel Wallerstein for their valuable comments, and to Newell Stultz for his assistance.

2. "Patron" parties and "parties of personalities" are terms employed by Thomas Hodgkin, author of *Nationalism in Colonial Africa* (London, Muller, 1956). "Cadre" party is used by Maurice Duverger in his *Political Parties* (London, Methuen, 1954).

3. Parties indicated with an * have gone out of existence.

4. Hodgkin, *op. cit.*, p. 144.

5. R. Rézette, *Les Partis politiques marocains* (Paris, Colin, 1955).

6. David E. Apter and Carl G. Rosberg, "Nationalism and Models of Political Change in Africa," *The Political Economy of Contemporary Africa,* Symposia Studies Series #1, The National Institute of Social and Behavioral Science, George Washington University, 1959, p. 8.

7. David Apter, *The Gold Coast in Transition* (Princeton, Princeton University Press, 1955).

8. Max Weber, "The Sociology of Charismatic Authority," *From Max Weber,* H. H. Gerth & C. Wright Mills, eds. (London, Routledge & Kegan Paul, 1952), p. 250.

9. Peter Worsley, *The Trumpet Shall Sound* (London, MacGibbon & Kee, 1957), p. 271.

10. Thomas Carlyle, "The Hero as King," *On Heroes and Hero Worship* (London, Ward & Lock, 1900), p. 262.

11. See Elliot Berg, "The Economic Basis of Political Choice in French West Africa," [*American Political Science Review*], Vol. 54 (June 1960), esp. Table I on p. 393.

12. Colin Clark, *The Conditions of Economic Progress* (London, Macmillan, 1951), p. 567.

13. From the electoral manifesto of September 5, 1945, issued by the *Parti Progressiste Soudanais* leader, Fily Dabo Sissoko.

14. Forerunner of the *Union Progressiste Sénégalaise.*

15. In 1958 both groups merged into the *Union Progressiste Sénégalaise.*

16. For further details, see Kenneth E. Robinson's excellent chapter "Senegal" in *Five Elections in Africa,* edited by him and W. J. M. Mackenzie (Oxford, 1960).

17. Sigmund Neumann, *Modern Political Parties* (University of Chicago Press, 1956), p. 404.

18. Hodgkin, *op. cit.,* p. 144.

19. Madeira Keïta, "Le parti unique en Afrique," *Présence Africaine,* February–March, 1960, pp. 19–20.

20. Dennis Austin and William Tordoff, "Voting in an African Town," *Political Studies* (Oxford), June, 1960.

21. *La Liberté,* PDG news,      December 22, 1955.

22. Traditional caste resembling medieval troubadours.

23. *Abidjan-Matin,* June 18, 1959. See A. R. Zolberg, "Effets de la structure d'un parti politique sur l'intégration nationale," *Cahiers d'études africaines,* October 3, 1960, p. 140 f.

24. Unless otherwise indicated, I recorded the citations in Africa.

25. *Condition Humaine, Bloc Démocratique Sénégalais** newspaper, November 30, 1948.

26. The forerunner of *Sawaba.*

27. *Democracy in America* (London, 1952), pp. 550–51.

28. The term is frequently used by the *Union Soudanaise* secretary general, Modibo Keïta.

29. *Official Report* (Conakry, 1959), pp. 43–4.

30. After 1957 the United Party.

31. "Common Sense" in *The Political Writings,* Vol. 1, Investigator Office (Boston, 1856), p. 33.

32. For a most interesting discussion of the new history of West Africa, see Immanuel Wallerstein's paper delivered to the 1960 meeting of the American Sociological Association, "The Search for National Identity," mimeographed.

33. Alexander Adandé, "In the Phase of National Reconstruction the Fusion of Parties Becomes a Categorical Imperative," address at the Congress for Cultural Freedom Conference, Ibadan, March 1959, mimeographed, F/413, p. 3.

34. Madeira Keïta, *op. cit.,* p. 9.

35. Julius Nyerere suggested this in "Africa's Place in the World," *Symposium on Africa* (Wellesley College, Wellesley, Mass., 1960), pp. 162–3.

36. *La Liberté,* November 23, 1954.

# PARTIES IN INDIAN POLITICS

## M. Weiner

India entered an age of mass politics in 1920 when Mahatma Gandhi launched the first national civil disobedience movement. Ever since, politics and government have been a part of the

Reprinted from *Party Politics in India,* 1957, by permission of Princeton University Press and Oxford University Press.

central core of Indian life. The popular coffee houses in Bombay, Calcutta, and the other urban centers are meeting places for the educated young and the politically minded, who are one and the same. For the educated young are as politically minded as were their parents a generation ago. Just as a generation ago their fathers entered the Congress movement, today's young people most often enter the opposition parties—the Communists, the Socialists, one of the Hindu communal parties, or one of the many Marxist groups. Here then is a conflict not only between two generations but within the younger generation itself. While the last generation of youth was united by the cause of nationalism, today's youth is divided by the varied ideas of what a national government means and how its power should be utilized.

## THE IMPORTANCE OF POLITICS

To gain an accurate perspective of political parties, the reader must first understand the intensity with which Indians participate in politics. Partly, the current importance of politics is related to the central role which the nationalist movement played in the lives of virtually all educated Indians. Large sections of the educated community were organized around the task of achieving self-government; the way to one's goals, including status and prestige, was through political rather than economic activity. National prominence was achieved not through sports or the cinema (although the ubiquitousness of the cinema has managed to thrust some film stars into national recognition, especially since independence) or even by amassing wealth (which could make one infamous) but rather by suffering and sacrificing for the national cause of independence. The need for such sacrifice no longer exists, but politics and sacrifice continue to remain prime routes to status and prestige.

This striving for status through politics is intensified by the fact that party workers in India come from urban areas, where traditional values have been disrupted and where the traditional social structure has been breaking down. Young party workers have often broken from the tightly knit organization of their village, their caste, and even their joint family. The party thus provides both an alternative set of values and an alternative social structure.

There are few outside loyalties to temper the intensity of party membership. Unlike party workers and members of interest groups in the United States and Great Britain, who are at the same time members of their family, business and church groups, trade unions, veterans' organizations, and so on, Indians do not generally have multiple group memberships. Party workers therefore tend to be uncompromising in their attitudes toward other parties. They are often more concerned with maintaining the identity of their group and its ideology than in increasing their prospects for achieving political power by working more closely with others. Indian parties are frequently torn by two desires: on the one hand they want to work more closely with other parties or even to merger in order to improve their electoral prospects, but on the other they fear that the identity of their group will be lost. The result is often a vacillating policy of uncompromising attacks against other opposition parties and passionate calls for unity.

Adding further to the intensity with which Indians take part in politics is the fact that job opportunities in business, social work, education, and even government service have not kept up with the growing number of university graduates. A study by the Lucknow University Anthropology Department showed that about 25% of the students who received their master's degree from Lucknow University in arts, science, commerce, and law between 1949 and 1953 are still unemployed. The survey also reported that about 47% of the liberal arts students, 51.4% of the science students, 7% of the commerce students, and as many as 85.7% of the education students said they joined the university to have the necessary qualifications for government service. About 51% of the degree holders concluded that university education is a "waste of time."[1]

Much of the political party recruitment, especially among the opposition parties, is from these educated unemployed—largely young people whose expectations are not being fulfilled and who consequently feel alienated from society. The opposition parties, with their *Weltanschauung* and their tightly knit organization, provide alternative outlets.

The importance of politics in the daily lives of educated Indians is also related to the fact that politics provides the language and symbols which serve as a unifying force. This proposition may first appear absurd and even contradictory when one thinks of the divisiveness of politics, the petty squabbles, the factional disputes, and the enormous ideological differences between political groups. None of this is irrelevant. No one can deny that politics divides. But it also unites those who have no other basis for union. Members of the educated elite who are otherwise divided by the traditional barriers of caste, language, and provincialisms of one kind or another, find in the symbols of politics a unifying link. Members of the Hindu Mahasabha, for example, whether they are Brahmans or Kshatriyas, from Bengal or Maharashtra, find in their language of Hindu communalism a unifying *culture* without which there would be no communion of feeling. The horsetrading of special interests, the logrolling and bargaining, which are so characteristic of American political parties, are not enough to unify a party in India, for a larger umbrella of values does not exist as it does in England or the United States. The sense of rootlessness and purposelessness which a Westernized elite feels can in part be mitigated through a language of politics and by the patterns of relationship which a political party can provide, but which the traditional forms of society no longer can.

Before 1947 the political struggle was between the British bureaucracy in India and the national movement; after 1947 the political arena centered around conflicts among Indian political parties. This remark no doubt seems commonplace to the Western reader, but it involves a phenomenon in Asia and Africa almost unique to those countries which lived for many years under foreign rule. In Thailand and Japan, countries which were not under prolonged foreign occupation, the response to the West came from an intelligentsia in the government. It was the bureaucracy, civil and military, which maintained a dominant position so that political struggles occurred *within* the bureaucracy. To the observer the political game was like stud poker, where the unseen cards were often most significant.

With the British in control of the bureaucracy in India, the "mediators" of the Western impact emerged from the professional classes—the teachers, the lawyers, the doctors—and the lesser government officials. It was from this group that the nationalist movement developed. The political struggle was thus against the bureaucracy, and the political arena was consequently open for all to watch.

With independence, there came to power a Westernized elite committed to creating a democratic, secular government, raising the standard of living of the masses, achieving a greater measure of social justice, and eliminating those features of the old social order which it felt to be anomalous. This elite set out to utilize the power of government to reconstruct society in its own image, and those in the society who cannot accept the new values are forced to wage their struggle in the political arena. In this sense the issue of Westernization is now even more of a political question than it was before.

## POLITICS AS AN URBAN PHENOMENON

Maurice Zinkin has given an incisive picture of the differences between Asia and the West in terms of the respective importance of the village and the city.[2] The civilizations of the West largely grew in the urban areas, such as Athens, Rome, Florence, and Venice, while in Asia, especially in India and Southeast Asia, civilization emerged from the rural areas. The old cities of India—like Delhi—were less centers of commerce and culture than they were centers of government. Bombay, Calcutta, and Madras are new cities, the product of Western impact.

The ability of the urban areas in India to be initiators of change is enhanced by the fact that being relatively new they have no historical tradition to undo. Out of the cities and the larger towns of India have come the personnel of politics. Even the political recruitment of young people from rural

areas takes place in the urban centers where they have gone to study or work.

It is often argued in India and outside that the crucial areas of the nation are the villages, where some 85% of the population lives; for there lies the antiquity of Indian culture, there is the greatest potential for discontent and revolution. But *satyagrahas* (civil disobedience movements) of peasants are frequently organized by Socialist, Communist, and communalist leaders who come from the urban areas. Peasant protest is often mobilized and directed by one urban elite in an attempt to weaken or destroy the political power of another urban elite, for the urban areas are the centers of parties radiating their influence out to the villages.[3]

## THE DEVELOPMENT
## OF POLITICAL PARTIES

There are many ways in which the development of political parties in India differ from their development in Great Britain and the European continent —not the least of which is that the struggle by parties for parliamentary institutions in India was not against an indigenous wealthy, aristocratic ruling class, but rather against alien rulers, thus permitting Indian big business, the intelligentsia, the urban shopkeepers, and the peasants to join together against a single enemy. But perhaps the single most important difference is that of *timing*. Parties emerging today find ready-made ideologies waiting for them, while parties of the nineteenth century had to evolve their own ideologies to suit prevailing conditions. But even more important in the matter of timing is the fact that suffrage was introduced into most European countries gradually and after prolonged struggles; the process of broadening the political base was a relatively slow one, in most cases allowing time for various groups to adapt themselves to new political rules. Britain is the classic case of the gradual entrance into politics of new groups—labor being the most recent—who accepted the basic democratic framework. In India as in other newly independent countries, universal suffrage has been introduced all at once in a society where interests are not clearly differentiated and organized. There is thus a measure of unpredictability in the behavior of these groups and consequently a degree of latency in Indian politics. So long as these groups have not organized themselves, they provide a fertile ground for organization by party leaders who seek to direct protest in ways that will gain political bnefit for their groups or themselves.

The *suddenness* of independence—in the sense that Indian political groups did not gradually take over the apparatus of government, but took power all at once in 1947—meant that there was little time for a gradual adjustment to an entirely new political system. Most of the opposition parties which emerged after 1947 existed before independence, but they were largely political groups within the Indian National Congress functioning in a common cause as part of a national movement.

The national movement itself passed through three stages of development: first it was a pressure group, then a national movement, and finally a political party. The Indian National Congress, created in 1885, was largely a pressure group which sought to influence rather than control the government on behalf of the special interests of its members. "Its outlook," wrote two historians,

> . . . was urban rather than rural; it had no organic connection with peasants, labourers, or country traders. . . . The great majority of those who attended the Congress were lawyers, teachers or journalists, that is to say, they belonged to the three new professions which had grown up under the British rule; a few Englishmen or Scotsmen gave substantial help in the early stages; the procedure was modelled on English practice; and the movement may justly be described as an attempt to influence the Government within the existing constitution.[4]

Until the 1920's the urban, professional intelligentsia which dominated the Indian National Congress had little communication with the masses of the country. The nationalist movement itself arose first in those areas where the Western impact was greatest: Bengal, Madras, the Punjab, and Maharashtra. The early Congress conferences were held in urban centers: Poona, Calcutta, Bombay, Karachi, Delhi, and Madras. British influence, wittingly or unwittingly, provided the impetus for a truly national nationalist movement. The unification of India by the British had facilitated the growth of a feeling of being "Indian." British higher education not only introduced Western liberal ideas and led to the emergence of professional classes, but also provided the language—English—whereby the educated elites of various parts of the country could communicate with one another. In the early days of the national movement there had been some mass participation, but it was largely confined to Bengal, which in 1905 in spite of the uproar of the Bengali population was partitioned by the British. The nationalist movement did not become nation-wide, however, until the 1920's when Gandhi successfully fused religious notions and political objectives and rallied the villagers behind him.

As a nation-wide nationalist movement, the Congress brought together a wide assortment of groups from business, labor, and the peasantry. Only communal considerations were able to substantially divide the national movement, with Muslims, Sikhs, Anglo-Indians, and Parsees maintaining their own organizations to act on behalf of their communities. The major opposition groups in India today were in pre-independence days part of the Congress fold:

the Socialists, the Hindu communalists, the Marxist leftists, and the Communists. Although Nehru and many other Congress leaders were deeply committed to parliamentary institutions, there were many in the nationalist movement who were not. The Communists, the Marxist left, and the Hindu communalists all participated in the national struggle without favoring the adoption of Western democratic political institutions. Such was the wide diversity of outlooks tolerated within the nationalist movement.

The Socialists, who became the second largest party in India after independence, first organized in 1934 as the Congress Socialist Party within the Indian National Congress. The Hindu Mahasabha, the largest of the Hindu communal parties in independent India, was never formally a part of Congress, but until the 1930's many of its members were also members of Congress. The Marxist left groups evolved out of the terrorist organizations which had been formed in Bengal at the turn of the century. Most of these groups functioned within Congress until shortly before the beginning of World War II.

Of the various pre-1947 political parties, the Communists have perhaps the longest record of opposition to Congress. The Communist Party of India was organized in 1924 and until the mid-1930's opposed Congress leaders, including Gandhi, as tools of imperialism. In 1934 the Government of India banned the Communist Party, but later in the '30's the Communists joined in a popular front with the Congress Socialists. When war broke out in 1939 the Indian Communists opposed it as imperialist, but completely switched their line the following year as the Japanese advanced through Southeast Asia. By supporting the war effort the Communists alienated themselves from Congress, which opposed the war and was at that time urging the British to "Quit India." At the close of the war in 1945, Congress expelled the Communists on the grounds that they violated its policy.

With the achievement of independence in 1947, the political setting in India underwent a drastic change. The Indian National Congress was now transformed from a national movement to a political party. This change was dramatically expressed in the new Party constitution which forbade Party members from belonging to any other political party. The Socialists, Communists, and others shifted their attack from the ruling British to the ruling Congress Party. A Constitution having been put into effect in 1950, the political parties began preparing themselves for the first national elections.

By 1951 four major groups of parties had emerged. One group more or less accepted the basic democratic, secular state provided for in the Constitution. This group included the Congress Party, the Socialist Party, the Kisan Mazdoor Praja Party, and several small state parties such as the Krishikar

Lok Party in Andhra. A second group rejected the Western-type parliamentary Constitution and advocated instead a model based on the Soviet or Chinese political and economic system. Besides the Communist Party of India, this group included the various Marxist left parties: the Bolshevik Party of India, the Revolutionary Socialist Party, the Peasants and Workers Party, etc. A third group also rejected the existing state, but turned instead toward the Indian tradition for its inspiration. In this group were Jan Sangh, the Hindu Mahasabha, and Ram Rajya Parishad, the Hindu communal parties. A fourth group could be characterized as "indifferent" to the Constitutional framework, being primarily concerned with some provincial or communal interest. The Sikh Akali Dal, the Scheduled Caste Federation, the Jharkhand Party, and the Tamilnad Congress were in this group. These parties not only made demands on behalf of their own communities; they were carriers of a group consciousness, sometimes communal, sometimes provincial, and in a few instances tribal.

## THE 1951 ELECTIONS
## AND THE ISSUES AHEAD

Somehow the Congress Party managed to survive the multitude of problems facing the new state after 1947. The normal difficulties involved in dividing the subcontinent into India and Pakistan were further complicated by widespread riots, violence, and the mass exodus of Hindus from Pakistan and Muslims from India. Furthermore, almost simultaneously with partition, violence and war broke out in Hyderabad and Kashmir. And in the midst of these birth pangs, the Communist Party of India launched its insurrection in Hyderabad.

In spite of these apparently insurmountable obstacles, the new Government of India continued to function. A strong administrative apparatus and a strong army, both legacies of British rule, stood behind the new government. But perhaps most important of all, the Congress Party leadership demonstrated that it could carry on, in spite of the assassination of Mahatma Gandhi in January, 1948. The Congress leadership was able to deal effectively with the Communist insurrection, bring peace to Hyderabad, control the refugee situation, integrate over 500 princely states into the Indian Union, and avoid war with Pakistan. Furthermore in 1950 the Constituent Assembly, with a Congress majority, approved a new Constitution, and India was declared a Republic.

Even with a stable dominant political party, however, there were portents of political difficulties. Independence had not brought the anticipated new era, and there was increasing corruption, disillusionment, and loss of *élan* in the Congress Party. Fac-

tional disputes multiplied. The Congress Socialist party, which had up to this time operated within Congress, withdrew and set itself up as an independent opposition party, and a few years later a large group of Gandhians in Bengal, Madras, Uttar Pradesh, and Malabar likewise withdrew from Congress. In addition there were growing regional pulls, expressed in the increasing agitation for reorganization of the Indian states along linguistic lines, which put strains both on the Congress Party and the government. And finally there was increasing recognition that the Congress Party was failing to recruit younger people and that no new leaders were developing inside Congress who could assume control when the elder Congress leaders withdrew from the political scene.

There was considerable curiosity and anxiety about the results of India's first national general elections based on universal suffrage: the largest elections ever held in a democratic state anywhere in the world. Although it was assumed that the Congress Party under Nehru would remain the major political force, there was still the question whether a major democratic opposition would emerge. From the point of view of traditional Western political notions about the function of political parties in a democracy, the growth of an opposition seemed desirable. This reasoning was based on at least two assumptions: first, that opposition parties, by providing an element of choice to the voters, are basic and essential to a democratic system; second, that the opposition would integrate those interest groups being neglected by the government and might be in a position to assume power and bring about a new public policy if the government failed to heed those interests adequately. The existence of a strong opposition, therefore, would serve as a check on the government and help insure responsibility in government. As the *New York Times* correspondent said several years later, there are many who "would like to see a second democratic party emerge strong in India, to provide stimulation and a feeling of 'running scared' for the Congress Party, to put forward new ideas and to give voters who are dissatisfied with the Congress Party a real choice."[5]

For those who looked forward to the growth of an opposition in India, a second question remained: Would there develop a two-party system as in the United States and Great Britain, an unstable multiparty system as in France, or a stable multi-party system in which compromises by various groups make stable government possible, as in Sweden? In short, what would be the relationship between the party system and political stability?[6] Whether an opposition which offered the prospect of alternative stable government would emerge in India remained an open question prior to the elections.

Prior to the elections the Congress Party issued its proposed Five Year Plan for economic development. This in effect became the election manifesto of Nehru's party. Nehru and the other Congress leaders toured the country promising a stable, democratic, and secular government which would aim to provide for the well-being of its citizens through a program of national development.

The opposition was badly fragmented. Fourteen parties entered the elections as national parties, fifty-one more as state parties, and an enormous number of candidates stood as independents. Many of these independents were former princes who, with the integration of the princely states into the Indian Union in 1950, had lost what remained of their effective powers. Others were powerful landlords or dissident members of the Congress Party who failed to receive their Party's nomination and who were therefore running as independents. Still others had started their own parties. A number of regional linguistic and tribal parties had entered the race, but partly because the claims of one linguistic and tribal group frequently infringed upon the claims of others, such regional groups offered little prospect of becoming a national opposition party. Then there were the various right-wing Hindu communal groups which had much in common with one another but which, unlike the Catholic parties of Europe, lacked the unity that an organized church might have provided.

The new Socialist Party made some effort to work closely with a group of Gandhian dissidents in Madras, Bengal, Uttar Pradesh, and Malabar who had broken from Congress in 1951 to form the Kisan Mazdoor Praja Party (KMPP or Peasants, Workers, and Peoples Party), but had little success. The various non-Communist Marxist left parties, which were largely centered in Bengal, also talked of some kind of united front, but by the time the elections came the front was confined to only a few groups.

There was a general lack of certainty among the opposition parties as to what the elections might bring. It was widely believed that the Congress Party would do poorly, and each opposition party thought that the mantle of being "His Majesty's Opposition" would fall upon it.

As a result of the elections the Congress Party scored an overwhelming legislative victory. Congress won 357 seats in a Parliament of 489 with a popular vote of only 45%.[7] In the state Assemblies Congress won 2,248 seats out of 3,283 with only 42.2% of the vote. In New Delhi the Congress Party formed a government with Jawaharlal Nehru as its Prime Minister; and in every state the Party formed a government, usually by itself but in several instances in coalition with independents or small state parties.

Of the opposition parties, only four received 3 or more per cent of the national vote, the total required by the election commission for recognition as a national party: Jan Sangh (a Hindu party, liter-

ally People's Party), 3.1%; the Communist Party of India, 3.3%;[8] the Kisan Mazdoor Praja Party, 5.8%; and the Socialist Party, 10.6%. In terms of parliamentary seats none of these parties did particularly well. But in the state assemblies several achieved some strength, and in at least three states, Madras, PEPSU (Patiala and East Punjab States Union), and Travancore-Cochin, Congress failed to win a majority of legislative seats.

Although the elections had resulted in the establishment of a stable government in New Delhi and in most of the states, and had demonstrated that national elections could be held peacefully in a country with an enormous illiteracy rate without all sorts of dire results, at least two consequences were disturbing. The first was that no national opposition party had emerged in a sufficiently strong position to provide the possibility of alternative stable government in the event Congress lost power. But this did not present any immediate difficulties. There were even some who argued that although a party system had not developed similar to that of a Western democracy (whether the United States, France, or Sweden), there were certain advantages to having a virtual "one-party democracy." It could, in fact, be argued that as long as there was a pressing need for rapid economic development planned by the state, such a program could best be carried out if a single party, with a minimum of opposition, led the country. If Congress and its leadership could organize the country around the Five Year Plan and minimize the many divisive tendencies in Indian society, many Indians felt that this was to the good. As long as free speech and the right of the opposition to organize exist and the ideal of a party system with a strong opposition remains, then the opportunity for such a system to develop remains open. Perhaps the process of getting non-Westerners to participate in a democratic framework could make most progress under the leadership of a single party which is capable of maintaining popular support even while allowing the opposition to operate. This, however, should be distinguished from a period of political "tutelage" in which one party maintains itself in power through suppression.

The Congress Party has been able, in fact, to maintain national political stability since independence by virtue of its dominant position and, at least for the moment, appears likely to continue to do so for some time. While there are advantages to such single-party domination, it is obvious that as long as the opposition has the right to organize, Congress cannot permanently remain in power. Moreover there are still no clear indications that the present leadership of the Congress Party has fostered the development of a younger crop of alternative leaders from within its own ranks; and it also remains to be seen what will happen when a new set of leaders do appear who do not have the prestige of being "the founding fathers." The real test of the stability of India's political system lies in the answer to the question whether power can be transferred to another group, capable of governing effectively within the democratic framework. This question must remain unanswered until Congress is defeated.

If this first disturbing feature for the moment appears to be remote, the second is nearer at hand. It concerns the impact of the party system on relations between the central and state governments. As long as India maintains a federal system, with considerabe power in the hands of the states (including agriculture, education, and public health), then relations between the center and the states can have far-reaching consequences. As Sir Ivor Jennings noted, ". . . one must put up with the inevitable consequences of federalism, one of which is the possibility of a conflict between the State and the Federal Government."[9] But can an underdeveloped country intent upon central planning for economic development afford the "luxury" of such conflicts? There is little doubt that conflict could stymie much of the development program. Paul Appleby in his report on public administration to the Government of India noted that there is in India "an almost complete dependence of the Centre on the states for administration of social-action programs."[10] And although there are ways in which the center can influence, if not control, state policy,[11] the effects are at best unpredictable and at worst deleterious to the development program.

The existence of widespread state-center conflict has thus far been precluded by one-party control of the central government and most of the states. There are, however, three conceivable developments in the various states that could affect state-center relations. First, it may be possible for an opposition party or group of parties to gain control of a state and provide effective government with a minimum of conflict with a Congress-controlled central government. The Praja Socialist Party or other pro-democratic groups, for example, once having won state power, could be expected to cooperate to a greater or lesser degree with a national Congress government. A second possibility is that a party or a group of parties might be able to assume power in a state and provide a measure of law and order, but be in direct conflict with the central government. A state government controlled by the Communists and other anti-democratic groups or possibly some of the Hindu communal parties would be an illustration of this. Finally, there is the possibility that no one party or group of parties could form a stable state government. Local law and order might then break down. Such a situation occurred in the state of PEPSU in 1952. It then became necessary for the central government to implement the emergency provisions of the Constitution and apply what is known as "President's Rule" with the center passing and administering laws for the state.

It was with more than passing curiosity, therefore, that the election returns in 1952 were scrutinized to judge the trend of party development in the various states. In Madras, the largest and most populous of the South Indian states, Congress returned only 152 legislators out of an Assembly of 375; in PEPSU, Congress returned 26 out of 60; and in Travancore-Cochin, Congress returned 43 out of 108. An anticipated post-election crisis in each of these areas did occur, but through a combination of political maneuverings within the states and the use or threatened use of emergency powers by the central government, it was possible to establish a stable government dominated by the Congress Party in each instance. Nevertheless in PEPSU and to a lesser extent in Travancore-Cochin, stability did not come until after a period of considerable uncertainty and disorder. Thus as long as the opposition parties remain splintered, of the three possibilities for party development in the states, experience suggests that the third is most likely to occur—that a Congress defeat would be followed by the emergence of a number of parties, none of which has so far proved capable of forming either a stable government or a stable non-Congress coalition government.

The future of the opposition remains perhaps the single most challenging political question in India today. The prospects for democracy in India depend upon many factors, not the least of which are the extent to which the aspirations of people for economic development and social change can be provided for, and the extent to which the Indian government can provide national unity and maintain law and order. If we are right in assuming that the future of parliamentary and democratic institutions in India depends in large part upon the long-range development of a political party system which can ensure stability, then it is essential that we understand how far India has thus far gone in this direction. It is necessary therefore that we take a look at the development of the opposition parties and the factors which have led to their fragmentation, and then assess the prospects for the emergence of a stable party system. It is toward these two questions that the following chapters are directed.

## NOTES

1. *Statesman,* November 27, 1955.
2. Maurice Zinkin, *Asia and the West* (London: Chatto and Windus, 1951).
3. This raises several interesting questions beyond the scope of this study: What is the present political relationship between the rural and urban areas in India? To what extent are the rural areas developing their own leadership and their own political organizations which may become a threat to the present dominant position of the urban leadership?

4. W. H. Moreland and A. C. Chatterjee, *A Short History of India,* 3rd edition (London: Longmans, Green and Co., 1953), p. 427. For a succinct account of the history of the nationalist movement in India see W. Norman Brown, *The United States and India and Pakistan* (Cambridge, Mass.: Harvard University Press, 1953), Chaps. 4, 5, and 6.

5. *New York Times,* January 2, 1956.

6. Political stability is used in this study *in the context of democratic values* (there can of course be stability in non-democratic societies too) and refers to conditions (1) in which one or a group of political parties controls the government and performs the minimum socially accepted functions of government for a reasonable length of time and (2) where change in the governing parties occurs within the legally prescribed democratic rules and is tolerated by the defeated groups.

7. All election statistics in this study are from Election Commission, *Report on the First General Elections in India, 1951–52, II* (Delhi: Manager of Publications, 1955), and Ministry of Information and Broadcasting. Government of India, *India, A Reference Annual 1953*

(Delhi: Publications Division, Government of India, 1953).

8. This official figure does not include the vote given to Communist front parties created in those areas where the CPI was under government ban. The unofficial estimate for the CPI and its allies is 5.4%. See Richard L. Park, "Indian Election Results," *Far Eastern Survey,* XXI (May 7, 1952).

9. Sir Ivor Jennings, *Some Characteristics of the Indian Constitution* (London: Oxford University Press, 1953), p. 69.

10. Paul N. Appleby, *Public Administration in India —Report of a Survey* (Delhi: Manager of Publications, 1953), p. 3.

11. The means by which the national government might influence state governments include power of the center to veto state legislation in conflict with national law, and, perhaps most important of all, the power of the center to take over the administration of a state and to make laws for a state when a Proclamation of Emergency is issued by the President and subsequently approved by both Houses of Parliament.

# ALTERNATIVE WAYS TO DEMOCRACY: THE EXAMPLE OF ISRAEL

## Amitai Etzioni

Each generation seems to work out its own definition of democracy. Since the totalitarian states have imitated many of the more external signs of democracy such as elections and party systems, an effort has been made to establish a definition which will clearly distinguish totalitarian from democratic régimes. There is a strong tendency to call a state democratic if the governmental power can be transferred from one party to another in a regularized way; that is, peacefully and in accordance with the rules of the constitution.[1] The party in office must not use its power to block the return of the other party or parties. Any attempt to do so is a violation of the rules of the game and is in itself an argument for a change of administration. In short, it is to the system and not to a leader or a party that the supreme loyalty of the voters is directed.

Reprinted from *Political Science Quarterly,* Vol. LXXIV, No. 2 (June, 1959), 196–214, by permission of The Academy of Political Science, Columbia University.

The frequent alternation of parties, it is further argued, keeps the government in harmony with the shifting distribution of power in society. Social changes quickly have their influence on the political situation and on the policies that are pursued. The equilibrium of the political system is maintained.[2]

It is obvious that this understanding of democracy draws heavily on Anglo-Saxon experience with a two-party system and the rule of law. But is the Anglo-Saxon form the only possible form of democracy? A priori this would hardly seem likely. It is the purpose of this article to describe what may be regarded as an alternative form, and to try to explain some of the political, economic, and social conditions in which it appears and is maintained.

We shall use the government of Israel as our example of a political system which is democratic and yet different from the Anglo-Saxon model. Among the basic features of the Israeli government are a multiple party system and coalition ministries in which one center party (Mapai) is always present and always stronger than the other parties. To leave this party out of the ministry is simply not a part of the accepted procedures of the system. The party is one of the political institutions of the country and is identified with the state in the minds of many voters. In fact, too, because of its long term of office it has permeated the governmental, administrative, economic and other institutions of Israel. Yet that country is democratic, for shifts in public opinion and in the distribution of social power lead to changes in governmental policy and the vital harmony between state and society is maintained.

Having analyzed the Israeli system in the main body of our paper, we shall devote some concluding paragraphs to a comparative note. Its purpose is to stimulate analysis of some other political systems that are also democratic but different from the Anglo-Saxon model of democracy.

# I. MAPAI: A CASE OF AN INSTITUTIONALIZED PARTY

## A. Mapai—a Dominant Center Party

An analysis of Mapai (Labor party) is the key to an understanding of the Israeli political system. Mapai gained more votes in all three elections to the *Knesset* (parliament) than any other party. Actually it obtained more seats than the next three parties combined. (See Table 1.)

Mapai has been the major party in all eight Israeli governments during the ten-year period following the establishment of the state of Israel. Usually it has held nine out of sixteen portfolios in the various coalitions, always including the key ones of prime minister, defense, foreign affairs, police, treasury, and education, leaving to other parties the post office, welfare, justice, agriculture,

interior,[3] and other secondary ministries. Thus, Mapai has been the dominating political force in the Israeli government.[4]

Mapai's control over the political life of the country goes far beyond a strong control of the government. Israel differs from other societies by having three major national political organizations, each with a "government" of its own. In addition to the regular government the Jewish Agency and the General Federation of Labor (*Histadrut*) have important political functions. The former is the major agency which recruits financial aid for Israel from Jews in the Diaspora and organizes migration to, and settlement in, Israel. The scope of its activities is well illustrated by the size of its budget, which was 211.5 million Israeli *lirot* (about 122 million dollars) for 1958–59, compared with the budget of the Israeli government, which amounted to 969 million Israeli *lirot* in 1957–58.

The political significance of the Jewish Agency will be clarified by examinations of the political significance of immigration. According to Israeli law new immigrants become citizens upon arrival in the country and immediately obtain the right to vote. Since the Israeli political parties have cognate parties in the Jewish communities abroad, regulation of immigration has direct political consequences.

The Jewish Agency is governed by a coalition of all the major Israeli parties except the Communists. As in the government of the state of Israel, Mapai has more representatives on the Executive Board of the Jewish Agency than any other party.[5] More than that, its members hold important positions, as for instance chairman of the board in Jerusalem, heads of the departments of settlement, of absorption of new immigrants, of education and youth.

## TABLE 1—Seats Gained by Parties at the Three "Knesset" Elections

| | 1949 | % | 1951 | % | 1955 | % |
|---|---|---|---|---|---|---|
| Mapai | 46 | 38.3 | 45 | 37.5 | 40 | 33.3 |
| Herut | 14 | 11.7 | 8 | 6.7 | 15 | 12.5 |
| General Zionists | 7 | 5.8 | 20 | 16.7 | 13 | 10.8 |
| Ahdut HaAvoda | 19 | 15.8 | 15 | 12.4 | 10 | 8.3 |
| Mapam | | | | | 9 | 7.5 |
| Hapoel Hamizrahi | | | 8 | 6.7 | 11 | 9.2 |
| Mizrahi | 16 | 13.3 | 2 | 1.7 | | |
| Agudat Israel | | | 3 | 2.5 | 6 | 5.0 |
| Poaley Agudat Israel | | | 2 | 1.7 | | |
| Communists | 4 | 3.3 | 5 | 4.2 | 6 | 5.0 |
| Mapai Arab parties | 2 | 1.7 | 5 | 4.2 | 5 | 4.2 |
| Progressives | 5 | 4.2 | 4 | 3.3 | 5 | 4.2 |
| Sephardim | 4 | 3.3 | 2 | 1.7 | .. | ... |
| Yemenites | 1 | 0.8 | 1 | 0.8 | .. | ... |
| Minor Parties | 2 | 1.7 | .. | ... | .. | ... |
| | 120 | 99.9 | 120 | 100.1 | 120 | 100.0 |

The third national political organization of extraordinary importance is the General Federation of Labor. Its special position in Israeli society has often been discussed.[6] The *Histadrut* is governed by an Executive Board elected by a national convention. The elections are organized according to the proportional system and representation is by political parties. The Board is a coalition government in which all the major *Histadrut* parties except the Communist participate. Mapai has an absolute majority in the *Histadrut* (see Table 2). In 1957, eight out of thirteen members of the Executive Board of this organization belonged to Mapai. Thus Mapai is not just the major partner in the government of the state; it is also the strongest political force in the Jewish Agency and the ruling party in the *Histadrut*.

Mapai domination in the political realm antedates the establishment of the Israeli state. The Jewish community in Palestine had a semiautonomous political status under the British mandate. A political organization was established in 1920 and later was formally recognized by the British government. While the organization officially had only education and welfare functions, attempts were made by the Jewish community, in its struggle for full political independence, to increase the functions and the significance of this organization. Its semiofficial parliament was called Assembly of the Elected[7] and the "government" elected by it was named The National Committee.[8] (See Table 3.)

Mapai originated in 1930 from a merger of two smaller parties. Since then it has become a major political party in the *Histadrut* (see Table 2) and an important political factor in the Zionist Congress. Mapai showed its power for the first time in the 1931 elections to the Assembly in which it obtained 43.7 per cent of the vote and gained control of the National Committee. From this election till the day a premiership was created in the first Israeli government, a Mapai member was the head of the National Committee. Thus it can be said that Mapai has been in office twenty-eight years and has never been replaced.

## B. Mapai—an Institutionalized Party

Does this mean that Mapai cannot be replaced? There are countries in which one party remained in office for similar periods (Democrats in the United States for twenty years; Liberals in Canada for twenty-two years, in one province—Manitoba —for forty-three years) and was ousted by legitimate procedures. Can Mapai be ousted in a similar way? While there is no unqualified answer to this question, a number of factors make such a change quite unlikely in the near future, short of a major economic crisis or an international rupture.

The multi-party system and the coalition structure of the government are important factors. We suggest *that if parties elicit strong ideological commitments and the center party is relatively large, no stable government can be formed without the center party.* Mapai is such a center party, with a "hard core" of more than 30 per cent of the votes. Thus Israel had a "Right" coalition—Mapai with General Zionists and other parties (December 23, 1952–January 26, 1954)—a "Left" coalition—Mapai with Ahdut HaAvoda, Mapam, and other parties (November 3, 1955)—and a center coalition—Mapai with the Progressive party and some religious parties (March 10, 1949–November 1, 1950), but never a government without Mapai. *There seems to be no basis for a coalition without Mapai.* The only way to create a government without Mapai which would have the confidence of the absolute majority of the

## TABLE 2—Political Composition of "Histadrut" Conventions, V-VIII, 1942-1955

| | V<br>April,<br>1942<br>% | VI<br>Jan.,<br>1945<br>% | | VII<br>May,<br>1949<br>% | VIII<br>Feb.,<br>1955<br>% |
|---|---|---|---|---|---|
| Mapai | 69.3 | 53.7 | Mapai | 57.06 | 57.54 |
| Hashomer Hatzair | 19.2 } | | Ahdut | | |
| Left Poale Zion | 5.8 } | 20.7 | HaAvoda } | 34.40 | 14.61 |
| Unity of Labor Party | .. | 17.7 | Mapam ) | | 12.54 |
| Haoved Hatzioni | .. | 3.0 | Progr. | 3.8 | 5.25 |
| Aliya Hadasha | .. | 3.0 | | | |
| Revisionists | .. | 0.2 | | | |
| Religious Workers | .. | 1.0 | Rel. Wkrs. | 2.0 | 1.96 |
| Yemenites | .. | 0.5 | | | |
| Unattached | .. | 0.2 | | | |
| General Zionists Workers | 3.5 | .. | Gen'l Zionists | .. | 3.01 |
| Proletarian Group | 2.2 | .. | Communists[a] | 2.6 | 4.09 |
| Total | 100.0 | 100.0 | | 99.86 | 99.80 |
| Valid Votes | 81,198 | 106,420 | | 130,670 | 410,435 |

a. Varying composition between 1949-55.

*Knesset* is by a coalition which would include parties of the Left or of the Right. In a country like Israel where ideological commitments to parties play an important rôle, such a coalition is not a realistic alternative.

The fact that parties other than Mapai have no realistic chance to become coalition leaders and must choose between permanent opposition and more or less minor coalition partnerships creates in them "irresponsible" tendencies. The term "irresponsible political behavior" is usually applied to extreme parties which have no or little chance of coming into office and therefore make promises to the voters and claims upon the government that they would not be able to fulfill, were they to obtain office. The Communists and Herut (extreme Right) come close to this type of total opposition party. But there is another type of irresponsibility which develops when one party seems to be a constant and dominant partner of coalitions. Other parties tend then to become irresponsible in the sense that they are ready to bargain about many issues of public interest in order to be included in the coalition and as a price for staying in it. As they have to choose between being an insignificant opposition or a minor member of the coalition, they often choose the latter. The religious parties in Israel have often followed such a pattern.[9] Irresponsible politics in turn causes some voters to shift to the major party which "does the job" and manifests responsible leadership. This validates the claim of the Mapai spokesman that there is no alternative to the party in office. Thus a vicious circle is created: one party remains in office for a long time; this creates irresponsibility in other parties; and this in turn strengthens the position of the party in office.

What are the social conditions on which this political structure is based? How permanent are those conditions? Would it be conceivable that in the next elections to the *Knesset* (in 1959) about 10 per cent of those who voted for Mapai in previous elections would vote for another party, thus undermining the basis of the present coalition system? Most well-informed political observers would agree that such a change can hardly be expected. The major reason rests on the assumption that, like many parties in office for a long period, Mapai has become so strongly institutionalized that it has a strong grip on a "hard core" of voters needed to maintain its superior position.

On the one hand, a party which remains in office for a long time often loses some public support because the necessity of taking certain action inevitably alienates some groups. For example, a responsible government frequently has to introduce measures which alienate large contingents of the voters without creating any special support from any group, as for instance, new taxes. Even if a party tries to avoid taking action on controversial issues, as Mapai does with the Israeli constitution and some religious issues, it alienates those groups which expect the party to take action. Thus, on one hand, being in office leads to the accumulation of enemies. On the other hand, holding office may have a positive influence cn future elections. The leadership of the state and that of the major party are often fused; people who identify with the state tend also to favor the leading party. The party tends to receive credit for any progress which is achieved during its régime. The opposition is labeled as a group of people who "only talk."

## TABLE 3—Constitution of the Four Assemblies of the Elected

| | I 4-19-1920 | | II 12-6-1925 | | III 1-15-1931 | | | IV 8-1-1944d | |
|---|---|---|---|---|---|---|---|---|---|
| | Seats | % | Seats | % | | Seats | % | Seats | % |
| Ahdut HaAvoda | 70 | 22.3 | 54 | 24.4 | Mapai | 31 | 43.7 | 63 | 52.9 |
| Hapoel Hatzair | 41 | 13.1 | 30 | 13.6 | Poalei Zion | 1 | 1.4 | .. | |
| Communists | .. | ... | 6 | 2.7 | | 2 | 2.8 | 21 | 17.6 |
| Yemenites | 12 | 3.8 | 20 | 9.0 | | 3 | 4.2 | .. | |
| Other Oriental Lists | 60a | 19.1 | 20 | 9.0 | | c | .. | .. | |
| Religious Parties | 64 | 20.4 | 19 | 8.6 | | 5 | 7.0 | 17e | 14.3 |
| Revisionists | .. | ... | 15 | 6.8 | | 15 | 21.1 | | |
| Var. Middle Class Lists | 67b | 21.3 | 44b | 19.9 | | 14 | 19.7 | | |
| League for Women's Rights | .. | ... | 13 | 5.9 | Aliah Hadasha | | | 18 | 15.1 |
| | 314 | 100.0 | 221 | 99.9 | | 71 | 99.9 | 119 | 99.9 |
| Registered Voters | 28,755 | | 64,714 | | | 89,656 | | 303,000 | |
| Valid Votes | 22,257 | | 36,737 | | | 50,436 | | 202,448 | |
| Valid Votes, per cent of Reg. | 77.0 | | 56.7 | | | 56.2 | | 67.0 | |

a. Includes: Sephardim, 54; Bucharim, 5; Gurgim, 1.
b. Ten lists in 1920, thirteen in 1925, three in 1931.
c. Sephardim votes included six Middle Class, five Revisionists, four Mapai.
d. Sephardim, General Zionists, and Revisionists boycotted the elections.
e. Only Hapoel Hamizrahi participated.

Party patronage is another factor. The amount of patronage available depends to some degree on the moral atmosphere and on the institutionalization of a civil service. But even more important is the amount of control which the political organizations have over economic activities. In Israel, as well as in many other newly developed countries, conditions encourage a widespread political influence on the allocation of manpower, capital, land, and power positions. The sources of foreign currency are of major significance in a small, expanding economy. The scope of government control over these sources is well reflected in the following figures. Compared to 28.4 per cent of income from exports and 4.3 per cent of income from private investment, which are only regulated by the government, about 65 per cent of the foreign currency income is virtually state income and is allocated and controlled by the government or by the Jewish Agency.[10] It is almost inevitable that partisan considerations have some influence when political organizations control the economy, and when this control is extensive, these considerations are very important. In such state allocations and controls, parties in power have an advantage over those in opposition.

The most important economic control which the Israeli parties exert on their members concerns place of employment. In an economy where the closed shop is the rule, parties control labor exchanges and trade unions. Parties also organize services for their members including health plans, housing projects, vacations, and recreation.[11] Thus all parties, especially the stronger ones, can expect to hold the allegiance of a large proportion of their members.

But in a régime where ideology plays an important political rôle, economic control is not sufficient. The parties attempt to secure ideological control by maintaining their own media of communication and by curbing the access of their supporters to communication media of other parties. All Israeli parties publish their own newspapers and exert pressure on their members to subscribe to these newspapers. The larger parties have publishing houses. Until recently, parties were quite influential in the school system. The separate party housing projects, vacation centers, and social clubs serve also to increase intra-party communication and to decrease inter-party communication. The members' *Weltanschauung* is constantly reinforced so that they will be ready to resist any "hostile" communication.[12]

In this sphere also the parties in office seem to have some limited advantages over other parties. Israel has no television; the single radio station is controlled by the government. The government has an elaborate information service headed by a Mapai member. This service usually does not communicate political ideology but it functions to increase the loyalty of new and old citizens to the state by emphasizing its achievements and its bright future. This inevitably has some political repercussions.

While the Israeli parties in general and Mapai in particular have considerable economic and ideological control over a good many of their members and supporters, this hold is far from being strong enough to make shifts of voters' loyalties impossible. Less than a third of the voters are party members, and in every election thus far at least 15 per cent of the voters have changed their party allegiances.[13] On the other hand, this very control gives each party a stable core and gives Mapai a hard core of 30 per cent of the electorate, which is sufficient to maintain its dominant rôle in the coalition system unless some serious crisis should occur.

About half of the voters who will participate in the next parliamentary elections have emigrated to Israel during the last ten years. Could this group cause a considerable change in the outcome of the election? Judging by past elections the answer is clearly in the negative. All attempts to establish new immigrant parties have failed. New immigrants are known to distribute their votes roughly in the same way as the old citizens.

The recent political changes in France illustrate the problem of a third form of institutionalization, namely, the investment of the parties in office in the Armed Forces, police, and other security agencies. These "instruments of violence" can be neutral in the political game and thus serve equally all parties which may come into power. If this is the case, they support the institutionalization of the democratic system. If they support parties in office, they increase the institutionalization of these parties and undermine the system. If they support moderate or, more likely, extreme opposition parties, they endanger the parties in office and the democratic system at the same time.

Mapai's position from this point of view has undergone a considerable change. In the pre-state period its control over the various underground forces was relatively weak, compared to its control over other national political organizations.

This difference between the power distribution in the civic political bodies and that in the underground forces sometimes caused "lack of subordination" of these armed forces to the civil authorities. When the state of Israel was established action was taken to change this situation. First of all, the Armed Forces have been de-politicized. Units which had political loyalties have been disbanded. Soldiers and officers are not allowed to be politically active. There has not been a case of "lack of subordination" since the establishment of the Israeli Defense Forces. Recently this came to a significant test when these Forces were ordered to withdraw from Sinai amid strong public protest.

De-politicizing of the Defense Forces has been considered an insufficient safeguard for the régime in a country where such Forces are so powerful. This may explain why today many of the top positions in the Defense Forces are in the hands of Mapai members or neutrals. Out of the five chiefs of staff of the Israeli Defense Forces during 1948–58, two have been active Mapai members before and after their service, two are known to be supporters of Mapai in their private life, and the fifth has never shown any special political inclinations. The names of generals and colonels are usually not published in Israel, but the government year book gives a list of twelve of the top commanders of the Defense Forces.[14] Most of them are known as members or close adherents of Mapai. The Israeli police commander-in-chief and his deputy are Mapai members; so are many of the higher officers. There is little information on other security agencies, but they seem to be staffed similarly. It is of interest to note that when, in January, 1952, a political demonstration by Herut (extreme Right) members broke through the police lines in front of the *Knesset,* an army unit was called to help.[15] This shows that the government, and first of all Mapai, can rely on the loyalty of the army.

## II. DEMOCRACY AND AN INSTITUTIONALIZED CENTER PARTY

The party in office has never been replaced in Israel and it is unlikely to be replaced in the near future. Still the changing power distribution in society corresponds to the changing policy of the government. What are the mechanisms which enable a democracy to function without replacing the party in power?

### A. Changes in the Composition of the Coalition Government

Mapai, like other parties in democratic countries, is quite sensitive to public opinion. Although its control over some of its supporters is quite extensive, Mapai can never be secure in its control over its followers. While it never lost its core support, its leaders feel that this was achieved only by the party steering a cautious course, based on a combination of responsible leadership with enough "flexibility" (opponents say "opportunism") not to lose the support of the voters.

Mapai has some difficulty in determining what the public wants. There are no by-elections to the Israeli parliament. If a member dies or resigns,

his party appoints a new representative. Since local elections usually take place on the same day as parliamentary elections, they cannot indicate public attitudes between elections. Experience has shown that other elections, as for instance to the *Histadrut* conventions, do not reflect clearly the outcome of forthcoming national elections and therefore they are not considered as reliable political indicators.[16] There is no Israeli Gallup Institute or any close equivalent which could serve as a means for assessing the public. Therefore, the main test for the policies of each government coalition comes with the general election to the *Knesset.* If the electorate then shows dissatisfaction with the government line, Mapai tends to change its policy and its partners in the coalition. Thus, while Mapai stays in office, the government policy may change considerably and in relation to changes in public opinion and pressures.

The first regular Israeli government (March 10, 1949–November 1, 1950) consisted of a coalition of Mapai, Religious United Front, the Progressive Party, and Sephardim. The government was under criticism from three major opposition parties: from Mapam (Left-wing party) in regard to the Israeli stand between East and West; from Herut (extreme Right) with respect to the defense policy; and from the General Zionists (Right wing) in the matter of economic policy.

As this was a time of mass immigration and rapid economic expansion, a strong inflation developed.[17] The government introduced a far-reaching system of control which included licensing of imports and exports, complete control over foreign currency, and government allocation of raw materials and of consumer goods. Nearly a thousand different products were rationed. Luxury items were highly taxed. Credit allocation was controlled by the government.

The General Zionists, a party of big business, exporters, importers, citrus plantation owners, and to some degree supported by small business men and artisans, objected to all this. The party advocated a liberalization of economic policy, that is, the curtailment or abolishment of governmental regulations and of various allocations. The ration system, which many loathed, was made the symbolic target in the political campaign.

In the elections to the second *Knesset* which followed, the public shifted its support to the General Zionists. While the General Zionists were a small party with 5.8 per cent of the seats in the first *Knesset* (1949), they obtained almost three times as many seats in 1951 (16.7 per cent) to become the second largest party. The other two opposition parties lost considerably (Herut fell from 11.7 per cent to 6.7 per cent and Mapam from 15.8 per cent to 12.4 per cent). Mapai lost only 0.8 per cent of its seats, but the lesson was obvious. Large groups of the public were not satisfied with Mapai's economic policy, and it adjusted to this situation in several ways. First, the party abolished some of the more disagreeable measures of control. Then, in December, 1952, the General Zionists were included in the government. Finally, a "New Economic Policy" was introduced which was a compromise between Mapai's policy and the General Zionists' ideas. Mapai economists pointed out that the changes in economic policy were possible now because the economic situation had changed. The change was brought about mainly by the reparation agreement with Germany. But it is clear that the election played its rôle. Although the General Zionists left the government at a later time and the economic situation changed again, Mapai never tried to return to the 1949–51 system of rationing.

A similar change took place after the elections to the third *Knesset*. The primary cause of conflict and adjustment was defense policy this time. During the days of the second *Knesset* (1951–55) the pressure from the Arabic countries increased by means of economic boycott, border incidents, and infiltration activities inside Israel. Israel reacted by retaliatory operations which were focused on the centers from which the Arabic activities were launched. The frequency and scope of these activities varied in relation to the pressure exerted by other nations on the Arabs and on Israel. Public opinion in Israel was split on these retaliatory activities. Herut and Ahdut HaAvoda (Left wing) demanded a more aggressive line and questioned the military and political expediency of limited retaliatory activities. All the other parties were for continuation of the moderate line.

The election to the third *Knesset* showed that the public now was more concerned with the defense issue than with economic problems and that it protested against the continuous insecurity. The public supported the extremists (or activists as they are called in Israel): Herut almost doubled its seats (from 6.7 per cent to 12.5 per cent) and became the second largest party in the *Knesset*. The other party which supported the activists' line also improved its position. Mapai lost a considerable number of seats (4.2 per cent) and so did other parties.

Mapai's reaction was as quick and as determined as in the earlier case. Ben Gurion reassumed the Prime Ministership and the Defense Ministry; Sharet—who supported the moderate line—resigned from the government. Since a coalition with Herut is inconceivable for Mapai,[18] a Left-wing coalition was formed on November 3, 1955 which included the Left-wing activists. When Nasser arranged his weapons deal with Russia and nationalized the Suez Canal only one year later, the Israeli government switched from limited retaliatory activity to broader military activity. In October 1956 the government ordered the Israeli Armed Forces into the Sinai peninsula. Thus again the government acted in accord with a new public trend. A new policy was introduced and a new coalition was formed.

Of course a change in public opinion was not the only cause of the change in government policy, but the election results had considerable influence. The objective situation was interpreted differently by moderates and activists. If moderate parties had gained in the elections and the activists had lost, Sharet might have remained in the Cabinet as Prime Minister and/or Foreign Minister and the policy as well as the composition of the Cabinet might have been quite different. It is not accidental that public support turned to the activists; the objective situation produced this support. Thus one can see the elections as one mechanism through which the policy of the government is adjusted to the situation and to the electorate wishes without a change of the party in office.

## B. Changes in the Inner Balance of Mapai

The study of factions and pressure groups within a party is of special interest from several points of view. First, these groups determine to a considerable degree the party's policy and the composition of party representation in the various political institutions. Second, the larger the party and the more interests and groups there are represented in it, the more some functions of the parliament, such as policy-making and consensus formation, are taken over by party organs. The party's higher bodies have to reach a working consensus among the various groups before party policy can be determined.[19] Mapai itself comes close to being a federation of groups.[20] The major groups are: an organization of collective settlements (*Kibbutzim*) which supports Mapai (about 97 per cent of the eligible population votes Mapai), an organization of cooperative villages (*Moshavej Ovdim*) (about the same ratio of support), the *Histadrut* group, professionals and intelligentsia, Mapai members in government administration and representatives of new immigrants. All these groups are represented in the Mapai Center (196 centers) and many of them in the Mapai secretariat (fifteen members, in March, 1958).

How does the federative structure influence the democratic process? Through it, those who support Mapai have a voice in the decision-making process in non-election years and without changing the party alliance. Thus, before Mapai changed its defense policy, the fight between moderates and activists was taken up in the Mapai Center, with Ben Gurion heading the activists section and Sharet the moderate one. Only after it was decided here by a majority vote that Ben Gurion's policies should be promoted did Sharet resign and Mapai offer the new policy to the whole government.

The functions, prestige, and voting power of collective settlements are declining, while those of the coöperative villages are increasing. For reasons discussed elsewhere, collective settlements still have considerable privileges and power.[21] But in the last years the cooperative villages have struggled for increased representation of their group. To some degree their demands have been met but the collective settlements are still somewhat over-represented. This is likely to diminish in the near future. Thus, changes in the social significance of groups are reflected in changes in their political power through change in their representation in Mapai's policy-making bodies.

Another group struggle which has aroused much public interest in recent years is that between *Histadrut* (trade union) leaders and Mapai economic experts concentrated in the Treasury. The economists press for enlarged investments in order to achieve an increasing degree of economic independence and strength. The trade-union leaders insist that this should be done without a considerable decrease in the standard of living of the workers. Till now the trade-union leaders have had the upper hand. One of the reasons why they are so influential is that they represent a much larger and better-organized group of voters than the economists.

Is group representation really democratic? First of all one should note that it is part of the democratic process in all democratic countries, especially in those where there is a two-party system, because fewer interests are directly represented on the party level, and more are represented on the faction level. It is more important to examine the way in which faction representation is determined. Even where there are officially controlled and supervised primaries, nomination is still open to much abuse. Oligarchic procedures in units which participate in the democratic mechanisms seem to be almost an "iron law." While there are no primaries in Israel, two thirds of the members of Mapai Center are elected by Mapai locals and one third suggested by the Mapai Secretariat and approved by the convention. The latter are in most cases group representatives, often elected leaders of their groups or organizations. New immigrants, intelligentsia, and youth representatives are frequently selected in less formal ways. Thus group representation in Mapai is quite democratic in a sense. It is an important mechanism through which powerful groups and Mapai's policy are maintained in balance.

### C. Structural Weakness of Mapai

Mapai's political power, which has been stressed above, is an important factor of the whole process of institutionalization. But the picture should be balanced by showing a major weakness of Mapai

which is important because it makes Mapai sensitive to group pressures and public opinion. Mapai is often seen as an omnipotent party, as a strong monolithic political body with branches in all the major centers. This description is misleading in one important respect. It does not take into account the federative nature of Mapai, in which the main power rests in each group and little in Mapai as a party. There is a powerful group of Mapai members in the trade unions, in the cooperative movement, in the three major cities, in the Treasury, and so on. But their relations to other Mapai groups vary all the way from close cooperation to open hostility. In most cases the relationships are highly voluntary because each group is very independent. The weakest group is the party bureaucracy which supposedly ties them all together. The party personnel is small in number, low paid, has little prestige and consists mainly of party representatives who failed to maintain a position in other organizations. Many Mapai branch secretaries are just clerks for party activities and mediators among the various local centers of power. The Mapai Center, itself, is a place where the various groups determine their relative power and work out common policies, not a center of a powerful party machine which has strong control over its representatives in various political organizations. This is an important reason why Mapai, with all its weight and power, when it comes to coordinated action on the national scene in opposition to other groups, is internally weak and highly sensitive to pressures of various groups.[22]

## III. A COMPARATIVE NOTE

Is Israel an exception to the "normal" democratic model or are there other countries which come close to her form of democracy?

The Swedish government in the last twenty-six years (since 1932) has seen a coalition government in which the Social Democratic party is the basic political partner. Since 1949, Germany has been run by a coalition government in which one party, the Christian Democrats, plays the role of the decisive partner. The situation formally resembles a two-party system because two parties, the Christian Democrats and the Social Democrats, obtain the majority of the votes, but many commentators agree that this is misleading since the class and religious structure of Germany does not give the Social Democrats a real chance to obtain much more than 35 per cent of the vote, which means that there is no alternative party to the CDU at the moment. The special importance of Adenauer for the maintenance of the system can be compared to the position which Ben Gurion holds in the Israeli system. While Ben Gurion has the charismatic rôle of the state founder, Adenauer plays a similar rôle as the one who restored the new German Republic to a respectable place among the nations. The coalition partners of the CDU are weaker than the partners of Mapai, especially since the CDU gained an absolute majority of the seats in the Bonn parliament (1957). On the other hand, nine years in office have been enough for the CDU to become considerably institutionalized. Group struggles within the CDU are an important mechanism of German democracy as well (Catholic labor, big business, Catholic and Protestant clergy, liberals, and others).

Another illustration is the French Fourth Republic which in some respects functioned similarly to the Israeli system. The MRP, like Mapai, participated in a large number and great variety of coalitions. The decisive difference between Israel and France is that the MRP was by far weaker than Mapai and therefore the coalition system never achieved the stability which the Israeli system has. No central party became institutionalized and the extreme parties on left and right were considerably stronger. The final blow to the system was given by power organization which had political orientations differing from those of the elected government of France.

Thus if coalition governments are formed on a continuum according to the strength of the center party, the Israeli and Swedish governments would be in the middle, Germany on one side, and the Fourth Republic on the other. There are of course other types of coalition governments without one center party, but a discussion of those would take us far beyond the scope of this paper.

Mapai is often compared to the British Labour party and the Social Democrats in the Weimar Republic. These comparisons have certain merits when one attempts to point out the ideological position of Mapai in an *abstract* continuum of political ideologies. Mapai subscribes to a Left-wing noncommunist ideology. But beyond that, the comparison is of little help. The British Labour party is one in a two-party system; it entered and left office several times in the last three decades, while Mapai became a highly institutionalized party.

The comparison to the Weimar Social Democrats is even less meaningful. The Social Democrats were not able to continue in office because, among other reasons, rightist forces were highly entrenched in the army, the bureaucracies and the judicial system. This is almost opposite to the situation in Israel. The center of the Israeli political spectrum is not liberal, as in so many Western societies, but social-democratic with an approximately even distribution of the more leftish forces on one side and conservative and liberal groups on the other side. More than that, for historical reasons which cannot be discussed here, the left-

of-center ideologies and groups have stronger political, economic, and prestige positions than the right and liberal forces. While socialist parties in Western societies are often parties of reform and change, Mapai is more representative of the Israeli values and social structure than any other party. To be a Social Democrat in Israel—and the same holds for many of the newly developed countries —means to be in conformity with the majority of the politically conscious members of society. It is like being a moderate liberal in the present Congress of the United States. Thus, in conducting a comparative analysis, we have to take into account not only the substance of political values but also the place of such values in the political spectrum of the society. What is quite revolutionary in one society may be rather on the conformist side in another society. The different place in the political spectrum is of great significance in view of the different political conditions with which revolutionary and reform parties are confronted as compared to those in which conforming and status quo parties are placed, disregarding the actual content of their ideologies.

Mapai can be fruitfully compared to other state founding parties which have become highly institutionalized in young nations, as, for instance, the Congress party in India, the Neo-Destour in Tunisia, the Convention People's party in Ghana, and the A.F.P.F.L. in Burma. Of course, there are considerable differences among these countries and between them and Israel, but they all seem to have in common a leader and a party with the charismatic rôle of gaining independence and establishing the state; left-of-center ideologies; state-regulated economies; a high degree of economic dependence on external sources (perhaps with the exception of Ghana); and control over the labor organizations, excluding the Communists.[23]

A comparative study of democratic societies cannot be carried out here. The main purpose of this paper has been to describe a democracy that functions through mechanisms other than the frequent alternation of parties in office. The concluding paragraphs are meant to suggest that such mechanisms can be found also in countries other than Israel and that a comparative study of these countries might throw light on the nature and organs of modern democracy.

## NOTES

1. For some relevant discussions, see Joseph A. Schumpeter, *Capitalism, Socialism and Democracy* (New York, 1950); S. M. Lipset, M. A. Trow, and J. S. Coleman, *Union Democracy* (New York, 1956);

Carl J. Friedrich, *Constitutional Government and Democracy* (Boston, 1950); H. H. Gerth and C. Wright Mills, *From Max Weber: Essays in Sociology* (New York, 1946), pp. 225–26, 242; S. N. Eisenstadt, ed., *Political Sociology* (Tel Aviv, 1955), pp. 28–30 (in Hebrew).

2. See Talcott Parsons, " 'Voting' and the Equilibrium of the American Political System," in Eugene Burdick and Arthur Brodbeck, eds., *Continuities of Social Research,* Vol. III: *American Voting Behavior* (New York, 1959).

3. The Interior Ministry has limited political significance in Israel because it has no control over the police force (which is under the control of a separate ministry), because its budget—like the budget of all ministries—is under scrutiny of the Treasury, and because the local municipalities have a strong tradition of political independence.

4. B. Akzin, "The Role of Parties in Israeli Democracy," *Journal of Politics,* vol. XVII, 1955.

5. The Zionist Congress elects two branches of the executive board, one seated in Jerusalem and one in New York. The Jerusalem branch is believed to have more political significance. Mapai had five out of eleven members, including the chairman, on the board elected by the twenty-third Zionist Congress in August, 1951. In New York, Mapai had two members out of eight.

6. See Margaret L. Plunkett, "The *Histadrut:* The General Federation of Jewish Labor in Israel," *Industrial and Labor Relations Review,* vol. 11, No. 2, pp. 155–182.

7. *Asefhat HaNivharim.*

8. *HaVaad HaLeumi.*

9. Amitai Etzioni, "Kulturkampf ou Coalition: Le Cas d'Israel," *La Revue Française de Science Politique,* vol. VIII, No. 2 (June, 1958), pp. 311–331—republished in English in *Sociologia Religiosa,* vol. 1, No. 4 (1958), pp. 3–27.

10. These figures represent the period of 1949–1956.

11. See Gerda Luft, "The Party That Shapes Policy," *The Jerusalem Post,* July 11, 1955, quoted by M. H. Bernstein, *The Politics of Israel* (Princeton, 1957), p. 71.

12. The manipulation of communication channels as a means of maintaining members' loyalties has been analyzed by Philip Selznick, in his *Organizational Weapon* (New York, 1952).

13. But note that most changes are among parties with similar ideologies. Thus while more than 15 per cent shift, only about 6 per cent or less shift from parties left of Mapai to parties right of Mapai or vice versa. Thus Mapai's superior and center position is maintained. See Table 1.

14. *The Government Year Book* (Jerusalem, 1958–59), p. 84.

15. *Ha'aretz,* Hebrew daily, Tel Aviv, Jan. 8, 1952.

16. For instance, Mapam lost 7.25 per cent of its seats in the *Histadrut* convention between 1949 and 1955 (in 1955 both splinters are counted together) but in elections to the *Knesset* in the same years it received the same per cent of the seats—15.8 per cent.

17. The amount of money in circulation tripled in three years (end of 1948 to end of 1951). Credit expanded in the same period from 80 million to about 150 million Israeli *lirot.* The consumer's price index jumped from 100 (September, 1951) to 178 (December, 1952).

18. Because of the strong ideological differences between the parties.

19. In cases where there is only one party as in totalitarian states, the factional struggle is an uninstitutionalized substitute for rivalry among parties. In some states in the United States where there is only one active party, the factional struggle is the most important form of political expression. Unlike the totalitarian countries, it is here institutionalized in democratic party conventions and primaries. See V. O. Key, *Southern Politics* (New York, 1949).

20. Factions have not been tolerated since 1944 when a faction split Mapai and created its own party.

21. See Amitai Etzioni, "Agrarianism in Israel's Party System," *Canadian Journal of Economics and Political Science,* vol. XXIII, No. 3 (August, 1957), pp. 363–375.

22. That unorganized voters or weaker groups lose out in this process is obvious, but this is a problem of democracy in general.

23. See S. M. Lipset, "Socialism—Left and Right—East and West," *Confluence,* vol. 7, No. 2 (Summer, 1958), pp. 173–192.

X

# X Comparative Politics and Political Thought:

# Past Influences and Future Development

David E. Apter

## I. INTRODUCTION

Today's ferment in the field of comparative politics is one of rediscovery as much as novelty. There is some novelty in our outlook if only because we cannot cast ourselves in the modes of thought characteristic of the elegant and classic period of natural law and natural rights. Our separation from past forms of analysis is not, however, unbridgeable. Consider for a moment how many of our primary concerns remain the classical ones and are deeply rooted in our intellectual vocabulary. Terms such as "democracy," "individualism," "freedom," "rights," and the like have lost none of their brightness, in spite of the disturbing opaqueness that has sometimes blurred the image Western man has of himself.

For these reasons, I should like to put our concluding remarks about comparative politics into a context of political theory. In the past political theory was a lively part of the intellectual life and philosophy of the times; today it has become less so. Has political theory, no longer a practical concern, become a repository for antique ideas, a treasure house perhaps, with its objects venerated rather than used? We think not. Eckstein has showed the connection between approaches to comparative politics and the events and developments of the political world. Here we shall try to show the relationship between political theory and comparative politics, for we accept the view that comparative politics is an important way to understand man's variety of symbols and ideas, as well as his infinite capacities for doing good and evil. His courage in repairing his errors is seen in the endless search for new solutions to the practical puzzles of daily life. And that is a matter of theory as well as action.

If this view is accepted, then the urgency of our need for valid knowledge about political institutions and their potentialities is greater than ever before. This urgency is created by the serious events thrust upon all—political scientist, politician, journalist, or citizen—by vast changes in world affairs since World War II. Heightened responsibilities have made more compelling a search for better theories and methods with which to treat our problems. Failure to understand contemporary politics often has the effect of causing us to view with some ascerbity those political institutions which we always cherished and to which we remain strongly attached. Are they not spun around by our antagonists almost, it appears, at will? Are they not forced to meet trials for which they are ill-designed? The result of melancholy crises in political faith is seen in our diluted attachments to political modes and, indeed, the larger failure of the West to withstand spiritually the *élan vital* of the Communist world. All this turns our troubled gaze to the nature of governments and societies in a compelling way.

Our belief that autocracy is always impermanent has been shaken by those totalitarianisms which have thrust themselves into the modern world after a long period in which the steady march of democracy was so consistent that constitutional government came to be viewed almost as the natural condition of man. Autocracy is no less "natural" than democracy. Our realization of this has now been extended to new nations and exotic regimes. Alternative mechanisms of government that result from the blending of ancient and modern institutions take on a fresh relevance. With political demands arising from the need to make economic innovations—to create new sources of wealth and to raise material standards of life—can political leaders in new nations build polities that effectively manage the tasks imposed? Can they do this democratically? Indeed, our own civilization is threatened less by matters of doctrine than by the fact that as Drogat has said, "Nous vivons dans un monde de prodigieuses inégalités, où un dixième de la population du globe dispose de 80% du revenue total."[1]

Thus, the practical problems of the modern world have brought vast changes in focus and interest to comparative politics. It is necessary to become less ethnocentric and parochial in our concerns. No longer can the ordinary problems of Western government occupy us so exclusively except as they yield their secrets to a wider knowledge of theory and practice in government. No longer can comparative politics indulge the preoccupation with special agencies of modern government as legislatures, committees, administrative tribunals, interpolations, political parties, interest groups, processes of lawmaking, legislative drafting, the selection and recruitment of leaders and representatives, and the other traditional concerns of comparative politics unless a wider set of theories give these a social meaning. Indeed, let us introduce here a theme to which we will return—namely, that comparative politics has suffered from so much specialization and so great a division of labor that, while it has been more or less apparent what political scientists do when they study foreign governments, it has been less obvious why they do it.

All this has brought on a veritable crisis of concepts as well as technique. If nothing else it is bewildering to know that the usual claim to science —specialized knowledge—can end in creating intellectual lacunae. But is specialization as such on trial? Becoming less specialized will not solve the problems of our field. Without more powerful working concepts and ideas, the evil of specialization is that it stifles the imagination. The scholar loses his grasp of the interconnectedness of the objects of his study in his passion for the mundane and the particular. Knowledge is not built merely by adding up details of information in the absence of a powerful tradition of thought and a ready practice of discipline. Whatever its standing as a science, comparative politics has too long suffered from this defect. Many political scientists have taken comfort from certain knowledge while remaining contemptuous or afraid of ideas. What is required is a long look backward into the past of comparative politics to give us a balanced view of the future. Accordingly we shall try to account for the present state of comparative politics by tracing its development from the beginning of the modern period. We shall also argue that freshness of spirit and a sense of original purposes is once again returning to the field as it finds ideas suitable to the problems we raised earlier.

## II. NATURAL LAW, SCIENCE, AND THE STATE

Modern comparative government begins in the seventeenth century and with a theoretical framework which consisted of three major parts, the first ethical, the second a view of man's nature, and the third a conception of the units of which human society is composed. The first was a belief in natural law with its attendent ideal expressed in the natural rights of man. The second was a concept of rationality. The third was individualism. The individual was the social atom of society. As a person, he had certain rights based upon the doctrine of natural law. Society, composed of separate and individual persons, had to devise ways by means of which those rights could be reconciled with one another. The major burden for such reconciliation lay with human rationality and the ability to reason. Through a knowledge of natural law, the individual could will a beneficent society by guiding his actions in the light of reason and exercising his own rights in such a way as to safeguard the rights of others. But reason alone was not enough. The mechanism that would facilitate this process was law. Law arose through legislation, and legislation was a process of government. Comparative analysis was thus a search for institutions of government most suitable for establishing those political conditions by which law and human reason were best achieved. By virtue of man's transition from a primordial state of nature to human society—the latter inevitably inequitable, with different styles, customs, and degrees of access to power and riches—law, equity and government were considered the critical factors that enabled the individual to achieve his natural rights and thereby exercise his rationality and individualism. Law and liberty, rule and freedom would come together to blend wisdom and prudence in a beneficent society. Thus it was that Montesquieu, for example, said:

Man as a physical being, is like other bodies governed by invariable laws. And as an intelligent being, he incessantly transgresses the laws established by God, and changes those of his own instituting. He is left to his private direction, though a limited being, and subject, like all finite intelligences, to ignorance and error: even his imperfect knowledge he loses; and as a sensible creature, he is hurried away by a thousand impetuous passions. Such a being might every instant forget his Creator; God has therefore reminded him of his duty by laws of religion. Such a being is liable every moment to forget himself; philosophy has provided against this by the laws of morality. Formed to live in society, he might forget his fellow creatures; legislators have, therefore, by political and civil laws, confined him to his duty.[2]

What then are the proper concerns of comparative government? Above all they are to seek out the universal properties of human rule and law that, though common in all societies, are varied in their applications and usages. A knowledge of such universals could provide a basis for constructing those institutions of government that best realize for individuals a state conducive to sound precept and property. Thus it is that the ethical view of man promotes a standard by which to evaluate human institutions.

Such a spirit infused throughout the work of the pre-Hegelian and pre-Comtian British and European thinkers. Not the state but the individual is the first concern; not the group imperative but the veneration of liberty best expresses and sets the standard of good government. Comparison is used to consider those choices of societal form and spirit open to each human group as it perfects its polity. Diversity is then a source of laws, natural and analytical, rooted in the nature of things and men, the knowledge of which makes positive man-made laws fitted to the needs of a particular time and place.

With such ideals and objectives, comparative analysis had a noble conception of the uses of inquiry. A tradition nourished by a Jefferson as a politician and a de Tocqueville as an observer, it is also a tradition to which in a somewhat different way contemporary comparative politics now seeks to return. Long diverted by the rhetoric and mystique of nineteenth-century universal theories—which often had grotesque consequences—comparative government is engaged in an attempt to return to its earlier elegance and purposes. The new emphasis upon science is thus an old one; it is a search for elegance of theory, clarity of thought, and the ability to predict political action and purpose in human affairs.

The nineteenth century with its biological and evolutionary thinking was, far more than the eighteenth century, a time for universal rhetoric. It was exploratory and at the same time doctrinaire. Man was substituted for God in the ultimate analytical scheme of things, with the result that man became mystical and God rational. Not only was thought less clear but also science was endowed with a sense of its own pre-eminence.

It is impossible to reflect on these tendencies without noting the vast changes in spirit and outlook that they involved. A gap exists between the period of the rationalists and the deists—those who believed in the idea that the perfectability of man lay with the perfectability of his political institutions—and the period of the romantics. From the one to the other is the whole way between science and scientism, reason and idealism, ethics and utilitarianism.

These views require further comment. We can define the three major nineteenth-century tendencies in political theory that deeply affected comparative analysis of politics as follows: the romantic idealist, with its ultimate emphasis on the superorganic state; the positivist, with its apotheosis of science; and the utilitarian, with its extension of the economic notion of utility to that of social groups (which differed from the eighteenth-century exponents of natural law by their notions of evolutionary progress).[3] Each made an undeniable contribution to contemporary politics. As well, for a time, each had a stifling effect upon it. Many of the controversies that continue to plague comparative politics are really polemics about the role of science and theory that originated in the nineteenth century. For this reason not a few of the arguments about these matters appearing from time to time in the journals seem curiously misplaced and obsolete.

The most controversial of the nineteenth-century approaches was the German school of romantic idealism—most controversial, at any rate, in a political sense, since the rise of German National Socialism has often been traced to it.[4] Its emphasis was upon the superorganic superordinate group, best expressed in the idea of the *Staat*. The state takes precedent over the individual, who has no legal personality outside the state. It is the state that endows the individual with his rights, his ideas, his obligations, and his sense of justice. This being so, the state can make claims both emotional and political upon the citizen in so far as it represents the spirit or *Geist* of the "tribe" and the unfolding of a divine conception of order. Law becomes *Staatsrecht,* the complete obverse of natural law.

The second tendency of which we speak was in many ways closest to the spirit of the enlightenment. This was the utilitarian. Unvarnished and sober, workmanlike but lacking in humor, the utilitarians were obsessed with the problem of reform. Comparative government became an earnest discipline. It tinkered with constitutional innovation, legal reform, aid for the laboring poor, and enlargement of the franchise.[5] The utilitarian emphasis differed radically from the *Staatslehrer* emphasis. There the lawyers and jurists in Germany were called upon to perfect the institutions of man and government. They did so by contemplating the ideal state as reflected in a constitution. The constitution and law itself became the almost Platonic form of reality behind the actualities of political society. It was in this light that the lawyers and jurists wrestled with the German Constitution of 1871 and the Civil Code of 1898. The utilitarians, on the other hand, less influenced by matters of theory, transferred comparative politics to the precinct of the politically minded social workers, who were conceptually more humble and were preoccupied with practical reforms.[6]

If the utilitarians reacted against the Continental idealists, such men as Green were rejecting both utilitarians and another great intellectual force, the third of the great philosophic traditions that, becoming pervasive throughout the Western world, deeply affected the work of comparative scholars. This third force was positivism. Its great flowering in France during the Second Empire coincided with a scientific renaissance during which France knew no peer in the natural sciences and in mathematics.[7]

It is, of course, Comte who is most associated with the Positivist philosophy—a philosophy that sought to reduce the nature of man to the status of laws in nature. All phenomena were subject to regularities. These regularities could be observed and identified by empirical observation. As such they were regarded as natural laws and hence linked to the same principles of order as galaxies, biological systems, or any of the natural phenomena subject to observation.

The special twist given by the Positivists, including Comte, Taine, Renan, and others, was the principle that science could establish standards of morality. If for people such as Green it was through the metaphysics of morality that the principles of society could be established, for the Positivists it was the other way around: to establish morality one had first to discover the laws governing man and society.[8]

The result was that science soon became "scientism." Rationality was transformed into mysticism and idealism. One could speak of the "church" of science, the cult of "system," and the worship of evolution.[9]

With respect to government, these ideas were reflected in a search for the laws governing the polity. As with the idealists of the German school, it was upon the lawyer and the jurist that the burden of such analysis fell. As in Germany, the study of politics and comparative government was a study of law—for the Positivists they were the laws governing nature as manifested in the laws governing man. Comparative theory turned to the past, to the analysis of Greece and Rome, in order to find those basic points of society, the analysis of which, it appeared, would reveal the essential qualities of the polis and the polity.[10]

Each of these three major nineteenth-century tendencies in philosophy tended to disrupt and confuse the study of comparative politics as compared with the earlier clarity and theoretical shrewdness of Hooker, Montesquieu, Pufendorf, Locke, or Hobbes. The religion of science in France came to have effects similar to the romantic idealism of Germany.[11] Both relied heavily on the system of law as the prototype of the polity, naturalistic in the case of the Positivists or idealistic in the case of the romantic idealists. The situation was otherwise in England, where law never developed into a power jurisprudence or a theory of the state, but remained the preserve of the practitioner.[12]

There are, of course, powerful exceptions to all these generalizations. Marx, although deeply affected by both the positivist and idealist traditions, skirted both by his emphasis on historical materialism. Other figures represent promontories of thought that jut out of the misty landscapes of romanticism or scientific scholasticism. Although a part of the Positivist tradition, Coulanges, Durkheim, and Pareto fought it as well.[13] In Germany, Tönnies, Weber and others were also exceptions; and one can almost regard Weber's *Methodology of the Social Sciences* as a *cri de coeur* for objectivity not for its own sake, as it has so often been misrepresented, but for the liberation of social thought from the juristic pontifications of the *Staatslehrer* school.[14] In England the lawyers performed the same function as the political theorists and sociologists on the Continent. Here Vinogradoff, Maitland, and Maine stand out.

What, then, were the effects of these three main traditions—the idealistic, the Positivistic, and the utilitarian—on comparative politics? The first two relegated comparative government to the jurist and the historian. Precedent and uniqueness were wedded in a contradictory synthesis of thought. In the third, comparative government was the concern of the reform-minded practitioner. True, in recent times Laski came forward with an effort to create theory out of reform, and Barker provides criticism and classical scholarship; but the first was not very profound and the other though profound was not theoretical.

The result was that comparative government virtually disappeared despite such exceptions as Ostrogorski's study of party politics or Mosca's concern with ruling elites. In its place there grew up the study of the uniqueness of various instruments of government. Specialization was a means of avoiding the metaphysics of the positivists and the idealists, on the one hand, and the glib generalizations of the utilitarians, on the other. Specialization, however, had the effect of cutting off comparative analysis from its philosophical roots, to say nothing of the works of those intellectual rebels in Europe who continued to innovate in the comparative analysis of society. These especially were lost to American political scientists, with the unfortunate result that the academic study of comparative government became increasingly learned, tedious, and dull.

## III. THE RETREAT INTO SPECIALIZATION AND THE RISE OF BEHAVIORISM

As a reaction to European forms of comparative analysis (which seemed utterly inappropriate and irrelevant to research) and in response to the need for suitable substitutes, descriptive knowledge about specialized political instrumentalities came to occupy the center of the field of comparative government. Rejection of the European traditions of the nineteenth century was not limited to the study of politics; it was also in keeping with a much wider American suspicion of European ideologies and theories. A descriptive approach required keeping one's head and looking past the welter of confusion, mysticism, and petty theorizing (which seemed to characterize European political thought) to the underlying reality of actions and mechanisms of governments. Closer to the utilitarian spirit than any other, the descriptive approach was hostile to theories and impatient of generalizations. Even in the period after World War I—with its sudden outpouring of constitutional formulas and the appearance of a large number of new states in the Baltic, Finnish, and Balkan areas, to say nothing of Weimar Germany—the emphasis was mainly upon detailed description of instrumentalities of government. A primary concern was prevention of absolutism, particularly of a monarchical kind. The view was widely accepted that if the constitutional forms of democracy were established, the rest would follow. Social and economic problems faced by a country could best be reconciled through a democratic legislature and an enfranchised populace. Thus, the devising of suitable mechanisms of government was all-important.

Instrumentalities of government become the critical focus of investigation, with wider social and political matters more residual. Implicit in this notion is the belief that the state has its own dynamics. Its inadequacies or failures can be dealt with by modifying constitutional mechanisms and instrumentalities of government. Theory results from an examination of instrumentalities; it is necessary to know in detail their functioning and scope.

The difficulty inherent in this approach arises because such detailed knowledge shows how uniquely adjusted is any institution in the social matrix of a country. It becomes awkward to generalize about the utility of governmental mechanisms. To make up for this deficiency, comparative government specialists relied heavily on "lore," phrased as propositions. One of the best studies of post-World War I democracies describes the practice of constitutional imitation and relies heavily on these "lore propositions." For example, a "natu-ral solution" to the problem of establishing a cabinet government is to combine a strong executive with the rule of a popular representative assembly. Another "lore proposition" requires an independent judiciary if freedom is to be maintained. Still a third "lore proposition" states that imperfections of constitutions do not matter if compromise and a determination to support it are present. These create tranquility in the community.[15]

Nor are such "lore propositions" restricted to constitution-making. In so far as government was managerial, description of how regulatory commissions, administrative courts, and other agencies operated resulted in much the same effect—the application of generalized wisdom to descriptive data. The sum total of agencies and mechanisms of government for a given country thus came to mean scientific description of the structure of government. Yet this approach disguises important theoretical problems such as those emphasized in Towster's *Political Power in the U.S.S.R.* Its descriptive completeness makes implicit a theory that social and political structures are contingent on the determinants of government actions—those determinants to be found within the matrix of government and its substructures.[16]

Commenting on this tendency among political scientists in the United States, Bernard Crick remarks that, "As 'scientific' I found them in fact more prone to narrow than to explain the field that I had conventionally thought of as 'political.' "[17]

If description in and of itself is an end in comparative politics, it is also a beginning. It is from the descriptive tradition that behavioral science in politics has its origin. If knowledge was in part based upon an increase in details, then research was the means of finding them. Research put emphasis on research technique and method. New concerns arose from the emphasis on research. More predictable criteria for reform measures were one basis of scientific interest.

A second basis was the new concern about political parties and their corollary, public opinion, that began to appear at the turn of the century. Realism, toughness, and a pragmatic concern for scientific techniques began to characterize the field. Pioneers in this approach were Lowell and Wilson, who raised questions about political institutions that required research beyond the legal and historical in order to find answers. F. J. Goodnow, A. B. Hart, and W. B. Monroe, with their intense interest in reform, also gave comparative politics a strongly empirical bias.[18]

A behavioral approach was also much stimulated by Graham Wallas, whose *Human Nature in Politics* aroused keen interest in the psychological aspects of politics. Charles Merriam, after his own involvement with reform movements, which included active participation in politics, became interested in its psychology.

In so far as the early science of politics movement was scientific enough to pass beyond mere description to theory in the attempt to find natural principles of politics there was a small but rapidly growing body of opinion that saw the superstructure of society as explicable, not in economic terms as Charles Beard or E. A. G. Seligman thought, but in terms of psychological drives.[19]

It was Merriam and his colleague, Harold Gosnell, who gave direction and impetus to this emphasis on psychology and helped to form and focus the interests of Lasswell. Through Lasswell such matters as public opinion, voting behavior, leadership and elites, and a host of other matters long divorced from the concerns of political scientists were made a part of the field. The emphasis on science and technique was expanded and the psychological orientation was extended until politics reached into the related fields where scholars were working on such problems as individualistic percepts, leadership, and authority.

Thus, if the retreat into specialization was at first antitheoretical, it was not antiscientific. Nor—as a matter of fact—was it in the long run antitheoretical. It developed its own theories. The narrow notion of science in politics concerned with the extension of "hard data" techniques to trends in behavior was the American answer to European theory, but it remained almost exclusively preoccupied with American problems. There remains a paucity of materials using behavioral methods and dealing with governments and institutions of countries other than our own.[20]

The point is, of course, that behavioral studies—whether conceived more or less purely in the tradition of psychology (or, as we prefer to consider it, concerned with motivation and perception as a basis for theory) or with the study of trends in aggregate behavior, such as voting behavior and public opinion—assume a knowledge of structural factors of society. The study of behavior can become effective only when general knowledge is in hand and can be taken as given, for knowledge of the context within which action occurs is essential if the action so analyzed is to have meaning and relevance. It is precisely for this reason that more broadly comparative work still emphasizes the artful selection of generalized variables.

The structural approach is an effort to find general properties of systems that limit the range of action open to individuals. It thus delimits gross behavior and is particularly useful for large-scale comparative studies. It seeks qualitative precision rather than quantitative, although the latter point is rather a matter of necessity than conviction. The behavioral school begins with the individual and his motivations. In so far as individual behaviors and motivations can be aggregated, general propositions become possible. In short, the structural approach establishes categories whereby action is itself limited and restricted by what Durkheim would have called "social facts." The behavioral approach emphasizes choices and motivations and infers structural limitations from the behavior of individuals rather than from the properties of collectivities.[21]

It was the institutionalists who first saw the need for both structural and behavioral science, and we can view their contributions in this light.

## IV. THE INSTITUTIONALISTS

The general characteristics of comparative analysis from the turn of the century to the post-World War I period can be restated as follows: 1. Comparative analysis became divorced from philosophy (and, indeed, philosophy itself became specialized in its subdivisions, particularly as the linguistic philosophers sought relief from metaphysical problems in a renewed emphasis on logical and conceptual precision). 2. A retreat from theory into descriptiveness led to the describing of how particular government establishments and mechanisms operated. 3. There was a compensating emphasis on specialization, particularly as the occurrence of social welfare governments in Europe helped to focus attention on new governmental activities with mechanisms including para-statal bodies and cabinet reforms.

There were, of course, prominent figures who held out against the tendencies. Among them were Bryce, Barker, Laski, Friedrich, and Finer. In the period following World War I they not only resisted the descriptive tendency but also helped to bring about major new developments in comparative studies that are only now gaining strength. First of all, each of these figures remained in some degree concerned with comprehensive theory. In varying ways they sought to add something to knowledge by the art of comparison. Without sacrificing scholarship, they sought to find the general in the particular.

Reacting both to the metaphysicians of the Continental tradition and the intellectual poverty of the utilitarians, the institutionalists nevertheless did not succumb to opposite extremes. They sought through empirical comparisons to find in certain key institutions and practices those underlying factors that were the ultimate derivatives of state power and that set the limits within which governmental actions were undertaken. What they share is an encompassing view of politics in which the political process is related to the wider coherence of social institutions. Thus, they attempted to indicate the political consequences of such institutions as religion, education, economic organization, and tradition. By this means they were able to relate leadership, ideologies, and political mechanisms, first in terms of single societies and then between societies.[22] Theirs was not a search for precision. Instead, their work was intuitive, speculative, and interesting. Friedrich's work on constitutional government or Finer's more extensive comparative treatment of modern governments, though written a generation ago, are still basic to any contemporary work in the field.[23]

What is so interesting about the institutionalists is that each to some extent continues in the tradition that he hoped to modify. Friedrich still bears the earmarks of the *Staatslehrer* tradition.[24] In some measure—for example, in his reliance on such crude factors as climate to account for political behavior or his plea for facts, facts, facts—Bryce remains a Spencerian witness. Nevertheless, he is refreshingly free from the romantic aspects of the naturalistic tradition of science. Asking whether or not profound differences characterize the human as distinct from the natural sciences, he replies to his own question:

The answer is that there is in the phenomena of human society one "Constant," one element or factor which is practically always the same, and therefore the basis of all the so-called "Social Science." This is Human Nature itself. All fairly normal men have like passions and desires. They are stirred by like motives, they think upon similar lines. . . . Human nature is that basic and ever-present element in the endless flux of social and political phenomena which enables general principles to be determined. And though the action of individual men may often be doubtful, the action of a hundred or a thousand men all subjected to the same influences at the same time may be much more predictable, because in a large number the idiosyncrasies of individuals are likely to be eliminated or evened out. Politics accordingly has its roots in Psychology, the study (in their actuality) of the mental habits and volitional proclivities of mankind.[25]

Thus, if human nature is the constant, then it is to the mechanisms and institutions through which it is expressed that we must look for answers to social and political problems.

Thus, in spite of tell-tale evidence of Positivist thought, Bryce derives his outlook primarily from his practical experience as a working politician. Inevitably, however, he is affected by the blending of ideas and beliefs that create those confluences of thought of which the intellectual ethos or the spirit of an age is composed, for only in rare cases can the ideas of a major thinker be uniquely traced to a single antecedent. So too with Laski, Barker, and Finer. The utilitarian influence in Laski is modified by the neo-Hegelians, such as Bosanquet and T. H. Green. Thus, Green, when speaking of the power of the ruler or the state says that:

When the power by which rights are guaranteed is sovereign (as it is desirable that it should be) in the special sense of being maintained by a person or persons, and wielding coercive force not liable to control by any other human force, it is not this coercive force that is the important thing about it, or that determines the habitual obedience essential to the real maintenance of rights. That which determines this habitual obedience is a power residing in the common will and reason of men, i.e., in the will and reason of men as determined by social relations, as interested in each other, as acting together for common ends. It is a power which this universal rational will exercises over the inclinations of the individual, and which only needs exceptionally to be backed by coercive force.[26]

Is this not the same blend of utilitarianism and socialism found in Laski? True, Laski specifically denies any higher morality of the state in itself, since he argues that:

The true end of the state is to maintain the legal principles which secure within its confines the predominence of the owners of the instruments of production; and what of common welfare it ever establishes is always subordinate to that major end. Social legislation is not the outcome of a rational willing and objective willing of the common good by all members of the community alike; it is the price paid for those legal principles which secure the predominance of the owners of property. It waxes and wanes in terms of their prosperity. It is a body of concessions offered to avert a decisive challenge to the principles by which their authority is maintained.[27]

In these terms the "good state" is that which is founded upon a proper distribution of properties and obligation, but even here the pre-eminence of the state is not entirely forsworn. Rather, it is limited to those showing a desirable egalitarianism. Hence, in Laski's marriage of utilitarianism and socialism, he relies less on reason than does Green and more on property relations. Laski compares specific governments in the light of their regard to the institutions that produce the greatest equality of access to authority and property.[28]

Of the five institutionalists it is Barker who remains closest to the earlier ideal of natural law and natural rights. While he brings to this early tradition a utilitarian test, individualism, liberty, and natural law remain his points of departure. When the functions of government are extended to secure fundamental rights more adequately, then the infringement of the state in social affairs is justified:

It is here that we may possibly find a limit, or a principle of limit, to the extension of our rights to the enjoyment of personal security. There is always a cost involved; and it is wise to count the cost in advance. The cost is partly financial, or a simple matter of money: it is partly also spiritual, or a more serious matter of control. The financial cost is that involved in the payment of contributions by the worker, the employer, and the general taxpayer, to meet the expenses of a system of joint or social insurance. The spiritual cost is that involved in the extension of the area of compulsory uniformity and administrative control. The double cost may be well worth the while: what is certain is that it must always be paid.[29]

With Barker the instrumentalities and forms of government must be viewed as they enhance the natural rights of man. The comparative analyst then explores the practical effects of the inherent paradox created when state intervention and control are extended in order to serve natural rights themselves. A standard of comparison derives from the paradox, to be studied not only in the mechanisms of government but also in the workings of institutions through which natural rights are expressed, including law, religion, property, and the like.

Of them all perhaps Finer comes closest to the utilitarian tradition:

> Government is composed of patterns of human cooperation; the allocation and forms of authority; and procedure. That is its anatomy. Its soul lies in choosing between alternative objects of happiness and choosing between duties and sacrifices, and effecting a proportion between them. It allows no complete rejection, but imposes a decision on a tolerable mixture of preferences, seeking and keeping power balanced against what other men and women are seeking. . . .[30]

These five institutionalists stand out against a field otherwise characterized by preoccupation with description and lore. Through them the early inheritance of comparative politics has come down to us. Taking their place beside those concerned with description, they form an important source for future development of the field.

From the descriptive and institutionalist approaches one can trace the beginnings of contemporary *behavioral* and *structural* analysis. It is these two approaches that are gaining currency today. *The structure may be defined as the relationships in a social situation which limits the choice process to a particular range of alternatives. The behavioral may be defined as the selection process in choice, i.e. deciding between alternatives.* Both stand on opposite ends of the same continuum and their point of contact is the choice process.


## V. STRUCTURAL AND BEHAVIORAL ANALYSIS

In order that we may be clear about the distinction being made here between the behaviorist and the institutionalist traditions, we must regard the distinctions between them on three levels: theory, method, and technique.

### Theory

The theoretical objectives of the behavioral tradition include (1) the most highly generalized—that is, those dealing with explanatory theories based on knowledge of human behavior itself—and (2) the most particularized—that is, those producing empirical theories of limited generalization and great precision. The explanatory theories of the structuralists are (1) less general than the behavioral, dealing with the properties of collectivities and the limitations they impose upon behavior, and (2) less precise and unique to a unit. In both the behavioral and the structural approaches theories are generalized directly from empirical analysis. We can cite as a behavioral theory an example from Lane. In describing the impact of mass media upon political action, we find the following highly generalized theory from which wide comparative inferences could be obtained.

> Political material is perceived and has an influence to the extent that it serves a need for the individual, i.e., if it provides (a) information useful in solving a career or other objective problem, (b) means of social adjustment to others, or (c) opportunity for the release of psychic tension.[31]

An even more comprehensive behavioral theory having comparative implications is to be found in Harold Lasswell's *Psychopathology and Politics,* as witnessed by the following formula: private motives displaced upon a public object, rationalized in terms of the public interest, produce political man.[32]

In contrast to a behavioral theory, an example of a structural theory is afforded by Selznick: commenting on the durability of values in society, he points out that a "weakening of values may characterize significant *segments* of a society before a radical decay is observable in the entire social body." The problem is the social vulnerability of a system to a militant organizational weapon, such as the Communist Party. "Put as a general rule we may say: Under conditions of political combat, those who have no firm values of their own become the instruments of the values of others."[33]

In order to consider by structural means the potentialities of militant political groups within a system, the political vulnerability of the society itself becomes the subject of analysis. Hence, several ranges of theory are possible. The first is the most general, dealing with the cultural and social factors which affect vulnerability. The second is the determination of a model type of subgroup, in Selznick's case the "organizational weapon." A third is the delimiting of alternative actions open to groups and individuals in the system, as limited by the previous two stages of analysis. The entire weight of the analysis can then be brought to bear on explanations of why a particular course of action was chosen, given the alternatives presented. In this sense structural analysis can be viewed as a kind of intellectual diamond cutting. The lines, planes, and potential fractures of the unit are observed. Just as the diamond cutter makes a prediction about how the perfect diamond will emerge from his strategic blow of the hammer on the rough stone, so the structuralist tries to predict how, in the face of a particular crisis or opportunity, the unit under observation will respond.

## Method

When we come to the methodological differences between the behavioral and the structural approaches, the effect of theory is pronounced. Structural concepts tend to be synthetic and less experimental than behavioral. Behavioral methods commonly employ a form of input-output model (similar to that used in mechanical and computer models) with the promise of quantification explicitly or implicitly a goal. Easton's general model of political systems is a case in point. "Inputs" are demands and supports that pose the problems to be dealt with by the matrix of the political system; "Outputs" are decisions taken.

The purer forms of behavioral analysis, as we have suggested, deal with the observation of motivation. Groups to which individuals belong are relevant in so far as motivation (and perception) are affected by such group membership. Theoretical explanations that have motivation as their object inevitably direct analysis to individual behavior. Where, however, behavior cannot be understood solely by reference to individuals as isolates or mere aggregates, behavioral theory broadens to include social groups. This trend has led to the development in behaviorism of approaches utilizing organizational theory and group analysis. Examining relatively small units, behavioral science can be extended to infer relevant factors of structure. Efforts to do this in political science are found in decision-making analysis, particularly in international relations, though such analysis has not been used very much in comparative politics so far.[34] More recently the conceptual focus of behavioral analysis has been to modify its original motivational emphasis and examine the interpersonal relations and social supports of action, including not only group properties but the tasks of the group and the sentiments of the members as well.[35]

The conceptual approaches used by behaviorists rely heavily on experimental methods utilizing a small number of variables, with the methods remaining closely integrated with actual techniques of analysis readily available to the research worker.

In contrast to the behaviorists, methods used by the structuralists vary greatly and tend to be tailored to the requirements of macrocosmic units— the more typical ones for structural analysts.[36] In general, the methods most frequently used by structuralists have involved ideal types; a form of analysis that was common in the historical sociological works of Weber, Tönnies, Sombart, Durkheim, and others. Whether or not ideal types actually represent "theories," they set forth a set of categories by means of which empirical material can be examined.[37] Particular ideal types have involved comparative bureaucracy (Weber), comparative

communities (Tönnies), and comparative societies (Durkheim). The structuralists rely heavily on comparative studies of large-scale units. The approach has been most usefully articulated by Radcliffe-Brown as follows:

*The Function* of any recurrent activity, such as the punishment of a crime, or a funeral ceremony, is the part it plays in the social life as a whole and therefore the contribution it makes to the maintenance of the structural continuity. The concept of function as here defined thus involves the notion of a *structure* consisting of a *set of relations* amongst *unit entities,* the continuity of the structure maintained by a *life-process* made up of the activities of the constituent units.[38]

Hence, the methodological approach inherent in structural analysis is the identification of the functional values of relevant aspects of social and political life in their relationship to the unit under analysis, whether a society, a government, a church organization, a trade union, or a political party. Recent efforts of structural analysis go beyond ideal types in order to demarcate a range of possibly relevant variables that, in their interconnectedness, cast light on the entire system under discussion. Structural methods thus employ comparison in two dimensions. One analyzes the changes over a period of time as they are manifested in a particular system. In this way, structural analysis may be used to compare the changes in organization and belief that have occurred in modern France, Britain, or the U.S.S.R. The punctuation points in time are usually revolutions, changes in regime or equally compelling or dramatic instances of events that indicate an alteration in the relationship of variables within the system.

Equally, structural analysis can be used as between systems in space—for example, in comparing countries or governments. Here the burden of comparison is in the analysis of the different ways variables arrange themselves from one system to the next. The method of structural analysis has as its first object the specification of those variables that are more significant than others and as its second purpose the specification of variables unique to each of the cases used for comparison.

Much comparative work in political science has been characterized by the structural method applied comparatively. The method has also been applied in other fields of the social sciences, particularly anthropology and sociology.[39]

The conceptual or methodological problems of behavioral and structural approaches, it will readily be seen, are different in their emphases. The former, more limited by their attention to techniques, tend to emphasize quantitative categories. Behavioral theories derive from that methodological treatment that, lending itself to more inductive methods, allows the building up of more general statements through repeated experiments. Structural theories derive from highly generalized statements about the functional and structural properties of a given class of system, they are more deductive and *a priori,* and they rely more directly on comparison among systems than do the behavioral.

### Techniques

Both the structural and the behavioral approaches employ a wide range of analysis, including interviews of various kinds, applied with varying degrees of efficiency. In addition, each can employ a range of mathematical and statistical techniques according to the skill of the analyst. The variations in techniques result from the nature of the material to be worked upon and the strategy employed. In general, however, the qualitative concepts used in structural analysis are more difficult to quantify, while much of the burden of method in behavioral analysis is in the development of concepts that lend themselves to ready quantification. In general, then, behavioral theory is limited by techniques of analysis available to the observer, while with structural analysis the techniques include intuitive skills as well as such tools as chi-squares or factor analysis.[40]

We can see that both the structuralists and the behavioralists begin at opposite poles of an intellectual continuum. Strung out at different positions along the continuum are most of the novel forms of comparative analysis today, while representatives of one approach or the other cluster around the two poles. In spite of efforts to reach out toward one another, they are often frustrated by their differing ways of treating problems. The behaviorists recoil in horror at the imprecision inherent in cosmic efforts of the structuralists. The structuralists scorn the behavioralists, who seem eternally preoccupied with precision at the expense of content and method at the expense of "real" problems.

How, then, can we usefully distinguish behavioral from and structural analysis? The most important distinction between them lies in the realm of theory. Is action to be explained largely in terms of motivation or in terms of organizational factors? For example, to analyze the behavior of Communists, should we describe their emotional commitments, their personality characteristics, and the perceptions they have of themselves, as Pye does so brilliantly in his *Guerrilla Communism in Malaya*?[41] Or should motivational factors be considered as given while the main determinants of action derive from the nature of a communist organization, its structure, its dynamic, and its group objectives, which "of necessity" insure a limited range of behavioral tolerance? For Pye structure is much less significant than it is for Selznick in his *The Organizational Weapon.*[42] Pye's work is clearly behavioral as we are using the term, while Selznick's is purely structural. Their theories, in part accounting for some of the same kinds of phenomena (although the emphasis is entirely different), are literally at opposite ends of the structural-behavioral continuum.

Another differentiating criterion relates, as we have suggested, to the size of units. Structural analysis lends itself to dealing with macro-units, that is, large-scale systems. The behavioral begins with individuals. A note of caution needs to be sounded here, however: it is possible to deal with individuals on a structural basis, as in *Gestalt* psychology, but it is equally possible to deal with aggregate behavior from a behavioral viewpoint. The best that can be said is that structural analysis lends itself to sorting out the properties of large-scale systems—and here we would include membership groups as inclusive as societies on the one hand and such secondary groups as trade unions, voluntary associations, and political parties on the other.

Structural analysis has been more characteristic of comparative studies than has behavioral analysis. The methods of comparison reveal the consequences of the presence or absence of structural variables, and in so far as structural analysis is "scientific," it is comparative. Few efforts at comparative behavioral analysis have been successful; for example, the examinations of authoritarianism made by Adorno and his associates in *The Authoritarian Personality* were not reproduced cross-culturally.[43] The reason is partly that many of the personality factors forming the substance of such analysis—that is, the nature of familial frustration, the mechanisms of socialization, and the like —may have different effects in another structural setting. If the Swiss authoritarian family is quite similar to the German, it is difficult to account for the quite dissimilar actions of their respective members. It seems clear that more knowledge of structural variables is required.

Finally, although behavioral analysis is much closer to experimental methods and is concerned more with individuals and small groups, its theories are more highly generalized than structural ones. This point will be discussed further.

There have been efforts to bring both the structural and behavioral forms of analysis closer together. It is not necessary that this be done; that is to say, there is no special virtue in bringing them together except as explanations provided by one approach leave questions unanswered that the range of analysis provided by the other may satisfy. Hence, closing the gap between the two is itself an important theoretical problem with important consequences for effective research.

## VI. CLOSING THE GAP

Two themes have run through this discussion. The first has dealt with the rupture in tradition that took place between the spirit and outlook and the problems and approaches of those early moderns associated with the development of comparative study of government in both its theoretical and practical aspects and those today who are wrestling with problems of government in a similar fashion in the face of diversity and challenge.

The second theme is the relationship between behavioral and structural studies. In our concluding remarks we shall try to show that both of these are significantly related to one another and that to resolve one is to resolve the other.

A third theme has centered around the problem of analysis of specialized mechanisms of government. The exploration of the social consequences of political machinery has been one of the core interests of camparative politics. If the instrumentalities of government are not to be seen simply as a reflection of social factors, what independent role can be charged to them and how can we best determine their potentialities in given societies? For it is the intermeshing of social needs with political machinery that represents the core interests of political science. From this relationship is derived our interest in decision-making, political stability, law and change, and political ideals. This orientation has led American political scientists to seek to determine more specifically the distinguishing and crucial ingredients of democratic government on the grounds that by providing those ingredients democracy will be assured. This quest is even more compelling today. If there is no one-to-one correspondence between political mechanisms and political forms, there is at least a close relationship between an ensemble of political mechanisms and political ideals. Can there be democracy without electoral systems and representative assemblies? Can there be popular decision-making without a stable framework of consultation with the people? Yet, alternatively, is it necessary to have more than one party, as, in fact, the political arrangements of the United States were conceived?

There are no simple answers to such questions. What is necessary is more than a certain knowledge of how the ideals of a people become translated into their concepts of legitimate government. Also needed are more adequate theories that can explain the complex motivations of people in their relation to government—theories that go well beyond the effective making of policy. Symbolic affiliations, identifications of the individual with a wide social group in countries where historic parochialisms prevail, and related matters may become as important in the comparative analysis of legitimacy and government as the actual identification of popular demands for decision-making. The degree to which a complex range of subgroups in a society provides psychological comforts and satisfactions required by individuals may substantially affect the role of government. Voluntary associations, taking up the slack

between citizen and state, may serve to provide a whole range of intermediate satisfactions for occupation, recreation, education, and the like. They may also be so blindingly absent that the state needs to intervene in all activities of life. Indeed, in many new countries, the state is not only the major ordering principle in social life but also the largest employer, the sole agent of social mobility, and the final arbiter of custom. Indeed, in some countries even the primary group becomes a political mechanism.

At both ends of the scale, behavioral and structural approaches have hammered away at these and related problems. Consider one of the recent efforts to analyze behavior and through it comprehend the social needs of individuals, Nathan Leites' *Ritual of Liquidation.*[44] Individual action in a highly structured social universe is the theme of this book. How the individual Bolshevik leader on trial identifies with his prosecutor and helps to undo himself is perhaps less significant than the renewed sense of belonging to the society provided by the act of self-relinquishment. The hunger for affiliation, the abdication of private standards, and other behavioral syndromes that made the events of the Moscow Trials of the 1930's so extraordinary begin to reveal latent propensities in all human beings when we begin to consider such problems as the individual's relation to the state. Leites attempted to recreate the motivational and perceptive aspects of the universe of the Bolshevik and to infer from that universe certain wider structural properties of the system. From motivation we proceed to structure, and from perception to action. As the picture of Soviet society and government begins to emerge, it develops not merely from the images the participants have of themselves as moral beings and their view of society but also from the ways in which the naked power of the state is revealed in the roles of prosecutor and defendant. Observing the role of the lawyers and the prosecutors, we see a microcosm of authority—the state squeezed into a courtroom. From motivation and perception to role, from defendant to image builder, one sees structure emerging from process in the wider context of past events.

Leites' book is a useful example of a behavioral approach that seeks to answer the question of how individual behavior both is reflected in the nature of the collectivity and helps to determine it. A volume that begins with the structural and moves to a few of the interstices of human motivation is Almond and Coleman's *Politics of the Developing Areas.* Advocating a functional and structural point of view, it attempts to delimit the area of the political from the other aspects of social behavior and to show how a functional core of analysis can reveal those differences in mechanisms of government that cannot be derived simply from an examination of the mechanisms themselves. Similarly, in the linkages between government and the individual, such problems as political socialization and recruitment take on a particular significance. Citing Hyman's work on political socialization, the authors not only react to the excessively rationalistic interpretations of emotional learning and political indoctrination, but also try to combine a rationalistic interpretation with those incorporating more unconscious psychological processes.[45] Thus, they seek to associate those building blocks of group activity with the larger context of politics by examining the political values and attitudes that are the shared inheritance of individuals:

The relationship between the political socialization function and the political recruitment function is comparable to the relationship between Linton's "basic personality" and "status" or "role" personality. . . . The political recruitment function takes up where the general political socialization function leaves off. It recruits members of the society out of particular subcultures—religious communities, statuses, classes, ethnic communities, and the like—and inducts them into the specialized roles of the political system, trains them in the appropriate skills, provides them with political cognitive maps, values, expectations and affects.[46]

Whatever its defects, the structural method attempts to use comparative treatment to exhaust explanation at a more general level before proceeding to a particular one. In this way it would ordinarily move closer to those concrete units of action in which the actual behavior of individuals becomes the subject of scrutiny. Two recent studies at the intermediate range between the structural, on the one hand, and the behavioral, on the other, show some of the work going on inside of the gap. One of these begins with the twin concepts of traditionalism and empathy. In the idea of the former there is also included the close relationship between ideas of tradition held by individuals and the social structure by which those ideas are expressed. Thus, a highly traditionalistic culture is resistant to change and innovation. What happens when people in a traditionalistic culture are exposed to the mass media? That is the question asked by Lerner in his *Passing of the Traditional Society,* and he shows that what does happen is based upon the ability of individuals to empathize new roles when their dimensions are sketched out through the impact of communications. Thus, through the transmission of knowledge of other roles, even the traditionalist can be weakened in his reluctance to consider himself in roles that he himself is not likely to play. In this case, beginning with a more behavioral orientation and using quantitative techniques, Lerner begins to raise questions about the durability of tradition in the face of individual abilities to empathize roles under the impact of mass media. That he has no general theory of structure but infers it from behavior is clear. It is equally clear, however, that

his approach is utterly appropriate to proceeding both to structural and behavioral theories. Lerner's book represents a significant effort to close the theoretical and methodological gaps between the behavioral and structural approaches.

Another such effort is Duverger's. Here the point of departure is frankly structural, but in *Political Parties* Duverger does not begin with an over-all structural analysis of any of the countries with which he deals, but rather attempts to deal at the subsystem levels with structural properties of differing kinds of political parties, electoral systems, and their effects upon regimes. It paves the way for more behavioral analysis of voting and the motivational factors that come into play when shaped by the structural propensities of the parties, governments, and electoral systems that he lays down. Here, too, there is an emphasis on quantitative techniques. As with Lerner, it is possible to move effectively toward the kind of comparative analysis that has been hitherto available only in studies of elections within single countries. It is just as possible to proceed to a more general structural level of analysis.

Some of the most important work that has been going on in an effort to close the gap between the structural and the behavioral has centered around the notion of "role." If we consider "role" as a functionally defined position in a social system, we are immediately struck by several of its characteristics. First, there is the fact that roles are socially conceived and, while played by individuals, are analytically separate from them. Secondly, individuals play a variety of roles. Thirdly, roles are institutionalized forms of behavior, so that rights and wrongs are associated with playing them. Fourthly, action, in so far as it is structured through roles, becomes motivated by expectations induced by roles themselves. "Role" then becomes the crucial analytical point that is both behavioral and structural at the same time. On the other hand, the membership groups of any society are themselves congeries of roles.[47] There are, however, other difficulties in using role analysis as a mechanism for linking the behavioral and the structural: it poses as many problems as it resolves. Nevertheless, for comparative analysis, it promises to open up a fruitful line of enquiry—especially in new nations, where much of the problem of nation building is involved in the establishment of new political roles that have behavioral as well as structural significance.

What, then, are the main lines of inquiry that have opened up in the contemporary forms of comparative analysis? We can briefly indicate some of them here. There is the continuing concern with the nature of functioning of political instrumentalities in respective societies. This has always been a major concern of those interested in comparative politics. Now it has been broadened and widened to include problems of social change and developing areas. On the structural side there has been an effort to introduce sociological methods into political science as a means of determining those social variables which affect the operations of government and shape the nature of demands on government. There has been interest in subjects that lie between government and society—political recruitment, the social backgrounds of political leaders, elite studies, problems of voting and nonvoting, and ideologies. On the more behavioral side, this interest has manifested itself in a concern over political socialization, the inculcation of values, the determination of discontinuities in culture and social status, and the effects of such discontinuities on political instrumentalities.

Another main line of inquiry has to do with accounting for the consequences of economic development and changing technologies. The central problem is the ways in which institutions adjust and adapt themselves to changing conditions. In addition to our traditional interests in problems of government such as legislative flexibility, there has emerged a concern with finding innovations in political practices capable of resolving problems of economic and political development. Especially on the behavioral side, we find concern with problems of cognition and efficiency: How is motivation toward group goals achieved? What are the standards of social behavior and motivation necessary to create those loyalties in the midst of changing perspectives that bring a satisfactory adjustment of structural and individual needs?

Between the behavioral and the structural a large number of problems traditional in comparative government remain central. While we observe a new concern with economic development planning and efficiency, we also seek knowledge of their consequences in the evolution of the state. Does it become more democratic or less? Is oligarchy a necessary consequence of organizational efficiency, and, if not, what alternatives are there? Theories about group behavior and individual perception must be blended with those dealing with structural propensities of the system as a whole.

Still another line of inquiry now developing deals with those groups that create roles intermediate between government and society. Voluntary associations, churches, trade unions, and social organizations are all politically important. Where they absorb the energies and activities of individuals and affect their jobs, their positions of power and prestige, and their incomes, government is involved in a substantially different way than is the case in countries where all organized aspects of life are somehow related to government. In the former instance political participation tends to be part time and residual; in the latter everything is politicized. What are the differences between highly politicized systems and those where voluntary associations and interest groups play a critical political role—as in modern France; those systems where voluntary associations are less politicized—as in England; and those systems where politics disappear into bureaucracy and voluntary associations become auxilliaries of the state? Put into a context of modern nationalism, conditions of politicization and the effects of extending pluralism that helped to create opportunities for nationalism and effective political parties are a major subject of inquiry. In some new nations—for example, Guinea and Ghana—there is a tendency toward bureaucratization and depoliticization. When single parties appear no longer separable from government, do they respond to larger social needs and fulfill individual demands and perceptions better than more pluralistic systems?

Finally, the comparative study of mass media and social communications has recently been opened. What have been the effects of mass media in creating standardized political responses and establishing political values? What is the role of mass media in terms of their manipulative implications? Is there a relationship between mass media and political conformity? Such questions are not limited to the West. It has been argued that the mass media are central transmission belts to men's minds and that the vast outpouring of literature that achieves the manipulation of symbols and the application of propaganda techniques to new nations has helped to create new desires and standards of life that result in pressures on governments. The mass media also provide an introduction to new roles, hitherto beyond the comprehension of an ordinary man.

Inquires into matters of this kind are centered around more classical problems. One is the analysis of change and stability, the intellectual mapping of the varieties of experience represented by changes from one type of system to another. A comparative study of revolutions is certainly one aspect of such analysis. A second is the comparative examination of traditions and traditionalism and the implications they have for future change. A third is the comparative study of political participation and a fourth the comparative examination of groups concerned with political socialization, such as schools and universities, trade-union organizations, and cultural organizations. Do they encourage disaffiliation and parochialism, or do they create commitment to the larger polity?

Ultimately, then, we return to still larger questions of political theory that it has always been a task of comparative government to explore. What are the political goals of differing societies, and how do these vary? Do they value liberty less and material welfare more? What political structures are the most suitable for certain given ends? Thus it is that the concerns of comparative theory are moral—just as government itself raises the issue of morality.

We accept the view that science and morality are indissolubly wedded. But what lies beyond morality? Action, of course. Science cannot determine morality, but it can be placed in its service. The next stage in comparative politics will produce, we venture to suggest, a new era of pragmatic theory and practical reform.

## NOTES

1. Noel Drogat, *Pays Sous-developpes et Cooperation Technique* (Paris: SPES, 1958), p. 12.

2. Montesquieu, *Spirit of the Laws* (New York: Hafner, 1949), p. 3.

3. Halevy says that, "According to Stuart Mill the idea of a theory of progress and of a philosophy of history was due to a reaction against the ideas of the eighteenth century, against the philosophy of enlightenment. This estimate is false: the Saint-Simonians and Auguste Comte owed their philosophy of progress to Turgot and Condorcet; and it is perhaps to Condorcet at least as much as Hartley, Priestly, and Godwin that James Mill from the earliest years of his literary production owed the doctrine which he held to be fundamental—that is, the doctrine that the human species is essentially perfectible, or capable of progress. Political economy was still thought of as a knowledge of laws, but those laws were no longer merely static laws, laws of equilibrium, but were also dynamic laws, laws of evolution or of progress." See Elie Halevy, *The Growth of Philosophic Radicalism* (Boston: The Beacon Press, 1955), p. 274.

4. Sir Ernest Barker remarks, "We have to confess that the cult of super-personal Beings has had some tragic results. It began with Herder's Folk-poetry and Folk-music; it grew into Hegel's Folk-minded and Savigny's Folk-right (the right or law which is just a particular people's sense of justice in its own particular phase of development). . . ." See Barker's introduction to Gierke's *Natural Law and the Theory of Society, 1500–1800* (Cambridge: Cambridge University Press, 1950), p. xvii.

5. In the United States this same utilitarian emphasis showed a predilection for reform mechanisms, such as initiative and referendum, proportional representation, and the establishment of a career civil service.

6. Nor were the influences of the utilitarians limited to English reform. The utilitarian point of view penetrated to India through the appointment in 1819 of James Mill to the post of assistant examiner of the East India Company. He was followed into the service in 1823 by his son, John Stuart Mill. Thereafter the tradition of evangelical reform, practical philanthropy, and successful mercantile enterprise so characteristically the utilitarian formula, became pervasive in shaping the character of the government of India. See Eric Stokes, *The English Utilitarians and India* (Oxford: The Clarendon Press, 1959). Among those who objected to this essentially anti-intellectual approach to prob-lems of comparative analysis were such figures as Bernard Bosanquet and T. H. Green. Both have been called neo-Hegelians. Both were in a very real sense looking for a more comprehensive theory that would enable them better to understand the mechanics of power. Treating the state, and indeed human society, as a moral order resulted in normative rather than empirical theory.

7. Charlton writes, "Having rapidly recovered from the interruptions of 1789 and the Reign of Terror, the sciences were expanding and triumphant. The foundation of the École Polytechnique (1784)—nursery of generations of scientists and thinkers, including Comte and Renouvier—and the reorganization of the Jardin du Roi (1793), the Academie des Sciences (1795) and the École Normale (1808) gave French science an impetus that never slackened throughout the century." See D. G. Charlton, *Positivist Thought in France* (Oxford: The Clarendon Press, 1959), p. 12.

8. This view was close enough to certain of the English utilitarians, particularly James Mill, Bentham and Spencer. One is tempted to call them positivists without general theories.

9. It is not surprising then that in the middle and latter parts of the nineteenth century the French positivists should suddenly discover the German idealists. Indeed, it was reaction to this misuse of history that gave rise to such works as Coulange's *Ancient City,* in which an effort was made to show how fundamentally Greece and Rome differed from the contemporary society of the nineteenth century and how whimsical and obscure those institutions became when regarded as prototypical of modern society.

10. See Fustel de Coulanges, *The Ancient City* (New York: Doubleday Anchor Books, n.d.).

11. See D. G. Charlton, *Positivist Thought in France* (Oxford: The Clarendon Press, 1959).

12. This remains true to this day. The Inns of Court are, in effect, "trade schools," where practitioners of law learn their craft. Laski once commented that in the United States far greater emphasis on legal theory characterizes the best law schools than is the case in England. See Harold Laski, *The American Democracy* (New York: The Viking Press, 1948), p. 585.

13. See Talcott Parsons, *Structure of Social Action* (New York: The Free Press of Glencoe, 1949).

14. As, for example, by Leo Strauss in *Natural Right and History* (Chicago: The University of Chicago Press, 1953), Chapter II. Aron points out that Weber "criticized bitterly the kind of *romanticism of Real-politik* which flourished in pre-war Germany." See Raymond Aron, *German Sociology* (New York: The Free Press of Glencoe, 1957), p. 90.

15. See Agnes Headlam-Morley, *The New Democratic Constitutions of Europe* (London: Oxford University Press, 1929), Chapter III.

16. See Julian Towster, *Political Power in the U.S.S.R.* (New York: Oxford University Press, 1948).

17. See Bernard Crick, *The American Science of Politics* (London: Routledge and Kegan Paul, 1959), p. v.

18. See in connection with comparative politics, A. L. Lowell, *Government of England,* two volumes (New York: Macmillan, 1908), F. A. Ogg, *English Government and Politics,* second edition, (New York: Mac-

millan, 1936), and W. B. Monroe and M. Ayearst, *The Governments of Europe* (New York: Macmillan, 1954).

19. Crick, *op. cit.,* p. 109.

20. There are a few European scholars working in the behavioral tradition.

21. It, is, of course, true that individual action can, and commonly is, treated from a systems point of view. This does not invalidate the distinction between behavioral and structural analysis. The one looks at individual behavior to explain the system, while the other looks at the collectivity in order to explain the individual. For a general discussion of the applicability of systems analysis for both behavioral and structural units, see J. Miller, *Towards a General Theory for the Behavioral Sciences,* in L. White, *The State ˙of the Social Sciences* (Chicago: University of Chicago Press, 1956).

22. Bryce puts his view as follows: "The fundamentals of human nature, present everywhere, are in each country modified by the influences of race, external conditions, such as climate and the occupations that arise from the physical resources of the country. Next come the historical antecedents which have given, or withheld, experience in self-government, have formed traditions of independence or submission, have created institutions which themselves in turn have moulded the minds and shaped the ideals of the nations." James Bryce, *Modern Democracies,* Vol. II (New York: Macmillan, 1921), p. 17.

23. To some extent Barker, Laski, and Bryce have faded from prominence. Bryce was rather theoretically primitive; and as his descriptions became out of date, his *Modern Democracies* was left to moulder on the shelves. Laski and Barker, primarily concerned with democracy and the innovations necessary for its survival in a world threatened by dictatorship, disseminated their ideas so widely, and yet were so completely unable to leave behind a cogent statement of their theories, that the contemporary comparative analysts now tend to ignore the debts owed to them.

24. Diluted by his earlier interest in Althusias and the beginnings of the modern period of natural law and by the modern sociological analysis of Weber and other experts on the study of bureaucracy.

25. Bryce, *op. cit.,* p. 14–15.

26. T. H. Green, *Lectures on the Principles of Political Obligation* (London: Longmans, Green and Company, 1941), p. 109.

27. H. Laski, *The State in Theory and Practice* (New York: Viking, 1947), p. 242.

28. See Harold Laski, *A Grammar of Politics* (London: George Allen and Unwin, Ltd., 1951), *passim.*

29. Sir Ernest Barker, *Principles of Social and Political Theory* (Oxford: The Clarendon Press, 1952), p. 246.

30. Herman Finer, *The Theory and Practice of Modern Government* (New York: Holt, Rinehart, and Winston, 1949), p. 6.

31. Robert E. Lane, *Political Life* (New York: The Free Press of Glencoe, 1959), p. 298.

32. See Harold D. Lasswell, *Psychopathology and Politics* (Chicago: University of Chicago Press, 1930). An extremely interesting study that indirectly deals with the problem of behaviorism in politics is Lucian Pye,

*Guerrilla Communism in Malaya* (Princeton: Princeton University Press, 1956).

33. See Philip Selznick, *The Organizational Weapon* (New York: The Free Press of Glencoe, 1960), second ed., p. 308.

34. The best discussion of this form of analysis and its implications for structural forms is George C. Homans, *The Human Group* (New York: Harcourt, Brace and World, 1950), *passim.* See also Herbert A. Simons and Allen Newell, "Models: Their Uses and Limitations," in White, ed., *The State of the Social Sciences* (Chicago: University of Chicago Press, 1956), pp. 66–83.

35. See Harold Guetzow, "Building Models about Small Groups," in Roland Young, ed., *Approaches to the Study of Politics* (Evanston: Northwestern University Press, 1958).

36. There is no theoretical reason that structural analysis cannot be applied to microcosmic units except that other forms seem more efficient.

37. Parsons argues that ideal types (as used by Weber) are not theories. Hempel argues that they are and demonstrates their logical similarity to certain theories in the physical sciences. See Talcott Parsons, Introduction to Max Weber's *Theory of Social and Economic Organization* (New York: The Free Press of Glencoe, 1947), pp. 12–14, and Carl Hempel.

38. A. R. Radcliffe-Brown, "On the Concept of Function in Social Science," in A. R. Radcliffe-Brown, *Structure and Function in Primitive Society* (New York: The Free Press of Glencoe, 1952), p. 180.

39. Its most recent and pertinent forms, however, show two related tendencies. The one is to use functional and then structural components in such fashion as to indicate those factors that are essential to the maintenance of the unit under analysis. This technique is ordinarily given the title of structural-functional requisite analysis. The second tendency is to examine structures not merely as derived from the observation of a given unit or comparatively, but rather in terms of their latent propensities for the unit. In this way, structural analysis is concerned with political dynamics, that is, the analysis of political change. For a full statement of structural-functional requisite analysis, see M. J. Levy, *The Structure of Society* (Princeton: Princeton University Press, 1952). See also Robert Merton, *Social Theory and Social Structure* (New York: The Free Press of Glencoe, 1949).

40. There is an increasing tendency for structural analysis, having achieved greater methodological precision over time, to apply statistical techniques.

41. Pye, *op. cit.*

42. See Selznick, *op. cit.*

43. T. Adorno, *et al., The Authoritarian Personality* (New York: Harper and Brothers, 1950).

44. Nathan Leites and Elizabeth Bernant, *Ritual of Liquidation; The Case of the Moscow Trials* (New York: The Free Press of Glencoe, 1954).

45. See Herbert Hyman, *Political Socialization* (New York: The Free Press of Glencoe, 1959).

46. See Almond and Coleman, eds., *The Politics of the Developing Areas* (Princeton: Princeton University Press, 1960), p. 31. For a critical evaluation of this effort see my review in the *Journal of Politics.*

47. As Parsons puts it, "Since a social system is a

system of processes of interaction between actors, it is the structure of the *relations between the actors as involved* in the interactive process which is essentially the structure of the social system. The system is a network of such relationships. Each individual actor is involved in a plurality of such interactive relationships each with one or more partners in the complementary role. Hence, it is the *participation* of an actor in a patterned interactive relationship which is for many purposes the most significant unit of the social system." See Talcott Parsons, *The Social System* (New York: The Free Press of Glencoe, 1951), p. 25.

# A Selective Introduction to the Literature of Comparative Politics

# A Selective Introduction to the Literature of Comparative Politics

This bibliography is not intended as a comprehensive presentation of the literature of comparative government. We desire merely to supplement the readings in a fashion that will round out the student's introduction to the literature and assist him in the early stages of his own researches in the field. In accordance with these aims, the bibliography has been subdivided into three parts.

Section I offers a selection of general works on foreign governments. This section is subdivided into the following areas: Europe, the Near East, Southern Asia and the Far East, Sub-Saharan Africa, Latin America, and Inter-Area Topical Studies. The works listed in each section are intended to provide a minimal introduction to the past and presently developing socio-political institutions of their respective areas. In these works the student will also find bibliographies that will assist his further study.

Section II contains a group of articles that parallel those included in the Reader. The student will find among these some that extend the interpretations applied by articles in the Reader to additional areas and others that offer contrasting interpretations of the events in the same areas. These articles have been chosen from among those published in the last ten years; the criteria of selection, in so far as possible, has been the quality of interpretation or stimulation rather than thoroughness of description.

The final section includes a list of bibliographies from which the student may supplement the suggestions of this bibliography. With these the student may begin his own research into comparative government and the process of confirmation and refutation necessary to the acquisition of further knowledge in the field.

## I. SOME GENERAL WORKS ON FOREIGN GOVERNMENTS

### A. Major European Governments

Beer, Samuel H., et al., *Patterns of Government: The Major Political Systems of Europe.* New York, 1958.

Finer, Herman, *The Major Governments of Modern Europe.* Evanston, Ill., 1960.

———, *The Theory and Practice of Modern Government.* New York, 1949. Rev. Ed.

Neumann, Robert G., *European and Comparative Government.* New York, 1960. 3rd Ed.

Robson, William A. (ed.), *The Civil Service in Britain and France.* New York, 1956.

#### 1. BRITAIN

Bagehot, Walter, *The English Constitution.* New York, 1928.

Blunt, Sir Edward A. H., *The I.C.S.* London, 1937.

Butler, D. E., *British General Election.* London, 1955.

Dicey, Albert V., *Introduction to the Study of the Law of the Constitution.* London, 1959. 10th Ed.

Finer, Herman, *English Local Government.* London, 1950.

Finer, S. E., *Anonymous Empire.* London, 1957.

Jeffries, Charles J., *The Colonial Empire and Its Civil Service.* Cambridge, England, 1938.

Jennings, Sir Ivor, *Cabinet Government.* New York, 1955. 3rd Ed.

———, *Parliament.* New York, 1958.

Laski, H. J., *Reflections on the Constitution: The House of Commons, the Cabinet and the Civil Service.* Manchester, England, 1951.

Mackenzie, Kenneth R., *The English Parliament*. Penguin Books, 1951.

McKenzie, R. T., *British Political Parties*. New York, 1955.

Stewart, Michael, *The British Approach to Politics*. London, 1938.

Woodruff, Philip, *The Men Who Ruled India*. New York, 1954.


2. FRANCE

Aron, Raymond, *France, Steadfast and Changing*. Cambridge, Mass., 1960.

Brogan, D. W., *France under the Republic*. New York, 1940.

———, *The French Nation: From Napoleon to Petain 1814–1940*. London, 1957.

Campbell, P., *French Electoral Systems and Elections, 1789–1957*. London, 1958.

Ehrmann, H. W., *Organized Business in France*. Princeton, N.J., 1957.

Goguel, Francois, *France under the Fourth Republic*. Ithaca, N.Y., 1952.

Leites, Nathan C., *On the Game of Politics in France*. Stanford, Calif., 1959.

Leuthy, Herbert, *France against Herself*. New York, 1955.

Litterdale, D. W. S., *The Parliament of France*. London, 1951.

Macridis, Roy C., *The De Gaulle Republic: Quest for Unity*. Homewood, Ill., 1960.

Pickles, Dorothy, *The Fifth Republic*. New York, 1960.

Tocqueville, Alexis de, *The Old Regime and the French Revolution*. New York, 1955 (paper).

Williams, Philip, *Politics in Post-War France*. London, 1958. Rev. Ed.

——— and M. Harrison, *De Gaulle's Republic*. London, 1960.


3. GERMANY

Brook, W. F., *Social and Economic History of Germany from William II to Hitler*. London, 1938.

Ebenstein, William, *The German Record, a Political Portrait*. New York, 1955.

Golay, J. F., *The Founding of the Federal Republic of Germany*. Chicago, 1958.

Halperin, S. W., *Germany Tried Democracy*. New York, 1946.

Kitzinger, V. W., *German Electoral Politics, the 1957 Campaign*. Oxford, 1960.

Neumann, F. L., *Behemoth*. New York, 1958.

Pinson, Koppel S., *Modern Germany*. New York, 1954.

Pollock, James K., *German Democracy at Work*. Ann Arbor, Mich., 1955.

Rauschning, H., *The Revolution of Nihilism*. New York, 1939.

UNESCO, *The Third Reich* (ed. J. H. Fried). New York, 1955.


4. ITALY

Banfield, Edward H., *The Moral Basis of a Backward Society*. New York, 1958.

Einaudi, Mario, and Francois Goguel, *Christian Democracy in Italy and France*. Notre Dame, Ind., 1952.

Finer, H., *Mussolini's Italy*. London, 1935.

Florinsky, Michael T., *Fascism and National Socialism*. New York, 1936.

Sturzo, Luigi, *Italy and Fascismo*. London, 1926.

Sprigge, Cecil J. S., *The Development of Modern Italy*. New Haven, Conn., 1954.


5. THE SOVIET UNION AND EASTERN EUROPE

Bauer, R. A., A. Inkeles and C. Kluckholn, *How the Soviet System Works*. Cambridge, Mass., 1956.

Brzezinski, Z. K., *Permanent Purge*. Oxford, 1956.

Djilas, M., *The New Class*. New York, 1957.

Fainsod, Merle, *How Russia Is Ruled*. Cambridge, Mass., 1953.

Gruliow, Leo, *Current Soviet Policies*. New York, 1953, 1957, 1960. 3 Vols.

Lasky, Melvin J., *The Hungarian Revolution*. London, 1957.

Leites, Nathan C., *Operational Code of the Politburo*. New York, 1951.

Lenin, V. I., *State and Revolution*. New York, 1935.

McClosky, Herbert, and J. E. Turner, *The Soviet Dictatorship*. New York, 1960.

Meisel, J. H., and E. S. Kozera, *Materials for the Study of the Soviet Union*. Ann Arbor, Mich., 1953. Rev. Ed.

Moore, Barrington, *Soviet Politics: The Dilemma of Power*. Cambridge, Mass., 1950.

Rostow, W. W., *The Dynamics of Soviet Society*. New York, 1953.

Towster, Julian, *Political Power in the U.S.S.R.* New York, 1948.

Trotsky, L., *The History of the Russian Revolution*. Ann Arbor, Mich., 1957. (Also abridged paperback.)

Zinner, Paul E. (ed.), *National Communism and Popular Revolt in Eastern Europe*. New York, 1956.


6. OTHER EUROPEAN AND WESTERN NATIONS

Brinan, Gerald, *The Spanish Labyrinth*. Cambridge, Mass., 1943.

Miller, J. D. B., *Australian Government and Politics: An Introductory Survey*. London, 1959. 2nd Ed.

Rustow, Dankwart A., *The Politics of Compromise*. Princeton, N. J., 1955. (Sweden)


B. The Near East

Arnold, Sir T. W., and Guillaume, Alfred (eds.), *The Legacy of Islam*. Oxford, 1949.

Barbour, Nevill (ed.), *A Survey of North West Africa*. London, 1959.

Bernstein, Mower H., *The Politics of Israel*. Princeton, N.J., 1957.

Bonne, Alfred, *State and Economics in the Middle-East*. London, 1955. 2nd Ed. Rev.

Coon, Carleton S., Caravan, *The Story of the Middle East*. New York, 1958

Eisenstadt, S. N., *The Absorption of Immigrants*. New York, 1955. (Israel)

Fisher, Sidney N., *Social Forces in the Middle East*. Ithaca, N. Y., 1955.

Gibb, H. A. R., and Bowen, Harold, *Islamic Society and the West*. Vol. I, pts. 1 & 2. London, 1950, 1957.

Kohn, Hans, *A History of Nationalism in the East*. New York, 1929.

Lacoutre, Jean and Simonne, *Egypt in Transition*. New York, 1958.

Laqueur, Walter Z., *Communism and Nationalism in the Middle East*. New York, 1957.

———, (ed.), *The Middle East in Transition*. New York, 1956.

Lenczowski, George, *The Middle East in World Affairs*. Ithaca, N.Y., 1956.

Lerner, Daniel, *The Passing of Traditional Society: Modernizing in the Middle East*. New York, 1958.

Lewis, Geoffrey L., *Turkey*. New York, 1955.

Longrigg, Stephen H., *Syria and Lebanon under French Mandate*. New York, 1958.

Rustow, Dankwart A., *Politics and Westernization in the Near East*. Princeton, N.J., 1956.

Warriner, Doreen, *Land Reform and Development in the Middle East*. London, 1957.

## C. South Asia and the Far East

### 1. SOUTH ASIA

Brown, W. N., *The U.S. and India and Pakistan*. Cambridge, Mass., 1953.

Callard, Keith, *Pakistan: A Political Study*. New York, 1958.

Desai, A. R., *Social Background of Indian Nationalism*. Bombay, 1948.

Griffiths, Sir Percival, *Modern India*. New York, 1957.

Joshi, G. N., *The Constitution of India*. London, 1954. 3rd Ed.

Lewis, Oscar, *Village Life in Northern India*. Urbana, Ill., 1958.

Marriot, McKim (ed.), *Village India*. Chicago, 1955.

Menon, V. P., *The Story of the Integration of the Indian States*. New York, 1956.

Moreland, W. H., and A. C. Chatterjee, *A Short History of India*. London, 1953.

Morris-Jones, W. H., *Parliament in India*. Philadelphia, 1957.

O'Malley, L. S. S. (ed.), *Modern India and the West*. London, New York, 1941.

Weiner, Myron, *Party Politics in India: The Development of a Multi-Party System*. Princeton, 1957.

### 2. SOUTHEAST ASIA

Emerson, Rupert, *Malaysia: A Study in Indirect Rule*. New York, 1937.

———, *Representative Government in South-East Asia*. Cambridge, Mass., 1955.

Furnivall, J. S., *Colonial Policy and Practice: A Comparative Study of Burma and Netherlands India*. New York, 1956.

Ginsberg, Norton, and C. F. Roberts, Jr., *Malaya*. Seattle, 1958.

Hall, D. G. E., *A History of South-East Asia*. New York, 1955.

Kahin, George McT. (ed.), *Government and Politics of South-East Asia*. Ithaca, N.Y., 1959.

———, *Nationalism and Revolution in Indonesia*. Ithaca, N.Y., 1952.

Pye, Lucien W., *Guerrilla Communism in Malaya, Its Social and Political Meaning*. Princeton, N.J., 1956.

Skinner, George W., *Chinese Society in Thailand: An Analytical History*. Ithaca, N.Y., 1957.

———, *Leadership and Power in the Chinese Community in Thailand*. Ithaca, N.Y., 1958.

Tinker, Hugh, *The Union of Burma*. New York, 1957.

Villa, Walter F., *The Impact of the West on Government in Thailand*. Berkeley, Calif., 1955.

Wertheim, W. F., *Indonesian Society in Transition: A Study of Social Change*. The Hague, 1956.

### 3. THE FAR EAST

*Annals of the American Academy of Political and Social Science,* "Contemporary China and the Chinese." January, 1959.

———, "Japan Since Recovery of Independence." November, 1956.

Fairbank, John K., *The United States and China*. Cambridge, Mass., 1957. Rev. Ed.

———, and Teng Ssu-Yu, *China's Response to the West*. Cambridge, Mass., 1954.

Latourette, K. S., *The Chinese: Their History and Culture*. New York, 1934.

Lattimore, Owen, and Eleanor Lattimore, *China: A Short History*. New York, 1947.

Levy, Marion J., and Shih Kuo-hong, *The Rise of the Modern Chinese Business Class*. New York, 1949.

Linebarger, Paul, Djang Chu, and A. W. Burks, *Far Eastern Governments and Politics*. New York, 1954.

Norman, E. Herbert, *Japan's Emergence as a Modern State*. New York, 1940.

Reischauer, Edwin O., *Japan, Past and Present*. New York, 1946.

———, *The United States and Japan,* Cambridge, Mass., 1957.

Rostow, W. W., *The Prospects for Communist China*. Cambridge, Mass., 1954.

Sansom, Sir George, *The Western World and Japan*. New York, 1950.

Scalapino, Robert A., *Democracy and the Party Movement in Pre-War Japan*. Berkeley, Calif., 1953.

Schwartz, Benjamin, *Chinese Communism and the Rise of Mao*. Cambridge, Mass., 1951.

Tang, Peter, *Communist China Today*. New York, 1957.

## D. Sub-Saharan Africa

*Annals of the American Academy of Political and Social Science,* "Contemporary Africa Trends and Issues." March, 1955.

———, "Africa and the Western World." July, 1956.

Apter, David E., *Ghana in Transition*. New York: Atheneum Press, 1963.

————, *The Political Kingdom in Uganda,* Princeton, N.J., 1961.

Bascom, W. P., and M. J. Herskovits, *Continuity and Change in African Cultures.* Chicago, 1958.

Carter, G. M., and W. O. Brown (eds.), *Transition in Africa: Studies in Political Adaption.* Boston, 1958.

Coleman, James S., *Nigeria: Background to Nationalism.* Berkeley, Calif., 1958.

Cowan, L. Gray, *Local Government in West Africa.* New York, 1958.

Duffy, James, *Portuguese Africa,* Cambridge, Mass., 1959.

Fortes, M., and E. E. Evans-Pritchard (eds.), *African Political Systems.* London, 1941.

Hailey, Lord, *An African Survey.* New York, 1957. Rev. Ed.

Hodgkin, Thomas, *Nationalism in Colonial Africa.* London, 1956.

Hodgkin, Thomas, *African Political Parties,* London, Penguin Books, 1962.

MacKenzie, William, and Kenneth Robinson (eds.), *Five Elections in Africa.* Oxford, 1960.

Thompson, Virginia, and Richard Adloff, *French West Africa,* Stanford, Calif., 1958.

————, *French Equatorial Africa.* Stanford, Calif., 1960.

Wallerstein, Immanuel, *Africa: The Politics of Independence.* New York, Random House, Vintage Books, 1961.

### E. Latin America

Alexander, Robert J., *Communism in Latin America.* New Brunswick, N.J., 1957.

Blanksten, George I., *Equador: Constitutions and Caudillos.* Berkeley, Calif., 1951.

Fitzgibbon, Russell H., *Uruguay: Portrait of a Democracy.* New Brunswick, N.J., 1954.

Haring, Clarence H., *The Spanish Empire in America.* New York, 1947.

Johnson, John J., *Political Change in Latin America.* Stanford, Calif., 1958.

Rippy, J. Fred, *Latin America, a Modern History.* Ann Arbor, Mich., 1958.

Royal Institute of International Affairs, *Latin American Studies* (a series of volumes). London, 1952, and following.

Schurz, William L., *Latin America, a Descriptive Survey.* New York, 1949.

Scott, Robert E., *Mexican Government in Transition.* Urbana, Ill., 1959.

Silvert, K. H., *A Study in Government: Guatemala.* New Orleans, 1954.

Tucker, William P., *The Mexican Government Today.* Minneapolis, 1957.

Whitaker, Arthur P., *The United States and South America: The Northern Republics.* Cambridge, Mass., 1948.

————, *Argentine Upheaval: Peron's Fall and the New Regime.* New York, 1956.

### F. Inter-Area Topical Studies

Almond, Gabriel A., and James S. Coleman (eds.), *The Politics of the Developing Areas.* Princeton, N.J., 1960.

Bowie, Robert R., and Carl J. Friedrich (eds.), *Studies in Federalism.* Boston, 1954.

Easton, Stewart, *The Decline of European Colonialism.*

Ehrmann, Henry W. (ed.), *Interest Groups on Four Continents.* Pittsburgh, 1958.

Emerson, Rupert, *From Empire to Nation.* Cambridge, 1960.

Human Relations Area Files, *Surveys of World Cultures.* New Haven, Conn.

Institute of Electoral Research, *A Review of Elections: 1954–1958* (29 countries). London, 1960.

Lipset, S. M., *Political Man.* New York, 1959.

McKay, Donald C., (ed.), *The American Foreign Policy Library* (series of background studies on various nations). Cambridge, Mass., n.d.

Mallory, Walter H. (ed.), *Political Handbook of the World, 1960.* New York, 1960.

Neumann, Sigmund (ed.), *Modern Political Parties: Approaches to Comparative Politics.* Chicago, 1956.

Northrop, F. S. C., *Meeting of East and West.* New York, 1946.

Rose, A. M., *Institutions of Advanced Societies.* Minneapolis, 1958.

Smith, Wilfred C., *Islam in Modern History.* Princeton, N.J., 1957.

## II. PROBLEMS IN COMPARATIVE ANALYSIS

### A. Methodology

Apter, D. E., "Africa and the Social Scientists," *World Politics,* 6(4) (July, 1954), pp. 538–548.

Aron, Raymond, "Esquisse d'un plan d'etude du federalisme," *B. int. Sci. soc.,* 4(1) (Spring, 1952), pp. 45–54.

Easton, David., "An Approach to the Analysis of Political Systems." *World Politics,* 9(3) (April, 1957), pp. 383–400.

Eisenstadt, S. N., "Communications Systems and Social Structure: An Exploratory Comparative Study," *Public Opinion Quarterly,* 19(2) (Summer, 1955), pp. 153–167.

————, "Primitive Political Systems: A Preliminary Comparative Analysis," *American Anthropologist,* 61(2) (April, 1955), pp. 200–220.

Lerner, D., I. Pool, and H. D. Lasswell, "Comparative Analysis of Political Ideologies: A Preliminary Statement," *Public Opinion Quarterly,* 15(4) (Winter, 1951–1952), pp. 715–733.

Neumann, F. L., "Approaches to the Study of Political Power," *Political Science Quarterly,* 65(2) (June, 1950), pp. 161–180.

Wittfogel, K. A., "Russia and Asia: Problems of Contemporary Area Studies and International Relations," *World Politics,* 2(4) (July, 1950), pp. 445–462.

### B. Autocracy

Adams, M., "Twenty Years of France," *Foreign Affairs,* 37(2) (January, 1959), pp. 257–268.

Aspaturian, V. V., "The Theory and Practice of Soviet Federalism," *Journal of Politics,* 12(1) (February, 1950), pp. 20–51.

Brzezinski, Z., "Totalitarianism and Rationality," *American Political Science Review,* 50(3) (September, 1956), pp. 751–763.

Duverger, M., "Parti unique fasciste et parti unique communiste," *Vie intellectuelle* (August–September, 1951), pp. 32–44.

Edinger, Lewis J., "Post-Totalitarian Leadership: Elites in the German Federal Republic," *American Political Science Review,* 54(1) (March, 1960), pp. 58–82.

Fainsod, Merle, "Controls and Tensions in the Soviet System," *American Political Science Review,* 44(2) (June, 1950), pp. 266–282.

———, "The Komosols—A Study of Youth under Dictatorship," *American Political Science Review,* 45(1) (March, 1951), pp. 18–40.

Herz, J. H., "The Problem of Successorship in Dictatorial Regimes: A Study in Comparative Law and Institutions," *Journal of Politics,* 14(1) (February, 1952), pp. 19–40.

Mecham, J. Loyd, "Latin American Constitutions: Nominal and Real," *Journal of Politics,* 21(2) (May, 1959), pp. 258–275.

Timasheff, N. S., "Political Power in the Soviet Union," *Russian Politics,* 15(1) (January, 1952), pp. 15–24.

## C. Political Problems of Social Change and Economic Development

*American Political Science Review,* "Cultural Requisites to a Successfully Functioning Democracy—A Symposium," March, 1956.

Apter, D. E., "Some Economic Factors in the Political Development of the Gold Coast," *Journal of Economic History,* 14(4) (1954), pp. 409–421.

Armstrong, L., "A Socio-Economic Opinion Poll in Beirut, Lebanon," *Public Opinion Quarterly,* 23(1) (Spring, 1959), pp. 18–27.

Badgley, T. H., "Burma's Political Crisis," *Pacific Affairs,* 31(4) (December, 1958), pp. 336–351.

Balandier, George, "Le contexte sociologique de la vie politique en Afrique noire," *R. Franc. Sci. polit.,* 9(3) (September, 1959), pp. 598–609.

———, "Le development industriel de la proletarisation en Afrique noire," *Afr. et Asie,* 20(4) (1952), pp. 45-53.

———, "Messianismes et nationalismes en Afrique noire," *C. int. Sociol.,* 14 (1953), pp. 41–65.

Binder, L., "Problems of Islamic Political Thought in the Light of Recent Developments in Pakistan," *Journal of Politics,* 20(4) (November, 1958), pp. 655–675.

Berg, Elliot J., "The Economic Basis of Political Choice in French West Africa," *American Political Science Review,* 54(2) (June, 1960), pp. 391–405.

Bertier, F., "L'ideologie sociale de la Revolution egyptienne," *Orient* 2(6) (1958), pp. 49-71.

Coleman, J. S., "Nationalism in Tropical Africa," *American Political Science Review,* 48(2) (June, 1954), pp. 404-426.

———, "The Problem of Political Integration in Emergent Africa," *Western Political Quarterly,* 8(1) (March, 1955), pp. 44–57.

Coon, C. S., "The Impact of the West on Middle Eastern Social Institutions," *Annals,* 24(4) (January, 1952), pp. 443–466.

Emerson, Rupert, "Nationalism and Political Development," *Journal of Politics* (February, 1960).

Firth, R., "The Peasantry of Southeast Asia," *International Affairs* (October, 1950), pp. 503–514.

Fitzgibbon, R. H., "Measurement of Latin American Political Phenomena: A Statistical Experiment," *American Political Science Review,* 45(2) (June, 1951), pp. 517–523.

Howman, R., "African Leadership in Transition: An Outline," *Journal of African Administration,* 8(3) (July, 1956), pp. 117–126.

Kilson, M. L., Jr., "Nationalism and Social Class in British West Africa," *Journal of Politics,* 20(2) (May, 1958), pp. 368–387.

Kroef, J. M. V. D., "Society and Culture in Indonesian Nationalism," *American Journal of Sociology,* 58(1) (July, 1952), pp. 11–24.

Levy, Marion J., "Contrasting Factors in the Modernization of China and Japan," *Economic Development and Cultural Change* (October, 1953), pp. 161–197.

Lipset, S. M., "Some Social Requisites of Democracy: Economic Development and Political Legitimacy," *American Political Science Review,* 53(1) (March, 1959), pp. 69–105.

Lockwood, William, "Japan's Response to the West," *World Politics* (October, 1956), pp. 37–54.

Nash, M., "Political Relations in Guatemala," *Sociological and Economic Studies,* 7(1) (March, 1958), pp. 65–75.

Pye, Lucien, "Communication Patterns and the Problem of Representative Government in Non-Western Societies," *Public Opinion Quarterly,* 20(1) (Spring, 1956), pp. 240–257.

———, "Eastern Nationalism and Western Policy," *World Politics,* 6(2) (January, 1954), pp. 248–265.

Shils, Edward, "The Intellectuals in the Political Development of New States," *World Politics* (April, 1960).

———, "Intellectuals, Public Opinion, and Economic Development," *World Politics,* 10 (January, 1958), pp. 232–255.

Weiner, Myron, "India's Political Problems: The Longer View," *Western Political Quarterly,* 9(2) (June, 1956), pp. 283–292.

## D. Politics: Elections, Parties and Pressure Groups

Beer, S. H., "The Conservative Party of Great Britain," *Journal of Politics,* 14(1) (February, 1952), pp. 41–71.

———, "Pressure Groups and Parties in Great Britain," *American Political Science Review,* 50(1) (March, 1956), pp. 1–23.

Campbell, D. and D. Donnison and A. Potter, "Voting Behavior in Drysden in October, 1951," *Manchester School of Economics and Sociology, Studies,* 20(1) (January, 1952), pp. 57–65.

Duverger, M., "L'influence des systemes electoraux sur la vie politique," *B. int. Sci. soc.,* 3(2) (Summer, 1951), pp. 342–370.

Ehrmann, H. W., "Pressure Groups in France," *Annals* (September, 1958), pp. 141–148.

Fall, B. B., "The Political Religious Sects of Viet-Nam," *Pacific Affairs,* 23(3) (September, 1955), pp. 235–253.

Finer, S. E., "The Lobbies," *Twentieth Century* (October, 1957), pp. 371–377.

Grumm, J. G., "Theories of Electoral Systems," *Midwest Journal of Political Science,* 2(4) (November, 1958), pp. 357–376.

Hamm, L., "Introduction a l'étude des partis politiques de l'Afrique francais," *R. jus. Polit. O. -Mer* 13(2) (April–June, 1959), pp. 149–196.

Kilson, Martin L., "Authoritarian and Single-Party Tendencies in African Politics," *World Politics,* 15(2) (January, 1963). pp. 262-294.

Lapalombara, J., "The Political Role of Organized Labour in Western Europe," *Journal of Politics,* 17(1) (February, 1955), pp. 59–81.

Lichtblau, G. E., "The Politics of Trade Union Leadership in Southern Asia," *World Politics,* 7(1) (October, 1954), pp. 84–109.

Padgett, L. V., "Mexico's One Party System: A Reevaluation," *American Political Science Review,* 51(4) (December, 1957), pp. 995–1008.

Tinker, I., "Malayan Elections: Electoral Pattern for Plural Societies?" *Western Political Quarterly,* 9(2) (January, 1956), pp. 258–282.

Weiner, M., "Struggle Against Power: Notes on Indian Political Behavior," *World Politics,* 8(3) (April, 1956), pp. 392–403.

## E. Bureaucracy and Local Government

Apter, D. E., "Some Problems of Local Government in Uganda," *Journal of African Administration,* 11(1) (January, 1959), pp. 27–37.

Eisenstadt, S. N., "Political Struggle in Bureaucratic Societies," *World Politics,* 9(1) (October, 1956), pp. 15–36.

Hailey, Lord, "Local Government Institutions in India and Africa," *Journal of African Administration,* 4(1) (January, 1952), pp. 2–6.

Hazard, J. N., "Soviet Public Administration and Federalism," *Political Quarterly,* 23(1) (January–March, 1952), pp. 4–14.

Hucker, C. O., "The Traditional Chinese Censorate and the New Peking Regime," *American Political Science Review,* 45(4) (December, 1951), pp. 1041–1057.

Jumper, R., "Mandarin Bureaucracy and Politics in South Viet-Nam," *Pacific Affairs,* 30(1) (March, 1957), pp. 47–58.

Kerlinger, F. N., "Decision-Making in Japan," *Social Forces,* 30(1) (October, 1951), pp. 36–41.

Merkl, Peter M., "Executive-Legislative Federalism in West Germany," *American Political Science Review,* 53(3) (September, 1959), pp. 732–741.

Ward, R. E., "The Socio-Political Role of the Buraku (Hamlet) in Japan," *American Political Science Review,* 45(4) (December, 1951), pp. 1025–1040.

## III. SOME USEFUL BIBLIOGRAPHICAL AIDS

UNESCO, Bibliography of works in Political Science.

———, Bibliography of works in Political Sociology.

———, Political Science Abstracts.

———, Sociological Abstracts.

American Universities Field Staff, Inc. *A Select Bibliography: Asia, Africa, Eastern Europe, Latin America.* New York, 1960. *A Study of Current Bibliographies of National Official Publications: A Short Guide and Inventory,* compiled by the International Committee for Social Sciences Documentation. Jean Meyriat, ed. Paris: UNESCO, 1958.